The Cottage Gardener

The Journal of Horticulture

THE COTTAGE GARDENER:

PRACTICAL GUIDE

IN EVERY DEPARTMENT OF HORTICULTURE

AND

RURAL AND DOMESTIC ECONOMY.

CONDUCTED

BY GEORGE W. JOHNSON, ESQ.

EDITOR OF THE "GARDENERS' ALMANACK," "COTTAGE GARDENERS' DICTIONARY," ETC.

THE FRUIT AND FORCING-GARDEN, by Mr. R. Errington, Gardener to Sir P. Egerton, Bart., Oulton Park.

THE KITCHEN-GARDEN, by Mr. J. Barnes, Gardener to Lady Rolle, Bicton; and Mr. T. Weaver, Gardener to the Warden of Winchester College.

THE FLOWER-GARDEN, by Mr. D. Beaton, Gardener to Sir W. Middleton, Bart., Shrubland Park.

FLORISTS' FLOWERS, by Mr. T. Appleby, Floricultural Manager to Messrs. Henderson, Edgeware-road.

THE GREENHOUSE AND WINDOW-GARDEN, by Mr. R. Fish, Gardener to Colonel Sowerby, Putteridge Bury, near Luton.

ORCHID CULTURE, by Mr. T. Appleby, Floricultural Manager to Messrs. Henderson, Edgeware-road.

THE APIARIAN'S CALENDAR, for the Management of Bees, by J. H. Payne, Esq.

THE POULTRY-KEEPER'S CALENDAR, by Martin Doyle, Author of "Hints to Small Farmers," &c.

ALLOTMENT FARMING. The last Number of each month is double, embracing Allotment Farming, and the Economy of the Cow-shed, Pig-stye, and Hen-roost.

THE PHYSIC-GARDEN, by a Physician.

HOUSEHOLD ECONOMY, by the authoress of "My Flowers."

VEGETABLE AND OTHER COOKERY, by a Lady.

DOMESTIC ANIMALS, by Mr. W. C. Spooner, M.R.V.C.

THE AVIARY, by a Naturalist and Bird Fancier.

VOLUME IV.

LONDON:

PUBLISHED BY WM. S. ORR AND CO., 2, AMEN CORNER.

MDCCCL.

TO OUR READERS.

WE were quite aware that it savours of rashness to promise of great things yet to be achieved, when we said, in our last address, that we felt assured that at the conclusion of our next volume our readers would not withhold from us their approbation. But we had full confidence in our "men at arms;" and now that "next volume" *is* concluded, we fearlessly look our readers in the face, and ask for the approbation we anticipated. Not one of the able minds devoted to the enrichment of our pages but evinces that its strength is unexhausted; and not one but continues in some mode to repeat, "My armour's on,—I would that the lists were wider;" and this is shown by what they have done from week to week, and from month to month. Then upon the merit of that strength which they have put forth we also fearlessly ask for approbation; for in no periodical in all our horticultural literature can be found such a mass of sound useful gardening information as within our "twopenny pages." We speak firmly upon this, because we have those best of testimonies—old friends continue with us, and a host of new friends come around us. One of the latter writes to us thus: "I hear from every quarter unqualified praise of your truly admirable publication, as well from brother clergymen as from other parties. I assure you the taking it in has become quite a connecting link between many people who would otherwise have not, perhaps, naturally been drawn together. It is a regular masonic sign—unmistakeable and humanizing."

It is from such testimony as this that the weary brain and the weary hand gather encouragement and strength; and we can assure our readers that both these are strengthened, and that week by week they will find evidence in our pages that the "masonic sign" has not lost any of its freshness, nor any of its power. Old features, we are confident, will be found worthy of the welcome they will receive; and there will be new features, we think, quite deserving of being admitted into fellowship with the old.

INDEX.

WOODCUTS.

WEEKLY CALENDAR.

M D	W D	APRIL 4—10, 1850.	Weather near London in 1849.		Sun Rises.	Sun Sets.	Moon R & S.	Moon's Age.	Clock bef. Sun.	Day of Year.
4	Th	St. Ambrose. Plum leaves open.	T. 56°—45°.	S. Rain.	31 a. 5	35 a. 6	1	23	3 5	94
5	F	Fieldfare last seen.	T. 57°—35°.	S.W. Fine.	29	37	2 18	23	2 47	95
6	S	Old Lady Day. Turnip Fly appears.	T. 53°—38°.	S.E. Fine.	27	39	2 58	24	2 30	96
7	Sun	Sexagesima on Low SUNDAY. Blackbird lays.	T. 55°—34°.	S.W. Rain.	24	40	3 33	25	2 12	97
8	M	Ringed Snake seen.	T. 51°—31°.	S.W. Rain.	22	42	4 1	26	1 53	98
9	Tu	Rook hatches. [Sparrow builds.	T. 41°—32°.	N.E. Fine.	20	44	4 28	27	1 36	99
10	W	Oxford and Cambridge Terms begin. House	T. 58°—34°.	N.E. Rain.	18	45	4 53	28	1 22	100

ST. AMBROSE, Bishop of Milan, who died on the 4th of this month, A.D. 397, was one of those characters of well-poised judgments who arise occasionally as leaders and beacons in the age they adorn. Instances of his moderation and candour are numerous; but one may be selected, because it is believed to be the origin of a wise but easily perverted proverb. At Milan it was customary to regard each Saturday as a festival, whilst at Rome it was observed as a fast. Ambrose was consulted as to the correctness of either practice, and his just reply was, "In matters of form only, and where no fundamental principle of rectitude is violated, it is proper to be guided by general custom: when I am at Milan, I do not fast; but when at Rome, I do as they do at Rome." From this is believed to have originated the common and somewhat dangerous saying, which has been thus versified:—

"When you are at Rome,
Do as they do at Rome;
When you are elsewhere,
Do as they do there."

In essential points Ambrose was as wisely firm: and his refusal to permit the Emperor Theodosius to enter the Milan cathedral, after his pitiless massacre in Thessalonica, has been not more lauded than the act deserves, and has been the chosen subject of more than one great painter.

METEOROLOGICAL PHENOMENA OF THE SEASON.—In the twenty-three last years, the average highest and lowest temperatures of the above days have been 55.8° and 35.3°, respectively. The greatest heat was 73°, on the 9th in 1814. During the above time and years, there were 94 fine days, and 67 on which rain fell.

RANGE OF BAROMETER—RAIN IN INCHES.

April		1841.	1842.	1843.	1844.	1845.	1846.	1847.	1848.	1849.
4	B.	29.642	30.309	29.553	29.534	30.053	29.916	29.702	30.033	29.656
		29.467	30.182	29.305	29.588	29.986	29.250	29.692	30.015	29.420
	R.	0.11	—	0.23	—	0.46	0.02	—	—	0.03
5	B.	29.436	30.355	29.917	29.735	30.041	29.222	29.745	29.099	29.656
		29.371	30.295	29.702	29.719	29.992	29.142	29.529	29.736	29.281
	R.	—	—	0.02	0.01	—	0.55	—	0.01	—
6	B.	29.748	30.186	29.842	29.947	29.914	29.058	29.855	29.653	29.509
		29.661	29.957	29.516	29.839	29.801	28.984	29.745	29.543	29.440
	R.	0.02	—	0.01	—	—	0.30	0.04	—	—
7	B.	29.781	29.907	29.453	30.047	29.915	29.156	29.837	29.501	29.514
		29.777	29.800	29.436	30 095	29.873	29.050	29.813	29.440	29.440
	R.	0.02	—	0.35	—	—	0.12	0.10	0 04	0.05
8	B.	29.779	30.199	29.473	30.399	29.872	29.411	29.625	29.160	29.429
		29.773	30.053	29.544	30.385	29.416	29.198	29.349	29.334	29.345
	R.	0.30	—	0.01	—	0.04	—	0.02	0.04	0.02
9	B.	29.908	30.331	29.702	30.480	29.068	29.799	29.775	29.543	29.536
		29.829	30.307	29.598	30.441	28.972	29.545	29.599	29.515	29.449
	R.	0.01	—	—	—	0.69	—	—	0.14	—
10	B.	30.020	30.358	29.921	30.386	29.118	29.835	29.900	29.483	29.564
		29.960	30.281	29.892	30.116	29.020	29.736	29.695	29.328	29.538
	R.	—	—	0.01	—	0.19	—	—	0.27	0.04

NATURAL PHENOMENA INDICATIVE OF WEATHER.—When distant objects appear more distinct or nearer than usual, it is a sign of approaching rain. The same, says Dr. Forster, has been observed of the mountains and hills in the West Indies, before the occurrence of the autumnal rains and tempests; and some of the most violent hurricanes of our colonies have been preceded by an extraordinary appearance of nearness in the distant mountains. In this country, also, showery weather is never considered to be past so long as the distant hills appear unusually near. This fact corresponds with the observation of Sir Isaac Newton, that the stars seem clearer and better adapted for observation in the clear intervals between showers, and just before a change from fair weather to rain.

THE HYACINTH being a prevailing flower of the season, we devote to it our first essay on the characteristic excellencies to be aimed at by the cultivator. We shall state what we consider would form a perfect flower; not with the idea that any will quite attain to such excellence, but because such standards enable the grower to judge which approaches nearest to the characteristics that a flower should possess to entitle it to be a successful competitor for a floricultural prize.

At the best, the Hyacinth is a formal-looking flower—there are too many straight lines about it,—yet at one time fashion made it costly, for there was a hyacinth mania as well as a tulip mania in the 17th century. It is not known to have been cultivated either in Holland or England before the latter part of the 16th century, but within about fifty years it had been widely distributed: numerous varieties raised, and enormous prices paid for favourite specimens. It was then as often called the Jacinth as the Hyacinth. Parkinson in his "Paradisus," published in 1629, mentions fifty varieties, but of these only three were double. Double varieties were so far from being estimated at that time that Peter Voorhelm, one of the largest of hyacinth cultivators at Haarlem, destroyed them as often as they appeared in his collection. Illness having one year prevented him visiting his flower-beds until the bloom of the Hyacinths was passing away, his attention was drawn to one double specimen, which though of no superior excellence, yet seemed alone blooming to welcome the convalescent. He cultivated it: increased it from offsets, and introduced it to flower fanciers. The taste for them prevailed; and for one, The King of Great Britain, which Mr. Voorhelm raised at the beginning of the present century, he obtained more than £100.

The first writer, of whom we are aware, who wrote fully and judiciously on the characteristics of a good Hyacinth, was Abercrombie in his "Universal Gardener," published during 1778. Martyn, Maddock, Loudon, and others, subsequently wrote upon the same subject; but less successfully, until Mr. Glenny took up the subject, and published his excellent little book upon "The Properties of Flowers." After perusing all these authorities, and after a careful examination of the

Prize Flowers at many exhibitions, we offer the following as

CHARACTERISTICS OF A GOOD HYACINTH.

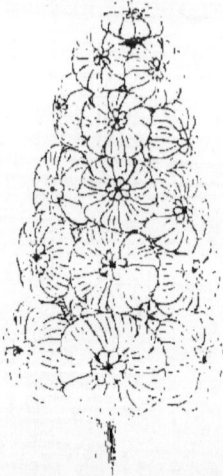

Size and Form of Spike.—To be a fine specimen, the spike ought to be at least six inches long, and two inches in diameter at the lowest and broadest part, tapering gradually up to a single pip, as shewn in our drawing. But form, or proportion, is the greatest merit; and the handsomest proportions for the spike are for its length to be twice the diameter of its lowest part, and for the whole spike to form a cone.

Size and Form of Pips.—The outline of each, looking at in front, should be circular; and, looking at in profile, it should be semicircular. In other words, each pip should be half a globe. To effect this, the petals (if the flower is single) require to be strongly bent back, or reflexed, so as to throw forward the centre. In double flowers it is not needed for the outer petals to be much bent back, as the semi-globular form in these is partly attained by the inner petals being imbricated, or lapped over each other in tiers, like the tiles on a roof. The lower pips should be large—an inch and a quarter in diameter is a superior size; and the pips of each circle should gradually diminish in diameter as they approach nearer to the summit. The petals should be thick, glossy surfaced, as if made of wax, and rounded at the end. Sharp pointed petals always injure the outline of the form of the spike.

The footstalk, or stem, of the spike should be straight, stout, and of height sufficient to raise the lowest part of the spike just above the points of the leaves. The footstalk of each pip should be gradually shorter as they approach nearer to the top; and each should spring from the stem at an angle just a little less than a right angle,

so as to aid the pips in adapting themselves to a conical form, and yet to keep their broad faces, or discs, full before the eye.

Colour.—What we say on this point is applicable to competing flowers of every species, for in all it should be esteemed as entirely subordinate to form and size. The reason for this is sound; for form and size, if no accident interferes, are superior just in proportion to the skilfulness of the cultivation. Colour, therefore, should have no further weight than to turn the scale in favour of the best coloured, provided that two specimens are equal in form and size. In the case of selfs—that is, flowers of one colour—the most uniform and brightest are best; but in flowers of more than one tint the colouring is best where the colours are distinct, and not clouded into one another.

Fragrance.—When flowers, such as is the Hyacinth, are of a kind yielding a perfume—if the rivals are equal in other qualities—we should award the prize to the most fragrant. It is even a criterion of good cultivation; for just in proportion to the flowering vigour of a plant is its fragrance. An over-luxuriant and a weakly grown plant have the fragrance of their flowers diminished.

The following list of Hyacinths embraces those which are of very moderate price, and yet, if well grown, are capable of attaining as high a degree of excellence as any that, as greater novelties, are of higher marketable value. The prices specified in our list are those at which the bulbs will be purchaseable next October:—

DOUBLE RED.	La Candeur, 9d.
Bouquet Royale, 1s.	Victoria Regina, 1s 6d.
Endracht, 1s.	DOUBLE BLUE.
Prince of Wales (splendid form), 3s.	Bouquet Pourpre, 9d.
SINGLE RED.	Lord Wellington, 9d.
Diebitsch Sabalskansky, 1s.	Prince Van Saxe Weimar, 1s 3d.
L'Ami du Cœur, 9d.	
Lord Wellington, 1s.	SINGLE BLUE.
DOUBLE WHITE.	Emicus, 9d.
Grande Monarque de France, 1s.	Grand Vidette (beautiful porcelain blue), 2s.
La Tour d'Auvergne, 1s 3d.	Orondates, 1s.
Ne Plus Ultra, 1s 3d.	YELLOW.
SINGLE WHITE.	Heroine (the best), 2s.
Grand Vainquer, 9d.	La Favorite, 9d.
	La Belle Jaune, 9d.

THE FRUIT-GARDEN.

VINE BORDERS IN-DOORS.—We believe we shall be performing a duty to one class of the readers of THE COTTAGE GARDENER in offering a few remarks on this head, for although advice concerning this subject has at times been offered it has been somewhat piecemeal.

The first consideration is *the depth of soil* necessary; the next drainage, the position of which, of course, will be regulated by the former. Now, seeing that *in-doors* the border will not be subject to the vicissitudes of the seasons like out-door borders, the maxims as to depth and texture which are considered imperative outdoors lose half their weight as to inside borders. Inside borders, too, depending as they must on hand-watering for their moisture, may possibly (unknown to the cultivator) become too dry beneath, whilst the surface appears damp. Under such circumstances, therefore, we think that a greater depth of soil becomes requisite in order that, should such a contingency occur, a greater extent and volume of root may be a compensation.

For out-door borders we do not advise a depth of more than two feet, and, had we to make an out-door border in such a humid northern county as Lancashire, we would by no means have it deeper than half a yard. This may alarm some folks, but we have experienced the benefit from such, and very frequently during the last 20 years had an opportunity of witnessing the difference between the deep and the shallow border.

For an in-doors border, then, we would advise 30 inches, or, if the proprietor is well assured of the texture of the soil, and of the certainty of a clever course of culture subsequently, he might allow a yard of depth, beyond which we should certainly consider the roots as too far removed from control.

We come now to consider the question of *drainage*, which is a paramount consideration, so much so that it will little signify what character the compost of the border may be of if this great point be neglected, or improperly performed. We are aware that there are some situations which would do entirely without drainage, nevertheless there is none but would be benefited by some provision for the escape of water; for it must be considered that the manures and other organic matters which are considered necessary in making a border, must, by decay, form a dark and unctuous kind of humus, and that this will be carried downwards in time until it forms a retentive kind of deposit, which without drainage is well known to be too retentive of moisture.

One foot in depth of imperishable materials—such as broken bricks, stones, the scoria from iron or other works, &c.—will suffice; but the character of the *subsoil surface* must be taken into consideration. This underground surface must slope to some one given point, in order to carry the drainage clear away. The best mode of making borders of this character is to build the front wall of the house on arches, *as open as possible*, and to make a provision *outside* as well, for the vine roots to pasture in, and this they will do readily—need we add, that such will increase their strength, and promote their permanency.

It is sometimes possible to form the inside and out-side borders on a uniform pitch or inclination; that is to say, as to the forming of the surface of the subsoil previously to setting the drains; and thus there will be a uniform incline from the extent of the border inside to its extent outside, through the arches. This is a safe and systematic plan; but it so happens, as in other cases, that the levels within and without cannot be reconciled, and of course the borders inside and out will not be on *precisely* the same level; be that as it may, an escape for the drainage *must* be provided.

The subsoil surface then being formed, and a main drain carried the whole length of the house, a foot of the materials in a coarse and open state may be placed on the surface, taking care that the main drain is somewhat below this surface level. The next thing is to provide something to fill up the inequalities of the rubbly material, otherwise the soil and sedimentary matter might eventually choke the drainage; and we are not aware that anything better can be used than cinders riddled clean; at least such is what we have been in the habit of using for years to fruit-tree bottoms in general. These may be spread at least two inches thick over the surface of the rubble, and be trod or rammed down firmly. Next, we would place a layer of small turfs, fresh cut from some sandy-soiled pasture; these need not be pressed close together; small interstices may be left between them, and a slight sprinkling of small cinders or charcoal may be scattered over the whole, and swept in the crevices.

The border is now ready for *the compost*, and as this is a point on which much difference of opinion exists,

we must indulge in a few remarks. Some first-rate cultivators insist on considering the vine as the most gluttonous of trees; and they provide not only ordinary manure in abundance, but the carcases of dead animals, bone manure, &c., &c. Now, for our own parts, we subscribe to no such opinion; these are, as we think, works of supererogation, if we may apply such a term. There can be little doubt that some of these expensive borders contain enriching materials sufficient for a score such; and why a thing of this kind is to be esteemed in proportion to the amount of prodigality evinced in its construction, we cannot imagine. We much fear that the importance attached to the circumstance of winning a medal at an exhibition has led to a most lavish expenditure; for mere size in these things is too often considered a superior test to quality. We are ready to admit that monstrosities may be produced for a year or two, whilst the trees are *young* and the border *new*. During such a period the freshness and porosity of the turf, or other inorganic matters in the borders, will counteract the evil tendencies of the enriching materials. But let a few seasons pass over such borders, and it will be seen that whilst other vines, on more simply constituted borders, are advancing and progressing annually, the others will be retrograding in a corresponding degree. Indeed, it could not be otherwise. Every good gardener knows the effect of using even too much dung in vine borders; how it eventually wars against the durability of the border. We have known old borders when broken up present a mass of black material below, which, in point of texture, might be taken for putty.

We consider that a mellow and sandy turfy loam from an old pasture is competent in itself to produce first-rate grapes, provided a proper system of top-dressing be resorted to. By proper system we do not mean heaping manure over their roots during the months of spring and early summer, to prevent the soil from borrowing heat from the atmosphere; but we will say more about *top-dressings* and *mulchings* on another occasion.

The following, then, is the compost we would recommend for an *inside* border:—Turfy loam, chopped roughly, six parts; mixed manures, half rotten tree leaves, &c., two parts; horse droppings (fresh), such as used for mushroom-beds, with litter amongst them, one part; charred materials, one part; lime rubbish, two parts. These materials to be thoroughly blended, remembering that both the chopping and the turning must be done when the materials are dry; and that the sooner it is housed after the last turning the better. We would also advise that a coating of littery droppings be strewed over the surface of the turfs in the bottom, before filling in the soil.

We have made use of the term *loam* as usual; and many of our readers have complained of the indefinite character attached to what the gardener terms "loam." It would appear, however, that there is some misconception about this affair. What gardeners, in their vague way of writing, in general mean by *loam*, is merely *maiden soil* containing much organic matter. This may contain five, ten, twenty, or fifty per cent. of the clayey principle; and in proportion as this prevails, in a like degree is the soil adhesive; and this adhesiveness is generally expressed in gardening technicalities by the terms *sound* loam, *strong* loam, *stiff* loam, &c. Still, the broadest signification has a reference to *maiden* soil, or soil that has rested for years, in contradistinction to old garden soil, which possesses less organic matter.

We would, however, have the amateur of limited means understand, that ordinary garden soil may be used in lieu of the loam, provided it is of a good staple. We would, in such case, advise that a little strawy, or littery manure, *fresh from the stable-door*, be mixed through the whole mass during the process of filling the border.   R. ERRINGTON.

THE FLOWER-GARDEN.

BEDDING PLANTS.—I said last week, that the *Sweet Alyssum* was the best white edging plant; but I forgot to say that the *variegated* form of it is the kind to which I give the preference. The Variegated Sweet Alyssum is, indeed, the richest edging to a scarlet, or blue, or yellow bed, of all the plants we possess; but some tastes might prefer *Mangles' variegated Geranium* before it; but as I keep strictly to white colours at present, that geranium cannot be admitted, on account of its pinkish flowers. The only drawback to the variegated alyssum is that it is not everybody's plant, like the original, as it must be preserved from year to year, by cuttings made in August, and secured from frost, like the verbenas. On the other hand, it is devoid of that powerful honeyed perfume for which the Sweet alyssum is discarded by those who dislike that kind of scent. Either of them is useful for second planting in July, after some other annual is done for the season; or, say a good successor to a bed of *Navel-wort*, or of the Great Cape Marigold, *Calendula hybrida*, alias, *C. pluvialis*: but the latter is a different plant, being the Small Cape Marigold. These two white flowering annuals are well worth growing, as they require only to be sown at once in the open bed; and the alyssum, being of the same height—a foot to 18 inches—would follow them, in an arrangement where height and colour were to be maintained. We gardeners do not encourage this style of planting, when we can put in a plant which will last through the whole season. We prefer it to a double crop in the same bed, but that is no reason why those who are fond of a variety should follow our example here. The *Calendula hybrida* is a particularly showy white plant for a bed as long as it lasts, and is only a foot high in the richest soil. It is one, also, that will easily transplant; and five or seven good plants of it thinned out of a bed would make a handsome patch in a mixed border. *White Clarkia* makes a delightful bed, but can never be used in a proper arrangement of heights and colours, because, when it is over, there is not another white of the same height to take its place; at least, not without waiting some time. A *White Petunia* or *Verbena* might pass for it; but, after all, that would only be a poor make-shift. This Clarkia must, therefore, be used without reference to this style of gardening, and when it is over a plant of some other colour must take its place. I shall once more remind you of making one bed, at least, of mixed *Clarkia*: introducing equal quantities of white and purple. A good-sized bed of them, thus mixed, any one may have for six-penny-worth of seed; and I engage to forfeit the good opinions of all our readers, if a single individual amongst them will not admire this bed.

PETUNIAS.—There are several good white petunias for bedding, but, with the exception of the old tall one called *nyctaginiflora*, I do not know one that could be got in the trade, as their names are so ephemeral. I must, therefore, pass them over, with one remark on that old one. It is the only one of them that can be relied on to come true from seeds; and the seedlings answer best on poor dry soils; but where the soil is rich and deep they grow too rank, and will not bloom so well as plants raised from spring-struck cuttings. A very dwarf white petunia is still a desideratum.

VERBENAS.—"I *wholly* dread" the verbenas, as we say in Suffolk, and so I left them out as long I could; but, fortunately for this week's article, they are rich in white bedders. *The Bride* and *White Perfection* being the best two which I have yet seen, and I have tried a hundred too many of them. *Miss Harcourt*, *Monarch*, and *Mont Blanc*, are the next best. *Princess Royal* kept her ground for three or four years, but is now discarded as only a fourth or fifth-rate variety. Then, there is the old *teucrioides* for those who delight in sweet perfume;

and there is another old one equally sweet but not so white: it is called *fragrans*, and *teucrioides carnea*, and I know not how many more names beside. *Carnea* is better than *teucrioides* for furnishing bouquets, as it is flat-headed, and comes in for a circular row in *those huge bundles of flowers* which are *fashionable*, but certainly *not tasteful* bouquets.

Where verbena beds are liable to *mildew*, the plants ought to be dusted once a fortnight, from the turn of Midsummer to the middle of August, with equal quantities of soot and flowers of sulphur. The sulphur is the real agent to arrest the progress of the mildew, but it looks ill for a while; whereas its own bulk of soot will give it somewhat of the same tint as the leaves of many kinds of plants. The way to apply the dusting is to make a little mop, with soft matting, about six inches round; tie it on the end of a stick 18 inches long; mix the soot and sulphur in a flower-pot saucer, dip your new mop in the mixture, and press it down that it may get a good pinch; then hold the mop in your left hand, and push it down among the plants until it is nearly touching the soil of the bed; then, with your right hand, strike gently against the handle of the mop, and the dust will fly in all directions, and reach the underside of the leaves, where it will be safe for some time from the effects of dew or rain; but the work should only be done on dry days. If this dose is applied twice before any symptoms of the mildew are seen, the chances are that it will not appear for that season; but the process is so simple, that to make sure of the remedy it would be better to continue applying it as late as August.

The *White Salvia patens* closes my list of white bedders.

SCARLET COLOURS.—I shall follow with this brilliant colour, because, of all the combinations of the colours of flowers, scarlet and white are, generally, the most pleasing. Here, again, if we begin with the lowest plants, we must recur to these puzzling *verbenas*; but they also are rich in scarlets, of many tints from orange to crimson-scarlet; and of all sizes, from *Boul de Feu*—which is so dwarf as to require to be grown in the very richest compost to get it to spread over the soil at all—to *Robinson's Defiance*, which is strong enough for field culture.

Boul de Feu (The Fire-ball) is still the best of the very low scarlet verbenas for a narrow bed, but requires to be planted in the richest soil. The first nine inches of the bed should be one-half very rotten leaf-mould or old dung. The colour is an orange-scarlet. The next best is *Inglefield scarlet*, or *fulgens*, which is a brilliant dark scarlet or crimson. By planting these two together in one bed, and alternately, the effect produced is much better than either of them alone; and this arrangement holds good with all the scarlet and pink verbenas, and with some of the purple ones. Indeed, three shades of these colours answer better; the only difficulty being to find plants exactly of the same height and strength; for unless they are so, the mixture cannot have a good effect. The whole bed should appear to a stranger to be made up with one plant only, and that one producing three shades of the given colour. The only other verbena that I could ever mix with Boul de feu and Inglefield scarlet is the old *Melindres latifolia*, which is more red than either of the other. These three may be mixed safely together; and, when the soil is rich and suitable for them, there is nothing in the whole range of flowers which will at all come near to them in brilliancy of colour.

Satellite and *Emperor of Scarlets* are two beautiful bedders, and both of them will associate in one bed, and produce a better scarlet bed than either of them by itself; and, for a large bed, the *Wonder of Scarlets* would come in for the outside row, as it is not so strong a grower. *Gladiator*, *Captivation*, and *Tweediana grandi-*

flora are three fine ones of an orange scarlet, with good habit, but their effect is not improved by being planted together. These are the best scarlets for ordinary beds of all that I have seen. *Robinson's Defiance* has the largest head of flowers of all the scarlets, but it is such a strong grower that ordinary people can hardly find beds large enough to do it justice, and it is not suitable for a small bed. I shall try it this season for a small bed, by way of experiment, under a different treatment from any that has been recorded for flower-beds; and I shall be much disappointed if the plan does not answer; and I should like to hear that others have made the same experiment, as it would be a great loss to let down such a splendid plant. I purpose putting it into a circular bed about a yard across, and to plant it 18 inches from plant to plant. As soon as the plants get a good hold of the soil, and begin to spread freely, I shall give the bed a good watering, pat down the soil rather firm, and then concrete the whole surface; this concrete I shall make with one spadeful of fresh slaked lime, four spadesful of rough sand, or fine gravel, and as much soot as will give it a dark colour like the ordinary soil, with mortar sufficient to form a thick mixture, which will be spread over the bed about a quarter of an inch in depth. If the colour does not please me, I shall sprinkle a little dry earth over the concrete while it is yet soft; and, by the time it is dry, it will "set" as hard as Roman cement, and no rain will get through it, but the bed will be moist enough for the roots all the season. My object in this experiment is to keep the plants from rooting at the joints, and thus compel them to feed from the original roots *only*. If the fore part of the summer should be wet, as is not at all unlikely after so much dry weather this spring, this plan will prevent this *Defiance* (a most vulgar name, by the way,) from getting the benefit of it.

GERANIUMS.—Scarlet geraniums are as plentiful as blackberries; and *Tom Thumb* is the best of them for small beds, but, like many more of them, it does not answer on some soils. I can make nothing of it, nor of the *Improved Frogmore*, which is the next best dwarf. Our calcareous light soil is inimical to the whole race of the Frogmore breed, to which Tom Thumb belongs.

D. BEATON.

GREENHOUSE AND WINDOW GARDENING.

LITTLE MATTERS: *Potting, &c.*—No great results can be expected in gardening when the operators can be induced to attend to certain things only, at particular times and seasons. Though many, therefore, may be inclined to smile at the vast amount of lore that was requisite for a gardener of the "ancient times," when almost every plant had to be sown and gathered, &c., under the influence of certain planets, and a certain day of the moon's age, it cannot be doubted, but that a portion of the assiduity and attention manifested by the knights of the spade *then*, would tell beneficially upon our practice and experiments *now*. Such matters as the potting and reshifting of plants require to be attended to at all seasons; and the delaying of such operations until several more plants may be attended to at the same time, is often productive of such results, that the doing of them at all becomes a matter of no importance. But whilst we hold that plants should thus be attended to, at all seasons, according to their requirements, still the spring time of the year—when branches and roots are receiving new vigour—may be considered the chief period when the greatest number of plants will thus require our good offices.

Geraniums for late summer and autumn blooming; *Fuchsias* that have stood in their last year's pots, and are now breaking freely; early *Annuals* that have been previously pricked off, and which are intended to be grown in pots, either in the window or the conservatory; *Epacrises* and *Heaths* that have done flowering, have been cut back and are now firm, having been kept close, beginning to break nicely; *Camellias* and early *Azaleas* that have finished flowering, and have commenced to make fresh wood; with all such plants as early flowering *Acacias*, *Correas*, *Cytisuses*, &c., will receive much benefit from being looked over, and obtaining what they require in the way of fresh soil, and more room at the roots.

We know that there is a diversity of opinion and practice among good gardeners, as to the time for fresh potting such plants as *Azaleas* and *Camellias*—some performing the operation, as we have advised, when the wood is beginning to grow freely, and others contenting themselves with doing so when growth is finished, and the flower buds are forming. So far as our own experience goes, we decidedly prefer the former method; having observed that the flowers are always finer than when the roots are disturbed late,—so much so, indeed, that, unless in extreme cases, instead of repotting *them* we should surface dress, and allow the plants to remain until the following season.

Having previously referred to the *soil*, which ought to be rendered open for the air to penetrate it, we will say nothing now, but that the degree of roughness and lumpiness in the soil should ever be in proportion to the size of the pot to be filled.

The Pots should be thoroughly clean. A nice plant has as great a diarelish for a dirty pot as a respectable labourer has for unchanged linen on a Sunday. Besides, there is no possibility of shifting the plant readily at a future time, if the pot is not scrupulously clean; for the ball will hang in detached pieces to the side of the dirty pot, instead of coming out at the slightest tap as whole and entire as a piece of cheese. Except in summer, pots should always be kept dry; and a wet day should be chosen to wash them thoroughly inside and outside, before placing them in their *appropriate* bins. This latter operation should be rigidly enforced, and a fine imposed for carelessness, as vast numbers of pots are broken from being put down in a higgledy-piggledy manner—large and small in one perplexing confusion.

The Blackheath Registered Pot is not only useful, but very interesting to amateurs when growing large plants, the bottom of the pot being nearly all moveable. When a block of wood is placed beneath it, so as to rest upon this moveable part, and pressure applied to the pot above, the ball is thus elevated so as to enable the examination of the roots to take place with much less risk of breakage and damage to the ball than when it is struck out in the usual way. Much stress has been laid by some upon soft-burned pots, but we are not admirers of them ourselves, as they generally soon get green and greasy. With care, most of those plants that the amateur delights in may be grown in hard china, and glazed earthenware vessels, in hard vases made of various compositions, of ground stone and clay, and even in those made of cast metal; but then in all such cases *particular* attention must be bestowed upon

Draining.—This should be attended to, not merely by placing potsherds, &c., at the bottom of the pot in the usual way, but turfy pieces of soil, lumps of charcoal, and broken pots and tiles must be mingled pretty freely along with the compost. In draining, in general, a number of pieces of tile, broken pots, &c., laid in a hollow manner over the hole in the bottom of the pot, will answer well enough where, from the position of the pot afterwards, there is no likelihood of worms gaining an entrance at the bottom. But where, from the future position of the plant, there is a danger that these—in other respects useful cultivators, but in a pot such perfect bores—should be likely to find an entrance, then the tile or potsherd should be placed with its convex side over the hole in the bottom of the pot, and then a number of pieces should be so arranged over it, and by *its side*, with a small handful of clean washed gravel or pebbles, or potsherds over them, and a little green moss, or chopped straw over all. The water will get down, and escape between the bottom of the pot and the tile, though a small worm would not be able to *wriggle* itself in. The chopped straw, or the moss, is necessary for this plan, as otherwise the water would wash down the fine earth, which concentrating around the potsherd with its convex side over the hole, the plant would be in danger of becoming water-logged. Our amateur friends should always endeavour to have a little green moss for this purpose, as independently of thus securing drainage it also acts as an equaliser of moisture—parting with water when excessive, but retaining a portion for a long time before it becomes quite dry. Those who wish to secure drainage and keep out worms more *neatly*, should have a number of little caps or bowls made of tin, zinc, or galvanised iron, from one inch to two or three inches in diameter and in depth, the bottom terminating in a convex point. By placing the open part or mouth of the bowl over the hole in the bottom of the pot, and surrounding the cap with drainage in the usual way, there will be no danger of the water not finding an outlet.

In *repotting*, the common method (and which for small plants cannot be improved upon) is to spread the palm and fingers of the left hand over the surface of the pot and soil, to turn the pot topsy-turvy, and holding its bottom, now uppermost, with the right hand, strike the side of the pot farthest from you on the side of the potting-bench; and while the ball of the plant rests in your left hand, the right hand puts aside the old pot, and is ready to assist in transferring the plant with its roots into the new soil. But before that is done, several things must be looked after. First—though you see no worms, notice if there be no worm tracks; because if there be, ten to one the sleek cunning fellow is ensconsed in the centre of your ball, and thence you must dislodge him, by boring through the ball with a piece of wire, or very thin wood. Secondly—observe the depth at which the plant previously stood in the pot, and do not place it deeper in the new, but rather scrape away a quantity of the surface soil, that you may be enabled to put a little fresh there. Hundreds of plants are killed by covering the stem of the plant too deeply; and thousands of forest trees meet with a lingering existence from the same cause. As a general rule—the *collar* of the plant, that is, the place from which roots and stem respectively start, should not be much, if at all, covered. Thirdly—observe whether the roots are densely matted on the outside of the ball; and what then? I can recollect the period, when in such cases he considered himself a clever fellow who could take his knife and slice off all such matted roots with as much gusto as the shepherd cuts up turnips for his sheep. This is bad. Gently disentangle the roots, and trace them out, so that they will form separate layers in the new soil you are going to give them. When traced out, jamming them all close together, as if you were fixing a gate-post, and the cutting them off in slices are alike specimens of barbarism. Fourthly—plants that have been shifted previously, and are merely to be grown on, require different treatment from those which have been standing during the winter in the pots in which they grew the previous summer. The first will want little done to the roots, and little soil to be removed, the old drainage being chiefly taken away. The others must have the roots examined, traced, pruned if necessary, and as much as possible of the old soil got rid of.

When the soil is all nicely packed about them again, the plants must be kept *close*, watered, shaded from

bright sun, and frequently syringed, to check transpiration, until they have fairly commenced making fresh roots and top growth. R. FISH.

HOTHOUSE DEPARTMENT.

EXOTIC ORCHIDACEÆ.

ROUTINE WORK FOR APRIL.—Continue to *pot* all plants that begin to shew growth; such plants as *Catasetums, Mormodes,* and *Cyonoches,* must now be growing, and ought to be potted forthwith. As the sun increases in power let the *shades* be let down earlier in the day; if the house is of the aspect we have described (that is, facing east and west) the shades should be let down on the east side as early as nine o'clock A.M. when the sun shines clearly—it may remain down till one, and then be drawn up; at 12 let down the shade on the west side, and draw it off as the sun declines. If the house is a lean-to facing the noon-day sun, the shade will neither be required so early in the morning nor to be kept on so long in the afternoon. On all dull days the shades will not be necessary at all; the grand object to aim at is to give orchids all the light possible without sunshine. The *syringe* may now be used pretty freely, as most of the plants are, or ought to be, growing rapidly. When the house is shut up, the shades drawn up, and everything set right to be left for the evening, then syringe the plants and every part of the house. Leave it hot and moist, and in the morning you will find your plants looking fresh, clean, and healthy. The *heat* may be increased now almost to the maximum; always remembering that the heat of the day ought to exceed the heat of the night 10° at the least; this gives the plants time to consolidate their growth, for if by great heat and moisture any plant is forced into growth as much and as fast as in the day, the apparent growth is not real; it is only, as it were, drawn out like wire; but let the plants have their night's rest and they will start strongly and freely during the day. *Water*, also, may be given in greater abundance, and more often, as the season advances, and the compost appears to dry more than in the dark short days. In the application of water much judgment must be exercised; the quantity required either from the syringe or watering-pot depending greatly upon the weather externally: if it be cloudy, rainy, and cold, so that no air can be given, the water will not evaporate so freely; and as the young shoots are very tender, if the water lodges in or near them for 24 hours it is almost sure to destroy them. The time has not come yet to give abundance of water; we shall not forget to remind our orchid-loving friends when it does arrive.

The warm weather will bring to life myriads of *insects;* these must be diligently sought for and destroyed. One of the most destructive, even to the most valuable plants—such as Aerides, Saccolabiums, Vandas, and the like—is a very small insect, which in its young state is white, but when full grown turns black; it is known amongst gardeners by the name of the *Black Thrip.* This insect congregates on the under sides of the leaves, old as well as young, and sucking out their juices causes them to turn yellow, become spotty, and eventually perish. There are no insects so difficult to destroy, though frequent washing of the leaves will prevent their increase. The following has been found to be a good method to clear the houses of this pest; it may be used successfully in the common stove also when the thrip is observed there:—Procure some flowers of sulphur (half a pound will be enough for a stove 50 feet long), as soon as the house is shut up mix the sulphur with a gallon of water, and with a common whitewash brush apply it to the warm pipes all round the house. Do this quickly, so as to have the greatest amount of sulphur vapour at once; then have some tobacco, or good tobacco paper, (the latter we find the most effectual) put some red hot cinders into an iron trivet, or a common garden pot will answer moderately well, put the tobacco paper pulled in pieces upon the cinders, and with a pair of small bellows blow at the cinders so as to raise a great cloud of smoke without blazing, which must be continued till the house is full. The trivet is an instrument made of sheet iron, standing upon three legs, in the form of a cylindrical garden pot, about seven inches across and nine deep, with a handle to it for the convenience of carrying it round the house. Should there appear any tendency to a flame, have a fine rosed watering pot handy, and sprinkle the tobacco slightly; this will prevent it bursting out into a flame, which would be very destructive to the leaves of the plants. These two vapours combined will destroy, most certainly, the thrip; but it will be necessary to repeat it the third night following to destroy any young ones that may be hatched into life in the interval; it will also effectually destroy the green fly, which sometimes makes its appearance in the orchid house. There are some other insects destructive to the young roots and flower shoots, the remedies for which we must give at an early opportunity.

FLORISTS' FLOWERS.

DAHLIAS.—Continue to put in cuttings of such as spring late; but, unless wanted for sale, by no means make too many plants; one or two of each variety to be kept in pots for next year will be very desirable, as these keep better than the large roots taken up out of the ground. The early struck cuttings should be repotted two or three times, so as to be stout plants to plant out as soon as the frosts are over.

PINKS.—The plants of this lovely fragrant flower will now be growing. The soil should be frequently stirred between the rows to let in the spring showers, do this with a small, short, three-pronged fork; taking care not to come too near the roots. Prepare sticks in good time to support the flower stems, so as to be ready as soon as they require it.

PANSIES that have been planted out some time will require the same treatment as the pinks; that is, the soil on the surface should be frequently stirred. This operation freshens the plants greatly, not only by allowing the rain to enter the soil freely, but also admits the air to the roots, which does them good to a greater extent than most cultivators are aware of.

RANUNCULUS.—In such severe weather as we have had lately, and in very heavy rainy weather, it will be desirable to shelter them with canvas covers. The soil, too, of the beds should be frequently stirred, or it will become baked and beaten on the surface, which will prevent the plants springing up freely.

TULIPS.—The same precautions must be used with these, and even to a greater degree, as they will be further advanced, and therefore in more danger from wet afternoons followed by a late spring frost. It is better always to be safe by constantly covering up every night, as yet, than to neglect one apparently fine evening and find them frost-bitten in the morning.

PICOTEES.—Last week we promised a list of the best selected kinds suitable for a new beginner, and we now fulfil that promise.

Red Edged.	per pair.	
	s.	d.
Ernest (Edmonds'), light edged, extra fine	5	0
Isabella (Wildman's), heavy edged, extra fine	5	0
Mrs. Bevan (Burroughes'), middling edged, very fine	2	6
Gem (Youell's), light edge, extra fine flower	5	0
King James (Headly's), heavy edge, small but good	5	0
Jenny Lind (Edmonds'), light edge, quite unique	5	0

Purple Edged.	per pair.	
	s.	d.
Enchantress (Mathews'), finest purple light edge, extra	3	6
Duke of Newcastle (Burroughes'), light edge, extra	2	6
Juliet (May's), heavy edge, an extra fine flower	5	0
Portia (May's), heavy edge, a good strong growing kind	3	6
Lady Chesterfield (Brindley's), heavy edge, extra fine	2	0
President (Burroughes'), heavy edge, fine	2	6

The above 12 picotees are really fine, distinct varieties, which any one growing for exhibition ought to procure. Scarlet edged and yellow picotees next week.

T. APPLEBY.

THE KITCHEN-GARDEN.

CABBAGE.—Some varieties of the early autumn planted cabbages may, through the late continuance of severe frost and drought, have a tendency to start into flower, instead of turning into or forming heads. When the weather becomes milder, such should be cut at once for present use; the stumps of them may be left, as these will produce a quantity of sprouts, and with some varieties such sprouts as form themselves into nice little cabbages, instead of seed sprouts, which are found useful in succession. The early cabbages we cut as fast as they become ready, clearing the stumps and bottom leaves for cattle, &c.; and when cleared, let the ground be prepared for Ridge cucumbers, Scarlet-runners, and Kidney beans, &c.

CAULIFLOWERS.—Those grown on some soils are infested, to an injurious extent, as soon as the hot weather sets in, with a little white grub, so numerous and destructive, that the prospect of a fine healthy crop is often blighted. Chimney soot and salt incorporated with the manure-water, and applied at this season, is the best preventive we can recommend. Plant out now in succession; prick off and encourage the growth of the spring sown plants, and sow another pinch of seed. Cauliflowers under hand-glasses should be well supplied with manure water. The glasses should be raised in due season; first, by forming with the spade a little ridge of earth all round for the glass to stand on, which forms a shelter as well as a basin for watering. Although the weather has been extremely severe, and nearly every night throughout this month from 2° to 8° of frost, with ice an inch thick sometimes lying unmelted throughout the day, notwithstanding the clear and sunny state of the atmosphere,—and the earth has been so deeply frozen that the plough has been stopped, more particularly on the 25th and 26th instants, on places where turnips had lately been fed off, nevertheless, with us the hand-glass cauliflowers, sown the beginning of October, which were grown through the short days in pots, and turned out on a kindly preparation of soil the first week in February, are now large strong plants, such as will produce good sized cauliflowers by the 20th or 25th of April. The good varieties of cauliflowers are worthy of considerable attention, as they may be produced in good supply throughout the whole year; and a handsome-shaped delicate white cauliflower we find as much esteemed by the kitchen folks as the double white camellia is by others.

AUTUMN SOWN CARROTS.—To push these forward they should be supplied with weak tepid manure-water, and be well surface stirred. Keep them shut up early if under glass, and in every way encourage them to make a rapid root-growth without too much top-growth; these are matters which may be easily managed by a little forethought and judgment.

CAPE BROCOLI should be sown in succession in small quantities, as old plants of this variety are worthless to plant out. A small sowing may now be made of the *Malta White, Wilcove, Walcheren, Chapple's White,* and *Late Purple* varieties, or of any other esteemed kinds.

ROUTINE WORK.—The present is a good season of the year to renew, replant, or make new plantations of *herbs*. The varieties of *mint* delight in rich, open, and rather light, moist soil, and should be planted partially in the shade; when the shoots have obtained the length of two or three inches they should be pulled up with a portion of root, and be dibbled at the distance each way from one another of about six inches. *Tarragon* requires a similar treatment. *Chives* and *sorrel* should be parted and replanted. *Chamomile* and *pennyroyal* should be planted in single shoots one foot apart. *Burnet, thyme, winter savory, sweet basil,* and *marjoram* should be sown. The last season's herb-bed should be top-dressed, and, where intended to remain, well forked; and *sage* should be pegged down and layered.

JAMES BARNES.

MISCELLANEOUS INFORMATION.

OUR VILLAGE WALKS.
(No. 24.)

I ALWAYS look with interest at the garden of a little cottage which stands at the entrance of the village near which I live. It belongs to a steady, industrious sawyer, who supports a widowed mother and sister, and who takes great pains with his allotment and this little garden. There are in it a nice row of gooseberry bushes, a little patch of raspberry plants, a bed for cabbages, onions, mustard and cress, &c.; in the proper season, a flower border, two or three plum-trees, a large plant or two of lavender, and a shed for the wheelbarrow; and yet it is so small, that the owner seems too large for his garden—as if one step would carry him over the paling into the road. Not a bit of the soil is neglected; all is doing its duty; and the produce invariably looks healthy and well. A fuchsia decorates a part of the cottage wall, and in the flowering season its bright crimson blossoms hang abundantly from the graceful sprays. A little petted cottage garden is a beautiful sight at every season; and the one of which I am now writing is never untidy, even in the winter. There is neatness in its desolation; and it seems to wake up from its needful rest sooner than any other garden in the neighbourhood. There is nothing at all attractive in its situation; the buildings and sheds near it are neither picturesque nor neat enough to be pleasing; yet this little garden is a pleasant object for the eye to rest upon as we pass by; and if it were ever to be built upon, or pass into careless hands, I should miss it exceedingly.

Some little cottages possess a strip of garden, which, although not by any means sufficient for the use of the family, might yet, by cultivation, produce much more than they do now. I do not think that gooseberries or raspberries are at all *desirable* for the *poor* man, where his garden is a small one. Unless they are grown in sufficient quantities to sell, they occupy the ground unprofitably, and should give place to vegetables. But I sometimes see nice little bits of ground yielding so little, that it may almost be called lying waste; and ground is so valuable in all cases, that not an inch should be suffered to lie idle, or carry less produce than it might be made to do. Cabbages, onions, and leeks, are so useful and wholesome, that they should be put in wherever they will grow. A good crop of the former is a help to the family in the summer, and a store of onions is a treasure for winter use. A basin of onion porridge is a warm, comfortable dinner or supper, to moisten and flavour the crust of bread; and in case of colds and coughs, taken at bedtime, it is an excellent remedy, healing and good for the chest. Leeks are extremely wholesome too, and afford a nourishing meal when well boiled; so much so, that they are highly esteemed and extensively grown in Wales, and might be a valuable addition to the poor man's garden in England, if they were better understood. I have seen tender young leeks served on a toast like sea-kale, and much liked by those to whom the flavour was agreeable; but in general they seem little considered or used. A little bed of herbs would be very useful too. A plant or two of white-mint, rue, horehound, sage, common mint, chamomile, rosemary, thyme, &c.,

would often turn to good account in case of sickness, and help a less thrifty neighbour. Indeed, chamomile should fill a little space itself, for it is so fine a medicine, and so excellent as an outward application, that it should occupy as much of the ground as can conveniently be spared. A herb garden would be a treasure in a village. How many little ailments there are for which the healing virtue of these simple plants is beneficial; and how often we pass from cottage to cottage in an unsuccessful search for them. The very smell of chamomile flowers seems to assuage pain, so well known are its soothing qualities to us all; and a large bag of them, dried for use, would ease many an aching face or joint, and save many a penny to the poor. Some plants of the valuable tutsan (of which I have already spoken) should be in every garden, to apply to cuts and wounds, if slight, and to severe ones also if medical aid is distant. It is a rich, ornamental-looking plant; as the foliage, during some part of the year, is of a brownish green, and in the autumn it becomes blood-red. The healing virtue of this plant is remarkable.

The cottager has not much in his power to do for his fellow men, when money or time are required. Of the first, he has none; of the last, his daily labour takes up the largest part; but a kindly heart will always try to do something, particularly when it serves, in simplicity, a Master who blesses the "cup of cold water" only "given in the name of a disciple." A herb-bed for the use of the sick is a work of love, not to be despised because it may *seem* trifling. A handful of chamomile flowers, or a cup of mint tea, may soothe the pains or cool the parched lips of a suffering fellow-creature; and is this, with a word of Christian sympathy to enrich the gift, a trifle?

There is some spare time for labourers, in the long days when work is over, that might be profitably spent in cultivating vegetables; and this makes it sad to see idle men and boys lounging in a village street, having nothing to occupy their evening hours. The allotments, indeed, where they exist at all, employ many who frequently toil on them till it is quite dark; and I have often heard the pleasant sound of the spade even by moonlight. But still, in a populous village there are a great number who really have no ground to till, except, perhaps, an atom of damp earth behind their dwellings. It would be a work of *rational*, doubly-beneficial charity—a means of doing unspeakable good—to let, or rent for the purpose of letting, to the poor pieces of land near every village; so that as many as possible, if not all the cottagers, should have a portion of ground to cultivate. Industrious characters would thus be materially assisted in providing for their families, and men of lazy habits *might* be encouraged to amend. I myself know an allotment tenant, who has held his quarter of an acre for upwards of twenty years. During the last seventeen, his wife has been a cripple confined to her bed, and unable to move without his assistance. Before and after his working hours, he has been engaged in placing her aching frame in easier positions; at his dinner hour he always came home to move her also; his nights were as weary as the days, from her painful restlessness; and yet *I know* that he has been on his land at three and four o'clock on summer mornings, to cultivate and attend to it. Should not all such men be encouraged? If boys were induced to rent and manage small gardens, it might be the means of keeping them from idle and wicked practices; give them early habits of industry, and an interest in honest employment too.

Gentlemen residing in a parish have much power to do good by promoting and encouraging garden cultivation; and the farmers, if they would but aid a good cause, might do a great deal, and benefit themselves in their turn. The rates—that perpetual source of vexation in almost every parish—might be diminished, or kept within due bounds by this system. And although this *ought* to be the last consideration when endeavouring to do good, yet we are compelled to admit that too often it is the first. Farmers are greedy of their land; but small portions let off would do such a world of good to so many, that they could scarcely regret them, and would feel happy in knowing they were at least trying to help the poor and needy. In "making money" we are very apt (to use a homely phrase) to "reckon without our host." We think it is our own, to do with as we please; forgetting that there is One who has a *first claim* upon everything we possess. "But ye say, wherein have we robbed thee? In tithes and offerings!"

Let *farmers* remember this; and when they grumble at the times and at the poor, let them remember, too, that "he that giveth to the poor, lendeth to the Lord!"

CHEESE-MAKING.

THERE are very few domestic operations which have not, in some form or other, been facilitated by the aids of modern science. The increased facilities, thus afforded, have extended even to dairy operations. Butter, cheese, and milk have all been better managed since the food of cows has been more correctly understood, and better varieties of roots introduced for winter keep. The progress of improvement has, of necessity, been far from rapid, because of the little correct knowledge generally possessed on the subject, and the very varying action of the food from even adjoining grass pastures upon the quantity and quality of the milk of the cow. This paucity of information has been peculiarly the case in the instance of cheese dairying; still something has been done: some few improved "cheese crumbs" have been recently gathered, and it is to these to which I propose to confine my attention in this cattle paper. As I had occasion to remark in another valuable periodical (Bell's Messenger), the art and mystery of cheese-making has been left chiefly (as in the olden time) to the care and skill of the dairymaid and the farmer's wife; and they have, in many instances, made observations and produced results which the philosopher has not always very successfully explained. Our ignorance, however, on these points affords us ample reasons for gathering together the little modern improvements which have been made in cheese-making in different localities. Produced from the milk of domestic animals, it will be well to remind the young dairy-keeper of what that milk is commonly composed. This has been given in a tabular form by Professor J. F. Johnston. One hundred parts of milk then contain—

	Of the Cow.	Goat.
Casein or curd	4 5	4 1
Butter	3 1	3 3
Milk sugar	4 8	5 3
Saline matter	0 6	0 6
Water	87 0	86 7

The Cheshire practice of cheese-making has been described at considerable length by Mr. H. Wright (Journal R. A. S., vol. vi., p. 102). From that essay the practical portion of the details may be gleaned. The operations in four different Cheshire dairies are given by him in a tabular form; No. 1 and 2 of these dairies were in Bucklow Hundred, No. 3 in Nantwich Hundred, and No. 4 in Eddisbury Hundred. The milk produced from these at two milkings, except No. 2, which was from four milkings, and the number of the cows, were as follows:—

	Date.	Cows.	Gals. of milk.
No. 1	Nov. 21	44	43
—	Aug. 17	48	112
2	Oct. 13	10	24
3	Aug. 18	26	56
4	Aug. 19	53	107

The temperature of this milk when the rennet was put in, and of the dairy-room in which the cheese was made, the salt used internally, and the weight of the cheese a day or two after making, were—

	Temp. of milk.	Temp. of Dairy.	Salt lb. oz.	Weight lb.
No. 1	83°	68°	1 1	55
2	78		0 4	
3		78	1 0	60
4	77	64 to 69	4 4	

The recent improvements which have been gradually introduced into Cheshire since the days of Dr. Holland, who long since described its agriculture, has been given by Mr. W. Palin (ibid, vol. v., p. 88). The first process of breaking down the curd in the cheese-tub is now generally performed by a breaker or curd-cutter, the dairy-maid alone walking round the tub, and pressing the breaker slowly through the curd at first, and more rapidly as she proceeds with her work, until it is reduced to small particles, when it sinks to the bottom of the tub. This practice supersedes the old mode of three women kneeling round the tub, and breaking the curd with their fingers. The next improvement is the curd-mill, which is for the purpose of breaking the curd after being drained from the whey in the cheese-vat, before finally putting it under the press, instead of the old tedious plan of again breaking it with the hands. The greatest improvement, however, yet effected, is by the introduction of a lever-press, which is self-acting, and may be used during the process of making. This invention renders unnecessary the previous custom of kneeling upon and pressing the cheese with a board, or two or three persons thrusting it with their hands, or pressing it for a time, before placing it under the heavy stone press. The great advantage of this machine consists in its being regulated by a small weight on the beam, by which the pressure upon the cheese can be increased or diminished at pleasure. It is also portable; and as warmth is very essential during the time of pressing, especially in cold weather, it can be conveniently removed to any warm situation. Artificial heat is now introduced into many cheese-rooms, either by means of hot-air stoves, or steam conveyed in cast-iron pipes through the rooms, for the purpose of forwarding the ripening of the cheese. By these means, large dairies, which formerly were scarcely ever marketable before April or May, are now sold as early as October or November.

In all dairy operations an attention to the temperature of the milk and of the dairy-room seems most important—an attention which it will be highly important to regulate by the thermometer. This seemed to be generally admitted at a recent practical discussion at one of the meetings of the Burton-on-Trent Farmers' Club, the report of which may be perused by the young cheese-maker with considerable advantage (Farmers' Magazine, vol. xxxi. p. 531):—"I have found," observed Mr. Gretton, one of the practical dairy owners who addressed the meeting, "that with a heat of from 82 to 86 degs. when the rennet is applied, the curd will separate from the whey; and I consider it desirable to use the lowest temperature which will insure the clearness of the whey. But as the curd is tender when gathered from milk at that temperature, I have adopted the plan of rendering it firm by pouring over it water or whey, heated to a given point. This method is often pursued, but seldom, I believe, with the exactness necessary to insure its constant success. All depends on the degree of heat at which the liquor is applied. My experience goes to prove that if the curd be raised to the heat of about 84 to 86 degs., it becomes sufficiently firm for all the ends it is desirable to attain.

"I believe that cheese-makers generally who scale the curd do not use a sufficient quantity of liquor for the purpose, and make it too hot; and in such cases it is obvious that a part of the curd which first comes in contact with the hot liquor will become raised very much above 84 degrees. I have therefore taken care to use a larger quantity of liquor at a lower temperature. The quantity of liquor which we use for curd, which yields 44 lb of dry cheese, is nine gallons, at a temperature of 94 to 98 degrees, according to the degree of heat of the curd in the pan.

"You will at once see that unless a thermometer be used, this operation would be liable to such a degree of uncertainty as would effectually prevent the cheese of one day being like that of another. I cannot, therefore, too strongly point out to you that this instrument ought to be an invariable article of furniture in the dairy. To reduce the milk from 98, at which heat it comes from the cow, to 82 or 84, at which we put the rennet to it, we have sometimes added cold water, and sometimes cooled part of the milk in shallow vessels. I have observed no ill effect from the addition of cold water; but, perhaps, when other conveniences are at hand for cooling the milk quickly, it may be advisable to use them in preference to cold water.

"Saltpetre is added to the milk after the proportion of half an ounce to 50 gallons. The time allowed before breaking up the curd is the same as I stated in my account of my first year's make; but instead of gathering by hand as we did part of the first year, a gatherer (the invention of Mr. Carington, of Creighton, near Uttoxeter) is used, with some alterations which I have made in it. I have enlarged the gatherer so as to make it fit the inside of the cheesepan, and have applied a screw instead of weights to compress the curd, and have added a small pump to remove the whey. This gatherer causes a saving of labour, and while it presses the whey from the curd, removes less curd and butter in the whey; I, therefore, recommend its use to all cheese-makers."

The different quality of cheese produced from different soils was alluded to at the same meeting, by Mr. H. Yates. On some soils there is certainly, as he remarked, great difficulty in making cheese of good quality, the poorest land usually producing the best cheese. The same management in Derbyshire which succeeds on poor land, yields heavy or sweet cheese on rich land. It is found in that county that a warm room up stairs, employed as a cheese-room, will render the cheese liable to sweetness. Another farmer who attended the meeting, making cheese from 90 acres of land, added, "it is only on 50 acres that my dairy-man can make good cheese;" when his cows are turned on to certain pastures, the cheese, it seems, in spite of all his care, will "heave." Mr. Bernays very justly thought that the quality of the cheese must naturally depend upon the age of the cow, the state of its health, the distance it has to traverse in search of food, and on the quality of the herbage. Pastures with a plentiful deep green herbage will yield a milk richer in butter than cheese, whilst the contrary is the case if the pasturage appear lean. The heaving of the cheese, the assembled farmers seemed to agree, is caused by a fermentation in the whey left in it; gases are formed which exposed the coats of the cheese. In some dairies, however, the heaving of cheese can scarcely be prevented. The difficulty, Mr. Gretton thought, arose from it not being easy in those places to get such a curd as will allow the whey to be well pressed from it. There is always great risk of heaving if the whey is not well pressed out. These practical observations will be of service to many a young beginner, and may not be without their use, even to the experienced owner of dairy farms. Their perusal, too, may serve to convince the general reader that there is no department of the farmer's very difficult vocation that does not require the exercise of much more vigilance and skill than is believed by those who are much too apt to decry what they cannot understand.   CUTHBERT W. JOHNSON.

LUCERN.

IN accordance with the wish of many correspondents, we have to state as our opinion, that Lucern is the most profitable crop that the cottager or any one else can grow for a supply of green food for his cow, horse, goat, and rabbits. It may be cultivated in any nook not over-shadowed with trees, though it will yield more abundantly if grown, as it well deserves, upon a portion of the main quarters of the allotment plot. On the merits of the plant we have lately seen a letter published by Mr. Moore, Curator of the Glasnevin Botanic Garden, at Dublin, and it is so applicable to our present purpose, that we shall quote it as follows:—

"Lucern appears particularly well suited for being cultivated on the light gravelly, or lime stone soils. It is also well adapted for the soiling system, which is every day becoming more general among the holders of small pieces of land—a class to whom I would beg specially to recommend a trial of Lucern. It is easy to cultivate, and will remain permanently in the soil for a great number of years, without losing any of its vitality or productiveness. The young plants soon arrive at a state of growth when they yield a good produce, which continues to increase during the first three years or so, when their vigour continues unabated for a considerable period, if the soil be not too damp or boggy. The portion of the Botanic Garden allocated for the agricultural plants is composed of a thin gravelly soil, where the Lucern has been growing at least eight years, without receiving any kind of manure, and it is now as vigorous as ever it was. It is, however, well known that Lucern is greatly improved by top-dressing; and I would consider it a plant particularly suited for being affected by those stimulating artificial manures which act quickly; but even without manure, it will afford to be cut four times in the season, yielding a good crop each time. The first before the end of April, which is a circumstance greatly in its favour—that being the season when food for cattle is most required. My reasons for recommending the cultivation of this plant to the small farmers are, because it will yield a larger quantity of nutritive green food for cattle than most of our other agri-

cultural plants; because it may be cut earlier than any of our other plants, Italian ryegrass excepted; because it is well calculated for being grown in small, compact patches, where the economical division of land is an object; because it requires less labour, and less manure than other green crops; and, finally, because it will remain permanent in the soil, and produce a good crop ten or twelve years in succession.

"The best season for sowing Lucern has been proved to be March, or very early in April. It may, however, be sown on land from which early potatoes have been removed after midsummer, in which case it will have well established itself before winter; and after the potato crop the soil will be in a favourable state for the growth of the Lucern."

The best time for sowing Lucern, as is stated by Mr. Moore, is during the first fortnight of April. Let the plot intended to be sown be trenched, and the seed sown very thinly in drills twelve inches apart, and one and a half inch or two inches deep. The easiest way of delivering the seed, is by putting the seed into a pint bottle and having a quill inserted through the cork. The seed may be sown very thinly and evenly along each drill by the aid of this very simple contrivance. Twenty-four pounds of seed will be sufficient for an acre. Thin out the plants to eight inches apart, and keep them constantly free from weeds. This freedom from weeds is most important; and to effect it, the hoe must be thoroughly used once or twice after every cutting. Do not wait until the whole plot of Lucern is mown before you begin hoeing, but hoe every square yard between the rows as soon as the scythe lays it bare. It should have a dressing of manure every spring, and the best way of doing it is to take off with the spade about an inch of earth from between the first and second rows, and carry that earth to be used for the last rows. Then sprinkle the manure between the first and second rows, and cover it with an inch of earth pared off from between the second and third rows, and so on until the whole is similarly treated. Never dig between the rows, for the plants are much injured by their roots being cut and disturbed. You may cut the Lucern twice the first year, and three times annually afterwards.[*] It is most hearty, or nourishing, just as the flower-buds appear, and whilst in flower. If sown early in April, the first cutting from it will be in the course of August.

The *soil* best suited to Lucern is one that is light, but not stoney, on an open, gravelly, or chalky bottom. It cannot endure stagnant water to its roots, and on a wet clay it will not succeed at all, though on clay well-drained it may be grown.

The *manures* which may be applied to it advantageously, besides common dungs, are soot, malt dust, and guano.

The *amount of produce* is difficult to define; but the first cutting of an acre has been known to keep two horses for seven weeks; the second cutting kept them for the same period; and the third cutting kept them six weeks, a few oats being given them daily besides, during the whole time. An average produce of green Lucern from a square root at one cutting, is said to be full 100 pounds; and this quantity is enough for a cow for twenty-four hours. She ought to have only a little at a time, as she will be apt to be hoven, or blown, upon it as much as if fed upon clover. Pigs are fond of it, but like it best whilst young.

Lucern is the *Medicago sativa* of Botanists, and is native of various parts of Europe. Its employment as a fodder was known to the Romans, and is mentioned by its earliest writers under the name of *Medic*, yet it was not until the time of Philip Miller, the author of "The Gardener's Dictionary," that much was known about it in England; and even now it is not cultivated so extensively as its productive nature deserves.   G. W. J.

HINTS FOR HUMBLE HOUSEHOLDS.

No. 1.

MANY of the evils of which the English poor complain might be greatly mitigated by a proper knowledge of that which conduces more or less to the comfort of every family—

Cooking.—There is no country in the world where the

---

[*] In Ireland, and other moist mild situations, or seasons, it may be cut four times.

people grumble so much, and no country in which they take so little advantage of the good so providentially provided for them. In Germany, France, and Scotland, the poor people chiefly subsist on vegetable diet—animal food being a luxury seldom tasted; but in England it is either a question of meat or nothing. In families of working-men when a piece of beef or mutton is achieved, at a sacrifice of many other things absolutely necessary, it is taken to the baker's, where it is wastefully prepared; there being no other way apparently known of cooking it in a savoury or satisfactory manner; while amongst our neighbours, the Scotch, if a small piece of meat is got once in the week, it is cooked in a manner which affords comparatively nutritious food either for a larger number of persons or for a series of days. In France the support of the working people is prepared much in the same way—in soup, or savoury broth; animal food being little used even in the making of potages. I fear, that the receipts I mean to append to these few remarks may not reach the class for whom they are intended; but there is scarcely any family in the middling ranks of life who have not some poor neighbours or dependants, and it is the assistance of these families I solicit to aid me in making known the following simple receipts. Simple as these are, however, they require in practice time and attention, for nothing can be done in cooking without attention; and here an objection may be urged, as the time of a working man's wife is valuable, hence her resorting to the baker's, or the cookshop; but even supposing she by her labour earns a few shillings a week, I am fully persuaded that by attending to the wants of her little household, cooking for her husband and children satisfying grateful meals, she might save more than she earns. Dry, unsubstantial food creates wants which the beer shop too readily supplies; and in a week, more pennies may be muddled away than would provide at least one good meal. I have known a family of six children fed by the mother on bread and butter for dinner; a complaint being made at the same time of its unsatisfactory nature, and that the children could eat it till they became hungry again! When the husband was in employment, and a dinner was to be obtained, baked meat was of course the solace for former privation; and this was a remarkably industrious, well-doing woman; but she knew no better; with her there was no temporising between poor and rich fare, when her husband was in work they had a "bit of meat," or pudding, or sausages, every day, but when he was idle, the loaf supplied the wants of the family. This is a very common case I apprehend.

Fish might also be more used, and with advantage, in the dietary of humble families. To the higher class of housekeepers in London, it is a comparatively expensive article of consumption; but they go to the dearest market, and generally at an early hour in the day, when good prices are demanded; but towards evening a tradesman's wife may buy in her next day's dinner for very little; and in almost every neighbourhood there are stalls, where a tempting variety may always be had at a moderate price. But fish, more than anything, wants nice cooking; and here the good helpmate of the working-man must shew her skill in the preparation; for the humid modes of dressing fish, boiling and frying, are by no means either the most economical or the most palatable.

FISH AND SAUCE.—Take a few whitings when they are cheap, or haddocks, and cut off the heads, tails, and fins, which put into a saucepan with a pint and a half or a quart of water, according to the quantity of fish you may have. Add to this an onion or two sliced, and some heads of parsley; boil it for an hour and strain it. Put an ounce of butter in your saucepan with a tablespoonful of flour; brown this well, taking care it does not burn; pour in the liquor, add some more parsley chopped, and pepper, and salt. Cut your fish into pieces, and boil it in this sauce for a quarter of an hour.

Cod, or flounders, or any other white fish, will be found equally good dressed in this manner.

BAKED FISH.—Whitings, or haddocks, or flounders, or cod, are excellent baked. Lay your fish in a pie dish, or oven-pan; sprinkle amongst it some finely-shred onion, chopped parsley, and pepper and salt. Put an ounce of butter, or dripping, broken into small pieces, amongst the fish, fill up the dish with water, and bake for three quarters of an hour.

J. W.

EXTRACTS FROM CORRESPONDENCE.

BEES.—Seeing at page 299 a communication from one of your correspondents respecting a box of bees in his possession, I venture to make the following suggestion to him:—I should allow the bees to swarm, and immediately afterwards I would stupify the bees by means of fungus, and then cut away one half of the combs; I should then return the bees to the box, and the following year, after swarming, I should repeat the stupifying of the bees, and cut away the other half of the combs. The hole in the top might be easily made during the time the bees are lying in a stupified state.—A SUBSCRIBER.

CELERY CULTURE.—In your number for 3rd October last you inserted a communication from me, in which I mentioned that I was in the course of testing the plan recommended by Mr. Nutt and Mr. Turner in THE COTTAGE GARDENER for rearing celery, and promised to let you know how I succeeded, and which I found to answer best. I have now to say that, although owing to my own absence during a material part of the process, and my gardener's want of experience in the management of a frame, the plants were put out in a weak spindly state, I never before grow such celery. The stems were not perhaps such as would have carried a prize at a competition, but they were fine, large, solid celery, some of them of three and a half inches diameter.

As to the comparative merits of the plans, I would certainly be disposed to give the preference to Mr. Nutt's if I were growing for competition, for the plants grown according to his directions were, upon the whole, the heavier. To save manure and trouble, however, and for the purpose of producing splendid celery for the table, I shall content myself with Mr. Turner's. I do not say anything of Mr. Barnes's plan, because it was very late in the season before I tried it, and with inferior plants, which came to no size.

While I have the paper before me I would strongly recommend such of your readers as may be planting out new gooseberries to apply to Mr. Turner for them, and to follow his directions for planting—see vol. i., p. 138 of THE COTTAGE GARDENER. I got a few plants from him about this time last year, and put them in the ground strictly as he advises; last season I allowed a very few of the berries to come to maturity, to see what they were like—and such thumpers! and this spring, after careful pruning and training according to his directions, I have very handsome miniature bushes, full of promises of fruit.—C.

HUMEA ELEGANS.—Should you think the following experiment worthy of a place in THE COTTAGE GARDENER, it may be of some use to others:—"About the 10th of September, I sowed seeds of this graceful plant in equal parts of peat, leaf-mould, and sand; placed them in a shady part of a warm greenhouse; but, as the seedlings got up, I brought them forward into a lighter place. They remained in their seed-pots until the middle of February. I then potted them off into two inch pots, using the same compost as before, and encouraged them to grow as much as possible. When these pots are pretty well filled with roots, I again shift them into pots two sizes larger, using one part loam, one peat, two of leaf-mould, and a little sand. As they fill these pots, I bring them into a cooler house; I again give them another shift, about the end of June, into pots suitable to their size. I place them in a cold frame for the summer, and bring them back into the house about the first week in October. There they soon begin to show for flower, and I then give them a good soaking of weak manure-water twice a week. By this treatment, I have them in flower by the end of November, and they last until late in the spring, and have a very pretty appearance in the back row of a house.—CHARLES LEVETT, Bury St. Edmunds.

POTATOES.—It may be some use to the excellent writer of "Our Village Walks," to be informed that there is an excellent plan for cooking potatoes, which she would do well to communicate to her poor cottage friends. It is almost universally practised in the northern counties of England, and obviates all the evils she mentions that arise from boiling them in water: I allude to the plan of cooking them *by steam*. A tin-pan, with a lid, is made to fit on a saucepan, and has its bottom pierced full of small holes; the saucepan is employed in cooking any article for dinner—say, making broth, boiling fish, or turnips, carrots, &c.; and at the same time the steam from it passes through the perforated bottom of the upper pan, and most beautifully *boils* the potatoes, without any of the soddening effect of water-boiling. The potatoes should first be peeled, and the peelings put into the pig's tub. By this plan two operations are conducted at once—a bit of meat may be boiling, and broth making, while the steam is cooking the potatoes above. The worst potatoes are much improved by this mode of cooking, and the good ones come out like a flour-ball.

If the authoress of the Village Walks would like to have a *potato steamer*, I shall be glad to make her a present of one, to try and shew to her poorer friends for whom she shews such a kind sympathy; for I agree with her that anything one can do to increase the comforts and economise the resources of the poor, is both a duty and a pleasure. In the south, where fuel is scarce, it is an excellent plan to boil potatoes by steam.

I agree with her in thinking that the potato disease cannot be accounted for, other than as a special visitation of Providence; but I believe it was much mitigated last year, and may be permitted by Him who causes the grass to grow to disappear altogether. I would advise her to urge on the allottees she alludes to, not to discard potato culture altogether; perhaps it would be safe to devote less space to it than formerly, but they still should grow some. By planting the early roots *at once*, they may get a crop of turnips after them; and I would say, for their information, that I last year saved a considerable portion of mine from disease by *pulling up the tops* as soon as I saw the haulm affected. One portion of my crop (the "Farmer's Glory"), as soon as I discovered the black unmistakeable patches on the stalks and leaves, was *mown with a scythe* close to the ground; another portion had the *tops pulled entirely up*; the person doing this placed his feet close to the stem of the plants, so that the tubers were not drawn out of the ground, or disturbed at all. A third portion of the crop was left untouched to see the difference. The result was, that the *untouched* part contained about a third part diseased potatoes; in the *mown* part about five per cent. were bad; and in part that had the tops entirely pulled up, there was not more than a couple of tainted potatoes in a bushel.—A FRIEND TO THE POOR.

SILVER CEDAR — POLMAISE — ARRANGEMENT OF FLOWERS.—I have to thank THE COTTAGE GARDENER, as the means of my having succeeded for the first time in blooming tree violets and crocuses, in moss, this winter; also, for having successfully turned out into the open ground, and *repotted*, some standard Fuchsias and a Brugmansia last autumn. I had never ventured to plant them out of the pots before, but shall never keep them in again.

I believe I owe all the hints that have enabled me to accomplish these little successes to Mr. Beaton's papers. I wish it might be any return to him to inform him, that the Cedar of Lebanon in my neighbourhood presents the same phenomenon as that described in his paper on the Silver Cedar, of the neighbourhood of Algiers. His mode of expression seems to imply, that he has never seen the receptacles of the cedar cones remaining on the branches, and looking like the teeth of a wooden rake set along them. In the case which habitually comes under my observation every year, the cones never fall whole, but scale by scale, leaving the receptacle fixed as before described. I have preserved a few cones of different species of such common firs as have come in my way, and have often looked for a whole ripe cedar cone to add to my collection, but have never found any thing but scales under the trees.

Perhaps some of your correspondents may like to know, that I have thrice succeeded in invigorating exhausted sea kale plants, by watering them occasionally, *when in full leaf*, with a solution of nitrate of soda—3 ounces to 8 gallons of water. It should never be applied *over* the plants, nor in *dry* weather. If left uncut the spring previous, the effect would be greater. Half the bed might be dosed one summer, and half the next.

I see one of your correspondents asks something in reference to a bed of mixed Fuchsias : I have long grown such, from love of variety, combined with want of space; but have come to a conclusion, that a much better effect would be produced, in the same space, by several small beds instead of one large one, arranged so that each should contain two sorts of a somewhat similar character. I have named some sorts I grow myself, and need hardly say, the stronger growing ones are used for the centre, *e. g.*, *Eppsii* edged with *Magnifica*, *Exoniensis* edged with *Globosa*, *Corralina* edged with *Buistii*.

I am also a great admirer of Peonies, and have a large bed of them edged with crocuses, of which I mean to prolong the interest by planting the interstices with summer flowering bulbs. [This is a very good idea. What summer bulbs do you intend using?]

I should be much obliged by your opinion of the following scheme :—I would propose building a "Fortune's pit," such as is described by Mr. Beaton, with the flue passing round the front and two ends, and the door in the back at the chimney corner, with the *addition* of a two-light frame to be heated by a pipe (with stop-cocks to be used at pleasure) from a boiler, over the fire of the Fortune's pit, which should be kept filled from the rain off the roof, having a waste pipe communicating with a slate tank inside the Fortune's pit, for watering, that to be also furnished with a waste pipe to prevent overflow. I also propose, that the fire and boiler shall be enclosed in a hot-air chamber, with an opening into the Fortune's pit—thus economising all the heat. This air in the chamber should be derived from an external opening, furnished with a regulator, on the principal of Dr. Arnott's stoves. It would be sufficiently moistened by the vapour from the boiler. Would its passing over the heated iron surface of the boiler make it injurious to plants? the stove might be brick, and a slate tank stand in place of the iron boiler, if there could be flanges made in it for the pipe.

The *fire* should be fed with air from a drain, passing under the whole length of the fortune's pit, with an open mouth at the extreme end of the floor, on the Polmaise principle, thus keeping up a constant circulation of air in the pit. This opening, and that of the hot air chamber, should be provided with means to close them at pleasure, and the drain should have a second mouth, external to the pit, to be opened when the other is closed, if the heat of the flue only be required. To make the scheme perfect, there should be means of making the smoke pass at pleasure through the flue round the Fortune's pit, or up a chimney direct from the stove; increase of heat being required for the frame, and not for the Fortune's pit, this I think could be contrived.—A FLOWER LOVER FROM CHILDHOOD.

[The arrangement seems good, and the principle of Polmaise is correct, but there are too many failures in its application for us to be justified in recommending its adoption. Many thanks for the information about cedar cones, but we are aware that the axis of these is persistent in this genus; and, also, that *Picea* is distinguished from *Abies* by a like feature: what Mr. Beaton said was, that the "Greek Courier" remarked, that the old cedars on Mount Lebanon did not exhibit the teeth-like remnants of the cones; and that no doubt is owing to the cones being so small, that the axis were hid amongst the foliage. We believe it is still undecided if the two cedars are distinct.— ED. C. G.]

SPRUCE FIR.—In the 69th number of THE COTTAGE GARDENER I see that, in the answer which you give to an inquiry made by one of your correspondents, you say that a spruce fir, if the top be cut off, will not form a fresh leader; I think it probable that this will be generally the case, but as a remarkable exception to the general rule once came under my observation I hope you will excuse me if I make you acquainted with it. You evidently do not mean, that a spruce fir if it lose a leader which is still in a growing state, or which is of only one year's growth, will not form a new one; for I am sure you know that, in that case, one of the lateral shoots which is of the same age with the lost leader, and which surrounds its base, will usually, perhaps always, replace it by taking a perpendicular direction; you plainly mean, that you have never seen a fresh leader produced by a spruce fir which has lost not merely a leader of one year's growth, but wood which is the growth of several years. It may, therefore, be not uninteresting to you if I state that, many years ago, I planted in a pasture some single trees, and among them a spruce, which when I planted it might be 12 or 15 feet high; its growth being checked by its being moved when it had attained this height, it bore, two or three years after I had planted it, a superabundance of cones upon the upper branches; the top being thus overweighted, a strong wind broke off a considerable part of the tree, the growth of perhaps four or five years. The fir thus mutilated was no longer ornamental, and I had condemned it to be cut down; how it came to be spared I know not, but I am glad that it was spared, for in a year or two I perceived that one of these, which were *now* the upper boughs of the tree, or rather of the stump, began to raise itself a little from its horizontal position, not forming itself into a curve, but apparently turning upon its point of junction with the trunk as its centre of motion. You may be sure that when I saw what was going on I no longer thought of cutting down the tree, but watched the progress of the ascending branch with some interest. It kept thus moving upwards year after year, while the rest of the branches retained their original direction (nearly horizontal), and at length it assumed a direction perfectly perpendicular, and united itself so accurately with the top of the stump that the place where it has joined itself to the stump is now hardly if at all discernible, nor are there any marks which would make the most attentive observer suspect that there is anything extraordinary in the growth of the tree. The fir is now a handsome and thriving tree, forming every year a leader a foot or 15 inches long. With this fact before you, you will perhaps think it right to advise your readers not to be hasty in cutting down an ornamental spruce because it has lost its top.—REV. EDWARD SIMONS, *Ovington, Norfolk.*

STOVE HEATING AND STRAWBERRY CULTURE.—I beg to refer to my communication published in THE COTTAGE GARDENER (No. lx., Nov. 22nd, 1849), and to say that, during the very severe weather which subsequently occurred, the atmospheric heat was found to be insufficient; or, rather, inasmuch as the atmospheric and bottom heat were supplied from the same source, the endeavour to increase the former beyond a certain point increased the latter to an injurious extent. I have since been enabled to remedy this defect, by putting up an Arnott's stove at the end near the door, with a four-inch flue of galvanized iron, and an evaporating pan at top. This fully answers my expectations, and I can thus get up any degree of heat required at a very moderate cost of fuel—say, at the season of the greatest consumption, under three-fourths of a barrel of coals weekly.

I lately perceived some queries in your "correspondents" department relative to strawberries, and as I have had considerable success in growing this fruit, I take this opportunity to say a few words thereupon. My bed is a ridge, sloping to the east and west, and about 100 feet in length, I have uniformly a good crop, probably due to attention being paid to the following method:—1st. Selecting the *earliest* runners only for propagation, and pinching off all subsequent runners. 2nd. Never injuring or removing any of the leaves unless decayed 3rd. Planting at such distances as that the plants when fully grown will not touch each other. 4th. Sheltering the roots in winter by layers of haulm, or waste litter, along the rows (the British Queen is especially impatient of frost). 5th. Top-dressing in March (when the litter is removed) with *very rotten* dung, gravel, and leaf-mould. 6th. Never allowing the bed to become actually dry while the strawberries are in bloom. Lastly, as to the most important part, *the soil :* I believe strawberries will never bear a certain crop if planted in a deep soil, or so as that the roots can get down so far as to be subject to constant moisture; in such case they will grow most luxuriantly in so far as leaves are concerned, but yield little or no fruit. On no part of my bed does the depth of soil exceed six inches, with eighteen inches drainage of stones and bricks beneath. The soil should be rich and light, and as little retentive of moisture as possible. From many trials I find that mentioned for "top-dressing" is the best.—R. GREEN, M.D., *Youghal.*

TO CORRESPONDENTS.

⁎ We request that no one will write to the departmental writers of THE COTTAGE GARDENER. It gives them unjustifiable trouble and expense ; and we also request our coadjutors *under no circumstances* to reply to such private communications.

BORDER IN VINERY (*H. B.*).—You will find a paper in the present number which meets your case. In planting the vines from the pots, be sure to loosen carefully the ball of earth, in order to liberate some of the principal ones from their coiled and unnatural position. Strew a thin coat of littery manure over the surface after planting, to supersede the necessity of watering for a few weeks.

DOUBLE AZALEA (*W. X. W.*).—We cannot tell whether it is a new variety from the two flattened and faded blooms we received.

HARDY CLIMBING ROSES (*Ibid*).—Six good roses for your pillars are *Amadis*, purplish crimson ; *Elegans*, crimson, streaked with white ; *Welty's Garland*, white ; *Bells Marie*, rosy ; *Obelr a de Rouwuuwne*, carmine ; and *Acidalie*, blush white.

JASMINUM NUDIFLORUM (*W. F. T.*).—This beautiful and fragrant winter-flowering plant is easily propagated by planting in August cuttings of the half-ripe young branches. It delights in a rich sandy soil. Your plant exhibiting flowers during the depth of the last winter, though there were no leaves, is an occurrence not uncommon in plants from northern China and Japan. The *Pyrus japonica* frequently does so.

BOTTOM-HEAT FOR POTATOES (*T. D. P.*).—When forcing potatoes, a bottom of 90° is most favourable.

MELILOTUS LEUCANTHUS (*A Subscriber*).—Will some of our readers inform us where this correspondent can obtain seed of the *Melilotus leucanthus.* Your mistletoe seed was sent in due course.

OLEANDERS (*W. H. G.*).—You will do right, as you propose, to shake all the old soil from these as soon as they start into growth this month, as they have been grown in very poor soil, and will not blossom this year, reducing their roots, and repotting them in more suitable soil.

LUCERNE (*Rev. A. Slight, R. L.*).—You will see that we have attended to your request.

MEDICAL QUESTION (*W. K.*).—We cannot undertake to answer this, or any other medical question.

DICTIONARY (*Novice*).—Wait a little, and we hope to introduce to your notice exactly what you require.

SULPHURIC ACID AND LIQUID MANURE (*A Bromley Curate*).—It is quite impossible to tell the exact quantity of sulphuric acid required for neutralising or fixing the ammonia in your liquid-manure tank, for it varies constantly in the strength and nature of its constituents; but, under similar circumstances, we know practical men who add three-quarters of a pound to every sixty gallons of the liquid compound from their water-closets, sculleries, &c.

RHODODENDRONS (*Rev. W. H. M.*).—You have a bed of these which have quite overgrown their space, and are so entangled together, that to cut them down to anything like a manageable size they must look bare stumps, without a leaf; and you ask if you must cut them, and how low down; and you have been told that they do not bear the knife. Now, all this testifies to demonstration the great need of a cheap periodical like THE COTTAGE GARDENER, to instruct the great body of our countrymen, and more especially the clergy, whose example is likely to be taken up by their congregations. Now about these rhododendrons; they are just as much under control as a geranium in a pot, will bear the knife equally well with the geranium, and may be cut to any height required, or be cut down to near the surface. Fix on the height you would like your plants to be—say three feet, four feet, or six feet, or any other height; then cut off the central shoots to that point, and the next branches below them cut so as to form the skeleton into a round shape. Every other plant in your bed we would so cut before the end of April, and leave the rest as they are until their bloom is over, and then cut them in the same way. For the centre of the bed you can use nothing so good as one of the tallest and best shaped of your rhododendrons; and from the time their growth is finished to this time next year you may remove any or all of them, to rearrange them, as easily as removing a pot plant from one pot to another; for their roots will carry enormous balls, which will secure the roots from all danger; nevertheless, give them a good soaking of water if you replant them. If you must have a different plant for the centre of the bed, get a strong one of *Magnolia conspicua*, which flowers very finely in the spring.

HOT-WATER PIPE FOR PIT (*T. D. P.*).—A two-and-half-inch pipe will be quite large enough to supply top-heat to a pit five feet wide and nine feet long, with bottom-heat supplied by a bed of leaves. Leaves, "of which you have a plentiful supply," will give you bottom-heat enough. *Gutta percha tubing* of two-inch bore is about 1s 9d per foot.

PEA SUPPORTERS (*I. S. Trundle*).—Those of which we gave a drawing at p. 271 of our first volume we used exclusively last season, and they answered admirably. The only alteration necessary is that they should be made to touch each other at the top, so as to form an inverted Λ, instead of being perpendicular, as represented in the drawing.

INCREASING APIARY (*S. J.*).—Buy swarms, by all means. They are quite mistaken who tell you that your bees will quarrel with the bees of strange hives. Bees from every county in England would be harmonious in the same apiary.

VARIOUS QUERIES (*Young Gardener*).—*Cactus*: Your cuttings will strike nicely; dry the bottoms first. *Greenhouse*. The temperature for forcing flowers and strawberries, 50° to 60° during the day, from 45° to 50° at night, is good—increase gradually from 5° to 10°. *Anemone seed*: Sown last autumn—we should be doubtful of. The *Acacia seed* sown at the same time are likely to do. You might give them both a mild bottom-heat. You must have patience with your luxuriant *Seedling Geranium*. If you starve it, ten to one but you would not be able to judge properly of the flower. Your error was in placing it in such a large pot—*nine* inches; one of four or five inches is quite large enough.

STANDARD ROSES (*E. F.*).—To train "standard and weeping rose-trees" along side of a carriage-drive, let the weeping ones have their main shoots trained down at regular distances all round the head, and that is easiest effected by passing strings from the top of the stake to a circle made on the ground, a yard or more from the stem, and tying the principal branches to the strings, and afterwards allowing the side branches from them to fill up the spaces to the shape of a parasol. The upright standards will merely require the shoots to be thinned out from time to time, and any of them that are growing too strong to be topped at midsummer, so as to have all parts of the head well balanced.

PARASITES (*A Subscriber*).—With the exception of some mosses and lichens, we have no real hardy parasites, except the mistletoe, worth cultivating. "Parasitic" and "Orchidaceous" plants are quite different in their way of living. The former feed on the juices of the plants on which they grow, the latter require only to be supported on trees, so as to enable them to feed on the air, and on dead vegetable matter in some instances. Some of the *dwarf ferns* might grow on your prostrate oak.

FLOWER-BEDS (*H. W.*).—All that relates to the flower-garden has been undertaken this season by Mr. Beaton, but he declines the responsibility of recommending how any given set of beds should be arranged as to colours. He has said—" to do this properly, is the most difficult point in gardening;" and to do it otherwise, on the advice of a public writer, would be like the blind leading the blind. You will have seen, however, at page 333, that Mr. Beaton would plant the two diamond-beds, Nos. 3 and 7 in your plan, with the same colour, and probably a white flowering-plant. Also the two small circles would be of the same colour, and that different from the colour of the four large fan-shaped beds, and from the large scarlet bed in the centre.

VINEGAR PLANT (*Rhyd y Gorn*).—Send your address to either of the parties named at p. 328.

FRENCH POLISH FOR BOOTS, &c. (*M. D.*).—Mix together, black ink, half a pint; gum arabic, two ounces; loaf sugar, half an ounce; and of vinegar and rectified spirit of wine, each two ounces; apply it to the boot with a sponge. We are told that this is a very superior preparation.

WIRE WORMS (*A Constant Reader and Improver*).—We wish we could give you a plan for destroying these pests in your allotment plot. Spirit of turpentine, as you suggest, would destroy them, but the expense and impossibility of getting it into contact with them forbid its employment. The ammoniacal liquor from the gas works, put on in large quantities, and stirred into the soil some time before sowing your carrots, might be effectual. The best remedy, however, is the mole; a few of these allowed to mine for a season unmolested in your allotments would destroy thousands; they look unsightly, but would not damage your crops so much as they would benefit them. We should adopt this remedy if our garden, like yours, was so infested with wire worms that "they will not allow a carrot to grow." High manuring, as you suggest, will not remove the evil. *Loam*; you will see that Mr. Errington explains what gardeners mean by this term.

COTTAGES (*Rev. H. Charasse*).—Thanks for your suggestions which we will not lose sight of. We cannot now advise upon emigration.

LONDON HORTICULTURAL SOCIETY'S MEETINGS (*M. B.*).—These are fixed for the present year to be on May 18, June 8, and July 13.

TREE ONION (*J. B. and J. R.*).—Send your addresses to H. S. Hodson, Esq., Botanic Garden, Bury St. Edmunds; he kindly offers to supply you.

BLACK SPANISH RADISH (*T. M. W.*).—This may be sown at the times when common radishes are sown; if in drills, let them be eight inches apart.

BEE FEEDING (*Ibid.*).—Give your bees *honey* diluted with a very little water; cover the feeder with a piece of green-baize, or something of the kind, to keep it of the same temperature as the hive, and with the cork-lining they will be sure to go into it. Sugar and beer, as you mention, is very unfit for food. If you have not a supply of honey, simmer for two or three minutes over a slow fire a pound of loaf-sugar in a wineglass-ful of water, and then add a spoonful of honey; next to pure honey this is the best food you can give them.—*J. H. P.*

HINTS (*Hortense*).—Pray continue the subject; what you have sent is very good. But pray *qualify* what you say about "judiciously cribbing"—we have just had some choice crocuses taken up by young gardeners to ornament their own plots! Can you not confide to us your address, that we may write if needful.

LYGODIUM SCANDENS (*E. N. P.*).—The dead patches on the leaves of this fern arise probably from the air of the stove, and the soil in which it is growing being too dry. Patches of this nature usually arise from the transpiration being excessive over the supply of moisture from the roots.

OUR VILLAGE WALKS (*Clericus*).—You will see that these have not yet concluded. You will oblige us by favouring us with your name, as the suggestion you make will be attempted probably.

BOTANY (*Amateur*).—The book upon the Natural System is a good one. Study it; read, and collect plants, and find out their characters; botanise with some one who knows the science. It can only be acquired by such means.

LAYING-DOWN PASTURE (*J. C. C.*).—Obtain leave to sow the grass-seeds on the barley *now*. The tenant will be benefited, and so will you eventually by hoeing the barley before sowing the seed, and bush-harrowing it afterwards.

NAMES OF PLANTS (*H. W.*).—Your plant is *Cineraria petasites*, the Butter-bur-leaved cineraria, and hardly worth cultivating in a small collection. Your description of the cactus agrees with that of *Epiphyllum Ackermanni*.

LONDON: Printed by HARRY WOOLDRIDGE, Winchester High Street, in the Parish of Saint Mary Kalendar, and Published by WILLIAM SOMERVILLE ORR, at the Office, No. 2, Amen Corner, in the Parish of Christ Church, City of London.—April 4, 1850.

WEEKLY CALENDAR.

M D	W D	APRIL 11—17, 1850.	Weather near London in 1849.			Sun Rises.	Sun Sets.	Moon R. & S.	Moon's Age.	Clock bef. Sun.	Day of Year.
11	Th	Small White Butterfly appears.	T. 47°—25°.	N.E.	Fine.	15 a. 5	47 a. 5	5 16	29	1 5	101
12	F	Song Thrush lays.	T. 51°—39°.	N.W.	Rain.	13	49	sets.	⊙	0 49	102
13	S	Stock Dove lays.	T. 51°—25°.	S.W.	Rain.	11	50	8a. 0	1	0 34	103
14	Sun	2 Sun. after Easter. Redbreast hatches.	T. 53°—32°.	S.W.	Rain.	9	52	9 14	2	0 18	104
15	M	Easter Term begins. Willow Warbler heard.	T. 50°—36°.	E.	Rain.	7	54	10 23	3	0 3	105
16	Tu	Blackcap heard.	T. 50°—34°.	N.	Fine.	4	55	11 39	4	0a.12	106
17	W	Frog Tadpoles hatch.	T. 47°—25°.	N.W.	Rain.	2	57	morn.	5	0 26	107

On the 5th of this month, in 1804, died one of the most classical writers in gardening literature, the Rev. William Gilpin. It would not be an easy task to select a character to place before our readers, and connected with the art we all delight in, so worthy of our study and our imitation as this amiable man. In early life he was a poor Cumberland curate; but having married his cousin, and their united fortunes being too small to maintain a family without some other addition than a curate's stipend, they removed to Cheam, in Surrey, and there successfully established a school for boys. It was successful in the fullest sense, for it enabled Mr. Gilpin to retire, after saving £10,000; and he had laid the foundation of the acquirements of pupils afterwards so well distinguished as Lord Bexley, Viscount Sidmouth, and Colonel Mitford, the historian of Greece. By this last-named pupil Mr. Gilpin was presented with the living of Boldre, in Hampshire, whither he immediately retired. Efficient as he had been as a tutor, he now became equally exemplary as a parish priest. It is recorded of him, by one who knew him well, that he was a blessing to those under his care. We feel the more assured that he was so, because we have in our hands his "Life of Bernard Gilpin," his great ancestor, "the apostle of the north," and his "Lectures on the Church Catechism"—works teeming with that gentle spirit that hopeth all things. He scarcely ever left his rural sphere of usefulness; and a plain tomb, beneath an oak in its churchyard, bears this record, which seems as if the last kind message from those beneath it:—

"In a quiet mansion, beneath this stone, secured from the afflictions and still more dangerous enjoyments of life, rests *William Gilpin*, together with the remains of *Margaret*, his wife, after living together above fifty years in happy union. They hope to be raised in God's due time,

through the atonement of a blessed Redeemer for their repented transgressions, to a state of joyful immortality, where it will be a new joy to meet several good neighbours, who may now lie scattered around them. He died April 5, 1804, at the age of 80. She died July 14, 1807, at the age of 83."

Mr. Gilpin's works entitling him to a place in our pages remain yet to be noticed; and these are twelve goodly volumes, in which his pen and pencil equally well pourtray the picturesque beauties he had observed in various parts of England. His faculty of describing such scenery was peculiar, and most effective; and Dallaway aptly describes that faculty as "painting with words." He was the guide well suited to the era in garden designing during which he wrote. Taste was just escaping from the imprisoning formalities of the Dutch and French styles of gardening; and those who were designers in landscape gardening needed some guide to point out what in nature deserved copying, and which of her features should be veiled. Gilpin was the well-suited guide; his works are full of excellent observations—he offers little of theory; but judiciously observing and selecting picturesque beauties, he very rationally insists that such are worthy of imitation. All his observations are illustrated by examples; and in addition to the natural English scenery from which he draws such contributions, he also brings before us, for the same purpose, descriptions of the grounds around the noblest "homes of England." His writings are most agreeable; and they powerfully aided the progress to correcter taste in garden designing.

Meteorology of the Week.—During the last twenty-three years, the average highest and lowest temperatures, on the above days, at Chiswick, have been 56.0° and 37.6°, respectively. The greatest elevation of the thermometer was 71°, on the 17th, 1814; and the greatest depression 20°, on the 16th, 1847.

RANGE OF BAROMETER—RAIN IN INCHES.

April		1841.	1842.	1843.	1844.	1845.	1845.	1847.	1848.	1849.
11	B. {	29.939	30.216	29.983	29.996	29.896	29.542	29.945	29.759	29.866
		29.923	30.137	29.871	29.914	29.365	29.337	29.794	29.663	29.691
	R.	0.01	0.01	—	0.16	0.05	0.10	0.12	—	—
12	B. {	29.969	30.194	29.949	29.958	29.770	29.607	29.796	29.340	29.819
		29.907	30.023	29.829	29.665	29.507	29.379	29.677	29.492	29.598
	R.	—	0.04	0.23	0.03	0.09	0.22	0.10	0.01
13	B. {	30.130	29.992	29.963	29.799	29.787	29.758	29.922	29.675	29.341
		30.077	29.957	29.797	29.689	29.354	29.509	29.541	29.540	29.218
	R.	0.06	0.08	0.02	0.10	0.02	0.01	0.45	0.12
14	B. {	30.083	30.025	30.005	30.026	29.559	29.715	29.947	30.009	29.533
		29.963	29.940	29.914	29.895	29.401	29.565	29.919	29.853	29.388
	R.	0.01	0.01	—	0.02	0.10	0.10			0.03
15	B. {	29.999	30.005	30.109	30.117	30.126	29.786	30.028	29.994	29.719
		29.751	30.852	30.091	30.019	29.560	29.500	29.906	29.881	29.548
	R.	0.05			0.09	0.05	0.05	0.01	0.38	0.06
16	B. {	29.762	30.147	29.992	30.187	30.275	30.027	30.096	29.960	29.785
		29.714	30.115	29.818	30.111	30.265	29.939	29.926	29.733	29.719
	R.			0.01					0.20	
17	B. {	29.945	30.189	30.048	30.048	30.323	29.952	29.894	29.693	29.776
		29.874	30.184	29.954	30.695	30.196	29.883	29.757	29.619	29.718
	R.						0.09		0.11	0.02

Natural Phenomena Indicative of Weather.—We lately observed that at the approach of rain distant objects appear nearer, so now we may record, that at such times *sounds from afar* come most distinctly to the ear. The saturation of the air with moisture increases its power of conducting sound, as well as its magnifying power. A Norfolk clergyman, writing to us relative to a recent note made by us on *the moon's changes*, says, "In this county the opinion of the effect of a Saturday's new moon is carried somewhat further than Dr. Forster's in the following saying in the vernacular:—

'Saturday new, and Sunday full,
Never war (was) fine, nor never wull (will):'

a saying which I believe is very frequently verified."

Insects.—"What is a *looper caterpillar*?" inquires a correspondent (*F. F.*); and we place our answer here because we intend at the same time to give as an illustration of our definition the portrait of a caterpillar very likely to be destructive of our gooseberry-tree leaves this season, if we are justified in arriving at such conclusion from the large number of the parent moths we saw last year. The first three segments of the body of the caterpillar of a moth or butterfly have each a pair of simple, short, and jointed feet. Behind these are a number of short fleshy tubercles, armed with small hooks, and called *pro-legs*. Caterpillars having these pro-legs on nearly every segment of their body crawl upon them all at once; but those having few pro-legs adopt a different mode. They seize fast hold with their six true legs of whatever they are walking upon, elevate the intermediate segments into an arch or *loop*, until they bring the hind pro-legs close to the true feet; they then disengage these and, retaining hold with their pro-legs, thrust forward their body to its full length, and repeat the effort until they reach their object. Caterpillars so moving are named *Loopers*. Their progress is well illustrated in the annexed drawing of the caterpillar and cocoon of the Magpie moth, *Abraxas grossulariæ*, a drawing and description of which will be found in our second volume, p. 193.

AN old writer has said, "I never took anything for certain that I did not receive a lesson that I had been presuming rashly," and we felt the full force of this observation after trying *Brown's Patent Fumigator*. We ridiculed the idea of doing that by a machine which could be done by lighting a whisp of tobacco rolled up in touch-paper; but as we invariably try before we condemn, we now have to confess that we "presumed rashly;" and we can confidently and strongly recommend it to our readers.

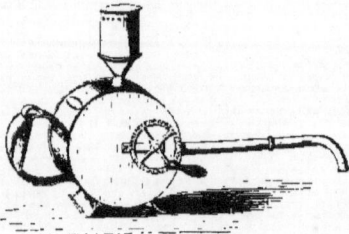

If a very small quantity (a quarter of an ounce) of tobacco be put into the circular vase at the top, and a red-hot coal upon the tobacco, the spout then be introduced through a slightly raised sash of the house, and the handle of the fumigator slowly turned, there will be such a continued and copious flow of smoke that the house, though a large one, will be filled in a very few minutes. It is the rapid and continuous production of smoke which renders this really an economical instrument, for it is quite certain that by its use less than half the tobacco is sufficient, compared with that required when its combustion is slower. For ladies, and other amateurs, it possesses this additional recommendation, that they need in no way be incommoded by the smoke: they stand outside the house to be fumigated, and not a whiff of the smoke escapes from the fumigator except that delivered by it into the house. It may be employed equally efficiently for fumigating pot plants, or bushes in borders; these need only be put under a tent, formed by driving a stake into the ground, and throwing a sheet or other covering over it, and the spout of the fumigator introduced beneath will sooner, and, consequently, more efficiently, fill the space with tobacco smoke than any other mode we know.

AT this juncture, when the cultivator of the soil must trust to his own clear head and his own right hand rather than to any aid from tariffs and restrictive duties, every suggestion for the profitable employment of his premises as well as of his soil deserves the most careful consideration. Now, among such suggestions is one for employing the stables and cowhouses on a farm for horticultural purposes, without interfering with their utility for the purposes to which they were originally devoted. This suggestion is one of the many beneficial results arising from the repeal of the duty on glass, by

which this material is rendered nearly as cheap as slates for roofing.

If our readers will refer to p. 91 of our last volume, they will find a question answered by us relative to the advisability of growing vines in a cowhouse with a glass roof. We there expressed our opinion that there is no obstacle to the success of the plan, and we are very glad to find that its spirited suggestor has carried it into effect. In a letter just received, he says—

"My new cowhouse, 90 feet long, is now glazed with Hartley's Patent rough plate, and the vines are planted. The rafters (had from Lewis of Stamford Hill) are 24 inches apart, so that the house is very light. The most ample means of ventilation have been provided all round the house, and along the whole ridge. The rafters were laid on just the same as for slating, and there are no sashes, so that the expense of this large house only exceeds by a few pounds a slated one. I think that even if the cows are kept in all the summer, the shade of the vines and ample supply of fresh air will prevent their suffering from heat.

"I purpose planting citrons and oranges on the wall of the feeding-walk.

"You shall hear of it again, from time to time. If it answers, I should think many farm buildings would be put up like it. I am at a loss for a name for it; some have called it 'The Combination House.'"

We shall be obliged by our correspondent reporting to us *frequently* how the plants progress, for it is an important experiment, and we should be glad to know how the leaves develop themselves, and how the wood ripens. We hope strict attention has been paid to forming the borders, for much depends upon this; and we should regret, supposing failure is the result, if it were doubtful whether that failure arose from the roots or the atmosphere of the house. With the arrangement for thorough ventilation we have no fear, however, that the air will be unsuitable; the slight exhalation of ammonia from cows' manure, and the little additional carbonic acid from their breath, will be beneficial rather than otherwise to the vines. We anticipate that the dust will be the greatest inconvenience and injury to them; and this will render necessary extra care for its prevention, judicious management of the ventilators whilst the litter is being moved, and the frequent use of the syringe at all permissable times.

As to a name for the house, we should have no difficulty in calling it the Stable-Vinery, or the Shippen-Vinery,—just as it may happen that horses or cows are kept under the vines.

WE have had so many inquiries relative to the culture of the *Himalayah Pumpkin*, that we think it best to give this one prominent answer. The best mode of sowing the seed is in pots of light, rich earth, any time during the present month; and plunging the pots in a gentle hotbed, or placing them in a warm greenhouse. The seedlings, when they have four rough leaves, will be ready for planting out in May, on a south border, or in any slightly sheltered quarter, and trained the same as cucumber plants. In May the seed may be sown in the open ground. The fruit may be cut when about seven inches long, for boiling and eating the same as the Vegetable Marrow, to which it is superior; or the fruit may be allowed to attain its full size and ripen, after which it either may be boiled and mashed like turnips, or be made into soup, according to the recipe we gave on a former occasion. Cooked in any of these modes it is excellent.

Numerous applications having been received by us for *Payne's Improved Cottage Hives*, and to inquire where they can be obtained at a cheap rate, we wrote to the inventor, and this is his prompt and very kind reply:—

"The man who makes my hives is a very poor man, although a very industrious one, living in an obscure village a few miles from this place (Bury St. Edmunds); sending his address will not effect the object desired I am afraid, but I will undertake to do as follows, and not think it any trouble, whilst I shall be serving two parties—the *maker* and the *user*. If a Post-office Order is sent me, at the rate of 1s 6d for each hive required, I will undertake to send from two to any number of hives, to any address or addresses that I may receive.

"They shall be sent from here (Bury) by rail, within four days, *at longest*, from the time of my receiving the order; and they will be precisely the same as those I obtained for you last spring."

We can answer for the excellence of the hives; and it remains, therefore, only for us to say, that any one requiring hives must write to "*John H. Payne, Esq., Bury St. Edmunds, Suffolk*," inclosing a Post-office Order, payable to him, for as many hives as are required, at eighteenpence per hive.

THE FRUIT-GARDEN.

Spring Frosts.—At the time we write, March 28th, we have the most astonishing frost for the period that we ever knew. The ground, also, has been covered with snow for twenty-four hours; the snow averaging at least three inches in depth. The ice on a sheet of water close by is an inch, or very nearly so, in thickness, and well it may be, for the thermometer was at 16° this morning at six o'clock, thus indicating 16° of frost. This is a *most extraordinary state of things*, and the sure consequence must be, we little doubt, the destruction of the apricot and gooseberry crop, at least, in this part of the kingdom (Cheshire). We are sadly afraid, too, that such weather is common to a great portion of the kingdom, from the circumstance of the atmosphere continuing in such a steady and unfluctuating character; the wind having been about N.W. by W. all the while. This is a very serious matter to thousands; for last year we had almost as severe a frost in April, and the bush fruit being nearly all in full blossom, the crop was mostly destroyed. Two years together! this is, indeed, most disheartening: let us, however, not despair, but look forward to more genial seasons.

We do not know how those who are averse to covering their fruit-trees will find matters, but we fear even for our peaches and nectarines, which are merely in the bud, although they are closely covered with Hulme's canvass. The pears are a splendid show this spring; we never saw such a profusion of bud before; and we look at ours with some confidence of a crop, for every tree we have—and there are some scores—are all well covered with spruce fir boughs; indeed, we had pears, plums, and cherries, nearly all covered some weeks since, in order to retard the blossoming period.

Aphides.—By the time this reaches our readers, it will be time to look out for these pests on the peach-trees, for the moment they are out of blossom, these destructive little rogues set to work. Let nobody fancy

they have deferred their usual visit; they are not particularly shy, and, indeed, we never knew a season without them. Our practice, therefore, is to syringe with tobacco water two evenings in succession. We lay the utmost stress on two consecutive evenings; for, in the first place, it is impossible, without a great waste of the liquor, which is somewhat expensive, to search every portion of the tree at one dressing; and, again, unless the liquor be exceedingly powerful, the larger insects will oftentimes revive again. A second application, however, with us totally extirpates them; or, at least, having thus carried matters, we seldom or never trouble ourselves about them through the summer. We may here *again* state the strength and character of the tobacco liquor. There is nothing like strong shag tobacco for this purpose; and we would advise the amateur who has only a few trees to use such; but where there are great lengths of walling to be gone over such proves a rather expensive item, and tobacco paper is resorted to.

We have before adverted to the great inferiority of the latter, as compared with the article sold under that name twenty years since; and we wish we could persuade all parties to use tobacco instead for one season, for the diminished demand for the tobacco paper would tend to stay the adulteration, which is so great, that tobacco paper *alone* is completely impotent in the destruction of the aphides. Three-quarters of a pound of shag tobacco, then, to a gallon of hot water, makes a liquid perfectly efficient. For two successive evenings, however, perhaps half a pound to the gallon would suffice. We use three liquids:—the one ordinary soap-suds, the second tobacco water from the paper, and the third liquid from shag tobacco, half a pound to the gallon. We allow a pound of the paper to a gallon of water. Thus prepared, we mix two gallons of soap-suds with a gallon of each of the tobacco liquids; and six large water pots of this mixture—or 18 gallons—suffices for a wall 240 feet long, nearly covered with peaches and nectarines. It is applied with the hand-syringe; and the operator after battering them one way to the end of the wall, returns and batters them again the reverse way, by which means scarcely a leaf is missed. Our trees are covered with canvass; and we choose a dry evening for the operation, applying the mixture about six o'clock, p.m., and drawing down the canvass immediately on the heels of the operation. The next day, also, we pull down the canvass in the event of sunshine or rain, in order that the effects of the liquid may not be too soon dissipated.

The Red Spider.—Having provided against the ravages of the aphides, we may as well offer a little advice about the red spider, which is nearly as great a pest as the former, and is almost sure to attack the peach and nectarine soon after the leaf is expanded. In former days, copious ablutions from the garden engine were resorted to every evening, than which nothing could be more prejudicial, robbing the wall of the heat which it had accumulated during the day, and which, indeed, constitutes the principal advantage of a wall. It, moreover, had a tendency to induce green and gangrenous matter on the shoots, through, we imagine, the sudden chill inflicted on the sap vessels. We confess to this bad practice until within the last twelve years or so, having, in early days, been taught to consider it indispensable; such is the force of mere prescription. In those days our peaches were like what too many are, even at this day; but since we discontinued the practice we have succeeded in peach culture to the utmost of our wishes, although living somewhat northerly. Sulphur, then, is a sure preventive; and, at the risk of being tedious, we deem it necessary to shew how we apply it; for although it has been before detailed, yet we must consider that not all of the present subscribers to The Cottage Gardener have taken in the work from its commencement, and this must be our apology for *this* as well as for *other repetitions*.

Some persons are content to dust sulphur on the leaves after they are attacked: our maxim is—prevention. We have found that sulphur made into a kind of paint as to consistence, it will adhere to the wall, and give out its fumes through a whole summer, so as to bid defiance to any injury from the red spider. Now this we have proved for several years; and although it may appear a little troublesome at first sight, as does every departure from an old and beaten track, yet in reality the amount of labour and material is not worth a moment's consideration. Our wall, 240 feet in length, employs a man a day and a half in applying the sulphur paint; who would not give three shillings in labour for an immunity of this kind? The sulphur is blended with thick clay-water, made by well-kneading a lump of clay until it is entirely dissolved, and of the consistence of paint. To this is added soft soap liquid, made by beating up about four ounces of soap to a gallon of water; a fourth part of this is amply sufficient. In later years, we have used in addition about a pint of soot to a gallon of the above mixture, in order to subdue the too bright tint of the sulphur, and to render it inconspicuous; and, probably, the soot also renders the mixture still more repellant. When this mixture is well blended, the operator applies it with a small painter's brush, painting every bare patch of wall which the brush will reach, and drawing an extra band or stripe along the bottom of the wall. So adhesive is this, that our last year's dressing is still visible; and so lengthened is its action, that the sulphur fumes may be plainly smelt until August, after which time it is not so very material if the spiders should commence operations; we never experience any injury worth recording. Let it be understood, however, that no engine-work must be practised after this operation; such would doubtless remove the paint from the wall. We *never* use engine or syringe, and we are not aware of any more successful peach culture in any quarter, and that, too, in a climate in which hot walls, a generation or two back, were thought indispensable.

R. ERRINGTON.

THE FLOWER-GARDEN.

BEDDING PLANTS: SCARLET GERANIUMS.—Specimens of two soils from Sussex were lately analysed by Professor Way, the Consulting Chemist to the English Agricultural Society, and found by him to be "exactly alike," both in their mechanical and chemical properties; yet the two samples were respectively from the best and from the worst wheat land in the county. This is sufficiently curious, if not puzzling; but not more so, I think, than that two plants raised from seeds out of one pod should vary so much in their natures, that one of them refuses to bloom freely, or even to put out its leaves kindly, in the same bed, or on the same kind of soil, where the other flourishes in all the beauty of its native race. Yet such is a fact, which certain seedlings of *Scarlet geraniums* have clearly established, and of which I have often remarked in these pages. Of these scarlet geraniums for flower-beds I said enough last autumn, but to those new readers who may not have that part of the work their names may be acceptable. *Shrubland Scarlet* is the strongest of them all, and has the largest truss. *Smith's Emperor* and *Superb*, *Prince of Wales*, and several other names are also given to seedlings of this variety which never fail to come true from seeds. I have reared hundreds of them from seeds, but never saw any variation, except in the leaf. The next largest trusser is a new one, sold last year by Mr. Ayres, of Blackheath, called *The Gem of Scarlets*. Conway's *Royalist* and Frost's *Compactum* are the two next largest trussers, both of them being well horse-shoe

marked in the leaf. The *Royalist* is, indeed, the best "horse-shoe" geranium I have seen. Our seedling *Punch* is a far better bedder and trusser than either of the above, except the Shrubland Scarlet, on our light soil, but on rich or heavy land it does no good. Nine or ten celebrated seedlings have passed through my hands, which do remarkably well in the places where they originated, and in many other localities, but I failed to establish them here. *Tom Thumb* is one of the number. On the whole, therefore, to give a good list of scarlet geraniums would be as likely to disappoint as to be of general use.

I have often said, one can hardly have too many scarlet geraniums; and I only know of one bed in a good flower-garden where they come amiss, and that is in the centre bed of a regular figure of any shape where the rest of the beds come all round it. No matter what beautiful plants and flowers may occupy the rest of the beds, the eye will pass over them and rest on the brilliancy of the centre mass. Besides, some shades of pink and purple, which might occupy any of the beds next the centre one, would be neutralised by the scarlet in it; a neutral bed should always occupy the centre round which the chief colours in flower-garden plants are to be arranged; and for such a centre bed I know of no plant more suitable than *Mangle's Variegated Geranium*. The flowers of this are small, and of a light pink shade, but the whiteness of the leaves drown the pink colour so far as to establish a neutral bed; and any colour may be placed next to this bed without imparing its strength, and yet we cannot call it a white bed. The old *Bouvardia* and the *Zauchsneria* would pass for small scarlet beds, and so might the old *Alonsoa*; but where scarlet verbenas and geraniums are much used, these things are too sober or subdued colours for a good arrangement of tints; and they are only fit for a miscellaneous assemblage of beds where no decided system of arranging the colours is attempted.

PURPLE.—I find this colour the most difficult to represent properly, either in shades of purple or strictly as a distinct colour. We have not a single true purple *verbena* yet worth planting as such, but they furnish abundance of shades. I thought, from a figure and description of the *Royal Purple Verbena* in "The Florist," that at last the desideratum was supplied, but I was deceived; and *Walton's Emma* is still the best purple verbena we have for a bed, but it is too dark for a real purple. The next best purple is *Heloise*, a beautiful bedding verbena, but still not a true purple. Plant either of these two best purple verbenas alongside of the light purple variety of the *American groundsel*, or the *petunia*, nearest to that colour, and you will soon see the reason I have for saying that we have no real purple amongst the verbenas. The original red or purple petunia, *P. phœnicia*, has not yet been improved on in colour for a bed in that family, though we have several as good and many better ones with darker or lighter shades of purple; but we have nothing better than a petunia that will do for a bed to last out the season.

We do not, in these days, call a plant fit for a flower-garden because it is a beautiful mass of colour while it lasts, which may not be longer than from a month to six weeks, unless it has other properties equally valuable in the eyes of a flower-gardener. One of the most essential secondary qualities of a flower-garden plant is to have creeping or very numerous fibrous roots, so as to enable the planter to remove it from place to place, either in the reserve garden before a place is open for it in the flower-garden, or from the flower-bed after it has done flowering. People who know little of those things will sit down and write you a fine story about the "facilities in these our days" for keeping up a succession of bloom, for a whole season, anywhere; all that you have to do is to remove everything as fast as it gets out of bloom, and fill up its place with something else brought forward on purpose in pots, or in the reserve garden; and really *on paper* it does seem very easy to do all this. But having for the last ten years paid particular attention to this branch of gardening—as much so, indeed, as any gardener in this country, and having also as much money allowed for carrying out my plans as most gardeners—I can safely repeat that this is the most difficult branch of our art, and the least understood by all our writers on gardening, myself among the number. The most successful results at flower-gardening are to be obtained by the *least number of plants*, provided that as many are used as will give all the principal colours of scarlet, purple, pink, blue, yellow, lilac, and white.

The most dwarf purple-flowering plant for this kind of gardening is verbena *Sabina;* and though not a good purple, it is still a very useful plant for the smallest bed. The best contrast to it in another shade of purple is *Lobelia unidentata*, also a very low plant for little beds. *Lantana Sellowii* is a reddish purple plant, extremely rich in a bed; and the same plants may be taken up on the approach of frost, and used for four or five years in succession. It seeds freely, can be got by cuttings as easily as a verbena, and delights in the richest soil if it is light. There should be a bed or two of this Lantana in every good flower-garden. *Phlox Drummondi*—There are two or three good shades of purple to be had from this beautiful annual, which is as good as any perennial for the flower-garden, as it blooms on from the end of June until cut by the frost. Where great stress is laid on having the best shades of colour, a few of the desired tints of this phlox ought to be preserved in pots, and propagated in the spring from cuttings. Indeed, this is the best way to deal with all the best varieties of it; and some of them are extremely pretty. But, in general, a packet of seeds will furnish a good bed. I sow this about the first week in April, in a little heat, for the seedlings do not rise so freely in strong heat. The old *Verbena venosa* is a good purple, but, like some of the purple petunias, the plant itself is coarse. If it is not quite hardy, it is the next thing to it, and that is a great recommendation. The best way to manage it for the flower-garden, is to fork out the roots every spring when the beds are being dressed; to cut them into six-inch lengths; and, after trenching the bed, to plant these pieces rather thickly.

COMBINATION OF COLOURS.—This verbena exemplifies, in a high degree, what I said about the necessity of taking the tint of the leaves into account in arranging colours in a flower-garden. Few would believe that a bright scarlet and a good purple would answer well together in the same bed, because the scarlet would be so apt to neutralise the purple. Thus, if you plant an equal quantity of the best scarlet verbena with *Emma* or *Heloise*, the best purple ones of the same creeping habit, you will find that two good colours are completely spoiled, or, at any rate, that the scarlet will carry the palm. If it were possible to mix a white verbena along with these, so that there would be one-third more white flowers than of scarlet and purple ones, an extremely pretty bed would be the result; but such arrangements can only be managed with cut flowers, and that is the easiest way to learn how to harmonise or contrast colours for beds. It is ten times easier and more safe than studying the colours from printed arrangements; and the way to do it is as follows:—Take the lid of an old box (the larger it is the better) and lay an inch of earth all over it of a darkish colour. I have used sand for this purpose, but it is treacherous; as the white or yellow sand gives the effect of its shade to the composition—dark brown loam is the best. Then, on a fine sunny day in summer, lay the board or lid on a plot of grass, or on a gravel walk, according as the flower-beds may be on the grass or surrounded by gravel. Take the flowers of two or more plants you wish to mix together, and some of the leaves of each plant; then make a flower-bed by sticking the flowers in the mould on the board, and a few leaves along with each flower or bunch of flowers. Now, about mid-day, step back three yards from your model bed, with the sun behind you, and if you see no fault in your composition, walk round to the opposite point, and look at it against the sun; if you are still satisfied, leave it till four, or half-past four, in the afternoon, and then look at it from the same points as before. The sun will then be striking sideways against the colours, and if there is any defect in the arrangement, it is sure to come out now. Yet be in no hurry to give it up—look at it next day *from the same points* between ten and eleven o'clock in the forenoon; and this should be repeated on a cloudy day before a final judgment is passed. It is unnecessary to observe that the colours may be arranged in any way one pleases on this board; but, *in all cases*, the leaves of the plants which produce the colours must be used, and why, I shall give an example next week.   D. BEATON.

GREENHOUSE AND WINDOW GARDENING.

DOUBLE CHINESE PRIMROSE (*Primula sinensis, flore pleno*).—Interesting as are the associations connected with the primrose race, and beautiful as the whole of them look, whether under the care of the skilful florist, under the protection of the forest brake, exposed upon the upland fell, or shedding some of the brightness of John Chinaman's land over our windows and greenhouses in the dull days of winter and spring, the division we have placed at the head of this article—though out shone by others in the splendour and richness of their colouring—is second to none in its *appropriateness* for floral adornment.

The single white and pink Chinese primulas, when well grown, are very pretty objects in winter and spring, especially when the colours are clear and distinct, whether the varieties are somewhat whole in the edges of the segments of the corolla, or, as more generally coveted, they are nicely cut and fringed. But though thus making nice pot plants, one drawback connected with them is, that they cannot well be employed in the forming of bouquets, as the flowers soon drop after their stem is cut; while the double varieties answer better than most plants for this purpose, preserving their freshness for a long period in water, and for a considerable time without any water.

Like the single ones, the double white and pink sport into several sub-varieties; the white sometimes being as pure as driven snow, and at other times containing a dash of blush, and even a 'tinge of green, in the centre of the flower; some being nearly whole in the edge of the petals, and others again deeply fringed, but all of them beautiful. The red is sometimes so dull in colour as to render it unattractive; it being less striking in such circumstances than a well-grown good coloured pink single variety. Partly on this account I have never done much with the red, but during this winter I saw some large fine coloured blooms that make me anxious to try such a variety, if at all presentable or procurable.

All these double varieties require similar treatment. I look upon the white as the most desirable, and, if anything, it is the most easy to manage. We seldom keep a plant above two years. Some of those in large pots measured within an inch of two feet in diameter, and during the winter have exhibited in the conservatory a dense mass of flowers. The plants might have been better had they obtained a better position and treatment during summer. To have even such plants next year you must commence with a nice healthy one-year-old plant *now*. If you resolve to commence from the beginning with a cutting *now*, you must be satisfied if you obtain such plants in the spring of 1852.

Propagation.—This is generally effected by cuttings which are taken off when the plants have done flowering, or the older plants are cut into pieces for that purpose. In making the cuttings it is advisable to strip off several of the lower leaves close to the stem, as if you leave any part of the petiole of the leaf it is apt to rot, and thus mould and destroy the cutting. In selecting cuttings from old plants, reject the hard bare part next the roots, and cut straight through nearer the leaves and top of the cutting, where the wood is softer and fresher, though ripe, and not spongy. The next thing to be done is to dry the base of the cuttings, and yet keep the top and leaves of the cutting green and flourishing. How do this? Nothing is more easy. Expose the ends of the cuttings for several hours to sun and air, but shade the tops, and give them a dash from the syringe. Those who dry the bottoms of other cuttings, such as geraniums, will find this worth noting. The longer that leaves can be kept green, the sooner will the cutting protrude roots.

In preparing pots for cuttings, means (such as those previously referred to) must be adopted for keeping out worms, as their entrance, by whatever means, is next to fatal to success. After securing the hole in the bottom, the inverting a small pot inside of a larger one answers well, as thus a hollow cylinder is formed through which the heat will have free access to the base of the cuttings. The bottom of the inverted pot should be on a level with the rim of the larger one, and the hole should be stopped with a potsherd or cork, so as to be removed at pleasure. The space between the two pots should be filled half-way to the top with drainage; above this the soil should be placed, consisting of equal portions of fresh loam, peat and sand, with a covering of silver sand on the surface, from one-eighth to one-quarter of an inch in thickness. Leaf mould, if it constitutes a part of such soil for propagating, should previously be dried and heated, to free it from insects. The cuttings being inserted as close as possible to the inverted pot, and well watered, are, when the foliage is *dry*, to be plunged in a nice sweet bottom-heat, such as will be found in the front of a cucumber or melon bed; and each pot covered with a bell-glass, or several of them covered with the top of a hand-light. In either case it will be advisable to *tilt* the one side of the glass at night, and replace it firm in the morning, which will prevent all danger from *damping*, and will also expedite the rooting process. Shading and watering must be given when necessary. When struck, shift separately into small pots, and give them a little bottom-heat again. As the summer proceeds, they will require a rather shady place; and would be better, if all the time they were kept under glass with plenty of air. If it is desirable to make a large plant from a cutting the first year, it would be advisable in reshifting it to keep it in a rather warm close atmosphere until September, when it should gradually be exposed to more air, and a lower temperature, in order to harden its wood, and set its flower-buds before winter. By giving a cutting, therefore, the treatment generally given to stove-plants, we have had fine plants the first winter. After being struck, and after the first shifting, the common routine of the greenhouse, or cold frame, will answer for them; but they will not grow so fast as when more heat is given them. In fact, with the exception of the time when they are in bloom, when they will stand beautifully for months in a cottage window, and when they are resting after flowering, they never seem to find fault with a highish temperature, provided they have fresh air, and during summer are not exposed to the mid-day sun.

With respect to those year-old plants that are to be

kept until another season, after being cleaned of all their flower-stems, &c., they are generally set in a shady place under glass, until May, or June. They are then shifted into larger pots, and kept rather close, and somewhat shaded until autumn, when, as in the case of their rival youngsters, they must be fully exposed to the sun, and more liberally supplied with air. If, after shifting such plants, an opportunity is afforded of giving them a gentle bottom-heat, whilst the tops are kept rather cool, the plants will increase rapidly in size and luxuriance. When I used to give them this bottom-heat, the plants were finer than I have had them since; but more care was necessary to get the wood thoroughly ripened in the autumn. During the winter months when in flower, and when resting for a time after flowering, any temperature below 50°, and not below 40°, will do. When growing they will enjoy what ranges from 55° to 75°.

The soil to flower them in may consist of equal parts of turfy loam, peat, and leaf mould, and half as much as of either of these of sand, charcoal, and dried lumps of cow dung, using it rough in proportion to the size of the plants and pots. During winter, pounded charcoal may be placed round the stems, to prevent them *damping*. When growing, water should be given freely; but during winter it will be wanted comparatively seldom. Weak manure-water will be of service during the growing season. Thus treated, they may be made to ornament the greenhouse and window from November to May.

Sowing.—Now is a good time to sow the single varieties for blooming in winter and spring.   R. FISH.

HOTHOUSE DEPARTMENT.

STOVE PLANTS.

GARDENIAS.—Though not so rich in colour as some of the Ixoras which we selected for first consideration, these are almost as beautiful, the pure white of their blossoms, garnished with their bright, glossy, handsome, green leaves, rendering them very attractive; and, in addition to their beauty, several species have a most agreeable fragrance. so much so as to have caused them to receive the popular name of the Cape Jasmine; a very erroneous title, for the sweet-scented species are natives of China. The two species cultivated in some nurseries round London and other large towns for the sake of their flowers, which are in great request for bouquets, are the *Gardenia florida plena* and *Gardenia radicans*.

In those nurseries we have alluded to, these two species are grown by hundreds to the greatest perfection. As they are so very beautiful and fragrant, we consider that no stove ought to be without them. Their culture is not so well understood as it ought to be, especially in the country; and as this treatment is different in some respects from that the rest of the family require, we shall describe it first, commencing with

The Winter Treatment.—Towards the end of summer all the Gardenia species of the two last mentioned species are put into a cold pit; here they receive only just water enough to prevent them from flagging; air is given every fine day, and the pit is securely covered up with mats and short litter every night through the winter; this throws them into a state of rest. They are quite hardy enough to bear such a temperature.. A week or two before it is intended to put a portion of them into heat they are taken out of the pit, and every stem and leaf carefully washed with a sponge; this removes their grand enemy, the red spider, besides cleaning the leaves from dirt and dust. They are then potted in sandy peat four parts, and one part decayed leaves, commonly called leaf-mould; then they are put into a pit heated with spent tanner's bark, and lined with stable litter, the wall of the pit being pigeon-holed to let in the heat of the linings. This moist heat suits them well; they flower and grow vigorously. The moist dung heat prevents the red spider from existing, and consequently the plants are of a deep, healthy green, and the flowers large and of a beautiful pure white colour. We have had plants of the *Gardenia radicans* with as many as 20 blooms open at once. As the flowers open the plants are removed into the stove, if the season is early; but the later blooming plants are removed into the greenhouse, where they continue longer in bloom than in the stove. After the bloom is over they are replaced in the cold pit again. Such treatment makes the plants produce a large quantity of blooms for the florists' shops; and as this method answers well on a large scale, of course it will answer on a smaller number. Our readers will only have to follow up the principles of first resting the plants, and then growing them on in a moist heat, to bring them into a clean, healthy state of bloom. Our orchid-growing friends may have them in bloom from December to May by bringing them in from the cold pit one, two, or three at a time, once in a fortnight or three weeks. This section of the genus contains the following varieties:—

Gardenia florida flore pleno (double-flowered).

" 　" 　*Fortuniana* (Fortune's Gardenia). This is a fine variety, lately introduced, with larger flowers and foliage.

" 　" 　*intermedia*. A dwarfer variety, and abundant bloomer.

" 　" 　*radicans latifolia* (broad-leaved). It has short broad leaves and large flowers, sparingly produced.

The rest of the genus require a somewhat different treatment.

Gardenia Stanleyana is a splendid plant of recent introduction; and is, when well grown, a truly magnificent object. It has handsome foliage and large flowers; the latter, numerously produced all over the plant, being six or seven inches long, having a tubular corolla spreading out at the end, so that the flower has a trumpet-like appearance; the ground colour is white, with spots of a chocolate colour. It takes three or four years to grow a plant to tolerable perfection.

Gardenia Devoniana is another fine species also recently brought to this country. It has flowered in two or three places, but not so finely as the preceding species. The flowers are about the same size, of a cream colour, produced upon dwarfer plants.

Gardenia Whitfieldia commemorates the discoverer of these three fine plants. The flowers of this species we have not seen. It has fine foliage and a somewhat stiff habit.

These three species of this noble genus require a culture different from that for the first section; and they are really worth cultivating even in small collections, especially the first named.

Soil.—Having a young plant well rooted, pot it in a compost of loam, sandy peat, and leaf mould, in equal parts, and place it in a warm corner of the stove, shading it from the sun. The first potting should not be into a large pot. It is better to be moderate in the removes, as the one-shift system of potting will not answer for these tender-rooted plants; shift them, therefore, gradually into larger pots from time to time, as they require.

Heat and Moisture.—Give them heat, moisture, and a close temperature, for, being natives of the hottest part of Africa, they can hardly have too much heat and moisture. The common stove is a few degrees too low in the spring, when the plants ought to be growing and flowering to perfection; here, again, the orchid house presents its friendly aid, and will assist the grower of these splendid plants much. Such cultivators as have the convenience of a pine stove will there find a con-

genial heat and moisture. Plunged in the warm bed, their roots will advance vigorously, seizing upon the food prepared for them with avidity, and throwing health and vigour into the plants. But we are running on too fast: these descriptions of the effects of good culture, and applications of such means as will produce magnificent specimens of these ornaments of our stoves, are exceedingly tempting subjects, but as we have not exhausted our theme we shall with pleasure resume it the week after next.

FLORISTS' FLOWERS.

Such a trying season for these objects of the florists' care has not occurred for several years; yet with moderate attention to warm shelters, unceasingly applied, the various tribes will have passed through the severe ordeal uninjured. We have nothing to add to our instructions of last week, for if they have been duly attended to the plants will be thriving in health and vigour, and will be in a state highly satisfactory to the cultivators. It is true, *Auriculas* and *Polyanthuses* will be rather backward; and it will be a matter of serious consideration whether it will or will not be desirable to hold the exhibitions of these spring flowers a week or a fortnight later than usual; should that be thought necessary, it is high time for the conductors of such exhibitions to let the exhibitors know that the time for the shows is altered to suit the late season. Such flowers will not bear forcing into bloom; this is a truth on which all florists will agree.

PICOTEES (*The yellow varieties*).—Agreeable to our promise, we now give a list of such as we consider worth growing, excepting, of course, such as we have already given, to which list we refer the reader.

	Per pair.	
Euphemia (Barraud's)	4s	0d
Amazon	2	6
Parsee Bride (May's)	3	0
Oddity (Rendle's)	2	0
Striata	2	6
Goldfinder (Wilmer's)	2	0

T. APPLEBY.

THE KITCHEN-GARDEN.

ROUTINE WORK. — If not already done, *asparagus* should now at once be sown; and new plantations of the last year's sown plants should be made as soon as they have made shoots two or three inches in length, as previously directed. Prick off the young *sweet basil* and *sweet marjoram* on a little heat; prick off also, in due season, the first sowing of *borecole*, and the other varieties of *kales*, in order to secure good, strong, and healthy plants for the planting out season. The present is still a good time for sowing the main crops of *carrots*; and young *cauliflower plants* should be pricked off, as soon as they can be handled, on a well-prepared bed. Sow in full crop the best varieties of *brocoli* and *savoys*, and the small varieties of *cabbage* for summer coleworts or greens, such as the best kinds of *York, Atkins' Matchless, Nonpareil, Shilling's Queen,* &c. Sow *Dwarf Kidney beans* and *Scarlet Runners* in a sheltered warm corner, or under hand-glasses, for transplanting on to warm borders as soon as the weather becomes a little more favourable. Make another sowing in pits or frames on a gentle bottom-heat. Supply those now coming into bearing with liberal soakings of tepid liquid manure. Plant in succession *Windsor Broad beans, Long Pods,* &c. Sow the late varieties of *peas* in succession. The *American Dwarf* and *Fan peas* may be sown as an outside edging to quarters, or on narrow strips; and some should also be sown on a north aspect, which will be found very productive when the hot dry season arrives. The above-named varieties are very suitable for those who have but a small garden, as they require very little room, being of the dwarf short-jointed kinds, and very prolific. The early peas should be stopped, or have their tops picked out, as soon as the first blossoms commence opening. Attention to this point will considerably advance their early podding. The soil about the main-sown summer varieties now coming up should be kept well stirred; should be earthed up in due season; and sticks, or some kind of protection, placed for keeping them upright, and preventing their being driven about by the wind. Sow *sea-kale* thinly in drills, one foot apart, and attend to the forced plants of this season. Thin the shoots, as required, at intervals, until thinned sufficiently according to the strength of the plants, leaving one, two, or more shoots to each.

Cucumbers.—Sow ridge varieties. Prepare the fermenting materials by thorough intermixings and frequent turnings; encourage those now producing fruit, by frequent application of tepid weak liquid-manure; stop the shoots regularly at each show of fruit; do not allow the vine to become too much crowded; but, at the same time, take care never to exhaust the plants by thinning too much at one time. It should be an almost daily custom thus to run them over—stopping, pegging, and regulating the vine, and setting and placing the fruit to grow straight. It is very easy to take out such portions of the vine as have become weak and exhausted, to make room for the younger and more vigorous parts. The same system should also be kept in view with regard to *melon* culture. The vine should never be allowed to become too much crowded, and then be thinned out extensively at once. Such extremes in management is often the forerunner of disease, canker, red spider, and thrip, &c., which should be avoided if possible. Sudden drafts of cold, when giving air, should be particularly guarded against throughout this month, or the prospect of a fine crop of healthy fruit may be very quickly cut off. Water should at all times be applied with caution and judgment, taking the advantage of applying it after a fine day, and when not very windy. Shut up early, take the covering off early in the mornings, and give air previous to the sun shining on the structure. If these instructions are attended to, neither disease nor vermin will be seen; but should any symptoms of canker at any time appear, from long continued dull, damp weather, apply immediately a slight dredging of fresh slaked-lime to the parts affected.

Broccolis.—All the different sorts of broccolis may still be sown (excepting the Purple Cape kind). Those who have not already done so, should prepare a good rich warm border for this purpose, and divide it into small beds—a bed for each kind. This is the best season for sowing the broccolis, Cape excepted, which for the general crop should be sown the first week in May; and should the weather then be very dry, the ground should be well watered previously to sowing the seeds, and a sprinkle given afterwards too.

Borecoles and *savoys* may still be sown, and *Brussels sprouts* too. The present is also a good season for sowing the general crops of the best sorts of Red beet.

Asparagus Beds should have had all their forking-up done before this; and if any are not raked off neatly, let it be done without delay, as the young shoots will now be soon peeping through where the earth is not too thick upon the crowns, so that the sun can penetrate it. A sprinkling of salt will be found very beneficial once a week during the cutting season. The alleys between the beds, forked-up neatly, would be a good situation for lettuce during the summer months. Cauliflowers are frequently planted in them, but this should not be, as cauliflowers are of too large a growth to plant in the alleys, which are rarely more than two feet six inches wide in the smaller gardens; but lettuces do well in such places.   J. Barnes & W.

MISCELLANEOUS INFORMATION.

HOME SUGGESTIONS.

By the Authoress of " My Flowers."

In commencing a series of hints on household management, I must earnestly solicit my readers to extend to me, in this department, the extreme indulgence I have experienced at their hands in one of a very different kind. On the subject of domestic affairs so much is involved, and so many able and experienced hands have been held out to help and direct inquirers, that I feel it almost impossible to fill the important post assigned to me either with benefit to others or the least credit and satisfaction to myself.

Real economy is *a principle*. It is, or ought to be, practised from the highest motives,—from the love and fear of God, and in accordance with the precept and example of our gracious Teacher, who commanded His disciples to " gather up the fragments that remain, that nothing be lost." It does not consist of scraping up with one hand and lavishing wastefully or *selfishly* with the other, but in firm and decided retrenchment in everything, however gratifying to the flesh, which can possibly be reduced or given entirely up. We are very apt to think, we have done great things when we have knocked off a few extra shillings in some way, where, perhaps, liberality would be most advantageous, while we are spending unnecessary pounds in others where frugality would be well-timed and of real account. The " right hand " and the " right eye " must be given up in things temporal as well as in things eternal; in fact there is nothing, however trifling, which we are called to do or suffer that does not involve a principle, and upon which a Scriptural rule cannot be brought to bear. It is difficult sometimes to be economical without being mean: from fear of one extreme the mind will fly off to the other, and in our utter corruption of heart we cannot be surprised to find this frequently the case; but when we do all things in obedience to a Divine Master, and with a single eye to His honour and service, we shall most generally find the right medium, or at least we shall commit fewer mistakes than those who are saving for the lucre of gain, or who are striving to keep up an appearance to the world that their means or circumstances do not warrant.

I commence by replying to the many correspondents who have addressed us on the subject of small means and reduced incomes, and whose situation in some cases is perilous and anxious in the extreme. I address myself, in the first place, to the husband and the father, because I am proud to say they are most difficult to deal with in matters of retrenchment and expense; and without their willing and full co-operation the self-denying wife and mother, with all her striving, can effect little.

" An expensive house," " an income alarmingly reduced," "precarious and uncertain" means, imply a position of distressing embarrassment, and call for prompt and vigorous measures. The only income which can be depended upon, in the case of one correspondent, is more than swallowed up by the rent and other expenses of the house alone, the remainder is insecure and fluctuating. The house, if it is possible—I mean if the tenure admits of it—should at once be let, and the *luxury* abolished. Even an "under-duty" pony must be fed; and the very simplest equipage draws on many useless expenses, the tax is probably the least of them. A small, cheap house, on the outskirts of the town, if the other *can* be given up, would be a radical reform and an important saving, so would the pony carriage. Is it *absolutely* "necessary for business?" or is it only very pleasant and very comfortable? One servant might be found sufficient to carry on the work of the house where the mistress is in health, and actively determined to meet the exigencies of her situation. A husband, especially if accustomed to see his wife in a position of ease and elegance, is distressed and agonised at the idea of seeing her reduced to the situation of, what he may call, "an upper servant;" but not even this affectionate regret must weigh one atom in the scale. The "three little mouths" will in a short time need more than *food*; and such expenses will then arise as the parents of *little* children do not dream of; for this approaching time the father must prepare; and if *he* will *lop* and *prune*, I will venture to say his wife will cheerfully bear her burden and labour of love. Every halfpenny of an uncertain income should be scrupulously watched, and laid by if possible—nothing of it should be spent that can possibly be saved.

Wine, and spirits, and beer, and meat, come also into the gentleman's list of essentials. The glass of wine after dinner, the warm brandy-and-water after a day of fatigue, the hearty meat breakfast and dinner, are things of such regular daily occurrence that they are not taken into the system of economy in many cases; but they are all expenses, and heavy ones, and are besides only luxuries. Meat once a day is quite sufficient for man's support: look at the man who labours for his daily bread, and who is dismissed if he does not do a "good day's work;" does he taste meat *once a week*, once a month,—I might, in nine cases out of ten, add, once a year? Let this silence the gentleman, at least when he is struggling to support a wife and children.

All visiting should be as much given up as possible; it leads to a thousand expenses, and in many cases it is of no benefit at all. *Friends* will always win their way, in spite of the little we have to offer; and such are indeed worthy of open hearts and arms; but the generality will do no real good, and much positive harm; and a busy mother and happy wife will have little time for the reception or return of formal visits. If the husband is but willing to be content with the society of his wife, and remember the asseverations he uttered "once upon a time," he will not be the less rich or happy as he struggles onward in his worldly course. The expense attending dinner company is too great for persons of small means; the mild term, "a few friends in a quiet way," sounds very cheap and plausible, but if we are *struggling* for life we cannot do it, at least we *ought not* to do it, however tenderly we place the pleasure before our eyes. The bills at the end of the week *will* be higher, economize as we will; and all who are obliged to take care of every penny well know that one friend coming in to dinner or tea *tells* in the weekly consumption.

Professional men are very apt to fancy they must keep up a certain appearance before the world, and see a certain amount of company, by which they often involve themselves deeply, and are kept in a state of anxiety and difficulty injurious alike to the mind, the body, and the temper. If a gentleman cannot command the means, it is in vain to say, "we must have," or "we must do so and so:" we *must not* have, or do, that for which we cannot, or are not sure of being able, to pay! Where incomes are uncertain they should be used with the most jealous care and caution. We know that we hold our *firmest* possessions only as "daily bread," bestowed meal by meal by the Giver of all good; but, still, when human probabilities themselves appear dangerously insecure, we ought, with the fullest and firmest faith in the tender mercy of an Almighty and pitying Father, to walk as wisely as serpents, and act upon the perfect example of Him who spake as never man spake— "It is written, Thou shalt not tempt the Lord thy God." We *do* tempt God when we act rashly, unadvisedly, disobediently; and *place ourselves* in situations of peril or distress.

With the utmost humility I lay these observations at the feet of the *lords* of the creation, because so much of *effectual* economy rests with them.

HINTS ON GARDENING FOR YOUNG PEOPLE.

In offering a few hints on the subject of gardening to the youthful readers of The Cottage Gardener, I must begin by disclaiming any intention of writing a regular treatise on the subject,—that is beyond my powers; all I wish to do, is to endeavour to encourage a taste for this delightful amusement in the young, and to let them see how easily, and with how little expense or trouble, they may succeed in rearing common flowers, and keeping their own little gardens neat.

I write for those who are *rather* past the age of digging up their seeds every second day to see if they are growing; though I will not deny having some sympathy with those who do so, for I did it myself when young; and I confess, even now I occasionally lift a cutting of pansy or pink to ascertain if they are beginning to take root. I have said, I will shew you with how little expense or trouble common flowers may be raised, but I write for those who think the *trouble a pleasure:* flowers will not grow, weeds will not disappear, unless we work, and work in right earnest too. Idle wishes will do as little good here, my young friends, as in more important matters; you do not hope to conquer your faults, to root out bad habits, to improve your characters, and to have the fruits and flowers of a Christian life grow up within you, by wishing merely! It is not one of the least recommendations of the delightful occupation of gardening, that it suggests many heavenly and profitable thoughts. Analogies are frequently drawn in Scripture from its operations, and it seems to me that it is "the sole bliss of Paradise that has survived the fall:" for Adam's occupation, before labour was laid on him as a punishment, was to dress and to keep the Garden of Eden.

I know few people, indeed, who do not like flowers, but I do know a good many who dislike the trouble of rearing them. At one time I thought the love of gardening was inborn in some people, and could not be acquired; but I have seen instances to the contrary, and have known persons who, though living in the country for years, cared not for gardening become fond of it, and devote much of their time to this fascinating pursuit. I take for granted, however, that the young readers of The Cottage Gardener have already a love of gardening; and like not only the flowers, but the labour of rearing them; and to such I would now offer a few hints.

Let your garden be your own property.—Sometimes young people have a border in the garden called theirs, or a plot of flowers near the house which they undertake to keep free from weeds, but they do not consider themselves as responsible for it. The gardener puts it in order if they neglect it; the gardener plants out geraniums, &c., in it, and lifts them at the proper time; the gardener, in short, has the chief charge, and it is not *your* garden. Now, what I would advise is this: get a bit of ground to yourself, no matter how small, and let it be understood to be your own, to do what you like with and in. It makes a great difference in your interest and sense of responsibility, as well as in your pleasure in working, when you consider the spot your own. I remember yet my own feelings on this point; and certainly my first garden had little else to recommend it. It was a dull back-green, in Edinburgh, with a narrow border on each side, and shut in by walls excluding almost all sunshine. But it was my own; for no one cared to attempt gardening in such a hopeless spot; but for years I spent many happy hours there, trying to get flowers to grow, and hoping always to succeed. Nothing did grow but some orange lilies and marigolds; and sometimes in one corner, where the sun shone, a few hardy annuals would flower; but it must indeed have been the love of the work itself that induced me to persevere, for more unsuccessful attempts never were made. I had an old-fashioned book on gardening, which I studied incessantly; it told me much I had no use for: hothouses and green-houses, pineries and vineries, were all described therein, but no "back-greens." There was no COTTAGE GARDENER in those days. From this experience I would say, in the second place,

Choose a good spot for your little gardens, if you have a choice.—At least get sun and air, for few plants will live in shade, and none will thrive without air. Do not, as I once did, take the first bit of border you find unoccupied, and commence gardening there. Think first, if flowers will grow in it. When (years after my early back-green gardening) I went to reside in the country, I of course renewed my gardening with fresh zeal, and, at first, was satisfied with getting leave to sow seeds, or weed anywhere, but I soon began to find this unsatisfactory, and thinking that in the country, flowers would grow in any part of the garden, I modestly accepted a little border bounding a small washing-green, where no one would interfere with me. I soon found, however, I had been too precipitate in my acceptance, for two or three trees shaded my border; and after the early spring months, when crocuses and primroses flowered well enough, I had few flowers, and those I had were pale and wan. Some alterations were making in the garden at this time, and I obtained possession of an empty border with a good exposure to light and air; thither I transplanted my chief favourites, and what between plants sent me by friends, and bits of things judiciously cribbed from the general garden, my border was soon filled; and for some years I worked away, gaining experience by my blunders, and making experiments—pleased when I succeeded, and undismayed when I failed. But I changed my garden again; and lest my young readers should accuse me of fickleness, I must briefly tell them the reason, and that will bring me to hint the third:

Expect and accept as little help as possible from the gardener.—My garden was backed by a thorn hedge, which of course required to be cut; I could not do this myself; and greatly annoyed I used to be, on coming out some fine morning to my garden, to find the gardener trampling down my border, and strewing it over with thorns. It did no good to me to have him put it in order again; I liked to do all myself; and I did not like that he should cut the hedge when he chose; so I longed for a spot where there should be "but one mistress and no master." Now, in offering you this last hint, I am far from advising you to be above receiving both assistance and advice from a gardener, but, in general, young people would do well in their little gardens to remember the old saying—" if you wish to be well served, serve yourself." The gardener is often too busy to attend to you, and you must wait his leisure, or, worse still, he knows and cares not where your treasures lie, and smash goes the spade through many a hidden cluster of snow-drops or crocuses, heedless of the little bit of stick you vainly thought a tally sufficient to warn him what was there.

Never mind at first being laughed at for your attempts at gardening: you cannot expect your gardens to look quite as neat as when kept by an experienced gardener; but your pleasure in them will be far greater, and by degrees you will improve in the mechanical processes of hoeing and raking. Digging the borders, I fear, must be left to the gardener, if you wish it done thoroughly, for this requires strength as well as skill. I know few pleasures greater than that of raking one's own garden in spring, when the clods have been softened by the winter's frost; and the bright yellow and purple crocuses look so gay when all the rough earth is raked smooth and even round them. I have grown quite accustomed to be asked in a tone of affected concern, "Why I let the poultry scrape all my garden over in that way?" but I go on, heedless of jests; if I waited for the gardener's help at this busy season, I might wait long enough ; besides I like doing it myself; and I therefore advise all my young friends to serve themselves, and rely on no one's help.   *(To be continued.)*   HORTENSE.

MUSHROOM SPAWN.

MUSHROOM spawn may be made in various ways, and is easily known by its smell and its small fine thread-like and hoary appearance. The smell is just the same as that of the common mushroom. It is to be often met with in manure heaps, and in fields, particularly where hay-ricks have been made, and the old thatch and bottoms have been thrown up into a heap to decay for manure. In heaps of manure that have been thrown out of an old cow-shed, where both horses and cows, &c., run into for shelter; and in the sweepings from horse-mill walks, thrown up into a heap in some dry corner, and allowed to lie for three or four months undisturbed, plenty of mushroom spawn is pretty certain to be generated.

If horse droppings, mixed with sandy loam, equal parts, and partly dry, packed in boxes or large flower-pots, with a small bit of good spawn in it three inches below the surface, all jammed in as solid as it can be done, and put in any heated structure, the whole bulk will very soon be found to be the best of spawn, if kept dry for five or six weeks.

Spawn may also be made in this way. Take one-third horse-droppings, one-third cow and sheep dung, and one-third sandy loam; let these ingredients be well mixed together, adding as much water as will make the whole something like stiff mortar. Spread the whole mixture out on a level bottom or floor in an open shed, from two and a half to three inches thick, and let it remain in that state a few days to dry; then let it be cut out into pieces about the length of common bricks, but a little wider—say an inch wider; let these pieces be so placed as not to get broken, and when dry enough to be handled about with care, and being a little more than half dry, pierce each brick about half through in

two places thus : that is, make the holes about an inch and a half in diameter, and place a small piece of real spawn in each hole, over which a portion of that taken out should be placed, something like sealing it over. After this, let the bricks be so placed as to forward their drying off as quickly as possible; and when perfectly dry have ready a quantity of well-prepared dry, husky, fermenting materials, and place from about six to nine inches thick on the floor of some rather warm shed, and on this place all the pieces in a regular manner, with open spaces; that is, the pieces on one row crossing the openings in the row beneath, just as brick-makers arrange their bricks to dry, and keeping the innoculated side uppermost, to prevent the spawn falling out, bringing the whole up to a point, so that the stack may not fall about. Then cover the whole with the before-mentioned kind of material, so as to give about from 50 to 55 degrees of heat, which will soon cause the spawn to run through the pieces. When this is observed to be the case, let the whole be stored away in some *dry, cold place* until required for use. These dry, light, hoary lumps will keep good for years in a dry place, but in a cold moist situation this spawn would soon perish; and if stored in a warm moist situation, the spawn will commence working or vegetating.—T. WEAVER, *Gardener to the Warden of Winchester College.*

BEES IN AN OLD HIVE.

A nameless correspondent in your 74th number, wishes to be informed how to act in the matter of his large box-hive, which gave two enormous swarms last summer, and weighed at the commencement of winter about 50℔, and which he desires to renovate and alter. The best plan by far, I believe, is that recommended by Dr. Scudamore, of Canterbury (of whose work I spoke favourably on a former occasion, see page 202), by which not only will the stock be saved, and an early harvest of honey be gathered in, but it may be made to swarm *twice before the 1st of June*, if the stock be in a healthy state, and the queen moderately prolific.

As soon as the *first drone* appears in the hive, a swarm may be got from it on the first calm and warm day, by turning the hive up at night, steadying it on a table, applying a box of the same diameter and form to its base, so exactly, that not a bee may escape, and tapping lightly, but quickly, against the sides of the *lower and full box*. In a very few minutes the queen and the major part of her subjects will have ascended into the empty box. Let two sheets of zinc, of *sufficient thickness*, be passed between the boxes, and let them be separated. The *new box* may then be placed on the *old stand*, where, as a new swarm, it will begin instantly to work, whilst the *old box* is removed to a *new stand* at as great a distance as possible from its former situation. Of course, if it be desirable to hive the driven swarm into any other box or hive than that into which it was driven, it may be knocked out of it the next day, upon a sheet spread on the ground, in front of the particular habitation destined for its reception, which must previously be set on the sheet, with one of its sides somewhat elevated from the ground by a stick or wedge, and the bees will quickly enter into it.

At the time this operation was performed—let us say it was done on the 3rd of May, the drones having appeared about a week—there ought to be a young queen in the hive *within about 15 days of her birth* (it may be less or more), in which case, as the young queen does not commence laying till five or six days have elapsed, it will usually happen, that not an egg has been laid in the hive for *three weeks*, or thereabouts; consequently, at the end of that time there will be but few unhatched bees of the old brood, and only a few eggs or very young grubs in the hive. Now, therefore, is the time (as soon as a warm day presents) for forming the *second* swarm, according to the method before recommended for the exclusion of the first, when almost every bee will follow its young queen, and the hive will be left deserted. Those which remain among the combs will be too few to annoy the operator, who may proceed to cut out the combs and *take what honey they contain*.

It *may* so happen, however, that the hive swarms *voluntarily before* the operator has driven them out by force. In the first instance, so much the better (though let him see that the swarm does not perish for want of food, because of ungenial weather) ; in the other instance, some little attention is required. Supposing, therefore, that a second *swarm* issues (which will *generally* be the case if the first swarm issued in the natural way, though rarely, when compelled to migrate) before the operator's assistance was rendered them ; it is clear that a third or fourth swarm may be thrown off within a few days, or at all events that a young queen will have been laying for a fortnight or more, so that the hive will be again filled with brood of all ages. In this case, I believe no rules can be laid down for the guidance of the hive owner, as it is doubtful whether he could so act, as to ensure at *this* season the attainment of his three-fold object, viz. : the preservation of his bees, the early harvest of his honey, and the breaking up of his hive. What I would advise, therefore, is, that if the hive should swarm a third or fourth time, these *colts* (as they are called) be united to some other and weak stock when the new and young queen will *generally* usurp the throne of her weaker rival, or be returned to the parent stock, (after fumigation of the colt to the destruction of its queen), which must be preserved as a working stock till the middle of August. It may then be fumigated or driven (as recommended before), and the bees so saved be united to some other stock ; *or, having been strengthened by the union of one, or two, or more tribes of expatriated bees, be returned to the old hive, after it has been emptied, cleansed, and altered, and fed liberally, and treated generously,* as I myself did a united colony of preserved bees last autumn, and which are now

(March 2nd) in full strength and vigour.* I would treat your stock in a similar way, supposing no swarms issued *after the second*, which, however, was thrown off *naturally* after the forcible ejection of the first swarm, because, ten to one, the hive will be full of brood of all ages.

While I am writing on this subject I wish to add a few words about my feeding-trough, which was described in your 74th Number. The "cylindrical tube of zinc" there mentioned, will be better made to *descend* half an inch into the hive, and to *ascend* not more than *one* inch into the feeder ; and it would be a great advantage and assistance to the bees if a *tube of wood* were made exactly to fit the inner side of the cylinder, about the sixth of an inch in thickness. The corks or wood affixed to the under side of the perforated zinc plate (*wood* would be better than zinc for this purpose *if* it could be prevented from warping) ought not to be more than a quarter of an inch thick, and it ought to be painted or charred with fire to render it impermeable by the liquor; otherwise it increases in weight, and the plate will be *flooded*—a thing carefully to be avoided at all times.

I will say a word about my apiary, according to promise, before I conclude, so that I may not trouble you again too soon. *All* my hives and colonies are in good health—the straw hives (D and E) being the *most* active. The result of my winter observation on the decrease in their weight is as follows :—

"A," 13th Nov., 19 ℔ ; 13th Feb., 14½ ℔ ; diminution, 1½ ℔ per month.
"B," 28th Sept., 25 ℔ ; 28th Feb., 16½ ℔ ; 　do.　　1½ ℔ 　 "
"C," 13th Nov., 25 ℔ ; 13th Feb., 21½ ℔ ; 　do.　　1 1-6 ℔ 　 "

By this it would appear that "B," which was the most numerous, consumed the greatest quantity of *food* ; but it must not be lost sight of that the largest consumption would have occurred in October and the early part of November ; last month it had diminished in weight only 1½ ℔, which seems to confirm this belief.—A COUNTRY CURATE.

THE CHOICE OF A HUNTER.

IN a paper on "The Choice of a Hackney," published in THE DOMESTIC ECONOMIST, we omitted to state an essential qualification which, however, in the eye of every horseman must have been fully implied by our other observations : we refer to that *sine qua non* in a hackney, *lean oblique shoulders*. The shape of the shoulder-blade should be well displayed, and not hidden under a mass of useless material which is found in heavy-shouldered horses. The withers should be high, and should gradually decline towards the back, which formation secures a proper resting place for the saddle, and prevents it slipping forwards. It also implies an extension of the *scapula* or shoulder-blade, the existence of which very much governs the proper action of the fore limbs, and causes the animal to be both a good walker and trotter, and at the same time secures *safety*, by preventing the fore legs from being placed too much under the body.

The observations which we have made under the preceding head, will very much break the ground for the consideration of the other subjects of our notice, and more particularly for that which will next engage our attention, viz., THE CHOICE OF A HUNTER.

Bearing in mind the many desirable qualifications which we have deemed essential for the hackney, it will be desirable to retain them, or as many of them as possible, in the hunter; but, in addition, we must have both strength, and speed, and bottom. For the two latter acquisitions, breeding is required ; and when this is combined with substance enough to carry from 14 to 16 stone, we have that magnificent animal which no other country in the world can produce, *the three-parts-bred hunter*.

The old hunter of the last century was a somewhat different animal. When the huntsman's horn was heard at peep of day, neither the horse, nor the master, nor the hounds, had any idea of a run of some thirty or forty minutes duration, during which a distance of ten or fifteen miles might have been traversed with the speed of the wind. The hound was a larger and slower animal, and consequently the great speed was not demanded in the horse; strength and endurance being for the most part required. The improvement of the speed in the horse and the hound kept pace with each other, as they were required to keep pace in the field ; but

* See page 202 of this year's volume.

with the difference that the horse having the weight of his rider to carry in addition to his own, greater speed was acquired in him; yet, without a sacrifice of substance.

We have said, that all the qualifications of the hack are desirable in the hunter, but it is rarely they are so possessed; for out of a stable of a dozen hunters it is doubtful whether we can find more than two really good hacks. One, perhaps, may be too sluggish in his slow paces; another may trip in his walk, though safe enough in his gallop; a third may be an indifferent trotter, or may have too short a neck, or may carry his head too straight, or too low. Any of these defects, though unredeemable in a hack, may yet exist in a hunter, accompanied with such marked excellencies as to render the possessor a first-class animal.

Strength, speed, and bottom, are the three cardinal virtues in a hunter; but these virtues may all be neutralized if the animal is either of a restive disposition, or of a hot, or irritable temperament. Of the two faults the last is the worst, inasmuch as it is incurable; for although an irritable horse will often make an excellent hack, or single-harness horse, he is perfectly useless as a hunter; for not only will he contrive to do three days' work in one, and thus require, perhaps, a fortnight to recruit, but he wearies the rider's arms in pulling at the bit, and endangers his head in rushing under the boughs of trees, or his legs in passing through gate-ways. The rider may esteem himself fortunate if he arrives home with merely the loss of a hat, or the skirt of a coat.

A restive or bad-tempered horse, on the other hand, may to a great extent be cured, by a good rider firmly resisting his evil propensities; for to sit a restive horse, is in great measure to cure him; and it is notorious that some of the most troublesome young horses have turned out the best hunters. A disposition to kick other horses is one of the worst vices of a hunter, as there are so many opportunities offered for the indulgence of the vice when a number of horsemen crowd together in a narrow lane or path-way, or at the "finish." A celebrated sportsman having an excellent mare with this unfortunate propensity, used when riding her to have a large label pinned to his back, on which in large letters was written, " SHE KICKS." It is not every one that would have the same consideration for his friends, or, having it, would submit to the singularity of such a mode of caution.

A hunter, therefore, is required to be steady and quiet with hounds, to have a good, though not too light a mouth, so as to bear a little pulling occasionally, which will ease and support him in a run; and this, with speed, strength, and bottom, will render him a valuable animal. It is extraordinary what large prices some hunters will realize; but it is only after some brilliant run that such sums are obtained. The writer has known an ordinary looking horse supposed to be bought dear at £40, afterwards sold for £100, then £150, again for £300. Another little animal, *at fifteen years old*, has lately realized £150 at a public auction; and these prices are very moderate as compared with the more aristocratic sums of £400, £600, and £800, which have sometimes been given.

Although the rarity of the possession of a combination of extraordinary qualities will often command such prices, yet we must observe, that there is no mistake so great as that frequently made in giving a very large sum of money for a horse, whose great reputation has been earned by such long continued services, as totally to incapacitate him for their further repetition. W. C. SPOONER.

VEGETABLE COOKERY.

THOSE who reside in the country can vary their dinners in a pleasant manner, by attending to their gardens, and having a succession of vegetables; and even in towns where vegetables have to be purchased it is still a piece of economy to have them. I do not mean to recommend such as are expensive, but the commoner sorts, such as carrots, turnips, parsnips, and onions; these are sold at a low price, and, if nicely cooked, they will be much relished both for breakfast and supper. Potatoes I need not recommend, they are fully appreciated, but still a few hints as to the method of dressing these universal favourites may not be useless. How much more comfortable it must be for those who go from home each day early in the morning, to follow their different callings, to have a nice hot mess of fried vegetables for breakfast instead of merely bread and butter, or bread

and cheese; the vegetables, if seasoned with pepper and salt, and fried in a little grease, will be most palatable, and will at the same time materially lessen the baker's bill. I observe many people who possess gardens are very ready to give to the pigs the vegetables that are not required for the dinner table, apparently forgetting that there are other meals to be prepared, and that although bread and butter are very good things, yet a change is always desirable, and that even in cookery "variety is charming." Where there are servants to provide for, vegetables will be found very serviceable; and the cook should be told to prepare some each day, particularly for the supper table.

Those who are able to gather their own vegetables should be careful to do so before the sun has shone long on them; they should also be used as fresh as possible. If they are obliged to be kept, put them into the cellar, or in some place where the sun cannot reach them; and put them on the bricks or the stone floor, not on the shelf; on no account should they be kept in water, as it makes them insipid and unwholesome. Cabbages, cauliflowers, brocoli, and all vegetables in which insects are liable to remain, should be thrown into cold salt and water before boiling.

BOILING POTATOES.—There is some attention required in boiling all vegetables, potatoes not excepted; cooks very often imagine such is not the case, and the consequence is that potatoes are constantly sent to table badly dressed, either crisp and indigestible or else boiled to pieces and full of water. Almost all sorts of potatoes are improved by being boiled "in their jackets;" they must be put into *cold* water (which is not the case with the generality of vegetables), into which a spoonful of salt has been put; when the water boils pour a little more cold water into the saucepan, in order to check it, and let it remain on the fire till a fork will pierce the potato easily; then strain the water off, and let the saucepan remain by the fire for ten minutes or a quarter of an hour, when the potatoes will have become dry and mealy.

ROASTING POTATOES.—A most excellent way of dressing them for supper is to bake them, or roast them as it is sometimes called; an oven by the side of the fire answers best for this purpose, but it can be well managed in an American oven hanging in front of the fire; they take nearly two hours to do them sufficiently, but then they require no watching, merely turning them at the end of the first hour. Eaten with a little butter or fresh dripping they make a very favourite supper dish, particularly with children.

FRIED POTATOES are also very nice; the best plan is to boil more than you require for your meal the day before, and when half done take a few out of the saucepan, and the next day they will be firm enough to cut into thin slices, which are to be put into a frying-pan in which there is some boiling dripping; fry them till they are nicely browned, and before putting them on the dish sprinkle some pepper and salt over them.

HASHED VEGETABLES.—Potatoes make a nice dish if mashed up with any cold vegetables, such as carrots, turnips, cabbage, spinach, or onions; therefore, save any vegetable which may be left from the dinner, mix them well together with some salt and pepper, and either put the mixture in the oven until it becomes very hot, or fry it.

ONIONS are most wholesome, and very sustaining. The poor should always be encouraged to plant them in their gardens. The large onion roasted in front of the fire, or fried in slices, is very good.

JERUSALEM ARTICHOKES may be parboiled and fried with the onions, using plenty of pepper and salt. Jerusalem artichokes require a very short time in boiling—a quarter of an hour is generally sufficient; their skins must be removed before they are put into the saucepan, and immediately they are soft enough the water must be strained off, or they will be watery.

CARROTS are very nutritious, and where it is possible they should be constantly seen on the table. Old carrots require boiling a long time, sometimes nearly two hours; half an hour is sufficient for young carrots. When you have a piece of boiled meat for your dinner always put the carrots into the same saucepan; it materially improves their flavour, and they become very tender. Carrots and *parsnips* must not be peeled before boiling, but merely scrubbed with a brush (kept on purpose for such work) and well washed.

TURNIPS require peeling. They must be put on in boiling

water with a little salt, and if field turnips they will take nearly an hour to boil; garden turnips take less time, but they are not so palatable as those grown in the fields.

CABBAGES are very generally liked; they require boiling from half an hour to an hour, according to their size. Great care must be taken that they are well freed from caterpillars; when first picked there are generally some in each head of cabbage. A large spoonful of salt must be put into the water in which they are boiled.

GREEN PEAS and FRENCH BEANS will very soon be plentiful, and when that is the case I should strongly recommend their making their appearance at your "festive board." Peas should not be shelled till just before they are put into the saucepan; or, should you be obliged to do so, put them into a basin, and over it place a wet cloth. They must be put into boiling water, in which has been dissolved a very small piece of soda and a lump of sugar. A few sprigs of mint boiled with them is observed to improve their flavour. Twenty minutes is generally sufficient time to allow for boiling them, but when done they will sink to the bottom of the saucepan.

Do not throw away the shells of the peas, but put them into a saucepan with some bones, onions, and herbs, and the soup when strained will have the flavour of green pea soup, though of course not so highly flavoured as when the peas themselves are used.

FRENCH BEANS are cut before boiling into long narrow strips. If prepared before you are ready to boil them, treat them in the same way as the peas; for if exposed to the heat after they are cut, their colour will be bad. A quarter of an hour is generally sufficient for them.

BROAD BEANS, when in season, are sold at a very reasonable rate; and if served with a piece of bacon, they make an excellent dinner. Half an hour is allowed for boiling them; and a bunch of parsley put into the saucepan with them is reckoned an improvement.

SPINACH requires attention in dressing, but when nicely cooked, it is an excellent vegetable. Each leaf should be picked and washed in two waters, then put it into a saucepan with a little salt and the least possible quantity of water, just enough to prevent the saucepan burning. Ten minutes is sufficient time to allow it to boil; drain it on a sieve, press it between two plates to extract all moisture, then beat it very smoothly with a little cream or butter, some salt, and a little pepper. Put it into a dry saucepan, and make it quite hot. Poached eggs are often served on it. It has a very pretty effect, and where poultry is kept it becomes an economical dish.

ASPARAGUS is tied in bunches before it is put into the saucepan; care must be taken that the stalks are all one length. They must be taken out of the water directly they are tender, or the colour will not be good. Twenty minutes is considered sufficient time to allow them to boil. A piece of rather thick toast, nicely browned, should be placed on the dish, and the asparagus on that. Melted butter must be handed round with the asparagus. The bundles should contain 25 heads of asparagus; three bundles are sufficient for a middle-sized dish.

STALKS OF THE WHITE BEET make a very good substitute for asparagus, and as it is in season when most other vegetables are scarce, it would be well if it were extensively cultivated. The stalks must be peeled before boiling, and tied in bundles the same size and length as asparagus. The leaves, also, of the white beet are a good substitute for spinach, and must be dressed in the same manner, only more time allowed for boiling.

BEET ROOT must be very carefully scrubbed and washed before boiling, not scraped, for if the skin breaks, the juice escapes, and the beautiful colour is lost or impaired. A small root requires an hour's boiling. When cold, they are sliced and eaten with vinegar, and, if approved of, oil and mustard. Beet-root is a capital addition to a bread and butter supper. These trifles should be attended to, for trifles constitute the happiness or misery of many a home. But at the same time, let us remember when inclined to be worried, that circumstances which now appear all momentous will ere long appear as "nothing," in fact, will excite our surprise and regret that we ever allowed our thoughts to dwell on such trifles. Remember this question—"What is a man profited if he gain the whole world, and lose his own soul."

C. A. M.

ARTICLES IN SEASON IN APRIL.—Meat: Beef, mutton, veal, lamb. Fish: Carp, cod, brill, eels, lobsters, mackerel, mullet, oysters, perch, pike, plaice, prawns, salmon, shrimps, skate, soles, tench, whiting, turbot. Poultry: Chickens, pullets, ducklings, rabbits, pigeons. Vegetables: Sea-kale, lettuce, parsnips, spinach; in very early gardens asparagus and cucumbers, small salading and radishes.

TO CORRESPONDENTS.

ERROR.—CLIMBING ROSES (W. X. W.).—In the list we gave at page 13, for Acidalie, which all flower cultivators know to be very dwarf, read Adelaide; but a still better is Princess Louise, creamy white, tinged with rose. The Gloire de Rosomene, we omitted to say should be planted with the other roses to keep the bottoms thick.

CANKERED APPLE-TREES (Mol Fos).—"Two apple-trees, growing in very different situations, have the bark die off close to the ground, excepting a piece about three inches wide. One tree (a French codling) grows in a damp, rich soil, eight feet from the brink of a fresh water river. The other tree (an early desert apple) grows on a dry, light soil, seven feet above the river. Both trees are of 25 years standing." Your trees are cankered from excessive moisture in the subsoil, into which the roots have penetrated. Your only remedies are to cut away all the deep striking roots, and to encourage the growth of surface roots, by mulching the surface, and not allowing the spade to come within six or seven feet of the stems of the fruit trees all round. The cankered places may be cut out with a sharp knife, and when quite dry, painted over with liquid Indian rubber, to exclude the wet and air. But you would act still better if you planted fresh trees on stations as directed by Mr. Errington.

LAWNS (E. L. H.).—By all means lay it down with turf. If this be well laid now, and care bestowed on rolling it, and watering it when needed, through the summer, it will not crack, unless the soil be very clayey. Do you require trailing or climbing plants for your arches? and what are these arches?

HERACLEUM GIGANTEUM (G. G. B.).—This is perfectly hardy. If sown last autumn, it will bloom in June, or July. Hardy annuals can be sown in an open border, and transplanted.

GOLDEN-CHAIN GERANIUM (A Young Lady).—We cannot tell where you can obtain cuttings of this. Can any of our readers ?

LEMON PICKLE (A Subscriber).—Scrape the insides out of two lemons, fill them with salt, sew them up, and dry them slowly in an oven. When they are dried, boil for five minutes a quart of vinegar in which have been put a dozen blades of long pepper; half a gill of mustard seeds; six cloves of garlic; and six shreds of ginger. When the vinegar is cold, pour it upon the lemons; let the whole remain in a warm, but not hot, place for three months. Then strain and bottle it, corking it close.

LIQUID INDIAN RUBBER (B. French).—You may make this, for painting over the wounds caused in trees by pruning, &c., by dissolving pieces of Indian rubber in naptha. The Indian rubber is easily cut into pieces, if you dip the sharp knife you use into cold water from time to time. Both naptha and diacholon plaister (ready spread) may be obtained of any chemist.

POTATO PLANTING (E. S. P.).—Planting so late, you must expect to lose half your crop by the potato murrain. However, as you have only "just taken possession," there is a reason for doing it now. But remember in future to plant in November, or to save your sets between layers of earth until February, and then plant. You need no other manure than lime, soot, and salt, spread over the ground, and dug in at the time of planting. Do not put guano nor any other rich stimulating manure.

RECIPE (Mrs. E. K).—Thanks. We shall be obliged by the recipe.

GREEN ALPINE STRAWBERRY SEED (A Constant Subscriber).—Can any one only inform our correspondent where some of this seed can be obtained?

DYEING WOOLLENS BLACK (A Lady).—Soak the articles in a solution of acetate of iron (obtainable at a chemist's) for twenty-four hours, and then for a similar time in a liquor made by boiling a pound of logwood chips and madder in a gallon of water. Cotton gloves may be dyed fawn or buff colour by dipping them into some of the last-named liquor only.

AYLESBURY DUCKS (E. J. H.).—Can any of our readers inform our correspondent where the genuine Aylesbury ducks can be purchased, and at what price?

TAYLOR'S AMATEURS' BOX HIVE (Ibid).—You will find a drawing of it at page 396 of our first volume. Our correspondent says, "I would venture to recommend a box called the 'Albert,' invented by Mr. Milton, of Great Marylebone-street. It is, in my opinion, formed on the most correct principle, and I have every reason to be satisfied with it."

BEES (Rev. W. B. A.).—"I have one common hive, two or three years old, without a hole at top; it swarmed twice last year, and will do so again, I conclude, this; could I with advantage cut out a two-inch hole, and put on a small hive or box, at the end of April? or had I better let them swarm, and hive them into one of 'Payne's Improved?' I should like your opinion of using Nutt's hives. I tried for several years, but I never succeeded. Could I not use the centre box (properly boarded at the sides), and have a small box at the top? Or is there really an objection to a square shape, on account of the condensed air falling from the flat top? We have 'heather' on the hills, but is it not a long way for the bees to fly,—it being some 500 or 700 feet higher than the village, and perhaps one, or one and a half, mile off? Would it be desirable to send the hives up to the heather when in bloom?" You may cut a hole in the top of your hive. See COTTAGE GARDENER, vol. ii., page 42: you will there see that a four-inch hole is necessary. If you look at our correspondence you will see that *Nutt's hives* prove failures almost everywhere. You may board up the sides of the centre box, and put a glass or box upon the top as you propose. Your hills are not too far off for your bees, yet removing your bees to the heather when in bloom would certainly be attended with advantage.

HOTHOUSE AND GREENHOUSE COMBINED (*W. F. Chapman*).—"I have just completed a greenhouse eighteen feet long and twelve wide, with front lights to open, and top ones to slide on rollers in the usual way. I wish to have a vine, and also grow greenhouse plants, to do which I have had a glazed division with doors, so as to form a hot and greenhouse, with two pits in front, one of which I propose to use as a cold frame in winter, the other to act the vine in : how to do so in the best manner is the knowledge I require. I have had the pit excavated three feet deep, and find the subsoil gravelly, and resembling lumps of iron ore. I have had the bottom lined with tiles, and have put on the top of them about six inches of brick ends; and my surface-soil is good. The aspect is about S.S.E., and heated by a flue, which runs along the north-west end, the front, and east end. The fire is at the back of the wall, in the north corner. I have no damper, as I consider it unnecessary, as the entrance is from the east end, and the chimney in the east corner ; so that when I require a strong heat in the hothouse, I can open the door or front lights in the greenhouse, to keep it the required temperature." We have no doubt that you will succeed, as you deserve to do. As one flue passes through and heats both divisions, you will obtain an advantage and a disadvantage: an advantage in being able to give more air in cold weather to your greenhouse plants, which will render them more healthy—a disadvantage, that if this is not attended to, your greenhouse will become too hot, especially at *night*, though you have partly taken precaution against this, by placing the greenhouse at the farthest end from the fire. Your flue running close to the front wall will also be of advantage to your pits in front; one for plants, the other for a vine to be planted in, and the head trained in one of the houses, or both. You have not said whether you intend covering the pit for the vine with glass, though, if you did, you might winter many things there that did not require much water, &c. There is only one defect we perceive in your preparing for the vine: with such a subsoil as you describe, you should have a *drain* somewhat lower than the bottom of your border, to prevent all possibility of stagnant moisture. Before placing your turf on the tile and brick ends, wash a little concrete among them, made of four parts drifts to one of lime, and plenty of water. Place only a layer or two of your sods above this; break and incorporate the remainder among your *good* soil—drift, lime rubbish, and rotten dung; but instead of using too much of the latter, obtain several bushels of *broken*—not bruised or ground—bones, which will give out their nourishment for years. Let the bottom and tops of your border incline at an angle of from 45° to 55°. The best kinds to plant will be Black Hamburgh and Royal Muscadine. They, as well as the other things you mention, can be procured from any respectable nurseryman.

HOVEA CELSII (*Hibernia*).—Your plant is in full bloom, nearly two feet high, all the flowers within four or five inches of the top, the lower part of the plant is without leaves or branches ; and you ask if you may head it down, and whether you can propagate by the top young shoots as cuttings? You should not cut it down too low, as the wood may be so hard it would not break freely. Cut back so as to leave a bud or two of your present flowering shoots. Cuttings of it are best formed from small side shoots ; but the part cut away, if young, will also succeed, if placed under a bell-glass, shaded, and at first kept cool, and afterwards put in a sweet bottom-heat.

BROMHAM HALL MELON (*A Subscriber*).—You may obtain six seeds for half-a-crown of Mr. Tiley, seedsman, 16, Pulteney Bridge, Bath.

CALENDARS (*I. T. Lawler*).—In these, *b* means *beginning* of the month, and *e* the *end*.

SEEDS (*Rev. H. W.*).—Thanks for those sent.

SAWDUST (*E. U.*).—Sawdust, we think, might be mixed with leaves in forming a hotbed, and would render its heat more permanent. Why not mix all together with the horse-dung? Leaves and dung should be mixed together for a hotbed, not placed one over the other.

VINES ON A SPAN ROOF (*T. W.*).—There is no weight in the objection to training vines up one side and down the other side of the roof. We do it ourselves successfully. Will you oblige us with a plan and description of your Shippen *vinery*—giving dimensions, &c.?

OXYGEN TO THE ROOTS OF PLANTS (*O. Stevens*).—This being beneficial when applied to them, *favours* our experience that earthing-up potatoes is injurious. The deeper these are buried the less the air can get to them. We are in favour of stirring the surface often.

HEATING GREENHOUSE (*A Subscriber, Normanby*).—It is quite possible to heat a small greenhouse (9 feet by 6 feet) by means of a flue or pipe ; but do not have it of metal.

PAYNE'S COTTAGE HIVES (*W. A. E.*).—See an editorial upon the price of these to-day.

MALE AND FEMALE BLOSSOMS (*R. Jackson*).—These are united in the same flower in all our cultivated wall-fruits, and no protection usually given prevents impregnation. The covering taken off in fine days permits the winds and insects to aid in the fertilization. It takes place even in our stoves and greenhouses.

CORRESPONDENCE (*S. N. V.*).—You think "more encouragement

might be given to correspondents." In reply to which we can only say that we are always most glad to receive communications, and to insert them as soon as we can find room. All letters must be addressed to "The Editor of THE COTTAGE GARDENER. Office, 2, Amen-corner, Paternoster-row, London."

HORSE WITH WEAK FORE-LEGS (*F. S. P.*).—You say of your horse:— "In cantering, I have not known it make a false step ; but in walking, it (some days) repeatedly bends the knee of the leg remaining on the ground while making a step ; and this takes place just when the weight of the fore body comes before the perpendicular. The sensation to the riding person is as if the beast was falling. The horse *rather* (what is called *stands over* when quiet : its feet and legs quite sound; but I fancy the near fore-leg is a little short in its step; but it is the off-leg the knee of which has the trick of bending." The animal is evidently not a proper one for a lady to ride. There is great weakness of the fore-legs ; and a sudden weight thrown on the fore-limbs, under which a horse with good firm legs would not succumb, would probably again bring the animal in question to the ground.—W. C. S.

WHITE FORGET-ME-NOT (*Flora*).—If you will favour us with your address, another correspondent obligingly offers to supply you.

COVERS FOR VOLUMES.—We cannot recommend binders. Any one can have the covers at our office, price 1s each ; and can have them put on by any binder in their neighbourhood.

LILIUM LANCIFOLIUM (*R. S.*).—This fine bulb requires very little water until the leaves are well up from the soil ; if the soil is not *dry*, it is enough ; and it does not require a great deal of water through the summer. A cool, airy house, with a south aspect, is best for it till midsummer ; and from that till the middle of August it will do better out of doors in a warm sheltered place.

SCARLET GERANIUMS (*S.*).—If you have wintered these in pots in a dry state you may now water them, so as to wet the whole ball, and keep them moist. As soon as you see them growing out back all the dead pieces, if any, down to a live bud ; and when leaves begin to open shake the plants out of the winter soil, and repot them in fresh compost. If they were kept out of pots you may now trim off their smallest roots and pot them at once, and give them water also.

TAGETES TENUIFOLIA AND SANVITALIA PROCUMBENS (*Ibid*).—The former is from 18 to 24 inches high, and the latter half those heights, according to the soil. Both are yellow.

JACOBEA LILIES (*Tooling*).—Although not yet growing, these are quite right. Allow them their own time, and, if the bulbs were properly grown last season, and are old enough, they will be certain to flower with you. You have only to keep the soil from getting dry till their leaves are a few inches high, then to water them freely, and as soon as their bloom is over to plant them out on a warm border, placing the upper surface of the ball an inch below that of the soil, and apply water in dry weather. Let them remain till the approach of frost, when they are to be taken up and kept dry over the winter.

OLD TREE AS A FLOWER SUPPORTER (*J. S. Trundle*).—If the pear-tree is not surrounded by other trees, you may plant any ornamental climber against it without any preparation. If the ground about it is full of roots from other trees, there is no better way of managing than sinking old barrels, in which climbers are nursed until they are strong enough to take care of themselves. Refer to what Mr. Beaton said about climbers in such situations, and select according to your own taste.

GERANIUM—TOM THUMB (*A. E. D.*).—You have been trying to preserve a small scarlet geranium (Tom Thumb) in a pot through the winter, after the plan given by Mr. Beaton, as adopted by Henry Moore. It has been kept in a dry room where there has been a fire for a few hours once a week, and no water given it. There is no appearance of any leaves at present. Take a knife and cut the bark here and there, and if the plant is dead the inside will be black, or nearly so ; but if it looks green or fresh it is all right ; and you may cut off any dead tops, and water it at once, and it will soon grow again. The same test is applicable to any other geranium, to ascertain whether it is alive.

NAMES OF PLANTS (*F. Giles*).—No. 1, we cannot name without seeing a flower ; 2, is *Cistus incanus* ; 3, is an *Azalea indica*; but we can say no more from merely seeing a few leaves.

INSECTS (*C. C.*).—The patch of eggs on a web is what may be termed the nest of the Vaporer Moth (*Orgyia antiqua*) ; they should be sought for and destroyed ; as the caterpillars from those eggs are very destructive to the leaves of wall-fruit, and of many flowers. (*C. A.*).—The grubs which have injured the roots of your vines and cyclamens, are the larvæ of some species of weevil, and probably of *Otiorhynchus sulcatus* or *O. picipes*. For a drawing of the first-named see page 125 of our last volume.

AQUATICS (*J. T.*).—Your letter, unfortunately, was mislaid, or it would have been answered sooner. Pray excuse the delay. There can be no doubt but small growing aquatics would do well on the shelves formed under the water in your pond. The pots should be as wide as the shelves will allow, and be filled with rich loam and mud. The plants should be firmly secured in the mould with small stones, to prevent the winds tearing them out of the pots. The larger aquatics might be placed in the centre, but not too thickly ; such, for instance, as the beautiful White Water lily.

LONDON: Printed by HARRY WOOLDRIDGE, Winchester High Street. In the Parish of Saint Mary Kalendar, and Published by WILLIAM SOMERVILLE ORR, at the Office, No. 2, Amen Corner, in the Parish of Christ Church, City of London.—April 11th, 1850.

WEEKLY CALENDAR.

M D	W D	APRIL 18—24, 1850.	Weather near London in 1849.			Sun Rises.	Sun Sets.	Moon R. & S.	Moon's Age.	Clock bef. Sun.	Day of Year.
18	Th		T. 50°—32°.	W.	Rain.	59 a. 4	59 a. 6	0 40	6	0 49	108
19	F	Alphege. Swallows first seen.	T. 50°—32°.	N.E.	Rain.	57	V11	1 34	)	0 54	109
20	S	Sun's declin., 11° 30' N. Song Thrush hatches.	T. 47°—26°.	N.	Rain.	55	2	2 20	8	1 7	110
21	SUN	3 SUNDAY AFTER EASTER.	T. 48°—27°.	W.	Fine.	54	4	2 53	9	1 20	111
22	M	Jelly Nostoc on lawns.	T. 48°—30°.	S.W.	Rain.	53	5	3 27	10	1 32	112
23	Tu	St. George. Squirrel builds.	T. 50°—38°.	S.W.	Rain.	50	7	3 55	11	1 44	113
24	W	Winchat first heard.	T. 50°—43°.	N.	Fine.	48	8	4 21	12	1 56	114

ON the 7th of April, 1797, died the Rev. WILLIAM MASON, author of *The English Garden*, a poem written to aid that better taste in the arrangement of extensive grounds, which, as noticed last week, Mr. Gilpin was at the same time advocating and advancing with prose and pencil. The first book, or canto, of this poem appeared in 1772, and the other three books between that year and 1782. The harmonious weakness of its blank verse we need not here exemplify, nor would it be criticism justly placed to shew causes for condemning the long episode of Nerina in the concluding book. We may more appropriately observe upon the gardening taste exhibited in the poem; and that the foundation on which he wrought is good may be judged from his definition of landscape gardening in three of its lines:—

> "The Art, which, varying forms and blending hues,
> Gives that harmonious force of shade and light
> Which makes the landscape perfect."

His condemnation of the old, formal style—

> " When, borrowing aid
> From geometric skill, they vainly strove,
> By line, by plummet, and unfeeling shears,

To form with verdure what the builder formed With stone "—

his pleading for adapting the plantations to the boldness or gentle slopes of the surface—for simplicity and a due regard to utility in all the decorations—are unexceptionably excellent. Indeed, the whole poem may be read with pleasure, and without any suggestion being detected inconsistent with good taste. This is saying that it achieves all that could be expected from it, and all that it could attempt; for practical directions written in poetry would be as little regarded by the gardener as by the lawyer are Coke's Institutes in verse.

He who was the advocate for taking nature as a model in gardening may be readily believed to be the author of that spirited satire, " An Heroic Epistle to Sir. W. Chambers," who had laboured to render attractive the puerilities of Chinese gardening. There is also some reason for believing that he was the author of "A Sketch from 'The Landscape,' a Poem, by R. P. Knight." This concludes the short catalogue of his works relating to gardening, but others were among his manuscripts. These were unfinished at the time of his unexpected decease; for he is one of the many instances that death may fly to us on a feather as surely as on a bowman's shaft. He wounded his shin when stepping from his carriage, and within two days the trifling wound had proved fatal. He was in his seventy-third year, and died—where he had lived the chief part of half a century—at his rectory of Aston, in Yorkshire.

METEOROLOGY OF THE WEEK. The average highest and lowest temperatures of the above days, at Chiswick, during the last twenty-three years, have been 58.6° and 38.3°, respectively. During the same period, 97 of the days were fine, and on 64 rain occurred.

RANGE OF BAROMETER—RAIN IN INCHES.

April		1841.	1842.	1843.	1844.	1845.	1846.	1847.	1848.	1849.
18	B. {	29.975	30.301	30.140	30.224	30.157	30.003	29.876	29.595	29.921
		29.924	30.091	29.980	30.194	36.101	29.993	29.790	29.306	29.861
	R.	0.14	—	—	0.01	—	0.02	—	0.31	0.38
19	B. {	29.995	30.199	29.960	30.281	30.081	30.197	29.813	29.354	29.464
		29.281	30.154	29.766	30.307	30.092	30.019	29.712	29.398	29.504
	R.	—	—	—	—	—	—	—	—	0.45
20	B. {	29 802	30.150	29.778	30.274	30.139	30.106	29.884	29.389	29.906
		29.562	30.092	29.690	30.106	30.072	30.072	29.742	29.304	29.564
	R.	—	—	—	—	0.03	—	—	4.39	0.01
21	B. {	29.904	30.140	29.849	30.197	30.108	30.049	30.027	29.507	29.295
		29.810	30.047	29.833	30.119	30.014	29.955	29.962	29.442	29.864
	R.	—	—	0.05	—	—	—	—	0.09	—
22	B. {	29.856	29.994	29.969	30.233	29.962	29.875	30.064	29.563	29.936
		29.734	29.899	29.815	30.124	29.924	29.851	29.950	29.447	29.762
	R.	—	—	0.03	—	—	—	—	0.09	0.22
23	B. {	29.545	29.901	30.043	30.234	29.851	29.815	30.024	29.679	29.683
		29.450	29.878	30.035	30.090	29.797	29.773	29.974	29.652	29.561
	R.	0.34	—	—	—	0.27	—	—	0.03	0.21
24	B. {	29.677	29.948	30.012	30.176	29.747	29.855	29.987	29.823	29.894
		29.552	29.921	29.990	30.070	29.707	29.746	29.962	29.619	29.704
	R.	0.15	0.01	—	—	—	0.05	—	0.08	—

NATURAL PHENOMENA INDICATIVE OF WEATHER. — When the surface of *the sea* is rough, and the waves, or " swell," rise without any wind sufficient to create them, a gale will shortly occur, and from the quarter whence the swell moves. We remember when voyaging to and from India, the commanders frequently and correctly foretold the occurrence of blowing weather from this indication. *Mock moons* (Paraselene) and *mock suns* (Parhelia) are usually followed by much rain and high winds.

THE first English author who notices THE AURICULA is old John Gerard. It is described and figured by him in his " Herbal," which appeared in 1597, and is there called the *Bear's Ear*, or *Mountain Cowslip*. He says there were then many sorts; giving drawings of eight:— the yellow, the purple, the scarlet, the blush-coloured, and several reds. Gerard gives it the specific botanical name of *Auricula Ursi* (Bear's Ear); but by Matthiolus and others it was named *Sanicula alpina*, from its supposed healing virtues and mountain birthplace. It was often called by ladies the French Cowslip.* Parkinson says it obviously belonged to the cow-

* It is very certain that auriculas were thus early much cultivated by French florists, for there is a poem in their praise, in a curious work published at Douay, in 1616, entitled " Jardin d'Hyver; " and with the verses are numerous drawings of the Auriculas, or " d'Oreilles d'Ours," as they are there called.

slip family, but Lugdwig was the first to arrange it there under the generic name of *Primula*.

Gerard says that the eight kinds he enumerates were then commonly grown in the gardens about London, but it is evident they were not much esteemed; nor is any notice taken of raising varieties from seed.

This neglect soon passed away, for Johnson, in his edition of Gerard, published in 1633, says that there were then a very great many varieties of these flowers growing in the gardens of Mr. Tradescant and Mr. Tuggie. Tradescant's garden was at Lambeth; and he, at the time Johnson wrote, was gardener to Charles I. Tradescant was a Dutchman; and there is little room for doubting, that, bringing with him that knowledge of floriculture for which his countrymen were even then justly famed, he applied it to the improvement of the Auricula, which in Holland had been neglected. At all events, the attention then paid to this flower in England was as great even as at present.

Parkinson, in his "Paradisus," published in 1656, says that "those who had been industrious in sowing the seeds of the several sorts" had so succeeded in raising varieties that he should not be able to enumerate them all. He describes, however, 21 varieties; and the drawing of one of these, "The greatest faire yellow Beare's Eares with eyes," shews that the florists had indeed much improved the flower; for, in the sketches given by Gerard and Lyte, the pips are small, and only four or five in a truss, but in this and others, given by Parkinson, the pips are large, and increased in number to from 8 to 13.

The raising varieties from seed was then well known, but regular canons for distinguishing a good flower were not yet established, as they probably were when the "Complete Florilege" was published by John Rea, Gent.: in the third edition of which work, printed in 1702, there are many varieties noticed, and named after their raisers.

Mr. Hughes, in his "Flower Garden," published in 1672, gives a short direction for its cultivation; and is the first writer on gardening we have met with who speaks of it as the "Auricula."

The cultivation of this flower continued to increase in favour; and it is the first of our show flowers of which canons were published in a separate work, whereby the superiority of rival flowers might be determined. The work in which these canons, or rules, appeared was written by Mr. James Thompson, a florist of Newcastle; and printed at that town, in 1757, under the title of "The distinguishing properties of a fine Auricula."

These, however, were not the first; for that fertile writer on such subjects, Richard Bradley, in his "New Improvements of Gardening," published in 1718, gives seven characteristics of excellence which are "required by skilful florists" to be possessed by this flower (Johnson and Slater's, The Auricula).

Abercrombie, writing in 1778, repeats these characteristics; and if we except "the top spreading flat," they briefly enumerate such as are still esteemed marks of superiority. "The flower-stem should be upright, tall, and strong enough to support its cluster of flowers tolerably upright; the cluster or truss of flowers should be large and regular, somewhat of a roundish form, all the florets being sustained on short pedicles, to form the truss close and regular; the florets should be large, and the top spreading flat and regularly around; and the eye of each floret large, circular, and bright."

Mr. Emmerton, who wrote on this flower in 1816, was the first to write more particularly on this subject; others corrected where he had erred slightly; and within a few years the collective judgment of the floricultural world, with some judicious emendations, were arranged and published by Mr. Glenny. This code, with some slight additions, we shall now republish from a little work which issued from the press in 1847.

As florists have several terms relative to the Auricula which may be not understood by every amateur, we

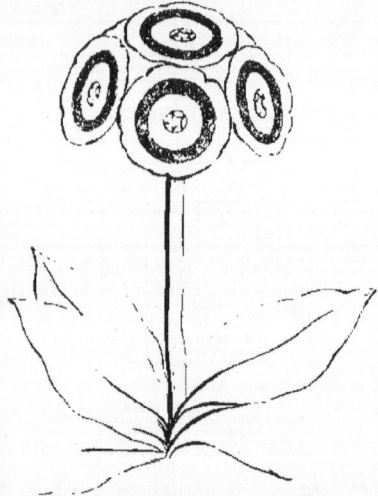

may as well explain that the *thrum* is a collective name for the parts of fructification in the very centre or *tube* of each flower. *Paste* is the white colour next round the edge of the tube, or *eye*, of the flower. *Ground colour* is the next colour to this on the petal, being the distinctive colour of the variety. *Edge* is the outer colour of all, forming the border of the flower. A *Pip* is a single flower, and a *Truss* is several pips, with their several footstalks springing from one stem common to them all.

The properties of the Auricula may be divided into two series; namely, those of the single pip, and those of the single plant.

The Pip.—1. Should be circular, large, with petals equal, firm, fleshy, smooth at the edges, without notch or serrature, and perfectly flat.

2. The centre, or tube, should not exceed one-fourth of the diameter of the pip; it should be of a fine yellow or lemon colour, perfectly round, well filled with the anthers, or thrum, and the edge rising a trifle above the paste, or eye.

3. The paste, or eye, should be perfectly circular, smooth, and a dense pure white, without crack or blemish, forming a band not less than half the width of the tube, and encircling it.

4. The ground colour should be dense, whole, and form a perfect circle next the eye; the brighter, darker, or richer the colour, the better the flower; but if it be paler at the edges of the petals (where they are parted into five) or have two colours or shades, it is a fatal defect.

5. The margin or outward edge should be a clear unchangeable green, grey, or white; and be about the same width as the ground colour, which must in no part go

through to the edge. From the edge of the paste to the outer edge of the flower should be as wide as from the centre of the tube to the outer edge of the paste. In other words, the proportions of the flower may be described by drawing four circles round a given point at equal distances; the first circle forming the tube, the second the white eye, the third the ground colour, and the fourth the outer edge of the flower, and the nearer they approximate to this (except that the ground colour and green or grey edge may run into each other in feathery points) the better the flower. The colours should not be liable to fly, as is the defect of Stretch's Alexander, the colours of which fade in three or four days.

Of the Plant.—1. The stem should be strong, round, upright, elastic, bearing the truss upright without support, and from four to seven inches high, so as to carry the truss well, but not too high above the leaves.

2. The length and strength of the footstalks of the pips should be so proportioned to the number and size of these that all the pips may have room to show themselves, and to form a compact semi-globular truss of flowers, not less than seven in number, without lapping over each other. The pips should be all alike in colour, size, and form, so as not to be easily distinguished from one another; for, otherwise, the unity and harmony of the truss will be destroyed, and although ever so beautifully formed, would appear as if taken from different sorts of Auricula. An Auricula ought to blow freely, and expand all its pips at the same time; for by this means the colours in them all will appear equally fresh and lively; whereas, in those trusses that do not open some of the pips till others have passed their prime, the whole appearance of the truss is impaired.

3. The truss is improved if one or more leaves grow, and stand up well behind the blooms; for it assists the truss, and adds much to the beauty of the blooms by forming a green background.

4. The foliage, or grass, should be healthy, well-grown, and almost cover the pot.—*Gard. and Florist,* i. 45.

We are of opinion that all these criteria are founded upon the dictates of correct taste; but, as these excellencies are never combined in one variety, and as some, being equals in many qualities, are mutually superior in others, the question constantly arises at Auricula exhibitions as to which variety has the preponderance of merit. Now, we are clearly of opinion that *form,* including in this the relative proportions of the colours on the pips, the half globular form of the truss, the number of pips, &c., is by far the most striking excellence in an Auricula. Next to this, we should place the harmony, or, as we should prefer, the agreeable contrast, or complemental association of the colours.

Of the Pairs.—Auriculas are usually exhibited two specimens together, or "in pairs." These should be of equal height and size in all their parts—leaves as well as blooms—for it is offensive to the eye to see a dwarf by the side of a tall-growing specimen. It is also desirable that the colours should differ—thus, a green-edged and a white-edged, a dark ground colour and a

light ground colour, should go together. But we do not attach so much importance to this diversity of colour as some judges do. We think it should have no weight further than that if two competing pairs are exactly of equal merit in other respects, the prize should be awarded to the pair of best contrasted colours. But the slightest superiority in any characteristic of the pip or truss, we think, ought to prevail over this mere matter of taste, for the other characteristics are evidences of better cultivation.

THE FRUIT-GARDEN.

VINE DRESSING.—There needs no apology for returning so soon to the subject of vine culture: this being the fruit which, of all others in-doors, concerns the greatest number of our readers; and now cheap glass and cheap bricks are to be had, we trust to see the day when almost every respectable tradesman will have his vinery—even in his work-yard, together with a shelf or stage for a few popular flowers. Assuredly our labours shall be so directed towards the simplification of matters, as to render vine culture quite easy to the most ordinary capacity.

At page 319, *root management* was adverted to; we now proceed to that of the *branches;* and we must divide the subject a little.

THE LEADING SHOOT OF YOUNG VINES.—When vines are newly planted, they are always headed back close, or nearly so, to the point where they are introduced into the house. This is a necessary course, for two reasons: first, they commence growth with more vigour in consequence; and, secondly, it is desirable that the first shoot should be uniform in character, and free from those crooked knots which point, during years after, to an untoward commencement. Every gardener, almost, prides himself on his young vines reaching the back of the house the season they are planted; and this they will do, be they ever so small, if under first-rate culture.

This pruned shoot, then, will "push" two, sometimes three, eyes; or it may be more; and many persons injudiciously disbud forthwith all but one leading one, in order, as they say, to strengthen the leader. Now, it does no such thing. The leader will be best strengthened by encouraging a speedy and healthy root-action; and to effect this a strong reciprocal action between root and top must first take place. Suffer, therefore, every bud that pushes to ramble in freedom for a month or so, and then means may be taken, *progressively,* to give the leader the pre-eminence. This must be done by first pinching off the point of the shoot to be done away; in a week or so the next surplus shoot may be pinched, and so on with others. These will soon begin to push out laterals, and such must be pinched similarly. These spurs, or snags, will thus appear like tufts or little vine bushes through the summer, full of healthy leaves, which, instead of drawing on the resources of the parent, will add to the general stock, and may, if properly situated, be made to bear in the ensuing spring.

The principal leader by this time will be so enlarged in capacity, as to be thoroughly prepared to carry out, for the rest of the year, that powerful reciprocity of action which fills the border with healthy roots, and the house with strong and sound wood.

As soon as the leader begins to acquire some strength, lateral shoots will be progressively developed all up the stem; and now a little judgment is necessary to know how to husband the resources of the tree, in fact, to encourage plenty of fibres in the border, by means of a healthy growth, and plenty of leaves; and yet to take care that the dormant buds which are to fruit the next year are thoroughly perfected, through a due exposure of the principal leaves to the light; for on the *main, or first-formed foliage*, will depend the character of the next year's produce, and, indeed, the solidity of the wood *itself*.

Gardeners differ in their practice as to stopping vines —not only the leaders but the laterals. Some will have every lateral cut or pinched away from a leading shoot the moment it appears; but why? we could never have explained. If the sole object was to produce several fine bunches for one year *only*, at the expense of the constitution of the plant, there would be some show of reason for such treatment. Nevertheless, assuming that one great point in vine culture is to get a strong frame-work of fibres in a sound border,—and that the amount, or extension of roots, in any given summer, bears a close proportion to the amount of foliage healthfully elaborating sap,—we say, it becomes a sound policy to expose all the healthy and early-formed leaves possible to the influence of the solar light. The close-stopping policy, we conceive, is better adapted to the latter portion of the summer, when the production of young and imperfect spray (which can never return to the plant an equivalent for the stores taken from it) has a weakening tendency, and somewhat interferes with the commencement of the "rest" period. Our advice, therefore, is—let the leader produce a few rambling laterals at the first without stopping; as soon, however, as a considerable extension of leader and development of lateral has taken place, and the latter are likely to become confused, let the stopping, or pinching, of the end of the laterals commence: beginning at the lower end, and stopping a pair or two; then waiting a few days longer before stopping another pair, and so on. We are perfectly aware that such will be considered bad practice by some good cultivators. Be it so; but let these prove—not by mere opinion, but by facts—that no other course is correct but *the close* stopping.

By the time that the young leader has nearly reached the back of the house (which will be, in many cases, about the end of July), the stem will have developed side spray at most of the principal leaves; and much of it will have been stopped; some, also, of those first stopped will have been stopped again and again; for we would not let any of them produce above a couple of leaves before we stopped them. And now the leader should be stopped; that is to say, when within about two feet of the back wall. We deem it necessary, when about to stop the leader, to suffer a little more rambling in the laterals for a week previously, to provide a vent for the ascending current of sap; otherwise a slight check to the root action might ensue, which would not be desirable. The leading point will soon break again; and our practice is, to let a couple or three of the principal buds at the top push and ramble considerably for about three weeks longer, by which time a considerable amount of strong foliage at the top is produced; and this we train right and left at the top of the house. After the end of August we permit no rambling, but close stop every lateral as soon as developed.

The amateur will naturally require a reason for so arbitrary a recommendation. It was before observed, that there is a period in the annual growth of the vine when the development of new foliage is a positive loss to the tree. The reason of this will be obvious, when it is considered that the rapidly decreasing light of our climate will not sufficiently aid the process of elaboration in such leaves, so as to enable them to compensate the parent plant for the drain from it in furnishing matter for their growth. Moreover, another and powerful consideration arises; the whole fabric or tissue of the plant has to be solidified, or, in technical language, "ripened." Late growths, then, are decidedly inimical to this process. We trust, therefore, that our less experienced readers will see at a glimpse how things stand,

and that the study of such vegetable phenomena will incite towards a farther and deeper investigation into nature's hidden secrets; for such studies, in the main, refresh the mind of man rather than weary it.

MANAGEMENT OF THE LEADING SHOOT ON ESTABLISHED VINES.—Here much depends on how far the main shoot has already ascended, and what the strength of the vine is. We think that—even provided the old wood of the leader has already reached the back of the house, or nearly so—it is well to suffer the young point to ramble unmolested for a few weeks, albeit it may crook and twist at the back wall. There can be little doubt that the extension of the main leader is very beneficial, as giving a greater impulse to the root than the side branches can do—it being generally so much more vigorous. However, stopped it must be after awhile; and by this time there will be abundance of foliage thoroughly developed all over the tree.

THE MANAGEMENT OF THE SIDE SHOOTS AND SPRAY.— This is, in general, well known, but we will give our practice. Almost everybody stops one joint beyond the fruit, and as to general circumstances, there seems no reason to depart from the practice. Cases, however, occur where much roof space remains to be covered; and then we would, by all means, after the first stopping, let shoots intended to fill such spaces produce three or four eyes at a time without stopping. It is our practice to let the spray grow rather freely after the first stopping, and until the vines are in full blossom; then we commence regular, *not close*, stopping, and continue it until the stoning of the fruit is nearly complete, when, if any more surface of roof is available, we permit it to become clothed with foliage. As soon as the fruit begins *to* change colour, *close* stopping is followed up, and continued until the fruit is perfect, when we see no harm in permitting the terminal points to ramble a little, provided it is not later than the middle of August.

R. ERRINGTON.

THE FLOWER-GARDEN.

BEDDING PLANTS: *Verbena venosa*.—With this plant I finished my notes last week, and before I dismiss this old and much neglected bedder, I shall recommend a way of using it in a *mixed* flower-garden, which, if I mistake not, will insure its being retained as a permanent plant, and not only that, but make the most interesting bed by the help of it that any one can use. I have had it the same way here for the last seven years, and I do not remember any one who has seen it that was not much struck with the beauty and novelty of that style of planting—I mean the mixed style of planting single beds, without reference to other beds in the neighbourhood—like the two Clarkias, which I have so often alluded to. I have another reason for bringing it forward to-day, to which I made some allusion last week, and that is, to shew how necessary it is to pay attention to the shade of green in the leaves of such plants as are recommended to be planted near each other, either for the harmony or for the contrast of their flowers. A want of this consideration is as apparent in all the arrangements that I have read of, as the disparity of the heights of many of the plants that are said to associate and assist each other in producing striking effects; and the reason I have in view in making these remarks, is "to shew cause" why I have declined to recommend to some of our readers how to plant certain arrangements of beds of which they sent sketches. When my own limited practice enables me to see glaring faults in the arrangements of those great masters, to whom I usually look up for instruction and advice, I cannot take any other view of the subject than that it is a most difficult one—even if I could not attest the fact from experience. Besides, I know several flower-gardens of note that no one can plant in such a manner as to produce a good whole, owing to the disposition of the beds with reference to the principal walks, and, also, for the want of some determined plan as to the different sizes of the beds themselves. It is thought by architects and landscape gardeners an easy matter to form a plan of a combination of flower-beds to suit a given locality; and one would think that a good draughtsman, with an artist's eye, could find little difficulty in laying down such a plan; and he might believe the same thing, and make his plan accordingly; yet the chances are, that when his beds are planted in the most judicious manner, or in the best possible order, the colours and sizes of the plants will admit of, the whole composition may not come up to the rank of a third-rate attempt. The truth is, unless one has such a thorough knowledge of all the plants that are suitable to form a good composition when combined together in various ways, as that he can tell you in the dead of winter their real colours, the tint of their leaves, their heights in rich and in poor soil, the time they usually come into and go out of bloom in a wet and in a dry season, no matter how proficient he may be in the art of drawing plans, he is not in a condition to lay down ten beds together without risking the danger of palpable mistakes. But I have said enough to warrant me in excusing myself from advising how to plant flower-beds which I never saw; and now we shall plant a bed with Verbena venosa, having deep purple flowers in upright spikes, and with dark green leaves. The plants, or rather the underground runners, we shall place at about a foot apart every way, and next May all the spaces between the verbena plants will be planted with a bright scarlet flowering plant; and, as a matter of course, these scarlet flowers will neutralise the effect of the purple ones; and so undoubtedly would be the case, provided the leaves of the scarlet flowering plant were of nearly the same tint as those of the verbena; but the leaves of my second plant are more than one-half pure white: it is the Old Scarlet Variegated Geranium; and the effect of these two plants thus managed I shall describe in the words of a gentleman whom I found one day admiring it a few years back: "By the bye, I have just written to her Grace the Duchess of —— to say that you have a flower-bed here which looks exactly like shot silk; I never saw such a charming bed!" Now, I hope all the old shrubbery borders in the country will be hunted out at once for this Verbena venosa, for it has been turned out of the flower-beds years since; and let all the nurserymen in the country be laid siege to for variegated scarlet geraniums, to make "shot silk" beds with this next summer; for if we do not strike while the iron is hot, the half of us may forget the thing altogether before another season comes round. This bed should not be placed near the windows, nor where you come close to it before it can be observed; not but that it will bear close inspection, for the nearer you come to it the richer it looks; but when friends come to see the garden, and observe it at a distance, it will puzzle them to make out what plants you have got in it. "What, in the name of goodness, have you got yonder?" is a common expression with strangers on viewing this bed at a distance; and away they run across the grass, wet or no wet; and the next observation you hear is, "Dear me, who would have thought that such common plants should produce this striking effect!" This bed, or one on the same principle—that is, having a rich display but not one decided colour—is by far the most suitable for a bed forming a common centre to a set of beds, as No. 1 in the annexed group; a very general way of forming clusters of beds, or small flower-gardens; not in circles or of the same size, how-

ever, as I have shewn them for the sake of simplicity; none of such beds need necessarily be a circle. In nine cases out of ten you see the centre bed in these groups planted with scarlet geraniums or scarlet verbenas, and their glaring brilliancy kills the effect of most of the colours in the other beds, unless, indeed, the other distinct colours in bedding plants, as blue, purple, yellow, and pink, are excluded, and white, light lilac, and gray, be used instead round the scarlet; but that could only be done in a very large garden, to exemplify one distinct kind of group, where many other ways of arranging flower-beds were adopted. In small gardens I like to see all the best and gayest colours brought together, and therefore the effect of the whole should not be lessened or even marred by placing the most glaring colour in the middle. I have been thus led to break in on the plan I proposed, of going on with the distinct colours before I said anything of mixed and shaded beds, by a correspondent (H. W.), who is answered at page 14. He sent a plan of his garden, which shewed the beds arranged from a central one; and he proposed to follow the common herd, and plant his master bed with scarlet geraniums. I shall, therefore, keep to these mixed beds a little longer.

PURPLE.—For the want of a real good purple among the verbenas I have tried many of them mixed, to see if I could make a better purple out of two or three shades of them, like the way of improving the scarlet ones, but I cannot boast much of these attempts. My standard plant for a real good purple is the lighter variety of the two purple Senecios, or American Groundsel. The very dark purple Senecio can only be matched by the dark purple verbenas; and with the exception of a few purple Petunias, I know so few plants that will match in colour with the light variety of Senecio, that I shall make a present of this volume of THE COTTAGE GARDENER to any one who will point out to me two leading plants exactly of the same purple, not to exceed twenty inches in height, nor be much lower than ten inches, and to flower from the middle or end of June to the end of September; Petunias to be excepted. Verbena Charwoodii is one of the best purple bedders, after Emma and Heloise; but there is a shade of red in it which is against it for a good purple. I have tried many of the dark crimson verbenas with it in equal proportions, but still I did not obtain a good purple bed; verbenas Louis Phillip and Barkerii were the only two which seemed to answer best with Charwoodii. It is not possible to make out how any verbenas would mix in a bed by putting out flowers of them together for trial: they must be seen growing together to judge of the effect properly, as the habit and strength of verbenas are so different from each other.

One more mixed bed and I have done with them to-day. Of all the neutral plants to be used in beds where a striking colour would not answer, the Heliotrope, or "Cherry-pie," is the best, for many reasons. Every one likes the perfume of it. It is one of the easiest plants to keep in winter; and comes from cuttings in the spring as easily as a verbena or fuchsia; and it lasts in flower till the frost cuts it; and it does not require rich soil. The only fault of it is, that it produces too many leaves, so that the bed looks too green. I had overcome this difficulty last season for the first time, and the plan was much praised. I tried four kinds of those verbenas whose flowers are of the same grayish colour as those of the heliotrope, and one called Duchesse d'Aumaule is the best of them. No one who plants a bed of Heliotrope should omit planting an equal number of plants of this verbena along with it. The verbena flowers will stand as four to one of the heliotrope, and a stranger could hardly detect the mixture at a yard's distance, and if he did there could be no harm. Those who object to the Heliotrope for a bed, might try this plan. The heliotrope will overrun the verbena in such a way that its shoots and leaves can hardly be seen, but the verbena's flower-stalks will push up regularly all over the bed.

D. Beaton.

GREENHOUSE AND WINDOW GARDENING.

It is no uncommon thing to meet with people whose philosophy, in relation to many of what are to them uncomeatable desirables, is merely a borrowed feature from the contracted wisdom of the fox, whose only consolation was to pronounce the luscious grapes "sour as crabs," after he had looked long and lingeringly and made many an unsuccessful leap to obtain the goodly prize. If there be one reader of The Cottage Gardener who owns such a spirit, one thing is certain, it has not been obtained from *its* pages. In common with hundreds more, I have derived great pleasure from the luminous papers of Mr. Appleby on the culture of orchids; and if a grain of something like impatient *foxism* nightmared my cranium, it had its origin neither from undervaluing the splendour of the objects themselves—for to see them is to admire them—nor for depreciating the talent with which they were and are introduced to our notice, because that is above our criticism, but from a painful regret that owing to our comparative *ignorance* of the groups, we were unable to gain that benefit from such lucid instructions that we otherwise would have done.

Several circumstances have convinced me that a kindred, and so far a favourable, sentiment (for to know our ignorance is rather a good omen) is felt by many of our friends, who may only have a small greenhouse, as well as by those who, by divisions, are endeavouring to concentrate several climates under one roof of no great dimensions. Without, therefore, intruding upon our friend Mr. Appleby's domains, we should like to tell our many readers, who have neither orchid-house nor plant-stove, how they may grace their conservatory, greenhouse, or window, with a beautiful terrestrial orchid for several weeks every season, *provided* they can manage to give it a higher temperature than the greenhouse for two or three months in the year, either in a vinery or any other convenience, such as a pit at work.

The *Bletia Tankervilliæ*, or *Phaius grandifolius* (for it is known by both names), is a native of China; is generally described as a stove plant, and has been a denizen of our hothouses for three-parts of a century. Its green broad lanceolate leaves, with its flowering stems, terminating in a beautiful spike, towering above them, render the plant very striking at this season of the year, when contrasted with the generality of plants in the greenhouse. For want of a better, it will furnish a good type of the orchidaceous family. The flower is whitish brown. The upper part consists of what appears to be five sepals, or petals—being generally described as three sepals and two petals. The lower part of the flower looks like a tubular monopetalous corolla, somewhat similar to a foxglove; but it is not tubular, but plain; though its being curved up gives it that appearance; it is merely the petal, called the *lip*, or the *labellum*, the wondrous development of which, in many other genera, gives to the whole order such a striking and wonderful appearance. Opposite this *labellum* petal is the front of the central *column*, in which the filaments of the stamens and the styles of the pistil are all joined together. The pollen masses are always opposite this *labellum*. In the present case you see nothing either of anthers or stigma; but, near the top of the column, you will observe a slit-like valve; insert the point of a fine pen-

knife, and turn up the cowl-like covering, and you will expose the pollen masses, lying over a viscid hollow tube, that answers the purpose of a *stigma*, if that is not more especially done by a small protuberance on which the upper part of the valve rested, called the *rostellum*. With many and great diversities as to the pollen masses, the appearance of the column, the form of the *labellum*, and the *apparent* number of sepals and petals in other genera, the Bletia forms no bad type of the orchid groups. Some woodcuts of some of the more striking of these, under Mr. Appleby's supervision, would at some future day constitute an additional reason for the gratitude of the subscribers, and render his dissertations more *universally* interesting.

From each bulbous-looking tuber now supporting its fine green leaves, and from one to several flower spikes, there will be seen sucker-like appendages issuing from the base in number generally proportionate to the size and strength of the tuber. As soon as the bloom is over, *these* must constitute the object of our attention, as we have got all in the way of bloom from the old tuber that we are ever likely to obtain. They are not, however, as yet useless, as the stored-up matter in the tuber assists the development of the suckers; and even the leaves should be retained as long as they keep green. In obtaining a plant, therefore, be not content with a little sucker, but insist upon having the old tuber along with it. Now, the common treatment of such a plant in a *stove* would enable you to get it fully grown before the middle of autumn; and then by keeping it cooler and drier, and re-introducing it to heat and moisture, the flower-stems would appear in mid-winter. Were you to keep your plant after flowering in the cool airy atmosphere of the greenhouse, growth would be too languid; and your plants, by the end of autumn, would neither be so strong nor so well matured as to warrant the expectation of fine flower stems the following season. Hence the importance of moving the plants when done flowering into a higher temperature and a closer atmosphere; such as will be found in a vinery, or forcing pit, or even a close cold pit, keeping them partially shaded for a time, but gradually exposing them to light and air; until, by July or August, they may be transferred to the greenhouse, cold pit, or even for a time to a sheltered place, full in the sun, out of doors; so that maturation may be thoroughly effected before the end of autumn, taking care to have them properly secured from early frosts. When growing they will relish a temperature of from 65° to 75° when gradually inured to it; and a little bottom heat they will also thank you for. Though the plants would thrive very well in the greenhouse during the winter, yet as there is nothing vastly attractive in them when out of bloom, we prefer transferring them to a vinery, which serves the purpose of an *omnium gatherum*, where gesneras, gloxinias, &c., are kept in a dormant state, the temperature being seldom below 38° or above 45°. Here they get scarcely any water at the roots, but the leaves are kept green by giving them a dash from the syringe on a sunny day, which so far checks evaporation. In the course of February the temperature is raised to start the vines, and when 60° becomes the medium temperature, the plants are top-dressed, and water given to the roots somewhat freely, and ere long the flower shoots begin to show themselves; and when they are expanding they are transferred at first to a warm corner in the greenhouse, to be placed in any desirable position after a few days. Those who have no vinery may give the increased temperature desirable for starting into growth, and starting into flower by means of a frame or pit.

Propagation.—Now, as to the time and the mode of potting or dividing the roots, upon principles which have previously been several times explained, it will be desirable to allow this to remain in abeyance until the young shoots have commenced to grow freely, encouraging them to do so by rich surface dressings, and clear manure water. The mode of potting must depend upon the object aimed at; for nice little pots, about eight inches in diameter, one old tuber with two or three young shoots will be amply sufficient; but where a great mass of flower stems is desired in a large pot or tub, a proportionate number of old and young shoots must be inserted. Though more striking from the great mass, yet by this method it is not often that the individual stems are so good as when few are grown in a smaller pot.

Soil.—This should consist of three parts lumpy peat, three parts fibry loam, one part of the following: silver sand, leaf mould, and dried cow dung, using plenty of drainage, and inserting pieces of charcoal. Before you start them into growth or flower, scrape away a portion of the surface, and top dressing with equal portions of cow dung, peat, and loam.

Water.—Let this be given liberally when the plants are growing; and, alternately, with pure water use liquid-manure made of soot, with a little lime to clear it. When the plants are in a dormant state, water should be nearly altogether withheld, but not so much so as to cause the leaves to droop or wither. We do not think this ever should take place until the bulbous tuber has finished its allotted purpose of growing and flowering.

R. FISH.

HOTHOUSE DEPARTMENT.

EXOTIC ORCHIDACEÆ.

INSECTS.—The destruction of insects that are injurious to plants is always desirable, and no less so to orchids than to any other tribe of plants. At page 6 of the present volume, the method of destroying the thrip was described; and we may here mention that the same means will destroy the green fly, and greatly check the red spider, which sometimes makes its appearance on the thinner-leaved species. As this is the season when all kinds of these destructive, though diminutive, enemies breed rapidly, and the food they like best (namely, the young tender roots and flower-stems,) is most abundant, every means must be used to prevent their ravages. After the thrip, the insects that are most injurious, and generally too prevalent in the orchid-house, are cockroaches, woodlice, small shell slugs, white scale, brown scale, mealy bug; and sometimes, though happily more rarely, the large shell slug or snail, and the black and grey common snails or slugs. This is a fearful host to contend with, yet by patience and industrial applications of the means of destruction, this host, though so numerous, may be nearly, if not quite, destroyed. We will now detail the means we have used successfully to arrest their progress, and finally banish them from amongst our favourite plants.

COCKROACHES.—The kind of cockroach that most commonly infests the orchid-house is a native of the warmer climates of the West and East Indies; and, no doubt, was first introduced into our hothouses amongst plants brought from these countries; but, more especially, they are imported amongst orchideous plants. We have seen cases of those plants completely destroyed on their passage by them. Whenever we receive a case of orchids, we always search very diligently for the cockroaches before taking a plant into the hothouse: looking diligently for the eggs as well as for the insects themselves. If a house is clear of them this precaution is very necessary, not only with regard to importations from abroad, but also to plants received from any nursery, or even private collection. They may be in the pots amongst the rough peat, or amongst the drainage; therefore, repot every plant that is received from any quarter, so that no breed

may obtain an entrance into the house clear of them previous to the new arrivals. Yet with every care and precaution some tiny ones will escape the keenest eye, and will soon grow larger, and propagate amazingly fast. As soon as their presence is observed or suspected, then use the means to entrap, catch, and destroy them we are about to detail. The common beetle trap is a box with sloping sides, and a glass funnel let into the upper side. Into this box put some crumbs of bread, mixed with coarse raw sugar. Place these traps (for more than one will be desirable if the house is large and the insects numerous) in the place where they have been observed feeding. If any are found in the trap in the morning, empty them into a vessel of boiling water, and so kill them at once. Set in different places amongst the plants glass vessels half filled with sugared beer; the insects will fall into them and be drowned; but these vessels must be placed near to something—the pots for instance—that they can climb up to the edge of the trap. Next cut some potatoes in two, and hollow out with a knife part of the inside; or slices of small turnips will answer the same purpose. Place these upon the peat or sphagnum in the pots and baskets, or even on the larger blocks. Every morning look these traps over, and crush all the insects you may find concealed under them. These are the best traps we know of to catch the small shelled-snails and woodlice. They answer the purpose also, in a measure, of feeding the insects, and so preventing them from preying upon the tender roots of the plants. Besides setting these traps, try to catch and destroy the insects by hand. And as, like beasts of prey, they prowl about seeking for food during the night, it is then they must be hunted for. Now, as the cockroach is an exceedingly shy and active enemy, we must look sharp, and be more active than he to catch him. The best instrument we ever saw for the purpose, was made of a long round piece of wood with a flat end, and that end stuck pretty full with needles, about three-quarters of an inch projecting. With this instrument in one hand, and a bull's-eye lantern or a candle in the other, the moment a cockroach is perceived dart your spears upon him, and nine cases out of ten you will impale the enemy. Crush him to death instantly, or, what is better, have some scalding hot water handy and plunge him into it. With an instrument of this kind we must plead guilty of having killed hundreds of cockroaches. Night after night the house must be diligently hunted over till the last enemy visible is destroyed. If after all this trapping, catching, and destroying, the plants are still found having their young roots eaten, and so their growths crippled, the last remedy to be resorted to is *poison.* The way in which this most destructive agent has been employed, is to mix lard, honey, and arsenic together, and stick small portions of it upon small rods, six or eight inches long. Sharpen the end where the poison is not, and stick them here and there into the pots. The insects will soon scent it, feed upon it, and be found next morning either dead, or in such a feeble state as not to be able to crawl away to their dens of concealment. Remove them out of the house, or the stench from their dead bodies will be disagreeably offensive. This method of destroying cockroaches was first adopted, we believe, by Messrs. Loddiges, in their large collection; and we were assured by one of the firm, that the first morning after the poison was placed amongst the plants more than half a peck of these destructive insects was gathered up. Care must, however, be taken that this mixture containing so deadly a poison does not touch the leaves of the plants. We have been assured by an eminent grower of orchids, that whenever that was the case the leaves became spotted, and eventually rotted away. The same grower suggests that the poison might be put in small shells—such, for instance, as the shell of the muscle—and laid upon the stages, or even upon the pots and baskets, and then there would not be so much danger of the poison being accidentally thrown upon the leaves, in moving the plants, as when it was placed upon the sticks. We think this idea a good one, and shall try it if we ever resort to such a mode of getting rid of cockroaches. We use here in the orchid-house, at Pine-apple Place, a liquid poison, which has cleared the house of numbers of these nightly marauders. It is made up for us by a druggist in the neighbourhood, but we do not know of what it is composed. All that we can say of it is, that it is a dark-coloured liquid in pint or quart bottles as we require it. It is rather sweet, and of a pleasant smell. We put it into bell-glasses, about half full, and plunge them up to the rim either in sand or moss. The insects plunge headlong into it by scores, and for months afterwards we see no more of them.

FLORISTS' FLOWERS.

Mild, genial weather has at last breathed its beneficial influence over the atmosphere of our beloved country; and the vegetable world, in gratitude for such a great blessing, is breaking forth its treasures and beauties to reward the cultivator, and do honour to the Giver of all good.

Now is the time for the florist to render all assistance to his much prized flowers. All the plants under glass will require more water and air, to encourage them to grow vigorously and send up strongly their flower stems, we allude particularly to *Auriculas* and *Polyanthuses*, which will, now that warmer weather has come in good earnest, be coming into flower very fast. *Carnations* and *Picotees*, in their blooming pots, will require water occasionally, if the weather is dry; they may be allowed with great advantage to have the benefit of gentle showers, for natural showers are far more beneficial than artificial ones, inasmuch as by falling from clouds the particles of water become more suitable food for all plants than water applied with either the water-pot or the syringe. *Dahlias.*—It is very probable that by the time these remarks are in the hands of our readers, it will be time entirely to cease taking off cuttings of dahlias from their old roots. Such as have produced shoots in such a way as to allow the roots to be divided, now is the time to perform that operation: take a strong knife and pass the blade through the crown of the roots, and divide them so as to leave a bulb or two to each division; these make excellent strong plants if well managed afterwards. Place each division in pots, put them in a frame, shade and water them, and by the time the planting season arrives they will be strong, excellent plants. Dried roots that have not been forced may now be planted quite safely in the open air, either in beds or amongst American plants, or amongst shrubs; when they will flower well if a shovelful of dung is put into the holes at the time of planting.

We must now finish our list of picotees; the classes that remain yet to be given are the red, rose, and scarlet edged.

RED EDGED PICOTEES.	per pair.
	s. d.
Duchess of Cambridge (Brooke's), an extra fine flower	2 6
Richard Cobden (Ely's), a fine, firm, beautiful variety	5 0
Isabella (Kirtland's), extra fine	5 0
Privateer (Lee's), ditto	2 0
Ne Plus Ultra (Matthews')	2 6
Isabella (Wildman's), very good	3 6

ROSE AND SCARLET EDGED PICOTEES.

Lady Alice Peel (Burroughes'), a light edged, beautiful, firm flower	2 6
Mrs. Trahar (Dickson's), also a light edge, the white very clear, petals evenly set, and a good form	5 0
Queen Victoria (Green's), extra	2 6
Proconsul (Gatliff's), a heavy edged, fine variety, strong	

	per pair.
	s. d.
grower	3 6
Venus (Headley's), a heavy edge, pod firm, never bursting, ground colour very pure	5 0
Eliza (Sykes's), also with a heavy edge; this, though old and low priced, is a variety of first-rate qualities	2 0

T. APPLEBY.

THE KITCHEN-GARDEN.

ASPARAGUS.—The time is now arrived for making young plantations, or, at least, it is time so soon as the young plants in the seed bed have made shoots two or three inches in length. In planting them, draw drills as previously directed, and place the plants regularly. Apply to the old asparagus beds, as the growing season has commenced, thin sowings of salt, taking advantage of showery weather, or just previously to rain, to apply it. A little and often is much better than applying large quantities, and throughout the growing season it may advantageously be applied.

JERUSALEM ARTICHOKES.—Where planted on ridge-trenched ground, should now have the ridges well forked or scarified over.

ANGELICA.—The surface of the earth about this plant should be kept loose; and, being a gross feeding plant, it should be liberally supplied throughout this month with liquid manure. A few plants if well attended to, will produce a large quantity of fine stalks.

KIDNEY BEANS may now be planted on warm dry borders; and those which have been sown under hand-glasses, or under other shelters, to make early plants, should be planted on a good rich, healthy soil, either in shallow narrow trenches, or in deeply drawn drills; to be protected with evergreen boughs, haulm, furze, boards, canvas, or some other easily comeatable material, at night. The same arrangements may be adopted with advantage with the *Scarlet runners*.

EARLY BROAD BEANS now coming into bloom, to facilitate their early podding, should have their tops pinched out. Another succession may be planted of the *Windsor* and *Long-pod beans.*

ONIONS, *parsnips, carrots, turnips,* and other spring-drilled crops should, as soon as they can be seen, have a short-toothed rake passed across the drills to break the surface of the earth. A fine dry day should of course be chosen, and immediately hoe, slightly, the whole of the surface between the rows, to keep an open healthy surface, preventing the progress of weeds and destroying the nursery for the larvæ of obnoxious vermin.

RIDGE CUCUMBERS and VEGETABLE MARROWS should be sown in full crop, in order to have sturdy plants for ridging out the beginning of May. Sow, also, the best varieties of FRAME CUCUMBERS and MELONS, that good plants may be always at command, for succeeding early potatoes, French beans, &c.

MUSHROOM BEDS should at this season be made in the coldest situations that can be found, but away from draughts, as the mushroom will not succeed at any season in a draught, or a windy situation. Slightly-made beds, with more loam than in the winter season intermixed, will answer very well at this season. Underground cellars, or caves, are famous for summer mushroom culture: keeping the beds without any external covering, and the floor often damped. Occasionally it should be damped with manure-water—in a tepid state, and clear—made from sheep, deer, or cow-dung; beds, which have some time been in bearing, should be assisted by liberal soakings of clear tepid manure-water, as above recommended.

[FEATHER-STEMMED SAVOY.—This excellent and prolific variety was raised by Mr. Burnes, being a hybrid between the savoy and the Brussels sprout. It is characterized, as the name implies, by having a multitude of sprouts produced upon its stem. Now is a good time for sowing it; and we know that Mr. Barnes always makes two sowings between the middle of April and the 10th of May; planting out the young plants in July, upon ground just cleared of peas, &c.—G. W. J.]

JAMES BARNES.

MISCELLANEOUS INFORMATION.

OUR VILLAGE WALKS.
(No. 25.)

THERE must ever be a feeling of solemnity within us when we stand upon the ruins of any building, however humble, that has once been the habitation of man. In a beautifully wild and woody piece of ground near my home, there are the remains of a little cottage garden, marked only by a large patch of snow-drops, and two box-trees, yet flourishing among the trees, and bushes, and fern now waving unconcernedly where the cottage used to stand. Not a relic of its simple walls remain: there is not even a mound to mark precisely the spot it occupied; but the shrubs and the flowers point out the position of the garden, once laying warmly open to the south, and perhaps fondly cherished by the cottage gardener of by-gone days. A private road only now passes by this quiet secluded spot; but in former times it stood on the verge of an extensive common, looking full upon a range of high downy hills, with the wild, fresh breezes sweeping round it, as they came laden with health from the sea. It is true, that every house and every garden we see—every building, every work executed by man's hand—may remind us of those who once lived, and wrought, " and builded and planted," and who are now passed from the world for ever; but a deserted garden,—a dwelling swept, as it were, from the face of the earth,—has a loud and peculiar cry; and we cannot help pausing to think and listen! It says to us, that "man is but vanity; his time passeth away as a shadow;" the frail flowers planted by his hand are longer-lived than he; "are not his days, also, like the days of an hireling?" We stand upon the very spot that was once ringing with many voices,—the home of beings as full of life and health as we are now,—where the business of this world was carried carefully on; and sickness and death were, perhaps, little thought of or feared. And now, the grass grows quietly upon the once cheerful hearth; and not a sound is heard but the sighing wind, and the notes of the careless birds! Has not a scene like this a word for the rich and the poor!

This day has been the first of real spring warmth, and how exquisite it is after the lingering cold of a hard winter! There has been a *something* in the shade that told of March, but the bright sunshine, the increased and richer song of birds, the cottagers sitting at work with their doors open to admit the genial air, and a sort of joyous sensation in oneself, marked the near approach of another summer. The fields were full of people; voices and whistlings arose on every side; and among the allotments great bustle prevailed—heaps of weeds were sending forth long trains of white smoke, and little carts were standing about here and there, with the harness hung over them, and the donkeys peacefully grazing in the ditch.

I cannot imagine that any country in the world can rival old England in these beautiful scenes of country life. Nothing, surely, can touch the sights and sounds that belong to a rural district in this "sea-girt home" of ours; and I always wish that at these lovely seasons of the year inhabitants of towns could escape from their long imprisonment, and pour into the country to enjoy a little of the sweetness and beauty of all *we* see; for even the country near a town never seems like the *genuine article*, such as we revel in among the woods and wilds. Then there is an interest in every person and thing among whom we live in a rural parish, which no doubt adds to the effect of the lovely scenery. Every field, every wood, every cottage, belongs to a friend or a neighbour; and there is pleasure in watching the progress or proceedings of those in whom we feel an interest. The lazily moving teams on the arable land are perpetual sources of admiration as well as interest. We often catch a *picture* in the various groupings of men and animals; and there is so much *nationality* in all that surrounds the plough that we can never tire of gazing upon it. Yet even amid the bursting beauty of spring we are called upon to remember, that " all is vanity!" we see, on the one hand, the ceaseless activity of worldly business, and on the other, "man goeth to his long home, and the mourners go about the streets." On passing out of the village street into a bye-path, I saw a simple funeral moving slowly across the church yard towards the porch: it was the last remains of *a cottage gardener*,—of him whose potato land had been so signally preserved from blight. He knew "that our Redeemer liveth!" he had felt Him to be "the Resurrection and the Life!" and he had for many years fre quented the courts of the Lord's house, which he was now entering for the last time!

At this most solemn season let us consider our ways. The funeral of a cottage gardener addresses itself loudly to some of us: it bids us prepare for that sure and certain hour which comes *at last* upon all men! We are now especially reminded that "death is swallowed up in victory,"—that the grave has no terrors for the Christian, because his Surety has risen in triumph from the tomb, "and ever liveth to make intercession" for us. Let the cottage gardener observe with deep solemnity, and holy joy, this glorious season. It is the seed time *now*: while life and health are spared to us, let us sow unto life eternal; for it will avail us nothing to dress our gardens, to till our land, to cherish our crops, and count our produce, if this is our only provision for the world to come. We often see labourers hard at work on Good Friday, while the church bell calls the flock to prayer. Ah! if masters would serve *their* Master,— if they would encourage their tenants, their workmen, and all belonging to them, to "seek *first* the kingdom of God, and his righteousness,"—how well it would be with all their worldly business! how well it would be with all "the things that belong unto their peace!" What will it avail us that "Christ hath died, yea, rather hath risen again," if our hearts are among the clods of the earth; if our hope stretches not beyond the "basket and the store;" if we mind only "earthly things?"

The passing-bell has a warning voice; the coffin lowering into the grave is a solemn sight; the rattling dust speaks loudly to us of time and of eternity! Let the funeral of a lowly cottage gardener awaken us to higher and holier things. It is a time for reflection; and from the simplest source we may draw a lesson of wisdom, good for our heedless hearts.

CUCUMBER HOUSE.

SEVERAL correspondents having applied to us for a description of the cucumber house noticed by Mr. Errington, he has furnished us with the following plan and particulars.*

As of first importance, we would recommend—an angle of about 45° for the roof; systematic roof covering at night in severe weather, and in order to economise fire-heat; and during intense sunshine shade for three or four hours in the day, to prevent an unnecessary drain on the powers of the plant; the amount of soil being necessarily somewhat limited. The hot-water pipes are best in a cemented trough, or an open gutter: one advance or flow pipe, *a*, of six inches diameter, to traverse the front, and at the end emptying itself into a metallic reservoir, just large enough to receive the orifice of the advance pipe and two return pipes, which need not be more than three or four inches diameter. One of the two return pipes to go under each bed of soil, as shewn in the diagram at *b b*.

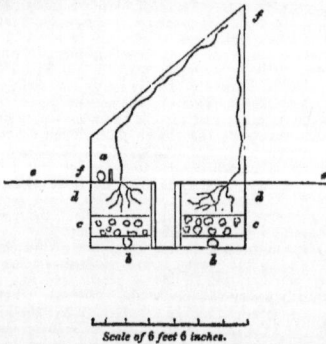

Scale of 6 feet 6 inches.

a Advance or flow pipe. *b b* The two return pipes. *c c* Stratum of broken stones to qualify the heat before entering the soil. *d d* Chamber of soil for the roots. *e e* Ground level. *f f* Sliders in front and top of house.

The back wall may have melons trained up it, and also pegged on the surface of the soil.

We lay the greatest stress on the pipes being capable of immersion in water, or in substituting open tanks. There may be sliders over openings into *b b*, to be drawn open when the bottom heat is too strong, and thus the atmospheric and the bottom heat and moisture may act reciprocally.

According to our sketch, the two beds of soil will be 30 inches wide each, and the central path half a yard, making the house six feet six inches wide; the length, of course, at the fancy of the owner. At *f f* some sliding or other ventilators ought to be provided, the front one pressing immediately over the advance pipe, and carrying warm and moist air through the house. Perhaps it will be necessary to raise the floor a few inches in order to cover the pipe, which must cross the walk at each end.—R. ERRINGTON.

HINTS FOR HUMBLE HOUSEHOLDS.

No. 2.

POTATO SOUP.—Put two or three ounces of dripping, or fat, into three quarts of cold water, and let it boil for a quarter of an hour; pare and cut in slices three pounds of potatoes, and soak them in boiling water for a few minutes; put them into the saucepan with two large onions sliced, one carrot cut into small pieces, and a few heads of parsley if convenient; season with salt and pepper, and boil the whole for an hour and a half. This will make an excellent dinner for four or five persons.

CHEAP VEGETABLE BROTH.—Take three ounces of dripping,

* Dr. L., of Bath, Clemens, and C. D., will please to take this in answer to their queries.—ED. C. G.

or fat, and boil as above, with three quarts of water; add a teacupful of barley when the water boils; cut down half a large cabbage, or, if middling sized, a whole one, two turnips, two large onions, and one carrot either cut or grated; boil the whole together for two hours; season with salt and a little pepper. This broth in winter will be found even more savoury by substituting leeks cut into pieces an inch in length, and well washed to free them from sand, and winter greens or savoys instead of turnips and cabbage.

LEEK SOUP.—This is a wholesome and excellent soup, and may be made as above, with fat or dripping, or any scraps or bones, but instead of barley take two tablespoonsful of oatmeal, or one of flour, and break it smoothly with a little cold water, and add to the soup half an hour before it is ready. Two hours and a half will be sufficient time to boil down the leeks.

It is almost needless to say that a pound of shin of beef, or a few trimmings or odd pieces, which are sold very cheap, or a quarter of an ox-head, or a marrow-bone well broken, any or either will be better than dripping or fat; but where meat of any kind is unattainable it may be easily dispensed with.

SHEEP'S PLUCK.—This, if well prepared, will make two dinners for a pretty large family. Wash the pluck well in several waters, and separate the liver from the heart and lights, which put on to boil with two quarts of cold water, a small teacupful of rice or barley, a couple of sliced onions, and a little parsley; boil this for two hours; take out the lights, &c., and put it aside for the second day's dinner. Put a small bit of butter or dripping in a pan, slice the liver, rub each slice over with flour, and fry it a nice brown; lift it out, or draw it aside, and put a cupful of the liquor of the broth in the pan, season with pepper and salt, and boil it up for a minute, and pour it over the liver. This, with the broth, will be one good dinner for a working man's family. Second day: mince the heart and the lights well; slice two onions and put them in a pan with a little piece of butter or dripping, and fry them till brown; put in the mince, two tablespoonsful of flour, pepper, salt, and a cupful of water, or of the broth of the previous day if saved, and let it all simmer for half an hour or three quarters; this, with a couple of pounds of potatoes boiled, will make a savoury, satisfactory meal. A lamb's pluck may be dressed in the same manner, only it will not go so far.

A POTATO STEW.—Pare and slice four pounds of potatoes, and soak them in hot water and a little salt for a few minutes; slice three onions, and put a layer of potatoes and a layer of onions and salt and pepper, alternately, into a baking dish; add an ounce of dripping or fat; fill up the dish with cold water and bake in an oven.

SAVOURY CABBAGE.—Take a large, firm cabbage, and wash it well in cold water; cut it down the middle and scoop a piece out of each half about the size of an egg; take a quarter of a pound of bacon and lay it in the hollow you have scooped out; close the cabbage again and tie it in a cloth, and boil it for two hours and a half, when it will be soft and pulpy; mash it up with salt and pepper. This, with bread, will be a satisfactory meal for several persons, and at a very small expense.

CABBAGE or CAULIFLOWER, when cheap, may be stewed (first parboiled) or fried, so as to make a wholesome dinner when meat is unattainable.

POTTED HEAD.—This, if well cooked and seasoned, is a very profitable and nutritious preparation. Get half an ox-head, and, if not too dear, an ox foot, but this may be dispensed with; wash the head well, and put it in a large pot with nearly two gallons of cold water. When it has boiled for four hours excellent *brose* may be made from it, by drying some oatmeal before the fire, adding a little salt, and pouring some of the liquor over the oatmeal; stir it up and eat it while it is hot; if oatmeal is not liked, crusts of bread may be substituted. When the head separates freely from the bones take it out, and strain the liquor; when the meat is cold enough to cut without tearing, cut it into small pieces and return it to the liquor; season well with salt and pepper and a little allspice, and boil all up together. This will keep, and warm up as excellent soup for several days, or, if a foot has been added to it, it will turn out and eat cold like brawn.—J. W.

FRICTION.
Addressed especially to those who neglect to grease their axles.

FRICTION, the great drawback on all mechanical power, is the resistance caused by two surfaces rubbing against each other; and the rougher the surface the greater it will be. For instance: suppose two files to be put face to face, it would require great force to slip them along one another; but if they were both polished surfaces like glass, they would pass easily. There is, also, another quality besides roughness, which is the attraction of cohesion, even where the surfaces are apparently smooth.

Two pieces of smooth iron in passing over one another exhibit more friction than if one was of iron and one of brass, or any other metal; and this is accounted for in the following manner. However smooth a surface apparently is, there is a sort of inherent grain in it, which fits into the grain of a similar substance, more closely than it would into a substance of a different texture; and for this reason, the moving parts of steam engines, and other machines, are generally made of two metals, that is, if the spindle of a wheel is of iron, the socket in which it works is of brass.

To determine the quantity of friction in two substances, the following method can be employed: one of the surfaces is laid down as an inclined plane, and the other is then placed upon it; the plane is now elevated till the upper mass begins to slide; the inclination of the plane, just before the sliding commences, is called the angle of repose, and of course the less this angle is, or the flatter the plane, the less will be the friction on these substances. It is this angle which determines the degree of sloping in the sides of hills composed of sand, gravel, or earth; as also in the sides of canals, embankments for railways, or the banks of rivers. If it were not for friction, we should walk on the ground or pavement as if on ice; and our rivers, that now flow so calmly, would all be frightful torrents. Friction is useful also, when out of the comparatively short fibres of cotton, flax, or hemp, it enables us to form lengthened webs and cordage; for it is friction alone, consequent upon the interweaving of the threads, which keeps them together.

There are several methods employed to diminish friction, such as making the rubbing surfaces of different materials. In watches for instance, the steel axles are made to play in diamond or agate holes; the swiftness of a skaiter depends much on the great dissimilarity there is between ice and steel; again, by interposing some lubricating substance between the rubbing parts, as oil for the metals, grease, black-lead, &c., for wood. There is a laughable illustration of this in the holiday sport of soaping a lively pig's tail, and then offering him as the prize of the clever fellow who can catch and hold him fast by his slippery appendage; the countryman, however, without having studied the theory of friction, shews a deep practical acquaintance with its laws, by rubbing the palm of his hand with sand.

Of all rubbing parts, the joints of animals—considering the strength, frequency, and rapidity of their movements—are those which have the least friction. We may study and admire the perfection found in them without being able very closely to imitate it.

Wheels are perhaps the most successful machines in combatting friction, by diminishing the distance rubbed over; for example—if a sledge were drawn along a road a mile long, there would be a mile of rubbing surface; but if the sledge were placed on wheels, observe the difference: the rubbing surface instead of being on the road, at the extremity of the wheel, is in the centre, at the axle; now as the axle is perhaps only three inches in circumference, and the wheel fifteen feet, each revolution of the wheel, although it will have taken the carriage fifteen feet along the road, has only caused a rubbing surface of three inches, or one revolution of the axle; and as the axle turns about 350 times in a mile, the rubbing surface would amount to only about ninety feet, instead of one mile—so that in drawing the sledge along the road, even supposing the road to be perfectly smooth, the resistance from friction would have been as much in ninety feet as from the wheel-carriage in one mile.

The broad old-fashioned conical wheel, with the lower spokes made perpendicular, and the upper part of the wheel hanging over, greatly augmented friction; for this wheel formed the frustrum of a cone. The circumference of the outside part of it would measure much less than the circumference of the side next the cart—the one being perhaps fifteen feet, the other sixteen; therefore as a turn of the large part of the wheel would carry the cart forward sixteen feet, and as the smaller portion is obliged to keep pace with it, the outer edge has actually been obliged to slide one foot along the rough surface of the road to keep up with the inner edge. Wheels of this description are not now much in use, though they are still occasionally to be seen.

Besides the saving in friction, the wheel-carriage has another advantage over the sledge, in overcoming any abrupt obstacle on the road, by the axle describing a gently rising slope or curve; the wheel, as it were, rising on an inclined plane, which gives to the drawing animal the relief which such a plane would bring. This kind of advantage is proportioned to the magnitude of the wheel, for the smaller wheel in order to surmount the same obstacle, has to rise in a steeper curve; a small wheel will sink to the bottom of a hole, where a large one would rest on the edges. The fore wheels of carriages are usually made small, because such construction facilitates the turning of the carriage, and not because, according to the popular prejudice, the large hind wheels of carriages and waggons help to push on the little wheels before them; but there is this slight incidental advantage, that in ascending a hill, when the horses have to put forth their strength, the load rests chiefly on the large wheels; and in descending, when increased resistance is desirable, the load falls chiefly on the small ones. In descending hilly roads, it is usual to take advantage of the resistance caused by friction, to prevent the carriage descending too rapidly; this is generally effected by putting the wheel of the carriage into a shoe, thus stopping its revolution, and causing it to rub over the surface of the road.

In France, the heavy lumbering diligence is provided with a piece of wood running across the carriage, just behind the wheels; this piece of wood is attached to the axle-tree by a strong screw through the middle of it; and in descending a hill the *conducteur* goes behind and turns the screw till he draws the wood close to the outside of the wheels, and by this means he can either entirely stop them, or allow them to grind slowly down the hill, which is the general plan, and a most delightful one it is, especially if the outside of the wheel is rough, or has lost a piece of its tire, which is by no means uncommon in French carriages. A machine on the same principle, but of very superior construction, is employed for stopping railway carriages, and is called a *break*.

C. F. GOWER.

HISTORY OF AN APIARY.
(No. 3.)
(*Continued from page 325.*)

I CONCLUDED my former letter with stating my resolution to give Mr. Nutt's system of bee management a trial. As soon, therefore, as the boxes, which had been placed at my disposal, were ready for the reception of their proposed tenants (after a good cleansing and smearing with honey), an early evening was fixed upon for the ejection of my unhappy bees (*unhappy*, as the sequel will shew) from their old domicile. I could have wished for a more suitable evening than that fixed upon; for the moon was high and bright in the heavens, when at about 8 o'clock we sallied forth, a large party of ladies and gentlemen, to witness or assist at the operation; but the season was so far advanced (it was already the 27th of August) that any further delay would necessarily have been fatal to the experiment. As it was, it was full late; but I hoped that the vicinity of heath-covered hills might yet, with the assistance of copious feeding, enable my bees to more than retrieve their losses. The gardener was the chief operator, assisted by myself and others; and the plan which I proposed to adopt for the transfer of the bees from the hive to the boxes, was the old-fashioned one of *driving*. Mr. Nutt, I was aware, strongly reprobates this system; but I had no puff-balls at hand; and on the whole it seemed to me the simpler operation, and I still adhere to it with the same persuasion.

As soon as everything was ready, I commenced the business by turning the hive, bottom upwards, and placing it in a pail to steady it, while the centre box, or "pavilion of nature," as Nutt calls it, was instantly placed over the mouth of the hive, and a sheet twisted into a loose kind of rope was hastily adjusted to the points of junction of the hive and box, as accurately as could be managed, so as to prevent the egress of the bees. As soon as this was tolerably well arranged, the gardener, sitting on a low stool, set briskly to work tapping with light sticks against the sides of the reversed hive; in a very few moments it was evident by the loud hum that the whole population was thoroughly aroused. Instead, however, of yielding to our requisition, we soon became aware that the bees had courage to defend their homes, and to stand by their queen; for, owing to the crevices between the hive and the box not having been stopped up with sufficient care—a difficult thing to do, as the one was round and the other angular—the infuriated insects issued forth in crowds, while the light of the moon pointed out to them their assailants. Then came a curious scene. The first to decamp were the female assistants, each literally with "a bee in her bonnet." The gardener followed next, after having stood his ground right manfully for awhile, in spite of several stings. I, too, though as yet unharmed, seeing small hope of success, and opportunely recollecting that old proverb, "He that fights and runs away," &c., had retreated in good time; so that hitherto the bees had the best of it. Again we returned to the charge, and were again repulsed; as the cloth became unfastened and gave way altogether, leaving to the bees a free passage, who were soon flying about in all directions. What now was to be done? The evening clearly was lost to us, and we must try again some other time, or give it up.

After letting the bees settle, I gently took the box away from the hive and rested it upon the old stool, while the gardener conveyed the hive itself to a distant part of the garden. There were many bees in both, and it seemed doubtful as to which the queen had chosen for a place of refuge. Curious to know the result of our efforts of the evening before, I was up betimes the next morning. The sun was already warm, and its rays were fierce throughout the day; while my poor bees, whom I cordially pitied, were passing and repassing from hive to box, and from box to hive, in great apparent disquietude. The ground, too, was strewed with many corpses, who had fallen bravely in battle the night before. As soon as evening came—most of them having returned to the hive, from which it was evident that the queen mother had not been dislodged—we resumed our efforts to transfer them to the box, but with no better success; though this time I applied the octagonal cover of Nutt's boxes to the hive, which, having a broad external base, was better fitted to confine the bees. None accordingly escaped; but tap as we might the queen would not ascend. Doubtless she and her subjects were congregated together beneath the ledge, presented by the base of the cover, there not being a clear and uninterrupted ascent into it, which is absolutely necessary to insure the success of the driving scheme. Very much disappointed at my repeated failure, I was again obliged to retire for the evening, heartily repenting of my scheme, and wishing I had let my bees alone. Again they were left till morning, when, having determined on a forcible ejection at all hazards, the gardener and I visited the scene of action, carefully protected by canvas screens, for the face and neck, and leather gloves. The sun had but just risen, and the bees were still dormant when the operation began. Discarding the square boxes, which had given us so much trouble, I took a common hive (the diameter of which at the base corresponded with the diameter of the old stock) and placed it carefully upon the reversed hive, which was poised in a pail as before; a cloth also was twisted about it, and the hive tapped. On this occasion we succeeded beyond expectation in the attainment of our object, as, after a very few minutes, the queen and the major part of her subjects had ascended into the upper hive. After a brief interval, this was taken off and placed upon a table at hand, while the bees which still adhered to the combs of the old hive were swept off with a goose feather. The combs were next cut out of the old hive on the spot, and removed quickly into an empty room at some distance from the garden. Of course during this operation the bees were very angry, but our defences were proof against their stings, though we were surrounded and attacked by thousands of them.

So far I had succeeded in dislodging the bees from their old dwelling, but much remained to be done, and I was sorely puzzled to know how I should get them into the box destined for their final location. As there were many bees who still resorted to the box, attracted doubtless by the honey with which it had been smeared, it struck me that, perhaps, if I suddenly shook the swarm out of the empty hive in front of the boxes, the heat of the sun would compel them to seek a refuge, and so that they might all resort to the box with which they had become partially acquainted two evenings before, and where some of them were still to be found. It was so done accordingly by a rude blow on the outside of the hive, and the bees fell out instantly in a body to the ground, where they soon congregated in a lump about their beloved queen. Overjoyed at seeing this, I quickly placed the octagonal cover (it ought to have been the centre box) partly over them, so as to shelter them from the sun, elevating it on one side with a stone from the ground. Attracted by the friendly shade, the whole swarm, to my great joy, put itself in motion, and quickly crept into the cover. Towards evening, as soon as the bees were quiet, I lifted it gently from the ground and placed it over the centre box, at the same time withdrawing the tin slide, which usually closes the communication between the cover and the box. Here, then, at last my long cherished wishes were gratified, and I had the inexpressible pleasure of seeing my bees safely housed—deprived of a comfortable home it is true, and of all their stores, but with much of the heath season before them, and, as I flattered myself, a careful master to boot. How it fared with them shall be told in due season.　　　　　A Country Curate.

EXTRACTS FROM CORRESPONDENCE.

Mushrooms.—The year before last I gathered a great number of mushrooms upon my asparagus beds, but last year there was not one to be seen, although the beds received similar treatment to the year before, excepting that I sowed salt over them last year for the first time. If, as Mr. Brownell states, salt is an article capable of producing mushrooms when applied to grass lands, why, may I ask, should it not have the same effect when sown on asparagus beds?—J. V. M.

[We cannot say why salt should not excite mushrooms into growth upon an asparagus bed as well as upon a pasture, if the mushroom spawn was there. Forking an asparagus bed, and exposure to frost, will effectually prevent mushrooms appearing a second year.—Ed. C. G.]

Since the above was written we have received the following from a Hampshire clergyman:—

"Mr. Brownell's letter respecting 'Mushrooms,' which appeared in your paper of March 21st, surprised me as much as it seems to have done you; and, as you invite any who happens to have had experience on the subject to contribute it, I beg to inform you that in the winter of 1847 I sowed some acres of pasture land with common salt, and have not seen, I think, a single mushroom since, whereas before the application of this saline dressing, some few mushrooms at least might be expected at the proper season."—J. T. P.

Flower Garden Plans.—It is with much pleasure that I find, on reading your number of 21st March, that Mr. Beaton has given us an example of the manner which he approves of laying out a flower-garden of limited extent. Now, as one example is better than 100 pages of letterpress devoted to the principles of the art in a general way, I trust we shall again be favoured with other and more varied designs. Having said thus much in approbation of Mr. Beaton's bringing an example before us, I hope to give no offence by differing from him in almost all that relates to the design which he seems to laud so much; very possibly my taste may be bad, or the divisions into which he says the triangles are again divided may give additional beauty to the figure, otherwise I cannot say it is at all pleasing. I am sorry the subdivisions were not added, as they would have made the plan more complete; however, by the subsequent remarks, I conclude those divisions to be figures all intersected by straight lines, with more or less of angular points. Now, what I find fault with is the monotonous feature which the whole presents; a number of beds all radiating from the centre may be excusable, perhaps, where the boundary presents a circle, but even the other figures might be found more pleasing. How much the figure of *X. Y. Z.* may be improved by judicious planting of flowers I know not, but I cannot bring myself to the belief that its appearance will be at all inviting in winter or spring, when nothing but the shapes of the beds are left to attract the attention.

As I consider this subject of much more vital importance than the assumed science (which I suspect ere long some will be giving a long name to) of harmonizing colours in a garden, in the latter case an error of one season can be rectified in the next, while the laying out of a piece of ground is expected to be a permanent feature. Now, as there are a great many suburban houses and others where it is desirable to make the most that can be made out of a small piece of ground, I think nothing can be really more useful than giving a series of plans or designs for doing so to the best advantage. I know the matter is beset with difficulties; and the great diversity there is in the public taste may deter some from staking their reputation on what, they may be afraid, another may assume; but I give Mr. Beaton credit for possessing sufficient moral courage to face it all; and he may rest assured that his labours will not fail to be appreciated by the thinking part of your readers, more so by giving us a few examples than if he established a code of artistical laws bearing on the subject.

Having vented my disapproval of the design of X. Y. Z., without, I hope, offending Mr. B., I by no means disagree with the style which it represents; on the contrary, for a small plot of ground adjoining a house, I think nothing can exceed the Dutch or embroidered beds of flower-gardening—not only for the display of floral beauties when in their prime, but, also, for their interesting and pleasing appearance when unadorned by such attractions—that I sincerely hope the matter will be followed out, either by Mr. B., or some one well versed in such matters; and I trust my hasty censure of the design of X. Y. Z., will not prevent any one venturing another, in that or some other way. Should no one reply to the invitation, I will, with your permission, send you a sketch of a garden of that description, applicable to a plot of ground containing 20 or more poles; but, should the subject not fall in with your wishes, I trust what I have hitherto said may not be taken amiss by any one.   S. N. V.

[We shall be glad to have the plan, but we cannot give many such, for the engraving them is expensive. Tastes differ so much on these points that variety is desirable.—ED. C. G.]

POTATOES FROM SEED.—The practicability of obtaining full and fine crops of potatoes from this source, the first season after sowing, may now be considered as beyond all doubt; and the chief care indispensable to insure success is, combining precocity with the cultivation of selected early kinds. From a single packet of our own selected seeds—value 6d—we have obtained seven bushels of fine-sized sound tubers, most of them fit for table.

On the impracticability of this object, with all due deference,

we are prepared to confute all prejudiced minds; and, as the practice is only in its infancy, a wide field for improvement, no doubt, is still open; and we shall feel pleasure in hearing from any competitors who may favour us with their correspondence for the public good.   HARDY AND SON,
                Seed Growers, Maldon, Essex.

[Now is a good time for sowing potato seed.—ED. C. G.]

DOUBLE ANEMONES (See THE COTTAGE GARDENER, February 28, 1850, page 303).—I was not aware they had *seed*; perhaps *semi*-double are meant. What occasions the anemone plant to run to leaf without producing any flowers? The leaves have a peculiar appearance, being much more fleshy, and with little spots on the underside, something like the *blossom* (I think it is) of the fern; and, if I mistake not, they have a peculiar smell. I am not sure of this latter though, for as I now pull them up whenever I see them, it may, therefore, be occasioned by my bruising those leaves, and that the others would smell the same if I treated them as roughly. I have given some of these plants to other persons, thinking that change of soil might benefit them, but they came up the same. I have lost many double anemones by their degenerating in this way, and I find the single ones do the same; but then I must say I have often neglected them, and allowed them to grow for several years without taking them up.   W. H. M.

[The really double anemones do not produce seeds we believe. It is very difficult to say what causes these to "run to leaf," and not flower. We have seen them with the blistered leaves and no flowers under various conditions; we should be glad to hear the opinions of some of our readers about this disease.—ED. C. G.]

REVIVING BEES.—I have no doubt what I am going to state must be well known to many, if not all, of your readers, but if a repetition of it draw attention from one to whom it was previously unknown, and so a handful of bee-hives may be happily saved, I, and you, will not regret the trouble. My hives stand south-west; and during the recent sunny days (with cold north and east winds strongly blowing) my bees were tempted forth; and I found one morning, to my dismay, the ground strewn with them in an apparently lifeless state. I picked them up, placed them under a glass shade before the fire, and, to my great satisfaction, I perceived first a leg move and then a wing quiver, until the whole mass was in motion. I then gave them some beer and sugar, and had very quickly the happiness of restoring many, in a perfectly strong and lively state, to their hive again.—TYRO.

TANNER'S BARK FOR PLUNGING.—Experience of many years has taught me that nothing can well be worse. It constantly generates a degree of heat and *steam*, which, in the winter, tends to mildew all cuttings, and even old plants. If used for plunging, it should be thoroughly spent and rotten, otherwise the pits are always damp, and the glasses require constant wiping.—W. G. C.

TO CORRESPONDENTS.

. We request that no one will write to the departmental writers of THE COTTAGE GARDENER. It gives them unjustifiable trouble and expense; and we also request our coadjutors *under no circumstances* to reply to such private communications.

ROCK PLANTS (*J. T.*).—You may select from the list given in THE COTTAGE GARDENER as many as you think you would want; or, send the extent of your pond and rockwork to Mr. Appleby, and he has consented to return you a proper list, and the prices of both kinds of plants.

CUCUMBER HOUSE (*Dr. L., Bath*).—We give a plan and description this week.

SMOKE-STAINED WALL (J. H.).—"An old vinery heated by flues in the back wall has been fitted up with hot-water pipes, and the fronts of the flues removed. The soot has been well cleaned away from the bricks, but these still pertinaciously refuse to be *whitened*; a rusty yellow prevails, although repeatedly limed. What appliance will neutralize the ammonia, or sulphur, or both?" If the case were our own, we should have the stained portion covered with a thin coat of Parker's cement. It would then take a coat of whitening, we think. Have any of our other correspondents been similarly situated; and, if so, did they succeed in obtaining a remedy?

RED SAND (S. D.).—If this be washed thoroughly, until no colour is imparted to the water, it might do for potting plants. But it is impossible to give a decisive opinion without seeing a sample.

CAMELLIAS (Mary Ormead).—These can be obtained of any of the florists who advertise in our columns.

COVERS (I. H.).—The cover for our third volume may be obtained at Liverpool, from Messrs. Orr and Co., North John Street, as well as at 2, Amen Corner.

A LOVER OF FLOWERS FROM CHILDHOOD.—Will you oblige the Rev. J. Lievre, Little Ashby Rectory, Lutterworth, by informing him whether he can have the same workman as you employed to erect a Fortune's pit?

THOULOUSE GEESE (A New Subscriber).—Will some one of our readers inform us where these geese, or their eggs, can be obtained?

RHUBARB AND RASPBERRIES (J. Bewicke).—Either guano or sulphate of ammonia may be employed to those, and will be especially beneficial to the rhubarb. Do not now apply them to your raspberries until they are in bloom.

MONTHLY PARTS (A Country Curate).—As we appear in weekly numbers, we cannot, prospectively, do more for the monthly parts than give in the last number of the month calendars of operations for the next month.

CAPONS (A Lady).—We cannot advise upon this cruel process. You will find information in Richardson's shilling book, "The Domestic Fowl."

HAIR FALLING OFF (I. T.).—Rub very fine salt down to the roots of your hair twice a week. We have known this simple remedy to be effectual. Never mind if your hair does become thin; most people of intellect are similarly situated.

BEE-HIVES (A Recent Subscriber).—You have painted Mr. Payne's cottage hive over the top as well as the sides, and ask, "Would there be any objections to my putting on top hives ten inches wide by seven deep? Is it very commonly needful to place three small hives on in summer?" You have no milkpan similar to those used by Mr. Payne, and ask, "Would a slate stone cut round, and projecting several inches beyond the hive, keep these sufficiently dry? Are Mr. Payne's small hives also painted? Should putty be used to stop any small crevices in the straw?" Ten inches by seven is too large for small hives—eight by seven is the proper size. Three small hives are required only for a very strong stock, and that only in an extraordinary good season. Zinc in the form of a milkpan, with a piece of stone or slate laid upon it to prevent its being blown off by the wind, answers very well; a flat slate is not sufficient protection. The small hives are *not* painted, nor need the large ones be on the top. *Use no putty.*

POMEGRANATE (J. M. S.).—The pomegranate generally flowers easily enough, trained like a peach-tree against a south wall, in good rich soil, on a dry or well-drained bottom. When it refuses to flower, as in your case, the reason, generally, either is that it grows too strong, or that it is half starved. If the former, root pruning is a remedy; and if the latter, the border must be enriched, or drained, or both. It flowers on the current season's growth, like the grape vine, and like it ought to be close pruned every spring. When pomegranates are kept in pots or boxes, to stand out in summer, they require the shelter of an outhouse in winter; and it is a safe plan to force them *gently* from April to the end of May, and then to inure them gradually to the open air; their flowers are then more certain, and they come earlier.

MYRTLE LEAFLESS.—W. F. says, "I have a fine myrtle standing about 3½ feet high; last spring one of the principal branches lost its leaves, and during the summer it died. This spring another of them has scarcely a leaf left upon it, though on raising the bark there is every appearance of life." We have two plants now in a similar state, brought on by the centre of the ball having been allowed to get too dry for a long time. We cut back the whole of the branches about one-half their length, and reduced the small side branches also, and put *the plant into a warm rinery.*

LIQUID-MANURE (M.).—Your plan of sowing three cwt. per acre of gypsum over your grass land, and immediately watering it with your liquid manure, is not a bad suggestion; but we should prefer mixing the gypsum with the liquid-manure in the tank; it would more certainly combine with, or fix, the ammonia. Neither would we apply "too strong liquid-manure" for the rain to reduce to a proper strength; we should prefer diluting it properly before applying it. Answers to other questions next week.

DOMESTIC ECONOMIST (R. C.).—Nearly all the subjects will be continued in our columns.

POTATOES IN SHADED GARDEN (Vulpis venator).—We fear that potatoes planted in a garden having "very little sun, except in the morning," would not be very productive under any circumstances; and planting them so late as the beginning of April will render them still more liable to be destroyed by the potato murrain. Answers to other questions next week.

DISTEMPER IN DOGS (Mouse).—What is thus commonly named, is really an inflammation of the mucous membranes of the animal's nostrils and windpipe; properly treated it is usually curable, but there is no specific cure. Each case should be treated according to its symptoms: if the dog is costive, give him, according to his size, from half a grain to three grains of calomel mixed with a similar quantity of tartrate of antimony; give this powder on a piece of meat or in milk; if the dog is sick or purged do not give the above medicine. Afterwards give twice a day, for two or three days, a pill made of powdered digitalis, 1 or 2 grains; antimonial powder, 3 or 4 grains; nitre, 4 or 6 grains. If the dog is weak, or much discharge from his nose, give twice a day a pill made of powdered gentian, 10 to 20 grains; ginger, 5 grains; powdered cascarilla bark, 10 to 20 grains. If, with these symptoms, there is purging or vomiting, add to the pill from one quarter of a grain to 2 grains of powdered opium. If the discharge is offensive from the nose, give a teaspoonful of yeast daily. If the dog is giddy, or there are other symptoms of his brain being affected, put a seton in his neck and in his loins. If the dog is weak give him broth and other nutritious food.—W. C. S. [Mr. Spooner will give, in due course, the characteristics of dogs.]

BEES (A Tyro Bee-Keeper).—Ventilation—we cannot give you advice as to this until we know whose system you follow. The direction to ventilate when the thermometer is at 76°, means when the thermometer *outside* the hive indicates that temperature; for a hive is always 76° within. You next ask, if box hives require constant protection? Boxes *must* be protected from wet; and when bell glasses are used these must be covered with an empty hive or box, and the milk-pan cover placed upon this. A May, or early June, swarm when hived into a straw hive *will* supply from 15 to 25 pounds of honey in a fair season, if properly attended to. Room must be given, and at the time, as recommended in THE COTTAGE GARDENER, vol. ii, p. 104.

IPOMŒA RUBRO CŒRULEA (M. D. P.).—"Can I grow this without risk of the red spider, by training it along a slip of wood three inches wide, well painted with clay, sulphur, and soft soap?" This is your question, and we think it is worth a trial. The only available article, so far as the spider is concerned, is the sulphur; and instead of depending too much on the paint, it would be desirable to renew the sulphur during the hot season several times. For your encouragement the writer may mention, that he has a peach-tree very near the cistern and hot-water pipes; and he has found boarding the trellis beneath, and using sulphur, has this reason, as yet, freed the tree from the red spider, to which it formerly was always more or less liable.

CUTTINGS OF ROSES AND LEMON-SCENTED VERBENA (Beginner).—There is no absolute necessity for bell-glasses for such purposes, though most plants will strike sooner with them if properly managed. The failure of those planted in pots, and set in frames, in a shady border, in the autumn, might be owing to several reasons: first, the want of drainage—the pots should have been half filled, instead of having a few sherds; secondly, the soil—half sand and half garden soil—would be too heavy if not previously well prepared; an addition of leaf-mould would have been an advantage: thirdly, perhaps the place was too shady; in spring and autumn we prefer a place exposed to the sun;—see what has been said by Mr. Fish, and also Mr. Beaton, lately; fourthly, were the cuttings well chosen? hard stems would hardly strike at that season, and young ones would require considerable care, to prevent an excess of moisture and an excess of evaporation. Read the articles referred to, which you will find in late numbers; and if there is anything abstruse, inquire again, and state shortly and clearly your difficulty. For your encouragement, we may tell you that you will strike cuttings of such things, and almost anything else, with a tithe of the trouble *now*, more especially if after being made a few days you can give them a little bottom-heat, and choose the nice young side shoots, cutting them off close to the stem, and with a nice *heel* adhering to them.

NUTT'S v. TAYLOR'S HIVE (A Subscriber).—You ask, what are the advantages and disadvantages of Nutt's and Taylor's bar hives? and what becomes (in Nutt's system) of the young queen which would otherwise go off with the swarm? Nutt's hives are too large, except for a very few districts; and the honey, *if any is ever obtained from them*, is always stained with pollen and brood. Taylor's are a much more suitable size; and the honey obtained from them is fine. The queen would be destroyed in the embryo state.

RUSTIC FURNITURE (Ibid).—There is a little book, with twenty-five plates, entitled, "Ideas for Rustic Furniture." Mr. Wright, bookseller, Haymarket, has a copy, we think.

NAME OF INSECTS (M. R.).—The insects you have sent, which were found close to a peach-tree, are a species of Millepede, *Polydesmus complanatus*. You will find a description of them at page 139 of our second volume.

LONDON: Printed by HARRY WOOLDRIDGE, Winchester High Street, in the Parish of Saint Mary Kalendar, and Published by WILLIAM SOMERVILLE ORR, at the Office, No. 2, Amen Corner, in the Parish of Christ Church, City of London.—April 18th, 1850.

WEEKLY CALENDAR.

M W D D	APRIL 25—MAY 1, 1850.	Weather near London in 1849.		Sun Rises.	Sun Sets.	Moon R. & S.	Moon's Age.	Clock bef. Sun.	Day of Year.
25 Th	St. Mark. Pss. Alice b. 1843.　Ds. Glo. b.	T. 69°—44°.	W.　Rain.	46 a. 4	10 a. 7	4　46	13	2　7	115
26 F	Lesser Whitethroat heard.　　　　[1778.	T. 69°—39°.	N.W.　Rain.	44	12	rises.	☾	2　17	116
27 S	Cuckoo first heard.	T. 61°—40°.	S.　Rain.	42	13	8a.23	15	2　28	117
28 Sun	4 Sun. after Easter.　Reed bunting sings.	T. 59°—32°.	W.　Rain.	40	15	9　29	16	2　37	118
29 M	Young Redbreasts fledged.	T. 66°—43°.	S.W.　Fine.	38	17	10　31	17	2　46	119
30 Tu	Martin first seen.	T. 66°—38°.	E.　Fine.	36	18	11　26	18	2　55	120
1 W	St. Philip & St. James.　Vine-leaves open.	T. 59°—49°.	N.E.　Fine.	35	20	morn.	19	3　3	121

On the 18th of April, 1802, died Dr. Erasmus Darwin, so well associated in the minds of all lovers of literature and botany with the title of his poem, *The Loves of the Plants.* Darwin from boyhood to the grave was more prone to the pleasures of the imagination than to those of inductive philosophy; and as this is demonstrated to have been so in his mature years by his writings, so does the following narrative shew how open to vivid impressions was his mind in youth:—Journeying from Newark, his native place, to enter upon his college education at Cambridge, he rested for the night at the house of two old bachelor brothers. They were delighted with the vivacity of the young student, and were rendered by it so painfully sensible that *they* were childless and solitary, that he heard one say regretfully to the other, " Why did not one of us marry !" The tone and the circumstances never allowed that sentence to fade from Darwin's memory, and it was the origin of that strong condemnation of an unmarried life which for ever afterwards he was so ready to utter. In due course he graduated in medicine at Cambridge; but even there he distinguished himself more by his poetical exercises than by his proficiency in science. It is needless to follow him in his professional career, which at first was unsuccessful, and in after years was never extensive. In 1778 he obtained a lease of a picturesque spot near Lichfield, called " The Cold Bath," where he established a botanic garden, and commenced writing on " The Loves of the Plants." Eventually he retired to the vicinity of Derby, and died there on the date above-named. He had often expressed a hope that the termination of life might come to him without pain, for thus he ever esteemed a greater evil than death. That hope was realised, for complaining of cold he seated himself by the fire, and died in a few minutes, without pain or emotion, in the arm-chair in which he had been placed. His " Loves of the Plants " formed only a part of a poem entitled *The Botanic Garden,* in which the physiology and classification of plants is told in harmonious verse, and illustrated with many notes, amusing though not profound. The digressions are many, and the flights of imagination widely discursive. These

flights are not always characterised by sobriety, but one deserves record in which he foretells the invention of steam-vessels and locomotive engines in these two lines—

> Soon shall thy arm, unconquered steam ! afar
> Drag the slow barge, or drive the rapid car.

Another work, still more entitling him to obtain the notice of the cultivator of the soil, is his *Phytologia, or Philosophy of Agriculture and Gardening.* This was published in the year 1800, and has the merit of being the first work devoted to the *science* of the arts to which it is relative. This, however, is not its chief merit; for, although many works have since appeared having the same science as their theme, yet Darwin's work has not been rendered useless by them. They, for the most part, repeat his opinions and his facts, further illustrated and confirmed by the discoveries of modern chemists and physiologists. It is a work which may be referred to yet for pleasure and instruction.

Meteorology of the Week.—At Chiswick, during the last twenty-three years, the average highest and lowest temperature of the above days has been 61.1° and 39.4° respectively. The greatest heat was on the 28th in 1840, when the thermometer rose to 81°, and the greatest cold was on the 25th in 1827, when it fell to 25°. There were 94 fine days and 67 on which rain fell during the period.

Natural Phenomena Indicative of Weather.—When *peacocks* scream more loudly, more frequently, and in a peculiarly elevated note, which those accustomed to them readily recognise, rain almost invariably is near at hand. If they utter their peculiar cry at night, the next day is usually wet. *Pigeons* returning slowly to their dove-house before their usual time, are said by Dr. Forster to indicate approaching rain. When the *Guinea fowl* (Pintado or Galena) utters its " come-back " cry more than usual, like that of the peacock, it fortells the coming on of wet.

Insects.—Every cultivator of wheat knows that this grain is liable to be affected with what is commonly called *the yellows.* These are small grubs or maggots found about the middle of June; and they adhere to the anthers, or male parts of the wheat blossom, as well as to the germen, or embryo grain; and they suck from this its milky juice, leaving it but little more than a shrivelled skin. These maggots are yellowish, have no legs, and their mouths are not detectable. They are the larva of the *Wheat Midge,* a minute insect, closely allied to the gnat, and called by some naturalists *Cecydomyia tritici,* and by others *Tipula tritici.* In our drawing this fly is highly magnified, for it is only about the twelfth of an inch long; and it may be seen in myriads during the month of June, in some years, hovering and flying about our wheat crops. It is of a reddish-yellow colour; carries its wings, which are milky white, horizontally when at rest; and when looked at from certain angles these wings exhibit the prismatic colours; the eyes are black; the head half-globular; the antennæ many-jointed, and hairy. It usually appears about seven or eight in the evening, but in the morning none are to be found upon the wing—yet they are resting upon the stalks of the wheat; and if these are shaken they are roused, and may be seen flying about near the ground. They deposit their eggs in the blossom of the wheat during the evening. The eggs are inserted by means of a long tube, or ovipositor, just within the corolla; and sometimes being unable to withdraw its egg-tube, the insect is detained a prisoner, and dies. In a field of fifteen acres, Mr. Kirby once found the grub of this insect so numerous as to justify the conclusion that they had reduced the crop twenty bushels. The Hessian Fly, *Cecidomyia destructor,* so destructive to the American wheat crops, is one of the same genus. It is that with the unfringed wings in our drawing.

RANGE OF BAROMETER—RAIN IN INCHES.

April		1841.	1842.	1843.	1844.	1845.	1846.	1847.	1848.	1849.
25	B. {	29.846	30.028	30.070	30.198	29.795	29.991	29.997	29.962	29.745
		29.550	29.946	29.648	30.062	29.532	29.784	29.951	29.827	29.728
	R.			0.30	—	—	1.46	—	0.01	0.03
26	B. {	30.180	30.055	29.677	30.040	29.589	29.818	29.786	29.972	29.836
		29.960	30.018	29.625	29.967	29.414	29.762	29.781	29.761	29.734
	R.	—	—	0.08	0.03	0.04	0.04	0.11	—	0.01
27	B. {	30.103	29.999	29.892	30.284	29.651	29.909	29.728	29.890	29.838
		30.078	29.959	29.674	30.203	29.620	29.885	29.513	29.793	29.650
	R.	—	—	—	—	0.42	0.03	0.01	6.10	0.04
28	B. {	30.132	30.059	30.779	30.359	29.589	29.988	29.696	29.844	30.000
		30.069	29.941	29.669	30.300	29.627	29.467	29.579	29.594	29.581
	R.	0.07	—	0.04	—	—	—	0.47	0.12	0.28
29	B. {	30.141	30.061	29.729	30.288	29.969	30.232	29.571	30.054	30.260
		30.096	29.881	29.677	30.199	29.875	30.193	29.528	29.999	30.176
	R.	0.01	—	—	—	—	—	5.30	—	—
30	B. {	30.171	29.925	29.929	30.277	30.041	30.298	29.794	30.171	30.291
May		30.091	29.809	29.784	30.243	30.075	30.207	29.667	30.001	30.208
1	R.	—	—	—	—	0.01	—	0.03	—	—
	B. {	29.998	30.007	30.140	30.469	29.995	30.285	29.844	30.139	30.141
		29.794	29.933	30.065	30.366	29.829	30.263	29.669	30.067	30.008
	R.	—	—	—	—	0.01	—	0.03	—	—

Himalayah Pumpkin.—Our supply of the seed of this vegetable is quite exhausted, owing to the unexpected number of the applicants. *Any one who saved seed from that with which we supplied them last year will oblige us by sending immediately all that they can spare us.* We shall retain for a week or two longer the envelopes sent us by various correspondents, in the hope that we may obtain a fresh supply of the seed. The Himalayah pumpkin may be sown in the open ground, on a south border, during the middle of May; and if the shelter of a hand-glass is given to the plants during the early part of their growth, they will be very little later in bearing fruit than those sown in April.

THE following act of liberality deserves this prominent position :—

EXHIBITION OF WORKS OF INDUSTRY OF ALL NATIONS IN 1851.

On entering the hall of a friend, recently, I was struck with the pretty appearance of a little rustic basket, suspended from the wall, from which growing plants were gracefully depending. On expressing my admiration, I was informed it had been brought from Antwerp, where great quantities were exposed in the public market-place for sale. The idea immediately occurred to me of the delightful occupation it might give to many of our ingenious countrymen in rural districts, whose odd time is often employed in the construction of those very clever but useless puzzles to be found in the dwelling of the herdsman or shepherd, in every imaginable and unimaginable form. Now, how much good might result to many a clever rustic by the direction of this ingenuity in a more rational and profitable channel. What stimulus it would give to the skill which produces these clever absurdities, had its possessors a knowledge of the demand which might be created, were their genius expended in the production of such wares as the pretty hanging basket I have alluded to, formed of the knarled and knotty branches of the oak, the yew, or any other durable wood, with or without the bark on; steeped in a preservative solution they would long withstand decay, and prove such interesting objects in a conservatory that nobody who possesses a plant house would be without them. I am the more convinced of this from having long grown plants myself in hanging baskets; and they present such pretty objects as to elicit universal admiration. Those I employ are of an open wicker-like construction, manufactured in dark brown German clay, but they are much too expensive for general adoption, their cost varying from 2s to 10s each ; but, pretty as they are, I think those of wood, of rustic construction, far preferable, as they look more *natural*, that is, they give the idea of a bunch of sticks suspended—as is often the case in the wild haunts of nature—on a branch of a tree, on which seed may have fallen and vegetated.

I am sure that these rustic baskets for orchidaceæ, and hanging plants in general, would meet with such universal approbation, that I am induced—if you will kindly take the thing in hand—to offer A PREMIUM OF ONE POUND, through the pages of THE COTTAGE GARDENER, for THE BEST SIX RUSTIC BASKETS for orchidaceæ or trailing plants, strongly formed of rough branches of oak, yew, or any durable wood, with or without the bark on ; *three to be formed to hang against a wall*, and *three for suspension* ; the sizes varying from 6 to 12 inches across. The mode of judging I leave entirely in your own hands, but would suggest that those obtaining the premium be forwarded to the Exhibition of the Works of Industry of all Nations, to take place in London in 1851.—WILLIAM SAVAGE, *Friary Cottage, Winchester.*

That nothing may be wanting on our part to promote the good purpose of Mr. Savage, any parties wishing to compete for his premium may send them, *carriage paid*, to our Office, No. 2, Amen-Corner, Paternoster-Row, London, on or before the last day of the present year. We shall have the competing specimens submitted to competent judges, who shall be named; and we will have the successful ones engraved and published in our columns, together with the name of the maker.

AT p. 330 of our last volume we concluded our observations upon the benefits derived by plants from oxygen being presented to their roots by the soil in which they are grown, and we will now resume our commentaries by observing, that the decomposing remains of animals and vegetables contained in a soil are highly absorbent of moisture from the air, consequently the more freely the air is exposed to those remains the more effectually are they enabled to deprive it of its moisture. By being freely exposed to the influence of the air, such remains, also, are more rapidly decomposed, which leads to a consideration of the practice of exposing soils as much as possible to the action of the atmosphere by ridging. &c. When a soil is either heavy or abounding in stub-born vegetable matters, as in heath lands, it cannot be too completely exposed to the action of the air; but to light soils, which are in general deficient in organic decomposing matters, chemistry would say that ridging is accompanied by evils more injurious than can be compensated by the benefits obtained : for such light soils are easily pulverized whenever occasion requires, are so porous as at all times freely to admit the atmosphere; and, therefore, by this extra exposure the vegetable and animal remains are hastened in decomposing, and much of their fertile constituents evolved in the state of gas, or carried away by the rains, &c., without there being any crop upon them to benefit by them. Thus theory argues, and practice certainly seems to support, in this instance, her doctrines. Switzer, one of our horticultural classics, says, " Rich, heavy ground cannot well be ploughed too often to make it light, and the better manure by killing the weeds ; as poor, light ground cannot be ploughed too seldom, for fear of impoverishing it."—(*Ichnographia Rustica* vol. iii., p. 237.)

The benefit derivable from the access of the atmospheric gases to the roots of plants, and the knowledge that fertile pulverized soil absorbs and retains from them moisture, explain why these plants are benefited by having their lateral roots kept near the surface, and by having that surface frequently loosened by the fork and hoe. This is no mere imagination of theory, for as long since as the days of Cato, half a century before the Christian era, the importance of pulverizing the soil was duly appreciated. " What is good husbandry?" inquires that writer. " To plough." "What is the second point?" "To plough." The third is, "to manure." In later days, Mr. Barnes, one of the best practical gardeners of the present age, in a letter to us, says,—" To secure good crops of carrots, parsnips, and onions, I make it a standing rule to trench the ground well in winter, throwing it into rough ridges, forking and turning it over during frosty mornings, which not only sweetens and pulverizes the earth, but eradicates insects, for I prefer a good preparation to early sowing; and practice has proved to me that a good season for sowing is any time between the 15th March and the 10th April. My practice is, sow everything in drills; hoe as soon as the plants can be seen breaking the surface, continuing the hoeing throughout the season at every opportunity when the weather will permit, but not during rain, or when the ground is full of water,—not for the sake so much of destroying weeds and insects, which are rarely to be seen if hoeing be followed up with spirit, but with a desire to keep one uniform pulverization and moisture throughout, which is the means of not only continuing the present crop in the greatest of health and luxuriance, but at the same time is making a beautiful preparation for the succeeding crop.

"I keep all ground, as soon as a crop is done with, well trenched, burying all the refuse I possibly can in a green state, casting the earth into rough ridges, tumbling those ridges over with a strong fork on frosty mornings in winter and spring, and during hot sunny days in summer; continually changing the crops; keeping the hoe at work at all seasons in suitable weather; and forking up all odd corners and spare ground without loss of time. By this management, I find the ground is always in good condition, and never tired by cropping; some judgment only being exercised in applying such properties again to the soil that have been taken from it, or that are likely to be required by the succeeding crop. To *rest*, or *fallow*, ground for any length of time is only loss of time and produce; more benefit will be obtained by trenching and forking, in frosty or hot sunny weather, in a few days, than by a whole season of what is erroneously called rest or fallow. Trench, fork, and hoe; change every succeeding crop; return to the earth all refuse that is not otherwise useful in a green state, adding a change of other manures occasionally, especially charred refuse of any kind, at the time of putting the crop into the ground. Every succeeding crop will be found healthy and luxuriant, suffering but little either from drought, too much moisture, or vermin."

All who have tried *charred vegetable refuse* as a fertilizer add their testimony to that of Mr. Barnes, that it is one of the best of manures. It is far more powerful, that is, it will produce a better crop of any kitchen-garden plant, than will an equal quantity of the same vegetable refuse uncharred. The reason of this appears to be, that charred, not carbonized, vegetable refuse decays faster than does the refuse uncharred; the earthy matters mixed with the refuse, also, become saturated with oxygen and carbonic acid during the process of charring, and these earthy matters, in which we include the oxide of iron which they contain, give out the excess of those gases to the roots of the crop. Moreover, charred refuse promotes the dryness, and, consequently, the warmth of a soil; for not only is that refuse dried by the process of charring, but the mucilage and other parts of it, which become moist during decay, are decomposed, and only the more solid parts remain, which drily moulder away during their putrefaction. That charred refuse does promote the dryness and warmth of a soil is readily perceived, if it be sown in drills with the seed. The surface soil over those drills is always drier than the other parts of the surface.

THE FRUIT-GARDEN.

WALL TREES, DISBUDDING, &c.—We have in previous numbers led the peach and nectarine cultivator through the planting, pruning, training, &c., of these fruits on walls, and we have shewn to him the modes of bidding defiance to the aphides and the red spider. We must now carry him forward to the principles of disbudding,

for this forms one important item in the successful culture of the peach and nectarine.

For the information of those who are for the first time trying their hand at the culture of these fruits, we may as well say why this disbudding becomes necessary.

In the first place, let it be considered what a vast difference exists between an ordinary peach-tree in its own climate, where it is unattached to a wall, and one under a course of training. The tree in its natural condition enjoys an amount of light, independent of sunshine, unknown to British skies; its limbs can stretch right and left, up and down, and bathe in the bright ethereal medium without hindrance; for light on all sides assists in the general elaboration of the secretions. Not so, however, the peach or nectarine sprucely trained on the south wall, of which the roots—if the doctrine of reciprocity between root and branch be admitted (and who can gainsay it as a principle)—should receive a degree of limitation equal to that of the branches. Here the tree derives all its light from one side, so that if two shoots spring together it is evident that the leaves of the foremost one will intercept the light from the other; and equally evident, that in proportion to the amount of shade just so imperfect will be the organization of those buds attached to the shaded branches. Thus, then, were a peach-tree left without disbudding it would become a thicket of useless spray, and the fruit would be exceedingly diminished both in size and flavour.

To remedy this, when the young shoots are about a couple of inches in length, which is generally the case by the time the trees have done blossoming, strip away the foreright shoots, that is to say, those shoots which extend outwards from the wall, and which at once shew that they are ill adapted for training to it; an exception may be taken where the tree is lean of shoots, for even a crooked or inferior shoot is preferable to a lost space on the wall. Next, let the operator, with a hammer in one hand, examine the trees carefully, and see if any young shoots have become lodged between the old wood and the wall; all such may be stripped away also, unless required to fill a blank, then the nearest nail must be eased with the hammer in order to give the young shoot more liberty.

These things carried out, the trees may remain untouched for a week; for a too severe disbudding performed at once is very prejudicial to the peach; we have known trees thus treated to become almost stationary, as to farther growth and enlargement of the fruit; but by disbudding at intervals nature gradually diverts the juices into fresh channels, and thus the tree is gradually led to submit and shape itself to the objects of the cultivator. After the lapse of about a week another examination may take place, and farther disbudding will be necessary. The hand of the dresser must now be applied with some judgment: selection becomes necessary. In the first place, in order that no confusion takes place in the work, the best way is to look over all the leading points, and as it is not good practice to suffer two or three shoots to grow side by side, all competing shoots within four inches of the terminal one may be at once stripped away, unless in the case of young trees, and where it is desirable to cover much walling in a limited time. Having disposed of this part of the matter, let the eye be turned to those shoots situated the lowest down in any given *fork*—by which term is meant, the angle formed by the divergence of any two limbs; these may be considered as *nursery shoots*, or as reserve stock, and the exciting these to develop themselves, and duly nursing them afterwards, constitutes one of the main features of the pruner's art. If a selection offers, choose a couple of the best and lowest, and pinch or stop the *very lowest* when about three inches long, suffering the other to ramble freely; if only one present itself, it must not be stopped until it begins to overtake the shoot next ahead, nor even then if but a weak shoot, for it will be necessary to suffer it to ramble in order to draw sap into it. Old gardeners in our younger days were wont to say, " stop it to strengthen it;" than which there could scarcely be a more vulgar error, for the strength of a tree may be speedily reduced by mere " stopping " alone.

Once more, then, the finger and thumb of the operator may rest for a week, and afterwards the whole of the tree must be looked over, and a somewhat general thinning out or disbudding may take place.

As, however, it is not easy with trees which produce much spray to ascertain precisely what shoots, and what only, should be reserved at this period, all of a doubtful character, instead of being stripped away, may merely have their tops pinched off, that is to say, provided they are overtaking their neighbours and tending to confusion.

About this period, what are termed *robbers* will begin to develop themselves in certain portions of healthy trees; these may be readily distinguished from the true bearing wood of the next year by their evincing betimes a tendency to branch into side spray ; these should all be pinched, or stopped, when about six inches long, for it must be understood that these greedy monopolists are fattening at the expense of all the subordinate shoots in their neighbourhood; added to which they call into being an undue root action, thereby lessening that amount of control which will always be possessed by the cultivator when trees are planted on sound principles, and the dresser knows what he is about. Indeed, it is entirely through errors in these matters that a necessity so frequently arises for root-pruning, and other such expedients to promote fruitfulness; we would have trees so managed as to be under the most perfect control, in spite of the waywardness of seasons; and this we know to be quite possible and comparatively easy,—all that is wanted is a sound knowledge of the constitution and habits of the tree in question, together with well digested ideas of the character of soils, especially their mechanical texture.

The "robbers" being stopped, the last of the principal spring dressing will have been carried out, and all this will bring the operator up to about the end of May, by which period the fruit will require thinning; but of this more shortly.

Let us remind our peach growers, once more, to give no quarters to the *aphides*, not even for a couple of days if possible.   R. ERRINGTON.

THE FLOWER-GARDEN.

BEDDING PLANTS *(Pink Colour)*.—We have a great variety of bedding plants of this colour, of which the often-talked-of *Saponaria calabrica* is the best for small and moderate-sized beds. This, as most of our readers know, is a hardy annual, but comes into bloom sooner if reared in a moderate hot-bed in the spring; and it has the good quality of being easily removed from the reserve-garden, where it may be kept until some of the May annuals have done flowering. Although it has been in cultivation for many years it is always scarce, for it ripens its seeds with us late in the autumn; and when September is wet we can hardly get enough of them to continue the breed. Notwithstanding all my care, I am often obliged to purchase the means of propagating this pot; and I have more calls for a pinch of its seeds than for anything else I grow. Therefore, when any one has grown it, the seeds should be carefully looked after.

There are three kinds of Catchflies *(Silene)* which make good masses of pink, but they do not last out the whole season. The lowest of them, and, indeed, the lowest pink bedder we have, is one called *Silene Shaftæ*; named, I think, after a person of that name. The

herbage of this Catchfly spreads on the ground; and the flower-stems do not rise above three or four inches. Like all of them, it seeds abundantly; and may be had from cuttings as freely as anything. It is, also, one of the nicest rock-plants we can select.

Silene pendula is the gayest May-flowering annual we have; and, in rich soil, ought to be transplanted three times in the reserve-garden before it is planted out for flowering, as the herbage is apt to come too coarse unless thus checked. It seeds itself about the borders in the autumn, so that we hardly ever lose it. When sown in the spring, in the reserve-garden—and it may be sown as late as the middle of May—and planted out in the flower-garden before midsummer, it will bloom until the frost overtakes it. For a pink edging round a large bed it is as well adapted as the *Virginian stock*, for when it spreads beyond its bounds, it may and should be clipped on the sides, and on the top also, as often as seed-pods appear, just as everybody manages the Virginian stock. If either of them are allowed to make seeds they go off the bloom directly.

Silene compacta is the next best of them, but is not so manageable as to cutting; but when sown late in April, or between that and the middle of May, it will bloom for three months—that is, in July, August, and September. But, if the latter month be dry, it will go off sooner; and that is the worst time of the season for flowers to fail us, as very few can then be had to fill up their places. The height of it is from 18 inches to two feet, according to the richness of the bed. The last of them is not quite so good as *compacta*, but is about the same size, and requires just the same management; its name is *regia*. The last three are very suitable for autumn sowing; and they have such a quantity of little roots that we can move them from place to place easy enough through the winter or spring, when the beds or borders are being dug or dressed.

The *Geranium* furnishes three sizes of plants for pink beds—very low beds—beds from 12 to 20 inches high, and some a yard in height. The *Pink Ivy Leaf* is the best and the oldest of them. It has a thick, smooth, green, shining leaf, trails on the ground, and is altogether a fine bedder. The Ivy Leaf puts me in mind that I missed a nice *purple* bedder of them—one in all respects similar to the common white ivy leaf, but with purple flowers, and a horse-shoe-marked leaf. The next-sized pink geranium is the green form of *Mangle's variegated pink;* and any one having this fine variegated geranium may soon have the green-leaved form of it from branches of the variegated one, which often sport into the green-leaved with a well-marked horse-shoe. If cut off as they appear, and preserved by cuttings, this makes really a fine bedder. Another recommendation of both varieties is that they never produce seeds, which much disfigure many kinds of geraniums. The tallest is one called *Salmon*, which is rather too light for a pink, yet comes in for a light shade of pink, and is one of the very best bedders of all the race of geraniums—that is, for a large bed; and it is one of the easiest to keep over the winter. Another good shade of reddish-pink is produced by the *Pink Nosegay geranium*. It is a fine tall bedder, but not quite so strong as the Salmon, which some nurserymen call *Salmon Nosegay,* but it does not belong to the Nosegay section at all. There are only three kinds of Nosegay geraniums: this pink one, a scarlet, and a lilac variety. The pink one has a peculiar bluish-gray tint in the leaf—nearly what we call glaucous, and a horse-shoe mark; the Salmon has also the horse-shoe form, but the rest of the leaf is light green. I reared many thousand cross seedlings, endeavouring to procure a good pink variety out of the scarlet section of geraniums without much success—*Cherry cheek* being the best one I obtained, and it is too sparing a bloomer for these days, but is beautiful for a pot variety. I have lately obtained a fine seedling in the way of *Judy*, but a better cherry colour, yet it is too red for a pink bed ; and *Lucia rosea* is too light for a pink—besides, the flowers do not well stand a strong sun. It makes a fine bed, nevertheless, if planted where the sun does not reach it in the middle of the day. Of the fancy or pelargonium section we have only one fine pink bedding geranium, the old *Diadematum*—the very gayest one can use for a bed. It is, indeed, the pink of the flower-garden ; and never seeds—I wish it would ! *Diadematum rubescens* is too red for a pink bed when we have so many.

The *Anagallis* furnishes one variety which, though not a real pink shade, is a beautiful thing for a bed. It is called *carnea* (flesh-colour) ; and, like all the anagallises, should be struck from cuttings early in the spring, as they are *miffy* things to get over a long winter. The best way to deal with them, is to keep a few plants of each sort in pots all the summer, plunged in sand or coal-ashes out of doors ; to let them flower till the end of July, and after that to cut off the flowering parts *by degrees*, as when the weather is hot and dry they are apt to die off if the whole head is cut off at once. As soon as the September rains come on they ought to be removed to some shelter, but not to be confined so early ; a glass frame, with a brick under each corner, is the best place for them, as long in the autumn as it is safe to leave them without danger from the frost ; and then a shelf, high up near the door of a greenhouse, is the best place to winter them. They keep best in strong loam, without any peat or leaf-mould ; and autumn-struck cuttings are not to be depended on, but in the spring they root like weeds, in a few days, if in a hot-bed.

Verbenas.—For several years we had no real good pink verbena for beds except *Miller's Favourite*, and, now, we have only two that surpass it—*Beauty Supreme* and *Duchess of Northumberland.* The latter is exactly in the way of the well-known *Favourite* (Miller's), with a deeper and better colour ; and if the two will mix well, as I believe they will, for I have not yet tried them, they will make a richer bed than either of them by itself. *Standard of Perfection* is, also, a good pink bedder, but is surpassed by *Beauty Supreme* ; and there is no improvement by mixing these two together, as I have done last season, and I have, therefore, rejected Standard of Perfection.

My list of verbenas last year amounted to 76 kinds, every one of which were grown here, so that I must know something of them. In one part of the garden we planted two broad borders, on either side of a walk, with the whole collection of verbenas, and many visitors admired them ; but I think that must have been from the novelty of seeing so many of them together ; I cannot say that I felt satisfied with them ; but I made notes of several names, which I think will make a tolerable show this season planted in the same way ; and I shall give these names when I write on " mixtures." Meantime, I must observe of purple and pink beds, although I have written of them in succession, that they ought to stand wide apart in the flower-garden, and have some strong colours put between them.   D. BEATON.

GREENHOUSE AND WINDOW GARDENING.

LITTLE MATTERS : WATERING. — And what about watering ? surely any one *may* water plants that has the ability to send the liquid out of the spout of a water-can by disturbing its equilibrium within. Aye ! *may*, just as every one who can handle a rake, and drive a spade into the earth with his stalwart tread, may be a full fledged gardener. Inattention to trifles, bold, assuming confidence, inflated self consequence, and high-stilted conceited importance, are ever the offspring, *not* of

knowledge but of ignorance. The most simple matters have depths in their philosophy, but when these depths are in a degree sounded, so that cause and effect are somewhat discerned, then simplicities become great ness, and greatness simplicity, because the connection between the one and the other is so far understood and known. Hence the great and the intelligent are the humble and the teachable, and no despisers of what are termed *little matters* ; having found that between the *simple* and the *magnificent* there is only, and scarcely, gradation in importance.

Thus, in the case before us, the most successful gardeners consider the watering of their pot plants no trifling matter. They will at once tell you that failures often take place, either by their assistants allowing the plants to become frequently too dry, or by drenching them whether they need it or not, or by giving them a dribble every day—in some respects the worst of the three treatments, as the gardeners may be deceived with the moist surface, and believe all to be right, while the bulk of the roots might as well be in the sands of Sahara. Simple as the operation seems, no sooner do our amateur friends get fairly launched upon gardening than they, too, begin to feel a sensation creep over them that, after all, there is some little difficulty about it ; and hence from such quarters one of the most puzzling questions put to the gardeners in the neighbourhood (puzzling because it cannot be answered just in a breath to either party's satisfaction) is, " How often should I water my plants ?" and part of what I am now going to write in reply is just what I have told to scores of sweet-toned, kind inquirers, whom it is a pleasure to have it in our power to oblige.

The first thing to be kept in mind is, that the vegetable, though similar in many respects to the animal, creation, chiefly resembles that portion of it that gets into a dormant state at certain seasons, and only requires a full amount of food when the functions of vitality are in full activity. This state of activity exists in the vegetable only when it is growing freely, and when by means of light and heat it is enabled to effect the decomposing, assimilating, and perspiring agencies. According to these circumstances, therefore, will be the amount of nourishing matter and water required, and the frequency of their application. Hence, were I to tell you to water so many times a week I should only lead you into a great error, as, when in a dormant state, a plant may not require water for months ; in cloudy, cold weather, even when growing, it may not require water for a week, while in warm, bright, sunny weather it may require refreshing twice a day. " But cannot you give us a little practical rule, more definite than such a general one ?" Yes—I might tell you to water your plants upon the same principle as you impart liquid to yourselves ; but here, again, you may be led into error, unless you could previously certify to me that you belonged to that wise class of people who drink *only* when they are thirsty, as otherwise the application of such a rule might be as fatal to the poor plants as the tippling of various fluids is ruinous to those who resort to it, and none the less though they be prepared to contend that what is their real bane is in their case the most valuable antidote. The rule, therefore, of most general application is, *to water thoroughly when you do water, so that the liquid will reach every root and fibre, and then wait patiently, without giving a drop, until your services are again required, and then, but not till then, repeat the process.*

The same principle applies to watering flowers or vegetables out of doors : a frequent dribbling on the surface, just as in the case of the flower-pot, does more harm than good. Thus, there is a vast storehouse of moisture in the earth, and the drier the surface the more will moisture be raised from beneath by evaporation and capillary attraction, and the fibres will imbibe that moisture as it passes. Keep moistening an inch or two on the surface, and what is the result? surface roots are encouraged, only to be parched up by the next day's sun; watering on the surface is again repeated, and a similar result takes place. Meanwhile, the lower roots are deprived of their accustomed moisture, for your mistaken kindness has put an extinguisher upon the capillary action that would have raised moisture from the interior of the earth, as if by a pump handle and sucker. Hence, in watering out of doors, first stir the soil, soak it well, and then, as soon as the surface is dry, stir it up and leave it rough, that the sun's rays may not hastily evaporate the moisture you have given. For good general cultivation, therefore, with established plants, give plenty of surface-stirring with the hoe and the fork, and then next to "a fig for the water pail."

But in the case of plants set in their pots upon a window-sill, or on the stage of a greenhouse, there is no under-moisture available, and, therefore, water must be given with even more care, as the dribbling on the surface will be attended with even more baneful results. In extremely dry and hot weather, shading and plunging the pots in damp moss will prevent the necessity of frequent watering; in such circumstances, also, more than in any other, top-surfacing with rich material, or the use of manured water, in the case of plants that will bear it, must be resorted to, otherwise the frequent watering will wash all the nourishing properties out of the soil.

The use of saucers for the pots to stand in would, at first sight, seem to answer the same purpose as the storehouse of moisture in the interior of the earth for plants growing in the open air; and though for some plants it is better to give them the water at the bottom rather than at the top, and though free-growing plants would suffer nothing from water being kept in these saucers in very bright, hot weather, yet, in general circumstances, and especially in dull weather, it would be prejudicial to allow the water to remain about any plants except those of an aquatic character. After watering, therefore, when the soil has become thoroughly wetted, and what has run through has been allowed to remain a short time in the saucer, in order to make sure of that thorough soaking, the water should then be emptied out of the saucers.

If from inadvertence a plant should have become so dry that the soil, by contracting, parts from the sides of the pot, then, instead of watering in the usual way, which would be of little use, as the water would escape by the sides and leave the centre dry, it is best to set the pot in a tub or pail of water and allow it to become thoroughly soaked, and then drained before replacing it upon the stage. "But how am I to know when a plant is so dry as to require this thorough soaking which is to reach every fibre?" Experience and practice alone can be your true guide; the very appearance of the plant will soon tell you, long before the leaves begin to flag, for that must not be allowed to take place from want of water, but as seldom as possible, for it is next to ruin to some plants. But the mere flagging, or drooping, of the leaf is no proof at all times that the plant is dry, as that will take place in a sunny day, after shady weather, from the plant being unable, all at once, to supply by its roots the demand made by evaporation upon the perspiring surface of the leaves; and here a sprinkle with the syringe over the foliage to check evaporation would be better than drenching the soil, moist enough already. Moreover, many plants seem to droop when they put their nightcaps on for a quiet doze, and in their case it is only necessary to wait for the return of day, which will soon revive them in a manner which no appliances of yours in such circumstances could ever accomplish. As a kind of physical guide to the knowing whether a plant wants watering, take the two following:—*First*. Accustom yourself to lift a pot when dry and when wet, and the difference of weight will soon enable you easily to decide in respect to any particular plant, whether it is dry or not. *Secondly*. Strike the pot sharply on the side as it stands with one of your knuckles, if the soil within be wet the sound will be dull, if dry the sound will be clear and sharp.

Temperature of Water.—In spring, autumn, and winter, the water used should be several degrees warmer than the atmosphere in which the plants are growing.

Time for Watering.—In winter, early spring, and *late* autumn, watering should be done in the morning, at other times in the evening.

River, or rather *rain water*, should, if possible, be used for all plants; and where that cannot be procured, spring water should be exposed to the atmosphere before being used.

Manure-water should be given chiefly at those seasons when growth is most luxuriant, and the secretions most abundant.   R. Fish.

HOTHOUSE DEPARTMENT.

STOVE PLANTS.

Portlandia Grandiflora (Large-flowered Portlandia : was so named in honour of the Duchess of Portland).—This is a noble stove plant with large deep green foliage, and fine pure white flowers, agreeably perfumed. They appear in pairs at the end of each shoot; and measure from four to five inches long, and from three to four inches across the mouth of the cup. The leaves are oval-shaped, six inches long when fully grown, and of a most beautiful light green. With tolerable management the plant forms a handsome bush. Though introduced so long since as 1775, it is yet a rare plant—a matter rather for surprise, considering that it is so beautiful, and is not difficult either to grow or propagate. We can only account for its comparative rarity by supposing, that cultivators of stove plants are ignorant, almost, of its existence, and quite so of its beauty and easy culture.

It is to make such fine plants more sought for by our readers that we write about them, for there are many plants occupying spaces in stoves that might be filled by better and handsomer plants. We would recommend to every cultivator a selection of the finest plants, rather than a collection of all kinds—good, middling, and indifferent. There are certain points or qualities in stove plants as well as in florists' flowers that render them worthy of the space and care bestowed upon them; and, unless a plant has the most, if not all, of these points, let it be discarded at once from the selection.

The *first* point is, that the plant should have fine flowers; either lasting a moderately long time, or be produced in succession for a considerable period.

The *second* is, handsome foliage of a pleasing colour. Some, indeed, have such fine variegated leaves (such as the *Crotons*, *Pavetta Borbonica*, some species of *Tillandsia*, and *Dracæna*) as to render them beautiful objects all the year round, though their flowers do not reach the first point of excellence.

The *third* point is, a good habit; that is, with moderate skill and care bestowed upon them to form handsome bushes, or little trees of an elegant shape.

Every stove plant ought to have, at least, two of the above qualities, to render it worthy of cultivation, especially where the stove-house is of small dimensions. The subject with which we commenced these observations, the *Portlandia*, possesses all three of these points in the highest degree; and, consequently, recommends itself to the grower of even a very limited quantity of stove plants. We shall describe its culture under three heads:—Propagation, Soil, and General Management.

Propagation.—It is always desirable to know how to increase a beautiful plant, because, if we have only one, it may die from unforeseen causes, such as accident, or disease; and the regret for its loss would be much lessened, if we had a young one or two to replace it. The best way to increase the Portlandia is by cuttings of the young shoots. Take them off, with a sharp knife, just below the second pair of leaves from the top. Cut off the two lower leaves, and then cut off the shoot horizontally, close to the node, or joint. Leave the two upper leaves entire. Insert the cutting in a pot, four inches across, half-filled with drainage, then sandy peat, with an inch of pure white sand at the top, level with the rim. Put the cuttings in by the aid of a small smooth stick. It will be necessary to water the sand with a fine rose watering-pot first, or the sand will fill up the hole before you can get the cuttings into their places. They will strike sooner if they are put in close to the side of the pot. Fill up the holes with some dry sand. Then give a gentle watering to settle the sand close to each cutting. This is very important, as the air is then excluded completely from the bottom of the cuttings. Place a bell-glass over them, taking care that the leaves are in such a position, leaning inwards, as not to touch the sides of the bell-glass. Plunge the pots in a gentle hotbed, either of tanners', or tempered stable litter, or tanners' spent bark; the last material is the best. Shade them from the sun, both by spreading on the glass of the frame either canvass or mats, and by putting sheets of paper over the bell-glasses; removing the shades as the sun declines. The best time for propagating is early spring. Should much moisture accumulate on the sides of the bell-glasses, let them be wiped quite dry every day till the cuttings show growth, when the wiping may be done only occasionally. As soon as they have made roots they should be potted into 2½ inch pots, and placed under hand-glasses, with moveable tops, for a month or six weeks, till they are fairly established; the shading to be continued till that takes place. Then remove the tops of the hand-glasses for an hour or two, early in the morning, replacing them during the day; lift them off again in the afternoon, and replace them during the night. This will harden them off till they are able to bear removal into the stove. By this method, which we have described rather minutely, most kinds of shrubby stove plants may be propagated. There are some exceptions which we shall notice when we treat of the plants that require a different mode of propagation.

Soil.—It is of the greatest importance to know the right kind of soil, or compost, a plant thrives *best* in. Numbers of stove plants do well in any light rich soil; our present subject delights in a mixture of light fibrous loam, sandy peat, and a very small quantity of vegetable mould. The proportions should be, the two first in equal parts, and one-eighth of the latter. The pots should be well drained with broken potsherds, in the usual manner.

General Management.—To form handsome specimens, follow the same plan as recommended for the *Ixora*, at page 347 of the third volume of this work. As the plants advance in growth, give them increased room for their roots, and fresh food to feed upon; but do not overpot them at any time, as this fine plant is not by any means a gross feeder, like Clerodendrums and other strong-growing stove shrubs.

Heat.—Place it in the warmest part of the stove, for, being a native of Jamaica—in the warmest valleys of that tropical island—it loves plenty of heat. When it is in flower it ought to be kept rather cooler, so as to prolong the bloom. Shade will be necessary whilst it is in flower, for the same purpose. As it thrives best in heat, plunging in the bark bed—where there is such a convenience—will be advantageous. In winter a cessa-

tion of growth will enable it to advance and flower the better in the spring and summer.

Water.—This plant does not require so much water at the root as most other inhabitants of the stove; in the growing season, of course, they require the most. Syringing over-head should be applied frequently during that season, but in winter both modes of applying moisture should be sparingly adopted. By attention to these minutiæ of culture, the amateur will succeed well in bringing to the point of excellence this noble stove shrub.

There is a species named *Portlandia coccinea*, but, from what we have seen of it, it seems to be a shy grower; but, if the blooms are as large as those of *P. grandiflora*, and of a fine scarlet colour, as the name implies, it must be a beautiful species indeed. We have some young plants of it, but have not, as yet, seen the flowers. The foliage seems to be much smaller than that of *Portlandia grandiflora*.

FLORISTS' FLOWERS.

THE warm weather, with which we have been favoured lately, has rapidly brought on these highly-valued flowers. It will be necessary, now, to shade such as have come into bloom, and even to remove them into cooler quarters. We allude more especially to *auriculas* and *polyanthuses*. There are few gardens but have a wall or a hedge, where these early bloomers may be placed on the north side of it; either under hand-glasses set upon something to elevate them three or four inches from the ground, or in small one or two-light frames tilted up in a similar manner. We prefer the frames, because they are more conveniently and securely covered up at night, to protect the tender flower from bleak winds, or even frosts, which may yet visit us. Those that are not yet in bloom may be continued in the original frame, or pit, to bring them forward. By thus retarding the early blooms, and forwarding the late ones, the chance of having a good stock in bloom at once will be greatly increased.

DAHLIAS.—The early-struck plants may now be placed on a bed of ashes in the open air, placing some hoops over them, and covering them up every night with mats to protect them from late frost. This exposure will strengthen them greatly, and enable them to grow freely and strongly when planted out for the summer.

PINKS.—We can only reiterate our instructions as to the treatment these favourites continue to require. Keep them clear of weeds, stir the surface frequently, and place neat sticks near to such as are beginning to spindle up their flower-stems. Tie loosely, so as to allow for the stems growing longer.

TULIPS.—We are happy to say, that the late cold weather has not materially injured the tulips, at least round London. They appear of the healthiest green, with stout leaves; and the flower-buds are beginning to appear very promisingly—at least, such is the case where the usual care and attention has been bestowed upon them. We can only say, continue that care still, as we are not yet quite safe.   T. APPLEBY.

THE KITCHEN-GARDEN.

ROUTINE WORK.—The present is a very busy and interesting part of the season. The seeds which have been committed to the earth, whilst in a healthy state, quickly produce strong plants, which will maintain their healthy luxuriance, if timely and methodical attention is given to surface-stirring, thinning-out, and, in due season, making up any little vacancies that may occur through the seed not having been distributed regularly by the sower, or through the depredations of birds, mice, insects, &c. If proper attention is paid to these little matters, an even luxuriant crop will be the result.

Weeds we will not even mention, well knowing, by many years' practice, that if our directions, as above given, are fully carried out no weeds will ever have the chance of appearing; as the soil will, at all times and seasons, remain in a healthy condition for every succeeding crop, without rest or fallow—only other terms for robbery and loss of time. Every one may, on reflection, be convinced that by allowing weeds to appear they suffer robbery and injustice to be committed on their growing crop; and prevent the due preparation of the soil for the succeeding one; besides adding considerable expense to themselves, as timely attention to surface-stirring and shallow hoeing, as soon as the plants can be seen above ground, does not take a tithe of the time and labour which the hoeing or destroying a crop of weeds requires.

Kidney Beans and *Scarlet Runners* may now be planted in full crop. It is the custom of some people to plant these as soon as they observe the first appearance of the swallow, which, in our opinion, is generally too soon by 10 days or a fortnight, unless, as previously directed, they are well provided for and protected. In this locality (Devonshire) the swallow generally makes its appearance from the 7th to the 9th of April; on the 7th of April this year we observed many on the wing over our noble lake; we heard the Cuckoo's mate on the 9th, the Ox-eye, White-throat, Black-head, or Merry Nettle-creeper, and the Red-start on the 10th. The first young rooks chirruped on the 4th, and in many nests previously to the 10th their young broods were on the chirp. In years gone by we used to observe in Surrey, Kent, Middlesex, and Essex, the first appearance of the swallows generally about the 17th of April, and the other welcome birds-of-passage at about the same date. In this locality the nightingale is not known, and the cuckoo is very rare, and stops but a short time with us, but the beautiful warble of the wood-lark throughout the winter, when mild weather prevails, and in early spring, is enchanting.

Borecole, kale, brocoli, or, indeed, any of the early-sown *brassica tribe,* should now have slight dredgings of charred dust while damp with the dew early in the mornings, to prevent the ravages of the fly, which this simple material will readily and effectively do; it acts also as a beautiful stimulant, causing at once a healthy luxuriance. As soon as they can be fairly handled thinning out and pricking the plants on a healthy piece of ground, not too rich, should be performed.

Capsicum plants and *Tomatoes* should be hardened off in readiness for turning out. *Early celery* should be pricked off as fast as the plants become large enough to handle, and another sowing made. Although it may be showery weather, yet if *cauliflowers, cabbage, artichokes, asparagus,* &c., are required of the finest quality, they must all be supplied with manure-water. In showery weather we always apply it liberally, as it may be given of much stronger proof, in less quantities, and consequently with less labour, while the earth is moist and rain prevails, at which time it is much more naturally distributed to the utmost points of the roots of growing vegetation, and does not require additional waterings from us to wash it in, as it does when *dry* weather prevails.

Cardoons may now be sown. A piece of well-trenched ground should be selected, and if not previously well manured, a trench should be thrown out, wide and deep enough for a liberal quantity of manure to be forked in, and the seed placed at 6-inch distances up the middle, to be afterwards thinned as the plants grow. *Sea-kale* must have a watchful eye kept over its crown. Thin the shoots little and often, as soon as they can be conveniently handled, leaving only the strongest, the number of which should be regulated according to the strength of the plants.

CAULIFLOWERS.—The early hand-glass crops that have been well attended to through the winter, with regard to airing and surface-stirring, should now have the spaces between the rows of plants well forked up and broken to pieces, moving the hand-glasses and their props out of the way during the time. When all are well forked up, set down a line, and mark out two-feet alleys in the centre between the rows of plants, and with a spade chop out the sides, and throw up as much earth as will bury the stems of the plants well up, keeping the sides towards the alleys three or four inches higher, so as to form a good trough or basin to receive the future waterings when required; and if the hand-glasses are not wanted for any other purposes of more importance for a week or 10 days longer, they may be lifted or propped up upon three flowerpots or half bricks, which will greatly assist in forwarding the growth of the plants.

Cauliflowers that have been spring planted out should have the earth well stirred with the hoe on dry days. The spring sown plants should be pricked out in succession on good rich borders, four inches, at least, apart every way.

Sow *Cape brocoli* for general crop the first week in May, and sow any little favourite sorts of *turnips* in cool situations—if a little shaded by trees all the better for summer crops. J. BARNES & W.

MISCELLANEOUS INFORMATION.

ALLOTMENT FARMING FOR MAY.

WE have been in the habit, hitherto, of addressing ourselves almost exclusively to the holders of very small allotment or cottage gardens—generally of from half an acre to as much as will keep a small cow. We see no reason, however, why we should stop at such very small holdings; knowing, as we do, that many plots of six, eight, or more acres, are held in the suburbs of our towns by parties who are not well versed in rural matters, and whose holdings are not obliged to be managed *precisely* as the ordinary farm. We hope, therefore, occasionally to be of service to such.

One of the first considerations connected with such holdings is, what line of policy to observe, situated as they are, in general, close to good markets, and where little or no expense, or risk, can take place in the transit of the produce. *Milk* and *butter* is of course a prime consideration at all times; *hay* from good upland, if well made, takes well, and is always in demand for high-fed horses; green cuttings of *rye, vetches, lucerne,* &c., is always of eminent service, either for home consumption or for sale. The worst of bulky crops, however, is that they require a good deal of cartage, if for sale; a thing to be avoided by small holders; for such incidental expenses eat up much of the profits.

Nevertheless, when a man holds some six or eight acres he will be necessitated to keep a horse; for he will not only be driven to plough occasionally, when spade labour is scarce, but his produce will require taking to market; and, moreover, if he be a clever and thrifty manager, he will soon be able to load back with town manure, which he will find it his interest to purchase.

There can be little doubt, that the most profitable way of farming such a piece of land would be to make the dairy the principal object; corn crops being held subsidiary to this. Indeed, we do not see what real necessity exists, under such circumstances, for corn crops at all; straw for bedding certainly must be had, but whether to increase the bulk of manure as a prime object, depends on the situation and size of the holding; for if, as before observed, in the suburbs of a thriving town, there need be no anxiety about manure, provided the holder manages well. He will, in general, purchase what *extra* manure he will require without feeling the expense. Straw, even for bedding, should be held as of secondary import; if it can be shewn (which we do think it can) that other things will prove more remunerative; and that land may be kept under culture for many years, without what is termed rest—that is to say, laying down in grass, for naked fallow is out of the question; *the pressure of the times will, before long, place fallows among the things that were.*

We have advised this much, in order to endeavour to direct the attention of the holder of such little farms to the necessity of reconsidering his whole policy; and, instead of going by any prescribed mode, to chalk out a system for himself, based on the circumstances before alluded to, together with a consideration of the demands of the locality; distinguishing carefully those which are temporary or fluctuating demands from those which are of a permanent character.

We come now to another and important item for consideration, and one which, as we think, should be woven into a system adapted to suburban farms. We here allude to a union, in some degree, of the more profitable portions of commercial or *market gardening* *with dairy farming*, which, for the present, we must term the case in hand. It was before observed, that great facilities offered themselves in such situations for obtaining manures; and we all know that, without a liberal manuring what is termed high culture cannot be carried out. The possessor of a few acres has not his attention divided, like the ordinary farmer in the country; his matters lay, as it were, all beneath his eye; and if a man thus situated should be enabled to devote his whole attention to some eight or ten acres, and proved skilful in appliances, how many of the more profitable vegetable productions might be not combine with the course of farming alluded to; each, too, playing into the other's hands, to use a common phrase?

KEEPING OF COWS, especially under a "soiling system," or, what we prefer, a modification of it, is necessarily productive of hot manure; and the latter might as well be employed in producing the early delicacies of the market gardener (which are generally high-priced) before putting on the land, as lie reeking away its strength at the cow-house doors, corrupting the air with fumes pernicious to the animal world, but exhilarating to vegetables.

Certainly, to go thus far, seems a departure from the *ordinary* objects of small farming, but we consider it as much a duty to furnish hints for progress as to give more calendarial matter. We had intended here to point to a rotation and course of culture somewhat in detail, but our limits are nearly attained; and it becomes necessary in this stirring month to pay particular regard to cultural matters. Perhaps it will be as well to deal with them successively, as in former allotment papers.

POTATOES.—Of course, all those who expect a full crop of sound potatoes have planted the whole by this time. Those who adopt the "lazy-bed" style, or what are called "bouts," or, in the vernacular of Lancashire and Cheshire, "butts," should be on the alert to destroy the first crop of weeds the moment they appear. In the counties above alluded to, this is done just before the potato sprouts are breaking ground.

Under the circumstances of culture there seems no reason to object to the practice, provided the soil has been well worked previously to planting. These people plant somewhat shallow, calculating on the additional "soiling," which is intended as a ready mode of destroying the first crop of weeds. As far as mere *annual weeds* are concerned this is accomplished; but one great evil attends this system—the couch grass, or "twitch," as the Derbyshire folks term it, is only scotched for a few weeks, whilst too many of the good country people imagine they are destroying it. After all, there is nothing like the drill system, for we have always considered that such well carried out is equal, if not superior, to a naked summer's fallow. Let us advise the allotment holder to stir the ground well, betimes, between his rows of potatoes, taking care that all cultural matters are complete before the stems begin to fall, and that at the last operation not a weed is left. The benefits of this will be found equally great to the succeeding crop, and a saving of labour will be the sure result in the end.

SWEDE TURNIPS.—In former allotment papers, remarks were made on the immense utility of using some exciting or stimulating mixture, in order to get the young plant out of reach of the fly as soon as possible. This, indeed, is the prime secret of a *safe* crop. The allotment gardener, at least, can carry out such practices, for the very soot of his chimney will come in for the purpose. Those who sow swedes *to stand* will have their young plants above ground shortly. As soon as they get out of the way of the fly, let them be singled out: that is to say, the first thinning, which is merely taking care that no two plants touch. The hoe should be passed nicely through them immediately, choosing a period neither wet nor dry for the operation. A seed bed of swedes, to succeed such crops as early potatoes, should be sown in the first week in May. These must be kept free from weeds, and not sown too thickly.

MANGOLD-WURTZEL.—Some persons sow this as early as the middle of April, and for field culture, and where land is more stubborn, it is well to do so. For allotments, however, under spade culture, where the soil is in better tilth, and richer, and where the young growth is more rapid, the first week in May is as good a period as any. The drills should be at least thirty inches apart, and the seed may be dropped in patches, one foot apart, putting about three or four seeds in a patch. By all means put some stimulating material alluded to at page 349. This will get the young plant rapidly out of the reach of slugs and the aphides, which sometimes make sad havoc, especially if the young plant is lazy through poverty of soil. We will say more about culture in our next.

PARSNIPS.—Will now be getting a nice plant, and culture becomes necessary. Let the rows be clean hand-weeded, and the plants singled out, so as that no two touch. Then the first dry day let the small hoe be worked through the young plants, stirring deeply; for we have found that disturbing, and even cutting away by deep culture, the stronger side fibres in tap-rooted plants betimes, has a tendency to cause the root to descend freely; a matter of some importance. Let the ground between the drills also be well cultivated and cleaned early.

CARROTS.—These, sown as advised at page 349, will soon be above ground. No crop requires more careful attention than this, the slugs are so apt to devour them, especially if near hedges or other covers. We advise, that the moment the plants are appearing every weed be completely removed, in order to be able to "take stock" with ease, at all times; and that a dressing, repellant of the slugs, be applied instantly, not waiting until they have commenced their ravages. We use cinder ashes from which all the dust has been ejected, and all the larger portions removed; in fact, our sample of stuff is about the size of turnip-seed. If such is carefully strewed among the young plants, we will guarantee them safe. If this is too tedious, some very coarse sand is good; some apply barley chaff. The best of the cinder ashes is, that they act as well in wet weather as in dry. The slugs cannot bear to travel over such cutting roads.

CABBAGES, GREENS, &c.—Of course the cottager has got a good plot of spring cabbages, planted in October or in February. Where those are planted as a principal crop, and are doing well, they may stand for sprouts; we would not advise cottagers, however, to encourage the practice, for their standing so long hinders rotations. Nearly all the cabbages requisite may be taken as "stolen crops," that is to say, from between existing ones, or some about to be sown or planted. We advise the allotment holder, therefore, to sow a pinch of cabbage monthly, in May, June, July, and August, choosing the dwarf kinds, such as the "Matchless." No doubt, green kale, savoys, &c., were sown in April, and it is well to make another sowing now. Those who want brocoli may sow a pinch now, and again in the end of the month. For this sowing he may choose The protecting, the very Late whites, and the Walcheren; in the end of the month, The capes, and Autumn white, or Granges. The thousand-headed cabbage should not be forgotten, especially by those who hold a greater extent of land than the mere cottagers.

SCARLET RUNNERS AND KIDNEY BEANS.—The former of these should be cultivated assiduously by the cottager; both must be sown directly, if not already done. Runners require deep and rich soil, and liberal waterings in dry weather, when in full bearing. Sticks of any kind, three or four feet high, will suffice, provided their tops are pinched the moment they reach the tops of the sticks.

GENERAL REMARKS.—Once more let us exhort the allotment holder to be exceedingly diligent. Let him first cast his eyes around, and compare the different conditions of those who try to employ every spare hour, and of those who lounge away their time, and then say whether a well-cultivated garden is not a stake worth playing for. A continual war must be kept up with weeds; your neighbour, perhaps, will tell you "it do'nt much matter," but do not believe him; make up your mind that every weed robs you of something. Select your weather carefully for the various operations, for on this much depends. A good cultivator watches the sky and its indications daily. No man ought to be more weatherwise than a good gardener or farmer. Above all things, look well to your manure; do not suffer its strength to run into the nearest ditch. Make a point of wheeling ordinary soil over the heap now and then, and occasionally throw that sometime made into a separate heap of a conical form, and case it over with soil to keep out rain.

In succeeding papers we will endeavour to pursue the subject with which this paper commences; and we shall in due time, come to consider corn crops, hay grass, pasturage, &c.

WHAT WE CAN DO, AND WHAT WE CAN DO WITHOUT.

By the Authoress of " My Flowers."

"A small country town where provisions are dear" is a very unfavourable situation for persons of small income, especially when they have, perhaps, been long accustomed to plenty, and unused to economy and care. But many are the families so situated; and it behoves us to strive to assist one another in the anxieties of making the most of a little, at a time, too, when all classes are

suffering from the depressed state of trade and agriculture, and no one knows how soon, or how fearfully, his own hour of trial may come.

The grand essential, I must unweariedly repeat, is to strike off every possible expense. It is, I know, a distasteful remedy, but the only specific. We may, indeed, practise rigid carefulness in many ways—in every way: we may lay in stores at the cheapest possible rate; we may leave off fires early, and take to them late; we may dismiss three servants at high wages, and replace them with others of a less expensive stamp; we may pick out the cheapest recipes from cookery books, and look narrowly after every scrap that is left from our breakfasts and dinners,—we may do all this, and it is important that all this *should be* done, but with this system of saving *only* very little will be gained at the end of the year. To economize, and be easy in mind, upon a serious reduction of means, we must give up superfluities, and even comforts: we must give up two servants out of three; we must reduce our bills by not purchasing our usual quantities, instead of being satisfied with articles at one halfpenny less per pound; we must give up all things that are dear, and substitute those that are cheap; and ceasing to consider altogether what we want, think only of what we can *do without*. A high-principled mind, vigorous, and self-denying, especially if sanctified by "the truth," will be enabled to perform wonders in the management of an income, compared to those who are lamenting their misfortunes, without beholding the Hand which bids the cruse of oil " stay;" and without cheerfully meeting and co-operating with those wants that are sent by our Heavenly Father, and therefore are the best for us.

"A genteel appearance" is an ambiguous phrase, which no two persons will probably understand alike; and therefore it is scarcely possible to lay down rules for maintaining it. My own interpretation of the expression is, living *strictly within* our income, at whatever sacrifice; preserving the neatness, cleanliness, and decorum of our homes, however simple and frugal may be the style to which we are reduced; and neither aiming to do as others do, nor becoming slovenly and indifferent because we cannot keep up the elegancies to which we have long been accustomed. A *gentleman* and a *lady* must be such, in whatever position they are placed by the wise decrees of Him who ordereth all things; and their own well-bred manners will throw a grace around the dignity of *honourable poverty*, which does in itself possess so much moral beauty when sustained with unrepining cheerfulness, that riches and grandeur sink into nothingness beside it.

I have, more than once, heard of instances where surprising cleverness has been displayed in the arrangement and management of a very small income. I *know* that a clergyman, with a wife and eight little children, maintains a most creditable appearance upon only one hundred pounds per annum, without noise, confusion, dirt, or dismay; but then the mother rises early, dresses all her children, and devotes herself to the duties of her arduous station with all her powers. I shall feel grateful to any of my readers, who may be so circumstanced, if they will kindly furnish me, through the Editor of THE COTTAGE GARDENER, such hints from their own experience as shall assist me, from time to time, in benefiting others in similar situations, but possessing less practical knowledge on these important points.

It is of the greatest consequence that *the mind* should be devoted to the duty we have to perform; this will not only sweeten the toil, but will enable us to make larger efforts, and to accomplish more difficult things. When young people marry upon *nothing*, or with very straitened means, the least thing they can do for themselves and each other is to carry cheerfully the burden they have vowed to bear; and if from a competent provision it has pleased God to lay upon us the sharp stroke of poverty, it is our first and most bounden duty to receive the affliction with child-like docility, and labour with our hands, if necessary, to supply our daily wants. Our Father has but recalled the things that are His own, to bestow when, and how, he pleases—" Wherefore doth a living man complain."

One of the most important steps to take in our daily routine is to establish early rising. By this means one servant will be able to do almost the work of two; and where the lady is called upon to undertake some, at least, of the little household offices so interesting to her to perform, if she loves her husband and her children, it will enable her to do everything during the early morning hours; and when her more affluent neighbours are just rising from their late breakfast, she will have gained nearly half a day upon them, and will be ready to seat herself beside the large basket of work, always over-flowing where children are concerned.

I will, in connexion with this subject, mention the good effects of early rising, from the practice of a family of near relatives, whose means were extremely limited. Seven o'clock was the hour of breakfast—an alarming intimation to some of my readers; and by that time their three children were dressed and hungry. The pretty cottage was in a state of perfect neatness long before dinner-time, and the lady busily employed with her needle, quite ready to receive her friends who were numerous and intimate, and who were yet wholly unsuspicious of all she had been engaged in since five o'clock in the morning. The maid servant was always the picture of neatness; the children were hardy, healthful, and well-ordered; and the little domicile of *real hospitality* was the admiration of all who entered it.

Late hours are mischievous in every way. They are ruinous to the health, to the comfort, and to the convenience of life. In a small establishment we are running all day after hours lost in the morning; and there is always hurry, confusion, dirt, and angry tempers, where there is much to be done, and no time in which to do it.

Solomon in his eloquent delineation of " a virtuous woman," alludes to her activity—" She riseth also, *while it is yet night,* and giveth meat to her household." It is impossible to retrench effectually without resolutely adopting early hours.

Before entering upon other details, I am anxious to enforce the most material points, and to assure my readers that if they will only resolve to attempt what I have already pressed upon their attention, they will find such sensible advantages accruing as will reconcile them to much which may not be quite agreeable to their tastes *at first,* but which will make the other departments of economy comparatively light.

A lady has so much in her power—always provided her husband will forego the *grand essentials* which appertain more especially to himself—that if she has only a " heart inclined to the testimonies of God," and a diligent hand, her home will be one of peace, and comfort, and orderliness, under many disadvantages. Let us all remember, that the blessing of the Lord is the one thing needful to us, whether in prosperity or in adversity; without it we may indeed "rise up early, and late take rest, and eat the bread of carefulness"—but our labours will not be sanctified, and our sleep will not be sweet.

THE POULTRY-KEEPER'S CALENDAR.
MAY.

By Martin Doyle, Author of " Hints to Small Farmers," &c.

Ducks.—The Rouen, Rhone, or Rohan duck—for it is called by all these names—is a common variety of the Dutch species; though, as Mr. Dixon writes, " we might just as well call them Thames or ' London ducks,' or ' Mr. Smith's

ducks'—it would puzzle most people to find in what they differ from the every-day brown, or white and brown, farm-yard duck." It has been supposed, but incorrectly, that the

tame duck is the domesticated offspring of the mallard. The old proverb—" we cannot expect tame ducks from a wild duck's nest "—expresses the true answer to that supposition. It is more likely to have been imported from the East Indies, where ancient travellers have found ducks exactly similar to ours. There are, however, among our tame ducks some breeds which very much resemble the mallard in plumage; but there is one certain mark by which the wild duck may always be distinguished from the tame—the blackness of its claws. It may be useful for cockney sportsmen in particular to bear this distinction in mind. A case in point will prove this. A gentleman of our acquaintance saw what he considered a flock of wild ducks, last winter, in a sedgy river within a few hours' drive of London. Their rich plumage, shaded with black, and purple, and green hues, and, more particularly, their distance from the poultry-yard, led him to the conclusion that they were wild. Fully convinced that six brace of mallards were in his power, bang went one of the barrels of his fowling-piece, and about half the flock met an untimely death. The remainder moved away, certainly not in the style of mallards; and bang went the other barrel, which completed the massacre. The sportsman, elated with his success, collected the victims of his error, and sent them in pairs—neatly ticketed, and marked "Game"—to his friends in the city, and, we believe, a brace to the owner, who recognised his tame ducks, which had rambled to the neighbouring river. If the fowler had been aware of the unerring test, according to Col. Hawker, for distinguishing wild ducks—viz., black claws—he would have discovered his mistake immediately after the slaughter, if not previously to it.

The Musk, or as it is more generally called, the Muscovy duck, might be found a suitable kind for the inhabitants of towns, as it has not the desire for water which other ducks have, nor is it of a gadding disposition. It is a dark-coloured bird, with a frizzled crest, and originally a native of South America. It is of a very dirty nature, and therefore would be quite comfortable in the puddle of a confined yard. Its peculiarity in not bathing like others of its species is remarkable. It will never go near the water if it can help it; but prefers the stable, or even the piggery, to the clearest stream. This is accounted for, according to Mr. Dixon, by the curious fact, that the feathers do not resist wet as well as those of other water birds. The quill and tail feathers become soaked and matted like those of a hen; so that if very long on the water, notwithstanding its being webbed-footed, it would sink and be suffocated. Its eggs are well-flavoured, and the flesh is delicate, if eaten when the bird is young; therefore, in the coming season, when ducks will be welcome with the approved accompaniment of green peas, it cannot reasonably be rejected, though we may doubt the expediency of recommending it in place of the other kinds which occupy our poultry-yards.

The White Aylesbury duck has a formidable rival for popular favour in the Rouen tribe. Mr. Baily, an eminent London dealer in useful and ornamental poultry, gives precedence to the Rouen in his list, in which three varieties only are named, viz., the Rouen, the Labrador, or Buenos Ayres, and the Aylesbury. For a drake of either of the two first-mentioned breeds he charges 10s, and for one of the last 6s 6d. On the other hand, the prize list of the Birmingham and Midland Counties exhibition of poultry for December next places the Aylesbury first, and the Rouen second, and names no other sort.

Yet the Labrador duck deserves some notice. From Mr. Dixon's invaluable work we learn the particulars respecting this variety. The Zoological Society received it from Buenos Ayres under this name; but in the south of England it bears the name of the Black Indian duck, which Mr. Dixon believes to be the true title, as all our tame importations are from the East. "The feet, legs, and entire plumage should be black—a few white feathers will occasionally appear; but I have had some birds," says Mr. Dixon, "that were immaculate, and such should be the model of the breeder. The bill also is black, with a slight under-tinge of green. Not only the neck and back, but the larger feathers of the tail and wings, are gilt with metallic green; the female also exhibits slight traces of the same decoration." It appears also—and this is a very curious distinction indeed, that the eggs which they lay at the beginning of the season are black, and that this discoloration, which gradually fades away, is occasioned by an oily matter, which does not enter into the entire shell, but may be scraped off with the nail. Their wild flavour causes them to be much esteemed; and as they are as easily reared as any other ducks, there seems every reason to suppose they will become general favourites, from their extreme beauty.

DUCKLINGS.—It is to be remembered, that ducklings designed for the table should not have access to more water than may suffice for drink and for toilet purposes. Meal of any kind, with or without potatoes, is the best substance for fattening them. The gross matter on which they would feed, if permitted to do so, would impart a strong and offensive flavour to the flesh. Ducks are pre-eminently suited to the circumstances of the cottager who has a garden, from their great hardihood of constitution, and the facility with which they can be supported where garbage of any kind abounds; yet, though they will eat garbage of any kind, and find a feast in a dead rat three-parts decayed, their flesh would be detestably offensive if fed during preparation for the table on any rank food. Under other circumstances, let them follow their instincts, and eat any filth they have a fancy for; there is no just reason for restraining the drake and laying ducks from the indulgence of their natural appetites, whether it be for eating dirty food, and all the snails and worms the garden produces, dabbling in puddles, or swimming in muddy ponds.

GREEN FOOD FOR POULTRY.—Since the commencement of spring weather, more particularly, the poultry in our yard eat fresh greens of all sorts with avidity, and in great quantities. They run to it with eagerness, though they have abundance; this shows that such food is natural, and, therefore, no doubt beneficial to them.

BEE-KEEPER'S CALENDAR.—MAY.

By J. H. Payne, Esq., Author of "The Bee-keeper's Guide," &c.

DELIGHTFUL, shining May! with what pleasure are we all looking forward to its arrival as the harbinger of summer, but especially to him who after a long confinement of six months to a sick room is its approach doubly welcome. Its sweet, balmy days will invite the convalescent to a frequent ramble in the fields without the risk of danger from pinching winds. And who has made so vast an alteration between January and May,—and who is it that speaks from the woods and from the fields "Arise, and come away! for, lo! the winter is past, the rain is over and gone, the flowers appear on the earth, the time of the singing of birds is come, and the voice of the turtle is heard in our land," but He who "spake, and it was done,—who commanded, and it stood fast!" Our little favourites, too, by this time will have commenced in good earnest all their operations; the by-gone winter to them has been a favourable one, and many stocks that are now alive and prosperous would have been dead long ago had it been a mild one.

I think I need not remind my apiarian friends that the time has now fully arrived for supplying boxes, glasses, and small hives, to those stocks which are not intended for swarming; for the manner of doing it I must refer to THE COTTAGE GARDENER, vol. ii., p. 41. Those persons, also, who are now about to commence bee-keeping (which I hope are not a few) must be preparing to make their purchases immediately, for the first May swarms are the only ones they should begin with; and such swarms, if properly managed, will by the end of July more than repay their proprietors the amount given for them, besides the possession of an excellent stock for another year; indeed, I never purchased one that did not. (See THE COTTAGE GARDENER, vol. ii., p. 104.)

FUMIGATION.—Much has been said and written to me lately upon the subject of fumigation, yet this is a process that I am not at all partial to; and, as far as my experience has gone, it is one which I have never yet had occasion to resort to in a single instance, for even in the most difficult operations I have always found a puff (and that a very little one) of tobacco-smoke to be all-sufficient. As I have said before, gentleness is the best protection; still, if by any little accident the bees should become irritated, a slight puff of tobacco-smoke quiets them at once. One reason for my not being partial to fumigation is, that I could never see the necessity for it; and another reason is, that all the bees which I have seen thus treated are sluggish and inactive for some days after the operation, besides many of them having been killed. Now, this in the early spring, or in the midst of the honey-gathering season, is certainly of great consequence, especially when we are told that a prosperous colony of bees will in a single day of the latter season collect from four to six pounds of honey.

TAYLOR'S IMPROVED AMATEURS BAR-HIVE.—I understand that a new edition of *Taylor's Bee-Keeper's Manual* will very shortly appear, in which mention will be made of the latest improvements in this hive; and I beg to say, in reply to the very many applications that I have had respecting it, that it is now made and sold, with the latest improvements, by Messrs. Neighbour and Son, 127, High Holborn, London, and by Mr. Baxter, cabinet maker, Bury St. Edmunds.

FEEDING.—An important circumstance connected with this subject has offered itself to my notice very recently, namely, that of giving bees food in a *solid state*. By this means very great trouble and inconvenience will be avoided, both to the bees as well as to their proprietors, for the former will be in no danger of drowning, and will also have a supply of food that they appear to like better than any that has ever before been given to them; whilst the latter will be spared the trouble of preparing those compounds usually recommended, many of which I have always considered to be very injurious to the bees, and more especially so when given in large quantities in the autumn. After many experiments by myself and some apiarian friends, it is found that of all other solids *barley-sugar* has the decided preference with the bees; they will take it before anything else that is offered to them, and the rapidity with which they dissolve it is quite surprising; it may be given either at the top of a hive, where there is an opening, by tying half a dozen sticks together and covering them with a box or small hive, or even with a flower-pot, or at the bottom, as in the common straw hive, by pushing a few sticks in at the entrance, for, unlike liquid food, it does not attract robbers nor cause fighting, although given in the day time. One of my friends supposes it to be the lemon flavour in the barley-sugar that is so pleasing to the bees, but I have within the last few days had some made without lemon, and when both kinds are offered to them at the same time the preference is given to the latter; I have tried the same also in liquid food, the lemon-flavoured is rejected for that without it. Another friend suggests it to be its deliquescent nature (that is, it becomes moist when exposed to the air), combined with its highly purified state, which in all probability is the true reason, for here are no crystals to contend with, nor any disposition to form crystals, of which both loaf-sugar and sugar-candy consist; and honey, even when crystalized, is useless to the bees, and is cast out of the hive by them. It is certainly most convenient to be able to push a few sticks of barley-sugar under a weak hive, and to know that by so doing they are made secure from want for a time. The idea of expense may be a consideration with some persons at first seeing barley-sugar recommended for this purpose, but upon inquiry it will be found that it may be purchased for less than a shilling a pound, and it may be made for sixpence, therefore it is not at all a more expensive mode of feeding than with loaf-sugar or with honey.*

PURCHASING SWARMS.—It will be better for those persons whose intention it is to purchase swarms, to select those kinds of hives they prefer, and to send them to the person of whom the swarms are purchased that the bees may be hived unto them; and it must be remembered that the swarm purchased must be removed to the place it is intended to remain in for the summer upon the evening of the day on which it swarmed; *this is most important,* for if delayed even till the next morning its destruction will, in all probability, be the result.

QUEEN WASPS are only now making their appearance, and should be destroyed as much as possible, for each one becomes the founder of a nest, computed to contain at least 30,000 robbers. The destruction of the queens, therefore, is important both to the gardener as well as to the apiarian, and I have found the syringe a very useful instrument in effecting this object; as soon as they are seen to slight discharge a syringe full of water upon them, which is sure to bring them to the ground, when they may be crushed easily with the foot.

ARTIFICIAL HATCHING.

THE art of hatching eggs artificially by the aid of ovens has been long practised in China and in Egypt; whilst of later years, in Europe, M. Reaumur, the celebrated naturalist, reduced the practice to a system, adopting any source of heat that would keep up a regular temperature of 96°. He also invented hollow covers (being low boxes lined with fur), which he named *artificial parents,* for the chickens to brood under. Since the time of M. Reaumur, we have seen one or more contrivances for hatching, in which the heat was supplied by a constantly burning jet of gas. Lastly, Mr. Cantello, of 4, Leicester-square, London, has invented an apparatus for carrying on artificial hatching upon a large scale. Some of the results of his experience he has published in a pamphlet, well worth the sixpence charged for it, entitled *A Practical Exposition of the Cantelonian System of Hatching Eggs, &c., by Hydro-incubation.* From this we will make a few extracts.

Mr. Cantello urges the importance of applying heat to the egg from above it; in which mode of application we do not see any importance, for under the hen, when sitting close, there is one uniform temperature, and she turns the eggs daily. Nor is Mr. Cantello entitled to the discovery "that the blood-heat of the feathered tribe is 106°," because many years ago, in the Memoirs of the Geneva Natural History Society, Dr. Berger stated, that the temperature of water-fowl is 108°, of domestic fowls, 107°, and of pigeons, 109° (*Thomson's Animal Chem.,* 629).

Turning Eggs.—"The fowl," says Mr. Cantello, "leaves her nest every day, in search of food, for twenty or thirty minutes; this must be imitated also, as the temporary loss of heat has the effect of causing the air at the butt end of the egg to diminish in bulk, and the vacuum is filled by a fresh supply, drawn in for the nourishment of the germ.

"The eggs must be moved three times a day—morning, noon, and night,—which prevents the adhesion of any part of the fluid to the shell, and also gives the small blood-vessels a better opportunity to spread around the surface of the egg. This is effected by nature: when the fowl leaves her nest, or returns to it, she naturally disturbs the eggs; and also, from any change she may make in her position while upon her nest; and also, as she pulls the eggs up against her sides with her bill; this has given rise to the supposition that she carefully turns her eggs."

* TO MAKE BARLEY-SUGAR.—Put a pound of the finest white sugar into a saucepan with a lip, together with half a pint of water; put it on a gentle fire and take off the scum as it rises; let it boil five minutes; strain it through a tammy (woollen cloth); return it into the saucepan and continue boiling it until the syrup has become thick, and that the handle of a spoon being dipped into it, and then plunged into cold water, the sugar upon the handle is found to be quite crisp; when this is the case the syrup is sufficiently boiled. On a marble slab, or a large china dish, well buttered, pour the syrup along in lines of the thickness the sticks are required; take hold of the sticks at each end whilst hot and twist them. The lemon flavour is given by dropping into the syrup ten drops of oil of lemon just before pouring the syrup upon the slab. Neither the oil of lemons nor the straining through the tammy are required in making barley-sugar for bees.

Act of Hatching.—The following is curious, and the result of observation :—

"Many persons have positively insisted, and some have gone so far as to say they have seen it, that the parent fowl breaks the egg at the proper time for the chicken to hatch. On the contrary, nature has provided the chicken with an apparatus perfectly adapted to procure its own exit; and if the smallest particle of the shell is broken, even after the chicken has forced open a hole, it will, in most instances, bleed to death—the whole interior surface of the egg being covered with a beautiful tissue of veins and arteries, which have served to convey nourishment to the little animal in an imperfect state. When the chicken has broken through the shell, it lays about twelve hours to gain strength from the atmospheric air, and to enable the lungs to become perfect in the functions consequent on breathing; the chicken grows in size and development from inhaling the atmosphere, and swells out from the interior; this forces the remains of the egg into its body by the naval, as also the intestines (which in a chicken are formed outside the body), and in like manner the blood filling the tissue of veins around the inner surface of the shell, is forced into the system, when the interior surface of the shell becoming thus in a manner free, the little animal makes another movement, as the head is bent down under the right wing, with the bill on the back, and the legs doubled up in front, gives a slight rotatory movement, and turns the body gradually round in the shell. At each movement, the instrument supplied by nature for the purpose * is forced to make a fresh opening. Thus, by a series of thrusts, the shell is cut about three quarters of the distance around, when the remainder breaks; the end of the shell then opens like the lid of a box, and the chicken finally pushes his way out, when, in a very few hours, he is able to stand or run alone,—the remains of the yolk and white of the egg, not used in his construction within the egg, serving for nourishment to the system until he learns to eat."

Carriage of Eggs.—"Much has been said relative to the injurious effects of the transport of eggs for incubation, and it has even been asserted that carriage by water is injurious. I do not say that an egg purposely shaken with violence will produce a chicken. This I have never tried; but I can say that they will hatch very well after an ordinary carriage of thirty or forty miles over country roads, provided they have been well packed. I have hatched many fine chickens from eggs which had travelled by rail one hundred miles, and by carrier sixty, having been bought previously in the market of a country town.

"Eggs are generally packed in straw, bran, or chaff; there is, however, a packing much superior to these, which I have adopted with success, viz., oats. This is, of all others, the most economical packing for eggs; for whilst the packer supplies the other at his own cost, he reaps several advantages from using oats. He charges the current price for his oats; he will have no broken eggs (a great item); the eggs are packed in smaller compass, and unpacked with a better appearance; they require much less time to pack, as the oats are thrown on in alternate layers with the eggs, fill up all interstices, and the two together form almost a solid body."

We have some other passages marked for extraction, but have selected enough to induce those who desire more information to purchase the work. To those who do purchase it, we are bound to add a caution against being led away by Mr. Cantello's calculation of profits. He presumes upon eighteen hatchings annually, whilst practical poultry-keepers say that it is useless to hatch in the winter months, for no care will enable the poultry attendant to rear the chickens. Again, Mr. Cantello's calculation of profit is founded upon rearing more than 81 chickens out of every 100 hatched, whereas we have seen an admission from him that 80 per cent is a safer ratio on which to calculate. Lastly, we have heard, but cannot speak from our own knowledge, of parties adopting his system and then abandoning it as unprofitable.

* A small sharp pyramid on the tip of the bill.

HEATING A SMALL PIT OR FRAME.

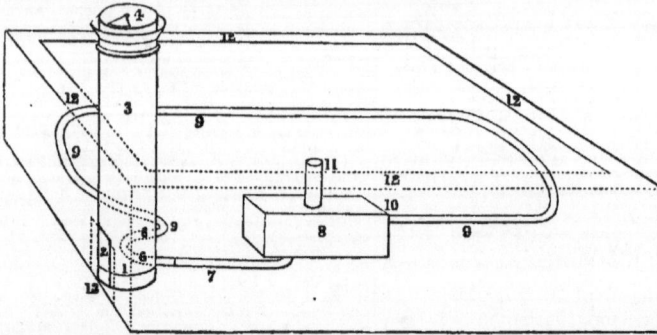

THE above is a sectional drawing of an apparatus I have invented for warming a large two-light frame, as a forwarding pit to a small conservatory. And as I am sure that my success warrants my recommending it to other amateurs who have the same dislike to manure-beds as myself, I send you an explanation for working the same, and I am satisfied that no mode can beat it for economy, both in first cost, and in keeping up a cheap and regular heat.

In the first place, the stove is a mere cylinder of sheet iron rivetted. It is four feet long, and has a ring inside at 1, for the fire-bars to rest on.

2 is a small sliding-door to admit air under the grate-bars, or to draw up higher than the bars if required.

3 is the cylinder itself, four feet long by eight inches wide, inside.

4 is the first cover with a draught hole in it, to be regulated by a sliding shutter or regulator.

The cylinder has a ring round it outside, four inches from the top, with a tapering edge that the conical top, 5, may fit close on.

5 has a two-inch pipe to conduct the gas out of the pit. This stove is fed with charcoal, by removing the lid, 4, and filling the cylinder, 3; and I may here say that this stove will burn 36 hours, but I work mine for 24 hours. It will sufficiently heat the air of any large two-light frame, and serves for heating the bed, or rather the under part of it.

6 is a one-inch copper pipe, conducted through the cylinder's side, bending, and placed four inches above the grate-bars at 1.

This copper pipe is joined to lead pipes about six inches from the cylinder's sides, the lower one, 7, coming from the tank, 8—a box eighteen inches by ten, by eight deep, covered with a slate. The other pipe, 9, makes the circuit of the bed, or, rather, is traversed backwards and forwards, and finally is led into the tank at 10.

Here, then, is an apparatus complete; and now for the main secret to be carefully observed by any one wishing to erect one. The pipe from 9 to 10 must on no account be *below the level* of the pipe, 7, 6 ; this is the grand secret, all the rest is plain.

Set the cylinder stove in one corner of the bed, or frame and bed; the tank 8, on bricks, as well as the pipes, 7, 8, 9 ; make a hole in the slate over the tank, 8, and set a draining-pipe upright, 11, so that the top of this pipe will be above the soil of the bed. This will give moisture and a gentle steam, which, if not desired, can be stopped with a slate or sod-cover. The drain pipe, also, is the place to feed the tank with fresh water. I filled up my pit with broken bricks, about six inches above the pipes, and then laid sods and bark on them, and thus obtain a nice bottom-heat.

I have placed my two-light frame on brick-work, two feet high, 12, and placed a small door at the part nearest the stove door, as shewn by the dotted lines at 13, for the purpose of admitting the draught to the fire, and removing the ashes when wanted. The fire-bars must not be more than three-eighths of an inch apart, or the fuel will be greatly wasted by dropping through before it is consumed. I have no doubt but that a patent for this machine would pay me, but I have not the time nor inclination to take one out, but wish to diffuse the knowledge of it through your valuable pages, and shall be glad to give any further explanation through the same medium.   W. X. W.

THE PHYSIC GARDEN.

By a Physician.

MALVACEÆ.—" The uniform character of this order," says Dr. Lindley, "is to abound in mucilage, and to be totally destitute of all unwholesome qualities." It is not, therefore, a matter of wonder that their virtues were so extravagantly extolled by the rude practitioners of former days : they found them harmless, consequently, they tried them for every malady, and wherever recovery followed the plant administered had all the credit of it.

Under the heads of the two species which I propose to describe, I shall mention the properties which really belong to them ; but before doing so, I must just refer to two other plants of interest in this order—one is the Hollyhock (*Althæa rosea*), from which all those beautiful varieties of this noble and majestic plant have been derived—ornamenting, as they do, our garden walls with their gay and stately aspect ; the other is the *Gossypium herbaceum*, from the heads, or seed vessels, of which is obtained that most valuable commodity, cotton. I may add, that that favourite garden flower, the *Hibiscus*, also belongs to this order.

MALLOW (*Malva sylvestris*.—Few persons could be found in the rural districts of England who do not know that common plant, the mallow. Its handsome lilac flowers, and numerous leaves, render it a conspicuous and picturesque object on almost every road-side ; and its curiously-formed seeds are often played with and eaten by country children, and called by them "cheeses;"

"Then sitting down, when school was o'er,
　Upon the threshold of the door,
Picking from mallows, sport to please,
　The crumpled seed we call a cheese."

The emollient properties which all parts of the plant, and particularly the root, possess have raised it high in the esteem of our predecessors. They used a decoction of it for the cure of nearly every form of inflammation, whether external or internal. It is of considerable efficacy in any irritation of the throat or the alimentary canal, as well as for bringing forward any tumours or swellings. The French, at present, use it to a much greater extent than we do: with them it is a favourite poultice; while we commonly use it as a fomentation. The common mallow is a most useful substitute for those who cannot procure the marsh mallow; but the latter possesses the properties of the former to a greater extent, and is therefore more generally used.

MARSH MALLOW (*Althæa officinalis*).—Like the plant last described, the marsh mallow yields from the whole herb, but especially from the roots, a plentiful, tasteless mucilage, which is salutary in most cases of irritation. That well known French lozenge, the Pâte de guimauve, is a preparation made from this plant; and is a very effectual remedy for coughs, hoarseness, or sore throats. Our less civilized progenitors used an equally efficacious, though ruder form, of prescription: they boiled the roots in water, with a little honey, or else in milk, and drank the beverage.

In diarrhœa, and other diseases where there is much irritation and inflammation, from one to three pints of the decoction may be taken daily with great benefit. Wounds and bruises are often treated with advantage with this fluid as a fomentation; and the juice of the plant, with linseed meal, makes an excellent poultice.

HYPERICINEÆ.—Although no wild or cultivated species of the order Hypericineæ are now used in medicine, by regular practitioners, yet there are three native English species which have long been accounted specifics in certain diseases, and these I propose to speak of.

The order contains no very remarkable plants. They all possess an abundance of a yellow juice, which resembles gamboge, and is slightly purgative. Most of them are bitter, and somewhat astringent, whence they have been used as febrifuges. The bright yellow blooms of various species of Hypericum, or St. John's Wort, are common ornaments to our roads and hedges; the fine golden colour of one kind, tinged, as it is, with red (*Hypericum pulchrum*), makes it a very striking object; and so numerous are the flowers upon a single stalk, that the poet Cowper has well spoken of it as

"all bloom; so thick a swarm
Of flowers, like flies, clothing its slender rods,
That scarce a leaf appears."

TUTSAN, OR PARK LEAVES (*Hypericum Androsæmum*).—The tutsan is the largest-leaved of any of our species of Hypericum, and is to be met with in the moist woods of some parts of England, though not very plentifully. It is, however, a very common plant in gardens, where its solid leaves and fine orange blooms render it a desirable and showy tenant.

It derives its former English name from a barbarous corruption of the French *la toute saine*—the leaves being formerly much used for fresh cuts or wounds. Its specific name is a compound of two Greek words, signifying *man's blood*—from the claret-coloured juice which the leaves give when squeezed; their scent then is very aromatic. This juice is said to possess tonic and astringent properties; but its application to the cure of wounds is the only use which I have ever made of it, and in this it is very serviceable.

ST. PETER'S WORT (*Hypericum quadrangulare*), ST. JOHN'S WORT (*Hypericum perforatum*).—The medical properties of these two plants are so little different, that they may be used indiscriminately for the purposes for which they may be required. As yet, however, it is not well known how they act upon the human system, and on this account I have been loath to experiment with them. Their taste is astringent and bitter, and hence they are probably tonic. They have been found beneficial in some inflammatory diseases of the kidneys, and have even been accounted as febrifuges; these, and some other testimonies to their virtues, would seem to entitle them to further trials.

To these plants some small interest attaches, from the superstitious notions which were formerly connected with them. A very discursive writer, about 100 years ago, in giving an account of different plants thus speaks of these: "If superstition had not been the father of tradition, as well as ignorance the mother of devotion, these herbs had found some other names to be known by; but we may say of our forefathers as St. Paul did of the Athenians—'I perceive in many things that ye are too superstitious.'" The St. Peter's Wort riseth up greater and higher than the St. John's Wort; and good reason too—St. Peter being the greater apostle (ask the Pope else!); for though God would have the saints equal, the Pope is of another opinion." The common people in France and Germany gather the St. John's Wort with great ceremony on St. John's day, and hang it up in their windows as a charm against storms, thunder, and evil spirits. It was also formerly carried about by the people of Scotland as a charm against witchcraft and enchantment; and in some parts they still believe that ropy milk—which they suppose to be under some malignant influence—can be cured by being milked afresh upon the herb. Both species are common in Britain.

THE HOUSEWIFE.

ON seeing a new series of papers commenced, the readers of THE COTTAGE GARDENER will naturally inquire, "What am I to expect from them?" "On what subjects are they to treat?" "What class of readers are they designed for?" I will, therefore, commence by explaining my wishes, and answering these questions. In the first place, the class of readers whose attention I hope to enlist, whose welfare I have at heart, and to whom I hope to be of some little assistance, are the wives and daughters of men in the middle and lower ranks of life. Women who work and labour during the day, perhaps not actually in gaining their daily bread, but in those offices which, although they do not bring money in, prevent its being wasted by having a needless number of servants to perform duties which every sensible person in that rank of life has a pleasure in undertaking. The subjects on which I intend touching are numerous, including various arts, which, if properly understood, would make a small income appear a tolerable one, by the air of comfort which would pervade the household where such arts were practised. Occasionally, I hope to treat on the management of a dairy, the cow-shed, pig-stye, and hen-roost, as well as on the more sedentary occupations, such as "making and mending." I trust, also, whilst pointing out the necessity of attending carefully to our earthly duties, I may be the humble means of reminding you that this world is not our "abiding city," that it is not our home, but that we are placed here to prepare us for that kingdom which has been promised to those who glorify their heavenly Father—"Whatsoever we do, let us do all to the glory of God." And let us all remember, that whether we read or whether we write, a day is fast approaching (to many of us how very near!) when we shall have to give an account for every idle word, and each misspent hour. Let us, therefore, work whilst it is called to-day. Let us remember, also, this precept, "Whatsoever thy hand findeth to do, do it with all thy might." This shews us that whatever we undertake should be done thoroughly—"If a thing is worth doing at all, it is worth doing it well." No pains should be spared, no trouble grudged, which will help to make the earnings of the husband or father last as long as possible.

The past winter has been a trying one both for farmers and labourers, but I hope many a heart has been cheered and "kept up" by the energy and forethought displayed by the manager of the household. A busy and, I hope, a better time is fast approaching, and the privations which many, I fear, have been forced to undergo, will be forgotten amidst the happiness and bustle of full employment. Let the wife of the labourer carefully save every *penny* that is not absolutely required for the daily wants of the family. In many villages a club is established, into which the poor can put a penny or twopence a week. At Christmas the savings are given out, and some money added to each member's subscription. This is an excellent arrangement for we all know how difficult it is to save any money the poor especially feel this. How often after a little hoard has been made does it disappear in a glass or two of "something bot;" and should the children happen to peep into the old jug, or under the cup in which the store of halfpence has been put, what shrill voices are heard all round begging for a cake or some lollipops. Therefore, take my advice, and if there is a penny-club in your neighbourhood, belong to it.

Having written thus far about my poorer friends, I think I had better devote the remainder of my allotted space to a few recipes on preparing the usual dinner for a labourer's family. The articles constituting the dinner vary in different counties, and according to what is grown in the "Allotment Gardens." In my part of the world, peas, potatoes, onions, and bread, with a little whey, butter, or dripping is, I am sorry to say, the usual fare. Meat is seldom touched, unless a pig is fatted; and even then the greater part of it is sold. A little management, a little knowledge, would improve this meal. A few pence expended on sheep's trotters, or scraps of meat, would turn the other ingredient into more nourishing diet, and the family would be fed in a comfortable manner, and without any extra expense.

SHEEP'S FEET, or TROTTERS as the butchers call them, contain a great deal of nourishment; they are usually bought all ready for dressing, and cost one penny each. Buy a couple of them next Saturday at market, and also 1 ℔ of damaged rice, the price of which is three halfpence. When you wish to dress them, proceed in the following manner:— Put a tablespoonful of dripping into your saucepan, with two tablespoonsful of water. Have ready to put in directly it bubbles some sliced onions and carrots. Keep them over the fire for three minutes, stirring it all the time, then put as much water as you require, and add the trotters and half the rice that you purchased. Cover the saucepan closely, and let it stew for three hours. Now for the potatoes! Wash them well, but do not peal them, they are always better and more wholesome when boiled in their "jackets." Put them into a saucepan *half full* only of cold water, with a little salt. When nearly soft enough, strain the water off, cover the saucepan close, and leave it on the hob for the steam to finish cooking them. By attending to these simple directions, you will have dry mealy potatoes. When ready to begin dinner, pour out your soup into a basin, keeping back the bones (which will again flavour a little onion broth). Help each person to some of the rice, and let the potatoes and bread be soaked in the broth. I am sure the whole party will agree that this dinner is a very great improvement on those they have been in the habit of seeing. A FRIEND.

WILD FLOWERS OF MAY.

As a new feature in THE COTTAGE GARDENER, we purpose to present our flower-loving readers with a monthly paper on native wild flowers, noticing particularly those peculiar to the month, and giving a detail of such facts relating to their history and properties as may be likely to find general interest. Among all the months in the year, no one is so richly adorned in floral garlands as the merry, merry month of May. The lap of "flowery May" is full to overflowing with the beauteous favours of Flora's hand. Her lovely gems are bursting into life and beauty all around us; they enamel the fresh green meadow; the placid stream reflects their fairy forms; the leafing woods shelter them from the noonday sun, and the mild breath of evening is made balmy by their fragrance.

In the hedges and bushy places the Traveller's Joy (*Clematis vitalba*) is already sending forth its fragrant blossoms, which, when they fade, give place to the not less beautiful seeds, with their long, silky, and feathery awns. This is a very ornamental plant for twining through bushy shrubberies, and decking old ruins, and, according to Smith, the seeds retain their vegetative properties for many years if kept dry. In the shady woods the Anemone (*Anemone nemorosa*) is in a glow of beauty, its pure white blossoms, which are gently drooping during moist weather, sometimes acquiring a tinge of purple. This acrid plant is dangerous for cattle, and we believe goats alone may feed on it with impunity. A few English pastures are decked with the handsome purple flowers of the Pasque flower Anemone (*A. pulsatilla*), a plant which is also very acrid, and blisters the skin, although its root is stated by Haller to be sweet. It was the good old Gerarde who gave this flower the name of Pasque-flower or Easter flower, and as he himself tells us, he was "moved to name" it so because of the time of its appearance: the flowers are reported to yield a green dye.

The rare little Mousetail (*Myosurus minimus*) is in flower as a weed in the fields and gardens. There are also various species of *Ranunculus* now in flower, a highly acrid family, and one which is to be guarded against above all others in cattle pastures. Curious enough, however, the roots of *R. Ficaria*, a tuberous-rooted species, whose dark, green, heart-shaped leaves, and glittering yellow flowers adorn many a wet and sunless bank, have recently been found to be edible, and may, by cultivation, become of some importance in an economical point of view.* The wood Crowfoot (*R. auricomus*) is also void of acridity. *R. arvensis* is the most acrid species, and three ounces of the juice have been known to kill a dog in four minutes, although it is noticed in Smith's "Flora" that cattle eat the herb greedily, and, therefore, ought not to graze where it abounds. The Marsh Marigold (*Caltha palustris*) gorgeously adorns the marshes with its large yellow flowers, and those of our readers who love to investigate into the natural resources of our country, may amuse themselves by pickling the buds instead of capers, for which they form a cheap substitute, and, indeed, both are very similar in appearance.

The Green Hellebore (*Helleborus viridis*) will be found exhibiting its dingy blossoms in places where it has escaped from cultivation, or been planted as cover for game. This, according to some writers, is now substituted by the practitioners in Germany for the true hellebore of the ancients (*H. officinalis*), and Haller gives all the reputed virtues of the drug to our plant. In England, however, Smith tells us that the *H. foetidus* is more frequently used "on the credit of the Greek Hellebore. The Baneberry (*Actæa spicata*) and Alpine Barrenwort (*Epimedium alpinum*) will now be producing their flowers at the few places where they occur—more particularly in Yorkshire. Neither of these plants are of great importance for their properties, but toads are said to be attracted by the fetid odour of the Actæa, and both are very attractive to the rarity-loving botanist: the Epimedium, especially, is one of our most beautiful wild flowers. In the neighbourhood of houses the Celandine (*Chelidonium majus*) is now appearing, with its brittle leaves and stems filled with a yellow juice, the medical virtues of which were supposed, according to Dioscorides, to be taken advantage of by swallows in curing their young of blindness: this has probably given rise to the name of the plant; but there is more probability in the suggestion of Dioscorides, that it arose from the circumstance of the plant's appearing and disappearing with these migratory birds. The herb has been used as a cure for jaundice; but, no doubt, the only recommendation it has consists in the yellow colour of the juice.

The Shepherd's Purse (*Capsella Bursa-pastoris*) is a continual weed in our gardens; and is, notwithstanding, a very remarkable plant, as being truly cosmopolitan in its character, occurring in almost every part of the globe. It is of little or no service in supplying the wants of man, and continually infests cultivated grounds; but its seeds and flowers afford a grateful repast to many of the smaller members of the feathered race. In dry sandy situations the *Teesdalia* is in flower, along with the beautiful little *Draba verna*—two humble plants of considerable beauty, and interesting to the botanist. The common Scurvy-grass (*Cochlearia officinalis*) ornaments the rocky coast with its white flowers, and will be sure to attract the attention of such of our readers as have gone to spend their summer vacation from city life by the sea-side. It is generally very abundant on the shore, especially upon moist maritime rocks; and will be readily recognized by its shining heart-shaped leaves and showy corymbs of white flowers. Smith dubs it a "smooth, sleek, and shining herb." The rare bulbiferous Coral-root (*Dentaria bulbifera*) is exhibiting its purple blossoms, accompanied by the little bulbs in the axils of the leaves, the production of which seems so to engage the energies of the plant as to prevent the

---

* At a recent meeting of the Edinburgh Botanical Society (April 11, 1850), Mr. McNab showed a specimen of ranunculus ficaria raised from roots which had been gathered in Silesia by the Rev. Mr. Wade, in August, 1846. These roots had been exposed over a large extent of country in Austria by heavy rains, and the common people gathered them and used them as an article of food. Their sudden appearance gave rise to various conjectures as to their nature and origin, and in the Austrian journals they were spoken of as if they had fallen from the sky. The small bodies were dried and used as pease by the inhabitants. Mr. McNab had tasted the dried specimens, as well as fresh roots of ranunculus ficaria gathered in this country, both of which, after being boiled, he found very starchy. There is no acridity in the roots, even in a fresh state.

production of seeds. The meadows are lively with the flowers of the different species of *Cardamine*, or Lady's Smock, one of which (*C. pratensis*) is the Cuckoo-flower—so named because its showy flowers appear in the meadows at the same time when the cuckoo's first voice is heard. The flowers get the credit of curing epilepsy, and are indeed "associated with pleasant ideas of spring; and join, with the white saxifrage, the cowslip, primrose, and harebell, to compose many a rustic nosegay."

The yellow rocket (*Barbarea vulgaris*) is now a chief ornament of the waysides and moist pastures; and although it has been recommended as a salad, we fear that *one trial* will be sufficient to convince any one that its offensively bitter foliage is ill suited for such a purpose. On old ruins the Wallflower (*Cheiranthus Cheiri*) is displaying its array of yellow blossoms; and in neglected corn-fields we find a profusion of the Charlock or Wild Mustard (*Sinapis arvensis*) giving them a premature golden hue. The Hairy Violet (*Viola hirta*) and the Marsh Violet (*V. palustris*) are both lurking in beauty among the long grass; and the wall-tops are covered with the different species of Pearlwort (*Sagina*), which are of little importance except in a botanical point of view. *Arenaria trinervis*, a great favourite with the botanist, now produces its little flowers resembling those of the chickweed, which may also be found, and in greater plenty.

This is the month for the flowering of the dusky Cranesbill (*Geranium phœum*), and the waysides abound with the little Dove's Foot Cranesbill (*Geranium molle*); both of them —although comparatively showy among native wild flowers— far behind the highly cultivated geraniums of our gardens in their array of gaudy blossoms. The common Wood Sorrel (*Oxalis acetosella*) adorns the old-tree trunks and shelving rocks in the woodlands; and

    " The yellow furze, like fields of gold,"

clothes the northern landscape in a glow of beauty, reminding us of the effect of such a scene on the sensitive mind of Linnæus, when he fell on his knees in profound admiration on first beholding it. Nor has the furze its glowing beauty alone to recommend it to our attention. That were indeed enough to claim for it the admiring eye of the poet and the naturalist; but our sturdy plant of prickles and flowers, deigns even to court the approval of the utilitarian eye. In the winter season the young shoots are extensively used as food for stock, and he who has wandered over furze-grown sheep-walks, can well testify to the liking of the woolly flocks for this shrub. The black Medick or Nonsuch (*Medicago lupulina*) may be seen abundantly in lowland sheep pastures and waste grounds, along with the more rightful tenant of the soil, the White Trefoil, or Dutch Clover (*Trifolium repens*). The Grass Vetch (*Lathyrus nissolia*) may be gathered sparingly in bushy places in England, and it has recently been added to the Scottish Flora, by a young Forfarshire botanist. The Wood Strawberry (*Fragaria vesca*) is abundant in the steep banks of the woods, where in autumn its small red fruit will be eagerly sought after by woodland wandering urchins. The Spring Cinquefoil (*Potentilla verna*) is also in full flower, adorning many a sunny bank with its rich golden blossoms. Some years ago, we, in another page, recommended this beautiful plant as very suitable for flower-garden edgings, and it has subsequently been proved to be admirably adapted for this purpose. The Burnet-leaved Rose (*Rosa spinosissima*) is producing its white blossoms on heathy and hilly places; and the Hawthorn or May (*Cratægus oxyacantha*), is in its glory. In parts of the country where this plant is extensively used for hedgings, or grows plentifully in a wild condition, the evening air will be perfectly loaded with its fragrance, while the large sheets of its snowy blossoms will give the scenery an inviting aspect, such as no other plant could give. The red fruit or haws (sometimes of a greenish orange hue), afford many a winter meal to the feathered-tribes of the hedgerows, and the rustic disdains not to catalogue the hawthorn berry as one of our best wild fruits. In the woods the various species of *ribes* will be observed in bloom, and in hilly pastures the granulated Saxifrage is in beautiful condition, being generally a common plant, although scarcely to be found in the Scottish Highlands, as well as some districts of England. The little clusters of pink coloured tubers of the roots are scarcely less beautiful than the large white flowers. The Wild-beaked Parsley (*Anthriscus sylves-*

tris) has already produced its umbels beneath the hedges, and the Sweet Cicely (*Myrrhis odorata*) perfumes the whole air with its powerful fragrance; the latter more particularly frequents the margins of streams and woodland fences, and is sometimes found by the ruins of an old cottage, or the crumbling walls of an old garden, often the last remnant of cultivation that adheres to the spot. The beautiful little Moschatell (*Adoxa moschatellina*) is a very general favourite, and may be sought for in moist shady places; and the Mistletoe (*Viscum album*) so long held sacred by our forefathers, may now be observed with its axillary flowers, clinging to the bough on which it depends for support. More interesting, perhaps, than any other we have mentioned, is the *Linnæa borealis*, now beginning to flower in its secluded habitats; in the words of Sir J. E. Smith, this "is the little northern plant long over-looked, depressed, abject, flowering early," which Linnæus selected to transmit his own name to posterity. Few could have been better chosen; and the progress of practical botany in Britain seems to be marked by the more frequent discovery of the Linnæa.—G. LAWSON, *Assistant Curator, Botanical Society, Edinburgh.*

        (*To be continued.*)

WHITE FLOWERS FOR BEDDING.

YOUR valuable coadjutor, Mr. Beaton, having finished his section of white bedding-plants, and invited the remarks of any one who might be willing to assist him in rendering his catalogue more complete, I venture to suggest a few plants which he has omitted, first premising that my knowledge only extends to their cultivation as mixed border flowers.

Saxifraga granulata, or Double white Saxifrage. This is neat, hardy, one foot high, and blooms freely in April and May. If set out in clumps in February or March, and taken up when done with, and removed to a reserve bed, they would answer for several successive seasons.

Double white Rockets (*Hesperis tristis*). There are two kinds of this plant, one a medium size, growing about 1½ foot high, the other 2½ feet, and usually called the Giant Rocket. I have grown both for years, but prefer the latter, owing to its larger spikes of flowers, and fuller habit. In addition to its brilliant whiteness it is remarkable for its delicate fragrance, and in this latter respect is preferable, near a drawing-room window, to a bed of white stocks, which of a close warm evening are apt to be overpowering. Separating the balls in the autumn, and retaining the young plants three or four together, they will bed out well the following spring.

White Feverfew. I do not mean the common sort usually grown in gardens, but a double variety, with flowers about the size of a halfpenny, and every petal well expanded, so as to resemble the double-blossomed cherry. They will bloom from June to November, and by nipping off the tops of the main stems, will throw out lateral ones, and be covered with flowers. A single plant stopped in this way in a pot forms a white dome, and hides it entirely.

Campanula. I have two of these, not mentioned by Mr. Beaton, growing from two to three feet high; one is shaped in the flowers like the Canterbury Bell, only not so deep; the other has the form of a fleet cup, and about two inches across; both are very showy, and renew their flowers if plucked off when faded; the former blooms with me from June into winter, the latter not quite so long. I do not know their scientific names, but they flower in bunches on the top of slender foot stalks. The white Canterbury Bell would surely do as a bedder; but I find it difficult to grow this plant of a pure white, owing to my soil having too much bog in it, which turns the colour to a French white, and sometimes pale blue; from this cause the dark varieties assume a deep purple.

Iberis or Candy Tuft. There is a perennial variety of this, but I allude to the *annual* sown in the autumn, and removed to the bed in patches, when, if the season be at all favourable, it will appear in spikes six to eight inches long. Spring sown seeds produce generally very ordinary flowers.

Will Mr. Beaton allow me to say that he has hardly mentioned one white flower that a bed could be got into bloom of before June. Now there are few hearts which are not gladdened at the appearance of spring flowers; ladies and even invalids are tempted from their warm rooms into the garden by these harbingers of a milder season; the feeling is inherent in our nature, and cannot something more be done to meet the want by having our *spring flower-beds* as well as our *summer ones.* I have known persons object to beds on a lawn, because, as they said, "the beds looked blank and monotonous six months out of the twelve." Might not the defect be, in some degree, obviated by introducing into two or three of the beds a *permanent plant?* and now that we are upon white colours, say, for example, the perennial double white anemone. I have seen clumps of these grown from four to six feet diameter looking like masses of snow. If patches were placed on a bed at proper intervals, they would in one or two seasons completely cover it; now, as white would be too much of a good thing for nine months consecutively, we might have yellow crocuses for February and March, the white anemone for April and May, and scarlet geraniums from June till November. The advantages of the bed would be these: as soon as the crocuses were off bloom, the anemones would cover them, and the former would have perfected their bulbs when replaced by the geraniums. When the geraniums were over, another set of bulbs, differing in colour, would be ready to come in for the following spring, and the beds could then be dressed for the winter. But the bed itself, covered with a carpet of green, would form a contrast to the surrounding beds of soil; and the different hues of the lawn, anemone and geranium foliage judiciously blended, might serve to heighten the picture.—S. P., *Rushmere.*

EXTRACTS FROM CORRESPONDENCE.

Carraway Culture.—As you write for the benefit of small allotment holders, as well as others, and as the proverb says, "a penny saved is a penny got," I am induced to send you the following:—In the spring of the year 1848, I sowed about a square yard of ground with carraway seeds, and the same year I got from it a tolerable supply of good seed. The next summer, 1849, I got 2 ℔ of excellent seed, besides calculating that I lost one-third of the produce by "being busy"—not collecting them in time. These were sown under an ash-tree, where nothing else would thrive; and as they are very useful in a domestic way—indeed, cottagers here (Herefordshire) are very fond of a few in their bread—the hint may be useful to them, as by growing a few, they may gratify their taste and save many a penny that goes to the shop; being also much superior in flavour. I drill them thinly in rows six or seven inches apart.—R. B. R.

Lilium Lancifolium.—In October last I repotted my bulbs of *Lilium lancifolium* (above a dozen) into pots of the same size as those in which they had very finely bloomed in the summer. I thought I had taken care to place the apex of the bulb in the centre of the pot (but three inches below the surface), but many of them have made their appearance very far from the centre (I suppose from my inadvertence or carelessness), so that I fear I shall run some risk of injuring the bulb when I put in the supporting stick. I therefore take the liberty of suggesting that, when the bulb is repotted, two or three slender sticks be placed round and outside of the bulb, half an inch distant from the bulb, and to be an inch or two above the surface of the earth; these will be a guide for the placing the tall supporting stick in the spring.

We are directed to be very sparing of water to these lilies until they advance in stem and leaf; I pray some of your very experienced associates to have the goodness to inform me what it is to be "sparing." I will suppose I have some pots 9 and 11 inches deep, and the same across, in each of which is a fine bulb of *Lilium lancifolium*, with a shoot from two to six inches high, how much water should be given each pot at one time, and how often repeated? and if the water is to be poured over or round the young plant, or over the whole surface of the earth, or close to the inside rim of the pot? If with one of Moon's water-pots, which pour out quite perpendicularly, and very finely, I pour over the whole surface of the earth half an imperial pint of water, it merely moistens the surface, and a very few inches below; if I use one pint of water it goes down to the bottom, and the drainage takes away any superfluous quantity. Now, will it not be better to use the pint, and not to repeat it but half so often as

if the half pint was used? and how *often* should this be done?—Dianthus.

[The suggestion to put sticks round the bulb at the time of potting is excellent, and should always be adopted. As to the watering, it is quite true that we gardeners are sad fellows in the way of explaining our meaning, but surely our instructions about these lilies have been very full. "To be sparing of water," means, that as long as the soil is just moist none is to be given; but, of course, the soil must be all wetted at every watering; but to state the quantity of water, or how often it should be given, might lead people astray, so much depends on the season, the state of the atmosphere, the kind of compost used, and the situation where the pots are placed. Our lilies get no water from November to March, and yet the soil is moist all the time, the pots being plunged in coal ashes, in a cold pit, under a north wall.—D. B.]

Large Produce of Potatoes. — Some correspondents having asked for more information relative to the large produce mentioned at p. 327 of our last volume, we wrote to our correspondent, and this is his reply:—

"By a rood I mean the common *digging rood* of eight yards square, containing, as a matter of course, 64 square yards. The return spoken of was certainly very great, and for that reason I appended *the note* to my communication. The potato under question I had from a friend, who could give no account how he came possessed of it; and seeing it grow in his garden I requested a few. He has lost the sort from careless housing in the winter, consequently I consider myself the only possessor of it. My friend's garden was a *cold, lumpy clay*, with nearly a *north-east* aspect; but under such disadvantageous circumstances I was aware, from the growth of the root, that it was worth cultivating. My garden being a good mould, with a sandy subsoil, and a *south by east* aspect, has brought out the crop spoken of. I cannot part with any of the seed tubers this planting season, but, if all be well, I hope to have a good quantity towards August and September next, when I will with pleasure furnish your correspondent with a few. It requires to be planted a full yard from row to row, from the luxuriant growth of the haulm, and 20 to 24 inches from plant to plant in the row".—Leighton.

Cochin-China Fowls.—The following information, obtained from a respectable and intelligent dealer in London (Mr. J. Baily, 113, Mount-street, Grosvenor-square), may interest some of your readers, as it answers the questions on the above subject at p. 301 of The Cottage Gardener. It appears from hence that the size and merits of these fowls have been exaggerated. Mr. Baily says, and he gives me permission to send you his observations, "I believe I have as pure Cochin-China fowls as any in England; and I am sure four-fifths of those kept are not more than half bred. I will endeavour to describe a pure bred fowl of this kind—small head, small comb, red face, yellow leg, slightly feathered, sometimes (but very seldom) five-clawed, large square bodies. The tuft of feathers on the leg is more distinct in some than in others, but where it projects too much I do not like it. The thigh should be covered with bushy feathers. The colour of the cock should have little or no variety, being of a reddish brown or a buff yellow, but one colour only; the pullet light brown, darker shaded round the lower part and sides of the feathers. But there are two more undoubted proofs of purity, the first and most important is the almost entire absence of tail. The cock has a small tuft of feathers, invariably black, and more like an ostrich than a cock; the hen has merely an apology for one, the feathers being the same colour as the body. The next proof is that the egg is of pinky cream colour, much resembling the Silver Pheasant's. I do not believe that they lay more than one egg a day; and though in my opinion they are the best fancy fowl that has been introduced for many years, the Dorking is quite as heavy, and if an average of numbers were taken I think a heavier bird."—D. Knight.

Pork v. Bacon: Weighing Pigs, &c.—I have not seen an answer to your correspondent, T. W.—"Which pays best, pork or bacon?" I can give a practical answer from my own experience and that of an extensive dealer in this neighbourhood. Fresh pork at 4½d per ℔ pays better than when just out of salt at the same price, because pork loses in salt at least ¼ of a ℔ from every stone of 14 ℔, besides the cost of salt, &c.; but bacon dried and sold at 7d per ℔ will pay best of all, and will fetch equal at least to 1d per ℔ on the whole more, if, as your correspondent says, trouble or labour is no object; but to salt and dry it will pay for all the labour involved. While I am on this subject I would say that we have a custom of measuring our live pigs to ascertain how they progress in feeding; the tape or string is passed under the belly close to the fore legs and brought up over the shoulders in a straight line; and the circumference thus ascertained is the guage—thus, a pig measuring 48 inches as above will weigh 14 stones, of 14 ℔ to the stone; and for every inch of increase in circumference will increase a stone in weight—supposing the pigs to be in good condition and of moderate size; but some very small breeds may not reach so much, while the very long breeds will sometimes weigh more by 2 ℔ to the stone. I had this winter a hog pig of a small sort; I bought it for a Berkshire; he fed well, and was very fat when killed, and measured 58 in., and weighed 23 stone 10 ℔, of 14 pounds to the stone—this weight includes the inward fat. I must add, that above, by weight, in all cases, means the weight of flesh the dead pig will yield. And we reckon a good pig when feeding should gain an inch per week until he ceases to gain; but he may cease for a week and be making inward fat. I always measure mine when they are eating with their heads down. Should you think the above would be useful to those who (like me) cannot weigh their live pigs, it is at your service.—JOSEPH BUTLER.

SMALL BAKED BREAD PUDDINGS (*Very Light*).—Pour boiling, on three ounces of bread crumbs and a morsel of butter, half-a-pint of new milk, cover them down with a plate, and let them remain until nearly cold; then add to them, by degrees, two large well whisked eggs, and an ounce and a half of sugar, with the slightest pinch of salt, and a flavouring of grated nutmeg, or of fresh lemon-rind. Beat the mixture up lightly, pour it into well-buttered cups, and bake the puddings *very gently* for half-an-hour in an American oven. Turn them out for table, and sift fine sugar over them. The proportions must be doubled when they are needed for a dinner of more than two or three persons.—E. ACTON.

EARLY SWARM OF BEES.—It is so unusual for bees to swarm in April, that I cannot refrain from informing you of a swarm which left the parent hive yesterday (Sunday) the 7th instant. The owner, a man named Hayes, a bee-hive and bee-hive-chair maker of Enfield, in the county of Middlesex, although one of the most skilful men I have ever known in the management of bees, could scarcely believe it possible when he was informed of the fact by a neighbour who had seen the swarm leave the hive, nor could he feel convinced of the reality until he had separated the group and taken up the queen. The whole swarm, which is a strong and healthy one, has been safely lodged in a new hive, where each bee seems to rejoice in its new and more roomy abode of industry. I observe you have directed attention to the management of bees in your very instructive periodical, THE COTTAGE GARDENER. I have no doubt many of your readers may look with astonishment upon the above fact, in confirmation of the truth of which I subscribe my name.—SENECA.

ANTS are very fond of travelling about peach-trees, and this alone creates a suspicion against them. And the fact is, that though the ant does not eat the leaves of the peach, it encourages the aphis which does so. I have myself seen ants carrying the aphides to the young and tender leaf of the peach. The ant eats what exudes from the aphis, and this is the reason the former takes care of the latter. It is an old saying—"Quod facit per alium facit per se" (That which a man does through another he does himself); and, therefore, the ant is injurious to the peach-tree. I know other people who have seen the ant employed in the way I have described.—REV. C. A. A. LLOYD, *Whittington, Oswestry.*

BEES, WEIGHT OF HONEY FOR.—We northerns are sometimes amused with the required weight of hives for *keepers* by your southern amateurs. Take an instance: In May, 1848, I bought a first swarm, a very large one, in a larger hive than usual here (common straw). At the beginning of July it threw off a strong swarm, and at the usual interval another. Early in autumn, the parent swarm weighed not less than 30 ℔, according to the estimate of a neighbouring bee-keeper, from merely lifting it. In December, the

same year, it had not an ounce of honey, and the bees had forsaken it altogether. I had not observed any quarrels or robbery. The two swarms were both very weak, containing not more than 3 or 4 ℔ a piece of honey. By hard feeding they wintered; and in 1849 each swarmed twice. But it was a bad honey year with us, and the four swarms were very poor—4 or 5 ℔ a-piece; the two parents probably 14 ℔ a-piece. By hard feeding they are yet alive and brisk. Moist sugar boiled in ale was their food. According to your south country notions, it would have been deemed folly *to try* to keep them alive. I wish Mr. Payne would favour us with his opinion on the points here touched on.—A CUMBRIAN.

TO CORRESPONDENTS.

*** We request that no one will write to the departmental writers of THE COTTAGE GARDENER. It gives them unjustifiable trouble and expense; and we also request our coadjutors *under no circumstance* to reply to such private communications.

CROCUSES AND OTHER BULBS (*H. E.*).—You must not move these until their leaves turn yellow at the end of the summer, if you wish them to bloom well next year.

VINES IN GREENHOUSE (*J. C——, Wakefield*).—Pray refer to Mr. Errington's two essays at pp. 33 and 153 of our second volume. You will there find every instruction—from planting the vine to ripening the fruit.

SALVIA NEMOROSA (*A., Worcestershire*).—This species of the Sage family is also known as *Salvia sylvestris*, but your specimens are certainly not of it, but seemingly of *Salvia Grahamii*. The *Melilotus leucantha* is also known as the *M. vulgaris* and *M. alba*, or White-flowered Melilot.

BINDING OUR PRESENT VOLUME (*Ibid.*).—There is no difficulty about this. Either cut off the page of advertisements, *not at the back but at the inner black line*, or tell the binder to do so. Your other questions will be answered next week.

ASPARAGUS BEDS (*C. J. P.*).—The insects you inclose are specimens of the Snake Millipede (*Julus pulchellus*), for an account of which pray refer to page 139 of our second volume. You will there see a doubt as to whether this insect is injurious to plants; and we shall be much obliged by your examining the roots of your asparagus-plants, and informing us whether you find any of these Snake Millipedes attacking them. We should incorporate a thick covering of quicklime with the surface soil; and give a manuring with common salt once a fortnight.

HOTBED (*An Invalid Subscriber*).—If your soil is dry it will not be liable to be chilled by excessive wet, and will, therefore, do quite as well, if not better, if formed in an excavation made in the soil. An answer to your other query next week.

IVY (*F. N. M.*).—Never mind the leaves having fallen off the branches of that planted last November. As the stems are green it will soon emit fresh foliage, but we do not know how it will succeed in the middle of London. You may divide your *Box* plants if they have more than one stem; if not, by cutting off a portion of the fibrous roots annually, you may keep them dwarf, so as not to require larger pots. The Chinese Arbor-vitæ is the *Thuja orientalis*; it requires no particular management, being quite hardy.

CURRY PASTE (*M. D.*).—Can any of our readers supply us with a recipe for making this? Our correspondent does not require a recipe for curry *powder*.

CHARRING SAWDUST (*T. Ellis*).—The best mode of effecting this is by mixing it thoroughly with earth, in the proportion of about two barrow-loads of sawdust to one of earth, to pile the mixture over some brushwood, to set light to this, and so cover up the fire that it shall only go on smouldering until the whole is charred.

MELILOT SEED (*Rev. F. W. P.*).—This sprouted very well. We are glad to hear that its flowers are such good bee pasturage. Many thanks for the Himalayah pumpkin seed. We have far more applicants for it than we can supply.

GALVANIC PLANT PROTECTORS (*Dianthus*).—These instruments for preserving plants from snails, slugs, &c., are circles of different diameters, from eight to twelve inches, made of zinc; two or three inches in depth at top is soldered, on, all round, a piece or circle of copper. On a snail or slug being attracted by the plant within this circle (for a circle is put round each plant in a pot, or out of doors in a border), he creeps up the zinc, but the instant he touches the copper rim he drops down—being completely *galvanised*. The vandyked zinc on the upper rim is merely for ornament. [The protector is only efficacious whilst the copper and zinc are bright, or unoxidised. A much more endurable and quite as efficacious a protector is a similar circle of zinc, with a horse-hair rope fastened round near its upper rim. The hairs form a chevaux-de-frise, which neither slugs nor snails can surmount. It remains good for years; and by nicking the rope longitudinally, a fresh palisading of hairs springs up.]

AYLESBURY DUCKS.—A correspondent, in answer to the inquiry of E. J. H., states, that the finest breed of Aylesbury ducks can be purchased of W. Dean, of Buckland, near Aston Clinton, Bucks. He gets, at the present time, for young *fat ones*, about 12s per couple; but for stock—*i.e.* breeding ducks—he recommends such as are not bred very early in the season, or old ones; his price for such, at a more advanced part of the season, would be from 5s to 6s. per couple; but his price is, of course, ruled by the London markets.

FRUIT-TREES IN KITCHEN-GARDEN (*B. Philadelphia, Norwich*).—The best plan to arrange fruit-trees in combination with vegetables is, doubtless, to make them a margin all round the plot, or nearly so. If you will search the earlier Numbers of THE COTTAGE GARDENER, you will find all these things thoroughly described in detail. Let us advise you to look well over those articles. Raspberry canes are frequently allowed to grow between the fruit-trees; we think them best by themselves, as they spawn or throw up suckers so. The length of stem of fruit-trees depends on the object. For rough dwarf standards two feet is amply sufficient for a dwarfing system, and no other is eligible in your little plot. As to kinds of fruit-trees, you cannot plant now; and you will meet with abundant information in our pages before the planting season. Your description of your subsoil—" sand, gravel, marl, and chalk "—is most humorous; surely you have plenty of choice. Always allow a tree or bush a certain space, however limited, unmolested by the spade.

OLD SEA-KALE PLANTS (*T. S.*).—Those which have spread their stalks very widely may be cut within one inch of the surface of the soil; and when the buds start by and bye, thin them out to two or three shoots from a crown, or even one if you want it very strong next year.

GARDENIA RADICANS (*Ibid*).—This may be kept in a greenhouse from which the frost is excluded all the year round; but to succeed well with it, it should have a warm moist atmosphere to start it into bloom. See what Mr. Appleby said about the genus lately.

CAMELLIAS (*Ibid*).—These kept in summer in such a house as that last-mentioned, and under vines not forced, will look greener than those set out of doors, and will perfect their wood and set their buds sooner; but then they should not be kept under the shade of the vines in the autumn, but rather be placed for a time in a sheltered place out of doors, though nothing is gained by keeping them too long exposed. If you prefer your plants to blow in spring instead of winter, the plants should be set out as soon as the buds are set.

VINE PRUNING (*Ibid*).—" Why is the spur plan of pruning preferable to the long rod system under glass?" We never said it was preferable in all cases. Fine crops are produced by both systems. One great advantage of the spur system is, that the space is made the most of, and more light admitted to the ground and plants beneath. *Solanum jasminoides* may be procured at most nurseries. We do not like mentioning names.

HEATING A SMALL GREENHOUSE (*J. N.*).—This you now effect by means of a flue round one end and the back, heated by a fire in the harness room, which stands at the back of the greenhouse; but the flue does not draw well, the front shelf is cold, and you propose having a hot water pipe all round the floor of the house, and also to go beneath the bark bed in the centre of the house, to be fed by an apparatus fixed in the harness room, and you ask our opinion as to recommending such a course, and we unhesitatingly answer yes, if you do not mind the trouble and expense. If properly done, it will be sure to answer; and you will be freed from the annoyance of cleaning flues, &c. The most economical method would be to have two turns of the pipe in the bark bed, on the same level as the rest round the house; but then you could not heat the bark bed without heating the house. The most complete method, therefore, would be to have a separate flow and return pipe for the bark bed, that you might heat it at pleasure, without heating the other parts of the house. In such a house, 11ft. by 11ft., a flow and return 3-inch pipe as far as the bark bed, with a double set of pipes there, in a chamber with the bark bed above, and slides in the side of the chamber to admit heated air into the house at pleasure, would be amply sufficient. Your own plan, however, having the pipe round the house, would keep all the walls in a comfortable dry condition, and diffuse the heat perhaps a little more equally. Unless you want a high temperature, the flue you now have ought to be sufficient for all common purposes, such as excluding frost, &c. We suspect the not drawing is owing to the flue and the furnace being too much on the same level. Before commencing operations, it would be worth while to see what sinking the bottom of the furnace from a foot to eighteen inches below the bottom of the flue would do.

HART'S EVERLASTING ROSE (*W. Thompson*).—This name is a gross imposition. It is merely the dry pericarp or seed-vessel of a species of *Mesembryanthemum*, which has the property of remaining closed up whilst dry, and of opening when wetted. " By an extraordinary provision of nature (by a wise provision of God would be a phrase more truthful), in some annual species of Mesembryanthemum, natives of sandy deserts in Africa, the seed-vessel opens only in rainy weather; otherwise the seeds might, in that country, lie long exposed before they met with sufficient moisture to vegetate." (*Sir J. E. Smith*.)

YARN-BLEACHER'S REFUSE (*A. B.*).—Your refuse is the same as that of the paper-maker (See vol iii., p. 136). It is too powerful to put upon grass land unless mixed with earth; and twenty bushels per acre put on early in the spring would be the best time and quantity.

SULPHATE OF AMMONIA (*H. N.*).—We have no doubt of this forming a good liquid manure for celery, lettuces, and other kitchen-garden plants; but we cannot say whether it would equal liquid manure made of guano; we fear that it would not. Try the experiment.

GRAVELLY SOIL ON CLAY SUBSOIL (*P. W.*).—There is little chance of improving your garden without draining; but if you could get up some of the wet clay on which the garden rests and burn it, then apply it as a top dressing of the surface soil from time to time, it would much improve it for vegetable crops; but fruit-trees cannot long live on such wet bottom. Mr. Rivers' dwarf trees on the quince and paradise stocks are the most likely to survive the longest. We should also mix a heavy dressing of the clay (unburnt) with the surface soil.

WINTERING VERBENAS (*Ibid*).—Your verbena cuttings, with " scarcely any water all winter," died from drought. The soil about their roots should not have been quite dry all the time. All cuttings made in the autumn require more or less water through the winter. It is only when strong old plants are kept that it is safe to let their roots become dry; but even old verbenas and petunias must have some water.

SEEDS OF ARUNDO DONAX (*G. H.*).—Can any of our readers state where seeds of this water reed can be obtained, and the best time for sending them to New Zealand? It is a native of France and Italy, where it is used for ornamental fencing, fishing-rods, &c.

ROUGH PLATE GLASS (*R. W.*).—We have no hesitation in saying that it is far preferable to sheet glass for glazing your greenhouse. See what we have said on the subject at p. 262 of our second volume.

SMOKY BACK GREENS (*Margaret Harvey*).—Even these inauspicious places in " Auld Reekie " may be induced to grow some flowers (see p. 34 of the present volume); but, even if yours is obdurate, it may grow pot-herbs; and, at all events, our pages will contain the other subjects you allude to. Thanks for the critiques.

SALT FOR ASPARAGUS (*C. J. P.*).—In a previous answer we think we have almost replied to your question. You cannot grow very fine asparagus unless you do manure the beds frequently with salt throughout the growing season. You may give liquid manure to asparagus beds all May and June with the greatest advantage. The drainings from stables, with an ounce of salt dissolved in every gallon, is excellent. You must not fork in manure now; you would destroy many of the shoots.

NITRATE OF SODA *Ibid*.—This has been found beneficial as a manure to carrots, cabbages, lawns, lettuces, and celery. One pound to a square rod or perch is a good proportion. In solution, half an ounce to a gallon. It is a good application to chrysanthemums and fuchsias the evening before the day of exhibition.

MOSS ON THE SURFACE OF POT-SOIL (*Ibid*).—We approve of this, not only because it looks neat and refreshing, but because it helps to keep the soil moist.

LOCAL SHOWS.—We cannot announce these except as advertisements.

COVERS (*F. Taylor*).—You can obtain these for any one, or all, of our volumes by applying to Mr. Ashley, bookseller, Newbury.

GOAT'S DUNG (*A Beginner in Floriculture*).—This answers as well as the dung of the sheep for making liquid manure. One peck of the dung to thirty gallons of water will be a good proportion. Tie the dung up in an old cloth before putting it into the water, and then the liquid will be quite clear.

BEES (*W. A. E.*).—Hive a swarm of bees into your hive full of comb. Never mind the old bee-bread and mites in it, for the bees will do what is necessary with both. Your seeing drones so early as the 13th of March and beginning of April, if they are last year's drones, is not a good sign for the hives, but they have in all probability been hatched this spring. Upon *Neighbour's Improved Cottage Hive* put the five glasses immediately, and if possible fix a small piece of guide comb in each glass; but the glasses will not be certain to prevent swarming. A hive the size they are now in will be too large to put under the glasses, and cover the parent hive; one-half the depth will be much better to prevent brood being put there.

CARNATIONS (*Verax*).—You may propagate these, as you state, viz., by slipping off their shoots and planting these shoots just in the condition they come off from the parent root, but these shoots do not root so easily as either layers or pipings.

WINTERING GERANIUM (*Ibid*).—When done blooming in July or August, shake off all the earth from their roots, cut them down, and repot them in smaller pots.

VASE IN CENTRE OF GRASS-PLOT (*A. R.*).—Scarlet geraniums are the most likely to suit your rustic vase, or the Double purple American groundsel, one of the very best vase plants we have. There ought to be a hole at the bottom to let the water escape, and to be drained just like a large pot; and in all vases the soil ought to be good light loam, and should be enriched with small doses of liquid-manure, as all plants in vases require to be regularly watered in some way.

CORONILLA CUTTINGS (*A. Lenny*).—These cuttings, made from the young shoots, will root freely, if put in now on a gentle bottom-heat, or even under a hand-glass in the open border later in the season. We are very much gratified to hear of your success with your verbena cuttings; whenever you meet with any difficulties with any plant, or method of culture, or with new experiments of your own, pray let us hear, and we shall do the best we can for you.

INSECT DESTROYER OF VERBENA CUTTINGS (*J. J.*).—We have never seen any of the worms (grubs?) you thus describe, and we shall be obliged by your sending us specimens. Have any other of our readers been similarly injured? " I have lost many hundreds of verbena cuttings from their being quite eaten through at the point where the stem enters the mould, by a very small white insect, hardly thicker than a hair, and about half the length of a cress seed. I have found it destroy entirely, the more delicate verbenas, even when planted in the borders, but its great delight seems to be cuttings. Pot after pot have been laid prostrate by it, in spite of trying covering the top of the pot with sand, different kinds of compost, and many other methods to prevent its ravages, but invariably, though every care has been taken, and the most healthy cuttings have been chosen, without the slightest trace of the insect upon them, in a few days they have all been eaten off at the point I have described. The only difference I have noticed, is that this insect does not seem to like the white verbenas so well as the coloured ones, and the scarlets it seems to prefer to all. I do not know the name of the insect, but though very small it is quite perceptible to the naked eye, and runs very fast."

MILDEW ON VERBENAS IN WINTER (*J. J.*).—Verbenas are very liable to this disease in winter, but if taken in time, sulphur will certainly prevent it, and the plan of using a little soot with ♃ seems an improvement; indeed we would advise that the whole stock of verbenas should be lightly dusted with soot and sulphur in October and November, before, the mildew appears, as prevention is better and easier than a cure.

HOTBED FOR CUTTINGS (*Amateur*).—A hotbed for cuttings does not require to be watered; but the surface of it is to be often sprinkled over in fine weather—pots, plants, and all—with a rose watering-pot. This keeps up a moist genial heat, so grateful to both young and old plants in the spring.

WINDOW PLANTS (*Ibid.*)—Geraniums, Heliotropes, Musk plants, Sweet-scented Verbenas, Tree Violets, Tree Mignonette, and many others noticed in our former volumes, will do " to mix with balsams in a window looking to the east." If the balsams are well grown, two of them would fill a very large window; after they come to that size they may be trusted outside the window. Low plants to fill in between the balsam pots are what we recommend, and to be sweet, to make up for size. We cannot give a plan for an arbour: we never yet saw a beautiful one.

TOOL HOUSE, POTTING BENCH, &c. (*J. N. C.*).—You say, "My idea at present is to have it of stout iron wire, arched in a semicircular form, and open at one end, and to train over it either ivy or some other climber that would keep out the rain (or nearly so). What ornamental climber would you recommend as an effectual covering; or can you advise some other better kind of construction, to form both a tool house and also a pleasant retreat from the heat of the summer's sun for such as are fond of books, &c." Your plan will answer perfectly well; and if you were to cover the top with asphalt pelt, to keep out the rain, you would have a complete, snug, retired place, for such purpose as you intend. A few fast-growing climbers, as the different species of Clematis, and evergreen climbing roses, would soon cover it. Then you might plant finer summer climbers, to supersede them in time—such as Lophospermum, Eccremo-carpus, Dolichos Lignosus, Cobæa scandens, the Canary Tropæolum, &c.

INARCHING VINES (*M.*).—We should say you might graft an *Esperione* vine, it being a hardy sort. Of your three proposals, we say by all means inarch the Esperione with a good branch of the Hambro', provided the root and border are good. Your Esperione, however, will carry a very limited crop, and each only on a few shoots—say six or eight good bunches, and those principally upwards. This will enable your inarched shoot to reach the back of the house this season, and to bear next. Your Esperione, moreover, should be close stopped all the season. Do not stop your *Muscats* in so prim a way as other grapes. Its majestic habit seems to scorn the snubbing which other vines are obliged to submit to. We will one day give a paper on the Muscat.

UNFRUITFUL CHERRY (*G. W. P.*).—Your cherry blooming profusely, but not producing fruit, is by no means an extraordinary case; but how to account for it is not so easy. We, too, have had cherries which when they grew old became totally barren, and, like many pears, continue to blossom abundantly—the blossom, moreover, appearing strong. On a close examination, however, we have generally, if not always, found the bloom minus the pistil or female organ, therefore not likely to set. Our friend Mr. Beaton is very likely to throw light on this interesting point. Perhaps thorough draining is not unlikely to benefit the tree.

CURRANTS DROPPING (*W. B.*).—You should watch and determine if birds or insects really attack your currants: this much you may at least ascertain. Soil excessively dry and poor might cause their falling, so might stagnant soil. Pray watch for the next three weeks.

WIREWORMS (*N. Brandreth*).—"The soil you have carted into your garden is swarming with wireworms." If we were in your place we should either cart it all out again or have it all sifted through a sieve so fine that the wireworms will not pass through the meshes, and have all that is retained in the sieve carted away. We know of no application that will effectually destroy the wireworm if it once gets into the soil. Spirit of tar, gas-lime, &c., will destroy them *if* they can be got into it; but here is the difficulty. Moles turned into the garden are the best resource against them.

FLOOR-BOARD OF HIVE, &c. (*I. A. E.*).—This should always have a very gentle slope, so that no wet will lodge upon it. Painting the straw is a protection against wet; but wet will never penetrate through it if the hive is well made. The best roofing over a hive is a milkpan turned bottom upwards. For the sake of appearance we have these painted slate colour.

SHIFTING YOUNG CARNATIONS (*A Young Amateur*).—It is indeed high time to remove these from the greenhouse; and you had better place them in a sheltered place for the first ten days.

OLD MYRTLES (*A Lady Subscriber*).—It is a good plan to keep old myrtles rather warmer than a greenhouse heat through April and May in each year, or until they make their growth, and then to inure them gradually to stand the open air in a south aspect. They require abundance of water all the summer, and by getting an early growth they are sure to bloom at the end of summer. It is also a good plan to turn them out of the pots or boxes into a warm south border, to water them liberally there with

liquid-manure, and to cut their roots partially, as we recommended for the *Brugmansias*, a short time before they are potted in the autumn. Mr. Gibbs, of Piccadilly, London, is the only importer of *Peruvian guano*.

HOT SOUTH BORDER (*M. A. H.*).—The jasmine and honeysuckle, which are established there, have complete possession of the border already; and, as in the case of planting young things near large trees, there is no way of establishing fresh plants in the same border with those two, except by plunging large pots or boxes to be filled with other climbers. These would need to be constantly kept moist for the first season. Try *Jasminum nudiflorum* that way. It is a beautiful flower against a house or verandah in winter.

ROOTS INVADING BEDS (*Ibid.*)—The only way to overcome the roots of trees getting into flower beds, is to cut a narrow trench outside the bed, and as deep as the roots go, and to fill it up with concrete made with lime and gravel, or cinder ashes, one part lime and five parts of gravel, &c.

STRAWBERRIES UNPRODUCTIVE (*A Constant Reader*).—You have tried various modes of treatment, yet you cannot obtain good fruit. Your soil is evidently not suitable for this fruit, for Keen's Seedling and the Elton, which have failed with you, will do on most soils; but the British Queen has failed in many situations, and in others, under the best management, can hardly be kept alive. Can you not trench a fresh bed for them; and use a quantity of burnt clay, and very rotten manure? We cannot recommend better varieties than the Elton and Keen's Seedling; and we have seen the *Downton* do well not far from you (near Malvern); but it, also, is a very choice about soil.

NARCISSUS (*J. F.*).—Your Grand Monarch Narcissus, having three healthy shoots, is quite right; and you will soon see the flower scape rising amongst the leaves. It is a hardy bulb, and will do to plant out in the border after it has *done flowering*.

MOCK ORANGE (*Ibid.*)—You ask us what this can be with " the seeds resembling those of the melon, but smaller?" We can only guess that it may be the orange-fruited gourd, which is sometimes called *The False Orange*.

TROPÆOLUM TRICOLORUM (*Ibid.*)—You broke the top off and repotted it, but no fresh shoots have appeared. Always plant them in their flowering pots at once. It will not start again, probably, till next September. Uncover it, and if you see no signs of growth let it get dry; but watch it through the summer, and whenever you see it offering to grow pot it afresh. You know the rest already. We have known the bulbs of this flower to lie dormant for a whole season without any apparent cause.

GLOXINIAS (*A Subscriber*).—It is best to pot gloxinias into their flowering pots at once; but the size of the pots ought to correspond to that of the bulbs, and you may for the small bulbs six-inch pots, and so up to nine, ten, or eleven-inch pots.

WATERING (*Ibid.*)—All plants ought to be watered " from above," and not by pouring water into the saucers.

AZALEA INDICA CUTTINGS (*Ibid.*)—This will propagate freely by cuttings by and by. When the young wood of this season is three inches long, slip a few shoots off here and there and put them in the hotbed, and if you can put a glass over them all the better.

SOWING HEATHS (*Ibid.*)—Their seeds may be put into a hotbed to hasten their growth, but as soon as you see the seedlings in leaf, remove the pans containing them into a cool airy place.

PRUNING PASSION FLOWER (*W. H.*).—If it is an old plant top all the last year's wood down to two eyes, unless you wish it to cover more space, in which case some of the shoots may be trained over it nearly their full length. The *inside of a greenhouse* should be whitened to increase the light. We cannot tell the name of your plant from such an imperfect description.

SOIL FOR ROCKERY (*Ibid.*)—A mixture of loam, sand, and peat, is the best general soil; but some species of rock plants require a modification of this mixture.

NAMES OF PLANTS (*Y. Z.*).—Your double yellow-blossomed Berberry is Mahonia (formerly Berberis) *aquifolium*. (*Desire Pontel*).—Your sprigs seem to be both from a *Leonotis Leonurus*; Polygala *cordifolia* and *Podalyria styracifolia* are greenhouse evergreen shrubs from the Cape of Good Hope, and the others are probably *Elichrysums*, but we cannot decipher their specific names, but they are all greenhouse evergreen shrubs. (*Crucifera*).—It gives us much and often useless trouble to send us a blossom squeezed flat like yours. If our correspondents are anxious to know the names of plants, they ought to facilitate our examination by sending a good bloom and a leaf in a box surrounded by damp moss. Your plant we think is *Iris rhinensis*, or Chinese Iris; and we are confirmed in the opinion by knowing that other persons besides yourself water it by pouring boiling water into the saucer of the pot in which it is growing.

GERANIUM LEAVES (*An Amateur*).—The edges of these which have been kept in a cool greenhouse all the winter, are turning black. This is a symptom that they require more moisture at their roots. Your Grizzly *Frontignan Grapes* do not ripen because they have not heat enough.

MELILOT SEED.—If "A Subscriber," who in our Number for April 4th wishes for this seed, will send his address on a ready-directed and stamped envelope to the Rev. Francis W. Pye, Blisland Parsonage, near Bodmin, the latter will send him some.

UNFRUITFUL CUCUMBER (*A Cumbrian*).—It is rather difficult, not knowing all the circumstances, to say why your cucumber plants produce blossoms yet no fruit; but the probable cause is that you give them too much water and keep them too cold. Non-impregnation we do not believe has anything to do with the failure.

CALENDAR FOR MAY.

GREENHOUSE.

Air admit freely in good weather; toward the end of the month have a good share at night. Annuals, &c., bring in from pits and frames when approaching the blooming state. Cuttings, consisting of nice stubby side shoots, will now root readily in a mild bottom heat. *Camellias*, epacrises, heaths, cinerarias, calceolarias, geraniums, &c. (see last month). Earth: stir the surface on pots and borders, and fresh dress where repotting or renewing the earth is not advisable. Sow seeds of the Orange or Lemon, and when of a suitable size let them be grafted or inarched—preferring the former and placing the plants in a moist hot-bed; any stocks raised late last season may be so used. For flowering in a dwarf state, and almost continuously, the Otaheite orange is valuable. Shifting into larger pots must be carefully proceeded with. Succession crops of *Achimenes*, *Gloxinias*, *Gesneras*, &c., must now be seen after. Salvias must be propagated for autumn and winter blooming. Hardy Plants should now be set in a sheltered corner, to make way for the importations from the pits and frames. Seedlings must be pricked off in time, or they will destroy each other. Water will be required oftener as the sun gains strength.

R. Fish.

FLOWER GARDEN.

Anemones, water well between the rows. Annuals (Tender), remove into another hotbed; pot, if not done in April; water gently, and give air as much as possible; prick out April sown. Antirrhinums plant. Auriculas done blooming, remove to N.E. aspect, where they will not have the sunshine after nine; offsets with roots, detach and plant, three in a pot; seedlings keep in the shade; water moderately in dry weather; auriculas to seed should be kept from wet. Awnings, or other shelter, continue over beds of tulips, e., now in bloom. Bedding Plants, be not in too great hurry to plant out; the middle of the month is time to begin any of the half-hardy plants. Biennials, sow, b., in rows, thinly. Bulbous Roots, generally, directly leaves decay, take up and store; seedlings shade through midday; (Autumn blooming), plant again after separating offsets, or else store until end of July. Carnations, remove side buds from flower stems; shade from meridian sun; water in dry weather; put sticks to, and tie stalks; sow. Dahlias, plant out, e. Dress the borders, &c., almost daily. Flowering Plants require staking, &c. Fuchsia, may be planted. Grass, mow and roll weekly. Gravel, roll, weekly. Hoeing cannot be too frequent. Hyacinths, take up and store as leaves decay. Mignonette, sow for succession, b. Perennials, sow, b.; propagate by slips and cuttings. Polyanthuses, part, shade, and throughout the summer; sunshine destroys them; sow seed of. Roses, watch for insect on, and destroy them; roses in groups keep them low; roses in pots may be planted out. Stake and tie up plants; seedlings thin. Tulips, remove seed-pods; take up and store as leaves decay; water frequently in dry weather. Wallflowers, sow, to bloom next year. Water-glass bulbs plant in borders as flowers decay. Watering, attend to in dry weather, especially to plants newly removed. At the commencement of this month, during showery weather, plant cuttings of *Double Wallflowers*, and *Pansies*; and divide the roots of *Neapolitan* and *Russian Violets*, transplanting in preparation for potting to flower in winter. *Half-hardy plants* may now be brought from the greenhouse and their other winter shelters, and distributed in the borders. Mild moist weather is most suitable for this work. The more tender *climbing annuals*, such as *Tropæolum aduncum*, and *Convolvulus major*, should not be planted out until the end of the month. Put in slips of double White and Purple Rockets, under hand-glasses, or near a wall on the north side. Cuttings of China roses plant in a shady place.

D. Beaton.

ORCHARD.

Disbud, and commence training all Wall or Espalier Fruit Trees through the month. Stop luxuriant shoots, e. Grafted trees of former seasons, continue to remove useless shoots from. Grafted Trees of the present spring, if growing, remove clay and loosen the bandages slightly at the end of the month. Budded Trees of last year, remove useless shoots from. Swelling Fruit of Apricots, Peaches, and Nectarines, thin out, lightly at first. Coverings, remove, m. Gooseberries, watch the caterpillar, dust them (if infested) when the dew lies on them with the powder of hellebore, a decoction of the common foxglove is also said to destroy them. Bandages loosen, where fruit trees are tied to stakes. Black Currants, water heavily if dry, e., also mulch. Strawberries, water well towards the end; also clean thoroughly from weeds, and place straw or grass for the fruit at the end of the month. Plant Alpines, e. Vines, disbud, stop, &c., e. Figs, disbud, e. Raspberries, thin away weak suckers, e. Cherries, watch for the black fly, and use tobacco-juice. Plums Trained, treat same as cherries for the fly. Mulching, see that all needy or newly planted trees are well mulched, three inches thick, e. Watering, let all fresh planted or heavy bearing trees be well watered towards the end if dry. Blights, watch the development of insects on every species of fruit, and act according to the advice in The Cottage Gardener in back numbers: remember that little more than half-a-pound of shag tobacco to a gallon of water will destroy every species of aphides. Walks, renew or dress, using salt with care if weedy. Borders, clean and dress all borders. Mow or otherwise keep down gross herbage in the ordinary orchard.

R. Errington.

FORCING STOVES.

Air, admit freely during the day. Bark Beds, renew if not done in March. Figs, first crop ripening, require abundant light before that period; syringe to destroy red spider; give less water, and ventilate freely. Insects, destroy by tobacco fumes or water; as well by clear, soot, lime, or even soap-suds. Kitchen-Garden Vegetables, as Kidney-beans, &c., introduce for succession. Leaves, clean occasionally, either with the sponge or syringe. Liquid-Manure, apply, clear and weak, to fruiting vines and other plants requiring vigour; especially to those in pots. Mushroom House, keep air in moist, also make a succession bed, b.; woodlice destroy. Succession Peaches (see March), thin finally. Pines, continue to treat as in March; shade during bright sun, and use liquid manure; shift when necessary, e.; suckers remove and pot. Red Spider is now apt to prevail; put sulphur upon the fires to drive away. Steam, admit frequently into house. Syringe every plant that will bear the treatment, especially Kidney-beans, to prevent the red spider and the thrips. Vines, treat as last month; thin grapes, and pin up shoulders of the bunches; water when dry; remove superfluous shoots, e.; temp. from 70° to 85°, with sunshine, and from 65° to 70° at night; in the late greenhouses, train up the rafters, stop and disbud. Sprinkle frequently about the house, and keep the pans full.

Melons, train and stop; set the blossom and provide successions; secure atmospheric moisture to repel red spider. Cucumber, stop frequently; plant out, ridge, m. Capsicums and Tomatos, pot off and harden, b.

R. Errington.

PLANT STOVE.

Achimenes, repot such as have started into large pans to bloom in masses. Amaryllis aulica, pot, to bloom in winter. Aphelandra aurantiaca, pot, or plunge in bark-bed. Begonias, repot, and grow on freely, to flower in autumn and winter. Clerodendrums, pot—for the last time—into very large pots, to bloom strongly in July. Cuttings of various woody and soft-wooded plants put in under bell-glasses, in heat. Erythrina crista-galli repot for the last time, and remove into greenhouse, to flower there during the summer. Gardenia florida and varieties, and Gardenia radicans, done blooming, remove into cold pit; and late crops of them place in greenhouse as they come into bloom. Gardenia Stanleyana, and others similar, syringe freely, to keep them clear from red spider; repot when necessary. Gesneras, now coming into bloom, tie out; that is, open out the shoots with sticks and mats, to show off the flowers. Gesnera zebrina, pot now, to bloom late. Give Air freely as the warm weather comes on. Gloxinias, repot into large pots, to form large specimens; young plants continue to force on to bloom late. Ixoras, tie out, and shift into large pots; keep them plunged in bark pit. Insects, fumigate, to destroy green fly. Syringe freely, to keep down red spider. Sponge the leaves of such plants as are subject to this pest. In extreme cases wash the leaves with strong soap-water. Seeds, sow, of all kinds worth growing, in shallow pots, in close heat. Stove Climbers keep well tied in, and within bounds by pruning freely. Water, apply plentifully, both at the root and on the walls, floors, &c., to keep up a moist atmosphere.

T. Appleby.

FLORISTS' FLOWERS.

Auriculas, done blooming, place upon coal ashes, in a cool place behind a north wall. Save seed from best varieties. Prick out seedlings in shallow pans—keeping them under glass. Seed may yet be sown. Carnations and Picotees, place sticks to, shade from hot sun; prick out seedlings. Dahlias, plant out; placing pots over them at night for fear of frost; place stakes to. Hollyhocks, mulch with short littery dung; place stakes to them in good time. Pansies now in flower shade from sun; put in cuttings of under hand-glasses, in a shady place: layer the long shoots in the same manner as carnations. Pinks, place sticks to; put in pipings of. Polyanthuses, treat exactly the same as auriculas. Ranunculuses, water freely between the rows in dry weather; stir the surface frequently. Roses, intended for exhibition in pots, shade from sun, water with manure water. Tie creeping roses frequently, but not too stiffly. Tulips still in flower shade deeply and effectually from sun. Take up early blooming bulbs and dry in the shade. Verbenas, plant out in beds.

T. Appleby.

KITCHEN GARDEN.

Angelica, sow. Artichokes, plant, b.; clean beds. Asparagus, keep clean; apply liquid manure. Balm, plant. Basil, plant out. Beans, sow, hoe, top. Beet (Red), thin; (White and Green), sow. Borage, sow. Borecole, sow, b.; prick out; plant out; hoe; leave for seed. Brocoli, sow, b.; plant; prick out. Burnets, sow and plant. Cabbages, sow; plant; earth up. Capsicum, plant out. Carrots, sow; thin. Cardoons, sow, b. Cauliflowers, take glasses from; sow, e. Celery, sow, b.; prick out; plant out; water; leave for seed. Chamomile, plant. Chervil, sow; leave for seed. Chives, plant. Coriander, sow; leave for seed. Cress (American), sow; (Water), plant. Crops, failed, replace forthwith. Cucumbers, prick out; plant out; attend to forcing. Dill, sow and plant. Dung, for hotbeds, prepare. Earthing-up, attend to. Endive, sow, e.; leave for seed. Fennel, sow and plant. Hotbeds, attend to; linings, &c. Hyssop, sow and plant. Kale (Sea), attend to blanching, &c. Kidney Beans (dwarfs), sow, b.; transplant from hotbeds, protecting them at night for a few weeks; (runners), sow. Lavender, plant. Leeks, sow; thin; leave for seed. Lettuces, sow; plant out; tie up. Marigolds, sow. Marjorams, sow and plant. Melons, sow, b.; prick out; ridge out; attend to forcing; thin laterals. Mint, plant. Mushroom Beds, make, b.; attend to those producing. Mustard and Cress, sow; leave for seed. Nasturtiums, sow, b. Onions, weed, &c.; sow for planting again in spring; (Welsh), leave for seed. Parsley, sow; leave for seed; (Hamburgh), thin. Parsnips, thin, &c. Peas, sow; top those blooming. Pennyroyal, plant. Pompions, sow, b.; ridge out, b. Potatoes, hoe. Purslane, sow; leave for seed. Radishes, sow; leave for seed. Rape, for salading, sow; (Edible rooted), sow, e. Rosemary, plant. Rue, plant. Sage, plant. Salsafy, thin, &c. Savory, sow and plant. Savoys, sow, b.; plant; prick out. Scorzonera, thin, &c. Sorrels, sow and plant. Spinach, sow; thin; leave for seed. Tansy and Tarragon, plant. Thyme, sow and plant. Tomatos, plant out. Turnips, sow; thin; leave for seed. Turnip Cabbage, sow. Watering, attend to, in dry weather. Weeds, destroy, as they appear.

London: Printed by Harry Wooldridge, Winchester High Street, in the Parish of Saint Mary Kalendar, and Published by William Somerville Orr, at the Office, No. 2, Amen Corner, in the Parish of Christ Church, City of London.—April 25th, 1850.

WEEKLY CALENDAR.

M D	W D	MAY 2–8, 1850.	Weather near London in 1849.		Sun Rises.	Sun Sets.	Moon R. & S.	Moon's Age.	Clock bef. Sun.	Day of Year.
2	Tu	Young Rooks fledged.	T. 68°—48°.	N.E. Rain.	38 a. 4	21 a. 7	0 15	20	3 10	122
3	F	Invention of the Cross. Yellow Wagtail arrives.	T. 74°—94°.	E. Rain.	30	23	0 56	21	3 17	123
4	S	Pettichaps heard. [seen.	T. 77°—47°.	E. Fine.	29	25	1 33	☾	3 24	124
5	Sun	5th or Rogation Sun. Latticed Heath Moth	T. 76°—45°.	N.E. Rain.	27	26	2 4	23	3 29	125
6	M	John Evan. s P. Lat. Greenfinch builds.	T. 62°—42°.	N.E. Fine.	25	28	2 30	24	3 35	126
7	Tu	Long-eared Bat seen.	T. 55°—36°.	N.E. Rain.	23	30	2 55	25	3 39	127
8	W	Easter Term ends. Turtle Dove heard.	T. 55°—39°.	N.E. Fine.	22	31	3 18	26	3 43	128

Scotland claims as her sons a large majority of the most celebrated horticulturists of modern days; and so marked is this, that we have heard as a humourous national toast, "The three exports of Scotland—gardeners, doctors, and black cattle." Now, one of the most known of the first of these valued exports is John Abercrombie, who died on the 2nd of this month, in 1806, at the good old age of fourscore. He may be said to have been doomed to gardening from his birth; for his father was a market gardener near Edinburgh, and from infancy he was employed in his father's garden. It was a pursuit in which he delighted; and to improve and to impart its successful practice to others engrossed his attention throughout his long career. His education was plain and slight, but it was bestowed upon a mental soil possessing the two best of qualities—a powerful memory, and sound sense. These enabled him to carry into effect one of the most useful practices that a young gardener can resolutely adopt—he wrote down each night such observations relative to gardening as he had made during the day. The treasures of useful knowledge which may be thus accumulated would surpass the belief of a cursory observer; and at the end of even ten years a fact jotted down per day would occupy a goodly volume of "three thousand facts." When Abercrombie became an author on horticultural subjects, he found the high value of his note-books; and though Weston has some grounds for saying that "the titles of many of his works are so copious and confused, that you can scarcely discover what you are to have, and they are like a piece of the same sort of meat dressed various ways," yet the meat is always

good. Let it be remembered, too, that the mass of practical information his works contain was obtained from actual personal experience; and with all its want of conciseness and deficient arrangement, yet a more original book than his "Every Man his own Gardener," first published in 1774, never issued from the press. Yet so lowly was his self-estimation, that he actually paid Mr. Mawe, then gardener to the Duke of Leeds, twenty pounds to allow his name to be attached to this publication. Success giving him confidence, he published various other works with his own name prefixed; and one of these, The Gardener's Pocket Journal, until lately passed through an edition of two thousand almost annually, from the date of its first appearance in 1791. It is needless to follow him through his various employments and vicissitudes, from his first employment in Kew Gardens down to his becoming a seedsman and nurseryman at Newington and Tottenham, where he died from an accident at the date we have specified. For the last twenty years of his life his principal refreshment was tea, taking it three times a day, and rarely eating fleshmeat. He was one of the earliest of "vegetarians," and frequently declared that tea and tobacco were the great promoters of his health. His use of tobacco was his only excess, and in this he was immoderate. His pipe—his first companion in the morning, and the last at night—has been known often to be in use for six hours without interruption. He never remembered taking physic until after the occurrence of the accident which caused his death, nor of having a day's illness before that which was his last, except once about twenty-three years previously.

Meteorology of the Week:—At Chiswick, during the last twenty-three years, the average highest and lowest temperatures have been 63.4° and 42° respectively. The greatest heat occurred on the 4th in 1833, when the thermometer rose to 81°; and the greatest cold was on the 5th in 1845, when it fell to 27°. There were 96 fine days during the period, and on 63 days rain fell.

Natural Phenomena Indicative of Weather.—When the Pimpernel, Wincopipe, or Poorman's Weather-glass (Anagallis arvensis), has its pretty little red flowers fully expanded in the morning, it indicates a fine day; and, on the contrary, if they are closed, rain will soon follow. Quarries of stone and slate, says Dr. Forster, foreshew rain by a moist exudation from the stones, or rather by a deposition of moisture upon them from the air. This seems analogous to the dampness on flagstones and stone steps just before rain, and during damp weather.

RANGE OF BAROMETER—RAIN IN INCHES.

May	1841.	1842.	1843.	1844.	1845.	1846.	1847.	1848.	1849.
2	B. { 29.674 / 29.540	30.022 / 29.062	30.104 / 30.004	30.432 / 30.335	29.957 / 29.921	30.208 / 30.195	29.743 / 29.577	30.077 / 30.066	29.936 / 29.854
	R. 0.25	—	—	—	—	—	0.03	—	0.60
3	B. { 29.766 / 29.715	29.967 / 29.854	29.891 / 29.778	30.013 / 30.138	29.980 / 29.878	30.063 / 29.932	29.898 / 29.788	30.101 / 30.074	29.816 / 29.797
	R. 0.30	0.02	0.06	—	0.01	—	0.15	—	0.01
4	B. { 29.569 / 29.480	29.907 / 29.892	29.766 / 29.508	30.132 / 30.090	29.895 / 29.791	29.856 / 99.791	29.868 / 29.858	30.165 / 30.133	29.849 / 29.829
	R. 0.70	—	0.16	0.61	—	—	0.02	—	—
5	B. { 29.571 / 29.399	29.885 / 29.530	29.676 / 29.552	30.050 / 29.913	29.885 / 29.822	29.724 / 29.544	29.769 / 29.721	30.166 / 30.159	29.618 / 29.781
	R. 6.16	0.16	1.20	—	0.03	0.03	—	—	0.04
6	B. { 29.774 / 29.496	29.422 / 29.376	29.623 / 29.343	29.867 / 29.791	29.986 / 29.061	29.546 / 29.404	29.744 / 29.710	30.089 / 29.922	29.643 / 29.813
	R. 0.02	0.12	0.32	—	0.18	0.13	—	—	—
7	B. { 29.706 / 29.528	29.388 / 29.197	29.538 / 29.501	29.868 / 29.792	29.649 / 29.589	29.740 / 29.565	29.663 / 29.569	30.045 / 29.993	29.968 / 29.889
	R. 0.16	1.22	0.06	—	0.30	—	—	—	0.02
8	B. { 29.561 / 29.491	29.796 / 29.392	29.572 / 29.551	29.947 / 29.944	29.457 / 29.430	29.931 / 29.730	29.611 / 29.334	30.112 / 30.096	30.016 / 29.994
	R. 0.16	0.20	0.57	—	0.01	—	0.15	—	—

Little has to be told of the history of The Polyanthus, the florist's flower on the characteristics of excellence in which we are about to offer a few comments. It is only a variety, but a very permanent one, of the Common Primrose (Primula vulgaris), and was so considered by our earliest writers on Gardening. Hence it is always difficult, and often impossible, to discern the varieties, if any, of which they had knowledge. Thus Parkinson's Paradisus, published in 1629, describes twenty-one kinds of Primroses and Cowslips, some of which are Polyanthuses; and from that time to the present we may say, as Abercrombie said in 1778, "the Polyanthus is one of the noted prize flowers among florists, many of whom are remarkably industrious in raising a considerable variety of different sorts."

Even in Abercrombie's days it was considered that,

" a Polyanthus must possess several particular properties to have admittance in their choice collections;" and we shall detail the "properties" that were then considered characters of excellence, because they are evidence that later authorities have done little more than particularize more precisely what our gardening ancestors had previously adjudged to be marks of merit:—" 1. The stem, or flower-stalk, shall be upright, moderately tall, with strength in proportion, and crowned by a good, regular bunch of flowers, on short pedicles (stalks), strong enough to support them nearly in an upright position 2. The florets (pips) of each bunch should be equally large, spread open flat, with the colours exquisite, and the stripes and variegations lively and regular. 3. The eye in the centre of each floret should be large, regular, and bright; and the anthers (by the florists called the thrum) should rise high enough to cover the mouth of the tube, or hollow part in the middle of the floret, and render it what is called *thrum-eyed.* But when the style elevates the stigma above the anthers, the eye of the tube generally appears hollow, shewing the stigma in the middle, like the head of a pin, the floret is hence called *pin-eyed,* and is rejected as an incomplete flower, although its other properties be perfect."

Maddock and others subsequently wrote upon these characters of excellence, and the results of their combined judgments, corrected by his own good taste, have been arranged as follows by Mr. Glenny:—

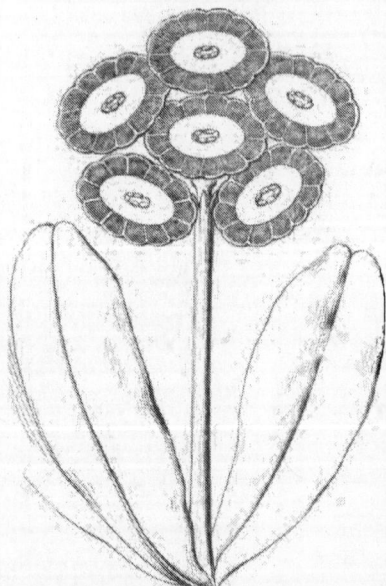

THE PIP.—1. This should be perfectly flat and round, slightly scolloped on the edge, and three-quarters of an inch diameter.

2. It should be divided in (five or) six places, apparently forming (five or) six flower-leaves, each indented in the centre to make it a kind of heart-shaped end; but the indentations must not reach the yellow eye.

3. The *indenture* in the centre of the apparent flower-leaves, should be exactly the same depth as the indenture formed by the join of these flower-leaves, so that it should not be known, by the form of the flower, which is the actual division and which is the indenture; in other words, which is the side and which the centre of the flower-leaf; and all the indentures should be as slight as possible to preserve the character.

4. The flower should be divided thus—the *yellow tube* in the centre being measured, the *yellow eye,* round the tube, should be the same width as its diameter; and the *ground colour* of the flower should be the same width: or draw with the compasses, opened to a sixteenth of an inch apart, a circle for the tube or centre; open them to three sixteenths,

and draw another circle for the eye, then open them further to five sixteenths, and draw a third circle for the ground or dark colour.* Beyond these circles there is a *yellow lacing* which should reach round every flower-leaf to the yellow eye, and down the centre of every petal to the eye, and so much like the edging that the flower should appear to have (ten or) twelve similar petals. The ends of these (ten or) twelve should be blunted, and rounded like so many semicircles, so that the outline of the circle should be interrupted as little as possible.†

5. The *tube* (one-fifth the width of the whole flower) should be nearly filled up with the six anthers, which are technically called the thrum, (have an elevated edge rendering it *trumpet-eyed*), and the flower should not exhibit the pistil.‡

6. The *edging* round and down the centre of the petals, formed by the divisions, should be of even width all the way, and uniformly of the same shade of sulphur, lemon, or yellow as the eye, and there must not be two shades of yellow in the eye.

7. The *ground colour* should be just what anybody likes best, but clear, well defined, perfectly smooth at the edge inside next the eye, to form a circle; and outside, next the lacing: a black or a crimson ground, being scarce, is desirable; but the quality of the colour as to clearness, rather than the colour itself, constitutes the property.

THE PLANT.—1. The *stem* should be strong, straight, elastic, and from four to six inches in length.

2. The *footstalks* of the flowers should be of such length as to bring all the flowers well together.

3. The *truss* should (rise from the centre of the foliage) comprise seven or more flowers, and be neatly arranged to be seen all at once.§

4. The *foliage* should be (dark green) short, broad, thick, and cover the pot well (but erect and clustering round, though lower than the truss).

THE PAIR, OR COLLECTION.—*The pair,* or pan of more, should comprise flowers of different and distinct colours, either the ground colour or the yellow of each being sufficiently different from the rest to be well distinguished.

The whole should be so near of a height as to range the heads of bloom well together.

The great fault of the polyanthus now, even among the best sorts, is that the divisions between the petals are so wide as to make the flower look starry, whereas there should be no more gap where the division is than is in the indentation of the petal itself.—*Glenny's Properties of Flowers.*

WE have received the following from Mr. Payne, and recommend his *Bee-keeper's Dress* to the attention of our readers, who ought to be as much obliged to him as we are for his gratuitous and kind attention to their wants.

"I have a similar account of a swarm of bees now before me, on the 7th of April, in the *Hertford Mercury,* probably the same as that mentioned by your correspondent. When bees swarm at this time, and earlier in the season, they are driven out of their hive either by famine, damp, mice, or something of the kind, but more frequently the former; and if the hive from which they came be examined, it will be found to be totally forsaken,—not a bee will be left in it.

I think that I have already sent away three dozen of hives since the publication of the last number of THE COTTAGE GARDENER, and have several now on order. I must, I suppose, hire a warehouse, and engage a clerk! I have, however, much pleasure in doing it. I only regret that I did not at the same time offer to send the *bee dress* that I mentioned in my last calendar with the hives, to those who wish to have it; for no apiarian should be without it; it is so exceedingly pleasant to the wearer, and answers the purpose of defence most effectually. I have induced a person here to procure a

---

* This measure is for a flower only five-eighths of an inch diameter, but it is the easiest to explain the proportions.
† All the passages in parentheses are our own additions. We greatly prefer an apparently *ten-*petaled polyanthus, for where there are twelve indentures the edge looks too much crimped.—[ED. C. G.]
‡ Some polyanthuses shew the pistil only, and are called pin-eyed; these are considered worthless.
§ We prefer them to be slightly convex.—[ED. C. G.]

quantity of the proper material, and to make them up, for which 3s is charged; and I find they will go free by post for another shilling."

Any person requiring a dress must write to J. H. Payne, Esq., Bury St. Edmunds.

THE FRUIT-GARDEN.

NEWLY PLANTED FRUIT-TREES.—We again advert to the propriety of paying much attention to such at this period, for by so doing a whole twelvemonth, as to the size of the tree, may be gained; and the importance of this, especially as to trees on walls or trellises, need scarcely be urged. In the first place, the waterpot must be put in requisition if dry weather ensue, especially if the trees have not been mulched. If the latter is the case, much slighter waterings will suffice, for the evaporation proceeds very slowly from soils mulched over. Many trees have been injured by overwatering in the latter case; and such, we imagine, is the reason why some persons are against the use of mulch. It must be confessed, that this process impedes, in some degree, the reception of the increasing warmth of the atmosphere, and so far may be considered a slight evil. This, however, we consider amply compensated for by the defence it constitutes against sudden droughts, which surely it requires no pains to prove, are exceedingly injurious to fresh planted trees; the roots of which, being in a weak or somewhat torpid condition, are ill calculated to bear farther check, and, indeed, need every appliance which can be furnished.

We should consider it good practice for those who have but a few trees to manage, and have plenty of time on their hands, to remove mulchings for a few days in the end of April or beginning of May, in order to suffer the soil about the roots to receive warmth from the atmosphere. This it would do in a week; and the mulch, which had been merely turned aside, could be restored to its former position. In all cases of watering such trees during the spring months, we advise that it be applied during sunshine, and, indeed, when the mulch has become warmed. This will carry a little warmth to the roots, instead of starving them, which very cold water would be sure to do. However, warmed water may be used, and this would be by far the best practice; in which case it should be from 70° to 80°. By the time this became filtered through the soil, it would be robbed of some 8° or 10° of its heat.

CARE OF THE FOLIAGE.—If this is important with established trees, how much more so with newly-planted ones. The utmost care should be taken to extirpate caterpillars, and indeed all insects, before they commit their depredations. If the aphides attack them, tobacco water or fumigation should be had recourse to; the latter process may be easily performed, by tacking a sheet or other covering before them. The sulphur paint should, by all means, be applied, especially to peaches, nectarines, and pears; for the latter often suffer much from the red spider. Syringing occasionally, provided the weather is warm, is of some benefit, as tending to a free and liberal development of the foliage; cleansing also from impurities.

DISBUDDING. — Newly-planted trees seldom require much assistance in this way, yet some little may become necessary. What are termed "maiden" trees are apt to produce a confused mass of shoots, especially strong young peach-trees; and it becomes sometimes necessary to remove ill-placed shoots. The better plan, as a general practice, is to merely pinch out the point of those supposed to be useless when they are about three inches in length; by these means the effect is not so stagnating as the root action; and, moreover, it is impossible to say, at an early period of the summer, what accidents may occur to the other shoots. The stumps or base of such shoots may be reserved at the winter's pruning, for in budding at the ensuing spring they will afford multiplied chances of making a selection, and carrying out the desired form or mode of training.

TRAINING.—Our favourite maxim with young trees of any kind intended for fan training, is to train a pair of shoots on each side, right and left, the first season, carrying one perpendicularly; and on this latter shoot we mainly depend for ultimately completing the fabric of the tree. Now this will, doubtless, appear unsound doctrine to some old practitioners; such a shoot they will be ready to imagine would lord it too much over its weaker neighbour. And so it would, but for some finger and thumb work.

This sort of handling was too little known in former days; winter pruning, done according to cut and dry prescriptions, reigned supreme; and the patience evinced by our old knights of the pruning knife, was not excelled by the labours of the mythological Sisyphus.

Let all amateurs, therefore, bear in mind that the central leader, or indeed any other portion of a tree, may be kept in the utmost subjection by summer stopping, through so simple a machine as the finger and thumb. We have grown peach-trees, years ago, in which a central shoot, and one of the most luxuriant, was left intentionally to prove the immense power of "stopping;" and by following up the process annually, for several years, the shoot remained alive, but was soon left behind by the very weakest shoots at the lowest portions of the branches.

This was an experiment only, but perfectly illustrative of the power of finger and thumb stopping, during the spring and summer, over that of the pruning knife during the winter season. This central shoot then, if healthy, may be kept as a reserve, or in order to multiply branches at pleasure; when such are needed, the centre may produce them unmolested; when the reverse, the stopping may occasionally be had recourse to. This principle may be applied to most of our fruits in a young state; and with it we see no reason to adopt any other mode of training, on the score of *real utility*, than the fan mode.

By the time this reaches the readers of THE COTTAGE GARDENER, it will be time to fasten newly-planted trees to the wall or trellis; for it will be remembered that such were recommended to be left rather loose for a few weeks, or until the soil settled. The bands or fastenings, nevertheless, should still have ample liberty, for the soil will still settle, and the tree must be permitted to settle too, or rifts may take place in the soil, together with derangement of the young fibres.

The young shoots from "maiden" plants need not be trained to form the lower portion of the tree the first year, but a half-way position between the horizontal or ground line and the central leader, or at an angle of from forty to fifty degrees. Thus, the central shoot, and the side ones requiring a separate course of treatment, will be somewhat apart; and the eye of the most unpractised, if they will observe what we have here said on the subject, will see at a glimpse how affairs stand.

What are termed "trained" trees, however, require a different course. Here sufficient shoots, or nearly so, exist to form the tree; and such must at once be trained precisely in the position intended as permanent; still, however, reserving a good central shoot, as in the case of the maiden trees, which shoot must, of course, be pruned back, in order to produce side-shoots. We may shortly offer seasonable advice as to trained espaliers; for what has here been observed has reference chiefly to wall-trees; although the principles of management are identical, the difference in application being in the main controlled or biassed by the form ultimately required.

We here repeat our advice about cleanliness. Insects must not be permitted to infest valuable fruit-trees, especially young ones.   R. ERRINGTON.

THE FLOWER-GARDEN.

BEDDING PLANTS.—I have said that purple and pink plants ought not to be planted near to each other; and the chief reason for that advice is the difficulty of meeting with many plants that are of the true colour, so that we are obliged to take the nearest shades to those we desire to represent them; and if the beds of purple and pink are neighbours, these shades will often neutralise each other, or come so near to the same colour as to confound the two, so that one can hardly tell where the purple ends or the pink begins—but both of them should always be represented in a good flower-garden where colours are arranged; as, notwithstanding the number of plants we possess, we can only make out five distinct colours after white in a good summer flower-garden, which is required to keep in bloom till the appearance of frost—pink, blue, scarlet, yellow, and purple—and if we confound the first and last of these, we are reduced to four colours. We have a dozen or more of shades (of which I shall write), but it is most difficult to get them into their proper places, owing to the manner in which the great bulk of our best flower-gardens are laid out; and then when you find a place for the right shade, the plants may be either too high or too low for those next to them; and without arranging the heights as well as the colours of plants, it is much better not to attempt this kind of arrangement at all. But let me not have all the *say* to myself, rather let me have the assistance of all our readers who have had some practice in planting according to heights and colours; and the simplest mode of testing our proficiency will be, perhaps, to suppose that we have a border to plant alongside of a walk; no matter how long this border may be, but let us say that it is ten or twelve feet wide, with a box edging between it and the walk, and that it is nearly level, or at any rate not more than six inches higher at the back. Now, let us say that we have six distinct colours in flowers, thus including the white, and even let us say lilac, if suitable plants can be found to produce it, when we shall have seven colours. I want to plant this border according to heights and colours with summer flower-garden plants, which will last in bloom from the turn of midsummer till the end of September, or, if the frost holds off, till the middle of October. My present arrangement does not include spring flowers, or those which only bloom from five to six weeks. The lowest plant must be planted alongside the walk, and one kind of plant is allowable for the whole row; the second row must not rise more than a few inches higher than the first, and its colour must harmonise with that of the first and third row; the third row may rise ten inches higher than the second row; and the fourth, fifth, and sixth rows may rise in like proportions, or a little more; but no one row is to be more than twelve inches higher than that in front of it, but every successive row must rise a little above the one before it; so that when the whole are in bloom we may have a sloping bank of flowers in a harmonious whole, every row being of one kind of plant, and, consequently, showing but one of the distinct colours. All I want is the name of the plant for each row, and the space of ground necessary to allow it to come to full perfection; the border being just twelve feet wide; and, to simplify the problem, I left out the violet colour, because I know we have no plant of that colour to suit this style of planting; so that out of the hundreds of plants yearly used in our flower-gardens I only want six kinds, and each to be of a distinct colour. I shall expect to receive these lists before the

end of May; and I strongly advise the exercise to young gardeners; but I shall be much deceived unless the best of them come from ladies in the country who have had some practice of ordering the arrangement of their own gardens. No one need sign his or her name to these "returns" unless they choose; and the whole must be first sent to the editor. I shall then comment on the suitableness or otherwise of each list, and surely we must all of us learn something from them. I am aware the thing is much more difficult than those who never tried the plan may suppose; but when done properly, there is no other way of planting a border so effectual to show the beauty of harmonising flowers; and it also involves the principle of planting any number of beds collected together into any regular figure, according to the highest style of flower-gardening. In short, it is the rudiment of the art.

Any one having but one flower-bed may represent this style of planting in it, provided the bed is a circle, and is large enough to contain six circular rows of plants in it, by placing the plant in our back row in the centre of the bed, and working down our other rows in circles to the edge of the bed. Again, the colours in the rows may be represented in different beds congregated together in a regular figure; and here is where the value of the different heights will be most apparent; for if one plants a bed of a tall blue plant, as Lupinus Hartwegii, and plants the next bed to it with Sanvitalia procumbens, a yellow of the lowest growth, although he may admire each bed by itself, the disproportionate size of the plants in the two beds will more than mar the effect; the two side by side would look ridiculous. The only way where a very low plant will associate with a tall one is, when a rich edging of one colour is placed outside a large mass of tall plants; and even here some kind of proportion ought to be preserved, by giving the edging plant a proportionate breadth according to the height of the tall mass; for to make all edgings of the same width, without reference to the size of those plants within the edging, would be a palpable blemish, if not absurdity.

One more request, and I have done with this border. I shall require from young gardeners, if they use plants generally raised from seeds for any of the rows, at what time would they sow the seeds so as that the plants would be in bloom—say by the first of July? and if they use trailing plants, as petunias, how do they propose to confine them to a single row without scrambling amongst the rows on each side of them? Of course, where one row of the desired height and colour would be too thin, owing to the upright habit of the plant, I shall allow two or even three contiguous rows of the same plant to be put in to make up a sufficient breadth of that colour: but you must state in inches the breadth you propose for each colour out of the twelve feet. I anticipate at least more than a hundred of such lists; and if I get *six different ones* out of that number, which will be in every respect suitable for the display I want, I shall be satisfied.

YELLOW FLOWERING PLANTS.—I have said so much about these last autumn, that I need hardly add more than the names of most of them, and that on the score that a good tale is not the worse for being twice told. *Tagetes tenuifolia* is the best habited plant for a bed of all we make use of, after the pink *Saponaria calabrica* and the yellow *Sanvitalia procumbens*; from eighteen to two feet, according to the soil, is the height of it, and it may be sown at once in the open ground; but, as it will transplant easily until it comes into bloom, the best way is to sow it in the reserve garden, and plant it out early in June when the May or spring annuals are over. The Sanvitalia, ten inches high, will also come in the open ground, and will transplant. Then come the yellow *Calceolarias*, and there are six good sorts of these, at least: Integrifolia, Rugosa, Rayii, Viscosissima, Corymbosa, and Amplexicaule; there are two good kinds of reddish yellow shrubby Calceolarias that would mix with Corymbosa and Viscosissima (say every fifth plant to be of these reddish brown ones), and I think they add to the richness of the bed without interfering with the colour of the mass—but that may be a matter of taste. The Kentish Hero will not come in, as a colour or as a shade; it is too brown, but it makes a splendid bed nevertheless. The *Orange African Marigold* makes a fine mass in a large garden, but is not suitable for small ones. The double clear *Yellow French Marigold* is very rich for a bed, and when kept over the winter from August struck cuttings, and planted in a soil not too rich, it has nothing of that coarseness about it which characterises seedlings. The same treatment as that given to verbenas will suit it during the winter, and it requires about the same attention as the American groundsel, for it is ticklish about damp. I believe I said that another gardener and I kept it in succession for eleven years by cuttings, and at first we had many mishaps with it, and always in the spring. The fact is, we used to begin it too early in the spring. The first of April is quite time enough to put it into heat to get a growth for cuttings, which strike like a weed. *Cereopsis lanceolata* divided in April like the little Campanulas, and once trained down to the ground in June, makes a fine mass for a large garden. The rest of the yellows will be noticed under "spring beds."　　D. BEATON.

GREENHOUSE AND WINDOW GARDENING.

BALCONIES.—How pleasant the ideas which the very word awakens! We scarcely think of a balcony, but there appear before our mind's eye fair and graceful forms, flitting among flowers, that are only less striking and lovely. If *ever* we can find an apology for a rational biped sublimating himself in the regions of *cigardom*, it is when, after the toils of the day, he whiffs the *weed* as he paces the balcony of his suburban retreat, ever and anon emitting a cloud over the Green-fly from his *own* fumigating apparatus, or uttering an exclamation of pleased satisfaction as the companion of his joys waters and tends the flowers, attractive by their beauty, and delightful from their perfume. A balcony without flowers in summer seems ever to speak of miserly, contracted, shrivelled bachelorism, bearing no impress whatever of the presence of those gentle, but powerfully influential beings between whom and the flowers of vegetation there is an attraction more binding than any mesmeric action. No wonder though some should inquire, "What are the best flowers to buy to adorn balconies at this season of the year?" though the locality of the inquirer, the present or future display of the flowers, and the object aimed at, as to the possession of floral beauty or floral rariety, should have been added to this otherwise concise inquiry, to enable us to make an appropriate answer. When the inquiry was made in April, some nice evergreen plants, mingled with flowering-bulbs, Wall-flowers (single and double), Heartsease, Hepaticas, Alyssums, evergreen Candy Tufts, Arabis, the Flowering Currant, Violets, &c., would be some of the most desirable for present display. But if a fine show of flowers during the remainder of the summer is the object of the purchaser, then he could not do better than obtain the necessary number of the common bedding-out plants as adverted to by our friend Mr. Beaton, such as Scarlet Geraniums, Fuchsias, Calceolarias, Salvias, Ageratums, Helitropes, Anagallis, Mignonette, Penstemons, Verbenas, Stocks, &c.

For producing a splendid effect, more will depend upon the skill and attention of the cultivator than upon the money spent in securing the plants. In a small balcony, "the bump of order" may be as strikingly developed as in a larger flower-garden; the principles of *adaptation* and *fitness* strike the mind, even of a common beholder, more forcibly than the mere assemblage of great masses. He may not be able to tell you *how* it is—but of the fact he is certain. I have seen an unlettered labourer jump with something like ecstacy at a combination of colour, all existing in the compass of a few feet; almost choking himself for words to express his delight, and yet quite calmly surveying, what I then thought a more perfect, because a somewhat more fashionable combination and contrast of colour. Men often acquire by something like intuition what they may lack the ability to demonstrate by reasoning. Harry More may never have thought there was anything wonderful in his treatment of the Scarlet Geranium; though when that treatment was unfolded in the words of a Beaton, tho way was made clear for that splendid plant flourishing in many a window, and decking many a humble balcony, where formerly it was a stranger. The ecstacy of the labourer taught me, that fine taste could be developed, and at once recognised, in the compass of a few feet as well, if not better, than in a few acres. Of course we are alluding merely to flowering-plants. Recognise and accept this idea, and there will be the cheerful working to make as much as possible of the little spot at home, instead of feeling a spice of envy because you cannot concentrate in that little spot the domains of a richer neighbour.

There is every room for improvement. Balconies in general when filled with plants, are a higgledy-piggledy affair. There the plants are in red clay pots, or huge green boxes, and stuffed, if growing freely, as if the less air and light they had the better. If plants are at all flourishing, their leaves will be the most cheerful green. But it matters not, whether in town or country, and whatever the colour of the house—stone, or red brick— the balcony in the majority of cases must be green. Why the colour should be different from the mansion, it always surpassed my comprehension to determine; unless it was for the purpose of telling every passer-by that the balcony was a mere accidental *after-thought* affair. As to the huge boxes, lengthy if narrow, we should prefer them to be of a dull stone colour, rather than fashionable green—that is to say, if we must have such things at all. Our readers who would aspire to please themselves, and delight their friends, by an exhibition of superior taste, would discard the whole paraphernalia of red pots, red gawky-looking saucers, and the sort of go-between—the bog-and-chicken-feeding trough-like boxes.

Bad as such contrivances are in a balcony, they become much worse when they are set upon the ground level, close to the walls of the mansion in the country. The gardeners, however, are much more to blame for this than amateurs. For years the string was harped upon, that a plant to be *healthy* must be grown in a porous, soft red burnt pot. A short time ago, we directed attention to the fallacy of the idea as a general principle; and some years since we mentioned, that the common plants, such as those grown in balconies, would do well enough even in iron, at least for one season, if *drainage* is properly attended to. For effect, therefore, a few raised or ornamental boxes, or baskets, or vases, would shame all such red pots or green boxes out of the field. Where there is the convenience, it is frequently desirable to have the main plants for the centre of such vases grown in pots and plunged in the soil or moss, with small plants to turn out around them. Where that does not exist, means should be taken to plant out those that will blow during the season. The advantage of the first system is, that whenever a plant gets a little shabby you can change it for another coming to its best. When this method is followed, it is necessary that the pot in which the plant is grown should be several inches less in diameter than that of the vase or basket; as then earth is not only introduced below the pot, but around its side; and into that part little trailers are planted to hang over the sides—generally of a colour contrasting with the main mass in the centre. The same system is adopted with pots or baskets intended to remain for the season. Contrasted with the old pot and box system, the advantages are chiefly these: the plants and their containing vessels present a more astistic appearance; the flowers are placed on nearly a level with the eye, or a little above, or a little below, where they can be more thoroughly and easily examined; and many little trailers just appear in their element and most striking beauty when thus festooning the sides of the vase or basket. How beautiful, for instance, is a mass of *scarlet geraniums* thus edged with the *White verbena*; and how more beautiful still, to see the lower scarlet flowers of the geranium blended with the blue *Lobelia speciosa* and *Grandiflora*, or the pretty *Anagallis Phillipsii*, while they garland the sides of the box or vase with their dense mass of flowers almost to the ground—presenting a power of rich colour which never can be obtained, unless when the plants are allowed to fall in a pendent position. And then how pretty a vase of *yellow calceolarias*, with an edging of *purple Senecio* blended with hangers of purple *verbenas*, or an old lilac, named *Pulchella*, which answers well for this hanging, drooping position. Another, not to go farther—there is the *Salvia patens*, so rich in its azure blue, which we had full in flower, and in the same vase from May to October, by merely giving the plant top-dressing, and manure watering. How nice it looks with *dependers* of the *Eschscholtzia*, or the *Tropœolum Canariense*; or for a change, the fine large red *Anagallis*.

"O, but"—says a friend—" it is all very well to speak of these raised boxes, and vases, but how are we humble folk to get them ?" We reply, that a neat ornamental wood box may be made out of the same wood, and at a no great degree of expense more, than is now necessary for the long green boxes—for they may surely be painted a stone colour, at least as cheaply as being daubed green; and not only may they thus be made of a stone colour, but so like the real article, that it will almost require examination to enable you to decide that they are not really stone. Thus—when *painted*, throw over as much as the paint will take on of dry silver sand, and when dry, it will have all the appearance of rough sandstone. The common pot may also be served in a similar manner; and though composition vases are still dear, there is no reason why the red ware common pot should not be made more artistic, which it will be, whenever there is a demand for a superior article; and then, when thus painted and sanded, they would answer the purpose, so far as gratifying the eye was concerned, as well as the more costly and valuable compositions. Even the common pot, when large, may be made somewhat elevated and artistic, by giving it a *plinth* of wood, painted and sanded, to rest upon. The plinth may be formed in the shape of a square box, with one side, that to go next the floor, open, and the upper side on which the pot stands with a circular hole to allow the drainage to pass, which may be received in a vessel placed in the plinth, and thus completely concealed. Some such temporary plinths have lasted with me many years. Pots so painted and sanded I have found to answer well for the generality of plants. R. FISH.

(To be resumed.)

HOTHOUSE DEPARTMENT.

EXOTIC ORCHIDACEÆ.

ROUTINE WORK FOR MAY.—The growing season for these plants has now arrived. They will require abundance of *moisture* both in the air of the house and at the root; a liberal supply must be given. Plants in baskets, such as *Stanhopeas, Gongoras, Aerides,* and *Saccolabiums*, should be taken down once a week and soaked in the cistern; the time they should be kept in the water will depend upon the state they are in. If very dry they will require half an hour to thoroughly wet them; if moderately moist in the centre a single dip, and out again directly, will be sufficient. Keep a good look-out for *woodlice*, and crush them as they rise to the surface.

As the sun will now be powerful, *the shades* must be let down whenever there is strong, clear sunshine; if this is neglected the leaves will turn yellow, the growths will be crippled, and the flowers will fade, besides, the moisture will sooner evaporate and the roots will lack support: all these evils may be prevented by a judicious use of shades.

Air and Heat.—The giving of air will depend upon the heat inside; refer to the table, and give air accordingly, always remembering to keep the night temperature lower than the day by six or eight degrees, or even more. Read attentively our remarks upon the mode of giving air. If the house is so ventilated that the air rushes into the house direct amongst the plants, hang up some gauze to break the current, so as to mollify it before it comes in contact with the plants. Continue to *pot* all plants that have not undergone that operation as they begin to grow. Several that were potted early in the year will be benefited by a top-dressing now; remove part of the old peat carefully, taking great care not to injure the young, growing roots, for they are very brittle, and as tender as young asparagus. In consequence of so much moisture the pots will begin to be covered with green scum; this is injurious to the health of the plants, and the pots must be washed frequently.

INSECTS: WOODLICE.—This tribe of insects is almost as destructive as the cockroach, but, happily, it is more easily come at and destroyed. In writing upon the destruction of that formidable enemy, mention was made of using sliced potatoes and turnips as good traps for woodlice and small shell-snails; we need only now remind our readers of those useful traps, and of the constant attention every morning to crushing any insects that may lodge under them. It will be necessary, also, to scrape off the skin that will form on the cut under side of each slice, or it will prevent the insects feeding upon them. Another excellent way of destroying these pests is that of sinking the pots and baskets up to the level in water; the woodlice will rise to the surface out of the compost to escape drowning, and then may be easily caught.

LARGE SHELL-SNAILS, and the common BLACK and GREY SNAILS, OT SLUGS.—When these obtain an entrance into the orchid house they are very destructive. About two years ago we had a very fine specimen of *Aerides odoratum major*, which one morning had the underside of two of its large leaves completely eaten away; search was made at night for cockroaches (they being blamed for the mischief done), but not one could be seen. The next morning two more leaves were eaten half through; the evil now became alarming, as the plant was, on account of its size, a valuable one, and we had had 25 guineas bid for it.' Again, at night, but an hour or two later, the search was renewed, and fortunately this time with success—an enormous shell-snail was discovered feeding very quietly, but voraciously, upon his dainty food; of course he paid the forfeit for his unwitting offences. There is no other way of catching these large enemies than looking out diligently for them at feeding time; the shelless snails may often be tracked to their retreats by the slime they leave behind on their track; but even these are best found if looked for by night with the aid of a lamp or candle.

WHITE SCALE.—This insect is also very injurious to orchids, by fixing itself firmly in one place, and by excluding the air and light, causing the part to decay. Where frequent washing with a small brush or sponge is neglected they increase at a fearful rate. The best means to destroy them that we know is to make a strong lather of soap, such as we use for shaving with; lay it on warm with a fine brush, working it into every crevice of the pseudo-bulbs and leaves of the infested plants; the soap adheres to the insects, stops up their breathing pores, and kills them.

BROWN SCALE.—Where this insect abounds it is almost, but not quite, as injurious as the white scale. If the plants are kept clean by frequent washing with a sponge, it will be a great preventive. Often smoking with tobacco is a good remedy, and the application of soap-lather as recommended above for the white scale.

MEALY BUG.—This is the most formidable of all our insect enemies to contend with. Where a house of any kind of plants has become very much infested with it, there is nothing in the shape of application will eradicate it entirely; in such a case, every plant must be diligently and carefully washed in every part; every pot must undergo the same purification; every particle of wood-work must be painted with at least two coats of paint; the walls whitewashed with hot lime. And whilst that is doing the cleaned plants must be placed in a warm pit, where some strongly-fermenting dung sends out its ammoniacal fumes, which help to destroy any insects that may have escaped the cleansing the plants have been subjected to. When the painting, whitewashing, and scouring, have been completed, let the house have abundance of air night and day for a week previously to replacing the plants in it. Perhaps some of our readers may say—Is all this necessary? Does this apparently insignificant insect do so much harm? We answer to both questions, most emphatically, Yes! We have seen in a house of grapes, the greatest part of the fruit rendered valueless by the mealy bug; the bunches glued together so as to be filthy and uneatable. The pine apple, too, we have seen so covered with this filthy insect as to be not fit for the table till it was scrubbed and washed as much as is required for a head of celery. We have seen plants so infested with it as to be all but killed, by having their leaves covered with its excrement. These are, it is true, but very rare cases; and the gardener who should so neglect his plants and fruits would now be justly disgraced and discharged; still, without diligent and severe methods of getting rid of these insects they would soon abound; though not, perhaps, to such an extreme extent as we have described above, yet so sufficiently so as to be very injurious to the plants, and not at all honourable to the cultivator. Therefore, whenever even a single mealy bug is discovered, let every plant be carefully looked over, and every insect destroyed. By this constant supervision, combined with using all the means we have described for the destruction of every kind of insect, the plants will be kept clean, and preserved from the destructive attacks of the host of insects that will, unless destroyed in time, prey upon them; thus injuring their health, preventing them flowering in perfection, and taking away all the pleasure that would otherwise delight the eye and gratify the mind of the owner.

We trust we have written enough about insects to prove to our readers that, though little taken individually, yet when by neglect they increase greatly in numbers, they are really formidable enemies to our favourite plants; consequently, we say, keep a strict look-out for, and constantly destroy, the intruders as they appear.

FLORISTS' FLOWERS.

The warm weather is bringing on all kinds of florists' flowers, as well as other products of the vegetable kingdom. The management necessary now will be to preserve flowers from fading, by using shades whenever the sun shines, and protecting plants from too much rain by canvas and glass covers. *Gentle showers* will be beneficial to all that are not actually in flower. Also to supply *stakes* to all flower-stems that need support, and keep the plants of all kinds clear of *weeds* and *insects*. In such showery weather as we have been favoured with lately, *snails* and *slugs* will be prowling about seeking for food; we have frequently found them underneath the pots of various plants, secreted in the holes of the pots: let such places be looked over, and the concealed enemy dislodged and destroyed.

Seeds of various florists' flowers may now be successfully sown in shallow pans or boxes, such, for instance, as *Auriculas, Polyanthuses, Carnations, Picotees, Pinks, Ranunculuses,* &c. Sow them in light, rich compost, and cover them thinly with finely sifted soil, placing them in a cold frame, and very slightly watering them; shade from sunshine, and give air in mild weather. By such treatment the seeds, if good, will soon come up, when more light may be allowed to them, till they become strong enough to prick out; that is, to transplant into similar pans or boxes, to acquire stronger growth. In this tender state of growth they are liable to great danger from *slugs* and *woodlice;* in a single night the greater part of a crop may be devoured. The best preventive is to place the seed pans upon a pot in a saucer of water; neither slugs nor woodlice can swim, therefore your choice seedlings are safe when set upon, as it were, an island.   T. APPLEBY.

THE KITCHEN-GARDEN.

AT this season pay good attention to the pricking out of all kinds of *kales, brocolis, savoys, cabbages,* and, indeed, of all the brassica family, as soon as the plants can be handled. If any have failed in coming up make another sowing; indeed, it is a favourable season for making another of *Grange's White, Walcheren, Early Cape,* and *cauliflowers,* &c.

Surface hoeing and *stirring* should be well attended to, as well as to giving liberal soakings of manure-water; late *peas* may be very much improved by such applications, and sowings should be made in succession of the late dwarf kinds, such as the *Fan Pea* and the *American Dwarf.*

POTATOES.—The earth about these should be well stirred and loosened in suitable weather; those which are shewing a number of shoots should be thinned to two or three of the strongest, an operation which may be performed either by hand or by careful hoeing. A multiplicity of shoots left is a certain indication of plenty of small tubers, and but few large ones. *Potatoes* in *pits* and *frames,* now nearly ripe, may, to save time, be taken up, placed in earthenware pots or pans, and covered with moderately dry sand, in order to keep them airtight for present use; and the lights taken off them may at once be turned to account for ridging out *cucumbers, melons, vegetable marrows, capsicums,* or *chillies,'* which should be grown along freely, so as to get strong enough for producing an abundant crop.

Ridge cucumbers, melons, and *vegetable marrows,* should now, also, all be got out. The strength of the bed made for them, of course, must be regulated by what can be spared at the present season with regard to fermenting materials, which are not only very scarce frequently at this time of the year, but are required for many uses. If a trench is cast out from two to three feet wide, and any kind of garden refuse, rakings, sweepings, and small prunings, are first placed in at the bottom, it is a considerable assistance to the prepared fermenting materials. If the fermenting materials consist principally of stable-dung, and a little *mushroom spawn* is placed on it previously to the soil being placed over it, a crop of mushrooms, provided the season is not too wet, will be produced from August to October.

SEA KALE.—The old beds that are intended to be cut from another year must have all the coverings cleared away, such as any remains of fermenting materials; and the covering-pots, of whatever kind they may be, should be all put away carefully, in a dry place if possible, if not wanted for any other purpose. Let all the crowns of the plants be examined, and if any should require cutting-in closer to the surface of the earth, or any that are already shooting forth should require to be thinned out, let this be done immediately. A few fine sifted coal ashes placed over the fresh cuts, either at the time of cutting the kale or in any other case, prevents the slugs working or boring down into the crowns, which they are very apt to do wherever a fresh cut is left to take its chance. The above remarks having been all attended to, take the digging fork and fork up the spaces

between the crowns, but taking the greatest care not to injure any of the roots. The fork may be used as expertly as the operator likes, but the following rule should be observed—narrow spits, broken up well, and as deep as it can be done without any injury to the roots of the plants.

The forward hand-glass crops of *cauliflower* should be attended to, with regard to forking between and making basins around them, according to the directions given in a previous number.

Broad beans may still be planted in cool situations; and the tall *Knight's Marrow peas* be sown in succession as the most profitable and best flavoured kind. Sow also *turnips* of any of the little early sorts, as well as *small salading* in succession.

For *turnip radishes*, red and white rooted, choose cool situations, and sow little and often.

Cape broccoli should now be sown in full crop. Let the spot where the seeds are to be sown be rich and good, and kept sufficiently moist, in order to encourage a quick growth.

Sage cuttings may now be planted out, if required, to any desired extent; and *Spear mint* may be planted out in open beds. Either cuttings or rooted plants will grow readily if planted out and well watered.

JAMES BARNES & W.

MISCELLANEOUS INFORMATION.

OUR VILLAGE WALKS.
(No. 25.)

THERE is great loveliness in wild uncultivated ground; it is almost always picturesque, and in defiance of a feeling of regret at its lying comparatively idle, I always admire it excessively. There is an ease and a natural grace in land that has retained somewhat of its original character; trees that have sprung up in it are often picturesque too, and the beautiful carpeting of heath that frequently covers the soil, looks well at every season, but particularly when its rich flowers literally paint the earth, and send up their amethyst-coloured dust when disturbed by the passer by. I have often heard my father describe this effect on the moors during his grousing excursions. Large tracts of land were entirely clothed with this brightly flowering plant, and clouds of this dust would arise like coloured smoke when the dogs were engaged in beating for the game. On those open districts, he said, the effect was singularly striking, and very beautiful.

The wild flowers and plants that love heathy situations are all full of beauty. The young self-sown fir-trees, that spring up in different places, give additional beauty to the scene; and there is always a dryness and pleasantness in the paths that cross this sort of ground that makes walking still more delightful. There are the remains of a large, wild, and beautiful common in my neighbourhood, which has been from time to time enclosed, cultivated, or planted; but in some places, large portions are still left untouched for the use of the poor; and beautiful they are. A ramble through these snatches of wild scenery in a warm, sunny, spring morning, is not easily described; but I shall content myself with intreating all those of my readers who reside near such healthy spots to turn their attention to them, and not pass them lightly by.

A cottage garden formed out of waste land like this has peculiar charms. Its shape and character have still a kind of wildness; and the blooming fruit-trees, the balmy row of beans, the gay border, and clustering

rose-trees, form a striking contrast to the uncultivated common to which it once belonged. How much may be done by cultivation! Is there not within each of us a wilderness? and how much may that barren land, by spiritual culture, be made to bear! Let us think of this, as we view with so much pleasure a smiling little homestead springing up from the bosom of a heathy moor!

The cottage gardener whose funeral I spoke of in my last paper, was once the possessor of a grant of land—if this term may be applied to so small a matter. It was a piece of waste land on the side of a rising ground, overlooking a valley and a village, yet with a northern aspect, and rather a stony soil. The man was then young and active, and he set to work at once. He built, with his own hands, a small two-roomed cottage, laid out his garden, planted his trees, and worked for his daily bread. When I first knew him, many years ago, he was an athletic carter, steady, kind to his horses, and diligent in his work. His bit of land had grown into a snug sheltered garden, his trees were in bearing, his laurels looked rich and bowery, and his little mud cottage in which he had brought up four children—who are all now in a far superior position to that which their parents occupied—was nestled among shrubs and rose-trees. As age advanced, he gave up his more active employments, and took altogether to gardening; tending his own piece of ground at his spare hours, and having a good knowledge of his business, he was in constant request. Difficulties, however, overtook him, and he was at length obliged to give up his own pretty home and retire to the village, where he passed the remainder of his life; still loving and cultivating a little spot of ground as well as his prosperous allotment. There were always pinks, hepaticas, fuchsias, and convolvuluses before his door, with a neat bed of cabbages, parsley, thyme, &c.; and many sorts of vegetables were raised behind his house: all good of their kind. It was a pleasure and a profit to enter the clean kitchen, where the old infirm couple sat quietly after the fatigues and anxieties of a long laborious life, and to witness their contentment and thankfulness under the privations that the aged poor most frequently suffer. He loved to talk of his former home,—of his garden, and his pleasure in making and watching it. But even the lowly and unknown cottager does not escape the sorrows that all flesh is heir to: his simple annals teach us, that "man is born to trouble as the sparks fly upwards;" that a wise and loving Father chastens his children for their instruction, wherever their lot is cast; and that no rank or circumstance can preserve us from the trials that belong to us, as a fallen race. Let us not seek to escape them in any country, or in any change of state. People are too ready to fancy that this or that situation or event would relieve or benefit them; but they are all mistaken. There is one situation, indeed, and only one, that insures both peace and safety—it is "the secret place," "the shadow of the Almighty!" That "refuge" and "fortress" guarantees our deliverance from every evil, or our quiet support under them. But in every other condition we have no defence—the palace and the cottage alike totter when built on the unstable sand; and neither the rich sheltering groves of the one, nor the fruit-laden trees of the other, can prop them up.

Now that the copses are clearing, I am particularly charmed with the beauty of the trees that are clothed with rich mantlings of ivy, standing conspicuously among their leafless companions, and increasing the loveliness of the spring scene. Yet I regret so much the mischief done to the trees thus encumbered, that I much wish every landed proprietor would consider the matter, and cause his trees to be stripped of this injurious decoration, for it is the ruin of timber, and, consequently, eventual loss to the landscape, as well as to the pocket. It is surprising to see the glee with which trees throw out healthy and vigorous shoots almost as soon as their stems are freed from the crushing encumbrance of the graceful climber, and the rapidity with which the dejected tree acquires a rich and ornamental appearance when it can freely breathe and expand once more. Some trees are beyond recovery when help is given, and in these cases, the ivy may be allowed to remain, especially in situations where picturesque objects are desirable, for there are few objects of more beauty than these. Many persons encourage the growth of ivy around their ornamental trees, and are not aware of the bad effects of its beautiful luxuriance. It is so rich and lovely, they cannot bear to hear even of its doing harm; but in a few years the mischief becomes apparent, when, perhaps, too late. Is there not a seeming fairness, too, in the outward bearing of ourselves and our fellow men that covers much that is corrupt within? Do we not, also, often encourage or permit ourselves in that which pleases the eye and heart, which is destructive to our spiritual growth, and if not "out off," will cause our souls to perish? We may learn a lesson from our trees withering amid the semblance of health and verdure, if we will listen to their teaching! Let us not close our ears to the whispering of the woods, as the early gales sing among the leafless boughs. Admiration of God's works is but half enjoyment: let us strive to understand and profit by them!

WILD FLOWERS OF MAY.

(Continued from page 59.)

In the woods the fragrant Woodruff (Asperula odorata) whitens the mossy carpet with its snowy flowers. The author of a little volume titled, "Wild Flowers of the Year," (published by the Religious Tract Society), says "its fresh leaves are almost scentless, but we have no native flower which so long retains its odour when dried." Withering says of it, "that its strongly aromatic flowers, when mixed with snuff, are also said to give to it the sweet odour of the Tonquin bean, without being, as that seed is, prejudicial to the eyesight—while the scent is more lasting." The scent of the leaves while drying very much resembles that of our garden Heliotrope or the grass Anthoxanthum odoratum (now in flower), which gives the delicious odour to new-made hay, and, like Woodruff, gives it out very powerfully while drying. Like Robin-run-the-hedge, and other plants of the natural order Rubiaceæ, the Woodruff has a rough feel arising from the presence of hooked bristles on the leaves and other parts, which in many cases make the plants stick to the clothes. Besides the Woodruff, but often in more moist situations, the not less fragrant Lily of the Vale (Convallaria majalis) is decked in its modest array, and certainly not less beautiful than when seen in the garden-border, or forced into premature bloom in the hothouse. The Dandelion (Leontodon taraxacum) lends its gaudy beauty to the adornment of the waysides, and will now afford an abundance of roots for the production of Dandelion coffee; nor should it be forgot that when the leaves are blanched they make a capital salad. In its wayside habitats it is frequently joined with the Coltsfoot (Tussilago farfara), which is now, however, almost entirely out of flower in the south. The Butter-bur (Petasites vulgaris) appears profusely on the banks of streams, and in wet meadows, ruining the undrained pastures to which it gains access, and choking up the drains of such as are drained. The Daisy (Bellis perennis),

"Whose home is everywhere—
A pilgrim bold in nature's care,"

is scattered with unsparing hand wherever our eyes can rest, and it calls at once to memory the many fine feelings and thoughts with which Wordsworth and Burns, and a host of other poets have invested the little gem. On the hills and heathy places the species of Vaccinium are in flower, and the V. Myrtillus or Bill-berry will soon afford the school-boy an abundant harvest. The Holly (Ilex aquifolium) is also a May blossoming tree; but its flowers are by no means so conspicuous as the red berries with which it is clad in winter. The Vincas (Periwinkles) are creeping through the bushes and long grass of the woods, adorned with their bluish purple flowers. The Lungwort (Pulmonaria officinalis), likewise grows beneath "the green wood's shade," and on account of its spotted leaves has received its name and been considered a cure for pulmonary complaints. In more moist places than it prefers, you will find the universally known and acknowledged emblem of friendship, the Forget-me-not (Myosotis), of which there are various species. The Field Scorpion Grass (M. arvensis) prefers dry places, such as wall-tops, and gravelly banks, but most of the species in this family are lovers of the cool shade or the streamlet's marge. One of the most beautiful is the Sylvan Forget-me-not (M. sylvestris), which often forms most lovely masses of blue in the shady woodlands; but perhaps the most beautiful of all is the Mountain Forget-me-not (M. alpestris), whose home is on the lofty alpine summits. M. palustris, which is considered to be the true emblem of friendship, is by no means a common plant, and some of the others are very often mistaken for it, even by botanists of acknowledged authority. The common Speedwell (Veronica officinalis) abounds in woods and pastures; and along with it, as well as by the waysides, will be found the Germander Speedwell (V. Chamædrys); its near ally the Mountain Speedwell, grows more rarely in the moist shady woodlands—these Speedwells, more especially the two latter, seem well entitled to a place in the herbaceous border. The common Bugle (Ajuga reptans) is one of the brightest ornaments of the woods, but not one of economical or botanical interest. The white Dead Nettle (Lamium album) is now abundantly in flower in many places, covering rubbish banks and waste places; its fœtid herbage is left to grow luxuriantly by browsing herds, but the plant is of some importance to the Apiarian, as the flowers yield an abundance of honey. There are also several other Labiatæ in blossom, not the least beautiful of which is the Ground Ivy (Glechoma hederacea) with its bright blue flowers peeping from beneath the hedges; in rural districts it is a popular cure for affections of the lungs. The large-flowered Butterwort (Pinguicula grandiflora) at once one of the rarest and loveliest of our native plants, has now produced its large rich purple blossoms; and the Primrose (Primula vulgaris); the Oxlip (P. elatior);

and the Cowslip *(P. veris)*, are all in the height of their glory, ornamenting every dell and woodland with their pale yellow flowers, and suggesting a thousand thoughts and associations of the most pleasing kind to every one except such as Wordsworth's hero, of whom the poet says—

> "A primrose by a river's brim,
> A yellow primrose was to him ;
> And it was nothing more."

The common Knot-grass *(Polygonum aviculare)*, in its varied forms abounds beside the habitations of mankind, appearing wherever human operations have disturbed the surface of the soil, or where human footsteps have effaced the original vegetation. The Sheep's Sorrel *(Rumex acetosella)* reddening the dry pastures with its unhealthy hue, tells of barren soils and meagre crops. The Dog's Mercury *(Mercurialis perennis)* frequents the closest shade of the woodlands; and the early browsing cattle that eagerly pluck its vernal herbage often fall victims to its poisonous properties. The weeping Birch, "with long dishevell'd hair," now delights the eye with its beauty, and throws its fragrance on the breeze; and a number of the willow family *(Salix)* are also richly adorned with their Catkins. The Cuckow-pint, or Wake-robin *(Arum maculatum)*, has now sent up its curiously sheathed flowers from among the arrow-shaped leaves on the shady woodland bank. It is a curious but well known fact that, all the species of Arum are very acrid, but entirely lose their acridity on being dried. Hooker tells us that the tuberous root of our native species affords an abundant starchy substance, which, if properly prepared, and the acrid juice expressed, proves an excellent substitute for bread-flour, and is sold for that purpose in great quantities at Weymouth and in Portland Island. The curious Herb-Paris *(Paris quadrifolia)*, and the more beautiful Star of Bethlehem *(Ornithogalum umbellatum)*, are also both in flower this month. The wild Hyacinth *(Hyacinthus nonscriptus)* adorns the green grass of the woodland with its cœrulean blossoms, and must be considered to be the true *hairbell* of the poets, and to have derived its name not from "occurring in places frequented by hares," but from the ringlet-like appearance of its drooping racemes of flowers, to which the poets have referred. Altogether, this flower is a great favourite with poet and proser, and is one of the most delicate gems of our woodland:

> "E'en the slight hairbell raised its head,
> Elastic from her airy tread."

Several of the earlier native Orchids have already produced their remarkable blossoms, mimicking the animal tribes; but the months of June and July are richer in these curious flowers, and we shall reserve our remarks upon their history till a future occasion. Many plants of the truly lovely order *Liliaceæ* are also in blossom: the Narcissus of the poets *(Narcissus poeticus)*, and the Pale Narcissus *(N. biflorus)*, join with their somewhat earlier ally, the "dancing Daffodil" *(N. pseudo Narcissus)*, in giving a lively loveliness to the woods and fields; and the Summer Snowflake *(Leucojum æstivum)* adorns the meadows with its snowy flowers, reminding us of the pale Snowdrop that came in mid-winter to cheer our flowerless paths, and tell us of the coming spring. Such is an account of the Wild Flowers of May. We have not, indeed, enumerated the whole of the wildlings that are to be found during the flowery month; that would have made our paper extend far beyond the limits assigned to it, and might, likewise, have rendered it of less interest with many of our readers. We trust, however, that these remarks may be the means of adding a relish to many a rural walk, and of directing many an eye, in an idle hour, to dwell upon the humble things of the waysides and forest paths that are often passed by unseen, uncared for, and unadmired.—G. LAWSON, *Assistant Curator of Bot. Soc., Edinburgh.*

DOMESTIC MECHANISM.

POLITICAL economy has long been practically studied, and undoubted benefits have resulted therefrom, but of late years a new science, more closely connected with the concerns of every day life, has sprung up, and is fast becoming of importance; it may be termed, that of social and domestic economy. Whatever may be the causes, it is certain that it is now the interest of all possessing, what may be termed, limited incomes to look well to their outlay; not only to endeavour in all things to avoid unnecessary expences, but to study closely the best means of "making a little go a great way." Too frequently, economists have contented themselves with attempting to save in large outlays, neglecting the consideration of the "little things about a house." For instance, a person may congratulate himself upon saving so much by adopting a proper method of cooking certain dishes, while he remains ignorant of the fact (or, at least, pays no attention to it) that, by certain mechanical arrangements, he might have succeeded in effecting a considerable saving in the article of fuel by which he prepared his meal. And the same may be said to be the case in many other departments.

If it be true that a "penny saved is a penny gained," and that it is worth while to gain a penny, it is no less true that it should be the endeavour of every one to pay attention to all means proposed to save even a penny. As the world is made up of little things, we hold that when attention is paid to small affairs, that a step in the right direction has been made. We have made these remarks, as we are aware that with many considerable apathy exists in connexion with improvements which they are pleased to call trifles. We trust that however unimportant any proposal at first sight may appear, it will be considered worthy of some degree of attention. It may not be exactly suited to all wants, but some useful hint may be derived from it that may be turned to good account.

We have elsewhere given a series of descriptions of improvements under the same title of the present article; we intend to continue giving such. We trust that the readers of THE COTTAGE GARDENER may derive some information therefrom, and may through them succeed in effecting some saving, in deriving some benefit from this branch of domestic economy. The season is fast approaching when the maintenance of continual fires will no longer be necessitated. Food, however, is required to be cooked, and many domestic arrangements require supplies of hot water. To supply such quickly, and without involving the necessity of kindling a fire in the grate, is the object of the following contrivance.

SUMMER WATER BOILER.—Take a tapered tin pan, as shewn in the cut, and place, running up the centre of it, a tapering tube: this must be open at the top and bottom, the top projecting above the lid of the pan. There will thus be a communication (water-tight) through and through the centre. Within two inches of the bottom of the tube, place a small grid made of iron wire. A tinsmith will have no difficulty whatever in constructing the whole concern; by simply examining the woodcut he will at once understand the minutiæ of its construction. The pan must be provided with a tight-fitting lid, with an aperture in the centre to let the narrow end of the internal tube pass through. This aperture should be no larger than necessary. By putting the pan in the fire-place, or the hob of the grate, and kindling a few pieces of sticks, turf, or charcoal, laid on the grid, the water in the interior surrounding the internal tube, will be heated, nay, boiled, in an amazingly short period.

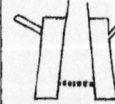

By using a contrivance made on this principle, five or six panfuls might be boiled before a common fire could be lighted. The expense of maintaining a charcoal fire for five or six hours a day would be very trifling. The whole affair will not cost half as much again as the price of the pan without the internal heating tube. The draught of the *tiny* fire may be increased by having the tube projecting further above the lid than is shewn in the cut. A handle and spout should be added for the convenience of lifting and pouring out. By the use of this, a very decided saving in fuel (not to take into account the trouble) will be effected in the summer months.   B.

BREWING AT HOME.

THOUGH an admirer of teetotallers, and always recommending, when practicable, the habit of drinking cold water, still, as there are some people who cannot work without the assistance of a glass of beer, and many others who *fancy* they cannot do so, I, therefore, think neither time nor space will be wasted if I make a few remarks on "brewing at home."

I dare say such a sentence will frighten many, and they will immediately exclaim, "Brew at home, impossible! I have neither coppers, coolers, mash-tubs, nor any of the hundred-and-one articles necessary for such an operation." Never mind, do not throw obstacles in our path, but read, learn, and practise! I must, however, tell you at starting, that it will cause extra trouble to the wife; but I am very sure there are few, if any, amongst the "wives and daughters of old England" who will grudge a little exertion when once they feel that by so exerting themselves they will benefit their husbands, children, and, consequently, themselves. And now let us see wherein the benefit of brewing at home lies.

In the first place it increases your comforts, in the second place it saves time, and thirdly it saves money—three very material points; but still, more than this, it removes many temptations out of a man's path. The habit of going to a public house, if only for one glass of beer, has been the occasion of many an after pang, many a heavy heart. That constant habit of even fetching your beer from the public house must waste much time, even if not tempted to drink it in the house instead of at home. Very often a child is sent to fetch it, and thus the young mind becomes early habituated to the sound of oaths and jests which every parent ought so carefully to screen their children from hearing, for who can tell the misery which arises from early acquaintance with vice? Early impressions take deep root, whether good or evil, and our hearts being so prone to sin, the evil habit which is imbibed with our early youth is more difficult to eradicate than the good, therefore, how studiously should each parent watch over the soul's welfare of his child, and not place him in scenes where he knows "sins abound."

I am sure, as I said before, when this is taken into consideration, trouble will not be withheld, but many will willingly try a plan which is likely to place temptation a little farther from their threshhold.

I will now tell you the articles necessary for brewing at home. Every cottage owns a large saucepan—one that holds about three gallons is a good size; this will answer the purpose of a copper. A tub will be the utensil for working the beer in; and if you cannot conveniently buy a small mash-tub, bore a hole in the bottom of a pail to allow the liquor to run slowly through. These three things are all that are really necessary; and now, as to the materials of the beer. Those who have been accustomed to drink brewer's beer will not, perhaps, at first like the pure malt and hops; their taste, however, will soon improve; or if not, they will find by adding to every two bushels of malt the following ingredients, they will obtain beer very similar to what they have always drunk:—" 3lbs sugar, boiled up once in a very little water, with one pennyworth of coriander seed, and one pennyworth of capsicum." Malt must be carefully chosen, the amber coloured is the best. It should not be ground, but merely crushed. Hops should be new; when good, they have a yellowish green colour. Soft water should be used, if possible, for brewing; and every article must be most scrupulously clean.

I will suppose you wish to brew six gallons of beer, and for that quantity you must have a pot which will contain four gallons of water. Have ready in your mash-tub one peck of crushed malt (be careful to have the hole in the tub stopped). When the water nearly boils, pour it on to the malt, stir it well for ten minutes, cover the pail over with a thick sack or piece of wood, and place it by the fire for two hours. Hold the pail over the tub, draw out the peg, and let the liquor run. Stop the hole again, and add to the malt two gallons more of nearly boiling water, cover as before, and set by the fire for an hour. Put the first strained liquor into the copper or pot, and add four ounces of good hops; boil for twenty minutes; strain it into a tub; return the hops to the pot, and add the second addition of wort, which has been standing by the fire; boil this half an hour; strain and cool this as you did the first; when lukewarm mix them together, and stir in ¼ of a pint of yeast. Skim it frequently during the day, and when it has stood twenty-four hours in the tub put it into a cask; leave the bung-hole open as long as any yeast rises, but when the fermentation is over, hammer the bung tightly in, and leave it for a week, by the end of which it will be fit for use.

One of the chief points in brewing is to attend to the proper heat the water has before it is poured on the malt. If it is too hot, it contracts the malt, and prevents the full flavour from appearing; the proper temperature is 180°, but as a thermometer is not a likely appendage to a cottage wall, the hand must be depended upon. You should just be able to draw your hand quickly through the water without experiencing pain.

There are several other methods of making beer, such as with potatoes, mangold wurtzel, and sugar, but I will reserve these for some future occasion, my present object being to tempt the cottager's wife to brew her husband's glass of beer. At the present time it will prove most economical, malt being cheap, and brewer's beer remaining at the same price.　　　　　　　　　　　　　　　A FRIEND.

ASPARAGUS.

At page 240 of THE COTTAGE GARDENER for January, 1850, some hints are kindly given of the Dutch method of cutting asparagus by Mr. Rushmere. Now the manner in which I have dealt with the asparagus beds, and my method of cutting for many years, are very different.

WINTER DRESSING.—In the first place, I never root prune the plants by throwing out deep trenches between the beds, as is too often done in very many cases; that is, by putting over the beds a good dressing of manure, then placing a line down the side of each bed and chopping off every root that has found its way into the alley. Very usually some of the best roots have thus run out into the alleys, which is not to be wondered at, for in the spring, say in the month of March, these beds in most gardens are forked over, and much of the soil and rough parts of the manure are worked back into the alleys again. This, of course, is a comfort to the poor roots that have been exposed throughout the winter to all weathers along the sides of these deep-dug alleys.

I have assisted often in the above sorts of work years ago, but for the last seventeen years I have not dug out a single trench between a bed.

When the stems are cut away in the autumn, the beds are cleaned, if weedy, and carefully forked up. A thoroughly good dressing of manure is put all over the beds equally, and when this is done the alleys are forked over too; whilst, for the sake of giving the whole a neat finish, a line is put down each side of the alley, the edges made up a little, and, perhaps, a few crumbs from the alleys may be thrown upon the beds, and the edges marked out with the point of the spade. The work is then done for the winter; and, of course, the asparagus beds neatly done in this way give the kitchen-garden a tidy appearance for the winter months.

SPRING DRESSING.—In the month of March these beds are again forked over carefully, the manure and soil well broken up and mixed together, and some of the rougher parts of manure, with all the rakings, are forked into the alleys after the beds are raked over nicely, and lettuces are there sown or planted in succession for the summer months.

CUTTING THE PRODUCE.—Now, although I have been a cultivator of the asparagus for so many years, I have never been an eater of this much esteemed vegetable, therefore the thought did not strike me about the best way of cutting it, until one day, some seventeen years ago, when I had an abundance of heads to cut from, all of good length above ground, I received orders for asparagus for a dish, and for another for soup. This latter dish was to be of heads all green. I well supplied the cook with heads green enough for her dish required, and her soup too; and a first-rate cook she was.

The next day, when I waited upon her for orders, we had a little talk about the green asparagus for the table, when she told me that the asparagus I had brought in the day before was the best that she had ever dressed for table—it was large, of good flavour, and the whole eatable. This was a good hint for me, for it opened my eyes greatly as to the management of the asparagus beds altogether. But the matter did not rest here, for my employers also soon found me out to praise the asparagus I was then sending them in. And thus have I continued ever since, year after year, continually receiving compliments and inquiries about it from innumerable friends of my excellent employer.

Of course, those who daily eat these kinds of vegetables must be the best judges of their quality; and in the act of cutting the grass or young heads in this way, *taking only the part above ground*, the operator can see what he is doing; and, however inexperienced he may be, he can cut a dish of asparagus without any loss. On the other hand, a person not used to this work, or with the usual long-handled, sawtoothed knife for cutting, would make sad havoc amongst the underground shoots in cutting a dish or hundreds for the market; for when thrusting the knife into the ground to cut one head, he would probably break off two or three others unseen at the same time. This old-fashioned saw-toothed knife I have not used since I have cut my asparagus above ground—that is, level with the surface of the earth; I use just what knife I may have in my pocket at the time, and it often happens that my penknife is obliged to be used, from having no other about me at the moment.   T. WEAVER,
Gardener to the Warden of Winchester College.

[We strongly recommend our readers to adopt Mr. Weaver's mode of cutting. Let the heads grow until they are six or seven inches above ground, and then cut them level with the surface. There is thus no waste—the whole is eatable.—ED. C. G.]

EXTRACTS FROM CORRESPONDENCE.

ARRANGEMENT OF FLOWER-BEDS.—Allow me to thank your correspondent, S. N. W., page 41, for the spirit in which he criticised the flower-garden in question; not that such consideration was necessary as far as D. Beaton is concerned, for if the critics will only keep their *hands off* him, I believe he is as impervious to pen and ink as the hide of a rhinoceros; and, moreover, he is one of the most *inconsistent* writers we have, for you have only to *prove* a case contrary to his most cherished opinion, and immediately he turns round and adopts your view as cordially as if no difference ever existed between you. It is provoking, however, that there is no standard by which to prove, not the difference between S. N. W. and D. B., but the difference between the new school of flower gardening and the rules applicable to the laying out of flower-gardens as they were planted before the present mode had existence. When I see the plan promised by S. N. W., I can tell in five minutes if he is a planter according to the present style as well as a designer; and if he is, I shall be very glad to assist him; and if he is not, I see no good that can come of disputing the point. The present position of flower gardening in this country is anomalous. We have a new school, which can hardly be said to have had existence in 1825, and its merits were not discussed in print before 1831 or 1832. It is true that Lady Grenville, of Dropmore, and the late Lady Cumming Gordon, of Altyre, in Morayshire, with some others, and unknown to each other, originated this school when Buonaparte was secured at St. Helena; but it has not taken firm root until within the last twenty years; and here we are now practising and studying in this new school without a vocabulary, a grammar, or a dictionary (and the old books only make our darkness more visible) the best plans according to the old style of planting. Dutch or other gardens go for little unless we can so modify them as to suit our present mode of practice. That this can be done, I have no doubt, but that it is a very difficult matter to do so, I equally admit. But to put the case so familiar as to come within the comprehension of all our readers, let us say that our different schools or styles of architecture are perfect of their kind; and let us suppose that a first-rate architect, who never heard or read of our domestic arrangements, were to design a mansion: such a house might exhibit the perfection of his art, but that would

be a poor compensation to the owner if he found, on taking possession, that his wine cellar was at the top of the house, and no provision made to reach it, and that his bed-rooms "had ground for their floor." Now all this might happen and the house still be a perfect specimen of architecture, and it is exactly so with designs for flower-gardens: they may or may not be suitable for a given style of planting, and yet be masterpieces of art.—D. BEATON.

MICE.—I see that the peas of one of your correspondents have suffered from mice. I have found the prickly *furze*, or *gorse*, quite efficient as a protection, sown in the drills with the peas.—REV. H. M.

SMOKE-STAINED WALLS.—Let J. H. mix in a bucket of lime-wash a quantity of fresh cow-dung (collected where the cattle are fed upon grass), and therewith give to the smoked parts a couple of coats; the walls will afterwards take a perfect white. It will be advantageous if the whitewashing at present on the walls were removed, as well as can be, before applying the above wash.—P. H., *Dublin.*

OX HEAD OR SHIN OF BEEF STEWED TO TURN OUT IN MOULDS.—Take half a bullock's head, or a shin of beef, and one cow heel, well cleaned and chopped in pieces, put them into a stewpan, with as much water as will cover it *well*; and when stewed till the meat leaves the bones, take the bones out and beat the meat small. Put the liquid it has been boiled in to it, with as much pepper, salt, cayenne, nutmeg, and mace as you like for seasoning. Put it into your pan again, until it thickens and will set, then put it into moulds or pots, and turn it out as you require it. It will keep for two or three weeks in cold weather. This is a most useful, economical, and pretty dish, and also very nourishing. For breakfast, lunch, &c., it is always ready; and for pic-nics, or taking on the moors, it is also well adapted. If you want an extra dish at dinner unexpectedly, you can warm a shape for a hash; and added to any broth, it makes a very tolerable soup. When turned out cold, it is a beautiful jelly.
Note.—The remains of a shape make an acceptable gift to a poor invalid, and can be easily carried.

SCALDED PUDDING.—Put a teaspoonful of flour into a large basin, then boil sufficient milk to make it the consistency of hasty-pudding. Pour the milk, *when boiling*, on the flour; let it stand to cool; then mix two eggs and a little sugar and cinnamon with it. Pour it into a mould, and boil for one hour. This is recommended by a physician as a very wholesome pudding for children and invalids. Add a pinch of salt. There is a good rule given for this by an admirable cook—
" *Sugar in all soups, and salt in all puddings except a custard.*"

PORRIDGE is eaten in Scotland by the child of the peer as well as the peasant, and considered most wholesome and nutritious. But the Scotch oatmeal is far superior, and quite different from any you can get here. The only way to ensure its being genuine, is to have a barrel or bag sent from Scotland. Boil it in water with a little salt for 10 or 15 minutes till quite thick, stirring it, and eat it with new milk. The same oatmeal makes admirable oatcake, baked on a girdle, or flat piece of iron, which is placed on the fire. Rice should be got by the hundredweight from Liverpool, or through a wholesale grocer, it is much cheaper.

GENTIANELLA.—The following may be interesting. About this time (April) last year I bought in the Liverpool market two plants of the blue gentianella *(Gentiana acaulis,* I think) just bursting into bloom; I put them in a sunny border in the garden, where they bloomed, after which—as an experiment, as I hardly expected them to bloom again, being shy flowerers, and transplanted at that season—I gave them a top-dressing of old manure and leaf-mould; but within a week after I noticed in THE COTTAGE GARDENER that they wanted rather poor soil, I therefore scraped away the dressing, and replaced it with light sandy peat soil; what was my astonishment in the middle of December last to find both plants bursting again into bloom, and I had them in bloom in the Christmas week. I feared that this would interfere with the usual spring flowering, but I am glad to say that both plants promise a brilliant show for next week. The soil of the garden is a strong heavy clay, thoroughly broken up, with peat soil and sand.—E. A., *Oxton, near Birkenhead.*

GOATS.—I perceive in your article on "Goat Keeping," that you state they will eat anything that is refused by any other animal. I kept three females and one male for about two years, and found them "more plague than profit." They were placed in an orchard, but would not eat the grass that was sour, but only such as the cows would feed from; nibbled the hedges, and in spite of all opposition would force themselves through. The milk is very rich, but not so plentiful as I was led to expect. The flesh of the kid is delicious. I had one female that produced three live and two dead ones at a birth. The male only barked the trees, and was not particular whether they were young or old. I have had much pleasure in recommending your work to several friends, who agree with me that it is the cheapest and best work of the kind ever published.—W. H. WHITE, *Thames Ditton.*

BEES.—You state (vol. iii., page 316) that raw sugar given to bees is useless; bees can only take it in the liquid state. I have two common straw hives, and have found from experience that bees *will feed* upon sugar, and make short work of *two ounces* at a time. In fact, they devour it in a similar manner that a parcel of flies would in a sugar basin. On the contrary, my bees, though tried repeatedly with ale and sugar, prepared as recommended in your periodical, would never touch it; but that sugar (and honey in a small quantity) dissolved in water was quickly consumed. — THOS. BROOK, *Hanover-street, Halifax.*

[You will observe in our last number that Mr. Payne and others have found that barley-sugar, which becomes moist when exposed to a warm, damp atmosphere, like that of the inside of a hive, is consumable by bees. Sugar also becomes moist in the same situation. We were, therefore, not wrong in saying that bees cannot partake of solid food.— ED. C. G.]

TO CORRESPONDENTS.

₌ We request that no one will write to the departmental writers of THE COTTAGE GARDENER. It gives them unjustifiable trouble and expense; and we also request our coadjutors *under no circumstances* to reply to such private communications.

WOOLLEN RAGS (*J. Derham*). — Thanks for your communication, which, with some notes of our own, shall appear next week.

BEES (*A Tyro*).—The ventilators need not be closed at night. Either a painted canvas covering or a thatched roof will answer as a shelter for your hives.

SUPER-PHOSPHATE OF LIME (*T. W. L.*).—To make this on a small scale you must mix together six pounds of bone dust, three pounds of oil of vitriol (strongest sulphuric acid), and a pint and a half of water. Sprinkle the water first over the bones and then add the acid; be careful, for it is very corrosive. Use a vessel large enough to hold more than twice the quantity. After the acid and the bone dust are united you may mix ashes with them, so as to enable you to spread the super-phosphate thus formed over your soil. The above quantity is enough for 150 square yards.

INDEX (*Ibid*).—You can have this through a bookseller for a penny, or if you send three postage stamps to our office you will have one sent free by post. The wool of the *dyed fleeces* can only be rendered loose by being washed with soap, beaten, and combed.

GLAZED ASPARAGUS BED (*T. H. B.*).—You ask how much earlier you would cut asparagus if you enclosed a bed with a brick wall and glazed lights, using these only in winter and spring? The asparagus would be about three weeks earlier than that in the open ground. You might keep carnations, auriculas, &c., in this protected bed during the winter, but you must have some place to remove them to early in March.

BUDDING (*J. Dawson*).—The reference in vol. ix. should be to p. 306 instead of 260. A work exactly suited to you is preparing, and will be announced almost immediately.

BULBS DONE FLOWERING (*P. W.*).—These must not be removed until their leaves turn yellow at the end of summer; they have now to prepare for next year's blooming. If economy is an object in your *bee-keeping*, buy Payne's Cottager's Hive; otherwise, Taylor's Amateur's Hive. If you refer to the indexes of our former volumes you will find Mr. Payne's Calendar for every month. Your other question must remain unanswered until next week.

PAYNE'S HIVES (*John Cockcross*).—You will find several drawings and full particulars of size, &c., from Mr. Payne himself at p. 239 of our first volume. The accompanying drawing shews the hive with the small depriving hive upon it. The large hive is nine inches deep and twelve inches in diameter, straight at the sides and flat at the top, with a hole in the centre of the top four inches in diameter; a piece of straw work like that of the hive must cover this hole, not fit into it, when the depriving hive is not over it. The small hive is seven inches deep, eight inches in diameter, flat at the top, with a small pane of glass let into the side, but

closed with a shutter, to observe how the bees are working in it. It is quite impossible for us to tell you the cost of carriage; ask the carrier.

SEEDS SOWN IN ELDER (*Louise*).—Never having tried the experiment we cannot give you the information, nor would we advise you to waste your time over such, at best, tasteless growths.

MELILOTUS LEUCANTHA.—If "A Subscriber" will send his name and address to N. S. Hodson, Esq., Botanic Garden, Bury St. Edmunds, this gentleman obligingly offers to supply him with the seed.

PORT WINE STAINS (*Emily Wyndham*).—Recent stains are removed by the following liquid. Mix together an ounce of powdered sal ammoniac and the same quantity of salt of tartar, put them into a quart bottle full of soft water, and shake until dissolved. Soak the stained part of the linen in a little of this mixture. Wheel *pedometers* measure accurately, but we do not know the price of them. The other question can be answered by any laundress.

BASS'S PALE ALE (*H. Beasley*).—Our correspondent will be obliged for directions how to brew this ale.

THE WORK TABLE (*Subscriber*).—We cannot answer questions relative to this.

MAGNOLIA GRANDIFLORA (*Zoe*).—A foot in depth of soil will be sufficient for this over the archway on which it is to be planted, as a greater and unrestrained depth of soil is within four feet of the place where it will be inserted.

VINES TRAINED ON ZINC (*A Tyro*).—It is very likely the rapid heat conducting properties of the metal which withered or scorched the grapes on your vines. We should say that the framework you propose to place between the zinc roof and the vines, need not be more than eight or nine inches from the zinc surface. You may so place it in divisions, that beginning with six inches it may be farther removed at an hour's notice, without derangement of the object sought. To pitch the roof would be a doubtful matter at the best; it would probably increase the heat.

UNFRUITFUL APPLE-TREES (*H. F. L.*).—You need seek little farther than the American blight for the cause of barrenness in your apple-trees. These pests require the very matter for their sustenance that should go to make healthy blossoms and to reinvigorate the roots. Pruning has nothing to do with it. You say "they are as yet free;" wait a few weeks and we doubt not the old enemy will reappear. Apply spirits of turpentine assiduously as fast as they appear—above all things, taking time by the forelock.

CROPS FOR FOUR ACRES (*A. Clarke*).—Really you are late in putting your queries. Four acres of light soil will keep a good deal of poultry certainly, and some pigs, but you say nothing about a cow. You may grow plenty of mangold and swedes yet, as root crops; and as for spring corn it will be surely getting too late to expect anything remunerative from oats or barley. Perhaps some buck wheat would assist in your plot. So much depends on the character and "heart" of your soil, that we can scarcely offer further advice now.

HEARTS-EASE FOR EXHIBITION (*Amateur*).—You ask how to cultivate these, the time liquid manure is used, and how often and also the time to nip off superfluous buds? This information fully given would occupy several columns, which is more space than we can spare at present. We will endeavour to give you a few hints, which your own ingenuity must carry out to the full extent. For soil and general management we must refer you to the places in our back numbers where the culture of the pansy or hearts-ease is described. We will only say here that they love a light moderately rich soil, an open situation, and a clear atmosphere; that is, an air free from the smoke of large towns. They produce the finest flowers planted in a bed (not in pots), but should be planted as early as February. Liquid manure, if the soil is right, is not required, but may be applied once or twice in a very diluted state a month before the exhibition. Nip off all flower-buds till within five weeks of the time you want them. Shade the flower during strong sunshine, and protect them from heavy rains. Gentle showers will not hurt them up to a fortnight before they are wanted for exhibition. Do not allow more than three or four flowers on a plant at once.

CRYPTOSTEMMA HYPOCHONDRIACUM (*Ibid*).—If this be the plant you mean, it is a hardy annual, of some beauty, growing a foot high, flowering in the middle of summer, of a yellow colour, and is a native of the Cape, and will grow in common garden soil. If you have got any seeds of it, we should be glad of one or two if you can spare them.

ACACIA CUTTINGS (*A Constant Reader*).—We are not surprised that your newly-potted struck cuttings of Yellow Acacia (*Acacia armata*, we suppose you mean) should perish in a heat obtained from *fresh* pig's dung. You should have potted and replaced them in the cold-pit. They would then have done well. Every other point of your management is quite correct. Try again, by all means; but avoid any heat to force them into growth after they are struck. Keep them close in a cold-frame after potting, and shade them from the bright rays of the sun till they grow again. You have failed this time by a too great heat in dung un-sweetened. It ought to have had frequent turnings over till the rank, injurious steam had evaporated, and become mild and sweet. We are surprised that even cucumber and melon plants have existed, much less grown, in dung so crude and unprepared.

CLIMBERS (*An Invalid Subscriber*).—It is too late now to plant out strong hardy climbers to cover your bower, unless you could procure them in large pots, as no doubt you could in some of the nursery gardens round Glasgow. *Clematis montana* (Mountain Virgin's Bower) is one of the best, and flowers beautifully in May; and then what can be better or sweeter than our own Traveller's Joy—or you might try those evergreen climbing roses which we so often recommend, and they are good stocks to bud others on to flower in the autumn.

VASE IN CENTRE OF BORDER (*S. S. J.*).—Mr. Beaton's condemnation of scarlet geraniums being placed in the centre of a bed, does not apply to a large vase so placed, and three feet high. Scarlet geraniums, and of these *Tom Thumb*, will be best for such a centre; but keep some subdued colours round it in the bed. *Tropaeolum canariense* would scarcely succeed to hang down the sides of the vase, unless it is very sheltered, for the wind would disturb it too much. In your larger vase, six feet high, and thirty yards beyond the smaller, on a grass mound backed by shrubs, plant *Calceolaria amplexicaulis*, or some other bright yellow calceolaria.

POT-BULBS (*E. P. Y.*).—Crocuses, hyacinths, and other hardy bulbs that have been flowered in pots this spring, may now be well watered, and the bulbs turned out into the borders or any spare corner, and see they do not want for water until their leaves fade at the end of summer.

FRENCH MARIGOLDS (*W. R. W. Smith*).—The treatment of the double marigolds will be given in a week or two by Mr. Beaton, when noticing the yellow bedding flowers.

CIRCULAR FLOWER-BEDS (*J. F. A.*).—This is divided into six equal parts. Plant 1 and 4 with two kinds of yellow flowering plants of the same height; 2 with a low scarlet plant; and 5 with a taller scarlet, to match it crossways; 3 plant with a white flower, same height as the plant in No. 2; and 6 may be a high white, or some undecided colour, as some verbenas are. For the actual plants, search Mr. Beaton's lists now publishing by us.

BALCONIES (*Vulpis Venator*).—You will see your inquiry has been attended to in to-day's publication. The query respecting a little garden, will also meet with attention ere long.

HEAT FOR CINERARIAS (*F. W. T.*).—To obtain a little mild bottom-heat for these flowers after Christmas, stable-dung would do very well, if well sweetened, and mixed with leaves; and more especially if a layer of dry ashes is placed on the surface. If leaves cannot be obtained, prunings, &c., to keep the dung open, will answer nearly as well. If well made and mixed, such a bed will keep heat a long time—there is much in the making. At that time the bottom-heat should not be above 60° at the highest; top temperature from 45° to 48°. Of course, this merely applies to those you wish to grow on quickly. Those to be merely kept must be much lower—from 38° to 45°

BEGONIA MARTIANA (*Ibid*).—Do not be uneasy though the tuber that has been two months in the stove has not vegetated, so long as it keeps fresh and sound. It must have a season of repose.

EUPHORBIA JACQUINIFLORA (*Ibid*).—We can see no reason why the cuttings that you had *dried* for two or three days did not strike, after being placed in a gentle hot-bed, unless it was owing to the cuttings being rather *spongy*, and your using nothing but sand. We should have preferred a little fine soil along with the sand; and that would have allowed a little more air to enter to the base of the cuting.

BEES (*T. M. W.*).—You have bees in a common cottage hive, and wish to prevent its swarming. You propose either to turn the hive, with the crown downwards, between the legs of a stool, and place another *flat-topped* hive over it, so that you may take away either the old hive, or the upper one, after next summer; or to take the crown of the old hive out, and place another hive over it; or to place an empty hive by the side of it, opening a communication between the two, and obliging the bees to enter through the new hive. Of the three plans you mention, that of inverting the hive is the worst, and that of cutting a hole in the top the best; but why not allow the bees to swarm, and put the swarm into the kind of hive you fancy? The swarm will supply you with from 15 lbs. to 20 lbs. of honey, above what the bees will require for winter store; and the *second swarm*, from so large a hive and strong a stock as yours is described to be, will, with a little help (and perhaps without it, if the season proves a good one), make a good stock for next year: you will not turn them to so good an account by any other treatment.

BLUE FLOWER FOR CENTRE BED (*E. E.*).—"A good *blue* flower for the small centre bed of three steep beds rising one above another" is, *Campanula garganica*, or *Anagallis Philippsii*, or *Cineraria amelloides*. The first is the best, and is the least trouble.

ROSES IN SHADES (*A Worcestershire Subscriber*).—Like you, we are often puzzled by the rose catalogues. It will be a most difficult thing to shade a bed of autumnal roses "from crimson " in the middle "to white " at the outside, that is, taking each shade between the two. All that you

can do this season can only be four good shades, namely, dark crimson, rose, blush, and white. The best roses for these are *Geant des Batailles*, three or five plants for the middle, then a row of *Baronne Prevost* and one of the *Duchess of Sutherland*, the third, or blush, *Souvenir de Malmaison*, the most charming of all the blush roses, and the *white China* outside as you propose. Next rose season you should visit the nurseries at Worcester, Cheltenham, and Gloucester, and choose out the exact tints you want, and the nurserymen will say how strong they are.

STRONG ROSES (*Ibid*).—There are very strong growers and the reverse in all the sections of the bush roses. The nearest to what you want for pink are *Mrs. Elliot* and *William Jesse*; but on your strong soil Mrs. Elliot will make shoots a yard long when once it is established; and you will have to transplant it, and others who may run up too high, every other year, and at the end of October.

CLIMBERS (*Ibid*).—You want three or four *strong*, hardy, but not common, climbers (not roses). We know of none better than those you have, unless you add the new *Yellow jasmine*, from China (*J. nudiflorum*), which will keep in flower all winter on your east wall. *Sollya* will not endure frost. *Ceanothus azureus* is one of the best evergreens to plant between the climbers; the frost will nip it, but not much, and the blue flowers are exquisite.

BROKEN COMB IN HIVE (*Gunthorpe*).—Having had the misfortune to knock down the centre comb, which now rests on the hive board and against the side of the hive, you ask, what you should do? and we reply—Let your bees *quite* alone; they will manage much better for themselves than you can for them. They will very soon work a piece of comb upon the top of the broken one, and attach it to the roof of the hive; and when done so, firmly, will eat away the part now resting on the floor board, so as to make a passage beneath it. The comb, being a centre one, is now full of brood, and must not be removed.

BEES (*M. F. G.*).—You need not feed your swarm as soon as you get it home. Leave them to themselves, and if the swarm be a good honey season, they will not require feeding at all. If they do, follow what is said in our last number about feeding with barley sugar. Your covering is unexceptionable. You may obtain Payne's "The Bee Keeper's Guide" through any bookseller. Its price is five shillings.

CAPE BULBS (*Mary Anne*).—If you will refer to page 100 of our first volume, and to page 250 of our third, you will find full information as to moving these from their native places.

BEES (*E. E.*).—All hives should now be got ready, for swarming time is arrived. Elm well-seasoned, and dovetailed across the grain to prevent warping is good for the floor boards. Mr. Payne has published a little Bee Manual for Cottagers. To destroy *worms* in lawns, see vol. iii, page 179.

VERBENA VENOSA (*F. P. D. H.*).—Any nurseryman can supply you with this plant, or with *Scarlet variegated Geranium*, as, if he does not possess it himself, he can easily procure it from a respectable London house. Let both be planted about the middle of May.

PETUNIAS (*Ibid*).—These should always be pegged down until they cover the bed—not after that; but Mr. Beaton will put you right about those at the proper time.

RUSTIC BASKET (*Ibid*).—*Tom Thumb* and *Improved Frogmore* are the best scarlet geraniums for your large rustic basket.

BITTER SEA-KALE (*Ibid*).—The steam from the fermenting leaves probably got access inside the pots, and so caused the bitterness.

CLIMBER FOR NORTH WALL (*H. M. T.*).—Ivy is the best covering for a north wall; and the fastest growing plants for it are those evergreen climbing roses which we so often recommend. We would plant them and the ivy now.

SPANISH JASMINE (*E. S. R.*).—We would by all means cut down this old plant, and leave a few of the present suckers at full length this season. The young shoots from the cut part will come up very strong, and you must "top" them here and there as they advance, in order to get side branches, and prevent a repetition of an old woody stem "full eight feet high."

NAMES OF PLANTS (*A Grateful Subscriber*).—Your plant is *Pulmenaria Virginica* (Virginian Lungwort), one of the most beautiful of hardy herbaceous plants. Always have a label fixed in the soil by it, to shew where it is, as it dies down below the earth's-surface. Your orange-shaped gourd is probably *Cucurbita aurantia*, or Orange-fruited gourd. (*I.S.D.*)—One of your plants is a young stem of Lily of the Valley; the flowers are those of *Arabia albida*; and the sprig of *Sedum palustre*. Your other questions we cannot occupy our space by answering. (*M. C. E.*).—Your plant is *Cineraria amelloides*: if you had sent a leaf with it much trouble would have been saved, as its flower is so much like that of *Kaulfussia amelloides*. Your other question next week.

RHUBARB FLOWER STALKS (*A Yorkshireman*).—Cut these down as fast as they appear, and never let the plants bear blossoms at all. An answer to your other query next week.

SAWDUST (*R. Hick*).—This, you say, is thoroughly decayed, and if so, it will make excellent manure for your flower borders, if applied in the autumn, or next spring.

LONDON: Printed by HARRY WOOLDRIDGE, Winchester High Street, in the Parish of Saint Mary Kalendar, and Published by WILLIAM SOMERVILLE ORR, at the Office, No. 2, Amen Corner, in the Parish of Christ Church, City of London.—May 2, 1850.

WEEKLY CALENDAR.

M D	W D	MAY 9—15, 1850.	Weather near London in 1849.		Sun Rises.	Sun Sets.	Moon R. & S.	Moon's Age.	Clock bef. Sun.	Day of Year.
9	Tu	Ascen. Holy Thurs. Burying Beetle seen.	T. 54°—49°.	N.E. Fine.	30 a. 4	33 a. 7	3 46	27	3 47	129
10	F	Daddy Longlegs appears.	T. 31°—42°.	N.W. Rain.	18	34	4 6	28	3 49	130
11	S	Reed Bunting appears.	T. 56°—30°.	N. Fine.	16	36	sets.	●	3 52	131
12	Sun	Sun. Aft. Ascension. Lily of Valley flowers.	T. 62°—41°.	E. Fine.	15	37	8a.11	1	3 53	132
13	M	Old May Day. Swift appears.	T. 62°—41°.	S.W. Rain.	13	39	9 35	2	3 54	133
14	Tu	Dot Moth appears.	T. 62°—47°.	W. Rain.	12	40	10 33	3	3 55	134
15	W	Hawthorn flowers.	T. 62°—49°.	N.W. Rain.	18	42	11 31	4	3 55	135

On the 10th of this month, in the year 1787, died Sir William Watson, a physician by profession, a man of deep scientific attainments, but chiefly deserving a notice in our columns for the account he has left to us of the remains of the gardens belonging to the Tradescants and Bishop Compton—subjects to which we shall more fully refer when jotting down our biographical notes of those horticultural worthies. Sir William Watson is one of the many instances afforded by our national annals of an individual winning his way to eminence and wealth, with no other earthly aid than his own good attainments and indomitable industry. It is a characteristic of our own blessed land, and never to be remembered but with an elevation of heart and of spirit, that in no other nation on the whole earth's broad surface is merit, however humbly born, so usually rewarded and advanced. So marked is this, that when Lord Chancellor Talbot was asked, "What are the best aids to success in life?" he replied, "Parts and poverty." The first of these requisites were Watson's in no small degree of excellence; and though poverty was not the lot attendant upon any portion of his career, yet, when he commenced life, to take a step in any profession was to take a step in advance. He was the son of a tradesman, and the apprentice of an apothecary, but very early distinguished himself as a cultivator of botany, and of natural science generally; and in 1745 he received the Copley Medal from the Royal Society, for his discoveries in electricity. From that period to the time of his decease one distinction followed close upon another; and though as a physician he had an extensive practice, yet as a man of honour and of varied high attainments he was still more widely and deeply esteemed. His success in the pursuit of several sciences teaches this lesson, which every student will benefit by imprinting upon his memory—"Examine with your own eyes—bring every alleged fact to the test of experiment." It was thus that Sir W. Watson pursued his way, cautiously and securely; and no reader of his numerous contributions to the *Philosophical Transactions* can fail of being struck with the truthfulness which characterises them; for they are almost entirely records of experiments, tried for the purpose of elucidating some previously doubtful fact. Such a mode of examining nature never fails of its legitimate object—the acquirement of truth; and to no pursuit is it more effectively applicable than to that of gardening. There was a time when writers on horticulture told their readers, and their readers believed, that if they sowed powdered ram's horns asparagus would spring up! Since then three centuries have elapsed; and such follies are not taught nor believed now, because those centuries have been the birth-time of continually varied and additional experiments on the growth of plants.

Meteorology of the Week.—At Chiswick, during the last twenty-three years, the average highest and lowest temperatures of the above seven days have been respectively 65° and 41°. The highest temperature during the period was 81°, on the 12th in 1833; and the lowest 26°, on the 15th in 1838. The number of fine days during the same time was 105, and on 55 days rain occurred.

Natural Phenomena Indicative of Weather.—If the *raven*, early in the morning, soars high in the air, circling round and round, uttering a hoarse, deep croak, it foretells fine weather. *Rooks* whirling round high in the air, ascending or descending in sudden and rapid spirals, indicate the approach of storms.

Behold the rooks, how odd their flight!
They imitate the gliding kite,
And seem precipitate to fall,
As if they felt the piercing ball.

'Twill surely rain; we see, with sorrow,
No working in our grounds tomorrow.

So the gathering together and returning home of rooks at unusual hours generally intimates the approach of rain. On the contrary, if they are noisy about trees, flying clamorously about, frequently leaving and returning to their nests, the return of fine weather is at hand.

RANGE OF BAROMETER—RAIN IN INCHES.

May		1841.	1842.	1843.	1844.	1845.	1846.	1847.	1848.	1849.
9	B.	30.097 30.008	30.094 29.992	29.861 29.504	29.962 29.933	29.490 29.483	29.974 29.863	29.839 29.757	30.222 30.153	29.992 29.070
	R.	— 0.10	— 0.03	—	—	—	0.03	0.04	—	0.06
10	B.	30.158 30.117	30.172 30.068	30.136 29.983	29.949 29.910	29.597 29.457	29.962 29.787	29.813 29.726	30.304 30.260	29.914 29.855
	R.	—	—	—	0.07	0.04	—	0.04	—	0.01
11	B.	30.064 30.003	29.996 29.842	30.184 30.165	30.060 29.931	29.849 29.805	30.003 30.058	29.681 29.591	30.220 30.278	30.101 29.837
	R.	0.01	0.06	—	—	0.08	—	—	—	—
12	B.	30.247 30.198	29.984 29.920	30.150 29.879	30.062 30.183	29.859 29.737	29.994 29.836	29.759 29.714	30.240 30.170	30.305 30.172
	R.	0.02	0.02	0.02	—	0.09	—	0.01	—	—
13	B.	30.330 30.314	30.078 30.073	29.904 29.856	30.335 30.309	30.171 30.043	29.734 29.713	29.834 29.821	30.175 30.137	30.035 29.728
	R.	—	—	—	—	0.03	0.21	0.02	—	—
14	B.	30.354 30.262	30.230 30.136	29.795 29.552	30.322 30.272	30.302 30.247	29.995 29.880	29.892 29.845	30.126 30.091	29.623 29.525
	R.	—	—	0.18	—	—	—	0.02	—	0.04
15	B.	30.194 30.043	30.337 30.341	29.509 29.497	30.305 30.285	30.278 30.274	29.968 29.859	30.123 30.059	29.966 29.781	29.571 29.529
	R.	—	—	0.14	—	—	—	0.19	—	0.27

Insects.—Every one is familiar with the Cheese maggot, or Hopper, but few of our readers, probably, are familiar with its history. A small, black, shining fly, not longer than an eighth of an inch, is very familiar to all those who are acquainted with the cheese trade. It is *Tyrophaga casei* and *Piophila casei* of naturalists. The female deposits her eggs in cheeses approaching to ripeness. The maggot from these eggs is one of those which have an extraordinary leaping power. When preparing to exercise this power, it erects itself upon its tail, bends itself into a circle, stretches out the two hooks appended to its mouth, fixes these into two cavities at its other extremity, contracts its body into an oblong loop, and then after a pause, during which it seems to concentrate its strength, it lets go its hold with a jerk so violent, that the sound of the hooks parting from the holes is plainly heard, and the leap is made rapidly, and to a great distance. Swammerdam saw one which did not exceed one-fourth of an inch in length leap out of a box six inches deep; so that if a man six feet high could leap with equal power, he could spring from the ground 144 feet into the air, or higher than an ordinary church steeple.

1, maggot preparing to leap; 2, larva, natural size; 3 and 4, fly, natural size and magnified.

Many of our readers are old enough to remember the ridicule with which the proposition to use bone-dust as a manure was received by the cultivators of the soil; and they must have heard, as we often have heard, the contemptuous query, "What! old knife-handles good for manure?" That ignorant prejudice has passed away; but another equally erroneous may arise in the mind of some of our readers, when they find that woollen rags as a manure are the subject of our present observations. We are led to make these by two letters from very different parts of England; one asking, "Why the Kentish hop-growers turn woollen rags into the soil of their hop-gardens?" and the other, which may serve in part to answer the query, is from Mr. James Derham, of Wrington, near Bristol. He says:

"What do you think of woollen rags for manure? In the lower part of this county (about Crewkerne) cultivators attach great importance to them. There are a great many field gardens there, and an immense quantity of *onions* are raised in the neighbourhood. No one thinks of sowing unless he has dug in woollen shreds. These are collected all over the county, and sold at so much per cwt. I was round there the other day (March), and saw many waggon-loads of them; and in one or two instances I saw them ploughing them in for *corn* (*oats*?). They tell me they put no manure besides; and if this really is a good thing, how very easy for many persons to accumulate a stock. I have a large heap myself, and should be glad to know your opinion as to the use of them. I have thought if they were first soaked for some days in liquid manure, it would *improve* them. Would they not do to apply to fruit-trees in that state?"

Soaking the rags in liquid manure would be a very good mode of applying the latter, and there is no doubt they would do well in combination; for the liquid manure would be for the immediate use of the plant, whilst the rags, being slow in decomposing, would serve it during the after stages of growth. They would do better for fruit-trees without being so soaked, for these trees, except when growing in very poor soil, require no stimulating like that afforded by liquid manure.

Woollen rags are by themselves, however, a good manure; and the willy dust, and other woollen refuse, so abundant in the great clothiery districts of Wiltshire, Gloucestershire, and Yorkshire, come within the designation of woollen rags; and as they slowly decompose in the soil, they all give out food highly useful to plants. During decomposition they produce ammonia and other matters soluble in water, every hundred parts being composed, like feathers, hair, &c., of about 50 parts carbon or charcoal, 7 parts hydrogen, 17 parts nitrogen, 24 parts oxygen and sulphur, and 2 parts of saline matters. These last contain carbonate of potash, muriate of potash, acetate of potash and lime, all of which' are salts, or bases of salts, useful to cultivated vegetables.

We can quote many practical authorities as to the value of woollen rags as a fertilizer. Mr. R. Slack, paper-maker, of Hayfield, Derbyshire, has used them for many years. He finds them good for *potatoes*; and adds, "for *hay grass* I have nothing that will produce so good a crop, spread upon the land in January, and raked off in April." *

Mr. J. M. Paine, writing in 1848, says that he had long been in the habit of using fifty tons yearly, paying for them in London from fifty to eighty shillings per ton; the dearest being those containing the most wool. Before putting on the land, they are cut into very small pieces (two inches square being the largest), and from one ton to half a ton per acre are sufficient. He finds them most beneficial to *hops* and *turnips*.

They are not so good when used mixed with lime; for although this decomposes them faster than when they are left to themselves, yet by such treatment the ammo-

* Our own experience tells us that woollen rags are most useful to *potatoes, strawberries, and raspberries.*

nia is driven off, in which their most active power is comprised.

We believe that the best mode of applying woollen rags to the soil is to mix them previously with the superphosphate of lime, made from bones. This contains sulphate of lime also, which will fix the ammonia of the rags as they decompose; and the phosphate of lime is a saline manure, in which the rags are deficient.

Mr. Cuthbert Johnson, in his excellent volume on "Fertilizers," says, that "woollen rags are a very durable manure, remaining dissolving in the soil and forming soluble and elastic matters for the service of plants for periods varying from two years on the heavy clays, such as those of the Kentish hop-grounds of the Weald of Kent, to three or four years on the light chalky soils of the valley of the Kennet in Berkshire. Of these rags. the consumption by the Berkshire and Oxfordshire farmers, but especially by the Kentish hop-growers, is very considerable. I am informed by an extensive dealer in these rags (Mr. Hart, White Lion-street, Bishopgate), that 20,000 tons, at the least, are annually consumed by the farmers of the south of England. Mr. Ellis, of Barming, Kent, purchased annually between four and five hundred tons, almost exclusively for his hop-grounds. The cottager, even, is interested in these facts, for every shred of an old woollen garment is available for his garden—is an admirable manure for his potato ground; or, if he has not a garden, the collectors of rags, who gather for the large dealers, will readily give him a farthing per pound for all he can collect."

Mr. Payne has written to us as follows:—

"If some of the large number of applicants for my *beehives* have to wait for them a little longer than they expected, the delay arises from the impossibility of having so large a quantity made at so short a notice. However, the season must be late, and they will all, I trust, be supplied in good time."

THE FRUIT-GARDEN.

MELONS.—We have to apologise to our amateur readers for having apparently slighted the subject of melon culture. The fact is, that so many things press in proportion to the space allotted to our labours, that some of our "irons must burn," to use a homely saying.

We are just in time to advise about a crop of late melons, which are more eligible for some families than the early ones, and which assuredly require some nicety of management. To grow melons in the months of July and August is not a matter of very great difficulty; very different, however, is it to obtain them in September, October, and even November: at which period both light and natural heat so rapidly decrease, and when the increasing and stagnating humidity of the atmosphere is anything but favourable to tropical fruits.

Those who possess melon and cucumber houses, or pits, with a source of heat independent of fermenting materials, have little difficulty; and such may continue to produce good flavoured fruit until near Christmas; for such kinds as the *Dampsha* will keep for weeks after they have been cut from the plant. We must rather address ourselves to those who have to fight their way with an ordinary frame and the use of fermenting materials only; and the latter, it may be, not over abundant. For such purposes there can be no better kind than the true *Beechwood*, the celebrity of which still remains unshaken. The *Hoosainee* varieties, however, and the *Ispahan* are excellent kinds, but we fear too tender for the amateur to try his hand upon.

Sowing.—Beechwoods, then, for the latest crop, should be sown in the early part of May. We will pass by their culture in a very young state, as that is very simple at that period.

Bed.—In making up a frame for ridging them out, it should, by some means, be built high. Many persons commit a great error in this respect; knowing that a very moderate amount of bottom heat will suffice at an advanced period, they forget that when the chills of autumn arrive strong linings will be requisite in order to revive the decaying bottom heat of the bed, and to expel stagnating moisture. To accomplish this properly, much depth of lining becomes desirable; and unless the frame is kept high to commence with, such cannot be carried out. We should consider at least four feet at back necessary for the height of the bed; and to allow for the sinking of the fermenting materials an extra foot should be added. We would, nevertheless, by no means build to this height with fermenting materials alone; for at this period such a course would assuredly endanger the roots by burning. Brushwood, or any rough material, might be carried up half the height at least, and the remaining portion should be composed of well sweetened manure and tree leaves, if to be had; finishing off at the surface with some half-rotten vegetable matter.

For *soil* we would recommend sound turfy loam; and the surface of the bed might have a good sprinkling of small charred material. This will tend to correct and dry the atmosphere of the frame, which, for late crops especially, is a most necessary point in their culture.

Training.—Much attention should be given to late crops, as to keeping the shoots well thinned and regulated; no crowding or confusion should be permitted; and the plants should, at all times during the fine weather, have abundant ventilation, in order to make them hardy and robust. This will the better enable them to endure the vicissitudes that assuredly await them at the approach of autumn. A bottom heat of seventy to eighty degrees will be better than a greater height of temperature, until the fruits have done their first swelling, which may be about the early part of August; by which time the heat will have much declined, as far as fermentation is concerned. From this period until the early part of September nothing will be requisite but to ventilate with freedom, and to syringe or sprinkle them on fine evenings at shutting-up time.

Linings.—We come now to deal with the declining temperature of autumn, and the consequent accumulation of pernicious damps, which can only be dispelled by a liberal ventilation; whilst the latter may not be permitted unless a lively heat be kept up in the body of the bed; and more especially in the upper part of the linings, which, for the most part, heat those portions of the frame or pit which impart atmospheric rather than bottom warmth. Now it is that our suggestion as to depth in the frame will tell; for width alone cannot accomplish what we feel bound to recommend.

Towards the middle of September, according as the heat of the bed and of the weather may indicate, those who undertake the somewhat perilous task of growing late melons in dung beds, must betake themselves to fermenting materials once more. The old linings must be broken up to the very bottom, and some fresh material applied; observing to use the most moderate in point of fermentative properties at the bottom, and increasing the fermentative power considerably next the sides of the frame or pit. Indeed, when above the bed level, using the most powerful hot manure, if available. And now the benefit of a little bottom heat, reinfused by

means of the linings, will be manifest; preventing the plant sinking into a state of torpidity, by keeping up a root action until the fruit is perfected.

A judicious yet free *ventilation* must still be practised; and if the frame has sunk, the back ought to be raised before applying the new lining, in order to give a steeper angle for the admission of the sun's rays. No watering will be requisite at this late period; nevertheless, it will be well, on fine afternoons, to syringe the foliage occasionally, in order to keep it fresh as long as possible; taking care that no more water is administered than can be dried away on the succeeding day.

The chief *watering* necessary is when the fruits are as large as hen's eggs, or nearly so. Up to this period, they should have been kept somewhat dry, or at least in a perfectly mellow state; *syringing* having been practised in all fine weather. When thus advanced, the best way is to give one thorough watering with warm liquid manure, which, if well performed, will, with the aid of occasional syringings, or light sprinklings, enable the plants to carry out the swelling process.

By the end of September they will require matting up at nights; still, however, leave a little air at back all night, in order that no damps be allowed to accumulate. To effect this, of course the lining heat must occasionally receive assistance by topping up, or otherwise.

By these means good melons may be obtained during October, and a great part of November, provided the hot manure can be spared, and due attention as to labour can be provided.

Clean glass must be secured to them; therefore, the lights had better be washed clean in the end of August; for all the light our skies afford will be wanted, and much more would highly benefit them. Another point, too, of good culture is to have them so inured to air and light during the heat of summer, that the lights should be pulled entirely off on all fine days—thus treating them as an ordinary ridge cucumber. This will be found to render the plants less susceptible of injury during the dull weather of autumn, and to impart a very high flavour.

We have been now speaking of their culture in dung beds; much superior, however, as well as more economical, is their culture by hot water in well contrived pits or houses, also more certain; and when the true economy of manures has been settled, we think they will generally thus be cultivated.　　R. ERRINGTON.

THE FLOWER-GARDEN.

BEDDING PLANTS: *Blue Flowers.*—The last colour with which we make distinct beds in an arrangement, is blue; and I have already treated of most of the best bedding plants of this hue, from the little *Lobelias* up to *Lupinus Hartwegii* and *Salvia patens*. This season I shall plant two large beds with those mixed lupines of which I wrote last March. I shall put three rows, or equivalents, in the middle; two rows of *Lupinus pubescens* outside that; and finish with a broad band of *Lupinus nanus*, which was sown in the beds about the middle of April. The other two were sown in boxes a month earlier. It matters not how early we thus sow all the large Lupines, such as these two, and the three kinds belonging to the *mutabilis* section, as if they should come into bloom by the end of May they never cease from blooming till they are overtaken by a smart frost.

I think that the *Lupinus pubescens* would succeed better than *Hartwegii* on deep, rich or heavy land; but here the latter never misses, and is particularly useful for large beds.

The first blue bed I ever saw (many years back) was made of *Cineraria amelloides*, a very old-fashioned looking thing, but one of the easiest plants in the world to keep in frames, and to increase. The flowers are borne on long stiff foot-stalks, which render them very suitable for the *bouquet* makers.

Amongst other things, we are noted here for keeping up to the fashion in *bouquets*; and when they are tastily made some of them look really very smart; but the makers are sad fellows to get the run of a flower-garden. I am obliged to have large masses of the most popular or suitable flowers for them reared in the reserve garden; and yet I often catch them trespassing; and then the usual excuse of some great personage "just coming in to-night," and something extra must be provided for the occasion, is sure to be urged.

I have not had a bed of this blue Cineraria since 1845, but I see a couple of them are marked for this season; and by way of a little polish I intend adding about one-third of *Lobelia ramosa*, for it will be recollected that this annual lobelia makes one of the finest low blue beds one can plant; and I make three sowings of it in pots—one in March, and two in April; get them up in a little heat, and then harden them gradually. I am not sure how this mixture will look, and I forgot to try them in cut flowers; but something I must have to render the beds richer than the cineraria by itself, although we fixed upon it on the recommendation of a gentleman who is celebrated for his fine gardens.

The *Salvia chamædrioides* is also a very old plant, but a very good one for a blue bed of no great size. It is next thing to being hardy, and creeps underground like spear grass, so that after you once get a bed of it by cuttings, you need never want it again—as by taking up the old roots at the same time as the Dahlias, and planting them in sheds or cellars, or any dry place away from the frost, you may keep it for a life-time. In the spring, that is, near the end of April, we take out the roots of this salvia, part them according to the stock we want, and then plant them either in sand under a cold-frame, or, what is as likely, plant them at once in their flowering-beds, and that is as good as any other way with the *Salvia patens*, and with the dahlias also, when one does not want a large increase from their roots. The best way to deal with this salvia in beds, is to plant the roots or plants rather close, or, say, not more than six to nine inches apart according to their size; and as they grow, to train the shoots round and round until the ground is matted with them. Their side branches from this net-work will rise in thick and close succession till the end of October; and the height under this management will be from a foot to eighteen inches, according to the richness of the soil. We need hardly remark, that all our salvias are partial to a rich pasture. Of all our blue beds, this has the darkest shade; and after all that has been sung and said on the subject, there is no way of bringing out the full effects of blue, purple, and pink flowers so successful as planting according to the shades in these colours. We can hardly meet with three plants with blue, purple, or pink flowers which are exactly of the same shade or tint. We have the blues from this dark blue salvia to the slate or gray bluish tint in *Isotoma axillaris*, of which I said enough last autumn to serve for one year at least; but I have another *new* bed to-day in this light blue tint, and an excellent bed to the bargain. It is made with *Selago corymbosa*, an old plant, it is true, and casts a reflection on us gardeners for our haste in discarding such useful plants after a few seasons, because we happen not to find out the proper mode of treating them at first, not only for the flower-garden, but for any of the gardening purposes. I believe the credit of introducing this new bed into our gardens is due to my worthy friend Mr. Smith, Curator of the Royal Botanic Gardens at Kew. The way to manage this blue bedder is to treat it as a biennial, that is, to sow its seeds one year, and to flower it the

following season; and this is a very good time to sow its seeds to come in next year; the plants can be taken up in the autumn, and kept over the winter with very little trouble; but although a soft wooded plant it does not readily yield a supply by cuttings.

Speaking of Kew Gardens, reminds one of the curious turns fashion takes in flowers, and in other things. Although they have the largest collection of plants in the country there, the most curious, rare, and expensive, and although they cultivate them in the first-rate style, since they have had proper accommodation, yet, they must have their flower-gardens, and plant them too, in the most approved style of fashion, just as I have been stating in those articles on bedding plants. Now, this is a very harmless and enjoyable way of amusing the public; and yet there are those in the high places of gardening who sneer at all the modern improvements in arranging flower-gardens, whether public or private; and who, assert that an *unskilful* race of degenerate gardeners have brought about such a state of things, substituting yards of this, that, and the other kind of verbenas, and scarlet geraniums, with "patches" of petunias, &c., &c., for hollyhocks, gilliflowers, and "herbaceous plants," which are all most beautiful in their way. So they are, sure enough; but a gardener of these days who could produce nothing better than these "good things in their way," might as well sing, "Bundle, and Go," and be off at once to New Zealand. They say a shoemaker cannot go beyond his "last;" and there are critics whose flights of imagination cannot reach above the range of their own natural atmosphere; but the "cant of criticism" looses its point in such hands. Out of the thousands of "beautiful plants" introduced into or indigenous to this country, very few, comparatively speaking, are found to possess the qualities necessary for the flower-garden, or for the purposes of high cultivation in any department of our craft—as any one a little versed in the subject may see shortly, at the first exhibitions of plants in the world, in the neighbourhood of London. I would give very little for the head and ears of a gardener who attended these great exhibitions of our skilful or *unskilful* efforts for a serious of years, who could not tell before hand not only the names, but the actual dimensions of eighty-five out of every hundred plants that will be staged in London this season for competition; notwithstanding that bushels of gold and silver medals have been offered and awarded, to stimulate the exertions of collectors and cultivators. No, like the flower gardener, we shall have nothing better than the old dish over again this season; but the flower gardener has the advantage of his "brother chip" of the exhibition tables, for he can cook many of his old dishes over again, and so produce a more apparent variety. The truth of all this, however, is simply this, that gold and silver can no more turn the tide of fashion, than skilful or unskilful gardeners, and critics, can change the nature of those plants they cultivate and describe; and it is very little to the point to say, that gardeners of any stamp are more potent than gold and silver. Seeing, therefore, that those things are so past our control, would it not be better for us to work each in his own calling, and endeavour to assist and please each other, rather than bandy about hard names, and ungracious epithets?

The principal plants for displaying the more distinct colours during the summer and autumn, have now been mentioned; those for the other half of the flowering season, or from February to the middle or end of June, there is no great hurry about for the present; and before I begin to enumerate those summer-flowering plants, which either produce no decided colour or which keep in flower only a month or two, I wish to recommend seeds of the following plants, chiefly annuals, to be sown between this and the 20th May, to come in either for beds or as auxiliaries for filling up vacancies as things go off in the autumn.

Alyssum (Sweet), always a useful plant to have a stock of at hand.

Aster (China)—To be sown about the middle of May in the reserve garden; to be transplanted there once or twice, or treated like celery plants in all respects, and not to be planted in the flower-garden till the plants show their colour.

Clarkias and *Collinsias*, always gay and useful, but will not remove after they are half-grown.

Convolvulus minor.—A most lovely summer flower, of which there are now many varieties. It makes a splendid bed for three months; will not transplant unless very young. Sow it where it is to flower, and place the tops of pea-stakes all over the bed as the plants advance, and they will soon be covered.

Convolvulus major.—Of this there are many shades of colours, from clear white to dark purple, and all of them are gay and useful for summer climbers.

Dianthus, or the Pink and Sweet William tribe, and the Indian Pink.—There are many nice little plants in this tribe for rock work, and for gay patches here and there, where room can be found for them.

Erysimum perofskianum.—This is a gay, tall, yellow annual, which will bear to be trained down; and will flower for three months; and also a good one to sow in the autumn.

Eucharidium grandiflorum.—This is one of our gayest little annuals, with purplish pink flowers; and a little bed of it is one of the gayest of the season, but it only blooms for five or six weeks.

Larkspurs.—These, again, are very rich in dwarf and tall plants of various colours; a bed or border of mixed dwarf larkspurs is extremely gay, and the tall ones not less so. The real blue branching larkspur is one of the most difficult to get and to keep true, without the purple tinge; and I would pull up all the shades of it to save seeds from the dark blue variety.

Malope grandiflora is a tall purple with mallow-like flowers, and will hold on for full three months.

Nemophila.—All of them are gay six-week annuals, which may be had from the end of April till the frost comes, by sowing them in the autumn, three times in the spring, and again in the first week in July.

Nasturtiums.—The common nasturtiums are very gay for edgings to beds when well managed, and will transplant until they are of a large size. They should be trained as a broad band, and their large leaves pulled off as often as they obscure the blossoms.

Salpiglossis.—Of this there are many shades, and they last three months or more in bloom, and are well worth a place in the flower-borders.

Stocks.—All the varieties of the ten-week stocks, if sown now, will come in useful in the autumn for filling up beds and borders.

Sultans.—The sweet sultans, particularly the yellow and the purple ones, make a good addition and variety in the flower-beds; and they may be sown till after midsummer for late autumn blooming.

Poppies, Persicaria, and *Sunflowers,* are also good old things for shrubbery borders; and so are *Zinnias,* and *Tvaria oculata,* and *Scabious,* all of which will be in time for autumn bloom, if sown before the 20th of May.

D. BEATON.

GREENHOUSE AND WINDOW GARDENING.

BALCONIES.—Since I adverted to this subject last week, I have had an opportunity of seeing a great many of these adjuncts in urban, suburban, and rural situations. In many of these, though the houses were coated with cement, and coloured, or painted, to resemble stone-colour, the railings and boarding of the balconies were of a bright green; the very diversity of colour attracting attention, and bringing up, not unfrequently, ideas of afterthoughtism and insecurity combined, and more especially the latter feeling, when no suitable balustradings, ornamental or otherwise, were seen; it being necessary for the complacent comfort of the observer, that *strength* should not merely exist, but that the elements of that strength should be *perceptible*—a fact which has led to many a necessary ornamental appendage in architecture that otherwise might have been unnecessary. But with all this incongruity, it was pleasing to observe that a better taste was finding its way, even as respects the prevalent colour of the balconies. In hundreds of yards of suburban balconies, where, a few years ago, *green* flamed in all its glory, the colour has been exchanged for dull stone, or sober bronze. In many of these balconies, too, vases and baskets had been exchanged for the long narrow boxes. But here, in some cases, the principle of harmony had been carried too far; for the walls of the house being painted, the pretty stone or composition vases had been painted too, which reduced them to the same level in point of appearance as would have been manifested by vases of burnt clay, of wood, or of iron, if equally painted; all of which would have looked better if liberally daubed with white sand when the paint was wet, which would at once remove the impressions of oily paint, which to our mind is rather incongruous with the growth of plants, and elicit the appearance and the associations of vessels of sandstone: not that we advocate, *in general*, anything approaching duplicity or deceit, even in appearance, but in the present case we cannot see the harm in hinting to our balcony friends *how* they may for the expense of a few shillings develop as pure a taste, as the titled lady may with propriety exhibit at the expense of as many pounds, by possessing the real *Simon-pure* article, and not a cheap make-believe vessel. As there is something in a name, so there is much in appearances, so far as the awakenings of feelings of pleasure are concerned; and, therefore, while upon the open balcony—even so far as the ideas of strength and solidity come before our notice—we would contend for having vessels intended for plants consisting *really* or *apparently* of stone; so upon the sill of the window outside, and especially inside, would we recommend, instead of the red pot, pots and vases of all beautiful shapes and colours, hard-burned, and glazed, or even the prettiest china; and for the encouragement of those who think that plants would not thrive in such vessels, I would state that some of the finest and cleanest plants in a window I ever beheld were grown in such vessels, the colours of which harmonised and contrasted with each other, as well as with the plants flowering so beautifully in them. Nothing but a prejudice in favour of soft, staring, red pots, could have reconciled ladies, who shew such refined taste in the choosing of the furniture, carpeting, painting, and drapery of their rooms, to place such incongruous vessels upon their tables or window-sills, when others, beautiful and diversified in form, and harmonious in colour, could have been used; and if too costly to come in contact with our rough gardening hands, so as to grow the plants in them, there could be no objection to setting the plants, with their common pots attached, inside of them when in their flowering state; and then a slight covering of green moss would not only perfect the illusion as to the plant growing in the beautiful vase, but would also, by its checking evaporation from the soil, render the necessity of watering a matter of less frequent occurrence.

But to return to our balconies—in London, and more particularly its suburbs, thousands of pretty *baskets* of wire-work, of all conceivable shapes and forms are to be seen, and at a very moderate price; the basket consisting chiefly of open wire-work, and the feet and legs formed of the same material. Such baskets, even in their present state, would be a great improvement on the pig-feeding-like troughs of boxes, as plants in flower might be set in them, the pots plunged in, and then covered with green moss; one advantage of which would be that one plant could easily be removed and replaced by another; and a second and greater advantage would be the ease with which plants could be tended and examined when placed upon a level with the eye, compared with the difficulty and uninvitingness of such an examination when the plants are struggling for existence upon the same level as our feet. The worldly-wise retail trades-man alike shuns a shop, where his customers would either have to rise or descend a step or two; knowing, that before they would give themselves the trouble to do so, they would pass by to a more considerate neighbour; a fact—this along with many more, involving a similar principle—which ought to teach our friends who would wish to diffuse the civilizing and refining influence from flowers which they themselves had experienced :—the *necessity* of placing these flowers in their balconies and boudoirs, as near the eye and the hand as possible; as the mere beholding of such flowers, and the close ex-amination of their beauties and structural organization, will be followed by sensations and consequences vastly different.

The first improvement in such baskets would be to change the flaming fashionable bright green into a sober bronze or dull stone colour. If the stone colour should be adopted, the second improvement would be to make the main supports of a stronger material, and bind them together with a smaller wire, so that when well sanded, the whole would resemble tessellated carved stone-work. The third improvement would be, to make from the continuation of the feet and legs, the framework on which to fix a vase or basket of zinc or galvanized iron, in which, after insuring means of drainage, the plants may be turned out into suitable soil. It would be easy to form several fillets round the vase, and to give it a grace-ful curved lip at the top, so as to make it very ornamental. The feet and supporting pillar might be encased in similar material, and all might then be painted to imi-tate stone or marble. Groups of threes or fives of such baskets or vases might thus be placed together, and thus transform our balconies into miniature flower-gardens. The green supporters would never be missed, for round the side of the vase we would plant running and creep-ing plants, such as *Maurandyas, Lobelias, Verbenas,* the smaller flowering *Tropæolums, Lophospernums,* &c., but generally of a colour to contrast with the main colour in the basket or the vase.

It is only for the lovers of flowers to say that they want such things, and our clever tradesmen will easily supply them; and in cheapness, in proportion to the de-mand. Mr. Savage has come forward to give an impetus to the forming of pretty baskets for plant houses. Will no one else step forward to encourage more artistic dis-play, combined with fitness for the end in view—whether composed of wood, iron, cement, or earthenware, as respects the vessels in which plants are placed in win-dows and balconies?

There is one purpose, however, for which we would tolerate a large square box or two in the corner of a balcony, and that would be for planting some strong growing creeper, to run and festoon itself among the railings, where the distance is too great from the ground to permit the plants being inserted below. For such a purpose, nothing answers better than the common *White jasmine,* the common hedge-row *Honeysuckle,* and some of the stronger *Clematis,* or hardy *climbing roses.* For summer decoration the *Cobæa scandens, Lophos-permum scandens, Tropæolum majus, T. peregrinum,* and

T. pentaphyllum, may be used, along with masses of *Sweet peas.* For such a purpose, and also for climbing around and garlanding a window, few things are more beautiful than the *T. pentaphyllum,* with its thousands of greenish red flowers.

SMALL FLOWER-GARDEN.—The same correspondent who inquired about balconies, also inquired about the laying out of a small front garden of 17 feet, which we presume means 17 feet each way. We can only allude to this *now.* Many methods might be adopted, and much in-terest created, by vases, baskets, raising the ground, using edgings of flint, box, &c. One of the simplest methods, however, and which would look well, would be to have a circle of six or seven feet in diameter in the centre, with four clumps equal in size, and similar in form around it, divided from each other and from the circle by gravel paths, of from two to three feet in width. Supposing, that the longer straight lines of the four clumps will be a fence of some sort or other, there *Sweet peas, Dahlias,* and a few strong-growing and climbing plants may be placed, and the front planted with those of lower growth. With the exception of these fence plants, the whole might be grouped, either with common bedding plants or with annuals, the latter only costing a few pence, if raised from seed. Were we to advise, we should say plant the centre bed with white, and the other beds in the order of colour mentioned—1, scarlet; 2, blue; 3, orange or yellow; 4, purple. Each bed might have different tints of the same colour, the lowest growing always next the path.   R. FISH.

                                Scarlet.
             Purple.   White.   Blue.
                                  Orange.

HOTHOUSE DEPARTMENT.

STOVE PLANTS.

CLERODENDRUMS.—For large and noble foliage, with high-coloured flowers in large panicles, there are no plants that surpass Clerodendrums; and, therefore, we now remark upon them, because in selecting stove plants for our fortnightly essays we endeavour to choose such as are really showy, fine plants, undeniably worth every care and attention the amateur and gardener can bestow upon them. Any one that has seen Cleroden-drums even moderately well grown, will agree with us that they are of the splendid character we have described above, at least such of the genus as we shall recommend for culture. We have already mentioned one species, the *C. splendens speciosissimum,* as a splendid climber, suitable to cultivate in the orchid-house, and it is equally well adapted for the same purpose in the stove; it is also very effective as a pot-plant for exhibition pur-poses. When trained either upon a balloon-shaped trellis, or a flat trellis, it produces its large bunches of rich scarlet flowers in abundance, rendering it an object fit either to be exhibited as a single specimen of superior culture, or to be one of a collection, however large or small. Independent of being used as an exhibition plant, it is well worthy of cultivating in this style as an ornamental object amongst other stove plants. With the exception of requiring a trellis to tie its slender branches to, it requires the same culture as we shall give presently for the shrubby species.

The following are the species worth cultivating; they stand in our list according to their merit, that is, the first is the best and the last the least worthy; but the degrees of merit are not widely different, as they are all good. Such persons as have the least room may try to obtain only the first or second, but where the cultiva-tor's means are ample in respect to room every one should be grown.

Clerodendrum Bethunianum (Bethune's Clerodendrum), has fine foliage, very large panicles of flowers, each with broad petals of a most dazzling scarlet colour.

Clerodendrum Kæmpferi (Kæmpfer's C.), a splendid species, producing a large panicle of scarlet flowers, rising very conspicuously above the noble foliage.

Clerodendrum fallax, also very handsome, sending up several branching heads of bloom of the finest scarlet colour.

Clerodendrum Devonianum, so named in compliment to that eminent patron of gardening, the Duke of Devonshire. It has fine branching panicles of scarlet flowers, but the foliage is not so large as that of the preceding.

Clerodendrum paniculatum (Panicled C.). Foliage very fine, of a rather glaucous hue, extremely large panicles of flowers of an orange scarlet.

Clerodendrum macrophyllum (Broad-leaved C.). This has the finest foliage of all the genus, produces large panicles of pure white handsome flowers, flowering very dwarf.

Clerodendrum fragrans flore pleno (Sweet-scented double-flowered C.). A very desirable species to cultivate on account of its fragrance; it produces umbels of white and pink flowers on small plants.

CULTURE.—This genus of plants may be propagated easily in the usual way, by cuttings of the young shoots placed in pots, under hand-glasses, in heat; but as they do not usually produce plenty of young shoots, they may be propagated successfully by cuttings of the roots. The way to manage this is to take an old plant out of the pot, shake off the soil, and cut off portions of the root, dividing them into pieces four inches long. Put these sections of the root into small pots singly, and place them in a propagating house, or in a hotbed; they will soon put forth new roots and shoots, and in one year make excellent plants. But the readiest way of increasing the four kinds first mentioned is by seeds, which are frequently produced freely; gather them as soon as they are ripe, and sow them in pans or pots plunged in a brisk heat. The March following pot the seedlings off, as soon as they have made two or three leaves, into small pots, singly; place them near the glass to induce dwarf growth, and repot them into larger pots as the roots fill the pot. This should be repeated three or four times during the summer, so that by October they will be in pots eight inches diameter, and be stout, stocky plants. They may remain in these pots till the February following, when they may be potted again, and placed in a higher temperature, have plenty of water given them, and be frequently syringed; by such liberal treatment they will grow surprisingly, and will require repotting again by the end of April. In these pots they should remain to flower in July, and will then be really magnificent ornaments to the stove till September. The same treatment of young plants raised by cuttings of the shoots or roots will have the same happy effect, but there is the advantage in raising seedlings of the probability of obtaining finer varieties.

WINTER TREATMENT.—The strong plants that have flowered so finely may be cut down after flowering, and be placed under the stages, where no water will fall upon them, giving them only just water enough to keep them alive. In the spring take them out of their resting place, turn them out of the large pots, reduce the ball and roots, repot them and plunge them in a gentle bark-bed heat; they will soon begin to grow, and most likely produce two or more shoots, but do not leave more than three to flower. Follow on the same generous treatment, by freely potting and liberally supplying water, that we have described above for one-year old plants; by thus treating two-year old plants, more head, or panicles of flowers, will be produced. After this second season of bloom it will not be worth while to

keep them any longer: let younger plants take their place.

SOIL.—As these plants are rapid growers, and in a short time develope a large amount of foliage and bloom, their food should be proportionably rich and stimulating; good fibrous loam, rough peat, and well decayed dung, in equal parts, is the compost they delight in; a sprinkling of sand amongst it to keep it open will also be useful; use both loam and peat in a very rough state, if there be fibrous lumps in each of the size of hen's eggs it will be all the better. Manure-water, well diluted, in the last stage of their growth, previously to flowering, will be useful, giving it every third time the plants require watering.

FLORISTS' FLOWERS.

Since we wrote last we have had a return of cold northerly winds, and slight frosts at night; we have had also some sunny days. Now, these changes from cold to heat, from dull weather to bright sunshine, imperatively calls upon the lovers of flowers to be on the alert to protect their blooms and plants from such extremes.

TULIPS.—These noble flowers are now the grand ornament of the florists' garden, and, with the exception of some early pansies, are the only flowers now requiring shade from too great sunshine. The old practical florist will be on the look out every morning, to observe whether the clouds will clear away to allow the bright sun to shine with unbroken splendour; if that is likely to take place, down goes the shade to protect his favourites, and preserve their fragile colours from fading too soon; our amateur friends will do well to imitate his doings, his foresight, and caution. Tulips will also require protection from cold winds and heavy rains.

T. APPLEBY.

THE KITCHEN-GARDEN.

GLOBE ARTICHOKES.—This excellent vegetable may be made productive throughout the greater number of the summer months. The old plants that have stood over from last season should have had their final thinning ere this; and also as many suckers planted out in succession as may be required for the new plantations. The strongest suckers left on the old plants, will, some of them, now be shewing their edible heads; and if these are well encouraged by the surface soil being kept well open, by slight forkings and hand scarifyings, with liberal soakings of manure water, an abundant succession of good, tender, well shaped and well coloured artichokes will be the result. The heads should be cut in good season, whether required or not; as, by allowing them to grow to a useless size, not only is the successional crop, which would be found so useful through the hot summer months, prevented coming to perfection, but the whole plant is exhausted for the future; whereas if they are cut when about the size of a small tea-cup, and well encouraged as above directed, a long succession may be expected; for generally, by good management, the artichoke will shew a number of heads in succession on the same stem. The earliest and strongest planted of this season's suckers, if managed as we recommend, will produce a succession for the autumn months. It is quite as essential to look forward and provide for the long days of summer, when heat and drought may be expected to prevail, as it is to provide for the short, dark, and frosty days of winter; for heat and drought may be observed, in some localities, at times very materially to limit the supply of good vegetables; and this, too, in places where, if a little forethought had been exercised, abundance would most probably have been the result.

SLOPING BANKS.—We find the sloping bank system, as we have elsewhere stated, very advantageous, not only throughout the summer but also in the autumn, winter, and spring. All our late sown peas are planted in single rows, as a protection and a partial shade to other crops. A row of late peas is, at the present season, sown on the summit of a large sloping bank in a deep drill, and the drill only partially filled up; that is to say, the drill is drawn, or a shallow trench cast out with a spade, deeper than is required to be filled up to cover the peas to their proper depth, so that there is, when sown and covered, a rill still left. As soon as the peas are up, their growth is first encouraged by frequently raking and stirring the surface soil, and as soon as three or four inches high they are mulched with half-decayed vegetable refuse, leaves, or short mulchy old dung linings, and the pea-sticks at once applied. The only after-management required are liberal soakings of liquid manure. The abundant production thus obtained is astonishing, and the quality so improved that the varieties are really not recognised by good judges.

On the north side of these sloping banks, or whichever way they may be formed, the shadiest or coldest side is selected for cultivating late *cauliflowers, Cape brocoli, lettuce, spinach, summer turnips,* &c.; each and all *sown thinly in drills,* to be thinned out and remain; on the sunny or hottest side, *Dwarf Kidney beans, New Zealand* or *Tetragonian spinach, vegetable marrows, gherkin cucumbers, capsicums, chillies,* and such other vegetables as require heat and shelter. All are, of course, duly encouraged by good attention to surface stirring and the application of liquid manure. The annual production by such management is wonderful. The *early celery* delights also in a warm situation; and a preparation made between two sloping banks in the valley appears to suit it well. Other ground between the peas, planted at wide distances, upon the same principle, as the spring crops come off, are famous for getting out the *autumn* and *white varieties of brocolis, kales,* and *borecoles, coleworts* and late *cabbages,* &c.; indeed, with a little forethought and method, all ground thus managed may be turned to most valuable account at all seasons.

JERUSALEM ARTICHOKES.—If these appear with more than one shoot to a plant, the superabundant ones should be taken off, as one good strong shoot to a plant will always produce more fine-sized tubers than if more than one is left. The earth about them should be well loosened with the hand drag.

CABBAGE.—Sow now the small compact varieties of *cabbage,* so as to have a store in hand in case of vacancies; a good supply of plants is always useful for producing successional crops of young greens and turned-in young cabbage.

CARDOONS.—Sow now in full crop; to grow them well a shallow trench, similar to a celery trench, should be cast out on a piece of ground which has previously been well trenched and manured; and, if it can be spared, a little well decomposed manure forked into the trench would be very beneficial. The seeds should be placed up the centre of the trench, about six inches or so apart, and covered from an inch and a half to two inches in depth; the plants should be thinned in due season, the standing crop encouraged by frequent surface-stirrings, and attention given to the application of liquid-manure, regulating its strength by the luxuriance of the plants. At all times liquid-manure should be applied to young plants well diluted of course, and well weakened down, or the effects produced will be as injurious as would be the giving strong beer and beef to a little child. The principle sowings of *celery* should be thus gently and gradually encouraged; and the plants, as soon as they can be handled, should be pricked out in succession on a well chosen piece of ground. The *early planted out celery* should have the same encouragement that is recommended for other crops with regard to surface-stirring and liquid-manure; the side suckers should at all times be kept cleared away.

ROUTINE WORK.—Plant out the early *basil* and *sweet marjoram,* and make a sowing also on a warm border; plant out *tomatos;* attend to the making out of any vacancies that may occur amongst the drill crop; attend well to the surface-stirring and timely thinning; make another sowing of *parsley* and *early turnips;* well protect the ridged out *cucumbers* and *vegetable marrows;* and, if cold winds or stormy weather prevail, keep the linings of the *frame* and *pit cucumbers* well topped-up in order to maintain one uniform heat; make successional sowings of the best kind of each, and attend regularly to the stopping of them, keeping the vine thin, and not allowing a glut of fruit to swell at one time, which will not only exhaust the plants, and cause deformity amongst the fruit, but the distress and poverty thus occasioned will be followed in time by vermin and disease.   JAMES BARNES.

MISCELLANEOUS INFORMATION.

MILK.

By the authoress of " My Flowers."

ONE of the cheapest and most useful articles of consumption in a family, particularly where there are children, is milk. In towns, where it is brought to the door, and doled out in small quantities at a high price, of course it must always be considered *dear;* but in the country, or in small towns, where it is perhaps possible to obtain it from farms in the neighbourhood, it will be found a most wholesome and valuable addition to the family-table in every way. Skimmed-milk is sold in the country at one halfpenny per quart, and at this price nothing can be so advantageous for children's food, both as regards cheapness and nutrition. A basin of boiled bread and milk is a simple, strengthening breakfast and supper, upon which every child will thrive; and if it is made properly, and the stomach will bear it (which is

not always the case), it is an excellent meal for grown persons, particularly those who are seeking to live in the cheapest manner possible. The bread should be *cut,* not broken, into the shape of large dice, and placed first in the basin—the *boiling* milk when poured upon it, in all its beautiful frothiness, presents as tempting an appearance to the eye as to the taste; and it is so nourishing, that invalids who can take only a few spoonful at a time, will thrive upon it.

Milk, and rice, and flour, all of which are cheap and nutritious, may be combined in various ways, so as to furnish economical dishes of great delicacy as well as usefulness; and it would be highly desirable that families living in country towns " where provisions are dear," should endeavour to effect an arrangement with neigh-curing farmers to procure milk on the cheapest terms. New milk is always dear, and is by no means necessary—good, unadulterated skimmed-milk from a farm is quite sufficient for general purposes, and for the means of those who are struggling for life. Let *this* always be borne in mind—it is a great assistance to us in domestic economy.

Milk, thickened with flour, and carefully boiled, is excellent either hot or cold, in which latter case it becomes a jelly; and if flavoured with bay-leaf, and sweetened with lump-sugar, it is almost as delicate as blancmange. The proportions are five tablespoonsful of flour to a quart of milk. The flour and milk must be mixed together in a basin, until as smooth as cream, and then poured into a delicately clean saucepan. It must be stirred one way, *without ceasing*, until it boils; if left to itself an instant, it either burns or becomes lumpy, and it should be as smooth as possible when properly done. It should be boiled until the underdone-smell of flour is quite gone, which will be easily understood by a little experience; the bay-leaves must be boiled in it, and taken out, of course, before it is served up. When done, it may be poured into a pie-dish, soup-plates, or small basins, if to be eaten hot; or into moulds to be turned out when cold; and in either case it is excellent. Sugar or treacle may be eaten with it.

This mode of preparing milk is so simple, that it may not have occurred to those who have enjoyed the luxuries of life; but even in that case I have known it eaten for breakfast, by a gentleman, who preferred it to any other delicacy for his morning meal. More or less flour may be used according to fancy, but the proportion given is the medium.

Rice is a very useful article in a family. There is a cheap and excellent kind sold as "broken rice," at 2d and 2½d per pound, which is quite as good as the whole rice sold at 3d and 4d. It is white and delicate, but it is sold cheap because it has been broken in the carriage, and is therefore sifted from the perfect rice, and sold by itself. It makes puddings, rice-milk, &c., and thickens soups as well as the unbroken grains would do.

Carolina rice is large, and white and fine, and swells quickly; but it is much dearer than the East India, or Patna rice, as it is sometimes called, and does not boil so light and dry when required for curry, and to eat with fruit or preserves.

Then there is another and still cheaper kind, but it is unblanched, and therefore not so delicate to the eye, although quite as good to the taste. This rice is sold at 1d. and 1¼d per pound, and if bought in large quantities it becomes even cheaper; for home consumption the colour is of little consequence. This rice requires a great deal more care in washing and picking than the finer sorts; but its only difference consists in retaining the skin, which is very much like that of the almond, before it is blanched. It is a most valuable food for the poor, and has been largely distributed among them since the failure of potatoes; but very frequently the poor are strongly prejudiced against that to which they have not been accustomed; and I know, in some instances, that they have received without much gratitude some pounds of brown rice, instead of the usual gift of potatoes. Others again, thankfully acknowledge its value; and say that a dish of plain boiled rice, with a little salt, and *perhaps* an onion, is a most comfortable meal, and a great help in their families; and not only "saves the bread," but satisfies the children sooner, and nourishes them too. East India rice does not swell so readily as the Carolina, and should be laid to soak in water as long as possible before it is dressed, when required for *baked* puddings; a day and a night will not be too long, but it is not always possible to give it so much time.

Rice should be purchased in large quantities when it is used freely in a family. By the cwt. or ½ cwt. it will be laid-in much cheaper than when a few pounds only are bought at a time.

Rice-milk is an excellent food for children; so is rice-pudding, both baked and boiled, with which treacle may be used instead of sugar. The three fine healthy children of a near relative of my own, were brought up entirely upon milk and rice, sago. &c., until they were four or five years' old. They never cared for meat, it is true; and children in general would probably prefer a more simple diet, if they were not, from their earliest years, accustomed to animal food. But in the instance to which I now allude, where means were small, and principle was strong, the boys were brought up in the simplest way; and their healthy appearance and milk-white teeth were the admiration of all who saw them, and bore ample testimony to the nutritious quality of their sweet and wholesome food.

Oatmeal is of too heating a nature for general use. It frequently produces eruptions and irritation of the skin, and I have known such effects arise from its use in gruel, if taken daily for a very short period. It is best even in gruel to employ flour; and this is a very good substitute for thick milk, if the stomach will not bear the latter, although of course not quite so agreeable to the palate. The occasional use of oatmeal cannot be objected to, but taken frequently, it often disagrees. Flour is so simple and wholesome, and so cheap, that we can scarcely substitute a better or more reasonable article for it, and when there is any possibility of injury arising to the health—that most important earthly blessing—we had better not attempt to try any experiments. I will, however, subjoin the method of making oatmeal porridge, used by the poorer classes of the Scotch and Irish, because it may be relished as an occasional meal. Oatmeal must be stirred into boiling water with a stick, a little salt added to it; and it must then boil on the fire for about ten minutes, being stirred all the time. If sufficiently done it will become like thick pudding, and should be eaten with milk. A little practice will discover the proportions as I find receipts lamentably deficient in quantities; but an experienced person will judge very accurately on these points.

THE DOMESTIC PIGEON.

In the endeavour to obtain for our readers trustworthy information relative to the varieties and merits of the domestic pigeons, we have found that those who possessed the requisite information were either unwilling or too idle to make it public. In this dilemma we referred to works which have been published in this country, and without a single exception, not one is in any of its departments satisfactory. In foreign literature we find works relative to the pigeon much superior, and from among these we have selected one which is the joint production of a practical manager of pigeons and of a naturalist too unknown to fame. This work contains not only the history, description, and drawings of each variety, but also enters fully into the particulars of their management, diseases, and other useful and most interesting to the pigeon fancier. It is entitled, "Pigeons of the Dove-cot or the Natural History and Description of Domestic Pigeons with the mode of establishing Dove-cots, &c., and securing Pigeons. By M. M. Boitard and ――――. The first of these gentlemen was for many years manager of the dove-cots and poultry establishments of the Duchess de Berri. We now commence a translation of this work

GENERAL HISTORY OF PIGEONS.

The pigeons combined with the multitudes in a numerous tribe of species in the systematic arrangement of all bewildering to naturalists. Thus, Linnæus, has allied with the sparrows (passeres). Brisson, Pennant, Temminck, and Latham, formed them into a distinct order; whilst others, and others have united them with the doves and fowls, making them a division of the Gallinaceous birds. Macgillivray has made them the single family in a separate order, that of *Gemitores*, or Cooers.

The generic characters of these birds are: a bill weak, slender, straight, pressed closely together at the sides, the bottom covered on both sides with an arched membrane, straight in front; a superior mandible swelled more or less towards the end, hooked, or only inclined at the point; oblong nostrils, open towards the middle of the bill, placed in a cartilage forming a membranous protuberance, more or less thick or soft; a tongue whole and pointed; feet short, mostly red, with uncombined nails; four claws, three before and one behind; the former are almost always quite free, but sometimes united at their origin by a small membrane; the wings long and pointed, or round and middle-sized; the body is fleshy and savoury; their food consisting of fruits, grain, and seeds, which they swallow whole; they build their nests in a simple manner on the branches of trees or in holes.

Pigeons, like the sparrows, are monogamious, that is to say, one female is sufficient for a male. They keep together during the whole of the breeding season, and both work in constructing the nest; they divide between them the cares of incubation (hatching), and the education of their young. These are fed for some time in the nest; they are born blind, and incapable of choosing their food, which the male and female bring to them alternately; in short, they do not risk quitting the cradle in which they have been born, until they are entirely fledged. The Gallinaceous, or fowl tribe, on the contrary, are polygamous, and in several kinds one male can serve for a great number of females. The nest for their rising family is made entirely by the hen; she lays a great number of eggs, covers them, and hatches their young without the cock appearing to take the slightest interest in her occupation. As soon as the chickens are hatched they can run about, quit the place of their birth, and know how to find their own food without the assistance of their parents. All these characters are more than sufficient to distinguish pigeons from the Gallinaceous tribe; but we shall also find reasons to separate them likewise from the class of sparrows. When these last drink, they take the water into the lower mandible of their beak, and make it run into the throat by quickly elevating the head almost perpendicularly; they all lay more than two eggs; they simply place in the bill of their young ones the food which they bring them; and lastly, they have not the faculty of inhaling air in large quantities. Pigeons, on the contrary, plunge their beak into the water when they drink, and draw in at one draught all the quantity of liquid that they require; they never lay more than two eggs; they feed their young by pouring into their throat, in a peculiar manner, the food prepared in their stomach; they can inhale a larger or smaller quantity of air, and retain it in their œsophagus (crop) as long as they wish. All this proves the interior organization to be quite different, besides which the singularity of their caresses, the nature of their plumage, and their inability to sing, separates them still further from this class of birds. From this it results that the pigeon should form, as Temminck, Le Vaillant, and other naturalists think, a separate order, and we may intercalate it between the sparrow and the Gallinaceous.

We know some pigeons which in the wild state feed on berries, and even insects; but they are generally granivorous, and all those that are reared in a tame state live on grain. Their food undergoes in their œsophagus, or crop, a maceration first, which renders the digestion more easy when it has descended into the stomach, or gizzard. This gizzard is lined with very thick and strong muscles, and is furnished within with a hard rugose or wrinkled membrane; it exercises a strong mechanical action on the food. Pigeons, like most other birds, swallow a certain quantity of small stones, which mixed with grain already softened in the crop, are rubbed together with it, and by their hardness help to reduce it to a nourishing state.

The lungs of all birds are single, closely attached to the sides and back-bone, and not enveloped in the inward skin of the ribs; they are pierced with holes, which permits the air to spread itself through every part of the body, as well as the cavities of the bones, but principally into some great bags placed in the breast and belly, by which means they can swell themselves considerably for the purpose of facilitating their flight, and producing that volume of voice which sometimes astonishes us. Pigeons have this singular faculty to a still more surprising extent, they can draw in and retain in their crop such a considerable quantity of air, that in some varieties their throat thus swelled is often as large as the rest of their body. The use of this strange organization is not yet known. Another singularity peculiar to these birds is, that at present no gall bladder has been discovered.[*]

It is believed that pigeons contract but one marriage in their life, unless this union is broken by some fatal accident, but this is very doubtful. It is true, that in a dovecot a male often keeps his wife during his whole life, because continually urged to enjoyment, he has no time to seek among the great number of his companions in slavery a free female which may be agreeable to him; but there is nothing to cause one to presume that in a state of liberty such is the case. As soon as the autumn commences pigeons unite themselves in numerous flocks, either to seek together some climate where the rigours of winter are more supportable, or to brave them in their native country. They remain there in large bands until the return of spring announces to them again the amorous season, when they couple, and separate from their companions to rear their brood in some wooded retirement. There is nothing to prove that at this epoch a male takes again the same female he had the preceding year. Be this as it may, every band is always composed of individuals of the same species, and we never meet with turtle-doves and ring-doves mixed together, or with the stock-dove. This observation is important, because it throws a little light on the history of the varieties of the dovecot.

Some pigeons choose a high tree, at the extremity of a secluded wood, to build on its branches, or in its trunk, a simple nest, composed of small sprigs and light sticks; others prefer the young underwood, the groves, the crevices of rocks, or even the deep holes in ruins and other old buildings. Their shapeless and almost flat nest is always sufficiently large to contain the male and female. They lay two eggs in it, which they cover alternately; and when they are hatched they divide equally all the cares that their offspring require. In their infancy they feed them with food reduced in their crops to a state of liquid pap, which has a singular analogy to the milk of the breast. The interior coats of the pigeon's crop are furnished with a great number of small yellowish glands; during incubation these glands swell in a perceptible manner, and when the young pigeons are hatched, a white liquor runs from them quite analagous to the milk of quadrupeds. It is known that with these last this liquor curdles in the stomach of the little ones, and by this operation becomes digestive; there is this difference between them and pigeons, that with these birds this first modification takes place in the crop of the father and mother, where this liquor mixes with a small portion of half-digested grain, and it is in this state they give it to their offspring in a very peculiar manner. For this purpose they place their entire bill in that of their parent, keeping it half open, while these bring the food up from their crop with a convulsive movement, which appears to be very painful, and is sometimes followed by dangerous consequences, as may be seen in our observations on the Large-throated or Pouter Pigeon. This operation is always accompanied with a quick trembling of the wings and body.[†]

DESCRIPTION OF THE DOVE COT PIGEONS.

FIRST DIVISION—DOVE PIGEONS.

FIRST RACE.

1. WILD-DOVE, OR ROCK-PIGEON: *Columba livia agrestis.*—The head, the top of the back, the covering of the wings, the breast, belly, sides, the upper and under coverings of the tail, are of a bluish ash colour; the sides of the throat reflect a golden green, changing colour according to the manner in which the light falls on them; the lower part of the back or rump pure white; the principal wing-feathers of a darkish ash colour, the others inclined to blue, all having two black spots, forming in connection two bands on the wings, and the tips are black, as well as those of the tail; the iris of the eye yellowish red; bill inclined to red; feet red, with black nails; length, twelve inches in a state of liberty, but thirteen, or even fourteen when domesticated. At all ages it is easily distinguished by its white rump. Several ornithologists look upon it as a separate species; others think it only forms a

* In this they also differ from Gallinaceous birds.—ED.

† We have thought it best to publish a description of the varieties and species by degrees, with the history and management, otherwise all the illustrations would come together at the end.—ED.

variety with the two following. Temminck, one of the authors who best understood these birds, only unites the dove-house pigeon to this, but he thinks that some varieties of the dove-cot might come from elsewhere. This bird, which is found in Africa, as well as far north in Sweden, appears in Europe in the spring, and departs in autumn. It inhabits the woods, builds on the branches, or in the holes of trees, and roosts habitually. If all domestic pigeons do not descend from this one, as some naturalists think, it is most certainly the origin of the stock of the dove-house; it soon becomes domesticated, and in one part of Asia they consider it an amusement to reduce it to this tame state. "All through Persia," says Chardin, "both wild and tame pigeons are found, but the wild are much more abundant. I think in this country they build the handsomest dove-houses in the world; there are more than three thousand round Ispahan. It is a great amusement to the inhabitants to catch these pigeons in the country, by means of some tamed and trained for this purpose; they fly in flocks all day after the wild ones, which they surround and decoy to the dove-house."

2. THE STOCK-DOVE: *Columba livia ænas*. — It differs essentially from the preceding, by having always a blue ash coloured rump; its head, throat, and all its under parts are also of this colour; the sides of the neck are of a varying green, that is to say, have a metallic reflection; the breast of a purplish colour; the top of the back of a brownish ash colour; a black spot on the two last secondary feathers of the wings; all the quill feathers of the wing and tail of a bluish ash colour, terminating in black, some white also is on the extreme beard of the lateral quill feathers of the tail; iris of the eye a reddish brown; bill and feet red; length thirteen inches in a state of liberty, and fourteen when domesticated.

We think that our dove-house pigeons descend from this one, as well as from the preceding, since they are found to resemble them both, and are nearly in the same numbers in all the pigeon-houses on large farms.

These birds, like the preceding, bear the name of wood pigeon, because they differ from the other domestic pigeons in their colour which is of a browner cast. They are never found in cold countries in the wild state, and only remain in temperate climates during summer. Towards the end of February and the beginning of March they arrive in large flocks in the south of France, and in the southern districts of Paris; they establish themselves in the woods, build in the trunks of trees, but never on the branches; they lay two or three eggs in the spring, and probably lay a second time in summer; they only bring up two each time, and return in the month of November, taking their route in a southern direction, probably they go through Spain to Africa, there to pass the winter. These birds roost, but not so frequently as the wild wood-pigeon. They become domestic with the greatest facility. Taken young and reared in a dove-house, they become attached to it; do not leave it again, and lay two or three times a year. They have often been seen to

come and fix themselves there of their own accord. Some of them even penetrate into the dove-cots, couple with the tame pigeons, and produce a posterity among whom no trace is found of the wild habits of their parents.

(*To be resumed.*)

DOMESTIC MECHANISM.

DINNER PITCHER.—Out of the many who dine "al fresco" in the fields, or like Trotty Veck, on the doorsteps of great men's houses in crowded cities, or like cabmen in their vehicles, how very few can say that their dinner or other meals, sent them by their "loving wives," are warm and comfortable. And yet, a little forethought and ingenuity can easily obtain this desideratum. Hot water is used in the houses of the wealthy to keep the dishes warm, why not use the same means for the comfort of the poor? The dishes frugal and cheaply got up should be given as warm as possible. In the inside of a proper-sized pitcher let the tinsmith fasten one of less dimensions, leaving a space of one inch or so between the two. At the upper side solder a flange, covering-in this space. At a part of this flange cut out an aperture half an inch in diameter, and solder into it a small brass screw cap. Through this aperture the warm water is poured just before the messenger leaves home. The meat in the inside pitcher is thus kept warm by the hot water surrounding it. A close-fitting lid should be made to close up the interior pitcher. For the purpose of withdrawing the water when cold, a brass screw cap (such caps cost only one penny) should be placed at the bottom of the pitcher. The figure at the left of the cut presents a contrivance placed in the lid of almost all such pitchers in America. Suppose the diameter of the lid to be six inches, a ring half or three-quarters of an inch deep, and three and a half in diameter, is soldered in the centre of it. This is used for holding salt, &c. As a cover for this a tin cup is made, the mouth of which can be passed tightly over the ring above-mentioned, and there fastened. This cup can be taken off at pleasure and used to drink out of. A strip of metal may be soldered to the side of the pitcher, down which may be passed the knife, fork, and spoon, and then the dinner-service of the "diner out" is complete.—B.

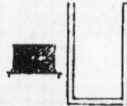

TO CORRESPONDENTS.

JASMINE NOT THRIVING (*A Yorkshireman*).—Your stunted jasmine is what gardeners term hide-bound, and that was caused by a sudden change when you planted it two years since. To enable it to make a fresh start, you must cut it down to within the last joint or two, and so get rid of the hide-bound portion. As soon afterwards as it begins to grow freely, water it once a week with weak liquid-manure to make up for lost time; never stop it all the season, but next October cut it down to a yard's length, and after that, it will branch out a beautiful plant.

CAMELLIAS KEPT TOO DRY (*M. S.*).—Your camellia is likely to get over the severe drying, but you must not enlarge the space for its roots; the chances are, that the pan is too large for it already. Keep it in-doors till the end of June, and never let it get quite dry again. Look at the roots next August, and let us hear how they look, and we shall advise you how to go on with it.

NAMES OF PLANTS (*W. X. W.*).—The two plants of which you sent the seed labels are not worth cultivating. *Hymenodictyon thyrsiflorum* is a tree, with very fine large leaves; and in India, its native place, is very handsome. The other is an Indian fruit of no use here. (*A Subscriber, Queen Mab*).—Your plant is *Doronicum austriacum*, or Leopard's Bane.

SULPHUR PAINT FOR WALL (*A. B. F.*).—In preparing this, as described at page 18, Mr. Errington puts four handsful of flowers of sulphur to a large garden water-pot (about three gallons). It is not easy to put too much sulphur.

SINGLE HORSE PLOUGH AND DIBBLING MACHINE (*Devizes*).—You can get the first from Messrs. Stratton & Co., Clarke-street, Bristol, and the dibbling machine from Dr. Newington, Knole Park, Frant, Faversham, Kent.

ERROR.—At p. 78, col. 2, line 11 from the bottom, for "*Sedum*" read "*Ledum*."

INDEX AND TITLE PAGE (*Dianthus*).—These, for our third volume, may be obtained through any bookseller. We charge for them *One Penny*; if you send three postage stamps, with your address, to our office we will send you a copy post free.

CHANGE OF NAMES (*Ibid*).—You complain, and very justly, of some botanists changing the name of our common heath from *Erica vulgaris* into *Calluna vulgaris*, and *Plumbago Larpenta* into *Valoradia Plumbaginoides*; and you add this query—"Whose adoption is necessary to their being acknowledged." To which we can only reply, that we know of no botanist with authority and judgment so acknowledged as to entitle him to create new genera, and to re-name species at his own discretion. There are some pests among naturalists who think their penetration is great in discovering some trivial distinction on which to argue for a new name. Respecting such men, great only in trifles, we will quote these words of the late Sir J. E. Smith:—"Those who alter names, often for the worse, according to arbitrary rules of their own, or in order to aim at consequence, which they cannot otherwise attain, are best treated with silent neglect. The system should not be encumbered with such names even as synonymes."

ANTS INVADING BEES (*Apis*).—To prevent the ants climbing up the leg or legs of your bee-stand, tie a piece of sheep's wool round each.

DISEASED LEAVES OF GERANIUM (*S. J. E.*).—The leaf sent seems perforated by some insect, but is too mashed by the post-office for us to be certain. Leaves and flowers should be put in little boxes that will endure the official blows.

ONIONS DISAPPEARING (*T. Fallon*).—Your onion seedlings on a rich suitable soil came up healthy, "but disappeared totally during one night and day." They must have been drawn into the soil by worms, or pulled up by sparrows; or both may have contributed to your loss. Water your ground with a solution of corrosive sublimate before re-sowing, and stretch threads of white worsted over the bed.

BROCOLI CULTURE (*C. Flok*).—You will find all necessary hints if you refer to the indexes of previous volumes. If you require information on any particular point, write to us again. We have put your note into good hands. *Liquid-manure* may be applied advantageously to peas and beans as soon as their pods are set.

BONE-BOILER'S WASH (*Ibid*).—This, which is "the water in which bones have been boiled, and when cold is like jelly," would be a good manure for turnips, cabbages, brocoli, and many other things, if poured over the ground, and dug in before planting or sowing. Such liquor contains a large quantity of animal and saline matters, and is, in fact, a very strong liquid-manure.

SOFTENING HARD WATER (*J. Toms*).—Your water is so hard that it injures your verbena and other greenhouse and frame plants. Do not add soda to it, but put an ounce of carbonate of ammonia (obtainable at the chemists) into each sixty gallons of the water. When it is quite dissolved, and has stood for a few hours, it will be ready for use. You can obtain guano of the company you name; their office is at No. 40, Bridge-street, Blackfriars.

CRICKETS (*S. A.*).—Every mode of destroying the cockroach, detailed at page 35 of our present volume, is equally efficacious against the cricket. Another way of trapping this insect is, to put into phials a little beer, and to place them on their side near the haunts of these insects. They creep in, but cannot escape.

WEEVIL ON APPLE-TREES (*W. M., Prescot*).—The weevil which you caught at night eating the bark from the shoots of your young apple-trees is the apple weevil (*Anthonymus pomorum*), of which you will find a drawing and many particulars at page 145 of our first volume.

GROWING MUSHROOMS IN BOXES (*H. I. B.*).—Boxes, two feet by four feet, and from nine inches to a foot deep, are a very convenient size for the growth of the mushroom. These boxes should be filled with horse-droppings, mixed with a little light rich loam, say two-thirds of the former and one-third of the latter, well incorporated together. These materials should be placed in a dry open shed, to be turned over several times to ferment until pretty dry and sweet. The whole being well mixed, dry, and sweet, fill the boxes to within two inches of the top, making the mixture as solid as possible. Then let them stand in the dry until the heat rises, when holes are to be made with a dibble six or seven inches apart all over the surface, and five or six inches deep. After two or three days, if the whole should be too hot, let the boxes remain in this way for several days longer, and the open holes will assist in letting off the excessive heat. As soon as the heat is a little on the decline, fill the holes with spawn, and if thought to be still too hot to cover over with earth, let them remain in this state any necessary length of time. When the heat has become gentle cover over the whole surface, from one to two inches thick, with light loam beat down solid and smooth. Keep the boxes in some suitable situation, according to the season. See page 35.

AURICULA PIPS NOT OPENING (*Herbert*).—Your auriculæ "half form their pips, and then these wither;" and from your statement we conclude that you did not keep your auriculas warm enough just at the time when they required most protection; that is, from the time they shew bloom up to the point when they ought to be in perfection. Your commoner kinds have flowered well, because they are more hardy. Also, are you quite sure that the cow dung you used to top dress with in February last was old enough and well sweetened enough? If not (which we strongly suspect), that is cause enough to prevent your flowers expanding; the too rich, crude food would poison the young roots, and prevent their taking up nourishment. Besides, you had too much dung and too little loam in your compost (half dung, quarter loam, and quarter sand). The proportions ought to have been reversed. We advise you to take off this too rich compost now, and top-dress again with a compost not so rich. See Mr. Appleby's weekly instruction on this subject.

VINE SCALE (*Ibid*).—You will do quite right to strip off carefully the old bark from your vines that harbours not *aphis* but *coccus*, or brown scale. The former generally inhabits the leaves and young shoots. Tobacco smoke is the effectual destructive agent for aphides. The coccus or brown scale will be nearly destroyed by peeling off the old bark, but you must be careful not to injure the inner bark, or the least wound will cause the vine to bleed just now severely. When the leaves are fully expanded there is no danger. Wait a fortnight before you water with liquid-manure.

OBTAINING NEW VARIETIES OF PANSY (*Amateur*).—It is not necessary to impregnate pansies in order to improve the breed. Bees and other insects do this effectually. Nevertheless, you may try it, but you may cover the flower you intend to operate upon before it opens, and keep it covered till the bloom drops off. Save seed from the best formed and brightest coloured flowers, and you will undoubtedly have some improved varieties. The best colour for a *pansy stand* is a *dark* green. The stand ought to slope three inches in a foot. The plate on the top of the tub to contain the calyx or flower cup of each pansy should be oval and sloping, and should be rather below the level of the board, so as to cause the flower to lay flat upon it. The best *time to sow pansy seed* is as soon as it is ripe. It need not be kept an hour after that. Therefore, the season of sowing will extend from June to September.

PERUVIAN GUANO.—We are requested to state that Messrs. Anthony Gibbs and Sons, of Bishopsgate-street, are the sole importers of Peruvian guano.

LIQUID GUANO (*C. T. F.*).—Dissolve an ounce of guano in each gallon of water, and let it stand still until quite clear.

BLISTERED PEACH-LEAVES (*W. S.*).—These do not arise from the wounds of the aphides, but from excess of stagnant moisture at the roots. If your borders were thoroughly drained, or your trees planted on platforms, you would have no blistered leaves. We shall be obliged by the report about screening wall-trees.

SWEDISH TURNIPS AFTER TARES (*Ibid*).—If you have a seed bed of swedish turnips, you may plant these upon the ground as fast as you clear it of tares, provided you pulverise the soil and manure it. Both your swedes and mangold wurtzel may be cleared off in time, to sow wheat in November as you propose.

WEIGHT OF EGGS (*Inkpen*).—Our correspondent says:—"Would you be kind enough to state what is the average weight of the eggs of the Aylesbury duck? I weighed some the other day and found that nine weighed 2 lbs., but I saw one belonging to a neighbour which weighed 6½ oz. It was badly shaped, and appeared to be *double yolked*. I have never had hens' eggs which weighed heavier than five to a lb., although a neighbour informed me that he had a Spanish egg which weighed nearly 4½ oz., but I did not see it. Are ducks' eggs considered wholesome food? I have had a prejudice against eating them." This is only a prejudice, for ducks' eggs are as wholesome as those of fowls; the only difference being that they are stronger in flavour, and larger. Can any of our correspondents tell what is the average or usual weight of an Aylesbury duck's egg?

TECOMA JASMINOIDES NOT BLOOMING (*An Ardent Amateur*).—This plant requires plenty of room; but the chief reason why we suspect your plant has not flowered is because you have been too kind to it, in nursing it so carefully in a stove. The pillar and roof of a greenhouse would suit it better. We think, however, you will succeed in the cool end of a stove, and by giving it plenty of air to ripen its shoots in the autumn. As your plant made shoots from one to two yards in length last autumn, it may flower on the side shoots, if the wood was well ripened. The stopping of the shoots would soon enable you to see, as their side shoots would sooner be thrown out. If it does not flower, you must make up your mind to give air in the autumn to ripen the shoots, or at once transfer it to the roof of the greenhouse, where the declining heat in the autumn, combined with a stinted supply of water, will accelerate the wood-ripening process.

DOUBLE FRENCH MARIGOLD CUTTINGS (*Verax*).—These are annual plants reared from seeds sown in the spring, and they die away by the end of the season; but by taking cuttings of them in August, we can preserve a given variety for many years. See what we said of them in the last weekly number.

EGGS (*Ibid*).—We believe that eggs will bear carriage without injury, if not treated with excessive violence. See page 35.

VERANDA (*M. M.*).—The shade caused by the luxuriant climbers in front of your veranda, and by the opaque roof, render the back wall unfit for any plants, except such as common ivy, and nothing can enable you to grow other plants, unless you cover the veranda with glass, or at least partly so, and the new rough plate is most suitable for such a roof. We often wonder how it is that those who can afford it do not use at least one-third glass in the roofs of verandas, and so get nice plants trained against the house as you propose.

GENTIANELLA NOT THRIVING (*Ibid*).—Your soil is too poor; it requires deep, light, rich soil; remove it to an open place in the kitchen-garden for a year or two.

PLANTS FOR AUSTRALIA (*M. C. E.*).—No plants can live in a the case, soldered close, for any length of time; living plants must have light, and that can only be given in such a voyage by a Wardian case. Such plants as you intend taking out would do much easier from seeds, and we would advise an assortment of all our popular half-hardy flowers to be tried that way, even if you should take the plants also.

LONDON: Printed by HARRY WOOLDRIDGE, Winchester High Street, in the Parish of Saint Mary Kalendar, and Published by WILLIAM SOMERVILLE ORR, at the Office, No. 2, Amen Corner, in the Parish of Christ Church, City of London.—May 9, 1850.

WEEKLY CALENDAR.

M D	W D	MAY 16—22, 1850.	Weather near London in 1849.			Sun Rises.	Sun Sets.	Moon R. & S.	Moon's Age.	Clock bef. Sun.	Day of Year.
16	Tu	Spotted Flycatcher appears.	T. 66°–50°.	S.W.	Rain.	9 a. 4	43 a. 7	morn.	5	3 54	136
17	F	May Fly appears.	T. 62°–49°.	S.W.	Rain.	7	45	0 20	6	3 53	137
18	S	Oxford Term ends. Midge appears. [fledged.]	T. 64°–47°.	W.	Rain.	6	46	1 1	3	3 52	138
19	Sun	WHIT SUNDAY. Dunstan. Broods of Starlings	T. 66°–50°.	W.	Rain.	5	48	1 32	8	3 49	139
20	M	WHIT MONDAY. Sailor Beetle appears.	T. 56°–50°.	S.W.	Rain.	3	49	2 1	9	3 47	140
21	Tu	Sun's declin. 20° 10' N. House Martin builds.	T. 71°–47°.	E.	Rain.	2	51	2 26	10	3 43	141
22	W	EMBER WK. Trin. Term beg. Oxf. Term beg.	T. 66°–45°.	S.W.	Rain.	1	52	2 50	11	3 40	142

ON the 19th of May, in the year 1794, died Thomas Hamilton, EARL OF HADDINGTON, who needs no other monument than the noble woods and plantations made by him about the family mansion, Tyninghame Castle, near Dunbar. He died in his seventy-fourth year; and for nearly half a century he wisely made his pleasures profitable by devoting much of his leisure to planting and the culture of trees. Nor was he contented with the selfish practice of what his own experience had taught him, but he communicated it to his countrymen, in a work published at Edinburgh in 1760, entitled, "A Treatise on Forest Trees." We have not the volume in our possession, but we remember referring to it some years since, and being pleased with the soundness and practical character of some of its contents. The Earl was one of the first members of our peerage who distinguished himself by the meritorious attempt to adorn as well as to subsidize his native hills; and his example—though at first neglected, if not ridiculed—was soon followed and excelled. He fully acted up to his family motto—"I perform, and I persevere;" yet the Duke of Atholl soon surpassed him in the extent of his plantations. One sentence tells the estimating consequence: these plantations have raised the Atholl family to the position of being one of the wealthiest of our peerage. The extent of the Atholl plantations may be estimated, in some degree, from the facts, that nearly ten thousand acres are occupied by larch alone, and that in 1820 a frigate was launched at Woolwich, and named The Atholl, from the circumference of being built of larch entirely from the Duke's plantations. His grace planted two hundred thousand annually; but in the course of 1819-20 he planted more than eleven hundred thousand. Let it not be supposed that Englishmen are behind their northern brethren in this praiseworthy pursuit; but, in testimony to the contrary, we must confine ourselves to the single instance of the Duke of Devonshire, who, in 1820, received a gold medal from the Society of Arts for having planted nearly two millions of forest trees.

The benefits derivable from planting need no eloquence to enforce. It has been well said, "Trees grow while men sleep;" they are always advancing into value; and we know more than one family who are now living upon the annual production from woods their parents planted. One warning word, before we close this comment. Let no one think that planting is digging a hole, and sticking a tree in it. Every soil is more suitable to some species of trees than to other species; therefore, select that which is appropriate: every tree loves to have a free loose soil in which its roots may wander; therefore, trench before you plant: and, lastly, every tree is injured by having stagnant water about its roots; therefore, drain before you plant.

METEOROLOGY OF THE WEEK.—At Chiswick, during the last twenty-three years, the average highest and lowest temperatures of the above seven days have been 65.3° and 44°, respectively. The greatest heat occurred on the 17th in 1833, during which day the thermometer rose to 86°. In the above period 99 of the days were fine, and during 62 days rain fell.

NATURAL PHENOMENA INDICATIVE OF WEATHER.—When sheep and herds turn their tails to the quarter whence the wind is blowing, and cease from pasturing, it is a tolerably sure indication that the approaching rain will be heavy and stormy. Sea-gulls flying far inland also indicate the coming on of tempestuous weather. Spiders crawling more abundantly and conspicuously than usual upon the indoor-walls of our houses foretell the near approach of rain; but the following anecdote intimates that some of their habits are equally the certain indication of frost being at hand. Quatremer Disjonval, seeking to beguile the tedium of his prison hours at Utrecht, had studied attentively the habits of the spider; and eight years of imprisonment had given him leisure to be well versed with its ways. In the December of 1794 the French army, on whose success his restoration to liberty depended, was in Holland; and victory seemed certain, if the frost, then of unprecedented severity, continued. The Dutch envoys had failed to negociate a peace, and Holland was despairing, when the frost suddenly broke up. The Dutch were now exulting, and the French generals prepared to retreat; but the spider forewarned Disjonval that the thaw would be of short duration, and he knew that his weather monitor never deceived. He contrived to communicate with the army of his countrymen; and its generals, who duly estimated his character, relied upon his assurance that within a few days the waters would be again passable by troops. They delayed their retreat: within twelve days the frost had returned—the French army triumphed, Disjonval was liberated, and a spider had brought down ruin on the Dutch nation.

RANGE OF BAROMETER—RAIN IN INCHES.

May		1841.	1842.	1843.	1844.	1845.	1846.	1847.	1848.	1849.
16	B. {	29.911	30.390	29.457	30.242	30.288	29.695	29.731	29.653	29.422
		29.674	30.307	29.356	29.661	30.234	29.360	29.581	29.482	29.383
	R.	—	—	0.67	—	—	0.54	0.09	—	0.02
17	B. {	29.632	30.278	29.671	29.964	30.138	29.218	30.001	29.494	29.576
		29.518	30.139	29.476	29.886	30.115	29.184	22.871	29.396	29.286
	R.	0.01	—	0.28	0.01	0.05	0.01	—	—	0.05
18	B. {	29.553	30.015	29.901	29.999	30.016	29.139	29.989	29.680	29.856
		29.531	29.911	29.796	29.927	29.851	29.023	29.785	29.352	29.457
	R.	0.02	—	0.04	0.02	0.17	0.17	0.02	0.01	0.01
19	B. {	29.674	29.807	29.893	29.997	29.814	29.645	29.902	29.706	30.000
		29.280	29.711	29.896	29.960	29.802	29.481	29.827	29.702	29.915
	R.	0.15	0.04	0.02	—	—	0.12	—	0.01	0.36
20	B. {	29.578	29.658	29.830	29.968	29.849	29.658	30.048	30.150	29.821
		29.243	29.645	29.682	29.982	29.841	29.444	29.841	29.753	29.721
	R.	0.06	—	0.44	—	—	0.26	—	0.05	0.64
21	B. {	29.647	29.724	29.649	29.926	29.764	29.949	30.134	30.353	29.838
		29.526	29.676	29.637	29.858	29.554	29.877	30.114	30.215	29.771
	R.	—	—	0.05	0.02	0.26	—	—	0.07	0.22
22	B. {	29.811	29.748	29.587	30.164	29.792	30.203	30.048	30.282	29.855
		29.507	29.674	29.653	30.146	29.694	30.120	30.004	30.242	29.743
	R.	—	0.01	0.09	—	0.02	—	—	—	0.20

THE rich, the gaudy, and the formal TULIP must engross our attention to-day. It has been styled "the king of florists' flowers," but he is so little to our taste that we would readily dethrone him to make way for any one out of many others. Its botanical name, Tulipa Gesneriana, retains upon our memory the fact that the Swiss botanist, Conrad Gesner, introduced it to general notice in Europe.

Gesner relates that he first saw the tulip at Augsburg, in the year 1559, and cultivated by Counsellor Hewart, a collector of floral rarities. This was not the flower's first introduction to Europe, for the specimen in question was from Constantinople, where it had been long known. From Germany, this flower reached England in 1577, being first cultivated by James Garret; and Parkinson, writing in 1629, says, " they are the pride of delight almost infinite," that he had 160 varieties, doubted not but that there were ten times as many, and that " no lady of any worth but was a delighter in them." Gerarde, some years before, states that Garret, one of his "loving friends, a curious searcher of simples," endeavoured to make out the number of the varieties; " but," adds old Gerarde, " he had not done this after twenty years, for each new year bringeth forth new plants of sundry colours not before seen; all which, to describe particularly, were to roll Sisyphus' stone, or to number the sands." In Holland, at the very same period, the rage for the tulip was really a mental phrensy. The ordinary business of the country, says Mr. Mackey, in his clever work upon popular delusions, was neglected, and the population, even to its lowest dregs, embarked in the tulip trade.

Ten thousand pounds were given for forty roots. One variety, named *Admiral Leifken*, sold for 440 pounds; and a *Semper Augustus* for 550. Yet we do not find that any particular perfection of colour or of form characterised these exorbitantly priced flowers. Rarity and the weight of the bulbs seem to have determined the value. In 1636, regular marts were established on the Exchange at Amsterdam, Rotterdam, Haarlem, and elsewhere, and gambling in tulip roots became a mercantile pursuit. All classes were engulphed in this seducing road to riches, and when the bubble burst, those who held tulips on speculation were ruined by the reduction of price. The government and the law courts were appealed to in vain, for the just reply was—you only suffer from having embarked in a gambling speculation.

During this mania, a merchant having given a herring to a sailor, who had brought him some goods, left him alone to his breakfast. The sailor seeing some tulip roots lying near him, and mistaking them for onions, ate part of one with his fish; and that bulb was so valuable, adds the narrator, that the sailor's meal cost the merchant more than if he had prepared an entertainment for a prince.

The same mania never prevailed to such an extent in England, but Mr. Mackay says that, in 1835, a tulip, named *Fanny Kemble*, was sold by auction for £75; and a florist in the King's Road, Chelsea, had one priced in his catalogues at 200 guineas; a price, we may readily believe, that never did more than appear in print. The florist conjured for spirits, but the spirits never came.

Many of our readers will be glad to have it explained that florists call tulips *seedlings* until they have bloomed; after this those preserved on account of their good form and habit, as well as the offsets they produce, are called *breeders*. After some years the petals of these become striped, and they are then said to be *broken*. If the striping is good, they are said to have a *good strain*; if it be inferior, they are described as having a *bad strain*. A *rectified* tulip is synonymous with a tulip having a good strain.

A *feathered* tulip has a dark-coloured edge round its petals, gradually becoming lighter on the margin next the centre of the petal; the feathering is said to be *light*, if narrow; *heavy*, if broad; and *irregular*, if its inner edge has a broken outline.

A *flamed* tulip is one that has a dark-pointed spot, somewhat in shape like the flame of a candle, in the centre of each petal.

Sometimes a tulip is both *feathered* and *flamed*.

A *Bizarre* tulip has a yellow ground, and coloured marks on its petals.

A *Byblomen* is white, marked with black, lilac, or purple.

A *Rose* is white, with marks of crimson, pink, or scarlet.

It is needless to follow the history of the characteristics of a superior tulip, as exhibited in the works of Rea, Abercrombie, Maddock, and others, for they have been revised and gathered together by Mr. Glenny in his "Properties of Flowers." With some slight alterations they are as follows:—

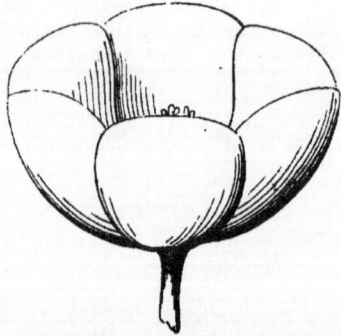

1. The cup when fully expanded should form, as nearly as possible, half of a hollow ball. The petals, six in number, must be broad at the ends, smooth at the edges, and the divisions where the petals meet scarcely showing an indentation.

2. The three inner petals should set close to the three outer ones, and the whole should be broad enough to allow of the fullest expansion without *quartering* (as it is called), that is, exhibiting any vacancy between the petals.

3. The petals should be thick, smooth, and stiff, and keep their form well.

4. The ground colour should be clear and distinct, whether white or yellow.* The least stain, even at the lower end of the petal, would render a tulip comparatively valueless.

5. Whatever the colours or marks upon a tulip, all the petals should be marked alike, and perfectly uniform.

6. The *feathered* flowers should have an even, close feathering all round, and whether the feathering be narrow or wide, light or heavy, it should reach far enough round the petals to form, when they are expanded, an unbroken edging all round.

7. If the flower have any marking besides the feathering at the edge, it should be a beam, or bold mark down the centre, but not to reach the bottom, or near the bottom of the cup; the mark or beam must be similar in all the six petals.

8. Flowers not feathered, and with *a flame* only, must have no marks on the edges of the flower. None of the colour must break through to the edge. The colour may

---

* *Ground colour* is that upon which the other colours are laid.

be in any form not in blotches, so that it be perfectly uniform in all the petals, and does not go too near the bottom.

9. The colour, whatever it be, must be dense and decided. Whether it be delicate and light, or bright, or dark, it must be distinct in its outline, and not shaded, or flushed, or broken.

10. The height of a tulip should be from 18 to 36 inches; the shortest is right for the outside row in a bed, and the tallest for the highest row.

11. The purity of the white, and the brightness of the yellow ground colours, should be permanent, that is to say, should continue until the petals actually fall.

THE FRUIT-GARDEN.

PINE-APPLE CULTURE MADE EASY.—We do not recur so often to this branch of our labours as some others, for it scarcely concerns the readers of this work so much as our commoner fruits. But the time approaches when this subject, being stripped of all complicated mystery, and the culture of them thrown back on first principles, a degree of simplicity will take place, both in the structures appropriated to them, and in the course of culture pursued.

We think it not too much to affirm, that *the pine requires less attention than any other hothouse fruit whatever.* "Why then," Mr. A. will say, "all this fuss about them?" We answer, because in their culture, people from the first have studied how to make their proceedings as artificial as possible. Let any one, for instance, as to structures, look back over the plans which for the last few years have appeared in some of our gardening periodicals for pineries, vineries, and other houses, heated by steam, hot-water, &c., and mark the complication which appears on the face of most of them. For our part, when we see a sketch of the kind, with nearly a score of references as to details, we turn from it with a sort of instinctive horror; for there appears concealed beneath the various gewgaws contained therein, such a fearful array of mason's, carpenter's, and smith's bills, as would make almost anything short of a millionnaire, give up in despair the culture of our noble in-door fruits. At the same time, a plan from a plain common-sense person, containing only half a dozen matters of detail (such things as a low house, a few pipes in a trench capable of holding water, and ample provision for ventilation) shall, in spite of all this paper finery, contain every essential for perfect culture—that is to say, if we take nature for our guide, instead of attempting to make her our slave.

Having thus far indulged in a few expressions of opinion, as to expensive and complicated buildings and apparatus, as being out of the reach of the million, and, indeed, altogether unnecessary unless for the purpose of display, we must be allowed to remark a little on the celebrated Hamiltonian method of culture; a method which we firmly believe will (in spite of a stiff adherence to old maxims), one day, be generally adopted, at least by the amateur, and the market gardener. Loudon long since prophesied, that a capitalist situated in such a place as Birmingham, or Newcastle-on-Tyne, will one day pour such a host of pine-apples into the London market, as will make the growers of Queens and Providences about the Metropolis reconsider their plans.

"But," says some one of these persons, "your Hamiltonian plans will not do for the *Queen, Providence,* and *Enville pines!*" Softly, my good fellow, this case is by no means cleared up yet. But admitting, for argument's sake, that such an opinion is *tolerably correct;* suppose

it can be proved to be just the thing for the culture of the *Black Jamaica,* and that such, well swelled, were to make their appearance in abundance in the London market during April or May, high-flavoured, and weighing from three to four pounds, would not such at three or four shillings per lb be as eligible for the Lord Mayor's table, or even that of the Premier himself, as a huge spongy Providence, Enville, or Queen, at eight or ten shillings per lb? But somebody will say, "Have you seen it done? have you done it yourself?" Be that as it may, we would merely remind the latter class of doubters, that most of the great projects which have been attempted to be stifled in their birth by bilious doubters, and those of a carping character.

At the same time it must be confessed, that two or three great essentials must be secured, or the project above alluded to, as to commercial gardening, could not be carried out: sufficient capital; a central situation, with coal and glass close to the elbow; no combination of inferior or collateral objects which might tend to hamper the main plan; and lastly, a clear view of the whole subject as a system. These, or most of these, no mere gardener can command. Let it not be supposed, however, that in all this there is the least mystery or difficulty. It is as simple as the culture of the Globe artichoke out of doors, which, indeed, it in some degree resembles, with this chief difference, that the pine requires a roof of some kind, and some artificial heat both at the top and at the bottom. Once properly planted by this system, the only labour worth recording for half a dozen years would be an occasional thinning of the suckers, and of course a regular attention to the fires.

We come now to the amateur's share in this question; and, indeed, the one which most intimately concerns the case in hand.

It may be taken for granted, that the majority of persons classed under the sweeping term amateur, are persons who have some profession, trade, or calling; and which circumstance gives them not that amount of the "ease combined with dignity" which the country gentleman enjoys. For this reason, then, we would have every amateur's gardening structure, whether hothouse or greenhouse, so planned, as to require no attention through the day, and indeed little at any other period. The heating apparatus so provided, that the servant lad or girl by feeding the fire once in twenty-four hours, and by adjusting the ash-pit door about three times during the same period, all things connected with artificial heat would be accomplished. There would then remain the matter of shading when necessary, and ventilation. If lean-to roofs characterize such houses, then, perhaps, the use of new rough plate glass might obviate the necessity of shading at any time, provided abundance of atmospheric moisture was present. And as to ventilation, we should not fear to continue it night and day, systematically, if, as before observed, the due amount of moisture could be secured, and a certain temperature guaranteed.

For the amateur, we are of opinion, that if the lean-to character *must be* adopted, what is termed the north light should be used; and, indeed, it would be a consideration, whether this north light should not be almost as large as the south one; or, in other words, whether a regular span-roof running east and west would not be a very suitable form, although we should prefer the same running north and south. Many places are so limited, that structures are obliged to submit in some degree to such limitation, as also to fall in with some pre-existing arrangement.

We can fancy, then, a house or pit combining the foregoing principles in some way, with a low and flat roof, a *thin* screen of canvass left on during summer, day and night, if trouble be an object; plenty of atmospheric moisture; a constant circulation of air (not draught); a bottom-heat of about eighty degrees all the summer, sinking gradually to seventy degrees in winter; and the plants planted out on the Hamiltonian plan. Fancy, we say again, such a house or pit giving little or no trouble to the amateur, who might lock the door on the Monday morning, and not open it again, if business press, until the following Saturday.

We should like one of Burbidge's boilers; and the lad or person who attended this would have to rake the fire clean and low every morning about seven o'clock; to fill the grate quite full of fuel, and to shut the ash-pit door close, or nearly so, leaving just as much air as would merely keep the fire in. At about three in the afternoon extra draught should be given; indeed from this hour until five, the fire might burn freely, for this is the period when the greatest amount of heat will be ever best applied by the forcing gardener; at five in the afternoon the ash-pit door would have to be placed on the same regulation as at seven in the morning; and this would complete all the fire routine during four-fifths of the year; all the rest would follow as a matter of course, the apparatus being complete, and all things well planned at first.

With the commercial gardener on a large scale, as adverted to at the commencement of these remarks, there would be an extension of matters, commensurate with the objects sought; and, indeed, his form of roof should be of a different character, in our opinion. We think that in all probability the ridge and furrow roof (the ridge running north and south) would be the thing; and we already fancy, that we see a plot of ground of some acres at Birmingham (that great central mart of commerce) occupied this way, in parallel lines; and all appropriated, by one grand and simple plan, to the production of pines for all our great markets. But whether with the commercial gardener or the amateur their culture is undertaken on the Hamiltonian system, every thing should be done that can be to render them permanent when planted out.

Amongst other items, perhaps the formation of the bottom they were to grow in for years would be the most important. Mr. Hamilton in his treatise (which every pine amateur should possess, who wants to study principles rather than mere rules) has shewn, long since, that the old-looking roots of pines, which our gardeners of the olden time were but too apt to despise, are, notwithstanding their ill-favoured appearance when dormant, real living organs, and capable of indefinite multiplication and subdivision; each simple dull-looking fibre being endued with power—if not disturbed, with returning warmth and light—to cater for the old stool, and thereby to assist in establishing the new colony of suckers, &c.

We had meant to have inserted an extract or two from Mr. Hamilton's letters, which we have permission to make use of; we are compelled, however, to waive them until another occasion.   R. ERRINGTON.

THE FLOWER-GARDEN.

FLOWERS IN VASES, RUSTIC BASKETS, &c.—For the last eighteen months I have intended to write a chapter on portable gardens, that is, the different modes of furnishing a flower-garden with vases, flower-boxes, rustic baskets, and the like; for, after all, these are so many flower-beds in another form.

By way of introduction, I may remark, that as a nation of gardeners we are singularly deficient in this style of decoration; and very probably the reason is, that our former meagre style of planting "herbaceous plants" in patches, here and there, as the landscape gardeners do their trees and shrubs, did not admit of being accompanied with such helps; but now that we have got, or rather are getting, into a more rich style of planting our flower-gardens, which style is very much heightened by these additions, when judiciously made, we must look the matter full in the face—make the best of it as it now exists, and then try whether or not it may be capable of greater improvement and extension.

RUSTIC BASKETS.—It falls in better with my present plan to begin with the most humble methods now in use—beginning with the rustic basket. The best rustic basket I ever saw was near the centre of the " Garden of England," that is about midway between the cities of Hereford and Worcester. It consisted of the bottom part of an old hollow oak or walnut tree, I forget which; it was neither round nor cornered; but one could not well see the shape of it owing to the rich mass of ivy which clung to it all round. The height was about a yard, and the diameter full three yards. This was filled brimful with scarlet geraniums; and if a row of the white-flowered ivy-leaf geranium had been planted round the outside of this natural basket, to form a white fringe between the large masses of scarlet geraniums and dark green leaves of the ivy, I question if a marble vase fresh from the Pentelican quarries could be made to look more rich.

They say that one good reason is sufficient for any thing; but there are two good reasons why we should turn over a new leaf in the management of flower-boxes, baskets, &c. The first, and most pressing, is the short time such things last when subjected to the alternate wettings and dryings of flower-pots; and the other is founded on the new way of keeping geraniums in a dry state over the winter, without disturbing the soil in which they grow from year to year: on Harry Moore's plan. It will be recollected, that I mentioned last year two large boxes planted with *Judy* geraniums, which are treated here after this fashion, and which improve from year to year. These two boxes are wintered in the conservatory; and this spring they are not to be pruned in the least degree; and if they flower well that way it will be an advantage, as this variety is not much stronger than *Tom Thumb*, and we want it to spread out wider than it could do for some years, after close pruning. These two boxes are turned outside early in April, annually, and they fit into two recesses close under the glass, so that a slight protection saves them from late frosts. Now, these boxes were made to suit the style of architecture of the conservatory, and were very expensive in the first instance; they are also handsome ornaments to the house in winter, placed on either side of the door as you enter; and sometimes to heighten their beauty, a few flowering plants in pots are stuck in between the old Judies. It will now appear plain enough, that this is an extravagant way of keeping old musty geraniums, if the system is managed in the usual way of drainage and a boxful of soil, which would rot these handsome boxes in four or five years. Instead of this, however, the mode is not at all extravagant, and the boxes may last for two or three generations, for aught we can tell at present; and on the same principle the most handsome and expensive pieces of room-furniture may be made for portable flower-gardens for drawing-rooms, or for any rooms, and for the outside of windows, or for accompaniments to architectural ornaments, or, indeed, for all the uses to which pots and common flower-boxes are put to at present. Ornamental flower-baskets of the most beautiful patterns may be made to suit this plan, and may last a lifetime; and an almost endless variety of Dutch and China tiles may now be bought of different shapes and sizes; and these may as easily be put up into frames as squares of glass, and these frames form beautiful sides and ends for flower-boxes; so that, in many instances, flower-cases fit for Her Majesty's gardens, may be made at much less expense than often is incurred in making strong common-looking boxes; and when we add to all this the certainty of such ornaments lasting our lifetime, surely it will be worth while to strain a point or two to get a few of them into our rooms and gardens.

I am no great admirer of what is called Wardian cases; they might pass muster in the house of a Mandarin in China, where such childish things are highly prized; but I cannot bring myself to believe that they are at all suitable to our stage of civilisation. At any rate, let us keep them out of country places, and confine their use to large towns and cities; and in place of them let this style of household gardening prevail, for it is applicable to all our requirements, to any order of architecture, and to every mode of house or room decoration! any recess inside or outside a window, up or down stairs, where there is plenty of light and air,—out about the doors, under verandas, along the terraces, on either side of a summer-house door, and, in short, in every conceivable way; and not only that, the plants may be changed in these boxes and baskets as easily and as often as if they were growing in pots; and, moreover, the plan is not a mere suggestion, for it has been in full operation here for some time, and is found to answer very well indeed, and like every thing else that is really useful it is a most simple arrangement.

It is no more than making all these flower-cases, whether boxes, or baskets, or stands, without bottoms. Yes, they are bottomless boxes; all our fancy boxes here in which we show off some of our best plants in the living rooms, and out on the terraces, are without bottoms. The sides and ends are made of ornamental wood, or painted in imitations, or made-up of exquisitely beautiful tiles of China-ware of different forms and colours. These are let into light-frames, just as we make glass-lights for a cucumber-bed; and sometimes the China or Dutch tiles, or coloured glass, are "backed," that is, placed in fancy patterns outside a light made box, and kept in their places with thin paste made of white-lead and oil. The whole side or end of a flower-box of this kind might be made out of a plate of looking-glass, or some of my old window friends may make a flower-basket out of the finest willows, and of any fancy shape they choose, and it will last as long as Sally's "work basket," which she has had since I was a boy; and every other contrivance between this frail basket and that looking-glass sided box may also be made to answer the purpose equally well. Who, then, would stifle beautiful little plants in glass bottles, or Wardian cases, when any kind of fancy furniture may be imitated in a flower-box, case, or basket?

But how are the plants to be supported all this time? Simply by giving them water when they want it. No! no! I do not mean that kind of support. But how are they to stand in a bottomless box, as you say they will do so easily? I never said such a thing; but I see what you mean. We make use of all this finery just in the same way, and for almost the same purpose, as others use "pillow-slips:" if there were no pillow-slips, the pillows must have been unfeathered every time they stood in need of the laundry-maid, just as flower-boxes of the common make need be taken to pieces when the bottom or sides are rotted by the damp mould; so that if they were made ever so handsome or costly, they could not last but a few years; hence the reason why this department of garden decoration has not kept pace with the other improvements of the day. With the aid of a few pillow-slips, or covers, one pillow will last no one knows how long, for I never saw a worn out pillow yet; and it is just the contrary with these fancy boxes, one of them will last as long as a pillow; and we can have a dozen rough-made boxes, and well tarred on both sides to hold the mould and the plants, and a zinc drawer attached to the bottom of each inside box to catch

and hold the drainage water, till the housemaids come round to take away such things; then, if we have twelve rough boxes for one slip or cover box, we could have a different set of flowers in each of them; and when one of these fancy cases stands in a recess under the breakfast-room window, and we have a friend come to see us who will prolong his stay to twelve days, we can shew him twelve arrangements of flowers, or twelve kinds of window flowers, all in daily succession, and apparently in the same box, for there is the motto and the family arms wrought in the side of the box next to us in stained glass, and the box cannot be mistaken; and the way to effect the daily change of plants, is this, the gardener has twelve rough boxes tarred as I have just said, and he sows or plants in them long before they are wanted in the house, or on the terrace, &c., &c., just as they do for the mignonette-boxes for the London windows. When he learns that the said friend is coming to visit his master, he will put one of his gayest boxes into the slip-box the first morning. It has four legs, or rather it stands on four stilts, which the carved legs of the slip-box cover and keep out of sight, and there is a vacant half-inch space between the side of the box and that of the case. There is a round hole in each end of the rough box near the top, and exactly in the middle, and the gardener has two hooks, something like "boot hooks," which fit these holes, and with these raises up or lowers down the rough plant-box, as the case may be, into or out of the beautiful slip-box. For the sake of a "little chat," Susan, the house-maid, will not object to help the gardener "of a morning" to remove and replace these boxes, especially if she takes a pride in her "profession," and wishes to see the rooms look smart when strangers come to the house. Out of doors we shall suppose more, if not better help, is at hand, and the boot-hooks are on a larger scale, and probably a couple of stout iron links are attached to the hooks, and also a large iron ring to each of them : through these rings a couple of handspikes, or stout poles, are made to pass, and by which very heavy boxes may be lifted or let down by a dozen strong men, should the weight require so much strength.　　　D. BEATON.

GREENHOUSE AND WINDOW GARDENING.

A FEW WORDS ON ANNUALS.—Times change, and men and customs change with them! In our younger days the sowing and the rearing of annually-sown flowering plants were occupations of high consideration. They then graced the lawn, took possession of the greenhouse in summer, added floral attractions even to the forcing departments, found a place on the balcony, and standing room on the window-sill. What has been termed "an age of improvement" came, and, like a ruthless invader who could bear no rival, swept them nearly all away. Gardeners can hardly be blamed, if blame there be. They, it is true, have originated the grandest and finest ideas as respects the development of their art: the grouping system without and within, with whatever advantage or disadvantage there is connected with it, is all their own; and its opposite, the fine specimen system, is a child of their own rearing; but, as *servants*, they must as a matter of duty carry out the tastes and the ideas of those who employ them. It matters not whether in their opinion the ideas of their employers be refined, original, and suited to the locality, or merely a servile imitation of what has been done in some great establishment, where circumstances are entirely different. In the different cases the pleasure of working will be dissimilar; but all that, in the latter case, the gardener can with propriety do, is respectfully to state his dissent, and the reasons on which it is grounded; and if that fails to convince, then faithfully to carry out the desires of those who employ him. In the case before us there was but little danger of dissent. Gardeners are as much if not more fond of variety than other people. It cost them but little to give up their old friends—the *Balsams*, and the *Cockscombs*, and *Egg-plants*, &c.—to make way in their greenhouses in summer for *Achimenes*, *Gesneras*, *Gloxinias*, &c.; though we think that a combination of the beauties of *all* would have rendered the groups more pleasing. Many of the hardy annuals, that used to lend such a grace to our conservatories in the winter and spring, are now seldom seen; but we question if their absence, because they were cheap and common, has enhanced the attraction of those structures, which are thus too often rendered merely and truly *green*-houses. For instance—will the *Scarlet Salvias*, and the many-coloured *Chrysanthemums*, in the beginning of winter be more dazzling because there are no large specimens of *Ageratums*, with their light blue flowers, to blend and contrast with the others, fine plants of which could easily be obtained from a pinch of seed sown in May or June, or cuttings taken in July? Or are the flowers of *Epacrises*, *Azaleas*, and *Camellias*, rendered more lovely because no such annuals as the *Collinsia bicolor*, with its delicate purple and white racemes of blossom, are now to be seen in their vicinity? We recollect having single plants of this two feet in height, and wide in proportion—a dense cone of blossom; and so delicate in their appearance, from the protection of glass, that some of the knowing ones imagined they were looking upon some splendid new plants; though all the care bestowed upon them was the dropping a few seeds, the value of the fractional part of a farthing, into a three-inch pot in September, thinning out the plants to *one*, pinching out the points of its shoots when three inches in length, transferring it to a six-inch pot, so as to fill it with roots before winter, protecting it from frost, and shifting again into rich light soil in January or February. Among many others that are worth recording, we cannot avoid mentioning that gem the *Nemophilla insignis*, which, under similar treatment, *except the stopping of the shoots*, will furnish fine masses if trained as a bush, but will look more splendid still when suspended as a basket, the trailing shoots studded with their inimitable blue flowers hanging in festoons for more than a yard in length. Spring and autumn are the periods for seeing this flower in perfection; the summer is too hot and bright for it, even out of doors. Great care is required in the watering of this and other succulent-stemmed annuals; and a good plan to prevent the possibility of rotting them with moisture is, in shifting them to leave them in their first small pot, after breaking its bottom and part of the sides, and then elevating the unbroken part, and that part of the ball inside, above the level of the new soil, and never watering the elevated part after the roots have taken possession in their new quarters. A similar method should be adopted when used for the centre or the sides of vases out of doors.

The discarding of annuals from the balcony and the flower-garden became even a more acceptable affair. The employing of tender plants for this purpose, that used to be seen only in pits and greenhouses, became not only fashionable, but the shrewd gardener at once saw, that in places in which his employers were absent during the spring months a great saving of labour would be effected; as, could he only manage to keep a portion over the winter, and then propagate from them in the spring, the chief part of his toils, as respects floral decoration, would be over by the month of June, and thus a breathing time of something like three months would take place before propagating time should again arrive. Besides being fashionable and aristocratic looking, it must be confessed that there is a compactness in beds of geraniums, calceolarias, verbenas, &c., which

few kinds of annuals as *generally* cultivated could imitate. Much as the heart of the gardener might cling to his old favourites, he could at length listen composedly to tradesmen and farmer's daughters styling them *weedy*-looking things. Even our cottagers pass by as worthless what they once would have coveted as a treasure. If we wish, therefore, to see our old favourite annual flowers in the best perfection, we must go to some fine place, where the family reside in the same mansion the most of the year, and where the presence of flowers is at all seasons deemed an essential of comfort. There annuals cannot be dispensed with, either in-doors or in the open air; and the sight of them when grown in perfection—either in spring, summer, or autumn—whether in pots, beds, or borders—would elicit the feeling, that in discarding them we were depriving ourselves of an element of pleasure.

We plead guilty to the not doing much with them ourselves of late; but we often think that the want of them, and the using for our flower-beds, balconies, &c.. nothing, scarcely, but the hardier compact greenhouse plants, is fast giving to our flower structures and our flower-gardens something of a stereotyped appearance: the variety produced being more a diversified combination of limited materials than that more pleasing and natural variety which is the result of combining and contrasting, in harmony, a great number of species dissimilar in colour, form, and manner of growth. In a small flower-garden, which consisted chiefly of a number of small circles cut in grass by the side of a walk, and in another place, where flower-gardening was confined to a sort of *go-between* a balcony and a terrace, and which was set off by vases at equal distances from each other—in both cases, in beds and vases, scarlet geraniums, kept with great care in a hay-loft during winter, were almost the sole decorative plant used. I could see the proprietors in both cases respectively expected to be congratulated for their skill and attention, both for preserving their plants during the winter and the beautiful appearance they then presented, which feeling I could cordially gratify; for let wise men say what they will, one of the best stimulants for renewed exertion is the receiving a little praise for what has been already done, provided that praise has been judiciously imparted, and not *pitched* on. But I could not congratulate them on their taste in having no other colour to sober down the flaring regimental-looking scarlet. Did these respectable people differ with me in opinion? No; they perfectly coincided, and allowed that edging their beds with different colours—or even having beds and vases of yellow, blue, orange, and purple—would not have detracted from but enhanced the brilliancy of their favourite scarlet; but they told me that they were alike young in gardening and meagre in finances—that they could afford a little time and labour, but they could not afford to lay out money in purchasing plants. Now, these are the very people who should patronise the despised annuals. For a few pence—supplied with the commodities of time and labour, and, in addition, a little judgment—they might have beds and vases to rival the finest geraniums, calceolarias, &c., or which, at any rate, would contrast and harmonise well with them; not only so, but they would be doing something to promote in themselves, and in their visiting friends, a superiority to that silly prejudice, that can see no beauty in a flower unless associated both with the distant in locality and the costly in money.

So much has already been stated respecting the height, colour, and habit of the prettiest of these flowers, that a list at present would be needless. We shall, therefore, sum up what farther we have to state in a few words; and first, as respects

Sowing.—To obtain early flowers, the most of the *North American annuals*, the *Candtufts*, &c., should be sown in the beginning of September, if in a cold exposed place; and in the end of September, if sheltered and warm, and the soil light. In both cases the seed should be sown thin, and the plants be defended from severe frost by evergreen boughs stuck in among them, but removed in fine weather. These plants may be lifted in pieces, and transferred to where they are intended to flower in April. Another method, quite as good, but requiring the assistance of a glass light or two, is, in the month of March, to remove the surface soil to the depth of a couple of inches when it is nice and dry. On the hard bottom, place two inches of rotten dung and leaf-mould; return upon the top of it the surface soil again, with the addition of a little light sandy matter, such as you may command. Draw this out in rows nine inches apart, in which sow the annual seeds rather thickly; cover up with the glass, give air freely when the plants are up, and they will lift in patches nicely in April and May, and never feel the removal. To succeed those obtained by either of these means, a second sowing should be made in the middle or end of May, in a rather shady place; but if a similar plan be followed, there will always be the necessity of shading the plants afterwards, which at such a season, especially out of doors, is a great eye-sore. It is best, therefore, to sow in large pots, and have the pots set on a hard bottom, so that they shall scarcely feel the removal. Discontented with every method, however, which I had heard of for keeping up a succession of bloom until the end of the season by annuals, I hit, some years ago, upon a very simple expedient, by which those even sown in the autumn, and especially those sown in the spring, were made to continue blooming all the season; an expedient that will just suit those who do not grudge the time, and feel a pleasure in always fingering and doing something to their plants; and that is, just picking off the seed vessels as fast as they appear. The great object for which the plant is aiming being the perfection of its seeds, the preventing of that will lead them still farther to strive for it, by producing fresh flowers, in which they will still farther be encouraged by surface dressings and weak manure waterings. By this simple means, the *annual* character, especially under protection in winter, may be completely lost. I once saw a mignionette plant many years old.

Planting.—The patches should nearly be as far from each other as the height to which the plant grows, or the length its shoots generally extend; and even then, when a fine mass is expected, the plants should be well *thinned*, as there is no comparison between plants having plenty of room and those left to struggle on in the patch in which they were first sown or planted. Almost all the hardy annuals may yet be sown for autumn decoration, and the thinning of them properly when up will enhance their beauty.

Staking and Tying.—Few of them will bear this when applied in the usual way. Unless carefully done, they look ungainly, weedy-like bundles. If well thinned, the shorter growing ones will be stiff and sturdy, that neither wind nor rains will hurt them; a few twigs stuck among them will render them more secure. For the taller growing ones, twigs larger in size, resembling small bushy pea-sticks, answer best. In a short time the twigs are never seen, but the shoots having grown through and become entangled in them, they preserve their natural defined character and outline, and yet are held so firm that it would require something like a hurricane to sweep them into bundles.　　　　　R. FISH.

HOTHOUSE DEPARTMENT.

EXOTIC ORCHIDACEÆ.

WE had the pleasure, a little time ago, of seeing the superb collection of orchids belonging to S. Rucker, Esq.,

of Wandsworth. Under the judicious care and persevering industry of that gentleman's gardener, Mr. Mylam, the plants were in the highest health. The veriest learner in orchid culture would at once have perceived that liberality in purchasing plants, and providing proper houses, and all other necessary means combined with skill and prompt application of all the points of culture, have caused the usual result—complete success. Four houses are devoted to orchids. The largest, a span-roofed one, is filled principally with Aerides, Saccolabiums, Vandas, Dendrobiums, and other Indian species requiring the highest temperature. This house is on the same plan as we have recommended, that is, with solid brick walls and a glass roof. This house is more shaded than usual, the shades being kept down nearly all the day, and almost every day. In it the plants grow most luxuriantly. We observed that rare plant the *Vanda Lowii* thriving beautifully in a basket filled with sphagnum; also the noble plant of *Vanda Batemannii* shewing a fine strong spike of its truly elegant flowers. Another house was filled chiefly with large Oncidiums, Cattleyas, Brassias, and other large growing plants of similar habit. Over the back walk was hung up a row of large Stanhopeas, and a large plant of *Acineta Humboldtii* finely in flower. This house is kept a few degrees of heat lower than the Indian house. The third house is devoted to such orchids as require the lowest degree of temperature. In it the natives of Guatamala, Peru, and Mexico have a habitation suitable for them; the heat maintained being still lower than that of either of the other houses. Lastly, a house recently erected is for the purpose of placing the plants in when in flower. This is a handsome span-roofed house, with spacious walks, a wide platform in the centre, and broad shelves on each side; the paths running down between the platform and the shelves. The plants as they come into flower in the other houses are brought into this, kept well shaded, and rather cooler. By these means, lasting much longer in bloom. The luxuriant health of all the plants, and the number in flower, as the list below will prove, shew that Mr. Mylam's system of cultivating these interesting plants is the right one. And we may venture to say, that all our instructions given in THE COTTAGE GARDENER correspond with his practice. We may remark, also, that all cultivators of large collections, who succeed well in growing them, follow nearly the same method, as far as their means will allow. In addition to the example of success we are now describing, we may mention Mr. Bassett, gardener to R. S. Holford, Esq., of Weston Birt; Mr. Williams, gardener to C. Warner, Esq., of Hoddesden; Mr. Paxton, gardener to the Duke of Devonshire; Mrs. Lawrence, of Ealing Park; Mr. Rae, gardener to J. Blandy, Esq., of Reading; Mr. Pass, gardener to T. Brocklehurst, Esq., of Macclesfield; Mr. Dean, gardener to J. Bateman, Esq., of Knypersly; and Mr. White, gardener to A. Kenrick, Esq., of Birmingham. These we may designate the great growers of private collections. Then the public gardens and nursery establishments in this country, and also on the Continent, all follow the same plan of cultivating orchids in houses of different temperatures, to suit plants from different countries and elevations. We mention this galaxy of examples to prove to our amateur friends the necessity of imitating, as much as possible, their practice in this particular point; but as they can not be reasonably expected to have so many houses for the purpose, they must try to place their plants in such positions in their house as will in some measure give them different temperatures.

To return to Mr. Mylam's plants; the following fine species were in flower when we called there:—

Acineta Humboldtii, having several spikes.

Ansellia Africana; two spikes, large and fine. The largest plant had just gone out of flower.

Calanthe ochracea; nice yellowish flowers, on several spikes.

Cymbidium eburneum. This is a rare and very fine species, with pure white sepals and petals, and the lip of a rich orange-yellow; flowers large and very fragrant, and lasting a long time in bloom.

Cypripedium caudatum (Tailed C.). A very curious and handsome species; the petals are lengthened out to the great length of 20 inches, hanging down from the main body of the flower below the edge of the pot. The colour generally is of a pale straw, with brownish spots inside the slipper-like lip.

Cyrtochilum maculatum; a handsome species with numerous flowers.

Dendrobium Devonianum; a most delicately beautiful species, the flowers of which are so elegant as not to seem "a flower of earth, but of heaven."

Dendrobium Jenkinsii. This pretty little plant had upwards of twenty of its beautiful orange-yellow blossoms.

Dendrobium nobile; a well known, beautiful species; an immense plant, with numerous flowers.

Dendrobium moniliforme; a beautiful, rosy-coloured species, with 10 or 12 spikes.

Dendrobium chrysotoxum (Golden flowered D.); very fine.

Epidendrum selligerum purpureum; dark flowers on a long spike; very fragrant.

Leptotes bicolor; had 40 blooms upon it.

Lycaste Harrisoniana; a good old species, well flowered.

Miltonia cuneata. Excepting *M. Karwinksii* this is the finest of the genus, with large, elegant, white and yellow flowers; several spikes.

Odontoglossum Cervantesii, O. major, and *O. roseum.* Beautiful plants to grow on blocks; they were well bloomed.

Odontoglossum pulchellum; growing in a pot, producing several spikes of pure white flowers, with the lip tinged with yellow, and spotted with crimson; delicately fragrant, and lasting long in bloom.

Odontoglossum cordatum; new and beautiful.

Oncidium Insleayi. Named in honour of the late G. Barker, Esq.'s excellent gardener. A first-rate species, with large yellowish brown flowers, spotted with crimson. This is one of the best of Oncidiums.

Phaius Wallichii; a noble species; the plant had five spikes of its large, handsome flowers.

Scuticaria Steelii; a fine plant, with several of its handsome flowers expanded. See its peculiar culture in a former number.

Trichopilia; this is a beautiful species not yet named. It had four flowers expanded; the sepals and petals are not twisted like *T. tortilis;* the lip is large, pinkish white, and spotted with crimson. Native of Costa Rico.

Such is the list of orchidaceous plants we saw all blooming at once, besides several other smaller species that we have not mentioned. The above are sufficient to show Mr. Mylam's great success in cultivating them.

FLORISTS' FLOWERS.

We have very little space left for our weekly remarks on these favourites, but we will try to find more room next week. The grand attraction is now the *Tulip bed;* continue to protect securely from frost, wind, and rain, to prolong the bloom as long as possible.

CARNATIONS AND PICOTEES.—Finish placing nicely painted sticks to these, tying very loosely, to allow the flower-stem to grow without cramping.　　T. APPLEBY.

THE KITCHEN-GARDEN.

THE severe frost at the commencement of this month will be found, we fear, to have made some havoc amongst the small seedlings just then making their appearance through the surface of the ground. Such matters as these should be carefully watched, and if any mischief has been done, no time should be lost in sowing again, otherwise disappointment will occur at a season when too late for the evil to be repaired. All the spring sown *brassica* family, especially, should be looked over with care, observing whether any failures occur, and if so what may be the cause; for the heavy drenching rains and hailstorms of April may have so much beaten the surface of the soil, notwithstanding the good preparation previously given, and the drying, parching days at intervals, may have so surface bound the earth that the tender plants may be unable to penetrate through it. Frosty nights at the same time also tend to retard, weaken, and even to kill many varieties whilst germinating and when quite in their infant state. These matters we have years ago ascertained, and have various plans in practice to remedy such injuries.

Now, to interfere with the surface of the soil whilst the seed is germinating, or the plant is really in an infant state, is so dangerous, that the remedy may possibly prove worse than the evil. We will, therefore, begin by supposing that a healthy seed-bed has been prepared, the seed sown, and all finished as they ought to be, after which, and previously to the surface of the earth becoming dried, a heavy rain falls: the next day the weather proving sunny, windy, and drying, the well-prepared seed-bed is found to be surface-bound, harsh, and so hard, that it is scarcely possible for the young plants to penetrate through it: the first remedy would be, if well performed, to surface-rake the soil; but if this is done in a thoughtless manner, with a heavy hand or a long-tooth rake, and that too at any time during the hot or drying part of the day, such treatment would of course be certain destruction to the seed, by admitting to it all the drying properties of the sun and wind; whilst, at the same time, if the operation be performed with care in the evening, or in the early morning whilst the crust is somewhat softened and modified by the earth's evaporation, a decided relief and benefit will be the result. Of course a worn down or short-tooth rake should never be put into unpractised peoples' hands for this purpose, or mischief will certainly ensue. Those who know well what they are going to do may be trusted with any rake that comes first to hand.

Now, for giving surface-bound seed-beds relief on a large scale, we adopt the following plan:—We have small wood rollers, from six to eight inches in diameter, and about five feet in length, with a small wooden frame and handle to them. A boy will roll over several acres of surface in the course of a day; and instead of binding the soil still harder, if taken in a proper state, these little light wooden rollers just crack and loosen the flaked and bound up surface, making it friable and healthy; giving relief to the young plants just about bursting up. If the surface has been quickly and very harshly bound up, we prefer the evening or early morning for performing these rollings; when, as before stated, the surface is somewhat softened by evaporation. Our practice also is, when needful, to have another boy to follow the roller with a hand-bush harrow, made merely of a few straight light bushes tied to a very light frame, with a short cross or T handle to draw it by. Thus, by a little management, an unkind surface-bound field, that will not allow the infant plant to penetrate, may be converted into a healthy surface, allowing every good seed the full liberty of producing a plant. These little contrivances, trifling as they may appear, often save great after-expense and disappointment. Such failures are to be observed in every locality; and, after waiting and watching for the plant, supposing the seed to be bad, or that the fly has taken the young plants as fast as they appear, the land has sometimes to be tilled again, and fresh seeded, and when it may happen too late for a full crop to be produced.

For large breadths of *cabbage, turnips, Swedes, mangold-wurtzel, clover*, &c., &c., when overtaken too quickly with storms or heavy rains, and quickly followed by a drying day, so as to bind the surface, we find that by carrying out the foregoing rules in a regular manner we have no failures, but always a production of healthy, strong, young plants; and we have no doubt but that thousands of acres might, every season, be saved by the same simple means, and a vast expenditure in seed and labour also saved, as well as the crop secured at its proper season. If the seed is weak and bad (which easily may be ascertained by sowing some to prove it on a little warmth, or in a sheltered corner in the garden, a few days previous to sowing the main crop), the seedsman should be made answerable for the loss. If attacked by the fly, by careful observation such depredations may easily be detected, and some remedy should at once be put into practice. A harrow made with green elder boughs is an excellent remedy (well dragged over the young plants) to drive away the fly. Charcoal dust and dry wood ashes sowed over the crop at night, or whilst damp with dew, is a still better remedy, as this not only drives away the fly, but also stimulates the plants so beneficially that they very soon grow out of harm's way.

ROUTINE WORK.—Attend well now to all growing crops, with regard to regular surface-stirring; choosing suitable weather for its performance. No one would, of course, think of disturbing the earth's surface whilst wet, but as soon as the soil is settled, and become a little dry on its surface, the oftener the operation is performed the less trouble it is to do, and the greater is the assistance given to the growing crops, and the more healthy is the soil for all succeeding crops; whatever manure may be applied to an unkind foul piece of soil, if the after surface-stirring is neglected, the produce will not equal a similar sized piece cultivated without any manure, where the surface-stirring is regularly attended to. Take advantage of showery weather to sow salt frequently, but with moderation; and also to apply liquid-manure to the *asparagus* beds. The same remarks hold good for the application of liquid-manure to all growing crops.

Garden beans, such as the *Long Pod* and *Windsor*, &c., should now be planted on a cold situation; if a north border, and the soil a stiff loam, so much to their advantage. *Dwarf Kidney Beans* and *Scarlet Runners* that are already up must be taken care of; and those transplanted, if the weather continues cold and unkind, must have dry dust shaken about them at night to prevent canker. Those who may have sown in succession for transplanting, are fortunate—since the weather has proved so cold—that plenty of good plants will be found very useful for forwarding their crop. To keep a succession of young *carrots*, they should be sown at three or four different times in the course of the summer. *Beet*, if not a regular plant, should be made out by transplanting. Make a small sowing of *endive*, as well as *parsley*; and also make or fill up any vacancies that may occur. If plants are saved for seed, take care that every thing is culled out which is not of a first-rate quality. The early *Dutch* and *Stone turnips* may now be sown pretty liberally. A bed of *Swedes* for transplanting may also be sown; and take care that the crowns of *sea-kale* are duly thinned, as previously directed; and also that the young seedlings are well cared for, duly thinned, and dealt with as recommended for other crops. A north aspect is now the best for getting *radishes* in varieties good and mild flavoured, and also for producing small sallads.

. JAMES BARNES.

MISCELLANEOUS INFORMATION.

OUR VILLAGE WALKS.
By the authoress of "My Flowers."
(No. 27.)

As *gardeners*, we certainly ought not to say any thing that may bring our profession into disrepute; yet I cannot resist the charm of wild scenery at any season, but especially in the months of April and May. It is more exquisite, far, than any thing a garden can present; because it is so *fresh*, so unstudied, so picturesque, in all its details, however small or insignificant; and it possesses, above all, the crowning charm of being thrown together by the hand of God, instead of that of man!

On emerging from a thick larch plantation, a few days ago, we opened upon a garden that bid defiance to our own, and every other in our neighbourhood. A copse had been cleared last year, which occupied a deep dingle, through which ran a little, rapid, narrow stream, in a deep channel, twisting and twining its way among roots of trees and broken ground, that gave great additional beauty to the little valley. Every atom of the ground "above, below, around," was carpeted with primroses, wood anemones—deepening from delicate white to purple,—violets, wild strawberry blossoms, and many other bright spring flowers, that sparkled like jewels beneath a cheering sun. The mossy edges of the stream; the gnarled roots that fringed it here and there; the hollows where primroses grew thicker and finer still; the stumps of trees mantled with ivy; and the standing oaks stretching out their rough arms with honest British independence, formed such a congregation of beauties and interests that, had I not possessed a companion, I must have uttered my feelings to the winds, for silence was quite impossible at such a time and place. Then there were such sounds! The rushing water; the concert of birds among the boughs, like so many Jenny Linds; the distant bleatings, and the soft accompaniment of the wild musical breezes, exceeded anything that could be devised by the taste and skill of man; and I am quite sure that if from that scene I had passed into the finest garden in England, it would have disappointed me. We are often troubled because we cannot make our own pleasure-grounds quite what we wish; we labour and expend a great deal of time and money in the attempt, and, I believe, when we have succeeded fully, we seldom relish our handiwork long; man's nature—and woman's too—sometimes delights in novelty, and when our gardens are *complete* they have lost their charm. But this is never the case when we go forth among the woods and fields and view nature in her beautiful simplicity. The finest garden "effect" dies before the burst of woodland wildness that sometimes surprises us in a secluded walk, and leaves nothing for the most fastidious taste to alter or reject. A bold solitary tree standing in a natural "clearing;" a forsaken chalk-pit, with a rich grouping of beech and spruce-firs springing up around; a deep dell, with the stony channel of a brook threading its way through fern, and briars, and broken banks—all these natural careless effects are so agreeable both to eye and mind, that nothing of the same kind that is arranged and invented can give us half the pleasure; and those persons who do not enjoy a country life, and country walks, and country beauties, lose an immeasurable amount of real enjoyment, both of body and mind.

This, too, is the period of the year when woodland scenery conveys a special lesson to our hearts. How often have we, in our beautiful rambles, really seen " the axe laid to the root of the tree," while the hand has paused, and the eye has once more narrowly scanned the unconscious monarch of the forest, and marked the best and most fitting place for it to fall. Ah, what an awful picture of *our own* position, as we stand in health and strength among our fellow men! I never see or hear the crash of a falling tree without an involuntary trembling: it is so striking, so affecting, so tremendously impressive; and does so loudly cry to our deaf and doting hearts as we walk " among the tombs " of this world in our ignorance and sin.

I particularly remember last year watching the fall of some fine spruce-firs that stood in my garden. They shaded my borders so completely from the sun, that I was reluctantly obliged to submit to their removal; and I stood by to see them felled. It spoke volumes to the heart. Bough after bough, that had so long and so gracefully bent beneath the breeze, fell to the ground, until the tall powerful stems stood stripped of their glory, bare and desolate, like the souls of men when their " vain pleas" are rejected, and they stand naked and helpless before the judgment seat of Christ! Then came the crash and the downfall; the saw at the root and the rope at the head did their work well. The once beautiful tree cracked, trembled, reeled, and fell!

Can any description more clearly and terribly pourtray the life and death of man—especially of him who "flourisheth like a green bay-tree"—than the sudden destruction which comes upon a noble tree, in all its healthful beauty, and lays it low? And yet how heedlessly we view these solemn and awakening sights! The passer-by who lingers to gaze, the woodman as he bends and labours at his work, little reck of the stroke which is, perhaps, at that very moment hovering over them to bring their powerful frames down to the gates of death; above all, they may little reck of the souls that animate those frames, perishing, in many cases, for lack of knowledge; and they may close their ears to the cry of the Baptist in the wilderness, and *refuse* " to hear the voice of the charmer, charm he never so wisely."

Let us, in our interesting walks at this lovely season, observe all that passes before our eyes, and lay it to our hearts. As we watch the mighty tree tottering to its fall, or see the young vigorous larch cut down in its early prime, let us remember that *we* " shall all likewise perish ;" and let us strive to " bring forth fruits meet for repentance," lest we " be hewn down and cast into the fire."

We cannot, in fact, snap off a twig, as we pass along, with its bursting buds so fresh, and green, and sweet, without marking the impress of the Hand Divine, and learning an instructive lesson. We trace the footsteps of the Lord on every side: upon the rising grass, the teeming fallows, the cottage borders; among the deep shades of the spicy woods, so full of fragrance in their early beauty; among the swelling blossoms of fruits and flowers; upon the wild open uplands, where the wind blows so briskly, and in the deep warm valley, with its nestling village, where the cool quiet stream enriches and beautifies the scene.

Let me urge such of my readers as may inhabit towns, or their suburbs, to take their evening walks, and spend as much of their leisure time as possible *quite* in the country. If they do but sit for an hour beneath a tree by a river side, and watch the sparkling ripple of " the cold flowing waters," the gay flies that dart across its surface, the sudden splash of the fish as it snatches its gaudy prey, and the rapid motions of the birds that frequent its banks, there will be ample food for deep and sweet meditation, and a broad well-filled page from which to gather evidence and tokens of God's love to his rebellious people. The language nature speaks, although uttered in whispers, is loudly heard by every *listening* heart; and there is so much companionship in her society, that sometimes the presence of our dearest friend would lessen our enjoyment. There is "a time " for all things, and certainly there is a time to *be alone*.

ROYAL BOTANIC SOCIETY'S EXHIBITION AT THE REGENT'S PARK.—May 8.

That there is no certainty in the affairs of this world is in nothing more frequently exemplified than in the weather for horticultural exhibitions. The cultivators devote their skill and care for months, nay for years, to exhibit their petted ones in perfection; and then, when the day arrives, the weather is unpropitious, and the lovers of flowers are prevented enjoying the sight of such pattern specimens of the blossoms of the world, grown to the highest pitch of excellence. Such was the case at the Regent's Park, on the 8th of May just passed. With but little intermission it rained all the day, and, consequently, the company, unlike last year, was exceedingly thin. Not more, we should think, than four or five hundred were present at any one time. Prince Albert, the Duke of Cambridge, the Duke of Norfolk, and other illustrious characters honoured the exhibition by a visit, and expressed themselves highly gratified.

The arrangement of the tents at these gardens is very advantageous to the visitors; for they are set down close to the entrance of one of them; and again, the large conservatory, with the spacious walks amongst and under the plants, is, even in the heaviest rain, a pleasant dry promenade. This " winter garden," as it is very happily named, is so large that it is capable of containing two or three thousand persons very comfortably. Hence the Regent's Park Garden both for the above reasons and being so near to the metropolis, renders it a convenient place for such exhibitions, let the weather be what it may.

There was a novel way of arranging the large collections of plants that had a very good effect. The tent devoted to them, instead of platforms of boards, as formerly, had terraces formed with green turf sides, and sand within to place the plants upon. The terraces were thrown up in circular forms of different sizes, each terrace holding a row of plants, the largest plants being placed at the highest points. By this arrangement each formed a splendid pyramid of floral beauty. This tent being on sloping ground had a very pleasing appearance, especially from the lowest point.

COLLECTION OF THIRTY STOVE AND GREENHOUSE PLANTS.

Mr. May, gardener to Mr. Lawrence of Ealing-park, brought his collection out in grand style, every plant being well flowered, and a perfect specimen of horticultural skill. This collection deservedly obtained the highest prize. Where all were so fine, it is almost invidious to select any for description, but our space will not allow us to describe every plant, therefore we must be content with the following :—

Pimelea spectabilis. This plant was 6 feet through, and 5 feet high, covered with its snowy blossoms in great perfection. *Polygala acumina,* well bloomed, the same size. *Chorozema Lawrenciana,* very full of flowers down to the edge of the pot : 4 feet by 4 feet. *Epacris grandiflora,* an immense well bloomed plant; 8 feet in height, 6 feet through. *Eriostemon buxifolium;* 6 feet by 6 feet. *Hovea Celsii.* This is a difficult plant to bring into a pleasing shape, but in this instance it was a handsome specimen, covered with its beautiful blue blossoms. *Polygala Dalmaisiana,* a handsome specimen, full of bloom; 3 feet by 3 feet. *Podolobium staurophyllum,* very well bloomed; 4 feet by 3 feet. *Gompholobium polymorphum.* Trained to a round balloon-like trellis, and full of flower; 2½ feet by 2 feet. *Ixora coccinea.* This favourite plant had upwards of twenty heads of its rich scarlet flowers. *Erica vestita rosea;* 3 feet by 2 feet; in fine order. *Gompholobium barligerum.* This is a fine exhibition plant, with large pale yellow flowers; 4 feet by 3 feet.

The only other collection of thirty, was exhibited by Mr. Cole, gardener to — Collyer, Esq., of Dartford. *2nd. Prize.* Several of Mr. Cole's plants were rather short of bloom, but will be better in a month's time. The following were in first-rate condition. *Erica propendens*, a fine plant; 3 feet by 2 feet. *Azalea Gledstanesia*, excellently well bloomed; 3 feet by 3 feet. *Leschenaultia formosa*, covered with its beautiful scarlet blossoms; 2 feet by 2½ feet. *Erica Cavendishii*, a noble plant, well flowered; 4 feet by 3½ feet. *Hovea Celsii*, well managed; 3 feet by 2 feet. *Azalea indica* (*Conqueror*), a rich well flowered plant; 5 feet by 4 feet.

COLLECTION OF TWENTY STOVE AND GREENHOUSE PLANTS.

1st Prize, to Mr. Green, gardener to Sir Edward Antrobus, of Cheam. This eminent cultivator has been a successful competitor for a number of years, and his productions this day shew that he has lost none of his spirit and skill. All his plants were excellent, but we can only mention a few of them. *Eriostemon buxifolium*, a handsome symmetrical plant, full of bloom; 5 feet by 5 feet. *Boronia pinnata*, full of its beautiful pink blossoms; 3 feet by 2½ feet. *Acrophyllum venosum*, a beautiful specimen of this handsome plant (which ought to be in every greenhouse, however small); 2 feet by 2 feet. *Leschenaultia formosa*; 2 feet by 2 feet. *Azalea indica alba*, an immense plant, covered with its snow white blossoms. *Gardenia Stanleyana*, a large plant, with upwards of 20 of its trumpet-like blossoms expanded. *Ixora coccinea*; the best plant in the whole exhibition; it had 35 heads of bloom upon it in first-rate order.

2nd Prize, to Mr. Taylor, gardener to — Costar, Esq., Streatham, Surrey. A well grown collection. *Adenandra speciosa*, an old plant well got up; 3 feet by 3 feet. *Adenandra fragrans*, do.; 3 feet by 2 feet; *Leschenaultia formosa*; almost every cultivator exhibited had fine specimens of this elegant plant; 2 feet by 2½ feet. *Ixora coccinea*, also a great favourite, with 14 large heads of bloom upon it. *Ixora crocata*, almost as handsome as the preceding, but of a more dwarf habit; 12 heads expanded, with 20 more to open.

3rd Prize, Messrs. Frazers, nurserymen, Lea Bridge. These gentlemen are well known excellent cultivators, and are coming out again with young plants in fine condition. *Erica Cavendishii*, fine; 3 feet by 2½ feet. *Leschenaultia Baxterii major*, a great improvement upon the old L. Baxterii; 2 feet by 2 feet. *Erica propendens*, a fine plant; 2 feet by 2 feet. *Epacris grandiflora*; 3 feet by 2½ feet.

4th Prize, Messrs. Pamplin and Son, Lea Bridge. These plants are much improved since last year. They had a good *Hovea celsii*; 2½ feet by 2 feet. *Euphorbia splendens*, a fine specimen of a handsome plant; 4 feet by 3 feet. *Podolobium staurophyllum*, well flowered; 3 feet by 2 feet. *Correa ventricosa*, very like *C. speciosa*, a pyramidal plant well managed. *Erica vestita alba*, a pretty grown specimen, well flowered. *Tropæolum Jarrattii*, full of bloom and very healthy; 4 feet.

(*To be continued.*)

NEW AND RARE GREENHOUSE PLANTS.

Messrs. J. A. Henderson and Co., of Pine-Apple Place, Edgeware-road, London, have furnished us with the following list, with their prices, of novelties and rarities for the present year. To those which we consider most desirable we have prefixed an *.

	s.	d.
Acacia grandis. Brilliant yellow flowers, with cut-leaved foliage thickly set on the branches	5	0
*Acacia oleifolia elegans. Drooping variety, the branches hanging down elegantly; flowers golden yellow globes. Flowers in autumn and winter	5	0
*Acrophyllum venosum. Serrated foliage, with spirea-like flowers, the young shoots assuming a crimson tint when expanding	5	0
*Burtonia pulchella. Flowers large and very beautiful, of a rich purple colour, with a yellow spot at the base of each petal	10	6
Blandfordia nobilis. A fine Australian plant, with pendant rich orange-scarlet tube-shaped flowers ..	10	6
*Boronia triphylla. The finest of Boronias with brilliant deep rose-coloured flowers, star-shaped	5	0

	s.	d.
Bossiæ Hendersonii. Dwarf erect evergreen shrub, producing inimitable orange and yellow flowers ..	7	6
Browallia Jamesonii. Rich orange flowers, neat foliage	3	6
Cantua pyrifolia. Yellow and white beautiful greenhouse shrub, flowering very freely	5	0
*Cantua bicolor. Neat box-leaved deciduous shrub, orange and red flowers	2	6
Chætogastra strigosa. Small foliage, abundant flowerer, each bloom studded all over with rosy pink spots	3	6
*Chironia glutinosa. Very abundant flowering species, with large bright rosy lilac flowers	2	6
Chorozema lanceolata. Like C. Dickensonii, with larger leaves, and a more robust habit	10	6
Chorianthus coccinea. New plant, very beautiful ..	3	6
Clematis indivisa (var. lobatus). Climber, with creamy white flowers, and peculiar handsome evergreen foliage	7	6
Conoclinium Janthinum. Blue Ageratum-like flowers, a beautiful summer, autumn, and winter blooming plant	7	6
Cuphea Donkellarii. New	5	0
*Daviesa glauca. A compact dwarf plant, abundant bloomer, with orange and yellow flowers	5	0
*Daviesa physodes. A glaucous shrub, with short racemes of flowers from the axils of the leaves, deep orange-red, beautiful	3	6
Daphne Fortunii. Deciduous shrub, producing its pale lilac flowers early in spring; very fragrant ..	5	0
Daphne Fioneana. Very fragrant; flowers in great profusion	5	0
*Dielytra spectabilis. Drooping raceme, four to five inches long, producing a profusion of delicate rosy pink flowers, somewhat keel-shaped, fine for early forcing	7	6
Dichosma spinosa. Dwarf compact plant, with slender foliage, producing a profusion of rich orange-bronzy flowers	5	0
Dillwynia glycinifolia. Delicate growing plant, having small leaves and orange and red flowers; a very elegant plant	3	6
Dillwynia sessiliflora. An abundant yellow flowering species, small drooping habit, exceedingly neat and pretty	5	0
Epacris hyacinthiflora candidissima. Large long hyacinth-like flowers, pure white, the finest of all the whole family of Epacris	5	0
Erica grande. Scarlet, colour of E. splendens, with fine E. vestita-like foliage, good habit, considered the best of Mr. Storey's new seedlings	30	0
Erica laqueata lutea. Short flower, well swelled and beautifully fluted, tinged with pink and green; flowers yellow orange; excellent habit	21	0
Erica regalis. A very striking variety when in bloom, from its double and triple whorls. For profusion and length of flower, for brilliancy of colour and robustness of growth, it is unequalled	21	0
Eriostemon cuspidatum rubrum. Large broad foliage, flowers white, tipped with pink	15	0
*Eriostemon intermedium. Small round leaves, blooms in great profusion for months; white flowers, tipped with pink in the buds	10	0
Eriostemon neriifolium. Foliage long and narrow, and most abundant bloomer, with white flowers tipped slightly with pink	7	6
*Eriostemon scabrum, or Philotheca australis. Pure white flowers, very conspicuous, with long heath-like foliage. Very elegant and abundant flowering plant	5	0
Erythrina Bidwillii. Colour a pure crimson, flowering in a very dwarf state	7	6
Enkianthus reticulatus. An evergreen shrub, with large white and pink Andromeda-like flowers	7	6
Fugosia hakeafolia. Large blooms of a reddish blue purple	5	0
*Gompholobium barbigerum. Moderate-sized shrub, flowers freely with large rich orange flowers; very showy	5	0

(*To be continued.*)

A FEW VERY CHOICE STOVE, GREENHOUSE, AND HARDY PLANTS.

We give this, with their usual price, at the request of "T. W.," and other correspondents. These are additional to Messrs. Henderson's list, which we have begun publishing:—

STOVE PLANTS.

	s. d.		s. d.
Allamanda grandiflora	5 0	Henfreya scandens	3 6
Aphelandra aurantiaca	3 6	Jasminum sambal	3 6
Clerodendrum splendens	4 0	Ixora odoratissima	7 6
" fallax	3 6	" grandiflora	5 0
Franciscea Hopeana	1 6	Ipomœa Horsfallia	5 0
" latifolia	2 6	" Waldeckii	3 6
" hydrangeæformis	3 6	Manettia bicolor	2 6
Hoya Imperialis	5 0	Rhyncospermum jasminioides	3 6
" belli.... 7s. 6d. to 10	6	Stephanotis floribunda	2 6

GREENHOUSE PLANTS.

	s. d.		s. d.
Tecoma jasminiodora	2 6	Boronia tripbylla	2 6
Zygopetalum Mackayi	7. 6	Brugmansia sanguinea (large	
Leschenaultia formosa	1 6	tree)	3 6
" biloba superba	2 6	Daphne indica rubra	3 6
(both beautiful)		" hybrida	1 6
Pelargonium tricolor	1 6	Epacris hyacinthiflora	0 0
" rosetta	2 0	" candidissima	0 0
" Maid of Anjou	1 6	Fuchsia—Comte de Beaulieu	0 0
" Annie	2 6	" Cassandra	0 0
Tropæolum Lobbii	1 6	" One in the Ring	0 0
" Jarrattii	3 6	Hovea ilicifolia	5 0
" Brachyceras	3 6	" Celsii	2 6
Trymalium odoratissimum	2 0	Kalosanthes coccinea	1 6
Azalea indica lateritia striata	3 6	" nitida odorata	2 6
" purpurea macrantha	3 6	Kennedya inophylla	3 6
" triumphans	2 0	" nannosa	5 0
Abelia floribunda (nearly hardy)	2 0	" Marryatta	2 6
Aphelexis macrantha purpurea	2 6	Primula attaica	2 6
" rosea	2 6	Mandevilla suaveolens ..	2 6
Boronia serrulata	1 6		

HARDY PLANTS.

	s. d.		s. d.
Clianthus puniceus	1 6	Stauntonia latifolia	3 6
Erica arborea	1 0	Tropæolum speciosum	1 6
" vulgaris pleno	1 0	" tuberosum	1 6
Gaultheria shallon	1 6	Weigela rosea 1s. to 2	6
" procumbens	1 6	Zauchneria Californica	0 0

HINTS ON GARDENING FOR YOUNG PEOPLE.

(Continued from page 24.)

I TRUST none of my young friends have misunderstood my last hint on serving themselves, so as to suppose I advise them to seek no counsel from the gardener, or to take their own way whether right or wrong. So far from that being the case, I give you, as my next hint,

Never be ashamed to ask if you do not know how to set about any work.—I believe few people who have taken any interest in the actual operations of gardening, are aware how very ignorant beginners (even when not young) are on the subject. There is, generally, a confused idea that it is very difficult to understand about gardening, and sometimes an amusing and amazing ignorance, as to the difference between roots and seeds, and as to the time for planting and sowing. In some there is a dread of daring to do anything that is not in "the book;" and in others, a daring to do and try all sorts of experiments, because they will not ask advice. I know a lady who got a plant of Primula farinosa (mealy primrose) from a friend who had brought it from its native dwelling in a marshy place; but as the lady who received it know little of plants, and did not ask advice how to treat the pretty little wild flower, it was planted in the warm sunny border before the greenhouse, and of course died in two days. I knew another who planted a bed of Ranunculus roots with the claws (or root ends) up; but she was excusable, as she had no one near to ask about them.

Try to have plenty of Common Flowers in your little Garden.—These are generally sweeter and make more show than the new and rare plants, besides being easier to cultivate. When what are called "florists' flowers" are cultivated, the object being to have fine blooms, quantity is sacrificed to quality, and auriculas, polyanthuses, pinks, carnations, &c., are only allowed to flower on one or two stems. But I suppose you wish your little gardens to look bright and showy, and occasionally, perhaps, you would like to pull a nosegay from your own flowers; and, for this purpose, freely flowering old friends, however common, are the best. Indeed, I dare say many of you have felt with me on going to see a fine collection of plants, that you are disappointed by the garden not looking gay; the plants may be rare and valuable, but the tallies were more striking than the flowers, and, except to a botanical cultivator, it was less interesting than a garden where common flowers grow in masses.

Endeavour to have a succession of flowers.—I believe my young readers will find this difficult at first, for most youthful gardeners have periodical fits of gardening, strongest in spring, but occurring at intervals through the summer when any bright or sweet flower catches their fancy, and a bit of it is begged for "my garden." Between these fits of zeal the poor garden is too often left desolate and waste, and the young gardener gets discouraged because her garden is dull while others are gay; and she fancies it is owing to the soil or situation, or any thing rather than to her own want of perseverance and forethought. I know nothing better for teaching young people, to follow good "Mrs. Think-in-time's" maxims, than the love and practice of gardening; for you must think and plan beforehand, and you must work at the proper time if you wish to succeed in having a succession of flowers. At first you will not know what flowers you should expect to follow each other, or how to arrange them, so as to make the gayest show; but keep your eyes open, look at every garden you visit for hints, mark down in a little book what flowers you see in bloom in other gardens during each month, and try to get some of each kind for your own little plot. Do not, however, in your eagerness to have some favourite flower which your have forgotten till you see it in blossom, transplant it in full flower to your plot; rather wait till the proper time for lifting it comes, which is generally in autumn; mark it down in your little book, and get it at the proper time. I must confess I am not yet cured of this childish trick of lifting plants in full flower, and sometimes when lifted with a ball of earth plants do flower on and look as if they never knew they had been lifted, but somehow next year they seldom flower so well, and I generally regret afterwards that I had not waited patiently till the plant had done flowering before I moved it.

Do everything in its proper time is as good a rule in gardening as in other things. I will try to suggest some common flowers in the order of their flowering, but as I can only give hints my young friends must study the garden and THE COTTAGE GARDENER for themselves, and get their plots into flowering order by dint of forethought and care. About the first common flowering plant I have in my little garden is the Winter Aconite, but its bright yellow flowers come out in such cold weather in February that I seldom see more of it than in a hurried morning visit to my garden. Then come bunches of Snowdrops and Crocuses, and before these are quite over my blue and pink Hepaticas are in flower; these last till about the end of March, when blue Grape Hyacinths and yellow Daffodils succeed them. I have also Wood Anemonies and a small white Saxifrage, and sometimes a bed of Hyacinths that had flowered last year in the house. April and May you can have no difficulty about, for primroses, cowslips, polyanthuses, auriculas, pansies, wood hyacinths, wallflowers, and gentians, are in flower; and jonquils and narcissus, if you can get a few bulbs of each, are delightful additions. In June I have some of the above named still flowering on, and, in addition, Tulips, some Phloxes, and White Roses; this early-flowering, old fashioned rose, I have heard called Prince Charlie's Rose, and I believe it used to be customary among the Jacobites to wear one of these roses if it could be had on the 10th of June, which was the prince's birth-day; if not in flower by that time (which it seldom is) a Guelder rose was substituted for

"The flower that I lo'e best,
The rose that is like the snaw."

Then come on gradually the annuals which you have sown in April and May; some of these your little gardens should never want; there is the pretty little blue Nemophila insignis, Lupinus nanus, and Virginian Stock, which each appear soon enough above ground to satisfy a young gardener, while mignionette, sweet peas, Clarkia pulchella, Venus's looking-glass, nasturtiums, and many others, will enliven your little gardens in July and August. There are several species of Campanula, too, which make a pretty variety, whether it be the tall Canterbury bells, or the intermediate-sized biennial, or the pretty little blue or white harebell. Then roses and pinks, and so many other plants are in flower that the difficulty for young gardeners is to select what their gardens will contain. By September and October, you will find a gradual falling off. African and French marigolds, China asters, and some late sown annuals will help you on; and then comes the pale michaelmas daisy, and the lingering Chinese rose, valued more, though perhaps despised, in summer's pride. Then, autumn wind and rain will do their work, and you must do yours; get in your bulbs, put all in order for winter, and live in hope till glad spring again brings forth your floral favourites. It must depend on the size of your gardens, of course, how many of those flowers I have named (and what a limited list have I given!) you can have; but try each month to have something in flower, if but one plant, and something coming on, and your gardens will never lack interest.

How to get Plants for your Gardens.—I find from a hint I have received, that there is some danger of my young friends misunderstanding an allusion I once made to "judicious cribbing," so I must take care, remembering that though I am arrived at years of discretion, and know pretty well what I may take a bit of out of the general home garden, all my readers are not to be supposed equally trustworthy. I would say then, in the first place, and gratefully would I say it, that I have never yet met the gardener, master nor man, who was unwilling to *give*, though I have seldom met one who was quite willing that any one should *take*. I have a fellow-feeling with them, for, though I delight to give roots, suckers, or slips to a friend, I know few whom I would intrust to go into my garden and help themselves. But though the young are in general told "not to ask for any thing," I think this good rule may be modified, in respect of plants and flowers. Do not ask for rare flowers, or for bulbs of value, or for what you see is scarce; but when you see a plant with runners creeping from it, or of a spreading habit, or with such fibrous roots that a little bit will grow, I do not think any one will blame you for asking for a portion of that plant, or will grudge giving it you; and it is wonderful how soon such *wee* bits grow into good-sized plants. When you do get a whole plant lift it, if possible, with a ball of earth about it; and at all events water it well, and shade it from the sun for a day or two. Damp, showery weather, with a cloudy sky, is the best time for transplanting growing plants; but I dare say you will not always choose to wait for that: so you must remember to shade and water your plants till they have taken root. A flower-pot inverted over them is a good plan, taking it off at night; but in default of that I often make an awning of a large rhubarb leaf, propping it up on four bits of stick. I have a good deal more to say on this head, about getting cuttings, sowing seeds, &c., but I must defer it till another opportunity, lest I encroach too much on these pages.   HORTENSE.

(To be continued.)

EXTRACTS FROM CORRESPONDENCE.

GENTIANA VERNA.—I send you one of our most beautiful alpine plants, *Gentiana verna.* I had it sent from Middleton, in Teesdale, Durham, about ten years since, which I believe is the only situation it is found wild in England. I had it sent early in the spring; I put a few plants in a pot, and set it in a frame, the rest were planted in the garden; they both flowered soon after those in the pot ripened seeds, the plants in the garden survived until next spring, but did not flower, and soon after died. I have since tried it in the garden, but it would not grow more than one season. I have never observed any seed since the first year I had it. On examining the flowers this spring, they appear to have neither stamens nor pistil; the flowers are all alike. I grow it in common garden soil, and treat it as a hardy greenhouse plant; soon after it is done flowering it is removed out to some shady situation, and housed again in September or October.

I have also been very successful in cultivating another beautiful British plant in pots, the *Andromeda polifolia.* I treat it as the above, only I grow it in peat. I have a plant of it now in flower in an 8 inch pot; it is about 18 inches diameter, and hangs beautifully over the edge of the pot; it has about 60 clusters of flowers upon it. The Gentiana and Andromeda are, now, two of the prettiest pot-plants I have.

I will feel obliged if you can inform me, in THE COTTAGE GARDENER, the reason why the organs of reproduction of the *Gentiana verna* are absent.—A. D.

[Many thanks for the specimens of, to us southerns, those rare flowers. It is more common for either anthers or pistil to be absent than for both to be wanting. In either case it very frequently arises from a too great development of root. If a potato produces tubers very early, it rarely produces any flowers at all; and if you wish to render an apple or pear speedily productive, you have to circumscribe its development of roots.—ED. C. G.]

TO CORRESPONDENTS.

*** We request that no one will write to the departmental writers of THE COTTAGE GARDENER. It gives them unjustifiable trouble and expense; and we also request our coadjutors *under no circumstances* to reply to such private communications.

GERANIUM LEAVES DISEASED (*Greus*).—We never saw leaves more severely affected with mildew and spot. The air of your greenhouse must be too damp and cold; and the soil is probably too retentive of wet. We should repot them, removing a great part of their present soil, and replacing it by some light fresh loam, and plenty of drainage. Dust the affected leaves with flowers of sulphur, and keep the air of the house dryer.

DRAINING (*P. W.*).—We will give some practical directions relative to this shortly.

DEPOSIT ON MARIE LOUISE PEAR (*L. A. C.*).—Send us a specimen in a box, so that the Post-office punch may not annihilate it.

TRANSPLANTING LARGE TREES (*H. H.*).—The best work on this subject is Sir H. Stewart's *Planter's Guide*, which can be obtained through any bookseller. As to odd numbers of *Loudon's Encyclopædia of Gardening*, if you write to Messrs. Longman & Co., Paternoster-row, they will give you every information.

FANCY GERANIUMS (*T. W. T., Leeds*).—You will be attended to before long; there is a difficulty in getting them to grow well in summer, they are such free flowerers. It is best to push them along in autumn and spring, when there is less direct light, and consequently less stimulus to the flowering process.

HEATING A GREENHOUSE (*B. D. Gale*).—We cannot satisfactorily dispose of your case in a passing notice. You might imitate the clever and ingenious plan of *C. P.*, page 355; but we think you would gain your purpose *much cheaper* by having a proper damper in your chimney. Contracting the fire-place, so far as removing some of the fire-bars, or filling them up solid, so that fuel might rest there without being exposed to draught from beneath; having also a proper ash-pit door, and having a smaller boiler, if the present one is too large, which we think far too much so for the pipes it has to heat. With these pipes you may keep out frost, but you could not force your pines, if, as we understand you, there are only two two-inch pipes, and these only round the front and end of the house; four at the least would be requisite. If you have shewn the boiler correctly, the pipes are not properly joined to it, for they seem in the middle, instead of being at the top and bottom. The keeping the water in the boiler, merely at the height of the upper pipe, would of itself lessen your boiler one-third; and we think, under all the circumstances, we would keep the water at that level, and make some little alterations in the fire-place, before going to the expense of a feeding-pipe, a metal plate, a hot-chamber, &c. The expense of adding two more pipes to the house, if you wish to force the fires, would be trifling in comparison. Write again, if you need more directions.

WINDOW PLANTS (*C. T. P.*).—Your fuchsias, geraniums, and cinerarias, should now have plenty of air; and in fine weather should be set outside to rusticate a little. Most of the begonias are rather tender, and like rich light soil. We do not know whether it be a begonia or not, by you calling it the *resurrection plant.* Send a leaf.

OLEANDER (*Ibid*).—This, which is just rooted, you must keep inside the window at present. If it grows well, you will obtain from it a panicle of bloom the following year. If the shoot was strong, and you could place it in a cucumber-bed in a nice heat, you might nip out its point, and when it broke allow two or three shoots to grow instead of one. Encourage them with heat until the end of summer, and then gradually harden them off, by setting the plant first in the window, and then out of doors, taking it in before frost. Your safest plan will be to encourage the present shoot you have got.

OAK-LEAVED GERANIUMS FOR BOUQUETS (*M. J. T.*).—The largest leaved geranium that we know of the oak-leaved kinds, is *Pelargonium glutinosum.* Of course the size of the leaf depends on the vigour of the plant. Most people have their favourites for surrounding *bouquets*, and for the purpose we know many use the *Pelargonium graveolens*, or the *Otto of rose*, and this is one of the best for such purpose. Perhaps Mr. Beaton will say which varieties he finds are preferred.

HEATING A SMALL PIT (*C. W. Estcourt*).—Our correspondent writes as follows:—"I was extremely interested by *W. X. W's* paper upon "Heating a Small Pit," for my great desire is to discover some cheap method of warming a small pit, without an expensive stove and boiler with its house and flue. There are, however, one or two points upon which I am greatly desirous of information. *W. X. W.* feeds his stove with charcoal, and says it burns for 35 hours. How much charcoal does the stove hold? How long after lighting the fire is it before the apparatus is heated? And how many hours a day is the fire lighted, in order to keep up sufficient heat when using the pit? Is the stove placed inside the brickwork? It seems to me that there must be a great waste of heat by using lead-pipes—lead being so bad a conductor of heat. And from having the tank under the bed at one side, that there must be an undue accumulation of heat just over it, as it presents so much larger a surface than the pipe. Besides this, the horizontal position of the copper-pipe in the cylinder is bad, inasmuch as the circulation would, I apprehend, be much accelerated by giving it a slanting direction through the fire. Would it not be practicable and much more advantageous instead of using lead-pipes, to make a shallow tank, either of wood, or cast iron, and let the copper-pipe lead directly into this tank? Would not, in such, the circulation be quicker; and would not the effect be greater; and would not the pit be altogether more complete; and scarcely, if at all, more expensive?" Will *W. X. W.* oblige us by answering these queries.

POTATOES (*Tyro, Plumstead*).—The leaf you have enclosed is blackened by frost and not by disease. This will not affect the crop much, the leaves at present being so young. Never mind your Ash-leaved Kidneys not being so forward as others, they will soon pass them when once they get above ground. The *peas*, of which you find the tops off and lying on the ground, have had their stems eaten through by slugs; hoe the ground near the rows and dust over it with quick lime, which will prevent their further depredations; the lime must be renewed after rain has fallen.

HEATING CONSERVATORY ON FIRST-FLOOR (*A. B., Camden Town*).—Have your boiler at A, and take care that the joints of your hot-water pipes are made very tight, or leakages from them will annoy you. We cannot give any estimate of the cost of your plan, nor recommend any one to do it. With so small an affair, and so situated, we should have the water kept hot by a jet of gas on the same floor with the conservatory.

BEES (*E. E.*).—You ask "If a swarm of bees is put into a hive placed on a doubling board (Taylor, page 98) will it require a second hive this season?" If it be a good and early swarm it will require another hive this season; and it should be supplied about 21 days after its being hived. It is not too late to obtain Payne's hives. You can obtain a folio case for THE COTTAGE GARDENER numbers as they come out, of Mr. Low, 169, Fleet-street.

ZAUCHSNERIA CALIFORNICA SEEDS (*T. M. W.*).—These should be sown in very light soil, and placed in a cold pit; common garden soil is by far too heavy for such very small seeds. Otherwise, the whole of your seeds, if they were ripe, would have vegetated.

FLOWER-BEDS, ARRANGEMENT (*C. W. L.*).—Your flower-bed, five and a half feet in diameter, with an Irish yew in the centre, and a row of crocuses and two rows of hyacinths round the outside, may be planted with geraniums, calceolarias, or verbenas, or with all three; and as it is always best to allow bulbs, as hyacinths, to ripen their leaves where they flowered, you might use any of those annuals which form good edging, and which could be transplanted as late as when the hyacinths were fit to move. More generally, however, all those spring bulbs are removed as soon in May as the weather will allow of half-hardy plants to be " turned out ;" and if they are removed in showery, or cloudy weather, taking great care not to injure the roots, and afterwards carefully watered till their leaves turn yellow, they take very little hurt. The beds are then dug, and are ready for a fresh crop.

NUMBER OF PLANTS FOR A BED (*Ibid*).—There is no rule necessary to determine the number of plants that will fill a bed of a given size, nor can we be of the least use to you, or to any one, under this head; but take an instance—we are now planting calceolarias at two feet six inches apart every way, and the beds are quite full at once; the very same kind of calceolarias we are planting not quite six inches apart, and the bed does not seem full, so that the number of plants depend entirely on their size. Every bed in a gay flower-garden ought to be planted as full as the stock of plants or the weight of the purse will allow of; *plant thickly, and thin in time*, is the proper rule.

FLOWER TO MIX WITH CRIMSON LOBELIAS (*Ibid*). — *Verbena leucrcoides* would make a good match, and the best contrast to your " deep crimson lobellias ; " at least a white flowering plant should be used. In the corners of your square bed large patches of *Gladiolus psittacinus* would look remarkably well, and suit the other plants as to colour and style of growth—and both should have equal consideration.

BEDDING-OUT FLOWERS IN POTS (*Ibid*).—Scarlet geraniums, fuchsias, &c.—indeed, all half-hardy plants—*may* be put into beds in their pots; and sometimes it is necessary to do so with some scarlet geraniums, to keep them in check in damp rich beds. The plan requires much attention, however; as if the balls once get thoroughly dry, no amount of water thrown on the bed will save them, as it will pass off as from the slates on a roof.

VERBENA VENOSA (*Rad*).—No other purple verbena or Stachy-tarpheta will do for mixing with the Scarlet variegated Geranium. Your idea that *Emma* would do, because it is a good dark purple, is an apt illustration of many of the closet arrangements of flowers that have been industriously recommended. It will not contrast pleasingly.

AZALEAS DONE FLOWERING (*Ibid*).—We suppose you mean the Chinese kinds. Plants of them getting bare below, with only leaves on the tips of the branches, are in a precarious state, probably, at the roots. Such require to be now pruned-in ; or say cut away two-thirds of all the bare branches, and stop all those that are not bare. See that the drainage is all right, and then assist them by a good moist heat of from 60° to 86° for the next six weeks.

MULBERRY BRANCH LAYERED (*J. H. F.*).—In May last was placed around one of a mulberry-tree's large branches a barrel about four feet deep, filled with clay : it held six or seven wheelbarrows full. The branch has roots in the clay already more than a foot long. Some persons advise

separating it from the parent stem when in full leaf; others, only ringing it, and separating it in the winter ; and our advice is asked. We should suffer the branch to become filled with sap from its parent before resorting to measures tending to a separation. Towards June we would merely score round the stem with a knife to begin with, and in the middle of July we would remove a strip of bark altogether—say about a quarter of an inch in width. We would then cut off the branch in the middle of October, and replant, tub and all. An excavation might be left for one year after around the tub, and the staves drawn away in the ensuing winter, and the hole filled up with good soil.

VINE BORDER (*T. W. L.*).—Your vine border soil is not bad after all : you will grow good grapes if you are safe from stagnant moisture. We should have preferred more loam and lime-rubbish in the mixture. The Bishop Stortford border will not last seven years longer if the quantity of manure used be correctly stated. The other portion of your arrangements are excellent ; and you can scarcely fail. You will have no success with oranges on the back wall, unless you confine your vines to the rafters on the spurring system.

RED SPIDER (X).—No syringing is employed by Mr. Errington to his wall fruit the whole summer. We do not, however, say that judiciously used it would not be beneficial. Mr. Errington wrote rather strongly, in order to deter from an abuse of the syringe.

INARCHING VINES (*S. G.*).—Vines are generally inarched on the old wood during the rest season. You may, however, inarch directly, using a young shoot in a young shoot, if possible. This is an operation that requires care. They will take almost any way ; but one point is to guard against bleeding.

ANSWERS (*E. E.*).—It is impossible for us to guarantee an answer to a query in any given time, for we never give a reply until we feel certain that it is accurate ; and before this certainty is attained we often have to consult authorities. The next Thursday but one after we receive a query its answer usually appears.

ACCENTING NAMES (*W. B. R.*).—We should accent the names if we could be certain of accuracy, but this cannot be secured in a weekly periodical ; and to be inaccurate, even occasionally, would be worse than leaving the names without accents. One of our objects in publishing *The Cottage Gardeners' Dictionary*, now preparing for the press, is to give a reference for accented names.

GINGER WINE (*M. A. C.*).—The correct receipt is as follows :—To make six gallons, boil together for one hour, and skimming whilst they boil, the peels of six lemons, nine ounces of ginger bruised, twelve pounds of loaf sugar, and six gallons of water. Let it remain until about as warm as new milk, then put in the juice of the six lemons, and four pounds of raisins cut small. Put all into a clean cask, and add three tablespoonsful of yeast or barm. Stir it daily for seven days ; then add half an ounce of isinglass dissolved in a little hot water, and a pint of brandy ; bung down the cask tightly, let it remain for six weeks, and then bottle it.

FUCHSIA MACRANTHA (*W. D.*).—Any London florist will supply it for about eighteenpence.

IRON STOVE FOR GREENHOUSE (*J. S. L.*).—We *never* thought an iron stove suitable for heating a small greenhouse, though we may have endeavoured to render our correspondent's intentions as little injurious as we could. It is not merely the gases from the fuel that are injurious, but those formed by the dust always floating in the air being burnt against the sides and tubes of the stove. No one can mistake the smell caused by this burning; added to which there is dust from clearing away ashes, &c.

WIRE-WORM IN COMPOST HEAP (*Ibid*).—You do not say what compost. If there is no objection, we should soak it thoroughly with ammoniacal liquor from a gas-work. If a small quantity, effect the soaking in a hogshead cask.

ASPARAGUS SHOOTS DECAYING (*C. T. P.*).—The specimens sent to us are quite decayed about three inches below the surface of the soil, and their tops curled round. We think this must arise from too much stagnant moisture in the beds. If this be so, the cure is to cut a trench between the beds three feet deep, and thence into some neighbouring ditch ; and lay draining pipes down, or to fill up the trench with flint-stones to keep the drain open.

MOON'S WATERING POTS (*A Lover of Gardening*).—Can any of our readers inform us where these are to be purchased, and at what price ?

WHITE FORGET-ME-NOT.—This grows abundantly in a garden near Ledbury ; and the kind owner offers to send it to any one who informs us that they require it. They must send their address and a stamped blank envelope.

NAMES OF PLANTS (*A Lover of Flowers from Childhood*).—Your specimen sent is *Berberis heterophylla*. We cannot guess at the other; please to let us see a specimen of the flowers, &c.

PEACH-TREE SHEDDING ITS LEAVES (*A Constant Subscriber*).—The probability is, that this tree in your hothouse has its roots too dry. Soak the earth in the pot thoroughly with tepid water, and take care to keep it moist. No two peaches on so young a tree should be nearer to each other on the same branch than nine inches. Answer to other question next week.

LONDON: Printed by HARRY WOOLDRIDGE, Winchester High-street, in the Parish of Saint Mary Kalendar; and Published by WILLIAM SOMERVILLE ORR, at the Office, No. 2, Amen Corner, in the Parish of Christ Church, City of London.—May 16th, 1850.

WEEKLY CALENDAR.

M D	W D	MAY 23—29, 1850.	Weather near London in 1849.			Sun Rises.	Sun Sets.	Moon R. & S.	Moon's Age.	Clock bef. Sun.	Day of Year
23	Tu	Greasy Fritillary Butterfly appears. [appears.	T. 69°—30°.	W.	Fine.	59 a. 3	52 a. 7	3 14	12	3 33	143
24	F	QUEEN VIC. B. 1819. Small Heath Butterfly	T. 75°—50°.	S.	Fine.	58	55	3 39	13	3 31	144
25	S	PRINCESS HELENA B. 1846. Bees first swarm.	T. 72°—50°.	N.W.	Fine.	57	56	4 7	14	3 35	145
26	SUN	TRINITY SUNDAY. Aug. 1st Archbp Cant.	T. 73°—48°.	S.W.	Fine.	56	57	rises.	☾	3 19	146
27	M	Ven. Bede. Garden Carpet Moth.	T. 77°—56°.	S.W.	Rain.	55	59	9a.19	16	3 13	147
28	Tu	Sand Piper first seen. [seen.	T. 58°—50°.	N.E.	Rain.	54	V11	10 10	17	3 6	148
29	W	K. CHARLES II. RESTORED, 1660. Stinging Fly	T. 75°—46°.	W.	Fine.	53	1	10 55	18	2 59	149

On the 29th, at Geneva, in the year 1829, died SIR HUMPHRY DAVY, the most distinguished chemist of the age, though no mental characteristic of his childhood threw a ray before prophetic of his future greatness. As a boy he was fond of poetry, and the fragments which remain of his early rhymes are above mediocrity; nor are these the only evidences that his mind was highly imaginative, and, seemingly, more prone to fanciful than to scientific efforts; even his first essays in science "on heat, light, and colour," most truly were brilliant fancies, bearing, as it has been said, "the stamp of youth and genius; for in them are the faults of the one and the redeeming qualities of the other." The boy was the epitome of the decaying man; for when disease imperatively forbade deep mental thought and minute research, the imaginative qualities of his mind resumed their activity; and the dying man of science and of poetry gave birth to that beautiful little volume, *Consolations in Travel, or the Last Days of a Philosopher.* It comes not within the purpose of our pages to trace minutely his general researches in chemistry, splendid, though, were their results, and beneficial as they were to mankind. It must suffice for us to say, that if Lord Bacon, the father of experimental philosophy, could revisit the earth, and was permitted to have placed before him the discoveries made by one of his disciples, those of Davy must be selected. Never were a chain of accurate experiments and close inductive reasoning more beautifully exemplified than in his researches concerning the metallic bases of the alkalies, the simple form of chlorine, and the qualities of flame. The last resulted in that blessing to the miner, *The Safety Lamp;* and which he has erected into the most enduring memorial of its inventor, by naming "The Davy." But we must confine ourselves to a notice of his researches relative to the cultivation of the soil; and here, also, he was most useful; for he was the first effectually to raise "Agricultural Chemistry" into a department of science. Very early in life, whilst yet an apprentice to Mr. Tomkin, a surgeon of his native town, Penzance, he made some experiments on the air disengaged by sea-weeds from the water of the ocean; experiments which convinced him that aquatic plants perform the same part in purifying the air dissolved in water, which land plants act in the atmosphere. These experiments gradually led him from Penzance to a scientific institution at Bristol, from thence to be Professor of Chemistry at the London Royal Institution, and ultimately to be President of the Royal Society. His earliest researches were connected with analyses of oak bark and other vegetable matters employed in tanning; and in 1802 he commenced a series of lectures

before the Board of Agriculture—a series which extended over ten years, and which were published by him with the title of *Elements of Agricultural Chemistry.* It is the first, and is still the best, work shewing the composition of soils, and how to analyse them; what is the food of plants, and how it can be best presented to them; what are their functions, and how the cultivator must regard these to promote their health. It is, in short, the application, in its most effective mode, of chemistry to the cultivation of plants; and we do not enter more fully here upon the importance and the benefits derivable from their combination, only because we shall have another opportunity for so doing. Constant mental exertion, and participation in metropolitan festivities, at length broke down his health, and he obeyed the advice to seek for its restoration in a milder climate and in total mental relaxation; but the cessation came too late, and in his fiftieth year he died as we have already related. With an extract from his last writing we will close our sketch. "Religion, whether natural or revealed, has always the same beneficial influence on the mind. In youth, in health, and in prosperity, it awakens feelings of gratitude and sublime love, and purifies at the same time that it exalts; but it is in misfortune, in sickness, in age, that its effects are most truly and beneficially felt; when submission in faith and humble trust in the Divine will from duties become pleasures, and undecaying sources of consolation; then it creates powers which were believed to be extinct, and gives a freshness to the mind which was supposed to have passed away for ever, but which is now renovated by immortal hope, and is the Pharos guiding the wave-tossed mariner to his home. Its influence outlives all earthly enjoyments, and becomes stronger as the organs decay and the frame dissolves; it appears as that evening star of light in the horizon of life, which, we are sure, is to become in another season a morning star, and it throws its radiance through the gloom and shadow of death." Such was the dying declaration of one of the greatest philosophers of modern days; such the attestation of exalted judgment, acute perception, and fervid imagination united in one mind. Can the scoffers at religion bring such a champion to the lists?

METEOROLOGICAL PHENOMENA OF THE WEEK.—The highest and lowest average temperatures of these days at Chiswick, during the last twenty-three years, have been 67° and 45.3° respectively. The greatest heat, 91°, was on the 28th in 1847; and the greatest cold, 29°, was on the 25th in 1832. Rain fell on 59 days, and 102 were fine.

RANGE OF BAROMETER—RAIN IN INCHES.

May		1841.	1842.	1843.	1844.	1845.	1846.	1847.	1848.	1849.
23	B. {	30.159 / 29.994	29.937 / 29.785	29.784 / 29.616	30.186 / 30.096	29.834 / 29.799	30.212 / 30.201	30.076 / 29.780	30.314 / 30.261	30.205 / 29.977
	R.	0.01	0.01	0.53	—	0.16	—	—	—	—
24	B. {	30.180 / 30.137	29.838 / 29.799	30.453 / 29.479	30.076 / 29.822	29.822 / 29.863	30.232 / 30.202	29.865 / 29.861	30.287 / 30.256	30.202 / 30.036
	R.	0.02	—	0.05	—	—	—	—	—	0.036
25	B. {	30.165 / 30.133	29.854 / 29.845	29.677 / 29.605	30.103 / 30.619	29.788 / 29.585	30.207 / 30.192	30.230 / 30.112	30.255 / 30.158	29.971 / 29.945
	R.	0.23	—	—	0.10	—	—	—	—	
26	B. {	30.076 / 29.945	29.823 / 29.767	29.597 / 29.547	30.206 / 30.156	29.685 / 29.610	30.136 / 30.115	30.242 / 30.103	30.196 / 30.031	30.013 / 30.003
	R.	0.01	0.20	—	—	0.27	—	—	—	
27	B. {	29.882 / 29.823	29.999 / 29.911	29.535 / 29.433	30.199 / 30.125	29.778 / 29.758	30.149 / 30.046	30.064 / 29.968	30.130 / 30.101	29.186 / 29.910
	R.	0.03	0.13	0.14	0.05	0.06	—	—	—	0.04
28	B. {	30.038 / 29.988	30.055 / 29.988	30.802 / 30.899	30.026 / 30.735	29.700 / 30.779	30.243 / 30.112	29.932 / 29.966	30.107 / 30.014	30.173 / 30.101
	R.	0.03	0.16	—	0.61	—	0.55	—	—	0.07
29	B. {	30.096 / 30.061	30.124 / 29.991	30.332 / 29.912	29.935 / 29.927	29.592 / 29.582	30.320 / 30.306	30.157 / 29.746	30.060 / 29.963	30.282 / 30.155
	R.	—	0.20	0.07	0.07	—	—	—	—	

INSECTS.—If the season continues as it has commenced, there is a probability that the gardener will never have to deplore a spring more productive of insect ravagers than the present. Slugs are the only vermin who seem in diminished numbers; for the severe winter and the dry March just passed have thinned their tribes, and kept the survivors in check. Foremost among

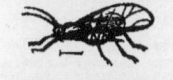

the insects from whom the gardener is now suffering, are the *Aphides;* these are thick upon our gooseberry and rose bushes; and we warn our readers to attack them the moment they are detected, for they multiply with almost incredible rapidity. The amount of injury they cause to a plant, by robbing it of its sap or blood, is pro-portioned to their number, and the time they are allowed to infest the subject of their attack; and the amount of that injury may be appreciated by the fact, that the hop-duty is often £468,000; but the hop-louse (*Aphis humuli*) frequently so destroys the crop as to reduce it to little more than £15,000. The green fly on our roses (*Aphis Rosæ*) is that of which we will now offer a few particulars. It is curious that these always are most abundant after the prevalence of easterly winds; and Mr. Jenyns observed in Cambridgeshire, during October, and Mr. White at Selborne, in August, myriads of aphides, in both instances, after the wind had been for some time easterly. So fast do they multiply, twenty generations being producible in one year, and the young at this season being born

alive and not from an egg, Reaumur has shewn that one female may be the ancestor of nearly six millions in five generations! It is needless to describe minutely the rose aphis. It is usually light green, with brown antennæ and legs, and transparent iridescent wings. They frequently change their skins; and these may be seen hanging about the leaves and shoots of the rose. The males may be known by a double row of black dots on each of their sides. The most effectual of all applications for their destruction is tobacco smoke; and the best mode of applying it is to cover the bush with a sheet, and fill the space enclosed with the smoke, by means of Brown's fumigator.

So numerous are the approvals with which the announce-ment of THE COTTAGE GARDENERS' DICTIONARY has been received, and so many are the relative suggestions and communications sent to us, that we are induced, for their better consideration, to postpone the publication of the first number until the 6th of July. In the meantime we shall be obliged by any of our readers sending us, without delay, a list of words which they may deem desirable to have explained, for we wish to have it especially a volume of reference for the amateur.

EVERY season is favourable to the abounding of some predatory vermin; for when man brought upon himself the doom to eat bread in the sweat of his brow, among the difficulties made attendant upon the cultivation of the soil most certainly was the guarding of his crops from such marauders. They are the gardener's most wearying foes, and far more difficult to vanquish than the thorns and thistles against which he has also to contend. During the present season weevils are vastly more prevalent than usual; and so many are the letters and specimens we have received, that we will give them one prominent and general answer.

One correspondent (*A Constant Reader*), writing from Mereworth, says—

"We were infested last season in some parts of this parish with a beetle, or bug, amongst our *filbert* plantations, which almost destroyed the crop; and this season they have appeared in ten fold numbers. They are not to be seen in the day, because they retire then to round the bottom of the tree's trunk, or under the clods near it, and there remain until night comes on; they then crawl up the trunk and seize upon the young buds or shoots, in some instances destroying the whole of its vegetation."

Now this insect, of which a specimen was inclosed, is the Red-legged Garden Weevil (*Otiorhynchus tenebricosus*), a drawing and description of which we published in the first volume of THE COTTAGE GARDENER, page 269. Similar specimens of this black-bodied marauder are before us, which had been found on the *peach* and *nectarine*, and on some *greenhouse plants*, by three other correspondents (*P. F., Gretorex, Contributor*). Now, to all of these we can give but one reply—Take an assistant bearing a lanthorn after nightfall, and with a quill feather in one hand sweep as many of the weevils as you can into a bason of water held in the other; next morning cover the surface of the ground round your trees, and close up to your walls, with a thick coating of gas lime. Where your trees stand singly you may also adopt the system pursued by the writer of the next letter, from which we will now give an extract.

This correspondent (*R. J. H.*) writes thus:—

"About a fortnight since I was dismayed at finding my small plantation of *roses* attacked by a brown beetle, in such numbers as leaves little room to doubt, that had they been undisturbed the trees would have been totally destroyed. Since first discovering these enemies I have picked over the trees after dark every night, and by this means have killed between 900 and 1000 on a small bed containing about 30 trees; but in spite of all my pains most of the buds are eaten out, and the young wood barked. Recollecting that a strong solution of soft soap was a preventive of some kinds of blight, I applied to each of my trees a plaster of this soap in a narrow band, at a different distance from the ground on different plants. Since this application I have killed several

of these enemies every night, but in no instance have I been able to find one above the barrier of soap; I am thus induced to hope that this remedy may prove a preventive of further mischief. My present short experience gives no great confidence as to the permanent success of the plan, as the unwillingness of the insect to cross the line may proceed merely from the unusual nature or smell of the substance to which in time it might become accustomed. I have never seen one of these bugs in the day time, but at dusk they begin to move out of the ground, and in a very short time are to be found at the top of the highest standards."

This insect we found to be the Furrowed Weevil (*Otiorhynchus sulcatus*), of which a drawing and description may be consulted at page 125 of our third volume. It may be caught at night in the same mode, and be destroyed by gas lime, as we have already advised for its near relative. To prevent its ascent up the trunk of a tree we should paint round this a band of gas tar, and if a similar band were made round each trunk, and on the wall, so as to enclose the branches of each tree trained on it, it would be similarly protective. Unboiled gas tar is very long before it becomes dry, and is not affected by wet; soft soap, on the other hand, is washed away by rain, and its surface hardens in dry weather.

THE FRUIT-GARDEN.

HARDY FRUITS.—The necessities of this period require that we offer a passing notice on most of our outdoor fruits; and our remarks although brief, are deserving immediate attention.

APPLES.—Those who are troubled with the *American blight*, will find it making unusual progress at this period. We believe that nothing is better than spirits of turpentine, which must be applied with a small-headed brush. Much care is necessary in the operation, for if flowers, &c., grow near the affected tree, a clumsy operator may do much harm by want of care. Moreover, the operations of the brush must be confined as much as possible to the precise spot where the blight is located; for we would not have our readers suppose that trees may be daubed over at random with so powerful a medicament. The application is best made by a young person, for the various and quick contortions of the body necessary, in order to hunt out the woolly little rascals, are not adapted to unbending frames of old labourers; and it is seldom the work is well carried out by these.

The amateur who has apple-trees of choice kinds under a course of training, should now look sharp out once a week, in order to guide refractory young shoots into the place intended for them, whatever the mode of training. By these means the trellis may be covered in half the time; for many a shoot may be made available by timely training, which otherwise would be thinned away amid the confusion which is sure to arise, if the disbudding and general spring regulation should get in arrears. Again, it is necessary to keep the root action under a proper control, for when this is too violent the trees speedily become unmanageable, and barrenness for a few years is the sure result; such barrenness lasting until the greedy tree has somewhat exhausted the soil. And herein is manifest the extreme folly of making soils too rich, or too deep, for a dwarfing system; there is not only a reckless waste of good compost in the original formation, but an annual loss for a length of time entailed on the unfortunate proprietor, besides the extra labour, and, not least, the chagrin at disappointed efforts.

It will soon be known whether there is a good "set" of fruit; if it should prove over abundant, let it, by all means, receive a judicious thinning in time, the extent of this to be regulated by the energies and age of the tree. If any young and choice trees set fruit before commencing a free growth, let nearly all the fruit be stripped off, merely leaving one or two to prove the kind. The exultation of some folks at seeing a dwindling tree laden with fruit, prematurely, is dearly purchased in the end; such trees are almost sure to be short lived; and no wonder, the very foundation of their constitution is undermined before they have fairly acquired sound wood.

APRICOTS.—Much attention will be requisite at this period, both as to stopping, thinning the fruit, training, and hand-picking the caterpillars, the offspring of the red-bar moth, which has been fully described in Number 71, page 252, of THE COTTAGE GARDENER. Stopping must be attended to most assiduously, not only in order that the resources of the tree be not drawn from their proper channels, but also that the true blossom-buds for the ensuing year be not shaded; for, as we have before observed, the apricot, coming as it does from the brightest climes of the East, needs not the shade of superfluous spray in our murky climate. We know not how our neighbours have fared, but we have a capital crop; and, perhaps, six times more have swelled off just beneath the broad coping than on other portions of the wall. Indeed, almost every blossom seems to have set in that situation, thus evincing the propriety of protection. Thinning for tarts, therefore, must have due attention, withdrawing all the small or crippled fruit where to spare, or those lodged between the shoots and the wall. The thinning must be done by degrees, for after so severe a frost as we experienced in March, it is not improbable that much of the fruit which even appears to swell freely may have been wounded, and if so, will turn yellow when the stoning process is proceeding, which is a severe crisis with most fruits, especially if unusual vicissitudes of weather occurred during the blossoming period.

Training must be duly attended to. The apricot is rather precocious in its growth, and the pinching of robbers, and the direction of the necessary shoots, require timely attention.

In picking the caterpillars, there is no better plan than uncoiling the foliage, where the lodgments shew the enemy has established his quarters, and crushing him in his den. Those who think this too tedious, may just squeeze the coils flat with the thumb and two foremost fingers; a little practice will soon enable the operator to perceive at a touch where the rogue lies. This latter, however, is a sadly mutilating plan, and as "there are no gains without pains," according to Dr. Franklin, let us advise our amateur friends to act like men of mettle in this affair.

BLACK CURRANTS.—Now is the time when, by a little perseverance, a crop of this useful fruit may be ensured. It has before been observed, that they cannot withstand drought, there is therefore no alternative but to water them liberally, on all soils not naturally retentive of moisture.

A coating of half rotten manure, which gardeners term mulching, is of eminent service; indeed, were we to cultivate them extensively for market, we should make a point of applying a top dressing of this kind every blossoming season. The moment they are out of blossom a heavy demand takes place on the roots; and coincident with this, the aphides so manage matters as to be prepared to attack the plant at the very period in which the latter could best dispense with their services. Hence, if drought occurs, the sap by a higher amount of elaboration becomes less watery, and the whole plant becomes a prey to these devouring little pests, which increase in power and rapacity in proportion to the necessities of the plant.

We have this week coated over the roots of our bushes three inches thick with a most economical material, being a mixture from old linings, composed of one-third stable manure, and three-parts of tree or shrub leaves. On this, immediately it is spread, we give a regular flooding of water; and we seldom take any further trouble over them, unless it be to syringe them with soap-suds, two evenings in succession, when just out of blossom. Indeed, but for this much pains, our land is so sandy that we should not gather a gallon from scores of bushes; as it is, we generally ensure a good crop.

STRAWBERRIES.—Here, again, the water-pot must be active, if drought ensues; no fruit is more injured by continued drought, and none more benefited by a timely and liberal application of water. Previously to the commencement of watering, all weeds should have been carefully eradicated, for the runners will shortly be out. Again, mulching is very beneficial to the strawberry, but such is not obliged to be rotten manure. The term mulching, we own, is an indefinite thing; let us hope that THE COTTAGE GARDENERS' DICTIONARY, which will shortly appear, will pave the way to a universal language in gardening—a thing much wanted. Strawberries should always have something put beneath them at this period, to keep the fruit clean, and to permit the air to circulate freely, in order to dispel all mouldiness and rot, should a bad summer occur. Clean straw (from the original application of which they perhaps derived their name) is most efficient for the purpose. Straw timely and properly applied is at once a protector of the fruit, and serves the purpose of a mulch, or, in other words, it is a screen, and has the effect of retaining moisture a long time in the soil beneath it. It intercepts the solar rays, and also prevents the radiation of heat, which latter not only carries off the ground heat at night, and at all periods when the soil is warmer than the atmosphere, but carries also moisture with it, thus robbing at once the soil of its warmth and its moisture.

Care, however, must be taken to guard against mice, especially if badly thrashed straw be used; for such we have known to attract a host of these rogues, before the straw had been down half a dozen days. It is best, therefore, to commence trapping or poisoning the moment the straw is placed. This we always do.

THE PLUM AND CHERRY.—The blue or purple aphides will soon be at work on the young wood. We have already adverted to syringing with tobacco water; the latter may be applied here just as with the peach. Where, however, time is no object, it is a very good plan to take a bowl of tobacco liquor and bend the young shoots betimes into it, over head; this will clean them for the season. We have cleansed ours tolerably well in former times, by syringing the trees with soap-suds, and then throwing dust all over the trees until they were encased in it, but it is a somewhat dirty plan.

DISBUDDING AND STOPPING.—Nearly all kinds of fruits under a course of training will require particular attention between this period and Midsummer, as to these processes. We would strongly recommend every amateur to provide himself with a pair of Mr. Turner's pruning scissors, which are the handiest and most efficient article we have ever seen. We carry a small pair constantly in the waistcoat pocket. His address is, "Neepsend, Sheffield."   R. ERRINGTON.

THE FLOWER-GARDEN.

MISCELLANEOUS FLOWER-BORDER.—After saying so much about summer flower-beds in masses of one colour, and before resuming the subject with reference to miscellaneous and spring flower-beds, I shall give a memorandum of plants in flower on a long border here, on the first of the present May; and I intend to kill two birds with one stone from behind this memorandum. In the first place it will prove, that a great show may be made in the spring, and indeed, at most seasons, with a very few plants judiciously selected. Secondly, it will shew that we are not altogether wedded to the massing system here, as some might infer from my letters.

This spring border is one hundred and twenty five yards long, is not much out of a straight line, and is divided into two equal lengths by some statuary. The width occupied by the spring flowers is from four to five feet, but the whole border is twenty feet wide in the narrowest part, and is used for many kinds of tall flowering plants, which cannot be used profitably in beds, and is, moreover, an excellent nursery for choice new shrubs for the first two or three years. The first few feet of it next to the grass, is devoted entirely to spring bulbs, and a few other plants, but the great bulk of the border is occupied by such bulbs as have been forced here for the last ten years, and which have so increased on our hands, that some of the varieties of early tulips and hyacinths are now planted by the hundred; and it may be worth while to mention that some of these have been now in the border five years without being disturbed, and three or four kinds of hyacinths have in that time degenerated to look like wild ones, while all the rest have improved every year, and this season some of them have the finest flowers I ever saw any where.

The depth of *soil* in the border is full two feet, with a very dry bottom, and the soil is a compost made on purpose, one-half of which is the natural dry sandy soil of the place, and the rest a soft spongy kind of peat, leaf-mould, and such vegetable refuse as one finds where the "rubbish heap" is made, or where all the refuse from the garden is wheeled to.

MANAGEMENT OF BULBS.—About this time in May, in each year, *the bulbs* which were forced last winter are collected from where they have been kept from cold winds since they were out of flower, and are taken to this border. Then the tulips are set down next to the tulip patches already in the border, the hyacinths and narcissus the same, until all are disposed of in their classes; but as no tallies or names are kept in the border, and the plants are out of bloom by this time, the planter has no guide how to plant the bulbs according to their colour, or their height, or their time of flowering. Some varieties flower three weeks earlier or later than the great bulk of the family. All that the planter is required to do, is to plant kind with kind. Now, this is a very odd way of planting, but it answers extremely well, and is the simplest way for gardeners in large places, where things of this nature are liable to be overlooked while in a dormant state; but I must explain. We shall say, that in 1845 a large quantity of these spring bulbs were collected from all parts of the establishment, and planted in this border in patches, from three to five bulbs being set in a patch, and sometimes more where there was a good stock of that sort, and sometimes one bulb only could be set to begin a patch, and all were planted according to their height, the lowest being in the front row, and from eighteen inches to two feet was allowed between the patches. In May 1846, the forced bulbs of that season were planted on this border "kind to kind," that is, all the tulips were planted in rings round the former patches of tulips, and quite close to them, and the other bulbs the same, so that no more patches could be counted than in the former season. In after years the same plan was followed, and now some of the patches have from twelve to fourteen bulbs in each, and in a few more years, if this system is pursued, many of the patches will meet. Now, it easily may be imagined what an odd mixture of colours these patches produce when they are all in bloom. A stranger would remark nothing particular in a border of hyacinths planted thus, only that each circle in a patch was of one colour, because all the hyacinths are nearly of the same height;

but, looking at the five years' accumulation of early tulips thus planted in rings, and in detached groups, or patches, the appearance might well surprise him. In the centre of a patch of tulips are three single *Van Thol* bulbs in bloom, not more than four inches high; then a ring of *Prince de Ligne*, a pure yellow, single, and seven inches high; then a ring of *Rex rubrorum*, or King of the reds, a double dark red flower, as large as a fist, and so top-heavy as to need the support of a stake; after that a ring of the *Golden Standard*, scarlet and gold; *Royal Standard* next, silver and crimson; and so forth. Not that the rings are planted in the way I put them here, but every ring is of one kind of bulb, and the different kinds of bulbs, as tulips, hyacinths, &c., are thus kept regularly apart, and that is all we aim at. The plan was first begun to save some of the best sorts of forced bulbs for cut-flowers, but it has answered so well, and is so simple, and takes up so little time, that it has risen to the dignity of "a mixed herbaceous border." If we choose to make use of them, there are many scores of bulbs in this border that may be forced again, but they answer so well for spring flowers, that we shall be loth to disturb them until they get more crowded.

Now, the idea that it is necessary to take up tulips, hyacinths, and such bulbs, every year, is quite wrong. Such a system is only a matter of convenience for the salesmen; the only use that it can be to private growers is, that unless the soil suits them one year, it can be changed for them the next. Indeed, the late Dean of Manchester, Dr. Herbert, who knew more about the different families of bulbs than all the best gardeners in England put together, assorted, long since, that it was of great use to many of the more delicate bulbs to be disturbed as little as possible, if the soil suited them; and that he found when the patches of bulbs increased by their own offsets to such a degree as to squeeze each other, they flowered best; and the reason he assigned for this was, that bulbs so congregated helped to drain the soil around them more perfectly than they could do in detached bulbs in the usual way. Bulbs, like some of the *Ixia* tribe, which are renewed annually from beneath the old bulbs, and thus deepen themselves in the soil every year more and more, will not come in under this rule; but we are now only considering such as are commonly called Dutch bulbs.

I have got another crotchet into my head, which was suggested by my experience with this very border, and it is this, that we are all wrong about potting these bulbs in October, so as to be more ready for removal at this season to get the beds ready for the summer crops, and that the old plan of taking up the bulbs carefully is the best after all; and I shall save a thousand pots every year by this single stroke, and have better flowers both in the bulb beds and in this border than I have yet had; and this is the way I shall go to work:—As soon as the beds are cleared in the autumn, those beds intended for spring bulbs shall be forthwith trenched two feet deep, and I shall suppose the beds to have been well manured with some suitable compost last spring, and that a crop of summer flowers has eaten up the strongest parts of this manuring, or, say, those parts that would now be disagreeable to our bulbs if the compost were laid on in October. Well, by trenching the beds, the remains of the last spring-dressing will thoroughly be mixed with the soil, and be thus rendered so mild and congenial for the bulbs, that they will root into it with great freedom; and it needs no prophet to foretell, that the more roots we have in a healthy pasture, the finer our bulb flowers will be. When the bloom is over in May, and we see a chance of a dull or rainy day or two, the whole of the bulbs will be taken up most carefully with a garden-fork, without breaking a single root if possible, then laid on their sides in a barrow or basket, and taken to the long border, then with a garden trowel deep cuts will be made outside the old patches, and the new comers will be planted in these rings, without in any way cramping their roots. The leaves of the old patches will hold up those of the newly-planted bulbs on one side, and four little sticks and a string of matting will keep them up on the outer side, and a good soaking of water will both settle the soil about the roots and set the leaves growing, just as if nothing particularly had happened unto them. It was a happy idea in theory to suggest the potting of bulbs that were to be removed before their growth could be finished. but in practice it is not nearly so good, or even attended with so little trouble, as the old plan when carefully performed; but, formerly, people did not understand the value of leaves as we are now taught, and all they did in May was to grub up their tulips, hyacinths, and other bulbs, when it was time to "put out" the summer plants, carry them to a reserve border, and lay them in by "the heels," or, in other words, cut a shallow trench across the border, and lay down the bulbs in the trench with their leaves leaning down on one side, and, in some instances, lying flat on the earth, and, as a matter of course, a few seasons of this rude treatment finished them. I have no room to detail experiments I made for the last three years to establish all this to my own satisfaction, but having strongly recommended the use of pots, I as firmly now advise the latter and more simple mode. A handy man may take up a bed of hyacinths or tulips, nacissus, and such like bulbs to-morrow, without injuring them a quarter so much as they would be if their roots were cramped in little pots all the spring; but after replanting them in rows, south and north, on a sunny border, let him hold up the leaves in their natural position, by passing a string up on each side of the row fastened to sticks. and then, if that does not hold them properly, let other strings be passed at short intervals across, between the two strings; but see that the leaves are not bundled together, so as to exclude the sun and air from them. Next week, I shall give the summer management of this border with a list of the bulbs in it.   D. BEATON.

GREENHOUSE AND WINDOW GARDENING.

FANCY GERANIUMS.—A correspondent (*T. W. T.*) inquires how he is to grow these beautiful and interesting plants, "such as *Anais, Queen Victoria, Ibraham Pacha, Statueski, Reine de Francais, Bouquet tout fait*, &c.; the time for inserting the cuttings; the soil; the temperature, top and bottom (if requisite); if to be cut down as other geraniums in the autumn; when to place them in their flowering-pots; the most approved form to train to, so as to get them large, say from eighteen to twenty-four inches in diameter, and one mass of bloom; the difficulty consisting in the facts, that the plants root so much at the bottom of the pot, with very few roots at the sides, and show bloom in the earliest stages, when the plants are extremely small, and when the bloom buds are pinched off again forming them, instead of growth and wood." As it has been deemed necessary that something more than a passing notice to these matters in the correspondents' column should be given, I shall be happy to render any little assistance in my power, merely premising that as there are now many beautiful varieties which I have not yet grown, the statements I may make will be freely open to emendations from those coadjutors and friends who may have had more kinds under their direct cultivation. I shall endeavour to meet the case, by making the inquiries the ground work of my remarks: and

First. *The time in which to take off and insert the cuttings.*—This may be effected at any period. A cutting

of a ten-shilling geranium plant is not to be slighted at any time; autumn and spring, however, are the best periods for striking these fancy geraniums, and so far as present and ultimate success are concerned, the spring is better than the autumn; not but fine plants may be produced from autumn-struck plants, as from some of the free growing kinds we have had plants as large as that desired by our correspondent in the following summer; but then there is greater risk of failures and disappointments. The reason of this is owing to the difference in habit of these plants when contrasted with the other favourite, but more succulent-stemmed geraniums. In the case of the latter, it is requisite, both for the ensuring of the breaking of the old plant when cut down, and also for the producing of healthy young plants from the cuttings, that the shoots should be well matured, by exposure to sun and air, and a diminished supply of water for some time previously. Fancy geraniums, from their profusion of blossom, their compact growth, and less succulent stems, require less of this *maturing* before the cuttings are removed; but if no attention to *maturing* the wood is given, then, in all likelihood, many of the cuttings will damp off at once; and even when they strike root they can only be preserved during the winter by keeping them in the most favourable circumstances, where all danger of damp and a stagnant atmosphere are provided against, by the ability to maintain when necessary a dryish atmosphere, and a temperature of from 40° to 45° in the coldest weather. If, on the other hand, the wood of the cutting is *over-matured*, that is, if its juices are highly elaborated, there is a likelihood that its organized material will be developed more in the production of bloom than of wood buds. This is still more likely to be the case if the young plants have been *starved* during cold weather in winter, by being shut up and covered for days in cold pits. The diminutive character, instead of being *accidental*, has now become *constitutional*. The stem from being hard, and having its juices so thoroughly inspissated, is quite incompetent to act as the vehicle for the transmission of fluids that would be necessary for a large-headed plant. As roots and branches act and re-act, relatively and co-relatively, upon each other, the stunted head is attended with few and diminutive root feeders. Of all stunted plants, there is nothing more discouraging than a stunted geranium. The cutting off the flowers, as our correspondent has done, will only prove a slight palliation of the evil—though when persevered in, and other points of good culture are attended to, fine plants ultimately may be gained. What would be good culture for free-growing plants, however, will not suit these stunted gentlemen: light rich soil is the thing in which they generally delight; but until you set the stuntedness adrift, you must use only the *light*, abjure the *rich*; employ small pots well drained, and keep the plants in a closer atmosphere than usual. Your object would sooner be gained by taking off a cutting or two, just in that state when the wood is neither soft nor thoroughly indurated. Properly treated it will soon shoot ahead of the old plant. Cutting the plant down to the surface of the soil, if it has got any roots of consequence, will also be attended with more success than doctoring the stunted head. The plant should be kept close, rather dry than damp, until the fresh shoots appear; then shaken out, and re-potted in the usual way. Foresters are well aware of the benefit of acting upon this principle; they do not stand picking and cutting the miserable twigs of a stunted young oak, that scarcely gets larger by inches in a twelvemonth; they cut it off close to the ground, and in a year or two they have a clean luxuriant plant, such as the original would never have been. Cuttings taken off in July or August, stopped when struck, potted into small pots, stopped and repotted again in October, and potted again in early spring, will make nice little bushy flowering plants the first summer; but if large fine plants are wanted, growth rather than bloom must be encouraged, by stopping and keeping the plants rather shaded, pinching back the tops, or cutting them down; removing the most of the soil, or only a portion, and repotting in July and August, just as the varieties are slow growing or the reverse, and early fine blooming plants will be obtained for spring and summer.

As we have said, however, we prefer spring-struck cuttings, as there is comparatively little danger of them getting into a stunted habit, and scarcely a cutting will fail of being made into a plant, while time will be saved. Cuttings may then be obtained from thinnings of the young shoots on established plants; or, better still, an old plant stopped in the autumn, should be left on purpose. It will stand comparatively hard treatment during the winter, but in February or March it should be put gradually into a moist atmosphere, and a temperature of from 45° to 55°, or a few degrees more. As soon as the young shoots are from one and a half to three inches in length they should be taken off close to the stem and properly treated; the strongest would bloom in the open air in summer if desirable; if potted, stopped, and re-potted in August, they would make nice little flowering plants during the winter, if a temperature not less than 45° is then given them, with fresh air. Similar plants—having their flower-buds removed, the points of the shoots pinched out, the shoots themselves trained into the desired shape, and repotted in September—will make nice flowering plants in spring and summer. For the end of summer and autumn others should be repotted in March and April.

Soil, and a few matters essential to success in propagating. —The soil should be light and sandy, free from worms and insects; one part peat, one part leaf-mould, one half part loam, one part pure sand, will answer admirably, with just an additional dusting of silver sand upon the surface; such a compost will neither be too close nor too open. If mere soil, &c., were present, the air would obtain too free an access to the base of the cutting when the compost became dry, and then the opposite evil would ensue from the moisture remaining too long around the cutting after watering, causing it to mould and decay. A similar effect would be produced by in-serting cuttings, as some do, wholly in *sand*; enough of air then would not be admitted, and thus a shanking-off would be liable to ensue, for the circumstances that would ensure the safety of a hard-wooded cutting would ruin a soft-wooded geranium. Then, if the cuttings are inserted into pots, these pots should be half filled with drainage, and the remaining portion with different layers of the prepared compost, reserving the finest for the surface. Before inserting the cuttings the pots should have been previously well watered, and the moisture allowed to drain away, as most of the waterings after-wards had better consist of sprinklings from the syringe. In *early autumn*, when the weather is still warm, and the sun's rays powerful, little or nothing in the shape of *bottom-heat* will be required; but the cuttings should be placed at such a distance from the glass that they may enjoy the *direct*, though *diffused*, rays of light; this will prevent the necessity of shading much to prevent flagging. The more direct though somewhat diffused light they will stand, the sooner will roots be pro-truded, and the more sturdy and healthy will the plants become. Of course they would require to be placed nearer the glass as the power of the sun declines. Every hours' shading, however necessary it be at times, is just so far encouraging the *mere* expansion upwards of what is contained in the cutting, without doing much for encouraging the protrusion of roots. In sunny weather they will require to be kept close, and receive frequent sprinklings from the syringe, to lessen their powers of evaporating their juices, but at night and morning air

may be given, and the sashes at times wholly removed. When propagating in spring the same course may be adopted, with one or two exceptions. First, as the presence of sun at that period is not so much to be depended on as in the autumn, the cuttings should be placed pretty near the glass, and shading in bright weather resorted to when necessary, as otherwise, in long continued dull weather, the cuttings would become weak and spindled. And, secondly, as the cuttings had been slightly forced before their removal from their mother plant, a little mild bottom-heat, of from 60° to 80°, would be of great service to them, giving them a top tempera-ture of from 50° to 60°. These, as we have already hinted, are the circumstances under which the finest plants are most easily produced.   R. FISH.

(To be continued.)

HOTHOUSE DEPARTMENT.

STOVE PLANTS.

ÆSCHYNANTHUS.—In the whole range of the floral kingdom, there are no plants cultivated for elegance and beauty that are more striking in appearance than the species that constitute the genus Æschynanthus. The most of them possess at least two of the grand pro-perties that all plants worth cultivating ought to have; our readers, no doubt, will remember them—handsome flowers, fine foliage, and an agreeable fragrance. Two of these the Æschynanthi possess in an eminent degree, namely, beautiful flowers, and handsome deep green foliage. Besides, this genus possesses another property to recommend it to the favourable notice of cultivators: a considerable number of the species will grow in baskets, or tied by the roots in a ball of moss, or even fastened to a block of wood covered with moss. In the nursery at Pine-apple Place, there is now a plant of *Æschynanthus ramosissimus*, or *parasiticus*, fastened to a block of wood, two feet long, covered with moss. The plant completely hides the block, and has on it more than 100 heads of its fine, scarlet, and dark anthered blossoms. Again, *Æschynanthus zebrinus* has its leaves beautifully barred with crimson, while *Æ. discolor* has the under side of its leaves coloured with the richest crimson-purple. When hung up either in a basket, or on a log, the leaves show off to great advantage. Another property these charming plants possess is, that on account of their trailing flexible branches, they answer extremely well to train round a balloon-shaped trellis. Cultivated in this style, we have seen specimens three feet high, and two feet through, covered with fine foliage, and in due season completely covered also with their beautiful tube-shaped scarlet and crimson flowers. All these charming and useful properties are sufficient to recommend this genus to the notice of every one pos-sessing even the smallest stove.

Propagation.—These plants may be propagated both by seeds and cuttings. Seedlings, however, do not come into flower so soon as cuttings, and as seeds are not cer-tain to be produced, we shall first describe the method of increasing by cuttings. Fill a pot, or pots, of a size to fit the cutting bell-glasses, with proper drainage, light com-post, and an inch of pure white sand at the top; give this a gentle watering to make it firm; then take cut-tings of half-ripened wood, cut them into two or three-inch lengths, trim off the lower leaves, leaving a leaf, or, at the most, two leaves at the top; then insert them with a small stick into the sand, placing the leaves in-wards, so as not to touch the glass. Then place the cutting pots either under hand-glasses upon a heated surface, or, what is better, plunge them in a bark-bed. They will soon put forth roots, and should then be potted off into small pots; put under hand-glasses till they are established, when they may be gradually hardened off.

to stand the light and air. The best time to propagate is in early spring; this allows time for a second potting, and the plants become strong and bushy by the autumn. We have frequently had plants flower the spring following that have been thus raised.

After-management.—When plants are a year old, they will be a right size to place in baskets to be suspended from the roof, either of the stove or orchid house. The baskets may be made of various materials, and of various forms. We prefer, as in the case of orchidaceous plants, to make them of wood; crooked branches of oak make curious fantastic baskets very suitable for these plants. Those who wish for neater baskets, may have them made of copper wire, or even of iron wire well painted. When the baskets are ready for use, line them first with moss, and then fill them with a light rich compost; make a hole in the middle, and place the plant in it. If the branches stand up too much, fasten them down with small neat pegs, so as to spread the branches equally on every side of the basket. They are naturally pendent, and will afterwards hang down of themselves. During the summer, let them have free supplies of water to encourage liberal growth, but do not allow them to produce flowers, as that will weaken them; *growth* must be the great desideratum the first year. In winter, keep them rather dry and cool; this will give them a rest; and the year following, if all be right, they will flower most profusely, and be really handsome objects.

If you choose to grow any on blocks, and as a curiosity it is really worth while, procure a piece of the branch of a tree, cover it with green flakes of moss, tying it on with small copper wire; then take one, or two, or even three plants (of different kinds if you will) and fasten them to the block, covering their roots with more moss, and tying them to the wood with more copper wire. If the branches are long and hang down loose, tie them up to the branch with more copper wire; after this they will require no more care, excepting duly syringing and occasionally dipping in tepid water. By this treatment they will form very beautiful objects.

The principal way, however, of cultivating these beautiful plants is in pots. To effect this to perfection it will be necessary to grow them on fast and strong by generous treatment, that is, frequently repotting in light rich compost till they are large enough to place a trellis to which to tie them : this trellis may either be formed with slender rods of willow or hazel, or, if the cultivator chooses to go to the expense, any wireworker will make it of any size or pattern.

The following are the species best adapted for baskets or blocks:—

Æschynanthus Lobbianus; dark scarlet.
　　" 　　*pulcher major;* scarlet.
　　" 　　*ramosissimus;* ditto.
　　" 　　*Boschianus;* ditto.
　　" 　　*radicans;* ditto.
　　" 　　*grandiflorus;* orange scarlet.
　　" 　　*zebrinus;* the flowers are not showy, but the foliage is beautiful.
　　" 　　*discolor;* ditto ditto.

The next are best grown in pots tied to a trellis—
Æschynanthus miniatus; rich crimson.
　　" 　　*longiflorus;* orange scarlet.

By this method they may all be grown excepting *Æschynanthus speciosus;* this is an upright, stout growing species, flowering at the end of each shoot in bunches of seven or eight flowers, of the finest orange colour. This is the finest of the whole genus, and ought to be in every stove, however small.

FLORISTS' FLOWERS.

We have at length really fine weather, and the amateur florist will take advantage of it to assist nature as much as possible in bringing these flowers to the greatest perfection.

AURICULAS and POLYANTHUSES may now be potted, the former in rich, light compost, and the latter in one with rather more loam in it. Now is the time, when the potting is being done, to increase them; take off all rooted offsets, and such as are pretty strong pot into 4-inch pots, but small ones may be put two, three, or four into the same sized pots, placing them close to the sides, at equal distances. When they are all potted, place them on the shady side of a low wall, upon a thick layer of coal ashes, watering them gently in dry weather, and keep a good look out for slugs and other destructive vermin.

CARNATIONS AND PICOTEES.—With a pair of sharp scissors clip out close all yellow leaves; by this means that pest the red spider will be checked, as well as a neat clean appearance given to the plants. Keep them loosely tied to the stakes, and water freely during dry weather.

DAHLIAS.—Towards the end of the month the strongest plants may be put out into their blooming quarters; they love a very rich soil and plenty of room; the situation, if possible, should be a sheltered but by no means a close one. Place the stakes, firmly driven down, previously to planting, as there is then no danger of bruising the roots, which might be if the stakes had to be driven in some time after the dahlias were planted. To secure them from late frosts, which may yet come upon us, cover them up every night with empty garden pots. Protect from snails by covering the surface near to each plant with rough, sharp coal-ashes, and water sometimes with lime-water if any slugs are observed.

PINKS are now growing freely, and must, without farther delay, have sticks put to them. Pipings should be taken of the stronger plants, and put in either under hand-glasses, upon a gentle heat, or be planted in pots filled with light soil, with one inch of sand at the top; place them in a gentle hotbed, shading from the sun till they begin to grow. By raising them thus early strong plants are obtained for next years' bloom.

T. APPLEBY.

THE KITCHEN-GARDEN.

If all our directions have been properly attended to in this department, there will remain at the present time but little spare ground unoccupied.

ANGELICA.—If enough has not already been secured for preserving, &c., apply good liquid manure pretty freely, in order to keep up a quick and vigorous growth, taking care that the seed-stalks do not make much progress previous to their being broken out, with the exception of one or two intended to be left for seed, as the plants very frequently become so much exhausted that some of them in consequence die.

BEET.—Observe in due time whether the plants have come up regularly, if not, the plants were perhaps too thick, and may be taken up and transplanted very advantageously; but *Beet* should not be *over* thinned, as it is liable to become too large by such treatment to be either handsome or useful.

The *Early Pea* ground if planted on sloping banks as previously directed, may have *Dwarf Kidney Beans* planted to advantage on the opposite side of the peas, that by the time the peas are ready to be cleared the French beans will have established themselves for a summer crop. The alley between each bank may then be forked-up and cropped with *Cape brocoli* between the beans.

CELERY.—Its growth should now be well encouraged, and a plentiful supply of plants in succession kept, pricked, and encouraged on kindly soil. The *Early Cauliflower ground* as soon as cleared, may at once be prepared for a main crop of *Celery* without much trouble, supposing the ground to have been well trenched for the cauliflowers, and liberally manured, as well as the surface kept well stirred; and if these matters were attended to at first nothing more will be now required than marking out trenches the desired width—say four or five feet wide, if a large crop of celery is to be produced economically on a small piece of ground. If a good portion of well decomposed manure, or cow, horse, sheep, or deer dung, can be spared, fork it in and well incorporate it with the soil. If these be not at hand, the growth of the celery may be encouraged by applications of liquid-manure.

CHERVIL, LETTUCE, &c.—Sow small patches of *Chervil* at this season on cold or north aspects, as it is liable in hot weather to run too quickly to seed. Sow a little *Endive* in succession, and continue to sow lettuce also in succession on rich healthy soil, to be thinned and hoed-out where they are sown, as transplanting in hot weather is likely to check and cause an early starting to seed. The *Victoria Cabbage Lettuce* is an excellent summer lettuce, as it will stand much heat without starting; but for a variety of the finest flavour and handiest for an every day lettuce throughout the whole year, none is to be compared with the *Hardy Brown Cos*.

ONIONS.—The onion crop ere this should have had its final thinning, and every vacancy have been made up, so that not one plant in any part of the rows may be missing. To encourage a luxuriant growth, surface-stirring should be kept in full practice, as long as there is room or convenience to work the hoe or hand-drag.

PARSLEY.—Sow in succession; fill up by transplanting any vacancies that may occur amongst the early sown; encourage its growth by applications of liquid-manure, or dredgings of chimney-soot in showery weather. The old parsley now started for seed, if intended to remain for seed, should have a cutting out, leaving no plants but such as are of the first-rate curled quality.

ROUTINE WORK.—Sow the early *Stone-Dutch* or *Red-top American Turnips* in succession of small patches, or single drills, where ground is not plentiful. *Spinach*, *Salsafy*, and *Scorzonera*, should be duly thinned, and the ground between the drills at all times kept loose by frequent hoeings and surface-stirring.

Mushroom-beds should be made in succession in shady quiet situations, such as sheds, cellars, or caves; old beds getting exhausted should be arrested by slight sprinklings of liquid-manure, applied, of course, in a tepid state, and with a fine-rosed watering-pot, and brewed from cow, sheep, or deer's dung.

Melons should, in every stage of fruit-swelling, be also encouraged by applications of liquid-manure, taking care that too many of them are not allowed to swell off at one time.

Ridge Cucumbers should be kept protected at night, whilst the nights remain so cold and uncertain; with us, in Devonshire, the frost has been intense—now, in the middle of May, at 4 A.M., everything drooping and ice bound. The month of May has been, thus far, one of the most unfriendly to vegetation that we ever remembered—ten severe frosty mornings occuring during the first fourteen days.   JAMES BARNES.

MISCELLANEOUS INFORMATION.

SOAP—CANDLES—SUGAR.

By the authoress of " My Flowers."

IT is advisable to lay in almost all articles of general consumption in large quantities, because they are always cheaper when purchased by the half or quarter cwt. Even in a town where everything can be sent for as it is wanted, and in the smallest quantity, it is far better to lay in a store of some particular things, on account of the saving in price. The only objection to this plan that can be offered—and it is, indeed, a very great one—is, that abundance is liable to cause waste and extravagance, by tempting us to exceed the quantities we have assigned for weekly or daily consumption. Now this is a point upon which we *may* act wisely and economically if we *chose*. If a lady will carefully and accurately *weigh out* from her own store-room, with her *own* hands, every morning, or once a week, which is perhaps a better period, the quantity allowed of every article, it matters not how large the stock in hand may be; but unless this is strictly done, and unless she scrupulously guard against extra-liberality, she will find herself a considerable loser at the close of the year. She must not allow herself to run to the store-room for a *"little* more sugar," or even *"one* extra spoonful of tea," if the weekly supplies run low. These are little things, I admit; but little things swell into large things if practised incautiously; and although a spoonful of tea in the week is scarcely noticed, yet the three months' allowance will come to an end much before its time, if this is indulged in. I am addressing those only who are really and seriously struggling to live on narrow means, and *without debt*, and therefore I shall not apologize for the minuteness and closeness of my suggestions. If the heart is large and liberal, the sparing hand will be guided by prudence, and not parsimony; and whatever springs from principle can never be called mean.

Tea, sugar, candles, oatmeal, Scotch barley, peas, rice, &c., may all be laid in in quantities; but they should be kept in a cool, dry place. Heat and damp are both injurious, but of the two extremes damp is the worst.

Soap should not be bought in very large quantities, because a great deal of its goodness is lost by long keeping. This is opposed to the generally received opinion, and to every Household Directory: but the advice was given by a respectable and experienced grocer, and it has been tested, and found correct. If cut into proper sized pieces, with a wire, and allowed to stand in an airy place for three weeks or a month, it will be in a much better state for use than if kept until all the oily property is exhausted, in which case it is like washing with a piece of stick. It must not dry quickly, but slowly, or it will crack.

The longer candles are kept the better; two years will not be too long. An airy, cool, dry place is best for them; the least warmth softens and spoils them. They should be laid in in March or October. Summer-made candles are never so firm and good as those made in cold weather; and if they can be kept for some months before they are used so much the better. The price of candles and soap rise and fall together; the chandler can always inform his customers when a rise in price is expected; and if the stock in the store-room is lessening it is best to renew it before the regular time, when there is a probability of the article becoming dearer.

The best sized mould candles for parlour use are

those called *short-fours;* they are not too tall for comfort, and their size gives a better light than that of long thin ones. For kitchen use "dips" of ten to the pound, or even twelve, are the best size. *Eights* have been tried, as being a thicker candle, but they do not burn an hour longer in *the kitchen*, and therefore do not go so far. Many persons use oil in preference to candles, as being cheaper; but from experience and close calculation nothing is cheaper than candles, if *carefully* used and looked after; and so much dirt and grease is engendered where oil is used, that the most scrupulous cleanliness is needful in managing it. This can rarely be reckoned upon in the household department, and therefore candles are, on every account, decidedly best. Where only one servant is kept it is requisite to avoid every unnecessary work, and nothing is so troublesome and so dirty as the care of lamps.

A careful mistress will look well to the management of candles, for a great deal of waste is sometimes unintentionally suffered, and they are an expensive item in the monthly book. Servants will often leave candle ends in the sockets, and throw them thoughtlessly away when cleaning the candlesticks. There should be a *save-all* to every candlestick in the house, and not an inch of candle should be thrown away. It is surprising how many candles will be saved in the course of the year by looking after the *odds and ends*. Even the black contents of the snuffers has its use; it is excellent for cleaning looking-glasses, well rubbed on with a piece of rag, and then polished off with a linen cloth. It brightens and cleanses the surface of the glass with very little trouble.

Sugar is a very expensive item in the week's account. It must be kept in a very dry, cool place, or it will turn into treacle. A great saving may be achieved by giving up its use in tea, and the right principle will be rewarded in time by the superior flavour of the tea, as well as by the decreased expenditure. This I know by my own experience: I gave up sugar in my tea, but not in the least degree on principle; I was exactly a month in becoming reconciled to the loss, and now I cannot take it even in coffee; the taste of sweetened tea is insipid in the extreme. Children should be brought up as much as possible without sugar, when means are small. It is not unwholesome, as some are led to think, but it is expensive and unnecessary; and a great deal more is used with puddings and pies than is at all required. Some sugars are very much sweeter than others, and go farther in consequence; this can only be ascertained by tasting them. The best moist sugar should look gravelly and sparkling—not dull and dead, like sand. East India sugars are not so sweet as those from the West Indies; and Brazillian sugar has scarcely any sweetness in it. The white sugars should be close, and very *sparkling*; if dull and *powdery* to the eye it is made from beetroot, and very inferior when used, although cheaper to buy. White sugar is often *said* to be as cheap or cheaper in the end than brown; it is more elegant and more agreeable to the taste, but on *strict* trial it will not be found cheaper, or so cheap. Gentlemen will often decide this point very comfortably to themselves; but if they will wisely give up the Commissariat department to their wives, I think brown sugar will be selected when the *second* stock of groceries is laid in. For preserves I think common cheap white sugar is decidedly the cheapest. It requires less boiling, less skimming, consequently less waste takes place, and the preserves keep better, and for a longer time; those made with brown sugar, unless boiled a long time, are very apt to mould, or ferment, and never taste so well. Three quarters of a pound of sugar to a pound of fruit is *quite* sufficient, for jam; jelly requires equal proportions; but on this point I shall touch in a future paper.

Let me recommend to the *anxious* economist the most rigid forbearance in sugar, as indeed in every thing that may be called a superfluity, and non-essential to the support of life. We use so many things from habit that are really not required, that it needs some little thought to determine what is a *necessary* and *lawful* article of food. If we gave our attention to this from an honest and holy principle, we should save immensely in many ways, and be able to "deal our bread to the hungry" too, and make many a "widow's heart sing for joy." Let us not save for ourselves only, but also for our "poor brother," that we may "open our hand wide unto him, and surely lend him sufficient for his need in that which he wanteth." This is God's own commandment.

ROYAL BOTANIC SOCIETY'S EXHIBITION AT THE REGENT'S PARK.—MAY 8.

(Continued from page 101.)

COLLECTIONS OF TEN STOVE AND GREENHOUSE PLANTS.

Generally these were well grown. The FIRST PRIZE was awarded to Mr. Croxford, gardener to H. H. Barnes, Esq., Stamford Hill. He had the best

Epacris grandiflora in the exhibition; 5 ft. by 5 ft. *Adenandra speciosa*; 2 ft. by 2 ft. *Leschenaultia biloba major*, 2½ ft. by 2½ ft. *Erica Hartnella*; 2 ft. by 1½ ft.

2ND PRIZE to Mr. Laybank, gardener to T. Maudesley, Esq., Knight's Hill, Norwood. The great attraction in this excellent collection was a plant of

Tropæolum tricolorum, trained to a trellis in the form of a pillar with a a rounded top. Every part, from the bottom to the top, was profusely bloomed. The pillar was 5 ft. high and 2 ft. diameter. *Zichya coccinea*, also trained to a round trellis and well bloomed; 2½ ft. by 2 ft. *Gompholobium polymorphum*; 2½ ft. by 2 ft. *Boronia anemonæfolia*; 3 ft. by 2½ ft.

2ND PRIZE to Mr. Stowe, gardener to — Baker, Esq., Bayfordbury, Herts. The judges awarded a prize equal with the last to this collection. The plants were all well grown, especially

Erica intermedia, a fine extra-well bloomed plant; 3 ft. by 4 ft. *Chorozema macrophylla*; 4 ft. by 3 ft. *Dillwynia floribunda*; 3 ft. by 2 ft. *Polygala oppositifolia*; 2½ ft. by 2 ft.

3RD PRIZE to Mr. Dennet, gardener to H. W. Gilliot, Esq., Clapham Common. The following were very good:—

Pimelea spectabilis; 2½ ft. by 2½ ft. *Chorozema Chandlerii*; 2 ft. by 2 ft. *Boronia anemonæfolia*; 3 ft. by 2½ ft. *Erica Sindryana*, a rather new, beautiful variety; 2 ft. by 1½ ft. *Epacris grandiflora*; 3 ft. by 3 ft.

A 3RD PRIZE also was given to Mr. Bruce, gardener to Boyd Millar, Esq., Clapham. Quite equal with the last; in it was a beautiful specimen of

Epacris miniata; 2 ft. by 2 ft. *Azalea speciosa*; 2½ ft. by 2½ ft. *Chorozema varia var. Chandlerii*; 2 ft. by 2 ft. *Leschenaultia formosa*, 2 ft. by 2½ ft. *Erica perspicua nana*, a pretty species; 2 ft. by 2 ft.

4TH PRIZE to Mr. Williams, gardener to Miss Traill, Bromley. We noticed, more especially, an immense

Erica vestita alba, well bloomed; 5 ft. by 5 ft. *Azalea indica* (Apollo); 3 ft. by 2 ft. *Daviesia latifolia*; 3 ft. by 2½ ft. *Dillwynia ericoides*; 3 ft. by 2½ ft.

A 4TH PRIZE, equal with the last, to Mr. Malyon, gardener to J. Brandrum, Esq., Blackheath.

Erica vestita alba, a pretty plant; 2½ ft. by 2 ft. *E. Beaumontiana*, 2 ft. by 1½ ft. *Ventricosa coccinea minor*, high coloured. *Chorozema Lawrenciana*; 3 ft. by 2 ft. *Oxylobium Pulteneæ*, small but good.

5TH PRIZE to Mr. Stanley, gardener to H. Bevens, Esq., Sidcup, Kent. A moderately well grown collection, but some in excellent condition, especially

Tropæolum Jarrettii; 3 ft. by 2½ ft. *Erica Cavendishii*; 2 ft. by 2 ft.

6TH PRIZE to Mr. Young, gardener to J. Barron, Esq., Denmark Hill, who had

Pimelea spectabilis, *Chorozema ilicifolia*, and *Cytisus Rhodopnæus*, well flowered.

AZALEAS:

The next class of plants that drew forth admiration were the collections of Azalea Indica. They were superior to any ever exhibited in these gardens before.

COLLECTIONS OF TWELVE GREENHOUSE AZALEAS.

The FIRST PRIZE was very justly awarded to Mr. May, gardener to Mrs. Lawrence. These were noble, beautifully flowered plants. The following were particularly fine:—

Azalea Lawrenciana; 5 ft. by 5 ft. *A. purpurea superba;* 5 ft. by 6 ft. *A. exquisita;* 4 ft. by 4 ft. *A. coronata;* 5 ft. by 5 ft. *A. lateritia;* 5 ft. by 4 ft. *A. speciosissima;* 5 ft. by 5 ft. *A. rosea superba;* 6 ft. by 4 ft.

2ND PRIZE to Messrs. Frazer. The judges must have had some difficulty in deciding between this and Mrs. Lawrence's collection, they were so nearly equal.

Azalea purpurea superba; 6 ft. by 4 ft. *A. refulgens,* a rich dark scarlet; 5 ft. by 2½ ft. *A. splendens,* an immense specimen. *A. Fielderii,* a large plant, with flowers of the purest white. *A. sinensis,* a good specimen of a most intractable species. *A. fulgens,* extremely glowing colours; 4 ft. by 3 ft.

3RD PRIZE to Messrs. Lane, nurserymen, Berkhampstead. The following were particularly fine :—

Azalea punctata; 4 ft. by 4 ft. *A. triumphans superba;* 5 ft. by 4 ft. *A. magnifica plena;* 3 ft. by 3 ft. *A. indica alba,* very large; 5 ft. by 6 ft.

COLLECTIONS OF SIX.

The FIRST PRIZE to that veteran, Mr. Green. A handsome well bloomed collection.

Azalea superba, a very large plant, full of flowers; 6 ft. by 5 ft. *A. rubra plena;* 7 ft. by 4 ft. *A. triumphans;* 5 ft. by 4 ft. *A. lateritia;* 5 ft. by 4 ft.

2ND PRIZE to Mr. Falconer, gardener to A. Palmer, Esq., Cheam.

Azalea bianca, pure white, with stout petals and a good form; 4 ft. by 2 ft. *A. variegata,* large and abundantly flowered; 6 ft. by 4 ft. *A. speciosissima;* 7 ft. by 3 ft. *A. lateritia,* extra fine; 5 ft. by 4 ft.

3RD PRIZE to Mr. Dennet, gardener to H. W. Gilliot, Esq. This collection was finely bloomed, but the plants were more unequal in size.

Azalea optima; 3 ft. by 2 ft. *A. exquisita;* 3 ft. by 2 ft. *A. refulgens;* 4 ft. by 1½ ft. *A. variegata;* 2 ft. by 2 ft.

These collections of Azaleas did great credit to all the contributors; they quite filled one side of one of the long tents, and the sight of them will not be easily forgotten by the visitors.

ROSES IN POTS.

To say they were fine would convey but a faint idea to our readers of the state of perfection they were brought to the Park. Messrs. Paul and Lane put out all their competing strength, but the merits of the excellent specimens were so equal that the judges determined it was a dead heat. Equal prizes were given to them. We have selected a few out of each that we judged to be the best.

COLLECTION OF TWELVE IN POTS.

Messrs. Lane and Sons, nurserymen, Berkhampstead.

Chenedolle, a splendid dark rose; hybrid China. *Baronne Prevost,* a shade lighter; hybrid perpetual. *Lady Alice Peel,* deep rosy carmine; hybrid perpetual. *Armosa,* bright pink; Bourbon. *Grant des Batailles,* splendid new dark rose, fine; hybrid perpetual. *Duchess of Sutherland,* pale rose, very beautiful; hybrid perpetual.

Messrs. Paul and Sons, Cheshunt.

Madame St. Joseph, a large flesh-coloured rose, very fine; tea. *Bouquet de Flore,* a rich deep rose; Bourbon. *Lady Warrender,* pure white, very double; tea. *Safrano,* yellowish, very fine; tea. *Madeleine,* pale flesh, edged with crimson; hybrid China.

2ND PRIZE to Mr. Francis, nurseryman, Hertford. This was a very good, well grown collection, evidently an improvement upon Mr. F.'s plants of last year; the best in it were—

Souvenir de Malmaison, a fine pale rose; Bourbon. *Paul Perras,* pale rose; hybrid Bourbon. *Augustine Mouchelet,* deep rose, centre carmine; hybrid perpetual. *Charles Duval,* deep pink; hybrid China.

COLLECTIONS OF SIX YELLOW ROSES IN POTS.

1ST PRIZE to Messrs. Lane, who had

Marie, a fine pale yellow rose; tea. *Queen Victoria,* much paler; tea. *Clara Wendell,* yellowish; tea. *Viscountess des Cases;* this is a good colour, but rather loose in the flower; tea.

2ND PRIZE to Mr. Francis, who had

La Pactole, very pale, almost white; noisette. *Pauline,* rather better; tea. *Safaterre,* a fine buff rose; noisette. *Princess Adelaide,* pale yellow; tea.

3RD PRIZE to Messrs. Paul, who had

Persian and *Austrian yellow;* these are really of a fine deep colour; Austrian. *Safaterre;* noisette. *Smith's yellow;* noisette.

COLLECTIONS OF EIGHT ROSES IN POTS—AMATEURS ONLY.

1ST PRIZE to A. Rowland, Esq., Lewisham, who had very good

Baronne Prevost, pale rose; hybrid perpetual. *Wm. Jesse,* purplish crimson; hybrid perpetual. *Queen,* rosy pink; hybrid perpetual. *Duchess of Sutherland,* pink; hybrid perpetual. *Specioza;* Bourbon.

2ND PRIZE to Mr. Terry, gardener to Lady Puller, Youngsbury, who had very good

Beauty of Billiard, crimson; hybrid China. *Paul Perras,* pale rose; hybrid perpetual. *Brennus,* fine crimson; hybrid China. *Souvenir de Malmaison,* flesh-coloured; Bourbon.

3RD PRIZE to Mr. Roser, gardener to J. Bradbury, Esq., Streatham, who had good

Paul Perras, pale rose; hybrid perpetual. *Mrs. Bosanquet,* blush; China. *Madame Laffay,* fine crimson; hybrid perpetual. *Chenedolle,* fiery crimson; hybrid China.

CAPE HEATHS.

The next class, in point of merit, exhibited in excellent condition were Cape Heaths, or Ericas. There could be no fault found with them; it was quite evident they had improved much since last year. Numbers of them we have met so often at the different exhibitions that we had become quite familiar, but some of them, like children, had almost grown out of knowledge, and all had become more fruitful in blossoms.

COLLECTIONS OF FIFTEEN CAPE HEATHS.

1ST PRIZE to Mr. Mylam, gardener to S. Rucker, Esq., Wandsworth. This collection was allowed to be the finest ever yet exhibited, every plant being quite healthy and full of bloom.

Erica elegans stricta, was a perfect beauty, both in form and colour; only 2 ft. high, but 3 ft. across. *E. vasiflora,* a large plant in the best order; 3 ft. by 3 ft. *E. favoides elegans,* most beautiful; 2½ ft. by 2½ ft. *E. suaveolens,* a fragrant species, very well got up; 2½ ft. by 2½ ft. *E. nudubilis,* a complete mass of flowers; 2 ft. by 2 ft. *E. tortilliflora,* a rare specimen, not quite in perfect bloom; 2 ft. by 2 ft. *E. Hartnellii,* very high coloured, full of flower; 3 ft. by 3 ft. *E. aristata major,* rather small, but excellent in bloom; 1½ ft. by 1½ ft. *E. ventricosa coccinea minor;* 3 ft. by 3 ft.

2ND PRIZE to Mr. Smith, gardener to W. Quilter, Esq., Norwood.

Erica elegans stricta, a fine plant, but not so full of bloom as the preceding; 2 ft. by 3 ft. *E. fastigiata lutescens,* a good specimen; 2 ft. by 3 ft. *E. Beaumontia,* a large plant, well flowered; 3 ft. by 3 ft. *E. favoides elegans,* finely bloomed; 2 ft. by 3 ft. *E. perspicua nana,* a large bush, completely covered with bloom; 4 ft. by 2 ft. *E. favoides purpurea,* novel and fine; 3 ft. by 2½ ft.

3RD PRIZE to Mr. Cole, gardener to — Collyer, Esq., Dartford. The following were the best—

Erica mutabilis, finely flowered; 2 ft. by 2 ft. *E. ampullacea vittata;* 3 ft. by 2 ft. *E. ventricosa superba;* 2½ ft. by 2 ft. *E. ventricosa coccinea minor;* 2 ft. by 2 ft. *E. vestita rosea;* 3 ft. by 2 ft. *E. Cavendishii;* 3 ft. by 2 ft.

COLLECTIONS OF TWELVE—NURSERYMEN ONLY.

The FIRST PRIZE was awarded by the judges to Messrs. Rollison, Tooting (the justice of this award was disputed by several connoisseurs, who declared, in our presence, that the second ought to have been first; it is certain Mr. Veitch's collection was generally better bloomed). Messrs. Rollison's heaths were large, fine specimens, and most of them finely in flower. We noticed the following :—

Erica fastigiata lutescens, a good specimen; 2½ ft. by 3 ft. *E. nitida,* a neat, well flowered plant; 2 ft. by 2 ft. *E. Beaumontia,* exceedingly well bloomed; 2½ ft. by 2½ ft. *E. Cavendishii,* a large, fine plant, in good health, but scarcely in bloom; 4 ft. by 4 ft. *E. viridis,* very rare; 2 ft. by 2 ft. *E. perspicua nana,* very fine; 2 ft. by 2 ft.

2ND PRIZE to Messrs. Veitch and Sons, Exeter. Handsome, well grown, and freely flowered plants, especially

Erica propendens, a dense bush, covered with flowers; 3 ft. by 3 ft. *E. ventricosa coccinea minor,* fine; 2 ft. by 2 ft. *E. depressa,* very finely bloomed; 2½ ft. by 2½ ft. *E. tortilluflora,* a well managed, finely bloomed plant; 2½ ft. by 2 ft. *E. mundula* and *E. perspicua nana,* both pretty little bushes, densely flowered; 2 ft. by 2 ft.

3RD PRIZE to Messrs. Fairbairn, Clapham. The following were excellent :—

Erica mutabilis, densely flowered; 2 ft. by 2 ft. *E. Syndriana,* a rather new heath, beautifully grown; 3 ft. by 3 ft. *E. suaveolens;* 4 ft. by 3 ft. *E. vestita alba,* very large, full of bloom; 4 ft. by 4 ft. *E. Beaumontia,* thin, but full of bloom; 3 ft. by 2½ ft.

COLLECTIONS OF SIX CAPE HEATHS—AMATEURS ONLY.

1ST PRIZE to Mr. May, gardener to — Goodhead, Esq., Beckenham. He had very fine

Erica mirabilis; 2 ft. by 2 ft. *E. vestita coccinea;* 3 ft. by 3 ft. *E. Cavendishii;* 3 ft. by 3 ft. *E. favoides elegans* and *E. vestita alba;* 2 ft. by 3 ft.

2ND PRIZE to Mr. Green. Well grown and freely bloomed, especially

Erica Hartnellii; 3 ft. by 3 ft. *E. vestita alba;* 2 ft. by 2 ft. *E. aristata major;* 2 ft. by 1½ ft. *E. sprengelii;* 1½ ft. by 1½ ft.

3RD PRIZE to Mr. Williams. He had in fine order

Erica ventricosa coccinea minor; 2½ ft. by 2½ ft. *E. propendens,* a large bush; 4 ft. by 4 ft. *E. fastigiata lutescens,* very large; 3 ft. by 3 ft.

(To be continued.)

ENGLISH CAGE BIRDS.

THE NIGHTINGALE.

INSESSORES DENTIROSTRES. SYLVIADÆ.

*Sylvia luscinia. Motacilla luscinia. Curruca luscinia. Phila-
mela luscinia. Philomel.*

THIS is, unquestionably, the most beautiful of songsters;
is most easily kept, and as easily captured. The time of its
arrival into this country, being one of our summer migratories, is about the middle of April. I have had two brought
me this day (April 18th); and before I give a description of
its mode of treatment, I shall endeavour to describe its mode
of capture, together with a rough sketch of the trap commonly
known as the "nightingale-trap;" for you must first catch your
bird before you keep it. The males arrive first, and the sooner
they are caught the better, for if caught after the arrival of
the female they are not so soon reconciled to confinement,
unless the female is placed with them; and as the bird is
only cared for, for its song, the female is not desired. The
trap is formed of thin pieces of wood shaped like *fig.* 2, with a

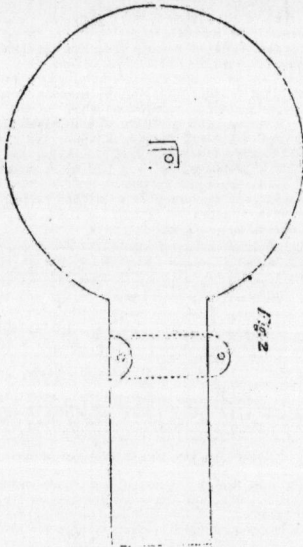

Fig. 3

Fig. 2

centre piece, *fig.* 5, fixed to it for the trap string to run through,

Fig. 5

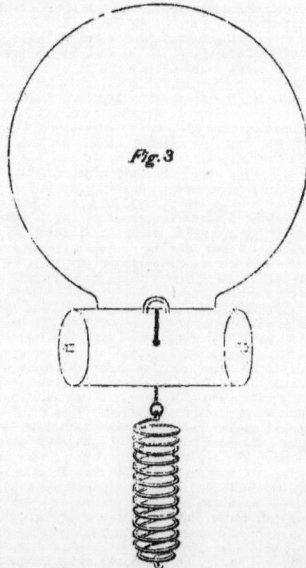

and having a piece of iron hooping nailed to the back, and turned
up at each side, to form the shoulders or receptacle for the
pivots of the wooden roller, as shewn in *fig.* 3. The wooden

roller is then made secure in the iron shoulders, giving it
freedom of play; a piece of string is then fixed to about the
middle of the roller, passed under the roller and attached
firmly to a spring, such as is used for bells, which is simply
a close coil of wire; this is firmly nailed to that part of the
handle of the base as is represented in *fig* 1. A wire is then

Fig. 1

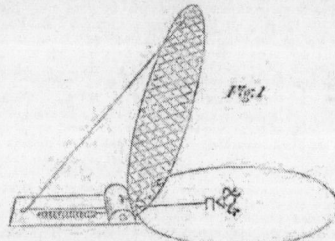

attached to the roller covered with very fine net, but loosely
covered, so that when it falls upon the bird will be so loose
as to allow its struggling without being pressed against the
board. A line is then attached to a piece of cork, or rather
a cork at one end, and the other passing through an eyelet
hole, such as a stair-rod eye, or piece of wire curved thus ∩,
is fixed to the upper portion of the wire as represented in *figs.*
1 and 4. The trap is set thus—by elevating the wire attached

Fig. 4

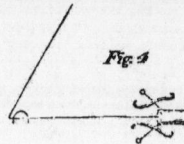

to the roller it stretches the spring by its revolution, the string is then passed through the block in the middle of the base, and having a knot in it to prevent its slipping back, is restrained by the cork slightly holding the string within the hole. Two or three pins are stuck into the cork, having impaled the larva of a beetle called a mealworm, to be found in mills, or a larva of any other kind of beetle, or the beetle itself will do as well. The trap is placed on the ground near the locality where the bird is either heard or seen, and in a few minutes he will descend from his perch to peck one of the worms, immediately upon the slightest touch down goes the trap, and the bird is caught. Being secured, and brought home either in the hat or pocket handkerchief, the first thing I do is to give it some water; and having procured its cage or aviary, turn it loose into either, taking care, if in a cage, to cover it up for a day or two, giving it so much light that it can see its food and perch, but so that it cannot see persons in the room. I then turn into its cage or aviary a quantity of cockroaches or black beetles, as they are commonly known by that name, alive in a large basin ; in the course of an hour or so, impelled by hunger, it readily takes to these insects and swallow one after another till satisfied; and mind you it will swallow sometimes three and four at a meal, and replenish itself in that way about every half-hour or hour; of course, a pan of water should also be given it. The next day I get some pounded hemp-seed ready, and also a small quantity of boiled bread and milk sufficiently thick to form a paste, I mix the boiled bread and milk and hemp-seed crushed together, and into this I stick the beetles, having first pinched their bodies so as to kill them, and stick them head foremost into this said paste, and leave them there looking like a plum-pudding, only not quite so nice ; the beetles, although deprived of life, move their limbs about convulsively while sticking in this paste, which the birds observing drop down from their perches and peck out the beetles, their rough thighs and legs dragging with them portions of the said paste ; this they readily swallow with the insects, and in a few days, should you be short of insects, the birds will feed on the bread and milk alone, having by this time acquired the *taste* and habit of going to the pan containing *that* food.

By feeding them in this way, I generally have them singing in less than a week. Should it, however, happen that no insects are to be had, I then mix up a paste formed of lean beef scraped fine and the yolk of an egg boiled hard, and opening the bird's beak gently poke a piece the size of a pea down its throat; this should be done every hour, and water given also by pouring a drop down its throat; but as beetles are to be had in almost every house, at any rate at every baker's oven, I never have recourse to cramming, which is very tedious, and often unsuccessful. Should you not have a supply of beetles to last, I, in addition to the beetles, stick small pieces of raw beef into the paste of bread and milk and hempseed ; and the bird will, in the event of no insects being at hand, sometimes take the meat, and sometimes the paste, separately ; but, as I said before, there is no trouble with the beetles. When once nightingales are reconciled to feeding, you have your song. And towards autumn, when insects become scarce, I feed them mostly on the scraped beef, and bread and milk, and crushed hempseed.

I will now transcribe portions of a communication made to me by the Rev. Mr. Cornish, of Totness, in Devonshire, some years ago, who was a most successful manager of the nightingale, which will close this paper; and I shall reserve my information relative to the diseases of this bird until when I speak of those common to birds in general.

I should observe that the top of the cage containing nightingales, or any species of migratory birds, should be covered with green baize, or flannel instead of wood, as they are apt to hurt their heads by flying upwards and beating themselves about, which is prevented by the baize, as this gives way to the impetus of the bird's attempt at flight upwards.

The Rev. Mr. Cornish says, " I have kept nightingales for more than thirty years, and they have sung with me in the highest perfection; indeed, one is at this moment (viz., Jan. 7, 1840) singing beautifully, accompanied by the Atracapilla, Alauda Arborea and many others. I may as well describe the food that is prepared for this charming songster; because this will, I have found, keep all the migratories in perfect health, with a little variety which I will mention when I come to

them in their order :—Lean beef parboiled, with an equal quantity of hard-boiled egg, chopped-up together very small; a little cracked hempseed, crumbled bread, and hard egg well mixed together, put into their tin pans or drawers; about as much as can be taken up with a sixpence ; this must not be mixed-up with the beef and egg, but put in the back part of their drawer distinctly by itself. The reason is this : the nightingale being rather lax in their viscera, generally this last food, particularly the hempseed, will have a contrary tendency, and keep them stronger. On this food I have kept several of these delightful birds seven or eight years, stout in song and high health. As I conclude, you wish to be informed of the particulars relative to their treatment; you must excuse me if I am or should be tedious. My birds are fed every morning about nine o'clock, at which time they have fresh food given them, and a sufficient quantity prepared that they may have some again at three o'clock p.m. Their sliders are covered with river sand, sifted, and also, which is *the grand secret* to keep them well, some old pounded mortar put on their sand. This last corrects anything wrong. Their sliders are cleaned every day; all their droppings removed, but clean sand only three times a week. I would recommend two sets of sliders, as the droppings from birds that eat animal food are offensive; the other may be washed and cleaned as mine are. Their water should be good and fresh."

[We have heard it argued that it is the air of Devonshire being unhealthy to the nightingale is the cause of its not being found wild in that county; Mr. Cornish's experience demonstrates that that cannot be the cause. It is more true, we fear, that in many districts this songster of the night as well as of the day, is becoming annually more scarce, and, if so, then some of our next generation may be liable to the Welchman's mistake, who, when asked whether he knew the night song of these birds, said, " Oh ! yes, but we do call them owls."[*]

The time of the arrival of the nightingale varies about three weeks. The Rev. Mr. Jenyns found that during twelve years, the earliest day of its song being heard in Cambridgeshire varied between the 8th and 28th of April.

We have always thought that the nightingale's notes were inimitable, but we quite agree with M. Audubon in his estimate of the following composition, which he thus introduces :—" One day, after partaking of a delicious breakfast of buckwheat cakes and sweet milk, under the roof of a peasant, I chanced to ask him what he knew of ' the nightingale.' ' Ah, monsieur! *that* is a bird which sings beautifully !' I then asked him whether he could tell what it says when it sings, and my host, after a customary scratching of the ear, rose, straightened himself, coughed, and in very decent musical tone sang this ditty—

Le bon Dieu m'a don - né une femme, Que j'ai tant, tant,

tant, tant bat-tue, Que s'il m'en donne une autre, Je ne

la bat-ter-als plus, plus, plus, plus, Qu'un petit, qu'un petit, qu'un petit'

It is a most true description of the expressions of the nightingale's notes, and marks the compass of the bird's voice, the emphasis on the different notes, and the terminating cadences most happily.—*Macgillivray's British Birds.*]

[*] The nightingale, says Mr. Blyth, in his excellent edition of White's History of Selborne, appears to migrate almost due north and south, deviating but very little either to the right or to the left. There are none in Brittany, nor in the Channel Islands (Jersey, Guernsey, &c.), and the most westward of them probably cross the channel at Cape la Hogue, arriving on the coast of Dorsetshire. They thence apparently proceed northward, any accidental stragglers being found beyond the third degree of W. longitude, a line which cuts off the counties of Devonshire and Cornwall, together with all Wales and Ireland, and by far the greater part of Scotland, in which last kingdom the nightingale has once or twice occurred to the eastward only of this meridian.

EXTRACTS FROM CORRESPONDENCE.

COCHIN-CHINA FOWLS.—When your notice of the Cochin-China Fowl appeared, many were the inquiries after this wonderful bird, and from the single answer given to those inquiries, it seemed as if Mr. Nolan, of Dublin, were the only person in the United Kingdom who had them to dispose of. I accordingly sent to him for some eggs, most of which proved rotten. This might probably be attributed to the distance they had to travel. Two of them, however, proved productive; but the chickens *were, and are, black, with black legs.* Probably there may be a cross of the Cochin-China in them, but from all I have learnt, they are not true. I have since obtained accurate information on the subject. The prices, too, of the London dealers are considerably less than Mr. Nolan's; indeed, a neighbour of mine bought a *Dorking cock* of a celebrated London poulterer, for 12s. Mr. Nolan's price is 25s. I told Mr. Nolan of my disappointment, and he has offered to make me reparation.—D. T. K.

[Regret that our correspondent has been disappointed, is all, unfortunately, we can offer him. Our columns are open to any dealer who chooses to advertise in them. When we wish for any particular breed of fowl, we buy full grown specimens, because we know how impossible it is for any dealer to be certain that no cross-breeding has impregnated the egg.—ED. C. G.]

CALENDARIAL INDEX.—From circumstances, I have had leisure to study THE COTTAGE GARDENER more thoroughly than most of your readers are likely to have done, and I have found it almost essential to the using it as a manual, to combine the index and the monthly calendar; at least, in the case of all those plants in which I was particularly interested. I enclose a specimen sheet of the memorandum book that has been the result. Do you think the publication of such a companion to your three first volumes, with space left for continuing it for future volumes, or for adding manuscript references at the discretion of the user, would be sufficiently profitable to entail no risk of loss at any rate? The volume might be used also as a reference to other works, by adding a column for miscellaneous references. Of course my book does not profess to be a complete index; indeed, it would lose some of its portable value were it so; the object being that each individual should select those portions of the work best suited to his taste or needs, without losing time in referring to the whole mass of information on any given subject.

OCTOBER.

	Vol. 1.	Vol. 2.	Vol. 3.	Vol. 4.	Vol. 5.	Vol. 6.
Geraniums......	152	368				
Scarlet ditto	234	90				
Bulbs planting..	34		17			

A LOVER OF FLOWERS FROM CHILDHOOD.

[This is an exceedingly useful suggestion, and we recommend its adoption by our readers. A book, with a page for each month, and ruled as above, would enable them easily to make a calendarial index for such plants as they especially regard. To publish such an index we fear would not meet with a demand sufficiently extensive to cover the expense, but we will not lose sight of the suggestion.—ED. C. G.]

TO CORRESPONDENTS.

₀ We request that no one will write to the departmental writers of THE COTTAGE GARDENER. It gives them unjustifiable trouble and expense; and we also request our coadjutors *under no circumstances* to reply to such private communications.

THE COTTAGE GARDENERS' DICTIONARY (*Kentoi Green*).—Our correspondent after stating his disappointments owing to his having no guide, adds:

"I see a remedy, if the proposed *Cottage Gardeners' Dictionary* is

carried out properly. The name of every plant should be given; its height and colour; its mode of propagation; if transplantable, and the best mode of doing so; nature of soil, &c.; for, in fact, editors should remember that they have ignorance to inform. You would smile at the odd mistakes I have made. To be sure knowledge is gained by errors, but then time is lost."

We can assure our correspondent that the work in question is intended to meet cases similar to his, and we think it will contain information on all the points he mentions.

DECAYED COW-DUNG (*E. L. T.*).—This desirable ingredient for many potted plants, must be prepared by yourself—though for immediate use you might obtain a little from some florist near to you. To prepare cow-dung properly, it should be gathered from a pasture piled into a heap under a shed, and be allowed to remain there undisturbed for two years, by which time it will be reduced in appearance to the state of a rich crumbly peat.

SAND (*Ibid*).—Next to silver sand, the fine drift sand in rivers is the best for potting purposes. Do you require *Cyclamens* for your borders, or for greenhouse culture?

CAPE JASMINE CUTTINGS (*B——k——B.*).—Now, and in June, is a good time for planting these. Select young shoots for the purpose that have no bloom upon them. Though this shrub (*Gardenia radicans* may grow in the open air against a wall without any other protection, as you say it does, in the south west of Ireland, we are of opinion that it will not bear similar treatment in any part of Lincolnshire.

EXCHANGE OF EGGS.—Mr. Henry Carter, Carleton-road, near Attleburgh, Norfolk, wishes to exchange a sitting of fifteen Dorking fowl's eggs for a few eggs of the Cochin-China fowl.

LIME AND STABLE MANURE (*C. B. C.*).—These should not be applied at the same time as a dressing to your kitchen-garden. The lime decomposes the ammoniacal salts of the manure, and sets free their ammonia. Gypsum in combination with the manure would be better, for the gypsum combines with, or "fixes," the ammonia.

STRAWBERRY FORCING (*John Roberts*).—It is quite impossible for us to say why you fail, unless we knew how you manage the plants. Read Mr. Errington's rules at pages 136 and 305 of our last volume, and if you follow them strictly you will not fail. We cannot write private letters.

ANEMONES BONE FLOWERING (*Isabella, Tottenham*).—You have a nice bed of anemones just gone out of flower. As some of them are double, we advise you by all means to take up the roots and gently dry them; that is, dry them in a cool room where the sunshine will not reach them. Prepare a bed of fresh, rich, light sandy soil sometime between now and August; about the middle of that month replant them. And with this treatment we think they must succeed. Sow seed, too, for fear of a failure.

ÆSCHYNANTHUS PARASITICUS (*A. B., Camden Town*).—You ask for the treatment necessary for this plant. It thrives best in a stove, but will do tolerably well in a warm greenhouse. It will grow in a pot trained to a trellis. The soil it requires is rather light and coarse, and should be well drained. It will also do well tied with wire to a long round block of wood covered with moss. See Mr. Appleby's remarks on the tribe in this week's paper.

CREEPERS FOR NORTH WALL (*Clericus*).—A north wall is a bad aspect for any creeper except ivy. You may try the following, but first drain the border well with brick rubbish. It is the cold wet earth that injures any plants on the north side of a wall, especially if shaded with shrubs:—*Ampelopsis hederacea* (Virginian creeper), *Clematis vitalba* (Traveller's Joy), *C. montana* (Mountain Virgin's Bower), *Rubus alba pleno* (Double-flowered Bramble). If you are not near a smoky atmosphere, you might plant some camellias in your drained border. Behind a north wall is the only place where camellias will flourish in this country.

SOFTENING WATER (*I. X.*).—For use with tea, &c., we know of nothing better than as much of powdered carbonate of potash as can be taken up with the point of a penknife, put into the tea-pot before pouring the water upon the tea.

LIQUID MANURE (*A Young Beginner*).—Why do you not refer to our indexes. Guano is better for the purpose than sulphate of ammonia made by adding oil of vitriol to gas ammoniacal liquor, though both are good fertilisers. If the guano is very strong, two ounces to a gallon of water is enough; of ordinary guano three or four ounces will not be too much. The London Manure Company, 41, Bridge-street, Blackfriars.

WEIGHT OF DUCK'S EGGS (*Elizabeth*).—Our correspondent says that the Aylesbury duck's eggs usually weigh three ounces. She says that she finds this duck a good sitter and a good mother. They are pure white, without a single coloured feather. You will find drawings and descriptions of it, and of the Spanish fowl, in our last volume. Eggs not hatching, but having half-formed chickens in them, were chilled probably at the time when the formation ceased. The exhibition of domestic poultry at the Zoological Gardens is not annual we think.

APPLES IN TARTS (*Legcolium*).—The best of baking apples still retain after baking the shape of the slices, but are so soft as to unite into a pulp with the least pressure. The shavings for bonnet making are made from the Lime or Linden tree.

HIMALAYAN PUMPKIN SEED (*J. Hampson*).—We have not enough to send even one seed to all applicants. We cannot do as you wish.

INSECTS ON ROSES (*Rosa*).—The caterpillars curled up in your rose-tree leaves can only be destroyed by hand-picking; and "the small green insect, about the size of a pin's head," is the green fly, or *Rose aphis*, of which see more in our first page to-day; tobacco-smoke is the best remedy. You cannot raise any particular *carnation* from seed; the seedlings will come different from their parent.

AYLESBURY DUCKS (*Rev. R. B.*).—Thanks for your attention. Our correspondent writes as follows, and his communication will give information to another enquirer. Those who complain of unfruitful eggs have too many ducks with the drake. We saw a brood a few days since of 13 pure Aylesbury ducklings from one sitting; only two ducks and a drake were kept by their owner. "I have found the eggs of this breed very uncertain in hatching (although fresh, and the drake was always with the ducks). On an average of nests, my first season of trial, not more than one in five produced ducklings. But, as I cannot imagine that any difference can exist in this respect between them and those of other breeds, I think it must have been from some error in management. Lately we have had rather better success, but not at all a satisfactory produce. I may notice that a few eggs (not used for sitting) have been of enormous size, one weighed five ounces and a half. While on the subject of poultry, let me ask your opinion on a disease in hens, from which my poultry-yard has suffered greatly this winter, and which I have not seen treated of in Richardson's book; I have been told it is congestion of the liver. Every case has terminated fatally. When first attacked the hens begin to mope, and to stand with their necks *contracted* into their bodies; they gradually waste away (the appetite all the time continuing voracious) to skin and bone, and then die. Nothing passes through them; I have given castor oil and calomel without effect." This we believe to be merely torpidity of the bowels, and we should give each fowl so affected a compound rhubarb pill, made according to the formula of the Edinburgh Pharmacopœa, in which this pill is made of rhubarb and aloes. Keep them warm, and supplied with plenty of clean water.

THE IDÆAN VINE (*Ibid*).—The lines you refer to in *The Lady of the Lake* are

" Where Ellen's hand had taught to twine
The Ivy and Idæan Vine."

By the last named plant Sir Walter Scott intended the Red Bilberry, Whortleberry, or Cowberry, which, in the language of botanists, is *Vaccinium Vitis Idæa*. Older botanists merely called it by the two last names. It is a native of Scotland, and its berries make the best of jelly to be eaten with venison.

HEATING A GREENHOUSE (*A. F. F.*).—Your plan only differs from that fully described at page 356, vol. iii., by the tube for supplying the fuel passing *through* the boiler, and as that answers yours probably will do so. At page 120 of our first volume full directions are given about the construction of a greenhouse; it will repay you for consulting it.

MYOSOTIS ALBA (*A. E. D.*).—Our correspondent wishes to know where she can obtain seeds of this plant.

LUCERNE (*P. P. H. H.*).—You must not sow this with your wheat, nor with any other crop, for you could not keep it hoed, which is necessary for obtaining good and permanent crops of it. Wait until the spring. You may sow turnips now, feed them off with sheep, and then sow wheat.

ROSE-TREE SUCKERS (*An Enquirer*).—Do not remove these now, but let them grow on until the autumn, when you may separate them from the parent trees, and they then may be planted where you please.

PURE PEAT (*Nemo*).—By this term (vol. ii. page 198) is meant peat unmixed with any other soil. Peat for gardening purposes is *not* that dug for fuel in fenny districts, but a sharp, sandy soil, mixed with the dead fibrous roots of heath; and is found upon Wimbledon and many other dry commons.

ANTS (*R. P. H.*).—We, too, are, and have been for years, "much troubled with ants;" and the best remedy we find is soot and hot-water poured into their nests and on their paths. The hot-water is not with a view to scald the rascals, but to raise ammoniacal vapour, which seems extremely annoying to them; for they will abandon a fortress on the second or third application. We also apply boiling water to them from a fine rose. A handful of fresh soot to two gallons of water is strong enough.

GLYCINE SINENSIS (*M. B.*).—By the best authorities this is the proper name of your plants which you say are "doing well, but not flowering freely." We should be loth to try experiments with a glycine that was promising; still, if you were to give it assistance with liquid manure once in ten days, from the first of June to the end of August, you would be very likely to get it into full bearing sooner and more surely. Good rich garden soil and a south wall are the other best auxiliaries.

ASPARAGUS (*Veras*).—We must not give opinions on what appears in other periodicals; but we may remark that editors are not responsible for the opinions of their correspondents; for they do not sit in judgment on these opinions, but to allow and obtain a fair hearing to each and all. If you put more faith in us, follow our directions; and we say most decidedly, do *not* cut the small shoots of asparagus. We have brought round many old, weak beds, by abstaining from cutting them. The reason is obvious: when asparagus produces these small shoots, or *sprew*, it is because the action of the roots is weak; and that weakness can be removed most readily by giving them rest, or abstaining from cutting.

DRIED GERANIUM CUTTINGS (*A Parson's Wife*).—As a set off against your disappointment with some plants, we are glad to hear that you have achieved a feat which has puzzled some good gardeners. We allude to your drying a cutting of a scarlet geranium last autumn, then potting it in January, and getting it to grow. You did quite right in stopping it when "five inches long." By and bye it will make a fine plant, although it did not "break" at the time you wrote.

CINERARIA SEEDLINGS (*Ibid*).—Your seedling cinerarias raised last autumn were starved. They should have been potted in January and again in March; but now, if you water them well and pot them next day, using rich soil, and pots two sizes larger, they will repay you yet. Repot your recent seedlings as fast as they fill each sized pot, and they also will bloom. Try some of both sorts in the open ground without the pots. The cineraria "white tipped with pink," of which you sent a leaf, is *Prince Albert*. None of this family like to be checked in any way; try some of these also in the borders.

NEMOPHILA MACULATA (*Ibid*).—This beautiful annual died with dropsy, induced by too much rich soil, water, and cold. It will raise from seeds in the open ground as freely as the blue one. You had better plant out the seedlings of it at once.

CUPHEA PLATYCENTRA (*Ibid*).—When young plants of this, struck last autumn, turn yellow in the leaves, the best way is to cut them down to the last two or three joints early in the spring, and they will spring up freely by the beginning of May. You should cut it back now, and the natural warmth of the season will be sufficient encouragement for it.

NEAPOLITAN VIOLETS (*Ibid*).—You are by far too kind a nurse, otherwise those "covered with buds" at the time of potting, would have bloomed safe enough. Did you not give them too much water?

VERBENAS (*Ibid*).—The severity of the winter was the cause of their death; but of course you will try the plan again and again.

WATERING (*Ibid*).—What is "plainly impossible," is not very probable to be achieved even by an editor! No one can say at a distance how much and how often a plant should be watered, although in our zeal we sometimes transgress the rule, and even now we are tempted to break the law to please you; but we had better escape by saying, follow the dictates of your own good sense.

RHODODENDRONS WEAKLY (*A. A.*).—Stable-manure is not a proper dressing for unhealthy rhododendrons; far from it—very rotten cow-dung would answer better; but we question the propriety of giving stimulants to any kind of plants in a sickly state. First, encourage plants to make new roots, by giving them a very sandy compost of earths or peat; and *then* begin with moderate doses of weak liquid-manure, and as the plants increase in strength, increase the strength of their food. Your rhododendrons having been sickly these three years, in stiff soil, will never recover without being cut down more than half way, and now is a good time; after that add some sandy peat, cover the bed with short grass or some mulching, and water them twice a-week with pond water till the end of the dog-days; and if it is possible to save them, depend on it that is the best way in your case, and give up all idea of stimulants this season.

PYRACANTHA (*Ibid*).—It will do for a south trellis on your stiff soil, if you give it a little light compost to begin with; and for other climbers take those evergreen climbing roses we recommend.

REMOVING BEES (*T. S.*).—If the bees are suffered to remain till the next day, there will be honey as well as combs in the hive; and when the latter is broken down, the former will run amongst the bees and kill them. The better plan will be to send them by the middle-day coach on the day they swarm, should they be early enough; but it would be better still to purchase a swarm in your own neighbourhood.

NUTT'S HIVE (*M. J. T.*).—The best plan would be to put two swarms into Nutt's centre box; you would then obtain a glass of honey from the top, and some in one, if not in both, the side boxes. The method of uniting, as given in page 104, vol. ii. of THE COTTAGE GARDENER, is very simple. If a swarm is put into each box they can never be united.

AURICULA SOWING (*W. H. G.*).—You may do this as directed for the polyanthus, at page 248 of vol. ii.; and the future management of the seedlings is the same.

PLUNGING POTTED PLANTS IN HOTBED (*R. Winn*).—It is worse than useless to do this when you have no frame. The action of the roots would supply sap far more rapidly than the leaves would have power to digest it; and this, together with the cold nights, would soon render them diseased. We cannot write private letters.

FEATHER-STEMMED SAVOY (*Billericay*).—Send us an envelope ready directed, and two postage stamps. Thanks for your suggestions relative to *The Cottage Gardeners' Dictionary*.

CUTTINGS OF FUCHSIAS (*W. T. Gidney*).—July is a very good month for putting in cuttings of any kind. Your plant is *Polygala cordifolia*, or Heart-leaved Milkwort.

NAMES OF PLANTS (*H. H.*).—Yours is *Daphne Pontica*. It will flourish anywhere in England in the open air, and preferring a cool situation. (*A Cottager*).—1. *Eupatorium corymbosum*. This will do for bedding in a poor soil. In a rich soil it grows too gross to flower freely. 2. *Polemonium cæruleum*, or Jacob's Ladder. 3. *Pulmonaria officinalis*, Common Lungwort. 4. *Trollius Europæus*, European Globe flower. 5. *Ornithogalum nutans*, Neapolitan Star of Bethlehem. (*T. M. W.*).—Your lentils, we think, are the seeds of the *Errum lens*. A subscriber, whose initials we have mislaid, sent us "a heath-like plant," with a white flower at the end of each shoot. It is *Fabiana imbricata*, usually mentioned as a greenhouse evergreen; but it is quite hardy, if grown against a wall. It is a native of Chili.

LONDON: Printed by HARRY WOOLDRIDGE, Winchester High-street, in the Parish of Saint Mary Kalendar; and Published by WILLIAM SOMERVILLE ORR, at the Office, No. 2, Amen Corner, in the Parish of Christ Church, City of London.—May 23rd, 1850.

WEEKLY CALENDAR.

M D	W D	MAY 30—JUNE 5, 1850.	Weather near London in 1849.			Sun Rises.	Sun Sets.	Moon R. & S.	Moon's Age.	Clock bef. Sun.	Day of Year.
30	Th	Corpus Christi. Swallow-tailed Butterfly seen.	T. 77°—53°.	S.W.	Fine.	52 a. 3	2 a. 8	11 34	19	2 51	150
31	F	Four-spotted Dragon Fly.	T. 79°—45°.	S.W.	Fine.	51	3	morn.	20	2 43	151
1	S	Nicomede. Common Elder flowers.	T. 78°—48°.	S.W.	Fine.	50	4	0 6	21	2 35	152
2	Sun	1 SUNDAY AFTER TRIN. Virginian Spiderwort	T. 78°—47°.	W.	Fine.	50	6	0 34	22	2 26	153
3	M	Common Red Poppy flowers. [flowers.	T. 75°—51°.	E.	Fine.	49	6	0 58	(C	2 16	154
4	Tu	Spotted Fly-catcher lays.	T. 81°—57°.	W.	Fine.	49	7	1 23	24	2 6	155
5	W	K. HANOVER BORN, 1771. Rye blooms.	T. 85°—57°.	W.	Rain.	48	8	1 45	25	1 56	156

LONGEVITY is a characteristic of gardeners; brevity of life, unfortunately, has been allotted to some of those who have been distinguished practitioners of their art, but these are exceptional cases to their usual length of days, and to these the REVEREND PROFESSOR MARTYN fully attained, for he died on the 3rd of June, 1825, in his 90th year. Although he ably performed during 64 years the duties of professor of botany at Cambridge, and although his *Language of Botany*, his *Plantæ Cantabrigenses*, and other botanical works, are efficient evidence of his knowledge in that fair science, yet still more widely and still more usefully were his labours diffused in his edition of *Miller's Gardeners' Dictionary*. This has been justly termed his "grand labour," and such a mass of valuable information does it contain, that amid our editorial difficulties when our eye rests upon its four goodly folios we take courage, for rarely have they failed to tell us what we wish to learn relative to the history and botanical characters of all plants known to gardeners previously to the present century. Even the directions for the culture of those plants are but little improved by subsequent practitioners; and the gardener or farmer who cultivated his crops according to the lights afforded him by *Martyn's Miller's Dictionary* would not be deemed a bad cultivator in any district of rural Britain, for it is a standard practical work, to which recent researches have provided ample additions, but which can never be superseded. The father of Mr. Martyn was a physician, and had resided for many years at Chelsea. It was there, he says, when writing in 1821 to a friend. " I was born, where my family lived in reputation during the greatest part of half a century, and I received the whole of my school education. I went under Mr. Roberry at five years and a half old, and continued with him until seventeen, when I removed to the university—having for about ten years walked about six times a-day between Church-

lane and Paradise-row. I knew and was known to almost everybody in Chelsea, which has of late years rendered it a melancholy walk to me, knowing and being known of nobody." He had now nearly reached the advanced age of fourscore years and ten, and his father having lived to be seventy, their united memories carried their personal acquaintance to the great gardeners and botanists of a century gone by. Sloane, and Ray, and Switzer, and Fairchild, had been either their contemporaries or acquaintances, and render their reminiscences more than ordinarily of high interest; but we must confine ourselves to one. Miller had dedicated his great work to his patron Sir Hans Sloane, and this seems to have recalled this giant of collectors to Mr. Martyn's memory. He says, " I beg leave to consider Sir Hans Sloane as one of my patrons. The condescension of the venerable and amiable old gentleman to me when a schoolboy will never be forgotten by me; and his figure is even now presented to my eye in the most lively manner, as he was sitting fixed by age and infirmity in his arm-chair. I usually carried a present from my father of some book that he had published; and the old gentleman in return always presented me with a broad piece of gold, treated me with chocolate, and sent me with his librarian to see some of his curiosities. It appears now like looking into other times." We will conclude by observing, that the pursuit of science did not render Professor Martyn a less efficient country clergyman. He died at his living of Pertenhall, and it is recorded of him, that " as a preacher of the Gospel of Christ, which he adorned by his life and doctrines, he was distinguished by strong sense, accurate knowledge of human nature, and comprehensive scriptural knowledge. Practical benevolence and charity were conspicuous traits in his character, and the exercise of them was confined neither to place nor party."

RANGE OF BAROMETER—RAIN IN INCHES.

May	1841.	1842.	1843.	1844.	1845.	1846.	1847.	1848.	1849.
30 B.	30.016 / 29.979	30.050 / 29.955	30.084 / 29.958	30.023 / 30.002	30.045 / 29.751	30.309 / 30.154	30.410 / 30.351	30.117 / 30.056	30.183 / 30.076
R.			0.03				0.02		
31 B.	30.042 / 29.995	30.155 / 30.110	29.854 / 29.813	30.035 / 30.001	30.181 / 30.156	30.178 / 30.130	30.471 / 30.449	30.049 / 29.823	29.999 / 29.970
R.			0.06				0.14		
June 1 B.	30.137 / 30.122	30.211 / 30.125	29.700 / 29.504	29.998 / 29.949	30.133 / 30.042	30.187 / 30.153	30.475 / 30.149	29.854 / 29.659	30.068 / 30.040
R.			0.08					0.08	
2 B.	30.177 / 30.107	30.261 / 30.169	29.305 / 29.224	29.971 / 29.953	29.951 / 29.761	30.210 / 30.188	30.450 / 30.399	29.417 / 29.309	30.162 / 30.075
R.			0.08					0.07	
3 B.	30.254 / 30.157	30.296 / 30.150	29.875 / 29.407	30.123 / 30.057	29.621 / 29.367	30.316 / 30.177	30.349 / 30.238	29.364 / 29.276	30.222 / 30.117
R.			0.08		0.06			0.03	
4 B.	30.357 / 30.300	30.112 / 29.965	29.639 / 29.223	30.147 / 30.037	29.607 / 29.616	30.178 / 30.165	30.244 / 30.222	29.638 / 29.465	30.101 / 29.939
R.			0.02		0.05			0.07	
5 B.	30.219 / 30.004	29.918 / 29.809	29.745 / 29.780	29.976 / 29.822	29.597 / 29.343	30.143 / 30.115	30.240 / 30.158	29.768 / 29.097	29.687 / 29.765
R.	0.03		0.09	0.06	0.08		0.01		0.24

METEOROLOGY OF THE WEEK.—At Chiswick, during the above seven days, the average highest and lowest temperatures of the last 23 years has been 70° and 45.5° respectively. On 65 days during the period rain fell, and 96 days were fine. The lowest temperature occurred on the 3rd of June, 1837, when it fell to 33°.

NATURAL PHENOMENA INDICATIVE OF WEATHER.—Dr. Forster very correctly observes, that though the obscured and enlarged appearance of *the Stars* denotes the approach of rain, because such appearance shews that the atmosphere is surcharged with watery vapour, as was long previously observed, and even by Virgil; yet it is nevertheless true, that previously to a change to rain, and while the barometer is sinking, some of the most clear skies are seen. On such occasions the stars' firmament is unusually clear and sparkling, and the Milky Way surpassingly light. This, as Sir Isaac Newton observed, is immediately before the change; rain-clouds soon form, and rain rapidly follows this excessive transparency.

THE PANSY or HEART'S-EASE, such as we see its varieties now in our gardens, is a creation of modern floricultural art. These varieties are all sprung from the trivial wild flower that bears the same name, and is found so generally in our fields. We have seen these introduced into the garden, and in its richer soil and warmer temperature attain a size gigantic, if comparison be made with its stature when in a state of nature. The seed saved from this cultivated plant produced seedlings differing still further, and more improved, from the wild original; and we have little doubt, if the experiment had not been interrupted, that by degrees, after two or three more generations of seedlings, the progeny would have been iden-

tical with the garden Pansy in its most improved form. We mention this in opposition to an opinion we have heard maintained that this flower is a hybrid.

In *The Gardener's Labyrinth*, published in 1586, under the authorship of H. Dethycke, it is simply mentioned as the Heart's-ease, which seems its oldest English name; but Gerarde, writing more fully ten years later, says it was also known as Pansies, Live-in-idleness, Cull-me-to-you, and Three-faces-in-a-hood. Let us indulge in a vagrant mood, and discourse more fully upon all these titles of affection,— all testifying, that even in earliest times it was a popular flower.

Pansies is a corruption of the French word *Pensées*—

thoughts,—a derivation Shakespeare admits when he makes Ophelia say—

"And there is Pansies, that's for thoughts."

Even the grammar here is not objectionable, for there is no doubt that Panseys, or Thoughts, was the name applied to the flower.

Live-in-idleness is not the name it usually received, even in Gerarde's time, for Shakespeare, his contemporary, writes thus of it:—

"Mark'd I where the bolt of Cupid fell:
It fell upon a little western flower,—
Before, milk-white, now purple with love's wound,—
And maidens call it Love-in-idleness.
The juice of it on sleeping eye-lids laid,
Will make a man or woman madly dote
Upon the next live creature that it sees."

A superstition that gives a clue to this name, popular even now in some parts of England.

Cull-me-to-you was a name inviting a gathering, and well suited for a love gift when modesty forbade a bolder invitation.

"No word spake she; and yet the flower
She threw, was 'Cull-me-to-your-bower.'"

Three-faces-in-a-hood alludes to the form of the flower, the under petals, over-hung by the two larger upper ones, bearing some resemblance to what the name describes. But some carried the resemblance even further, and one old herbalist writes indignantly—"This is that herb which such physicians as are licensed to blaspheme by authority, without danger of having their tongues burned through with an hot iron, called an herb of the Trinity."

Whichever name be selected for this our favourite flower, we recommend it especially to our readers. The beauty and long succession of its blooms, the endless variety of these, the fragrance of some, and the cheapness of all, recommend it strongly for more general cultivation, and with an assurance that it will give *heart's-ease* to the grower.

It is but recently admitted among Florists' Flowers;

and we think that Hogg, in 1833, was the first who wrote upon it as belonging to the class; and he begins by saying, "Several florists have *lately* turned their attention to the culture of Heartease." Many have written since upon the characteristics which belong to it when really a superior flower, but Mr. Glenny has gathered together all the good suggestions of his predecessors, adding others of his own, and we reprint them with such alterations as we consider desirable.

1. Each bloom should be nearly perfectly circular flat, and very smooth at the edge; every notch, or unevenness, being a blemish.

2. The petals should be thick, and of a rich velvety texture.

3. Whatever may be the colours, the principal, or ground colour of the three lower petals, should be alike whether it be white, yellow, straw colour, plain, fringed, or blotched, there should not in these three petals be a shade difference in the principal colour; and the white, yellow, or straw colour should be pure.

4. Whatever may be the character of the marks or darker pencillings on the ground colour, they should be bright, dense, distinct, and retain their character, without running or flushing, that is, mixing with the ground colour.

5. The two upper petals should be perfectly uniform, whether dark or light, or fringed, or blotched. The two petals immediately under them should be alike; and the lower petal, as before observed, must have the same ground colour and character as the two above it; and the pencilling or marking of the eye in the three lower petals must not break through to the edges.

6. If flowers are equal in other respects, the larger, if not the coarser, is the better; but no flower should be shown that is under one inch and a half across.

7. Ragged or notched edges, crumpled petals, indentures on the petal, indistinct markings or pencillings, and flushed or run-colours, are great blemishes; but if a bloom has one ground colour to the lower petal and another colour to the side ones, or if it has two shades of ground colour at all, it is not a show flower. The yellow within the eye is not considered ground colour.—*Glenny's Properties of Flowers.*

THE FRUIT-GARDEN.

PEARS.—Believing, as we do, that two-thirds of the readers of this work esteem good pears in the winter dessert, it will become a duty to recur somewhat frequently to their culture; for of all our fruits the pear seems best fitted to adapt itself to the controlling power of man. This arises in a great degree from its natural longevity and hardihood.

In former days the culture of this fruit was very imperfectly understood, all being comprised in a prim system of winter pruning, which sought more to enslave nature than to assist her. Such an effort ended as might have been anticipated by a mind unfettered by the customs of a bygone age. The trees proved uncontrollable in spite of the neat spurring system of those redoubtable sons of the soil, with their cut-and-dry recipes.

In due time it occurred to the minds of many that the action of the root was a point for consideration, and that there really might be such a thing as an over-powerful action of root; and that this quondam friend might, under certain circumstances, assume the attitude of a foe. Not all who plant pears plant for their heirs merely; these are days of quick return in the commercial world, and, indeed, everything British seems likely to partake of this character. No wonder, therefore, that horticulture comes in for its share.

The late Mr. Loudon, in his popular magazine, was the first to open a medium for the free exchange of gardening opinions; and here was an arena furnished in which the lovers of progress in horticulture might exchange opinions freely, and wherein old and time-honoured opinions might be submitted to the test of science.

In those days, a Mr. Robert Hiver, whose whereabouts, we fancy, never came to light, wrote a paper on fruit-trees, which at once dealt a severe blow at prescriptive routine; and we well remember what an impression it made on many ingenious friends in the gardening way, by the boldness and originality of the opinions held forth. Mr. Hiver went at once to the fountain head; he showed by past experience that although expensive borders of compost, and laborious systems of winter pruning, looked very elaborate and pains-taking on paper, that they had ever failed in attaining the object in view; and that to understand the subject aright, we must "begin at the beginning," or, in other words, take a lesson or two from the school of nature. The dubbed thorn in the hedge was brought into comparison, both root and branch, with the unpruned, unmolested thorn-tree, covered in profusion with its crimson treasures; here it was made manifest that a prepared compost below, and severe mutilation above, had certainly made a good hedge, but by no means been productive of haws.

In a very short period the whole question of fruit culture underwent a severe scrutiny; and although many a poor wight had the mortification afterwards to find his elaborate paper enclosing a patch of butter, still he might have the gratification to consider that he had kept the question warm, and furnished to others, if not genuine ideas, at least the germs of them.

From those days to these in which we are living, both science and practice have been brought to bear continually on this matter; and the subject of the present narrative has fallen in for an unusual share of consideration on both sides. One rather remarkable doctrine was long adhered to by the *old school* gardeners. They held, that what is termed "stopping" had a tendency to strengthen the tree. Now, if such were right, the practice of the present day of stopping over-gross shoots, in order to weaken them, is fearfully wrong. The idea was, however, absurd; trees strengthen by enlargement and extension; and stopping is surely averse to such extension.

At this period the trained pears require and deserve more attention than most of our trained fruit-trees, their tendency to produce spray being almost unbounded during the month of June, especially if planted in soils too deep, or too rich. Rainy periods, too, exercise considerable influence over pear-trees, especially young ones, which in many cases seem capable of taking in almost as great an amount of watery matter as some of our willows. All this points plainly to the necessity of severe restriction at the root.

With regard to thinning and stopping the spray, where trees are in a healthy medium state, the best practice is to rub away at once all gross robbers which are not required to cover the nakedness of the branches. These, if suffered to remain until their succulent leaves are developed, will have called an undue amount of new and gluttonous fibres into being; for we may rest assured, that as the top is so the root is, or soon will be. In all

ordinary cases the production of spray is a tolerably sure index. After disposing of the above shoots, the whole of the spray should undergo a revision, and where crowded a thinning out must take place betimes, if only to admit light freely to the embryo blossom-buds on the natural spurs; for these will already be in course of organization, and light is indispensable. If a very severe thinning-out becomes necessary, we advise an immediate *root-pruning*. It may alarm some persons to talk of root-pruning in June, and certainly, where there is fruit swelling on the tree, the process requires some caution. A very small amount of curtailment will suffice at this period; indeed, opening a trench at the very extremities of the roots, or any portion of them, and suffering it to remain open for a few weeks, will alone produce the desired result. Without such precautions the cultivator will only be deceiving himself; but be it remembered, we are speaking of pears which have been improperly planted—that is to say, planted without a sufficient amount of root control.

In thinning out the young spray (preparatory to what we have termed, in previous papers of THE COTTAGE GARDENER, the tying-down system) regard must be constantly had to the character of the young shoots, as we have often urged. Even as early as the month of May at least *two* distinct kinds of wood may be distinguished, varying somewhat in colour in various kinds, yet still retaining some characters in common, the principal one of which is, shortness in the joints, or the part between two buds, termed by botanists the internode. The earliest made wood is generally the best, because most mature, and probably through its monopoly of the *true* sap of the former year; for be it understood that much of the late made spray—commonly termed "watery wood"—is the mere production of the sudden impulses communicated by rainy weather, bringing into a state of solubility manurial or organic matters existing in the soil, and facilitating the extension of the young fibres, by softening down obstructive matters.

As much, therefore, of the young spray must be disbudded as will admit a fair portion of sunlight to all parts of the tree; and this done, the remainder had better be suffered to grow unmolested for a few weeks; for any stronger proceedings would cause many of the embryo fruit-buds for future years to burst; and this it is that causes many gardeners to leave their trees in a rude state until late in the summer—thus damaging the welfare of the fruit-buds as to shade, for fear of their being over-excited by a too sudden influx of sap. How plainly this shows the want of a proper amount of root control, which has been so repeatedly urged in the pages of THE COTTAGE GARDENER.

Let us press on those who have trellises or walls to cover, and training by system to carry out, the propriety of attending in due time to the early growths of their young trees. The loss of a year or two, or of many square feet of expensive walls or trellises, is an object of too much importance to be overruled by a short-sighted economy.　　　　　R. ERRINGTON.

THE FLOWER-GARDEN.

SPRING BULBS.—The leaves of all our spring bulbs are now in their full prime, digesting food suitable for the production of blossoms next year. Yes, next year! We often plume ourselves on our skilful management of forced bulbs in pots, because we seldom fail of having them "very fine indeed this season;" and it seems almost unkind in a public writer to disturb this prevailing opinion of our own proficiency; and I should be the last to mention it, had it not been that at this season we are all of us liable to overlook or neglect the proper treatment of these bulbs, by cutting off their leaves to make room for other things, or by removing them care-lessly from the flower-beds and borders to the reserve-ground just at the very time when the necessary supply of matter, for giving a fine bloom the following year, is being stored in the bulbs through the agency of the leaves. This explanation reveals the fact—for a fact, and a great one too, it certainly is—that the bloom of this spring was not altogether due to the care we might have taken of the roots or bulbs since we potted them last autumn, but rather to the care that was taken of the leaves last May and June. If it were not so, we could not bloom them so fine in moss and in water-glasses as in a good compost. Therefore, " it stands to reason," as we say in the country, that if we wish for a good crop of flowers from spring bulbs next year, we must ripen off their leaves with great care now; and this is the proper time to give liquid manure to such bulbs.

In the spring border which I mentioned last week, the bulbs have had it all their own way these three, four, and five years back; and all those that were forced here this winter and spring are now added to them in rings as formerly. The first eighteen inches of this border is occupied in summer with the blue *Nemophila;* the seeds being sown first in a row four inches from the edge, and again fifteen inches from the edge; but this cannot be in a continuous row, because the patches of bulbs come in the way. Therefore, only the spare ground between the bulbs is sown; but the sowing is continued in a straight line; and by the time the bulbs' leaves are all dead—say between midsummer and the beginning of July—the two rows of *Nemophila* spread themselves so as to meet in the middle; and just in this middle, and at this very time—the first of July—another row of Nemophila is sown to succeed the first two rows, which in our case are put in on the first of May, " or thereabouts." To come in sooner, they might be sown as early as the last week in March; but we do not want them in bloom here till about the middle of July, and we sow accordingly. The sowing for autumn succession of this Nemophila succeeds best when done in the first week in July. Sometimes there will be a blank of a fortnight or three weeks between the time when the first-of-May sowing is done blooming and the commence-ment of that of the July sowing; but as that blank occurs near the end of August, the loss is not felt when every other bed and border is in full prime. Seven or eight degrees of frost does not harm the blue Nemophila; and I have seen it peeping out through four inches of snow in November, and still full of bloom.

From early in May, when most of the spring bulbs are over, and before the Nemophila comes in, all the spare places on this border are occupied with a very bright pink annual, only a few inches high, and which is so accommodating as to be easily removed from place to place until it is in full bloom. I mentioned it the other day as one of the catchflies, *Silene pendula.* There is not a brighter plant in England for the flower-garden in May than this; and, strange to say, not one of which the management is less understood, or, at least, less attended to. It sows itself in the autumn; and on very poor or very light land it may be removed into the flower-beds in March; but on rich, or damp, or heavy soil, it should be transplanted from the seed-bed in February, and again in March, also in April, and finally in May, as the flowers are just beginning to open. All this moving is to check the luxuriance of the leaves, and may be performed, of course, in the reserve-ground; or, what is better, make up a bed for it of very poor stuff early in the spring in the reserve-garden, and there let it remain till the beginning of May, when it may be planted anywhere, either as a rock, vase, bed, or border plant. I must really apologise for such minute details for what is, after all, a mere weed—but a very pretty one; and I have seen it so badly used as to cause its con-

demnation altogether, and that not a hundred miles from St. Paul's, where one would expect to see a better sys tem in play.

The Editor and Mr. Appleby, with their florist friends, will think it strange enough to hear that *Rex rubrorum* is my favourite red tulip, and that I have a hundred of them on this border, and as many of the following *Prince de Ligne,* fine single yellow; *Aimable rouge,* a very dwarf single red; *Turnsole,* orange and yellow; *Marriage de ma Fille,* variegated; *Golden standard, Royal stand ard,* and *Claremond,* red and rose; and *Purpur Croon,* or the Purple Crown. This last is an extraordinary fine tulip of the early and forcing class; and if prices were given for the largest and strongest tulips, this would be sure to come in first. I am almost certain that this and Rex Rubrorum, with probably many others, should not be taken up more than once in six or seven years. No doubt the finer tulips of the florist class would soon run riot if thus left undisturbed in a congenial soil; but let this early flowering class have beds or borders of deep, light, rich soil, and depend upon it we shall beat the Dutchmen out of the market, for them at least. The *Duc Van Thol,* single and double, do not seem to do so well, at least they have not improved so much as the others. Out of a great number of sorts the above are the best for forcing; and really, when one sees how simply cast-off bulbs may be usefully employed in a garden, it does seem unaccountable how people can afford to be so extravagant as to let them slip through their fingers.

Of *Hyacinths* we flowered about a thousand in this border, but not more than twenty or two dozen sorts, every one of which were first forced. We also flowered six hundred hyacinths, in pots plunged in some beds and borders near the house. The latter were as good as " mixed hyacinths" generally are; but they were beaten over and over again by the same sorts which were not disturbed for the last five years in this spring border; and two sorts only revert to the wild state, because, as I suppose, the soil does not suit them. Nobody can say how long a Hyacinth bulb will live; and I believe I have already told that a gentleman in this neighbour-hood has four bulbs, which he bought in Haarlem in 1822, and they flowered this year as strongly as ever, and his flower-beds and borders are half filled with their progeny, besides distributing many bulbs every year to his friends and neighbours. I could never make out that one hyacinth is better than another for forcing; and I believe it is all moonshine to say otherwise. It is true that the dealers put certain marks to them in their lists to show that this sort is more suitable for water glasses, that for culture, and so forth; and some years I have been so wicked as to take the very opposite sorts for the same purposes—from which, and from other actual experiments, I am led to believe that we often allow ourselves to be swayed more by the dictates of—no-matter-what—rather than be guided by natural laws, or the tests of practice and experiments. Therefore it is that I shall forbear giving a long list of the best hyacinths for spring borders and for forcing.

Not so, however, with the next family—the *Daffodils,* of which there are vast numbers very difficult to deter-mine or describe as species, or seedling varieties; but for forcing I have them reduced to five sorts: the *Double Roman* being the earliest; then *Grand Monarch,* fol-lowed by *Soleil d'Or, States General,* and *Bazelman Major.* These, with six other sorts of *Narcissus,* which do not force well, are all that we cultivate of this family, or rather which we do not cultivate at all, but let them do for themselves, and that they do right earnestly; for their tops are now so heavy that we are obliged to tie them up.

The single and double *Jonquils,* of which there are smaller and larger varieties, belong to the last family, being a species of daffodil, they increase like chives, and are excellent for cut flowers.

Several varieties of the *Crown Imperial* bulbs, backed-up this border in a line of patches, between which a good selection of *Pæonies* are planted. These Pœonies come in as the Crown imperials go out of bloom, and before they are quite over the *Bulbous iris* comes in. This is one of the best for cut flowers, and its long spike may be cut off as soon as the first bloom is bursting the bud. *Christmas rose* in patches, *Snow drop, Snow flake, Star of Bethlehem*, but no *Crocus, Poppy*, and *Wood anemones, Turban ranunculus*, with *Erica herbacea*, make up the rest of this spring border; and they show, conclusively, that to grow large quantities of a few selected very common things is the way to make a fine show, in contradiction to the old rule of having " a collection."

D. BEATON.

GREENHOUSE AND WINDOW GARDENING.

FANCY GERANIUMS : *An additional word on Cuttings.*—In adverting last week to the time, &c., of taking cuttings, no notice was taken of the propriety of *drying* the base of each cutting a little before inserting them in the suitable soil. They do not require this so much as the more succulent groups of the family, but still they are all the better for it. There is, however, a little secret as to the manner of doing this. A gentleman amateur employed as a writer in a leading horticultural periodical, gave specific directions about shading the cuttings of geraniums after planting them, and drying the cut ends before inserting them ; but in the process of drying the poor leaves became so flagged and withered, that the cuttings afterwards would have got on rather better without them than with them, roots and leaves being *then* respectively protruded—chiefly, however, at the expense of the matter stored up in the cutting, just as is seen developed in the case of cuttings inserted in a border out-of-doors. This gentleman seemed much surprised that batches of these succulent plants were fit to be potted off or transplanted that were cuttings ten days before, and that without a paraphernalia of shading and unshading ; whilst others were being inserted with their bases dried to his heart's content, and yet every leaf was fresh and vigorous. His cuttings had been treated according to his own system for a month, and were showing but little signs of vigour, and all, or chiefly, owing to the injury done to the leaves. The drying of the base of all succulent cuttings is useful, because it prevents that free absorption of moisture that would be apt to issue in the disagreeable process termed "damping-off." With the *fancy* group this drying had better take place in the *shade ;* and whilst the root ends are exposed the tops and leaves should be sprinkled with water, and covered with a leaf to prevent evaporation. The less succulent varieties may thus be exposed for a few hours, the more succulent for a longer period. Any absorption of moisture that will be inhaled by the leaves will be different in its effects from moisture absorbed by the base of the cutting. The more healthy the leaves are at first, and the more vigorous they are maintained afterwards, the sooner will roots be formed. No after-care can compensate for inattention to this simple matter at first. Our seeming digression will not be without its use, as with many this will be a chief time for obtaining and inserting cuttings. The hints as to keeping the leaves fresh will be applicable to all cuttings. When brought from a long distance, in whatever way carried, unless in a close box, they will be apt to suffer ; and thousands of cuttings among our amateur friends are lost in their endeavours to restore them, as

many for this purpose place them in a vessel of water, and when the leaves raise their heads they imagine that all is right, and success certain, though the distending of the stem with mere water is ever apt to produce a damping-off *dropsical habit.* The best plan is to restore the vigour to the leaf, by making *itself*, and part of the stem, instead of the cut end. the points of absorption ; and this is most efficiently done by laying the cuttings down in a damp place, and sprinkling their tops with water.

Having adverted to the soil necessary for propagation, we now proceed to indicate

3. *The Soil suited for their growth.*—This should be light and rich ; the following, with good drainage, will answer admirably :—Two parts light brown fibry loam ; one part heath soil ; one part leaf-mould, well decomposed, and dried so as to exclude all insects and worms ; one part cowdung, two years old, and dried ; one part silver sand ; one part small, but not dusty, charcoal.

Cowdung is the best manure to incorporate with the soil, but it should be at the least two years old, and well dried before using it. It is not to be supposed that every amateur can have all these ingredients at his elbow ; but we believe the nearer he approximates to them the greater will be his success. Sandy loam—such as that procurable from a road-side—with either a little leaf-mould or cowdung, will grow them very well. One thing, however, should be borne in mind by the uninitiated—the change from the soil used in propagating and that for growing should not be *sudden :* the calf is not at once transferred from its mother's milk to oil-cake. In vegetation, transitions likewise must be gradual. The first soil for potting, after propagating, should be light rather than rich, the richness being added by degrees.

4. *Temperature.*—Unless when cuttings are struck in spring, bottom-heat will be unnecessary. During the first potting *then*, a mild bottom-heat will be an advantage, as they will grow the faster. Cuttings taken off in the end of summer, and nearly in autumn, will require no bottom-heat, but merely to be kept close ; and should be potted off and well hardened, by standing upon boards before winter. Housing, or placing under glass, should be effected *earlier* than with other kinds, as they are very impatient of cold drenching rains. During winter they should be near the glass, and have plenty of air, and a temperature from 40° to 45°, using as little fire-heat as possible. Those intended to continue blooming during the winter, will require a temperature of from 45° to 50° ; a few degrees more will benefit them, if joined to light and air. In a warm conservatory they answer well for winter blooming. When kept at a temperature of 40° the flower-buds will not open. Plants intended to bloom early in spring and summer, should have a temperature of 50° during the day, in the end of February and beginning of March, with 45° at night—as it is desirable to grow the shoots before hot sunny weather comes. These as they grow ought to be well trained, and then hardened by exposure to more air and sunlight before the flower-buds appear, which will cause them to come more vigorous and strong. Altogether, in the matter of heat, they require rather more *coddling* than even their rivals, the fine prize varieties, and a great deal more than the hardy scarlets.

5. *Cutting down the plants in the autumn.*—This should be done early, that the plants may have time to break and ripen their short shoots before winter. Few, unless some of the strongest varieties, such as *Nosegay*, will bear cutting down so close as the prize geraniums ; as if the stems are very hard they do not break fresh buds freely. The more weak growing kinds, such as *Anais* and *Ibraham Pacha*, ought never to be cut down at all, but merely to be thinned of all the blossom shoots and buds, and encouraged to grow instead of to bloom, by

keeping them closer afterwards, and in a moister atmosphere. Even the strong growing kinds which may bo cut down, should not be so much dried previously as is suitable for other geraniums. After being cut down, or merely shortened, according to the habit of growth, the plants should be kept drier at the roots than usual, until they break afresh; though, as we have already said, a moist atmosphere will be an advantage, obtained by sprinklings from the syringe, and damping the walls, and a slight shading. If the pots in July and August are fully two feet from the glass, the shading will not be necessary. For nearly all purposes we prefer *diffused* light to *shaded* light; but in late autumn and early spring, light is so valuable that we would have the plants as near the glass as possible, though when the sun burst out we were forced to shade in consequence.

6. *Potting and placing in flowering-pots.*—Much that might have been said upon this head has already been adverted to. To obtain early flowering-plants in April and May, plants raised from cuttings early in the spring, repeatedly stopped and shifted, and prevented flowering, should bo finally stopped in the end of July, and put into their flowering-pots in August, after removing a part of the old soil, thinned and trained out into the desirable shape, kept close until the roots are working freely in the new material, and then hardened by exposure to air before setting them in their winter quarters, which must be done before they are subjected to heavy autumn rains. Plants that have bloomed in spring and summer should be cut *down* or merely stopped and deprived of their flowering-buds in July, taken out of their old soil when fresh growth has commenced, have their roots slightly pruned before repotting in smaller pots, encouraged to grow by a rather close, moist atmosphere, and transferred to their blooming-pots early in September. Successions may be obtained by preventing flowering, and repotting in January, February, and March, and they would thus keep on flowering until the spring-struck plants would be ready to come in in winter. Eight inches is a good medium size for blooming-pots.

7. *Training.*—This is all a matter of taste; round flattish cones look very nicely; a cone more pyramidal in its outline, might look better. Unless with the stronger growing kinds, great height could not be reached except with old plants.

8. *Watering.*—This must be given according to the general principles previously referred to. When making their wood, weak manure-water from a solution of cow-dung will be useful, but it should be desisted from when it is desirable that the wood should be hardened before the formation of the flower-buds. When these are formed the manure waterings may again be resorted to. Though the small growing kinds will not want water so often as the strong growing kinds, the want of water will be more injurious, and allowing them to flag repeatedly will be next to fatal.

9. *Insects.*—They, like their congeners, are exposed to hosts—green, red, and grey. The best prevention is good cultivation, and a liberal use of the syringe when growing. If a *red spider* appears, syringe with sulphur-water, laying the plant upon its side, and keeping it in the shade for a day, dipping the head of the plant repeatedly in clear water, and syringing it again before restoring it to the house. If a *thrip* is seen, adopt the same course, only using weak laurel-water instead. If one *green fly* is seen, you may calculate on scores not being far off; smoke at once, but gently; it is always safest to repeat the dose often. If you patiently wait until you see scores of either of those insects upon a leaf, you may as well turn the plant to the rubbish-heap, as give yourself trouble, and incur expense for tobacco, &c.; for when so bad, the cure and the disease will prove nearly equally fatal, so far as being gratified with the sight of a luxuriant plant is concerned. R. FISH.

HOTHOUSE DEPARTMENT.

EXOTIC ORCHIDACEÆ.

WHEN we first began the course of orchid culture, it was proposed to give lists of such as are proper to grow in baskets, on blocks of wood, and in pots. We feel quite sure such lists will be useful to all growers of orchids, but more especially to amateurs and young beginners And in order that those lists may be still more useful, we shall give short popular descriptions, such as will enable the amateur to select the most desirable plants in proportion to the size of his house or houses, and the extent to which he chooses to go in purchasing them. We shall also give the price at which each may be procured at any respectable nursery; such prices being for medium-sized plants. As we consider of orchids, as well as any other tribe of plants, it is far better to grow a few really good species with handsome flowers, or with very sweet scent, to compensate for the lack of bright colours, we shall only name such as are really worth growing, either on account of the beauty of their bloom or their agreeable fragrance.

PLANTS REQUIRING BASKETS, OR WHICH THRIVE BEST IN THEM.

Acineta Barkerii (Barker's A.).—A handsome species producing long spikes of yellow flowers. Native of Mexico. The flower-stems push through the bottom of the basket, and hang down frequently a foot or eighteen inches below it. 31s 6d.

Acineta Humboldtii (Humboldt's A.).—This is also a noble species, flowering in the same stylo as the preceding. The flowers are larger, of a deep chocolate, spotted with reddish crimson. Native of Venezuela. 42s.

Acropera Loddigesii (Loddige's A.).—A curious and pretty plant, producing, when well grown, numerous pendulous racemes of pale yellow flowers, spotted with purple; each flower being curiously formed so as to look something like a boiled cockle. 10s. 6d. There is another species named *Lutea*, but it is not so handsome. 10s 6d.

Aerides affine (Related Air-plant).—The whole of this genus is exceedingly lovely. This species is of the most delicate rosy hue. The racemes of flowers are frequently branched, and sometimes two feet long. Native of Sylhet. 63s.

Aerides Brookii (Sir R. Brookes' A.).—This is perhaps the most lovely of this lovely tribe; it grows strongly, and flowers freely. The foliage is handsome, of a glaucous (milky green) hue. The colour of the flowers is varied, from a bright purple labellum to white in the sepals and petals. It is also very fragrant. Native of Bombay. 42s.

Aerides maculosum (Spotted Air-plant).—Bright green long leaves with light coloured flowers, spotted all over with purple, and a large purple blotch on the labellum. This is a dwarf growing species, with an exquisite fragrance when in flower. Native of Bombay. 105s.

Aerides odoratum (Fragrant Air-plant).—This old species has several first-rate qualities to recommend it. It flowers more profusely than any other, it grows more freely, lasts longer in bloom, and has the finest fragrance of perhaps any plant known. The flowers are of the most delicate flesh-colour, tinged with rose. Native of the East Indies. 42s.

Aerides quinquevulnera (Five-spotted A.).—A strong growing species, producing generally two spikes of flowers on each stem. Each sepal and petal has a distinct purplish lilac spot near the top, thus bearing five spots, hence its specific name; the ground colour is white speckled with purple, the top of the lip is green, the two side lobes pale pink, and the middle lobe of a deep crimson. It is slightly fragrant, and is a fine species. Native of the Philippine Isles. 105s.

Aerides roseum (Rose-coloured Air-plant).—This is a lovely species, with the stems and leaves spotted slightly with brownish purple; a dwarf grower, with flowers of a rich rose colour. Native of Java. 105s.

Aerides tesselatum (Chequered Air-plant).—A scarce species, with flowers lined and streaked with green, white, and purple. Native of the East Indies.

Aerides virens (Deep-green Air-plant).—The leaves of this plant are of a lively green; ground of the flower delicate peach, spotted with rich purple; labellum or lip spotted with crimson; very fragrant. Native of Java. 63s.

Such are the characteristics of this truly lovely genus. It will be observed they all come from the East Indies, and consequently require the hottest house. The baskets should be filled with sphagnum, or white bog moss, which should not be pressed down tightly. Whilst the plants are young and small they should be suspended near the roof, but when large they may be set upon pots elevated, so as still to be near the glass. There are plants of *Aerides odoratum* in some of the best collections so large as to measure five feet high, and four feet through. We have seen a specimen with more than sixty spikes upon it.

(To be continued.)

ROUTINE CULTURE FOR JUNE.—During this month, orchids, with very few exceptions, will be growing vigorously, and will require a proportionate increase of moisture. The first thing every morning let the pipes, walls, and paths be thoroughly wetted, so as to create a large volume of *atmospheric moisture*. Then look over the plants in pots, and water freely all that are growing and appear dry, observing that *Cattleyas* and *Laelias* require less water than most of the others. Examine the baskets of *Stanhopeas*, and of similar plants, and if found to be light and dry let them be dipped up to the leaves in a cistern in the house, the water to be new milk-warm. Let the peat or moss be thoroughly wetted. The *syringe* must then be used freely, especially to the plants on logs. By the time this is done, the sun, on fine mornings, will be shining brightly. The *shades* then must be let down to protect the leaves from its strong burning rays. The *thermometer* in the India house may be allowed to rise to 85° the maximum, and then air ought to be given by opening the ventilators, care being taken that no strong current of cold air passes directly upon or over the plants. Lay this down as a law, like that of the Medes and Persians, which altered not, that *the plants must be dry once a day*. By letting in the dry air of the external atmosphere this will be effected. Towards the middle of the afternoon you will find the paths and walls, and the plants, completely dried. Then close the ventilators, wet the walls, &c., and renew the internal moisture to the air. This will, as it were, be giving the plants their second supply of food for the day. In the evening syringe the blocks, and close up the house in a comfortable moist state for the night. Allow the temperature to fall during that season of repose, and in the morning you will find the plants looking happy and comfortable, and growing freely, to reward you for all your care. During the whole of this month this daily treatment must be faithfully followed.

Should any of the early growing species have fully formed their annual growth, place them in a situation by themselves, either in the same house or, which is far better, in another cooler and drier house. Plants that are in flower would preserve their bloom much longer if they too could be placed in a similar situation; but as soon as they are out of flower, if they have not fully completed their yearly growth, let them be removed into their moist quarters again.

FLORISTS' FLOWERS.

PANSEY.—These cheerful flowers will now be in grand feather, and if intended for exhibition will require shading from the midday sun, and protecting from wind and rain. We are very partial to layering the long strong shoots, as they, by obtaining a fresh supply of feeders, thrive amazingly, besides affording a supply of nice cuttings from the centre. Put in cuttings of all the sorts worth propagating, in the way we have often directed; that is, short cuttings placed under a hand-glass in a shady place, but not under the drip of a hedge or trees.

PINKS.—This class of florists' flowers are particular favourites with us; we think them a very genteel race, and then they smell so sweet! They are now preparing to reward us for the pains we have bestowed upon them, by sending up their slender flower-stems, calling forth more care to protect them from wind and heavy rains, which otherwise would mar their beauty greatly. Pipings, as they are termed, may yet be put in, either under hand-glasses or in pots placed under glass upon a gentle hotbed.　　　　　　T. APPLEBY.

THE KITCHEN-GARDEN.

CAULIFLOWERS.—Select and mark for seed a few of the handsomest and finest quality, that is to say, those that have short thick stems, and well-shaped smooth leaves, with the flower showing milk-white and perfectly firm; free from spot, blemish, or frothiness. Spring-sown plants, which have been pricked out, should be taken up with a trowel, and planted in rather cold and shady situations at this season, such as on the north side of late-sown peas, between the asparagus-beds, when ample room has been allowed, or on a north border. Another sowing should also be made, if there is space to spare, at this season. It is best to sow thinly in drills, and to hoe out for the crop to remain, without transplanting; or a part of the plants may be taken up carefully, when thinning, and planted, as the check thus given would secure a succession if well supplied with water. Chimney soot-water, with soapsuds, is a capital stimulator for cauliflowers, as well as a protection against the destructive maggot to which this excellent vegetable is so liable throughout the summer months.

SEA-KALE.—To secure good sea-kale for the next winter and spring, it must be attended to at this season. In the first place, if the crowns have not had their final thinning of all small and spurious shoots, no time should be lost in performing this operation; and that too with great care, so as not to break about and loosen the shoots intended to remain, or their leaves. The soil about them, as previously directed, should, whilst there is space not covered with its foliage, be constantly loosened by hand-scarifying, and manure-water should be applied in abundance. Any kind of sewerage or cesspool-water is valuable for this purpose; or any liquid brewed from the excrements of pigs, poultry, horse, cow, deer, or sheep, to which soot and salt added is an improvement. Guano-liquid is also well known as a good stimulant, but if any of the first-named manures are procurable, the expense of guano may very properly be saved; as we consider no work well done, at any time or season, if waste of any kind is permitted, and if those things which we have at command are not turned to good account. Economy in every respect must always be placed foremost in the mind's eye. Soot and salt may at all times be added with certain advantage to any of the Brassica family; and *asparagus* and *sea-kale* especially delight in it. The stronger the plants are, of course, the stronger the liquid may be applied. No one would allow a child to make use of beef, beer, and brandy, in which a brewer's drayman, or other strong hearty working biped, taking 16 or 18 hours of daily exercise, might indulge.

ROUTINE WORK.—Supposing ere this the earliest bank of cabbage to be cleared of its leaves and stumps, and all turned to good account, the ground should be forked up into ridges, if not already done, and on the summit of the bank a row of *Scarlet runners* may be planted, to be dwarfed by stopping to four feet sticks, or string, and stakes. A row or two of *Dwarf kidney beans* should be planted on the warmest side; and a row or two of the *Dwarf Fan*, or the *American dwarf pea*, sown on the coldest and most shady side; or a row or two of *lettuce* seed may be drilled in, to thin out, to stand for crops. See that the main crops of *carrots, parsnips, onions,* and *early turnips,* are thinned to a sufficient distance; and that every vacancy is filled up by transplanting, taking the best plants from where they can be spared, and performing the operation with care,—very little check will then occur. Hoe and hand-drag, or scarify, the soil between the rows in suitable weather as often as possible.

Sow the early variety of *turnips* in succession a little and often. *Radishes,* in variety, and *small salads* should at this season be sown also in small portions, often repeated, and in a kindly preparation, on a northern aspect, if tender fine-flavoured salad is required.

MUSHROOMS.—If abundant gatherings of short-stemmed firm weighty mushrooms are wished, care must now be taken. A cold situation, shady, and free from draught, must be maintained; and a kindly evaporation, by often sprinkling the floors of the shed, or cave, or other structure, with cold water; the beds of course excepted, as they should at all times be sprinkled very lightly with *tepid* water, about milk warm; and a little clear liquid manure intermixed with it, brewed from sheep, deer, or cow-dung.

MELONS and CUCUMBERS, in a fruit-bearing state, should be well encouraged also with liquid-manure.

JAMES BARNES.

MISCELLANEOUS INFORMATION.

OUR VILLAGE WALKS.
By the authoress of "My Flowers."

THE first appearance of a swallow is a harbinger, indeed, of spring: yet I was forcibly reminded, a few days ago, of the well-known proverb, that "one swallow does not make a summer:" for nothing could be more dreary and wintry than the day in which I first observed these favourite birds skimming, like lightning, over the water, as I passed along the banks of a fish-pond, quite unprepared for the sight of anything connected with summer skies. The cold, bleak east wind was blowing strongly, and there had been two days of heavy rain; the bursting trees looked chilled and comfortless, and the springing grass was so soaked with wet that it drooped heavily to the earth beneath its burden, and the beautiful May flowers, just opening, seemed as if they had mistaken the season, and were blooming in dark November. Yet in spite of all these discouragements, led by their wondrous instinct, came the swallows; and cold and wet as it was, they seemed to promise that sunshine would soon appear. Their rapid and graceful movements always please; and they sometimes wheel and sweep so near us that it seems as if we could almost catch them in their sportive flight. It is remarkable, that nothing should be positively known of their winter residence; they go, and they come again—but whither they go, and whence they come, has never been fully ascertained. The hand of God guides them across the waste of waters to sunnier climes; they have no compass by which to steer their course; they can take no "observation," nor trace their way by the glittering stars; yet they go straight and safely to their appointed place; and at the fitting time they return to their former habitations. What a reproach to the dull and senseless heart of man is conveyed by means of the migratory habits of birds! "The turtle, and the crane, and the swallow observe the time of their coming; but my people know not the judgment of the Lord." They obey the instinctive impulse given by the Creator, and they go and come at His command; but *we* resist the influences of the Spirit of God—we are not "obedient to the heavenly vision," and we shut our eyes and hearts against the commandments of the Lord.

It is amusing and interesting to watch the proceedings of the swallows when they take possession of their summer home. The curiously constructed nests seem formed by magic; and when the feeding period begins it is really wonderful to see the rapidity with which the parent deposits the supply, as he skims past the entrance of the nest: he scarcely appears to touch it with his beak, and the most observant eye cannot perceive the action.

Their fondness for the haunts of men, and their confiding disposition, surpasses that of the rook. I have seen their nests pulled down day after day, when forming them close to an entrance door, and yet the little persevering creatures resolutely built them up again, until bunches of furze or thorns were so fixed to the spot as effectually to baffle their attempts. What a beautiful picture of peace and holy security the social habits of the swallow offers to our restless, troubled hearts! "And the swallow" hath made a "nest for herself where she may lay her young, even thine altars, O Lord of hosts!" Let us remember, as we mark the clay-built nests clustering around our roofs, that "Blessed are they that dwell in thy house; they will be still praising thee."

Among the varied beauties of country scenery at this season water meadows have their charms; and have added considerably to the interest of some of my walks and musings. In the spring they appear to particular advantage, because they are so richly green, and instead of being laid under water they are now flooded with sheep; and the perpetual bleating that rises from the flocks is ever musical to the ear and heart. I could sit for hours looking down upon the valley, with its silvery intersections, its stunted pollards, the quiet stream that flows through it, with a railway by its side, and beyond these symbols of stillness and motion, upon the milk-white flocks that spread themselves over the deep green subdivisions of the ground; for there is so much scriptural interest and meaning, as well as beauty, in all that belongs to a flock of sheep, that we can never tire of watching and listening.

It is quite impossible to see them clustered together, feeding "in green pastures," by the side of "still waters," "resting at noon" beneath the shade of spreading trees, and in the evening quietly following the shepherd, as he goes before them to the fold, without such inexpressible emotion as neither pen nor tongue can describe. They picture forth so exquisitely, and fully, "the footsteps of the flock" of Christ on earth; and as such, address our hearts so pointedly and powerfully, that among all the glowing imagery of the Book of God, nothing brings us so closely and immediately into contact with the promises of Christ.

I have often watched sheep feeding quietly and carelessly, scattered over a large field, apparently quite unprotected and alone A sudden alarm has aroused them, and they have rushed together in terrified confusion, bewildered and helpless. In an instant, from the shelter of a hedge or tree, starts the shepherd! He was near, although hidden from their eyes; "asleep," it may be, in the heat of the day, but his ear quickly alive to the movements of his timid charge. What a picture of Him who watches with Almighty care "the sheep of His hand." We may not perceive His presence; he may be, as it were, "withdrawn," but He "neither slumbereth nor sleepeth;" and He has Himself declared that He "giveth His life for the sheep." The wolf may come—dangers ghostly and bodily are ever hovering around the "little flock"—but the Good Shepherd has said to them, "fear not;" "no man is able to pluck them out of my hand."

Let us take courage and comfort in these assurances, for we all need them—we are all wandering in devious paths—and no poor, helpless, silly sheep can be so helpless, or so silly, or so ignorant as man. When we ramble through the beautiful scenes of nature, and mark the different objects that meet us at every turn, we find constant food for thought, instructive as well as delightful; and if we apply to our hearts what passes before our eyes, it is astonishing how many lessons we may learn and what deep teaching we may receive.

Whatever our Great Teacher has selected to convey His heavenly meaning to our darkened minds, is specially fraught with instruction; and He has selected so many beautiful but simple incidents and objects for this gracious purpose, and so many belong to all nations, as well as to the one sanctified by His bodily presence, that we can scarcely look out upon the face of nature without being reminded of His Word. Let it ever be impressed upon our hearts.

ALLOTMENT FARMING FOR JUNE.

THE time has at length arrived when vegetables will, or ought to be, in their most active state, and when not a day may be lost without a corresponding amount of pecuniary loss in the ensuing winter. There are those in the world who are constantly in the habit of saying, "it don't matter;" now this "don't matter," we beg to say, in the majority of instances, is the sure precursor of failure. A swarm of young weeds has invested the young carrot crops; a chance occurs of getting them out betimes in favourable weather; they are neglected, and a rainy period commences; in a few days the plants are nearly smothered, and, moreover, become "drawn" with whitened stems. Fine weather again prevailing, they are rushed upon eagerly as being in arrears; and now their half-bleached and delicate stems are suddenly exposed to intense sunshine, the consequence of which is that they become stunted through a contraction of the delicate sap vessels, and a check is hereby sustained which the plant never entirely recovers; need we add that the crop proves unsatisfactory, and the cultivator, forsooth, imagines that the ground was to blame—was too poor—and, of course, votes an extra amount of manure in the ensuing year.

It is, indeed, pitiful to see how lightly three-fourths of cultivators regard weeds. Many fancy that when they are once drawn out that all is right again, and that no harm has ensued; at the same time many such persons are ready enough to thin out portions of the crop as robbing their neighbours, whilst the rivalry of the weeds is slighted, the character of exhausting the soil scarcely being imputed to them—they are supposed to live entirely on the air. Let us, therefore, advise our allotment friends to be very much in earnest this summer, and then let them say at the approach of the ensuing winter whether or no they have found a benefit in a cleanly course of culture.

GENERAL MAXIMS.—In all cases of drill crops under allotment practice, by which practice is meant that on plots of ground in much finer tilth than farming lands in general are, it is well to precede the hand-weeding and singling out in the drill by some culture between the drills, provided the weather is suitable. We generally use the Dutch hoe for this purpose, but there is nothing like the fork or spade for those who can find time, and who do not begrudge a little labour, especially if the weather prove showery. When the weeds between the drills are decayed, the necessary operations in the drill will be readily seen. The first proceeding in the drills should be to draw all the earliest weeds, and the next is to rough thin the plants if necessary; not, however, a final thinning, which is termed singling, that is, so reducing their numbers as that no two plants touch.

These things done, most crops will be benefited by a hand-hoeing with the small hoe, and for this process the land should be in a condition between wet and dry, rather inclining to the latter, for a twofold purpose has to be served—pulverisation and the destruction of weeds. It will be seen that we have been speaking of general principles of culture, applicable to most of our drill crops; we must now descend to some necessary details of a specific character.

SWEDE TURNIPS.—By this time the Swedes will be above ground in most parts, and a seed bed will have been provided, as a guard against failure. We must refer to the general principles of culture, as previously adduced, and if the fly should become seriously destructive it will become a consideration whether to break the whole plot up and recrop, or otherwise to repair blanks by transplanting. The latter is generally preferred, and, indeed, is generally the soundest policy, for there is no crop which can at this period supply the place of Swedes as a store root; common turnips, such as the Tankard, the White Round, or Dale's Hybrid, will succeed as far as time is concerned, but the great misfortune is they will not keep like a Swede.

POTATOES.—We regret to say that at the time we write the old disease has again shewn itself, in a neighbouring garden, amongst some early kidneys which have been protected. We do not name this in order to cause our readers to suppose that we feel the same amount of alarm as when the disease was rampant; much better things surely may be anticipated. The hoe, or other cultural implement, must be well plied between the drills, and a little soil drawn to the stems, where there is danger of the produce becoming greened through light and air. Where they form part of a system of mixed cropping, combined in alternate rows with such things as mangold, or Swedes, or other root crops, their stems should be gently drawn aside occasionally by means of a fork or pointed stake, or the young plant may be overpowered. We need scarcely say that cultural operations are well repaid with the potatoe; no root pays better for timely attention. If the late crops should happen to fail in places, the best plan is to fill up the blanks in good time with Swede plants.

CARROTS.—We can add little to the remarks at page 51. This crop requires some dainty handling; above all things let not weeds overpower them. A sowing of the Early Horn kind may yet be made; such, however, must not be considered as adding to the store roots for winter and spring, but as a luxury for the allotment holder's table during October and November; they have the merit, however, of keeping him from his store carrots of the larger kinds, which should not be used until after Christmas if possible.

PARSNIPS.—In addition to our advice at page 51, we may add that the final thinning must be completed, if not already done; they should not be closer than five inches from plant to plant. Hand-culture between the plants with the small hoe, when they get a few inches high, will, by breaking the side forks, cause the tap root to descend. Deep culture between the rows is also eminently advantageous, as with most other root crops.

COMMON TURNIPS.—Good full crops of these may be obtained by sowing in the early part of June; it often happens, however, that a few of the Dutch kind may be stolen from narrow borders where nothing else will grow. A drill or two in such situations may be sown without digging; thus treated they produce neat and good eating turnips, with a small amount of leaf. For a winter and spring supply to the allotment holder's family, the middle of July will be a proper season.

JERUSALEM ARTICHOKES.—These should have their stems thinned out. We seldom leave more than a couple, but we have heard persons affirm that a single stem will produce more than a couple; of this we are not thoroughly assured, although, of course, the distance at which they are set biasses the whole affair. A little deep culture between the rows will be of much benefit, and they should have one thorough hand-weeding when they are nearly a foot high; or the hoe may be plied, not cutting too deep.

ONIONS.—These are a valuable allotment crop, and some cottagers make a good deal of them. We think hand-weeding preferable to thinning with the hoe, for we find the hoe to loosen them, and render them liable to be thrown down with storms. These must receive their final thinning soon, and if blanks occur a showery time should be taken advantage of to fill up all gaps by transplanting. We would not advise them to be thinned beyond five inches apart; the onions will not, of course, be exhibition ones, but they will be a fuller crop, and will keep better. A sprinkling with soap-suds every washing day in June will tend to secure the crop from the onion fly, and to enrich the soil.

LEEKS.—A valuable cottager's crop; to grow them fine they are best in a trench, like celery; a double row in each trench, well manured. Planting should not be delayed beyond the second week in June. Surely our cottagers in general cannot know what a delicious dish these afford when highly cultivated or they would plant more. When about three parts grown they should be soiled up, as celery, but not quite so deep.

CABBAGES.—As these are cut let the leaves, at least once a week, be collected for the cow or pigs. Some spring sown ones may be introduced amongst any standing crops, or to fill gaps; they will be very useful in August and September. A good sowing of the dwarf kinds at midsummer, or a little before, will produce fine autumn coleworts; these should not be missed.

GREEN KALE.—We need hardly say that this is the most useful green for ordinary purposes at present known; we consider it the first consideration with the allotment holder, and he should not fail to plant a considerable quantity in the course of June.

SAVOYS.—A patch of these, forward plants, should be planted in the early part of June; they will grow nearly as large as the Drumhead cabbage if the soil is good, if poor the green kale will prove more hardy.

BROCOLIS.—A drill made rich, like for celery, might be sown with Cape brocoli in the first week of June, to stand where sown; this is a much superior plan to transplanting with the Cape kind. A few seeds should be dropped in patches every 15 inches, and when up they must be singled out. A few Walcheren brocoli plants may be planted out in the middle of the month, and a few plants of cauliflower. Whatever late spring brocoli is needed should be got out in the middle of the month.

SCARLET RUNNERS.—Let these be well staked betimes, and it is a good plan to apply a mulching on each side the row; the stakes need not be above a yard in height of necessity, when they get to the top pinch off their heads.

DWARF KIDNEY BEANS.—Let a little soil be drawn to their stems when six inches high; storms are apt to do serious mischief without this precaution.

BROAD BEANS.—A good soiling up is of much benefit to this crop, which is a very useful one to cottagers. As soon as a good bloom is opened let the tops be pinched to help the swelling.

PEAS.—These, of course, are soiled up, and staked; nothing is necessary but to keep them clean. If any marrowfat kinds overtop their stakes let their heads be pinched off.

LETTUCES.—A few of the Bath cos may be sown in the middle or end of the month; they will not prove a profitable crop, however, until the middle of July. These will be thrown on the cool of autumn again, and will produce full sized lettuces.

SPINACH.—In the end of July some of the round kind may be sown; this, like the lettuces, will not yield a bulk of produce until the second week of July.

FILLING UP BLANKS.—This, we are sorry to say, is a labour that may in all seasons be anticipated with one crop or the other; and it becomes a consideration whether to fill up with the same or to select some other. Swedes may be filled with Swedes, or with any of the dwarf cabbages; Mangold may be made up with Swedes, or with cabbage; Parsnips with cabbage or mangold; and as for Carrots, almost any other crop is too heavy in its growth for the habit of the carrot. Perhaps lettuces transplanted would do as little harm as most things; if, however, the carrot crop is very bad, the best way is to dig it up, and recrop with cabbages or Swedes, or common turnips.

In all cases of transplantation we need scarcely say that the ground should be clean, and that the process be carried out either during rainy weather or immediately after it. When there is a heavy foliage on the plants about to be transplanted it is well to cut a portion away, perhaps for general purposes we may say a third; this, however, depends upon the character of the weather as well as size of the plants. Let not any of our readers cut their plants to a mere stick; we have seen Swedes overgrown in the seed bed, with every particle of leaf cut away—nothing but the stalks left; those who do so have not a single idea of the character and office of the foliage of plants.

COLLECTION OF REFUSE.—We have but space to say—make a point of looking over allotment grounds at least once a week, for refuse vegetable matter for the cow or pig, during the summer; those who have a good extent will do well to make it an almost daily affair. There is an old saying, that "what is done at any time is never done;" there is nothing like being as systematic as possible in all such matters.

THE POULTRY-KEEPER'S CALENDAR.

JUNE.

By Martin Doyle, Author of "Hints to Small Farmers," &c.

PIGEONS.—In June and July pigeons are at the height of their breeding season, whether choice fancy kinds, or mere mongrels, or dove-house sorts for the supply of the larder. If your neighbours do not make any objection to your keeping pigeons, you will find them a very interesting kind of poultry to keep. The pigeon, like the Guinea-fowl, is faithful to one mate; and one of these affectionate couples will have, with proper food and management, seven or eight pair of young ones in the year; and these squabs (as they are in elegantly called) are very good for roasting, or for pies, when nearly fledged. The parent birds feed the young ones, so that pigeon rearing causes no trouble. For the cottager's purposes pigeons, however, are little suited, because—though, as Mr. Cobbett has judiciously remarked in his Cottage Economy, they are an object to delight children, and give them the habit of fondness for animals, and of setting a value upon them—they are not very profitable; "for the man to be trustworthy towards a teem, the boy must have been kind and considerate towards animals; and nothing is so likely to give him that excellent habit as his seeing from their very birth animals taken great care of, and now and then having a little thing to call his own." When they are kept by cottagers some pretty kind should be obtained, with a view to selling the offspring as pets.

GEESE.—The gander and goose should both be well fed now, and secured from interruption, that the eggs may be fertilized properly for the second brood of the year.

TURKEYS.—In June and July the second batch of turkeys will be out, and under our care. Those young birds which are designed to be eaten in February, March, and April next, will have to meet the severity of December and January with less established constitutions than their elder brethren which will be slaughtered for use at Christmas. They will require, therefore, especial care: feed them with extra liberality and frequency. The grand secret in rearing turkey chicks is constant feeding—every half hour, if possible—with something fresh to tempt their appetites. By the time they are the size of partridges they will consume an enormous quantity of lettuces and green onions, which should be provided for them and cut up, but not too small. A mixture of animal with vegetable food seems to be the diet better suited to them than any great quantity of grain, during their very young and growing state. Great benefit will be found from having a worm-heap, or dunghill filled with worms and grubs, from which a spadeful or two may be thrown now and then to the delicate chicks. Any person who keeps a pony, or grows cucumbers, may make a worm-heap with the out-castings of the stable and the hotbed—but this cannot be done in a moment; it should have been put together in the last autumn, at the very latest. You can, however, prepare one now for the next year. Warmth at night, and protection from wet by day, are matters of necessity for turkey poults.

DUCKS.—Your pond should now be swarming with duck-lings. As every honest contrivance by which the num-ber of poultry can be multiplied may be resorted to, we shall mention what an experienced friend has suggested. If two hens be set on the same day on duck's eggs, by smuggling away from one hen the brood which she had hatched, and giving it to the other hen also, and then com-forting the bereaved bird with a batch of hen's eggs, a brood of chickens will be obtained also. This certainly appears to be somewhat cruel. To sit fifty-two days in succession is no small trial of the patience of the deceived hen, yet her maternal longings will in the end be gratified; and we must suppose, that if she found the long sitting very irksome and contrary to her inclination, she would not continue on the nest. She will have some reward in having a brood of chickens to nurse instead of ducklings, which would cause her much vexation of spirit when they, disregarding her warning voice, would indulge in aquatic sports; and the other hen, to counterbalance her shorter time of sitting, has a double family of step-children to plague her in the sup-posed case.

GUINEA-FOWLS.—The distinction of sex, which we have not before stated, is accurately described by the Rev. Mr. Dixon: "An unerring rule is, that the hen alone uses the call note, 'come-back, come-back,' accenting the second syllable strongly, from which they are generally in Norfolk called 'come-backs.' Of all known birds, this, perhaps, is the most prolific of eggs. Week after week, and month after month, sees no, or very rare, intermission of the daily deposit. Even the process of moulting is sometimes in-sufficient to draw off the nutriment the creature takes, to make feathers instead of eggs: and the poor thing will some-times go about half naked, in the chilly autumnal months, like a fowl that had escaped from the cook to avoid a prepa-ration for the spit, unable to refrain from its diurnal visit to the nest, and consequently unable to furnish itself with a new great-coat." As Guinea-fowls, like pigeons, go in pairs, and are most faithful to each other, it is of course necessary to have a male for every female. The Guinea-hen sits twenty-eight days. According to the same author, a bantam hen is the best step-mother for Guinea-fowls, and can cover nine eggs, as the natural mother is too wild in her habits to be a good nurse of chicks. These are delicate little birds, and require much care when young, and often die with hardly any previous appearance of sickness. They do not mope and pine for a day or two, like young turkeys under similar circumstances, and then die; but in half an hour after being in apparent health they fall on their backs, give a convulsive kick or two, and fall victims, in point of fact, to starvation. The grubs and worms of the worm-heap are specially needed for them, unless they have liberty of going with their nurse to some orchard or field, where they may themselves procure insects in abundance. A free range they naturally require, and when once reared are very hardy and self-supporting. Rearing them is a capital lesson (inde-pendently of the value of the birds when raised) for in-struction in the art of rearing poultry, and for acquiring a knowledge of the natural history of birds, which can be best learned by personally attending them, and observing their habits.

A great secret in rearing the more tender poultry is, besides feeding them very frequently during the day, to feed them not only very late in the day, which is easy to do, but very early also, which lazy persons find more difficult. "Shake off dull sloth," and meet the dawn of a summer's day, or take care that your poultry-maid does so for you. This and the next month should exhibit the good results of the forethought you have been exercising during all the previous months of the year. For instance, everlasting layers should have been provided for those families in which the consumption of eggs is considerable. But it is almost too late now to remedy the deficiencies which may have existed in such particulars, though warning may be taken as to the better management for the ensuing season.

Beware of the tribe of fowl-stealers. These fellows feather their own nests at the expense of the honest poultry-keeper twice in every year—viz., at Christmas, when under the covert of darkness they make a heavy booty of fat turkeys, geese, fowls, &c.; and, secondly, about this season, or a little later, when with a very innocent look they seem to be about gathering watercresses, or herbs for some cure, and contrive to bag whatever poultry they can lay hands on.

THE BEE-KEEPER'S CALENDAR.—JUNE.

By J. H. Payne, Esq., Author of "The Bee-keeper's Guide," &c.

I AM much pleased to find that my offer in the pages of THE COTTAGE GARDENER to procure the *Improved Cottage Bee-hives* for those persons who are desirous to obtain them, but whose distance from this place renders it a rather diffi-cult matter to accomplish, has been so largely responded to; and should some of my very numerous correspondents have thought the time long before their hives reached them, it has, I beg to say, arisen entirely from the number of applications received, and the difficulty in having so great a number made in so short a time. However, as the season is, swarms cannot be early this year; so that they will all be supplied in good time I trust; for unless a very considerable change in the weather takes place, and that also immediately, swarms must not be expected before June.

In my own apiary I have not yet seen any drones, nor have I heard of any having made their appearance in this neigh-bourhood (now the 13th of May), which is already much later than their usual time of appearing, and which will make swarming, and the honey gathering season also, late; but still, on this account, it may not be the less abundant; the honey harvest very seldom extending beyond three weeks, and whether it commences in June or July makes but little difference. The honey, perhaps, gathered in June is rather the best colour.

For the method of placing *bell-glasses*, boxes, or small hives upon stocks in the improved cottage hives, see THE COTTAGE GARDENER, vol. ii., page 41; and for the general treatment of swarms, taking honey, expelling the bees from the glasses, &c., &c., see page 104 of the same volume.

I observe in the classified list of objects which may be ad-mitted to the *Exhibition of the Works of Industry of all Nations*, to be opened in London on the 1st of May, 1851, under the head "substances used for food," that *honey* is mentioned. This notice, I feel assured, will not fail to bring a host of competitors; and should the ensuing season prove a favourable one, many very interesting specimens will, I doubt not, be brought together from all parts of the king-dom for exhibition. Now, it must be remembered that the excellency of a glass of honey depends not so much upon its size and shape, as upon its colour and quality. It should be as free from colour as possible, which a glass filled in June is sure to be, provided it be begun and finished in from four-teen to twenty-one days. Any glass containing brood, or even the cells in which brood has been hatched, be it other-wise ever so handsome or so well filled, cannot be considered fine; therefore, when guide-combs are fixed in glasses (which is always very desirable), it is necessary that they should be of the finest quality and of the purest whiteness; for although the bees have the power of fixing them to the glass, and, in some measure, to alter their form, the colour must remain the same.

Very many stocks of bees have died this spring, leaving a considerable quantity of honey in their hives, some even as much as fourteen pounds, and without any appearance of disease or probable cause for their leaving. It has arisen, I should imagine, from the death of the queen, and that at a time when there has been neither eggs nor larvæ in the hive. In cases of such desertion, I have always recommended to have the mouth of the hive carefully stopped, and a swarm hived into it at the earliest opportunity; that is, if the combs

* This useful little volume is only priced 4s.; we quoted a wrong price lately.—ED. C. G.

are clean, of a good colour, and not more than two or three years' old. Now, had there been either eggs or larvæ in the hive at the time of the queen's death, the bees would have exercised the power which they possess of making from them another queen, and would have remained in the hive; but finding that impossible, they, in all probability, *swarmed* and joined some other stock. A friend writing to me from Devonshire lately, gives the following very interesting account of this process :—"My large box contains now *an artificially raised queen*. They lost their former one last year. I gave them a bit of brood in a glass, at top, late in the season (before the drones were all gone, however), and watched them daily, that is to say, half a dozen times daily for sixteen days, when their queen came forth, and has proved a most fertile one, for it is the most populous family I have. They constructed the cell seven hours after I gave them the bit of brood. I saw them begin it and finish it; take a grub out of a cell, place it in the royal cell, and nurse it assiduously. Had I not given them this brood, the colony would have been extinct long ere this, for they had no brood suitable at the time." He concludes by saying, "I have down in my bee-book many interesting observations on my hives of this nature, but it would only be tiresome to relate them."

I have just been looking over the fourth edition of *Taylor's Bee-keeper's Manual*, published yesterday by Groombridge and Sons, it contains upwards of thirty fresh illustrations, and a very considerable quantity of additional and highly interesting matter; and I beg to say to the very many inquiries that I have had respecting the late improvements in his *Amateur's Bar-hive*, that a full description and explanation of them is also given. The book should be read by every amateur apiarian. It was said of the last edition "that it was one of the best, cheapest, and most easily-referred-to works on the subject;" and the present one, with all its additions, is published at the same price.*

THE PHYSIC GARDEN.

By a Physician.

HIPPOCASTANEÆ.—In this beautiful though very small order I have but one species to mention, and, as it is a good type of the rest, I proceed at once to speak of it :—

HORSE CHESNUT (*Æsculus Hippocastanum*).—I know of no tree which, when in bloom, affords a more magnificent spectacle than the Horse chesnut; nor is the pleasure conferred by it confined alone to the *eye* : the *nose* is delighted by its fragrance, and the *ear* with the stirring hum of the bees that are attracted by the nectared sweets contained in its blossoms ; and last, not least, the *mind* is led to the contemplation of the perfections of that wonderful Being who could design such a noble object, and to the reflection that it should imitate the conduct of the busy insects, in devoting its whole energies to the fulfilment of those duties for which men were placed upon earth.

The fruit, or rather the seeds, are much valued in the south of Europe as food for fattening sheep : and they have been used by some persons as a substitute for coffee. Like the acorn they possess an astringent principle, which exists likewise in the bark; and this latter part of the tree has been recommended as a valuable febrifuge in intermittent and other fevers. This property has also rendered a decoction of the bark serviceable in some cases of gangrene, in which particular it resembles a nearly-allied tree, the Tinguy, which is similarly employed in Brazil, to heal sores in horses caused by stinging insects.

AMPELIDEÆ.—As is my custom, having but one plant to allude to in this order, I commence at once my observations on the

VINE (*Vitis vinifera*).—Those who take an interest in tracing the history of any plant from the earliest period at which we have any record of it, will not perhaps meet with one that will prove more ancient, or more generally useful and instructive, than the vine. It would be foreign to my purpose here, to enter into such a subject, but it is one which would well repay any who can devote the time to it, supplying them with much valuable information connected

with history, civilization, progress in the arts and sciences, and also the manners and customs of nations since the days of Noah, who is the first person mentioned as having used the vine.

Neither is the use and abuse of the juice of the grape so much my theme as the medical properties which the vine possesses, and the mode of employing them to the relief or cure of man, in a state of sickness.

If the branches of the vine be punctured in the spring, the sap will exude in the form of drops, and these, commonly known as "tears," are a popular remedy in France for diseases of the eye—their value however, is very doubtful. The leaves are astringent and acid, and a decoction of them is a very efficacious lotion for sore mouths, and is likewise sometimes taken internally to stop diarrhœa. "The ashes of the burnt branches will make teeth that are as black as a coal, to be as white as snow, if you but every morning rub them with it." The fruit, however, is the most important part of the plant, though more so domestically than medically. The skin and seeds of grapes are indigestible, but, according to Dr. Cullen, the pulpy or fleshy part of the sweet varieties are the safest and most nutritive of summer fruits. When eaten freely, they prove slightly laxative ; and in inflammatory and febrile complaints they are a most delightful and valuable agent in allaying thirst, and diminishing feverish heat. Those, who on account of affections of the lungs are compelled to seek a warmer climate, are recommended by Sir James Clark to try the effect of a " course of grapes," as a remedy in high estimation in several parts of the Continent.

When dried, grapes are denominated *raisins ;* and common raisins, the sultanas, muscatels, and other sorts, together with the fruit called by grocers, currants, are all dried fruits of one plant, the ordinary vine ; but assuming these different characters, partly from varieties in the plant produced by climate and cultivation, and partly from the mode of curing them. Raisins are more sweet, mucilaginous, and laxative. than fresh grapes, but from their containing less acidity are less cooling and refreshing.

We come now to the most important of the products of the vine, namely, the fermented juice of its fruit—wine.

If it be taken in moderation, wine acts as a beneficial stimulant to the whole system. To a person in *perfect* health, its reasonable use can be in no way prejudicial ; while on the other hand, very deleterious effects are likely to result to those who have their vital powers in any manner impaired. People who are dropsical, or subject to gout, or maladies of the digestive organs, are likely to aggravate these complaints by the use of wine. But wine is also a tonic, as well as a stimulant, and on this account it becomes a most valuable medicine in the latter stages of fever, in order to support the system under the languor and torpor which is the general consequence of such an attack, to invigorate the spirits, and to induce sleep. Sherry is the wine most commonly employed medicinally, on account of the small quantity of acidity in it. Madeira is a more stimulating wine, and is to be preferred for invalids and elderly people, where the additional amount of acid which is contained in it is not objectionable. This would render it improper to be used by those who have gout ; and a similar reason makes port wine improper in such cases. There is, however, more astringency in this latter wine than in any other, which constitutes it a valuable medicine in relaxed conditions of the stomach, subject of course to the above objections.

If wine be exposed to the air, a chemical change takes place in it, and it becomes converted into vinegar ; and this fluid when purified by distillation forms acetic acid.

ROYAL BOTANIC SOCIETY'S EXHIBITION AT THE REGENT'S PARK.—MAY 8.

(*Continued from page 114.*)

ORCHIDACEÆ.

COLLECTIONS OF TWENTY FIVE ORCHIDS.

1ST PRIZE to Mr. Williams, gardener to E. Warner, Esq., of Hoddesden, Herts. The weather was so unpropitious that there was no competition for this grand prize (15£). Mr. Williams' collection, however, was thought worthy of the

---

prize by the judges. His plants were well grown and in fair condition. He had fine

Dendrobium macrophyllum, with 11 spikes of its beautiful fragrant flowers. *Maxillaria tenuifolia,* a large mass, with scores of flowers upon it. *Cattleya Skinnerii,* 6 spikes of its beautiful flowers; 1 spike had 9 flowers upon it. *Cattleya citrina* had 2 of its fine lemon-scented flowers. *Cattleya mossiæ superba,* 5 large flowers. *Oncidium papilio major,* 3 flowers like butterflies. *Phalænopsis grandiflorus,* 7 flowers. *Phaius Wallichii,* 5 spikes. *Dendrobium cærulescens,* many spikes.

COLLECTIONS OF FIFTEEN ORCHIDS.

1st PRIZE to Mr. Plant, gardener to — Schroder, Esq. Very nearly, if not quite, as fine a collection as the preceding one. The best plant in it was the elegant

Saccolabium guttatum, with three spikes expanded. *Vanda cristata,* with 9 of its curious flowers in bloom. *Calanthe veratrifolia,* with 12 spikes. *Dendrobium densiflorum,* 9 spikes.

2nd PRIZE to Mr. Franklin, gardener to Mrs. Lawrence, Ealing Park. This collection had many rare and good plants in it. We can only mention a few of the very best.

Dendrobium moniliforme, 3 ft. through, and a mass of flowers; a fine specimen. *Chysis bractescens,* 7 spikes of its large pure white-wax-like flowers. *Vanda insignis,* a good plant, with 2 spikes of its fine bronze yellow flowers. *Dendrobium nobile,* a large mass of stems and flowers.

COLLECTIONS OF TEN ORCHIDS.

1st PRIZE to Mr. Dobson, gardener to E. Beck, Esq.

Dendrobium nobile, a large finely-bloomed plant; 5 ft. by 5 ft. *Cattleya Skinnerii,* very high coloured; 7 spikes. *Epidendrum crassifolium,* 12 spikes.

2nd PRIZE to Mr. Woolley, gardener to H. B. Ker, Esq., Cheshunt. A fine specimen of that fine old plant

Phaius grandifolius, 9 spikes. *Lycaste Harrisonii,* 14 flowers. *Cyrtochilum filipes,* 4 spikes.

NEW ORCHIDS.

1st PRIZE.—Messrs. Rollison exhibited the new and rare *Cypripedium Lowii,* with 2 of its large curious flowers. They are of a brownish yellow colour, with dark spots; the petals are drawn out, one on each side, about five inches long.

1st PRIZE.—Messrs. Veitch had a small plant of *Saccolabium miniata,* considered equal to the last.

2nd PRIZE.—Also *a new Dendrobium,* with pale spotted flowers of medium size; something like D. aquem.

2nd PRIZE.—Also another *Dendrobium,* like *D. Pierardii,* but more strongly marked.

In specimens of orchids, Messrs. Lucombe, Pince, and Co., of Exeter, had a noble plant of *Dendrobium cærulescens,* 6 feet high and 4 feet across; obtained a first-class prize.

PELARGONIUMS.

The weather had considerable influence upon this class of plants. They were neither so numerous nor so fully expanded, except in one or two collections, as we might have expected had the season been more favourable. Notwithstanding this there was a very fair show of these splendid flowers.

COLLECTION OF SIX IN 11 INCH POTS.—(Open to all.)

1st PRIZE to Mr. Parker, gardener to — Oughton, Esq., Roehampton.

We noted a few of the best in each collection, and, therefore, shall write them without any further preface.)

Negress; dark. *Zanzumim;* light. *Resplenden;* dark. *Adonis;* light. *Rosy circle;* light.

2nd PRIZE to Mr. Gaines, nurseryman, Battersea.

Emma; light. *Negress;* dark. *Gazelle;* light.

The rest of this collection wanted a fortnight longer to bring them up to the mark.

COLLECTION OF TWELVE IN 8-INCH POTS.—(Amateurs.)

1st PRIZE to Mr. Cock, amateur, Chiswick.

Salamander; dark. *Pearl;* light. *Rosamund;* light. *Mont Blanc;* light. *Bertha;* light. *Mary;* dark. *Orion;* dark. *Gulielma;* light. *Forget-me-not;* dark.

2nd PRIZE to Mr. Robinson, gardener to J. Simpson, Esq., Thames Bank, Pimlico.

Negress; dark. *Cassandra;* dark. *Gustavus;* dark. *Rosetta;* superb light. *Camilla;* light. *Gulielma;* light.

3rd PRIZE to Mr. Staines, amateur, Maida Vale.

Norah; dark. *Minna;* dark. *Negress;* dark. *Gulielma;* light. *Pearl;* light. *Forget-me-not;* dark.

COLLECTIONS OF TWELVE IN 8-INCH POTS.—(Nurserymen.)

1st PRIZE to Mr. Dobson, gardener to E. Beck, Esq. This collection was in excellent condition.

Pontiff; dark. *Gustavus;* dark. *Chloe;* dark. *Agatha;* dark. *Mont Blanc;* light. *Blanche;* light. *Cuyp;* dark.

COLLECTIONS OF SIX FANCY PELARGONIUMS.—(Amateurs.)

These beautiful plants were exhibited in great perfection. The competition was very severe.

1st PRIZE to Mr. Robinson.

Fairy Queen; light. *Queen Superb;* light. *Empress;* light. *Madame Meilles;* dark. *John Superb;* dark. *Anais;* dark.

2nd PRIZE to R. Mosely, Esq., Pine-Apple-Place, Maida Vale.

Lady Flora; light. *Lady Rivers;* light. *Nosegay;* dark. *Anais;* dark.

3rd PRIZE to Mr. Staines.

Nymph; light. *Statviska;* dark. *Madame Meillez;* dark. *Queen Victoria;* light.

SEEDLING PELARGONIUMS.

A considerable number of seedlings were exhibited, but only one obtained a prize. It belonged to E. Beck, Esq., Isleworth.

Beck's Rosa: lower petals a glowing scarlet, upper petals dark blotch; well defined edges, with the same colour as the lower petals; size moderate; a very desirable flower.

Mr. Beck had also a very good seedling, named *Incomparable,* almost as good as Rosa, but not quite so good a form.

Mr. Hoyle exhibited a seedling of merit, named *Eclipse,* which, when better grown, will be thought much of.

CINERARIAS.

COLLECTIONS OF SIX CINERARIAS.

1st PRIZE to Messrs. Henderson, Pine-Apple-Place. The best were

Speciosa, Cerito, Edmondia, and *Husseyana.*

2nd PRIZE to Mr. E. G. Henderson, Wellington Nursery, St. John's Wood.

Matilda, Effie Dean, Adela Villiers, and *Flora Mac Ivor.*

3rd PRIZE to Mr. Ivery, Peckham.

Prime Minister, Gem, Beauty of Peckham, and *Edmondia.*

3rd PRIZE, equal with Mr. Ivery, to Mr. Robinson, gardener to J. Simpson, Esq., Thames Bank. His best were

Newington Beauty, Husseyana, Edmondia, and *Amanda.*

SEEDLING CINERARIAS

Were exhibited in quantity, but were sadly deficient in quality. The following obtained prizes :—

Lady Hume Campbell; form good; petals broad; disk dark; ground colour white; petals tipped delicately with rich blue. A very pretty variety. Mr. E. G. Henderson.

Madame Sontag; form perfect; petals broad; dark disk; ground colour white; petals tipped broadly with deep lilac; size large. Mr. E. G. Henderson.

Jetty Treffiz; form excellent; blue disk; white ground; broad petals, each elegantly tipped with the most vivid blue.

PANSIES.

COLLECTIONS OF TWENTY-FOUR PANSIES.

Considering the unfavourable season, the pansies exhibited were very respectable.

1st PRIZE to Mr. Turner, florist, of Slough. We select the following as being the best, and worth growing.

Commodore, Optima, Duke of Norfolk, Lucy Neal, Bellona, D'Israeli, Climax.

2nd PRIZE to Mr. Bragg, of Slough.

Duke of Norfolk, Thisbe, Rainbow, Ophir, Premier, D'Israeli, and *Lucy Neal.*

CALCEOLARIAS.

CALCEOLARIAS—COLLECTION OF SIX.

1st PRIZE to Mr. Stanley, for

Sebastian,* Beauty Supreme,* Enchantress, Chancellor,* Solicitar-General, Mussonii.* Those marked * were the best.

CACTI.

COLLECTIONS OF SIX TALL CACTI.

1st PRIZE to Mr. Green. Amongst them were fine plants, with large rich flowers, of

Formosa, Ackermannii, and *Coccinea grandiflora.*

SINGLE SPECIMENS OF SUPERIOR CULTURE.

1st PRIZE to Mr. May, gardener to Mrs. Lawrence, for *Pimelea spectabilis;* a most extraordinary plant, measuring 9 feet across and 6 feet high.

2nd PRIZE to Mr. Lane, for a very fine specimen of *Rhododendron Gibsonii;* 6 feet high, 5 feet through, with numerous flowers.

3rd PRIZE to Messrs. Veitch and Son, for *Boronia Spathulata;* a good plant well bloomed; 3½ ft. by 3 ft.

4th PRIZE to Messrs. Rollison, for *Epacris miniata.*

4th PRIZE to Messrs. Veitch and Son, for *Fuchsia spectabilis.*

5TH PRIZE to Messrs. Lucombe, Pince, and Co., for *Hoya imperialis*; a large plant with three heads of bloom upon it.

NEW AND RARE PLANTS.

1ST PRIZE to Messrs. Veitch for *Medinilla bracteata*; very large foliage, and racemes of flower; they are of a dull red colour. The bracts are pale rose, with deep rose-coloured veins. Likely to be a fine conservatory plant.

2ND EQUAL PRIZES were given to Messrs. Veitch and Son, for *Dielytra spectabilis*. Messrs. Lucombe, Pince, and Co., for a new *Rhododendron—Bianca*, pure white; for a new heath, named *E. Hanburyana*, light crimson; for two new heaths, named *Ruckerii*, large reddish flower, and *Cinnabarina*, brilliant crimson. To Messrs. Henderson, Pine-Apple-Place, for *Pimelea Weippergiana*, for *Pimelea Verschaffeltiana*; both of a neat habit, and likely to prove useful ornamental plants; and for *Acacia grandis*, fine foliage, and flower of a dazzling orange colour.

3RD PRIZE to Mr. Stanley, for a new broad-leaved *Hovea*, with blue flowers.

Mr. Wood, of Norwood, exhibited a large collection of hardy variegated plants; and Mr. Williams, gardener to C. Warner, brought a finely-grown large collection of British ferns, for neither of which was a prize awarded!

LONDON HORTICULTURAL SOCIETY'S SHOW AT CHISWICK.—MAY 18TH.

WE never witnessed a more gorgeous display of that singularly beautiful tribe of plants the *Orchidaceæ*; they were produced in really magnificent condition, both as regards number and excellent condition. The *Azaleas* were in splendid order, as were the *Heaths*, and collections of *Stove* and *Greenhouse Plants*. The *Pelargoniums* also shewed an improvement upon those shown at the Regent's Park ten days previously. In *Roses* we could not detect any improvement; though still very fine several specimens were evidently past their prime. There were more of single specimens of superior culture exhibited than usual, and in better condition. In new and rare plants, as our report will shew, there were several useful and interesting specimens exhibited. The great wonder of the day, however, were two specimens, from the gardens of the Duke of Devonshire and the Dowager Duchess of Northumberland, of that magnificent water plant the *Victoria regia*, of which we shall give a description hereafter. *Fruits*, as might be expected so early in the season, were but thin in numbers, but there were some good *pines*, *grapes*, and *strawberries* placed upon the tables.

This, and similar exhibitions, exemplify the great benefit of emulation. Without such a stimulus to exertion would there ever have been such noble examples of skill exhibited? If all exhibitions of garden produce were ever to be extinct, we might safely prophecy that the culture of fine specimens would in a very few years be superseded. Hence the public, and gardeners especially, ought to be grateful to such societies as the London Horticultural and Regent's Park Botanic Society for opening, continuing, and promoting, as they do so liberally, such exhibitions of horticultural industry and skill. We might expatiate much upon this theme, and allude to the great stimulus that will be given to human industry in all branches of science at the forthcoming grand exposition in 1851, but our space forbids, and we shall content ourselves with heartily wishing success to all horticultural exhibitions.

COLLECTIONS OF TWENTY EXOTIC ORCHIDS.

1ST PRIZE to Mr. Mylam, gardener to S. Rucker, Esq., Wandsworth. This collection was, without exception, the finest ever seen; every plant was a picture of beauty and skill. Our brief description of the best of them is arranged according to their respective merits, the best being first; and we shall follow the same plan in noticing the plants in all the classes.

Saccolabium præmorsum, an extremely fine, well grown, and freely flowered plant, with 18 of its lovely racemes of flowers. *Saccolabium guttatum*; 18 spikes. Equally handsome but not so large a plant. *Dendrobium Devonianum*; 11 spikes, one of which had 30 flowers upon it. Decidedly the best plant ever seen of this charming species. *Dendrobium formosum* had 15 of its large white and yellow handsome flowers upon it. *Dendrobium densiflorum*; 10 spikes, and many more to open. *Aerides affine*; 12 spikes, a large plant; there were at least seven more spikes to open. *Cymbidium eburneum*; this rare and beautiful plant had four of its large fragrant blossoms fully expanded. *Cœlogyne Lowii*; also rare, with its cream-coloured flowers and a large rich brown spot on the lip; had three spikes numerously flowered. *Chysis bractescens*; five spikes, a large plant. *Vanda cristata*; a large healthy plant, with 20 flowers. *Vanda teres*, eight feet high, with six spikes. *Vanda tricolor*; two spikes, 12 flowers on each. *Vanda suavis*; two spikes, one had 14 flowers. *Phalænopsis amabilis*; one spike, with five branches, averaging five flowers on each; an uncommonly fine plant. *Phalænopsis grandiflora*; very large, pure white flowers, with five spikes.

2ND PRIZE to Mr. Williams, gardener to C. Warner, Esq., Hoddesdon. This collection was a remarkably well grown one; several of the plants in it were exhibited at Regent's Park; we refer our readers to our account of them in that report. We noticed the following in addition:—

Dendrobium fimbriatum; a fine plant with 12 racemes. *D. nobile* and *D. cærulescens*; large masses, thickly bloomed, 4 ft. high and 4 ft. across. *D. Jenkinsii*; a little gem, with 40 flowers. *Lælia cinnabarina*; one spike, with 11 of its rich orange scarlet blossoms upon it. *Epidendrum aurantiacum*; seven spikes.

3RD PRIZE to Mr. Rae, gardener, to J. Blandy, Esq., Reading. In this fine collection of well grown plants were:

Cattleya Skinnerii; 13 spikes, very well coloured and numerously flowered. *C. mossiæ*; 20 large fine flowers fully expanded. *Phalænopsis amabilis*; seven spikes. *Oncidium guttatum*; two long branched spikes with hundreds of rich coloured blossoms. *Scuticaria Steelii*; this rare plant had two of its large beautiful flowers expanded. *Epidendrum Stamfordianum*; five spikes.

4TH PRIZE to Mr. Franklin, gardener to Mrs Lawrence, Ealing Park.

Vanda insignis; a noble plant, with two spikes of its beautiful flowers. *Cyrtopodium punctatum*; one tall spike with 12 branches of its curiously spotted, handsome flowers. *Dendrobium densiflorum*; seven spikes, a large handsome plant. *Chysis bractescens*; five spikes, rather past its best. *Cattleya mossiæ*; seven spikes. *Vanda teres*; two spikes. *Dendrobium nobile*; a good, well flowered plant. *D. Dalhousieanum*; rare, with several flowers.

COLLECTIONS OF FIFTEEN EXOTIC ORCHIDS—NURSERYMEN.

1ST PRIZE to Messrs. Veitch and Son, Exeter. A splendid collection of well grown plants.

Vanda suavis; a very large plant, with six spikes of its lovely flowers. *Dendrobium nobile*; large and well flowered. *Cattleya mossiæ*; 14 flowers. *Dendrobium Devonianum*; a large mass. *Grammatophyllum multiflorum*; three long spikes, numerous light green and brown flowers. *Oncidium sphacelatum*; large mass. *Aerides affine*; a good plant with two spikes.

2ND PRIZE to Messrs. Rollison, Tooting. Messrs. R. exhibited again, in good condition, the rare

Cypripedium Lowii, with two flowers upon one stem. Also a fine plant, with very large flowers, of *Epidendrum Stamfordianum*. *Leptotes serrulata*; a rare gem even in orchids. A good plant of *Saccolabium guttatum*, with two spikes. And a fine *Oncidium sphacelatum*, densely flowered.

3RD PRIZE to Mr. Dobson, gardener to Mr. E. Beck, nurseryman, Isleworth.

Dendrobium nobile; in better order even than at Regent's Park; an immense plant, 5 ft. by 5 ft. *Oncidium ampliatum major*; a fine plant but scarcely in bloom. *Epidendrum vitellinum*; a beautiful scarlet-flowered species, one spike. *Dendrobium densiflorum*; 10 spikes. *Oncidium stramineum*; two spikes, a pretty species.

COLLECTIONS OF TEN EXOTIC ORCHIDS.

1ST PRIZE to Mr. Carson, gardener to W. G. Farmer, Esq., Cheam. In this collection there were several unique plants, especially the following:—

Acineta Humboldtii; a very large fine specimen, with seven spikes expanded, and many more to open. *Cattleya Skinnerii*; nine spikes, with numerous flowers. *Lacæna bicolor*; a very long spike of its curious handsome flowers.

2ND PRIZE to Mr. Blake, gardener to J. Schroder, Esq., Stratford.

Saccolabium guttatum; a nice healthy plant, with three spikes. *Angulos*; a new species; very handsome flowers, with three spikes; cream-coloured, spotted with rose. *Calanthe veratrifolia*; a fine plant, with 12 spikes. *Oncidium papilio*, the far-famed butterfly plant, the large variety, with three flowers.

COLLECTIONS OF SIX EXOTIC ORCHIDS.

There were five collections exhibited, in every one of which was some striking, good plants.

1ST PRIZE to Mr. Kinghorn, gardener to the Earl Kilnorey, Orleans House, Twickenham.

Oncidium ampliatum major; two large spikes very densely bloomed. *Dendrobium cærulescens*; a good plant, with numerous spikes densely bloomed. *Phalænopsis grandiflora*; one spike, with the extraordinary number of 15 flowers upon it, all in perfect condition.

2ND PRIZE to Mr. Ivison, gardener to the Dowager Duchess of Northumberland, Syon House. He had also a fine plant of

Oncidium ampliatum major, not quite so well flowered. *Dendrobium densiflorum* ; a large mass, with seven spikes expanded, and many more in bud. *Oncidium altissimum* ; numerous long spikes, much branched, and densely flowered.

3RD PRIZE to Mr. Green, gardener to Sir Edmund Antrobus, Bart., Cheam. Mr. Green had a large plant of

Dendrobium nobile, with high-coloured flowers ; and *Phaius grandifolius*, a large plant, with numerous spikes.

4TH PRIZE to Mr. O'Brien, gardener to G. Read, Esq., Burnham, near Bridgewater. The most remarkable plant in this collection was the rarely-seen

Epidendrum rhizophorum, with its beautiful scarlet flowers. Also a good specimen of that beautiful species *Dendrobium Devonianum*.

5TH PRIZE to Mr. Gerril, gardener to Sir John Cathcart, Bart., Cooper's Hill, near Egham. In this collection was the wonderful

Stanhopea tigrina, with two of its strange large flowers fully expanded. Also a good *Dendrobium densiflorum*, with 10 spikes of flowers expanded ; and a good spike on the fine old orchid *Brassia maculata*.

SINGLE SPECIMENS OF ORCHIDS,

Showing superior culture, were very scarce. Only one obtained a prize, and it well deserved it.

1ST PRIZE to Mr. Cole, gardener to H. Collyer, Esq., Dartford.

Dendrobium calceolare; a plant 8 ft. high; well clothed with flower-spikes.

NEW ORCHIDS.

1ST and 2ND PRIZES to Messrs. Veitch and Sons, Exeter, for

Bolbophyllum Lobbii; named after the indefatigable collector Mr. Lobb. This is a really handsome and exceedingly curious plant—pale yellow and bronze spotted; a curious triangular-shaped lip: under-side of the sepals exceedingly beautiful, spotted with crimson. The sepals bend forwards, petals backwards; 3 inches across. *Dendrobium transparens*, like *D. pierardi*, but deeper-coloured spots.

(To be continued.)

NEW AND RARE GREENHOUSE PLANTS.

(Continued from page 101.)

Messrs. J. A. Henderson and Co., of Pine-Apple Place, Edgeware-road, London, have furnished us with the following list, with their prices, of novelties and rarities for the present year. To those which we consider most desirable we have prefixed an *.

	s.	d.
Gompholobium versicolor. An upright twiggy shrub ; flowers large and beautiful, of a rich deep scarlet orange	5	0
Gompholobium venustum. Low growing shrub, with rosy purple flowers	7	6
Gastrolobium gracilis. Dwarf compact shrub, studded all over with bunches of rich orange yellow flowers	5	0
*Helichrysum proliferum Barnesii. The free flowering variety, very dwarf, with crimson flowers	3	6
Helichrysum purpurea macranthum. Rich everlasting purple and pink flowers, good habit and elegant foliage	0	0
Helichrysum macrantha roseum. Rich rosy pink, very large flowers, with lighter foliage	3	6
Hemiandra pungens. Rich green foliage, of a dwarf compact habit, lilac flowers, forms an excellent low bush	5	0
*Hovea chorozeniifolia. Lovely blue flowers, with holly-leaved foliage. Has the best habit of all the Hoveas	7	6
Hovea pungens major. Rich blue flowers; a very lovely plant	5	0
*Ipomea pandurata. Large flowers, of a bluish French-white colour, with a deep purple eye. Climber	3	6
Lapageria rosea. A beautiful new climbing plant, with scarlet bell-shaped flowers		
Leschenaultia arcuata. Low shrubby plant; flowers large, of a sulphur-yellow; a very elegant and graceful plant	5	0
*Leschenaultia biloba superba. A stout growing shrub, of a good habit, producing abundantly its large rich blue flowers ; a fine variety	2	6
Leptospermum bullatum. Small myrtaceous foliage, bearing an abundance of snow-white flowers	5	0
*Mitraria coccinea. Dwarf compact evergreen shrub, with brilliant scarlet tubular flowers	5	0
*Mirbelia florabunda. Lilac large flowers, remaining a long time in bloom. The rarest and most beautiful of all the Mirbelias	3	6
Melaleuca purpurea. Dwarf evergreen shrub, bearing small tufts of crimson flowers. An elegant little gem, quite new	7	6
*Pimelea Nieppergiana. Lemon cream-coloured flowers and abundant bloomer, with exceedingly neat foliage	5	0
Pimelea Verschaffeltii. A pretty and distinct plant, with broad glaucous foliage, and white heads of flowers and yellow stamens	5	0
*Pimelea Hendersonii. Rosy pink flowers, considered the most beautiful of all Pimeleas	3	6
Pleroma elegans. Rich purple flowers ; very large blooms produced in great profusion	3	6
Rhyncospermum jasminioides. Evergreen climbing shrub, with white flowers delicately fragrant	3	6
Rhododendron Javanicum. Large bunches of rich orange-red flowers	15	0
Statice imbricata. Lilac-blue flowers, foliage imbricated, exceedingly elegant	7	6
Statice frutescens. Lilac flowers, compact habit; better than S. arborea; rich green foliage	7	6
Stylidium scandens. A new climbing variety, very beautiful	7	6
Stenocarpus Cunninghamii. Fine handsome glossy oak-leaved foliage, exceedingly handsome flowers; colour, orange-scarlet	10	6
Styphelia tubiflora. Beautiful winter-flowering shrub, with long fringed red flowers	3	6
Swainsonia Greyana. Large flowers of a handsome purple colour	3	6
Tacsonia mollissima. A beautiful climber, with rich green foliage and very long rosy flowers	3	6
Telopia speciosissima. A beautiful rare Australian plant, with peculiar handsome foliage, and heads of deep crimson flowers	10	6
Tritonia aurea. Rich orange-red, sends out lateral branches, with a profusion of its rich flowers	10	6
Tropœolum azureum. Climbing plant, with pale azure flowers	5	0
*Tropœolum Dickerianum. A new species, very beautiful flowers; scarlet and green with dark blue spots	7	6
Tropœolum Smithii. Orange and yellow ; of a climbing habit; fine plant	7	6
Veronica Andersonii. This is a very interesting addition to our autumn-flowering plants. When the blooms first open they are of a violet-blue colour, but they gradually change to pure white. Very distinct and new	10	6
Viburnum macrophyllum. Dwarf flowering evergreen shrub, with bunches of white flowers like Laurustinus, only blooming when a few inches high	21	0
Ziebya longepedunculata. Rich scarlet orange flowers; a profuse bloomer; climbing	3	6
*Ziebya pannosa florabunda. This exceedingly beautiful plant is of a climbing habit, having bunches of orange-red flowers, very brilliant in colour	5	0

DUTCH FLOWER-GARDENING.

WHEN I ventured on a difference of opinion with Mr. Beaton, regarding the merits of the plan of the flower-garden of *X. Y. Z.*, inserted in THE COTTAGE GARDENER, p. 332, vol. 3, I was in hopes the remarks there made would have called up designs from other parties, applicable to a plot of ground such as I guess the one of X. Y. Z. to be ; but as no one has yet replied to the invitation, I now, with some reluctance, send you a rough sketch, which though it may be exceeded in beauty by many others, is, I trust, an improvement on the Union-flag-like plan Mr. Beaton lauds so much. Now, as there is an endless diversity of figures in this kind of gardening, and the beauty is much increased by being extended, I hope the annexed one will not be censured for being small, as I expressly made it so in order to meet the case of such a one as *X. Y. Z.*—it numbering the same quantity of beds as his, exclusive of the centre one, which I believe, in his case, was a fountain. It may, therefore, be regarded as one of a set of rivals to *X. Y. Z.'s* figure, of which I could easily contrive many others, but hope some one else will do so, being of opinion that for a limited piece of ground there is no method so well adapted for a floral display in summer, or an interesting appearance in winter, as Dutch or geometrical plans of which this is only a limited sketch, capable of being varied in many ways. Even the largest plans are not (I think) complete without something of the sort. I imagine an arrangement of 50 or 100 beds in various tasteful figures, bordered with box, and walks of uniform width between, placed in such a situation as to be seen from an elevated position, as a terrace, balcony, up-stair window, or any place where the whole figure at once can be distinctly seen, and it need hardly be asked what opinion will be given. True, there are some who aspire to what they call a close attention to Nature, who despise everything in which symmetry forms a part; but even these are rapidly becoming converts to the opinion which makes a pleasure-ground picturesque in the true sense of the word, and not grotesque, as the attempts to imitate a forest or extended landscape on less than an acre of ground too truly imply.

Whilst on this subject, I will make a few remarks on what, I think, ought never to be lost sight of in this description of gardening. When a good view from above cannot be obtained, and one nearly horizontal must serve, never allow much intricacy in the figures, for although it may look very pretty on paper, you will find, when it is laid out and planted, the beauty of the outline will be lost; and, what is worse, the points of beds that may seem jutting into their neighbours, will appear as forming part of such, and thus a confused mass of flowers will present themselves instead of clearness and distinction. I beg to put particular stress on this point; but, where the principal view is from an eminence, where the whole of the internal walks, and the beds when in flower, can be distinctly seen, then you can exercise your own taste in the matter. Ever bear in mind, however, that walks ought in all cases to be of uniform width, which puts a task on your ingenuity, in order to get the various ornamental figures you wish to introduce fit into each other.

It may be proper to add, that grass need not be totally banished from this kind of gardening; a circular centre-piece of turf, with a vase, sun-dial, or piece of sculpture on it, looks very well; as also does a broad margin, say four feet wide, surrounding the whole, and dotted in proper places with vases or plants, which can be retained in symmetrical appearance, as clipped box, Irish yew, Yuccas, standard roses, and the like. Slopes and terraces form useful adjuncts to this kind of gardening, with their accompanying appendages—flights of steps and broad walks.

And now for the planting—that very serious undertaking I say serious, because Mr. Beaton seems afraid to stake his reputation by giving us an example, which, as I before said, would have conveyed a more clear idea than a whole volume of letter-press, from which so many inferences may be drawn, that I am induced to give my opinion also; at the same time I do it in such a manner as, literally speaking, nails my colours to the beds (instead of the mast); not that I think they are the best that can be, but that others in criticising them may do so without using that vague description of generalities which leads to very inaccurate conclusions. For my part, I confess, I do not see the utility of investing the mere planting of a few flower-beds with the importance that of late has been attempted to be put upon it. But I will keep to my case, and observe, that one great error seems to be run into, of arranging the colours so as to centre in one harmonious whole at one point or centre; the fallacy of which is easy to explain. A flower-garden is not like a portrait: it ought to present equally agreeable views, sideways or upside-down—a fact which writers seem to have forgotten; but my meaning will be best understood by reference to the annexed list, as being the plants with which I advise to plant the accompanying design:—

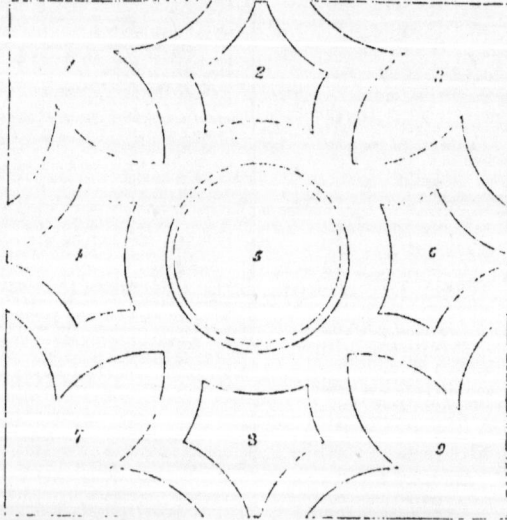

No. 1 Scarlet geranium (Tom Thumb).
  2 Verbena, a white variety.
  3 Petunia, a purple (say Phœnice).
  4 Anagallis, or Lobelia (blue).
  5 Heliotrope.

No. 6 Cuphea strigulosa.
  7 Calceolaria viscosissima.
  8 Verbena, crimson (Hendersonii, or Charlwoodii).
  9 Silver-edged geranium.

In giving the above list, it is by no means supposed to be the very best that can be contrived; what I mean to explain is, that in looking over the whole, no two beds should appear on a line of the same colour: thus 7, 4, and 1; 1, 2, and 3; 3, 6, and 9; 7, 8, and 9; 7, 5, and 3; 2, 5, and 8; 4, 5, and 6; and 9, 5, and 1, ought all and each to represent colours differing as much from each other as possible; some beds, as 2 and 6, might be of the same colour, because in regular lines they do not come in contact with each other, which 2 and 8 would do; and I do not think the intervening of one solitary bed sufficient between colours exactly alike. Such is my opinion; and as the majority of flower-gardens are surrounded by walks, it is imperative that they look equally well on all sides. Where flower gardens are planted in masses of one colour, attention to the above simple rules is all that can be well carried out, and all that has been written on the subject beyond that only tends to confuse the planter.

Some years ago I saw a series of beds which were planted under the direction of one who was thought a great authority in such matters, and certainly a worse display, on the whole, could not have been made by an unlettered labourer. That failure, as well as some others in the same way, led me to believe, that the difficulties in getting plants of the required size, colour, &c., combined with other uncertainties, were such, that quite as good, if not in many cases a better result attended planting in an almost indiscriminate manner. In support of that opinion, I may quote those landscape writers' own words who so strongly advocate desultory planting in other things, yet affirm so much mystery (for I will not call it information) on the subject of floral display.

In conclusion I beg to say, I do not arrogate to myself that the opinions above given are all just, only let us have discussion, and prove I am wrong or ignorant. I am glad to see Mr. Beaton recommending mixed beds again. I always thought they were too hastily condemned some years ago, but, as that is his province, I shall wait until he has done before saying anything, as I should only, perhaps, be repeating what he had written the preceding week. I will, however, if required, send you a sketch of a geometrical garden applicable to grass, and some other subjects less treated on by your able coadjutors.   S. N. V.

[We shall be very glad to hear from you on any subject; and Mr. Beaton, we are sure, will read your paper with interest, for our prime object is the attainment of truth in all that concerns the homes and gardens of the British islands. We shall be glad of your address, in strict confidence.— ED. C. G.]

THE SEEDLING CULTURE OF THE POTATOE.

It is somewhat remarkable, that amongst all the various opinions that have been expressed relative to the potato disease, very little has been said of the seedling culture of the plant, as the means of mitigating its devastating influence. And although some of our oldest cultivators can bear testimony that the potato, like other plants, has been subject to different diseases and attacks of blight for a great number of years—a fact also well-known to their ancestors—still they have failed to assist nature in her work.

Some writers have asserted, that the potato disease is caused by the gaseous exhalations of the earth; others, that it is a blight, an insect (Aphis vastator); while some have stated that it is entirely atmospheric; and some that the plant is wearing out, and in time will become extinct. Now, taking a philosophical view of the question, I will ground my argument upon the last named cause, "that the plant is wearing out," by stating that it is not altogether unfounded, although it is in some degree fallacious to suppose that one plant should become extinct more than another; while the all-wise Creator has provided the means of perpetuation for every living thing, both animal and vegetable, upon the face of the earth; and with such means placed at our disposal, there is good hopes to suppose that the health and cultivation of the potato may be resuscitated, and the disease if not totally exterminated, greatly reduced in its effects.

Now, I regard this wearing-out of the plant as its old age, just the same as that an old man or woman are not so well able to withstand the attacks of disease as youth; although infants and children have their complaints, and often die, and

so do young plants. We all know, that have any knowledge of horticulture at all, that old plants are more subject to disease than a healthy vigorous young one, and weak sickly plants are more subject to the attacks of insects than the more robust. By way of example. The carnation is very subject to a disease called canker, which is caused by too much wet or damp, but do we ever find it among a batch of seedlings? very seldom! and only then when it is an extraordinary wet season, or under very bad management. And were it not for the assiduity of the florist in constantly keeping up a succession of new seedling varieties, the old ones in course of time would become diseased and die, while others would degenerate back to the original Clove gilly-flower Again, let us consider what has been done for the dahlia, through the untiring perseverance of the florist, in the prosecution of seedling culture; compare the beautiful varieties of the present day with those of ten or fifteen years back, of which many are still in existence. And as such a wonderful improvement has been made in flowers, is it not reasonable to suppose that the same improvement could be made in roots also?

Now, the dahlia, like the potato, is a tuberous-rooted plant, consequently more analogous; and I will here remark, that I have long been of an opinion, that dahlias and other tuberous-rooted plants have been subject to a disease similar to that of the potato. When taking up my roots last autumn, I observed that of a fine root of *Sir E. Antrobus*, the tubers were covered with brown specks and blotches; and this rotted during the winter, although under the same treatment as the others from which I have now a numerous and healthy stock. Now, let me return to the point from which I started, namely, the old age of the plant, and ask whether any one who has written upon the potato disease has ever thought of the durative periods of existence of plants? The duration of plants, like the life of animals, varies according to its species. " The days of man shall be threescore years and ten." (I suppose the average life of man to be about forty years), the horse so many, the sheep so many, and so on; and with plants we will begin with the annual of one year's duration, the biennial of two, and the perennial lasting a number of years, but we are not to suppose that all perennials last the same number of years alike. No! hence the inference between them and animals; some perennial plants last four, five, and seven years; others ten, fifteen, and twenty. But does any one know the average duration, or life, of the potato? It is very doubtful! and when a favourite variety is obtained, it is grown year after year from the tubers, until the vital energies of the plant are exhausted, and it then follows the course of all things in nature; no one having bestowed a thought for the perpetuation of the same by means of seedling cultivation.* Now, what do we arrive at, and what has the sowing of potato seeds to do with the disease? I will tell you. That by a steady perseverance in seedling culture, there would always be in the market a regular supply of one year old tubers, young ones, not tainted with disease, so that an abundant and sound crop may be expected; especially if the prescribed rules of the new system of potato culture be attended to. In reference to the seedlings, the most simple and easy plan that could be adopted would be to sow the seed thinly in frames on gentle heat, about the beginning of April; and when the spring frosts are over to plant them out into fresh ground—a light hazelly loam without manure. But I think I hear some persons say, "what a deal of trouble!" and in answer to them, I say that it amounts to a mere nothing, when compared with that of the dahlia; and perhaps some of the readers of THE COTTAGE GARDENER will be greatly astonished when I tell them that our large growers plant as much as three, four, and five acres of land with dahlias only. I think there never was a subject connected with horticulture against which so much prejudice exists, as that of the potato question; but it is gradually wearing away; and I am happy to find that Messrs. Hardy and Son, of Maldon, Essex, are in possession of such information, as to be able to convict of error the most prejudiced of minds; and that those gentle-

* This is not quite correct. There are several reports of experiments in raising potatoes from seeds, in which the seedlings are stated to have been affected with the potato murrain as much as old potatoes were the same season. But we agree with our correspondent in thinking more extensive trials desirable. We should like to have some seedlings raised from seeds obtained direct from the wild plants in South America. Here could be no inherited disease.—ED. C. G.

men invite the opinions of the many. But for the seedling culture of the potato to be successfully carried out, it must receive a stimulus in the form of a society. And when we consider what has been done for floriculture and horticulture by the two great societies of this country, and agriculture by the Royal Agricultural; also the improvement that has been effected in the pansy or heartsease, by the combined means of similar associations; and while we have cucumber, melon, dahlia, pink, and lastly, chrysanthemum societies, which are springing up in all parts, why should we not have a potato society? It is true, that occasionally a basket or two of very early grown ones may find their way to some of the floral exhibitions, and also some large specimens to some of the agricultural meetings; but we want a society formed for the improvement, the seedling cultivation of the potato; and endeavour to eradicate this disease, if not entirely to have it under control, and keep it in subjection.

I would suggest that a central one be established in London, and branch societies in all parts of her Majesty's dominions. Furthermore, I feel persuaded that if Her Most Gracious Majesty or his Royal Highness Prince Albert were properly applied to, they would feel proud at becoming the patrons of an institution established for the better cultivation and improvement of so useful and staple a commodity as the potato, and upon which to a certain extent depends the well-doing of nations, more particularly Ireland.—G. HASKER, *Ball's Pond, Islington.*

THE DAIRY.

A DAIRY is always an object of interest. The first request, when showing our possessions to town or country friends is, "Let us see the Dairy." And certainly a well kept dairy is a pleasing sight. The excessive cleanliness, the coolness, the neatness, the sweetness, is delightful, even to those who have been born and bred in the pure air of the country; what must it be then when life has been passed amidst the turmoil, the heat, and the smell of a town! Should you happen to pay a visit to a farm-house whose mistress is not famed for cleanliness, walk into the dairy. You will be pretty sure of meeting nothing there to disgust or annoy you, for cleanliness in that department becomes a matter of pounds, shillings, and pence. Butter cannot be sold unless it is good, and that it will never be if cleanliness to the nicest point is not attended to.

If possible, a dairy should face the north. The window and door should be opposite each other, in order to have a current of air through the dairy. The flooring should be either brick, stone, or slate. The shelf also, on which the pans are placed, should, if possible, be made of slate or stone. *China* is used in "show dairies," ("model" dairies I suppose they are now called), but of course that is beyond the means of any, except the favoured few. Wood, by so quickly absorbing liquid, is very objectionable for shelves or flooring; but should it be found in a dairy, *plenty of soda* must be dissolved in the water with which it is washed, or it will always retain a disagreeable smell. I object to the wooden milking-pails even; infinitely preferring tin; and as to milk standing in pans made of wood, it is wholly inadmissible. Earthenware, tin, or glass pans are easily kept clean; and the cream rises in them better than in the wooden ones. Zinc trays are much used in large dairies, and even those made of lead, but I do not like their appearance.

Now, having said thus much on the "properties" of a good dairy, let us follow the milk from the time it is taken from the cow until it appears at table in the form of butter.

When a cow is milked great care should be taken that every drop is drained from her; the last "droppings" are always the richest. Let it be carried quietly and steadily to the dairy, where it must be strained into the pans appointed to receive it. In summer it may be skimmed in twelve hours; in winter the milk should stand twenty-four before it is touched. Each milk-pan should be skimmed twice in summer, and, if possible, three times in winter. The cream when skimmed should be put into a deep earthenware pan, which pan should, in hot weather, be put into a pail of cold water. If your dairy is a cool one, churning twice a week will be sufficient; if not, it must be done three times. Before putting the cream into the churn, wash the churn well with cold spring water in summer, and with hot water in winter. From an hour to an hour and a half is the usual time cream takes before the butter comes; very much, however, depends on the weather, the kind of churn used, and the amount of attention bestowed on the cleanliness of the dairy.

When the butter is taken from the churn put it into a shallow tub, pour cold water on it, and beat it thoroughly, wrapped in a cheese-cloth, rolled in the form of a ball. This cloth being very porous absorbs the butter-milk; but care must be taken that it is constantly washed in cold water which must be at hand for that purpose. The water in which the butter is lying must be frequently changed, until no appearance of milk is seen: during the last washing some salt must be mixed with it. When the salt is well beaten in, the butter is ready to be made into shapes, either of half a pound, or into small pats. Should it be very soft when made up, put it into spring-water, in which a little saltpetre has been dissolved. If you require butter for salting, attention must be paid to its being perfectly dry, and free from every drop of water. Many people prefer beating it with a porous cloth, to extract the butter-milk, instead of washing it in water. The salt which is used should be of the finest quality. Before mixing it with the butter it should be pounded quite fine, and dried before the fire; the usual proportions are 5 lbs. of salt to 50 lbs. of butter. The inside of the tub in which the butter is to be placed should be washed with a mixture of salt and water; and whilst damp, rub the sides with salt, and sprinkle some at the bottom. When the butter has been well mixed with the salt, press it into the tub as tightly as possible, and fill it full; sprinkle some salt at the top, and tie it down with a bladder. In some counties this method of salting butter is carried on to a great extent, but in situations where a ready sale is found for fresh butter it is seldom practised.

There are several ways in which skim milk may be turned to account; the most usual are, fattening pigs on it, or making skim-milk-cheeses. Some, however, should always be either given or sold to the poor around you. The practice is much appreciated, and adds materially to the comfort of our poorer brethren: "He that hath pity on the poor lendeth to the Lord," "And look, what he layeth out shall be paid him again," are the words of "the wise man." And true indeed they are, for if we look on the poor as "messengers of the great King," we shall do them all the good in our power, for the sake of the King's Son, who sends them to us, in order to try our love for Him; and the payment we shall receive for these imperfect services is such that it fills our mind with astonishment, and we are ready to exclaim with David—"Lord! what is man that thou art mindful of him, and the son of man that thou so regardest him?"

A FRIEND.

EXTRACTS FROM CORRESPONDENCE.

BLANCHING RHUBARB.—I know that any simple contrivance for gardening purposes is acceptable to some of the readers of THE COTTAGE GARDENER, and I am, therefore, tempted to describe the mode adopted here for growing rhubarb. I am not kitchen gardener enough to know whether it is of general practice. Just when the rhubarb is about to start, they drive three stakes or slips of board about three feet long into the ground, round each plant, so as to be about two feet, or two feet six inches, out of ground, and slightly inclining together at the top. Round these stakes they twist hay-bands, fastening off the ends by twisting them amongst the hay, so as not to get loose, and leaving the top open. By these means the rhubarb is drawn up; if it is not drawn too fast, you obtain a great length of stalk; and when you want to cut, away you slip the hay-bands off the top altogether, like a chimney-pot; and then, having cut what you want, put it on again like an extinguisher, with no trouble at all. Of course the hay bands should reach close to the ground.—C. W. ESTCOURT.

SQUIRRELS.—A late contributor accuses the squirrels of gnawing off the top twigs of his spruce firs. I have my walks and plantations strewn with these fragments; but if your correspondent will take the trouble to examine these twigs, he will find that in far the greater number of instances the pith has been excavated by an insect (probably *Cossus piniperda*), which has gnawed its way out through the bark at the joint below; and thus weakening the branch in that part, has caused that the rough winds break off very numerous branches at that weakened part. No doubt squirrels will do mischief, but the most part of this is not their work. —W. P. T.

WRITING NAMES ON POTS.—I potted some hyacinths in October last, and wrote the names under the rim of the pots in *blue ink*, and sank them in an open border; and find, on taking them up after a lapse of five months, and washing the pots prior to placing them in my window, that the names are as distinct as when first written.—GEORGE HODGEDES, *Tavistock.*

BOILING JERUSALEM ARTICHOKES. —They must be *first peeled*, and thrown into cold water till you set them on to boil. Let them boil till quite tender, put them in your dish, and pour melted butter over them. It is very simple, but if not put first into cold water they will look black.

BOILING WATER FOR VALLOTA PURPUREA.—As the benefit of watering the *Vallota purpurea* with boiling water, poured into the *saucer*, may not be generally known, I beg to mention it. I had it second-hand from a Scarborough cottager, who told the secret of its flowering so invariably well in that locality. The *Calla Ethiopica* I find also to delight in similar treatment.—*Brentingby Cottage.*

COCHIN-CHINA FOWLS.—Mr. J. Bailey, of Mount-street, has done good service to your readers in giving so minute and clear a description of the Cochin-China, in answer to the questions at page 301, of vol. 3, of THE COTTAGE GARDENER; and being a respectable and intelligent dealer such communications have more especial value. I beg to give you the communication of another respectable and intelligent dealer on the same subject. " I have had in the same clutch of Cochin-China, birds with a high serrated comb, and those with a small double comb ; the wattles large ; legs not very long ; the legs are frequently yellow. I have had the Cochin-China of various colours; the majority dark brown in the hens, and dark red in the cocks; sometimes black breasted and red, like the game-cock. I should prefer a single colour in the plumage, but do not think it is always so. The tail feathers are frequently brown."

I cannot help recommending to poultry-keepers a work lately come out, entitled " Domestic Fowl, by J. J. Nolan, of Dublin." I do not know any work which gives such clear and accurate descriptions of all the various breeds of poultry, with very good and accurate engravings of each. With such book no one could be at a loss to determine any breed, though they had not seen it before ; and it is by no means dear, being only 3s.—W. J.

TO SOFTEN HARD WATER.—When the hardness proceeds from the bicarbonate of lime (which is very frequently the principal, and always in great part, the cause), it may be softened by a cheaper ingredient than carbonate of ammonia, or soda. Add a little quicklime to the water. The lime decomposes the bicarbonate of lime which is dissolved in the water, taking from it one of its two equivalents of carbonic acid, and leaving the residue of the substance in the state of proto-carbonate of lime, which state the fresh added lime and the equivalent of carbonic acid thus subtracted from the bicarbonate also themselves acquire. This proto-carbonate of lime is a ponderous and insoluble salt, and sinks to the bottom of the fluid, leaving the superincumbent water pure and soft. To the inexperienced it appears an absurdity to propose, that water which is hard from being overloaded with lime should be rendered soft by adding more lime ; but such is the case. Those of the poor who have no access to any but hard water for washing may much economize their soap by softening the water with lime before they wash.— PENNY-WISE.

PRUNING DAHLIAS.—Observing that Mr. Beaton has requested some suggestions on the subject of bedding plants, although it may appear presumptuous on my part to offer any suggestion that may be worthy of his adoption, nevertheless, feeling myself to be indebted to his writings for much information, I therefore gladly take the occasion to testify at least my desire of complying with his wishes. With a view to obtain something like a uniform standard of height in the growth of Dahlias, my practice has been to bring forward somewhat earlier those plants that attain the greatest height, and then to cut out portions of their leaders (according to the vigorous habit of the plants) and to train the lower shoots upwards. To the plants of weaker habit, a little liquid manure is occasionally given in their earlier stages to promote their growth; and by these means, at the flowering season, a more uniform height in all the plants is obtained than by any other means that I could devise.—T. O.

[We shall be glad of your suggestions relative to grape vines.—ED. C. G.]

SMOKED BRICKS—PAINTING GREENHOUSE INSIDE.—The only and the cheapest way to prevent stains arising from smoked bricks, is to give the parts affected a coat of oil paint, and when dry the whitewash may be applied without the least fear of a recurrence of the evils your correspondent complains of. My greenhouse (30 feet by 16 feet) I oil paint, and find it in every respect preferable to whitewash. I employ a workman, to whom I give 2s. 6d. per day, and find my own materials ; consequently, the first cost is very little more than whitewash ; and when taking into account its durability, superior neatness, and cleanliness, and the greater light and heat imparted, it is positively cheaper. The fine, and the walls immediately in connection therewith, I whitewash, to avoid the smell that would otherwise arise when the house is under heat. Let any of your readers who have not hitherto adopted my plan try oil painting, and the whitewash brush will be for ever discarded. For the information of any who may be disposed to adopt my recommendation, I would observe that I first prepare the walls with a coat of size and whitening, laying it on warm (this is equal to a coat of oil paint), after which I give two coats of oil paint, and the work stands for years. As every crevice is stopped, no retreat is left for the spider and its numerous companions in mischief.—A SUBSCRIBER.

HERACLEUM GIGANTEUM.—Messrs. Hardy and Son, Maldon, Essex, inform us that they have already leaves on some two-year-old plants five feet broad and five feet long. They say it is a most majestic plant, and that last year they grew it fourteen feet high. Mr. Moore, the Curator of the Chelsea Botanic Garden, states that it is appropriate to the bold openings of rude or wilderness scenery. It blooms in June or July, and its umbels of white flowers are a foot across.

BEDDING-OUT PLANTS.—Would not *Campanula Lorei* make a good purple bed ? I saw a very pretty bed last year of the *double white feverfew*, which Mr. Beaton has not mentioned amongst his white bedders.—A LOVER OF FLOWERS FROM CHILDHOOD.

HAIR FALLING OFF.—You give advice to some correspondent who complains of losing his hair. Allow me, from experience in my own and other cases, to recommend the use of the following receipt, and to add an earnest recommendation *on no account* to be persuaded to have either the head shaved or the hair unusually cut close :—1 drachm of white wax, 1 ditto of spermaceti, 2 oz. oil of almonds, 2 drachms essence of cantharides ; essential oil to scent at pleasure. The whole to be dissolved together in a gentle heat, and stirred and beaten till quite cold.—M.

MACAW LAYING EGGS.—Many useful hints have been given to increase this propensity. I have a large scarlet Macaw (Psittacus Macao), which has laid during the last few months 20 eggs, and promises to continue her labours. Can any of your correspondents inform me how I can put a stop to this ? It weakens the bird, and makes her restless and irritable. All accounts which I have seen state that they breed but twice in the year, laying two eggs each time ; if so, we have a new ornithological fact. May not the circumstance be attributable to disease ?—S. P., *Rushmere.*

TO CORRESPONDENTS.

. We request that no one will write to the departmental writers of THE COTTAGE GARDENER. It gives them unjustifiable trouble and expense ; and we also request our coadjutors *under no circumstances* to reply to such private communications.

HEATING SMALL PIT.—In answer to *C. W. Estcourt* we are obliged by this reply from *W. X. W.*:—"The stove cylinder (page 56) holds about two bucketsful of charcoal. A few hours would be sufficient to warm the bed ; but I have kept a *constant* fire in my stove, so that I might ensure a regular and constant heat. The amount of heat is controlled by the damper in the first lid. The stove is placed *inside* of the brickwork in one corner of the frame, and the square tank is in the *centre* of the bed. I should have added in my first communication that it would be the best to place the stove in the south-east corner of the frame, and to bring the top of the stove through the glass at the corner, so that it may be fed without removing the lights ; and this also will keep out any charcoal dust from the plants. By placing a small sliding ventilator in the side of the frame, near the surface of the bed in the corner near the stove, and another at the top or higher end, a constant draught of warm air would flow over the bed. My reason for using lead pipes was, that they are easily bent into a turn ; and my reason for using pipes instead of an open trough is, that I wanted my bed for forcing roses, or greenhouse plants, and was afraid of too much moisture ; indeed, it has proved too much as it is for my Zauchaneria cuttings. My copper pipe is perpendicularly placed in the fire, the upper pipe returning through the side of the cylinder about eight inches above the lower or feeding pipe."

HARDY FERNS (*Ibid*).—Write to Mr. Appleby, at Messrs. Henderson's, Pine Apple Place, Edgeware-road, London.

PROTECTION TO HIVE (*P. W.*).—As you have a straw cap over it, you need not put on any pan or other covering.

GENTIANA VERNA.—The Rev. D. T. Knight, Earls Barton Vicarage, Northampton, wishes to know where he can procure a plant of this, of *Andromeda polifolia*, and *Primula farinosa*: can the correspondent who obliged us with specimens of the two first-named assist Mr. Knight ?

WEEVIL DESTROYING SCARLET THORNS (*H. Berkell*).—The specimens you sent were the Furrowed Weevil, *Otiorhyncus sulcatus*.

DESIGNS FOR ARBOURS (*H. J. Sanders*).—We are sorry that we cannot aid you. Common arbours any one can make and cover with honeysuckles, traveller's joy, and climbing roses ; and anything superior we never yet saw that was not odiously ugly.

COTTAGE GARDENER'S DICTIONARY (*T. Fallon*).—Your best mode of taking it, residing as you do in a remote part of Ireland, will be to have it in monthly parts through your nearest bookseller. It will not contain anything about bees ; for these buy the three first volumes of THE COTTAGE GARDENER.

BALSAMS (*S. C. C*.).—These which have "withered just on a level with the earth in the pot," have damped off ; that is, the stems have become ulcerated and decayed where putrefaction is always most rapid, just where the part is exposed to violent changes from wetness to dryness. Your balsams have too much water, too little warmth, too little air, and too little light. Cover the surface of the soil with a little silver sand ; the errors of themselves suggest the requisite remedies.

SEA-KALE (*W. B. G.*).—Never let it throw up flower-stems, but cut these down as soon as they appear. The very fact of your plants throwing up these stems, shows that they were strong enough to have been forced this year.

CORN SALAD (*E. A.*).—This is also called Lamb's lettuce *Valerianella olitoria*. It is one of the oldest of salad herbs. It likes an open situation, and light rich soil. Sown in August and early in September, the plants will be usable in winter, if mild ; otherwise, early in the spring. Sow in drills six inches apart, and cover half an inch deep. Gather the leaves whilst quite young.

HEATING SMALL STOVE (*D. A. P.*).—A preceding answer is a reply to the chief of your queries. The pit of W. X. W. will do for growing cucumbers. We should use a cast iron pipe over the fire ; it would be as effectual, and last longer.

ERROR.—Page 94, vol., iv. line 21 from bottom, read, "(if not disturbed) with returning light to cater, &c." The words are all correct, but they are punctuated so as to make them read unintelligibly.

BEES (*C. C.*).—Your bees " are bringing out a great many grubs and fully-formed white bees." This is frequently done when the stocks are at the point of starvation, and the weather is bad. Before this reaches you, unless feeding has been attended to, the bees may have all perished. The warmer weather we hope has prevented such a catastrophe.

PREMATURE SWARM (*Ibid*).—Our correspondent says, " Last year I hived a large swarm into a full-sized hive, which appeared so full that a day or two after I put on a glass, which the bees immediately took possession of, but did not work in ; and on the eighth day from their being hived I saw them throw off a swarm ; and a large one it was. What could have made them swarm when they had room, and none of the young brood could have been hatched ? " In all probability two swarms united without your knowledge, and after eight days separated.

PARROT FEATHERLESS (*S.*).—Your parrot has plucked out all its feathers ; can any of our readers tell of a remedy ? We know a cockatoo which is similarly featherless, and the owner is advised to give it no animal food, and to bathe it in an infusion of tobacco in water, taking care that the liquor does not go into the bird's eyes.

INSECTS (*S. G.*).—The "worms" you sent are one of the species of Snake Millepedes, of which you will find a drawing and description at page 139 of our second volume. It is very doubtful whether they are injurious to plants.

CUTTINGS (*F. C.*).—Those you enclose are correctly prepared. By "cuttings with a heel" to them, are meant cuttings with a piece of the old wood from which they spring attached. You will have found in Mr. Beaton's papers lately an answer to your inquiry about removing the *leaves of bulbs* done flowering. We may say briefly, however, it should never be done until the leaves turn yellow.

HAUTBOIS STRAWBERRY (*An Original Subscriber*).—The fruitful blossoms of these have a green diminutive berry in their centre. The unfruitful have only stamens. Do not destroy these, for if you do the fruit will not set.

CONTRIBUTIONS (*J. D.*).—We shall be very glad to receive the account of your recipes and experiments. The communications you object to are just those which many of our readers desire to have mingled with those which you admire. We will answer your questions next week ; but in future write briefly, and do not put many queries into one letter.

CINERARIAS IN A WINDOW (*A Subscriber*).—Your plants having bloomed once will not bloom this season again, though by cutting them down, thinning out the suckers when they appear, leaving only a few of the strongest of them, fresh potting afterwards, and encouraging with manure waterings, they would come into bloom in the autumn. As you have neither pit nor greenhouse, you may keep them over the winter in your window ; but for this purpose you had better turn out your plants when they get shabby into a bed out of doors, surrounding each ball with a spadeful of light rich soil, and planting rather deep. In September lift several of the best rooted and strongest suckers from each stool, insert them separately in small pots in light rich earth, or several of them in larger pots, and before cold rains or the least frost come, remove them inside your window, and give air at all suitable times during the winter. Your success will be more sure, if you can make or get for yourself a moveable table to set them on, with hoops and a cover to be used for the various purposes as described in last volume, under the auspices of *Mrs. Think-in-time*.

SALVIAS, PENSTEMONS, AND LOBELIAS (*Ibid*).—These may all be safely planted now.

PROPAGATING (*An Improver*).—Read attentively the articles by Messrs Beaton and Fish. Cuttings of hardy plants will do better now under a hand-light than when placed in a hotbed. Shading will be necessary, unless the glass is placed in a shady place. Fuchsias, and the hardy plants you name, would have been more quickly struck in a hotbed in February or March, more especially if they had been kept in a cold-frame for a short time after being made. The balsams had better be sown in the cucumber-box. The placing of such things as wall-flowers, &c., there now, would be liable to bring insects among your cucumbers. Though for your encouragement, if you choose to try, we may mention that at midsummer we have struck such things by plunging them on a strong bottom-heat in a third of the time that they could be rooted under a hand-light. "Slow and sure," would, however, be your best motto at present. *Moss roses* do not succeed well as cuttings.

HEATING TWO PITS (*S.*).—These are each twenty-six feet by seven feet four inches, divided into four compartments, and so as to have bottom-heat and top-heat in any or all at command, with steaming *ad libitum*. We have several times stated what boilers of a certain size can be procured *for*, and *pipes* at so much per foot, according to their size. We do not feel warranted to do more in the way of *estimate*, as the cost will depend upon matters of various kinds, such as the locality, carriage of the materials, being very different according to the position of the parties, being near or distant from a foundry and water carriage. As to heating with one furnace, and one boiler, that can easily be done, as one boiler of fair size would do three or four times the work. You may then heat the pits altogether, or separately, either as two separate pits or as four—not being able to heat the farthest compartments from the boiler without heating these nearest to it—by means of valves for the pipes, and slues for the tank. As cheapness and effectiveness are alike your object, we would advise you to do similar to what we are now doing ourselves. Upon the top of your boiler fix a T pipe, which will give you two flows instead of one—take one of these to a cistern inside your pit, higher than you wish your highest heating pipe to be. In this cistern have two other holes, supplied with valves or plugs, to three holes let pipes be attached, make one of these the flow pipe for your top-heat, the other the flow pipe for the bottom-heat, the return and flow joined together at the farthest extremity by a semi-circular bend, being placed either horizontal to or beneath each other, both returns being joined to the main return at the bottom of the boiler. By this means you can heat each range of pits separately, and top or bottom, just as you like, but only in two compartments. If you wish to make four, you must consent to lay out several pounds more for stop valves, &c., in the middle of each. Having a flow and return pipe at the bottom, bottom-heat is easily secured by surrounding such pipes, somewhat hollow at first, with clinkers, brickbats, and pebbles at top, or washed gravel, above which you may place your soil, &c. A few funnels left communicating with the pipes below, or pans fixed to the pipes above, will always enable you to steam as you like.

CAMELLIAS (*Mr Williamson*).—Your only chance of recovering these Camellias with such yellow leaves, and having only a greenhouse, is to put them in the warmest part, syringing them frequently ; keep them close, and a little shaded in bright sunshine, and examine the roots when shoots are freely produced. You will see from the calendar to-day that you can scarcely manage all that with other flowering plants in your house, unless you can continue to shut off a little space by means of a screen for them, and if they are favourites the trial would be worth while, and if the plants are not too far gone you would be rewarded.

GUERNSEY LILY (*A Subscriber*).—To make, or try to make, the bulbs bloom this summer which did not flower last season, but have now several yellow leaves, we should plant them out in a warm sheltered corner, and in a nice rich light compost. You say nothing of the treatment given.

ARRANGEMENT OF FLOWERS (*A Lover of Flowers*).—You have a large circular bed filled with roses, &c., and you have six smaller oblong beds around it. These you wish to plant with low bedding plants of the colours specified. We recommend for *White*, Campanula garganica alba, or a White Verbena; *Pink*, Saponaria Calabrica; *Blue*, Salvia chamædryoides, Cineraria amelioides, or Lobelia ramosa; *Yellow*, Sanvitalia procumbens, or Tagetes fragrans, a single dwarf marigold; *Purple*, American Groundsel, Dwarf Penstemon, or Verbena Emma; *Scarlet*, Tom Thumb Geranium.

SANVITALIA PROCUMBENS (*Ibid*).—This sown now in heat will be in bloom by the first of August.

PREPARING WAX (*J. Carter*).—You will find full directions in our second volume, p. 285.

MANDEVILLA SUAVEOLENS (*Ibid*). You should have pruned this in March; but it must be left alone now for this season. It is too late to take cuttings from *Hydrangeas*, to change from pink to blue.

PRUNING HOLLIES (*C. J. P.*)—You may prune them now, but the first week of May would have been a better time.

LAURESTINUS GROWN TOO LARGE (*Ibid*).—From the middle to the end of May is the best time in the year to cut down or prune Laurestinuses, and they bear the knife as well as the rhododendrons or the willows; they may be pruned a few inches, or feet, or may be cut close to the ground. Your Laurestinuses, which are overgrown and getting bare, in a flower-border, we would prune thus:—Choose four, five, or more of the strongest and barest shoots, and cut them to within one foot of the ground, and they will soon shoot up as thick as grass; the next strongest cut to two feet, and the smaller ones let alone till the cut ones furnish leaves enough to hide the bare stems, then you may cut out all the weak ones; and at this stage, or say before the middle of August, cut away all the roots that run more than two feet from the outside of the plants, by opening a trench a foot wide, and as deep as the roots are; this trench fill in with fresh soil, not too stiff, and your plants will do for many years—better than they have done lately.

CALCEOLARIA: KENTISH HERO (*Verax*).—Doctors do not disagree in this instance. Our coadjutors agree that this calceolaria *will* root in the autumn, but *more freely* in the spring—that is all. You will find the reason for *cutting the large roots of geranium* fully given in our first volume, page 152. A *list of annuals* has been given repeatedly, if you refer to our indexes. Mr. Beaton has given the treatment of nearly all the best of them, but will say something more about them soon. Our *Himalayah pumpkin seedlings*, like yours, look very weakly. The last packet of *Custard plant seed* reached us safely; and pray accept our thanks, though too tardily given.

POTATO-LEAVES TURNED BLACK (*T. M. F.*).—This occurred on the 2nd of May, and was caused by the night frosts. The stems will come up again. There is no preventive except covering over the leaves slightly with straw or other litter when frost is expected. If the leaves and stems are not far advanced when thus destroyed the plant is not much weakened.

MULCHING (*P. W.*).—A paper shall be published on this most useful practice.

ROTATION OF CROPS (*Ibid*).—Presuming that your land is good, we do not see why your rotation—"Rape, sheep-fed; then wheat, with grass seeds for six years, all fed with sheep, and each piece in rotation broken up for potatoes"—should not answer. You will have plenty of rest, with six years' sheep pastures; and the soil will be in prime heart when broken up; and produce splendid potatoes; which might, if necessary, be taken two years successively, thereby, with high culture, clearing the land thoroughly. Rape is extensively used in some parts of the Continent, as green manure ploughed in. Your's sheep-fed, although a "stolen crop," will benefit the soil much.

DISBUDDING (*A Constant Subscriber*). — Do not remove all shoots between the buds at the forks and the terminal ones. The question of removing or of leaving a shoot depends entirely whether there is room for it. Common sense is as much wanted as science in this matter. When you find one young shoot inconveniently pressing on the heels of another, immediately nip off his head, and fear not.

PEACH SHEDDING ITS LEAVES (*Ibid*).—It is probably overcropped. The tree is not of long standing, and has not a strong root-action; indeed, the latter is speedily paralyzed by an over-crop in young trees. How should it be otherwise? The fruits need all the exercise of the elaborative powers; what then is to carry out that reciprocity so absolutely necessary to a lively vital action or reciprocation between root and leaf; or, in other words, how is the root to become strengthened? Perhaps, you have the red spider. The webs you mention carry suspicion with them.

NAMES OF PLANTS (*Amateur, Thame*).—Your plant is Veratrum nigrum, a very strong fibrous rooting plant. The roots spread some distance round the crown of the plant; and the cause of yours not blooming is, very probably, that these are cut pretty much in winter or spring dressing the borders. We have the same plant standing at the back in a plantation, not over shaded by anything else, and where it has stood for the last ten years undisturbed. It was a strong plant when planted in that place, and has flowered eight seasons out of the ten. Sometimes it throws up one very strong flower-stem, and sometimes three or four flower-stems, all very strong; but last February the plant was moved, and although it was taken up with much care, it fails to flower this year. The plant sends up fine, tall, branching flower-stems from four to five feet high, producing an abundance of glossy flowers as black as rocks.

It is a polygamous plant, having three sorts of flowers on the same plant; that is, some blossoms contain only male organs, some only female organs, and some contain both. (*H. H.*).—Your *Frimula* is P. *nivalis*. (*I. C.*).—We do not know the seeds, but will try them, and state the names of the produce. (*L. W., Blackburn*).—Your plant is *Cotoneaster microphylla*. (*Clericus Anon.*).—Yours is *Correa alba*, not a very showy species. Its cuttings root readily if planted in sand and peat, with a little bottom-heat.

FUCHSIA MACRANTHA (*R. G. R.*).—This is a shy bloomer, but a beautiful looking flower. Every lover of flowers likes it, although it blooms almost before it has its leaves well out. This we shall turn out immediately into the open ground, to be lifted in the autumn. Owing to its succulent tuberous roots it should be well drained, and be sparingly supplied with water at all times in the winter months. *Fuchsia serratifolia* does best out-of-doors in the summer months, either plunged in its pot or turned out of it, and lifted up carefully just before the frosts, and replanted in a pot with plenty of drainage, and kept in the cool for a few days, something as Mr. Beaton directed for scarlet geraniums last autumn. *F. speciabilis* is something in the same way, and we would treat it similarly. Plants treated in this way make noble specimens, and flower most of the winter and spring.

HOTBED JUST MADE (*W. H. G.*).—Keep the glass close for a day or two, or until the heat is well up; then water liberally, and ventilate freely; the watering to be repeated after a few days, or at least before the frame is got to work. We will one day give a paper on this important subject.

WHITE FORGET-ME-NOT (*W. Cooper*).—It can be grown in pots, and on rockwork too if duly supplied with water.

FIR CONES (*Aber Fennar*).—Do not plant them whole; bore a hole at the end and drive in a wedge, which will split them open. Sow the seeds in a light soil, without bottom-heat.

CARDOONS (*Odo*).—No wonder that you found the *roots* of these "unpleasant to the smell, and to the taste more so!" The stems should be earthed-up and blanched, like celery, and the stalks of the inner leaves when blanched, stewed, or used in soups or salads.

CATERPILLARS ON ROSES (*J. Egremont*).—Hand-picking, we fear, is your only remedy; try dusting thickly with white hellebore powder, and oblige us by reporting to us the result.

DEPOSIT ON PLUM-TREE BRANCHES (*L. A. C.*).—The little brown skinny bags you sent are the females of a species of *Coccus*, or scale insect. The sooner they are destroyed the better, for they are full of eggs, and the young will soon be hatched.

SALVIA NEMOROSA (*A Worcestershire Subscriber*).—It is a hardy herbaceous perennial, and will grow in partially shaded places.

SPOTS ON CUCUMBER LEAVES (*Ibid*).—They are a species of fungus. Dust them with flowers of sulphur, and keep the air of your frame more dry; that is, ventilate more freely, and give less water.

BEES (*E. P.*).—"At page 305, vol. i., Mr. Payne, in detailing his system of managing bees, says, 'I usually put on a bell glass first, and, when partially filled, I raise it up, and place between it and the parent hive the small hive or box before mentioned.' Now, neither in the drawings nor in the descriptions of the small hive or box is any mention made of a hole at the top: be pleased to inform me hereon, giving *the size of the hole*. In the same communication mention is made of 'ADAPTING-BOARDS:' be pleased to inform me of their use, and what is meant by '*inside of mahogany*.'" When the box is used for placing between the bell-glass partially filled and the parent hive it has neither top nor bottom, the adapter only is placed between it and the bell-glass, and another adapter is also placed between the box and the parent hive; it a small hive is used instead of a box, a hole of two inches in diameter must be cut in the top, but should a glass be preferred to either the box or small hive, they may be obtained of Messrs. Neighbour and Son with a hole at the top of a suitable size. By using the adapting-board the small hive or glass may be placed upon a hive of any shape, and their removal when filled is greatly facilitated, especially when two are used. "*Inside mahogany*" is a typographical error; it should be read, "*made of mahogany*."

CALENDAR FOR JUNE.
GREENHOUSE.

AIR, admit freely, to all the hardier plants, such as cinerarias, calceolarias, &c., as the cooler they are kept the longer they will bloom, and the freer they will be from insects. The HARDIER PLANTS should now be placed out of doors, in a sheltered place, to make room for fresh importations from the pits; and here arises the great difficulty in the case of those who have only one house, as the plants removed, intended to be kept for another year, would have been all the better to have been kept in until the fresh wood was made. Many winter-flowering things, such as *Daphnes, Cytisus, Heaths*, &c., may now be set in a sheltered place out of doors, and safely kept; but they will neither bloom so fine nor yet so early as they would have done had they been kept longer in the house. Another difficulty arises from the wish to make this single greenhouse suitable for plants in bloom, requiring a cool atmosphere; and plants done blooming, such as early *Camellias* and *Azaleas*, that require a high temperature, and a moist atmosphere, to enable them to make their wood and set their buds early. Any greenhouse may now be used admirably for this purpose, merely by shutting it up early in the afternoon; syringing the plants at the same time, and giving but little air during the day; but then this would soon ruin the health and appearance of such things as calceolarias, &c., in bloom; though it would answer well for bringing on large fuchsias and geraniums for succession. Hence the importance of screens, &c., for securing different temperatures. Cuttings insert, and pot off when struck; many of the first struck will make fine plants for autumn and the beginning of winter. Climbers—many tender annuals, such as Thunbergia and Ipomea, may now be introduced, either upon pillars or trellises. Cleanliness must be particularly attended to. No plants can be healthy with yellow or dust-encrusted leaves; and the sight of such is always a speaking reproach. The system of picking off every yellow leaf that presented itself as you went round with the watering-pot would prevent the woe-begone aspect which yellow-leaved plants always wear. Grafting may still be done, in the case of myrtles, oranges, Daphnes, camellias, &c.; but, as it is getting late, you must try and obtain scions from retarded plants, and then place them in a gentle hot-bed, and keep them close until the union is effected. Oranges and Lemons should have the blossom thinned and impregnated, where fruit is wanted. Seedlings of all kinds prick off. Shift everything that requires it, for all vital action is now rapidly progressing. Watering will be required oftener; and, in small pots, at times twice a-day. Manure-water may be given liberally, to promote luxuriant growth when wanted.

R. Fish.

FLOWER GARDEN.

Anemones, take up as leaves wither: dry and store. Annuals (Hardy and some Tender), plant out to remain, in showery weather best; some (hardy) may be sowed, b. Auriculas, continue shading; plant offsets; prick out seedlings. Baskets or clumps, form of greenhouse plants. Beds, attend diligently to recent planted; water and stir them in dry weather. Biennials and Perennials, sow, if omitted, b. Box edgings clip. Bulbous Roots (Tulips, Jonquils, &c.), not florists' flowers, remove offsets from; dry and store; may transplant some, or keep until autumn; (autumn flowering), as Colchicums, &c., take up as leaves decay, separate offsets, and replant, or not until end of July. Carnations, in bloom, attend: aid the bud-pod to split with a pair of narrow sharp-pointed scissors; bandage buds, to prevent bursting, with Indian-rubber rings, or tape; water every second day; tie to supporters, &c.; prick out seedlings; make layers; pipe. Chrysanthemums, plant out to layer next month. Cyclamens, transplant. Dahlias, finish planting out, b. Dress the borders assiduously; neatness now stamps a gardener's character. Fibrous-rooted Perennials, propagate by cuttings; shade and water. Flowering Plants generally require training and support. Grass, mow, roll, and trim edges. Gravel, weed, sweep, and roll. Hedges, clip, e. Leaves and stems decaying, remove as they appear. Liquid Manure, apply occasionally to all choice flowers. Mignonette, plant out; sow, b. Mimuluses, plant out. Pæonies (Chinese), water freely with liquid manure, or they will not flower finely. Pink Seedlings, prick out; make layers. Pipings (or cuttings) of Carnations and Pinks may be planted. Potted Flowers, dress, stir earth, and water regularly. Ranunculuses, take up as leaves wither, dry and store. Roses, bud, lay, and inarch; fumigate with tobacco to destroy the aphis or green fly; Roses out of doors, wash with tobacco-water. Salvia Patens, pinch down centre stem to make it bushy. Seedlings of Perennials and Biennials, transplant. Seeds (ripe), gather in dry weather. Seed Vessels, remove, to prolong flowering. Water, give freely and frequently to all newly moved plants, and to others in dry weather; early in the morning or late in the evening is the best time. *Brompton Stocks* and *Moss's Intermediate* should be sown on a north border. They will require to be potted in September, and sheltered in a cold pit or greenhouse during the winter. Peg down *Salvias*, and, for a time, until the layers are rooted, cut off the flowers. Verbenas, peg down to cover the beds sooner. Tulips, continue to shade to prolong the bloom, b.; towards e. expose them to full sun to ripen the bulbs; take off seed vessels for the same purpose. Slips of Double Wallflowers, Sweet Williams, and Rockets, put in, either under hand-glasses or under a north wall or low hedge.

D. Beaton.

ORCHARD.

Apricots, thin for tarts. Apples, search for caterpillars. Currants, stop watery wood. Currants (black), water if dry. Cherries, free from aphides. Disbud all trained trees. Figs, thin the young wood, and stop. Gooseberries, free from caterpillars. Insects in general, try to extirpate. Mulching practise where necessary. Peaches, thin both wood and fruit, and stop gross shoots. Plums, cleanse from aphides, and disbud. Pears, disbud, and stop. Raspberries, thin suckers. Strawberries, water if dry, clear runners, and put something to keep fruit clean. Strawberry (Alpine), clear runners from, and water. Stopping practise constantly, where necessary. Thinning practise, both with fruit and wood. Training commence, and continue. Vermin destroy. Vines, thin shoots, and stop. Watering attended to.

R. Errington.

FORCING STOVE.

Cucumbers, keep thinned and stopped. Cherries, water liberally, and cleanse from aphides. Capsicums shift finally, and place in a warm situation. Fire-heat dispense with as much as possible. Grapes thin, and tie shoulders of the late ones. Grapes ripening, remove a few laterals. Liquid Manure apply where size and strength are required. Melons, attend to setting, water freely when swelling; thin the vines frequently, and attend to linings. Nectarines treat as Peaches. Peaches disbud and stop gross shoots; apply liquid manure, and thin fruit. Peaches ripening, remove those leaves which shade the fruit. Strawberries, turn out healthy plants from forcing-house; they will fruit in September. Shading, practise with delicate things, during intense sunshine. Vines, attend to disbudding and stopping. Ventilate freely. Watering, neglect not.

R. Errington.

PLANT STOVE.

Æschynanthes, put in cuttings, pot into large pots and train round a trellis; place in baskets to suspend from the roof of the orchid-house. Amaryllis aulica and varieties pot and plunge in a very gentle heat. Achimenes, repot and shade. Begonias, propagate, and finish potting. Bilbergias, divide such as have bloomed; repot young plants. Caladium bicolor, repot, and grow on, to cause it to make large leaves. Clerodendrum, one more shift. Climbers, tie in, wash to keep clean. Dichorizandra ovata and its allies, pot and grow on. Eranthemum pulchellum, raise in quantity to bloom in winter. Gesnerias, pot, and grow on to increase their bulbs; put in cuttings of. Gloxinias, pot seedlings, and young plants; place them in heat, a hotbed is the best. Gardenias, done blooming, place in a cool pit to rest. Hedychiums, place in large pots to bloom. Ixoras, put in cuttings; pot young plants and specimens; tie the latter out to allow young shoots to spring up in the centre. Luculias, place out of door for a month. Insects, destroy diligently. Musas, either plant out in a bed, or put them in your largest pots; put short dung in lumps on the surface. Nepenthes (Pitcher plant), pot, and plunge in bark-bed, or plant them upon a warm flue, covering it first with moss. Potting may now be done throughout all Stove plants; they will require no more this year. Syringe the walls, and water freely during bright days. Syringe the plants generally at least once a day. Stove bulbs, done flowering, place in cold-pit, giving no water to induce rest. Water, apply freely to the roots of most kinds of Stove plants.

T. Appleby.

FLORISTS' FLOWERS.

Auriculas, finish potting and placing in summer quarters; seedlings transplant, and as soon as strong enough put into small pots singly. Carnations and Picotees, place in their blooming quarters; commence layering as soon as the annual shoots are long enough. Dahlias, finish planting, b.; stake and tie early to secure the plants from wind. Prick out seedlings, and Pot late struck cuttings in four-inch pots, to keep them in through the winter. Irises, in flower, protect from sun, wind, and rain. Pinks, tie to slender sticks to prevent the pod-buds bursting on one side, put round them a strap of India rubber or bass mat, before the flower opens; finish piping. Panseys, now in bloom, protect from sun, wind, and rain; continue to put in cuttings; save seed and sow immediately. Ranunculus bed, water freely, stir the soil when moderately dry; protect the flowers from sun, wind, and heavy rain. Tulips, early kinds, when the leaves turn yellow take up and dry gradually. Turn over composts, and procure fresh loam and peat. Weeds, carefully eradicate from every pot and bed in the garden.

T. Appleby.

KITCHEN GARDEN.

Alexanders, earth up in dry weather. Asparagus beds, sprinkle with salt, and stir with some pointed implement which can be used readily among the plants; no weeds will appear if salting has been attended to. Basil, plant out in good rich warm borders; attend to watering, &c. Broad beans, plant for late crops; let the soil be rich, and if the weather be very hot, give a thorough watering at the time of planting. Beets, thin out, and fill up any vacancies by transplanting; do this in dull weather, and water well. Borage, thin out from eight inches to a foot apart. Borecoles, of all kinds, prick out four to six inches apart. Brussels sprouts and Brocoli, of all sorts, both prick out, and plant out finally, in particular such as the Purple Cape and Walcheren. Cabbages, sow; prick out; and plant out finally, and earth stir. Carrots, finally thin out. Cauliflowers, prick out; plant out in succession; let those in forward growth be well basined up to receive plenty of water; those that are heading-in should be looked over occasionally, and a few of their leaves inverted down over the young heads, to preserve them of a fine white colour. Celery, prick out, and plant out finally. Cucumbers, plant out under hand-glasses, for pickling, &c.; keep the glasses close a few days, until the plants are become established, in particular if the bottom heat is not very much; when established, let them be inured to the open air steadily; those in pits and frames should be weekly attended to, stopped, thinned out, and top-dressed. Endive, make a small sowing of both sorts—Batavian and Green Curled—for early crops. Garlic, Shallots, and Under-ground Onions should be full-grown and fit to take up, dried off, and stored away for use. Herbs, of all kinds, should be cut when in flower for drying and distilling. Jerusalem Artichokes, keep free from weeds with the hoe. Dwarf Kidney Beans and Scarlet Runners, sow for late and last crops; should the weather be very dry at the time of sowing, give a good soaking of water, which will cause them to vegetate quickly; attend to sticking and earth stirring often. Leeks, thin out, and transplant. Transplanting, always do in the evening, and well water. Lettuces, sow often in a situation where they are to finish their growth; place a stick to those intended for seed; tie up in dry weather; a few at a time, according to the consumption. Melons, lose no time in planting out for the late crops; look daily to those setting their fruit; attend to this setting the fruit, and topping the shoots, about eleven o'clock in the forenoon every day; attend to earthing, &c., about three in the afternoon of a warm day, after which, sprinkle the plants over with water, and shut up early. Mint beds which were made last month surface-stir the earth. Knotted Marjoram, plant out in warm borders. Onions, thin out, and transplant, to fill up vacant spaces. Parsley, sow, and thin out. Parsnips should be finally thinned out eight to ten inches apart. Peas, sow; Tall Knight's Marrows may be sown in the early part of this month, but sow any of the early kinds towards the latter end of the month, such as the Early Warwick, &c; should the weather be dry, well water at the time of sowing; attend to hoeing and sticking. Radishes, sow often in cool situations in rich soil. Savoys, plant out finally, and prick out for future plantings. Vegetable Marrow, plant out. Thyme, plant out seedlings. Use the hoe freely in dry weather. Take advantage of dull or wet weather for planting, or pricking out.

T. Weaver.

London: Printed by Harry Wooldridge, Winchester High Street, in the Parish of Saint Mary Kalendar, and Published by William Somerville Orr, at the Office, No. 2, Amen Corner, in the Parish of Christ Church, City of London.—May 30, 1850.

WEEKLY CALENDAR.

M W D D	JUNE 6—12, 1850.	Weather near London in 1849.			Sun Rises.	Sun Sets.	Moon R. & S.	Moon's Age.	Clock bef. Sun.	Day of Year.
6 TH	Landrail first heard.	T. 66°—51°.	N.E.	Fine.	47 a. 3	9 a. 8	2 7	26	1 45	157
7 F	Nightingale's song ceases.	T. 71°—50°.	N.W.	Fine.	47	10	2 32	27	1 33	158
8 S	Honesuckle flowers.	T. 66°—42°.	N.E.	Fine.	46	11	2 9	28	1 23	159
9 SUN	2 SUN. AFT. TRINITY. Dagger Moth appears.	T. 62°—43°.	N.E.	Fine.	46	12	3 34	29	1 13	160
10 M	Silver Moth appears.	T. 60°—42°.	N.E.	Fine.	45	13	sets.	☉	1 0	161
11 TU	ST. BARNABAS. Common Mallow flowers.	T. 65°—37°.	N.E.	Fine.	45	14	9a.21	1	0 49	162
12 W	Trin. T. ends. Redbreast's second brood hatch.	T. 57°—46°.	N.W.	Fine.	45	14	10 16	2	0 36	163

ON the 3rd of June, 1740, died JETHRO TULL, the inventor and the unwearied advocate of drill-sowing and frequent hoeing—the greatest improvements which have been introduced into the modern practice of tillage. The saving of seed effected by this practice is no small consideration; for let it be remembered, that millions of acres are annually sown to grow food for man and his assistant animals, and that by drilling more than one-third of the requisite seed is saved. But this is of trivial importance when compared with the facility that drilling affords for the destruction of weeds, and loosening the soil by the hoe. Every weed, living as it does upon the same food as the cultivated plants among which it grows, is really a robber depriving them of a certain portion of their nourishment, and rendering them less vigorous by depriving them of light and air proportionate to its own size. On the importance of loosening the soil we need not further insist, for we have repeatedly explained that importance, and our coadjutors almost weekly advocate the benefits derivable from the practice. Before Tull's time thick sowing broadcast, and the scanty employment of the hoe, were the established mode; and when Tull adopted and published a work recommending a practice totally the reverse, though many came to see his "new system of husbandry," yet they for the most part came to deride it, and his very labourers thwarted him in "his new-fangled ways." Yet he wrestled firmly and undauntedly against all difficulties; and so nobly does he stand forth in every period of his life, that we must glance over its promisest passages, and hold them up to the cultivators of the soil, to cheer as well as to warn. Tull was educated for the legal profession, but acute disease drove him from a sedentary life, but not into idleness. During his travels in search of health he directed his attention to the agriculture of the countries through which he passed; and finding that they never measured their vineyards, he rashly concluded that all plants might be

similarly cultivated. On returning to England he occupied his own farm of Prosperous, at Shalborne, in Berkshire, and commenced that warfare, to win success against adverse circumstances, from which he only ceased when he rested on his death-bed. If any cultivator despairs over a thin and hungry soil, let him take courage, for Tull won crops from a soil of the same character; nor let him be subdued though sickness enervate him, for Tull was afflicted with agonising diseases, yet was never cast down. The tradition of his neighbourhood is, that when confined to his couch by his incurable maladies, he carried on his experiments in boxes placed before his windows—sowing his seeds and trying his surface-stirring processes with all the enthusiasm of an inventor. If stupid, prejudiced, and perverse servants encumber and thwart the cultivator, this, too, was Tull's fate; and, like him, let the cultivator meet such obstinacy and ignorance with a firmness that will defy all opposition. He is still spoken of by the old labourers of the district as being a man whom it was impossible to oppose with eventual success; and the secret of his triumphs over peasant prejudice is told in this his own apothegm, "There is more than a rent odds in saying to the husbandry servants, Go and do this, or Come, let us do it." Like many other inventors, he arrived at some conclusions not justified by his experiments; and among these errors was the opinion that hoeing and pulverising the soil might supersede the use of manure altogether; but he lived to see his mistake, and, which is still more worthy, to acknowledge it. Our space warns us to conclude, and we will do so in the words of Mr. Cuthbert Johnson, who well appreciates his merits: "Tull lies buried without even a stone to indicate where such a benefactor of agriculture reposes. His grave is even undetermined; and if he died at Shalborne, there is no trace of his burial in its parish register. The tradition of the neighbourhood is, that he died and was buried in Italy. His deeds, his triumphs, were of the peaceful kind with which the world in general is little enamoured; but their results were momentous to his native land. His drill has saved to it, in seed alone, the food of millions; and his horse-hoe system, by which he attempted to cultivate without manure, taught the farmer that deep ploughing and pulverisation of the soil render a much smaller application of fertilizers necessary." That the biography of Tull is no scanty is to be regretted, and is the more surprising because his son, John Tull, was a writer, and a man of enterprise, to whom England was indebted for the first introduction of post-chaises, and the establishment of fish-markets in London.

METEOROLOGICAL PHENOMENA.—During the last twenty-three years, at Chiswick, the average highest and lowest temperatures of the above seven days are 71° and 48.9°, respectively. The greatest heat occurred on the 7th in 1846, when the thermometer rose to 90°. On 63 days rain fell, and 96 days were fine.

RANGE OF BAROMETER—RAIN IN INCHES.

June		1841.	1842.	1843.	1844.	1845.	1846.	1847.	1848.	1849.
6	B.	29.981	30.038	29.861	29.934	29.860	30.064	30.073	29.859	30.109
		29.923	29.915	29.799	29.714	29.575	30.035	30.846	29.787	30.090
	R.	0.01	—	0.17	0.02	—	—	—	—	0.47
7	B.	29.956	30.217	29.896	29.933	29.654	29.078	30.108	29.867	30.137
		29.921	30.163	29.671	29.862	29.796	29.883	29.989	29.788	29.920
	R.	0.02	—	0.23	—	0.25	—	0.02	—	—
8	B.	29.974	30.244	29.407	30.857	30.200	29.871	29.835	29.894	29.996
		29.958	30.304	29.256	30.001	29.897	29.805	29.743	29.756	29.892
	R.	—	0.10	0.03	—	—	—	0.01	0.01	—
9	B.	29.947	30.318	29.642	30.409	30.855	29.835	29.865	29.891	29.916
		29.911	30.163	29.346	30.083	30.335	29.772	29.767	29.623	29.792
	R.	—	—	0.01	0.01	—	—	0.05	0.27	—
10	B.	29.815	30.160	29.937	30.110	30.365	29.995	29.854	29.627	29.728
		29.609	30.064	29.749	30.034	30.269	29.912	29.676	29.476	29.668
	R.	—	—	0.34	—	—	—	0.05	0.95	—
11	B.	29.775	30.190	30.045	30.186	30.235	30.195	30.017	29.811	29.851
		29.637	30.133	30.015	30.143	30.151	30.149	29.960	29.730	29.797
	R.	—	—	—	—	—	—	—	—	—
12	B.	29.973	30.263	30.014	30.166	30.165	30.222	29.971	29.784	29.933
		29.867	30.244	29.959	30.080	30.141	30.125	29.845	29.515	29.223
	R.	0.01	—	0.29	—	—	—	0.78	—	—

INSECTS.—At this season of the Glow-worm's appearance, a few notes relative to its habits may be acceptable. It is the Lampyris noctiluca of entomologists. Both male and female are about half an inch in length,

MALE.   **FEMALE.**

of a blackish colour, with legs of dirty red hue. The male is winged, but the female is quite destitute of the means of flying. Our drawing represents both the sexes. It is the female only which emits the brilliant

phosphorescent light so famed in poetry as well as duller prose. This light proceeds from the under part of the abdomen, and from near its tip, and the insect has the power to vary its intensity. White says, of two specimens he kept, "these little creatures put out their lamps between eleven and twelve, and shine no more for the rest of the night," a fact not unknown to Shakespeare, the poet of nature, who says,

"The glow-worm shews the matin to be near,
And 'gins to pale its uneffectual fire."

The light they emit seems to arise from phosphorus secreted by them, for M. Latreille states that they sometimes explode if confined in hydrogen gas. It is usual to suppose that, like Hero, the glow-worm lights her lamp as a guide for her lover; but a more probable, though less poetical, opinion is, that the light serves to discover to the insect its prey, for its eyes are beneath its head, as the light is also beneath its tail, and can by a slight bending be made to cast its illuminating power forwards. The glow-worm's light is rarely bright after the middle of July. Both the perfect insect and its larvæ seem to feed on snails and slugs.

RESUMING (from page 45) our observations upon the light afforded to gardening by other sciences, we will commence by observing, that the benefits derived from keeping the roots of plants near the surface of the soil are more apparent in fruit-trees and other perennials than in our annual crops, inasmuch as that the roots of trees being thus kept within the influence of the solar rays, always vegetate early, and ripen well their young wood. The quantity of oxygen absorbed by the roots of growing plants is very large; being, in the instances of the radish, carrot, and others, not less than their own bulk in the course of twenty-four hours.

Digging, hoeing, and trenching are the practices employed for facilitating the access of the air to the roots of plants, by rendering the texture of the soil loose and easily permeable.

Very few people ever consider in detail the expenditure of labour required from the garden labourer when digging. It is a labour above all others calling into exercise the muscles of the human frame; and how great is the amount of this exercise may be estimated from the following facts:—

In digging a square perch of ground in spits of the usual dimensions (seven inches by eight inches), the spade has to be thrust in 700 times, and as each spadeful of earth, if the spade penetrates nine inches, as it ought to do, will weigh on the average full seventeen pounds, eleven thousand nine hundred pounds of earth have to be lifted; and the customary pay for doing this is 2½d. !

As there are 160 perches or rods in an acre, in digging the latter measure of ground, the garden labourer has to cut out 112,000 spadefuls of earth, weighing in the aggregate 17,000 cwt., or 850 tons; and during the work he moves over a distance of fourteen miles. As the spade weighs between eight and nine pounds, he has to lift, in fact, during the work, half as much more weight than that above specified, or 1,278 tons.

A four-pronged fork, with the prongs twelve inches long, and the whole together forming a head eight inches wide, is a more efficient tool for digging than the common spade. It requires the exertion of less power; breaks up the soil more effectually; and does not clog even when the soil is most wet. It is less costly than the spade, and when worn can be relaid at a less expense.

The following table shewing the results of the experiments of M. Schluber, exhibits the comparative labour required in digging various soils, and the same soil in various states. Thus if to penetrate with a spade, when dry, grey pure clay, required a force represented by 100, then to penetrate an arable soil in the same state would require a force equal only to 33, or about one-third; so in a wet state the clay would adhere to the blade of the spade with a force equal to 29·2 lbs. the square foot, while the arable soil would only adhere to the same surface with the force of 6·4 lbs.

	Firmness when dry.	Adhesion to a square foot of iron when wet.
Siliceous sand	0	3·8 lbs
Calcareous sand	0	4·1
Fine lime	5·0	14·3 lbs
Gypsum powder	7·3	10·7
Humus	8·7	8·8
Magnesia	11·5	5·8
Sandy clay	57·3	7·9
Loamy clay	68·8	10·6
Brick earth	83·3	17·2
Grey pure clay	100·0	27·0
Garden mould	7·6	6·4
Arable soil	33·0	5·8
Slaty marl	23·0	4·9

The preceding observations and facts are applicable to hoeing, an operation beneficial in consequence of its loosening the soil, as much, or more, as by its destroying weeds. Moisture abounds in the atmosphere during the hottest months, and it is absorbed and retained most abundantly by a soil which is in the most friable state. Professor Schluber found, that 1000 grains of stiff clay absorbed in twenty-four hours only thirty-six grains of moisture from the air; whilst garden mould absorbed in the same time forty-five grains; and fine magnesia seventy-six grains. Then, again, pulverizing the soil enables it better to retain the moisture absorbed. This We demonstrated some years since, and the reason is, obviously, because a hard soil becomes heated by the sun's rays much more rapidly than one with a loosened texture. The latter is better permeated by the air, which is one of the worst conductors of heat. We are glad to find our opinions confirmed by so practical and so intelligent a man as Mr. Barnes, gardener to Lady Rolle, at Bicton Gardens, Devonshire. He says (Gard. Mag., Sept. 1843), " I do not agree with those who tell us, one good weeding is worth two hoeings; I say, never weed any crop in which a hoe can be got between the plants; not so much for the sake of destroying weeds and vermin, which must necessarily be the case, if hoeing be done well, as for increasing the porosity of the soil, to allow the water and air to penetrate freely through it. I am well convinced, by long and close practice, that oftentimes there is more benefit derived by crops from keeping them well hoed, than there is from the manure applied. Weeds, or no weeds, still I keep stirring the soil; well knowing, from practice, the very beneficial effect which it has.

" Raking the surface fine, I have almost wholly dispensed with in every department. By hoeing with judgment and foresight, the surface can be left even wholesome, and porous; and three hoeings can be accomplished to one hoeing and raking. Much injury is done by raking the surface so very much. It is not only the means of binding and caking the surface, but it clears the stones off as well.* The earth, in its natural state, has stones, &c., to keep it open and porous, &c. If the earth be sufficiently drained, either naturally or otherwise, and the surface kept open, there is no fear of suffering either from drought or moisture."

Exposing the soil in ridges during the winter is usually

* A finely pulverised even surface cakes after rain much more than a surface rather rough.

practised by gardeners for the purpose of destroying predatory vermin, but it is also beneficial by aiding the atmosphere to pervade its texture, which texture is also rendered much more friable by the frost. M. Schluber says that freezing reduces the consistency of soils most remarkably, and that in the case of clays and other adhesive soils, the diminution of this consistency amounts to at least 50 per cent. In hoeing clay he found it reduced from sixty-nine to forty-five of the scale already stated, and in the ordinary arable soil from thirty-three to twenty. He satisfactorily explains this phenomenon, by observing that the crystals of ice pervading the entire substance of the frozen soil necessarily separate the particles of earth, rendering their points of contact fewer.

THE FRUIT-GARDEN.

DRAINAGE, MULCHING, &c.—It may not appear a very opportune period to many of the readers of this work to discuss drainage matters, but the fact is, this question is mixed up with the top-dressing or mulching affair; and from letters recently received from correspondents, it is manifest that, however well each of these practices are understood in themselves, they are not so conjunctively, or in the relation they bear to each other under peculiar or trying circumstances.

One correspondent complains of his peaches "withering in their young shoots, losing their buds, &c.;" and at the same time observes, that having lately taken to mulching, *alias* top-dressing, he thinks it probable such practice may have occasioned the evils. Our correspondent nevertheless adds, further, "perhaps, as my soil is wet and undrained, mulching keeps the warmth too much from the roots;" and again, "my soil is of a gravelly nature at top, with a light brick clay below."

Now, as we are persuaded that hundreds—it may be thousands—are similarly situated, it appears a very good opportunity to chat over the principles and practices of mulching or top-dressing, and also of wet or dry subsoils, as connected with surface culture.

It is really astonishing that the immense importance of drainage should yet be ill appreciated, seeing how many fine after-dinner speeches and quires of paper have been devoted to this thrice-told tale; fully exemplifying the poet's satire—

"Truths would you teach, and save a sinking land,
All hear, none aid you, and few understand."

It is so with the oft mooted case of draining: nothing is more easy, or more common, than to find a multitude of false impressions as to cultural practices, owing to this one great enemy beneath—*stagnant moisture.*

It is surely well known at this time of day, that two bodies cannot fill a given space at once; and that, consequently, if the interstices of the soil are water-logged that the atmosphere cannot get free access. Now this is not a question of the mere conveyance of the food of plants; it is that and a something more, which, perhaps, at certain periods is even more important,—*a question of bottom-heat in its relation to the atmosphere.* Let no person suppose, that whether the ground heat in the neighbourhood of the roots of a fruit-tree is 50° or 60° in the month of May is a matter of indifference; no, it is one of those *vital* questions which every one interested in cultural matters should take care to master betimes: having done so, he may carry out all surface operations with the assurance that if any man can command success he can, and that if he fail the blame will not attach to him.

The practice of *mulching* is old as the hills; it will be found strongly recommended in Monsieur de la Quintinye's book of more than a century ago; and, indeed, in gardening books of much older date. Not that this is a proof that it is right, and cannot be abused; it merely shows that it has been submitted thoroughly to the test of experience, and has been much resorted to by men of science as well as of practice.

At the same time it has its bounds, both as to *circumstances, quantity,* and *time of application.*

As to the first, a moment's consideration would show that to place a thick coating of mulch over a sour bottom of undrained clay, is to cut off the last main chance of escape the stagnant moisture within possesses, viz., by evaporation upwards. Such escape prevented, what remains but that all chance of acquiring a proper amount of ground heat through exchange with the atmosphere is cut off; and the anomaly presents itself of a bottom-heat some eight or ten degrees below the average of the atmospheric warmth—a condition which all fruit-bearing trees abhor, for nature did not so intend it.

It is, we believe, a well attested fact, that in most climes the average amount of the bottom-heat through the year exceeds that of the atmospheric average by at least two or three degrees; what, then, may we expect if we reverse this natural average to any extent? Now this bottom-heat, for so we must term it, is not only a stimulus to activity in the vegetable kingdom, but it also, in all probability, acts as a *protection* to plants; and we can scarcely do better than quote from the "Theory of Horticulture" in confirmation of such views:

"That the warmth of the soil acts as a protection to plants may be easily understood. A plant is penetrated in all directions (all?) by innumerable microscopic air passages and chambers, so that there is a free communication between its extremities; it may therefore be conceived, that if, as necessarily happens, the air inside the plant is in motion, the effect of warming the air in the roots will be to raise the internal temperature of the whole individual; and the same is true of its fluids. Now, when the temperature of the soil is raised to 150° at noonday by the force of the solar rays, it will retain a considerable part of that warmth during the night; but the temperature of the air may fall to such a degree that the excitability of a plant would be too much and suddenly impaired if it acquired the coldness of the medium surrounding it; this is prevented, we may suppose, by the warmth communicated to the general system from the soil, through the roots, so that the lowering of the temperature of the air by radiation during the night is unable to affect plants injuriously, in consequence of the antagonistic force exercised by the heated soil."

So, then, we see that what is termed bottom-heat is a provision of nature for the purposes before specified; and we trust it will be understood that thorough drainage, by keeping the soil emptied of all excess of moisture, places it in a condition to receive and renew that amount of heat from the solar rays which had been lost during the previous winter; and the soil being less liable to sudden changes than the atmosphere, proves a store-house of sure reliance.

We have thus shown that whatever prevents the soil from attaining its proper relation in warmth to the atmosphere is likely to prove injurious, especially in spring; and we now proceed to show that there are cases wherein mulching may be not only harmless but of immense benefit. Trees recently planted, and those on soils comparatively shallow and thoroughly drained, require a steady supply of root moisture; and when a period of drought, accompanied by much heat, or even of drying winds, occurs, trees thus situated are sure to suffer, if some extra attention be not paid to them. Watering, of course, immediately suggests itself, but this is an operation frequently requiring an inconvenient amount of labour; and, moreover, unless the water is in a tepid state, its utility, as sometimes applied, is somewhat questionable.

Under such circumstances it is that we advocate mulching; but where there is doubt of a proper amount of porosity in the soil, or a fear of water lodgment below, or in cases of very adhesive soils, we own that mulching should be resorted to with some caution. As to the matter of temperature in the soil, little harm need be apprehended from applying it in the course of the month of May, for the ground has by that period acquired a sufficient amount of warmth from the atmosphere to carry on the purposes of vegetation.

To all those, then, who have doubts on the subject, and who can find time to water and duly attend to their trees, we would say—do not mulch until May, and then only in cases where injurious droughts are apprehended. At the same time it is necessary to observe, that we practise mulching systematically with most fruit-trees; but then the trees in question are on shallow soils, possessing a dry and sound subsoil of clear red sand. On such we mulch newly planted fruit-trees in November, in order to prevent any sudden and injurious vicissitudes; for, strange to say, what prevents the soil from becoming too hot in summer prevents it from becoming too cold in winter. We mulch all fruits carrying unusually heavy crops in May, in order that sudden droughts should not affect them injuriously, and also to the end that all rains passing to the roots should be compelled to carry with them an extra amount of nutritious properties from the manure.

Again, we mulch at various periods merely to encourage *surface roots;* being assured that fruit-trees are ever more prosperous the more the latter are encouraged and protected. But then, be it remembered, that we never dig near to such trees, and that most of our fruits are planted on the platform system, with a depth of only fifteen inches to two feet of soil, as the case may be. Our peaches and nectarines were mulched over four inches deep in the second week of May, and a thorough soaking of water immediately applied; they have now (May 26th) made nearly enough wood for the whole summer.　　　　　　　　　R. ERRINGTON.

THE FLOWER-GARDEN.

PROPERTY OF ROOTS.—There is one property belonging to the roots of many trees which is seldom taken into consideration, either in laying out a new flower-garden, or in planting in or around an old one. Yet, of all the difficulties incident to flower-gardening, those which arise from this property, or peculiarity, in the roots of certain fine trees are the most difficult to contend with.

I happened to be in the company of some scientific people the other day, who I found, on joining them, were in "deep consultation" on this very subject—the properties of roots; and an observation that was made by one of the party, a practical man, tickled in my ears for two or three days afterwards; owing, as I suppose, to its originality—for in these days of reading and writing one seldom hears or meets with an original idea. Before the tickling faded away, I fixed on the subject as a good text to write a lecture on tree roots for THE COTTAGE GARDENER. I need scarcely say this practical man is a good gardener. He and one of our greatest architects, together with a lady and gentleman high in the gardening world, seemed much perplexed, at the time I joined them, about a certain beech-tree, under whose full spreading boughs they were sheltered; not, however, like Virgil's Tityrus, from the heat of the sun, but from a keen easterly wind. As far as I could make out, this beech-tree was very much in the gardener's way, and he could

see no great harm in having it removed, root and branch —a feat in which the architect seemed very willing to assist him; but the owner of the tree (and *he* might be proud of it) thought very differently, and seemed to have it settled in his own mind that, come what would of new fancies in architecture and in gardening, this fine old spreading beech-tree should be spared to shelter and shade the owners thereof for the next two or three generations. But he, the said owner, knowing that whatever the result of the consultation might be, it must be paid for in hard cash, had no great objection to see the gardener and architect come into a mutual collision, if there is such a thing, about this tree; inferring all the while that a spark thus produced, though on the old principle of steel and flint, might not only save the beech-tree, but redound to their own credit and fame in after generations, and to his own comfort and pleasure in the mean time. I found also that it was a settled point with them all, that some kind of ornamental and permanent fence must pass under the boughs of this beech, and within five feet of the trunk. The architect had much objection to allow this fence to be constructed of such materials as came under his department of the "fine arts," and the "practical man" could not perceive how a live fence could be established under and on either side of such a tree "anyhow." The arguments for and against this dead or "alive" fence brought out, I should think, the greatest portion of all the light which vegetable physiologists have hitherto employed in examining and describing the properties of the roots of large trees in general.

I could see that my friend the gardener was, by this time, well nigh losing the day, and that a hedge of tree-box, seven or eight feet high, at once must and would be planted on this disputed site; and whether this box-hedge should be planted by the gardener or by the architect was all that remained to be settled, when the gardener exclaimed, "Man alive! the roots of the beech would not only come to the surface of the new border for the box the very first year, but they would go up to the top of the tree itself and down again on the other side, take a new lease, and thus girdle the tree like a girl's skipping rope." This was now and sufficiently startling to all of us, but I believe he was not very far wrong.

I have since learned that they have decided on the following ingenious plan:—A trench eight feet wide is to be opened in front of the beech-tree, and within five feet of its trunk. This trench will be as deep—or a little deeper—as the roots have gone down. The whole of the soil within the influence of the roots of the beech is to be carted away, and a four-inch brick wall, built in cement and carried up to the surface of the ground, is to keep back these voracious roots from a new border, in which large box-trees or bushes are to be planted next August or September, according to the state of the weather, as thickly as they can stand, and then to be dressed or pruned on one side into the shape of a hedge. Before the new soil is put into the trench, the bottom is to be strongly concreted with a slope from the brick division; and should the roots pass under the wall, they are met and stopped by the concrete.

Now, any gardener of common experience can see the impossibility of establishing a live hedge close to a full-grown beech, ash, or elm tree or trees, without some such expedient as that resorted to in this instance, because the roots of these and similar trees will immediately occupy whatever good soil may be used to plant the hedge in; so that the newly planted things have no chance but to pine and starve by inches. Hence the reason for my own tar-barrel system for planting climbers and choice plants against old trees, or in the front of established plantations. What shall we say, therefore, if our own flower-beds just planted with care and the choicest things we could procure for them, happen to be within the reach of the roots of old trees? Why! we need say no more than that all the gardeners and watering in the kingdom could hardly compete against such odds. The shade of tall trees is bad enough, but when their roots find their way into flower-beds the consequence is soon told. You may trench and turn, and turn and trench over and over again, add new soils, stimulants, and what not, but all to very little purpose. The more you prepare the beds for flowers, the faster they are in the possession of these intruding roots. I have had to do with this kind of annoyance as much as most gardeners; but I never yet met with a case I could not cure, if I had sufficient money to go to work with; and I always went on the principle of cutting off all communication between the roots and the flower-beds, but with cheaper materials than bricks and cement, like my friend the "practical man."

On thin dry soils, and on heavy undrained clay, this kind of warring against immediate neighbours is not at all a difficult operation, because in the former case rambling roots are compelled to run near the surface, and a trench a foot wide and, perhaps, not more than 18 inches deep, opened just a little beyond the bed or beds, and filled with concrete, generally settles the matter for many years. A couple of careful hands, to whom this kind of defence is entrusted here, say that if all our trenches were reduced to one uniform standard of a foot deep and twelve inches wide they would reach from here to—I am afraid to say how far, for people will talk wide, even of narrow trenches, and it will be enough if I say we have many of them which keep back the roots very effectually, and one small fancy garden of about 30 little beds is entirely surrounded by a deep trench filled in this way, and some parts of this trench are seven feet deep, and the shallowest part of it is a yard deep and full two feet wide, because the men could not work so deep in a less width. Our manner of filling up these trenches with *concrete* is simple enough; we take so many cart-loads, or barrow-loads, as the case may require, of the finest chalk—that which the frost crumbles down from the face of a deep bed of chalk is the best and easiest to work,—and for every load of this we put five loads of unsifted gravel, both chalk-gravel and pure white sand being close at hand; a layer of nine or ten inches of the chalk is first thrown in, then a quantity of water, sufficient to make a soft puddle, into this six inches of gravel is thrown, and a man on each side of the trench follows with long poles, with which they poke the gravel and chalk-mud until they are well mixed; after that true proportions of one chalk and five gravel are thrown in, with water enough to keep the whole very soft; indeed, so soft that one of the poking sticks may be thrust down a yard through the mass with very little effort. In summer it takes a week to dry this kind of concrete, but after it is once dried it sets as hard and close as cast-iron, and a castle might be built over it; and yet, where rough coal-ashes and lime would be cheaper than chalk and gravel, they would form a still harder concrete, and seven parts of cinders to one part of lime would then be about the proper proportions.

Where the whole side, or end, of a flower-garden is exposed to the roots of neighbouring trees, instead of cutting a circle round each bed, or some particular beds, to keep them back, the cheapest way will be to run a trench in the shortest direction round the outside of the garden, or part of it if that will do. I know so many nice flower-gardens that are entirely ruined by the roots of old trees, and that might thus be effectually relieved from such invaders, and at a very small cost, comparatively speaking, and, moreover, I find the comfort of the plan so enjoyable myself, that I cannot recommend the plan too strongly.

Between old tar barrels, new barrels made of elm staves, and concrete trenches, we set all the old trees at defiance in this garden; and in a few days I shall make a new bed—and, may be, a set of new beds, for when one finds time to begin fancy things in a garden the difficulty is to know when and where to stop—in the close vicinity of some old trees and large Portugal laurels; and I know we shall have to cut through large roots in digging out the beds, but concrete will make short work with them. These new beds—that is, if we make more than one of them—are for an entirely new bedding plant, a most noble plant to the bargain, and a most novel bed it will make no doubt; and I speak of it thus early that all those who can afford it may have the chance of an equal start with myself. And lest some should suppose that this is like calling "chick, chick," before the eggs are hatched, I must remark that this very noble bedding plant has been fully proved in Suffolk to be really a good thing, and no one need be apprehensive of the bed answering well. This new bed should be made where a dark mass of foliage comes in behind it, and, if possible, it should be seen from the living rooms; and if it could be so placed that it could be viewed *not against* the sun after midday, all the better. What gardeners call " with the sun," and "against the sun," is this:—on this side of the line when one looks due north at midday the sun is striking against the back of the head, and the person is said to look "with the sun;" and if he turns the other way the light, or rays of the sun, strike him full in the face, and he is looking "against the sun." Now the best situation for the bed I contemplate is where one could see it from the windows, looking " with the sun" at four o'clock in the afternoon, and with a dense mass of foliage behind it. The bed will be splendid in the autumn; in the forenoon the shade of the trees and shrubs behind it will throw a softness into the mass that will really be most charming, and altogether I anticipate a very favourable opinion of this bed, once we get it fairly afloat.

The old *Datura,* or *Brugmansia arborea,* is the plant I have in view for this new bed; it has been already sufficiently proved to be as capable of being left in the ground from year to year as the fuchsias or any other half-hardy plants. With it I propose to plant, and recommend others also to plant, the red and the yellow sorts of *Brugmansia ;* and next week I shall give all the rules that I think necessary for managing this and similar plants under this system.   D. BEATON.

GREENHOUSE AND WINDOW GARDENING.

AZALEA INDICA: HINTS ON SHADING, ARRANGING, &c.—These beautiful plants must be treated according to the state they are in, and what you expect from them in future. We fear that, to some of our readers, we may seem to be harping over an old tune, and laying ourselves open to the imputation of giving " Cauld kail, het, again"—the usual designation given in Scotland to hearing a sermon a second time, either in a similar or a different place of worship. I have little faith in the old adage—" A good story is none the worse for being twice told," especially if I should be the narrator. My reason for adverting to these plants again, arises from the desire to meet the case of the many inquiries that have lately been made respecting Azaleas.

First, then, with respect to those *plants now in bloom* or just coming into it, if it is desirable to prolong the flowering period, they should be kept shaded, and as cool as possible. A place out of doors, against a north wall, and covered with glazed calico, if not with glass, would just be the situation for them. A greenhouse kept moderately hot, to forward fuchsias, and the early-blooming azaleas, soon would destroy the beauty of those later-blooming ones. Even in one small house, heated by one flue, or set of pipes, various degrees of temperature and humidity in the atmosphere may easily be maintained, by means of divisions ; and keeping these divisions differently, as respects shading and air. The knowledge of this would often obviate the necessity, in heating by hot water, of increasing the expense by reason of stop-cocks, or valves, for every division, however small. The amateur, therefore, who wishes to have his azaleas early and late (and no tribe is more worthy of having their beauties prolonged), or who would wish to pursue a similar course in the case of any other favourite family of plants, should resolve upon having a division in his house, however small; which, even if of glass, will be no great consideration now, as regards expense, unless for the door and other wood-work. One department, then, could be applied to the *cultivating* of plants, and the other chiefly to the *exhibiting* of them in bloom. Of course, the warmest end of the house would require to be devoted to the purposes of culture ; and even there, by a difference of air at one end, much difference in temperature and atmospheric moisture can be maintained. Plants when in bloom, even if somewhat tender, will remain in bloom much longer if kept cool and airy, insects prevented from access by gauze netting, and shaded from bright sunshine.

In great as well as in small gardens much advantage would be gained by the plants, and an additional interest awakened, by having blooming plants and growing plants separate from each other, at least to a great extent. Even the difference exhibited by contrast in passing from the one to the other would create a feeling of pleasure, from the very fact, that the distinction was *marked* and *defined*. When flowering plants are sprinkled somewhat regularly over the surface of a house, or stage, with green and growing plants between, the feeling produced is more that derived from viewing varieties combined in regular confusion than associated with the delights derived from a felt harmony of parts. I lately saw two houses of plants : one consisted of geraniums in full bloom, the other of geraniums, calceolarias, azaleas, &c. ; a few in bloom, the others growing and showing bloom-buds : no mingling and commingling of the contents of the two houses, as is generally done by many of our friends, so as to make all places look gay—sticking a flowering plant here, and another there—would have produced such a satisfactory result as the mere contrast in the present instance elicited. "Oh ! but," says one of our readers, "such an arrangement would be so *unnatural :* it is not at all like what we see in our meadows, our hedgerows, and woodland brakes and fells—those brakes which that amiable lady in THE COTTAGE GARDENER, whose writings you so much admire, praises so eloquently and well." No ! but not to enter into this pleasing question at present, I will content myself with stating, that a plant-house is not a wild brake or heath. It is an artificial erection for a particular purpose ; and ought, in everything within, to bear the impress of an arrangement *different* from what exists in external nature ; except, indeed, in those colossal piles of glass which are *yet* to be erected, where meadows and fields are to be enclosed, and woodland scenes in Australia, or tropical scenes from warmer latitudes, are to be pourtrayed ! and where pots, and boxes, and baskets, would be as much out of character, with the style of art attempted, as they are perfectly in keeping with the *not more artificial*, but the more *apparent*, art represented in our greenhouses.

But then, again, there is the shading from bright sun, necessary to keep azaleas and other flowers long in bloom, and also to assist them when growing and making their new wood ; and this I find to be a troublesome and expensive affair, and if neglected the plants are more susceptible to injury than if they were never shaded at all. Bunting, fastened by one side to the roof, and by the other to a round pole, with a wheel at one end for holding the rope, and either or not connected with a pulley-wheel, answers remarkably well; but, then, my man "Friday" pulls it up and lets it down with such a jerk, that in a few months, if not weeks, it is pretty well in ribands ; and, then, when in despair I have turned to mats—in the placing, fixing, and removing them—more glass was broken than the plants were worth, so that, being obliged to be from home a great part of the day, I am next to hopeless as to succeeding with my greenhouse, unless a cheap and secure method of shading could be adopted.

A *very* cheap method, which we were among the first to use, though not a very pretty looking one, but not a whit more unsightly than dirty mats, consists in dissolving a little whitening in a pail of water (not lime, mind, that injures paint), and then throwing it over the roof with the syringe : a very little whitening will be sufficient, or it will look ugly. As we have not much dull weather in the heat of summer, except what is accompanied by rain, the whitening would seldom want removing or replacing, except when washed off by these natural means. Dipping a whitewashing brush into the mixture, and quickly and evenly drawing it down each row of glass, would look neater ; but in both cases your liquid must be just coloured with the whitening. Try a bit, and let it dry, to satisfy yourself before doing a whole house, as it is much easier to over-do it than under-do it. But if neatness and suitability combined be your object, and you do not mind a little time at first, I have found nothing better than common size, or glue, put on the glass quite hot as thinly as possible with a brush, and then slightly daubed with the points of a dry brush as you proceed. The glass should be dry, but the sun not shining strong. In ordinary occasions it will last until the heavy rains of autumn ; will be quite inconspicuous, unless you come close beside it, but will blunt the force of rays of light sufficiently to suit tender growing as well as flowering plants. If you want it *denser*, a little whitening dissolved in it would suit your purpose ; but the last thing will leave a greyish-white appearance on the glass. Always put it on outside.

We make no apology for these several digressions, though I wish I could have made them shorter. They will be *generally* applicable, as well as suitable to Azaleas. Without shade, or keeping them at a distance from the glass, they neither can be preserved in bloom late nor forwarded so as, without *forcing* in winter, to produce their flowers from January to April, and continue doing so from year to year. Different views are held by first-rate gardeners as to the period when different operations should be performed ; but these differences would be greatly reconciled were it seen that the difference consisted less in *principle* than from looking at the object from different points of view. Thus, for instance, in the disputed matter of *potting*, some would say pot and repot at any time ; others, pot immediately when growth commences after flowering ; and others again, and equally good growers, say pot only in the autumn, when the new wood is ripened and the buds are set. Now I consider all these directions good, provided the circumstances of the plants are duly attended to. A lanky-looking plant should be cut down, placed in a high temperature, say from 60° to 70°, and potted as soon as the fresh shoots begin to break. Plants flowering from Christmas to April, when cleared of their flowers, should have the first and strongest shoots produced stopped, to insure a more plentiful, as well as a more equal, as to strength, supply of young shoots, as upon them the next season's blooming depends. When these begin to break freely, the plants should be examined and repotted, or merely top-dressed, as may be seen necessary ; placed in a vinery at work, or set in the warmest end of the growing department of the greenhouse; and, besides watering, giving them frequently a dash from the syringe; and especially looking after the jumping fellow, the thrip. When the shoots get nearly full-grown they should be exposed gradually to more air, and when well hardened set out of doors in a sheltered place, exposed to the sun, but sheltered from rains, and the pots protected from the heat, by any of the methods several times referred to. These plants, if removed to the greenhouse before very cold nights in autumn, will commence swelling their buds in the middle of winter.

Plants blooming in May and June, and intended to do so in future, should be treated somewhat differently. Growth should be encouraged, the shoots be ripened, the ends of the shoots plumped, so as to show that the flower-buds for next season are set; and then the roots, as soon as possible, be examined and repotted, not giving large shifts however. Those of this class that made their wood early, as some kinds do, almost cotemporaneously with the flower-buds expanding, I have treated just as I have recommended for early flowering ones, and with the best results. But supposing we adopt the different methods according to these different circumstances, the principles of action are identical; and are these:—First, the propriety of not repotting a plant until the fresh growth commences. Second, the necessity of having a pot full of roots before the flowering season comes, if the flowers are wanted fine and large. Now plants flowering at an early period, and intended so to flower again, would not like being potted after their buds were set, for two reasons: first, the pots would not be filled with roots sufficiently early; and secondly, from the increased range of food given, there would be a danger of the shoots, ripened or nearly so, starting again into growth, and thus spoiling the spring display of flowers, which is avoided by shifting early; as then the strength of the new compost is thrown into the new shoots, and the coolness of autumn, out of doors, and a north aspect, if there is the least sign of danger, will prevent a second growth. In the second case, the late flowering ones are encouraged to make their new wood sooner than if retarded with a shift; and then being shifted as soon as the buds are set in autumn, they have got the fall of the autumn and the whole of winter to fill the pots with roots, while plenty of air is admitted to their tops.

Several matters might be summed up and referred to, which we barely name.

1. *Azaleas*, and *camellias* likewise, require to be encouraged *after blooming* by a higher temperature, and in order to produce their new growth.

2. This encouragement may as well be given in the end of a common greenhouse, shut off on purpose, or with less air given, as under the shade of vines, or any other place.

3. In encouraging this growth, Azaleas, even the strongest growing, should only have clear waterings; anything else ought to be weak indeed. A solution of very old cow dung, from its cool nature, seems to answer best. Camellias, on the other hand, will drink guano water, or any other manure solution, like topers, though it should not be strong.

4. In *potting*, *Azaleas* like lumpy heath mould best, with silver sand, and pieces of charcoal to assist drainage. Peat and loam in equal portions do well for *camellias*, with a sixth part of very rotten cow dung.

5. In potting *Camellias*, we prefer doing it earlier than even for Azaleas, as, if done late, and bloom is wanted early, the flowers will be small. Rather than repot late in autumn, we should top-dress, and repot the following season. With top-dressing, and manure waterings, and good drainage, they will flourish for years in the same pot.

6. In choosing sorts of Azaleas, look to the lists at the Metropolitan shows.

7. In buying plants, get them young, stubby, in small pots, and even these not crammed with roots.

R. FISH.

HOTHOUSE DEPARTMENT.

EXOTIC STOVE PLANTS.

GESNERACEÆ—a family of plants that for beauty and usefulness is almost invaluable. When we first began gardening, some thirty years ago, they were scarcely known. In 1759, a plant, the first of the order, named by the great Linnæus—*Gesnera tomentosa*, was introduced from South America. It was followed by *Gesnera tubiflora* in 1793; and that again by *Gesnera acaulis* in 1815. A still older plant of the same natural order exists to this day, namely, *Gloxinia maculata*, so named by Heritier; and which was introduced to Europe so long ago as 1739. No other Gloxinia reached this country till 1815, when the beautiful *G. speciosa*, the parent of numerous hybrids, was introduced. In 1816 two more species of Gesnera reached us, named, severally, *G. aggregata* (since lost) and *G. bulbosa* (still grown). From 1820 to the present time the importations were constantly adding to the stores of these beauties of our hothouses. When the late indefatigable Mr. Loudon first published his "Hortus Brittanicus," the now large family of Achimenes, belonging to this order, was totally unknown. Since that time, by the labours and persevering endeavours of such collectors as G. A. Skinner, Esq., who resided for several years in Guatemala, and Mr. Hartweg, the London Horticultural Society's collector, these beautiful plants were introduced, and increased both in number of species and quantities of each, so that at this present time there is not a plant stove in the three kingdoms without more or less of them in cultivation. Several genera, besides, have been added to the order, so that it is now a pretty extensive one, as the list we shall give presently of them will prove.

In one respect this tribe of plants has a great advantage over most others. By proper management some species or other may be kept in flower nearly all the year round. In the Kew Gardens we witnessed *Achimenes picta* and *Gesnera zebrina* in the finest bloom in the January of this year; and they were likely to continue until others were brought forward to succeed them. The grand season, however, for bloom of the whole family is from June to October, just the season when greenhouses are most deficient of bloom, excepting from annuals, such as balsams, cockscombs, and the like. During these months they are, if moderately managed, the greatest ornaments of both stoves and greenhouses.

Culture.—Commence early in January to start a portion of them into growth, by potting, and placing them in a moist heat. The best compost for them is a light turfy loam that has been frequently turned over to sweeten, and half-decayed tree-leaves, in equal parts, with as much sand as will give the compost a sandy character. For the stronger-growing species of *Gesneras*, *Gloxinias*, and *Achimenes*, the addition of one-eighth of very rotten dung will be useful. Drain the pots well, and proportion their size to the size of the roots. The genera *Gesnera* and *Gloxinia* will, when three or four years old, have tubers as much as from four to six inches in diameter. They then require pots full three inches wider than the tubers. Shake off gently all the old soil, trim off all dead roots, and work the compost in amongst the living roots, leaving the crown of each tuber just level with the soil.

The scaly roots of *Achimenes* may either be placed singly in 3½ inch pots, to be repotted after they have filled them with roots, or they may be, if plentiful, potted in wide shallow pots, five, or six, or more, in each, according to the fancy of the cultivator. Either way they will flower admirably, if properly managed as to heat and moisture. The latter method saves the trouble of repotting, but the single bulbs form the neatest plants. Give no water after potting in the moist compost for a week or two; place them in a gentle heat. A moderate hotbed of well-sweetened dung, covered with coalashes or tanners' bark, will answer the best for them at this early season. This potting ought to flower in May. The next batch may be set to work in the same manner the first week in March; the next in May; and the last in July. These two latter pottings will not require any heat, but may be placed after potting in a cold pit, where the natural heat of the season, if they are kept moderately close at first, will be sufficient to bring them slowly on. These two latter pottings will consist chiefly of the different kinds of *Achimenes*, and *Gesnera zebrina*, with the varieties of *Achimenes*, especially *A. picta*. They are intended to bloom through the autumn and winter months in the warm stove and orchid house, which they will ornament greatly when there are few other plants in bloom.

Water.—The application of this is a matter of importance to all plants, but to this tribe more than to most others. In the early stages of growth it must be given sparingly, and never over the young and tender leaves, especially in the morning. If the leaves are wet with water, or even dew from the steam of the fermenting materials employed to stimulate them into growth, the sun will be apt to discolour them, and the growth will be crippled. Avoid, therefore, wetting the leaves as much as possible, and water chiefly in the after part of the day. Shade also early, and give air so as to allow the steam to evaporate, and the tender leaves to dry. When the season is more advanced, and the leaves more mature, a gentle syringing in the afternoon will be beneficial. One point must be attended to at all seasons, and that is, to keep them near to the glass, to induce short vigorous growth. If they are placed far from the glass their leafstalks will be drawn up, and will be weak and unsightly.

Winter treatment.—As soon as the flowering season is over, whether early or late, the plants ought to be put to rest. We have experienced it to be a good plan when the plants showed evident signs of exhaustion, to place them out of doors in a warm sheltered place in the garden. This applies only to such as have done blooming as early as July. To prevent them receiving too much moisture, which would have a tendency to start them into premature growth, we lay the pots or pans on one side. As soon as the leaves and stems are quite yellow, cut them off, and place the roots in a cool shed till the frosts begin, when they should be removed into their winter quarters, the best of which is under the stages of the stove, where they may remain till the potting season returns, care being taken that they are kept quite dry. Later potted plants, the blooming season of which extends to autumn and winter, should be set to rest by withholding water, and placing them out of the reach of frost. Attend to this—*let such as go to rest the first be started first.* They will have obtained a habit of early growth, and their early rest will give them the power and desire to start again at the usual season they have been accustomed to. This is a law of nature which cannot be infringed with impunity. The fruit cultivator is fully impressed with its truth. His vines, peaches, &c., that have been by degrees brought into early habits, are the most easily stirred in active growth the following season. It is so also with flowering plants of every kind, and by none more so than the order of Gesneraceæ.

(*To be continued*)

FLORISTS' FLOWERS.

Spring and summer in our climate do not come at any particular day, week, or even month, but visit us in fits and starts. Sometimes we have a week of cold dry weather, succeeded by showers of rain, and occasional warm sunny days; these again are sadly too often succeeded by cold days, and frosty nights, varied by windy stormy ones, accompanied by hailstorms, heavy long continued rains, and cold easterly winds. It is this uncertainty of weather that calls forth all the forethought and untiring vigilance of the florist, to guard against the bad effects which those disastrous changes bring upon his favourite plants. He has stood in need this season of all these careful attentions, or, if they have been neglected even for a single day and night, the woeful effects of such neglect will now be visible. Let even such as have carefully tended and watched their choice flowers, by no means relax their attention now. Read over and practise all the points of culture we have weekly endeavoured to enforce.

TULIPS.—The glory of these noble flowers is fast departing for another season; and they seem to say—"Take care of us, or we shall be unable to feast your eyes and gratify your mind another season. To strengthen our roots cut off all our seed vessels; protect us from heavy rains; lift up gently such of us as seem unwilling to go to rest with our fellows; leave us in the ground till our leaves turn yellow; and then take us up and lay us in a cool place to dry." Such is the language the imaginative tulip fancier will say his highly prized departing friends would use, could they speak. And we say, act accordingly We say this to the new beginner; the old staunch experienced grower will not need our advice.

T. APPLEBY.

THE KITCHEN-GARDEN.

CAULIFLOWERS.—Plant liberally in shady situations, and make a couple of good sowings this month, the produce of which will come to hand at the end of summer, and in the autumn. *Coleworts*, too, should be sown at twice, liberally, this month, so as to have at command a supply of good plants to put out in succession on the early potato and other spare ground.

CELERY should now be well encouraged. Prick and plant out in succession, keep the early plants well surface-stirred, and free from suckers; particularly bear in mind that you must neither plant nor prick the plants too deep; they should not be buried deeper than their seed-leaf, or collar; indeed, deep planting is a serious detriment to the kindly progress of vegetation of every kind. *Celery*, as every one knows, is a gross feeding and thirsty plant; and to produce it of an extraordinary size, of good quality, the principal essentials are a good, rich, well pulverized piece of ground, which has been well trenched and liberally supplied with good manure, well inter-mixed amongst the soil, and the plants never allowed to become dry; the lack of moisture in dry weather being likely to render the celery pipy and tough; too much water can hardly be applied to it. Our system, when we wish to produce a large supply of celery from a small piece of ground, is to choose a well prepared piece, as above described; and supposing it to be eight feet wide, a shallow trench five feet wide is cast out up the centre, the plants are put in the crossway of the trench, in rows from a foot to eighteen inches apart, the distance being regulated according to the time of planting, whether late or early, or whether it is required to be grown of a large size, &c. The number of plants in each row is also regulated by the same rule, and varies from five to eight. The surface of the soil between the plants we generally lightly mulch with decayed refuse leaves, or short decayed manure of any kind; the advantage of which is, that any quantity of water may be applied without the soil becoming surface-bound. By following these principles, every facility is afforded for surface-stirring, watering, and applying the earth for blanching; and a large quantity of celery may thus be obtained on a small piece of ground, of a good size and excellent quality, with less expense than by any other means.

WATERING.—At the present season, when dry weather may be expected to prevail, there is no doubt but that in many instances much benefit may be afforded to growing crops by the judicious application of water, and when watering is performed it should be done systematically, or more harm will be caused than good. Our method, when we set about watering, is to choose dull or cloudy weather, if such prevail, or the late evenings and early mornings; and to apply the water in great abundance, if we apply it at all; taking care to apply it to all except seed-beds, without wetting either the leaves or foliage of the plants or crops. We also apply it without any rose on the water-pot, thrusting, instead, a spray or a branch of heath from an old broom, into the spout or nozle of the water-pot; and with a pot in each hand held close to the surface of the earth the water is quickly and softly dispersed amongst the growing crops without surface-binding the soil.

ROUTINE WORK. — *Artichokes, cauliflowers, celery,* *cabbages, beans, peas,* and all kinds of kitchen-garden crops, are the better for being slightly mulched for the next three months, should dry hot weather prevail. And if ground can be spared a planting should be made of *Brussels sprouts* and *Dwarf savoys. Cape brocoli* and the *Walcheren brocoli* should be planted in succession.

POTATOES.—We shall no doubt soon hear some outcry respecting the disease of this vegetable, the extent of which so much depends on atmospheric influence. We are sorry to observe all through the spring, the old enemy still lurking about, though we are happy to say only to a very trifling extent, compared to that of former years. By pulling up a few potato stalks and closely examining them at the base where the disease first commences, there will be found, if any disease exist, small punctures, advancing into brown ulcerated gangreen blotches; but up to the present time we have not found amongst any of our early-taken-up produce one tuber thus effected—all having been excellent both in crop and quality.   JAMES BARNES.

MISCELLANEOUS INFORMATION.

TEA DRINKING.
By the authoress of " My Flowers."

TEA is usually considered an expensive enjoyment, and so indeed it is; but when coffee and cocoa are recommended as substitutes, on account of their cheapness, I believe on a close calculation they will be found to fail; at least we have tried the experiment unsuccessfully in our own family. If herbs are collected and infused, there is no doubt that a great expense would be avoided in giving up tea; but if foreign produce must be resorted to, tea is certainly the cheapest in the end.

A small quantity of tea, carefully managed, will form a much more agreeable meal for a family than a small quantity of coffee: we can drink rather weak tea with less distaste than weak coffee, and there is a flavour, even then, that is pleasant. Coffee is really disagreeable unless it is tolerably strong; and it cannot be renewed like tea. Although coffee is considerably cheaper per pound than tea, in fact it *may* be bought at less than half the price, yet requiring to be used so much more freely it becomes *much* dearer in the end. It is a heating, stimulating beverage also, when taken constantly, and will not agree with many persons, yet it certainly is the most delicious of all, when well made and strong; and when taken during or after fatigue it is far more reviving and strengthening than wine or beer. Still it is not a cheap re-freshment when used as a meal in the family. When it is bought, it should always be in the berry, and fresh roasted if possible. When wanted for use, the berries should be placed in an oven, or before the fire, to become gently warm before they are ground, which should take place only just previous to being made into coffee, and the mill should be a coarse one. Coffee should not be ground fine; and it is even said that when beaten in a mortar the flavour is improved; but this is a more tedious and troublesome process, and I cannot vouch for its truth. A small quantity of very strong coffee poured into three parts of a cupful of boiling milk is the best and pleasantest way of taking it for breakfast; and where milk is plentiful and cheap it may not be an extravagant plan; but tea is cheaper.

Cocoa is a nourishing article, but not a cheap one. The patent soluble cocoa at eightpence per pound is extremely convenient, because it is made so quickly and easily; but unless it is tolerably strong it is not very palatable, and a pound is very soon gone. It is certainly cheaper than coffee, however, and if it agrees is pleasant and strengthening; but as a *family* meal it will not be found to answer. Many things may be economical for one person that become seriously ex-pensive when required for a party. Cocoa nibs are perhaps the cheapest mode of preparing it. Two handsful of the nibs should be placed in a middle-sized tin coffee-pot, and allowed to heat gradually until it boils *gently*, at which point it must be kept for two or three hours. When the cocoa has been used the pot should be filled again with water, and allowed to simmer gently in readiness for the next meal. When become weak a handful of nibs should be *added* to those already in use, and so on, until the vessel becomes too full to hold the quantity of water required.

The old nibs must then be taken out, and a similar process take place as at first. A little experience will direct the proper quantity to be used, and the degree of strength required, which can easily be added to or diminished. It is the *lightest* preparation of cocoa, which is very frequently heavy for the stomach; and where the health is delicate it is used with very beneficial effect.

Many persons will say, and perhaps think, that high-priced tea goes further than cheap. I have often heard, that tea at four and even five shillings per pound is cheaper in the end than that which costs three and eightpence: but there is theory in this idea. No one ever puts in less tea because it is higher in flavour; or if they do, it is so *little less* that it does not in the least degree atone for the additional price. Highly-flavoured tea is a most delightful beverage, but do not let us deceive ourselves into fancying that we are economizing by indulging in it. Teas at the same price will occasionally vary in flavour and quality, and sometimes we may meet with an inferior kind; but we must not on this account be induced to pay an extra sixpence per pound, when we are really *striving* to the utmost to live within very small means. If we give way on one point, we shall certainly be as weak on another, and another, and another; and the monthly bills that are "only a shilling or two higher than they ought to be," will swell into importance at the close of the year. If it is pos-sible to purchase tea at one of the old established tea ware-houses in London, a far better article will be obtained at a lower price than can be bought in country towns; and by laying in half a year's consumption at once, or even more—if money can be paid down—the expense of carriage is trifling.

A teaspoonful of tea for each person, and one for the tea-pot, is the old-fashioned recipe for making it; but much less will suffice for economists. By allowing it to stand long, and close to the fire when there is one, the strength will be more fully drawn out, and less will do. The common black tea-pot is the best for tea-making, and is preferable to metal, and even silver; besides, it can be placed near the fire without injury, and is easily replaced.

I have already observed, in THE COTTAGE GARDENER, that by the Chinese themselves sage-leaves are so highly esteemed as a substitute for tea, that they were in the habit of giving the Dutch four pounds of tea for one of sage, so great was their preference for that herb. Now this fact is worth our consideration. Why should we disregard and neglect a luxury so highly prized by the very people who possess the fragrant and delicious tea-plant? Is it not worth while to try if we also can like what is thought by others so very agreeable? What an advantage it would be to some of us, if we could grow and prepare our own breakfast beverage! What a blessing to those who are fond of a warm and pleasant infusion for their morning and evening meal, and yet are seriously inconvenienced by paying so much for tea! The leaves should be dried gradually in the shade, and used in that state. There is do difficulty in the cultivation of this plant; and its very wholesome properties were well known in the earlier ages. The old Roman adage alone would give it value in the eyes of many—"Can a man die, if he has sage in his garden?"

Young tender strawberry-leaves, picked from the stalks, and dried in an airy shady place, form a good substitute for tea also. When perfectly dry they may be kept in canisters or bottles, and used in the same way. Very young leaves of rue, dried, and used with the strawberry-leaves, in the proportion of one-twelfth of the former, give the flavour of green tea.

The following herbs are said to be agreeable, used for the same purpose:—Equal quantities of septfoil, balm, wild marjoram, and agrimony; one-fourth part of each of these—black currant leaves, cowslip flowers, and red roses. As each herb or flower is procured, cut them into small bits, and mix with the rest. Let them all be carefully and completely dried, and then put them into canisters for use.

An immense saving would be effected in this way, if we could only reconcile our taste to home-grown tea. I can fully enter into the sorrows of those who enjoy their tea, at the thought of giving it up; but it is a real expense where a family is large and increasing, and if it can be spared, the duty of close and sincere economists is, to resign it. A stout, steady principle of right regards little things as well as large; and, when based on the Rock of Ages, will enable us to ride rough-shod over everything that stands in our way.

LONDON HORTICULTURAL SOCIETY'S SHOW AT CHISWICK.—MAY 18TH.

(Continued from p. 133.)

COLLECTIONS OF TWENTY STOVE AND GREENHOUSE PLANTS.

1ST PRIZE to Mr. May, gardener to Mrs. Lawrence. The following were either new to the collection or much improved since shown in the Regent's Park:—

Leschenaultia biloba major, covered with its lovely blue blossoms; 3 ft. by 3 ft. *Podolobium trilobatum*, 4 ft. by 3 ft. *Erica intermedia*, with scores of pure white flowers; 3 ft. by 3 ft.

2ND PRIZE to Mr. Cole. The following were in addition, or much improved since we saw them in Regent's Park:—

Aphelexis macrantha purpurea, densely bloomed; 3½ ft. by 3½ ft. *Adenandra speciosa*; 2½ ft. by 2½ ft. *Chorozema Henchmannia*; this difficult-to-grow plant was in fine condition; 3 ft. by 3 ft. *Azalea indica* (three varieties on one plant); 3 ft. by 3 ft. *Erica Cavendishii*, a noble plant; 2½ ft. by 3 ft.

COLLECTIONS OF FIFTEEN STOVE AND GREENHOUSE PLANTS.

1ST PRIZE to Mr. Green, gardener to Sir E. Antrobus, Bart.

Azalea variegata, a splendid plant; 6 ft. by 5 ft. *Azalea rubra plena*; 6 ft. by 5 ft. *Erica depressa*; 2 ft. by 2 ft. *Sphenotoma gracile*; 2½ ft. by 2½ ft. *Aphelexis sesamoides*; 2½ ft. by 2½ ft.

2ND PRIZE to Mr. Carson, gardener to H. G. Farmer, Esq.

Epacris grandiflora, finely bloomed; 6 ft. by 6 ft. *Azalea Smithii coccinea*, a pyramid of flowers 6 ft. high. *Pimelea spectabilis*; 5 ft. by 5 ft. *Francisceen macrophylla*; 20 heads of bloom. *Bossiæa linophylla*, a drooping, graceful plant, covered with bloom; 5 ft. high. *Gardenia Fortunii*; this plant was much admired; the flowers were large, pure white, very double, and numerous.

3RD PRIZE to Mr. Gorrie. Finely bloomed plants; the Azaleas were particularly excellent.

Eriostemon buxifolius; 6 ft. by 5 ft. *Azalea variegata*; 7 ft. by 5 ft. *A. lateritia*; 3½ ft. by 2½ ft. *A. lateritia alba plena*; a pyramid, 7 ft. high. *Zychia villosa*, finely trained and full of flower.

4TH PRIZE to Mr. Taylor, gardener to J. Costar, Esq., Streatham.

Adenandra speciosa; 3 ft. by 3 ft. *Aotus gracillimus*, a graceful, drooping plant, densely bloomed; 3 ft. by 3 ft. *Epacris lævigata*, white, 2 ft. by 2 ft. *Adenandra fragrans*, pink, and very handsome; 3 ft. by 2 ft.

5TH PRIZE to Mr. Ivison. Our readers may be surprised that such a collection should be placed fifth, but the differences between each were so small that it must have been no easy task to determine which should have been first and which last.

Gardenia Stanleyana, with scores of its large trumpet blossoms upon it; 5 ft. by 7 ft. *Euphorbia splendens*; 3 ft. by 5 ft. *Eriostemon neruifolium*; 5 ft. by 5 ft. *Azalea indica alba*; 5 ft. by 3 ft. *Aphelexis sesamoides*; 2½ ft. by 2½ ft. *Indigofera decora*, should be in every greenhouse; 2 ft. by 2½ ft. *Siphocampylus microstoma rubra*; 2 ft. by 2 ft.

COLLECTIONS OF TEN STOVE AND GREENHOUSE PLANTS.

1ST PRIZE to Mr. Malyon, gardener to J. Brandum, Esq.

Erica ventricosa coccinea minor; 2½ ft. by 2 ft. *E. Beaumonia*; 2½ ft. by 2 ft. *Aphelexis humilis*; 3 ft. by 2 ft. *Azalea Woodsii*; 3 ft. by 2½ ft. *Erica elegans*, a well bloomed young plant.

2ND PRIZE to Mr. A. Stuart, gardener to T. Higgins, Esq., Norwood. This collection did credit to a new exhibitor.

Tropæolum tricolorum, well flowered, and trained in a novel style. *Podolobium staurophyllum*, very fine. *Zychia longipedunculata*, a new species, neatly trained and well flowered. *Erica intermedia*; 3 ft. by 3 ft. *Eutaxia myrtifolia*, a fine plant, but injudiciously trained.

3RD PRIZE to Mr. Speed, an amateur, Edmonton. Good plants, but much disfigured by being excessively staked.

Erica hybrida; 3 ft. by 3 ft. *Pimelea Hendersonii*; 2 ft. by 2 ft. *Azalea indica phœnicea*; 4 ft. by 3 ft.

COLLECTIONS OF SIX STOVE AND GREENHOUSE PLANTS.

1ST PRIZE to Mr. Kinghorn.

Leschenaultia formosa; 2 ft. by 2 ft. *Azalea indica optima*, a mass of bloom. *Erica ampullacea*. *Tremandra verticillata*, a pretty plant, with violet coloured blossoms.

2ND PRIZE to Mr. May, gardener to — Goodheart, Esq.

Erica Cavendishii; 2½ ft. by 3 ft. *Aphelexis macrantha purpurea*; 3 ft. by 3 ft. *Chorozema Laurenciana*, a handsomely trained plant. *Francisceen villosa*; 3 ft. by 2½ ft.

3RD PRIZE to Mr. Stanley, gardener to H. Bevens, Esq., Sidcup, Kent.

Erica Cavendishii; 2 ft. by 2 ft. *Epacris grandiflora*; 3 ft. by 2 ft. *Francisceen Augusta*, a fine variety; 2 ft. by 2 ft. *Pimelea spectabilis*; 2 ft. by 2 ft.

COLLECTIONS OF TWELVE GREENHOUSE AZALEAS.

1ST PRIZE to Mr. May, gardener to Mrs. Lawrence. As these were nearly the same plants as we described on a late occasion, we must refer to that report.

2ND PRIZE to Mr. Green. This collection would certainly have been placed first, had they been all sides alike; they were certainly better flowered, and the flowers were larger and brighter, but the one sided system of growing them was fatal to their taking the first place.

Azalea exquisita; 6 ft. by 5 ft. *A. optima*; 4 ft. by 2½ ft. *A. Gledstanesii*; 8 ft. by 5 ft. *A. triumphans*; 4 ft. by 3 ft. *A. lateritia*; 6 ft. by 6 ft. *A. præstantissima*; 5 ft. by 4 ft. *A. sinensis*; 5 ft. by 3 ft. *A. rosea punctata*; 6 ft. by 4 ft.

3RD PRIZE to Messrs. Lane and Sons, nurserymen, Great Berkhampstead.

Azalea mirabilis. *A. Lucomagista*. *A. duplex superba*. *A. Broughtoni*. *A. picturata*. *A. triumphans superba*.

COLLECTIONS OF SIX GREENHOUSE AZALEAS.

1ST PRIZE to Messrs. Frazer and Sons. The same as those at Regent's Park.

2ND PRIZE to Mr. Carson. Among these were

Azalea speciosissima. *A. lateritia*. *A. alba*. *A. splendens*.

COLLECTIONS OF TEN CAPE HEATHS—No restriction in the size of pots—NURSERYMEN.

1ST PRIZE to Messrs. Fairbairn, Clapham. Nearly the same as we have described lately, excepting

Erica mutabilis; 2 ft. by 2 ft. *E. favoides purpurea*; 2½ ft. by 2 ft. *E. propendens*; 3 ft. by 3 ft.

2ND PRIZE to Messrs. Veitch. The following were different, or much improved since we saw them in the park:—

Erica depressa. *E. tortillæflora*; 2 ft. by 2 ft. *E. Florida*, very beautiful, and pale flowered; 3 ft. by 2 ft. *E. perspicua nana*; 3 ft. by 3 ft. *E. ventricosa tricolor*. *E. tricolor*, the original species; 3 ft. by 3 ft.

3RD PRIZE to Messrs. Rollison. The few below were additions, or improved since the 8th.

Erica pragnans superba. *E. Beaumontia*. *E. mutabilis*. *E. ventricosa coccinea minor*. *E. primuloides*. *E. Andromedæflora*.

COLLECTIONS OF TEN CAPE HEATHS IN ELEVEN-INCH POTS—
NURSERYMEN.

This was a new feature in the regulations for exhibiting
heaths; the design being, no doubt, to give little growers an
opportunity to exhibit; but no sooner was the Society's intention made known than our veteran heath growers, using the
one shift system, were as ready to compete with their usual
antagonists, and all others, as if they had known of the new
arrangement for two years instead of one year.

1ST PRIZE to Mr. Fairbairn, who was first again in this
class. His *Erica aristata major* was a perfect little gem.

2ND PRIZE to Messrs. Veitch. These gentlemen had a
beautiful rare heath, *Erica peziza*, of a clear white; each
flower appeared as if it were covered with hoar frost.

COLLECTIONS OF TEN CAPE HEATHS IN ELEVEN-INCH POTS—
AMATEURS.

1ST PRIZE to Mr. Smith, but nothing new, except a plant
of *Erica aristata Macnabiana*, a variety with large flowers
and brilliant colours.

2ND PRIZE to Mr. Roser, gardener to J. Bradbury, Esq.,
Streatham. This new exhibitor of heaths had his plants in
excellent style.

Erica ovata, E. gelida, and *E. campanulata florida* were unique
plants.

PELARGONIUMS.

COLLECTIONS OF SIX IN ELEVEN-INCH POTS.

1ST PRIZE to Mr. Cocks, Chiswick.

*Forget-me-not, Rosamund, *Pearl, *Salamander, Bertha*, and *Orion*.

2ND PRIZE to Mr. Parker, gardener to J. Oughton, Esq.,
Roehampton.

*Forget-me-not, *Negress, Orion, *Pearl, Rosy Circle*, and another.

COLLECTIONS OF SIX NEW PELARGONIUMS IN EIGHT-INCH
POTS.

1ST PRIZE to Mr. Cocks.

*Pictum, Rosamund, Mont Blanc, Salamander, *Mars*, and *Centurion*.

2ND PRIZE to Mr. Robinson, gardener to — Simpson,
Esq., Thames Bank, Pimlico. Very well bloomed plants,
consisting of

*Gulielma, *Negress, *Pearl, *Armida, Orion*, and *Forget-me-not*.

COLLECTIONS OF SIX IN ELEVEN-INCH POTS—NURSERYMEN.

1ST PRIZE to Mr. Gaines, Battersea. A well bloomed collection, consisting of

*Emma, Cotherstone, *Ackba, Pearl, Negress*, and another.
(Those marked thus * were the best.)

The other collections did great credit to the growers, but
they were nearly all the same kinds as were exhibited at
Regent's Park. (See our account of them.)

COLLECTIONS OF SIX CAPE PELARGONIUMS.

These are exhibited to show the Pelargonium in its native
state.

1ST PRIZE to Mr. Parker.

Pelargonium elegans, P. flexuosum, P. holosericeum, P. tricolor, and
P. Blandfordianum.

2ND PRIZE to Mr. Staines.

*Pelargonium bicolor roseus, P. Blandfordianum, P. Ardens, P. flexuo-
rum, P. quinquevulnerum*, and *P. bipinnatifidum*.

ROSES.

COLLECTIONS OF TWELVE ROSES IN POTS—NURSERYMEN.

1ST PRIZE to Messrs. Lane and Sons, Berkhampstead.
This collection was in splendid condition; the best we noted
were

Emperor Probus, blush; hybrid China. *Chenedolle*, dark rose, hybrid
Bourbon. *Moire*, yellow; tea scented. *Countess Mole*, marble rose;
hybrid Bourbon. *Lady Alice Peel*, crimson; hybrid perpetual. *Paul
Perras*, rosy crimson; hybrid Bourbon. *Coup d' Hebe*, delicate rose;
hybrid Bourbon.

2ND PRIZE to Messrs. Paul, Cheshunt. The finest roses
in the collection were *Madame de St. Joseph*, a delicate,
flesh-coloured, tea-scented rose; and *Paul Joseph*, a fine
dark rose.

COLLECTIONS OF TWELVE ROSES IN POTS—AMATEURS.

1ST PRIZE to Mr. Terry, gardener to Lady Puller, Youngsbury.

Mrs. Bosanquet, Lamarque, Smith's Yellow, Charles Duval, and
Lamarque.

2ND PRIZE to Mr. Roser, gardener to J. Bradbury, Esq.

Wm. Jesse, Madame Laffay, Marjolin du Luxemburgh, and *Belle Amelie*.

COLLECTIONS OF SIX CALCEOLARIAS.

1ST PRIZE to Mr. Gaines.

Panther, Baron Eden, Nil desperandum, Maid of Orleans, Regulator,
and *Astarte*.

COLLECTIONS OF SIX CINERARIAS IN SIX-INCH POTS.

This we consider to be anything but a wise regulation, for
how could it be expected that fine plants, in good bloom,
could be grown cramped up in six-inch pots!

1ST PRIZE to Mr. E. G. Henderson, Wellington Road,
St. John's Wood.

Alboni, Attila, Camilla, Wellington, Cerito, and *Angelique*.

2ND PRIZE to Messrs. Lane.

Blue Superb, Cerito, Attila, Poperina, Countess, and *Grand Master*.

COLLECTIONS OF SIX RHODODENDRONS.

1ST PRIZE to Mr. Gaines. These are noble, fine, and
handsome shrubs, the growth of which cannot be too highly
encouraged. Mr. Gaines's plants, though finely bloomed,
were not in good forms, but if the Society continues to give
prizes for these really lovely objects, no doubt they will be
brought to perfection in every commendable property.

SPECIMEN PLANTS.

1ST PRIZE to Mr. May, Ealing Park, for his monster *Pimelea spectabilis*. 2ND PRIZE to Mr. Glendenning, for *Hoya Imperialis*. 3RD PRIZE
to Mr. Edmonds, gardener to the Duke of Devonshire, Chiswick, for
Rhododendron Gibsonii, 8 ft. high, with numerous flowers. 4TH PRIZE
to Mr. Kinghorn, for a large plant of *Erica Cavendishii*. 5TH PRIZE to
Mr. Mylam, for *Erica rusiflora*, a unique specimen. 6TH PRIZE to
Messrs. Veitch, for *Mitraria coccinea*.

NEW OR RARE PLANTS.

1ST PRIZES were awarded to Mr. Paxton, gardener to the
Duke of Devonshire, Chatsworth; and to Mr. Ivison, gardener to the Dowager Duchess of Northumberland, for specimens of that wonderful aquatic plant *Victoria regia*. The
leaves were 5 ft. diameter, and more than 15 ft. in circumference. The flowers, when fully expanded, were more than
a foot across, or 3 ft. in circumference. There were three
leaves exhibited, one being upside down—showing the ribs
of the leaf in strong relief; each rib diverged from the
centre, and measured a full inch in depth. It is, indeed, a
wonderful vegetable production.

Prizes were given also to Messrs. Veitch and Son for a new
Rhododendron, with small foliage; white flower, with yellow
anthers shaped like a jessamine bloom. The flowers are
produced in bunches; are tubular-shaped, with a spreading
border, and very fragrant, named *R. jasminiflora*; and for
Stylidium ciliatum.

To Messrs. Noble and Standish, for a new *Viburnum*,
named *plicatile*, producing flowers much like the well-known
double Viburnum Opulus pleno, or Guelder Rose.

SEEDLING FLORISTS' FLOWERS.

There was no prize offered by the Society for this class of
plants, yet several parties, eager to exhibit their novelties, sent
a considerable number. Mr. Hoyle, Reading, had several
seedling PELARGONIUMS. One, named *Ajax*, was a promising
flower: the lower petals of a rose colour; the upper dark
blotched with a rose rim; good form, and free bloomer.
Rubiola, scarlet, with dark blotch, very fine. We shall hear
of this again. *Cristine:* prevailing colour rose; white eye,
upper petals dark crimson, edged with pale rose. Mr. Bell
had a useful kind named *Little and Good*, with nicely-formed
flowers.

Seedling CINERARIAS were plentiful. Messrs. Henderson,
Pine Apple-place, sent *Jetty Treffiz:* a light flower, with BLUE
disc. *Lettice Arnold:* a red flower, good form; and *Constance:*
light blue self, of good form. These three are really good
kinds worth growing.

Mr. E. G. Henderson sent his *Lady Hume Campbell*, the
same as was exhibited at Regent's Park: and *Madame Sontag*,
a light flower, deeply edged with blue; both excellent flowers.

Seedling CALCEOLARIAS were not so plentiful, and of very
medium quality. The best was from Mr. Kinghorn. His
Miela was a pretty flower of good quality, straw coloured,
with spots of crimson.

FRUITS.

In this class the exhibitions were far from numerous. There
were some good Pines, Grapes, and Strawberries, both in pots
and dishes. In Peaches and Nectarines the show was meagre,
indeed, only one dish of each being present.

1ST and 2ND PRIZES for *Providence Pines* were awarded to Mr. Davis, gardener to Lord Boston; weight, 8 lb. 4 oz., and 8 lb. 5 oz.

3RD PRIZE to Mr. Snow, gardener to Earl de Grey; weight, 7 lb. 8 oz.

MARKET GARDENERS.

1ST PRIZE to Mr. Davis, Oak Hill, Barnet, for a *Providence Pine*; 7 lb. 2 oz.

Grapes.—Heaviest bunch, Mr. Fleming, gardener to the Duke of Sutherland; Black Hamburgh; 1 lb. 7½ oz.

Mr. Davis, Oak Hill, for ditto; 2 lb. 3 oz.

Melons (the heaviest and the best-flavoured) :—
1ST PRIZE to Mr. Fleming, for a hybrid green flesh.

Apples and Pears of the previous year:—
1ST PRIZE to Mr. Snow. These were excellent—fresh, large, and good; especially the pears.

Cherries in dishes :—
1ST PRIZE to Mr. Ingram ; 2ND PRIZE to Mr. Fleming; both fine well-ripened fruit.

For *Strawberries* (both in pots and in dishes), the 1ST PRIZE to Mr. Snow.

TIRYDAIL SHIPPEN VINERY.

Scale four feet to an inch.

THIS combination of the cow-house and vinery has already been prominently noticed by us at page 16 of the present volume, and we shall now only add the explanatory references to the above drawing.

a The ventilator, extending the whole length of the house.

c Iron bars instead of purlieus.

d Sliding ventilators in back wall.

e Stone shelf for strawberries.

f Shelf for pot-vines.

g Water-trough.

h Feeding-trough, made of flag-stones set on edge.

i Hurdle false-floor for the cows to rest on.

k Concrete floor.

l Drain of iron open guttering.

m Vine border.

n Drainage of the border.

EXTRACTS FROM CORRESPONDENCE.

PASSION-FLOWERS.—I take blame to myself for not having sooner replied to Mr. Errington's request about the Passion-flower (see vol. iii., page 343). After the appearance of the older *Tacsonia*, about twenty years since, I had a strong pull at these passion-flowers, with a view to effect a cross between any of them and the Tacsonia, but I did not succeed. However, I gained some insight into their economy, which enables me to answer Mr. Errington. Botanists, as far as I am aware of, have not put much stress on the arrangement of the seed organs in these flowers, which stand alone in the division of plants to which they belong—in the disposition of their stamens and pistils—the Irids, or Ixia tribe, being the only parallel to them in the other grand division of the vegetable kingdom ; and it will be remembered that I mentioned last year, that the chief feature by which Irids were distinguished from neighbouring fa-

milies was the ungallant position of the stamens standing up with their backs turned to the fairer sex—the pistils; and in my hurry I then fell into a mistake, by saying that the Irids alone, among flowers, were so unmanfully disposed. But here, among all the passion-flowers I examined, the same phenomena occurs, and even more markedly than in the irids ; for in the passion-flower both sexes "look asklent and unco skeigh," or, in plain words, the males not only turn their backs on the virgins, but the latter pay them in their own coin by looking in a different direction; and if all this is not a *phenomenon*, what shall we call it ? Those who have little acquaintance with the inside arrangement of these flowers will, perhaps, understand it better from the following description. In the centre of a Passion-flower a column is set up without a pedestal, and afterwards a pair of pedestals, one above the other, are added, and placed against the bottom of the column. From the upper pedestal fine full grown men generally, but sometimes only four of them, stand up all round the column with their backs turned towards it; and, of course, their faces are looking to different points of the compass. These five men are the stamens, whose height, together with the length of the column, differ in different kinds of passion-flowers. In the *Purple-fruited* one, referred to by Mr. Errington, the height of the men exceeds that of the column by head and neck; and the apex or top of the column stands in a line with the top of their shoulder-blades. On this apex is placed the berry or seed vessel, in the shape of an egg, and on the top of which stand three nymphs—the pistils. When the flower opens upwards these ladies look up straight to the zenith; but when the flowers are pendulous, as is more generally the case, they look towards the earth. In either position the two parties stand head to toes, that is, the heads of the stamens reach to where the pistils are attached to the seed vessel, and by their fixed position it is impossible for either to see each other. Now, "if all were known," it would very probably be found, that the old story about the Spanish monks having mistaken this arrangement for emblems of the crucifixion was only a mere moonshine; and that the more probable reason the holy fathers had for naming this a passion-flower, seeing the attitudes of the parts representing the sexes so very *unpassion-like*, and on that account more in accordance with their own better sense in such matters. If that was really the case, and I see no reason to doubt it, the foolishness of worldly wisdom could hardly be better exemplified; for in the very next stage of the Passion-flower the tables are turned—prudish coquetry gives way to a softer passion. The virgins bow themselves round in the direction of the sentinels, "to meet them half way," and the latter in their turn lean back their heads for the embrace. No wonder, therefore, that honest men like the Spanish monks, and our friend from Cheshire, should be deceived and puzzled by "such fancies." However, we must give Mr. Errington credit for wishing to clear away all impediments to such mutual understanding.—D. BEATON.

GERANIUMS FOR BOUQUETS.—*Gravcolens* is the original name for the true *Rose-scented geranium*, which is the best of all leaves with which to encircle a bouquet. The little *l'ariegated oak leaf*, as we call it, has sported from Gravolens. The leaves of *Pelargonium radula* are sticky, and look like small ferns mixed with the flowers in a bouquet. These are much sought after; also very small-leaved varieties of the *Citron-scented geranium* with the *Rasp-leaved* or *Skeleton-leaved*, of which the scientific name is *Bipinatifidum*—long enough at any rate.　　　　D. BEATON.

CANARIES.—It may not be generally known that the canary, so prized and petted within doors, is perfectly hardy, and will stand the rigour of our severest winters. About ten years since I purchased in the spring nine young canaries, and placed them in a small summer-house, with a wire front, fitting up the interior with a few rustic conveniences for their accommodation. In two seasons they increased to 40, when I reduced their numbers, and they have since flourished remarkably well. They cover the wires during rain and snow to obtain the benefit; are in full song ten months out of the twelve; and an aviary thus formed, is an interesting, an ornamental addition to a flower-garden.—S. P., *Rushmere.*

GRAVEL WALKS.—Those who are about to form new gravel walks, should be cautioned how they use the refuse lime from gas-works, as a substratum for the top layer to rest upon. A friend of mine adopted this plan to destroy the worms, and the result is, that all the stones on the surface are coated with various colours of green, blue, indigo, &c., so as entirely to destroy the freshness of the gravel; even the minuter particles are impregnated with them; the effect is curious, but the walk, so far as appearance is concerned, is spoiled.—S. P., *Rushmere.*

TO CORRESPONDENTS.

** We request that no one will write to the departmental writers of THE COTTAGE GARDENER. It gives them unjustifiable trouble and expense; and we also request our coadjutors *under no circumstances* to reply to such private communications.

HARD SEEDS NOT VEGETATING (*A. W.*).—Old seeds of some Acacias, and many other plants, will require to stand several minutes in boiling-water before they are sown, to accelerate vegetation. We had a quantity *Martynia fragrans* seeds of our own sowing, a fine flowered half-hardy

annual, since 1845, and tried "all means" to get them up, with very partial success, till this spring, when we put them in a cistern which connects two sets of hot-water pipes, for five days. This cistern was not far from the boiler, and the water in it was nearly 200° on two nights, and all the time from 120° to 180°. We then sowed twenty of them, and seventeen came up in about twelve days. Your *Tacsonia* seeds have no vitality in them, for if they had, and were ripened in this country they ought to be up in ten days. We have often met with full-grown seeds both of *Tacsonia* and *Passion-flower* from our own sowing, which wanted the life germ, and such instances are not at all rare. But we believe the seeds of none of the family will require, or endure, the hot water cure.

SCANDIX BULBOSUM (*M. Webb*).—What used to be called *Scandix bulbosum*, is now referred to *Cherophyllum*, to which also the common chervil herb belongs; and your plant may be sown in the open border at once, and receive the treatment of the commonest border plant; but after all it is a mere weed.

GARDENER'S RIDDLE (*Annie*).—The following is what you allude to:—Why is a gardener the most extraordinary man in the world? Because no man has more business upon *earth*, and always chooses good *grounds* for what he does; he commands his *thyme*, is master of the *mint*, and fingers *penny-royal*; he raises his *celery* every year, and it is a hard year indeed that does not produce a *plum*. He meets with more *bows* than a Minister of State, and makes more *beds* than the French King, and has in them more *painted ladies*, and more genuine *roses* and *lilies*, than are to be found at a country wake. He makes *raking* his business more than his diversion, but, unlike other gentlemen, he makes it an advantage to his health and fortune. Distempers fatal to others never hurt him, for he thrives most in a *consumption*; and he can boast of more *laurels*, if possible, than the Duke of Wellington.

FLOWER-GARDEN (33).—Your plan of breaking up the grass next autumn to renew it, is excellent; and if you are fortunate enough to get seeds true to name, and free from weed seeds, early next spring will be time enough to sow them. To convert a portion of the ground into a kitchen-garden would be an easy matter, by running a trellis across from walk to walk, and by covering the trellis with evergreen climbing roses; and the end next the road and farthest from your house would do well for a kitchen-garden, *provided* you would root up the "laburnum, very tall poplar, horsechesnut, large japonica, and the two evergreens" of which you do not know the names. However, if the ground belonged to us we would rather supply you with vegetables from Covent Garden market than allow you to touch any of those trees and shrubs; but we would devote that end entirely to beautiful flowering shrubs, and leave the grass in it as it is, until you see the effects of your renovation in the flower-garden end. Dig up all the flower-beds along with the turf, they are positively ugly. Then, after levelling the ground, get some one on the spot to give you a plan for the new beds. No one at a distance can guide you safely, if he has a conscience.

OPENING THE FRONT LIGHTS OF A HOUSE ALL AT ONCE, AND CHEAPLY (*T. W. L.*).—You think Harwood's plan too expensive. We are not sure if we know it, though many methods may be adopted, especially in a new house. We have seen the same principle as that which we believe may be seen at Dropmore in operation, with the best effect. A flat iron rod is fixed, but so as to move along easily on the front of the house inside the sill. Upon this is fixed, for every window to be opened outwards, pieces of iron still narrower and thinner. The straight end being fixed along the bar so far, and the segment of the circle end fixed to the window—as when the bar is moved along, the pressure will cause the window to open from a part of an inch to its full extent at pleasure. The end of the bar for the length of the window is locked and moved by a racket wheel. It is usual to have the front sash divided into two, and then one division opens to the east, and the other to the west, but for that purpose there must be two flat iron rods, and a racket wheel at the separate ends of the house. A more simple method still, is to have half the sashes in front fixtures, and the moveable ones to slide behind the fixed ones, instead of opening out with a similar bar and racket wheel; all you have to do is to join each moveable sash to the bar, by means of a stout iron pivot. Turning the wheel will *set them all in motion*.

WARDIAN-CASE (*Legolium*).—There can be no doubt but your Wardian-case made in the form you mention will answer for a time. To suppose that ferns thrive and live longer in a Wardian-case than in a proper stove, is absurd. Ferns, like most other plants, love a free circulation of air, light, and moisture, freshly applied. The wires you intend to set up in the case will no doubt be useful to hang something upon, but do not try orchids; they will disappoint you. Lycopodiums or Epiphyllums of a dwarf kind will answer better. Let your ferns in the same case have a little air sometimes. It is a great mistake to think they require no air in those cases. Therefore, dispense with the sand and water in the grooves. Let the inside be lined with zinc, it is better than lead.

TAYLOR'S HIVE (*W. T. L.*).—Your second swarm, if hived into Taylor's upper box and placed upon the stock-box having the first swarm in it, will *not* unite, but, in all probability, fight until one is destroyed, and consequently the other much weakened. Unite them as directed in page 104, volume ii. of THE COTTAGE GARDENER, and not a bee will be killed. The process is very simple, and may be done in a minute.

ASPARAGUS SHOOTS CANKERED (*A Subscriber*).—The shoot you sent to us was cankered or ulcerated all round within the soil, and so deeply ulcerated as to destroy the sap vessels. Consequently the growth was prevented. We should think that your soil requires draining; and we should not give liquid manure, but salt about once a month, and in the autumn a good coat of well rotted manure and charred refuse.

POTATOES NOT EARTHED-UP (George).—If any of the tubers are close to the surface, cover them about an inch in depth with earth. Applying such a depth of soil even generally is desirable, to prevent the upper tubers from becoming green, and is very different from earthing-up. It is quite impossible for us to say why your sitting-hens uniformly have added eggs, whether you have them from your own layers or from elsewhere. The nests must be in fault, we should think. Are they damp, or incommodious? At all events alter them. Put them down on the ground, or raise them so as to be different from what they are at present. Jennings's Indian Rubber Tap will not bear much pressure, and the Indian rubber lining, we hear, requires frequent renewal; but Mr. Jennings says he has removed this objection. His direction is, 29, Great Charlotte-street, Blackfriar's-road, London.

WEEVILS ON ROSES (J. S. S.).—These are the Otiorhynchus sulcatus, or Furrowed Weevil. See what we said on the subject at page 106.

BEE-FEEDER (W. Whitear).—Your fountain bee-feeder is very good when it is absolutely necessary to feed bees from the outside and through the entrance. We will give it a trial.

FROSTED ROSES (R. Wrench).—We, too, have lost roses to a severe extent by the frost at the end of March, which was more severe on the 27th than the frosts of 1838 and 1841. Nothing that we know of can now be done for them, but to wait patiently in hope that the Midsummer growth may push some eyes or buds, which to all appearance are now dead.

SOILS FOR FLOWERS (J. D. S.).—Ageratum Mexicanum is an annual, but may be kept as a perennial by cuttings, and will grow in any kind of garden mould that is not too poor. The Yellow Acacia requires a very good open porous soil, such as one-third peat with two-thirds loam, with a little sand. Calceolarias, same soil as the Ageratum; Cyclamens, the same as the Acacia; and the Gaillardias, dry good common garden soil.

RHUBARB WINE (W. Camberwell).—May and June are good months for making this. Five pounds of the stalks of Rhubarb, sliced and mashed, added to each gallon of cold water. Allow the mixture to remain untouched for three days, then pour off the liquor; add three pounds of loaf sugar to each gallon; allow the mixture to ferment in an open tub for four or five days, and when the fermentation has ceased draw off the liquor into the cask, and allow it to remain until March, when all fermentation will have finished. Then rack off, and add three pounds more sugar to each gallon. This is said to make so good a wine, that a Mr. Stone, of Bradford, in Wiltshire, took out a patent for the process. Another recipe is as follows:—Add to every pound of stalk, sliced and bruised, one quart of cold water; let the mixture stand three days, stirring it twice a day; then strain and press, and to every gallon of liquor add three pounds of loaf sugar; cask it, adding a bottle of brandy to every five gallons; suspend by a piece of string a lump of isinglass in the cask, and stop it close. In six months, or when the sweetness is sufficiently diminished, bottle for use.

VINEGAR PLANT (E. A. E.).—The vinegar made by this is excellent. You will find a drawing of it with a description, recipes, &c., at page 94 of our second volume.

PLANTS FOR BALCONY (A. Y. Z.).—You will find a list of these at pp. 60 and 68 of our present volume. Go to any florist with that list in your hand, and select for yourself.

NEW CHEESE (B. H., Fulham).—To make this, or, as it is often called, Bath cheese, for no other reason that we could ever learn than because it is not made there, you must proceed as follows:—To each quart of new milk add half a pint of cream; warm the mixture to 80°, and stir in then just enough rennet to coagulate or curdle it. When the curd is formed, place a cloth over the perforated bottom of the mould, then fill it with curd by the aid of a skimming dish, and cover the ends of the cloth over it. As the curd shrinks, add more curd until the cheese is of the desired thickness. During this process, a piece of board to fit within the mould must be kept upon it, and a pressure of half a pound. When the cheese is thick enough, turn it out into a dry cloth, return it into the mould, and put on a pressure gradually increased from one to two pounds. At night, turn it into another clean cloth, sprinkle it with a little fine dry salt, and if enough drained place it on fresh leaves of the nettle or strawberry, and cover it with the same. Turn the cheese and change the leaves every morning. In a fortnight it is fit for use.

COTTAGE GARDENERS' DICTIONARY (S.).—Thanks for your hints; you will find most of them carried out. We cannot give estimates, however, you might as well ask a builder to give you the prices of plants.

GOOSEBERRIES DISEASED (X. X.).—Your gooseberries and have hardened on one side have been injured, probably, by the severe frosts early in May. Some water is softened by mere exposure to the sun, but it is only that of which the hardness originates in calcareous salts (salts of lime) held in solution by carbonic acid gas in the water. The warmth of the sun drives off the gas, and the calcareous salts fall to the bottom of the vessel.

SCOUR IN CALVES (T. W. L.).—The best medicine for them is, prepared chalk, two drachms; powdered opium, ten grains; catechu, one drachm; powdered ginger, half a drachm given in thick gruel once or twice a day.—W. C. S.

MILK, TO ASCERTAIN ITS PURITY (S. D. K. T.).—You ask for a simple mode of ascertaining this, and we regret that we know of none. The richest of cow's milk contains 96 parts in every 100, and the poorest

90. If you were to evaporate 100 grains to dryness, and found less than ten grains remained, you might justly suspect that water had been added.

PROPAGATING THE MULBERRY (Ibid).—You may do this as you wish from one of its large branches. You cannot follow a better plan than that detailed at page 104 of the present volume. It is quite impossible for us to say with precision how much house sewage is enough for an acre of ground; it depends upon the number of inmates, and many other contingencies. If your sewage contains one pound of fertilising matter in every ten pints, you may put on twenty tons per acre, and repeat the application once a month throughout the summer.

SOOT AS A MANURE (J. O.).—You say this mixed with salt and applied to potatoes was a failure. How, and in what quantities did you apply them? We knew a man who dibbled holes, put in the sets, then filled up the holes with salt, and was the sworn enemy of salt as a manure, because the sets he had pickled did not grow! If we were about putting soot upon turnips in a rich soil, we should sow it over them immediately they appeared above ground.

VERBENA VENOSA (A. A.).—We see that this plant is marked one shilling in the catalogue of Messrs. Henderson, Pine Apple Place, Edgeware-road, London; but you may get it at the same price of any florist who advertises in our columns.

NAMES OF PLANTS (L. R.).—Your plant marked A, is a species of Lonicera; and B, Alyssum saxatile. (Mabinogian).—Yours is Lonicera Tatarica, or Tartarian Honeysuckle. (A Subscriber, Evesham).—1, is Spiræa opulifolia, or Guelder-rose-leaved Spiræa. 2, Nemophila phacelioides. 3, Prunus padus, the Bird Cherry.

EXHIBITING FUCHSIAS (Northumbria).—If you have three moderately well and equally grown fuchsias fit for exhibiting in a stand of three, we should not displace from these Scarlatina reflexa, to substitute for it your noble specimen of Fuchsia serratifolia. The gardeners are quite right in advising you to have uniformity of size. But you should certainly exhibit F. serratifolia as a single specimen, and the judges may award you an extra prize; for a specimen of this "seven feet high, beautifully furnished, and well-bloomed," is not to be seen every day.

VINE TRAINING (W. D.).—Your Black Hamburgh against a wall having two branches about four feet long each, you bent each down horizontally, and left only two buds on each branch to grow, intending next winter to cut out two and leave the other two for fruit bearing, and so every year; but you find the buds have shot up about six inches; they are throwing out fruit. You are taking a wise plan with your young vine, but pinch off the bunches of fruit by all means.

KEEPING A COW (P. P., A Poor Curate).—You wish to know the most profitable way of tilling one-third of an acre of land, for the support of a cow. The soil and situation of your land, to us equally unknown, renders any precise answer impossible. If your land is grass, and you can water that grass, or, still better, irrigate it with the sewage of your house, improved in quality by admixture with cow-dung, or any other rich organic manure, and can add to the bulk of this by diluting it with pump-water; and if you soak the land with this as soon as the grass is cut for your yard-fed cow, you will, with proper care, get four or five capital cuttings of grass per annum; and, as a cow cannot be fed better than upon cut grass and hay, there is no extent of produce equal to this. We are trying this ourselves, and it promises to work admirably. If you cannot thus irrigate or water your land with liquid-manure, try lucern (and the produce of this is much increased by irrigation); keep it clean, and dress it with one cwt. of gypsum (it will cost 1s 6d). If you expect, that by growing any description of roots you can better support your cow, sow the land with carrots (red, if the soil is suitable, and white if it is heavy, and with Swedish turnips, in equal proportions—changing the ground every year; but if you can manage the grasses in the way to which we have alluded, there is nothing equal to that for weight of produce. There is one cow, the returns from which were very large, that was kept as follows. The plot, to supply the green food, was rather less than half an acre. In summer, per week—3½ bushels of grains, 1½ ditto of bran, and the produce from 10 perches of red clover and rye-grass, 9 perches lucern, 17 of white clover and cow grass, 18 of red and white clover, 10½ of lucern, and 2½ of carrots—Total, 1 rood, 29 perches. In winter she had per week, grains 8 bushels, bran 4 bushels, hay ½ cwt.

STICKS ACROSS A HIVE (A. H. G.).—You say, "I shall have to send my hives every year to the moors, say 50 miles; and I am told by several bee-keepers, that sticks across the hive are a great help in keeping the comb up." The objections to sticks across the hives are twofold; for they not only cause much unnecessary trouble to the bees in the construction of their combs, but render the extraction of these almost impossible, which in the depriving system become necessary; but if it be absolutely necessary to remove the bees 50 miles every year, it is more than probable that without sticks the combs would be broken down, and the bees destroyed.

SOW PIGGING TOO SOON (W.).—We are inclined to attribute the evil to some innate defect in the sow, and not to mismanagement. Moderate exercise and moderate feeding is most desirable for breeding animals, but after parturition the food should be more nutritious. We do not approve of many Swedish turnips for breeding-sows.

LONDON: Printed by HARRY WOOLDRIDGE, Winchester High-street, in the Parish of Saint Mary Kalendar; and Published by WILLIAM SOMERVILLE ORR, at the Office, No. 2, Amen Corner, in the Parish of Christ Church, City of London.—June 6th, 1850.

WEEKLY CALENDAR.

M D	W D	JUNE 13—19, 1850.	Weather near London in 1849.			Sun Rises.	Sun Sets.	Moon R. & S.	Moon's Age.	Clock bef. Sun.	Day of Year.
13	Tu	Small Blue Butterfly appears.	T. 67°—34°.	N.E.	Rain.	44 a. 3	15 a. 8	11 1	3	0 34	164
14	F	Young Swallows fledged.	T. 78°—40°.	N.E.	Fine.	44	15	11 36	4	0 11	165
15	S	Ivy casts its leaves.	T. 78°—42°.	E.	Fine.	44	16	morn.	5	0bef2	166
16	Sun	2 Sun. Aft. Trin. Young Redstarts fledged.	T. 69°—46°.	N.	Fine.	44	17	0 6	6	0 14	167
17	M	St. Alban. Sweet William flowers.	T. 72°—40°.	N.W.	Fine.	44	17	0 33	7	0 27	168
18	Tu	Tadpole's first feet seen.	T. 75°—41°.	W.	Fine.	44	17	0 57	8	0 40	169
19	W	Meadow Brown Butterfly seen.	T. 66°—43°.	S.W.	Rain.	44	18	1 21	9	0 53	170

On the 18th of June 1835, aged about 73, died WILLIAM COBBETT, one of the most useful men who has lived during the present century. If he had never written any other works than the *Letters of Peter Porcupine* and his *Political Register*, however we might have admired the purity and power of their language, they would not have entitled him to a notice in our pages; nor would his *Grammars* have strengthened his claim to our notice, excellent though they are, and beneficial though they have been. But he has another title to be noticed by us—he was a cultivator of the soil from childhood—wrote most attractively upon the subject—and from being a day labourer in Kew Gardens raised himself to the position of a member of the legislature of his country. His father, an agricultural labourer, possessed a small patch of ground near Farnham, in Surrey, and it was there that Cobbett was born; and passed his childhood; and of how he passed it, we shall allow him to be himself the narrator.

"At eleven years of age my employment was clipping box-edgings and weeding beds of flowers in the garden of the Bishop of Winchester, at the castle of Farnham, my native town. I had always been fond of beautiful gardens: and a gardener, who had just come from the King's gardens at Kew, gave such a description of them as made the instantly resolve to work in these gardens. The next morning, without saying a word to any one, off I set with no clothes, except those upon my back, and with thirteen halfpence in my pocket. I found that I must go to Richmond, and I accordingly went on, from place to place, inquiring my way thither. A long day (it was in June) brought me to Richmond in the afternoon. Two-pennyworth of bread and cheese, and a pennyworth of small beer, which I had on the road, and one halfpenny that I had lost somehow or other, left three-pence in my pocket: with this for my whole fortune, I was trudging through Richmond, in my blue smock frock and my red garters tied under my knees, when staring about me, my eyes fell upon a little book in a bookseller's window, on the outside of which was written, 'Tale of a Tub; price three-pence.' The title was so odd, that my curiosity was excited. I had the three-pence, but then I could have no supper. In I went, and got the little book, which I was so impatient to read, that I got over into a field at the upper corner of Kew Gardens, where there stood a hay-stack. On the shady side of this I sat down to read; the book was so different from anything that I had ever read before, it was something so new to my mind, that though I could not at all understand what I have always considered a sort of birth of intellect. I read on till it was dark, without any thought about supper or bed. When I could see no longer, I put my little book in my pocket, and tumbled down by the side of the stack, where I slept till the birds in Kew Gardens awaked me in the morning; when off I started to Kew, reading my little book. The singularity of my dress, the simplicity of my manners, my confident and lively air, and, doubtless, his own compassion besides, induced the gardener, who was a Scotsman, I remember, to give me victuals, find me lodging, and set me to work. And it was during the period that I was at Kew that the present king (George the 4th) and two of his brothers laughed at the oddness of my dress, while I was sweeping the grass-plot round the foot of the pagoda. The gardener seeing me fond

of books, lent me some gardening books to read; but these I could not relish after my 'Tale of a Tub,' which I carried about me wherever I went; and when I, at about twenty years old, lost it in a box that fell overboard in the Bay of Fundy, in North America, the loss gave me greater pain than I have ever felt at losing thousands of pounds."

We need not touch upon the causes of that visit to America, but we may content ourselves by observing that he there devoted himself to the cultivation of the soil; and upon his return he endeavoured to introduce the Maize, or as it is now frequently called "Cobbett's Corn," among our field and garden crops. He published a treatise on the subject, entitled *Cobbett's Corn Book*, promising by its means " to see it growing in every labourer's garden, and to see every man of them once more with a bit of meat on his table and in his satchel, instead of the infamous potato." In this he failed, as all must fail who do not consider beforehand whether the climate of a country agrees sufficiently with that of the region from which they propose to bring emigrant plants. More useful works were his edition of *Tull's Husbandry*, of which he said, " from this famous book I learned all my principles relative to farming, gardening, and planting;" his *English Gardener*, written on the principle that " every young man should be a gardener, whatever else may be his pursuit;" *The Woodlands*, "taking every tree at its seed, and carrying an account of it to the cutting down and converting to its uses;" and *Cottage Economy*, of which he was justified in saying, " beyond all description is the pleasure I derive from reflecting on the number of happy families this little book must have made." But we are warned to conclude. We have said that Cobbett was a most useful man, and he was so because he addressed himself directly, and in strong, plain language, on strong, plain facts, to the common sense of his countrymen. He wrote for the multitude, for the multitude of his own times only, and for no other multitude than that of the British Isles. To these, and for these, no man could or did write so effectively; and this was his strong, his only firm footing, which when he left, he invariably stumbled and fell. But he is gone; and it has been scarcely too strongly said—

Now in the quiet lone churchyard,
    Beside the growing corn,
Lies gentle nature's stern prose bard—
    Her mightiest peasant born!

For Britons honor Cobbett's name,
    Though rashly oft he spoke;
And none can scorn, and few will blame,
    The low laid heart of oak.

METEOROLOGY OF THE WEEK.—At Chiswick, from observations during 23 years, the average highest and lowest temperatures of the above days are 73.4°, and 51°, respectively. The greatest heat, 93°, was on the 19th, in 1846; and the lowest, 36°, on the 15th, in 1841. On 70 days rain occurred, and 91 were fair.

NATURAL PHENOMENA INDICATIVE OF WEATHER.—Dr. Forster says, that when soot takes fire more readily than usual on the back of the chimney, or on the outside of pots and kettles placed on the fire, it indicates approaching rain; that it is similarly foreboded if the soot falls on the ground after being carried into the air from the chimney; or if it falls down the chimney into the grate. The last phenomenon is readily explained, because soot absorbs moisture from the damper air as rain approaches, and thus becoming heavier breaks away from its slender attachment to the chimney walls. Smoke frequently serves as a similar indicator. Those accustomed to smoke a pipe early in the morning observe, that when the smoke hangs a long while in the air, and smells more strongly than usual, rain is not far off; and a good hunting day always follows. When the smoke from a chimney mounts up straight into the air, it is a sign of settled fine weather; but when it sinks towards the ground rain soon follows.

RANGE OF BAROMETER—RAIN IN INCHES.

June		1841.	1842.	1843.	1844.	1845.	1846.	1847.	1848.	1849.
13	B.	30.049	30.293	30.843	30.003	30.157	30.096	29.776	29.919	30.118
		29.944	30.153	29.792	29.940	30.186	30.094	29.592	29.499	29.997
	R.	—	—	0.14	—	—	—	0.03	0.12	0.01
14	B.	30.047	30.094	29.874	30.020	30.120	30.105	30.068	29.974	30.175
		29.906	30.012	29.907	29.999	30.050	30.141	29.560	29.924	30.115
	R.	—	—	0.18	—	—	—	0.34	—	—
15	B.	30.097	30.048	29.969	30.045	30.038	30.343	29.721	29.833	29.909
		29.993	29.989	29.959	30.009	29.995	30.155	29.589	29.770	29.791
	R.	0.01	—	—	—	—	—	0.18	—	—
16	B.	30.386	29.995	29.960	30.197	30.844	30.320	29.758	29.822	29.776
		30.111	29.990	29.931	30.168	29.794	30.296	29.566	29.748	29.750
	R.	—	—	—	—	—	—	0.13	0.09	—
17	B.	30.079	30.084	29.979	30.153	29.814	30.314	29.589	30.040	29.975
		29.973	30.058	29.972	29.925	29.771	30.343	29.576	29.754	29.924
	R.	—	—	0.04	0.19	—	—	0.03	—	—
18	B.	29.788	30.041	29.929	29.757	29.857	30.310	29.792	29.992	30.065
		29.605	29.886	29.823	29.670	29.789	30.145	29.613	29.865	30.038
	R.	0.34	0.12	0.01	0.05	0.05	—	0.09	0.87	—
19	B.	29.990	29.769	29.934	29.856	30.032	30.106	29.955	30.142	29.905
		29.597	29.598	29.894	29.994	29.994	30.084	29.879	30.063	29.923
	R.	0.08	0.34	0.01	0.03	—	—	0.01	—	0.02

If we wished to produce the most powerful evidence of what the florist's skill may effect in the course of some ten or fifteen years, we think we should select THE CINERARIA, and exhibit drawings of what were considered first-rate flowers even as late as 1840, by the side of the best specimens of the present day, such as *Madame Miellez*, from a sprig of which our illustration is taken.

The *Cineraria cruenta*, or Bloody-leaved Cineraria, was introduced into England as long since as 1777, from the Canary Islands; and this, we have little doubt, is the parent of the beautiful varieties which are now the most unfailing ornaments of our greenhouses in the winter and spring months. *Cineraria lanata*, or Woolly Cineraria, a single and larger-flowered species, introduced from the same islands in 1780, and *Cineraria populifolia*, or Poplar-leaved Cineraria, probably had something to do with the parentage. The two first-named have purple, and the Poplar-leaved has red flowers. Would not a still greater diversity of colours be obtained among the offspring if *Cineraria geifolia*, which has yellow flowers, and *Cineraria gigantea*, or some other of the white petaled species, were one of the parents?

The earliest raiser of varieties of the Cineraria was Mr. James Drummond, Curator of the Botanic Gardens at Cork, in 1827; and he then stated that he annually cultivated many. Cinerarias were his great greenhouse favourites; and he says, "except in cases when it becomes desirable to preserve any particular variety for its superior beauty, I prefer raising the *Cineraria cruenta* every year from seeds, which the plant perfects with me in the months of April and May. Care should be taken to select the finest varieties, and those which produce the largest and finest heads of flowers. The plants must be attended to daily when ripening their seeds, as the flowers retain their beauty until the very day the seeds are scattered with the wind,—a remarkable and valuable property in this fine winter flower."

It is needless to follow the steps of the various florists who soon crowded the market with varieties, for they were all more or less star-like, thin, pointed-petaled, and in other ways inferior. Mr. Glenny, somewhere about the year 1844, was the first to point out the characteristic excellencies the flower can be made to attain; and which excellencies if not possessed by a specimen should exclude it from the prize list.

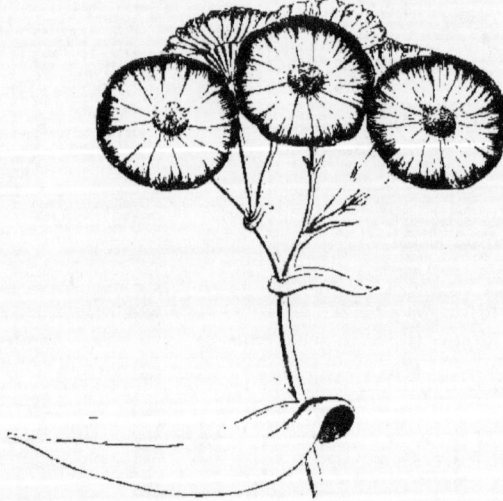

1. The petals should be thick, broad, blunt, and smooth at the ends, closely set, and form a circle without much indentation.

2. The centre or disk should rise boldly, and almost equal to half-globularly, above the petals, and be not much more than one-fifth of the diameter of the whole flower: in other words, the coloured circle formed by the petals should be about twice as wide all round as the disk measures across.

3. The colour of the petals should be brilliant, whether shaded or self; or if it be a white, it should be very pure. That of the disk should harmonize with that of the petals.

4. The trusses of flowers should be large, close, and even on the surface,—the individual flowers standing together with their edges touching each other, however numerous they may be.

5. The stems strong, and not longer than the width across the foliage; in other words, from the upper surface of the truss of flower to the leaves where the stem starts

from, should not be a greater distance than from one side of the foliage to the other.

6. The leaves should be broad and healthy. No worse symptoms of bad cultivation can be apparent than the leaves being stunted, discoloured, and showing other symptoms of having suffered from insects.*

THE FRUIT-GARDEN.

STRAWBERRY CULTURE.—Anything connected with the culture of this much-esteemed fruit is, doubtless, at all times acceptable to the holders of small gardens; and as we have received several queries connected with this subject, we shall be doing something towards answering them by going fully into their culture.

SOIL.—A deep and mellow loam is most suitable; and by loam we do not mean fresh or maiden soil, *merely*, from the fields, but a soil which to the quality of uniformity of colour adds a texture of a slightly adhesive character, yet not so much of the clayey principle in its composition as to prevent its being readily disintegrated by the spade when in a condition between wet and dry. There are many gardens of a very sandy or even gravelly character; we have seen these at times so loose, and, in consequence, so poor, as that a great portion would slip off the spade in the act of removal. It is almost unnecessary to observe, that such are not loams; and that they will deserve the title commonly applied to them of "hungry soils." And, indeed, they may well be termed hungry, for apply what manure you will it is soon gone; its properties are carried through to the subsoil with every shower, or evaporated by its exceeding porosity and tendency to acquire an undue amount of heat. A good and sound loam, on the contrary, proves a more severe medium of filtration, and compels the waters to pay toll on their passage, holding, in fact, the chief of the manurial properties in a state of suspension as they become disengaged, and thereby proving a sure storehouse of food to the roots.

No success of a permanent character can be expected on the loose shingly soils above alluded to; and it will be by far the best and truest economy to begin by correcting their staple. Marl is an excellent material; clay, powdered or burnt; ditchings which have become mellowed, especially if from clayey districts; and even pond-mud. Any or all of these may be used; but the very best material of all are the furrowing clods from clayey soils, if obtainable; these thrown in a heap with a little manure in layers, for half-a-dozen months, form the finest dressing imaginable, and, indeed, adapted for almost any garden purpose whatever.

With regard to soils in which the clayey principle predominates, of course a very opposite mode of proceeding becomes necessary. Such should be thoroughly drained, if necessary, in the first instance; and this would be well performed in the month of October. By the end of November any surplusage of water would be carried away, and the next thing should be to trench and ridge it for a winter's fallow; before doing so, however, something to ameliorate the texture of the staple should be added. Sharp sand, of any colour, of course will immediately suggest itself; next we would point to cinder-ashes, or, indeed, any ashes; then we may add lime rubbish: any or all of these mixed might be applied as a dressing before trenching, taking care that during the operation they were well commingled with the soil. The ground being thus handled should be thrown into ridges, in order to mellow with the frost, and in the first dry weather in the early part of February the plot should be levelled down, and planting may proceed.

*The above are chiefly from Glenny's *Properties of Flowers*.

PLANTING.—Now we do not say that we advise February as the *very best* time for planting; we are speaking with reference to soils which require an amended staple, for amending which some seasons are better than others, and the planting out period *may*, therefore, become a secondary consideration. Those, therefore, who anticipate such a course, will surely provide plants in the previous summer; for nothing more would be necessary than to plant some of the *earliest* runners that could be obtained in rich beds in July, at about seven or eight inches apart; these will remove with a ball of earth, by means of a trowel, in February with full success, as we have ofttimes proved. Having disposed of the questions concerning the correction of the staples in the two extreme cases, of over-sandy soils and those in which the clayey principle prevails, we may safely leave it to our readers to determine to which kind their respective localities incline, and to modify their proceedings accordingly. The only thing further needed being that useful function called *gumption*, which, being a sort of vulgarism, we had better translate as, common sense.

DEPTH OF SOIL.—And, now, as to depth of soil really *necessary*, or merely desirable. A great warfare it would appear is constantly raging on this very point, in one part or another; for, strange to say, as soon as a victory is won, and the matter seems closed in one quarter of the gardening world, it breaks out anew in a second portion: so that the gardening writers of the year 1950 are quite as likely to have their hands full of such business as those of 1850, unless the world becomes less inquisitive; but we are not assured that this is the tendency of things as at present manifested. We have heard of an amateur, recently, who has taken it into his head that the soil for strawberries should be at least three or four feet deep. Now, we are far from having any aversion to a liberal depth, for such has much to do with the stability and permanency of the crop; but we are always sorry to hear of such extreme opinions, for they frequently deter others from pursuing their culture who are less fortunately situated. Any one possessing fifteen inches of such soil as we have previously described, may rest assured that he can produce first-rate crops—other points of culture being good.

NEW PLANTATIONS.—We come now to the consideration of making new plantations—a proceeding if not carried out finally in July, must at least receive attention at that period; for plants must be prepared or provided, and the earliest runners *alone* are adapted to produce a full crop. In order to obtain good and very early runners, some special culture becomes necessary forthwith. A portion of the old crop should be set apart for this very purpose; that is to say, as much as will be requisite to produce the desired quantity; and by special culture is meant, that some half rotten manure or vegetable soil should be spread over the ground about to be occupied with runners. The exterior of rows is generally devoted to this purpose, as the interior is too much shaded, whereby the plants become "drawn."

If the strings are already out, they must all be carefully turned aside, in order to apply the mulch; and, where this is placed a couple of inches thick, the strings should be placed carefully down again; training them a little, and loading them with a stone or lump of hard soil, in order to hold them fast until roots issue from them, which, with due attention, will be in ten days or a fortnight. In the mean time the waterpot must be in frequent use, for on keeping them always slightly moist depends at once the rapidity of their rooting, and the strength of the plants.

When the fruit is in course of ripening, *not a foot* must be set amongst these young aspirants for future plantations: all gathering must be performed from the other side; and weeds similarly eradicated—by-the-bye such should be carefully extracted the moment they appear.

Thus cultivated, there will be a stock of lusty young plants by the early part of July. And now the cultivator must make up his mind as to the course of culture he should pursue; but as the full discussion of the various modes, with their reasons, would prove too long for the present paper, we must beg to waive it for about a fortnight or so; when, if all be well, we will grapple with the remainder of the subject in all its known bearings.

VARIETIES.—Something may, however, be added about kinds; and, for our part, notwithstanding all that has been said about new kinds, we feel it a duty to keep the eye of the amateur, or the small gardener, fixed on a few good old sorts, which have kept their ground against all competitors. These are the *Keen's Seedling*, the *British Queen*, and the *Elton*.

Now, it must not for a moment be supposed, that we so hedge in the amateur as to dissuade from the culture of all others; by no means: let the new kinds, after receiving some respectable attestation as to their merits, be tried by all means; only let the main reliance for the present be placed on those above-named. They form an excellent sequence; are most abundant croppers; noways delicate or shy; and the Elton, if cultivated in a special way, which shall hereafter be described, will continue bearing freely until nearly September, when *Alpines* will carry forward until the frost. Thus may good strawberries be secured for at least four months; all this, however, requires that many persons pursue a very different course from their present mode of culture; and it shall not be our fault if a decided improvement in the growth of this valuable fruit does not take place.
R. ERRINGTON.

THE FLOWER-GARDEN.

FLOWER-BEDS.—I have said if S. N. V. (see page 133) was a planter as well as a designer of flower-beds, I should be glad to assist him to arrange a plan in which the present style of flower-gardening might be represented; and if he was not a planter, that no good could come of our disputing about the matter; now that his plan and planting is before me, I say at once that we had better not follow the subject any farther, for I am quite certain we cannot agree, and I should be much out of my element in disagreeing with any of our correspondents, and more particularly with S. N. V. Yet I am pushed up into an angle, and escape is impossible, and what to do puzzles me. If I give my opinion on the shape of his beds, he will be very angry with me; and if I pass on and say nothing, he will say I have been discourteous. Now here is a pretty position for a man to get into in this hot weather! Perhaps, after all, the best plan will be to say, good humouredly, that every gardener who has written about flower-beds for the last 15 years has condemned the plan of sharp angles, which are sharper in the four corner figures—1, 3, 7, 9—in this plan than in any plan that has been before the public for that time—as far as I have seen. Well, then, as all our gardeners agree in condemning sharp angles and long narrow points, because they cannot fill them as they would, I need not say anything about shapes; indeed, I do not put any stress on the shape of a flower-bed farther than that I quite agree with all the gardeners, and conductors of the gardening press, in condemning the whole host of stars, diamonds, and all other sharp angled figures which designers *will* push into books. My own part, therefore, will lie in the planting of them.

I find six distinct colours in bedding-plants—yellow, purple, scarlet, blue, pink, and white; and in each of these, again, I find three sizes of plants—very low plants, medium sized plants, and tall plants; and I want a set of beds in which I can present to the ladies the whole of these; and if I do it—even without a neutral bed, or, as gardeners call it, "in bare bones"—I must have either six beds and three sizes and kinds of plants in each, which is impracticable except in two or three instances, or else 18 beds and one kind of plant in each—that is, a tall white plant in one bed by itself, a medium sized in the next, and a low white in the third, and so on with the rest. These 18 beds, then, are "the bare bones" of a flower-garden, I care not in what style it is planned; and without these 18 beds in these degrees a flower-garden of the first class will no more represent the simple groundwork of our present stock of plants, than a vessel without masts and rigging will represent a man-of-war.

Now these 18 beds may be so planned, I suppose, as to arrange round a common figure in the style of S. N. V.; but if so I do not know how to do it, not even with the help of half-a-dozen neutral beds. There are nine beds in S. N. V.'s plan and five colours only; the two verbenas *Hendersonii* and *Charlwoodii* are only shades of purple, not crimson flowers; the *Heliotrope, Cuphea*, and *Silver-edged Geraniums*, are neutral beds—that is, there is either as much of the colour of the leaves as there is of the colour of the flowers, or the flowers themselves are not distinct colours; and, to do justice to his planting, two neutral colours should not follow each other, as 9 and 6. All variegated plants are neutrals, as, if the variation is well marked—as in the variegated geraniums—a bed of them will answer any where, or in any composition, for a white or white flowering plant; and that is the secret why they do so beautifully as an edging to a mass of scarlet geraniums. Of Silver-edged geraniums I cannot make out which he intends, as his planting differs from the usual way of planting that style of garden. These kinds of figures are generally planted thus—1 and 9 to be of the same colour, and the plants as near as possible of the same height; and 3 and 7 the same, but they are purple and yellow; and 9 must either be lilac, pink or scarlet, opposite 1, which is scarlet. There are scarlet variegated geraniums, two lilac ones, a variety of the old scarlet variegated, and the oak-leaved variegated, and two pink variegated (Mangles's and the Ivy Leaf), also one which never flowers, *The Dandy*, all of them beautiful things for beds, but still as neutrals. Then bed No. 2 is white, and its opposite, No. 8, purplish, or say crimson, quite the reverse of the usual way; and so with 4 and 6,—a deep blue and a neutral of three tints; I cannot make out the principle of this planting. The *Heliotrope* in the centre is excellent, and just as it should be; but in so small a garden most people would prefer the *Silver-edged geranium* for the centre bed; and I would prefer the *Cuphea*; but as there is no accounting for taste I shall let that pass. Now, as the common way of planting is departed from, and that I cannot make out the principle of the composition, there is no standard within my reach by which to criticise, therefore I give it up.

About twenty years back the late Mr. Loudon began to give plans of little flower-gardens of the same style as this, in the *Gardeners' Magazine;* and we have had many of them in different works since. Gardeners call them by a funny name, *Merrymanias*, because, as they say, you have a fountain, a sun-dial, a vase, or a bed in the centre, and on either side duplicate beds, as a clown paints his face—patch for patch. But let gardeners say what they may, this is the best way to show off a certain number of the best flowering-bedders; but I hold it to be quite impossible to show the heights, colours, and shades of all the leading families of flower-garden plants that way, as it is now attempted to be done in the first-rate large gardens. I am only a pupil in the fancy myself, I knew very little about it twelve years back, when many gardeners were well nigh through this part of their education; but my lot has been another than that of many of my brethren during this time; for I entered on this part of gardening almost without any prepossessions of my own; got under an indulgent instructor, and one of the highest *artistes* in flower-gardening in this country, and with all this and my own mistakes, I have learned just enough to see faintly what flower-gardening will be a few years hence on a large scale. But, as I said before, I can find no instructions, or rules, or plans, which go beyond a mere section of the art, and principally in this style of S. N. V.'s—that is, a group of figures arranged round a central one, and chiefly planted with flowers of distinct colours; and the best example of this style that I ever saw, is in the last May number of the *Gardeners' Magazine of Botany*—that is, the best formed beds, the easiest to walk amongst, and the best way of planting them.

A gentleman with a lady on his arm walking amongst flower-beds full of sharp points, is one of the most unenviable positions one can imagine. The lady's attention is so taken up with the flowers, that she is in danger of treading on these sharp points at every turn; and he, poor man, must keep his eye on these "points" to save the lady from, perhaps, a tumble down.

Now, about X. Y. Z. (volume 3, page 332); I also fear he will be angry with me for not giving the sizes and shapes of his flower-beds, and with S. N. V. for calling them "union flag-like," without seeing them. The ground-plan of the garden of X. Y. Z. is only given, without any beds; that ground is divided into triangles, and I know full well that is one of the worst shapes to get a set of beds into, and be free from sharp points; but the beds were so well managed that there was not a sharp point in any of them, and yet the sides of them next the walks had straight lines; and, moreover, there were thirty-two of them, not one of which had a single fault, as far as the outline is concerned; and that of S. N. V. has only one bed out of nine free from fault—the middle circle. All the rest have starry points, the worst of all faults, and one which every writer on gardening, from Dr. Lindley to D. Beaton, has condemned years ago; and if this letter will do no more good, I hope it will warn young artists against making sharp pointed figures for such beds. Corner figures, or beds in a square piece of ground, like 1, 3, 7, 9, in this plan, seems to be the most difficult for designers to manage, for in nine cases out of ten they either have sharp points and deep narrow recesses, as in this plan, or their sides next the walks do not correspond with the lines of the walks themselves. These two errors are self-evident, and cannot admit of a dispute. Taste, fashion, and principle, I care little about; they are words which only weaken any argument; taste and fashion turn about like weather-cocks, and what one man calls a *principle*, another, whose judgment has equal weight, says is no principle at all, or is the most *unprincipled* thing in the world. Mr. Loudon had three ways of managing the outlines of such corner figures better than any one I recollect, but I have no time to refer to the figures. I quite agree with S. N. V. that this geometric style is the best for small gardens; and for the largest I would prefer it, and not only so, but unless I am very much deceived, a flower-garden to exhibit the whole force of flower-gardening plants, cannot be arranged well but on the geometric plan; and, I repeat it, that the smallest of this kind of flower-garden cannot be complete under eighteen beds, and those beds to be in three different sizes. But I disagree entirely from S. N. V. in considering it a point of excellence to be able to see the outlines of a given figure in winter, or at any other time; and yet that may be a matter of taste, and one man is as much entitled to his taste as another; and, as I said before, I can see no good in following the subject in this way

any further. And now I regret the offer I made to assist S. N. V. until the subject is better understood among designers and planters, myself among the rest; and I hope no one will be displeased at what has been said by either of us. I can afford to sail comfortably under the "union flag plan," assigned to me by S. N. V.; and I hope he will excuse my apprehension about the ladies walking amongst sharp angled flower-beds.*

BRUGMANSIAS.—Here is a subject on which all of us will agree—a new flower-bed fit for an emperor. It had been the practice for many years amongst gardeners, to plant out half-hardy plants in sheltered places, and to keep them alive there as long as they could, by covering them in winter; but the system, agreeable as it is, had given rise to an extraordinary delusion, which took hold of our minds, and from which some of us are not quite free yet. This delusion supposed a power in the art of gardening that could change the nature which was stamped on the vegetable kingdom at the creation—so that a plant from a hot climate could be wrought upon in such a way as would enable it to bear up against the rigours of a hard winter in our latitude, and this art was and is called *acclimatizing*,—but we have no such power. One of the coral-trees, *Erythrina crista galli*, was an early favourite with acclimatizers; and if they had succeeded in converting it to a "hardy shrub," we should not now think so much about it as we do, although it is one of the finest things that can be shown in the flower-garden when it is in full flower. But, unfortunately for the flower-gardener, it will not answer his purpose better than a good annual of the month or six flowering class; and when the flowers are gone he cannot move it with safety to make way for a succession; not so the Brugmansias, white, red, and yellow—they will flower on like the scarlet geraniums till cut off by the frost; and then may be cut down to the surface of the bed like fuchsias; and if the wet and frost is kept from them till the return of the next summer, they will push up again "stronger than ever," and flower most gorgeously for, no doubt, many years. I said this is not to be proved now, for it is, beyond a doubt, already. The thing has been done most effectually, and I have great pleasure in recommending others to do likewise. Those who do not know the nature of these Brugmansias, or old Daturas, must be told that no soil is too rich for them, nor can well be made so; a great depth of bed is also essential to their doing well; a yard or so of the same compost as Mr. Errington would use for a grape-vine is about the right thing for them. Like all half-hardy plants, a dry bottom they must have, for damp is more hurtful to them than cold; but, of course, frost must not reach them. It will be said, why not have heard of this while the garden "was in litter," last winter, that one might make a bed on purpose for them? The first reason is this: the oldest plants in the country ought to be selected to begin with; and old Brugmansias are turned into dark sheds and under stages in winter, and look so besmutted, that no one could find half heart enough to give the nurserymen a reasonable price for them; and the next reason is, that many people are so extravgant as to make a very large bed at once, so as to get rid of the trouble of renewing it for some years to come, and that would not suit the Brugmansias half so well as to enlarge their beds by degrees, as they filled, or exhausted, the old soil; and now, when the gardens are in full order, is just the right time to make, or begin to make, up their beds for them, as no more will be done than one can help,—only just enough to serve for this season. Then, take three

* Here the subject had better terminate, for our pages are too limited in number to afford room for controversy of any kind. Our two friends have each good-humouredly advocated their peculiar opinions; and we hope to hear from them both very often for many years to come; but in future they will oblige us by advocating their own ideas and stating their own experiences without reference to each other. We say this because we are well-pleased with the controversy as it now stands.—ED. C. G.

of the oldest plants within your reach, one of each colour, and make three circular little beds for them on the grass in a suitable corner, and not far from tall evergreens, to make a back ground for them. Make these beds in the points of a triangle, and a yard from centre to centre ; put three barrow-loads of the good compost in each bed, and then plant out the Brugmansias, and the work is done for this season. Recollect that all the soil that can be removed from the roots of all old plants, to be "turned out" without breaking them, should be shook off before planting; and if the plants have large tops, they may be pruned staghorn fashion; that is, the top parts and all the large leaves cut off. As soon as new leaves are at work, give a heavy watering—a whole potful to each—say twice a-week; and when the flower-buds appear, soot-water, or any liquid manure, will do them much good. Their flowering this year will be nothing to what it will be when the old sticks are got rid of, and fresh succulent stems come up directly from the roots next year, and for many years to come ; then, the beds will be enlarged till they meet, which will be in the third or fourth season. **D. Beaton.**

GREENHOUSE AND WINDOW GARDENING.

Plant Structures.—"What is the difference between a greenhouse and a conservatory ?" is a question often put, and to which it is difficult in a few words to give an explicit answer. Hence the difficulty of replying to another question which comes to us nearly as often—"Whether should I, in the few limited feet I can command, erect a greenhouse or a conservatory? and how should I arrange it internally so as to yield the greatest amount of pleasure?" which just brings us back to the propriety of distinguishing between the two terms, for, though used indiscriminately, and often synonymously, the different words ought to convey different ideas; for, allowing that a greenhouse may be termed a conservatory, it does not follow that a conservatory is always and necessarily a greenhouse. The primary meaning of the word, *conservatory*, is merely a place where a thing or being is kept in circumstances suitable to its nature; and thus, *fish* in a pond, *birds* in an aviary, *natural objects* in a museum, &c., are as much in conservatories as are plants from tropical or more temperate climes, when kept in glass structures suitable to their healthy existence.

As a new Gardeners' Dictionary is being brought out, the settling of terms and definitions will be an object of some interest. The term greenhouse is applicable to all gardening structures in which tender plants are cultivated; but since we have plant stoves for plants from tropical regions, orchid-houses, vineries, peacheries, pineries, &c., all of which may be used for many purposes, but the main object of each of which is generally understood, it would be advisable to restrict the term *greenhouse to those structures which contain plants so comparatively hardy, that they require protection only during the colder months of the year.* The term *conservatory* is more high sounding, and carries with it something more of *dignity*, especially when the possessor enthusiastically describes its treasures to one who has not had the privilege of seeing it, and whose mind may therefore be left in pleasing suspense whether the wonderful place covers a few square feet or the large fractional part of an acre. The term also conveys a higher degree of the *comfortable*, for though in a north-easter in February, alike sufficient to pinch nose and finger-ends, we should just expect the *cold* to be prevented intruding into the *greenhouse*,—we should expect something of the cosiness of the snug parlour to be realised in the *conservatory*. Hence, on account of

the prevalence of this idea, we should be satisfied if plants are green, without much of growth or of floral attractions, in a greenhouse in winter ; while under the more *aristocratic* name of *conservatory* we should expect to find plants in bloom at all seasons—the blooming of plants in winter requiring quite different circumstances from what is requisite *now*, as adverted to last week, coolness and shade being not more essential for preserving the bloom in summer than heat and light are necessary for a similar purpose in winter. Plants that may be kept healthy in a temperature of from 35° to 40°, will not open nor expand their bloom freely if in a lower temperature than from 40° to 50°. Hence, again, arises the difference between a *cold* and a *warm* greenhouse; the first a structure for preserving plants in winter for ultimate effect during spring and summer, the second for the same purpose also, but combined with the growing and blooming of plants in winter.

Suppose we carry our definition of distinctions a step further, and have a *cold* and a *warm* conservatory—one in which plants are merely kept from the contingencies inseparable from our climate, and the other in which plants are grown and bloomed, and to which plants in bloom are brought from other still warmer structures; then we have only one more distinction to make before we answer the question of many amateurs, as to whether a conservatory or a greenhouse would be the most suitable for them—and that is a broad demarcating line to separate greenhouses from conservatories. Now this we believe would easily be done were we to term all plant-houses greenhouses in which the plants are cultivated in pots, baskets, vases, &c., with or without stages ; and were we, on the other hand, to term all such *structures conservatories* in which the plants were either planted out upon beds of soil, or plunged with their pots into it, so as to present that appearance.

Now, keeping this definition in mind, for all single small structures possessed by amateurs we unhesitatingly recommend the cultivating of the plants in pots or vases, in preference to planting them out; thus making their plant-houses greenhouses, instead of conservatories. There is only one matter in which we would depart from this rule, and that would be in the case of *creepers*, which grow more freely when planted out, require less trouble, and even then interfere not at all with the general arrangement. I am aware that large plants turned out permanently would give less trouble to a gentleman or lady, when the time was comparatively limited that one or the other could afford to bestow upon such objects. But even here it would soon be found, that what gives little trouble imparts but little pleasure. The nobleman who owns a *town* of glass-houses, may with propriety have many of these planted out with permanent plants, because in the very extent in the different points of view selected, in entering his plant-houses from different ends, there would always be pleasing change and variety ; but this variety would soon be unseen and unfelt in a house, say thirty feet by twelve. The objects, however healthy, would soon pall the appetite from this very sameness—everything like a stereotyped appearance being incongruous to our feelings, as lovers of floral beauty, and lovers of change and variety. The same principle holds good, though not in such a striking degree, in flower-gardens, especially when of small extent.

An enthusiastic amateur who had applied some years ago in a friendly way for assistance in laying out a little spot—and who generally makes a point of having an hour or two of gossiping every May, as to how he is to fill it for the succeeding season—called the other night to have his annual consultation ; and was told for his trouble, that I thought I should be obliged to act in future as the lawyers do, who never give their advice for nothing. Well, he described how beautiful it was last season,—so beautiful indeed, that your correspondent (S. N. V., page 134, but who has got into such good hands, that we refrain from putting our finger in the pie, though persuaded that none of us are more obliged than Mr. Beaton himself), if he had seen it would have owned that many methods, and some superior to his own, may be taken for producing a harmonious whole. " Well then," says I, "why don't you have the same thing over again, if it was so pleasing to yourself, and so enchanting to your friends." "Oh!" says he, "that would never do ; every one of my friends would say—' Ah ! umph ! just the same as last year ! nothing new, either in the materials or in their arrangement!" Now, if an amateur wishes to get tired of his little plant-house, we advise him by all means to turn a few good plants out of their pots, that he may have the dis-satisfaction of viewing them every day, exactly in the same position. The prettiest object will then become tame and insipid. Now, in a greenhouse with the principal plants in pots, a fresh house may be made, if desirable, every week by a fresh arrangement and combination of the plants ; and hence the charm of such houses to amateurs with limited means.

"Oh ! but," says an objector, "we can't see how you should speak so authoritatively on such subjects, whilst great men act differently ; for there now, I go at least once to some of the great floral shows every year, and in a conservatory I don't know how long nor yet how high, but which is a perfect mountain to my mole-hill concern, there is not only a broad shelf all round the house supplied with plants in pots, separated from the bed in the centre by the main pathway, but on the bed itself ; along with those plants planted out, are, or were, many plants in pots and tubs introduced as ornaments and fill-gaps. And surely the superintendents of such concerns must have as good, or rather superior, pretensions to taste as yourself." No doubt, and vastly superior ! But these superintendents are more anxious to recognise the properties and capabilities of plants, than the principle of harmony in their combination ; and hence, much as we admire what such able men have done and are doing, it will not be felt as any detraction from their high and just claims if we state, that in the carrying out their object, the arranging of the plants in harmonious combination formed but a small part of their study ; and that, therefore, those who go to such structures should examine the capabilities of the plants rather than the mode of their arrangement.

We have already not disapproved but recommended the planting out of creepers in the greenhouse. We would have no great objection to having the surrounding shelf in front supplied with pot plants in a conservatory, because in walking round we could, if we thought proper, look only at the shelf ; and then, in returning, look only at the bed ; though we think, that a more agreeable feeling would be produced by not seeing anything of a pot in the house ; but nothing should reconcile a man of refined taste to the beholding, in the main bed of the house, a higgledy-piggledy mass of plants growing in beds, and others standing in tubs and pots. Every pot and tub brought there ought to be plunged, that the plant may appear to grow out of the soil. We can seldom successfully follow out two ideas at the same time ; and, therefore, every pot in such circumstances at once dispels the pleasure of the illusion. The finest specimen of tropical or Australian vegetation growing in the bed of a conservatory, loses its charm when tubs and pots are paraded in its neighbourhood. Therefore, for promoting unity of idea, ease for examination, the greatest amount of pleasure, the largest degree of variety and change, we recommend those with limited space to grow all their tender plants in pots or vases. With a few hours' labour, plants may then easily be thrown into fresh groups and combinations ; so that the person who walked through

the house the day before, would scarcely recognise it to be the same. A flower-garden upon the grouping system must remain much the same for the season, but a greenhouse thus managed may be changed every week, and with increased pleasure to all concerned.   R. FISH.

HOTHOUSE DEPARTMENT.

EXOTIC ORCHIDACEÆ.

LIST OF ORCHIDS REQUIRING BASKETS—(Continued).

Angræcum eburneum (Ivory A.).—A noble plant, with leaves frequently eighteen inches long. The flowers are of a greenish white ; the lip of the purest white, and highly polished like ivory. Placed in a basket filled with sphagnum and pieces of charcoal it thrives well. Being a native of the hot climate of Madagascar ; it requires the highest temperature. It is rare. Price 310s.

A. caudatum (Tailed A.). — Sierra Leone. Leaves when healthy, one foot long ; petals and sepals whitish ; lip erect, pure white, and from it hangs down a long tail of a greenish white. This is also a rare and beautiful species. Requires the same treatment as the last. Price 31s.

A. bilobum (Two-lobed A.).—This is a lovely species. The way to treat it is, first to grow it on a log till it becomes strong, and then to place the log with the plant upon it in a basket filled with the same mixture as directed above, leaving the log and plant elevated a little out of the moss. The flowers are of the purest white, tipped with pink ; fragrant and numerous. It is a desirable plant. 42s.

A. apiculatum.—This is very like the preceding one, excepting being larger in all its parts. The same treatment also suits it exactly. 42s.

Chysis bractescens—Guatemala. Sepals and petals pure white, like polished ivory ; the lip has a large blotch of yellow. Pseudo bulbs, when fully grown, more than a foot long ; very stout and pendent. The flowers are produced at the same time as the young shoots. They are large, frequently measuring three inches in diameter. A handsome species, flowering in May. 63s.

C. aurea (Golden C.).—Venezuela. As the specific name imports, the flowers of this species are yellow. The lip is marked with crimson veins. The pseudo bulbs are longer and not so thick as *C. bractescens*. 63s.

C. lævis (Smooth C.).—Guatemala. Flowers cream colour, with a blotch of yellow on the lip. The treatment this genus requires is to place them in baskets filled with rough pieces of fibrous peat, mixed either with broken potsherds or small pieces of charcoal, or even pieces of willow wood. The plants should be a little elevated above the rim of the basket. They require abundance of water when growing, but when the pseudo bulbs are fully grown they should be kept dry. They will do well in the cooler house.

Cirrhæa.—Though the species of this genus do not possess showy flowers with bright colours, yet as they produce them numerously on long racemes, they are worth growing.

C. bractescens (Bracted C.).—Brazil. White sepals and petals ; lip fleshy and of a yellow colour. Flowers produced on long racemes. 42s.

C. lævis (Smooth C.).—Brazil. Sepals and petals yellow ; lip spotted with brown. 42s.

C. Loddigesii.—Brazil. Sepals and petals greenish yellow, striped with red. 21s.

C. tristis (Sad C.).—Dull purple, shaded with blood colour ; lip dark purple ; flowers very fragrant. 21s.

C. Warreana.—Red, yellow, and dark purple flowers. This genus also will flourish well in pots, but on account of the drooping habit of the racemes of flowers they look best cultivated in baskets filled with the same compost as required by *Chysis*. 21s.

Dendrobium amœnum (Lovely D.).—Nepal. In this large genus there are several fine species that are of a decided drooping character, which renders them very proper plants to cultivate in baskets. *D. amœnum* is of that habit, and consequently should be grown in that way. It is a most lovely species, with white, yellow, and green flowers ; but is very rare. The baskets should be filled with the same compost as for *Chysis*. 115s.

D. Cambridgeanum (Duchess of Cambridge D.).—Khooseea Hills, India. A very splendid species. Sepals and petals of a rich yellow ; the lip has a large blotch of rich crimson. Grow it for the first year on a block of wood ; when fairly established place the block in a basket filled with rough peat and potsherds, keeping it well elevated. 63s.

D. chrysanthum (Golden D.).—Nepal. A fine species, which every orchid grower ought to have. Sepals and petals of the richest golden yellow ; the labellum lip has two spots of brownish purple, and is beautifully fringed at the edge. Decidedly of a drooping habit. 21s.

D. Devonianum (Duke of Devonshire's D.).—Found by Mr. Gibson on trees on the Khooseea Hills. The flowers are exceedingly beautiful, with various colours. Sepals cream colour, shaded with pinkish purple ; the petals are broader than the sepals ; pink, with a deep purple stain at the end ; the lip is broad, finely fringed ; the end rich purple with two spots of rich orange on each side of the column. It is impossible to find words sufficiently to do justice to the beauty of the flowers. Until very lately this species was very scarce, the price of a plant being at least ten times its weight in gold. Good plants may be had now for 63s.

D. macranthum (Large-flowered D.).—Manilla. Sepals and petals pinkish lilac, with purple veins ; labellum very long, purple, and covered with down. The fragrance is so powerful as to be quite overpowering. A strong growing plant, with long, pendulous, pseudo bulbs. When growing it requires abundance of water, both at the root and from the syringe over the leaves ; is well suited for basket-culture, in rough peat. 42s.

D. macrophyllum.—Very similar to the last species, but with brighter colours ; requires the same treatment. 42s.

D. Pierardii (Monsieur Pierard's D.).—East Indies. Though more common, this species is well worth cultivating, being a quick grower and free flowerer. The sepals and petals are of a delicate rose colour ; the labellum of a beautiful pale yellow. 10s 6d.

D. Pierardia, var. *latifolia.*—This is a much finer variety, with broader leaves, stronger pseudo-bulbs, and much larger flowers. 21s.

D. pulchellum (Pretty D.).—Sylhet. This species will do well tied to a block, or even hung up in moss by itself ; but it thrives best in a basket filled with sphagnum and rough pieces of peat, elevated a little in the centre above the basket rim. Sepals and petals white, tipped with green and marbled with rose ; the labellum beautifully fringed, with a spot in the centre of bright orange red. 10s 6d.

D. sanguinolentum.—A very beautiful, pendulous species ; requires the same treatment as *D. pulchellum.* Sepals, petals, and labellum fawn colour, tipped with a large spot of violet, and a scarlet spot in the centre. 42s.

Gongora.—Though this genus is not estimated very highly by large growers of orchids, yet the species are well worth growing, both on account of their fragrance and the very curious forms the flowers assume. The racemes of flowers are often of great length, frequently from two to three feet long, which renders the cultivation of them in baskets the best mode of showing them to advantage. One part of the flower somewhat resem-

bles the head of Mr. Punch. We shall enumerate a few of the best varieties.

G. fulva (Tawny Yellow G.).—Demerara. Rich orange, spotted with crimson. 21s.

G. maculata (Spotted G.).—Demerara. Sepals brown, spotted with purple ; petals pale purple, spotted with dark purple ; lip green, spotted with pink. 15s.

G. maculata, var. *tricolor.*—Peru. Clear yellow, banded with brown ; lip white. 21s.

G. atropurpurea (Dark purple G.).—Trinidad. 10s 6d
(To be continued.)

FLORISTS' FLOWERS.

Now is the grand season for planting out *Petunias, Verbenas,* &c., to furnish flower-gardens ; but as this department belongs to our able coadjutor, Mr. Beaton, we only just allude to it. Such of our readers as intend to exhibit these charming flowers in pots must be on the alert, and continue to give them every due attention. Give moderate supplies of water, and keep the plants tied out, so as to form nice round bushes ; keep them clear of green, fly by frequently smoking them with tobacco. Should the *red spider* appear, attack him earnestly with a wash of sulphur. Shade from hot sun, and protect from heavy rains, but gentle showers will do good. Pinch off all the flowers till within six weeks of the exhibition day.

Polyanthuses must be now repotted in a strong compost, and placed on the north side of a low wall or hedge, but not so as to allow the drip from either to reach them. We have kept them very healthy by putting pans under each pot, during very hot weather, to keep them cool and moist.

Pinks will be greatly benefited by a thin covering of either very rotten dung or leaf-mould spread all over the bed ; this covering, besides enriching the soil, prevents it from cracking, and keeps it cool and moist.

Dahlias.—It is high time to finish planting out even the last new varieties. Continue to keep them well tied up to the stakes ; a single windy night or day would do them great mischief. Prune off all the lowest branches of the strong, early-planted varieties, to strengthen the principal leading shoot.   T. Appleby.

THE KITCHEN-GARDEN.

Asparagus cutting should now be slackened ; cut only the finest shoots, allowing the remainder to grow on, taking care by all possible means to encourage a luxuriant growth by constant surface-stirring and applications of good manure-water, with soot and salt added in small portions. Mulching with half-decayed dung, leaves, short grass, or any available article, is also a good system at this season.

Routine Work.—Plant a few *broad beans* in a coldish situation ; keep those in bloom stopped by pinching out the points of the shoots. Plant also a few *dwarf kidney beans* and *scarlet runners* in succession. Constantly *surface-stir* the early-growing crops, and mulch between. *Peas.*—The late and tall-growing kinds should be stopped, which will cause them to branch and keep up a succession of pods ; late growing kinds should still be sown. A good breadth of the most esteemed dwarf kinds of *cabbage* should now be sown, for late summer and autumn *coleworts* and *greens.* Full crops of *borecole, Egyptian* and *Buda kale,* also some of the early kinds of *brocoli,* should now be put out. These may be planted ' to great advantage between peas and beans, when managed as we have directed ; they will thus be furnished with shade until well established, by which time those crops will be ready to clear away, and the cabbage family will have the full enjoyment of the sun and air. Sow a small portion of *spinach* in succession, in order to maintain a regular supply of such as is good until the *New Zealand spinach* is able to supply what is requisite. Spinach should be kept in succession, that as soon as a crop is started for seed another crop should be coming in. *Carrots, parsnips, potatoes, onions, scorzonera, salsafy,* and all kinds of root crops cannot be too often surface-stirred; this is the true means of encouraging a luxuriant and healthy growth, and of maintaining the same, besides its being such a kindly preparation for every succeeding crop.

RHUBARB.—Desist from gathering any more for this season. Apply bountifully good liquid-manure, and encourage the greatest possible luxuriance, and then there will be no fear of another season's bountiful supply. Such kind of encouragement also must not be forgotten with *Sea-kale,*—one of the most esteemed and best of all vegetables, if well managed. A good portion of salt should always be dissolved in the liquid-manure, of which it is particularly fond.

CAPSICUMS and CHILLIES, now strong and well established in pots, may be turned out on a warm border, or where vacancies occur between fruit-trees against the wall, and to which they must be trained. If by the middle of September they should have not produced ripe fruit enough, take them up with a ball of earth, repot them, shade them in a frame, pit, or hothouse of any kind for a few days, and keep them under glass. They will hardly feel the moving, and will produce abundance of either green or ripe fruit, whichever may be most required for use, all winter and next spring.

TOMATOES.—Keep their shoots thin, and trained into such vacancies as can be spared for them, taking care to stop all side shoots down to the blossom showing growth. Abundance of fruit, either green or ripe, may thus be obtained all through the season, either for pickling, preserving, or for sauce.

RIDGE CUCUMBERS.—Attend well to their training and stopping; mulch over the whole bed, and if any kind of charred materials or mow-burnt hay can be spared to surface it with, so much the better.

JAMES BARNES.

MISCELLANEOUS INFORMATION.

OUR VILLAGE WALKS
By the authoress of " My Flowers."

How delightful it is to be once again watching the bursting forth of the spring buds and flowers! To find the beautiful woods once more robing themselves in verdure; and to observe daily less and less of the distant views, revealed so fully by the barrenness of winter. The days of spring are sometimes so warm, that it is a comfort to rest on a stile, or a fallen tree; and a never-ending book is always open before us when we give our minds to the objects we see around. The prostrate "stick," on which we are seated, may in itself awaken a deep and interesting train of thought, and tell us many things. A MS. has been placed in my hands, which is so full of interest and instruction, and conveys it so agreeably to the mind, that I am sure I shall gratify my readers more by transcribing it than anything would do which I could place before them.

"Few things in existence are regarded with such utter contempt as the morsel of wood lying at our feet; and yet what a history and what a moral are attached to it! In the Mosaic history of creation, and so early as the eleventh verse of the first chapter in the Bible, the first objects named after the formation of the heaven and the earth, light and water, are ' the grass, the herb yielding seed, and the fruit-tree;' and these were the productions of 'the third day.' How important an influence has this particular substance exercised over the moral and physical nature of man ever since; and, indeed, it may be remarked, that no other created substance has at all affected *both* the moral and physical condition of mankind. In the garden of Eden, abundantly supplied as we know it must have been with everything to administer to the joy and necessities of our first parents, the most striking objects in it, in their view, must have been the *two trees*—' the tree of the knowledge of good and evil,' *and* ' the tree of life.' Although on the fall of man these were removed from his vision, yet the Almighty permitted every variety of tree, and shrub, and flower, to greet him in humbler forms in the external world; and not merely for purposes of utility, but even of ornament and beauty. The fruit of a tree was the permitted instrument of man's fall. The first instruments of tillage, and the first weapons, offensive and defensive, [the consequences of that fall] in all parts of the globe, have been found made of wood; with this the first altar burned; and, pursuing the Mosaic history, as this same material may be considered to have been instrumental in the Fall, so it was plainly conducive to the safety of the human race in the ' ark of gopher-wood ' (or cypress-tree,), which Noah was divinely instructed to prepare,—the largest and most important vessel ever constructed, and admitted, from its proportions, to be of most extraordinary aptitude both for capacity and for natation. On the subsidence of the deluge, the first material substance presented to Noah was the branch of a *tree*.

"We cannot, within our scanty limits, dwell at any length on the various applications of wood in the history of mankind. Tubal-cain was the first artificer in metals, but it seems as if all men had an intuitive knowlege of manipulating wood and stone. Referring, however, to the Sacred Volume, who can fail to think of ' the fire and the wood ' in Abraham's sacrifice; the blood on ' the two side-posts, and on the upper door-post of the houses wherein the passover should be kept; the patriarch leaning on his staff; the ark, and the various utensils of the altar service; Moses' rod; the ' weaver's beam;' the ' bow drawn at a venture;' and the fragment of wood, wherewith the idolater ' maketh for himself a god ? ' And, without any remarks as to the application of wood for all the purposes of arts, and arms, and of humbler utility, how can we be wholly silent on the glories of the Temple? This stupendous fabric of surpassing beauty and splendour was constructed chiefly, as we are told, of ' timber of cedar,' and ' timber of fir,' from the forests of Lebanon. Following on in the path of Holy Scripture, how frequent are the allusions to the trees of the wood, in the parables and teaching of our Saviour, himself being, as was supposed, ' the carpenter's son !'

"But what can we say when our thoughts dwell on ' the accursed tree,' which sustained the Saviour's blood-stained body until life had fled ? As in the earliest ages the ark had been instrumental in saving the lives of Noah and his family, so the unconscious wood became again the chief instrument in effecting the salvation of his believing descendants. And here it may be well to remark, that although the gopherwood is expressly mentioned as the species from which the ark was constructed, the exact material of which the cross was made is left hidden in darkness; probably to save it as well from undue veneration as from holy abhorrence."

I shall conclude this MS. in a future paper. What a range of thought it opens up to us of things dear to the Christian's heart! If we thus reflected, how large a volume might be comprised in one single walk! and yet what a chaos is the mind most frequently, even as we gaze on the finest scenery! The bold and beautiful undulations of the ground—the rocky or chalky hollows among the hills—the cool green valleys that refresh the eye—and the broad mirror that sometimes spreads itself among them, all offer to us inexhaustible subjects for reflection and deep enjoyment; yet are they admired but too often as objects of simple beauty, and disregarded as themes for "wonder, love, and praise!" We step with indifference, too, upon plants, and stones, and fragments of wood—all full of deep instruction! We have seen them day after day, and are weary of looking at them.

The masses of dead fern that still cover the ground in some wild woodland spots add beauty to the scene. The rich green mosses glow among the crisp brown foliage; once tall and graceful, waving with every breeze,—now lying crushed and sapless on the ground, like the leaves that mingle with it! It is beautiful, and instructive too, to see through the stems of trees, the relics of summer loveliness, while the bursting beauties of spring are again returning to us; there is such quiet thoughtfulness in a woodland scene, and so many objects of affecting interest to attract us. Here and there an old mossy stump catches the eye, rising from among the beds of leaves and fern; a young seedling tree springing up gaily beside it, to beautify and enrich the earth for a time, and then perish for ever; a deep-green shady spruce fir stands in an opening, clothed with its broad waving boughs; and a rich snowy May-bush decorates the scene with its fragrant clusters. These and a thousand beauties besides delight us in wood scenery. Trees are endless sources of enjoyment; they are beautiful in their youthful vigour, and still more beautiful in their decay. The old, gnarled, hollow stem, with its few straggling boughs still green, is a study to the eye, and a deep teacher to the heart, as it stands sternly, yet affectingly, before us. It tells us, that " the strong shall be as tow;" and that "if a man live many years, and rejoice in them all, yet let him remember the days of darkness, for they shall be many."

Let us take warning by the trees of the wood! Our glory and strength will as surely and as utterly depart from us as from the beautiful ruin before us; for in this world of sin and sorrow " all is vanity." We may send out our " boughs unto the sea," and our " branches unto the river," but unless the Lord God of Hosts " turn us again," and cause His " face to shine" upon us, we shall not " be saved." Let us remember this !

WILD FLOWERS.
JUNE.

MAY, *poetically* speaking, and according to the literature of our time, is *the* month of flowers ; but certain it is that in reality rosy June far outstrips her fair predecessor in the number, the variety, and the gaiety of her floral productions. With May come the *early* flowers—the firstlings of summer time ; but June unfolds the more matured beauties of Flora, in all their gorgeous colouring and variety of forms ; and although the earlier gems are all the more welcome for their early coming, they are eclipsed entirely by the bright array by which they are succeeded, and which at once claim our unqualified admiration.

Already are the hedge-rows and the waste way-side banks gaily adorned with wild Dog-roses, which will be of equal interest to the ordinary observer, whether they agree or disagree with the particular specific characters assigned to *Rosa canina*. We shall not venture upon the utterly impracticable project of detailing the various forms which the Dog-rose assumes, and which some botanists consider as species, while others reduce them to the subordinate rank of varieties; for we are well aware that no one has done much to elucidate the metamorphoses of *Rosa*, without pricking his fingers to very little purpose. The bright and showy blossoms of the hedgerow roses add quite a charm to our country walks, for there are few objects at once so truly beautiful and so conspicuous in the summer landscape. The flowers when they fade give place to the well known rose-hips, which the reader will connect with many pleasing incidents of school-boy wanderings. Nor is it the school-boy alone who relishes this wild fruit; for many of the songsters that cheer us in sylvan solitudes, and add such a charm to the enjoyment of natural scenery, are chiefly supported throughout the early part of the winter by the way-side rose-hips. They are also used in the preparation of conserves, although not'nearly so much so now as in days of yore ; for they were greatly esteemed by the " cooks and gentlemen" of Queen Elizabeth's time. To the gardener the wild Dog-rose serves an important purpose ; he finds that the fine hybrid and other delicate varieties of roses grow weakly when on their own roots, and he accordingly calls in the aid of the robust plant of the hedge-row upon which to bud his favourite kinds ; and this is the plant *universally* used for that purpose, the tall clean shoots of one year's growth being chosen. The leaves of the Dog-rose are frequently spotted with a small parasitic fungus, *Uredo rosae*, of an orange colour ; and another fungoid production sometimes distorts and swells the bases of the young branches. The branches are sometimes ornamented with what are familiarly known as " Robin Red-breast's Pincushions," the production of an insect.* Various kinds of our wild roses throw off a fragrance from their leaves, especially in the evenings, when they are moist with dew; but the one especially gifted with this property is the true Sweet Briar, or Eglantine of the poets; the *Rosa rubiginosa* of botanists, which although chiefly abundant in the South of England is more or less found all over the country, and may be frequently observed blooming in beauty beside the door of the way-side cottage.

The meadows and the margins of running streams are now richly fragrant with the odoriferous Meadow-sweet (*Spiraea Ulmaria*), aptly styled the *Queen of the Meadows*. The numerous creamy flowers are produced in *cymes*, and the Meadow Queen is a very conspicuous object indeed in the summer meadows, and well entitled to preside over the gay assemblage of floral beauties with which they are adorned. In low lying moist situations, where this plant occurs in great profusion, its scent is often quite overpowering during the blooming season, more especially in the evenings when the atmosphere is loaded with moisture. The author of the " English Flora" remarks, that " the taste of the herbage, like the scent of the flowers, is aromatic, resembling the American *Gaultheria procumbens;* nor is it unlike the flavour of orange-flower water; dried sloe leaves partake of this flavour (and are sometimes used in the adulteration of tea in this country); and hence we trace it to the perfume of green tea, and the delicious odour of the Chinese *Olea fragrans*, a plant in no respect allied to our Meadow-sweet." In dry hilly pastures and rocky places a near ally of the Meadow-sweet will be found coming into blossom towards the end of the month—we mean the *Spiraea filipendula*, or common Dropwort, which, notwithstanding its name, is by no means a *common* plant in this country, and becomes particularly rare when we seek for it towards the north. The flowers of this species are even more beautiful, and scarcely less showy, than those of the former plant; and a variety with double flowers often forms a very ornamental object in the herbaceous border. The leaves, also, are exceedingly elegant, of a dark green hue, and beautifully pinnate, being chiefly radical, or springing from the root, only a few small ones clothing the stems. The roots are very curiously *beaded* with hard swellings, and although the whole plant is powerfully astringent, Linnaeus remarks that the dried knobs of the roots, beaten or ground into meal, afford no despicable substitute for bread.

In hedges and fences the common Elder (*Sambucus nigra*) now unfolds its cymose clusters of cream-coloured and faintly scented flowers, which soon give place to the blackberries. Smith remarks, "It may be observed that our uncertain summer is established by the time the Elder is in full flower, and entirely gone when its berries are ripe. These berries make a useful and agreeable rob, of a slightly purgative quality, and very good for catarrhs, sore throats, &c. The inner bark is more actively cathartic, and is thought beneficial, in rustic ointments and cataplasms, for burns. The dried flowers serve for fomentations, and make a fragrant but debilitating tea, useful perhaps in acute inflammations, but not to be persisted in habitually. An infusion of the leaves proves fatal to the various insects which thrive on blighted or delicate plants; nor do many of this tribe, in the caterpillar state, thrive upon them. Cattle scarcely touch them, and the mole is driven away by their scent. Both the *varieties* have usually whitish berries, of a less disagreeable flavour than the recent black ones; but the latter are best for medical use. A wine is often made of them, to be taken warm, with spices and sugar; and they are said frequently to enter into the composition of a less innocent beverage, artificial or adulterated port." In moist shady grounds, by the margins

---

* *Rhodites rosae* or Rose Gall Fly. The mossy swelling or gall it causes is also called Bedeguar. It protects the larvae of this insect.

of streams, the Water Elder is also in flower, the *Viburnum Opulus* of botanists, the Guelder Rose of our Gardens.

In our paper on the floral wildlings of May, we referred to the numerous tribe of native Orchids, some of which were then in flower; but we deferred any remarks upon them till the present occasion. Many of them are now in full bloom, and although they do not aspire to the truly remarkable forms and gaudy colouring of their brethren in the tropical forests, yet there are many of them very conspicuous objects in our native Flora. The following are the species in flower during the month of June:—Green-winged Meadow Orchis (*Orchis Morio*), Early Purple Orchis (*O. mascula*), Lax-flowered Orchis (*O. laxiflora*)—a Jersey and Guernsey plant; Dark-winged Orchis (*O. ustulata*), Marsh Orchis (*O. latifolia*)—sometimes found with *white* flowers; Spotted Palmate Orchis (*O. maculata*), Fragrant Gymnadenia (*Gymnadenia conopsea*), Green Habenaria (*Habenaria viridis*), White Habenaria (*H. albida*), Butterfly Habenaria (*H. bifolia*), Green Man-Orchis (*Aceras anthropophora*), Green Musk-Orchis (*Herminium monorchis*), Spider Ophrys (*Ophrys arachnites*), Fly Ophrys (*Ophrys muscifera*), Lady's Slipper (*Cypripedium Calceolus*). The last-mentioned, besides being one of the rarest and loveliest of native orchids, is one of the most interesting of our native plants. Many of the species derive their names from their remarkable resemblance to members of the insect creation, as will be observed by a glance at the above list of species now in flower; but appropriate as some of these names are, we fail to admire their aptness in such cases as that of *Aceras anthropophora*, where the tiny flower known under that name bears as much resemblance to a man as it does to a mammoth, a mole, or a mountain.—G. LAWSON.

(*To be continued.*)

HISTORY OF AN APIARY.
No. 4.
(*Continued from page 40.*)

YOUR readers were informed in my last paper of the successful transfer of my bees to their new dwelling, of which they occupied the upper story. I longed to see them in their proper place, but after what had happened I really had not the heart to disturb them again, so they were left to their own devices. To my infinite delight, however, on the third morning I discovered that they had spontaneously descended in a body to the "pavilion," not a bee being left in the cover; doubtless they had found the inconvenience of climbing to an attic so high and so remote from the entrance. It was certainly an act of deliberate choice which indicated a wonderful instinct and sagacity, for they abandoned a beautiful piece of comb in which they had already stored honey. This I took from them, and deposited in my small museum as the first-fruits of future spoils, after I had carefully closed the communication between the pavilion and the box. *Now* I had no alloy to my satisfaction on account of the success of my experiment so far; and, as with a liberal hand I supplied the bees from day to day with honey, and beer and sugar, everything went on prosperously up to the time of my return to Oxford about the middle of October. I left them with about eight combs, filling nearly half the box, the construction of which I had watched with great interest through the back window; my observations being facilitated by the help of a small hand-glass, which I held in such a manner as to reflect a strong light into the interior of the hive. The honey with which I supplied them was partly furnished from the surviving stores of the old hive; these were indeed, miserably small, not exceeding a pint and a half in all. A very great consumption no doubt had taken place during the three days excitement consequent on our repeated attempts to dislodge the bees, yet there must originally have been too little to stand them in provision through the coming winter, so that they must have perished without copious feeding; this thought consoled me much afterwards.

Previously to my return to Oxford I added one or two other colonies to my apiary, upon each of which I experimented with the most sanguine zeal. The discovered poverty of my own stock led me to conjecture that my neighbours' bees were probably in no better condition than my own, and to hope that, being transferred to my care, I might save them, while amusing myself as well. Going round the village, therefore, I persuaded a bee-master who resided close at

hand to give up to me the lightest of his hives; it was accordingly transferred to my garden, and so late as the 6th of September its occupants were driven as before into a straw hive with a wooden top, constructed after Mr. Cotton's plan, as recommended in his "Letter to Cottagers." It was, unfortunately, a great deal too large, being calculated to accommodate a first-rate May swarm. On this occasion the operation of driving was very speedily accomplished; within an hour from the commencement of the operation, which was performed by broad daylight, at 6 o'clock in the morning, the bees were on their stand, and the old hive broken up and destroyed; not half-a-pint of honey was discovered in it, though there were plenty of bees! At this time I committed a grievous mistake in moving my first hive to another part of the garden and locating the new hive in its place, as there was much fighting for many days between the new comers and the old "habitans," who revisited their former well-known quarters, which greatly weakened my hives, at a time when not a labourer could be spared. Apparently, however, all went on well—I had yet to learn by *experience*. Looking into this hive from the bottom on the 11th, just five days after, a beautiful piece of comb disengaged itself from the roof and fell down; it measured full five inches in depth, and was weighty with honey. The damage, however, was soon repaired, and by the 12th of October they had formed six combs of various sizes stretching across the top of the hive.

On the 11th I procured another hive from a second neighbour. It was a July cast, and was in a miserable condition; there were several drones in it, no queen, and a mere cupful of workers,—of course I could do nothing with these.

About this time a lady-friend of mine, hearing of my successful experiments, desired me to procure for her a colony to a single box-hive which had been presented to her some time before. In obedience to her wishes I purchased a fine populous stock on the 17th of the same month, and drove it the next day. This hive was located in the window of an empty room, where I had the opportunity of watching them at all seasons and supplying them liberally with food. By October 12th they had constructed and stored five combs, but I was in fear for them. On one occasion on opening the drawer of this hive, to give a fresh supply of honey (all my hives had feeding drawers at the bottom at this time, but I have since discarded them altogether, preferring *top*-feeding), I perceived, to my great joy, that the queen had got imprisoned and was in my power; I quickly siezed her, with two or three of her subjects, and put them under a tumbler, where I inspected her, and showed her to several people. The behaviour of the bees to their queen was most attentive and respectful. At the end of nearly an hour I returned her to the hive, pushing her in at the mouth, when she was quickly surrounded and drawn in by a vast concourse of her subjects.

It only remains for me to give the result of my first year's experience as a bee-keeper. No one could doubt the issue of my foolish experiments,—foolish, not in themselves, but because of the lateness of the season. They all perished of hunger, one after the other; not a bee being found alive after March, nor a particle of food in the cells. The longest to survive was the first colony, who lived till the middle of that month, and was cut off by a frost at last. After my return to Oxford I found that no care was taken of them, no food, or very little, supplied, and my favourites perished in consequence.—A COUNTRY CURATE.

DESTROYING THE RED SPIDER.

I AM induced to give you my plan of *attempting* to get rid of that pest, the red spider, which no doubt many of your readers are troubled with. I see recommended, to dust with flour of sulphur; this I have found of no avail. I took a leaf with a couple of the marauders on, and put it under a strong magnifying glass; I then saw them very busy spinning a web, under which were numerous eggs, along the main fibre of the leaf. I then dusted them over with sulphur, and two hours afterwards they were still lively, therefore I think this would be of no avail, as, if noxious to them, they would naturally crawl to another leaf. I have, therefore, found the best plan, either to wash each leaf with a sponge, or use a brush (for instance, a fine-haired tooth-brush); this is a tiresome job, as the pest is always under the leaf, and bad to get at without stooping. Now for my plan, which I find very expeditiously accomplished. I cut an inch board 12

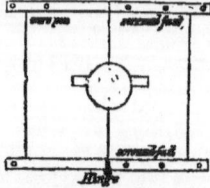

inches square, and cut a circle out of the centre about 2½ inches in diameter; also a cross cut on each side of the circle, to admit the stems of the plant if spreading. I then saw it in two, one half of which I screw to two strong ribs of wood; I then fix a hinge at one end (a piece of gutta percha is as good as anything), and near the other end put a wire pin as a fastening. I fix a cord to each corner of the ribs, one having a slit to admit the cord without letting the knot pass through, and a wire pin to fasten it. I fix this wooden supporter on the pot, and turn it wrong side up, and then hang it on a hook in the centre of the greenhouse doors when open, the four cords being joined in the centre like a ring. I have then the plant inverted, and can get round it and see every leaf; and after washing with a sponge can give it a good syringing with a watering-pot without disturbing the mould, which, if not near the edge of the pot, I put a piece of tow to prevent the ball moving. As my long yarn may not be explicit I send you a sketch.—EVESHAM.

THE DOMESTIC PIGEON.
GENERAL HISTORY OF PIGEONS.
(Continued from p. 88.)

YOUNG pigeons, like turtle-doves, come into the world covered with a light, or nearly white, down, which disappears entirely sometime after the body is fledged. It is not until this has taken place that they risk quitting the nest, and that their parents forsake them to recommence laying. They do not, however, stray far from the place where they have been reared, but remain in the neighbourhood until the time for migrating arrives, when they unite themselves with their family to the first band that passes in their sight, and go together to seek in the South, perhaps in Africa, some hospitable land sheltered from the rigours of winter. Buffon, like the naturalists who have followed him, draws a delightful picture of the manners of these birds, which needs only truth to make it admirable. " All," he says, " have qualities which are common to them: the love of society, the attachment to their kind, a gentleness of manner, reciprocal fidelity- and the inseparable love of the male and female. Their cleanliness and the care they bestow upon themselves show a desire to please, of which their graceful movements are a still greater proof. No ill humours disturb their lives; no disgust, no quarrelling : they employ their whole time in the service of love, and the care of their offspring, equally dividing every laborious duty, the male, anxious to participate in, or even take upon himself, the maternal charge, regularly covering in his turn both the eggs and the young ones to spare his companion the trouble, and to place that equality between them on which the happiness of every lasting union must depend." Yet these pigeons partake of the vices of society, for it often happens that after having been coupled for a longer or shorter time, a female grows weary of her mate, whose caresses she at first refuses, and some days after forsakes him altogether, attaching herself to the first that offers, without any apparent cause for such caprice. Such infidelity is more frequently among the females than the males, who, however, seldom fail to profit by the kindness of some other female, who, without quitting her own male, bestows also her caresses on him. The result is, that the amateur who calculates on a breed of any particular kind, is greatly astonished to find his young pigeons valueless, and of a crossed breed. Sometimes, but more rarely, the male entirely abandons his wife, and returns all her caresses with blows. These disorders may take place all through the year, but they are most frequent during the moulting season, that is to say, in August and September. The amateur must watch these false couplings very carefully, so as to remedy them instantly; for if he leaves these birds to follow their own inclination, or is negligent about them, he will have in the end nothing but degenerate and mixed varieties, incapable of pleasing the eye or taste, and entirely valueless. It sometimes happens, also, that a pigeon—this model of constancy and chastity—is not only unfaithful to his companion, but obliges her to live together with a preferred rival. He watches both of them, and with blows compels them, at least in his presence, to remain faithful to him; but the result of this bigamy is, that being unable to attend to the cares of two broods at once, he suffers, wastes away, and sometimes dies the victim of his own inconstancy. Besides which, the eggs being badly covered, the little ones are always thin and sickly, if they do not perish young, or even before they are hatched. These inconveniences are remedied by means of a breeding cage; but it frequently happens that a bird persists in the caprice which has caused it to forsake its mate or female, and resolutely refuses to couple with it again. A young female frequently obstinately refuses to couple with the male which has been given to her, in spite of every means the amateur may employ; and the only plan then is to set her at liberty, and leave her to make her own choice according to her fancy.

It will be no matter of surprise if she at once chooses the most unfit, and to her own size, the most disproportioned pigeon, and oblige him to couple with her by her importunate advances; but, happily for the preservation of pure races, these examples are very rare. Sometimes a young female, after having refused coupling, attaches herself without choice to several males, and lays her eggs alone, that she may not be compelled to devote herself to one companion only. When a male becomes old or infirm, his wife rarely remains with him, and the others constantly refuse to match themselves with him. It sometimes happens, however, that his companion having grown old with him, does not forsake him; but, taking any passing lover that may chance to offer, she produces a family of bastards, which the male is obliged to take care of as if they were his own. " And this state of things," says M. Vieillot, " may last until extreme old age; for even when these birds lose the power of flying and walking, such is the wisdom and power of nature, they still retain that of deglutition, fatiguing as it is, and they can still cover the eggs and feed the young, which enables the amateur to preserve, without infringing the laws of economy, those old birds to which, from their beauty, or any other cause, they have become attached."

When a female feels an antipathy for the male with which she is wished to couple, she stedfastly refuses his caresses; nothing can please or cause her any emotion ; squatted in a corner of her prison, ruffled and pouting, she only moves to eat and drink, or to repulse her companion's caresses with rage.

DESCRIPTION OF THE DOVE-COT PIGEONS.
(Continued from page 89.)

3. THE FUGITIVE ROCK-PIGEON : Columba livia fugiens.— This resembles very closely the preceding one, but differs from it in its plumage, which is generally paler and more of a slate colour; as well as in the white part of its back, which extends much further than in the first; and in the irregularity of its colours, which vary individually—a certain mark of a more ancient domesticity; and, finally, in the difference of its manners when living in a free state. Some among them are found to have the iris grey, and black heads. That drawn by Frisch is white, with the head and tail red; their bill is generally black or lead colour, and their heads blackish or of a red tinge.

This pigeon never roosts; it avoids shady places and the silence of the forests. It generally inhabits the holes of walls in old buildings, or even the clefts of rocks. Many years since some pairs took possession of holes which exist under the arches of the Pont-Neuf, in Paris, and there brought up their progeny in the midst of the tumult of the capital. It is evidently a bird escaped from our dovehouses, whither it frequently returns. It does not generally live more than eight years, and is not fruitful more than the four first, after which the laying insensibly diminishes. In our dovehouses it commonly lays two or three times a year, and the greater part lay four times in the southern parts of France, commencing in May, and continuing every month until August inclusive, if left to themselves, and but little care taken of them; but they often lay six or seven months without interruption, if they have an abundance of food.

In dovehouses that are well kept, many young pigeons are even found in September and October; and these broods are called "stolen." These fugitive pigeons are smaller than the dove-cot species, do not lay so often, and are never naturally so fat. They provide for themselves, feeding on every kind of seed which the fields offer them, both cultivated and uncultivated, without being any expense to their owners. There are other kinds which never leave, or at least wander but little into the country, consuming a great deal, and requiring more attention. However, the dove-cot pigeon, the carrier, and the tumbler, easily acquire the manners of the fugitives, and seek their food in the fields.

By particular attention fugitive pigeons have been brought up in some dove-cots, and made as productive as the others, even as many as eight or nine broods a year being obtained; but this is useless, because this kind being smaller, the produce is always of less value, whilst the expense is nearly the same.

(To be continued.)

EXTRACTS FROM CORRESPONDENCE.

LABURNUM WITH PURPLE AND YELLOW FLOWERS.—I send you a very beautiful vegetable curiosity, which I have just gathered from a tree in my grounds, and which I think ought to rank amongst the much-talked-of wonders produced by the Chinese gardeners. I know not if such specimens have been often met with; but most gardeners are aware of the phenomenon occasionally exhibited by the Purple, or Hybrid Laburnum, of a tendency to throw out branches of the Common Laburnum and the Purple Cytisus, being the original parents from whence the hybrid is derived; and once or twice I have seen on the same tree, flowering branches both of the hybrid itself and those of its two parents; thus presenting a very motley assemblage. This is a curious fact in vegetable physiology which I have never heard clearly explained; nor am I acquainted with any other hybrid that ever plays such a freak. The specimen I now send you, however, carries its eccentricity much further; for you will observe that one half the flowers in the same racemes are those of the Yellow, whilst the other half are those of the Purple or Hybrid Laburnum. These different flowers are not mixed at random, but one side of the raceme is composed of purple and the other of yellow flowers. On the same portion of the tree are many entire racemes of hybrid flowers, but none entirely of laburnum. One half the tree, I may add, consists of a large branch of Purple Cytisus, thrown out a year or two ago during the progress of growth. Altogether, I look upon my tree of motley flowers as a great curiosity; and if you, or any of your readers, are desirous of another specimen, I shall be most happy to send them one. —S. H. H., *Greenside.*

CHINESE PRIMROSE.—The following method of growing a very useful winter flowering favourite, *Primula sinensis*, may perhaps be useful to some of your amateur readers. Sow the seeds in the first week of June. As soon as the seedlings show two rough leaves, prick them out into pans an inch apart; and as soon as they begin to fill up their inch of room in the pans, transplant them out into beds prepared with some light moderately rich soil, in a rather shady corner of the garden, giving plenty of water when necessary. They will grow away here, and make beautiful plants to be taken up and potted in the autumn. The above, I think, is a better plan than growing them in pots all the summer, as they are apt to get neglected or pot-bound. I had plants eighteen inches in diameter covered with flowers, last winter, treated in this manner.—J. L. MIDDLEMISS, *Gardener to A. Potts, Esq., Bentham Hill, Tonbridge Wells.*

THE COTTAGE GARDENER.—Let me again thank not only you, but all the writers and answer seekers of THE COTTAGE GARDENER. It has been—and I hope will continue to be—the greatest source of enjoyment to me that ever I knew. Until the appearance of the publication I had never grown a flower: it started me off; and I now have growing, and in excellent health, heaths, epacrises, azaleas, boronias, cinerarias, geraniums, fuchsias, &c., in a greenhouse—gesnerias, gloxinias, achimenes, vincas, Thunbergias, ixoras, torenias, justicias, begonias, eranthemums, &c., in stove, and a variety of plants in frames, &c. Until the autumn of 1849 I *never struck a plant of any description.* During the summer I bought and had given me the parents of all the bedding stuff I now possess. I struck and potted off in small 60's some twelve or fifteen cuttings of each sort. I put them into heat early in January, took the cuttings when ready, and placed in large 60's, as Mr. B. directed; and can say, that in many pots with thirty cuttings in them not 2 per cent. missed striking, and none more than 4 or 5. I have now potted off 1000 to 1200 pots of them, leaving about twenty pots of cuttings, in case I should want. This part of the gardening operations is, I think, the most exciting; I am very fond of it. I should have much liked to have seen Mr. B. during his six weeks propagation. I had a pit light made (under which I struck my cuttings) of Hartley's patent rough plate glass. I never in any instance shaded them.

I am about to enlarge my stove. It will be a span-roof, running east and west. I am about to use this last-mentioned glass for it.—AN AMATEUR.

TO CORRESPONDENTS.

COWS FOR EIGHT ACRES (* *).—You will have seen in our paper last week that by soiling, that is, cutting the food for a cow and feeding her in a yard, half an acre, with grains, &c., is ample to supply her. This requires high farming and a constant succession of crops. We do not know the quality of your soil, nor the locality; but we think that your four acres of permanent upland pasture, two acres of dug ground for Lucerne and roots, and two of lowland meadow for hay, ought to support twelve cows; but then we should break up a large portion of the upland pasture to grow roots, cabbages, &c., for winter supply.

WHITE FORGET-ME-NOT.—We have received a large number of stamped envelopes with applications for this flower, and we have forwarded them all to the party at Ledbury who so kindly offered to supply them. The applicants must have patience, and they will doubtless receive the plants in due time. This must be taken as a general answer to those who have written to us a second time.

ANTS (*A Subscriber*).—We have never recommended quassia for destroying these insects. We believe that a little weak ammoniacal liquor from the gas works, or a little diluted spirits of hartshorn, poured into their haunts two or three times, within a day of each other, would destroy many, and drive the others from your conservatory.

OLEANDERS (C. J. P.).—These are just coming into flower, therefore water them daily abundantly, and keep their saucers full of water. After the summer growth is finished, put them out under a south wall; then, and when you return them into the house, remember they will require very little water from September until March. *Liquid manure* made from cow-dung may be given advantageously, once a week, to Heliotropes, Begonias, Scarlet Geraniums, and Fuchsias, just coming into blossom.

THICKENING THE HAIR (*Ibid.*)—Our correspondent has sent us the following recipe as "infallible" for this purpose:—Mix equal parts of olive oil and spirits of rosemary, add about a sixth part of oil of nutmegs, and a few drops of essence of bergamot. Rub the roots of the hair well with this every night.

VINES IN A FORCING-HOUSE.—For growing vines in pots, the only secret is high culture, with occasional "stopping." The former consists in starting from the "eye," growing them strongly, and exposing as much surface of leaf to the light as possible; and, in the succeeding season, pursuing similar principles to those in vogue in the ordinary forcing vinery. The full detail of those proceedings will one day form the subject of a paper.

STRAWBERRIES (*Eastoniensis*).—The first part of an article on strawberries appears to-day, and will assist you. The second will shortly appear, and will, we think, dispel your doubts. In the meantime we fear that low temperature has injured the *British Queens* during the winter. This impatience of extreme cold is the only fault of the Queen. We do not conceive that it signifies much about breeding from runners from barren plants; it was otherwise with the hautbois class some years since cultivated, but does not equally apply to ordinary strawberries. Pines, and indeed other gross kinds, are easily rendered barren by a too liberal

THE COTTAGE GARDENER.

application of manures. The British Queen is a good bearer under proper culture.

MELON GROWING (*A Farmer's Daughter*).—Let us refer you to a paper on their culture at page 80, in the number for May 9th of this year; you will there find every one of your inquiries, or nearly so, answered. Your soil would be better with some of your father's furrowing clods mixed up with it, rough chopped; but pray do not riddle your materials. Let us advise you to burn your riddle. *Cantaluques* may do, but we prefer the *Beechwood* varieties. Take care your bed is cooled down with water if too hot. Four plants in a two-light frame. Begin by a liberal ventilation, and continue increasing it until the plants will by and bye bear the lights off in the day, like cucumbers.

DAMSON-TREES NOT BEARING (*Y. O. U.*).—The fruit you say sets well, but never ripens; and the trees appear as if scorched. We have little doubt that your greatest enemy is the red spider after all. Dust the trees immediately with flour of sulphur, so shaking it beneath the leaves as that it may ascend in a fine cloud and lodge principally in the bark of the leaves. Or you may make a solution of soft soap, three ounces to the gallon, and add four handsful of sulphur to each gallon, then syringe the trees all over, especially the under side of the leaves. We live in a damson country, and have had twenty-three years' experience of damson culture. We have known trees nearly destroyed by Red-spiders in a hot summer, and the poor country folks feeling persuaded that their red appearance was merely the effect of heat!

VINES (*A.*).—Your vine is "far north"—the wood requires to be more ripened. Until you carry out this principle, it matters not whether you stop at two or six eyes. See that the root is right. Follow up former culture, and above all, pray let the glass sash be done forthwith.

QUEEN WASPS (*Tirydail*).—All those you enclosed were queen wasps. If gardeners have not looked as sedulously after these as you and we have, it is probable that wasp's nests will be more than usually abundant this year. Eighteen queen wasps were killed in May upon one quickset hedge in our garden.

INSECTS (*J. Vincent*).—The thread-like worm you enclosed is *Gordius aquaticus*, frequently found upon garden beds after rain : very little is known about its habits. Your *Crown Imperials* will bloom next year; moving them last year whilst in bloom prevented their blooming this year. Their roots were injured and disturbed just at the time they were employed in storing up matters for the next year's productions. (*Verna*).—The minute insects from the bark of your rose-trees are a species of *Bark Mite* (*Acarus*). Soak the bark with ammoniacal liquor from a gas-work; this will destroy them.

EAST INDIAN SEEDS (*J. C. P.*).—The seeds from Calcutta, of which you sent us a list, are not worth the paper they are packed in. They are as good as these collections generally are from thence, and from Delhi; the plants producing them are fine things enough in the East, but of no use here.

ROSE STOCKS (*W. D, W.*).—We believe no rose will succeed well on the sweet briar.

GODETIAS (*Ibid*).—These should not be topped, because they do not branch out well after the operation; and a portion of the succession of bloom is lost by stopping.

LAWNS (*Eugenia*).—The best way to keep a lawn "particularly fine and smooth" is, first, to spud out all the broad-leaved plants from among the grass, and also any strong coarse grass itself; doing this either in the autumn or in the spring; then in summer to roll it once a week, and mow it the next day. Wood ashes is a very good top-dressing for lawns; and the daisy rake will keep the daisies from seeding, and prevent them spreading that way; but it will not eradicate the old plants. The daisy rake is a very useful tool.

SOWING FLOWER SEEDS (*Ignoramus*).—As a general rule, all pot plant seeds ought to be sown in light poor soil, well drained and lightly covered, and without any reference to the kind of soil the plants prefer when they are potted off. The *Marvel of Peru* comes under this rule; and when the seeds are good they come up in a slight hotbed in about three weeks. Neither they nor any other seed "rot before they germinate." How could a rotten seed germinate?

SNOWDROPS (*Ibid*).—Soil for their seeds as above. We believe they do not vegetate under twelve months; but we never sowed any snowdrop seeds. Can any one of our readers tell who has?

PEACH-TREE BLIGHTED (*T. D. P.*).—If you mean by that very vaguely used term "blight," that your tree is "in a most miserable state" from the aphis or green fly upon it, fumigate it with tobacco-smoke, and syringe it occasionally with tobacco-water. *Hamilton's Treatise on the Pine Apple* can be obtained through any bookseller; it is published by Mr. Masters, Aldersgate Street; its price is about four shillings we think. Pine Apple prices vary in price. Mr. Errington will give a description of a good pit for growing them some day.

CINERARIA (*T. Mc M.*).—The specimen you sent was pressed quite flat, and withered. We cannot judge of a flower's merits unless it comes to us perfectly fresh, well packed in a box, and surrounded by damp moss.

PEACH AND NECTARINE LEAVES BLISTERED (*M. R.* and *A Subscriber from the Commencement*).—You drained your border and yet this occurs. We can only reply that there is still too much moisture at the roots; these are probably too deep below the surface, or have struck down into a wet subsoil. We should open the ground and cut away the deep descending roots, and encourage the production of others near the surface.

PANSY (*W. J. W., Hull*).—Your pansy seems of good form, and is a deep purple self, but so crushed that no one can judge of its merits. See what we say about "Cineraria" to another correspondent.

APRICOT LEAVES FULL OF HOLES.—The "perforations like shot holes," are the result of the gnawing of the larvæ of some of the small moths belonging to the race of Tortricidæ; such as *Ditula angustiorana*. See a drawing, &c., at page 81 of our third volume.

NAMES OF PLANTS.—We shall be obliged by our correspondents not sending to us wild plants, as we wish to confine our pages to information connected with those in cultivation. (*M. R.*).—Yours is a common weed, *Apargia hispida*. (*Constant Reader, Mereworth*).—Yours is *Lycopodium clavatum*, or Common Club Moss. (*A Subscriber, Bury St. Edmunds*).—Yours is *Lonicera tatarica*, or Tartarian Honeysuckle.

DAPHNE PRUNING (*H. D.*).—Your hardy Daphne is probably *D. pontica*, and will bear cutting in; and you may so treat it now if you please without any injury.

SEED (*W. D.*).—Thanks for the Coriander and Persian Lettuce seed; we will attend to your request relative to the latter. We have not one Himalayah Pumpkin seed left.

STEEL PENS (*Rusticus*).—The best mode of keeping these clean and uncorroded, is to put them into a vase kept constantly full of water, so that no part of the pen whilst not in use is exposed to the air.

BEES IN OLD BELL-HIVE (*J. L. M.*).—You had better leave these in their old habitation, and put a swarm from them into one of the Improved Cottage Hives. You may cut a hole in the top of the old hive, and put on a small hive or bell-glass; but the best time for doing this is at the end of April.

BEES IN AUSTRALIA (*M. J. J.*).—Whether bees to a colonist in Australia would be profitable, see THE COTTAGE GARDENER, volume 3, page 173. It would be folly to hazard the risk of taking them out, when they may be obtained so readily there. The proper time for putting the cap, or small hive, upon a swarm put into an Improved Cottage Hive, will be from 18 to 21 days after its being fixed. See COTTAGE GARDENER, volume 2, page 104. We can give you no directions respecting the method adopted by "a gentleman who always deprives his bees of the early honey, and allows them during August and September to collect for their winter use." It is a plan we do not recommend.

MOTH (*Eliza*).—The specimen caught in your greenhouse is the Eyedhawk Moth (*Smerinthus ocellatus*). It is not rare. Its caterpillar feeds chiefly on the willow, but is also found upon the leaves of the apple, peach, and other trees. The most expeditious mode of killing insects is to put them into a wide-mouthed bottle or jar, closely corked, in which a good number of *œil bruised* laurel leaves have been previously placed, and covered with a thin layer of cotton wool. The prussic acid with which the air in the bottle is impregnated, destroys the insect almost instantly.

GERANIUM LEAVES SCORCHED (*N. M. G.*).—The geranium-leaves you have enclosed, which are dead and brown across their middles, are what gardeners call "scorched." If you give them air earlier in the morning, or even leave the top-lights a little open all night, so that the upper surfaces of the leaves may be dry before the heat of the sun comes powerfully upon them, you will have no more such disfigured leaves. Your plants are the more liable thus to suffer, because you have been obliged to push them on freely, which makes them more tender, and loose textured.

BLUE ANAGALLIS (*A Subscriber*).—It depends on your own judgment or fancy, and not on the anagallis, whether it is best "pegged down" or "left to grow upright," as it, and most plants of that habit, grow equally well both ways.

DAPHNE CNEORUM (*Ibid*).—This is an extremely pretty plant while in flower, and worth all the care you can bestow on it; but it requires neither manure, liquid-manure, nor shelter from frost. It is perfectly hardy with us even as far north as Caithness, and is not improved by stimulants. It is very choice, however, with respect to soil—a very sandy loam suits it best; and it comes from layers as freely as a willow by merely covering the young shoots an inch or two in the ground, without any other preparation; and this is a very good time to do so, and a better time when it is done flowering.

CYCLAMEN SEED (*T. T. G.*).—When the seed pods burst, the seeds are ripe. The autumn is the proper time to pot cyclamens that have been summered in the open borders.

SPARAXIS VERSICOLOR (*Ibid*).—Your sparaxis plants, which have flourished without blooming, and now withering, are going on well; let them die off and remain dormant till the autumn. They were not flowering bulbs; if they were, they never miss flowering. Those you took up to see how they were will not flower next year; pray be not so curious next time.

CRASSULA (*Ibid*).—If the roots of your long-legged plant are good, cut it down to within four inches of the pot as soon as the flowers are over; and after it starts or grows again into young shoots about an inch long, shake all the soil from its roots, and begin afresh with it in a small pot and new compost. Every morsel of the tops, "long legs and all," will do for cuttings with little or no trouble.

LONDON: Printed by HARRY WOOLDRIDGE, Winchester High-street, in the Parish of Saint Mary Kalendar; and Published by WILLIAM SOMERVILLE ORR, at the Office, No. 2, Amen Corner, in the Parish of Christ Church, City of London.—June 13th, 1850.

WEEKLY CALENDAR.

M W D D	JUNE 20—26, 1850.	Weather near London in 1849.	Sun Rises.	Sun Sets.	Moon R. & S.	Moon's Age.	Clock bef. Sun.	Day of Year.
20 Th	Q. Vict. Access. Young Greenfinches fledged.	T. 75°—50°. W. Fine.	44 a. 3	18 a. 6	1 44	10	1 6	171
21 F	Q. Victoria Proclaimed. Longest Day.	T. 72°—48°. S.W. Fine.	44	18	2 10	11	1 19	172
22 S	Sun's declin. 23° 27' N. Six-spotted Burnet Moth	T. 72°—46°. W. Fine.	45	19	2 40	12	1 32	173
23 Sun	4 Sun. aft. Trinity. Wheat flowers. [seen.	T. 85°—52°. S.W. Fine.	45	19	3 13	13	1 45	174
24 M	Nativity John Baptist. Mids. D.	T. 89°—46°. N.E. Fine.	45	19	rises.	☾	1 57	175
25 Tu	Common Wasp abounds.	T. 79°—53°. S. Fine.	45	19	8a. 53	15	2 10	176
26 W	Privet Hawk Moth seen.	T. 75°—51°. W. Fine.	45	19	9 34	16	2 23	177

On the 19th of June, 1820, died Sir Joseph Banks, Baronet, and President of the Royal Society, another of those instances, now less rare than formerly, of a man preferring th labours, both mental and physical, attendant upon the most active pursuit of natural history, rather than the ease and seductive indulgences placed at his command by inherited wealth. In boyhood he was uncharacterised by any peculiarity but good humour, and the love of british sports; and it was not until fourteen that his tutor ever detected him perusing a book during the hours when recreation was permitted. That first instance is memorable, and may be told in his own words. "One fine summer morning I had bathed in the river as usual with the other boys, but having remained long in the water, I found when dressing all my companions gone. Walking leisurely along a lane, the sides of which were richly enamelled with flowers, I stopped, and exclaimed involuntarily, 'How beautiful.' After some reflection, I said to myself, 'It is surely more natural that I should be taught to know all these productions of nature rather than Greek and Latin; but the latter is my father's command, and it is my duty to obey. But I will make myself acquainted with all these plants for my own pleasure.'" From that time he commenced learning Botany; and, for want of more able tutors, submitted to be instructed by the women employed in gathering herbs for the London herb shops. When at home for the ensuing holidays, he found in his mother's dressing-room a book in which all the plants he had met with were described and engraved. This was Gerarde's Herbal; and it was over this huge folio—which, despite its size, he had taken to school—that his tutor found him poring. This love for natural history increased as he advanced to manhood, and became his cherished occupation. His father being dead, he persuaded his mother to reside at Chelsea, near to the well-known garden of the Apothecaries' Company; and whilst here he was apprehended on suspicion of being a foot-pad, the pursuers of the felon having found young Banks in a ditch beneath some underwood, and turning a deaf ear to his assurance that he was only botanising. We shall not follow him through his adventures in his voyage round the world with Captain Cook, nor to Iceland with Dr. Solander, much less shall we touch upon complaints made against the preference shown to natural sciences more than to the mathematical whilst he presided over the Royal Society; but we will pause to enumerate the benefits he effected, all springing from his love for and knowledge of the departments of science which he preferred, and we shall do so by quoting the words of one of his biographers. The African Association owed its origin to him, and Ledyard, Lucas, Houghton, and the unfortunate Mungo Park, all partook of the care which he extended to the enterprising traveller. He devised the means of carrying the Bread-fruit from Otahetie, and the Mango from Bengal, for cultivation in the West Indies. He transferred the fruits of Persia and Ceylon, also, successfully to the West Indies and Europe. The establishment of our Colony at Botany Bay originated entirely with him. In the affairs of the Board of Trade, and of the Board of Agriculture, he was constantly consulted; and he took a leading part in the management of the Horticultural Society; and he was indefatigable as a trustee of the British Museum, to which institution he bequeathed his scientific library and his foreign correspondence. His writings relative to cultivated plants were numerous, and highly interesting, among them being dissertations on the mildew in wheat, on the Native Country of the Potato, and on the cultivation of strawberries, figs, and American cranberries, at Spring Grove, his residence near Hounslow. Here, under the care of Mr. Oldacre, his gardener, the cultivation of his kitchen-garden, especially in the forcing of mushrooms and pine-apples, became markedly eminent. It was the birth-place, also, of one of our best summer kitchen apples, the Spring-grove Codlin. Death did not close his useful and generous career until he had attained his eightieth year; and most truly may it be said of his whole manhood, "His time, his wealth, his influence, his talents, an incomparable library of works on science and art, knowledge and judgment to advise, generosity to assist, all, in short, of which he possessed, he made the patrimony of the studious, not of his own country alone, but of the whole world!"

Meteorology of the Week. At Chiswick, from observations during the last twenty-three years, the highest and lowest average temperatures of these days are 72.6° and 50.7°, respectively. The greatest heat, 93°, occurred on the 22nd in 1846; and the greatest cold, 37°, on the 25th in 1835. On 60 days rain fell, and 99 days were fine.

RANGE OF BAROMETER—RAIN IN INCHES.

June		1841.	1842.	1843.	1844.	1845.	1846.	1847.	1848.	1849.
20	B.	29.759 29.794	29.734 29.566	30.160 29.956	30.041 29.972	30.117 30.083	30.181 30.097	29.954 29.872	30.130 30.075	30.139 30.095
	R.	0.02	0.01	—	0.01	—	—	0.01	—	—
21	B.	29.959 29.769	29.670 29.640	30.128 29.984	29.980 29.751	30.082 29.991	30.199 30.061	29.900 29.740	30.065 30.063	30.118 30.030
	R.	0.26	0.01	—	—	—	—	—	—	—
22	B.	30.059 29.994	29.757 29.725	30.045 29.984	29.797 29.759	30.014 29.935	29.987 29.849	29.717 29.637	30.019 29.966	30.165 30.011
	R.	0.01	0.29	—	—	—	0.59	—	—	—
23	B.	30.028 29.812	29.823 29.767	30.051 30.027	29.789 29.742	30.126 30.094	29.644 29.577	29.646 29.433	29.839 30.591	29.941 29.822
	R.	0.40	0.01	—	—	—	0.06	0.36	0.44	—
24	B.	29.741 29.639	29.679 29.420	30.011 29.987	30.051 29.642	30.034 29.797	29.517 29.401	29.623 29.580	29.633 29.560	29.994 29.880
	R.	0.49	—	—	—	0.21	—	0.02	0.04	—
25	B.	29.543 29.494	29.805 29.585	29.962 29.906	29.566 29.513	29.868 29.799	29.543 29.497	29.835 29.543	30.897 29.631	30.979 29.907
	R.	0.04	0.03	—	0.02	0.09	—	0.06	0.04	—
26	B.	29.774 29.805	29.915 29.574	29.986 29.845	29.784 29.718	29.856 29.776	29.681 29.647	30.192 30.014	30.016 30.011	29.980 29.919
	R.	—	—	—	0.12	—	0.09	0.01	0.01	—

Insects.—One of the greatest pests of this season are the Gad-flies; and they who, like Jacques, deduce "sermons from stones, and good from everything," may aptly moralise upon the frantic terror evinced by animals powerful as the horse and the ox at the mere buzzing sound of the wings of an insect scarcely an inch long—a buzzing discomforting even to man, and acquiring for the insect the popular name of "The Breeze." The species we have selected as an illustration is the Ox Gad-fly, Tabanus bovinus. It resembles a large fly, with large greenish eyes, and its abdomen spotted with white longitudinally. At the sound of its flight, as well as at that of another species, (Œstrus boris, terrified herds, with their tails erect, or stiffly stretched out in the direction of the spine, gallop about their pastures, make the country resound with their lowings, and fear to rest until they have plunged into water. The Zimb, an African insect, is probably a species of this family. Bruce describes it as attacking cattle so fiercely, that, unless immediately protected, they forsake their food, and run wildly about the plains, dreading even its very sound, until they die, worn out with fatigue, fright, and hunger.

Very much against our inclination, and we are not sure that it is not contrary to our interests, we have resolved to postpone the publication of the First Number of The Cottage Gardeners' Dictionary until Thursday, the 3rd of October. The present is a season so fully employing our various coadjutors, that they cannot devote to the work so much attention as is desirable, if we resolved to commence publishing at once, and to continue the publication of a number on every successive Thursday. Purchasers of the Dictionary will not regret the postponement under these circumstances; and the knowledge that the work will be improved, reconciles us to the delay.

WE have a long array of new works before us, all requiring, because deserving, notice; and for fear that they should accumulate until they become a hopeless pile and labyrinth through which to pick and wind our way, let us address ourselves to the pleasant task, and write more fully the opinions we jotted down as we perused them.

"The History of British Birds," by the Rev. F. O. Morris, is one of a class which we always hail with extreme pleasure—original, accurate, and cheap—within the reach of every one, and a guide every one may rely upon. The first number (price only one shilling!) contains four portraits, most excellently drawn and coloured, with six times as many pages of biography, of four of the largest birds of prey which have been found wild in the British Islands. First is the *Griffon Vulture*, with his wary and expectant look, like some legatee we have seen, watching for death symptoms in him who has written the "I give and bequeath." But one such Vulture (we are speaking now of the bird, not of the legatee) has been caught in the British Islands. "A single specimen," says Mr. Morris, "an adult bird, in a perfectly wild state, was captured by a youth, the latter end of the year 1843, on the rocks near Cork harbour, and was purchased for Lord Shannon, for half-a-crown, by whom, when it died, it was presented to the collection of the Dublin Zoological Society." Next are a pair of *Egyptian Vultures;* and never, again, was there a better illustration of Lavater's comparison of the animal with the human physiognomy, for these at once call to mind a vicious old man. A pair of them was seen in Somersetshire, and one was shot in the October of 1825. The third portrait is of that "compound of the characteristics of the vulture, the hawk, the predatory gull, and the raven,"—*the Erne*, or Sea Eagle. Lastly is given *the Golden Eagle*, which "seems to have established a prescriptive right to the proud appellation of 'the king of the birds;'" as the tiger, in the corresponding predatory class among quadrupeds, has obtained that of "royal." "It is, on the whole, extremely intractable; one, however, is related to have been tamed at Fort William, near Belfast, by Richard Langtry, Esq., which would come at its master's call; and another is mentioned by the late Bishop Stanley in his 'Familiar History of British Birds,' as having been so thoroughly tamed as to have been left at perfect liberty, neither chained nor pinioned. Of this freedom it would often avail itself, and after an absence of two or three weeks would again return. It never attacked children; but on one occasion, it is supposed from its master having neglected to bring it its food, it assailed him with some violence. Of young pigs it would occasionally make a meal. After having been kept safely for ten or twelve years, it was unfor-

tunately killed by a savage mastiff dog. The battle was not witnessed, but it must have been long and well fought. The eagle was slain on the spot, but he did not die unrevenged, for his antagonist, very shortly afterwards, expired of its wounds. We hope to renew our notices of this work, for it is of interest equally to the naturalist and the mere reader for amusement.

"A Treatise on the Theory and Practice of Landscape Gardening, adapted to North America." By A. J. Downing. This is just one of the books which a stay-at-home Englishman should read to brush away from his opinions that film of prejudice which invariably envelopes the innocent bigotries of the untravelled. Among these is an idea that no cultivated landscape scenery can equal that of "his own green isle;" and so far as the fresh verdure of its grass, and bits of rich, happy, home scenery are concerned, he is right—quite right. We have dwelt in many climes, and can testify that in no other land we have visited have we seen anything to compare for quiet beauty to

> "The cottage homes of England,
> Which by thousands on her plains,
> Are smiling o'er the silvery brooks,
> And round the hamlet fanes."

But though there is none of such scenery in other lands, yet they have their exquisite beauties for which we should in vain look for parallels in England. Never shall we forget our first visit to the Botanic Garden of Calcutta, for there did we, for the first time, feel the force and the justice of Bishop's Heber's exclamation—"I now can realize what its was to dwell in the Garden of Eden." Our climate, our vegetation, give no examples with which imagination can construct such grand masses of form, fragrance, and colour. So in America, we confess to having had our prejudices against her gardening; we have always thought that where there was no aristocracy of class, there, in gardening, would be no aristocratic habits and tastes. And so far it seems we were right; for Mr. Downing says—"In the United States, it is highly improbable that we shall ever witness such splendid examples of landscape gardens as those abroad. Here the rights of man are held equal; and if there are no enormous parks, and no class of men whose wealth is hereditary, there is, at least, what is more gratifying, the almost entire absence of a very poor class; while we have, on the other hand, a large class of independent landholders, who are able to assemble around them, not only the useful and convenient, but the agreeable and beautiful in country life." The result, we believe, is correctly foretold—"in half a century more there will exist a greater number of beautiful villas and country seats of moderate extent in the Atlantic States, than in any country of Europe, England alone excepted."

It is quite true that these States can never have the same kind of beauties in their landscape gardening as we have in England; all must be on a larger and grander scale—giant forest-trees, inland seas instead of lakes, and rivers miles in width and thousands of miles long, are features to which the garden designer has to adapt his plans and his vistas. Let us take as an example what Mr. Downing says of Blithewood, the seat of R. Donaldson, Esq., near Barrytown, on the Hudson. "The natural scenery here is no where surpassed in its enchanting union of softness and dignity—the river being four miles wide, its placid bosom broken only by islands and gleaming sails, and the horizon grandly closing in with the tall blue summits of the distant Kaatskills. The gently varied lawn is studded with groups and masses of fine forest and ornamental trees, beneath which are walks leading in easy curves to rustic seats, or to openings affording most lovely prospects. As a pendant to this graceful landscape, there is within the grounds scenery of an opposite character, equally wild and picturesque—a fine bold stream, fringed with wooded banks, and dashing over several rocky cascades, thirty or forty feet in height, and falling altogether a hundred feet in half a mile." We need quote no more; it is with such gigantic materials that the American landscape gardener has to compose, and we can assure our readers that the results are correspondingly bold and striking. But it is not for these alone that we recommend the book for perusal; but, on the contrary, because it is full of instructive lessons, profusely illustrated, relative to the arrangement and management of the garden designer's three grand elements of composition—the ground—the water—and the wood.

Our allotted space is filled, and we must postpone until next week the further examination of our "candidates for honours."

THE FRUIT-GARDEN.

[Absence from home prevented Mr. Errington preparing his observations for this department.]

THE FLOWER-GARDEN.

FLOWER-BEDS. — Summer flower-beds, in masses of one colour, being made up chiefly with half-hardy plants and late spring-sown annuals, the plants are only just now beginning to feel their freedom, having got a good hold of the ground. The *Verbenas*, where they are extensively cultivated, are the first to show the care and success of the propagators, as they are first in bloom. It is provoking to see a white, a lilac, or a bluish flower opening in a bed which was to be all scarlet, besides the comfortable assurance that the mischief does not end there, but must extend to other beds or borders, as Verbenas and most flower-garden plants are propagated and nursed in quantities together in one pot; so that one tally, or number stick, set in in the wrong pot any time in the spring, will often throw thirty or forty plants of a wrong colour on the planter's hands; and the first symptom of any such derangement is looked to with a jealous eye. In all cases where gardening can be carried on systematically, he who makes the cuttings should have the after-management of them until they are finally planted out in the flower-beds, so as to be fully responsible for the accuracy of the tallies, or, which is the same thing, the respective colours. But it so happens here, as if to prove the adage, that what one preaches he does not always practise, when I assist the propagator in making, or "potting" off, cuttings when he is very busy in the spring, all the consequences of misplaced tallies are sure to be laid to my charge for

that season, or for that particular family of plants I may have had through my hands; and, to save *my credit*, the first wrong placed plants which show their bloom are sure to be pulled up, contrary to my orders; and this is what I want to impress on others—not to look to the "credit" of any one, but rather to look to the appearance of the flower-beds in the meantime; and as accidents will happen among tallies with the most careful, and these accidents are sure to come to light sooner or later, by far the best plan will be not to pull up the wrong plants at this stage, though they may be an eyesore to the planter. What I insist on here, is to let such plants be stripped of their flowers as fast as they appear in bud, and the shoots stopped for two or three weeks longer; and by that time the neighbouring plants will have advanced sufficiently to cover the ground, and all misplaced plants may then be safely rooted out without leaving gaps, as they would in the first instance.

PEGGING-DOWN.—This trailing growth of the Verbenas brings me to the first stage of summer dressing the beds. All plants which trail on the ground, or grow sideways, like Verbenas, must be trained or tied down, to fill the more open spaces, so as to get the soil in the beds covered as soon as possible. This training in our forthcoming dictionary will be called "*pegging*," because, in former days, the training was effected with little hooked or forked pegs; but there are many ways of "pegging" without the use of pegs at all; and one of the simplest with Verbenas is to take hold of a flower truss in bud, make a hole with a stick, or with the two fore-fingers, and poke the truss down in it. The shoot is then held in the right position at once, and without knowing how the thing was done, no one could make out that the shoot did not naturally grow in that position from the first. Unless the surface of the bed is very loose indeed there are many plants, such as *Petunias*, trailing *Geraniums*, and the like, which may be trained after the same fashion, being kept in the right direction by means of a leaf here and a leaf there buried in the soil. The footstalk of the leaf, like the flower-stalk of the Verbenas, being still attached to the plant, it holds down a shoot just like one holding a pig by one ear. This may be called the simplest, or cottage mode, of training. The next higher in the scale, is a plan of training invented some years since by one of our fashionable gardeners, and consists of doubling thin strips of matting, of four or five inch lengths, round the shoot, and then burying both ends of the matting in the soil. In large places, or where large quantities of training matting is required, the ends of the new mats bought in the autumn are reserved in little bundles for this purpose, when the mats are being tied, and boys split the strings into the smallest threads, or shreds, on wet days; so that a trainer, with no more matting than he can hold in one hand, can fasten down some thousand shoots. Another way is, to have bundles of short sticks, say of six-inch lengths and as small as can be got, and stick them down slantways against the shoots and branches of many plants. Two such sticks so placed opposite each other, will have the parts above ground crossing one another, like the letter X, and form a very strong holdfast. The very tops of the fuchsia shoots might be put by for this purpose, as I suppose that no cottage gardener is so extravagant as to burn or cast away his annual crop of fuchsia stalks, for they are the handiest things possible for staking many things; and all the dressing they require is to cut them into the required lengths and sharpen one end. Then, at this dressing, thousands of little tops are discarded as useless; and a man is sent to the fields and hedges in the height of summer, for whole days, to look out "pegs" to do what the fuchsia tops would have done much better, unless one chooses rather to work on the old plan of training "by hooks and by crooks."

MIDSUMMER GROWTH.—Very many beautiful half-hardy shrubs, *roses, &c.*, have been sadly cut by the last spring frosts; and the best way to treat such is to look them over after the turn of midsummer, and have all those parts which do not show a strong second or mid-summer growth cut back to a healthy shoot, otherwise we shall have a bad foundation for the growth of future seasons. I have a capital thermometer here, which I keep out on purpose for the stokers to regulate their fires according to the weather; and for the last ten years I have checked this glass with those used in the London Horticultural Society's Garden, and during that time there has not been more than three degrees between them. When the air is very still and frosty, their glasses show three degrees more cold than mine, but with a brisk easterly wind in winter my glass is the lowest. Now, this glass of mine stood as low as six degrees above zero, indicating twenty-six degrees of frost on the morning of the 27th of last March, with nearly two inches of snow on the ground, and the damage done here was more than in the hard winters of 1838, 1840, and 1841. So that here, at any rate, we have plenty of mid-summer pruning, and some lessons to the bargain. The *Plumbago larpentæ* stood out uninjured with no pro-tection, and so did *Clematis tubulosa*—a recent intro-duction from China, for which prizes were given last year at some of our provincial meetings as a greenhouse plant. It seems as hardy as *Fuchsia gracilis*, and *Zauchsneria Californica*; the frost only killing the tops. The beautiful *Mandevilla suaveolens* seems to be of about the same hardiness as the old *Eccremocarpus scaber*, and may, therefore, be trusted against a south wall, and covered with some thatch from frost. I had many of the little wild *Cape Pelargoniums* on a protected border, not one of which was hurt last winter; and mixed with them were many sorts of our fashionable florists' ones, every one of which was dead before Christmas. So that improving the breeds of ge-raniums does not harden their constitution, but the reverse.

Speaking of geraniums in this the height of *the crossing season*, let me urge on cross-breeders to try to get us a set of good bedding sorts, with very small leaves, and distinct colours. Pure whites and lilacs we are very much in want of, and the large loppy leaves of the fancy sorts are altogether unsuitable for bedding ones. Between one thing and another, I shall not be able to cross much this season, but from what I have done I am quite satisfied of the possibility of originating a section for bedding with very small leaves, and large clear-coloured flowers The best new seedling of this season which I have seen, has clear white flowers about the size of those of *Queen Victoria*, and much after the same shape, but the largest of the leaves could be hid under a shilling; but I did not learn if the plant is a perpetual summer bloomer like the Queen, but I believe it is. I have seen another seedling from the fancy sorts, which takes after the habits of the florists' Pelargonium, of great beauty; the flower is quite round, the back petals of that deep shade peculiar to *Ibrahim Pasha*, a clear white eye, and the front petals light salmon. It is, therefore, beyond a doubt that the Pasha and *Anais* are capable of imparting their shades to the better forms of the old sorts, although at first every breeder thought this cross would be worthless, seeing the clouded and speckled seedlings which the first two or three crosses brought to light. I would recommend breeders to discard *Anais* altogether, and employ *Ibrahim Pasha* instead, and always as the mother plant; for there is not much truth in the idea, that "breeding in and in" will deteriorate the offspring—not at least the flowers; and if the leaves could be rendered smaller that way, it would rather be an advantage; but I have little faith in that either.   D. BEATON.

GREENHOUSE AND WINDOW GARDENING.

BEGONIAS.—An amateur "having a little greenhouse in which vines are cultivated, together with a mis-cellaneous collection of plants, will be glad to know what Begonias may safely and successfully be introduced." To meet his case, and that of many more who wish to have as much variety as possible in their little green houses, we shall make this inquiry the handle on which to suspend a few remarks upon the treatment this beau-tiful family requires in such circumstances, merely pre-mising that such was the treatment successfully pro-secuted by ourselves, when destitute of a stove or a hot-house for plants, in which structures the Begonias may be more easily cultivated, and be rendered very orna-mental during the winter months; while in the green-house and vinery they can only be expected to show off their attractions in the summer and autumn.

The genus was named in compliment to a French botanist. It consists chiefly of herbaceous and tuberous-rooted plants, and succulent stemmed under-shrubs, with a few that have a climbing character; Mr. Hartweg having found some that thus mounted the stems of trees from twenty to thirty feet. The leaves are curious and unique, showing almost at a glance the family to which they belong; being *obliquely cordate*, owing to one side of the leaf at the base extending much farther than the other In some, however, such as the *hydrocotylifolia*, this ob-liquity is nearly lost, and the succulent foliage covering the surface of the pot looks nearly as round as the leaf of the common nasturtium. The flowers are produced in cyme-like spikelets, and are frequently very beautiful. The male and female organs are in different flowers just similar to what is seen in the cucumber and melon. The whole family is chiefly found in the West Indies, East Indies, and South America. Few of them, there-fore, will flourish in a cool greenhouse, if kept there all the season. A temperature as low as 35° for any length of time in winter, would kill them altogether; more especially if great care is not taken to keep them dry. The increased temperature in such houses, from the advance of the season, would not come sufficiently early to start them into growth, so as to make fine flowering plants during the summer. If kept in a temperature of 45° during winter, and then started in a hotbed in March, similar to Achimenes, fine plants will be obtained for blooming in such houses during summer. Hence, in the absence of a stove, a vinery, or a greenhouse, used as such is much better suited for their cultivation than a greenhouse. In the warmest end of such a house, if even under a stage, but near where the fire enters, and with the pots on their sides, or if standing protected from drip, a medium temperature of 45°, and from that to 50°, can easily be maintained, without detriment to such plants as Geraniums, Calceolarias, Epacrises, &c., the medium temperature for which would be some-what lower. In such a temperature there will be no danger of starting the vines, and the tuberous-rooted and succulent stemmed Begonia will be safe. Many kinds that have permanent, though not very succulent stems will even retain their leaves; though that is not a matter of much consequence. When a little extra heat is given to break the vines, and again to set the fruit when in bloom, the Begonias will show signs of vitality; and then should be watered, receiving as much formerly as would be sufficient to prevent them being thoroughly dried; and that is best done by surrounding the plants with a damp substance, such as moss, instead of applying the water directly to the soil. Shortly after growth has commenced the plants should receive what pruning they require; and then, before long, be repotted, getting rid of as much of the old soil as possible, and replacing it with new; and as soon as the plants will stand the sun giving them an open place, with a little but not a thick shading. The shading obtained from *climbers* in a warm greenhouse, or in such a house with vines not too thick on the roof, is just the thing that suits them. If treated with light rich soil, plenty of water, and a manure solution frequently, the plants will grow with great rapidity, and soon reward you by masses of their pretty blossoms; keeping on flowering generally until the cold nights of autumn, when you must bid them adieu for the season. Before stowing them away in their winter quarters, try and set them right in the sun for a few weeks, and refrain from watering, that the tissues may be consolidated. In a house kept from 45° to 50° during the winter, some kinds will bloom freely all the winter, such as *obliqua ;* but for the general collection you must be content with blooming them in summer, unless you have a plant stove. For the preparing for this summer's blooming of these plants, Achimenes, Gloxinia, &c., nothing is better than a vinery, or a greenhouse used as such; all that is necessary being a sheltered spot, or rather a cold pit, to remove the hardier plants to when the temperature is increased.

But now comes the difficulty. I have glanced at how the plants should be managed in such circumstances, and this I can do with confidence, but the instancing of the species most suitable is quite another thing; not because these species require different treatment, farther than will be apparent from the character of the species as a herbaceous plant, or a succulent under-shrub, but because of the great difficulty of being sure of giving such a name, that the collector may depend upon obtaining the "Simon Pure" indicated; for, either owing to the carelessness of botanists, or the ignorance and stupidity of us cultivators, the whole genus seems a mass of confusion; some of the prettiest species receiving almost as many names as the gardens in which they are found, while these names are either not to be found in catalogues, or are contradictory to the definitions there given. For instance, there is a Begonia (and the only one I have seen) grown in cottage windows, rather coarse looking, large leaves, brownish green above, crimson veined below, herbaceous, fleshy, tuberous rooted, and hardy enough to bear rather rough cottage treatment, as I have seen it frequently there for at least fifteen years past; and yet this old plant has I know not how many names, being termed *bicolor, diversifolia, heracleifolia, mutabilis, discolor, Evansiana,* &c., the latter being, perhaps, the most current, only, according to the catalogues, it should have white flowers, while our favourite rough gentleman has pink ones; and rough though he be, so rough as to be discarded by our fastidious friends who will not give house room to such a common thing, we, nevertheless, place it here first in our list; because when forwarded as we have indicated, and potted in equal portions of loam, leaf-mould, and rotten cow-dung, the plant four feet in height, and the mass in the pot nearly as much in diameter, standing upon a stage, or in a vase above rather than below the eye, with leaves like cabbages, showing the purple of their under sides, and masses of the long pedunculed cymes of pink blossom hanging over them, it then becomes an object so far from despicable, that ladies of refined taste have stood before it and exclaimed, "Beautiful!"

2. *B. nitida.*—The name given in this neighbourhood to one of the very best of the group, with thick shining pale green leaves, and beautiful large pink or flesh-coloured flowers. This species in the catalogues is marked white. This is one of the prettiest ornaments of a plant-stove in winter. Soil for this and the following, equal portions of peat, leaf-mould, and half portions of sand and cow-dung. Plants kept in a conservatory are just now showing bloom and breaking, but rather lanky. Young plants forwarded in a vinery are in bloom.

3. *B. obliqua.*—Pink; not so showy as the last, but hardier; flowered all the winter in a conservatory; temperature from 40° to 45°, with a rise of 10° for sun heat.

4. *B. manicata.*—Pale pink; very pretty.

5. *B. hydrocotylifolia.*—Rather pretty; leaves are studded over the surface of the pot: they and the numerous flower-stems rise from thick tuberous short shoots.

6. *B. parvifolia* (sometimes *floribunda* and *semperflorens*).—White; a little gem: for a limited space the best of all; an evergreen shrub in the stove, deciduous under the treatment we are speaking of; leaves small, as the name implies; flowers small, but in vast abundance. Plants that stood in the back of a vinery, in a medium temperature of 40°, so woe-begone in their appearance that many would ask, what we kept such things for?—after being pruned, potted, and assisted by the increasing heat of the vinery, are now nice little bushes, 2 feet in height, and more in diameter; a dense mass of bloom, and with moderate care will continue so until the month of October.

7. *B. sanguinea.*—Small white flowers; the underside of the large leaves crimson; little attractive except for the leaves.

8. *B. argyrostigma.*—Also termed *punctata* and *maculata,* owing to the white spots on the leaves, which are its only attraction; the flowers being small and white, and produced in no great profusion.

9. *B. fuchsioides.*—Scarlet; one of the prettiest; flowers produced upon dependent twigs, making it resemble a fuchsia. Should, therefore, be grown with one or more upright stems; does not like being cut down; must be kept in the warmest possible place in such circumstances during the winter, so as to preserve the stems entire. If the leaves are browned, or if even many drop off, that is of little consequence, provided the wood has been *hardened* by exposure to the sun in the autumn; for shortly after growth commences the flowers will also begin to be produced. The plant, if well-grown, is always beautiful to look at, but as the flowers are not produced in large panicles they must be numerous to render the plant a floral attraction.

10. *B. coccinea* (sometimes *rubra*).—Scarlet. The flowers are small, but produced in large panicles, and of such a vivid rich colour as to make it a desirable acquisition. It is rather *tantalizing* to tell our friendly amateur, that this will be one of the worst to manage in his greenhouse vinery. In such circumstances I only succeeded once to my satisfaction. The plant was the growth of several years. In the end of summer it was kept close to the glass, and water was gradually withheld in autumn; during the winter it had a temperature seldom below 45°, and oftener near 50°. When the vines showed in the spring, the flowers of the Begonia came with them, and continued for several months a mass of bloom. It is of little use cutting such a plant down, unless when growth is desirable, as, unlike such sorts as *parvifolia,* and *blanda,* &c., which flower on the year's wood, the Coccinea chiefly blooms on the wood, or rather the extreme points of it, formed during the preceding season.

11. *B. blanda* (also termed *lucida*).—A very pretty species, with shining leaves; may be treated as a herbaceous plant; has large white flowers, seldom grows high, and should have been placed after Parvifolia.

We think that from this limited number a small collection may easily be made. I have already referred to watering and soil, but forgot to say that Coccinea should have more peat than any of the others. All the kinds are easily *propagated,* either by divisions of the root or by cuttings, which should be dried at the base before inserting them in sandy soil, and covering them with a bell-glass. Many of the species also produce seeds in abundance, and these will bloom in the second year, and some of them the first season.   R. FISH.

HOTHOUSE DEPARTMENT.

EXOTIC STOVE PLANTS.
GESNERACEÆ: ACHIMENES.

Propagation by Cuttings.—The young tops of these plants will strike easily if put in sand, under a bell-glass in heat, and potted off as soon as rooted. *Gesneras, Gloxinas,* and other families of this order, will sooner make blooming plants by the same method. If the cuttings are put in as early as March, they will flower well the same season, and succeed the old plants in blooming: thus prolonging that season till late in the autumn.

By Division.—The roots of *Achimenes* and some *Gloxinias,* that is the perennial roots, are scaly. Each scale, if detached and placed in pots of light earth, and slightly covered, will make nice plants, that will flower next year. We have occasionally divided the large bulbs or tubers of *Gesneras* and *Gloxinias,* exposing them a short time to dry up the wounds; but unless they have grown inconveniently large, or are very scarce, this practice is needless, as they increase so freely by cuttings. They may also be increased *by leaves,* either whole or cut into small pieces. For new varieties this is an excellent method. The leaves, if put in whole, should be managed exactly like cuttings. If a bud be taken off the stem with the leaf, that bud as soon as roots are formed will push forth; but if no bud is taken off, the leaf will form a tuber at the bottom of the leaf stalk, and that tuber will send up young shoots in the spring. It is a curious circumstance, that a leaf should have, as it were, the power without a single bud to form a tuber; nay, more curious still is the fact, that the smallest portion of a leaf, provided there is a vessel in that portion, has the same power, though in a less degree; and this is the more remarkable when we consider the kind of leaf. It has abundance of sap in it, so much so, that it might be expected to rot almost instantly. No doubt life is preserved by the leaf, or portion of a leaf, being placed in a situation where evaporation is prevented, that is under the bell-glass.

By Seeds.—To obtain new varieties seeds must be saved. This has been done already to a great extent, especially in the large family of *Gloxinia.* Bright colours have been obtained, but the great desideratum yet to be achieved is to obtain fine form, substance, and magnitude. The properties of a good *Achimenes* or *Gloxinia* should be: first, a good shape—that is, the flower should be quite round at the mouth of the tube; the edge quite smooth, and not at all reflexed or turned back. The flower-stem ought to be stout—able to support the flower well up above the foliage. It should support the flower so as to show the inside markings, spots, or shades. The flowers ought to be produced numerously, so as to have, at least, six flowers open at once. The colours should be clear, distinct, and bright; the spot or blotch, if any, should be well defined. Where the spots are small and numerous they should be on the lower part of the flower, so as to be distinctly seen. Lastly, the flower should be large and of a good substance. All these properties are pretty well exemplified in the variety of Gloxinia raised at Pine Apple-place Nursery, named *Gloxinia grandis,* and in the variety of Achimenes raised by some continental florist, named *Achimenes longiflora alba.*

RAISING VARIETIES.—Excellent as these varieties are, we have no doubt the persevering industry and skill now so much in exercise amongst the lovers of flowers will soon produce much finer varieties. Our amateur friends who have time and space cannot do better than amuse themselves by raising seedlings of these charming ornamental flowers. In order to increase the probability of obtaining superior varieties, the seed should be saved from the best flowers, such as possess the properties described above; and if the pollen of one superior variety be dusted upon some other possessing some desirable property, either of colour, form, or size, the object will be more certain to be achieved. If the anthers of the plant intended to bear the seed be removed before they shed their pollen, the produce will be the more certain to have the desirable properties of the male parent. To prevent bees or other insects carrying to another plant the pollen of inferior flowers, cover the one operated upon with some fine gauze. All these precautions having been taken, nip off all other flowers on the plant; allow no water to fall upon the seed-vessels, and place the plant near to the glass. When the seed is ripe the seed-vessels will burst; it must then be gathered, and dried gently, and put away in a dry drawer, in a room where no frost can reach it. About the middle of February will be a good season to sow it. Prepare some shallow, wide, clean pots; fill them half full with potsherds, place some siftings of peat upon them, and fill up the rest with a compost of loam, peat, and very rotten vegetable mould, in equal parts, adding one-sixth of fine white sand, mixing them well together. Make the surface smooth and even with a round, flat piece of wood. Then sow the seeds thinly and equally on the surface, and sift through a very fine sieve the thinnest covering imaginable of the compost upon them—the thickness of a wafer will be enough. Water them with the finest rose watering-pot, and place them in a warm stove near the glass, shading from very bright sunshine. The seedlings will soon come up, and as soon as they can be transplanted, prepare pots similar to the seed pots, and prick out the seedlings in them half an inch apart. As soon as the leaves begin to touch each other, transplant them again singly into thumb-pots, one inch in diameter, in the same compost, and replace them upon the shelf near the glass. Be careful in watering, as they are very apt to damp-off at this critical period. Prepare now a gentle hotbed of one or two lights, or more, according to the quantity of seedlings; and as soon as the heat is moderated, place upon the dung a thick covering of coal-ashes. By the time this is ready the seedlings will require repotting into $3\frac{1}{2}$-inch pots, well drained in the same compost. Place them upon the coal-ashes thinly, so as to allow room for the next potting. Great care must now be taken to shade them from the early sun in the morning, as the steam arising from the hotbed will, during the night, have clothed the leaves with dew, and half an hour's bright sun would scald them. They should have a covering of mats during the night; and if the steam is very strong, tilt the lights behind with a thin piece of wood, to allow it to escape during the night. Give air also during the day, but so as not to allow the cold winds to blow in over the plants. As soon as the pots are moderately filled with roots, repot them into 5-inch pots, in a rather richer compost, by adding a little more leaf-mould. Continue the same attention in regard to watering, giving air, and shading. In these pots they may be allowed to flower, which they will do about the month of July. Such as may prove deficient in all the good properties will serve admirably to flower during the later months in the stove or greenhouse, and when the bloom is over may be thrown away; but such as promise to be of first-rate excellence should be kept in the frame a little longer: the removal of the commoner ones will give them more room to expand their leaves, and will allow them to have another shift into a little larger pots.

Winter Management.—All the kinds—whether established favourites or good new varieties—should, as soon as the blooming season is over, be placed in a situation where no water can reach them. We keep them very well under the stages in the stove, or in a warm greenhouse, where the thermometer never is allowed to fall lower than 40°. As soon as the leaves turn quite yellow they should be cut off close to the tuber, taking care not to injure it. In this state of rest they must be allowed to remain till the season returns at which they were started into growth the previous year.

(To be continued.)

FLORISTS' FLOWERS.

CARNATIONS, PICOTEES, AND PINKS.—The two first in pots, and the latter in beds, would be greatly benefited by a top-dressing of rich compost: remove a portion of the old soil, and replace it with the fresh, taking care not to disturb the root. Now is a good season to thin the buds, especially of the pinks: leave the most promising one on each stem of the pinks, and two—or at most three—on the carnations and picotees. Some of the strongest of the latter may now be layered; for by doing this thus early a good stocky plant is secured for the next season.

RANUNCULUSES will be greatly benefited now by a plentiful supply of water. If this is neglected just now the bloom will be indifferent. Every third watering, mix a portion of liquid manure amongst the water—it will strengthen growth and heighten the colours considerably.   T. APPLEBY.

THE KITCHEN-GARDEN.

ASPARAGUS.—The cutting of asparagus will now be brought nearly to a close, with the exception of those who have old beds, and intend to destroy them as soon as this season's cutting is expired, instead of allowing the plants to remain till next season's forcing. To secure abundance of fine heads next season, this is the time to give the beds every possible encouragement, by the application of salt sown a little and often when showery weather prevails. During dry hot weather, if it is considered necessary to apply water for the assistance of the plants, give liberal soakings of manure-water with salt dissolved in it; it is by far the best method. Mulching and surface-stirring should be also well attended to. The ground cleared of old asparagus and trenched over is a famous situation for planting some of the varieties of *brocolis* and *borecoles*, or a crop of late *cauliflowers*. Sow at this season liberally of *cauliflowers*, for obtaining abundance of plants for successional production throughout autumn and winter. This being one of the most delicious and useful of vegetables, we continue to plant it in every corner we have to spare from July to the middle of September, when we commence storing them in temporary-built sheds for the winter's use. As soon as the head of the cauliflower shows itself, then, in the dry part of the day, the plants are pulled up by the roots and tied into bunches of from four to eight, and hung up to the roof of our sheds, where they keep very well, and are found very useful all winter.

STORING SHEDS.—To give an idea of such home-made sheds, or *lenhays*, as they are called in Devonshire, we save any kind of refuse, such as all kinds of evergreen prunings, bean-stalks, artichoke-stalks, asparagus-stems when cut in autumn, furze-hedge trimmings, &c., and these are dried, bound up into small faggots, with two withes, and stored. Rough poles, saw-pit scantlings, or any kind of refuse wood are also stored until the time comes round when a shed is to be put up in some corner. A few old stems of trees also have been stored, or thick clumsy saw-pit slabs, for posts to form the shed with to the required size, and to support the roof; some of the scantlings or poles are nailed to the outside of them, when fixed about three feet apart, and enough of those bundles are placed close together to fill up the sides and ends, with the exception of the door-way, to make it close and warm. These bundles are either tied to the nailed scantlings, or other scantlings are nailed in on the other side of the bundles, which keep all in tight together. The best and closest of the bundles are selected for covering the roof, over which a thin thatching of straw or reed is placed. A handy labourer and boy will, in a very short time, finish snugly an erection of this kind. The floor of such a shed is a good situation for storing potatoes, carrots, parsnips, and turnips in sharp winter weather. In summer, such places are excellent for mushroom-culture. A flap-window is placed either in the side or at the ends, for admitting light and air; and a snug, convenient, useful store is thus erected with but small cost.

SHALOTS and GARLIC should be tied up in small bunches, harvested as soon as ready, and hung up in a shed or other open-roofed situation to dry gradually; and the ground they have grown on will be found an excellent situation for sowing *cauliflowers*, *colewort*, *endive*, *lettuce*, &c., or for pricking out any of the winter stuff. Between the earliest potatoes may now be planted a crop of *Savoys*, or some other winter crop. *Turnips* sow in succession; thin those already up in due time, and encourage the growth by oft repeated stirrings. If attacked by the fly, sow dry wood ashes over them early in the morning, and draw elder-boughs over them in the heat of the day. *Collect* horse, cow, sheep, or deer *dung* where convenient, and some good holding *loam*, and well incorporate them together for making a *mushroom-bed*, taking care to put enough loam to modify the heating of the dung, which is the most essential matter to attend to in mushroom-bed making, for a strong heat not only dries and parches up the materials, but destroys the spawn.   JAMES BARNES.

MISCELLANEOUS INFORMATION.

ECONOMIZING.

By the authoress of " My Flowers."

A REMARK in the letter of a very interesting correspondent has struck me forcibly, as being exactly what I have so often felt, and which is indeed a painful and embarrassing fact— " to pursue economical plans well, one should have plenty of money, and time too, to set the machine going!"

Now it may seem a contradiction or an absurdity to say, that to economize well, we should have plenty of money; and, perhaps, *plenty* may be an expression too strong for the occasion, but it is perfectly true that we must have *some*.

The parents of three children possessing five hundred per annum may live with economy upon three; those who possess three hundred per annum, may live upon two; but when they are so situated as to possess scarcely one hundred per annum, exclusive of house-rent, and that " a lottery, and dependent upon others," how are they to trim and steer their little bark among the rocks and shoals of a pitiless world? Not by economizing, but by *renouncing*. When we have a tolerable income, we can manage it with care and discretion;

we can choose the least expensive articles, and carry on our household affairs in the least expensive way; but when our income is so very small, our only refuge is to give up every thing that can be given up, and bring ourselves into such a compass as not only to feel that we are not spending one unnecessary shilling, but that we are actually living within our means. What can we look forward to, when we know that we are, every year, exceeding our income, although it may be by a trifling sum? *That* bill must be paid with next year's money, and consequently our next year's income will be just so much less than it was before. This *must be* the case, if we do not keep strictly within bounds, and if we have no kind friends to aid us in our difficulties; and then, again, how can a delicate mind bear to *make itself* a burden to even the kindest friends? When we are not doing our strictest, most self-denying duty in this matter, we cannot feel that we are submitting to the will of God, or receive without remorse the bounty of others.

It will be my endeavour to obtain, from some of the best and most experienced managers, such scales of expenditure as will enable persons of small income to adapt their consumption to their means in some degree; but in those scales which I have hitherto examined I find, that in the case of a family with three children *no servant* is allowed when the income is less than £150.

One of our correspondents, in whom we feel a lively interest, possesses "nearly an acre of garden," for the cultivation of which the services of a man are required, who is useful also in other ways "connected with the house." As many other of our readers are very possibly situated in a similar manner, we will venture to suggest a retrenchment, that may perhaps be distasteful to the feelings, and *at first* to the judgment, but which will, we think, be found of some decided benefit, if the trial be made; it is, to give up the enjoyment of the garden,—of the kitchen-garden, at least; to let it, and dismiss the man. At the lowest computation of wages the regular weekly payment will be seven shillings, which by the year will amount to £21 5s 10d; but in most cases, particularly in the neighbourhood of towns, the wages are higher than these.

The purchase of vegetables all the year round will not amount to more than one-half of this sum, and most probably to much less, when they are prudently and economically managed; and thus a considerable sum in a small income is at once obtained, besides the rent of the ground, which although it may not be much, is still something, and everything in such cases should be considered. With " a good, superior" servant in the house to overlook all things, a boy or a woman might be employed for a couple of hours in the morning to clean shoes, knives, &c., and to perform the little morning offices required, which would be a far cheaper plan than that which is now pursued.

A relative of our own has adopted the plan of giving up the expense of a garden with complete success, even where the labour of a man is still required in the managment of land. In *this* case the relief is felt; how much more, then, when the man can be entirely dispensed with? *Unless* a garden can be made to pay its own expenses, those of the labourer, and to supply the family too, it is an *outgoing*, and, in the circumstances we are alluding to, should be resolutely given up.

May I also suggest to our most kind correspondent, that where a conveyance can be hired the pony and carriage might be resigned. "Pleasurable excursions" with those we love are indeed delightful, but they must not be indulged in at the expense of that which is right; and so serious an item per week as a labourer's wages will make a striking alteration in the year's account.

Let this suggestion be seriously considered where so much depends upon *retrenchment*. It is wonderful how many things are considered "indispensable" until they are given up; and then we are amazed to find how well and quietly we go on without them, and how little we really miss them. This is no theoretical remark, but one grounded upon actual experience; and we feel sure, that where a conscientious desire exists to conform to those circumstances which a Gracious Father sees to be good for us, and in which His Hand has placed us, all things will be possible and even easy to be done.

The best way to set about a reform is to make it at once, boldly and resolutely, and adapt ourselves to it; we shall find

the effort far less than we expected, and the consequences great; whereas, if we do anything by halves, we are not the less inconvenienced, and the result will be unsatisfactory. There is, of course, always a degree of awkwardness on first beginning a new household system: it does not immediately work well; little alterations require to be made in the various parts, so as to fit them conveniently to each other,—and this takes a little time and skill; but it should on no account lead to vexation of spirit, or despair. All things will right themselves in time, where sound principle, firm resolve, and good temper, grapple with the foe. Godly fear and trust will make many rough places plain, and we need them both, in all their fulness, even in the *seeming* quiet of our own homes. A wife and mother may have little of the external world to cope with, but she has to "guide the house, and give no occasion to the adversary to speak reproachfully;" and this is in itself a mighty charge; but it will not be beyond the power of any one who takes "of the water of life *freely*."

Where a husband and wife combine cordially in their efforts to economize and renounce, all *human* means are in their hands; they have then only to seek and *expect* the promised blessing upon all who do the will of God.

HOUSE-DRAINAGE.

The theme which is the object of this paper has only of late years seriously engaged the attention of the English public; the very subject is, in fact, unattractive and distasteful,—all discussion, therefore, upon the vital evils of its neglect, has been in consequence too much avoided; it was left entirely to the architect, or the bricklayer; and in few instances, till a very recent date, have their arrangements betrayed either sufficient care or even knowledge of the subject. This state of things is the more remarkable, from the obvious evil of bad drainage, to which in so many houses our senses must bear testimony, especially in the dwellings of crowded localities. It is here that the evil commonly exists in its most aggravated form; but it is not confined to towns,—it is met with, in a modified degree, in country houses and in cottages: often in these the evil may not be so great as in suburban dwellings, but then the remedy is much easier—the excuse for inattention, if possible, less. In many of these a self-acting trap, or valve (which may be bought for a few pence), by preventing the passage of the gases of putrefaction, cures the nuisance; in others, the re-laying of the pipe-drain, originally placed without a sufficient fall, accomplishes the desired object. These little modern improvements require, for their application, only a little common sense: they do not need any considerable engineering skill, or material expense. But, if the householder is in doubt as to the origin and cure of such a dangerous nuisance, as that to which I have alluded, how readily can he now consult those who have in most towns now paid very considerable attention to the subject. These things should make us all, indeed, promote, in every way in our power, the progress of sanitary improvement, of systematic house-drainage, and of the consequent employment of workmen, well acquainted with the best principles and detail of their business. Let no one object to this on the score of any imaginary invasion of his independence, or interference with his right thus to neglect his own comfort and health, as well as to endanger that of his neighbours and visitors.

Such false and injurious conclusions have thus strongly been alluded to in a late able *Report of the Survey on House-drainage*:—"It is only when the overflowing cesspool, or the choked-up drain, is no longer bearable, that the mitigation of the evil is forced upon him (by the services of the scavenger). And from year to year is this unwelcome visit repeated. Nor is this all; yet more unwelcome visitors—sickness and disease—force their way in by the same channels in spite of him; and those are happy who escape the most unwelcome visitor of all—death: too often prematurely summoned to these scenes of neglect and apathy."

Of the close connexion between disease and bad drainage there is abundant testimony. Dr. Southwood Smith observes (*Report of Commissioners on Public Health*, page 9):—"It appears that the streets, courts, alleys, and houses, in which fever first breaks out, and in which it becomes most prevalent and fatal, are invariably those in the immediate neighbourhood of uncovered sewers, stagnant ditches and ponds, gutters always full of putrefying matter, and privies, the soil of which lies openly exposed, and is seldom or never removed." And he proceeds to remark (page 4):—"The operation of these peculiar causes is steady, unceasing, and sure; and the result is the same as *if twenty or thirty thousand of these people were annually taken out of their wretched dwellings and put to death*, the actual fact being that they are allowed to remain in them and die. It has been stated, that the annual slaughter in England and Wales from *preventable* causes of typhus-fever, which attacks persons in the vigour of life, is double the amount of what was suffered by the allied armies in the Battle of Waterloo." "I particularize *fever*," he adds, in a subsequent page of the Report, "because fever is the most obvious and the most rapidly fatal of the diseases arising from the neglect of sewage, ventilation, and cleanliness; but it would be a very inadequate view of the pernicious agency of the poison unceasingly generated in these filthy and neglected houses, to restrict it to the disease the most obviously produced by it. Its indirect action is highly noxious, though the evil is not so manifest. It is a matter of constant observation, that even when not present in sufficient intensity to produce fever by disturbing the action of some organ, or some set of organs, and thereby weakening the general system, this poison acts as a powerful predisposing cause of some of the most common and fatal maladies to which the human body is subject. For example, the deaths occasioned in this country by diseases of the digestive organs, by inflammation of the air passages and lungs, and by consumption, form by far the largest proportion of the annual mortality. Now, no one who lives long in or near a malarian district is ever for a single hour free from some disease of the digestive organs. But disordered states of the digestive organs not only constitute in themselves highly painful and even fatal maladies, but they lay the foundation of several other mortal diseases."

It is hardly necessary to strengthen this testimony by any additional evidence. I shall merely add, therefore, an extract from the evidence of the excellent Dr. Arnott, who, when speaking of the increasing progress of the typhus-fever in Glasgow, observed (*Report*, page 47) that the medical attendants stated, that "it was the most severe amongst the labouring classes, even although the individuals were apparently somewhat robust, *if their habitations were dark, damp, filthy, and unventilated;*" and he continues (page 50):—"Our inquiries gave us the conviction that the immediate and chief cause of many of the diseases which impair the bodily and mental health of the people, and bring a considerable *portion prematurely to the grave*, is the poison of *atmospheric impurity*, arising from the accumulation in and around their dwellings of the decomposing substances used for food, and in their arts; and of the impurities given out from their own bodies."

As relates to house-drainage, and the defects produced by its neglect upon the health of the inhabitants, the Commissioners afford an impressive summary when they say (*Ibid*, page 17):—"The medical witnesses have brought before us facts in support of their strongly-urged and unanimous opinion, that no population can be healthy which live amid cesspools, or upon a soil permeated by decomposing animal or vegetable refuse, giving off impurities to the air in their houses and in the streets. They state the necessity of preventing all accumulations of stagnant refuse in or near houses; and of substituting a system of house-drainage and cleansing, aided by the introduction of better supplies of water into the houses."

Amid, then, all the ever-occurring objects which require the vigilant attention of the housekeeper, let him place in the first class, the construction and preservation of a good system of house-drainage! Such an effort, he may rest assured, in spite of the repulsive nature of some of its details, will be rewarded by not only a freedom from annoyance, but by the increased comfort, and health of body and mind, of all those who are the members of his family circle.

CUTHBERT W. JOHNSON.

EGGS AND POULTRY.

Eggs are just now very plentiful, and should therefore be used as much as possible in every household. In cottages where meat seldom finds an entrance, what a luxury is an egg! and even on tables where dainties are usually seen, the egg still holds a foremost place. I wish many more of my humble readers would keep poultry, and thus be enabled to have a change of diet, which is so satisfactory both to the palate and the health. There are many ways of dressing eggs besides that of boiling them, though that method, from giving the least trouble, is the one usually adopted. There are, as I dare say you have often heard, "two ways of doing every thing," and it is certainly the case in sending eggs on the table. What can look nicer or more tempting than a snow-white egg; yet how often you see them discoloured, and looking anything but agreeable. To prevent this, if the eggs are from your own hen-roost, pay great attention to the nests; change the straw directly it becomes dirty; this will generally secure your obtaining eggs clean and white; should you however happen to have any that are stained or discoloured, wash them in *cold* water before putting them into the saucepan. Unless this is done the stains will remain, and the consequence will be, that a most uninviting dish appears at your table. Perhaps many of my readers will smile at my directions as to egg boiling, and say they think themselves lucky to have an egg for breakfast without quarrelling with the way it is done; but, remember, "if a thing is worth doing at all, it is worth doing well."

Summer is the season of plenty, and consequently of cheapness, and the thrifty dame will take advantage of this, and provide such things for the sustenance of her family as are not to be had in the winter. If you have more eggs than you wish to consume, put them by till Christmas time. There are several ways of keeping them fresh, but I never tasted them so good as when kept in lime-water, which is very easily made in the following way:—Break the lime into small pieces and pour over it some boiling water, stir it well, and when it is quite cold put the eggs into it. Be careful that the water quite covers them, and keep them in a cellar, or some cool place. I have heard of eggs kept in this manner being as good at Christmas as when they were put in at Whitsuntide. I intend trying it this year; but I do not recollect the proportion of lime to the water; perhaps some of my readers could inform me? Bran is a very good receptacle for eggs; great care must be taken that it is quite dry, and the top layer must be three inches, at least, in thickness, in order to exclude every breath of air. Another plan is to "smear" them with fresh butter or lard. This is, I believe, an effectual but a very troublesome operation.

Poached eggs require a little more attention during the dressing than the boiled egg does, but it well repays the trouble; and a couple of poached eggs with a few potatoes will make an excellent dinner or supper for those who are unaccustomed "to fare sumptuously every day." A wide saucepan or stewpan is the best utensil for poaching eggs in. Put into it a quart of water, set it on the fire, then break each egg separately into cups, when the water boils let the egg drop gently into it. In three minutes the white will have settled round the yolk. Put a spoon or skimmer carefully under it, let it drain for a moment, and then place it on a piece of hot toast on some mashed potatoes. If the cottager is fortunate enough to possess a flitch of bacon and a couple of hens, he may provide himself a dinner "fit for a prince." Fried eggs and bacon is a most excellent dinner; and when you remember that in many cases it only requires a little exertion, a little energy, to procure these, you are surprised on being told that nothing is tasted for dinner but vegetables or bread. Look how many gardens are almost uncultivated—how many "bits of land" lying waste—which if dug and planted would enable you to keep a pig, and poultry; for poultry thrive and lay eggs as well (or nearly so) on a vegetable diet—if allowed at the same time the "run of the road"—as they do when pampered and fed upon barley and oats. A little management, a little forethought, a little exertion, and perhaps a little self-denial, would make our cottage homes more cheerful and more peaceful. Surely the wife (at any rate) would think this an advantage! Even in a worldly point of view, how pleasant it would be to see the husband returning after his day's work to assist his wife in cultivating their little garden, instead of loitering at the public-house, and returning late at night, cross and out-of-sorts with himself, and every one about him—and, in a spiritual view, how very superior! For though temptations are around us, and evil thoughts abound amidst every occupation, every scene, yet how happy must that cottage home be whose owners are employing their time in a profitable manner—remembering that God has given a talent to each, and with this command, "Occupy till I come;" and though our Lord may appear to delay his coming, it is sure and certain; and on his arrival we shall have to deliver up the accounts of all our time, our thoughts, our actions! Surely if our thoughts rested on this subject a little more our conduct would be widely different! "By their fruits shall ye know them."—A Friend.

THE LONDON HORTICULTURAL SOCIETY'S FETE.
CHISWICK, June 8.

The exhibition was better than an average one, and again showed what skill and industry can do when spurred by the kindly spirit of emulation. For the benefit of such of our readers as had not the opportunity of witnessing such a grand display of horticulture, and to record the names of the chief successful candidates, we shall give as brief a description as the nature of the subject will allow. We shall, as usual, commence with that class of plants which were exhibited in the greatest state of perfection, considering the difficult nature of their culture, and the great skill displayed to bring them to that state.

EXOTIC ORCHIDS.
COLLECTIONS OF TWENTY.

1st Prize to Mr. Mylam, gardener to S. Rucker, Esq., Wandsworth. Though only a month has elapsed since we had the pleasure to notice Mr. M.'s collection of 20, yet on this occasion, from the rich stores at his command, he produced nearly 20 fresh plants, and all in perfection. We can only notice a few of the best.

Dendrobium formosum, a lovely plant with 19 flowers. *Odontoglossum Karwinskii;* a rare orchid with long spikes of rich dark-coloured flowers. *Odontoglossum citrosmum;* this is a beautiful species with a lemon scent; 5 spikes numerously flowered, three of them were branched. *Barkeria spectabilis,* a splendid specimen with eight spikes of its lovely blossoms; several of the spikes had 12 flowers on each. *Cattleya violacea;* had six spikes of its beautifully coloured blossoms. *C. candida;* 6 spikes, many flowers on each. *C. intermedia;* 10 spikes, with many flowers on each. *Angræcum caudatum;* two long spikes, one had eight flowers fully expanded. *Vanda cristata;* a fine plant, with 20 flowers.

2nd Prize to Mr. Blake, gardener to J. Schroder, Esq., Stratford Green. This gentleman's orchids are evidently improving fast. The collection exhibited this day was excellent, the plants well grown, and in splendid bloom.

Saccolabium guttatum; a large healthy plant, with eight freshly-bloomed spikes of flowers. *Aerides Schroderii;* a new variety with a beautiful deep rose lip, rather reflexed; numerous flowers. *A. Larpentæ;* another new variety, with the lip considerably elongated. *A. odorata;* a large plant, with eight spikes. *Phalænopsis grandiflora;* 15 flowers beautifully expanded, one spike not open. *Calanthe veratrifolia,* with 12 spikes of its snow white blossoms. *Aerides affine;* three neat spikes of its lovely rose-coloured flowers. *A. maculosum;* very rare.

3rd Prize to Mr. Williams, gardener to C. Warner, Esq., Hoddesdon. This was a very unusual position for this excellent cultivator to be placed in, but his plants were not so good as usual, owing, as we were informed, to several of his best not being quite in bloom; still, the following were excellent:—

Odontoglossum citrosmum; two spikes. *Brassia verrucosa* (the best of the genus); nine very fine spikes. *Epidendrum aurantiacum;* five spikes of its orange-coloured blossoms. *Cælogyne Lowii;* one spike with 13 flowers. *Dendrobium Devonianum;* two spikes well flowered. *Aerides crispum;* four spikes.

COLLECTIONS OF FIFTEEN EXOTIC ORCHIDS—NURSERYMEN.

1st Prize to Messrs. Veitch and Son, Exeter. It is really a circumstance to be surprised at, that these gentlemen can manage to send such delicate plants so great a distance in such fine order. The delicate, satin-like blossoms of the *Sobralia macrantha* were as fresh and uninjured as if they had travelled only as many miles as they had hundreds. We particularly noted as fine

Saccolabium præmorsum, with seven very fine long spikes. *Sobralia macrantha;* 14 magnificent flowers, measuring 5 in. in length and 4 in. across. *Dendrobium Devonianum;* a large mass with numerous flowers. *Oncidium ampliatum major;* very strong, four large spikes. *O. sphace-*

latum; seven fine spikes. *Lacæna bicolor;* three long spikes. *Aerides affine,* with a long spike, 15 in. *A. crispum;* a large plant with four spikes. *Dendrobium transparens;* a dwarf species, numerously flowered. But the gem of this collection was the rare, beautiful, and seldom flowered *Cattleya aclandia.*

2nd Prize to Messrs. Rollison, Tooting. A fine, well-grown, and beautifully flowered collection, especially the following :—

Huntleya violacea; 8 flowers, a large good plant. *Cymbidium pendulum;* a desirable species, with three long spikes. *Dendrobium moschatum;* nine spikes. *D. formosum;* a variety with longer pseudo-bulbs and longer, more obtuse lip. *Oncidium lucidum guttatum;* one spike 7 ft. long, with numerous branches; another 4 ft. long, also much branched; this is a desirable variety. *Stanhopea tigrina,* with several of its strangely formed flowers. *Aerides affine;* four good spikes. *Dendrobium Devonianum;* five spikes. *Aerides odoratum;* 19 spikes; a fine plant.

3rd Prize to Mr. Dobson, gardener to E. Beck, Esq., Nurseryman, Isleworth : a collection of great merit.

Aerides crispum; a noble plant; one spike had six branches upon it each branch as long, and with as many flowers upon it, as are usually seen on a single unbranched spike : there were five other spikes upon it. *Epidendrum Phæniceum;* a rare and beautiful species; one spike of its beautiful, richly-coloured blossoms. *E. vitellinum;* another beautiful, rare species, with two spikes of its orange-scarlet blossoms. *Oncidium stramineum;* two spikes; very neat and pretty. *O. roseum;* a neat plant, with long spikes of pretty rose and crimson flowers.

COLLECTIONS OF TEN EXOTIC ORCHIDS.

1st Prize to Mr. Carson, gardener to I. W. Farmer, Esq., Nonsuch Park, Surrey. The best plant in this well grown collection was

Aerides odoratum; very large, in perfect health, and finely flowered, having upon it 25 spikes of its fragrant beautifully tinted blooms. *Acanthophippium bicolor;* a large mass, with numerous flowers. *Cypripedium barbatum;* five flowers.

2nd Prize to Mr. Franklin, gardener to Mrs. Lawrence, Ealing Park. This collection contained that rare and delicately beautiful plant, the

Oncidium pulchellum; sepals pale flesh, petals rosy pink, lip large, and spread out; flesh colour at the base, with a large brownish yellow spot on the upper part; many flowered.

We noticed the following also :—

Trichopilia tortilis; a large mass, with numerous flowers. A *Stanhopea* named *oculata,* with two large black blotches on the column (we doubt this being *S. oculata*). *Phalænopsis grandiflora;* three spikes, with numerous flowers.

SINGLE SPECIMENS OF ORCHIDS OF SUPERIOR CULTURE.

1st Prize to Mr. Bassett, gardener to R. S. Holford, Esq., Weston Birt. It is impossible to convey to our readers an idea of the extreme beauty of his plant of *Camarotis purpurea.* It was 4 ft. high, and 2½ ft. through, covered with its truly elegant spikes of purple flowers. There were more than 200 spikes in beautiful perfection upon it.

2nd Prize to Mr. Cole, gardener to H. Collyer, Esq., of Dartford, for

Dendrobium speciosum; a noble plant, with 17 long spikes of pale yellow flowers.

(To be continued.)

NEW, RARE, AND CHOICE STOVE PLANTS.

Messrs. Henderson, Pine Apple Place, London, have sent us the following list and prices :—

	s.	D.
Achimenes Ghaisbreghtii. A charming species, with orange scarlet flowers, having a whitish throat.....	3	6
Achimenes fimbriata. A fine large bold Gloxinia-like flower, white, deeply spotted, with yellow throat ; very distinct...	3	6
Achimenes Jayii. A pretty variety, very dwarf, abundant bloomer, colour rich violet purple...	3	6
Achimenes Jaurequi. Habit of A. longiflora, fine white flowers, with carmine eye, and a stripe of the same colour extending half-way down each petal; very distinct...		
Achimenes Mountfordii—has bright scarlet flowers like the old A. coccinea, but much superior	3	6
Adenocalymna comosa. A fine climbing plant.....	5	0
Æchmea fulgens. Crimson and blue flowers, succeeded by handsome fruit or seed-vessels, of a fine scarlet : lasts a long time in beauty.	10	6

Æchmea fulgens discolor. Exactly like the preceding, except that the under side of the leaves is of a fine glossy purple. 10 6

Æschynanthus speciosus. A stout upright growing species, bearing on the end of each shoot a head of 6 or 7 orange scarlet flowers, large and handsome, lasting a long time in perfection. A most beautiful plant that should be in every collection. 3 6

Æschynanthus longiflorus. A beautiful plant of more slender habit than the preceding, and darker coloured flowers.............................. 3 6

Æschynanthus radicans. Desirable on account of its small neat foliage, and deep red flowers: very suitable for suspending from the roof, tied up to a ball of moss or in a fancy basket................. 3 6

Æschynanthus miniatus. Handsome deep crimson flowers, produced most abundantly.............. 3 6

Agalmyla staminea. An extra fine plant, with large fine foliage, and bunches of splendid scarlet tubular flowers. Like a Gesneria, suitable for growing on branches of wood, in a basket, or in pots. Will do well in the Orchid House, or in a moist stove..... 10 6

Allamanda Schottii. A half climber of robust habit, flowers large, of a deep yellow striped with rich brown streaks in the throat..................... 5 0

Allamanda Parsensis. Like A. cathartica, but has much larger flowers. 7 6

Allamanda grandiflora. Buff yellow, suitable, for pot culture, small foliage, and neat habit............. 5 0

Anguria Warsewiczii. Handsome foliage, with large corymbs of orange vermillion flowers blooming very freely ....

Aphelandra aurantiaca. Flowers in winter and early in the spring. It has dense spikes of bright scarlet orange flowers, which remain a long season in beauty............................... 3 6

Balsamia latifolia. Vivid green foliage, with bright pink flowers produced very profusely. Blooms nine months in the year........................ 2 6

Batatus Waldeckii. A climbing plant of great beauty, having rich green foliage and white flowers with purple centre, flowering all the summer........... 5 0

Begonia albo-coccinea. Large almost round foliage, red underneath, scarlet and white flowers: a very elegant desirable plant. 3 6

Begonia cinnabarina. A new Bolivean species, remarkable for its large bright scarlet orange flowers. The flower stems are of a rich crimson colour; handsome foliage tinged with red at the edge: the finest of all Begonias........................... 10 6

Begonia luxurians. Very handsome and graceful, palm-leaved foliage, with large corymbs of bluish white flowers: the stems both of the plant and leaves are of a beautiful purplish crimson. A very distinct variety or species..................... 7 6

Begonia fuchsioides. A free flowering elegant species, with flowers like a fuchsia...................... 3 6

Chirita Moonii. Flowers large, bluish lilac, with a stripe of yellow down the centre, leaves sea-green.. 5 0

Campylobotris discolor. A handsome plant of dwarf habit, with green and purple velvety foliage; petioles and stems of a carmine colour, flowers rich scarlet.

Centradenia floribunda. Very handsome and dwarf habit, with dark red coloured wood, producing large corymbs of bluish and pink flowers.............. 5 0

Cinnamomum aromaticum. The true cinnamon. The leaves if eaten possess the flavour.......... 10 6

Clerodendrum Bethuneana. Flowers rich scarlet with white spot, large branching panicles; a noble species quite new............................... 15 0

Clerodendrum Kæmpferii. Scarlet flowers and large leaves, a showy species. 5 0

Clerodendrum macrophyllum. White flowers on a large upright panicle; foliage bright glossy green, very large. Handsome and distinct............. 7 6

Combretum latifolium. Fine foliage, with dense racemes of scarlet flowers...................... 5 0

Croton variegatum longifolium. Leaves long, drooping, and richly variegated, very ornamental. 5 0

Cyrtoceras reflexus. A plant very nearly related to Hoya. Flowers waxy white and greenish yellow; a free flowering useful plant..................... 3 6

Cyrtolepis longifolius. Neat lively green foliage, with large corymbs of pure white flowers............. 5 0

Cyrtanthera aurantiaca. Fine green foliage, with bunches of rich orange flowers 7 6

Dipladenia crassinoda. A beautiful climber; flowers large bright rose with golden eye, foliage rich green; should be in every collection.............. 5 0

Echites atro-purpurea. A neat climber, with deep chocolate flowers; very desirable................ 5 0

Echites nobilis. A half climber, with rich rosy pink flowers, which are produced in succession for a long season............................... 7 6

Echites splendens. A beautiful climber, with beautiful large delicate rosy flowers. Will answer well either to plant out or grow in pots................... 3 6

Eranthemum albiflorum. A half shrubby plant, bearing panicles of snow white flowers............ 3 6

Francisca confertifolia. New; large flowers and very fragrant. 7 6

Franciscea Augusta. Bluish lilac flowers, produced in large trusses: free flowerer............... 3 6

Franciscea latiflora. Flowers lilac purple changing to white, very large and fragrant................. 3 6

Gardenia Stanleyana. Flowers trumpet-shaped, 5 to 6 inches long, creamy white, spotted with chocolate: a free flowering and noble species.............. 3 6

Gardenia Devoniana. Very fine, somewhat like the above, but of a dwarfer habit, with a large trumpet-shaped flower, white and fragrant.............. 5 0

Gardenia Fortuniana. Like G. Florida pleno, but with flowers much larger, more double, and deliciously fragrant........................ 3 6

Gesneria Merkii. Flowers rich scarlet crimson, produced freely even on young plants: a very excellent species................................. 3 6

Gesneria macrantha purpurea. A dwarf habit, free flowering, of the richest scarlet with a tinge of purple on the lip........................... 5 0

Gesneria picta. New; a beautiful plant; orange scarlet flowers produced in winter and spring..... 3 6

Gloxinia carminata splendens. The best of all the dark red varieties. 3 6

Gloxinia grandis. Beautiful and distinct colour, delicate creamy white, with a very dark rich crimson throat, large size, and the finest form of all Gloxinias 5 0

Gloxinia Fyfiana. Flowers perfect bells, standing upright instead of hanging down, white tinged with blue and thickly spotted in the throat. Singular and distinct............................ 3 6

Gloxinia labiata. Something like G. grandis, but rather darker and not so large: a nice variety..... 3 6

Gloxinia Professor-Decaisne. Pale red, and pure white throat............................ 5 0

Gloxinia Touchlerii. A peculiar variegated and striped flower, scarlet and lilac intermingled............. 3 6

Gloxinia Wortleyana. Flowers light blue, with white throat delicately spotted with light purple; an elegant variety........................... 3 6

Gloxinia Passinghamii. Flower large, of the deepest purple and violet, the best of all the dark varieties. 3 6

Guzmannia tricolor. Like a smooth-leaved variety of the pine-apple tribe, with a beautiful spike of three-coloured flowers, quite a gem in its way.......... 10 6

Hindsia longiflora alba. A handsome variety, bearing clusters or corymbs of pure white flowers, like a Jasmine. Fragrant..................... 5 0

Hindsia violacea. Large pale violet blue flowers, rich green foliage. 5 0

Hoya Bella. This has been well described as " an Amethyst set in frosted silver;" a more lovely plant cannot be conceived. It is also delightfully fragrant. 7 6

Hoya imperialis. One of the most superb stove climbers we have, with fine handsome foliage and large chocolate and white flowers.............. 7 6

Henfreya scandens. A climber with rich dark green

foliage and spikes of white flowers, blooming early in the spring. ... **s. d.** 3 6

Ixora coccinea superba. A fine variety, with fine orange scarlet blossoms, superior to the old fine species. ... 7 6

Ixora Griffithii. Leaves large flowers borne in a compact cyme, rich yellow and orange; a noble species. ... 5 0

Ixora salicifolia. Elegant long foliage, with cymes of orange flowers. ...

Ixora Javanica. Another handsome addition to this fine genus, with noble foliage and handsome pinkish orange flowers. ... 5 0

Jasminum toscanum. A very double white Jasmine, tinged with pink: it has a delicate perfume equal to the orange. ... 7 6

Luculia gratissima. Rosy pink flowers in heads like the Hydrangea; very fragrant. ... 5 0

Luculia Pinceana. Pure white blooms of the most delicate perfume, changing to cream colour tinted with red. ... 5 0

Liebigia speciosa. Herbaceous and low-growing flowers, drooping; colour white blue and yellow.. 3 6

Lycopodium cæsium arborea. A beautiful new plant introduced from Calcutta by H. B. Kerr, Esq., in 1849.—Obtained a prize at the Chiswick Show. This is truly a tree Lycopod; the leaves are much brighter coloured than L. cæsium, and it will grow to 10 or 12 feet high: very ornamental. ... 10 6

Medinella Sieboldiana. A very handsome plant of dwarf habit, much neater in growth than M. speciosa, with large heads of white and rose-coloured flowers.

Medinella speciosa. A beautiful plant with large handsome foliage and fine spikes of pink flowers, succeeded by equally handsome bunches of purplish berries, which are very ornamental for a long time. 7 6

Moussonia elegans. A fine Gesnera-like plant, with orange and scarlet flowers in bunches blooming in winter. ...

Napoleona imperialis. Flower resembling a passion flower, of a nankeen colour changing to blue; an evergreen attaining the size of a little tree. ... 5 0

Nematanthus Morrelliana. The handsomest of the tribe, and a profuse bloomer; colour rich crimson with spotted throat. ... 5 0

Pavetta Borbonica. Leaves dark green, beautifully mottled with white: a very handsome plant. ... 15 0

Pharbitis ostrina. An elegant twining plant with purple flowers, suitable for pot culture. ... 5 0

Physianthus auricomus. A climber with racemes of creamy white flowers, profusely produced and powerfully perfumed. ... 5 0

Portlandia grandiflora. A fine evergreen shrub, with large pure white Brugmansia-like flowers, which contrast well with the stout large rich green leaves. It is a very free bloomer and deliciously fragrant.. 21 0

Puya Altensteinii. Flowers ivory-white, which issue out of beautiful crimson sheath-like bracts. ... 5 0

Quassia amara. Graceful foliage, with a branching spike of red flowers ... 10 6

Rondeletia speciosa (var. major). A great improvement on the species, having larger flowers of richer hue ... 5 0

Roupellia grata (syn. Strophanthus Stanleyana). Cream-coloured fruit, fine foliage, with very beautiful flowers ... 10 6

Salpixantha coccinea. This plant has a beautiful habit, fine glossy bright green leaves; the flowers resemble an Epacris, being of a deep bright crimson ... 7 6

Siphocampylos manettifolia. Compact close growing plant, with scarlet tube-shaped flowers, tipped with orange ... 3 6

Siphocampylos microstoma rubra. Crimson flowers and handsome foliage ... 3 6

Siphocampylos glandulosus. Fine foliage, with flowers of a peculiar light purple beautiful colour ... 3 6

Solandra lævis. Very large trumpet-shaped flowers, of a creamy white; a noble plant ... 7 6

Stachytarpheta aristata. Long spikes of rich blackish purple flowers, exceedingly beautiful ... **s. d.** 5 0

Stiftia chrysantha. A beautiful shrub; the flowers are of a rich feathery orange; very showy ... 10 6

Thyrsacanthus strictum. Rich foliage, with spikes of scarlet flowers. ... 5 0

Tillandsia Zebrina (syn. Vriezia splendens). The leaves are elegantly marked in bands of chocolate colour; the flowers white, springing out of scarlet bracts

Tillandsia Morrelliana. Handsome graceful foliage, the underneath side striped with powdery white, with a spike of flowers out of scarlet bracts of a deep azure blue. Decidedly the handsomest of the tribe ...

WILD FLOWERS OF JUNE.

(Continued from page 106.)

By the month of June the northern mountains of our land are one universal glow of purple, with the bright blossoms of the common Heather (*Calluna vulgaris*), which although better known for its celebrity in the realms of poesy, than for its use in supplying the more essential bodily wants of mankind, is by no means useless in this respect: it forms the thatch of many a mountain cottage, and the woody roots are extensively used for fuel in mountanous districts. The botanist who has explored our native alpine Flora well knows that,

> "Of this old Scotia's hardy mountaineers
> Their rustic couches form, and there enjoy
> Sleep, which beneath his velvet canopy
> Luxurious idleness implores in vain."

And there is another use still to which this noble plant of the mountain is put to in Scotland, and a use, too, which does not show in a very favourable light the regard with which the natives view the pride of their land, and its glorious scenery: we refer to the use to which the heather is applied in the making of rough brooms for cleaning back courts and the clay floors of lowly homes; and, indeed, many a time have we admired the beauty of *heather-besoms* in *full bloom* hawked from door to door through the streets of Edinburgh, and other Scotch towns, at a penny a piece.

On the lower hills, and in situations less lofty in elevation than those which the heather prefers for its home, there is a shrubby plant higher in stature, and scarcely less lovely in appearance when clothed with its gorgeous array of golden flowers—we refer to the common Broom, the *Cytisus scoparius* of De Candolle, "the lang yellow broom" of the Scottish bard, which is likewise applied to such practical purposes of housewifery, as the sweeping of the kitchen floor, and the court yard. Nor is this its only use in rural districts; the very powerfully purgative qualities of the young shoots recommend them to attention in rustic practice as a remedy in cases of dropsy, and the medical profession recognise the plant for its properties.

The cultivated fields will now be adorned with many of those annual plants denominated by the farmer the vile pests of the farm, but looked upon with a more tender eye by the admiring naturalist, whose enthusiastic admiration is not checked by one thought of light crops, low markets, nor the baneful influences of "free trade." Among these field-flowers, first of all in our list comes the *Camelina sativa*, or Common Gold of Pleasure, anent which we may make no farther remark, as "The ridiculously pompous English name seems a satire on the articles of which it is composed, as yielding nothing but disappointment." Towards the middle or latter end of the month, the Corn Blue-bottle (*Centaurea cyanus*) begins to show its cœrulean flowers.

> " The blue CYANUS we'll not forget,
> 'Tis the gem of the harvest coronet."

And already have the fields assumed a premature yellow hue, by the flowers of the Wild Radish (*Raphanus raphanistrum*) and the Wild Mustard (*Sinapis arvensis*)—one of the most troublesome of field weeds.

> " O'er the young corn the CHARLOCK throws a shade,
> And clasping tares cling round the sickly blade."

The *Agrostemma githago*, or Corn Cockle, is likewise a very elegant field flower, and although not now so plentiful in our fields as it has been in times gone by, yet it may still be found in tolerable abundance in some districts, although it is certainly a weed of the most intolerable kind, notwithstanding the beautiful flowers which it raises among the rising ears of corn. Its numerous black seeds prove highly detrimental to the grain, from which it is difficult to free them when the plant grows among the crops. It is said that the name, *githago*, is derived from the Celtic *git*, or *gith*, the name of a peculiarly large and black seed. The white Campion, too, the *Lychnis vespertina* of the scientific world, is a gay flower in the summer fields; and although a rare plant in some parts of the country, is of abundant occurrence in others, and ranks as a farm pest. Its gay white flowers are not, however, confined to the fields, and in our evening walks along the lanes and hedgerows we are frequently greeted by its odour-breathing flowers—for it is only to the moist evening air that this plant gives out its fragrance. On dry sunny hedge-banks and in hay-fields it often occurs in the greatest profusion; but is, in every respect, an evening flower; for besides giving out its odour to the evening air, the pure white flowers become very conspicuous in the dim twilight, when other flowers have either closed their petals with the close of day, or are obscured from view in the absence of the bright sunshine, to which they owe much of their beauty. The Red Campion (*Lychnis dioica*) is considered by some botanists to be only a variety of the white flowered plant, but chooses different situations for its growth than those preferred by the latter, being chiefly confined to the woods. But what of the remainder of the field pests? There is the numerous family of Crowfoots (*Ranunculus*) bursting into bloom and beauty, and some of which we referred to in our papers on the wild flowers of May. Among the field species now in flower, may be mentioned the Upright Meadow Crowfoot (*R. acris*), which abounds in pastures and by the margins of fields; the Creeping Crowfoot (*R. repens*), readily known from its creeping shoots, and which is likewise profusely scattered through the pastures and by the waysides; the bulbous Crowfoot (*R. bulbosus*), often a frequenter of dry pastures and rocky places; and the Corn Crowfoot (*R. arvensis*), the most deadly cattle-poison in the family. In shady places, and especially in woods, the common Columbine (*Aquilegia vulgaris*) will be found in the character of a wild flower; although its right to rank as such is exceedingly problematical, seeing that it only occurs in situations where it is likely to have escaped from gardens, or been planted. Nor have we aught to say in favour of *Aquilegia's* exotic relatives—the Field Larkspur (*Delphinium consolida*), or the poisonous Wolf's Bane, or Monk's Hood

(*Aconitum napellus*), both of which are now to be gathered in blossom, although not indigenous to our country. In waste places, and in dry corn-fields, embankments, &c., the long prickly-headed Poppy (*Papaver argemone*) and the common Red Poppy (*P. rhœas*) will be found scattering their evanescent petals upon the breeze; and the Welsh Poppy (*Meconopsis Cambrica*) will be observed more rarely in shady woods and by cascades, in various parts of England, Wales, and Scotland, although in the northern kingdom it only occurs as a naturalized plant. But we must draw our notes on the wild flowers of the month to a close, although conscious that we have not enumerated half of the myriad gems that have opened their bright corollas to the sun-beams of joyous summer-time—

> " For who would sing the flowers of June,
> Though from grey morn to blazing noon,
> From blazing noon to dewy eve,
> The chaplet of his song he weave,
> Would find his summer daylight fail,
> And leave half-told the pleasing tale."

> G. LAWSON, F.R.P.S., &c.

DOMESTIC MECHANISM.

WATER FILTER.—Procure a box made of zinc or wood, with water-tight joints, provided with supports or legs, and a pipe and crane at its lower extremity. Suspend in the inside of this a large flower-pot, or zinc receptacle; if the latter, the bottom should be punctured with small holes. The bottom of the inside receptacle should not be nearer the bottom of the outer box than two inches. In the inside of the flower-pot, or inner receptacle, place pieces of broken flint, clean tiles, or pebbles; above this, spread a layer of coarse clean sand; then, above this, pieces of coarsely pounded charcoal, and finish with a layer of finely pulverised *peat* charcoal, or other charcoal will do as well. The water to be filtered passes through the successive layers of filtering material to the box below, and rising up therein, can be drawn off at pleasure; by regulating the flow of water into the inner receptacle by a crane on the pipe supplying it, any required degree of quickness may be obtained. The cut will sufficiently explain the construction.

KITCHEN SUMMER GRATE OR FIRE-BOX.—The following contrivance has been adopted with considerable success, both as regards the economization of fuel and the facility with which a fire is kindled in it. Make a circular case of plate iron, 9 or 12 inches in diameter, and 9 or 10 inches high—a larger according to fancy; provide at the distance of one inch from the bottom, a grating—made cheapest out of a perforated circular plate of iron—and above this cut out spaces, so as to form a species of open bar-work. At the top, but in the side opposite to this bar space, cut a square flue, or chimney aperture, as shown by the black space in the cut—to this a short length of pipe may be attached, say of 12 or 18 inches in length. A lid should be provided to cover the top, but so made as not to obstruct the aperture to the flue. A boiling pan or kettle may be made to rest on the top, which will soon be boiled by the heat beneath. This box being placed on the empty grate, or on the hob, or oven top, a little bit of stick will soon kindle the contained coals, and if the lid is put on the draught will be materially increased. We have used one which cost one shilling, which burnt most capitally—boiling water, roasting potatoes, &c., and, what was of considerable advantage, using up the veriest refuse of the coal-cellar.—B.

TO CORRESPONDENTS.

*** We request that no one will write to the departmental writers of THE COTTAGE GARDENER. It gives them unjustifiable trouble and expense; and we also request our coadjutors *under no circumstances* to reply to such private communications.

DRAGON ARUM (*M. E. von D.*).—By this we presume you mean *Arum dracunculus*. It is a native of the south of Europe, and is quite hardy, at least it blooms freely in a light soiled open border at Winchester without any winter protection. It would do the same, we think, near London; but certainly if planted out beneath a south wall. Moving them in the spring has made your plants of it look sickly, for the bulbs produce roots very early, and these were injured by being taken up. Turn your plants out of the pots into a warm border at once, without disturbing them, and place a label by their side, so as to know where they are, for they die down early, and may get injured by the spade, or trowel, in putting in other plants.

BLIGHT ON GREENHOUSE PLANTS (*Ignoramus*). — Your plants "covered with blight, and some appearing a mass of insects," have been grossly neglected. Watering and steaming now is of no use, but tends to aggravate the evil; for the increase of insects, like that of other animals, is promoted by the abundance of their food, and the more plants are watered and steamed, the greater the amount of sap which they contain, which is the food of the blight or aphis. Fumigate your plants for two or three successive evenings with tobacco smoke, syringing them each following morning. If the blight arises from the aphis, this will remove the enemy. Let us know the result. If the treatment does not succeed, the insect must be the thrip.

ROUP IN FOWLS (*A Poultry Keeper*).—This we have always considered very nearly resembling glanders in the horse, and if it is allowed to reach that stage when there is an offensive discharge from the nostrils and eyes, the bird usually dies. We should like to know the effect of minute doses of sulphate of copper given in this disease. At present, immediately symptoms of the disease appear, separate the bird from the other fowls, keep it warm, very clean, and give it tepid water to drink. Mix together two parts of powdered gentian, and one part hydriodate of potash; make it into a mass with a little lard, and give a pill as large as a pea every night and morning. If you try sulphate of copper, mix a quarter of a grain in a little gruel, and pour it down the bird's throat every morning.

FLOWER-GARDEN (*An Amateur*).—We have to apologise for the delay (A. B.), but we have hesitated some time as to engraving the plan. Your new garden is extremely pretty and exceedingly well planned, and your arrangement is very nearly to our mind. We would place the Ageratum in the opposite corner bed, No. 8, to the Heliotrope bed, No. 1, and place the Cuphea in bed No. 9; as the Lobelia is too dwarf between the two verbena beds. We would plant any other diamond bed under the half standard Roses, with the blue Lobelia and the Ivy-leaf Geranium, either pink or white, in the other diamonds, and train some of the shoots up the stems. The diamonds are large enough for the roses, and next year you can raise the turf all round them, and place more good soil for the roses, without enlarging the sizes of the beds. We can hardly believe that you have learned so much from our labours. You have not too many roses. As your span roof is to be east and west, we would use the rough plate glass only on the south side, and British sheet glass on the north side; the latter will give more light, and you will have no shading required. You have proved that the rough plate is most excellent for propagating pits.

GOOSEBERRY BORERS (*J. Turner*).—The berry borers sent were crushed from the corks being loose. Two appear to be the larvæ of the winter moth (see THE COTTAGE GARDENER, vol. I., page 53), and the other is the larva of some tortrix, which it is impossible to determine until the moth appears. Can you oblige us with more specimens in a stronger box?

BEES HIVED INTO A BELL-HIVE (*A Constant Subscriber*).—At the end of three weeks after the hiving of your bees, you may cut a hole at the top of the hive and put on a box, or glass, or small hive (see THE COTTAGE GARDENER, vol. II., page 104). You must not separate your two hives placed one on the other at this season. The best time for doing it will be in February, on a fine day; the bees will then be all in the upper hive. As they are at present, you will, in all probability, have neither swarm nor honey from them.

PREVENTING BEES SWARMING (*Z.*). — You ought to have placed another small hive between the one now on, and the parent hive, as soon as you had discovered any appearance of want of room, as directed for swarms, page 104, vol. II., of THE COTTAGE GARDENER; and sometimes, for a short time, even a third small hive must be supplied in a similar manner before the upper one is sufficiently filled to be taken off. Continue to kill queen wasps as long as you can see them, for their nests are not yet formed, or, if formed, not sufficiently forward to survive the loss of the queen. With Underwood's Wasp Catcher, you would be able to capture those about your hives (see advertisement on cover of THE COTTAGE GARDENER). The "Manual for Cottagers," published by Mr. Payne, was expressly done so for gratuitous distribution; and every copy has long since been given away. For "the manner of preparing honey and wax," see THE COTTAGE GARDENER, vol. II., page 285; but it must be remembered that only honey in the combs is admissible at table; and, besides, when drained it fetches only half the price. For instruc-tion in bee management, let the cottagers read the pages of THE COTTAGE GARDENER, kindly lent them by those who wish to increase their comforts and their love of home. Honey in the combs, in small hives of from 8 to 12 lbs., has always a ready sale and at a good price, either in London or in almost any large town. We know several kindly disposed and influential persons in different villages in the kingdom, who will take the small hives of honey of the cottagers and send the whole produce of their village in one package to some respectable honey warehouse in London,—either Neighbour and Son, Fortnum and Mason, Milton, or some such house; and, by so doing, obtain for them the best price. Your small hive, put on on the 16th of May, should have had another placed beneath it and the stock about the 1st of June; and then, as soon as perfectly sealed up, taken away. The straw hives and cover, figured in "Taylor's Bee-Keeper's Manual," pages 35 and 37, were sent him by Mr. Payne; and we doubt not but, if applied to, Mr. Payne would have some made for you. The zinc covers are manufactured by Messrs. Deane and Dray, 11½, Bunhill-row, St. Luke's, London. Hives do equally well without a shed; if you prefer a shed yours is certainly one of the best kind.

SOOT-WATER (*H. M.*).—One gallon of soot to ten gallons of water, prepared as recommended by Mr. Savage in our seventieth number, may be, as you say, "the colour of dark sherry," without being too strong. The ammoniacal salts extracted from the soot by the water are the chief cause of benefit.

NIPPING-OFF THE TOPS OF POTATO-STEMS (*W. E. J.*).—This we know to be a bad practice if done during an early stage of their growth, for it only induces the stems either to produce side-shoots, or the set to emit more stems; either of which fresh productions are hindrances to the early production and large size of the tubers. Nipping-off the flowers we consider a good practice.

GOOSEBERRY CATERPILLARS (*T. M. W.* and *T. O. U.*).—Every kind of these we find are destroyed by dusting over them and the bushes generally with white hellebore powder. We apply it by the aid of a common cook's dredging box. You may get this powder of any chemist; and for such a purpose he ought to let you have a pound for a shilling. Your other questions shall be answered next week.

SNAILS (*T. O. U.*).—You may keep these from creeping over the wall from your neighbour's ivy, by having a hair rope stretched along the wall on your own side. It makes a *chevaux de frize* which they cannot surmount. A less permanent barrier would be salt strewed in a continuous line along the top of the wall.

NAMES OF PLANTS (*H. H.*).—Your plant was so damaged that though we have shown it to several botanists we could not, any of us, recognise it. Send us another specimen in flower, and protected by a box. (*B. V.*).—The leaf you sent us, given to you as "Mexican Kex," is, we think, that of *Heracleum giganteum*. (*Fanny H.*)—Your plant is *Abutilon striatum*.

COBŒA SCANDENS (*A. Subscriber*).—This, as well as *Maurandya Barcleyana*, do best when planted out in the border beneath a warm wall.

LANTANA CROCEA (*Ibid*).—This is propagated by cuttings planted in sand under a bell-glass, and plunged in bottom-heat. Propagate it in March for summer, and in August for winter.

STANDARD ROSE (*Ibid*).—This "planted last November throws up strong suckers from the roots, but the bush scarcely grows." Remove the suckers immediately they appear, and water with liquid-manure.

MIGNONETTE AND TEN-WEEK STOCKS (*Ibid*).—For blooming in winter sow these during July, and transplant the seedlings into small pots.

POTATOES PRODUCING TUBERS BUT NOT STEMS (*Ibid*).—When the eyes, or buds of the set which produce the stems, are from accident, or other cause, prevented developing themselves into stems, a wise provision of the Creator for the preservation of the species enables the parent set to give birth to numerous young tubers.

VERBENA VENOSA (*C. G.*).—To bloom this at the same time as the old Scarlet Variegated Geranium in May, you must bed out strong plants of the Verbena in March. Apply to Messrs. Henderson, Pine Apple Place.

BEGONIA (*An Amateur*).—Will see that his inquiry has been attended to.

HEATHS (*Margaret*).—The Heaths done flowering should be cut down freely if strong growing. If of a less strong habit let the pruning be done more sparingly. Do not repot until fresh growth has commenced. See an article on the *Epacris* lately published by us. Something else will probably appear upon the Heath before long.

CRASSULA (*Erina*).—We are sorry we cannot detect the cause of the spot on the leaf, unless it was burned by a lens formed in the glass; and it does not present that appearance. You did not use the soft soap lather too hot, for if you did, the edges of the leaf might afterwards present the scalded-like appearance. Unless the plant is a large one, and a great favourite, you had better discard it; as the restoring it to a state of health would cost more trouble and expense than rearing a young healthy one.

LONDON: Printed by HARRY WOOLDRIDGE, Winchester High-street, in the Parish of Saint Mary Kalendar; and Published by WILLIAM SOMERVILLE ORR, at the Office, No. 2, Amen Corner, in the Parish of Christ Church, City of London.—June 20th, 1850.

WEEKLY CALENDAR.

M D	W D	JUNE 27—JULY 3, 1850.	Weather near London in 1849.		Sun Rises.	Sun Sets.	Moon R. & S.	Moon's Age.	Clock bef. Sun.	Day of Year.
27	Th	Cuckoo last heard. [seen.	T. 78°—47°.	S.W. Fine.	46 a. 3	19 a. 6	16 a. 8	17	2 35	178
28	F	Q. Victoria coronation, 1838. Wasp Beetle	T. 76°—48°.	N.W. Fine.	47	19	10 37	18	2 47	179
29	S	St. Peter. Water Chickweed flowers.	T. 73°—48°.	S. Rain.	47	19	11 3	19	2 9	180
30	Sun	5 Sun. aft. Trinity. Great Horse-fly seen.	T. 63°—51°.	N.E. Fine.	48	18	11 26	20	3 11	181
1	M	Orange Lily flowers.	T. 79°—57°.	S.W. Fine.	48	18	11 48	21	3 23	182
2	Tu	Visit. B.V.M. Oxf. Act. Cam. Com. Rooks roost	T. 72°—55°.	W. Fine.	49	18	morn.	☾	3 35	183
3	W	Dog Days begin. [on their nest.	T. 73°—58°.	W. Rain.	50	17	0 10	23	3 46	184

It is not alone by being guides upon the road which leads to eternal life that the clergy of our land are aiders of our happiness. If this were a fitting place, we could tell from an experience of twenty years of village life in how many minor, yet important, circumstances, the ministers of the gospel, with their families, dotted about the British islands, are so many centres from which are diffused, from day to day and from year to year, the growing information and amenities of society. Nor is this an advantage, or blessing, emanating from them only in modern times: whenever and wherever there has been a fixed source of religious instruction, it has invariably been also the source of general improvement in the arts of life. It has been usual to look upon the monasteries of the Middle Ages as institutions of unmixed evil; but even they were not so; and however debased was their Christianity, yet they were the nurseries of the arts and sciences, and storehouses of the knowledge and improvements of the past, held sacred when all else was subjected to dispersion and destruction. Among the arts thus cherished and improved, gardening has ever been one; and we could tell of many monks who were as skilled in vine culture as they were fond of drinking deep of the juice of its berries. Records of their vineyards, orchards, and flower-gardens still remain; but we will tell of another ecclesiastic who emulated their vices without any fellowship in their vices.

Henry Compton, Bishop of London, is one of those characters on which no one can dwell without gratification; for in no period of life not only did he never fail in the performance of his duty, but never did he cease from striving to effect every possible good within his power. He was born in 1632, the youngest son of the second Earl of Northampton, and inherited the courageous spirit of his father, who died in the battle of Edge Hill whilst fighting for Charles I. He was but ten years old when the battle of Edge Hill was fought, and was, for the sake of security, in the royal camp during that blood-stained day. After the Restoration, he accepted a cornetcy in a regiment of horse, but soon gave up the profession of arms and was ordained a minister of the church. Here he rapidly obtained preferment, and, finally, in 1676, became Bishop of London. He was emphatically known as "The Protestant Bishop," during that era of the struggle for ascendancy between the members of the Reformed and of the Romish church. We have no space sufficient for tracing even an outline of the efforts and labours which earned justly the popular title bestowed upon him, for we must particularise his acts for the advancement of the art which especially entitle him to notice in our pages. So ungrudging of expense was he for the encouragement of horticulture, that he enriched the gardens and greenhouses of his palace at Fulham to an extent which rendered them remarkable not only for excellence of cultivation, but for containing a greater variety of plants than any other gardening establishment in England. Of exotic plants he possessed more than 1000 species. To his taste for horticulture was united a knowledge of botany, not usual among the elevated in rank of those days. He was a great encourager of Mr. London, who had been in his service, and who, under his patronage, established the Brompton Nursery—the best of its period. The Bishop was one of the first to promote the importation of ornamental exotics; and not only delighted in encouraging their cultivation, but also that of kitchen-garden plants. He was particularly fond of the Kidney bean, and introduced many of its varieties. Every department was under his own general superintendence; and having especially directed his attention to ascertaining the climates of the countries from which his favourites were imported, he soon was enabled to cultivate in his open borders many plants which had been considered too tender to be exposed to our seasons without protection. Death was sent not to him until he had passed his eightieth year; and when he was thus released from his labours on the 7th of July, 1713, he left behind him the reputation of being one of the few who, whatever part they have to fill, always act correctly. It is quite true that many virulent assaults upon his character and conduct are to be found in his contemporary literature, but they are attacks all to be traced to evil sources, and in every instance probably would have received the same worthy comment which me made upon one libeller: "I am glad of his attack upon me, for he has given me an opportunity of setting you a good example in forgiving him."

Meteorology of the Week.—At Chiswick, the average highest and lowest temperatures of these days, from observations during the last twenty-three years, are 73.6° and 50.6° respectively. The greatest heat, 93°, was on the 27th, in 1826; and the greatest cold, 37°, on the 30th, in 1848. On 67 days rain occurred, and 94 days were fine.

RANGE OF BAROMETER—RAIN IN INCHES.

June		1841.	1842.	1843.	1844.	1845.	1846.	1847.	1848.	1849.
27	B.	30.128	30.213	29.776	29.885	29.760	29.797	30.960	29.925	29.969
		29.951	30.143	29.676	29.823	29.462	29.699	30.240	29.776	29.943
	R.	0.10	—	—	—	0.15	0.01	0.01	0.02	—
28	B.	30.061	30.274	29.593	30.016	29.761	29.850	30.955	29.889	30.076
		29.773	30.128	29.599	29.949	29.236	29.800	30.348	29.807	29.992
	R.	0.55	—	0.01	—	0.16	0.03	—	0.02	—
29	B.	29.817	30.078	29.797	30.055	29.937	29.814	30.967	29.758	30.079
		29.743	29.989	29.754	29.926	29.897	29.796	30.253	29.619	29.019
	R.	0.07	—	—	—	0.04	—	—	0.01	0.02
30	B.	30.093	29.933	29.910	29.936	29.856	29.978	30.372	29.645	30.186
July		29.927	29.791	29.873	29.850	29.838	29.888	30.294	29.539	29.916
1	R.	0.01	0.80	—	—	0.05	0.02	—	0.08	—
	B.	30.080	29.840	30.002	29.955	29.966	30.014	30.284	29.783	36.180
		30.040	29.737	29.923	29.899	29.572	29.973	30.274	29.450	29.991
	R.	0.06	0.25	—	0.34	0.13	0.04	—	0.04	—
2	B.	30.123	29.848	29.995	29.841	29.824	30.074	30.969	29.876	29.999
		30.085	29.830	29.964	29.832	29.776	29.988	30.189	29.838	29.964
	R.	0.81	0.05	—	0.23	0.06	0.01	0.01	0.67	—
3	B.	30.125	29.961	29.992	29.876	29.928	30.165	30.147	29.813	29.745
		29.289	29.896	29.967	29.809	29.540	30.129	30.040	29.738	29.567
	R.	0.04	0.01	—	0.14	0.01	—	—	0.29	0.01

Insects.—With no creature is the gardener more familiar than with the Earth Worm (Lumbricus terrestris); and yet there is no other of which, in general, he possesses less knowledge. Let us bring before him a few of the most interesting facts in its history. When boring, the worm insinuates its pointed head between the particles of the earth, among which it penetrates like a wedge; and the fore-part of the body being fixed by the spines, of which there are four pairs on each segment (see b in annexed drawing), the hinder parts are then drawn forwards by a shortening of the body. This swells out the fore segments, and forcibly dilates the passage into which the head has been already thrust. The spines upon the hinder rings then take a firm hold upon the walls of the hole into which they have been drawn, and the effort is again repeated so long as onward progress is desired by the worm. If it be cut into two equal parts when in motion, each part will continue to move for a time, but only the fore half will continue to live. This forms a new tail, and soon shows but few signs of injury. If the division be made near the head, the body remains alive, and will form a new head, but the old head dies. On more than one occasion we have advocated the cause of the worm, and we will now quote from an eloquent and truthful writer his concurring observations. This animal, destined to be the natural manurer of the soil, consumes on the surface of the ground, where they would be injurious, the softer parts of decayed vegetable matters, and conveys into the soil the more woody fibres, where they moulder, and become reduced to a simple nutriment fitting for living vegetation. Beneficial as these creatures are, by giving a kind of under-tillage to the land, performing the same loosening below that the spade and the hoe effect on the surface, and thus admitting the air and the moisture,—and beneficial as they are by drawing leaves and other decaying matters into the earth, yet they are sad tormentors to the gardener, and occasion, in some situations, the loss of more young plants than even the slug, by drawing in their leaves, and thus inverting our nurslings. Yet, if these depredations do at times excite our ire, we must still remember the nightly labours and extensive services of this scavenger and manurer of the soil. The worm-casts are produced by the digestive process of the worms, which take into their intestinal canal portions of the soil through which they burrow, extract part of the decaying matters it contains, and eject the rest in a finely divided state. In this manner a field manured with marl has been covered, in the course of eighty years, with a bed of surface earth averaging thirteen inches in thickness (Carpenter's Zoology). a, the perfect worm; b, the fore-segments magnified, shewing the spikes directed backwards; c, egg, inclosing two young ones; d, young worm escaping from the egg.

A RECENT decision in a Common Law trial has roused the fears of more than one of our readers, who either have been using, or are wishing to use, the saw and the pruning knife pretty freely in their gardens. One gentleman (*R. F., of G.*) asks, "May I not lop off a large branch from a lime which totally obstructs the view from my library window?" And the reply we now make to him we make to all who inquire of us how far they may venture to lop their landlord's trees, *Ask of him permission before you commence operations.*

The facts of the trial in question are briefly these:—A gentleman occupying a house, which has a small garden before it, in St. John's Wood, lopped so extensively an Acacia, a Birch, a Laburnum, and a Weeping Willow, for the purpose of obtaining a view of the high road, that his landlord estimated the depreciation of his property to be one-fourth of its rental of £3 per week. The tenant maintained that he had made the trees handsomer; but the jury gave the landlord £30 damages, and beyond all doubt they were right in their decision. Very few persons would consider a residence improved by having it exposed to view from the high road; but if it were otherwise, no man either according to law or to reason (and they are not always synonymous) has a right to make any permanent or long-enduring alterations of another's property, without first obtaining his consent.

The law has ever been scrupulously and wisely protective of everything growing in our gardens and orchards; for, were it otherwise, every such inclosure might be ravaged by the mattock and saw of any tenant, however brutally insensible to vegetable beauty. As long ago as the time of Sir Edward Coke—for even then his contemporary, Lord Bacon, had acknowledged "gardening as the purest of earthly pleasures"—it was determined that a tenant is liable to be sued for waste, if he cuts down *any* fruit trees in the garden or orchard he holds; and a similar decision has been in cases where trees of *any* kind have been cut down which afforded a defence or shelter to the house.

Many persons seem to think, and most erroneous is such an opinion, that they may plant and uproot in the garden they rent without any other control than the dictates of their own fancy. Now we have already seen that tenants have no such right relative to the trees they find planted at the time they enter upon the premises. But, the law wisely goes further than this, and says that tenants, not being nurserymen, shall not remove *any plant*, even which they themselves have inserted in the soil they hold, if, by so doing, they depreciate its value; and we will quote as an instance the case in which a Mrs. Mackie, having planted a large quantity of box edging, attempted to have it removed when her tenancy of the garden expired. Her counsel in arguing that she was entitled to remove the box said, "The question is whether any damage results to the freehold? Could not a tenant remove flowers which he had planted in the ground?" To which three judges thus replied:—"*Mr. Justice Littledale.*—No. *Chief Justice Denman.*—A border of box is intended to be perma-

nent. *Mr. Justice Park.*—It might as well be contended that a tenant could take up hedges."

Now this, again, is not only law but good reason. If a tenant cuts out the soil into borders and beds, edging these with box, this edging can by no possibility be removed without disfiguring the garden, and depreciating the rentable value of the property. It is doubtful whether the dictum of Mr. Justice Littledale is to be taken as literally ruling that a tenant has no right to remove *any* flower that he has planted in the soil he rents. We think this doubtful, because, as Lord Kenyon observed in another case, "In modern times the leaning has always been in favour of the tenant, in support of the interests of trade, which is become the pillar of the state. What tenant will lay out his money in costly improvements of the land, if he must leave everything behind him which can be said to be annexed to it?"

The rule established by all the decisions seems to be, that the tenant has no right to remove, or to alter extensively, the trees and plants he finds upon the land; and that having once planted trees, shrubs, or other plants, he has no right to remove them, if, by so doing he depreciates the value of the property. Thus in another case Lord Ellenborough ruled that an action would lie against the tenant of a garden for ploughing up strawberry beds, although it may be usual for the incoming tenant to pay the out-going an appraised value, and the tenant who ploughed up the strawberry beds may have paid the former occupier accordingly.

We have endeavoured to explain, and to offer as a warning to our readers, the law relative to such cases; but, to avoid litigation, it is always much the wisest course to have *an agreement in writing, signed by the landlord,* giving the tenant permission to remove plants, &c., which he may have inserted during his tenure of the property.

ON the tenth of this month the friends of the cultivators of the soil had to deplore the death of Mr. James Smith of Deanston, a man who in various public efforts had rendered no mean service to agriculture; and his labours to benefit mankind were not confined to the enrichment of the soil; he struggled, and successfully too, to remove from ill-cultivated lands their stagnant water; and yet he was equally energetic in his attempts to promote the cause of sewage irrigation. He well knew how intimately connected with an increased attention to the health of the animal world, is the application of the results of better house drainage, and more copious supplies of water to the enrichment of the soil. He was born at Glasgow, on the 3rd of January, 1789; and was, therefore, in the 62nd year of his age.

His career, thus briefly sketched in the *North British Mail,* is full of interest to every one who regards, even with only moderate attention; the good objects to which we have alluded:—

"His death took place at Kingencleuch, the residence of a cousin of Mr. Smith, near Mauchline, in Ayrshire, where he was staying for a temporary period. Although the infirmity attendant on advancing years had been for some time creeping gradually upon him, he had continued to maintain his usual health, and on Sunday night went to bed apparently not the least indisposed. Next morning, when called by his servant, it was found that during the night, his sudden and unexpected decease had taken place. At first it was ascribed to apoplexy, but as there were none of the usual evidences to confirm the supposition, it is presumed that the proximate cause of death was over-exhaustion, the result, perhaps, of a long journey of some thirty or forty miles, which Mr. Smith had undertaken on the previous Saturday. Mr. Smith has been most generally known for his improvements in agriculture, and his experiments in subsoil ploughing, thorough draining, the application of sewage manure, the manufacture of tile-drains, &c. But, as a civil engineer, his name in scientific circles is also most favourably known. Of the originality of design, and the powers of mind, which he so displayed in the prosecution of this favourite pursuit, sufficient evidence is afforded in the construction of the celebrated water-wheel of such large dimensions at the Shaws Water cotton-mill, Greenock, and of a floating-bridge at Gargunnock, on the Carse of Stirling. That he was also possessed in a marked degree of that *pervidum ingenium* which by some is placed among the national characteristics, has been exemplified by the invention of various agricultural implements, and other mechanical contrivances in connection with cotton-spinning, &c., exhibiting a singular amount of ingenuity. As further illustrative of this, and also as proof of the fact that up to the last his vigorous intellect continued unimpared, it may be mentioned that at the time of his death he was taking out a patent for a "sheep dip," of a new composition, and intended to supersede the system of "tarring" at present in use. This is a subject to which Mr. Smith had lately devoted much attention ; and it was no doubt the cause of much satisfaction to him to find, from experiments made a short time ago on the estates of his Grace the Duke of Montrose, that his invention even more than surpassed the anticipations that had been formed of it, in accomplishing the end in view; and we have no doubt that this discovery, when introduced, will be duly appreciated by that portion of the community for whose benefit it was contrived. Mr. Smith was a member of the Glasgow Philosophical Society, to whose Transactions he contributed several important scientific papers. He had been latterly engaged in reporting to the Board of Health on the sanitary condition of different districts in England."

THE FRUIT-GARDEN.

Strawberries.—These are now ripening, and where colouring has not already commenced free applications of water will be of immense benefit, unless the weather prove rainy. Indeed, if colouring has already commenced, and the crops appear somewhat scanty, and many are wanted for preserving purposes, it is better to sacrifice a little in point of flavour than to run short in quantity. Of course, a portion may be reserved for the purposes of the dessert.

As connected with this matter, the superiority of soils of some depth over those which are shallow, becomes manifest. Every inch extra in depth may be considered as enabling the plant to endure several days more of drought; and this applies not only to the strawberry, but to almost every crop both in the garden and the farm.

It is hoped that the readers of THE COTTAGE GARDENER have taken the precaution of putting some straw or other material beneath their plants, to preserve them clean. We generally use clean new wheat straw; some persons use the short grass from the lawn, but this is not to be recommended, as in the event of a rainy July—which in the average of seasons perhaps is to be expected—the grass harbours myriads of slugs, as also wire-worms, which in some districts are exceedingly prejudicial to the crop. We do not see why ordinary slates, such as those rejected from old roofs, should not be procured and laid by for the very purpose. These would be of an imperishable nature, and if the operator in placing them carried a basket of stones, or broken brick, and placed one beneath each corner of the slate next the plant, the surface of the slate would present an incline, from which moisture would at all times readily escape.* Mr. Roberts's tiles, which we see advertised, are no doubt good things, but too expensive to be within reach of the million. We would rather direct attention to ordinary materials within reach of everybody.

Much attention should be paid to protect the ripening fruit from birds and mice. In this part of the country (Oulton Park), so numerous are the blackbirds and thrushes, that we are obliged to gather every one we can lay hands on each afternoon, especially when they first begin to ripen, for the birds will be at them soon after three o'clock every morning, and take all that are about half ripe. This is sad work, but where a considerable extent is grown (and we have a quarter of an acre) it is impossible to cover with nets. Such, however, are used-up for preserving purposes; and those for the table are planted near to the houses, or other situations where there is a continual movement going on, and whither the birds seldom resort.

The *Elton* and *Alpine* strawberries, for late purposes, should at this period receive liberal waterings; and all runners should be trimmed clean away from the Alpines after this period. Indeed, all runners not required for planting should be kept trimmed away from *all* the kinds, at *all* times, for they doubtless rob both the plant and the soil, and tend to produce confusion as well as intercept the light from the mother plants; the latter is the most injurious robbery of all; for if the runners are cleared away, the exterior leaves of the parent plants drop, and the whole of the foliage slightly descends in succession; and by this means the crown of the plant is exposed equally to the light with the rest. When, however, the plant is hedged-in with coarse runners, the interior leaves are huddled together, and abortive or weak blossoms are the sure result.

We do hope that none of our readers will resort to the barbarous practice of *cutting off the leaves* of their strawberries in the end of summer ; a more absurd practice does not exist, condemned at once by every principle of physiological science, and by long practice. Because, forsooth, crops have been produced in spite of this practice, persons of hasty conclusions have taken a fancy that the practice is good. In doing so, not only is one portion of those valuable secretions which give plumpness to the bud and complete the organization of the future blossom cut away, but the protection of the half decayed foliage, which nature has wisely ordained

* We use slates ourselves, but put them flat upon the surface.—ED. C. G.

as a shelter in northern climes, is at one fell swoop destroyed, and the hitherto protected bud placed entirely at the tender mercies of the northern blast, and the withering frosts of a long period of extreme low temperature.

We have little doubt that a part of the failures so often complained of with regard to the *British Queen*, is attributable to this very error. The labourer, or jobbing gardener, of the suburban villa, is anxious at the end of summer, or when the leaves have fallen, to make a general cleaning: a very commendable course to be sure. Now it so happens, that half decayed strawberry leaves do not carry a very fresh appearance, albeit so useful as protectors. Away, then, goes the clothing of the poor strawberries in the general clearance; no distinction is made between the proper removal of dead and useless asparagus stems and the useful strawberry leaves. Look at all our best gardeners, and see what care they take over their strawberry pots for forcing. Surely they do not take all this trouble for nothing?

PEACHES AND NECTARINES.—The disbudding, according to former advice, having been duly carried out, the fruits will now be in that stage termed, by practical gardeners, "stoning;" and not to stay here to explain what we would willingly fancy the largest portion of our readers already understand, we will merely point to the prospect that exists of a universal mode of expression, or, perhaps, it might better be said of understanding and accepting these plaguy conventionalities, through the medium of *The Cottage Gardener's Dictionary*. For our own part, and as connected with the fruit department, we beg to say, that all "the secrets of our prison-house shall be disclosed," every technicality explained, to the gaze of the meanest gardening groom. But "let us return to our sheep," as the French say.

We have before advised somewhere that a good deal of stopping, or pinching if you like so to call it, be practised on peaches and nectarines, especially in northern districts. It has, also, been shown repeatedly how this stopping has a twofold tendency: viz., to ripen the wood by checking over-vigorous root action, and also to equalise the strength of the tree, by "cutting off the supplies" from the gross shoots, and by consequence throwing the surplus on to the weaker shoots; the latter, of course, left unstopped to the end of the season.

If our advice has been followed, the gross shoots have been pinched long since, and by this time a host of lateral or side spray will have been developed from their sides. How to manage this has been fully discussed in previous papers; but we may repeat, that it must be kept duly thinned out; for one leader and a pair of laterals, one right the other left, is as much as will in general prove of any benefit to the tree, except in the case of young and luxuriant trees. In the latter case, as much may be trained-in as space can be found for; remembering, that as soon as they have produced length enough for the ensuing year, that the tops of all the superior ones must bè pinched off; this, as before observed, will cause the inferior parts of the tree to increase in strength, and by such means assiduously attended to, the strength of a tree may be balanced to a nicety.

TRAINING.—If not commenced, no delay should be permitted, especially with young trees. The leading shoots in most cases should be secured, for fear of injury from storms; and these "laid in," the next strongest shoots may be fastened, the operator at the same time keeping a watchful eye on the condition of the tree, and removing all superfluous spray which is likely to shade the best shoots.

The above remarks apply, in the main, to nearly all our trained fruits; still, as there are some special matters which should be pointed out, we will endeavour to return to the subject shortly.   R. ERRINGTON.

THE FLOWER-GARDEN.

SINCE I last wrote I have been sight-seeing in and around London, where competition, in almost everything one can think of, runs higher than on any other part of the globe of equal extent,—from a cabbage to a pine-apple, and from the sowing of a seed to the last stage of the ripening of the second generation thereof. All is done there under the stimulus of competition, so that instead of being a nation of shopkeepers, as Napoleon asserted long ago, we are rather a nation of gardeners—from Her Most Gracious Majesty downwards, "in country and in town." But country-people, and especially country-gardeners, should "go up to town," at least once a-year, to see some of the wonders produced by all this competition; to meet old friends, and make new ones; to exchange notes and ideas, and to rub off the rust and prejudices which are almost inseparable from a private country life. There is a class of gardeners, and of others, commonly called "the strong-headed," and they of all people in the country should be advised to go and see the New Houses of Parliament and London Bridge. No matter how hard or how soft, how dull or how refined and intellectual a head may be, let it but find its way to London, and there it is most sure to meet its equal; and then, to know that we are, after all, but one out of a common herd is a very good and effectual way to keep us humble—say, humble cottage gardeners.

Last year when I was in London I kept looking up to the windows and balconies as I went along, to see what new arrangement I could spy out for "window-gardening," but this season there was little in my head but flower-beds and bedding-plants; and amongst other things I got a promise of a good purple *Verbena*, at last, from one of the best flower-gardeners in this country, or in any other; and he agrees with me, that *Emma* and *Heloise* are not good purples, nor shades of purple. I also heard, that a verbena called *Voltaire* is the best striped one of this season; and some of our readers may not be aware that *Eclipse* and *Clotilde* are the best striped ones of the older sorts.

Of *Geraniums* which I did not mention in my former lists, I saw the *Gooseberry-leaved* used as an edging to a large bed in one of the flower-gardens belonging to the Royal Botanical Garden at Kew. It was very wrong of me to have forgotten this beautiful edging geranium, for I have used it some years; and a most interesting plant it is for an edging, or for very small beds; and it is very easy to keep over the winter, although it looks very delicate. The flowers of it are the smallest of all our geraniums, but they are bright scarlet, of a starry shape, and so thickly produced that they soon make a bright mass. Here, also, I saw a large bed of a fancy geranium called *Nosegay*. It belongs to the old *Yeatmanianum* breed, with reddish front petals, streaked, and the back ones dark. It makes a good neutral bed, as does *Bouquet tout Fait*, which is of the same breed, and of which there was a good bed in the new flower-garden in front of the new conservatory at Kew. This is the first time I have seen this new flower-garden, and being in a public establishment I can refer to it with the greater confidence as an example of a very judicious system of planting such figures. It is a terrace garden, divided across the middle by a broad walk—the figures, or beds, in one division being a repetition of those in the other compartment; and the colours of the beds in one division are repeated in the other, but with different parts of the same height. The scarlets are represented in one of the divisions by *Tom Thumb*, and in the other by *Diadematum rubescens*, which is tallied there *Diadematum superbum*,—a wrong name, for *rubescens* has the priority, being an old name given, I believe, by Sweet, who was a great authority in such things. Of these scarlets there are four corner beds in each division; and the only improvement that I can suggest on the mode of planting is that each bed should be of a different kind of plant, to make a greater variety, as in that case there would be eight scarlet flowering plants, instead of the two already mentioned. Instead of the four beds of *Diadematum rubescens*, I would have only one of it; and in the cross corner opposite I would plant *Diadematum*, which would exhaust the scarlets in that breed; and in the other two opposite corners I would have *Lady Mary Fox* and *Rouge et Noir*. The last is the strongest of the four; and if it threatened to rise higher than its fellows, I would *partly* train it down to the ground. In the other division, where *Tom Thumb* is used, it would be more difficult to get four low kinds of the true scarlet breed. Any of the many dwarf seedlings belonging to the *Frogmore* section would only be a repetition of *Tom Thumb* itself; but my own seedling called *Judy* would make a good match for *Tom Thumb*, and though a shaded scarlet, is sufficiently high-coloured for the purpose. These two would be planted cross-cornered, and the other two corners with a well marked *Horse-shoe* kind, or kinds, if two such could be had of so dwarf a habit as to match the height of *Judy* and *Tom Thumb*, but I do not know any seedlings of such marked characters. Perhaps some one will be so good as to let us know of such a one. And for the fourth bed, rather than repeat Tom Thumb or Judy, I would use one called *Lucida*, which would answer well for height and colour, but the leaves are much crumpled, and the shoots streaked with a light colour; but the height and the colour being preserved, that would only add to the variety produced. Most gardeners would prefer the present arrangement, which is the easiest mode; but ladies who visit their own gardens daily would prefer my plan, which has a greater variety of plants; and, with the single exception of keeping on good terms with the cook, there is nothing more judicious for a gardener than to follow out such fancies as ladies prefer in the flower-garden. Whatever tune they like best he should learn to whistle it, and that would carry him safely over many scrapes.

The other colours used in this garden were all represented in low growing plants, and one peculiarity, which I have often insisted on in these pages, is well carried out here, namely all the central beds throughout the two compartments are of subdued colours, or nearly neutral. Those who have been in the habit of planting the centre beds of regular figures with the highest colours, should see and study the much better effect produced here by a contrary arrangement.

Altogether, I was much pleased with the planting of this new flower garden. The garden itself is not yet finished, and therefore not open to criticism on the design; besides I am not fond of that kind of criticism, and never indulge in it, unless it is forced upon me. I wish they had allowed a couple of acres for a complete flower-garden on the other side of the large conservatory, in sunk pannels, as the American ground is now laid down, so that we might have *one* national flower-garden worthy of this great gardening country. They say the Botanical Garden and Collection there are better than anywhere else; fine news no doubt to a few half crazy philosophers who see as much beauty in a toad-stool as I see in Mr. Hoyle's new seedling geranium *Ajax*,—the finest thing to my eye that Mr. Hoyle has yet produced; but what interest can the great body of the people who visit Kew take in hard names, masses of weedy-looking "herbaceous plants" in clumps, and beds of strange forms? How many ladies go there to study "the beauties of nature" in the botanic arrangement? Not one of the ten thousand who will spend an hour taking notes of the few ornamental plants in the new flower-garden, small as it is.

D. BEATON.

GREENHOUSE AND WINDOW GARDENING.

GLOXINIAS—CULTURE IN A GREENHOUSE VINERY.—As a sequel to the article on Begonias, we beg to recommend the addition of these still more compact and beautiful plants—and plants, too, that will require even much less trouble than the Begonias. In such a situation as a greenhouse in winter, changed into a vinery in summer, and the vines made the principal thing for that period—the hardier plants being either removed to turf or other pits, or placed out of doors,—the Gloxinias will be just in their element,—will blossom more freely than in a regular moist plant stove, and if their leaves are not so luxuriant as when placed in a stove, they are free from that shrivelled, woe-begone appearance which they are apt to assume when placed on the airy shelf of an un-shaded greenhouse. The less airy situation, the higher temperature, the shade of the vines, in such circum-stances just suit our little favourites; and for those of our readers who wish to combine in their small houses the *floral* and the *horticultural*, there can be no com-parison between a compact plant of Gloxinia densely covered with its pretty blossoms, and a lanky geranium, or a spindly balsam, or even with any except the prettiest and dwarfest of the achimenes, while the trouble required is not greater than that required for the latter, and much less than that requisite for either of the two former. In such circumstances, under vines, geraniums, and balsams, &c., &c., will get *drawn*, and loose their sturdy look; but if the shade is not too dense it will be the very thing for the Gloxinia. We frequently use them for ornamenting a cool glass-covered verandah, and there they stand for months during summer, but then there is the opportunity of shading during bright sunshine. In a range of forcing houses with upright glass in front, upon a narrow shelf close to the front glass, we have a row of Gloxinias, and even here, not-withstanding the shade of the vines, we deem it ad-visable to *size* two or three squares from the bottom of the upright sash, as mentioned lately, that the bloom may be longer preserved. Of course, under such circum-stances the Gloxinia can only be cultivated during summer; in winter we must be content if we possess its tuber—its flowers must be given up to the possessors of regular plant stoves.

Like many more of our most beautiful and accomo-dating plants, the Gloxinia belongs to the group of Gesner-worts, and received its name in compliment to *Gloxin*, a celebrated botanist. The flowers are more like, and are more nearly allied to, a *Foxglove*, than any other of our common plants. The blossoms, therefore, are not only beautiful, but the four stamens are arched, joined, and key-stoned together by the anthers. All of them are low herbaceous plants, with bulbous tuberous roots, with some special exceptions, for some varieties of *Cartoni* will grow to a height of several feet, and so will the old species of *Maculata*, while *Maculata* and *Tu-biflora* (if synonymous with *Gesnera tubiflora*) have not bulbous, but scaly imbricated tubers. None of the species or varieties have much or any scent, with the exception of *Maculata*, which has a very pleasing scent resembling that of mint.

REST PERIOD.—The main points of culture, as respects all the species, are identical; embracing chiefly a period of *rest* and a season of *growth*. During the *rest*, the tubers are allowed to become *dried*, but not *shrivelled*. Hence the propriety of keeping them in the pots in which they grew during the previous season. After starting water must be given, gradually increasing its quantity until the plants are in full leaf, when they will require a large supply. With the exception of garden hybrids, most of the species are natives of South Ame-rica. Exposing the tubers, therefore, to a low temperature would be fatal. If kept dry, and not colder than 45°, the tubers will be safe. I have had them considerably lower than that, but the game is not a safe game to play at. In a greenhouse vinery, where the temperature may range from 35° to 45° in winter, the pots should be turned on their broadsides, and placed in an inconspicuous position at the warmest part of the house. I have frequently kept them, and always safely, in a shed where the furnace of the house was situated. There is less danger if the leaves have been well ripened, and the tuber in consequence firmer, before storing. If the soil should be apt to get too dry during winter, we prefer throwing some water *about* the pots instead of *in* them. Some would recommend our amateur friends to take the tubers out of the pots, and keep them in bags in a cosy corner—near the *ingle* in the parlour. But though this would do, neither care nor labour would be saved, and there would be the danger of getting a fleshy juicy tuber as attenuated as a shrivelled mummy. One advantage, and a great one, arising from keeping the tubers in the soil in which they were grown, is the preserving of their freshness, even though the soil be dry, unless it be so near the heating apparatus as to be baked. To prevent this in a cool house, we have covered the pots with boxes, such as empty tea-chests, &c.

GROWING PERIOD.—Towards spring the tubers will begin to push from the cluster of buds placed in the centre; then, but not till then, should they be repotted. If you do scarcely force the vines, the plants would be all the better then to forward them a little in a cucumber frame after potting, taking care, however, that no sun strikes the leaves while there is condensed moisture upon them. They may then be taken back to the vinery when the general temperature there approaches 60°. In want of the accommodation of a hot-bed, we have made a temporary one, near where the flue enters, or the boiler is situated, just to give them a start. If you do not put fire to your vines until April, something of these means must be taken to give a fine display of bloom in June. If you keep a temperature of 45° during winter, and commence increasing it for the vines in the beginning of March, your Gloxinia plants will want no such coddling; they will progress along with the vines, and reward you with their blossoms for several months from the end of June, and earlier if previously assisted.

As soon as the shoots have sprung from a little to an inch we like to repot them; and at that early season it is advisable that the soil should be *heated* a little, to prevent a sudden check. We prefer removing almost entirely the old soil, but saving what few fibres may be fresh and growing. The size of the pot will depend upon the size of the tuber, and whether you pot upon the *one* or the *successive* shift system. We prefer the latter for those that are small, and the former for those that are large. An 8-inch pot will contain a large plant, from which, in several kinds, you may have from 60 to 100 blooms expanded at once. Be careful in potting to keep the tuber or bulb near the surface, only slightly covered. Equal portions of leaf-mould, peat, and loam, with half a portion of silver sand, will grow them well; but they will succeed better if to this is added half a portion of old dried cow-dung, and half a portion of *small*, but not *dust*, charcoal. All the materials, except at the surface of the pot, should be rough, and the pots well drained. Water should be given carefully and rather sparingly at first; when in full growth and bloom they will require it often and liberally. A manure solution will not then be distasteful, but it should be of a cool nature, such as that formed from two-year-old cow-dung, with just a little lime to clear it. When done blooming, and before storing it past, the plants should stand full in the sun under glass, and receive less and less water, that the roots may be well ripened.

PROPAGATION.—They may be propagated easily by seed, leaves, and, cuttings. Seeds sown early in spring will produce flowering plants the following season; few may bloom the same season. Garden hybrids are thus produced by cross-breeding; leaves taken off are inserted by their footstalks will form tubers that will bloom the following season. If there is a bud when the leaf is separated from the shoot, the tuber will be the stronger. In rare kinds, a score or more of plants may be made from a single leaf. In this case, all the reticulated nerves on the back of the leaf should be notched with a sharp knife, and this underside of the leaf should be fastened to damp sand on the surface of a well-drained pot, and a bell-glass put over it; unless from the strongest nerves, the tubers formed will be small, and, therefore, will not bloom so early as when only one tuber is formed from a leaf. This, altogether, is a pretty experiment for young beginners. In strong plants, the shoots produced will be more numerous than you can find room for; and these thinnings made into cuttings, and treated with a little heat and shade in the usual way, will make nice little flowering plants for the end of summer and the beginning of autumn.

I shall conclude with mentioning a few desirable kinds:—

Maculata—one of the oldest; looks best when only one large tuber is used; purple.
Speciosa—blue; compact growth.
S. pallida—pale blue.
S. Cartoni—pink; several varieties under the same name, one very strong growing; the best has light blotches in the segments of the corolla.
S. alba—white; pure; compact.
Caulescens—light purple; large flowers.
Maxima alba—white and blue; compact, beautiful.
Discolor—lilac, blue; a poor thing, but the leaves are pretty.
Leuchonerva—flowers similar, but better and more abundantly produced; the leaves beautifully veined with white.
Passinghami—violet; large fine flowers.
Rubra—red; one of the best; there are several varieties, such as *maxima, superba*, &c., but for general usefulness they are little superior to the species.
Handleyana—white and red, similar to *Alba coccinea* and *A. sanguinea*, if not synonymous; all of them are excelled by
Grandis—of similar habit, but not yet common.
Fyfiana—white, with bluish margins; the flowers have the peculiarity of standing upright; very pretty; a little shy.
Carminata splendens—carmine; good and large.
Teuchleri—pinkish-red, dashed and blotched with bluish-purple; a most beautiful thing when it comes true, but very apt to produce pinkish-red blossoms. I have now a plant with a number of stems, and on only two of these shoots do the beautiful and desirable blossoms come. I would recommend more than the usual proportion of heat for this variety.

BEGONIAS.—As a note in addition to the article of last week, allow me to recommend the *Begonia cinnabarina*, in the possession of the Messrs. Henderson, of Pine-apple-place,—a bright orange, different, therefore, from all others, and likely to suit the greenhouse in summer; if not, our friend Mr. Appleby will correct us.

R. FISH.

HOTHOUSE DEPARTMENT.

EXOTIC ORCHIDACEÆ.

PLANTS THAT REQUIRE BASKETS—*(Continued from p.* 169).

Lacæna bicolor (Two-coloured L.).—Guatemala. This is not a plant with showy flowers, but is worth cultivating, because the spikes are long, frequently as much as two feet, and the flowers are set thickly upon it. The foliage is handsome; colour a pale greenish buff; the petals have three violet-coloured stripes; the labellum white, with a dark purple spot in the centre. Place it in a basket lined with moss and filled with rough fibrous peat. The Mexican house will suit it best. 21s.

Odontoglossum citrosmum (Lemon-scented O.).—Mexico. This is a most lovely species, with flowers of a delicious lemon-like scent. The colour of the flowers is very delicate—pure white in the centre, shaded off to the edge with rose. The racemes are, when well grown, more than a foot long. They are decidedly of a pendulous habit, hence we recommend them to be grown in baskets. Fill these with fibrous, rough pieces of peat, and place the plant in the centre. When growing keep it well supplied with water. The Mexican house is its proper habitation. It is a free grower, flowering in June. 31s 6d.

Saccolabium Blumei (Dr. Blume's Bag-lip flower).— Java. This is a most beautiful species. A casual observer would take it for *S. guttatum*, to which fine species it is nearly allied. The racemes are more pendulous, and thicker; the individual flowers are a little larger, and the spots more confined; ground colour pure white. The sepals and petals have a bright streak of violet below the apex; the labellum or lip is blotched with the same colour, but the tip is white. This is a scarce and expensive plant. 168s.

S. denticulatum (Toothed Bag-lip flower).—India. Though not so handsome as the last, this species has much to recommend it. The flowers are produced on short footstalks, and are arranged in corymbs; each corymb having five or seven flowers upon it. Sepals and petals greenish yellow, spotted all over with red. The lip is large, with a yellow pouch expanding into an open white margin. We have a plant in a basket with more than twenty corymbs of flowers in bloom at once. In that state it is really a pretty object. 42s.

S. guttatum (Spotted Bag-lip flower).—East Indies. A truly elegant species, which no collection, however small, ought to be without. The flowers are produced on long drooping racemes, often eighteen inches long. We have seen a plant in the collection of orchids belonging to J. Blandy, Esq., of Reading, with twenty-five of these elegant racemes of flowers upon it. This is probably the largest plant in cultivation. It is supposed to be one of the first of the kind introduced into Great Britain. The ground colour of each flower is pure white; the sepals and petals are dotted all over with dark rose colour. The labellum has a blotch of purple in addition to the spots. 105s.

S. præmorsum (Bitten-off Bag-lip flower).—East Indies. Also a very fine species with long pendant racemes of flowers. The sepals and petals are white, stained with a delicate rosy lilac; the lip is more highly coloured. This species is extremely rare. 210s.

S. ampullaceum (Flask-shaped Bag-lip flower).—East Indies. We have very lately been gratified with a view of the lovely blooms of this new and rare plant at Messrs. Loddige's. The colour of the entire flower is of the richest crimson rose. The flowers are produced on short racemes; the flower-stalks and short branches gave them quite a distinct character. It was a lovely object even among its beautiful relatives. Being so new and rare and slow to increase, the price is necessarily high. 420s.

S. miniatum (Red-lead-coloured Bag-lip flower).—Java. The flowers of this species are small, and produced on short racemes, sometimes branched. The colour is pleasing, and the plant altogether a gem of its kind. 105s.

This closes our list of the best species of Saccolabiums. The culture they succeed best with, is to place them in baskets in proportion to their size. The *S. denticulatum* and *S. miniatum* are small species, and will thrive well on blocks till they become moderate-sized plants, when they may be placed in small baskets, but keeping them upon the blocks till they decay. The other species may be put into baskets in proportion to their size. Fill the baskets with moss (sphagnum), and place the plants in the centre, tying them to a stick till they are established. They root very freely, and the young roots will soon work their way to the outside of the moss, clinging partly to the wood of the basket, and part of them will hang down into the warm moist air of the Indian house, which must be their habitation. They require plenty of water during the hot months of growth, but should be kept moderately dry and cool during the winter, to give them an annual rest. They will grow and thrive in one of these baskets for two years, and must then have a larger basket and fresh moss to grow in.

Scuticaria Steelii (Steel's Whip-plant).—Demerara. This plant has very long leaves; they are round like the lash of a whip, whence its name. The flowers are large, of a cream colour, and beautifully striped with reddish brown. It thrives well on a block, but better if the block is plunged as it were on one side of a basket in moss. The flowers are produced on short footstalks at the base of the long leaves. It is a desirable plant, and loves a damp moist atmosphere. 42s.

Stanhopea aurea (Golden Stanhopea).—Guatemala. This genus is the most remarkable of the whole tribe; the flowers are large and of the richest colours, and freely produced. The *S. aurea* is a fine species. A writer on it has said, "Imagine a plant, of which the flower is the size of *S. insignis*, the form of *S. venusta*, the smell of *S. oculata*, and the colour of *Maxillaria aromatica*, and arranged on a spike two feet long, and the reader will have a tolerably distinct conception of this beautiful thing." The sepals, or outer floral leaves, are pale orange-dotted, with small spots of light purple; the petals, or inner floral leaves, are of a deeper orange, with darker spots; the lip is dark orange, with a blotch of dark purple on each side. 21s.

S. Barkerii (Mr. Barker's S.) is like *S. Wardii*, excepting the spots. It is very fragrant. 31s. 6d.

S. Bucephalus Quito.—This is a fine rare species, very delicately fragrant. The general colour of the flowers is yellow, with two dark spots at the base of each petal, and thinly spotted all over with crimson. The sepals, also, are spotted with the same colour; the lip is of the deepest orange. 42s.

S. Devoniensis (Duke of Devonshire's S.).—A beautiful species; sepals and petals yellow, with deep crimson brown blotches. The lip is white with few spots, and a deep purple stain over half the lower part. 21s.

S. eburnea (Ivory S.).—Brazil. This is the same as *S. grandiflora*. The flowers are of the purest white; the lip is like ivory, polished and shining, and on being touched the resemblance to that substance is still greater. It is a beautiful species. 10s. 6d.

S. graveolens (Strong-smelling S.).—Peru. The scent of this fine species is so strong as to be disagreeable if approached too closely. If the flower be handled, it will taint the fingers even for a considerable time; but if it be hung up at some distance from the walk, so as to diffuse the scent, it is not disagreeable. The sepals and petals are of a most delicate straw colour; the lip and central parts of the flower are of a clear apricot colour; the upper part is like yellow ivory. It is a free bloomer. 15s.

(To be continued.)

FLORISTS' FLOWERS

AURICULAS.—The plants to flower next year should be growing strongly, and accumulating the power to produce fine blooms. The care they require now, is a constant supply of water during dry weather, and protection from heavy rain. The true lover of flowers will take care of them quite as much when they have ceased to give him the pleasure of seeing them decked with floral beauty. He will bestow this care, in the hope of seeing their loveliness in increased amount the following year. Small plants, that were detached from the large ones at the time of potting, should now have another shift into larger pots. With this treatment some of the strongest may be expected to bloom the next spring. Seedlings should also receive a due share of attention. Such as have been pricked out into pans and have made four or five leaves, may be shifted into pots 3½ inches wide, singly; or three may be put into 5-inch pots till they bloom. We have practised the method with seedlings of planting them out in one or two light boxes in the proper compost, and allowed them to bloom there, planting out in the border the common ones as soon as they were proved, and transplanting such as were judged to be worthy of a farther trial into pots, singly. The raising of new kinds from seed is a delightful amusement, which, we trust, our amateur friends will treat themselves with as much as circumstances will allow.   T. APPLEBY.

THE KITCHEN-GARDEN.

An abundant variety and supply of good winter and spring vegetables depends so much on a proper system of cropping for the next few weeks, that no space of ground should be left uncropped. *Cauliflowers, brocoli, Brussels sprouts, borecole,* and *kales* of the best varieties, *colewort,* &c., should be abundantly planted; not a space must be left vacant. Many of these vegetables may be planted to advantage between the rows of the *peas* and *beans.* As soon as the crop of the latter is gathered they should be cleared away, and the ground be well hacked over with the spud mattock, or strongly surface-scarified; an operation which will be but little trouble, if the surface of the soil has been attended to as previously directed. If the soil is not in good case, in consequence of not having been well manured when the winter or spring trenching was performed, apply some liquid-manure to the plants when established in the soil.

SPINACH. — A sheltered and good piece of ground should now be chosen for sowing the winter spinach when the time arrives. So much depends on the preparation of the soil for securing an abundant winter supply of this useful winter and spring vegetable, that it is well worth while to take some pains in preparing for its culture; and a small piece of ground, well chosen, may be made to produce a very large quantity of its fine healthy leaves. A spot of the early border, pea-

ground, or old strawberry-ground, intended to be destroyed, should be ridge-trenched, exposing the soil as rough as possible to the influence of the sun and air; continuing, in the after-management, to frequently fork and hack it over, until it becomes, by the 10th or 12th of August, as well pulverized as an ash hill.

Some of the ground also, where the strawberry-crop is to be destroyed, may be prepared for sowing *colewort,* and the principal *cabbage* crop, as well as *lettuce, endive, Rampion, winter onions, late radishes,* &c., as it will be found fresh and healthy for sowing seed and raising plants, as well as for general cropping. Sow the *Early Dutch, Early Stone,* and *Early Red-top American turnip,* all of which are quick in coming in, and of a very good quality when they do come. The fly, which in this locality is very plentiful and troublesome this season, will require to be well looked after, if a healthy even crop of turnips is to be obtained; dusting them over early in the morning with charred dust or dry wood ashes, both of which are famous protectives against those depredators, as well as stimulants of the first quality to the plant. Branches of the common elder, put into a light frame, and drawn over the turnip crop in the heat of the day, is also famous for driving away the fly. The previous-sown crops of turnip, if not well watered occasionally, will be hard, strong, and useless for culinary purposes.

POTATOES.—The ground of the early and second early potatoes, between each row, may now be planted with any kind of winter vegetables, such as *savoys, borecoles, cattle cabbage,* &c. The potatoes afford for a time a slight shade and protection, and by the time the potato-haulm is taken up these kinds of plants are established; and the forking-out of the potatoes when ripe affords considerable advantage to the progress of these winter crops; after which, when rain prevails, and it is considered needful to stimulate their growth, a small portion of guano or liquid-manure applied will cause great luxuriance.

RIDGE CUCUMBERS should be encouraged by having the earth's surface about them mulched, the vine or shoots kept occasionally stopped, trained, and pegged down, and a good soaking of manure-water applied when hot weather prevails.   JAMES BARNES.

MISCELLANEOUS INFORMATION.

OUR VILLAGE WALKS.

By the Authoress of " My Flowers."

THE MS. of which I gave the commencement in my last paper concludes thus:—

" Passing onward to the every-day occupations of life, how curious it is to reflect that the trees of the forest, sometimes greatly enriched by cultivation, have, in all ages and in every climate, been made instrumental as well for the maintenance as the destruction of human life. They have at one time supplied food, shelter, clothing, and luxuries of every kind; at another, the instruments of death—the fire and stake of the martyr, his cross, and his earthly crown. Well might Wordsworth say

" ' There is a spirit in the woods.'

It would be a vain thing here to attempt to particularize all the various, useful, and necessary applications of this substance. It is found in every climate—each of which produces an indigenous supply, according to the wants of man—equally available for savage as for civilized life. What can we say of its various qualities of hardness and softness, its lightness and its weight, the rapid growth of some kinds, the slow growth of others, its tenacity, its brittleness, its beauty

of texture, colour, odour, and fibre; the medicinal qualities of some varieties, together with the almost endless diversity of its products of fruit, flowers, leaves, bark, gums, roots, and berries? Or what shall we say of the modes in which timber is almost tortured by man for his own purposes? Think of the application of steam to make the stubborn log bend; the process of Kyanizing, charring, and galvanizing to preserve it from decay; the extraction of its sap and resins, and then the injection of liquids through its pores to give it solidity and weight; its adaptation to arts and manufactures, not only for the shelter, preservation, and conveniences of life, but also as one of the component parts of gun-powder for its destruction!

" Although it is well known that a large portion of England was originally little else than one continued forest, yet it is believed that only a very few kinds of timber were really and strictly indigenous in our soil, indeed for purposes of workmanship it has been said there were but three, according to the old legal adage and distich—that

" ' Oak, ash, and elm
Are timber throughout the realm.'

But it is not merely on the surface of our country that we possess such invaluable treasures of this material; if we go to the coal districts of England, how vast and inestimable are the supplies of fossilized wood, which we find beneath the verdant turf, stamped with vegetable formations of endless variety—some of which are most plainly discernible, as in the more recent transitions from wood to coal, in the works at Bovey Tracoy, in Devonshire.

"In the progress of civilization and of population in different parts of England, many large tracts of forest have wholly disappeared, causing at the same time a complete displacement of some valuable manufactures. For instance, in the early history of Sussex, we find that the eastern parts of that county were celebrated for their extensive iron manufactures. The iron work of the monument of Henry III., in Westminster Abbey, was cast in Sussex, and the first iron ordnance was cast there. But the Sussex forges all ceased with the destruction of the timber in the forests above the iron ore; there being no accompanying stratum of coal to provide the means of smelting.

" It is no less wonderful to observe—in connection with this subject—the extraordinary manner in which human knowledge is permitted to be available, in adapting itself to the changes brought about by the active interference of man with the gifts of nature. It is manifest that in this country, at least, we have greatly destroyed or diminished the growth of timber; hence we have, by the application of science, provided substitutes, and some of a most wonderful character. Who could have conjectured, only a few years ago, that some of our swiftest sailing ships would be built of iron ? that the wooden water-pipes of London and other cities should be exchanged for iron; and that for the smaller descriptions of tubing, gutta percha, and even India rubber should be substituted; and that our doors, and roofs of wood, and even articles of furniture may give way to materials of glass; while entire houses are built for exportation or domestic use, of iron alone—wood being deemed either valueless, or comparatively useless?

" These changes in the material used in manufactures have also led to others in the arts of life, and one of them of high celebrity in the Middle Ages, the art of carving in wood, is dwindling into insignificance; and the elegant carvings of Gibbons, at Chatsworth, Hampton Court, and other places,—and the ' storied urns,' cups, and vases of Benvenuto Cellini throughout Europe, are now rivalled or surpassed by compositions of plaster, lead, or papier-mache, cast in moulds, and produced in the sheds of a builder's yard, or in a cellar in Drury Lane !

" And thus the ' wood, hay, and stubble' of this world are in a state of perpetual vicissitude, under the permission of the Almighty, and the application of man."

Let us meditate on these interesting facts during our daily rambles. They will lead our minds to much that may instruct and benefit us; and we shall never want an object to call them to our remembrance. The tall graceful tree, with its rich summer foliage, will utter them; the prostrate trunk, stripped of its spreading boughs, and lying in mighty helplessness, will repeat them; and even amid the cheerlessness of towns and cities we may be taught them by the chips that feed our fires.

How mercifully does a gracious Father provide all things necessary for man, and adapt his wants and tastes to those things that nature produces ! And how sad it is to see and feel the readiness and dexterity with which we apply and benefit by His gifts and mercies, and the slow, guilty reluctance with which we pray and praise ! O let the teeming earth with all her beauties and her treasures " praise the Lord !" and awaken our sluggish hearts of stone to praise Him too ! Let every work of man; every new, and useful, and wonderful invention; every grand and vast conception carried out and formed for the use and good of our fellow men, "praise the Lord;" for he alone teaches the cunning artificer, and guides his hand, although man in his self-sufficiency "thinketh not so," and gives himself the praise.

Let the whole earth, and everything that hath breath, "praise the Lord !"

ALLOTMENT FARMING FOR JULY.

AT this period everything will be in its highest vigour; and now it is that cultural matters, where necessary, should be carried out with the utmost assiduity.

Having recently travelled through districts abounding in small gardens, and some containing allotments, we must confess to a great amount of astonishment, at the dirty and ill-cultivated state of many of these holdings, indeed, we may say of the majority of them.

The allotments are, on the whole, by far the most creditable; and this arises probably from the fact, that such plots have a more direct interest taken in them by the proprietors : thus plainly evincing how much good might be accomplished if our landed proprietors generally would either themselves, or by means of their agents, keep a strict eye on these things; and occasionally give a helping hand, in the way of seeds or plants from their gardens; or advice and books, as the case might be.

We are willing to believe that THE COTTAGE GARDENER has been of much service in this way; and it may be presumed, that the *Dictionary* will be of still further use, as (being alphabetically arranged) instant reference may at all times be made on any subject, about which the least doubt exists.

The spirit of competition fostered by our local horticultural societies has been of considerable use in this affair as an adjunct, and it would seem to be a most desirable thing that such should be much extended; for many thousands are deterred from competing, through the distance at which they happen to live from such societies. For this reason we think that the principle of offering prizes for the best cultivated plots, to be determined by visiting judges, ought to be much extended; but care should be taken that such judges should be well qualified to decide, both in point of real experience and in integrity of purpose; for we have, more than once, known tradesmen from our towns selected for the purpose who understood not the bearing of the matter, and who, indeed, felt no real sympathy with the allotment-holder or cottager.

To return to cultural matters, we will begin with

THE POTATO.—By the time this reaches our readers, we trust they will be enjoying abundance of early potatoes, which is, indeed, an inestimable blessing to the ordinary cottager; for however much the policy of encouraging the cultivation of the potato may be doubted, we feel persuaded that the English cottager will stick to them as long as a leaf remains.

We would advise small holders to keep a strict eye on their Early Kidneys, or others for seed in the ensuing year. Such should never be mixed with the ordinary stock. The best way is to take them up a little before they are " dead ripe;" not, however, to prevent curl merely, but to prevent their sprouting again too soon. We have known the *Ash-leaved Kidney*, when very lightly soiled, to become greened, and to sprout before taken up for seed, especially if an early and partial ripening had been induced by hot and dry weather, and warm rains had supervened. The reasons, therefore, for an early removal from the ground will be manifest. The later crops of potatoes must be well looked to at this period; every weed must be eradicated forthwith. Care must be taken in hand-weeding not to tread upon, or throw down, the haulm, for this is productive of much injury to the crop. We advise a thorough stirring of the soil *between* the drills; the deeper this is stirred the better. Any blanks that may occur should be immediately filled after the cleaning process is complete: we do not know of anything better for this purpose than the swede turnip.

CARROTS.—We gave pretty full advice last month about this very useful root. We have advised deep hoeing when the plant is getting a few inches high, even between the plants in the drills, we now add that of deep culture *between* the drills, like the potato. If the grub occurs extensively, it will become a consideration whether to break them up entirely, or to endeavour to patch them. The latter case has been dealt with in previous papers; the former, if necessary, gives rise to a question as to what is the most eligible crop. This the allotment holder must decide according to his prospective wants, choosing that crop which will not only prove of utility when gathered, but which also requires but a short period for its culture; for it must be kept in mind that there remains but ten or a dozen weeks, at the most, for any given crop to perfect itself in. Of course, any of the winter-green family will be eligible, and if greens instead of root crops are preferred, few things can excel the green-kale, or savoy. If roots are preferred for pig-feeding, or for the cow, why nothing can exceed the swede turnip; and if the soil is too poor, and the season somewhat spent, any of the ordinary turnips may be sown. We have before observed, that fine young Horn carrots may be produced from a sowing made in the beginning of July on good mellow soil.

PARSNIPS.—These will need little further culture; weeds, of course, being eradicated, a good stirring with the hoe will be beneficial.

SWEDES.—These having been duly thinned out at about eight or nine inches apart, the future course to pursue is to pass the hand-hoe through them, not stirring too deep between the plants. Deep culture, however, between the drills is, in common with other root crops, of much importance. Need we add, that weeds must be kept cleared away at all times.

MANGOLD requires the same cultural operations as the swedes, after singling them out to about ten or twelve inches apart. Our practice is to soil them slightly up the bulb when about three-parts grown, or rather when side fibres begin to show themselves above the ground level.

ONIONS.—The final thinning must take place now. We are no advocates for great distances in this crop, finding, from experience, that a somewhat thick crop, by lessening the size of the individual onion, gives them better keeping qualities. They, moreover, come to hand sooner, as to their ripening,—a thing of much importance in the north. If the grub has much thinned their ranks, something should be introduced amongst them which will not smother them. We are not aware of any better plan than sowing or planting lettuces, which cannot be produced too abundantly where a pig is kept. The latter may be almost entirely supported by this crop in summer, letting them run up a little towards seeding, to increase both bulk and quality.

SHALLOTS.—As soon as these begin to loosen their hold, they must be removed forthwith to a dry situation—one, indeed, where rain can never touch them. We have known them rendered very firm by throwing them beneath the bee-bench for a few weeks. The housing of this crop must be done successively as they ripen.

CABBAGES.—All that are become solid and white should be used up either for the family, the cow, or the pig. By this means they become more profitable, as they soon produce good sprouts. Cabbages may be considered as ceasing to yield profit the moment they are full grown. Those sown in April or May should be got out between existing crops or on borders; and in the first week of July a liberal sowing may be made to produce good autumn Coleworts; such may be planted on the onion ground the moment the crop is removed, using a little manure near the surface. The dwarf sorts are best. We use the Matchless entirely.

GREENS.—Under this head we include the savoy, green kale, Brussels sprouts, or indeed any other of the Brassica family. We cannot point to the proportion of each, or whether it is expedient to grow all; we may merely say, that July, above all the months of the year, is the most proper for securing a good planting. Where early peas are being removed, the ground may be profitably occupied with these things. It need scarcely be added, that the whole tribe are partial to manure, but if the ground has been manured in the previous winter, there will be no occasion for more at present.

COMMON TURNIPS.—These may be sown any time up to the end of August, choosing for late sowings the Dutch or Stone. We merely point to these as a secondary consideration, or as a matter of convenience; for the swedes and mangold are of more importance as keeping roots.

LEEKS.—A planting of these in the early part of July, well manured, will give a supply until the succeeding June.

We now take leave of our cottage friends for the present, and may merely observe, that during summer the hoe and the waterpot, occasionally, are very profitable implements, if used in good time; and above all we must repeat, that cleanly culture, or an early freedom from weeds, is the grand point in allotment farming or gardening. Deep and frequent culture if not of equal import, is the very next; indeed, as cultural affairs they almost comprise all that can be said as to summer work.

THE POULTRY-KEEPER'S CALENDAR.—JULY.

By Martin Doyle, Author of " Hints to Small Farmers," &c.

FOWLS HATCHING.—It is very doubtful whether it be judicious to give the eggs of any of the gallinaceous birds for hatching after the middle of July at the latest. Supposing that a hen sits on the fifteenth of this month, the brood will not be hatched until about the fifth of August. Though it is natural that a hen should feel the instinctive desire to sit in autumn as in spring, and would, in the warm countries from which fowls originally came, bring forth two broods as a matter of course in the year, it is to be remembered that the temperature of our climate causes a material difference in this respect, at least as far as the hardihood and success of the second brood is in question. About Midsummer is the most desirable time for the second course of incubation to commence. Late broods of fowls, turkeys, and Guinea fowls, are all extremely uncertain, and dependent on the chance of a fair or foul autumn following. The temperature of any given locality, no doubt, will cause some difference in this respect. The poultry-keeper who lives in a cold wet region where an early winter sets in, and where chilling mists and fogs prevail in the autumn, cannot, with any reasonable expectation of success, rear late broods of the birds just enumerated; yet, in other parts of the United Kingdom, where the autumnal are frequently more mild and dry than the summer months, the breeder of fowls need not be discouraged from gratifying the longings of any hens that feel the desire for incubation, even to the end of July or later. It is to be calculated, that a late brood, if they do survive the severities of our climate, are worth a good deal of money in spring. Experience, then, as to the average kind of weather in the autumnal months, in any particular district, and of the usual effects upon the poultry which are there hatched at an advanced period of the year, can best determine the question, when the last broods may, with a fair chance of success, be brought forth?

Though so many more fowls and other poultry are reared by the peasantry of Ireland than by those of England, it is a fact, that coops—for the occasional confinement of the hen and the protection of the chickens, so common in England—are scarcely known in many parts of Ireland. The reason probably is, that the floor of the cabin in the latter country is the privileged place of retreat for young poultry, when they require shelter from a passing shower or from strong sunshine. In fact, a cabin itself is the coop, but as its scale is too large for the purpose required, and inconvenient in some respects, the true coop is a desirable substitute. We accordingly give here a sketch of one of the most approved construction and dimensions.

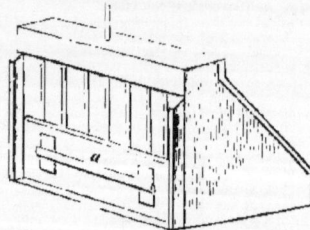

By confining a hen some hours in the day to the coop she is prevented from rambling into danger, and yet has the liberty of enjoying fresh air, and the pleasure of seeing her chicks run in and out through the bars, and returning to her when her voice warns them to seek shelter, on the approach of a shower or of any other danger, with her in the friendly coop, and remain there under her wing until she thinks fit to let them issue forth again. The instincts of the young birds will generally induce them to obey her voice, even though it be that of a step-mother. At night they may be closed in by means of the shutter, *a*.

But those who prefer a certain moderate to an uncertain large profit will act more wisely in placing duck's eggs under hens, and goose's eggs under turkeys, that are manifesting a strong desire to sit during July and August. The turkey-hen is a very assiduous nurse, and will sit upon the eggs of

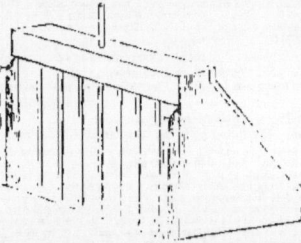

a goose or of any other bird as willingly as upon her own, or those of any other turkey. As it is, however, natural for her to sit at least thirty days, it is better to place the eggs of a goose, which require the same period of incubation; though, no doubt, the turkey-hen, if she were employed to hatch chickens, would not be uncomfortable at finding them libe-rated from the shell ten days sooner, which would enable her to stretch her legs, and enjoy the self-importance of a step-mother so much sooner.

The art of poultry-rearing is useful abroad as well as at home; to British residents in foreign lands as well as to the inhabitants of the United Kingdom.

TURKEYS.—At Calcutta, turkeys are now reared in great abundance for the supply of the tables of the British, at which these noble birds are considered almost indispensable. We suppose that it is very easy to rear turkeys in the warm climate of India, and that second, and perhaps third, broods of many tribes of the gallinaceous order are a matter of regular course among the poultry-keepers there.

The importance of giving abundance of food to young tur-keys, and, indeed, to all the young of poultry, cannot be too frequently urged. "The demands of nature for the growth of bone, muscle, and particularly of feather, are so great, that no subsequent supply of food can make up for a fast of a couple of hours. The feathers will still go on, and grow, and grow, and grow, and drain the sources of vitality still faster than they can be supplied, till the bird faints and expires from inanition. I have even fancied that I have seen a growth of quill and feather after death in young poultry, which we had failed in rearing. The possibility of such a circumstance is supported by the well known fact of the growth of hair and nails in many deceased persons. This constant supply of suitable food is, I believe, the great secret in rearing the more delicate birds, turkeys, guinea fowls, pheasants, &c.; never to suffer the growth of the chick (which goes on whether it has food in its stomach or not) to produce exhaustion of the vital powers for want of the necessary aliment. Young turkeys, as soon as they once feel languid from this cause, refuse their food when it is at last offered to them (just like a man whose appetite is gone in consequence of having waited too long for his dinner), and never would eat more, were food not forced down their throats, by which operation they may frequently be recovered; but the little guinea fowls give no notice of this faintness till they are past all cure, and a struggle of a few minutes shows that they have indeed out-grown their strength, or, rather, that the materials for producing strength has not been supplied to them in a degree commensurate with their growth."*

Turkey chicks, when they are "shooting the red," that is, when the feathers about the head and neck are becoming reddish (which change takes place when the birds are about two months old) require especial care as to feeding; after their constitutions are once established, less attention as to the quality of the food is necessary, as we have already had occasion to remark; but this one rule should be always ob-served, never to allow young turkeys, or the young of any poultry, to be hungry or become thin; inattention to this

* Dixon.

rule is the cause of much of the mortality which prevails among poultry.

GEESE.—Though goslings will find much satisfaction in eating every sort of vegetable, even nettles if chopped up for them, it would be miserable economy to withhold from them a due allowance of meal and grain. Such large frameworks as their's require proportional feeding. When they are ram-bling about on commons, care should be taken, yet, to keep them from dabbling in ponds or ditches. The cramp, which is often so fatal, may be avoided by observing this precaution as well as by reasonably good feeding; for the cramp may be occasioned by debility of stomach.

Mr. Cobbett boasted of having the most tender, and best flavoured, and altogether the finest geese in England, by buying goslings at this season, and confining them in a pen well supplied with straw. In one trough he had water, in the other oats. This, with lettuces starting to seed or in a sound state, and cabbages, were their entire food. After ten days he began to kill a bird or two every week until October; and he calculated that the oats for each bird did not cost more than one shilling—when oats were much dearer, too, than now. In short, he saved half the market price of geese by that simple management. The garden supplied half the requisite food.

THE BEE-KEEPER'S CALENDAR.—JULY.

By J. H. Payne, Esq., Author of "The Bee-keeper's Guide," &c.

UNLESS June shall have proved a more favourable month for our little favourites than May has been, I am afraid that instead of receiving from them a supply of honey it must this year be reversed, and we must afford the supply, or we shall have no bees another season. Amongst my own bees I have not yet seen a drone, nor have I heard of any having been seen but in one apiary in this neighbourhood. I have heard of two attempts at swarming; the numbers were very small, and in both cases the bees returned to the parent hive, and, in all probability, it was poverty that induced them to leave it. In looking over my hives yester-day, the 10th June, I find the combs of many of them to be as bare of bees as they were in February, which circumstance I never remember having witnessed before. It is usual for us at this time to see our glasses filling fast, and to be thinking about giving additional room, but I have not yet even put on a glass, nor shall I for some time to come.

WASPS.—I see that Mr. Underwood, of the Haymarket, advertizes his "wasp catchers," and I am quite sure that it is needful for us all to use every means in our power for the destruction of those sad enemies to our bees, and in this season more especially as "prevention is always better than cure," that object is attained by capturing the queen wasp at this time, and, indeed, as long as they can be seen. Some persons recommend shooting them; I have always found a garden-syringe to be a very useful thing, for if filled with water and discharged at them, it seldom fails to bring them to the ground—but it matters not by what means so that they are destroyed.

UNITING SWARMS.—The necessity for uniting swarms this year, I think, will be apparent to every one at all acquainted with bee-management, and, indeed, in some cases of return-ing swarms; but this cannot be done with any chance of success but in a bar-hive, and there the operator is sure to succeed, the manner of performing the operation will be as follows:—As soon as the swarm has left the parent hive, proceed immediately to open the hive and take out the bars one by one, and cutting from each comb every royal cell that is seen upon it and replacing the comb again in the hive. The cell in which the queen bee is born is entirely of a different construction from that of either the drone or the common bees. The cell of the latter is placed horizontally in the hive, and that of the queen is placed perpendicularly; that of the common bee is an exact hexagon, and that of the queen circular; besides, the cell of the queen is always fixed at the sides of the combs, and generally upon those near the middle of the hive. This operation of removing the royal cells will take about five minutes, and when done, return the swarm immediately to the hive; the old queen which led it off finding by this process that there is no royal brood left in the hive to succeed her, will not again attempt to leave it. Persons who have never practised this method will be surprised to find how easily it is accomplished, for the parent hive will at this time be found to be almost depopulated from the numbers that left it in the swarm and those that are out collecting. In some cases the help of a puff or two of tobacco-smoke may be useful, should the few bees left be angry, or the operator feel at all timid. The readiest way of returning the swarm will be to lay a board upon the floor-board of the hive, and parallel with it, upon which, by a smart and sudde nmovement, shake the swarm, and as nigh to the entrance of the parent-hive as can be done conveniently, and with the finger, or a piece of wood, guide a few of the bees to the entrance, and the remainder will follow immediately.

Gloomy Prospects.—The last week or two have been most lovely, but certainly not propitious for bees. They have not worked with their wonted vigour. There has been a visible languor and dullness about them, accompanied by a disposition to attack any one who approached them; the same thing has been observed in many places. The accounts which I have had from various counties are not by any means encouraging. One gentleman writing from the neighbourhood of Chester, says, "A cottager here had a swarm, on the 20th of May they continued inactive for some three or four days, dwindling gradually to nothing; the same person had a well-stocked hive completely demolished by the bees of his own or some other apiary. Another cottager had a swarm on the 19th, rather small; they became restless, and were found all dead the next morning. A third cottager had a stock which made an attempt to swarm, the queen was found five roods from the hive, to which place she was returned; the hive has since died." I have myself seen several stocks that in March and April appeared to be doing remarkably well, but, since that time, have rather decreased in numbers than otherwise; the brood appears to have died in the cells after having undergone the change to the perfect insect, and is brought out dead and shrivelled by the few living occupants of the hive, and this process appears to take up a very considerable portion of their time; the ground in front of some of these hives is strewed with young bees that have, to all appearance, died in the cells.

THE LONDON HORTICULTURAL SOCIETY'S FETE. CHISWICK, June 8.

(*Continued from page* 178.)

COLLECTIONS OF TWENTY STOVE AND GREENHOUSE PLANTS.

1st Prize to Mr. May, gardener to Mrs. Lawrence, Ealing Park. The resources of this cultivator are really astonishing. We can only notice such as were exhibited for the first time this season.

Coleonema rubrum, an immense plant, 4 ft. by 7 ft. *Epacris grandiflora*, a large bush in fresh condition, 6 ft. by 8 ft. *Polygala acuminata*, densely flowered, 5 ft. by 8 ft. *Leschenaultia biloba major*, 3 ft. by 2½ ft. *L. formosa*, 3 ft. by 2½ ft. *Pimelea Hendersonii*, very fresh and full of bloom, 3 ft. by 3 ft. *Chorozema ovata*; this beautiful and difficult plant was very healthy and densely bloomed: scarlet, purple, and yellow flowers; 2 ft. by 2 ft. *Sphenetoma gracilis*, a large plant covered with its heads of pure white flowers; 3 ft. by 3 ft. *Allamanda grandiflora*, a large plant with 30 flowers upon it of the most exquisite colour; 6 ft. by 5 ft. *Erica bergiana*, very finely bloomed; 3 ft. by 3 ft. *Adenandra fragrans*, a lovely plant with numerous pink flowers; 2 ft. by 2 ft. *Ixora coccinea*; 30 heads of scarlet flowers; 2½ ft. by 2½ ft.

2nd Prize to Mr. Cole, gardener to H. Collyer, Esq. This collection was much improved. Nothing but the immense size of Mrs. Lawrence's plants enabled that collection to obtain the first prize.

Allamanda Schottii; 6 ft. by 5 ft. This species is a grand improvement upon the old *A. cathartica*, the flowers being larger and finer-coloured. We had one measured, and its dimensions were 5½ in. long by 5 in. diameter. *Dipladenia crassinoda*, a fine plant with high-coloured flowers; 6 ft. by 4 ft. *Pimelea Hendersonii*; 3 ft. by 2½ ft. *Aphelexis spectabile grandiflora*; 2½ ft. by 2½ ft. *Ixora crocata*, a handsome plant, with numerous orange-coloured blossoms; 2½ ft. by 2 ft. *I. coccinea*, with large heads of scarlet flowers, very numerous; 3 ft. by 2½ ft. *Sphenotoma gracile*, very well bloomed; 3 ft. by 3 ft. *Clerodendrum paniculatum*, had two spikes, much branched, of brilliant scarlet flowers. *Pimelea decussata*, a large plant, rather fading, 6 ft. by 4 ft.

COLLECTIONS OF TWENTY STOVE AND GREENHOUSE PLANTS—NURSERYMEN.

1st Prize to Messrs. Frazer, Lea Bridge. The few we mention were placed in exchange for such as had gone out of bloom.

Rhyncospermum jasminoides, a beautiful slender climber, with heads of pure white sweet-scented flowers, very like jessamine blooms. It was trained in a pillar-like manner, and was densely covered with flowers; 5 ft. by 2 ft. *Epacris grandiflora*, a large plant; 4 ft. by 5 ft. *Chorozema varium elegans*; 2 ft. by 2 ft. *Azalea indica, var. prestantissima*; 3 ft. by 3½ ft.

2nd Prize to Messrs. Pamplin, Leyton. There were several good heaths in this collection, and

Vinca rosea, 2 ft. by 2½ ft.; *Vinca rosea alba*, of the same size.

COLLECTIONS OF FIFTEEN STOVE AND GREENHOUSE PLANTS.

1st Prize to Mr. Green, gardener to Sir E. Antrobus, Cheam. We noted as being fresh in this collection:—

Allamanda grandiflora, a large plant with numbers of fine golden yellow flowers. *Rondeletia speciosa major*, 4 ft. by 3 ft. *Erica depressa*, very dense; 2½ ft. by 2½ ft. *E. tricolor Wilsonii*; 2½ ft. by 2½ ft. *Epacris miniata*, large and freely bloomed; 3 ft. by 3½ ft. *Leschenaultia formosa*; this is a favourite plant with the exhibitors, very few of the collections being without it; indeed, it is well adapted for the purpose; 2½ ft. by 2½ ft. *Ixora coccinea*; 25 heads of its gorgeous blossoms. The same remark applies to this charming plant. 3 ft. by 2½ ft. *Aphelexis spectabilis grandiflora*, 2½ ft. by 2 ft.

2nd Prize to Mr. Gorrie, gardener to Sir J. Cathcart, Bart. The following were fine plants:—

Erica vestita albida; 4 ft. by 4 ft. *Vinca rosea* and *V. rosea alba* each 2½ ft. by 2½ ft. *Gloxinia carnea superba*, excellent, 2 ft. by 2 ft. *Erica ventricosa superba*; 2 ft. by 2 ft. *Epacris miniata*, 3 ft. by 2½ ft.

COLLECTIONS OF TEN STOVE AND GREENHOUSE PLANTS.

1st Prize to Mr. Carson, gardener to F. G. Farmer, Esq., Nonsuch Park. We noted especially

Allamanda cathartica, neatly trained, pillar-fashion. *Leschenaultia biloba superba*, covered with deep blue flowers. *L. formosa*; 2½ ft. by 2½ ft. *Sphenotoma gracile*; 2½ ft. by 3 ft. *Ixora coccinea*, with 12 large heads of flowers; 2½ ft. by 3 ft. *Polygala oppositifolia*; 2 ft. by 3 ft. *Medinilla speciosa*; this is a fine stove plant, with handsome large foliage and large racemes of pink flowers. In this instance there were 12 racemes upon the plant. 2½ ft. by 2½ ft.

2nd Prize to Mr. Taylor, gardener to J. Costar, Esq. We noted the following as being remarkable:—

Azalea indica variegata; cone-shaped, covered with bloom; 5 ft. by 3 ft. *Aphelexis spectabilis grandiflora*; 2 ft. by 2½ ft. *Erica Westphalingia*; 2½ ft. by 2½ ft. *Pavetta caffra*; a desirable plant. This had thirty heads of pure white flowers on it. *Erica Cavendishii*; 2½ ft. by 2½ ft.

There were five other prize-takers in this class, but our limits must confine us in each to a notice of the 1st and 2nd.

COLLECTIONS OF SIX STOVE AND GREENHOUSE PLANTS.

1st Prize to Mr. Kinghorn, gardener to the Earl Kilmorey, Orleans House, Twickenham. A good collection of well grown plants, especially

Erica Cavendishii; *Azalea Gledstanesii*; *Epacris grandiflora*; *Leschenaultia formosa*; and a fine bush of *Tetratheca verticillata*.

2nd Prize to Mr. May, gardener to E. Goodheart, Esq., Beckenham. The best were

Pimelea Hendersonii; 2½ ft. by 2½ ft. *Erica Cavendishii*; 3 ft. by 2½ ft. *Acrophyllum venosum*; 2 ft. by 2 ft. *Aphelexis sesamoides*; 3 ft. by 2½ ft.

COLLECTIONS OF CAPE HEATHS

Were numerous and in fine condition. This class of plants is well adapted for exhibitions, and the different societies do wisely to encourage their production.

COLLECTIONS OF TEN.

Mr. Smith, gardener to J. Quilter, Esq., of Norwood, obtained *the first prize*. We have only space to notice a few of the very best.

Erica Westphalingia; *E. Bruneoides*; *E. perspicua*; *E. Cavendishiana*; *E. vestita rosea*, and *Alba*; *E. metulæflora*; *E. suaveolens*; *E. ventricosa coccinea*; *E. Bergiana*; and *E. elegans*.

2nd Prize to Mr. Mylam, for

Erica tricolor, var. *Wilsonii*; *E. Cavendishii*; *E. ventricosa grandiflora* (Henderson's); *E. ventricosa hirsuta alba*; *E. jasminiflora*; *E. halicacaba*.

NURSERYMEN.

1st Prize to Mr. Epps, Maidstone. A very fine collection of handsome, well grown, and densely bloomed plants. The rarest and finest was a large specimen of *Erica splendens*, the best ever seen.

2nd Prize to Messrs. Rollison, of Tooting.

COLLECTIONS OF TEN, IN ELEVEN INCH POTS.

These, though small, were very beautiful plants, and profusely bloomed.

1st Prize was taken in this class also by Mr. Epps. 2nd Prize to Messrs. Rollison. 3rd Prize to Mr. Cole.

Mr. Epps exhibited three *seedling heaths* of great promise, especially one named *E. tricolor Eppeii*, a variety with large inflated tubes, deep pink half way up from the base, and the rest pure white.

COLLECTIONS OF HELICHRYSUMS, OR APHELEXISES.

1st PRIZE to Mr. Green, for

H. sesamoides ; H. humilis ; and *H. sesamoides purpurea.*

2ND PRIZE to Mr. Young, for

H. macrantha roses ; H. prolifera ; H. macrantha purpurea ; and *H. humilis grandis.*

SPECIMEN PLANTS

Were exhibited in considerable numbers, and were very creditable to the growers.

1st PRIZE to Mr. May, gardener to E. Goodheart, Esq., for

Aphelexis purpurea ; and *Erica depressa.*

2ND PRIZE to Mr. Ivison, for a handsome plant of the charming *Indigofera decora.*

NEW PLANTS.

1st PRIZE to Mr. Ivison, for

Bejaria Lindenana ; a fine pink flowered species, scarcely in bloom.

2ND PRIZE to Messrs. Garraway and May, for

Achimenes grandis ; a deep purple variety of *A. longiflora.*

(*To be continued.*)

ROYAL BOTANIC SOCIETY'S SHOW.
REGENT'S PARK, JUNE 12.

Such a number of happy faces seeking pure pleasure we never witnessed before. The exhibition was certainly the best we have seen, taking it as a whole, and, combined with the plants in the American ground, together with a rich display of fruit, afforded such a treat to the visitors as will not be easily forgotten. The exhibitors must have had great pleasure in hearing their productions so justly praised by such a numerous and respectable company. The effect will be, we have no doubt, that not only will they strain every nerve to keep the remaining exhibitions of this year up to the mark, but the display of those beautiful productions of horticulture will in 1851 be greatly in advance of all previous ones.

As by far the greater number of the plants and fruits were the same as those exhibited at Chiswick the previous Saturday, our notices of each collection will be very brief.

COLLECTIONS OF TWENTY-FIVE EXOTIC ORCHIDS.

1st PRIZE to Mr. Mylam, gardener to S. Rucker, Esq. In addition to the fine plants Mr. M. had at Chiswick we noted

Aerides odoratum ; a large plant with very many spikes of its lovely fragrant blossoms. This plant was 4 ft. high, and 3 ft. through. *Anguloa Clowesii,* with three large flowers. *Paphinia cristata ;* a rare and beautiful species ; several flowers. *Aerides Schroderii ;* a manifest improvement on *A. odoratum,* to which it is allied. *Odontoglossum Lindleyana ;* well bloomed.

2ND PRIZE to Mr. Blake, gardener to J. Schroder, Esq., Stratford. Nearly the same as were exhibited at Chiswick, yet in excellent order.

COLLECTIONS OF FIFTEEN EXOTIC ORCHIDS.

1st PRIZE to Messrs. Rollinson, Tooting. The following were not shown before :—

Acineta Barkeri, with a long spike of golden yellow flowers. *Coryanthes macrantha ;* a wonderful flower, almost impossible to describe. *Barkeria spectabilis ;* a respectable specimen.

2ND PRIZE to Mr. Franklin, gardener to Mrs. Lawrence.

Odontoglossum hastatum ; a very desirable species. *Epidendrum cistum ;* very pretty and fragrant.

COLLECTIONS OF TEN EXOTIC ORCHIDS.

1st PRIZE to Mr. Carson, gardener to L. W. Farmer, Esq., Nonsuch Park. In addition to the fine plants exhibited on the 8th, a fine plant of the lovely *Epidendrum phœniceum.*

2ND PRIZE to Mr. W. Barnes, gardener to R. Hanbury, Esq., The Poles, near Ware. We were very glad to find this veteran once more exhibiting, and we trust he will continue, for a better grower of plants does not exist. We shall notice this collection more in detail, because this is the first time for three years that Mr. Barnes has exhibited.

Cypripedium spectabile. Seldom has the lover of orchids such a treat as this plant afforded. It was in perfect health, was 1½ ft. high, and 1½ ft. through, and had 25 of its beautiful flowers fully expanded. *Saccolabium guttatum ;* a good plant, with four spikes. *Oncidium phymatochilum ;* a delicate flowered species, with numerous flowers. *O. altissimum ;* a very long spike, neatly trained. *Phalœnopsis grandiflora ;* a strong plant, with four spikes, and many flowers.

(*To be continued.*)

DESCRIPTION OF THE DOVE-COT PIGEONS.
SECOND RACE.
(*Continued from page 167.*)

MIXED PIGEON : *Pigeon Mondain ; Columba admista.*—We shall not treat here of the innumerable varieties that this race of pigeons presents, because none but the first and third are constant, and reproduce individuals like themselves. The *mixtures* owe their origin to the confusion of all races abandoned to themselves, crossed and mixed together by chance ; in consequence of which one cannot assign to this group any strong and exclusive character. All that can be said of it is, that we must connect with this section all those which do not belong to a pure or, at least, determined race. They partake of every form and every size, and their plumage, varied or uniform, may have one or several of the colours common to the pigeon. They sometimes have a filament round the eyes, but more frequently they are without it ; sometimes they are shod ; that is to say, they have feathers on the tarsus,* as far as the commencement of the claws, which are quite free from them ; sometimes their feet are naked, or without feathers. The plumage of these birds is not only without uniformity from individual to individual of the same variety, but it is not even regular on the same one ; for example, we see some with one wing white and the other black, or even half the covering shaded with one colour, whilst the other half is of another. The females resemble the males.

Although these pigeons are, in consequence of all these reasons, disdained by the amateurs, they are quite as prevalent as the other kinds ; and this is easily accounted for ; for birds that are the most valuable and of the purest races, are placed in the hands of a negligent man ; they will soon mix, lose their purity, and produce nothing but *mixtures*, which will be so much the more worthless, as they may have been produced by a greater number of crossed breeds ; for they will have some characters belonging to most of these races, without having any one in particular. In compensation for this, what they lose on the side of beauty and purity they gain with regard to fecundity ; for we know that the more the races are crossed, the more productive the mongrels are. Therefore, those who regard interest more than beauty, and above all the gourmand, esteem them highly, in consequence of the quantity of young pigeons they annually produce.

If they are kept in small numbers in a dove-cot, where each pair can occupy in turns two or three baskets, they will hatch almost every month through the year ; that is to say, they will make eight or nine nests in the year, which is the most satisfying result one can expect from any species.

The *mixtures* are not particular as to food or lodging. They subsist very well on every kind of grain with which poultry are generally fed, such as buckwheat, beans, maize, wheat or pollard, rye, and barley ; still the better they are fed the more they produce ; and I have often seen that the seed of cow-grass gives them a kind of diarrhœa, makes them cold, and causes them to lay soft eggs. They are equally content in a dove-house, a dove-cot, a stable, and a box or locker two feet square ; they will even build in a simple cage. They easily become accustomed to noise, and even to the tumult of populous places, and fear less than others shade, bad air, and unwholesome smells.

We shall only mention three varieties here, because they are constant. The first is, above all, remarkable for its figure, and also because it has been known and described by ancient authors. This first variety and the third are more delicate than the others.

4. LARGE MIXED PIGEON : *Pigeon gros Mondain ; Columba admista crassa* (White-rumped pigeon). Latham.—A red filament round the eye. Very large and heavy, sometimes attaining, says Buffon, the size of a small fowl ; but if this bird has not degenerated since the time he wrote, this is a little exaggerated. Its plumage is varied, or uniform, of every colour. It produces very little, and is not much sought after, because it has the fault of breaking its eggs, which it crushes with its weight while sitting on them to hatch.

---

* The tarsus among birds is that part of the foot generally covered with scales, which is commonly called the leg, and which commences at the end of the claws, and is articulated or joined to the heel, which is called the knee by as common an error.

5. MIDDLE-SIZED MIXED PIGEON: *Pigeon Mondain Moyen; Columba admista Media.*—Of all pigeons these are the most

common; at the present day, all the economical dove-cots, where they do not seek to possess pure races, are inhabited by them; and they, with the stock-dove, furnish the markets. We shall not give their characters, because they consist precisely in not having any; only they are smaller than the preceding, and generally larger than the following. The facts related of the generality of this race apply particularly to these. They are of every colour, with or without crests, rough-footed or not, and their numerous varieties cannot be described, because they are the produce of mixings infinitely combined. Their distinctive character can only be their size, which equals that of a pullet three months old.

6. BERLIN MIXED PIGEON: *Pigeon Mondain de Berlin; Columba admista Berolini.*—This pretty variety, brought from Prussia in 1808, has a red filament round the eyes; the plumage of a beautiful black, streaked with white, and a row of small round and white spots, like pearls, on the wing. I have seen these handsome birds in the Paris Museum of Natural History; but I do not know whether they are bred here, or whether they are very productive.

(*To be continued.*)

THE DOMESTIC PIGEON.
GENERAL HISTORY OF PIGEONS.

(*Continued from p. 166.*)

THE jealousy of pigeons, and especially of the males, is unbridled; and they occasionally beat their unfaithful females with an exasperation that is only equalled by the fury with which these defend themselves; and it is only after numerous battles that they succeed in bringing their capricious companions back to constancy. They are not only jealous of their own wives, but they are, also, so of others; and are always ready to interfere with the caresses of a strange couple whenever an opportunity offers. This is frequently followed by a struggle, in which they display a rancour very opposite to that idea of gentleness which authors are pleased to give us of their character. They are even cruel and unmerciful enough to kill the young defenceless pigeons that have, by any accident, been precipitated from their nest. It may be concluded, therefore, from what we have just said, that the gentleness, the chastity, and all those virtues that have been chimerically attributed to these animals, exist only in the brilliant descriptions given of them by some writers.

"It is easy," says Buffon, "to domesticate unwieldy birds, such as the cock, the turkey-cock, and peacock; but those that are light and that fly rapidly require more art to subdue them. A low thatched building, enclosed, is sufficient to contain and rear our poultry in, but towers and high buildings made on purpose, well plastered without and furnished with numerous cells within, are requisite to attract, retain, and lodge pigeons. They are not really either domestic, like dogs and horses, or prisoners, like hens; they are rather voluntary captives, or fugitive guests, who only remain in the lodging offered them so long as they are pleased with it, and they find therein an abundance of food, an agreeable dwelling, and all the necessary conveniences of life. Should they be displeased or want anything, they quit the place and disperse for the purpose of removing elsewhere; there are some which even prefer the deep holes in old walls to the cleanest pigeon-hole in our dove-houses; others, which dwell in clefts and the hollow parts of trees; others, again, which appear to shun our habitations, and cannot by any means be attracted to them; whilst, on the contrary, we see some which dare not leave them, and which it is necessary to feed round their pigeon-house, which they never leave." There is no bird existing whose species is so multiplied and so widely extended as the pigeon; it is found in the southern and temperate parts of the two Continents, and even in very cold climates, whither, doubtless, they have been transported. They thrive best, however, in temperate or even rather warm climates, where they increase much quicker than in cooler latitudes, and produce more valuable varieties. The dove-cot pigeons are known from the earliest antiquity; it appears that even in the time of Aristotle they had attained a high degree of perfection; since that ancient preceptor of Alexander the Great said, in his History of Animals, that these pigeons produce ten or eleven times a year, and those in Egypt as many as twelve. In the time of this philosopher, however, there were none known but those that we call at the present day the dove-cot, and none of those that now stock the large pigeon-houses. He neither distinguishes the differences between the divers domestic pigeons, nor mentions their numerous varieties, which, perhaps, at that time only existed in small numbers. The Romans, doubtless, were greater amateurs than the Greeks; for Pliny speaks of several varieties, and particularly of the great pigeons of Campanie, in Italy, for which the fanciers paid a high price. The common value of a pair of these Italian pigeons was four hundred Roman pennies, which, at the present time, would make about 60 shillings, the ordinary price of our handsome races. Others paid very considerable sums for these birds; they bestowed upon them their titles of nobility, related their origin, and reared them in towers placed on the tops of houses and palaces.

Great differences exist in the form of these birds, which would be sufficient to establish several species, if they did not produce together fruitful individuals capable of perpetuating their race. The bill varies its proportion according to the varieties; in some we see it very thick, in others very delicate, long or short; the partitions of the nostrils very thin, or covered with a thick membranous cartilaginous or fleshy protuberance. Their voice is sometimes a mournful and tender cry; with others, it resembles the sound of a drum. The noise they make with their voice is expressed by the word *cooing*; in the male, it is always more full, longer sustained, more frequent, and stronger than in the female. The ruling colour of their plumage is grey, or a greyish brown, but the domestic state has more or less altered these colours. They love to wash and roll in the dust to free themselves from parasitical insects, with which they are frequently inconvenienced. After this operation they generally dress their feathers, which they like to keep very clean. Their flight is rapid and long, especially when pursued by the sparrow-hawk, the kite (their most cruel enemy), or other birds of prey. Notwithstanding their being very quick-sighted and possessing great sensibility of hearing, and although the organs of these senses are always in a state of activity, they frequently become the victims of these voracious creatures, who employ against them both their arms and stratagem.

HINTS ON GARDENING FOR YOUNG PEOPLE.

How to get plants for your little plots.—In resuming this subject, I shall next say a few words on the subject of cuttings; these you may ask for without danger of being thought greedy, and if you succeed in striking them yourself, you will value those plants more than any you have. In the days of my youthful gardening, I and many others had an idea that only certain plants would grow by cuttings; and in my old book there was a list of such, most of which I could not obtain. The first cuttings I ever struck were some sprigs of lavender, and I still remember the pride and pleasure I felt when these sprigs struck root and actually grew. Then how I used to long for cuttings of anything that would grow; and how grateful I would have been for bits of geraniums or fuchsias, had such come in my way. Once I received a bouquet with some sprigs of heliotrope in it, I stuck them into a flower-pot, and covered them with a tumbler, and, to my great delight and surprise, three out of the five slips struck root, and I had, for the first time, the pleasure of giving away a rooted slip of my own rearing. Now-a-days, I think every plant seems to be capable of propagation by slips or cuttings; and though many require more time, skill, and pains than juvenile gardeners have to bestow, yet there are many sweet common plants you may thus propagate, and get your borders filled. Pansies root easily in a shady place without any glass over them—so will pinks; then you may make cuttings of the hardy fuchsias, of penstemons, snapdragons, and many others. The common red flowering currant strikes root almost whether you will or not, but it grows too large for little gardens, though you might amuse yourself by striking cuttings to give away. If you have the convenience of a hotbed, of course cuttings will strike root sooner and more securely; but then you must trust to the gardener, for I think few young people are aware how difficult a hotbed frame is to manage till they try, and kill all their cuttings with over-coddling. There are small frames to be got cheap, with glass on one side and zinc on the other; these shade as well as shelter the cuttings, and keep them in an equal temperature. But, I dare say, many of the young readers of THE COTTAGE GARDENER have no assistance, and can get none from either gardener or frames: well, do not despair, bring a good will to the work, and you will succeed. Choose a shady spot, shaded, if possible, by a wall rather than by trees or shrubs, dig the ground well, and rake it smooth, insert your cuttings, and gently press the earth round them; keep them moist, and do not be in a hurry to dig them up to look for roots, and I think I may promise that enough of your cuttings will take root in a few weeks to repay your trouble and rejoice your hearts. When they begin to grow at the top, you may hope all is going on well at the root; and some moist day, soon after, you may take your trowel and transplant them into your own garden; shade them for a day or two if the sun is powerful, and I hope many of you, even this autumn, may have the satisfaction of thus filling up blanks in your little plots.

As to seeds, I have spoken already of sowing annuals, but you may get some pretty additions to your stock by sowing biennials in beds, apart from your little gardens, and planting out such as you require in the places where you wish them to flower. I suppose you know that biennials do not flower the year they are sown, but the next; so you need to consult Mrs. Think-in-time in this matter; and if you want wall-flowers, stocks, snapdragons, foxgloves, and many others, you must remember to sow them this year, and wait patiently for next summer to see them flower. Those of you who have an opportunity may also get many pretty wild flowers that will transplant from the woods and fields, and grow in the garden. Wood anemones, wild hyacinths, saxifrage, primroses, and foxgloves will all transplant easily; and I do not know any excursion more delightful than setting out on a fine spring day with a basket and trowel, and bringing home a supply of wild plants for the garden.

Make a good selection of flowers.—I do not mean by this merely what I said before about having your gardens gay each month; but what I mean is to select such plants as from their size and manner of growth are suitable for small gardens. Large plants take up too much room, and also exhaust the soil round them; for instance, hollyhocks, dahlias, and flowering shrubs, though beautiful in a large garden, are too large and greedy for little plots; while low-growing plants—such as lily of the valley, and sweet-scented violets, that require to be grown in masses to have any effect—are also unsuitable. Many plants spread themselves so fast by their roots that they require to be taken up every year, and separated, but this is a pleasant part of your work; so I would not cast out all spreading flowers—by the division you get two or three plants out of one, and you have also the pleasure of planting them in a new bit of your garden, and making a variety by this means. You must remember, however, to watch plants that have this habit, both for your own sake and theirs, and check them in time, lest they encroach too much on their neighbours. Many of them run thus out of bounds to get fresh soil, when they have exhausted that near them; you will observe in these plants that the outside portions look stronger than the middle part. Mimuluses and garden Forget-me-not both grow in this way; but if you lift them in autumn, separate the roots, and replant them in a fresh place; I think you will rather prefer plants that you can thus increase to those that remain more stationary. There is a campanula, however, which has this trick of spreading so that it is a perfect nuisance, and more difficult to eradicate than even bishop's-weed, or goul-weed, as some call it. I have turned it out of my garden in vain, for its small fibres have got in among the roots of other plants; every thread of root and bit of stalk grows, and it is a perpetual work to hoe it up and weed it out.

Plant your flowers at regular intervals.—A little formality makes small gardens neat; and by placing your large plants in the back row, then smaller ones in the next, and little low-growing flowers in front, you will both see them all to more advantage and have more room. Do not plant your flowers one behind another, but let those of the second row come between the spaces of the first: thus, * * * * and keep them as nearly as possible at regular * * * * intervals.

Dress.—There is no doubt that a lady's dress is not one very well suited for gardening; all we can do to obviate its disadvantages is, we will still I fear find, that actual work in a garden does not improve its appearance. A large apron and gloves are some protection; but what I have found better is a dark skirt; this can be put on and taken off as easily as an apron: it protects the dress better and allows more freedom in kneeling on the ground or pushing through the shrubs. Gloves are indispensable; they should be made to come half way up the arm, so as to protect the sleeves and to prevent the earth getting in at the wrist. I believe these gauntlets are used as riding gloves for ladies; the kind I have are what used to be called York tan, and I got a glover to affix gauntlets to them. The advantage of this is, that as the glove, especially the right hand one, wears out before the upper part, you can renew the glove at a trifling expense, and sew it yourself to the gauntlet. I have seen ladies make gauntlets of strong unbleached linen fastened to the glove; this is quite as effectual for protecting the dress and for preventing that sun-burning of the wrist which is the frequent fate of lady gardeners. A shawl is perfectly inadmissible as gardening costume; but a polka jacket is convenient when the weather does not admit of your going out without any additional wrappings. I may also give a hint, that when a polka jacket is worn and work is to be done, it is a good plan to open a few hooks of the gown behind, unless my readers are very fond of sewing hooks and eyes daily on their dresses.

Give, if possible, daily attention to your garden.—I am aware that while young people have their studies to attend to, the time allotted for amusement and recreation cannot always be devoted to the garden; but even as a recreation, gardening requires regular attention; and, indeed, I believe most who have tried it as such, find the danger of its becoming too absorbing a pursuit, and encroaching on the time devoted to higher duties. I dare say you have all read of gardens that never had a weed to be seen in them, because the owner went round every morning and pulled them up as fast as they appeared. This sounds well, but I doubt its practicability. There are often weeks of fine weather when the borders, if once hoed and raked, remain neat and free of weeds; but let a wet day or two come, and on revisiting your garden it looks as if it had been sown over with little green leaves; and how are you to get them pulled up during a morning's walk? Still, daily attention will do much; it will prevent work accumulating on your hand till you know not what to begin first, whether weeding, or transplanting, or tying up; and then you put off doing anything till you have time for a good day's work; and if you have, as you ought to have, other and more important duties to attend to than your gardens, a good day's work in them is an enjoyment not easily attained. Try, therefore, to do a little every day, and be very particular about neatness and order in your little domain, remembering that whatever is worth doing at all is worth doing well. Finally, my young friends, never forget that you have work of a higher kind assigned you by the Lord of the vineyard, even to labour to keep your souls as a well watered garden, where no sins are willingly permitted to grow, and where He has promised to bestow the aids of His Spirit as showers and dew upon the tender herb, to enable you to bring forth much fruit to His glory!—HORTENSE.

[You must not say, finally, "good bye" to us! We, and our readers, have derived too much gratification from your hints for us not to request that you will very soon greet us again.—ED. C. G.]

ENGLISH CAGE BIRDS.
THE BLACKCAP WARBLER.
INSESSORES DENTIROSTRES. SYLVIADÆ INSECTIVORA. *Sylvia Atricapilla ; Curruca Atracapilla* (Blackcap, Black-capped Fauvet) ; *Motacilla Atricapilla.*

This bird ranks next to the nightingale in song, and, like the nightingale, the males arrive here first. They are easily distinguished by their jet black head, for that of the female is of a chestnut brown. These birds are more hardy than the nightingale, and less insectivorous, for they feed largely on our summer fruits, as witness our currant-bushes and raspberries. On its first arrival the blackcap betakes itself to the ivy, where, securely hidden from observation, it obtains its food from the ivy-berries; and when satiated, pours forth its loud and melodious strains continually. It is often mistaken for the blackbird, so loud are its notes. It is an extremely shy bird, and very difficult to catch. Its capability of enduring cold is shewn by the fact of my having had one of these birds, and a lesser whitethroat, in my large aviary, having a northern aspect, but surrounded by buildings (and thus far protected), during that most rigorous winter, 1837-38, in which the thermometer stood at 18 degrees, as on reference to my diary I find it so noted on the 20th January, 1838. If the bird be fresh caught, it should be placed in a cage, and covered over for a day or two, in order that it may be sooner reconciled to captivity, and supplied with the berries of ivy, or hempseed, or fruit, such as currants, or even grocer's currants that have been rendered plump by placing them for some time in hot water, and of course with water. Owing to the difficulty of procuring the old birds, I have generally resorted to the expedient of rearing them from the nest, which I have done successfully by feeding them on the paste of bread and milk, and hempseed crushed, and well mixed together, adding now and then an insect of some kind, and fruit, such as strawberries, raspberries, or currants. When able to feed themselves, they have fed on the nightingale's food already described, and have thriven exceedingly well; I will, nevertheless, give you the Rev. W. Cornish's method as well as my own. He says, "My next favourite of the summer birds is the Atricapilla, being the healthiest and most lively of all the tribe, and their song most sprightly. I have six of them—three I have had for eight or nine years in perfect health and song. To these birds I give a small portion of beef and egg—say one-third ; the remainder, bread, egg, and hempseed, chopped up together. The other tin drawer is filled every day with German paste, of which they are very fond. I had almost forgotten (he says) that the garden warbler and the blackcap *must have* every day a little fruit—it is indispensably necessary for their health ; a small bit of soft apple, or of baked apple, and in the fruit season a few *red* currants, raspberries, strawberries, or a little of any nice ripe fruit. They must have it, or pine for it and droop : *no song without it.* I captured them in a net that covered my red currants, stealing my fruit, about three autumn's since. I mention this time because it is the best season of the year for capturing them, when they have done moulting, and submit to captivity most readily. Their food should be the fruit they have been purloining, put into a drawer with moistened bread, egg, sugar and milk. In taking out the fruit they find the other food palatable. A few very thin bits of raw beef put in with the other meat would reconcile them to their new situation. I captured three blackcaps by this method. The currant-bush, or bushes, should be perfectly covered, leaving an aperture at one end of the net. The birds always fly to the opposite end to which they entered. This part of the net should have a hole, which must be kept tied up till you find some captive in it. Now tie up the hole by which the birds entered, and open the other end and take your birds. There is no cruelty in this mode, as the little pilferers are luxuriating on your fruit all the time they are within it."

I shall conclude this paper with a receipt for the *German paste,* which is made as follows : 1 lb. of wheaten meal, 2 oz. of fresh butter, 4 oz. of brown sugar, 3 hard-boiled eggs cut up very small. Put the meal, butter, eggs, and sugar into a wide saucepan, over a clear slow fire, and keep stirring it to prevent its burning, and when it becomes dry keep stirring it till it becomes crumbly. When this is ready (N.B., it must not be *burnt,* as this would be injurious to the birds) put a pint of cracked hempseed to the mixture, and mix them well together. While the process of baking is going on a penny-worth of saffron must be added to it, and mixed with the rest. If kept in a dry place it will be good for months.—W. RAYNER.

[The song of the blackcap is a compound of the robin and thrush, but softer, more mellow, and more modulated than that of the latter, and of more compass than that of the robin. It arrives in England early in April. It is rather more than six inches long, and nine inches and a quarter across the wings when opened out. The male has its upper parts light yellowish-grey, the head black, lower parts ash-grey, paler behind, and tinged with yellow; wings and tail greyish-brown. Female similar, but with head reddish-brown. Its nest is built in the fork of some shrub, and formed of dried stalks, usually goose grass, put together with a little wool, and sometimes a little green moss on the outside ; the inside is lined with fibrous roots, and over them sometimes a few long hairs. The eggs, four or five, are very broad oval, 8½ twelfths of an inch long, and 7 twelfths broad, greyish-white faintly mottled and freckled with purplish-grey, and a few streaks of blackish-brown (*Macgillivray's British Birds*). No one can refrain from admiring the rich melody of the blackcap's song, and it is one of our most frequently heard birds, for its chief places of resort are our orchards and gardens. It is one of the few birds which seem to have to make a violent effort in giving utterance to their song, and during this effort the throat is very largely distended. In Cambridgeshire, Mr. Jenyns says, that this bird's note is usually first heard about April 16th, that its eggs are first found about May 19th, and that its song ceases about the 27th of July. It is one of the most shy of birds, yet it feeds with such delight, and with an appetite so insatiable, upon the currant and raspberry, that when engaged on this banquet it suffers itself to be looked at, and forgets for the moment its usual timidity. It finishes its feast here with the Jargonelle and other early autumn pears, and then leaves us for other fruits and milder climes.—*Journal of Naturalist.*]

THE MUSCAT OF ALEXANDRIA VINE.

As many inquiries have been made concerning this inestimable grape, we will offer the chief information we possess relative to its management ; and in order to throw light on the subject, it will be well, as a preliminary, to observe, that amongst the several difficulties which beset its culture that of getting it to answer in a house containing other kinds stands prominent. It is well-known, also, that it is what is termed "a shy setter;" that is to say, the impregnation of the blossom by means of the fertilizing pollen is very uncertain under our present course of culture.

By some it is considered a shy bearer: this, we think, arises from the circumstances of its enormous size and highly concentrated flavour.

With regard to its shy setting, opinions differ much as to the *real* cause. Most of our best gardeners insist that it requires a very high and very moist temperature ; and, indeed, past experience would seem to confirm the opinion, or else why should it be found so difficult to succeed with in houses of a mixed character, especially if plant-houses? which, of course, are much more moderate in point of temperature than our stoves.

An opinion prevailed, some years since, that all our grapes required this close kind of treatment when in blossom; and Mr. Paxton (if we remember right) was the first to attempt to show, that if the practice was right in principle it was carried to an undue extreme. In casting our eyes over the vegetable kingdom generally, we find plants so constituted that by nature the pollen or male dust of the anthers can only be rendered capable of impregnation through the medium of heat, combined with a comparative *absence* of moisture. As with all rules, numerous exceptions may be expected to occur; our climate varying so exceedingly as to the relation which the amount of atmospheric moisture bears to the heat, and both of these, it may be added, to the intensity of light.

On a close examination of the blossom-bud of the vine, especially of the Muscat, it will be found that the organs of fruitfulness are encased in a sort of vegetable coat of mail. Now, this coating has a peculiar mechanical construction, and has also important functions to perform; and some vigour of constitution, combined with a favourable state of atmosphere, is necessary to cause it to expand freely. Now, however correct Mr. Paxton's idea might be as to vines in general, it is tolerably certain that an exception must be made in the case of the Muscat of Alexandria vine. We believe that for this a much greater amount of atmospheric moisture is necessary than gardeners commonly imagine. We are the more confirmed in this opinion from the fact, that early forced Muscats, or at least those in forcing houses possessing tan-pits, have, in general, been found to "set" better than those in the *ordinary* vinery. Now, it does not require much argument to prove that a very great amount of atmospheric moisture is present at all times under such circumstances, yet there is no doubt that the amount far exceeds what is usually believed, especially when the houses are closed. We know a respectable gardener, now retired from business (and who sits by us whilst we write), who has been a most successful grower of the Muscat, and whose practice was to encourage a vast amount of atmospheric moisture, so much so, that he affirms that he has had his houses in the month of January or February actually suffused with steam during bright periods. We, therefore, have no doubt that a deficiency of atmospheric moisture is one of the principal causes of the bad setting of the Muscat grape. At the same time it is necessary to observe, that a considerable amount of *heat* is necessary for this vine; and by this we do not mean any absolute amount, but that the Muscat requires more heat than our ordinary grapes. To state any specific amount would be both unnecessary and impossible, as it is a relative affair; but we should say that 65 degrees, or nearly so, is requisite at an early period—say in January; and that as much as 80 degrees may be indulged in during the months of April and May. In our opinion, one most material point in Muscat culture, and to which we would beg to draw attention, is the amount of foliage necessary to the well-being of the Muscat. There are those who will persist in as close a stopping of this prince of grapes as of our ordinary and smaller kinds; this we think exceedingly wrong.

Whoever studies the general character of this vine will see that nature never intended it for a dwarf. There is something gigantic and princely in its very growth—something which seems to indicate a desire to receive little assistance from the hand of man. Indeed, when we take into consideration the immense size and the splendid flavour of this noble berry, it becomes obvious that nothing but the most perfect elaboration (accomplished by an ample amount of surface in the perspiratory organs) can render the Muscat what it is capable of being made—the finest grape in the world. There can be no doubt, therefore, that what is termed "close stopping" is unfriendly to this vine; and it is totally inexpedient to resort to extreme measures as to stopping; in fact, we say encourage all the foliage you possibly can find room for.

How often have we heard gardeners of small experience remark, that their Muscats would not bear equally well every year. And why? Three parts of their vine borders are made on false principles; and where there is not a powerful and safe root action it is vain to expect crops of this grape. To those who are thus situated we would say, be sure and exercise great moderation as to the amount of the crop. If you *will* have a heavy crop under such circumstances, be assured that it will be at the expense of the next year's success. In such an event, the best way is to allow the tree to make a vast quantity of extra wood during the resting year, if such must be. By these means a considerable amount of fresh fibres will be created in the borders, and these will tend to a renovation of the constitution of the tree. We feel that we have by no means exhausted the subject, and must recur to it again at some future opportunity.—R. ERRINGTON.

HISTORY OF AN APIARY.

(Continued from page 165.)

You will have a very bad opinion of me, if you suppose that the ill success of my first bee experiments in the least degree damped my ardour as an apiarian. On the contrary, I was prepared to renew those very experiments another year, though doubtless in a different manner; and I have since repeated them with much success. At all events, the year 1845 saw me no longer a novice in bee matters. I had served an active apprenticeship, and had gained no inconsiderable amount of experience, especially as to the *rationale* and best manner of performing the very useful operation of *driving*, without understanding which a bee-master cannot be said to have *command* of his apiary. Moreover, I had a tolerably accurate and particular acquaintance with every part of the economy of bees, derived from a diligent perusal, or rather *study*, of a great variety of bee-books. Still I had much to learn, and many disappointments to undergo; for the climate of this country is, I should say, about the most unfavourable of all climates for bee cultivation, and to this must be attributed the comparatively little progress which it is notorious has been made in this branch of rural economy. It is no easy matter to become a successful bee-keeper in England. Mr. Taylor, in his preface to his very useful book, has well styled the tyro aparian's path "usually a rough and uncertain one," so rough, indeed, and uncertain, that three out of every five persons who take this study up, even warmly, will be found generally to relinquish it with disgust at the end of a few years. The causes of failure are usually an insufficient beginning (I mean, starting with only *one* stock), want of enthusiasm or perseverance, negligence or ignorance of the fundamental rules of the science. While in America or Australia* it is almost incredible of how large an apiary *one hive* may become the original in a very few years; in England a similar hive may stand year after year without change, apparently strong, and yet unprolific in both swarms and honey. A stock at the time of purchase may have a three or four-year-old queen, who dies some time in our long winter, before there is brood wherewith to replace her; the winter may be mild, and the spring cold and late, and no honey gathered till the end of May—such was the case this year, for instance, in our neighbourhood at least (Herefordshire), and many stocks have perished in consequence, or are spoilt for the current season—a rainy summer may follow, or a very dry one, neither of which afford much honey; in short, there are a thousand casualties to be feared with which the more fortunate bee keeper of other countries is unacquainted, but which tend to dishearten the English cottager. To be a successful apiarian it is necessary to have sufficient knowledge of bee matters to be able to meet all those difficulties; it is requisite to be initiated thoroughly into the mysteries of judicious feeding, and to understand somewhat of that improved system of bee-keeping by which the great honey harvests are secured at those favoured but rare seasons when they occur, and the most is made of indifferent years; while, at the same time, the acquisitive propensity is held in check, so that if *much* is taken as legitimate spoil, there is yet *enough left* to support the prosperity of the hive. Difficult, however, as unquestionably is the science of bee-keeping, it is not beyond the reach of persevering attention, and the very difficulties only serve to enhance the pleasure and gratification of the bee-master. I think it is Mr. Payne

* In a late work on New South Wales, whose title I have forgotten, I read the following astonishing account of the increase of a stock of bees: "In the district Illawara, near Sydney, one hive has been known to have multiplied to 300!! in the course of three years!"

who somewhere very justly observes, that " no one who pays a fair amount of attention to the management of these very interesting insects, will willingly relinquish the keeping of them." Due attention, and a fair degree of intelligence and perseverance, is sure to succeed. It is only indifference, neglect, or ignorance which finds the difficulties which have been enumerated insurmountable; and it deserves to do so. Now, is any *intending* bee-master a reader of this paper? I would urge him, *very strongly*, not to grudge a little expense at the outset, but to stock his garden with, at the very least, *two strong* hives—*Experto crede.* My own apiary was at a standstill during four entire years, because I had only one stock to begin with. Had I purchased *two* hives instead of only one, I might now have many more, and much more interesting details to bring forward than are actually at my command. By laying a good foundation to the apiary, there will be so many more chances of success, neither will the loss or failure of one hive cause much distress while another thrives *ad libitum.*

I must pass over briefly the four years succeeding the year 1844, lest I be tedious to the reader, as my note-book is almost barren of interest touching that period. In March, 1845, another hive was bought from the stock of a long established bee-keeper in the place, who always kept on hand a large winter stock, though destroying them according to the old plan. There was much activity apparent in my new colony; pollen gathering went on well, and the population rapidly increased, so that there appeared every reasonable probability of strong and early swarms. Due preparation was made accordingly; a set of boxes, not unlike Mr. Taylor's improved White's hive, was constructed in good time, at considerable expense, and other hives of straw were in readiness, but April passed, May and June slipped by, and July came, and yet no swarm, though masses of bees depended for weeks together from beneath the floor-board. Provoking and vexatious as was this disappointment, there was no remedy. A general break-up of our family party at the beginning of July, and a continental tour of three months, saved me, perhaps, from despairing of success. A probable cause of my disappointment was, doubtless, the very unfavourable summer of that year; for so carefully did we watch, that I am persuaded the swarms did not escape us.

During my tour, I kept my bee eyes open; but I saw no hives either in Belgium or Germany, as we travelled rapidly from place to place without seeing much of those countries, till we settled down in a charming retreat in the heart of the Black Forest. No sooner, however, did I enter Switzerland, than they abounded everywhere. It was not uncommon to see 20 or 30, or even 40, hives ranged systematically on shelves against the walls of the picturesque cottages. Honey, too, presented itself at every breakfast and tea-table; a regular item in the bill of fare, as every traveller knows. I much regret that I did not make enquiries as to their method of bee management. The fellow-countrymen of Gelica and Madame Vicat ought to be able to instruct a stranger; but my stay was short, and my visit hurried, in that interesting country. A COUNTRY CURATE.

SALTPETRE AND CUBIC-PETRE AS MANURES.

I HAVE not observed that any one of your coadjutors or correspondents has recommended the use of a manure which, in this part of the country, and, I believe, in many other districts, is used extensively and beneficially in agriculture, especially upon those soils which are commonly called " hot soils :" I mean saltpetre (nitrate of potash), or another salt, which seems to be equally efficacious, and which is much cheaper, namely cubic-petre (nitrate of soda). I am not a farmer, but I can from experience bear witness to the good effect which either of these salts produces upon many garden crops.

The soil of my garden is rather gravelly, and therefore rather hot, but not very poor; the adjoining land, which is of the same quality, produces, when fairly cultivated, about three quarters and a half of wheat per acre, and usually about five quarters of barley, and good crops both of clover and turnips. Some of my garden crops are also very good, especially peas, beans, French beans, both dwarf and runners, carrots, parsnips, and spinach, brocoli, &c.; cauliflower, and other plants of the cabbage tribe, are good, but do not grow very large, especially in a dry season. Potatoes, before they were infected by the mysterious disease which has attacked them for the last five or six years, were in general of a good quality, and by no means deficient in quantity; and the early varieties are still pretty good. Endive grows to a very large size, though in order to check its luxuriance I use no manure for that crop; many of the plants are, I think, not much less than eighteen inches, or perhaps two feet, in diameter. But to some crops the soil of my garden is not favourable; strawberries, especially, do not grow luxuriantly, and produce but little fruit; other plants run to seed prematurely, for instance, lettuces and celery. Now, either saltpetre or nitrate of soda appear to mitigate, if not entirely to correct, this defect. They seem to promote the growth of the leaves of plants, and to check the growth of the flower-stems. They may, in my opinion, be applied with advantage, at least on hot soils, perhaps upon all soils, to crops of *lettuce, celery, spinach, brocoli, cauliflower,* and other crops of the *cabbage* tribe, and I think to any other plants which do not grow so luxuriantly as they should do. Above all, either of these salts seems to be most beneficial to *onions.* And I will add, that till I used saltpetre, my *radishes* were hardly fit to eat,—they were tough and hot; but since I have used it they have been mild and brittle, or (to use a common expression), they have " eaten short." I cannot say that I have been altogether able to overcome the propensity which lettuce and celery have, on my soil, to run to seed; but, perhaps, this evil might be removed by a more liberal use of the salt. I believe I might safely use it more freely than I have done hitherto. I understand that the farmers use a hundredweight upon an acre, and I believe they apply that quantity twice in the season. I also usually give my crops two doses, each of half an ounce to a square yard. I administer the first dose when the plants, either springing from seed or after being transplanted, have begun to grow rather rapidly : for instance, in the case of radishes, when they have formed two or three rough leaves. That the salt may be scattered evenly over the beds, I mix it with a good quantity of sand or very dry mould.

I saw in one of your late numbers that one of your correspondents wishes to obtain the seeds of *Melilotus leucantha:* if that is the plant commonly known by the name of Bockham clover, as I suppose it is, I shall perhaps be able to supply him with a few seeds, as I have two or three plants. If he wants it for agricultural purposes, I fear it will not be of much use to him. It has been tried in this neighbourhood, and has not been found to answer. If it is suffered to blossom, the stalks are as hard as sticks; and even when it is cut before the flower-stalk begins to grow the cattle do not like it; I believe some absolutely reject it.—REV. EDWARD SIMONS, *Ovington, Watton, Norfolk.*

HEATING BY FLUES.

HAVING, at pp. 282 and 313, of vol. 3, explained my views regarding the heating of plant and other houses by hot-water pipes, I now take up that much despised yet ever useful *smoke flue,* the merits of which are too often forgotten when we listen to the appeal of the advocates of hot water, independent of the still more recent yet nearly defunct Polmaise system; so that, while we have every novelty which ingenuity can devise in the way of attracting attention to the two latter plans, the poor old flue scarce finds a friend. If we go into an old structure and admire the productions there displayed, and inquire how the house is heated, we are told it is only a flue; an emphasis resting on the word " only;" as if the merits of the various good things there seen so early, was due to other causes, or rather in spite of the means employed. Now how does this happen? Is heat abstracted from a substance of hard-baked clay, as flue-covers generally are, less genial to vegetation than that arising from cast iron, presuming the amount in both cases to be alike? I confess I cannot see in what way the mild moist heat we are told hot-water pipes afford, can differ from the heat that would be dissipated were those pipes filled with hot smoke instead of hot water—the close air-

and-water-tight joints not allowing any escape; and if we had the same amount of heat, I cannot see where it would differ in its component parts from heat derived from confined water, inasmuch as both substances are alike shut out from access to the atmosphere of the house, that we must look to other causes for the difference which exists.

In the first place, smoke is seldom honoured with a cast-iron pipe to travel its rounds in, neither is it necessary that it should be so, when a cheaper material can be had. The only place where I did see it in use, seemingly acted no better than an ordinary brick flue; and as its great expense will ever prevent its being generally adopted, I will, in the present chapter, endeavour to compare the merits of a good ordinary smoke flue with that of a well-arranged boiler and pipes, and make such remarks as a long course of experience has placed within my reach; so as to enable the amateur, about building a greenhouse or a grapery, to judge for himself which of the two systems will most likely suit him. I put Polmaise out of the question, because it seems abandoned by all but those who committed themselves so much by lauding it, as to be unwilling to retract their opinion.

Before comparing the two competing systems, it may be better to say a few words on smoke flues, as disappointment sometimes arises from them; but very little need be said. Generally, circumstances over which we have no control fixes the place where the stoke-hole is to be. When a choice exists, let it be as much as possible exposed to the open air. The best acting fires I ever had of that description had no shed or roof over them, and, by the nature of the plan, were not at all sunk below the surface; but it is generally necessary to sink the fire hole, that the smoke in its course may first ascend a little, otherwise travel on a level. It is very unwilling to dip downward on its first formation, but after once entering the flue and travelling some distance it may be made to descend then very well, only such descent had better be gradual and not in sudden perpendicular falls. There are many cases, as the crossing of a door-way, when it is necessary to sink the flue. In that case let it be done gradually as an inclined plane; and be not satisfied by making the bottom of the flue in that way, but let the top, or cover, be made so likewise, because smoke invariably floats on the top or upper side of the flue, and I think but seldom expels the whole of the atmospheric air over which it rolls. Now, as such is the case, a sudden obstruction, as a mass of descending brick-work, offers exactly the same impediment to its onward course that a mill-dam does to that of a river, save that the latter is irresistible; but the accumulation in both cases is the same, and in the case of the flue offers a powerful check to the impetus which directs it forward. Therefore, smooth it off; and if the appearance requires it to assume a perpendicular fall, let that be done by building upon the flue so made the required height. It will so much certainly impair its efficiency by burying the heat, but if every other circumstance be favourable, little loss will be felt.

For the same reasons as above let all the corners or turns be rounded, so that every facility be made for the quick circulation of that heated air we so often call smoke; and when it has travelled its rounds let it have a few feet of upright chimney through which to make its final escape.

In the erection of a flue use the best bricks. The end nearest the fire of the side-walls of the flue ought to be half brick thick, that is, 4½ inch work; the remainder may be brick on edge, and only those near the fire need be fire-bricks; the covers also near the fire ought to be of that material. Cement, or what bricklayers call "compo," ought not to be used. It does not stand the fire well. A flue, about 9 inches wide inside by about 12 inches deep, will be ample size for most purposes, and

one much less than that will not be found to answer well long. I may as well add, that flues of all kinds ought to stand above the level of the ground-work of the house, and not be buried under the walk, as is too often the case. Of course, many circumstances place its direction in a certain way inevitable; but when a choice can be made let it be as much as possible exposed, only not so as to endanger its taking harm from its improper use as a stand for plants, without duly guarding it by a trellised shelf resting on iron bearers, or such like.

Amongst the many supposed advantages hot-water pipes has over a flue, the consumption of fuel is one; yet the difference is often over-stated. I do not deny but that a well constructed hot-water apparatus will heat a given space with less fuel than a flue will do under some circumstances, but there are cases again the reverse,— where a large old house, indifferently glazed, is heated with hot water, it will be found almost impossible to maintain a forcing heat, unless there be a great number of pipes employed: the reason is obvious. Water will not heat beyond the boiling point, 212°, it passing then off as vapour; now a flue may be heated much beyond that, but such cases are of rare occurrence, and I only refer to an extreme case to illustrate my views, that unless an ample provision of pipes be made a flue is safer in a severe frosty night.

That flues use more fuel in a general way I at once admit, and having had a considerable share of experience in the management of both plans, I should say that such difference may amount to one-half; it is not very easy to make calculations of that kind with any degree of accuracy, but certainly it does not exceed that; the amount of labour and attention is certainly much less on the side of the flue than on that of those fantastic contrivances of boilers, but on well constructed apparatuses the attention is about alike.

In regard to the quality of the heat evolved, there is much difference of opinion; certainly where a flue has been long out of use, a disagreeable smell arises when the fire is first lighted, doubtless as offensive to ourselves; but it is soon all right again, and if one or two ventilators be thrown open, the place is soon sweet. The reason of such a rank smell is the dissipation of those vaporous gases which are generated by heat applied to the damp brick-work; that hot water pipes are free from that evil is certainly a point in their favour, yet it must not be valued too highly.

Acknowledging the above two points to be in favour of hot water, let us examine the claims of the flue, and, the first thing, compare the respective cost of the two; and I am certainly within the mark when I say, that the flue will not cost more than one-tenth or one-twelfth of the other system, and that is a very important matter. It is of no use being told you will save it all in the end by the less fuel wanted; I have known an apparatus of that kind cost as much as would have built a flue, and supplied it with coal for twenty years; and that was not an unusual case. If the amateur be building a small house, and decide on having pipes, &c., he may rest assured the heating apparatus will cost him as much as the house altogether (provided there be no architectural ornaments, &c., about it); and if he be building two moderate-sized ones, the cost of boiler, &c., being less, will probably be about two-thirds of the expense of the whole of the work. I mention these matters because I know many people forget the expense of heating when they take the building matter in hand. Now, suppose a greenhouse was wanted, 30ft. by 15ft., and about 12ft. high, let us say that such a house cost £80, now it would seem foolish to throw away £60 or £70 more in an apparatus to heat it the few times that it might be wanted in winter to keep the frost out, when the same purpose could be effected by £5, or, at the most, £8;

the after-labour, &c., being quite as much in the hot water case as the other, and much more so if any of those whimsical contrivances, miscalled boilers, be attached, that the after-attendance of flue-fires need not create any alarm.

In respect to the dry heat arising from a flue, I have never felt any inconvenience from it, because that can be rendered as moist as that from the pipes, perhaps more so; a few pans of water set on the covers, or if the latter be scooped out in the making so as to hold water, which I have seen some times done, every purpose of a moist heat is served. And in regard to a flue retaining its heat during the night, I have no hesitation in saying, a well-contrived one will do so quite as well as the best hot-water apparatus. I well remember in my younger days keeping a grape-house in the early spring months up to 70° by a flue, yet never attended it after nine at night, or before six in the morning, and very rarely was the thermometer more than one degree below or above the fixed point; of course, practice only teaches the way of such things—merely looking on and giving directions will not do—nothing else than using the shovel and coal-rake can convey a good idea of the care or trouble of these matters. But gardening now-a-days does not require such exact working of a thermometer, in fact that instrument may be safely dispensed with, except for experimental purposes. Now, although I have had some tolerably good working hot-water affairs under my hand, I could never ensure such a uniform continuance of heat; yet it is fair to say, that no inconvenience arises from a slight fall towards morning, provided it be not too much.

From the above it will be seen, that for all structures where heat is required no further than to exclude frost, a flue is all that is wanted, provided the interior arrangements offer no impediments in the way; and likewise for a great many forcing purposes a flue will be found as useful as the other; but where bottom-heat is required for Hamiltonian pine pits, and such like, I question whether a flue would be found to answer; and where a course of pits are in regular working the whole year, pipes might then be most advisable; but for any solitary house or pit, I think a flue would serve all purposes wanted; even in vineries or houses expressly used for forcing grapes, I have found flues act quite as well as pipes, more especially if assisted by a large body of fermenting material inside.

In conclusion, let me warn the amateur, whichever method he adopt, to take care to have the furnace large enough; more than half the failures of the boiler contrivances are by making so small a place for firing, just as if combustion would go on in such a Lilliputian scale; also let the ash box be capacious; there is no need for a door then; they are seldom used, and are only in the way of cleaning out, &c., and any tendency the fire may have of burning too quickly away is easily remedied by thrusting the hot fire near the throat of the flue at making-up time, and placing the coal or coke behind it, i. e., nearer the door; a few ashes between, or over all, likewise checks combustion, but these matters will soon show themselves to the stoker, whose trade, like all handicrafts, can only be learned by himself using the tools.　　　　　　　　　　　　　　S. N. V.

EXTRACTS FROM CORRESPONDENCE.

Tobacco Fumigation.—Permit me to submit the following plan for fumigating plants, which may be found useful from its economy:—Take the nozzle of the waterpot, put an ounce of tobacco and two or three ignited fuzees, or red hot cinders, into it. Insert the tube of the kitchen bellows, filling up the space between the tube of the nozzles of waterpot and bellows with rag, and blow gently; the smoke comes out freely. One

objection is, you get a good quantity of smoke over your own clothes. I have tried this and found it answer.—E. P.

Fishes Drinking Salt Water.—It may not be an absurd question to inquire, if fishes drink sea or salt water? Some may say, what else can they drink but the water in which they swim? Plausible as this sounds, the experiments of Sir E. Home, and the trite expression, that "sea fishes are fresh," tend to show they do not drink salt water, or if they do it is changed by a process which cannot be explained. I think, however, that Mudie, copying from the great anatomist referred to, mentions that the salt water is converted into fresh as it passes through the gills of fishes before it is drunk. If such be the case it is really curious, for I believe there are no means yet discovered to convert salt water into fresh except by evaporation. But it is very natural to allege, that sea water enters into the stomachs of fishes when they are in the act of swallowing their food, if so, it must be in very small quantities, for their inside is as fresh as their outer bodies or skins That these are not salt is beyond doubt, but the reason why they are so is very wonderful. It is, however, surmised, that fishes do not drink nor even swallow water, but that it all passes out at their gills without entering their stomachs. Be that as it may, I content myself with observing, that perhaps all sorts of sea animals have the power of repelling salt, if I may so express myself, in a similar way as the feathers and felt of water-fowls do water. Perhaps the slimy matter on fishes serves the same purpose; and it may be owing to the difference in this singular property that fresh water fishes die instantly in salt water, and the same happen to sea fishes in fresh water.

Professor Forbes, in his very interesting account of star-fishes, states, they die instantly when dropped into cold fresh water; but, perchance, the same result would be obtained if they were put into fresh water of the same temperature as the water at the bottom of the sea.

The fact of some kind of sea fishes living part of the season in rivers, &c., is not fatal to what I have said; for these take good care not to enter fresh water suddenly, but linger a while at the mouths of rivers in brackish water, in order to prepare their bodies for the fresh climate; and the like happens on their return to the sea. Although hardly connected with this subject, I may remark, that all sorts of sea weeds are salt; and, perhaps, so would be a live trout or pike if dipped into the sea, but not a living herring. But I question how it would be with the herring if dead a while. It has occurred to me, if fishes have the power to convert salt water into fresh as hinted at, it may be worth inquiring if seals and all other air-breathing animals drink salt water? Those who have kept tame seals can easily tell what sort of water they drank. The best account I know of one of those sea-dogs is that which was kept by a party in a fort on the small isle of Garvie, in the Firth of Forth. It was not only tame, but would follow its master's boat to Leith Harbour, and back a again, a distance, perhaps, of six or seven miles. This most singular trait in the character of the seal has nothing to do, of course, with what we are told concerning seals following boats, attracted by music in them. That such is the case there seems little doubt; at least, I have seen seals, near the place referred to, pop their heads above water, apparently to listen to the blithesome sound from the sharpening of my scythe on a fine summer morning.— J. Wighton.

Parrot Losing its Feathers.—Although I am unable from experience to recommend any outward application, yet from having long and successfully managed one of the more tender paroquets, I would suggest that the bird in question is suffering from a heated and over stimulated state of the blood, which of course acts upon the skin, as our hair is apt to fall off after fever or inflammatory attacks. In a state of nature the parrot tribe live on fruits, seeds, and grain; it must, therefore, be a great mistake to give them meat, or chicken bones to pick, as I have seen them permitted to do. I have had my king paroquet five years from the time of his first moulting; and his diet has been constantly hemp-seeds in fresh bread and milk—his tin being scalded every morning. If his bread be crusty, or not sufficiently soaked, he evinces his displeasure by throwing it beyond the bars of the cage, the floor of which is daily strewed with coarse sand. This is most important, as, like the common fowl, parrots require the assistance of some hard matter in the digestion of their food. They should also frequently be furnished with the means of bathing: in cold weather the chill must be taken off. I open the cage door frequently, and allow its inhabitant to fly about the room for some minutes, after which he gravely marches in again, seemingly well contented with his exercise. He has also an iron wire swing within the cage, the motions of which he well knows how to accelerate or retard by the rising and falling of his feet. In winter nights we cover him carefully, and place him near the fireplace; if he appear shivering and dull I mix up a little sugar with a broken peppercorn, and force him to take about half the corn in twice as much sugar. His beauty is remarkable, and his health, even when moulting, excellent. Peas in the pod, apples, gooseberries, cherries, and strawberries, are very wholesome to refresh and cool the birds. The enclosed feather will prove how healthy mine is, as, though it is a cast one from his yearly moult, it is as clean and vigorous as a new one.—A LOVER OF THE BRUTE CREATION.

TO CLEANSE THE ROOTS OF THE HAIR, AND PREVENT ITS FALLING.—Take a cup of salad oil, (a small teacup), and put it in a Bain Marie over the fire; add to it the size of a walnut of bees-wax, and when quite melted and mixed take it off the fire. As it cools, stir in a little bergamot, or any other perfume. The wax of the honeycombs without any preparation is the best, as a little honey is beneficial.

ON PROPAGATING FLOWERS OF DIFFERENT COLOURS.— Reading lately an article on Chinese gardening, it is there stated, that "some join two slips of different colours, in each of which, towards the bottom, they make a long notch, almost to the pith, and afterwards tie them together with packthread, that they may remain closely united; by these means they obtain beautiful flowers, variegated with whatever colours they choose." The article in question was on the culture of the *Parthenium*. Now this process is different to grafting (the uniting of a scion to a stock) and to inarching (the uniting of two stocks by approach). What is the name of the practice? Where is it treated of? and, is it attended with success? I can find nothing in THE COTTAGE GARDENER on the subject, and should be very glad of any hints for performing the operation.—S. P., *Rushmere*.

[It is quite certain that two slips fastened together in the way mentioned would *not* unite. The author must have been unacquainted with his subject, and must have mistaken inarching or grafting for the process he describes. It is quite possible for colouring matter of the scion's leaves, &c., to be imparted to those of the stock on which it is placed.—ED. C. G.]

TO CORRESPONDENTS.

⁎ We request that no one will write to the departmental writers of THE COTTAGE GARDENER. It gives them unjustifiable trouble and expense; and we also request our coadjutors *under no circumstances* to reply to such private communications.

MANY QUERIES (*W. Thompson*).—Your jasmine is *Jasminum revolutum*, a stove evergreen climber, native of Hindostan. Your evergreen shrub is *Euonymus Japonicus*, and will thrive with you in the open air in light loam, with a little peat mixed, if in a somewhat sheltered situation. For the *Azalea Indica* no soil is better than peat alone, and the drainage of the pots should be good. We have nothing to do with providing plants; you can ask Messrs. Henderson, if you choose, about those you name (*Erica cubenodes* and *Statice crinia*). Turn out your *cinerarias* at once into a bed in the open air, planting them deep in rich light soil, watering them at the time and when necessary. In August, divide each stool into as many parts as there are strong suckers, and if these are potted singly into light rich soil, and treated as directed at page 99 of our third volume, you will find they will bloom freely. The hard, almost opaque, *drops* on *vine branches* are exudations, and symptomatic of vigour and excess of sap rather than of disease. Give your vine all the light and air you can.

COCHIN CHINA FOWLS (*C. C.*).—Your letter is an advertisement, and cannot be inserted unless paid for.

SELTZER WATER (*E. B.*).—This is prepared artificially, by adding to each gallon of the softest water one scruple of carbonate of magnesia, one drachm of dry powdered carbonate of soda, and four scruples of common salt. When these are dissolved in the water, saturate it with fixed air by the aid of a soda-water machine.

MUSHROOMS (*Delta*).—These can be grown in a shed. The directions at pages 36 and 96 of the present volume will give you the other information you require. If you want any further particulars, write again. We do not know a pink *Eschscholtzia*; you must have mistaken the name.

GLORY PEA (*Ibid*).—This, which you received from New Zealand, is the *Clianthus puniceus*. It is a half hardy evergreen, with beautiful crimson flowers, and will bear plunging in the border during summer. An answer to your other question next week.

WHITE BEET (*M. O. L.*).—This is a species (*Beta cicla*), and sometimes called *spinach beet*, because its leaves are boiled like spinach. Leave the plants about nine inches apart. The stalks of this may be used as asparagus, and are much improved by being earthed-up and blanched like celery. *Green beet* is only a variety of the white, with greener stalks and leaves. The *Thousand-headed cabbage* and *Brussels sprouts* are totally different.

SUCCESSION OF FLOWERS (*W. M. H.*).—You have two beds in a small geometric garden; one of blue nemophila, the other of the *Nemophila discoidalis*, but they have come up very thinly, and have a shabby appearance. You wish for something to replace them, so as to bloom with verbenas, &c., this summer. Any of the *dwarf blue Lobelias* will replace the blue nemophila, or *Cineraria amelloides*, or the *Swan River daisy*, or the *little blue Campanulas* Mr. Beaton has often mentioned. *Nemophila discoidalis* is a poor thing, and only fit for a collection of curiosities, so that any plant of the same height will do in its place—say *Silene Shaftæ*.

SIZE REQUIRED FOR A KITCHEN-GARDEN (*H. H. H.*).—It is not an easy task to say how much ground would be required to supply a given number of persons with vegetables, for some persons are greater eaters of them than others; and there is such great difference in soils, some being much more productive than others. There is also much difference in the cultivators of the soil, some obtaining nearly as much again as others would off the same plot of ground, by system and good management. Making allowance for all these circumstances, as near as can be estimated, we should say, twelve square perches to each head in a family (exclusive of servants), but rather more than less.

CLIMBING PLANTS FOR A SOUTH VERANDAH (*A Young Beginner*).— Bourssault elegans, crimson purple rose. La Biche, creamy white rose. Ayrshire Queen, dark crimson rose. *Felicia perpetuelle*, white rose. *Miller's climber*, crimson rose. *Lonicera flexuosa*, light red honeysuckle. *Clematis Hendersonii*, blue. *Clematis Azmanula*, white. *Periploca Graca*, purple. *Jasminum officinale*, common jasmine, white. *Passiflora coerulea*, blue. *Bignonia radicans*.

WEIGELA ROSEA (*Ibid*).—This has been found hardy in many places.

PANSY SEED (*Ibid*).—We cannot recommend a dealer where you had better lay out your five shillings for a packet. No regular grower will send out what he thinks his best.

STRIKING PINKS, &c. (*An Enquirer*).—This will not be accomplished so early, nor yet so well, by using an inverted pot over them, instead of a bell-glass; though by taking off the pot in the afternoon, and replacing it before the sun is strong in the morning, you may thus rear pinks and other soft wooded plants. We are surprised the *Tropæolum canariense* does not, with you, answer out of doors, as it is hardy enough in most places. Have you secured it properly as it grew, as it is easily broken?

BEES TURNED REGICIDES (*G. A.*).—"On the 1st instant, a last year's first swarm threw off a first swarm; it was hived and set up the same night, and has continued hard at work ever since. This morning about eight o'clock, the queen was found on the ground in front of the hive (she was not there at seven), one of her fore legs was half gone, and her wings were very ragged; she was twice placed on the floor-board (she could not fly), but on both occasions she was ejected as soon as she had made an entrance. Has she been turned out in consequence of age, or for what other reason? Are the young queen bees full-grown and full-sized upon issuing from the cells, or do they increase much after impregnation?" Old age was, in all probability, the cause of the queen's being ejected from the hive. Had you given the number of days between the time of their swarming and your finding the queen, we could have spoken with more certainty; but in all probability there was a queen in embryo in the hive at the time of your finding her. The young queens are very nearly full-sized upon issuing from the cells.

BEES (*A Young Amateur*).—Had you placed a piece of guide comb in the glass, as directed at page 43, volume 2, of THE COTTAGE GARDENER, your bees would in all probability have worked in it. It is always advisable to do so. We do not know where you can obtain the *Mummy raspberry*.

RETURNING SWARMS (*W. Christian*).—"Some bees, in a set of collateral hives, threw off a swarm on the 31st of May, although the side box (in which they had just began to work) had been given them. The swarm was returned again to the side hive, where they went on very well for about ten days, when they swarmed again, and have been doing the same every day since, sometimes going back of their own accord. A bell-glass was also put on the middle box, so that they had plenty of room if they chose to accept of it." See our advice as to returning swarms at page 216, vol. 2, of THE COTTAGE GARDENER. In a bar hive it may be done with the *certainty* of success. See as above. Perhaps if you had ventilated the centre box they would not have swarmed; but this is what Mr. Nutt does *not* recommend.

APRICOT UNFRUITFUL (*T. O. U.*).—Cut away any tap roots in autumn, and apply a surface dressing of loam and manure to encourage surface roots. This may bring into bearing your apricot which blossoms every year without producing a single fruit.

VINE TRAINING (*W. H. G.*).—We do not know what answer you refer us to. As a general principle, grapes are only allowed to grow on shoots considered permanent. Still, like other matters, many exceptions occur.

Your inquiries concerning *hot-beds* shall have attention in due time. We are always on the look-out to discover the wants of amateurs.

MUSCAT VINE (*M.*).—Your muscat affair before long. We do not understand your clipping affair; please to be a little more explicit on this head; also, "as to outside the house." Do you mean the root or top? Please to remember that without much heat good muscats cannot be produced. No grape requires or will endure more. We advise you to leave at least six or seven eyes beyond the bunch, if room can be obtained. As to reserving the old shoot, it is a matter of fancy chiefly. Vines on the spurring system should, from their first growth, have a regular number of spurs established as growth proceeds. This done, the shoot may be considered permanent. Many, however, prefer to bear the muscat on the cane.

PINE-PITS (*T. W. Lawford*).—Keep your ridge and furrow roof as low as you can, to obtain head room. As to the cheapest plan, your carpenter must settle that with you. We should doubt the power of your one pipe to heat 500 gallons. Your water would, doubtless, circulate if made hot. Why not carry the steam at once round the house, without anything intermediate? We are not, however, well assured that we understand your sketch. An angle of about 45° to 50° would, we think, be suitable.

FRUIT PACKING (*Tirydail*).—We will give a paper on fruit packing before long.

FRUIT TREES (*E. R.*).—If we understand you aright, your soil is too rich as well as too deep. You will do well to take up all such young trees in the end of October, and to replant them in a proper way. You may put any crops on the border for the present which do not require spade culture. We would recommend *Shipley's apricot* for hardiness, and the *Moorpark* for flavour.

ROOTS FROM VINE-STEMS (*M., Minehead*).—Roots having protruded from the vine-stems, we suffer them to remain; at the same time, it may be considered undeniable evidence of a rather too great amount of atmospheric moisture in the house. The fermentation from the tan must be considerable, and from frequent sprinklings increase moisture much. We think you would do well to use little or no water when you close in the evening. If you do use it, you ought to encourage a current of air all night. Vines abhor excessive confined damp.

NAMES OF PLANTS (*T. M. W.*).—We believe your plant is *Solanum macrantherum*. (*Juvenlus*).—Your plant is *Linum flavum* (Yellow flax). It is propagated readily by cuttings.

CALENDAR FOR JULY.

GREENHOUSE.

AIR admit freely night and day, unless when stormy; make an exception, however, in those cases where growth is still desirable. There shut up early, and use the syringe morning and evening. BUD and GRAFT oranges, camellias, azaleas, climbers, &c. CUTTINGS make and plant, placing them in cool pits at a distance from the glass, or in a mild bottom-heat, according to their requirements. Dress and keep everything neat. CALCEOLARIAS give manured water; fumigate when necessary; cut down early blooming; thin the pods of those left for seed, as one pod will give hundreds of plants. GERANIUMS, cut down the forwardest; tie and train successions; prepare for early supply of cuttings. HEATHS, cut down and prune when done flowering; give plenty of air to those in flower; shift those starting again after being pruned; and propagate by seeds, and by cuttings in a pit under hand-glasses. Examine all PEAT PLANTS as respects water, for if dried up several times, death is next to certain, your only chance is to set the pot or tub in water until all is saturated, and then allow it to drain. SEEDLINGS of all kinds prick off as soon as up, or they will be apt to *fog* off at the surface of the soil. SHADE when necessary; it is better in bright weather than more air or delugings of waterings. SHIFTING must be attended to with all successions, such as fuchsias, geraniums, balsams, cockscombs, &c., and free-growing, quick-blooming plants, as Achimenes patens, and coccinea. Tropæolums, and other twiners and climbers, must be trained and fastened daily. One of the prettiest ornaments for a window is the Tropæolum pentaphyllum; when done flowering, keep in dry earth until they vegetate. WATER must now be given with great judgment, especially to newly shifted plants that have been transferred from a small to a large pot. In general circumstances, there is now as much danger from want of water, as in winter there was the danger of giving too much, and giving it when not required. All bulbs that have finished flowering and growing are an exception; as soon as the leaves get yellow, they should be encouraged to get into a state of rest as soon as possible by withholding water. Those that have their leaves yet green should be assisted with water, until the bulbs are mature.

R. FISH.

FRUIT-GARDEN.

APPLE ESPALIERS, train thin and stop. APRICOTS, pick off caterpillars, and train. CHERRIES, cleanse from fly and protect from birds. CUCUMBERS, thin and stop frequently, and reserve specimens for seed. CURRANTS (red and white), prune back all side spray and top. CURRANTS (black), water freely. FIGS, thin out the wood, and stop. GOOSEBERRIES, exterminate the caterpillar; thin out where bushes are overloaded. MELONS, train, stop, thin, set fruit, and water freely when swelling the fruit; also syringe on fine afternoons. NUTS, remove superfluous spray from the interior of the bushes. PEARS, remove waste shoots, stop, &c., according to advice previously given; thin fruit if too thick. PEACHES, make a final thinning of both fruit and wood; stop gross shoots wherever found. PLUMS, beware of the fly; stop and thin. RASPBERRIES, thin suckers, and stop when more than five feet high. STRAWBERRIES, keep down runners, and water late kinds. VINES, remove extra laterals from those ripe, and continue stopping late grapes; water border, if dry and sound beneath, in dry weather.

R. ERRINGTON.

FLOWER GARDEN.

ANNUALS (Tender), bring out from frames; dress; give fresh earth; stake and tie. ANNUALS, transplant generally. AURICULAS in pots, dress and water frequently; seedlings transplant; old plants repot, e. Box edgings clip, b. BUD roses, jasmines, &c. BULBOUS ROOTS, take up (see June); seeds, sow. CARNATIONS, attend to (see June); shade and shelter during hot weather; water freely, and give liquid-manure. CHRYSANTHEMUM suckers separate and plant; lay. CUTTINGS of most herbaceous plants will root now, and of all the scarlet geraniums, if planted on a south border, b. DAHLIAS require support and pruning. EDGINGS, clip. EVERGREENS, prune; seedlings, prick out. FLOWER-BEDS, stir surface often; train; stop and often regulate the plants, to get a uniform growth and bloom. GRASS, mow and roll often. GRAVEL, weed and roll. HEARTSEASE, plant slips, e.; water freely. HEDGES, clip. HOE and rake at every opportunity. LAYERING carnations, &c., may be performed, b.; water freely; transplant rooted layers. LEAVES, decayed, remove as soon as seen. LIQUID-MANURE, give occasionally to flowering shrubs. MIGNONETTE and a few other quick-flowering annuals may be sown, b., for autumn. PIPING of pinks, &c., may be still practised, b. PELARGONIUM cuttings plant, b. POLYANTHUSES, seedlings, transplant; roots of old, part. ROSES, bud and layer, b. SEEDS, gather as they ripen. STAKE and tie up plants wherever necessary. TRANSPLANT, b., from the reserve garden in damp or dull weather. WATER freely, not only the roots, but over the foliage.

D. BEATON.

ORCHID HOUSE.

The same treatment, as to watering, syringing, and shading, as directed for last month, should be followed through the whole of July. AIR, give abundance of during the day; and, when the weather is very hot, even during the night. MOISTURE, keep the walks and walls constantly flooded with water. DIP baskets and logs at least once a-week during this hot month. If any have formed their PSEUDO-BULBS for the season, place them in a cool house. The NEW HOLLAND SPECIES when in that state may be placed in a sheltered place out of doors, protecting them from rain.

T. APPLEBY.

PLANT STOVE.

ACHIMENES will now be in flower, water them only at the roots. AIR, give in great abundance, night and day; more, of course, in the day than in the night. ÆSCHYNANTHUS done blooming place in a cold pit to rest, giving but little water. BEGONIAS, pot off, and keep growing, to flower in winter. ERANTHEMUMS, repot, and grow on for the same purpose. To CLERODENDRUMS coming into flower give liquid-manure. GARDENIAS going out of flower keep cool. GESNERIAS and GLOXINIAS now in flower refrain from syringing. CUTTINGS of the two last-named may yet be put in. IXORAS, pot for the last time this season. INSECTS extirpate most diligently. At this warm time of the year they breed prodigiously. REPAIRS, such as glazing and painting, this is the best season for. YOUNG STOVE PLANTS will be much benefited by being placed for two or three months in cold frames. HOT WATER PIPES, see too, and repair. If necessary empty the water out of them.

T. APPLEBY.

FLORISTS' FLOWERS.

AURICULAS, look to, and keep clear of slugs and weeds. CARNATIONS, layer, shade, and keep free from insects. DAHLIAS, mulch and water freely; tie to stakes, at least, once a-week. See that old ties do not strangle the shoots; thin their branches. FRAMES, repair their glass, and paint. PICOTEES attend to, the same as carnations. PINKS, pot off pipings of choice sorts, three or four together, in 5-inch pots. RANUNCULUSES, refrain from watering. TULIPS, take up all, and dry gradually at the beginning of the month. VERBENAS, put in cuttings of the best as they come into flower. WEEDS continually eradicate.

T. APPLEBY.

KITCHEN-GARDEN.

ALEXANDERS, earth up in dry weather. ASPARAGUS, discontinue cutting; keep clean from weeds. If salting has been attended to, none will appear; but earth-stir with some pointed implement. BROAD BEANS, save seed from the best kinds; a small planting may be made of the *Early Masagan* kind in an open south border, and well watered at the time of planting should the weather be dry. BORAGE, sow, and thin out a foot apart. BORECOLES, plant out and prick out; in all cases well water at the time of planting. BROCOLIS, treat the same. CABBAGES, plant out; sow seed about the 20th of the month, in an open situation; should the weather be dry, well water previously to sowing. CAULIFLOWERS, plant out; supply those that are forward in growth with plenty of water; invert a few leaves over the heads of those turning in. CUCUMBERS, attend to daily as to thinning, topping, training out, top-dressing, and watering. The hand-glass crops, fork up the earth round about their roots, allowing them sufficient room to run out freely. ENDIVE, of both sorts, make a good sowing toward the middle of this month, and plant out previously sown plants. KIDNEY BEANS (dwarfs), at this late season, should be sown in open warm borders. MELONS, attend to earthing-up late planted-out crops; do such work in the afternoon; shut up close; setting the fruit is best done about 10 or 11 o'clock in the forenoon; give plenty of air to those ripening off their fruit; be sparing of the water among the ripening fruit. ONIONS, well thin out, weed, and earth-stir; press down stiff-necked onions as they advance in growth. PEAS, at this late season, sow early kinds in open warm situations; well water at the time of sowing in dry weather. VEGETABLE MARROWS, train out and thin out. PEAS, save seed from the best favourite kinds. In all kinds of PLANTING-OUT, take advantage of dull weather, and water well at the time of planting. Make good use of THE HOE in dry weather, in cutting down weeds and earth-stirring. I never like to see the rake used much in the kitchen-garden.

T. WEAVER.

LONDON: Printed by HARRY WOOLDRIDGE, Winchester High-street, in the Parish of Saint Mary Kalendar; and Published by WILLIAM SOMERVILLE ORR, at the Office, No. 2, Amen Corner, in the Parish of Christ Church, City of London.—June 27th, 1850.

WEEKLY CALENDAR.

M W D D	JULY 4—10, 1850.	Weather near London in 1849.		Sun Rises.	Sun Sets.	Moon R. & S.	Moon's Age.	Clock bef. Sun.	Day of Year.
4 Tu	Trans. of St. Martin. Wood Leopard Moth seen.	T. 67°—42°.	W. Fine.	51 a. 3	17 a. 9	0 34	24	3 47	185
5 F	Cambridge Term ends. Chaffinch's song ceases.	T. 76°—45°.	W. Fine.	52	17	1 0	25	4 8	186
6 S	Old Midsummer's Day. Oxford Term ends.	T. 79°—48°.	S.W. Fine.	53	16	1 31	26	4 18	187
7 Sun	6 Sun. aft. Trinity. Th. à Becket. Glow-	T. 96°—52°.	W. Fine.	53	16	2 7	27	4 28	188
8 M	Lappet Moth appears. [worm shines.	T. 88°—59°.	S.W. Fine.	54	15	3 53	28	4 38	189
9 Tu	Yellow Underwing Moth seen.	T. 84°—49°.	N.W. Fine.	54	14	sets.	●	4 47	190
10 W	Shore Beetle seen.	T. 84°—45°.	N.E. Fine.	55	14	8 a. 53	1	4 55	191

On the 7th of July, 1799, died William Curtis, who as the originator of *The Botanical Magazine* will never be forgotten either by the botanist or the gardener. He was born in 1746, at Alton, in Hampshire, and at the age of fourteen was apprenticed to his grandfather, an apothecary of the same town. It so happened, that his new residence was adjoining the Crown Inn, the ostler of which, John Lagg, though of slender education, had, by the aid of Gerard's and Parkinson's huge folio volumes, obtained a knowledge so complete of plants, that not one could be brought to him of which he was unable promptly to tell the name. The impression made upon the mind of young Curtis, by the fact of this deep and useful knowledge being acquired by one so unlearned, was never to be obliterated. He devoted himself to the same study; and pursuing it with that energy characterising his efforts in after life, he soon acquired a practical knowledge of all the plants natives of the neighbourhood, and especially of those possessing medical virtues. There is no doubt that John Lagg was a most able guide and teacher in the acquirement of this knowledge; but whoever will turn to the folios we have named, and will reflect, that their unsystematised pages were those only to which he could refer for aid, will the more readily perceive what praise was due to him for his pursuit of knowledge under such difficulties. They were difficulties which we, who have but to stretch out a hand and bring before our eyes such books as Henfrey's *Rudiments of Botany*, Smith's *Introduction to Botany*, Lindley's *School Botany* and *Vegetable Kingdom*, are not well situated to appreciate duly. However, young Curtis forced his way through the cumbrous masses to the information he sought for; and when he reached London, in the course of his medical studies, soon found the advantage of his hard-earned knowledge of plants. Dr. Fordyce gladly employed him as botanical demonstrator, to aid him in his lectures on the science, at St. Thomas's Hospital. This gave him and the essentials to success in life—confidence in his own powers—and led him by degrees almost insensibly into that path in which he nobly earned both fame and independence. He began by giving public lectures on botany; and a few of his pupils still survive, and can remember the pure delight attending upon their excursions with their tutor, and the joyous good humour with which he commented during dinner upon the specimens they had gathered in their morning ramble. He had the good

sense to discern, that though science is lovely and loveable for its own sake, yet that science unapplied to the arts of life is but a fruitless flower. Therefore, whilst he wrote on botany he also published such works as "Practical Observations on the British Grasses," "Directions for the Culture of the *Crambe Maritima*, or Sea-kale," combining also with his botanical researches the study of entomology; and thus was enabled to supply valuable information, not only relative to the habits of plants, but also respecting the insects preying upon them. It is amusing to know, that where now stands that mass of densely populated houses known as the Grange Road, Bermondsey, was situated Mr. Curtis's first Botanical Garden; and from the plants he there assembled he began to publish that series of portraits of British plants known as the *Flora Londinensis*. The Grange Road Garden becoming too small to contain his rapidly accumulating species, he moved to another, now equally unsuited for the purpose—namely, Lambeth Marsh, near the Magdalene Hospital; and it was not until the increased population of the neighbourhood rendered the air there too smoke-impregnated for his plants' welfare that he moved to his last resting-place, Brompton, in Middlesex. In a pecuniary sense the *Flora* was a failure, for its sale never exceeded 300 copies; nor is this a subject for surprise, because it was expensive, and suited exclusively to that very limited class, the botanists. For each botanist that can be named, every one can enumerate a thousand lovers of flowers; and to embrace a circulation among these he commenced publishing in 1787 his *Botanical Magazine*, the first of this class of our periodical literature, and consequently the most long-lived; for it still continues its monthly appearance, and has extended to between seventy and eighty volumes. Upon the death of Mr. Curtis the editorship was given to Dr. Sims, who was more than slightly assisted, we believe, in the performance of his editorial duties by the late Mr. Bellenden Ker. In 1827, his share in the magazine was purchased, and the management confided to Sir James Hooker, assisted by Mr. W. Curtis, then of Glazen Wood, Essex, and a relative of the original editor. It is now under the sole control of Sir James, aided only by Mr. Smith of the Kew Gardens, who furnishes the directions necessary for the culture of the plants delineated. We will conclude this necessarily imperfect notice by saying of Mr. Curtis, in the words of one of his friends, "Somewhat of elegance and neatness pervaded whatever he took in hand. The form of his mind was pourtrayed in his garden, his library, his aviary; and even a dry catalogue of plants became from his pen an amusing and instructive little volume. His delicacy never forsook him, nor would he willingly adopt the coarse names given to plants by some of the older botanists, though accepted by Linnæus himself. In short, this amiable member of the Society of Friends was an honest, laborious, worthy man,—gentle, humane, kind to everybody, a pleasant companion, a good master, and a steady friend."

RANGE OF BAROMETER—RAIN IN INCHES.

July	1841.	1842.	1843.	1844.	1845.	1846.	18	1848.	1849.
4	B. { 29.999 29.963	29.770 29.696	29.975 29.836	29.638 29.596	30.109 30.053	30.154 29.990	30.011 29.949	30.137 29.948	29.702 29.697
	R.			0.81					
5	B. { 30.264 29.929	29.823 29.652	29.717 29.643	29.568 29.576	30.186 30.161	29.763 29.696	29.946 29.900	30.186 30.121	29.973 29.772
	R. 0.59	0.11	0.16	0.00		0.24			
6	B. { 29.805 29.635	30.161 30.103	29.836 29.751	29.279 29.949	30.007 29.996	29.539 29.448	29.996 29.930	30.085 29.969	30.097 30.078
	R. 0.03			0.66		0.13	0.02		
7	B. { 29.985 29.639	30.009 29.826	29.946 29.913	29.995 29.929	29.965 29.943	29.875 29.744	29.855 29.737	29.876 29.849	30.065 29.995
	R. 0.08	0.89	0.14	0.13	0.61		0.02	0.03	
8	B. { 29.898 29.742	29.804 29.511	29.941 29.876	29.931 29.856	29.969 29.940	29.950 29.764	29.929 29.835	30.063 29.963	30.129 30.038
	R. 0.61	0.48	0.94		0.01	0.08	0.06	0.33	
9	B. { 29.949 29.939	29.719 29.685	29.977 29.954	29.906 29.850	30.001 29.978	29.569 29.541	30.115 30.016	29.999 29.742	30.275 30.233
	R. 0.08	0.03		0.15	0.16	0.02	0.36		
10	B. { 29.926 29.492	29.894 29.854	29.954 29.935	29.967 29.890	29.814 29.721	29.987 29.734	30.131 30.129	30.268 30.003	30.375 30.535
	R. 0.36				0.02	0.39			

Meteorology of the Week.—At Chiswick, observations during the last twenty-three years show that the average highest and lowest temperatures of these days are 75.5° and 52.3° respectively. The greatest heat observed, 95°, was on the 5th in 1846. During the period there were 109 fine days, and 59 on which rain fell.

Whenever we meet with new and pleasant acquaintances, the desire to know their parentage and previous history comes upon us spontaneously; and this form of inquisitiveness extends to flowers; for we never yet saw a beautiful one without wishing to know where it came from, and when it was found. Nor are we singular in this thirst for the biography of plants, as is testified by the cluster of inquisitive admirers who gather round the collections of Cape Pelargoniums, neglectful for the time of their more brilliant and more robust offspring, the Pelargoniums of the Florist. Thus, at the Chiswick Gardens on the 8th of last month, we had some difficulty in obtaining an uninterrupted view of the Cape Pelargoniums then gathered together. Among them were *P. elatum*, white and purple; *P. glaucum*, white and red; *P. quinquevulnerum*, purplish; *P. roseum*, pink; and *P. tricolor*, white and purple; species all cultivated in our greenhouses before the commencement of the present century, and from which and others we shall mention presently, bearing flowers equally insignificant, have descended, by means of various cross impregnations, those large, brilliant-flowered, and broad-leaved varieties, so strikingly ornamental in our floral collections.

Some of our contemporaries have fallen into the mistake of supposing that *Geranium*, now *Pelargonium*, *triste*, the earliest introduced of the Cape species, may have had something to do with such parentage, but this is more than improbable, for *triste* is one of the herbaceous species. If we turn to Abercrombie's Dictionary, published in 1778, we shall find that the shrubby Geraniums then common in our greenhouses were, *zonale*, the horse-shoe, both with green and variegated leaves; * *capitatum*, the rose-scented; *fulgidum*, the flaming-red; *inquinans*, the mallow-leaved; *papilionaceum*, the pea-flowered; *cucullatum*, the hood-leaved; *vitifolium*, the vine-leaved, or balm-scented; *gibbosum*, the gouty-stalked, with columbine leaves; *carnosum*, the fleshy-stalked; *betulinum*, the birch-leaved; *peltatum*, the shield-leaved; and *acetosum*, the sorrel-flavoured. In these we can see the germs of those colours, forms, and habits which now characterize our most-favoured Pelargoniums.

We believe that Mr. Fairchild, who died in 1729, was one of the earliest improvers of this flower; and we have before us the reports of many of his experiments, and among them one of a successful attempt to inarch "A Geranium with variegated leaves upon a Geranium with a scarlet flower, from whence it is reasonable to suppose all the arborescent Geraniums will take upon one another." It is certain that varieties had much increased between the time of Fairchild and 1800; for the Rev.

* We think this was the chief parent of our varieties.

Mr. Marshall, writing in this year, enumerates of the Horse-shoe Geranium alone, the "green-leaved, variegated, silver-edged, silver-striped, gold-striped, pink, two scarlets and a purple, and one large scarlet, or *grandiflorum*."

The increase of newly imported species continued, as well as of new varieties; and some of them were so markedly beautiful, that they attracted the attention of many nurserymen and amateurs; for it became evident that they were so capable of improvement and variety as to be entitled to a place among florists' flowers. Sir Richard Colt Hoare was one of the amateurs who first addressed himself especially to this pursuit; and so markedly successful was he in his efforts to improve the flower, that one section of the genus was named HOAREA in honour of him. After the lapse of five or six years, the number and consequence of these flowers had sufficiently increased to enable Mr. Sweet to commence, in 1820, the publication of a work devoted entirely to Pelargoniums. This was his *Geraniacea*; and though it is a culpable confusion of varieties and species, yet it is a book of beauty and authority, enabling us to trace the gradual improvements effected in this flower; and in the last volume, published in 1830, there are some varieties, such as *Dennis's Rival*, which are very little less excellent than the best prize flowers since exhibited by such cultivators of them as Cook, Catleugh, Thurtell, Foster, Garth, Beck, and Hoyle.

No one, that we remember, published any criteria worthy of notice, whereby to test the merits of a Pelargonium, until Mr. Glenny did so about eight years since in the "Practical Florist." Those criteria, with some alterations, we now republish.

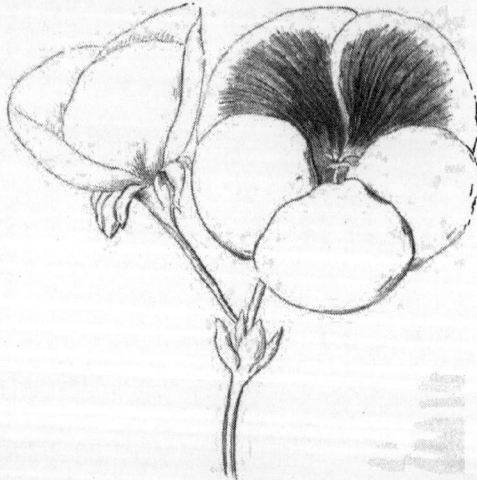

1. The petals should be thick, broad, blunt, smooth at the edges, and lie close on each other, so as to appear whole or one-petaled, rather than a five-petaled flower.

2. The flower should be large—two inches diameter is a good size,—circular, higher at the edges than in the centre, so as to form rather a hollow, though by no means a deeply-cupped bloom, without puckering or frilling of the petals; and where these lap over each other, the indentation caused by the join should be hardly perceptible.

3. The colour should be bright and dense; the spots on the upper petals should be boldly contrasted with the ground, and the darker the better: both upper petals should be alike, both side petals alike, and the lower petal uniform.

4. All white grounds should be very pure; and the colours on the white, no matter what they be, should be decided, well defined, and not flush into the white.

5. The spots on the upper petals, or the marks in any other, should not break through to the edge.

6. The general flower-stalk of the truss should be straight, strong, elastic; carrying the blooms well above the foliage. The foot-stalks of the individual flowers should be stiff, and of sufficient length to allow the flowers to show themselves in an even head, fitting compactly edge to edge, and forming a uniform bold truss.

7. The truss should approach to a semi-globular form; each flower presenting its face fully to view. Each truss should have at least five flowers, and we have one now before us, of *Constellation*, which has eight. There should be a truss at the end of each shoot.

8. The plant should be shrubby in its habit, the foliage close, and of a rich bright green, the joints short, strong, and able to support themselves in every part without assistance.

After seeing the Pelargoniums at the great metropolitan exhibitions, as well as the seedlings of the year, we regret to have the conviction forced upon us, that their cultivators are making the great mistake of sacrificing too much for the sake of obtaining high or dark coloured flowers. Florists breed from parents thus distinguished in preference to those having as prime characteristics stoutness of petal and roundness of form. Inferior offspring must be the consequence; but, leaving form and substance entirely out of consideration, we still consider dark-coloured flowers far less desirable, because much less pleasing to most eyes than those of fairer tints. We believe the most popular, and we think the most beautiful flower that could be bred, should be in other respects like *Pearl*, but with its two upper petals dark crimson.

THE FRUIT-GARDEN.

FRUIT-PACKING.—A little advice on this subject may prove of some interest, both to the young gardener, the amateur, and the cottager: it being often imperfectly understood, or too carelessly practised.

In former days our fruits travelled by coaches, or by the ordinary road-waggon, but now principally by steam; and it is to modes of packing adapted to that kind of transit that we would now invite attention. By the former mode of travelling, the box or basket was subjected to a loose jolting action; by the latter, it undergoes a perpetual jarring; and although the action of the steam-carriage is by far more uniform than that of the old coach, yet these little jars, unless provided against by good packing, are very damaging to tender fruits, or those with a thin skin and a soft pulp.

The kinds of materials to pack in are the first consideration; and here we may observe, that whatever the kind be, it is, as we think, absolutely essential, that it be of an elastic character, and at the same time possess a kind of strength or soundness which, after travelling many miles and enduring many hard knocks, shall yet preserve its elasticity somewhat unimpaired. Thus, as an example, fine grass from lawns which have been mowed *several* times, or some from beneath the shade of trees, in a dry state, is a very tempting-looking material, and looks soft as silk; but for general purposes the second cut from upland mowing will be found far preferable, as longer preserving its elasticity.

Closeness, not to say tightness, in packing is the great essential; the one great maxim to bear in mind is this, PRESSURE IS BETTER THAN FRICTION. We well remember calling on an old schoolfellow, about twelve or fifteen years since, to advise with him as to the best mode of packing peaches; for at that period we grew the finest peaches in England; for a few years we had the honour of beating all competitors or nearly so, our fruit at that period averaging as much as eleven ounces, and sometimes nearly reaching thirteen. The schoolfellow alluded to was the late Mr. David Dulley, who kept the large fruit-shop in Covent Garden, formerly occupied by the late Mrs. Grange. The axiom about "pressure, &c." was, he assured me, the best advice in few words that could be given; and we have for many years had ample opportunity of proving the truth of Mr. Dulley's advice.

His opinion was, as to material, that few things excelled soft hay, or, as the Londoners term it, "rowen;" such being for the most part the second cut or aftermath from grass lands of a somewhat finer character than ordinary. Nevertheless, he did not confine all fruit-packing to this material alone, but merely pointed to it as at least a useful adjunct in *all fruit*-packing.

At the same period we called at Gunter's, in order to get their opinion; there we were told, that sawdust or bran were capital materials for peach-packing; the former from white and flavourless wood, such as the lime, horse chestnut, &c., &c. The soundness of the last advice has always appeared questionable, especially as to railroad travelling; the sudden and severe jerks on which would seem to require that some body of a more yielding character should be placed around the fruit.

Some persons are very partial to the use of cotton, wool, or "wadding;" some to dry and thrashed moss; others use paper shavings from the stationers; the latter being for the most part the edgings removed from writing paper during the squaring or finishing process we suppose. These paper shavings are, indeed, a truly good article, and perhaps are better for grape packing than any other material.

Having thus "broken the ice," as far as first principles are concerned, we must now beg to be a little more explicit, and to come home at once to the details; we must crave our readers' patience whilst we pack three ideal boxes of strawberries, grapes, and peaches.

STRAWBERRIES.—Having provided a shallow box or tin of three inches in depth, clear inside measure, we will place, at least, one inch of dry thrashed green moss over the bottom: moss from which, after thrashing, all dirt and dust have been completely ejected. This must be pressed as close as hands can make it; indeed, made firm and equal. And, now, let a piece of fine and soft cap-paper be placed double, and perfectly even, for a bed for the strawberries. One of the best strawberry-packers we ever knew used to place a layer of nettle-leaves (which had been gathered two or three days and become very pliant) over the cap-paper; and exceedingly well it answered. These things done, let the same mode of packing, reversed, proceed, until the box is quite full; so that the topping-up will be a facsimile of the bottoming, only, as before observed, reversed. And now we may fairly nail down or close the lid, and rest assured that they will travel well—from the Land's End to London.

GRAPES.—We must now change our tactics, for we shall of course require both a deeper box and a stronger material; the latter partly on account of the much increased weight, and consequently pressure. Grapes pack best, as we think, in a sort of diagonal position—not quite flat, but nearly so; of course the stalk end in the ascendant. The box being ready, and sufficiently roomy—four inches deeper than the bunch when in its recumbent position—two inches at least of the white paper shavings may be placed in the bottom, tucking them somewhat close, but not tight. If any of the paper remains in masses, as cut from the quires, it must be separated into individual strips. The best way now, in our opinion, is to surround each bunch as they are placed in the box with silver or tissue paper; this must be placed gently, and somewhat loosely, round the bunch, avoiding carefully all friction; and now a little extra paper shavings may be so placed as to form a sort of nest for the bunch, and this so managed, as that when the bunch with its paper is laid down there will be no occasion to move or to handle it again. As they are thus successively placed, a little paper must be introduced here and there as a wedge, or prop, to prevent the bunch from slipping.

When the bunches are very large, or possess huge shoulders, some little pillows or cushions may be introduced between them and the body of the bunch; occasionally these may be formed by enclosing small portions of the paper shavings in the silver paper, thrusting such in any situation where a great weight of berries are likely to infringe on each other. The bunches being all thus placed, some more of the little cushions may be thrust here and there over the *general* surface, so placing them as to render it impossible for the bunch to move in any direction. The surface being thus brought level, nothing remains but to fill up the box with the paper shavings, taking care that it is *quite full*, so that the lid in fastening down will have to be compressed a little. The thrashed moss may, if necessary, be substituted for the paper shavings; we are not aware which is best, but confess to a partiality for the shavings; such, however must not be coarse—the finer the better, and from thin white paper.

PEACHES.—For these, we think the soft or rowan hay not to be excelled. We have repeatedly sent the large peaches before named to the Chiswick exhibitions, with scarcely a blemish; and as such were much admired by the public, and on one occasion their packing made the subject of a leading article in the *Chronicle*, we cannot do better than detail the precise mode of doing so on those occasions.

The boxes were made exactly eight inches in depth; this allowed two inches of the packing material below the fruits, and two inches, or nearly so, above: thus, four inches at least were allowed for the thickness of the peach. Our boxes were partitioned-off into cells, measuring about five inches square on the surface; one, of course, apportioned to each peach. In the bottom of each of these was placed the two inches of rowan hay, pressed close, and shaped in a concave manner, so as to form a nest for the peach to descend into. Some squares of silver paper and cap paper were now provided; and taking first a square of cap paper in the left hand, another of the silver was placed in it; the right hand then quietly placed the peach on the centre of the paper in the palm of the left hand, and now the right hand was employed to gently twist the four corners together.

Thus imbedded, the peach was lowered into its cell, and so on with the whole. The next proceeding was to take a long-bladed knife—one of the ordinary dinner knives—and with this to tuck in the soft hay in a wedge-like character, until each cell was full, *close, but not hard.* Of course the top of the box received the two inches of rowan; and the box lid was obliged to be slightly compressed in nailing down, the hay being applied rather liberally.

Now, we do not mean to say that these are the only rules for fruit packing—fruit of a tender character we mean; but we do mean to say that they travelled well by these modes; and a hope may perhaps be indulged in, that our detail of the proceedings may assist in furnishing useful ideas on the subject of fruit packing amongst the uninitiated, for whom in a great degree it is our duty to write. It may be observed, in conclusion, that such things are not always confined to single layers; many of our country gentlemen or noblemen who have extensive gardens and forcing establishments have tin cases adapted to the reception of several layers; of course the packing of each layer is comported to the same system—each layer is complete in itself.

As opportunities occur, we shall feel it a duty to return to the subject, and must then descend to easy modes of packing our common fruits.

R. ERRINGTON.

THE FLOWER-GARDEN.

LAPAGERIA ROSEA.—Those who have friends or connections at Valparaiso might easily receive this beautiful plant from thence. It is one of the most beautiful flower-garden plants one could possess, and is called in that part of the world "Copigua;" but it was named, botanically, many years since, by Ruiz and Pavon, two Spanish botanists, who wrote a work on the plants of Peru and Chile, called "Flora Peruviana." There is also some account of it given in a work called "Narrative of the Wreck of the Challanger," on the coast of Patagonia. It was introduced to the Royal Botanic Garden, at Kew, two or three years since, where I saw the plant the other day, and I could compare it to nothing but to a Smilax, a common prickly herbaceous climber which has been in our shrubberies time out of mind. The flowers, which are large and hanging down, are of a deep rosy-red colour, and look very much like those of some of the twining *Alstrœmerias*, now called *Bomareas.* The roots are in bundles, just like those of asparagus, and of the same quality as sarsaparilla. The fruit is a berry, and good to eat—at least they eat them about Conception and the southern parts of Chile; they also send branches of the plant in flower as presents from Conception, as far north as Valparaiso; and they are said to last in flower some weeks hung up in the rooms, and are known as *Copigua flowers;* so that one might easily hunt them out by these descriptions, and, unless we get large importations of the roots or seeds, the plant is likely to be scarce and dear with us for some time.

I believe it will be almost, if not altogether, hardy with us. I have been hunting after this beautiful plant these six or seven years. I wrote to Capt. G. Broke, R.N., about it when he was on the Cape station, expecting then that he would have been sent from hence round to the coast of Chile, but I have failed, and now I hand over these notes on it to all whom it may interest.

SILVER CEDAR.—This is another fine plant about which I have been very anxious to learn something. It will be recollected that I wrote of it last spring, that it grows on the southern ranges of the Atlas chain, between Morocco and Algiers; and it has been supposed to be only a variety of the Cedar of Lebanon. I am now satisfied in my own mind, however, that the two are as distinct from each other as are the spruces of Norway from those of the Himalaya range—*Abies excelsa* and *Abies morinda*. I examined some hundreds of plants of both these cedars the other day, at Mr. Low's nursery, at Clapton, near London,—some in the seed pots, some a year old, and so on up to plants five or six years of age. The Silver Cedars of the latter age were plants raised from seeds in Algiers, brought to France, and from thence to London; and their rate of growth appeared to be in regard to the Cedar of Lebanon in the same proportion as that of the Deodar Cedar of India. The silvery hue was conspicuous on the young wood of all these plants from the Atlas, while out of some hundreds of the Lebanon plant not one produced that kind of gray we call glaucous. If, therefore, the Silver Cedar will grow with us as freely as it does in the south of France, it will soon become as popular as the Deodar Cedar, and a good companion to it in avenues and other places where such trees are in request.

Roses.—Hybrid perpetual roses, and all other roses, ought now, or as soon as may be, to receive three good heavy waterings in succession with strong liquid manure " as brown as a berry," and only a couple or three days between each watering. This will enable the summer roses to make a better and an earlier growth, after flowering, to flower from next season. It often happens, that after a heavy crop of flowers these summerlings are overtaken by a long drought, and owing to these two demands upon their strength they languish and look ragged a long while, and then make a late growth in the autumn, which never ripens half enough, of which the consequence is not seen or felt till the following June, when we say this is, or has been, " a bad rose season;" whereas the state of the plants, or of the weather, or of the attendance they received in the previous autumn, ought to have had so much of the blame. Great fanciers do not let their perpetual roses bloom much until the bulk of the summer ones are over; and the stopping to subdue the first flowers causes so many young shoots to come up where the plants are vigorous, that they cannot all flower very strongly unless they are helped with two or three good soakings of strong manure water, and that, too, to be repeated again in August and September—say the first or second week in each month. This kind of watering is much more effectual than if the bushes are only once watered every other week, as it is now well known, that however strong liquid-manure is, or how often applied, if the land is deep, and well worked, and drained, it is capable of retaining the goodness from the water as it passes through it. The recent experiments of Professor Way, chemist to the English Agricultural Society, are conclusive on this point.

Flower-beds which were planted properly last May will now, or very soon, require to be thinned out. What I call " planting properly" is, that the whole surface be as much covered as possible at the first planting, and more particularly the sides, which can hardly be planted too closely. When the stock of plants are too limited to allow of this liberal planting, the next best mode is to have recourse to spring-sown annuals, and to fill up in rows, or in broad patches, between the permanent plants; and as the latter are now spreading freely, these temporary helps must be removed gradually, that is, a few at a time. The most surprising thing I saw round London the other day, were some flower-gardens planted as we used to plant larches and firs in the Highlands, thirty years since, that is, so many feet apart each way; many of these flower-beds are not yet covered. Now, after having discarded and written down, as it were, the use of nice little annuals about London, it does seem curious how they can reconcile their notions of flower-beds half filled, and more like fields in the country getting their preparations for the turnip crop

than like beds for flowers at midsummer. I must qualify this, however, by the remark, that in some of the places I visited the planting was even more liberal than in the country; but these instances seem the exception, not the rule generally followed.

The proper way to act where summer half-hardy plants are scarce is this, and even where no scarcity is known, it is a good plan. The beds being ready in April or May, let the summer plants, as *Verbenas, Petunias, &c*, be planted in regular rows, and at such distances as will allow of their getting too crowded before the end of July, and particularly the outside row next the grass or gravel; the least spreading plants should have a free space of at least nine inches between them and the edge of the bed, and a foot is not too much for most of them; for unless the pruning or cutting is done with great care, the sides of the beds will look badly. Then, the beds being so far planted, let regular rows of annuals be transplanted from the reserve garden in the intervening spaces. These will flower and look very gay from the end of May till this time, when the permanent plants will be so far spread as to require a thinning of the annuals. *Virginian stocks* in full bloom will easily transplant for this purpose, and so will *Sphenogyne speciosa*, the prettiest of all yellow annuals whilst it lasts; *Navel wort*, white; with the purple and white *Candy tuft*; *Calendula hybrida*, white; all the *Clarkias, Collinsias, Godetias*, with *Eucharidium grandiflorum, Cochlearia acaulis*, and many other low things, would easily transplant in the same way, and after good waterings would make a gay assemblage, and render the beds not only full of plants but also with distinct colours, while the summer plants were getting established. Surely with a little more expense and forethought we might keep up a show of flowers in the early part of the summer, and not be annoyed as at present with raw, naked, or half covered beds. The objections which may be urged against this mode are, that such things would not look well at first planting, and that the annuals would impoverish the soil too much for the permanent crop; but all this is only moonshine. I have adopted the plan, and have seen it done by others over and over again. When the annuals are removed, let their places be well stirred with a hoe or fork, and let a few canfuls of liquid manure be poured on the exhausted parts, and instead of robbing the beds they may rather be enriched under this system. When we hear of so much having been gained by the disuse of annuals, and see beds only half filled for the best part of the summer, it is difficult to reconcile ourselves to the truth of the assertion.　　　　　　　　　　D. Beaton.

GREENHOUSE AND WINDOW GARDENING.

Vines in a Greenhouse.—Some months ago we directed attention to this subject, and would now advert to a few matters that should be attended to by our less experienced friends, believing that there are few plants, the successful culture of which are more an object of worthy ambition, among those who own a glass-house, however small; that the associations connected with it over yield a source of elevated pleasure to the contemplative mind; and that independently of the delight, approaching a proud satisfaction, of being able to place a cluster of the luscious fruit, of their own rearing and tending, before their visiting friends, there is something of the paradisiacal restored in the very thought of " sitting under their own vine."

Stopping the Shoots, &c.—The fruit being produced upon young shoots of the present season's growth, which started from the mature buds on the young wood of the previous season, it is usual to stop all these young shoots, except the terminal or leading one in a young vine, at one eye or point beyond the fruit; and where the spur system is practised, to stop those shoots which may not show fruit at a similar length; as, if allowed to grow longer, their shade would injuriously affect the others. As a general rule, this cannot be bettered. When vines are weak, however, it is advisable to allow the shoots to grow a few joints farther, if there is room, in order to promote a more vigorous root action—the profusion of roots, and the extension of branches, or the increasing the number or the size of leaves, ever acting as relative and correlative to each other. Hence it is also advisable, in such cases, not to cut off part of a shoot, but in due time merely to nip out its terminal bud, as thus less of a check will be given to the system. When the shoot thus nipped is found too long for the space, it may be gradually shortened, when the first-formed leaves have so increased in size, or the laterals left are so numerous, that the reciprocal action between the roots and top may be maintained without any great check to the system, though a joint or two at the end of the shoot be removed. In very vigorous vines, where from the size of their leaves much more space is requisite for their full expansion to light, the bearing shoots may be stopped one inch or so beyond the bunch, taking care, however, to give full exposure and justice to the leaf situated close to the bunch, as then it will be sufficient to maintain a requisite flow of nutriment to it. When it is desirable to strengthen the base end of a young vine, the terminal bud may be nipped out with advantage when the shoot is from three to six feet in length. This will cause the free protrusion of laterals, which, according to the room, must again be nipped at the first, second, or third joint. The development of the secondary or lateral shoots will strengthen the main stem, and increase the size of the buds in the axils of the leaves, upon the same principle, that the more numerous and extended the branches and leaves of a tree, the more bulky will be its timber. In this case, however, a compromise must be made in the early part of autumn between mere growth and fruitfulness, by removing these laterals by degrees, and leaving only the primary leaf at each joint, so that the juices may be more perfectly elaborated; otherwise the buds, though strong, will be apt to be pointed instead of being round, and more productive, in a following season, of wood than of bunches. In thus nipping out the terminal bud of a young shoot, to increase its strength at its base, some of the buds near the point will start into growth, and of these the strongest must be selected as the leader. This fresh-formed part will not be so strong as if no stopping had taken place; but that is a matter of less moment, as in a young vine that part will be cut away in the winter pruning; while, as we have seen, additional strength and vigour will have been transferred to the base of the rod, where it is most required. Without something of this kind being done, it often happens that the strongest wood, and the best swelled buds, are situated on the extreme ends of the shoots which are pruned away during winter, without being of any other advantage than swelling the contents of the rubbish or charring heap.

This stopping and pruning must be regulated in accordance with the system of culture, as respects the plants being treated upon the long rod, and the succession rod, or what is termed the spurring system; because all the shoots produced and retained during summer upon established vines—and all, with the exception of the leading shoot in young vines—are cut down in winter to one or more buds. In either of the first cases, unless where there is plenty of room, laterals need not be allowed to remain upon the stopped fruitful shoots; and towards autumn they may be deprived of all the buds in the axils of their leaves, as they will be cut away altogether in winter, and, in fact, any time as

soon as fruit is removed; while laterals should be encouraged upon the main shoots, for producing in the following season, gradually removing them in the autumn, and even disbudding the points of the shoots, for reasons already given.

On the other hand, when the spur-system is followed, and it is the best of all for a greenhouse, because involving least shade, laterals should be encouraged, but *chiefly* at the base of the young bearing shoots—those nearest the end next the fruit being first removed; and then in autumn, when there is no danger of starting the smaller-looking buds at the base, those from the point downwards may be picked out, leaving the leaves untouched, and thus a greater proportion of organisable matter will be lodged in the buds and wood ultimately left, than otherwise would have fallen to their share. Under such treatment, winter pruning may be effected shortly after cutting the fruit, or as soon as the leaves turn yellow.

Under such a disbudding, encouraging, and removing lateral system, vigour and fruitfulness are alike encouraged. Under such management, other circumstances being favourable, so great is the quantity of organisable matter stored up in the main stem, that fruit will show from whatever part shoots are produced; so that even *spur* pruning is dispensed with; some first-rate cultivators, at the winter pruning, cutting off all close to the main stem. From such cut parts, buds that were latent are developed during the increased temperature of spring; from these one or two are selected, and the others rubbed off, and when these have fruited they are cut clean off in a similar manner. Let not young beginners, however, try such a system without clearly seeing through it in all its bearings. Several have already burned their fingers by recklessly adopting it; and the chief cause of failure arose from leaving part of a young shoot upon the end of the main one, from which all the young shoots had been closely cut off. As the sap would flow more copiously into its natural prepared channels than into those which required to be aroused from inertness, the consequence was, that the buds on the shoot left broke and grew with unusual strength, while no stopping or doctoring afterwards could tempt the juices to find an exit by the latent undeveloped buds. Those, therefore, who, seeking the pleasure of excitement in something new, would try the smooth whip-handle system of pruning, had better see that not one truly developed bud was allowed to remain.

Thinning the Fruit.—This should be done early, as soon as the berries are the size of half-grown green peas. The sooner they are cut out, the better will it be for those that are left. The thinning should be regulated by the average size that the berries of the respected kinds arrive at. At this season, and especially in a greenhouse, something more should be done, as, if left thick and firm in the bunch, the berries are apt to mould with damp in autumn. While close bunches, therefore, may be a desideratum for the early part of the season, they should hang looser in the autumn, so that the air may percolate freely through them. In thinning, cut out the centre berries, leaving the outsides; use sharp pointed scissors, and a hooked stick for holding the bunch, that you may have no necessity for touching it with the hand.

Air and Temperature.—During the summer and beginning of autumn the temperature of our climate will be sufficient under glass, with plenty of air during the day, shutting it off as the cold nights of autumn arrive. In cold weather in September, a little fire will be more effectual for ripening the wood than half a dozen such fires in the end of October; but then a portion of air should be admitted all night. This is always a safe course to follow, as, if shut up, and the sun strikes upon the house before opened, the berries are frequently disfigured by being covered with deposited moisture, while the close and sultry atmosphere elongates and weakens the footstalk of the berry, and is thus one of the predisposing causes for the evils of shanking, shrivelling, &c.

Watering.—This will be required at the root in dry weather; manure-water of any kind and quality they will greedily devour. This, if not more successful, is more refined to men's general feelings than filling a border for vines with rank garbage—such as the carcases of animals of all sorts and sizes. As to watering over head, we recommend the disuse of the syringe and engine as soon as the buds are fairly broken. Moisture in the atmosphere may sufficiently be maintained by watering the stages and floor of the house. If that great pest, the red spider, makes his appearance, he should be dislodged by lighting a fire in a dull night, and painting the flues and pipes with a solution of water and flowers of sulphur. If in a flue, be careful that you put none of the sulphur near to where the flue enters, as it ignites at a comparatively low temperature, and then will kill everything green in the vegetable way.   R. FISH.

HOTHOUSE DEPARTMENT.

EXOTIC FERNS.—A correspondent having asked for information on the culture of these most interesting plants, we are induced to make our reply to our correspondent a general one, for the benefit of such of our readers as either now, or may hereafter, cultivate these beautiful ornaments of our stoves. We know from experience that the love of them is on the increase, and no wonder, for their beauty and delicacy are unquestionably great. It is not the least recommendation of them, that a large number of them will grow in situations where most other plants would not exist; that is, in the deepest shade under other plants, and on shelves at the back of a lean-to house. With these few preliminary remarks we proceed to describe their culture.

Soil.—Ferns love a light rich compost composed of fibrous loam, turfy peat, and rotten leaf mould; the whole broken well with the hand and thoroughly mixed with a considerable amount of silver sand. For very small plants it will be desirable to run the compost through a sieve with a moderately small mesh. For large plants it is desirable to use it without sifting.

Drainage.—This point of culture is almost of as much importance to ferns as to orchids. They will not thrive long in a sour ill-drained soil. The best material to drain with is broken potsherds, the larger pieces at the bottom of the pot, and then a layer of the smaller ones, covering them with some moss or rough siftings of the compost. Some of the more delicate kinds will thrive better if the compost is mixed with the smallest potsherds. This will keep the soil porous throughout; a point of consequence to these delicate rooted plants.

Potting.—The spring time of the year is the best season for potting; and as the plants fill the pots with roots, they ought to be repotted in the middle of summer. Free growing kinds may require potting three times in the growing season. The operator must be guided by the requirements of the plants, as to the number of times potting would be advantageous to them.

Watering.—The strong species require abundance of water during the growing season. At all times they must never be allowed to become quite dry. In this point they considerably resemble the tribe of Heaths, for if once allowed to become thoroughly dry, their death is almost certain. It is desirable, then, to attend closely to their demands for water. They delight, also, in a moist atmosphere. Hence the climate of the orchid-house suits them admirably, especially in the spring months. In this house they will be useful to fill up a space that without them would be void and naked. We have mentioned frequently that there are considerable numbers of orchids that are best cultivated in baskets, and so grown they necessarily require a large quantity of water whilst in a growing state. Now, the drip from these baskets will be considerable, and the orchids in pots will be injured, almost to death, by such dripping of water on their young growths. Not so the ferns, they will bear it with impunity, excepting the more delicate kinds. This place under the orchids in baskets, therefore, may be very elegantly and very effectively filled with the stronger growing species of ferns, and the drip from the orchids in baskets, or on logs of wood, will be advantageous to them.

General Management.—In winter give a moderate supply of water; remove all decaying fronds (the branchy leaves), and refresh occasionally by a top dressing. In spring pot the plants, and increase the quantity of water at the root, syringing them occasionally during hot weather. In summer we have found it advantageous to remove them into a deep cold pit, shading them with mats from the sun. In this situation they obtain a stout strong growth, which enables them to bear a diminution of heat through the non-growing months of winter.

Like all other large families of plants, the Ferns are best in a house devoted to their culture alone. In the Sheffield Botanic Garden, a house of considerable dimensions is assigned principally to this beautiful tribe of plants. In this house they are, or were very lately, cultivated in such a manner as to assimilate in a great degree to their native solitudes. Rustic arches, formed of branches of trees, were covered with the smaller species; and the stronger ones were planted in the soil; their luxuriance of growth showed that they were quite at home. The growth was greatly aided by a trickling fall of water into a small pool, over which rustic arches were thrown, covered with the elegant forms which those lovely plants assume. A somewhat similar mode of growing them may be seen in the garden of J. Anderson, Esq., of The Holme, Regent's Park. Ardent lovers of plants will find the culture of Ferns in a house expressly devoted to them a source of great enjoyment. Ever varying, ever new, is the appearance of these plants.

Propagation.—A considerable number of the species of Ferns are easily propagated by division. They send forth a creeping rhizoma, or root-shoot, which puts forth roots for itself; and may then be divided with a sharp knife from the parent, potted into small pots, and kept in the shade till established. Others produce on the leaves a kind of knot, which, when tolerably matured, may be cut off with a portion of the frond, and placed upon the surface of the soil in a pot covered with a bell-glass. In this situation the knots quickly put forth roots, and become independent plants. There are, however, several species that neither put forth a running rhizoma nor leaves capable of producing plants. Such unmanageable fellows must be humoured in their habits. The only mode in such cases to increase them is by seeds, or sporules, whichever they may be; but as it is an undoubted fact, that young ferns do spring from these, it is of little consequence whether we call them seeds or plants in embryo sporules, as they are termed in the language of botanists. It is from this dust-like substance that young plants are produced when in a proper situation. In moist hothouses ferns spring up spontaneously from these seeds or sporules, in every situation that is damp and shady. This we must imitate when we wish to increase any particular species.

Very lately we saw a successful bit of this kind. In the gardens at Kew there is a propagating house for woody stove plants. There is a platform in the centre, and two narrow shelves at the sides; underneath these shelves a second shelf has been put up, and covered with a rather strong loam. Upon this a quantity of the sporules of that rare and beautiful fern *Gymnogramma chrysophylla*, or Golden-leaved Fern, had been scattered early this year. We visited these famous gardens about a fortnight since, and found this shelf covered with young plants of this rare and beautiful fern. This was a lesson to be conned over deeply, and put into practice as nearly as possible, to obtain the same results.

(To be continued.)

FLORISTS' FLOWERS.

CHRYSANTHEMUMS.—This fine autumnal family will now require considerable attention. As they come into flower when the beauties of Flora are, for the most part, departed for the season, they are on that account, as well as for their intrinsic beauty, well worthy of the assiduous and never-tiring care of the florist. Though a green-house plant in the more northern parts of the kingdom, and therefore belonging to our good friend Mr. Fish, yet we opine they are truly a florist's flower; and, therefore, we trust he will excuse us saying a few words about them.

Such as are intended for exhibition—for with such we only have to do—should have the needful attention paid to them at this particular time more than any other. Fine blooms can only be obtained by leaving only two or three on each plant; and the plant must be strengthened by re-potting frequently, and watering with liquid-manure once every ten days. Begin this assisting process early, to strengthen the plants, and there will be almost a certainty of success. Keep them clear of green fly by frequent smoking or washing with tobacco-water. These aphides, if allowed to prevail, will prevent the growth, and finally destroy the flowers. T. APPLEBY.

THE KITCHEN-GARDEN.

PLANTING.—All kinds of vegetables should at this season, whilst dry hot weather prevails, be planted in the evening, and be well watered at the same time. The dribbling system of applying water is of little use. Let a good soaking be given, and have done with it.

A great advantage will at this season be found by all those who have followed out directions with regard to sloping banks, and the regulating the pea and other summer crops, as directed, at sufficient distances, to afford ample room for the winter cropping, as well as a partial shade.

CELERY in all stages of growth must at this season be well irrigated with water, if it is required to be produced of good quality.

ROUTINE WORK.—The principal routine at this season to be kept in practice is the application of abundance of water to all growing crops, if parching weather prevails: and the well mulching, and surface-stirring, and preparing the soil for the autumn and winter cropping.

CUCUMBERS—whether in the frame, pit, or in the natural ground—will require stopping, pegging, and regulating in a methodical manner; applying occasionally, also, liberal soakings of manure water.

MELONS.—As soon as the first crop is clearly cut off, lose no time in again giving all possible encouragement to the plants, in order to ensure their making a luxuriant growth—stopping, setting, and encouraging the setting and swelling of the fruit as soon as possible, according to our previous directions. JAMES BARNES.

MISCELLANEOUS INFORMATION.

THE EYE OF THE MISTRESS.
By the Authoress of "My Flowers."

In the management of a small income we must scrupulously study to save in the smallest, as well as the largest, concerns of a household, and endeavour to make every arrangement to accomplish our important object.

It is a very good plan, if room can be found for the purpose, to set apart a closet for the wholesale articles of consumption, such as are laid in for some weeks or months, and to weigh out, every Saturday or Monday, the proper quantity of each for the week's supply, to be placed in a cupboard, for convenient daily use. The cupboard of a chiffonier in the sitting-room will answer this purpose for articles that do not omit an unpleasant smell; and this will, perhaps, somewhat lessen the trouble of the mistress of the house, and prevent a good deal of running about; but the kitchen cupboard is the most convenient for this purpose. The shop, as the store-closet may be considered, should then be resolutely closed till the following week; and in this way a strict watch may be kept over every item, and no unnecessary expenditure allowed. But unless the mistress of a family can depend upon her own firmness of purpose, she had much better give up the smaller saving to avoid the greater loss, and order in from the grocer, &c., a weekly supply of the articles required. A store-closet should be dry and cool, and at a distance from the sitting-rooms; because candles and soap will sometimes create a disagreeable effluvia, particularly when first brought in.

The keys of the store-closet and the cupboard should never leave the hand of the mistress; her eye should be over everything, and her judgment exerted in the simplest and most trifling concerns; for, with the best intentions, servants never economize so fully, or manage stores so prudently, as the mistress herself can do. I have known excellent servants, of unblemished integrity, strongly attached to the family they lived with, and sincerely anxious to save expense in every way, yet extremely deficient in management, and thoughtless about what seemed trifles, but which kept the weekly bills at a higher figure than they needed to have been. Candles are carried about the house, flaring themselves away, when the work might have been done by daylight; or two or three are left burning needlessly about the kitchen and offices; or they are lighted by being poked into the fire, instead of a match or splint being employed. Soap is left swimming in water and wasting, instead of being put into its proper place the moment it is done with; house brooms are used in the kitchen and spoiled before their time; housemaid's gloves, black-lead, brushes, &c., are thought so little of, that they are knocked about without the smallest concern, and destroyed in half the proper time, thereby considerably increasing the consumption, and of course adding to the bill.

These remarks may, by many, be deemed trivial, but to the class of economists whom I am anxious to assist they will prove to be of moment, if they are really desirous of clipping away every superabundant expense, and looking carefully to every little department of household economy. It is never mean to prevent waste with the largest income; we are but stewards of that which our Lord has committed to our trust; and with the small means many families possess, it is an imperative duty to look closely and narrowly after everything that is used in the house. Honest, sensible servants will never object to be closely watched. They will place themselves in their mistresses' situation, and be satisfied that they would do exactly the same if their circumstances were reversed. Where servants dislike being strictly looked after, they are either disposed to do that which is evil, or they are ignorant and self conceited, and fancy that their mistress suspects their honesty, when she is only guarding against thoughtless waste. Knowing, as we all do, the plague of our own hearts, we cannot and ought not to be surprised and indignant at the evil we find in others, particularly where education is always deficient, and where precept as well as example is too often sadly injurious to the infant mind. But, by strict attention on the part of the master or mistress, much mischief may be prevented, and a great deal of good effected, particularly where servants are young enough to be trained and taught. Really good, trustworthy servants are so rare, that we must not write so much for those who possess them, as for those who possess them not.

The eye of the mistress should be in every place, and never really withdrawn from her household at any hour of the day. Where method is observed, which is of the first consequence, she should know every duty of every servant, and when, as well as how, it ought to be done. By this means she will be able, very nearly, to know what is doing in the offices, while she is seated at work, or instructing her children, or taking necessary exercise. If all is scramble and irregularity, the bell may be rung when the maid-servant is just mixing the pudding, or the dinner things may be washing up at the hour when visitors are most likely to call. With one servant, these embarrassments may be avoided by sensible arrangements and a little steady perseverance; and the importance of this is in reality much greater than at first sight we may be inclined to suspect.

Ladies who have been accustomed to the comforts and elegancies of life, may think it enough to enter their kitchens once a day, to order dinner, and glance superficially around; but when the difficulties of life rise up before us, we must renounce its elegancies, and consider only how we may make the most of "such things as we have." When the lesson— the mighty lesson—be content, is learned by heart, "the pomps and vanities" of the world shrink into their real nothingness, and how comparatively easy is the onward path! We must not be ashamed to make the kitchen and its concerns special objects of our attention, not simply as regards the actual eating and drinking, but as involving so much of the economy, respectability, and peacefulness of our dwellings. We all know and feel that our educated minds and tastes do not prefer this branch of duty; and that it obliges us to do and say much that is foreign to our dispositions and painful to our feelings; but, besides that, in all stations it is woman's peculiar work to "look well to the ways of her household;" where means are small, it is a peremptory obligation, to be strictly and religiously fulfilled. As such, whether the mistress of a household is suffering from reverse of fortune, or is but pursuing her accustomed path of prudence and self-denial, her close attention to apparent trifles, her watchfulness over the hourly proceedings of her servants, and her frequent visits to the domestic offices, are a holy and beautiful portion of her walk in life—a section of her duty to God and man.

I am not now drawing an imaginary portrait; the original is daily before me; and although I have none of my own practical experience to offer, yet I am even less likely to overstate facts, and unintentionally mislead, because I am not blinded by vanity, or led ignorantly to fancy my own ways the best. I am, happily, so situated as to see the working of systems guided by other hands and governed by other minds; and I beg, once for all, to disclaim any further merit in these papers than that of putting the experience of others into what, I trust, may be found a convenient form. That they have met the approval of some of our correspondents, is a source of the deepest gratitude to Him who is the Author and Giver of all good.

MY FARM-YARD.

THE subject of the farm-yard has lately been rather neglected by my pen, not so, though, by my thoughts; for as the summer advances the poultry-keeper's cares multiply.

POULTRY.— Brood after brood succeed each other with great rapidity until the yard appears alive, so numerous are its inhabitants. By far the safest plan when chickens are hatched is to keep the hen under a coop for the first three weeks; this prevents her dragging her young brood over the wet grass, which occasions cramp and many other diseases to which young poultry of all sorts are liable. Rearing

poultry requires a good deal of patience and attention, at least, to be a successful rearer of it; and what can be more disheartening, "in a small way," than to find the young things dying off! which is always the case unless trouble is taken with them. "If a thing is worth doing at all, it is worth doing well," is certainly true concerning poultry rearing. The great secret is to feed them often, and a little at a time. The old nurse's saying, of "children and chickens are always a picking," is a very true one as regards, at least, the latter; for if you carefully watch a brood of young chickens you will observe they are always scratching about and picking up something—it may be a seed, or an insect, or a worm. Thus, nature points out the proper management; for, of course, if the hen is under a coop she cannot obtain food for them, and therefore it must be placed within their reach at various times during the day.

DUCKS I have always found more difficult to rear than chickens; for they are very greedy, and often eat so much that they become suffocated. They stray a long way from their mother (if she is confined) in search of their favourite food, which is slugs; they are therefore very desirable assistants to the gardener, and as they do not scratch up the earth they are most useful, particularly in a flower-garden. In moderation nature's food must be beneficial to them, but then they should not be fed to the same extent as when unable to cater for themselves. Boiled potatoes, damaged rice, and barley-meal are all equally good for young poultry of all sorts. Ducks are particularly calculated for the poor man to keep, if he lives near a pond or ditch; for they require very little feeding, and are contented with the refuse of any vegetables. Cabbages boiled, chopped-up, and mixed with the skins of potatoes, they will eat greedily; young nettles also, if boiled and mashed up, they like much.

How much more comfortable would the cottager's life become, if he exerted himself to procure some, if not all, the little luxuries recommended in THE COTTAGE GARDENER. What a pleasant picture of English cottage life it is, when, on taking your evening walk, you pass a cottage "neat and clean," a little flower-garden in front, some rows of potatoes, carrots, onions, in the back ground, half-way up the garden two or three neat straw hives tenanted by the "busy bee," from whom the owner takes many a lesson. Walk on a little further and you will come to the pig-stye and the house in which some ducks roost, and a goat rests after the fatigue of searching for herbage from the bare common. The rabbit hutch, too, is not forgotten: there it is in the other corner, with its useful and pretty occupants. Such cottage arrangements would make many a heart beat with pleasure, and not without good cause, for although outward appearances are apt to deceive, yet you may be pretty sure that the owner and arranger of such a little arrangement is a happy and an industrious man. I think, also, from cultivating habits of self-denial, and "learning wisdom" from all around, he will (if hitherto a "stranger to the fold") become not a "hearer only, but a doer of the word." That he will do all to the glory of God, and that he will remember that all the good things which he receives, though they appear to the natural eye to be the result of his own carefulness, his own forethought, are in reality the free gift of the Almighty, and therefore He should have the "first fruits"—even his whole heart. "Seek ye first the kingdom of God, and all these things shall be added to you," are the words of our blessed Lord himself, and therefore if we have faith "as a grain of mustard seed," we shall believe—and not only believe but we shall practise. I am quite sure I am not wrong in stating, that when a cottager has truly the love of God in his heart, his home will be one of comfort, neatness, and cleanliness.—A FRIEND.

THE LONDON HORTICULTURAL SOCIETY'S FETE.
CHISWICK, JUNE 8.
(Concluded from page 195.)

AZALEAS.

This season being now advanced, the collections exhibited though past their best, yet were respectable.

1ST PRIZE to Mr. Green, gardener to Sir E. Antrobus, for Apollo; Decora; Variegata; Coronata; Lateritia; Optima; and Rosea Punctata.

2ND PRIZE to Mr. May, of Ealing Park, for Fulgens; Decora; Minerva; Variegata; Coronata; and Gledstanesii.

TALL CACTI.

These were exhibited only by Mr. Green, but his collection was in fine condition, being large plants and beautifully bloomed. He deservedly obtained the first prize. The collection consisted of

Cereus Egertonii—a splendid variety; *Cereus speciosissimus*; *Epiphyllum Ackermanii*; *E. Jenkinsonii*; *E. rubrum coccineum*; and *E. Russelianum.*

COLLECTIONS OF ROSES IN POTS.

We cannot help remarking, that this part of the exhibition was rather the worse for wear—neither the quantity of bloom nor its freshness was so fine as in May.

NURSERYMEN.

1ST PRIZE to Mr. Lane, Great Berkhampstead. The best in it were

Souvenir de Malmaison. Compte de Paris. Souvenir d'Ami; a beautiful new rose. *Souvenir de Meillez;* a handsome kind. *Victoria;* and *Elisa Sauvage.*

2ND PRIZE to Mr. Francis, Hertford. In this lot we noted as good

Mrs. Elliott; Las Casas; Mirabelle; La Pactole; Viscomtess des Cases; a fine yellow. *Smith's yellow Noisette;* an old variety, but still charming when, as in this instance, well bloomed.

AMATEURS.

1ST PRIZE to A. Rowland, Esq., Lewisham. A very fair collection. We can only notice

Aspasia; a neat variety. *Mrs. Bosanquet;* a useful kind. *Coup d' Hebe. Compte de Paris. Blanchefleur;* a chaste and beautiful kind, very much admired.

2ND PRIZE to Mr. Roser, gardener to — Bradbury, Esq. Nearly equal to the last. In it was

Eugene Beauharnois; a fine rose. *Devoniensis;* a much admired variety. *La Reine;* and *Marjorlin de Luxembourg.*

3RD PRIZE to Mr. Terry, gardener to Lady Puller, Youngsbury. Several of the above mentioned kinds were in this collection, and also

Fulgens; a rich crimson or scarlet rose. *Duchess of Sutherland;* a well known favourite. *Princess Maria.*

PELARGONIUMS.

COLLECTIONS OF SIX, IN EIGHT INCH POTS.

1ST PRIZE to Mr. Cock, Chiswick, for six well managed plants, consisting of

*Gulielma, Centurion, *Mont Blanc;* light. *Orion;* dark. *Sikh;* dark. *Rosamund;* light.

2ND PRIZE to Mr. Black, gardener to E. Foster, Esq., of Clewer Manor, near Windsor. Well grown plants, but scarcely in full bloom. They were

Victory (Foster's); dark. *Ariel (Foster's);* light. *Gipsy Bride (Foster's);* dark. *Constance (Foster's);* dark. *Narcissus (Foster's);* dark. *Alonzo (Foster's);* a fine variety; dark.

3RD PRIZE to Mr. Staines, of Maida Vale, for

*Alonzo, *Pearl, Victory, Rosamund, Orion,* and *Negress,* dark.

4TH PRIZE to Mr. Robinson, Pimlico, for

Pearl, Orion, Negress, Forget-me-not, Gulielma, and *Rosetta,* light.

COLLECTIONS OF SIX, IN ELEVEN INCH POTS.

1ST PRIZE to Mr. Cock. These were large and finely flowered plants of

*Rosamund, *Pictum, *Salamander, *Pearl, Centurion,* and *Thisbe.*

COLLECTIONS OF SIX, IN EIGHT INCH POTS.—NURSERYMEN.

1ST PRIZE to Mr. Beck, of Islesworth, for fine plants of *Rosalind, Emily, Delicatissima, Prince Arthur, Mont Blanc,* and *Star.*

2ND PRIZE to Mr. Bragg, of Slough, for

*Centurion, Gulielma, Pearl, Phyllis, *Norah,* and *Marion.*

COLLECTIONS OF SIX, IN ELEVEN INCH POTS.

Only one collection exhibited by Mr. Gaines, of Battersea, who obtained the 1ST PRIZE for

*Gulielma, *Model, *Miss Holford, Negress, *Emma,* and *Aspasia.*

COLLECTIONS OF SIX FANCY VARIETIES.

1ST PRIZE to Mr. Robinson, for six excellent, well bloomed, and finely shaped plants, namely:—

*Fairy Queen, Queen superb, *Madame Meillez, Statuiska, *Reine des Francais,* and *Anais.*

2ND PRIZE to Mr. Gaines, for

*Orestes, Priam, *Hero of Surrey, Odoratum, Magnificum, *Elegans,* and *Reine des Francais.*

3RD PRIZE to Mr. Ambrose, Battersea, for

*Madame Meillez, Magnificum, Anais, Defiance, *Jenny Lind,* and *Ibrahim Pacha.*

4TH PRIZE to Mr. Staines, for

*Jehu superb, *Statuiska, *Madame Meillez, Queen, Bouquet tout fait,* and *Yealmannianum grandiflorum.*

(Those marked * we considered the best.)

CALCEOLARIAS.

COLLECTIONS OF SIX.

These were in considerable numbers, and in good order. Mr. Franklin, gardener to Mrs. Lawrence, had the best, but his were disqualified on account of the size of the pots.

1ST PRIZE to Mr. Gaines, of Battersea, for

Baron Eden, Astarte, Nil desperandum, Panther, and two others.

2ND PRIZE to Mr. Glendinning, who had

Lady Grey, Full Moon, Homer, Mulberry, Marquis of Abercorn, and *Lord Cockburn.*

3RD PRIZE to Mr. Stanley, gardener to H. Bevens, Esq. He sent

Sebastian, Solicitor-General, Chancellor, Beauty, Attraction, and *Canary.*

THE SEEDLING FLORIST FLOWERS were placed in a small tent by themselves; a very proper and convenient arrangement, giving those visitors who cared for such things a good opportunity of viewing them, and studying their points of excellence.

In PELARGONIUMS, Beck's *Major-domo* is a flower possessing much merit, and will be an exhibiting flower next season. Mr. Morris, gardener to — White, Esq., sent a seedling named *Peerless,* a scarlet ground with a dark spot, which promises well.

Mr. Hoyle exhibited several good seedlings, but none better than we already possess, though *Chieftain* and *Ajax* will, we have no doubt, become favourites, especially the latter.

Messrs. Lee sent their seedling AZALEA, *Symmetry,* a larger and handsomer variety than *A. lateritia.* This obtained a prize.

Mr. Gadd's PETUNIA, *Violacea,* is worth growing on account of its form and peculiar violet colour.

MISCELLANEOUS SUBJECTS.—Under this head there were several fine things exhibited, especially *Nepenthes sanguinea,* from Messrs. Veitch. A very fine variety with pitchers a foot long, and four inches in diameter, of a dark reddish brown colour outside, and mottled with darker colour inside. This obtained a prize.

Mr. Ivison sent a large plant of *Nymphæa cærulea,* which was in bloom. This also had a prize, as had a large mass of that curious and rare fern, *Platycerium grande,* from the same.

A prize also was given to Mr. Salter, of Hammersmith, for a large tray of *Irises,* of every hue under the sun.

Mr. Hoyle, Reading, exhibited a beautiful seedling, *Epiphyllum,* named *platypetalum;* a variety of excellent form, broad petals, and a rich dark crimson colour. It very deservedly obtained the silver Banksian medal. Mr. Beck sent a beautiful plant of the curious *Gloxinia Fifyana;* and Messrs. Garraway and Co., Bristol, sent a collection of six *Amaryllises.*

FRUIT.

Considering this was a June show the fruit was by no means abundant, though there were a few good pines and more good grapes than at the last show; also, the peaches were a little better, and so were the strawberries and melons. The prizes were awarded as below.

PROVIDENCE PINES.

1ST PRIZE to Mr. Chapman, gardener to J. B. Glegg, Esq., Chelford, Cheshire. Weight 9 ℔ 11 oz.

2ND PRIZE to Mr. Davis, gardener to Lord Boston. Weight 8 ℔ 3 oz.

3RD PRIZE to Mr. Slowe, gardener to W. R. Baker, Esq. Weight 6 ℔ 11 oz.

MARKET GARDENERS.

1ST PRIZE to Mr. Davis, Oak Hill. Weight 6 ℔ 12 oz.

BLACK HAMBURGH GRAPES.—AMATEURS.

1ST PRIZE to Mr. Frost, gardener to Lady Grenville, Dropmore. Very excellent fruit, well ripened, and of a good colour.

For the heaviest bunch of grapes (*Black Prince*), weighing 2 ℔ 8 oz.—

1ST PRIZE to Mr. Chapman, gardener to J. B. Glegg, Esq.

PEACHES.

1ST PRIZE to Mr. Robertson, gardener to the Marquis of

Waterford, Curraghmore, Ireland, for *Royal George*. Mr. Robertson's peaches were the finest we ever saw; well swelled, large size, quite ripe, and perfectly coloured to the bottom of each fruit.

2ND PRIZE to Mr. Chapman, Chelford, for *Gross Mignon*.

NECTARINES.

1ST PRIZE to Mr. Chapman, Chelford, for *Scarlet Nectarine*.
2ND PRIZE to Mr. Foggo, for *Elruge*.

MELONS—HEAVIEST.

1ST PRIZE to Mr. Munro, gardener to Mrs. Oddie, Colney House, for *Munro's hybrid Egyptian Green Flesh*, weighing 7 lb 8 oz.

BEST FLAVOURED.

1ST PRIZE to Mr. Fleming, gardener to the Duke of Sutherland; *Hybrid* between Housainee and Ispahan.

STRAWBERRIES.

1ST PRIZE to Mr. Busby, gardener to S. Crawley, Esq., Luton, Beds, for *British Queen* strawberries, excellently coloured and perfectly ripe.

IN POTS.

1ST PRIZE to Mr. Elliott, gardener to J. B. Boothby, Esq., for *British Queens*.
2ND PRIZE to Mr. Toy, for *Kean's Seedlings*.

FIGS.

1ST PRIZE to Mr. Foggo, for *Brown Turkey*.

ROYAL BOTANIC SOCIETY'S SHOW.
REGENT'S PARK, JUNE 12.

(*Concluded from page* 195.)

NEW ORCHIDS.

1ST PRIZE to Mr. Franklin, for
Odontoglossum hastilabium; a fine species, with large flowers produced on a spike two feet long; sepals and petals yellowish; lip broad, with deep rosy purple blotch.

2ND PRIZE to Mr. Barnes, for a well-grown plant of
Barkeria melanocaulon; a very desirable species, allied to *B. spectabilis*.

COLLECTIONS OF THIRTY STOVE AND GREENHOUSE PLANTS.

1ST PRIZE to Mr. May, gardener to Mrs. Lawrence, Ealing Park. The following were additions to this fine collection :—

Abelia floribunda; 3ft. by 3ft. *Adenandra fragrans*; 2ft. by 2ft. *Azalea fulgens*; 3ft. by 3ft. *Dillwynia floribunda*; 2ft. by 3ft. *Gompholobium splendens*; a beautiful golden-flowered species, 1ft. by 1ft.

2ND PRIZE to Mr. Cole, gardener to H. Collyer, Esq. The additions were

Allamanda grandiflora. *Azalea lateritia*; finely bloomed, 3ft. by 3ft. *Clerodendrum Kæmpferii*; 3ft. by 5ft. *Dillwynia rudis*; 2ft. by 2ft. *Ixora crocata*; 3ft. by 2½ft. *Polygala cordata*; 3ft. by 4ft.

COLLECTIONS OF TWENTY STOVE AND GREENHOUSE PLANTS.

1ST PRIZE to Mr. Green, gardener to Sir E. Antrobus. In addition was a well-grown plant of
Gardenia Fortunii. This is a decided improvement upon *G. florida*. The blossoms are nearly twice the size, and the foliage larger, and the habit better.

COLLECTIONS OF TEN STOVE AND GREENHOUSE PLANTS.

1ST PRIZE to Mr. Carson, gardener to W. J. Farmer, Esq., Nonsuch Park. In addition to the handsome plants already noticed were

Leschenaultia biloba grandiflora; 2ft. by 2ft. *Allamanda cathartica*; 6ft. by 2½ft. *Dipladenia crassinoda*; 4ft. by 2½ft. *Aphelexis humilis*; 2½ft. by 2ft. *Polygala oppositifolia*; 2ft. by 3ft.

2ND PRIZE to Mr. Barnes, for equally fine plants of
Æschynanthus boschianus; 4ft. by 2½ft. *Dipladenia splendens*; a fine specimen, 3ft. by 3ft. *Ixora grandiflora*, *Pimelon Hendersonii*, and *Tetratheca verticillata*, &c., &c.

3RD PRIZE also to Mr. Laybank, gardener to T. Maudesly, Esq., Norwood. We noted as particularly good

Pimelea decussata; 2½ft. by 2½ft. *Chorazema varium*; 1½ft. by 1½ft. *Leschenaultia formosa*; 2ft. by 2½ft. *Hoya carnosa*; an old plant, too much neglected, 3ft. by 2ft.

CAPE HEATHS

Were exhibited in considerable numbers, and in fine order. The competition was very severe.

COLLECTIONS OF FIFTEEN.—AMATEURS.

1ST PRIZE to Mr. Mylam, gardener to S. Rucker, Esq. We can only notice a few :—

Erica Cavendishii; 3ft. by 3ft. *E. elegans stricta*; 2ft. by 3ft. *E. halicacaba*; 2ft. by 2ft. *E. tricolor rubra*; 2ft. by 2½ft. *E. tricolor speciosa*; 2ft. by 2ft. *E. tricolor Wilsonii*; 2ft. by 3ft. *E. mutabilis*; 1½ft. by 2ft.

2ND PRIZE to Mr. Smith, gardener to W. Quilter, Esq., Norwood.

Erica Cavendishii; 3ft. by 4ft. *E. bergiana*; 3ft. by 3ft. *E. vestita coccinea*; 2ft. by 2ft. *E. metulæflora*; 2ft. by 1½ft. *E. suaveolens*; 3ft. by 4ft. *E. perspicua*; 3ft. by 2½ft.

COLLECTIONS OF TWELVE.—NURSERYMEN.

1ST PRIZE to Messrs. Rollison, of Tooting. Fine plants; extra well-bloomed, especially
Erica Grieswoodiana, *E. inflata*, *E. grandiflora*, *E. ventricosa grandiflora* (Henderson's), *E. tricolor mirabile*, *E. pregnans superba*.

COLLECTIONS OF SIX.

1ST PRIZE to Mr. Dennett, gardener to S. Gilliot, Esq., Clapham.

E. Cavendishii; 4ft. by 4ft. *E. florida*; *E. tricolor Lecana*, &c.
2ND PRIZE to Mr. Green. These were remarkably well coloured.

Erica ventricosa grandiflora; *E. tricolor Wilsonii*; *E. elegans*; *E. tricolor Lecana*; and a nice plant of *E. Massonii* not quite in bloom.

SINGLE SPECIMENS, SHOWING SUPERIOR CULTURE.

Were not numerous, but were mostly remarkable for being new plants. Equal prizes were awarded to Mr. Cole for
Roupelia grata, a rather promising plant, known in gardens as *Strophanthus Stanleyana*.

To Messrs. Veitch, for
Escallonia macrantha, a handsome new hardy shrub, and for *Mitraria coccinea*, also very handsome, and said to be hardy.

To Messrs. Lee, Hammersmith, for their beautiful CACTUS, named *Cereus Lecana*.
2ND PRIZE to Messrs. Veitch, for
Dipladenia unophylla, a handsome species, but rather shy to bloom.
3RD PRIZE to Mr. Ivison, Syon House, for the handsome *Curcuma cordata*, a rare plant.
4TH PRIZE to Mr. Macqueen, for a neat specimen of the new handsome
Lycopodium cæsium arboreum.

NEW PLANTS.

1ST PRIZE to Messrs. Henderson, of Pine Apple Place, for their beautiful new
Begonia cinnabarina. This is the handsomest of all the tribe, with crimson flower-stems and orange-scarlet blossoms.

Prizes of equal value were awarded to Mr. Laybank, for a pretty new species of *Gompholobium*; and to Mr. Ivison, for his new *Bejaria*.

2ND PRIZE to Messrs. Henderson, for their new
Gloxinia, named *grandis*; a variety we noticed lately in describing the properties of a good Gloxinia. It is something like *Gloxinia albo sanguinea*, but much larger, better formed, and with brighter colours.

To the same firm, for
Schizanthus retusus albidus, a new annual of great beauty.

The Regent's Park Botanical Society offered prizes (very judiciously we think) for plants used in the arts, medicine, &c., or remarkable for handsome foliage. The consequence was, the production of several interesting plants. A prize was awarded to Mr. Mason, gardener to G. Vivian, Esq., of Calverton Manor, near Bath, for a nice plant of the Peruvian bark-tree (*Cinchona calysaya*). Also to Messrs. Veitch, for a small plant of the Mangosteen (*Garcinia Mangostana*). An extra prize was awarded to Messrs. Rollison, for *Bischoffia Javanica*, a plant with very fine foliage.

EXOTIC FERNS.

A collection of twelve species, exceedingly well grown, were exhibited by Mr. Williams, from the gardens at Hoddesden, for which a second prize was awarded.

BRITISH FERNS.

A collection of thirty came from the same place, and obtained the first prize. 2nd to Mr. Smith, gardener to J. Anderson, Esq., Regent's Park, Bath. Collections were exceedingly well grown—so much so, as to create surprise that such specimens could possibly be so fine.

FLORISTS' FLOWERS.

PELARGONIUMS.

The display of these really ornamental plants was very great. They occupied the entire of one side of one of the long tents, and it is not too much to say that there was not a faulty plant among the whole. A better, if so good, a show of them, in our opinion, was never seen at any previous exhibition.

PELARGONIUMS IN EIGHT INCH POTS.—AMATEURS.

1ST PRIZE to Mr. Cock, Chiswick, for a collection of twelve new and distinct varieties.

Forget-me-not, Star, Centurion, Salamander, Mars, Pearl, Orion, Rosamund, Sikh, Cruenta, Gulielma, and Grandiflora.

2ND PRIZE to Mr. Black, gardener to E. Foster, Esq., of Windsor, for

Alderman, Lamartine, Lalla Rookh, Armida improved, Norah, Victory, Constance, Gipsy Bride, Alonzo, Ariel, Narcissus, and Conspicuum. These were all Mr. Foster's own raising, and were in beautiful order.

3RD PRIZE to Mr. Staines and to Mr. Robinson; the judges not being able to say which was best. Mr. Staines showed

Marion, Lamartine, Negress, Forget-me-not, Pearl, Victory, Orion, Rosamund, Star, Alonzo, Lalla Rookh, and Norah.

Mr. Robinson had

Gulielma, Star, Forget-me-not, Chimborazo, Pearl, Orion, Negress, Gustavus, Sundown, Rosetta, Superb, Cassandra, and Sir Walter Raleigh.

NURSERYMEN.

1ST PRIZE to Mr. Dobson, gardener to E. Beck, Esq., for *Symmetry, Star, Emily, Emilia, Delicatissima, Governor, Rosa, Mont Blanc, Agatha, Centurion, Sarah, and Cuyp.*

2ND PRIZE to Mr. Bragg, of the Star Nursery, Slough, for *Princess, Centurion, Phyllis, Marion, Conspicuum, Lalla Rookh, Corregio, Norah, Narcissus, Gulielma, Bertha, and Pearl.*

3RD PRIZE to Mr. Gaines, of Battersea, for *Centurion, Adonis, Nobilissima, Negress, Sikh, Model, Grandiflora, Mrs. Beck, The Nun, Gulielma, Crusader, and Grenadier.*

FANCY PELARGONIUMS.—AMATEURS.

1ST PRIZE to Mr. Robinson, Pimlico. He had this time *Anais, Bouquet-tout-fait, Statwiska, Jenny Lind, Empress, and Magnifica.*

2ND PRIZE to Mr. Staines, for *Yeatmanniana grandiflora, Queen, Statwiska, Madame Meillez, Jehu superb, and Bouquet-tout-fait.*

NURSERYMEN.

No first prize awarded.

2ND PRIZE to Mr. Ambrose, for *Reine de Francais, Formosa, Magnifica, Jenny Lind, Fairy Queen, Picturata.*

3RD PRIZE to Mr. Henderson, St. John's Wood, who had *Queen Victoria, Anais, Amelia, Alboni, Mrs. Loudon, and Fairy Queen.*

And another 3RD PRIZE to Mr. Gaines, for *Anais, Reine de Francais, Gem, Rosetta, Priam, and Orestes.*

ROSES IN POTS.

The show of these beautiful flowers was certainly better here than at Chiswick.

AMATEURS.

1ST PRIZE to Mr. Terry, gardener to Lady Puller, for *Barrone Prevost, Souvenir de Malmaison, Brennus, Rosetta, Madame Hardy, Robin Hood, Coup d'Hebe, and Comtesse Mole.*

2ND PRIZE to Mr. Roser, gardener to H. Bradbury, Esq., Streatham, for *La Reine, Miss Glegg, Beauty of Billiard, Duchesse of Burcleugh, Marquess, Rosetta, La Dauphine, Mrs. Elliott, and Eugene Beauharnais.*

NURSERYMEN.

1ST PRIZE to Messrs. Lane, of Berkhampstead, for *Devoniensis, Courier, Souvenir de Malmaison, Paul Perras, Miss Glegg, Great Western, Madame Plantier, Chenedolle, Comtesse Mole, Souvenir d'Ami, and Meillez.*

2ND PRIZE to Messrs. Paul, of Cheshunt, for *Duke of Cambridge, Barrone Prevost, Madame Nevard, Charles Duval, Mrs. Bosanquet, Leopold de Beaufremont, Belle Maria, Wm. Jesse, Niphetos, Madame Laffay, Paul Perras, and Augustin Mouchelet.*

YELLOW ROSES IN POTS.

1ST PRIZE to Messrs. Lane, for *Fellonia, Persian Yellow, Queen Victoria, Clara Wendall, Harrisonii, Smith's Yellow, Viscountess de Cases, and Lea's Yellow.*

2ND PRIZE to Messrs. Francis, for *Persian Yellow, Smith's Yellow, La Pactole, Viscountess de Cases, Pauline Plantier, and Harrisonii.*

COLLECTIONS OF SIX CALCEOLARIAS.

1ST PRIZE to Messrs. Henderson, of Pine-apple Place, for *Parkmount Beauty, Incumara, Umbrosa coronata, Lowre, and Le splendens.*

2ND PRIZE to Mr. Callough, gardener to Mrs. Griffiths, Avenue Road, for

Curreglayed, Lord Fullarton, Athliste, Catherine, Earl of Rosslyn, and Marion.

3RD PRIZE to Mr. Franklin, gardener to Mrs. Lawrence, Ealing Park, for *Isabella, Queen Victoria, Elegance, Earl of Rosslyn, Earl of Dalhousie, and Lord of Islay.*

PANSIES.

1ST PRIZE to Mr. Turner, Slough, for *Lucy Neal, Queen of England, Ophelia, Marchioness of Lothian (Seedling), Constellation, Climax, Viceroy (Seedling), Goliath, Mrs. Beck, Sambo, Bellona, Mr. Beck, Garratt's Seedling, Addison, Lord Harding, Thisbe, Supreme, White Sergeant, Milton, and Jenny Lind.*

SEEDLINGS.

Certificates of Merit were awarded to Mr. Beck's PELARGONIUM named *Incomparable*; a splendid scarlet ground; the upper petals with a dark blotch on each, well defined, and edged round broadly with the ground colour. To Mr. Smith, for his FUCHSIA named *Inimitable*; a fine light variety, the tube and sepals blush white, and the corolla of the brightest scarlet; the sepals reflex boldly, showing off to great advantage the fine scarlet corolla. To Mr. Bragg, for a PANSY, named *Joseph Hunt*; a large promising variety. To Mr. Ayres, Blackheath, for a seedling FANCY PELARGONIUM, named *Formosissima*. To Mr. Ambrose, for another named *Prince Arthur*. To Messrs. Henderson, Pine-apple Place, for a CALCEOLARIA named *Mrs. Stanley*; yellow ground, beautifully and distinctly marked with crimson. To Mr. Epps, Maidstone, for his new ERICA named *Erica tricolor Eppsii.*

FRUIT.

There was a tolerable display of fruit, of considerable excellence; but we have no room to notice even the winners' names.

VICTORIA REGIA.

Mr. Ivison, gardener to the Duchess Dowager of Northumberland, Syon House, sent again a flower and two leaves of the far-famed *Victoria regia*, for which an extra prize was awarded.

EXTRACTS FROM CORRESPONDENCE.

RANUNCULUSES : SELF-MANURING, &c.—A bed of ranunculuses was the sole extravagance in which my father indulged in his garden, though every thing in it—from these choice pets to the untended lilies of the valley which carpeted a shady corner under a hedge, and from his grape vine, which he pruned himself, to his savoys and parsley—was a delight and luxury to him. My father has rested many years from his labours, and with him the home and garden in which we delighted have passed away from us; but long even before that the ranunculus roots had been destroyed by an accident while out of the ground, and were deemed too costly to be replaced.

Though never without a garden of my own, or an eye for my neighbours' beds and borders, I happen not to have seen a ranunculus from that time till this year, when half-a-dozen blooms kindly sent me by a friend have redeemed the race from my childish recollections, which were by no means very favourable to them ; moreover, they have drawn exclamations of admiration from sundry friends who have, ordinarily, no eyes for flowers.

I know nothing of what should be the properties of a good ranunculus, but I am quite sure that my six blooms would be pronounced to be execrably bad by a florist; nevertheless these—and much worse than these—would be an ornament to any garden, and the pride of many such as mine; and as I look at them I cannot help thinking of the hundreds and hundreds of roots raised as seedlings, condemned, and thrown away, because they do not possess the qualifications needful to perfection. An edging (even of single ones) would be beautiful round one of my beds; but the cost of any quantity of those advertised is quite beyond my means. Why should not Mr. Tyso, and other great growers—not only of ranunculus, but other florist's flowers—sell those of no value, to put out singly into the market, by the pound or hundred, at a price which would be remunerate them for all trouble expended on them, and for the loss of the manure they would produce when thrown on the rubbish-heap; this would enable the cottager almost, and certainly thousands of amateurs, to share in otherwise forbidden pleasures. I am far from undervaluing the florist's art; but why should any source of pleasure in the world be wasted? and there is more pleasure to be derived from bad flowers than from none. There would be no fear of the popular taste in flowers deteriorating, even were our small gardens inundated with bad flowers. The beauty of a good flower makes itself felt at once to the most unpractised eye, and the taste for flowers, *per se*, would spread with the increased ease of gratifying it.

For myself, I am bent on having some ranunculuses in my garden next year, if only a patch; for the sight of them has recalled a host of memories as bewitching, and almost as pure, as their own painted petals. Will you kindly tell me whether I may hope that they will flower if planted in my common garden soil, which is as unlike a buttercup loam as may be, being light and sandy? Should I give them the sunniest or shadiest spot? and will rotten hotbed linings, or vegetable mould, and spring waterings help them? I have no other luxuries, and little time to devote to them, but should be quite content if the blooms came at all, though as different from Mr. Tyso's treasures as the tulips of a cottager's patch from their stately kindred at Mr. Groom's.

Speaking of Mr. Tyso's throwing his rejected ranunculuses on the rubbish-heap, reminds me that you have not mentioned the subject of self-manuring in THE COTTAGE GARDENER. I remember a story of a vine-dresser, too poor to buy manure, who was, in consequence, on the point of giving up their culture, but could not resist one more trial, and for want of anything else, dug in about their roots, as far as it would go, all the prunings of the vines, old and new, he could collect; and the produce of those, so treated, enabled him to hold out a helping hand to the remainder.

When a girl, boasting only a corner in the home-garden as my own, I pulled up the withered bines of my major convolvoluses one autumn, and tossed them into a summer-house to await my leisure to garner their seeds; my leisure, or my pleasure, never came till sowing time, when, having gathered and shelled till I was weary, yet not liking to waste any of my store, I dug a hole and stuffed the bines and the dead pods remaining on them into it, trusting that some would come up—as they did; no thanks to my treatment, for I did not know in those days that air was necessary to the vegetating of a seed, and buried the whole pretty deeply. Such magnificent convolvoluses—plants and flowers—as came from that patch I have never seen before nor since; but I recommend every one who can keep the haulm of any annual in any quantity apart from other manure to try the result of a less rough experiment on the same plan. I now always chop up the tops of my asparagus when withered, and return them to the bed, and so also the prunings of my roses, but the amount of manure furnished is too small to produce any apparent effect. Has the plan ever been tried in any of the great rose or gooseberry gardens?—A LOVER OF FLOWERS FROM CHILDHOOD.

[Mr. Appleby will give some timely notes upon ranunculus culture. "Self-manuring," or manuring plants with their own refuse, or the refuse of their species, is good practice; but plants usually require more ammoniacal matters to be applied to their roots than can be furnished them by their own refuse alone.—ED. C. G.]

A PARROT BECOMING FEATHERLESS is caused by over-feeding with unnatural food. Parrots in a wild state feed on fruit and vegetables; and the more simply fed in a state of confinement the better: they must not have either meat to eat or bones to pick. It is a skin disease, similar to mange in quadrupeds, that causes them to bite off their feathers. The remedy is, ¼ oz. liver of sulphur dissolved in half a pint of water, applied warm with a brush every day, until a cure is effected, and the bird placed in a warm apartment until perfectly dry.—AN OLD BIRD FANCIER.

EGGS IN LIME WATER.—"A Friend," in No. 90 of your COTTAGE GARDENER, wishes to know the proportion of lime to water for keeping eggs. 1 lb of lime to a gallon of water is the quantity; and it is important that the lime should be quite fresh—*i.e.*, quick-lime.—I. F. E.

BLANCHING CELERY.—The mode in which I cultivate celery being pretty successful (indeed, I am looked-up to hereabouts as a model celery grower—no great praise, however), I am induced to mention it, as I have not seen it alluded to in your pages. I plant and prepare the ground for it, and

give it liquid manure, pretty much as you direct, and earth-up very gradually at first; but when the plants have attained some strength, instead of earthing-up I lay long bands of *clean straw* along both sides of the row, merely leaving the leaves in sight, and throw a little soil on the outside, to prevent the wind blowing away the straw. As the celery grows, I add more straw, &c.: this prevents the possibility of any earth getting into the centres; and it eats crisp and cleaner than any I ever saw.—FLORA

TO CORRESPONDENTS.

*** We request that no one will write to the *departmental writers* of THE COTTAGE GARDENER. It gives them unjustifiable trouble and expense; and we also request our coadjutors *under no circumstances* to reply to such private communications.

PEONY FROST-BITTEN (*A. W.*).—When in full bud last April your peony was nipped by the frost, and the stems have since gradually decayed, and are now dead. Leave it alone, and if the roots have not been injured it will shoot up again, perhaps this autumn, but certainly next spring.

GUANO FOR EXHAUSTED KITCHEN-GARDEN (*W. W. H.*).—For digging into this it would be prejudicial to employ more than the usual quantity of one pound to every ten square yards. It is too highly stimulating, or, in other words, too rich in ammoniacal salts, if genuine, to permit its being added to the soil in large quantities without injuring the next crop. To an exhausted soil we should recommend the addition of super-phosphate of lime (four ounces to every 10 yards), and some slowly-decomposing vegetable matter, such as decayed sawdust, or decayed tanner's bark (20 or 30 tons per acre), as well as the guano. This is supposing that you have no stable-manure.

SUPER-PHOSPHATE OF LIME (*S. L. of C.*).—In preparing this, the bones should be broken into fragments not larger than a sixpence; sprinkle the bones with the *water* and then pour on the acid. If you wish to apply it in a liquid state, more water must be added *after* the bones are dissolved. If the oil of vitriol is of the strongest kind you ought not to fail in preparing the super-phosphate, if you follow the directions given at page 62, vol. i. The mixture is best spread over the soil, and dug in before planting or sowing. On no account should it be poured over the crop. *Lime-water* is not used as a manure, but for the destruction of slugs, &c.; and is best applied through the rose of a watering-pot. It is hardly fair to ask our correspondent for "the philosophy of the recipe," for thickening the hair, given in our 89th number. Did you ever ask a medical man to give "the philosophy" of his remedies, and obtain from him a satisfactory reply? Such things are empirical; they are found to be useful, but it seems vain to ask, Why?

EDIBLE-ROOTED RAPE.—*A Subscriber* wishes to know where he can obtain some seed of this?

TEMPERATURE OF POULTRY HOUSE (*A Half-pay Naval Officer*).—"To ensure a supply of eggs through the winter," you have introduced steam-pipes into your hen-house, and wish to know the temperature to be maintained? You, of course, will only require artificial heat during the winter and early spring, and we should recommend it to be from 64° to 76° during the day, and about 54° at night; for animals as well as plants are benefited by less stimulus during the hours of rest. Will you oblige us with a sketch and description of your hen-house and your mode of warming it?

MUSHROOM-BEDS (*C. Palmer*).—Nos. 46 and 66, which contain the long particulars you require, will cost you sixpence, and can be had through any bookseller. The mode of growing mushrooms in a cellar are the same as those given in No. 66. You have done right as far as you have gone.

CAULIFLOWER PLANTS (*Ibid*).—These, just planted, have their roots attacked by grubs. Water those which are not yet attacked with lime water, in which is dissolved common salt; not more than one ounce in each gallon.

MANY QUESTIONS (*Ibid*).—Pigeons' dung is one of the richest of manures, and will do for any kitchen-garden crop. Leave your *Pæony* roots undisturbed. They did not bloom this year, probably owing to their being disturbed. The *drainings* from your stable, mixed with four times their quantity of water, will do for your asparagus, cabbage-worts, celery, lettuce, and all other plants cultivated for their leaves. Cut away the *suckers of your plum-tree* as fast as they appear; there is no other remedy. *Rhubarb* likes neither a heavy nor a light soil; mix them together, and make a moderately tenacious loam, which it *prefers*. It is quite impossible to say what a *red soil* is, without previous examination.

THE COTTAGE GARDENERS' DICTIONARY (*X. Y. Z., No. 2*).—Thanks for your suggestions. It will be completed in about forty-five weekly numbers, to be published on as many successive Thursdays.

BOX-EDGING (*Ibid*).—The best months for planting box are September and February; yet some planted during wet weather last April is growing strongly. Small rooted slips are employed, and are planted against the perpendicular side of a small trench along the edge of the border or bed they are desired to bound. The best month for clipping box is June, and it should be done in showery weather.

VINEGAR PLANT (*H. O. N.*).—In No. 35, you will find not only a description but a drawing of the Vinegar plant, and directions for its use.

FRUIT-TREE BORDERS (*Flora*).—These should not be cropped, but only the weeds hoed off, and the surface in spring and autumn pointed over, two or three inches deep, with a garden fork. Digging is the very worst treatment applicable to a fruit border.

BLISTERING OF GOOSEBERRY LEAVES (*Ibid*).—The red blotches on the fruit and the red blisters on the leaves are, probably, occasioned by frosts occuring when they are fully charged with moisture during their early growth. It is a good practice to take off the ends of the gooseberry shoots affected with the green fly, or aphis; but it is not true that the aphis becomes a caterpillar!

FLOWERS FOR BEES (*Ibid*).—See what we say on this subject at page 316 of our last volume. The broad-leaved plant you refer to, perhaps is *Borage*, which yields much pasturage for bees.

MENDING INDIAN-RUBBER GOLOSHES (*Ibid*).—Fill the small holes by means of Indian-rubber dissolved in naptha; and to prevent further similar injuries, have a leather sole sewn upon them. A classed *list of Tulips* is given at page 57 of our first volume.

WHITE FORGET-ME-NOT (*Hoffield*).—The party kindly supplying these has no more at present; but if you will send your direction on a stamped envelope, it shall be forwarded, and you will have a plant in your turn we have no doubt.

GRUBS IN TURF (*Frederick*).—These which travel from the turf to "your flower-beds in thousands, and destroy the roots of Cyclamens, &c.," are the larvæ of the common Daddy Long Legs, *Tipula oleracea*. Gas-lime and quick-lime are both said to be fatal to them. See Vol. ii., page 61.

DELAY OF SECOND SWARM.—*J. A. E.* says: "I have for four days been expecting a second swarm from a common cottage hive. The first issued on the 2nd of June; on the 15th I heard three notes of the queen's piping, and consequently expected a swarm on the following day; on the 16th I heard three notes again, and again no swarm followed; on the 17th I heard one note, repeated at long intervals; on the 18th I could hear none. I have now given up all idea of a second swarm, and intend to cut out the top of the hive, and put on a cap (one of Mr. Payne's small hives)." It was in all probability the cold we had at the time your second swarm should have come that prevented it, and caused the young queens to be killed. You have done quite right by cutting a hole and placing a small hive upon the stock, as the season is, you will be a gainer by their not swarming a second time; your stock will be all the better, and a second swarm would have been of little value, indeed, none beyond that of uniting to some weak stock.

REMOVING SMALL HIVE.—*M. A.* says: "Perceiving that the bees did not close up the cells in the small hive put upon a last year's swarm, as it had been on thirty-two days, I proceeded to move it as follows:—I placed a large sheet of pierced zinc between the adapting board and small hive. I then removed the small hive to a distant part of the garden, and placed it on a dish with room for the bees to escape, but perceiving an hour after that they had not left the hive, I caused a little smoke to be inserted from the bottom without effecting my object. An hour later, finding they still adhered to the comb, and that no confusion occurred in the parent hive, I took the hive into a dark room and proceeded to draw them out as I could, with a potato stalk. Much time had now elapsed, and the weight of the combs caused some to give way. I then, gently, with a skimmer, removed them one by one, and placed them in a colander, when to my surprise I found one large comb filled with brood, some of which were on the point of hatching, and many came out during the process. To-day I purpose breaking the comb, and draining the honey, but whether the comb in which the brood is can be made of any avail, I know not. I ought, perhaps, to remark, that the hive swarmed on the 9th inst. The adapting board and sheet of zinc got, unfortunately, removed in the progress of the work, and I placed a flower-pot saucer upon the top of the hive, an old straw one, in which I had cut the hole about a month since. I placed a small hive on the 7th inst. on another old stock. How should it be treated? The stock I expect will swarm shortly." Your small hive should have remained until the *combs were ceiled*, and if room was required another small hive should have been given them, placing it between the parent hive and the one you removed. Upon discovering brood in it, it should have been immediately returned; and its containing brood was the reason of the bees not leaving it. Cells containing brood are very easily distinguished from those containing honey; the cieling of the former is spherical, while that of the latter is plane; had there been no brood in your hive the bees would have left it in a few minutes. *In future use no smoke*. Place a second small hive upon the other old stock you mention; putting it between the one now on and the parent hive, as directed at page 104, volume 2, of THE COTTAGE GARDENER. The comb in which you found the brood is valueless, except for returning to the parent hive, which might easily have been done.

BEES (*A. α.*).—We have never recommended either doubling boards or side hives. We should say, in about 16 or 21 days take out the cork from the top of your hive, and place over the 3-inch hole a bell-glass or small hive, first putting a piece or two of guide-comb into them. Taylor's ventilator (which appears to be the most effectual one), may be placed in the small hive. The glasses are sold with ventilators in them. Your hives are in a very proper situation. If you are anxious to obtain the largest quantity of honey at the least possible expense, we say, use *Payne's Improved Cottage Hive*, and follow *strictly* the directions already given in our pages for its management. The hive you mention, with five glasses, is a pretty toy, but you must not expect *profit* from it. Transfering stock is *altogether* bad practice; not one in ten ever succeeds; were they let alone, they would supply swarms for many years.

PREVENTING SWARMING.—*A Constant Reader* says: "Having heard that room might be given (to prevent swarming) by placing a butter-tub underneath the hive, and opening a communication when necessary, I did so, with a very strong and healthy hive; and having a pane of glass previously inserted, I soon saw the tub perfectly full of bees, and concluded they were working into it, as they always appeared lively and busy, till after about 10 days I fancied I perceived, on a narrower inspection, the bottom of the butter-tub strewed with dead bees; and on removing the hive to ascertain, I took out a full quart of dead bees. Can you in any way account for this? There was no appearance of dissension, or any disease; and it could not be want of air, as the tub was by no means air-tight, light being perceptible through all the cracks. There was no commencement of comb, although they had been in possession of the tub a fortnight. I have now added caps to two of my hives, and though they are filled with bees—as full as possible—and have been for a week, I can perceive no sign of any comb, or any appearance of their being at work." Never again attempt to give your bees room after "the tub fashion;" it is well you found only a few and not all dead that went into it. In giving them room at the top of the hives, by placing small hives upon them, you have done quite right; had you done so at first, your small hives by this time would in all probability have been filled. It was, perhaps, cold that killed them; for a constant current of cold air was passing through the cracks of the tub into the hive, to supply the place of the heated air that was passing out of it. If your caps are filled with bees, they are working in them; the glass where you can see their combs is the last part of the hive they will come to.

WEST INDIAN SEEDS (*A Lady Subscriber*).—We have often heard of and sowed seeds of a *Yellow Convolvulus*, or *Ipomæa*, and also of a *Yellow Pea*, from different countries, but we never saw a good example of either; nevertheless, we would sow those you have from Jamaica. *Veronia* is a local name, and not known to us.

COBŒA SCANDENS (*J. B. Storey*).—This is a half-hardy perennial climber, bearing purple flowers, and blooming in August.

ASPARAGUS (*H. M. Ferns*).—Do not despair, your asparagus is young. It will be better next year, if you give it plenty of liquid manure and salt this summer. Mr. M'Glashan, of Dublin, will get you the covers and indexes.

MILDEWED PEACHES (*An Amateur*).—The white spots on the fruit of your Royal George Peach, which gradually increase and, becoming confluent, at length nearly cover the whole fruit, is the mildew, the agent of mischief being a parasitic fungus. Flowers of sulphur and quick lime slacked, mixed in equal quantities and dusted over the fruit, is said to be the best remedy. The sulphur does not impart any flavour to the fruit. Prevention is better than cure. Paint your wall over with a mixture of clay and sulphur, cut away all the roots that sink deeply into the soil, and promote the production of surface roots by applying mulch to the border. The Royal George and some others are more liable than the Noblesse to be attacked in this way.

HERACLEUM GIGANTEUM (*G. G.*).—This does not require either propping or liquid-manure. *Sea-kale affects*, if growing well, will be benefited by the application both of liquid-manure and salt.

SUN-BURNING AND FRECKLES (*A Traveller in the Sun*).—To prevent these, dissolve half an ounce of citric acid, two drachms of sugar, and one drachm of borax, finely powdered, in a quarter of a pint of water, and apply to the skin before going out.

ROCKERY (*R. A. L.*).—We will have an essay on this subject, if possible, next week.

GNAT BITES (*T. Lindsay*).—To prevent these very irritating punctures the hands and face may be moistened with citric acid, dissolved in water; and to relieve the irritation after being bitten, apply, repeatedly, spirit of hartshorn to the place. Thanks for your gratifying note.

NAMES OF PLANTS (*Mary*).—Your little yellow flower is *Cheiranthus alpinus*, or Alpine Wallflower. The other is a species of *Silene*, or Catchfly, but the specimen was too small for us to determine its specific name. (*Augusta*.)—The seeds from the Italian sailors is *Lunaria biennis*, Honesty, or Moon-wort. Do not take up your *Globe Artichokes*, but remove all the suckers but two or three from each stool yearly. (*Questior*.)—Your plant is *Abutilon striatum*. (*H. W. Hargreaves*.)—How could you suppose it possible to tell the name of a *Fuchsia* from a single leaf? We must have a sprig with flowers on it carefully packed in a box. (*F. W. S.*).—Your *Geranium* seems to be a variegated variety of the old Rose-scented. (*G. A.——S. N.*).—Your plant is *Astrantia maxima*, or Largest Masterwort. (*M. E. S.*).—1. Polygala vulgaris. 2. Pinguicula vulgaris. 3. Euphrasia officinalis. 4. Myosotis alpestris. 5. Salix caprea. 6. Euphorbia Helioscopia. 7. Mercurialis perennis. (*J. N. Q.*)—Your tree is the Sycamore, *Acer Pseudo-Platanus*, which sows itself like a weed. Remove your young trees as soon as possible after Christmas. Cutting through their roots all round now will facilitate the operation.

PEA-FOWL REARING (*J. F. E.*).—We have sent your note to Martin Doyle.

LONDON: Printed by HARRY WOOLDRIDGE, Winchester High-street, in the Parish of Saint Mary Kalendar; and Published by WILLIAM SOMERVILLE ORR, at the Office, No. 2, Amen Corner, in the Parish of Christ Church, City of London.—July 4th, 1850.

WEEKLY CALENDAR.

M D	W D	JULY 11—17, 1850.	Weather near London in 1849.		Sun Rises.	Sun Sets.	Moon R. & S.	Moon's Age.	Clock bef. Sun.	Day of Year.
11	Th	Elephant Hawk Moth seen.	T. 94°—47°.	E. Fine.	57 a. 3	13 a. 8	9 33	2	5 5	192
12	F	Magpie Moth seen.	T. 91°—52°.	N.E. Fine.	58	12	10 7	3	5 12	193
13	S	Hoplia Argentea seen.	T. 81°—48°.	E. Fine.	1V	11	10 36	4	5 20	194
14	Sun	7 Sun. aft. Trinity. Drinker Moth seen.	T. 81°—52°.	N.E. Fine.	1	10	11 2	5	5 27	195
15	M	St. Swithin. White Horehound flowers.	T. 75°—49°.	N.E. Fine.	2	9	11 36	6	5 34	196
16	Tu	Blackbird's song ceases.	T. 81°—51°.	N. Fine.	3	8	11 49	☽	5 40	197
17	W	Burnished Brass Moth seen.	T. 69°—49°.	S.W. Rain.	4	7	morn.	8	5 46	198

In a very secluded village church-yard of the county of Hampshire, and at the head of a grave, overgrown with the greenest and softest of grass, stands a stone bearing no other inscription than this—

G. W.
26th June,
1793.

A brief memorial, yet not unfitting. It marks the last resting place of him who wrote *The Natural History of Selborne*—of Gilbert White; of whom every feature in the vicinity recalls the remembrance; for each of those features was pourtrayed by him with truthfulness, and are, therefore, unchanged. In words he delineated nature as he found her; and, unlike the fashions of the world, her garb is the same in 1850 as it was just a century before; at which date he left Selborne to be admitted a Senior Proctor of Oxford. Thus that village, of which the natural productions and antiquities he has immortalised, Gilbert White needs no memorial, for when we have found the grave in which he rests, and know that that grave is in Selborne Churchyard, we feel that it is all as it should be. The eye would require an effort to confine it to any inscription, though penned by his playfellows, the Wartons; for that eye involuntarily turns to the old trees, and Nore Hill, and the Hanger Copse, and "the deep lanes," and the epitaph springs unbidden to the lips, for it is written on the memory and on the heart—" And this is *White's Selborne!*" White was not a gardener, but he loved plants, and insects, and birds; and he mingled with them, and jotted down a narrative of all their ways naturally, therefore, eloquently; for he who writes or talks of what he loves, thinking only of his subject, and not of how he shall write or talk of it, will ever be eloquent. In this is the charm and the strength of his volume,—a volume which never wearies, which makes the lover of nature more enamoured still, and wins from the veriest worldling a wish to ramble, and watch, and tell of her goings on in quiet places. White (he is one of those intimates of all to whose name no one can prefix Mr. was well fitted for the task he undertook; the aspect of every tree, of every stream, and of every rood of ground, as it changed its colour with the season, were knowledge intimately his, for brief indeed was the space during which he had been absent from Selborne between the dates of his first and last breath, which were both inhaled within its boundary. Four lines of his verses—for he was a poet too—tell us of his birth-place.

" Nor be the parsonage by the muse forgot ;
The partial bard admires his native spot ;
Smit with its beauties, loved, as yet a child,
(Unconscious why), its scapes grotesque and wild.''

RANGE OF BAROMETER—RAIN IN INCHES.

July		1841.	1842.	1843.	1844.	1845.	1846.	1847.	1848.	1849.
11	B.	29.572 29.266	29.960 29.511	30.160 30.009	29.880 29.860	29.792 29.533	30.140 30.082	30.161 30.132	30.417 30.380	30.342 30.325
	R.	—	0.02	—	—	0.71	—	—	—	—
12	B.	29.594 29.878	30.026 29.886	30.147 30.065	29.950 29.670	29.946 29.997	30.142 30.078	30.170 30.105	30.448 30.439	30.343 30.357
	R.	0.02	—	—	0.05	0.07	—	—	—	—
13	B.	29.719 29.630	30.252 30.143	30.040 30.022	29.995 29.404	29.946 29.811	30.063 29.717	30.195 30.184	30.423 30.366	30.213 30.302
	R.	0.02	—	0.07	0.53	0.01	—	—	—	—
14	B.	29.796 29.570	30.237 30.388	30.069 30.048	29.670 29.530	29.895 29.884	29.771 29.864	30.169 30.137	30.310 30.198	30.202 30.199
	R.	0.07	—	—	—	0.06	—	—	0.04	—
15	B.	29.742 29.546	30.388 30.252	30.117 30.048	29.926 29.659	30.059 29.959	29.997 29.813	30.140 30.116	30.260 30.225	30.135 30.125
	R.	1.46	—	—	—	0.03	—	—	—	—
16	B.	29.877 29.894	30.175 30.003	30.094 30.191	29.994 29.949	30.045 30.006	29.703 29.504	30.047 29.923	30.205 30.230	30.116 29.990
	R.	0.01	—	—	—	0.07	0.02	—	—	—
17	B.	30.018 29.820	29.594 29.789	30.242 30.143	30.022 29.848	30.020 29.974	29.311 29.406	29.984 29.916	30.171 30.122	29.964 29.725
	R.	—	—	—	—	0.04	5.06	0.86	—	0.47

Insects.—So numerous have been the inquiries as to the nature of the thread-like and intricately-twisting worm which has occurred abundantly since the rains following the hot weather, that we are induced here to insert a drawing and notice as a general answer. It is the *Gordius aqueticus*. It belongs, like the leech, to the class Suctoria, or suckers; scarcely exhibits any marks of articulation on its body, and has no distinct respiratory organs. Its colour is pale brown, and being found in such a twisted form, as already noticed, suggested its name after the inventor of the Gordian knot. The mouth is a simple pore at the fore extremity of the body, which is conical ; but the tail being forked, as represented at o, has often been mistaken for its mouth. Its habits are little known, but we are inclined to think it one of the friends of the gar-

So few and brief are the known facts of his biography, that even within our brief space we may comprise the whole. His father was "John White, of Selborne, Esquire," and his mother, "Anne, daughter of Thomas Holt, Rector of Streatham, in Surrey ;" and he was born on the 18th of July, 1720. The routine of his education proceeded at a school in Basingstoke, under the vicar of the place, Mr. Warton, best known as the father of two sons, one of whom became Master of Winchester School and the other Professor of Poetry at Oxford. In December, 1739, White was admitted a student of Oriel College in that University, took his Bachelor's degree in the October of 1746, and was elected a Senior Proctor in April 1752. Such are the few dated events of his life of which a record remains. He returned to his native village ; officiated occasionally as its curate; refused to leave it, though tempted with the offers of rich College livings ; and died there, at the date so briefly chronicled on his gravestone, being at the time Master of Arts and Senior Fellow of his College. But we have his imperishable monument in our hand ; a volume, brief as it is, that has been more effectual than any other in rendering Natural History popular ; a volume always pleasing, always fresh, because its sketches are from nature ; unconnected, yet founded on the best of all systems—the systematic pursuit of truth. Neither did truth often escape from a pursuer so unwearied, for we think that no one has contributed so large an amount of original and truthful information concerning the instincts and habits of our native animals. By publishing that information he tells us that he hoped to induce " a more ready attention to the wonders of the creation, too frequently overlooked as common occurrences." How entirely that hope has been realised each generation which has since passed, or is now passing away, has borne general and ready testimony. But had he failed in his kind and pious effort,—"if," as he says, "I shall not be successful in any of these my intentions, yet there remains this consolation behind—that these pursuits, by keeping the body and mind employed, have, under Providence, contributed to much health and cheerfulness of spirits, even to old age." Let our readers dwell upon this testimony of one of the most truthful let them impress this testimony upon the minds of their children ; and let us be believed when we add, as our experience, that if they succeed in planting in their offspring a love of Natural History, they have by so much endowed them with the materials of many hours of never-regretted happiness.

Meteorology of the Week.—The average highest and lowest temperatures during the above seven days, from observations made at Chiswick during the last twenty-three years, are 74° and 52° respectively. The greatest heat observed was 94°, on the 17th, in 1834 ; and the extreme cold, 41°, occurred on the 13th, in 1849. There were 106 fine days, and 55 during which rain fell in the period.

Phenomena Indicative of Weather.—When the *Swallow* flies low and skims over the surface of the ground or of the water, frequently dipping the tips of its wings or bill into the latter as it glides along, we may conclude that rain will soon occur. The two reasons for this lowness of flight may be, that at such times insects are more busy near the earth's surface, and that the rarity of the air then renders flying more laborious in proportion to the height to which a bird soars. *Swans* flying against the wind, says Mr. Forster, portend rain ; and, he adds, that he frequently noticed this sign and its fulfilment. Other musical instruments having catgut strings, never emit such perfect tones when the air become damp just before and during rainy weather. Neither will they keep so well in tune, for the catgut continues to expand in proportion to the moisture of the air.

dener, for two parties observed one escape lately from the body of a beetle, which they found writhing on the ground.

POLITICAL themes are excluded from our pages, and too grateful are we for thus escaping from the anger, malice, and uncharitableness almost inseparable from their discussion, voluntarily to risk a departure from the exclusion even in a single instance. If we resolved sometimes to relax from our rule, one such relaxation should be for the consideration of the present condition of the cultivators of the soil. But we will be proof against even this temptation, and we will go no further than to acknowledge, what all the world knows, that the said cultivators are complaining that they are labouring under great distress. We will not venture to state the proofs which they offer to show the amount of that distress, nor the evidences which those who deny the existence of the distress have adduced. We will not thus venture, because, though Justice herself guided our hand, and though Truth herself trimmed our lamp, still one party or the other would say, "it's pretty plain in which direction *that* is prejudiced." Now, as we are no partizans, we will not subject ourselves to any such suspicions; but, as we have a few relative observations and statements to make, we will suppose—and nothing more, —we will suppose the distress does exist; and we will further suppose, that we had (which is consonant with truth) this question placed before us, "What can be done, with wheat at 40s. per quarter?"

We should reply, as strictly within our province, that three things can be done. In the first place, not because the most important, but because it comes forcibly upon us in connection with an admirable discourse we heard delivered yesterday on the text, "Bear ye one another's burdens." In the first place, we think that landlords should reduce their rents. It is quite true,—as more than once has been observed by a landlord or his representative,—it is quite true, that if wheat had risen instead of having fallen, the tenant would not have paid more rent; but the cases are not parallel. The parallel case is this:—Suppose a landlord, owing to that rise of prices, was on the brink of ruin, would his tenants agree to an advance of ten per cent. upon their rental to aid him? We think they ought; therefore we think the same equity presses upon him when the circumstances are reversed. There is no law to compel either party to help the other to bear his burden, but there is the voice of duty, which is entitled to as much respect as any section of the statute book.

In the second place, "what can be done," is for the cultivator to reduce his expenditure by scrupulously eschewing every outlay, however trivial, that is not needed. We can tell him, from evidence that cannot mislead, that for the mere *essentials* of living, a family of five, with their two domestics, need not exceed £120. In what the non-essentials amount to, is comprised the expenditure upon which economy may be effectually exercised; and we here include dress, because it is one of those items beyond all others that can be effectively tested by the inquiry, "What we can do, and what we can do without." What the cultivator of the soil can do

without, of whatever nature, it is his imperative duty to refrain from; for if there is one equity more palpable than another, it is that which says, he should be self-denying who requires another to be self-denying for him. The reduction of expenditure is to be carried, without any reasonable complaint, much further than many of our readers may imagine; and we have within a bow-shot of us one of the most successful of merchants, who says, "I have succeeded because, even when I began life, I never allowed my expenditure to exceed my income."

In the third place, "what can be done," is for the cultivator to improve his tillage. This may be an unpalatable lesson, but we are convinced of its practicability and necessity, and we speak our conviction boldly. Many of our readers will sneer at the doctrine, but when the same doctrine was uttered to an Irish peasant who turned up his potato ground by the aid of a horse attached to the plough by his tail, that peasant sneered also, and even required an Act of Parliament to compel him to use traces. There are those alive who have witnessed the improvement of our stock, the introduction of drill husbandry, the due rotation of crops, the use of swedes and mangold-wurtzel, the application of artificial manures, and the employment of deep drainage; yet, before these improvements were effected, was there a farmer alive who would not have ridiculed the advice to improve his tillage? We are well assured that it is still open to great and highly remunerative improvements; and as facts are antagonists that even the stoutest yeoman is puzzled to overthrow, we will offer a few for him to wrestle with. They are introduced to us by the following letter from our Publisher, and if they fancy he is not a straightforward, trust-worthy character, let them obtain a contrary conviction by having five minutes conversation with him in Paternoster-Row:—

"I observe many communications are addressed to you, requiring information as to the best and most profitable mode of employing, and the results that may be expected from the skilful management of a few acres. As applicable to these inquiries, I enclose you a copy of an account furnished me by a distinguished member of the Corporation of London, which will answer many of the questions put to you by those correspondents, and which will probably satisfy some of your agricultural friends that there is still hope for them, if they employ their means with skill and energy.

"The crops to which the accounts relate, I can testify were the finest I have ever seen; and it is well known in the neighbourhood that the produce was as here stated. The situation being within six miles of London, is, of course, most favourable both for markets and manure, but otherwise for labour; and the only objection I have heard raised to the account is, that the charge for manure is insufficient. Be that as it may, and making a considerable allowance on that score, it does not show farming to be without its prizes in the lottery of life.

"*June* 21, 1850.   YOUR PUBLISHER."

EXPENSES ON 6½ ACRES OF LAND FOR THE YEAR 1849.			
	£	s.	d.
To twice ploughing 1½ acres of land, @ 12s per acre	1	16	0
11 sacks of potato plants, @ 12s	6	12	0
Cutting and planting	1	0	0
Hoeing and moulding	0	15	0
Ploughing 1 acre three times	1	16	0
Carrot and wurtzel seed	0	4	0
Planting and thinning wurtzel	0	9	6
" cleaning carrots	0	7	6
Hoeing wurtzel three times	0	15	0
Taking-up and trimming	1	0	0
3 bush. of seed rye	0	12	0
Double ploughing 4 acres for oats	4	16	0
2 qrs. of seed oats	2	12	0
Drilling, harrowing, and rolling	1	5	0
Scaring birds	0	16	6
Harvesting oats	2	0	0
Threshing 53½ qrs. of oats, @ 2s 9d per qr.	7	7	1
20 loads of manure, @ 10s	10	0	0
Rent, @ £4 per acre	26	0	0
Rates, taxes, and tithe	4	0	0
	£74	3	7

RETURNS OFF 6½ ACRES OF LAND FOR 1849.			
	£	s.	d.
By 1 acre of rye cut green	9	0	0
1 " potatoes sold on the ground	24	0	0
Turnips off same ground	8	0	0
1 ton of potatoes for house use	5	0	0
4 sacks of plants	2	0	0
6 " chats for pigs	0	18	0
1½ ton of carrots	2	10	0
18 " wurtzel, @ £1	18	0	0
53½ qrs. of oats, @ £1*	53	10	0
17 loads of straw, @ £1	17	0	0
Returns	139	18	0
Expenses	74	3	7
	65	14	5
Interest on capital, wear and tear of carts, &c.	5	14	5
	£60	0	0

THE FRUIT-GARDEN.

ROUTINE WORK PECULIAR TO THE SEASON.

PRESERVATION OF FRUIT.—At this season a very watchful eye is necessary duly to secure the earlier fruits, about which so much care has been bestowed during a long and untoward spring. The anxious housekeeper will be thinking about her preserves; for the stomach must be gratified as well as the eye; and without the products of the garden, the minds of, at least, the natives of the British Isles would be ill at ease. Foremost in this category, the depredations of *birds* may be alluded to. It is of little use to ask a gardener to be merciful on this subject; our splendid *British Queen strawberries*, and our *Fastolff raspberries*, as I think, deserve a better fate than to be gulped down by impudent blackbirds, whose mellifluous notes, however gratifying, may be nurtured in a more economic way.

Of course, most of the readers of this work are on the alert betimes, in order to defend their fruits; nevertheless, as we write for young as well as old, it is a duty to caution against the depredations of these crafty foes.

At the risk of being thought cruel, we must say, that few things are more effectual for destroying the throstle and the blackbird than iron traps, such as are used for rat-catching, only of a very small size. Such may be purchased for about eightpence each; and a single cherry or strawberry will suffice for a bait. The tops of garden walls are a very safe situation in which to place them; here they should be fastened at one end. They answer quite well on the ground near to the crops they are intended to protect; but care must be taken or the fowls, or some pet dog or cat—not to say young people may be injured by them.

Much attention is also necessary as to *the weather*; for in some seasons it is difficult to get strawberries thoroughly dry, and they will not be satisfactory for preserving purposes if gathered when damp. In rainy periods, therefore, a greater frequency in the gatherings becomes necessary, and all other work should be laid aside when proper fruit can be secured. As a general principle, both strawberries and raspberries should be carefully looked over every afternoon: for the greatest amount of depredations committed by the birds is generally from half-past three until five in the morning.

Alpine strawberries should now be well watered during dry periods; drought being very injurious to them at this period, when they are forming those strong trusses which are to produce fruit in September and October; when, if good, they become useful assistants in the dessert.

Apricots will soon be ripening, and as *earwigs* are most destructive vermin to this valuable fruit, a look-out must be made and the enemy destroyed. We are not aware that any plan is better than placing bits of linen rags in clusters, in the lower parts of the tree; here they take refuge at certain periods, and under certain changes of the atmosphere; a day or two's observation will soon exhibit their habits to a sharp observer. Old shoes, with a wisp of soft hay in them, or what are termed "thumb-pots," with hay placed sideways at the bottom of the trees, or even in the larger forks formed by the branches dividing, will act as very good traps; whilst our great carnation growers will tell you of bean-stalks, or even the heads of tobacco-pipes.

The wood of the apricots should be carefully nailed down, or otherwise trained, just before the ripening period. The apricot fruit probably enjoys the direct action of sunlight more than any of our cultivated fruits; and no wonder, when we consider the climate it comes from. Let finger-and-thumb stopping be exercised over all young apricots in course of training; we mean, in stopping those grosser shoots which, in gardening phraseology, are apt to "run away with the tree."

Another point of very great importance is, to have all lateral *breastwood* of later growth stopped, before it can produce any injurious effects as to shade. Be assured, the little spurs (on which the principal dependence must be placed for ensuing crops) need not the shade of their coarser neighbours; such may keep up a smart root-action in their behalf, but at the same time it must be remembered, that they are averse to the perfecting of the blossom-bud.

VINES.—Nothing sooner runs wild than the grape-vine, whether in-doors or out; especially in the latter case. No success can be expected, even in the most favourable parts of Britain, from out-door vines smothered with useless spray; the vine-dresser, therefore, should be on the alert, weekly, from the early part of May until the end of July, or nearly so, pinching, stop-

[* The oats being very fine in quality, part of them were sold for seed, at (we believe) 30s.—ED. C. G.]

ping, disbudding, &c., as the case may be: the prime object being to get the *wall* itself heated by the solar rays. Such heat is given out, as we have before observed, during the night; and it need scarcely be said, that the benefit is immense, for it must be obvious to the most uninformed, that it is a matter of some import, as to whether a thermometer placed amongst the shoots be 55° or 60°. Of course, the vine-dresser will attend to the general principles of thinning in the bunch; and also of the berry, if fine fruit is desired.

Towards the end of the month the earliest *Peaches* will require thinning in the leaf, for although the chief of the swelling may be carried out most beautifully by means of the moderate shade afforded by the leaves, yet it is essential that the sun should at last shine on the fruit itself. This renders the fruit high-coloured, and high-colour and flavour generally go together in the peach; and herein it forms an exception to some other fruits, especially the grape; for those will colour under the most intense shade, formed by a thick canopy of its own umbrageous foliage.

We would never, however, remove the peach foliage until the fruit has nearly completed its swelling—say about one week before it is ripe; and even then we do not advise any wholesale plucking away of the leaves. Our practice is, to pinch away portions of the leaves immediately over the fruit, just enough to let the sun shine on about a third or a half.

The first training, as previously advised, of all the principal or leading shoots, will have been carried on by all parties who are in earnest about their affairs, and we must now advise a further advance in *training*, in order to facilitate the admission of light in an equal way to all portions of the trees. In fact, there can be no reason why every shoot, considered permanent, should not be instantly trained close. It has been before observed in these pages, that when peach or nectarine trees are managed by system, not a shoot need remain but what is necessary in the ensuing spring. This is, of course, presupposing that the trees are free from insects, and that they are safe at the root; or, in other words, are in soil adapted to their habits, and on a sound subsoil. Those, however, who have doubts on such subjects must admit of a compromise; must proceed by "a middling sort of system," by which, indeed, hard though the words be, two-thirds of the wall peaches and nectarines are managed in this kingdom.

Currants (Red and White).—Those who mat up, or otherwise cover, these in order to retard them, should do so the moment the berries change colour. It is well, however, to do this at twice—once immediately, and the remaining portion a fortnight hence. Those done the earliest, should be occasionally uncovered—say once a week—for a day or two, in order to acquire, at a slow pace, both colour and flavour; for those will not be so high flavoured as those which are encased when all the berries are matured. They will, nevertheless, keep longer, provided a little attention be given.

Our readers are aware that *Gooseberries*, and, indeed, all other fruits, with scarcely an exception, may be retarded on similar principles; viz., by first slightly retarding the ripening; and, secondly, by retarding ripeness itself. The latter by far the most important affair, about which we shall say a little more as the autumn advances.

FRUIT ROOMS.—To talk of the fruit room in July may appear, at first sight, a far-fetched theme. We name it here to suggest, that all parties get their fruit rooms—the place we mean for their winter stores—cleaned out immediately, in order that all destructive fungi, or their spores, may be nipped in the bud; at least, all those which fester on the remains of decayed pieces of fruit,

or shrivelled specimens, which may still remain in holes or corners.

Let no one suppose that these are mere ceremonious proceedings; depend upon it, all fruit rooms are the better for *a thorough scouring-out* once in the year—in the John Bull fashion—we mean with plenty of soap and water, and also that great essential of English cleanliness, a liberal amount of what the country-folk, in their homely vernacular, term "elbow grease." This course not only removes impurities from the shelves, but from the very floors. If there be but a slight amount of stagnant damp existing, it generates a host of fungi in the form of a mere crust, which, by arresting evaporation, engenders a corrupt atmosphere. Washing, then, and a most liberal and attentive course of ventilation, are of eminent service during the succeeding autumn and winter; for the fruits themselves may, in their *own* nature, breed fungi.   R. ERRINGTON.

THE FLOWER-GARDEN.

AFTER all our planting, and writing, and new modes of filling the flower-garden for many years, we must confess that the largest number of our best flower-gardens are not what we might and could make them, from the middle of May to this time. When the flush of "spring flowers" is over, a sudden check is allowed for the next six weeks, to give time to the half-hardy and fashionable plants of this department to establish themselves; and for the sake of an autumnal display, we forego the great show which annuals alone, under our present system, can produce in June, or until the newly "turned out" things fill up the beds and are in bloom. When we have a warm May and a dripping June things are sooner righted, but this season the cold spring lasted later into May than usual; and, although we experienced a good planting-out season, with refreshing showers, the stock was hardly disposed of before a drought and dog-days' heat ensued, and with them watering-pots, ragged grass, and a general languidness all over the gardens. Add to this, the damage sustained by half-hardy shrubs and climbers, and by a great portion of our best roses from late spring frosts, and we shall not have much to boast of for the June of this year. But now the worst is over, and the flower-gardener has reached that period at which he has more leisure and less anxiety than at any other time of the whole year. The chief work now will be to train out and regulate all the trailing plants, such as *Verbenas* and *Petunias*, where the beds of these are not already covered. Trailing plants which run into each other in the autumn, and are liable to be beaten down with rain and high winds, should now have some supports placed amongst them. Petunias, in particular, are much benefited by this early attention; and the small spray, or the tops of pea-sticks, are good things to give them the necessary support. Begin with small sticks for them, not more than a foot or 18 inches high; and as they are covered longer sticks may then be added; and if these are placed equally all over a bed of this kind, no wind, however high, can damage them afterwards.

Stakes, of suitable sizes and lengths, will also be in demand now for *Hollyhocks*, *Phloxes*, *Dahlias*, and other tall plants. Most people put down the stakes for the dahlias at the time they are planted out: the worst of which plan is, that small birds take a fancy to perch on the tops of such naked stakes, and then disfigure the plants below them with their dung, which is annoying to the gardener, and prejudicial to the health of the leaves and plants themselves. But there is a simple way of preventing all this, which I can confidently recommend; which is, to stick a pin in the very top of the stake, and then no bird can or will sit on the pin or by the side of it, supposing the stake to be flat on the top. Nothing can be more simple or effectual than this.

Then comes the thinning and training of such *edging plants* as are reared from seed: as the *Virginian stock*, *Sweet alyssum*, common *Narsturtium*, *Convolvolus minor*, and the like. The highest plants of these should now be cut on the top, so as to get up the edging all of one height. Some of the side branches will also be the better from a clip, to keep the whole in a trim, neat fashion. Then, where such plants are too thick, some of them must be pulled up; for if they stand too thick they will not last so long without going to seed; and it is one point of good management, in a regular flower-garden, that no seeds be allowed to come to maturity. The reserve ground, or places out of sight, should be the seed-nursery. As the common *Narsturtium* will grow in any soil, rich or poor, it is a better edging-plant in many places than the *Musk mimulus* when used for the same colour. Where a bright yellow or orange yellow edging is wanted, or is suitable, no better plant than this nar sturtium can be used; and there are three or four varie ties of it which do well mixed together, and all of them will transplant, I believe, at any age; at any rate, such as are now scrambling about from self-sown seeds, or in a seed-bed sown last April, may now be safely removed to any other place, and transplanted in a row round a bed or beds. All the preparation that is necessary for them is, to cut off most of their largest leaves, and to water them well for the first week or ten days. Where they have been sown purposely for an edging, all the attention they require now, is to train the shoots round and round, or along, in the spaces they are intended to occupy. This training when them is effected simply by placing little bits of sticks against one side of the shoot, or by burying a leaf here and there to hold them in the right position, and as soon as the flowers are produced so thickly as to make a show; the large leaves must be cut off every ten days, or fortnight, for the rest of the season; and that does not seem to affect them in the least. Indeed, the whole secret of making very beau tiful beds or edgings of them is, to keep down the leaves regularly from the time they come into bloom. I do not mean, of course, that every leaf is to be removed at any one time,—only enough of them to allow the flowers to be free and easily seen.

The *Convolvolus minor*, of which there are three or four beautiful varieties, particularly a large dark bluish purple one with a clear white eye, is peculiarly well fitted for edgings, or rows, as it keeps in flower the whole season, and is as gay as any plant I know. But they require to be watched constantly, as they are so prone to scramble away when they are not wanted. They must be kept within bounds by the use of sticks, which, however, must be so placed as to be out of sight, and their tops should all be trained or compelled to grow one way. Then, as they grow on, they cover each other, and nothing is seen but the flowering ends. They must not be touched by the knife, or stopped in any way, as they do not branch out afterwards. They are often marked in books as growing only a few inches high, but that is a great mistake. I have seen them grow ten feet high; and a pretty picture they made. The seeds were sown in an outside circle round a large bed of *Red salvias*, with the intention of confining them down for a bright edging; but the bed was so rich, and the Salvias were strong old plants, and grew away enormously, with out ever showing a disposition to flower till very late in September; and this Convolvolus minor was let loose amongst them and soon overtopped the Salvias all the way round, and were one mass of blossom from top to bottom for three months; and at last their tops collected in a hyramidal heap in the centre of the bed; and if they had been supported in that position by a strong stake, the whole would have looked unique for the rest of the

season; but the wind blew them down among the Salvias, which by this time began to push out their flowers from amongst the Convolvolus; and if one had tried to make such a bed by careful training, ten to one if the thing would have looked half so well. Now, if instead of the Salvias, some bushy sticks, such as we use for peas, were put in to support them, there is no doubt but a very showy bed might be produced that way also. I have heard of a bed being made in the same way by planting two-year old *Maurandias*, which soon covered the sticks, and made one mass of bloom all over the surface; but I never either saw or tried a bed that way.

Another plant that would be very likely to answer well after the same manner, and look remarkably well, is *Tropæolum pentaphyllum*. The tubers of which should be taken up and kept dry all the winter, and planted out any time after the middle of March; and if set four inches below the surface their young tops would take no harm from late frosts, and they would come up very strong as soon as the season was warm enough for them. Then to begin with dwarf sticks, and go on with taller ones as the shoots advanced, as we do with Petunias, I should have no fears about getting a novel and interesting bed that would flower from July till the frost came; and this plant stands a good smart frost before the shoots or flowers are injured. Indeed, we have plants of it here which remain in the ground from year to year without any protection; but for a bed I would prefer taking up the roots every autumn, and keeping them in sand away from the frost all the winter.

There is a newer one of these pretty *Tropæolums*, called *Speciosum*, with red flowers; and many gardeners have been sorely puzzled how best to grow it for the last two or three years. It is a hardy, and, I believe, nearly as strong a grower as the last; and the only secret to grow it to perfection, if the soil is all right, is to plant it behind a north wall where the sun cannot reach it. We are often applied to for climbers to suit a north aspect, and here is one of the prettiest summer climbers in the kingdom, just ready at our elbows for this very purpose; and not only that, but it is foreign to its nature to grow half so well in any other way. A deep, rich, light soil will no doubt suit it best; but if one were now to make choice of a place for a plant of this where the soil is too hard, or too strong, or otherwise unsuited for so fine a flower, all that would be required is to dig out a large hole for it, say two feet deep, and as much in width, then to put six inches of broken lumps of peat, with two or three handsful of stones or charcoal lumps, and then fill up with a compost of one-half light sandy loam, the rest of leaf-mould and peat in equal proportions, and then plant out this Tropæolum and water it well. The chances are, that a plant now looking sickly and half starved in the sun, would so recover itself before the end of the growing season, as to become a splendid object for many years to come in similar situations; but in case it should not prove quite hardy, it had better be taken up for the winter.   D. BEATON.

GREENHOUSE AND WINDOW GARDENING.

RESTORING NEGLECTED PLANTS. — Among a mass of inquiries, this week I deem it advisable to give this prominence to those of a gentleman who has lately pur chased a small greenhouse, but the plants in which are in a sad neglected condition; believing that restoring old unhealthy plants to a state of vigour will be as generally interesting as detailing the most approved method of managing them, when they are in a state of health and luxuriance.

Camellias that were wintered in a cold pit, removed thence to the greenhouse, but have produced no flowers,

e branches being long and straggling, "is it too late
prune? and what water should be given?" It is
ot yet too late to prune, if you can give them good
eatment; and we would recommend you to do so, even
you should not have so many flowers the succeeding
ason. The culture of the Camellia has been several
mes referred to, but chiefly as respects plants in a
oderate state of health. For soil, propagating, time
potting, &c., we refer you to previous numbers. We
ily mean at present to tell you how to make these
raggling, woe-begone, barren plants healthy and flower-
roducing. Some of the best of them may be submitted
similar treatment, *without* cutting them down, and then
ou may safely calculate upon having flower-buds formed
pon the points of their present shoots; but in either
se you must not expect flowers until late next spring.
lants intended to bloom about Christmas must have
eir fresh wood formed early, and growth nearly
nished by July. Supposing that you can command
othing but your house or pit, in one or the other your
lants should be placed, and kept as close, and moist,
nd hot as they will bear, shading when the sun is
right, but removing the shade in good time, that the
in's rays may heat the place well before the evening.
Vith sun heat, the temperature may thus be allowed to
inge from 70° to 85°, or even a few degrees higher,
ntil the old shoots throw out young ones, when of
ourse more air would gradually be given, and thus the
mperature be reduced. The cutting back may either
e effected at once, before submitting them to this treat-
ent, or, if the shoots are very straggling, and it is
esirable to keep up a circulation of sap, and yet effect the
urpose of forming a bushy head, then these straggling
hoots may be bent and tied down as much as possible,
that the organized sap may make passages for itself
y means of the lateral buds at the bends. Your object
light thus be effected without giving a sudden check to
e system, a thing of less moment in the case of a
igorous young tree than in one old and worn out,
here a check of this nature is almost as likely to end
death as in increased vigour. In both cases, in unison
ith the close and high temperature from sun heat and
ven from the flue, if necessary, success will greatly
epend upon keeping the atmosphere saturated with
loisture, by dusting the stems of the plant, and syring-
ig the paths and walls of the building; taking care,
owever, that though the soil at the roots is moist, it
lust not be *puddled*. In using the syringe thus freely,
leans must be taken, therefore, to prevent the water
illing upon the soil in the pots. By this method you
ill succeed moderately, if your plants are fairly supplied
ith healthy roots; and in that case no repotting should
ake place until the young shoots have grown from half
n inch to two inches in length. If the roots are bad,
r the soil fine and quite worn out, the plants may be
ansferred to light sandy soil, and to smaller pots; but
he cutting-in of the branches and repotting should not
o resorted to at the same time, if it can be prevented.
he above system will answer if carefully attended to,
ut not so surely as if in addition you could give the
lants the assistance of the heat and moisture arising
rom sweet fermenting materials. Those who have pits
rill have no difficulty in doing so, as, if not high
nough, a cucumber box may be set upon it. It would
equire a thickness of two feet of dung—or dung and
eaves in a sweet state—to maintain a fermenting power
ong enough to suit this purpose. I have already stated,
hat one of the best means for an uninitiated person
nowing whether such a fermenting mass is sweet or
lot is to observe the drops of dew collected on the sash
ars in a morning, that have been placed over such a
ed: if clear as crystal, nothing, with due care, will be
armed; if of a dirty yellow colour, trust the bed with
lothing.

Now some, like the gentleman whose case we are considering, may have camellias and other plants in this
straggling, merely-existing state, and yet have no pit or
frame in which they can place them to have the advantage of this fermenting mass of manure. In such
circumstances we have made a temporary house of old
doors, boards, tarred cloth, &c.; and when no lights
could be got, have used glazed calico, and with the best
results. The calico would enable you to dispense with
shading, which you must attend to if lights from a pit
or frame are used. The genial heat and moisture,
along with invigorating gases thus rising from the fermenting materials will cause the plants to break fresh
buds more quickly and strongly than by any other
method. If the pot is full of roots, do not plunge it in
the dung, &c., or even set it upon it, without the inter-
vention of a board as a nonconducting agent. But if
the roots are so bad that you have been forced to repot,
then the pot may be plunged, to encourage the fresh
protrusion of healthy roots; but care should be taken
that the heat at the roots is never more than from 80°
to 85°. As roots and shoots are formed, the temperature
and the moisture should be gradually reduced, and the
plants be hardened to stand in a cool greenhouse during
the winter. From the first-produced shoots flowers may
be obtained, and the others will grow freely, to reward
you fully in the second season.

Hoya carnosa looks sickly—leaves thin. An analogous
case has lately been referred to. Keep it in the warmest
end of the greenhouse, and exposed to the sun, at least
whenever the leaves will bear it; also give moisture at
the roots during the summer; but in its sickly state,
instead of deluging there, syringe frequently over the
foliage; and towards winter allow it gradually to become
rather dry, re-watering and syringing again when the
warmth of spring returns. Like most tender succulent
plants, growth must take place under plenty of light in
one season, in order to ensure abundance of bloom in
the season ensuing.

Cacti.—" How treat *C. Jenkinsonii* coming into bloom?
Those that have not flowered, should they be repotted?
And how know when they have finished their growth?"
This matter has also been several times referred to. In
addition, and as it meets several cases of inquiry, we
add—First: water the Jenkinsonii while in bloom, and
for some months afterwards. When done flowering,
prune the plant, clearing it from its oldest stunted
shoots. Set it as near the glass and as fully exposed to
the sun as you can; water it duly when requisite, and
if at times with manure water, all the better. By the
end of July, or a little later, place it out of doors close
to a wall, where the sun's rays will strike hard upon it.
Allow it to remain there until the cold nights of autumn
give warning to protect it in-doors; but previously to
that, by means of tiles or wood, protect the roots from
autumn rains; and when once restored to the house,
give no more water all the winter, unless it be very
shrivelled indeed; and when warmth again returns
with the spring your plant will begin to show its flower
buds; when moisture, both by watering the soil and
syringing the top, must again be given—doing the latter,
however, sometime before resorting to the former. Some
kinds, such as *Cactus speciosissimus*, require less pruning,
because they bear flowers freely upon the old wood of
several years' growth; but, nevertheless, they require
even more attention in exposing to the sun in summer,
and keeping dry in winter.

Secondly: As to *repotting*—the Cactus does not require it so often as many other plants; but if the drainage is bad, and the soil soured in consequence, the sooner
they are overhauled the better; and for such purposes
three parts sandy loam, one of lime rubbish, one of
peat, one of old cow-dung, and one of charred turf, will
answer well; performing the operation after blooming,

or earlier if the plant has not bloomed, that the pot may be well filled with fresh roots before winter, keeping the plants rather close after potting, the same as is done with other plants. Top-dressing with rich soil—such as equal parts of cow-dung and loam—will, however, keep large plants healthy for years, if the drainage is all right. As to knowing when their growth is finished, that is a difficult matter, as with proper stimulants the most of the flowering kinds would continue to grow on; but if heat and moisture were applied to cause them to do so, there would be abundance of size, but no flowers. To obtain the latter we sacrifice part of the former; and after a certain growth has been effected we do not ask ourselves whether we should like more, but is there as much as we can hope to mature. The hardening, instead of the extending system, should commence, if possible, by the middle of August.

Vines.—See a paper of last week, also Mr. Errington's able observations; and if that does not suit write again.

                           R. FISH.

HOTHOUSE DEPARTMENT.

EXOTIC ORCHIDACEÆ.

PLANTS THAT REQUIRE BASKETS.—*(Continued from p. 189.)*

Stanhopea guttulata (Small-spotted S.); Guatemala.—The whole flower is pale yellow, and every part prettily spotted with crimson and brown; flowers medium size. 21s.

S. insignis (Noble S.); Trinidad.—A handsome species, of which there are several varieties. The sepals and petals of the original species are pale yellow, spotted with purplish red. The lip is nearly white, spotted and blotched with dark purple. The varieties are *S. insignis purpurea*, with more purple spots; and *S. insignis aurea*, with a more golden colour pervading the flowers. All of them are delightfully fragrant. 15s.

S. Martiana (Von Martius's S.).—A very distinct and beautiful species. The sepals are of a clear transparent straw colour, faintly spotted with blood-red spots in clusters; the petals white, with large spots of bright crimson; the labellum is a clear ivory white. The horns of this part of the flower are of great size and strength, the extreme end being lengthened out and twisted in a most extraordinary manner; no other Stanhopea has such appendages. 42s.

S. oculata (Eyed S.); Mexico and Guatemala.—The ground colour is of a beautiful pale yellow, spotted with small rings of purple; at the base of the lip, on each side, there are two large eye-like spots, whence its name. Very fragrant. 15s.

S. oculata, variety *Barkeriana* (Barker's Eyed S.); Mexico.—Larger flowers and deeper colours than the former species. It is a very desirable variety. 21s.

S. quadricornis (Four-horned S.); Spanish Main.—The sepals and petals are deep yellow, spotted with red; the lip at its base is rosy crimson, softening into greenish white; the point is clear yellow; the lip has four horns of stout substance like ivory. It is deliciously fragrant. 21s.

S. saccata (Bagged S.).—The lower part of the sepals and petals is swollen out into an appearance like a bag, whence its name. They are pale yellow, regularly speckled; at the base, where the bag-like form is, the colour is of the most brilliant orange. This is a small flowered species, but it blooms profusely. 10s 6d.

S. tigrina (Tiger-spotted S.); Xalapa and Guatemala.—This is the handsomest and largest flowered of the whole tribe. The ground colour is red, spotted and largely blotched with deep chocolate. The appearance of the flower is very startling, looking like some monstrous animal's head. The scent, at a little distance, is very agreeable. It flowers freely, generally in pairs. 21s.

S. Wardii (Ward's S.).—This is a handsome species, with flowers of a fine yellow produced on long spikes, and spotted thinly with rich brown. The lip is of a dark blood colour, encircled at the base with a ring of bright orange. 21s.

CULTURE.—The peculiar manner in which these very singular plants produce their flowers, points out the necessity of growing them either in baskets or on logs of wood. They send their flowers directly downwards, frequently through the bottom of the basket. On logs they flourish pretty well for a year or two; but afterwards, for want of due moisture and support, the pseudo-bulbs become smaller, and unable to produce flowers so large or so numerous; but in baskets there is such a supply of food for the roots, that they make larger pseudo-bulbs, and the number and size of the blooms is greatly increased. Shallow baskets are preferable to deep ones; four or five inches deep will be sufficient for the largest plants. As the plants grow larger by spreading themselves over a large surface, the propriety of enlarging the baskets laterally, every way, is naturally pointed out to the attentive cultivator. The centre will, in course of time, become barren of young pseudo-bulbs, in which case it will be necessary to cut through the rhizoma, or attaching root-stalk, and to remove an old bulb or two. The portions so divided will soon send forth new shoots, and so supply more equally, in every part, flower-spikes, and thus increase the beauty and effect of the plant when in bloom.

We have already described the kind of baskets we consider the best, and also the material to fill them with; we will, however, repeat, that the baskets should be filled with rough pieces of very fibrous peat, the size of each to be in proportion to the size of the plant. During the season of growth they must be plentifully supplied with water; and the most effectual way is, by dipping the baskets and compost in tepid water until the whole mass is thoroughly moistened. As soon as the pseudo-bulbs are fully grown water must be withheld, and the temperature of the house considerably lowered.

Stanhopeas are very accommodating, they will thrive well in either the Indian or Mexican house. In the former they will require more moisture than in the latter. *The greater the heat the greater the moisture*, is a rule without exception to all kinds of orchids in a growing state. Great heat without a corresponding increase of moisture, both at the root and in the atmosphere of the house, is positively injurious, weakening the plants to a great degree. Such of our friends as may possess only small plants of this beautiful genus will be glad to read the account Mr. Paxton gives, in the *Magazine of Botany*, of the successful mode he adopted to produce a fine plant:—

"On the 20th of May, 1837, I received a very small damaged plant of a new Stanhopea. I allowed it to get perfectly dry; it was then potted, and placed in a strong bottom-heat, with a strong heat above; the plant began to grow in about a fortnight, and at the end of July had perfected a small bulb. The plant was then kept dry for a fortnight, and was again placed in a strong bottom-heat; and in a temperature never lower than 70°, but often in the day-time amounting to 90 or 100°. By the end of September it had perfected a second bulb, considerably larger than the first. The plant was again dried on a hot flue for a fortnight, and then removed to a larger pot, and elevated a little above the surface; it was again re-plunged into a strong bottom-heat, and by the end of December had perfected two more bulbs, making four since the commencement. I should here observe, that the plant had but one bulb when I received it. The plant was now dried for a month, then re-potted and placed as before in a strong bottom-heat; about the first week in April it had made two more bulbs; the process of drying was again gone through, and the plant placed in a strong heat. It has on it now nine bulbs, made in the short space of 15 months. The plant was cultivated with some others of a similar size in a house that could be kept very hot."

Such is the very clear account of a mode of culture by which a small plant may in a very short time be made into a large one. Mr. P. does not state whether the plant so treated flowered during the period, neither is it necessary he should; sufficient it is, that a plant can bear such a treatment to induce the cultivator to practise it as nearly as possible. If the plant makes fine strong pseudo-bulbs the flowering follows of course, as surely as any effect follows a cause. When a plant has become strong enough to flower, there will be no necessity for such strong and frequent forcing into growth; once a year for growth and rest will be quite sufficient.

Vanda Batemanniana (Bateman's V.).—This is a truly noble plant, of exquisite beauty. It was sent home by Mr. Cummings, several years ago, from the Phillipine Islands; and flowered first at J. Bateman's, Esq., Knypersly, and was named in honour of that distinguished cultivator. It has since been flowered by Mr. Mylam, the successful gardener to S. Rucker, Esq., Wandsworth. The beauty of the plant and the grandeur of its flowers render it an object of great interest to the lover of orchids. Unfortunately for its general distribution it is very scarce, there being not above five or six plants in the country; and the plant being very shy in sending out offsets necessarily keeps it scarce. Messrs. Rollison, Tooting, sent out their collector last autumn to the place where Mr. Cummings found it, with express instructions to search it out and collect a quantity of it, if possible, and send them home. If he is successful, of course they will be more plentiful, and cheaper.

V. cristata (Crested V.); Nepal. — This is a very splendid plant, producing its flowers at the axils of the leaves. They are of medium size, and are produced on long peduncles (flower-stalks). The sepals and petals are whitish; the lip is large, and spotted and striped thickly with dark brown. They continue in bloom a long time; very desirable, but rare. 210s.

Mr. Rucker's plant is nearly three feet high; the stem is stout and robust; the leaves are about 15 inches long, arranged in a flat manner on each side of the stem; the flower-stems are produced out of the axils of the leaves, rising nearly upright to the height of three feet; the flowers are produced on the stem at regular intervals, but rather thinly; they are large, measuring 2½ inches in diameter; the underside of the sepals and petals is of the most brilliant crimson, and the upper side is white, streaked with crimson; the labellum is similarly marked; altogether rendering it a truly gorgeous, and lovely flower. Add to which, it lasts a long time in bloom, and has a faint, though very agreeable fragrance. We are almost afraid to mention the price. Very lately we sold a small plant with three roots and four small leaves for *fifteen guineas*. A good strong plant would fetch at least double that price. Such a price will give our readers some idea of the value set upon this truly aristocratic plant by its present possessors.

(To be continued.)

FLORISTS' FLOWERS.

CARNATIONS AND PICOTEES.—These July flowers will now be unfolding their beauties to please the cultivator, and reward him for his twelve months assiduity and care. The grand points to attend to now, are shading, watering, and tying both the stems and buds. To enjoy their beauty fully, and to the greatest advantage, a regular carnation-stage with a roof of canvass sufficiently high to walk under comfortably, and made impervious to rain, is indispensable. Such a stage, and so covered, we described in the 1st volume of THE COTTAGE GARDENER, and we beg our readers to refer to it. The shade will preserve the flowers from the exhausting rays of the sun, as well as from wet, besides protecting the cultivator and his visitors. Watering is still necessary, especially now that the natural showers from the clouds are prevented from falling upon the earth in the pots.

To prevent the buds from bursting on one side more than another, place round each a ring of India-rubber. These rings may be procured of the proper size at any India-rubber manufactory at moderate prices, or if they cannot be had in country places, tie round each bud a strip of bass matting, so as to allow the bud to expand. With a sharp knife slit open such sides of the calyx, or flower-cup, as will not open naturally. Picotees generally do not burst on one side, because they have fewer petals than Carnations. To show each flower to advantage, procure some stoutish brass or copper wire, form a ring at one end, slip it under the flower, and thrust the other end into the stick to which the flower-stems are tied. This will bring the flower into such a position as to show it to the best advantage to the eye. Cards of pasteboard also should be placed under each flower to keep up the under petals. This will give them a firmness for the exhibition table, but ought to be removed previously to being exhibited. We are amongst those who strongly disapprove of any artificial means to support a flower on the stands on an exhibition day. All these minute points, trivial as they may seem, must be attended to by the florist that desires to bring his flowers to the highest point of perfection.

T. APPLEBY.

THE KITCHEN-GARDEN.

PREPARATION OF THE SOIL. — Every opportunity should be taken, whilst we have length of days, with the heat of a powerful sun, to ridge-trench all spare pieces of ground immediately they are cleared of any crop, exposing the surface in as rough and open a manner as possible to its influence. Between crops of all kinds where there is sufficient room for forking and surface scarifying, it should be done as often as possible; for this not only assists the present growing crops, but also prepares the ground for their successors.

If showery weather prevails, continue to apply sprinklings of salt to the *asparagus* plantations; *Globe artichokes* should be examined, as sometimes, after a dry hot time, they will produce a quantity of spurious suckers, which will exhaust and rob the principal suckers that are producing their heads, if not duly thinned. Sow also *borage* now; and all winter cropping should be well attended to this month; such as the *borecoles, brocolis, Cape brocolis, cauliflowers,* and *coleworts,* should be put out plentifully, as well as Brussels sprouts and *savoys.* Another liberal sowing should be made of some of the best and dwarfest kinds of *cabbage* for planting out, for *coleworts* or winter greens; and a good piece of ground should be well prepared for sowing the first cabbage crop, about the middle of the month. The *Matchless, Nonpareil, Shilling's Queen,* and the *York,* are all known to be good and compact varieties, when procured true to their kinds. There are also many other good varieties; indeed, in almost every locality some favourite variety may be found. Those who may have ground to spare, may plant a few more garden *beans* of any early sort; *dwarf kidney beans* and *scarlet runners* may also be planted; any of the early varieties may also still be sown. The *American dwarf* and *Dwarf Fan peas* are very good varieties for sowing at this season, as they require but little room, and may be sown at two feet distance, or as an edging to a quarter. The seed of both *beans* and *peas* may be quickened by first soaking them for twelve hours.

Endive and *lettuce* should be sown in succession, and plantings made of those already large enough. A small sowing of *spinach* should be made for autumn consumption, and a kindly preparation made on a warm border, or sheltered rich quarter, for the *winter spinach*. *Herbs* of all kinds, as fast as they come into bloom, should be cut or gathered while dry. *Lavender* should not be too forward previous to cutting, or much of its blossom will drop of. Make another sowing of *parsley*, and transplant some of the strongest and most curly into pots, to get well established for the winter.

The root crops, such as *beet, carrots, parsnips, onions, horseradish, salsafy, scorzonera, &c.*, should by this time have had their final thinning; and as long as the hoe or hand scarifier can be got amongst them, it should be employed continually.

JAMES BARNES.

MISCELLANEOUS INFORMATION.

OUR VILLAGE WALKS.

By the Authoress of "My Flowers."

Our walks are now enlivened by the bustle and fragrance of innumerable hay-fields; and what animation there is in the scene! The labour of hay-making is more pleasing to the eye than that of the harvest; its groupings are more varied and picturesque, and the sounds that accompany it are more lively and joyous. The position of the reaper is one of uneasiness and fatigue, while that of the hay-maker is erect, and frequently relieved by change of action. This may, perhaps, account for the cheerful voices and merry laughs of the different groups, as they turn and toss the hay; for there is comparative silence in the corn-fields, in spite of the deep and thrilling interest that attends it.

The hay-harvest, with all its beauty, endeared to us as it is from our earliest childhood, is one of the very few agricultural scenes that is not associated in our minds with Scriptural interest; there is no mention in the Sacred Writings of such a provision being required or made for the wants of the animal creation. The burning influence of the sun, the absence of wintry seasons, and the rich fertility of the soil in eastern lands, may have rendered this process unnecessary or impossible; at all events, we have no intimation of it, or allusion to it, in the books of the Old Testament. Thus, although we may in every case receive spiritual improvement from the simplest incident that passes before our eyes, yet the hay-field is singularly deficient in this sweetest and holiest interest. The waving crops of autumn, the piled-up shocks that succeed them, even the dry and barren stubble when all has been gathered in, has a word of solemn instruction to the passer-by. We can scarcely perform an operation in the farm or garden, without feeling that we are practising and exemplifying customs and allusions conveyed to us by the Word of God, and common in the days when the Creator veiled His glory, and visited the earth as man. We feel that they are sanctified, by His having used them to impart instruction to the unenlightened minds of His disciples, and our enjoyment in them is, therefore, heightened a thousand fold; but when we are contemplating our sweet English hay-field, no Scriptural recollections increase its charms, no Bible story, simply and exquisitely told, rushes into our minds: we are reminded chiefly of the days of our youth, when the enjoyment of this peculiar season was so great, the smell of the hay so pleasant, and the houses we made in it were so sweet and snug. I have little doubt but that all my readers look back with a smile, and, perhaps, a sigh, to those days of childish glee, when the few sorrows they felt were not more severe than when a wet day occurred during hay-time, or the summons to bed was sent after them, before the last waggon load had been carried in.

Still we may gain instruction as we watch another generation playing as we have done before them. Are we not still children, nay, I may say, idiots, in our advancing years? Are we not still thoughtlessly amusing ourselves with the trifles of a passing world, like children in a hay-field? Still sporting in gladness of heart, or mourning over some blighted hope, but *all* with reference to the world in which we live, to the time which hath an end, to the things that "are seen," and that will all soon perish for ever! While we pride ourselves on our intellectual powers and mental acquirements, let us remember that in spiritual things we are less than children; and let us strive, "while it is called to-day," to put away childish things."

How full of beauty is the whole face of nature at this time. The rains over which we were grieving a few days ago "are ended and gone;" but they have enriched and refreshed the soil, and have caused bud and blossom to swell into richer luxuriance. The hedges—my favourite hedges—are decked in all their simple loveliness, and the graceful, wild creepers are now encircling the stems and boughs with such thick and beautiful wreaths, that the garden cannot boast of anything more agreeable to the eye. An evening stroll is delicious when the cool breeze has sprung up, especially on the banks of a river, where we can sometimes enjoy the musical dip of the oars as a boat quietly glides by. I am enjoying this luxury now, and I delight, too, in watching the gallant spring and plunge with which a noble dog takes the water—the white foam sparkling round him, and his long shaggy black coat shining and dripping as he stands anxiously waiting for another stick to be thrown in.

There are few situations so utterly devoid of beauty and interest as not to afford us pleasure at this charming season of the year. If we simply observe a glowing sunset, what a train of thought arises, and how quickly our minds are led on from admiring its outward splendour, as it sinks among gold and purple clouds, to that "excellent glory" of which—although the grandest of all natural objects—it is but the type and shadow. Even that sun—that splendid orb of fire—whose lustre the eye cannot bear, shall be "ashamed" when that day shall dawn in which "the Lord of Hosts shall reign in Mount Zion, and in Jerusalem, and before his ancients gloriously."

The song of birds, too, although not so full as during the preceding months, greets us delightfully in our evening walks. It is rather singular to remark the sudden way in which it ceases at night. We have sat on the lawn listening to the full chorus around until night has closed quietly in: but still all was vocal, until in one instant, as if by general consent, the concert ceased, and we have been almost startled by the sudden silence. It seemed as if all had joined in a final hymn of praise, and when that ended their daily work was done.

The nightingale has just ceased to add its full liquid notes to the general harmony; after the 20th of June it is heard no more. In the garden of the friends with whom I am now staying, it seems unusually social. I have been accustomed to hear them in the woods, among the tall trees of the distant grounds, and occasionally nearer to the house, but here they sang among the garden shrubs, close to the windows, and when we were sitting at work on the lawn, they warbled immediately over our heads. I saw one day a little quiet-looking bird resting on the branch of a weeping ash not yet in full leaf, and it was so close to us, that we could perceive its throat swelling with the fulness of its voice, which was remarkable in so small a creature. This was the far-famed Philomel of the poets, uttering those plaintive notes so highly and universally extolled. I confess that the nightingale does not please me so much as I know it ought to do. It has no *song*. It repeats the same full, musical note, with surprising power and delicacy, and there is a plaintive sadness that attracts us in its tones; but it does not *sing* like the blackbird, the thrush, the lark, or even the robin. There is *subject* in their strains; but the nightingale harps upon one string, if I may so express myself, which, with all its sweetness, disappoints me. As one among the feathered choir, and as prolonging its music after other birds are still, the nightingale is delightful; but as a sole musician, I prefer one of the less valued performers.

While speaking of birds, I must notice the nest of a golden-crested wren which was brought in a few days ago, cemented so wonderfully to the drooping sprays of a Red Virginian Cedar as to be quite concealed from every eye but that of a shool-boy. It was a deserted nest, the young birds being fledged and gone. The bough was cut from the tree with the beautiful little nest suspended safely among the sprays, like a small round bag, formed of moss, and wool, and feathers, exquisitely woven together, so as no hand on earth could weave them. It was impossible to look at it without wonder and delight, and a feeling deeper and more exquisite still; for does not a work like this, made without hands, constructed only by the beaks of two little birds, exalt the power and goodness of Him, without whom even man can do nothing, and who alone enables the dumb creation to exhibit such wondrous skill? A bird's nest is, at all times, an object of peculiar interest and delight; but I have never seen one so beautiful in its form and position as that of the golden-crested wren.

CHEAP DINNERS.

A VERY tempting title, truly! I hope the results will prove as tempting to the palate! A few months ago, every receipt, headed with the magic word "cheap," was read with avidity, and not only read, but it was tried and adopted. Now, since our prayers have been heard, and most mercifully answered, the same eagerness for cheapness is not evinced; and I fear some, who had learnt in the season of scarcity a few lessons in economy, are now returning to their old bad habits, and indulging in indolence or expences which are unsuited to the station in which it has pleased the Almighty to place them.

It is the imperative duty of every mistress of a family to see that the "master's" earnings are expended in the most profitable manner. This requires some little knowledge,—some little forethought, but "where there is a will there is a way;" and the art of feeding a number of hungry mouths on a scanty pittance, in a satisfactory and comfortable manner, though a difficult matter at first, will, if the heart is in the work, soon be accomplished; and by means of great economy, both in buying and using articles of food, great cleanliness, and a "cheerful countenance," our cottage homes would soon become scenes of happiness and contentment; public houses would be abandoned, and our churches and schools frequented.

When meat is at a low price, I think it very much better economy to buy a little for each day's dinner than to feed the family on vegetables and bread alone; but then the meat must be made into soup—not eaten. In this way all the vegetables that are mixed with the soup become not only more palatable, but more nourishing.

FISH STEW.—If any of my readers live by the sea-side, how many nice dishes may be made from the inhabitants of the "briny deep!" Hake, conger eel, and several other coarse fish, are sold at very low prices, and make a nice dish dressed thus :—Put into a saucepan two quarts of water; have ready, sliced, four onions, two carrots, two turnips chopped very fine, a little parsley and a few herbs. Buy a couple of pound of fish, cut it into slices about four inches long, put it into the saucepan with the vegetables, and stew it for three-quarters of an hour. When done, mix a little flour very smoothly and add it to the broth; boil it all together for ten minutes, and it is ready for table. This also makes a good dish, if, when it has stewed a quarter of an hour, it is put into a pie-dish, and a crust put over it, and baked.

SHEEP'S-HEAD AND "PLUCK" (as the liver and lights are called) is a favourite and economical dish. The pluck should be chopped up and well mixed with onions and potatoes (the latter having been previously boiled), and then fried with a little fat. The head should be boiled, and when eaten with plain boiled rice it is a nourishing and delicate dish for an invalid. The brains should be taken out and mixed with the liver which is in the frying-pan. The water in which the head has been boiled must be carefully put by until the next day, when, after all the meat has been picked from the head, put the bone into the water, and boil it for an hour with plenty of vegetables, particularly onions. Boil with it some split peas or damaged rice (a pound of which can be bought for 1½d.), and you have another wholesome dinner.

RICE is an article which is very much neglected by the poor; and it is, I think, a great mistake on their part. It is easily prepared, very wholesome, and very cheap. A large rice pudding made thus is very good :—Wash one pound of damaged rice: put it on to boil with very little water; when it begins to swell, add a quart of skim-milk, a little fat, and a quarter of a pound of treacle: pour it into a pie-dish or basin, and bake it in a slow oven for two hours. It will be soft enough if it only remains in the oven half an hour, but it is improved by standing in a cool oven for the two hours. A few gooseberries or currants are additions which are much prized by the little ones; and those children who are accustomed to see fruit on the trees and withstand the temptation of touching it should be encouraged by partaking of it at the dinner-table. Do not forget to commend them for thus obeying their parent's wishes, and at the same time remind them, that trusting in their own strength they will fail; but looking to the Saviour for his grace, they will withstand the various temptations to which childhood, youth, and manhood are liable; and at last will receive that crown of glory which is prepared for those who love and, consequently, serve God here. A FRIEND.

RHODODENDRONS.

WE are much obliged to *A Constant Subscriber* for bringing these flowers under our notice. We agree in thinking that the truly magnificent display of Rhododendrons in the exhibition of American plants at the Botanic Gardens, in the Regent's Park, is well adapted and well timed to draw public attention to the many beautiful varieties of these charming shrubs. No doubt the effect will be an increased demand for them, and we have great pleasure in complying with the request to give a list of the finest varieties. We agree also that those splendid varieties are not known so much as they deserve to be. The beauty of the show in the Regent's Park this year is beyond all praise. It was truly a fairy scene. Our readers that had not the pleasure of seeing them, can form no idea of such a display of floral beauty. Several of the standard *Rhododendrons* measured 12 feet diameter, and were one mass of bloom. The hardy *Azaleas* and *Kalmias*, especially *K latifolia*, were equally splendid, though not quite so large.

The following is a very select list of hardy Rhododendrons :—

	s.	d.
Amethyst—pink shaded; large flowers; free bloomer	7	6
Adonis—rose; large truss	10	6
Album elegans—fine blush	5	0
Atro-rubrum—fine crimson..	10	6
Alexandrina—pure white; very dwarf	10	6
Brilliant—bright rosy lake	10	6
Blandyanum—deep rosy crimson; extra fine	21	0
Captivation—rosy crimson, black spots	31	6
Cerito—deep purplish rose	10	6
Coriacea—deep pure white; fine habit	10	6
Candidum—pinkish white; fine truss..	3	6
Delicatissimum—waxy blush; do..	3	6
Decorum—rosy crimson	3	0
Elegans—deep rose; fine truss	10	6
Eminent—rosy lilac; fine foliage; free grower	5	0
Fair Rosamond—fine rosy flesh; beautifully spotted	10	6
Geraldine—deep pucy purple	7	6
Helena—rosy red; a fine variety	10	6
Ivanhoe—deep claret; free bloomer	10	6
Jeannie Deans—rosy flesh colour; finely spotted	10	6
Metaphor—very smooth rose; good form, and fine truss ..	10	6
Nobleanum bicolor—deep rose; white throat; a fine variety..	21	0
Othello—dark purplish crimson; free bloomer	10	6
Pictum—pinkish white; densely spotted..	3	0
Queen Victoria—deep claret; fine compact truss	10	6
Rivenum—deep crimson; black spots	21	0
Standishii—violet; black spots; fine	21	0
Towardii—rosy lilac; spotted; fine shape. The largest and most perfect flower and truss ever seen	21	0
Ververicarum—purplish lilac; immense trusses; large double flowers	21	0

WILD FLOWERS OF JULY.

THE natural order *Umbelliferæ* (*Apiaceæ* of Lindley) is a conspicuous one in the month of July, as some of the most gigantic of the tribe produce their large umbels of white flowers. Several of the species of this order are highly poisonous, but many of them have been transplanted from their native soil to the kitchen-garden with great success, and some of these we shall briefly notice. First, then, there is the *Daucus carota*, or Wild Carrot, which occurs abundantly by waysides, and in pastures and waste places; but we dare say it will be more familiar to the majority of our readers in its culinary character, when its Latin title is exchanged for that of Altringham, or Early Horn Carrot. Scarcely less useful is the fusiform root of *Pastinaca sativa*, when cultivation has caused it to assume the form of the garden parsnip; and the aromatic seeds of the common caraway (*Carum carui*), as well as those of the coriander (*Coriandrum sativum*), are well known for their kitchen, confectionary, and pharmacological uses. In speaking of the Scottish Lovage (*Liguticum Scoticum*), a July flowering umbelliferous plant, which luxuriates on the bare maritime rocks and promontories of the northern portions of Britain, Sir James E. Smith remarks (*English Flora*, II., 82)—"The herb is eaten, either crude or boiled, by the natives of Scotland and its isles. The flavour is highly acrid, and, though aromatic and perhaps not unwholesome, very nauseous to those who are unaccustomed to such food." We are sorry to be unable to bear testimony to the edible qualities of liguticum, for, accustomed as we have been since days of infancy to see the sea-weed cast upon the shore used as food (quite horrifying, no doubt, to the English epicure), yet an instance of Lovage eating has never come under our observation. We presume that our coast countrymen have, in these luxurious days, acquired a *taste* for better fare; but the fact recorded by Smith is interesting alike to the historian and the botanist. We have still another sea-side umbellifer to add to our list of culinaries, that is the Sea Holly (*Eryngium maritimum*), which is now producing its dense heads of *blue* flowers on the sandy coasts; we have the authority of Linnæus for the value of this plant, and he recommended the blanched shoots to be used by way of substitute for asparagus. Sir W. J. Hooker (*British Flora*, I., 133) mentions that the roots are well tasted when candied, and they are considered stimulating and restorative, having been so employed in the days of Shakespeare.

But what of the dangerous species? There is the common Hemlock (*Conium maculatum*), a very powerful medical plant, growing to the height of from three to five feet, the hollow glaucous stem being covered with purple spots, and somewhat shining. We have also the Fool's Parsley (*Æthusa cynapium*), whose lurid green hue bespeaks it to be suspicious; Smith well remarks that the few long, pendulous bracteas, under each partial umbel, distinguish it from all its tribe. The Waterdropworts (*Œnanthe*) are looked upon as more or less poisonous, and, indeed, the Hemlock Waterdropwort (*Œ. crocata*), a species whose roots frequently, but not always, contain a yellow juice, is considered to be perhaps the most virulent of British plants, although, curiously enough, it is sometimes innocuous; we find it recorded that Ehret, the celebrated botanical draughtsman, experienced a giddiness from the mere scent of the plant. Concerning the Water Hemlock, or Cowbane, (*Cicuta virosa*), a considerable difference of opinion seems to exist amongst authors of authority, some considering the herb to be fatal to horned cattle and other quadrupeds as well as to mankind, while others hold that, although a deadly poison to man, cattle may eat the leaves with impunity; in fact, the poisonous qualities of the *Umbelliferæ* do not appear to be at all clearly understood. Professor Balfour has some useful and interesting remarks on the subject (*Manual of Botany*, § 893)— "In regard to the poisonous species of this order there is still much to be learned. They appear to vary according to the soil and climate in which they grow; some species, generally reputed poisonous, have been found by Dr. Christison to be quite innocuous when gathered from localities in the neighbourhood of Edinburgh. The most important plant of this section is *Conium maculatum* (Hemlock), the *κώνειον* of the Greeks; it is a biennial plant, found abundantly in Britain, and distinguished by its undulated ridges, smooth purple spotted stem, and the peculiar, mouse-like odour of its leaves when being dried. Every part of the plant, especially the fresh leaves and green fruit, contains a volatile oleaginous alkali, called Conia, which acts as an energetic poison; to this substance the effects of Hemlock on the animal frame are due, and care is required in the preparation of the leaves and fruit in order to retain this active principle. A few drops of Conia will kill a small animal; it acts on the spinal cord, producing paralysis, with slight convulsive twitches, and its fatal effects are attributed to asphyxia, produced by palsy of the muscles of respiration, without convulsions or coma. Hemlock has been employed medicinally to allay pain, more especially in cancerous and neuralgic affections. *Œnanthe crocata* (Hemlock Dropwort, or Dead Tongue), and a variety called *apiifolia*, have been long looked upon as poisonous; the roots have been mistaken for parsnips, and fatal effects have been thus produced. It would appear, however, that these poisonous qualities are not invariably present, for Dr. Christison found that the roots of this plant when growing in a sea-side locality, near Edinburgh, were innocuous; it remains to be determined if the climate and locality have any effect in modifying the properties of the plant. The same remarks may be made in regard to *Œnanthe phellandrium* (Water Dropwort) and *Cicuta virosa* (Water Hemlock, or Cowbane), which seem to vary as regards their poisonous properties. *Æthusa cynapium* (Fool's Parsley) is another plant in the order reputed poisonous. It has been stated, that the roots of parsnips during the spring of the second year, on the approach of the flowering season, occasionally produce a poisonous matter."

Before leaving the Umbelliferæ, we must mention a few other species of general interest which are now in flower, viz., the Cow Parsnip, or Hog-weed (*Heracleum sphondylium*), the largest native species, and a very coarse plant, but one which is much relished by cattle, and especially hogs; it is reported to be very nourishing and wholesome for them. The upright Hedge Parsley (*Torilis anthriscus*), and its near ally the *T. infesta*, the fruits of which are curiously clothed with hooked bristles; the wild Beak Parsley (*Anthriscus sylvestris*), a beautiful plant, which flowers from April to the present time in the woods and under the hedges, and sometimes in more exposed situations; and, lastly, we shall note the Shepherd's Needle, or Venus's Comb (*Scandix pecten*), whose small white flowers are by no means conspicuous just now, but the large, somewhat beak-shaped fruit which follows the flowers readily draws attention on the harvest-field.—G. LAWSON, F.B.S., &c.

(*To be continued.*)

EXTRACTS FROM CORRESPONDENCE.

FUCHSIA CULTURE.—It may appear presumptuous in a person who has only cultivated Fuchsias about three years, to offer an opinion contrary to Mr. Beston, and many other experienced gardeners, who, I find, always recommend these beautiful plants "to be cut-in," early in spring or February. Now, I would say cut them down—aye, down to the last eye, at that time, and you will have plants of symmetrical forms, which I never saw when "cut-in;" for you have invariably long *woody* stems; and they never break equally. I cut down most of my plants last December (as I had to be absent till March), and I find they did quite as well as if they had been operated upon in February. They remained under the stage in the greenhouse all winter, and of course were kept nearly dry. The house has not had a fire since the frost left us. They began to break about the beginning of March, and were potted when they had shoots a few inches long; and now some of the strongest growers— *Corallina*, *Exoniensis*, &c.—are from 5 to 6 feet high, and without a *blind eye* from bottom to top, and shaped like a cone, and beautiful plants. The weaker sorts are from 2 to 3½ feet high. It is true, it makes them rather later in blooming, as they are now only just out; whilst some of those that were "cut-in" have been in bloom some time; but what a difference in the appearance of the plants! the latter have no shape at all, and look like men with one arm. My young plants, i.e., this year's cuttings, I shall keep *just* growing all winter, in order that their leading shoot will not die, which in my opinion always spoils the plants.

Fuchsias are my favourite plants, and nothing, *to me*, looks more wretched than ill-shaped bushes. I dare say what I have written you will consider stuff and nonsense, but I have never seen this plan recommended ; but always "cut-in," "prune-in," &c. I have my strongest plants in No. 2 pots, and in a strong and rich compost, and give them weak *guano* water twice a week ; their foliage is beautiful, and they are covered with flowers and buds, and short-jointed, having been kept as near the glass as possible. Several of the *Corallinas* send forth three branches at each joint, which I have not seen in other sorts. This is a beautiful out-door plant in a sheltered spot, and will grow to 9 or 10 feet in height in one season, in a rich soil. I find I commence this *pencil* note on half a sheet of paper, which I hope you will excuse. Allow me to add my testimony as to the great value, at a trifling cost, of THE COTTAGE GARDENER ; and that it may flourish like a Fuchsia, is the sincere wish of ONE WHO HAS DERIVED BENEFIT FROM IT.

LAUREL-LEAVES AND THE GREEN FLY.—I do not remember to have read, either in your pages or elsewhere, that the prussic (or *hydrocyanic*) acid contained in the leaf of the laurel effectually destroys the green-fly. It is known to kill wasps ; and a muslin bag filled with a few leaves thrust into the mouth of the nest, and covered with a turf, would probably destroy the colony with much greater certainty and rapidity than turpentine. This led me to conceive that the fumes would be equally injurious to the more delicate lungs of the green fly : and I was not disappointed. I placed three or four laurel leaves, *well crushed and bruised*, under a bell-glass, on the surface of the earth in a pot. I inserted some cuttings from a plant which were well covered with green-fly. In a few minutes there was a visible commotion among the settlers of the colony ; and in a few minutes more they were all dead. Not a single survivor remained. I then removed the bell-glass to ascertain whether they would recover, but not a single movement took place. Ten minutes, or a quarter of an hour, will be quite sufficient to exterminate them. Upon a small scale, where plants can be thus enclosed, I look upon it as a very superior remedy to the smoke of tobacco, more especially where a greenhouse adjoins a sitting-room, as in my own case. But upon a larger scale, for a whole house, I do not see how it could be applied. Here Brown's fumigator would not be an available instrument, I fear. Some of your more ingenious correspondents may, perhaps, devise some mode of applying the principle more extensively ; if so, I hope they will communicate the result of their attempts. Care should be taken to cut the leaves into small pieces, and to bruise them very thoroughly, in order that the noxious fumes may be more readily emitted. I have tried this frequently, and it never fails. But although it effectually kills the insect, it does not at the same time detach them from the plant ; they must be washed off afterwards with a gentle syringe.—C. P.

SHALLOW PLANTING.—I live on a strong soil, and the substratum is what we call "catbrain," which is a mixture of whitish clay, gravel, pebbles, and sand. Some years ago, I found my apple-trees all canker and fail, when the roots got into this subsoil. I planted some young apple-trees on a plan which I then fancied was new, by first digging the holes to receive them, and then by putting a common glazed earthenware milk-pan at the bottom of each hole under each root. A friend of mine afterwards planted a young orchard, by placing the roots upon the *surface* of the land ; he then supported the stems by a strong stake, and carted soil round, that is, *upon* the roots. By this means, the trees hitherto seem not to have found the noxious subsoil, but the roots have probably struck along the surface. This was the notion I had when I obstructed the descent of the roots by the milk-pan, the sloping sides of which I fancy threw the roots upwards again. A square flag-stone would have been the safer process, as the force of the roots, when the trees grew large, might break any fragile material.—A WORCESTERSHIRE MAN.

EFFECTS OF THE GRAFT ON THE STOCK.—Mr. Evans, of the Edinburgh Experimental Garden, recently directed the attention of the Botanical Society to a curious instance of the effects of the graft upon the stock, which had occurred in a tree at Morningside House, the residence of Mr. J. Deuchar. The tree in question is *Pyrus aria*, grafted upon *P. aucuparia*

as a stock. Its entire height is 18 feet, and the stock forms a clean trunk to the height of 4 feet, where the union of the graft and stock is conspicuously shown. At 13 inches from the base of the trunk there are shoots of *P. aucuparia*, and at the height of 1½ feet *branches of P. aria appear* (being 2½ feet *below* the point of junction), while farther up the trunk a branch has been accidentally taken off, which is believed to have been *P. aucuparia*.

WISTERIA SINENSIS.—This beautiful plant blooms in the spring, before unfolding its leaves, and often so early that the blossoms are cut off by frost ; this spring, however, the check was given before the flower-buds were set, and though June 1st, it exhibited nothing but naked branches, it is now coming out in full perfection. *Query.*—Can any mode of culture be adopted to retard the development of the plant, say for a month, until the spring frosts are over ?—S. P., *Rushmere*.

TO CORRESPONDENTS.

*** We request that no one will write to the departmental writers of THE COTTAGE GARDENER. It gives them unjustifiable trouble and expense ; and we also request our coadjutors *under no circumstances* to reply to such private communications.

SUCKERS OF PINE-APPLES FALLING (*Delta*).—Your suckers of Pines grown on the Hamiltonian system must have sticks, but they must be weak, through bad roots, to fall down. Cannot you, also, thrust some new tan amongst their stems. For summer and early autumn, we recommend the best sorts of *Queens* ; for late purposes, and through the winter, nothing can exceed the *Black Jamaica*. You will see a paper on Pines shortly.

BEES NOT STAYING IN HIVE (*W. Speed*).—You say that the swarm put into a clean hive without any smearing of the inside remained ; whilst the swarm also put into a new hive, but the inside of which "was well smeared with honey," suddenly took flight and were lost. In future do not smear your hive ; if you refer to former numbers you will see that we deprecate the absurd practice.

SECOND SWARMS (*J. B. P.*).—"Mr. Payne says, that if a first swarm goes off, a second (or cast) will certainly follow. Now, on the 31st May, two strong stocks threw swarms, and since the seventh day I have assiduously listened every evening to hear the piping of young queens, and examined every morning to discover any royal nymphs or young queens cast out ; neither has happened, nor has a second swarm departed." Yours is certainly an exception to a general rule. The cloudiness of the weather just at the time of throwing off the second swarms, and the general unfavourableness of the season for bees, must be considered as the cause. It will be in vain to look for second swarms now, and as the season is, perhaps it is much better not to have them : should, however, your stocks be seen to cluster at the mouth of the hives, put a small hive upon each of them.

ICE-HOUSE (*Delta*).—Nothing more has been done to the ice-house you name, nor to the way of managing it, and it answers very well indeed.

BROMPTON STOCKS (*F. W. T.*).—Mr. Beaton told us last year that he never saw such fine Brompton Stocks as are grown about Ipswich ; and we know that many cottagers in Suffolk, who do not possess even a hand-glass, succeed with them as well, if not better, than many who coddle them in pots and cold pits through the winter. Some people succeed in getting an early crop of fine cauliflowers by keeping the plants in pots over the winter, while others grow only "button heads" that way. Sow your Brompton Stocks now, and try one-half of your seedlings in the open ground, transplanting them to their final places next March, and please let us hear the result. We never pot or shelter ours, and they do pretty well.

STEPHANOTIS FLORIBUNDA (*F. W. T.*).—Your cuttings of this will readily root in a hotbed under a bell-glass, any time from March to August. Those short growths which are produced near the bottom of the plant make the best cuttings for amateurs, and March or April is the best time to put them in.

LIQUID-MANURE FOR FUCHSIAS, GERANIUMS, &c. (*C. J. P.*).—What it should be made from, and what its strength, will depend upon what you can get. Deer-dung, sheep-dung, and cow-dung, after they have lain some months to sweeten, are good, either separately or unitedly for this purpose. A good shovelful will be enough for a dozen of gallons. Soot, also, is a valuable fertiliser for such plants. A small handful will be sufficient for six gallons of water. A little lime will clear it, but rob it also of a portion of its ammonia. Guano and super-phosphate of lime are the cleanest and easiest used. Three ounces of the former, or four of the latter, will do for four gallons of water. Even these you must give to your plants alternately with clean water.

CACTUS BONE BLOOMING (*Ibid*).—Do not keep it dry yet, but encourage it to grow until the autumn. See what Mr. Fish says in another part of the paper.

GARDENIA FLORIDA PLENA (*Florida*).—The plant which has become so "melancholy looking," by loosing its leaves, and dropping its buds, and is now standing in a sunny warm greenhouse, and syringed every evening, should be duly supplied with water, and allowed to remain there until the side shoots begin to break, when it should be cut back, and the young shoots encouraged to grow so as to form buds for the next season's blooming. This breaking and cutting back should have been effected before potting, but as that has been done, it cannot be helped. You will accomplish your object more effectually, if you could set your plant in a pit or frame, kept close and moist; and if there was a slight heat from sweet dung, all the better. During winter a temperature of 45° will suit it, but in spring, just as fresh growth commences, you must return it again into a moist heat (and if from sweet dung it will vastly enjoy it), if you wish your flowers to be large and fine.

CYCLAMEN SEEDLINGS (M. B. L.).—These on a south balcony would be better if slightly shaded; the leaves do not grow large the first season; but you should have more of them. We are obliged by you numbering our queries; it saves time and space, and we will answer them accordingly. 1st. The seedlings do not require bottom-heat, nor yet to be put in a cucumber-pit. 2nd. Continue watering until the leaves begin to fade, then place them in a cold-pit, where they shall neither be dry nor wet, because if too dry the tuber would be shrivelled; and keep them from frost during winter. 3rd. We prefer keeping them in pots, as the earth prevents them getting too much dried.

COLD-PITS (Dido).—Your brick-pits, covered with cucumber-frames, will answer admirably. A cold-pit is one where no artificial heat of any kind is used. The protection the plants receive being given solely by coverings. During summer and spring, these pits, when not covered, are still a great protection to plants by their walls. Gardeners use many simple contrivances for serving the purpose of such pits. There will be no danger of your plants damping-off in summer, and if deep sunk you must guard against it in winter, by drainage, &c., and sending off the surface water. See an article by Mr. Fish in last volume.

MANDEVILLA SUAVEOLENS (Ibid).—This you may train over an iron globe trellis; but it will give you more trouble, and less satisfaction, than if you planted it out, and trained it over a pilaster or an arch in your greenhouse, provided the average temperature in winter was from 40° to 45°.

COAL-ASHES FOR PROPAGATING, INSTEAD OF CLEAR SHARP SAND (Veras).—We should like better to hear of its success than to try it with anything rare and valuable. Charcoal-dust is a very different thing, and that we often use; but the cuttings should not remain long in it after they are struck. In almost any neighbourhood a little sharp sand might be washed out of the drift of the roads, more especially after a heavy rain, and with little more trouble than sifting fine coal-ashes, impregnated with sulphur. You may be successful, but at present we join your gardener in ominously shaking our heads.

CALCEOLARIA : KENTISH HERO (Ibid).—We have no doubt that a little manure water would benefit it, but do not give it too strong. It is the real " Hero " of all calceolarias for bedding, and sustains the high character given to it by Messrs. Beaton and Fish. It seems to thrive best in a stiff loamy soil.

PLANTS IN A WINDOW (W. R. J.).—We can hardly conceive how your plants do not open their blossoms. Have they been regularly watered? The plate glass and the facing the south might hurt them; but you say that you give plenty of air, which ought to neutralise these. A thin muslin shade might be tried, or, better still, the plants should be set outside. We have an idea that, after all, want of water and want of air may be the cause of your disappointment. A short period of bright sun, without air or shade, would soon shrivel your cinerarias, more especially if the soil was dry.

ROSES FOR FORCING IN POTS (A Half-pay Naval Officer).—If you had told us what roses did not succeed with you, and when you wanted them in flower, we should very likely have better met your case. Many of the Bourbon, China, and Tea-scented force well in a general way; the following are some of the best :—Tea-scented—Belle Allemande, Bougere, Devoniensis, Eliza Sauvage, Nephitos, Sofrano, Triomphe de Luxembourg. China—Abbe Mioland, Cramoisie superieure, Fabvier, Mrs. Bosanquet, Napoleon, Belle de Florence. Bourbon—Armosa, Augustine Marget, Bouquet de Flora, Paul Joseph, Queen, Souvenir de Malmaison, Proserpine. Perpetuals—Crimson Perpetual, Duchesse Prevost, Dr. Marx, Duchess of Sutherland, Madame Laffay, Mrs. Elliot, La Reine, William Jesse. Hybrid China and Bourbon—Charles Duval, Coupe de Hebe, Fulgens. Gallica — Boula de Nauteuil, Rouge eblouisante. Moss—The common Moss, Celina, Unique de Provence. These will, however, require a little difference in their treatment.

PLANTS FLAGGING AND ROTTING OFF (Henry).—As you are so successful in propagating, you ought to be equally successful in rearing your plants after potting. We think your pit a better place for establishing such things than a shady part of the greenhouse, though either ought to do. You have no doubt watered and shaded; but you have erred in keeping them so close as to have the thermometer up to 70° and 80°. This would render your fresh potted things weak, and with shade it would prevent their rooting. In such circumstances, when shade is essential for a short time, give air at the back and front to keep down the temperature for such things as myrtles, verbenas, salvias, primulas, fuchsias, &c. We would also recommend you not to sift your soil too fine. Let us hear from you again. Read the articles of Messrs. Beaton and Fish on propagating.

DOUBLE FLOWERS—IMPREGNATING FLOWERS (Mary H.).—These matters will meet with attention ere long; the inquiries can scarcely be answered shortly enough for this place.

VERBENA SEEDLINGS (Ibid).—These now only two inches high will scarcely bloom early enough for producing seeds this season; but the plants or cuttings from them, if worthy, may be kept over the winter. Seedsmen generally sell seeds of these plants as well as others.

CACTUS (Ibid).—The keeping hot water in the saucer has little or nothing to do with its blooming—that will depend entirely on the treatment it received the previous season, in getting its wood well ripened, and then resting the plant by keeping it dry during the winter. With your limited convenience, the application of hot water would be time enough in April, and then much should not long stand in the saucer. You will find something suitable in to-day's paper.

D will see that his request has been attended to.

SWARMS DESERTING HIVE (W. H. W.).—We know of no other reason for your swarms having three or four times left their hives, except is be from their being dressed. Mr. Payne says, in page 42, vol. 2, of THE COTTAGE GARDENER, " Let there be no sugared ale nor honey put inside the hive, but let it be as clean and dry as possible." The ridiculous practice of dressing the hive, by drenching it with beer, honey, fennel, &c., frequently compels the bees to leave it. In future, use a new, clean, and dry hive, and we think your bees will not leave it.

TREE ONION (E. Sargent).—The directions already given in THE COTTAGE GARDENER, vol. 3, page 296, are so excellent, that little more need be said as to the management. The stalks should be, as you say they are, throwing out their proliferous heads of young onions (for which reason it is called Allium proliferum). The stalks should be kept tied up, or supported with stakes, as their heavy heads are in most cases too weighty for their stems. This should be done with some care; make a tie first to the stake, so that the material used do not slip down the stake, and then carefully round the stalk of the onion, allowing plenty of room for the stem. When full grown, which is readily known by the appearance of the heads of little bulbs, and the yellow colour of the stems, toward the last of July or August, then collect the bulbs borne by the stems, and dry them as shallots or other kinds of onions are dried for storing. We can only recommend you to get some Vegetable Marrow plants from some gardener in your neighbourhood, to supply the place of those you have lost.

BITS OF THE HARVEST BUG (Zero).—To prevent its attack, we have heard that bathing with a weak solution of sal ammoniac the parts liable to be attacked, and allowing it to dry on, is effectual. Bathing the bitten parts with spirit of hartshorn is a speedy cure.

COCK OF DORKING BREED (L. C.).—It is very unlikely that the dealer sold you a capon. Keep him and feed him well for a few weeks. If you have the same cause for complaint, write to the vendor and ask him to exchange him for another. Wash the eyes of your fowls with cold water, into which a very little brandy has been added.

NAMES OF PLANTS (F. W. S.).—The leaf of Geranium seems to be a variegated variety of the old Rose-scented. (A Subscriber, Bury St. Edmunds).—Your plant is Hieracium aurantiacum, or Orange Hawkweed. (F. F.).—Silene quinquevulnera. (J. D. S.).—Your shrubs, 1. Ledum latifolium. 2. Rhododendron ferrugineum. It is impossible to be certain of names from such bits as you send, but we think the others are, 1. Dianthus diminutus. 2. Erysimum cheiranthoides. 3. Cuphea strigulosa. 4. Cuphea platycentra.

BEES, GIVING ROOM TO (M. J. J.).—Although it has been recommended not to give fresh room after July, yet it is frequently necessary to leave some of the capes already on till the end of August, and even later. Should brood be seen in them, and this season is will be more especially necessary, if your hives are very full, give another small hive in the manner directed at page 104, vol. 2. Your bees strewed about are evidence that they have been fighting. Do not alter the entrance, and have but one.

BEES (W. Y.).—The comb-knife is made in Sheffield, and sold at Bury St. Edmunds; the price is 3s 6d; Mr. Payne will purchase one and send you on receiving a post-office order for that amount. The glass should have been put on first, and when full a small hive placed between it and the stock (see page 104, vol. ii., of THE COTTAGE GARDENER); now it must be a small hive put between. When a small hive is full, it should never be removed until another has been placed between it and the stock, and allowed to remain a week at least; and not then, unless the cells are all sealed up. A small hive cannot be put advantageously on an old hive that has swarmed and is to be transferred. Transferring is bad; put a swarm next year into Taylor's hive, you will gain time by so doing. At page 340, vol ii., the stupified bees were put to a strong stock—putting them into an empty hive is quite another thing; they may possibly be kept alive by copious autumn feeding. Fine honey in small hives fetches in London from 1s 2d to 1s 4d per lb.; in large hives it is not saleable.

LIQUID-MANURE FOR RHUBARB AND ASPARAGUS (A Beginner).—Use your house-slops, including those from the water-closet. A household of five persons produces about 500 gallons per week. It is quite a mistake to suppose that this is offensive, even if merely passed through a coarse sieve.

REFUSE HOPS (Ibid).—There is no doubt that these would ferment and give out heat sufficient for bottom-heat in a pit, but they would require more frequent renewal than tan.

OILY REFUSE (*B. Smith*).—This, which saturates cloths employed for wiping machinery, and is extracted from them by means of soda and soap, might be employed as a manure by pouring it over vacant ground just before its being dug, and four gallons to a square yard would not be too much probably for cabbages and other strong vegetables. We shall be happy to hear from you at all times.

HONEY-COMB (*Z.*).—This should be sent to London *in* the glasses, boxes, or small hives, in which it was worked. The glasses, &c., to be inverted, packed in a case, well surrounded with straw. The small hive should not have been removed by you until the cells had all been sealed ; the number of drones indicated the strength of the hive. If the bees wanted room, another small hive should have been placed between the stock and the one already filling, as directed at page 104, vol. ii., of THE COTTAGE GARDENER, and all would have gone on well. We never recommend transferring bees from one hive to another. We recommend Taylor's *single* box hives ; they are sold by Messrs. Neighbour of London, and by Mr. Baxter of Bury St. Edmund's, a full description of which is given in Mr. Taylor's "Bee-keeper's Manual," at page 43. The *zinc shades and covers* are made and sold by Messrs. Deane and Dray, 119, Bunhill-row, St. Luke's, London.

ROSES PEGGED-DOWN (*An Admirer of the Letter and Spirit of the Cottage Gardener*).—We do not approve of pegging-down roses, because it does not improve the bloom or keep the plants dwarf, as the next growth is sure to come up from the bottom, and not from the sides of the shoots laid down. We support such branches as are overloaded with flowers, and plant so thickly as to cover the beds the first season.

CAMELLIA RETICULATA (*Ibid*).—It was over-potted, and is only re-covering from the bad consequences. You can do nothing with it now, to improve the nakedness of the shoots. See to the drainage, and grow it on until the beginning of the next growing season,—say next April. Then you may safely cut in all the shoots to a few joints each, and it will most likely make three or four shoots to one ; at any rate you will get rid of the nakedness, and have some fine shoots.

PLANTS (*Sabrina*).—Your plants are *Elæagnus parviflora;* a pretty strong bush, not more than half-hardy; north of London. *Buddlea Lindleyana*—the same, but will do against your south wall, and will soon cover it ; it is a thirsty plant. *Calycanthus macrophyllus*—a stout hardy (?) shrub for the borders. *Deutzia staminea*—a hardy border shrub, but not much to boast of. *Jasminum nudiflorum*—we have over and over again recommended this new winter flowering jasmine ; look in our indexes. *Daphne Fortuni* and *Forsythia viridissima*—you will also find in former pages all that is known of them. *Chirita sinensis* is a very little stove plant, or for a vinery or hot pit. We see by your list that these plants were sent to some one by the London Horticultural Society ; and we mention the fact in order to recommend the Society to write on the labels what kind of plants they send, and how to treat them, as they very properly do with their seed packets. We are too frequently called on to rectify this neglect.

GRASS (*A. Bennett*).—Grass, by which we understand you to mean *turf*, is not easily established on a "perpendicular" face—say of a bank, but the thing is not impossible. Our own turf "on the flat" is now as brown as a berry, after a six weeks' drought, with the exception of one slight shower; and all our natural grass banks are burnt up, but the grass is not killed. No means that we know of could save newly laid turf on steep banks under such circumstances, and it is a dangerous experiment at any time.

WOODBINE (*Ibid*).—Your newly planted woodbines were no doubt hurt by the late spring frost; you had much better cut them all down now like the other two, and water them well to the middle of September, and at the end of next October or March cut the young growths down to a few joints, and give them a few waterings with liquid-manure next summer.

ARTIFICIAL ICE (*F. F.*).—This is produced by placing water in a vessel (of metal is best) and plunging it in the following mixture :—five pounds muriate of ammonia (sal ammoniac), five pounds nitrate of potash (saltpetre), and 16 pounds of water. All the vessels and the water should be as cold as possible, and the operation should be conducted in a cellar or other cold place.

GREEN ALPINE STRAWBERRY (*Ibid*).—Can any reader supply our correspondent with a few ripe berries of this strawberry for the sake of its seed?

KEW GARDENS (*S. T.*).—We believe that servants, whether in or out of livery, are admitted into these Gardens.

CABBAGES NOT HEARTING (*Rusticus*).—These being "planted in a nook overtopped by high elms" is a very evident reason why your cabbages only produce "large leaves ;" the shade from the elms above, and their roots below, would ruin any crop. Cabbages require a rich soil and an open quarter. Thanks for your gratifying note.

WILD PARSLEY (*Ibid*).—When this or any other weed has got into grass land we know of no better mode of destroying it than to let it grow up until the seed is formed, and then to root it up with a dock-spud, and to put a pound of salt into the vacancy.

INDIAN SEEDS (*T. E. Q.*).—We cannot say what they are, but we shall sow them, and if we recognise the seedling we will let you know.

LIST OF PLANTS (*Devonian*).—Lists of the best bedding and border herbaceous hardy plants are in preparation, and will be given in the course of the autumn. Plants at the prices named can be had of any London florist.

IRIS GERMANICA (*Ibid*).—Do you not mean the endless varieties of the bulbous Irises, Xiphium and Xiphioides ? We dare not commit ourselves by giving a selected list of such ephemeral varieties ; but as they are so easily grown as Crocuses, and nearly as cheap, they are within the reach of all, and any one can choose his favourite colours out of the collection.

ROCK-WORK (*R. A. L.*).—This is a very difficult undertaking to construct *well*, and we might refer you to some of the early numbers of THE COTTAGE GARDENER in which we wrote fully on Rockeries for Alpine plants and Ferns, but as your's is a peculiar situation, and there may be others similarly placed, we shall endeavour to shape our reply to meet the case in question. The formal rock-work having been " demolished," and some larger and better stones or pieces of rock procured, information is requested as to the mode of forming the work. From the appearance of the ground in the lithographic print sent, we judge the situation of the artificial rock cannot be better placed than in the place marked on the plan. The grand object in all such imitations ought to be to form it as like nature as possible. Some parts should be bold and projecting, others should be more retired, and gently sloping, the strata should be of one character, that is, the veins of rock should all point one way, not crossing each other. In fact, observe a natural rock and imitate it as much as possible. The great object of an artificial rock is, however, to grow Alpine or other suitable plants. It will be necessary to leave wider vacancies between the stones than is quite natural, such spaces will soon be covered with the plants, and be no disfigurement to the general effect. We recommend the general outline of the face of the rock to be in the form of a half-moon, broken into irregular shapes ; some erect, bold and projecting; some even hanging over; and others of a less abrupt character sloping gently upwards, and in this part the principal compartments should be left for plants. A gravel walk should surround the whole, and, if convenient, it would be a good feature to form a small piece of water in front, beyond the walk. In this a few aquatics might be cultivated, and would have a pleasing effect, especially if the whole was entered upon through a shrubbery, so as to come upon a visitor by surprise. The embankment against which the rocks lean may be either of good soil or of clay. In the latter case, provision must be made for soil to cover the clay for the plants to grow in. The top of the bank should be planted with pyramidal shrubs, and a few Swedish Junipers, and a Deodar Pine or two, with some Arborvitæs, would materially heighten the idea of an Alpine region. Care, *great care*, must be taken not to plant any plants that have creeping roots, such for instance as the various mints. If these are planted they will soon overrun the more stay-at-home plants and destroy them. In large rock-work a few dwarf shrubs might be planted with uncommon good effect, such as the dwarf Rhododendrons, Daphnes, Cistus, Helianthemums, and numerous others. These, with their pendent branches overhang some point or projection, and take off and soften the outline of the work with the happiest effect. Sedums and Sempervivums serve to fill up the dry places of the work, and never become too large. Any shady parts of the rock will be suitable for the growth of Ferns. The walk might pass round one end, and join the carriage-drive as you suggest, with great propriety. The end of the rock-work should not be seen from any part of the ground, nor from the dwelling-house ; neither should it be under the shadow of large trees. We trust these few hints will be of some use to you, and should be happy to give any further information you may require. Pray read what is said at page 89, of volume i.

SMALL GREENHOUSE (*O. P.*).—To heat a small greenhouse use a brick flue, running either in front or under the stage, whichever is most convenient. The whole of the flue may run along above ground on brick-on-edge supporters, and the return may run upon top of the other; so that where the fire-place is there may be the little chimney also. The best way to deal with such a *brick pit* as you speak of (nine feet by six feet) would be take out all the old fermenting materials, and make the inside thoroughly clean, and form a boarded stage of any height that might suit the plants intended to be placed in it for the winter. The greenhouse would contain a large number of plants, if the best use be made of the room ; and in this house it would be advisable to keep such plants as geraniums, and other tender plants, because a little fire could be lighted in November and December, to dry off damps, &c., whilst the dry, airy-bottomed pit will do for myrtles, calceolarias, petunias, and many other such-like things. The sooner the flue is put in the better, so that the materials may be dry before the winter.

TANNERS' BARK (*Ibid*).—This, like other fermenting materials, should be turned over three or four times to sweeten, until nearly half decayed, before it is put together for heating a pit. But, unless the bark is cheaper than dung or leaves, or both, we prefer the latter well worked up and mixed together. Tan is the most pleasant to plunge pots into, and gives out a lasting steady heat ; but the dung and leaves will do this, and be most useful when done with for other purposes.

MANY QUESTIONS (*J. D. S.*).—Do not crop your fruit border at all. Move *raspberries* in November, and plant their roots six inches below the surface. All your other queries will be found answered, if you refer to our Indexes and Calendars.

LONDON: Printed by HARRY WOOLDRIDGE, Winchester High-street, in the Parish of Saint Mary Kalendar; and Published by WILLIAM SOMERVILLE ORR, at the Office, No. 2, Amen Corner, in the Parish of Christ Church, City of London.—July 11th, 1850.

WEEKLY CALENDAR.

M.W.D.	JULY 18—24, 1850.	Weather near London in 1849.			Sun Rises.	Sun Sets.	Moon R. & S.	Moon's Age.	Clock bef. Sun.	Day of Year.
18 Th	Whitethroat's song ceases.　[Moth seen.]	T. 73°—50°.	S.W.	Rain.	5a. 4	6s. 8	0 15	9	5 51	199
19 F	Sun's declination, 20° 13' N. Humming Bird	T. 73°—44°.	S.W.	Rain.	7	5	0 43	10	5 55	200
20 S	Margaret. Goat Moth seen.	T. 73°—47°.	S.W.	Rain.	8	4	1 16	11	5 59	201
21 Sun	6 Sun. Aft. Trinity. Musk Beetle seen.	T. 69°—44°.	W.	Fine.	9	3	1 52	12	6 2	202
22 M	Magd. Sedge Warbler's song ceases.	T. 69°—56°.	S.E.	Fine.	11	2	2 34	13	6 5	203
23 Tu	Turtle Dove last heard.	T. 67°—48°.	S.	Rain.	12	0	3 24	14	6 7	204
24 W	Swallow-tail Moth seen.	T. 67°—45°.	S.W.	Rain.	13	vii.	rises.	☽	6 9	205

On the 25th of July, 1904, at the residence attached to his office of chief superintendent of Kensington Gardens, died WILLIAM FORSYTH, who merited much for his acquirements as a horticulturist, but whose good fame, we think, is more than jeopardised by his pretensions to a discovery and a reward to which he was not entitled. He was born some time in 1737, at old Meldrum, in Aberdeenshire, and was there early initiated in the horticultural arts, but completed his pupilage by being placed, during 1763, under Philip Miller, at the Chelsea Garden of the Apothecaries' Company. At Miller's recommendation, he obtained the head gardenership to the Duke of Northumberland, at Sion House—a situation which he resigned in 1769 to succeed his old master in the curatorship of the Chelsea Garden. He retained this appointment until 1784, and then resigned it upon succeeding Mr. T. Robinson in the office of the Royal Gardener at Kensington and St. James's. He held this appointment until his death, publishing during the tenure of his office, "Observations on the Diseases, Defects, and Injuries in all kinds of Fruit and Forest Trees, with an account of a particular method of cure invented and practised by the author," 1791; and "A Treatise on the Culture and Management of Fruit Trees," 1902. In 1904 we have seen he died; and but for one circumstance, the testimony of his friends that he was "benevolent, unaffected, modest, and worthy," might have been inscribed without comment beneath his portrait. We are told that from the year 1768 down to 1789 he devoted much time to the cultivation of fruit and forest trees, but especially toward the discovery of some composition to remedy their incidental diseases and injuries. He laid claim to success in his research after this sanitative composition; for we have seen that he published "an account of a method of cure invented and practised" by himself; and government gave him £1500 for the discovery. They proposed to double the sum upon certain facts being established by him; but in the meantime Mr. Knight, the late president of the Horticultural Society, stept forth in the discharge of a distasteful public duty—to dispute Mr. Forsyth's title to any reward. We have had occasion to examine minutely into the merits of the contest, and regret to have arrived at the conclusion, that the composition Mr. Forsyth employed was borrowed from Hitt, and other writers upon the cultivation of trees; and that the cures he alleged to have effected were not of the extent or importance certified. Mr. Forsyth's plaister for healing the wounds and restoring to vigour decayed trees, was as follows:—One bushel of fresh cowdung; half a bushel of lime rubbish, that from ceilings of rooms is preferable, or powdered chalk; half a bushel of wood ashes; one-sixteenth of a bushel of sand: the three last to be sifted fine. The whole to be mixed and beaten together until they form a fine plaister. Now, there is nothing in this compound sufficiently differing from others recommended by his contemporaries and predecessors to entitle him to call it his invention; but supposing that an arbitrary difference in the proportions of the constituents suffices to sustain such claim, still what can be said in defence of his assertion, that this composition has filled with young wood the hollow trunks of timber trees, and that he had in his possession parts of the trunk of a tree in which the new wood, by the efficacious power of his "poor tree's plaister," had been made to incorporate with the old; and that trees so cured were rendered as fit for the navy as though they had never been injured? New wood and new bark may be induced to grow over old wood, but no power, no application, will induce them to unite to it. It is quite true that Dr. Lettsom, Dr. Anderson, and others, who ought to have been more circumspect, certified that Mr. Forsyth's statements contained "nothing more than the truth;" but they afterwards either acknowledged that they did so on evidence that ought not to have been deemed sufficient, or that they meant no more than to testify in favour of "the utility" of Mr. Forsyth's plaister. Of this there can be no doubt, because every application excluding the rain and air from a tree's wound is of great "utility." It is also quite true that Mr. Forsyth received a parliamentary grant of money, but it was granted upon inconclusive evidence; and, as Mr. Knight observes, affords a much better proof that he was paid for an important discovery than that he made one. The whole of the correspondence on the subject, between Mr. Knight and Dr. Lettsom, can be referred to in the 74th and 75th volumes of The Gentleman's Magazine, and may be read as a warning how literary controversy should not be conducted. Dr. Lettsom had rashly attested to the truth of that of which he was not a competent judge, and had not the noble candour to seek a fair examination; whilst Mr. Knight poured forth insinuations and charges in a wrathful tone, very unbefitting either a philosopher or a gentleman.

METEOROLOGY OF THE WEEK.—During the last twenty-three years, from observations at Chiswick, it appears that the average highest and lowest temperatures of these seven days are 73.1° and 52°, respectively. The greatest cold observed during the time, 40°, was on the 24th in 1838. There were 82 fine days, and 79 days on which rain fell, during the period.

INSECTS.—Whenever surveying the works of his species—from the minute perfection of the chronometer, marking with faultless regu-

RANGE OF BAROMETER—RAIN IN INCHES.

July	1841.	1842.	1843.	1844.	1845.	1846.	1847.	1848.	1849.
18 B.	29.742 / 29.684	29.903 / 29.829	29.975 / 29.794	29.762 / 29.718	30.091 / 30.096	29.450 / 29.394	30.036 / 30.037	30.088 / 29.913	29.741 / 29.622
18 R.	0.02	0.56	—	—	0.22	—	—		0.06
19 B.	29.813 / 29.796	29.842 / 29.754	29.743 / 29.700	29.891 / 29.723	30.058 / 30.030	29.326 / 29.374	29.893 / 29.853	29.776 / 29.499	29.608 / 29.521
19 R.	0.07	0.01	0.02	0.39	—	0.23	0.01	—	0.22
20 B.	29.699 / 29.493	34.735 / 29.690	29.735 / 29.690	30.174 / 30.067	30.041 / 29.955	29.995 / 29.933	29.870 / 29.856	29.512 / 29.999	29.677 / 29.525
20 R.	0.20	0.19	0.01	—	0.34	—	—	0.07	0.14
21 B.	29.565 / 29.456	29.864 / 29.718	29.818 / 29.682	30.275 / 30.237	29.521 / 29.968	29.905 / 29.883	29.679 / 29.847	29.758 / 29.677	29.922 / 29.931
21 R.	0.10	0.01	—	—	0.04	—	—	0.21	
22 B.	29.838 / 29.794	30.128 / 30.506	29.808 / 25.513	30.190 / 30.044	29.235 / 29.921	29.243 / 29.673	30.107 / 30.030	29.836 / 29.812	36.055 / 29.959
22 R.	0.69	0.08	—	—	0.05	—	—	—	
23 B.	29.999 / 29.915	30.197 / 30.133	29.781 / 29.457	29.999 / 29.919	29.210 / 29.965	29.886 / 29.895	30.238 / 30.193	29.684 / 29.619	29.758 / 29.356
23 R.	0.01	—	0.06	—	0.05	—	—	0.38	0.40
24 B.	30.133 / 30.095	30.118 / 29.927	30.128 / 30.015	29.948 / 29.916	29.924 / 29.906	29.793 / 29.425	30.149 / 30.016	29.963 / 29.863	30.519 / 29.439
24 R.	—	—	—	—	—	0.32	—	0.08	1.15

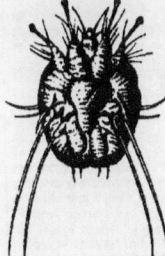

larity the progress of time, to the flying leviathan of the railroad, which almost keeps pace with that progress rendering neighbourship nearly universal—a man inclines to feel elevated with a consciousness of the power of his species, we know of no better antidote than to direct his thoughts to the almost invisible Acarida, by which his property, his health, and even his life, are destroyed. The Acaridæ, or Mites, are everywhere around and about us. The Harvest Bug (Leptus autumnalis) is a mite that will soon be afflicting us with an irritation scarcely less tormenting than that suffered by those who are infected with the itch. This disease is also caused by a mite (Acarus scabiei), represented in our wood-cut, and of which the very aspect is demoniacal. We might enumerate many other similar pests; but we will conclude our notice of this class by observing, that with death by dysentery is associated another mite, Acarus dysenteriæ. Our property is even more subject than our persons to be injured and destroyed by these minute creatures. The Red Spider, so destructive to our plants, and figured in a former volume, is a mite (Acarus tellarius); flour is apt to become uneatable from the inroads of another (Acarus farinæ); the strawberry is infested by the Gamasus baccarum; our cabinets of specimens fall a prey to one of the same tribe; and even our old cheeses are consumed by the well-known Acarus siro, represented, as magnified, in the annexed outline figure. What ground for boasting, then, has he whom the very mites prey upon and subdue?

The object of every subscriber to *The Gardeners' Benevolent Institution* must be to secure a maintenance to as many as possible of *aged* gardeners of good character, incapable of work, and in other respects destitute. We lay an emphasis on *aged*, because it is quite impossible for this Institution, with restricted means, to admit as pensioners even middle-aged men. A disabled gardener at fifty is likely to live for more than twenty years, and however we may compassionate his early decrepitude, whether from blindness or other cause, yet we must remember that there are many more in conditions equally pitiable, with the superadded claim of extreme old age. A gardener at 70, probably, will not survive five years, therefore the pension granted to one man of fifty would during the time of his benefitting by it have gladdened the hearts of four men of past threescore and ten, during the last years of their descent to the grave. If, then, to secure the greatest amount of benefit be our object, one rule that we should adopt for guidance in the employment of our vote, is *to bestow this upon the oldest* of the claimants, otherwise equally entitled to our preference.

Secondly, as entitled to an influence for our vote, we admit *the length of time that the candidate has been a subscriber to the Society's fund*. We do not place this first, because we think that from an Institution supported so largely by amateurs and others who will never require to receive an annuity in return, a man who has supported himself until 75 without recourse to its funds, is more entitled to receive a pension than a man at 65, who has subscribed a few shillings to these funds; and so strongly do we feel on this, that we should never allow any weight to the circumstance of a candidate being a subscriber, unless he had been so for at least five years.

If each subscriber would give his vote to the individuals pointed out in each list of candidates by these tests, he would have an unanswerable reply to all solicitations for his vote, and he would act in the way all must desire, namely, in the way to enable the funds of the Society to effect the greatest amount of benefit.

We strongly recommend the Society to adopt some rule forbidding any one being eligible to an annuity until he has attained the age of sixty. When he attains this age we should also recommend, if he is then quite unable to work, and has been a subscriber for twenty years or more, that he should succeed without election to the first vacant pension. The title to such succession should be in the order of priority settled by the number of years the candidates may have been subscribers; a 22 years subscriber to succeed before a subscriber of 21 years; and the latter before one of 20 years.

Water, every one knows, is a necessary of life, and the knowledge is as general that hard water is very disagreeable when employed for washing, but not one of our readers, probably, ever minutely examined the consequences of using this hard water for drinking, cooking, and other household purposes. It is one of those occur- rences of every day life which we meet with, deprecate, and submit to: we grumble, but are not sufficiently aroused to make an effort to remove the evil. We would earnestly endeavour to dispel this apathy, for the consequences are largely, very largely, injurious to the health and the purses of those who thus submit; and we do so the more confidently, because our attention has been recalled to the subject by a most interesting *Report by the General Board of Health on the Supply of Water to the Metropolis*. A report drawn up chiefly by Mr. Chadwick, and which is only equally creditable with other similar documents, indicative of his ability and judgment.

Now, with regard to the influence of hard water upon the health, it appears from the universal testimony of medical men from Hippocrates down to the day on which we are writing, that it has a tendency to constipate the bowels of the drinker. "Hard water," says Dr. Todd Thompson, "under whatever name found, should be excluded." Dr. Sutherland says:—

"Having lived for a number of years in Liverpool, a town which has a supply of very hard water for domestic use, my attention has for a length of time been called to the fact, that the continued use of this water has a somewhat peculiar effect on the digestive functions in certain susceptible constitutions. There are so many local causes of disease in the town, which may be left behind by going to other more favourable localities, that it is not very easy to state positively how much injury may be done by the quality of the water alone, but after some experience and observation, both in myself and others, I arrived at conclusions which I frequently expressed several years ago, and which nothing has since occurred to alter, and these are, that in the class of constitutions referred to, the hard water tends to produce visceral obstructions; that it diminishes the natural secretions, produces a constipated or irregular state of the bowels, and consequently deranges the health. I have repeatedly known these complaints to vanish on leaving the town, and to reappear immediately on returning to it, and it was such repeated occurrences which fixed my attention on the hard selenitic water of the new red sandstone as the probable cause, as I believe it to be, of these affections.

In these opinions he is sustained by the testimony of Drs. Heberden, Paton of Paisley, Leech and Cunningham of Glasgow, Wolstenholme of Bolton, and many others.

Dr. Playfair enforces his conviction that hard water is injurious to human beings, by referring to its effect upon animals. He observes that,

"Horses have an instinctive love for soft water, and refuse hard water if they can possibly get the former. Hard water produces a rough and staring coat on horses, and renders them liable to gripes. Pigeons also refuse hard water if they obtain access to soft. Cleghorn states, that hard water in Minorca causes diseases in the system of certain animals, especially of sheep. So much are race-horses influenced by the quality of the water, that it is not unfrequent to carry a supply of soft water to the locality in which the race is to take place, lest, there being only hard water, the horses should lose condition. Mr. Youatt, in his book called "The Horse," remarking upon the desirableness of soft water for the horse, says, 'Instinct or experience has made the horse himself conscious of this, for he will never drink hard water if he has access to soft; he will leave the most transparent water of the well for a river, although the water may be turbid, and even for the muddiest pool.' And again, in another place, he says, 'Hard water drawn fresh from the well will assuredly make the coat of a horse unaccustomed to it stare, and will not unfrequently gripe or further injure him.'"

To sum up the whole, there is no doubt with medical men that health is promoted by employing—and that for invalids one great aid to recovery is by the use of—"the softest, lightest, and purest of water." Every one has heard of the sick and the weakly resorting to Malvern to drink its renovating waters, and our readers will be startled, and feel more forcibly what has been said, when we add, from the report before us, that "at Malvern the spring water in the highest reputation for medicinal quality, is *a water only remarkable for its purity.*"

Next week we shall show the consequences of using water for household purposes.

THE FRUIT-GARDEN.

STRAWBERRY PLANTING.—Although much was said about this useful fruit at page 157, yet something more may be added as advice to those who are about to make more plantations, for doing which the present period is, perhaps, superior to all others, as a matter of principle. The pricking-out runners on reserve beds is an expedient generally resorted to from necessity; the ground in such cases being occupied with summer crops. We do not wish to be understood as advising the cottage gardener, or the amateur to aim at planting now, to the exclusion of other and useful objects, merely because planting them in July in permanent situations is considered the best practice. We would, as general advice, recommend the reserve beds, and for two reasons : first, in order that the owners of small plots may be enabled to make the most of what ground they have ; and secondly, because if "pricked-out" in reserve beds, as we shall recommend shortly, they may (if spring business should press unusually severe) *remain* in the reserve beds, and produce a most satisfactory crop.

As, however, practice differs much in strawberry culture, and also in order to give the question a full consideration, it may be observed, that market gardeners and others, who cultivate them extensively, generally make a point of taking a good crop of some other kind from between each pair of rows, during the autumn of the season in which they are planted; whilst at the same time, in nine cases out of ten, a full spring crop of some kind has preceded them. Now all this points at once to the propriety of determining a year, or nearly so, beforehand, where the succeeding plot of strawberries shall be ; in order that the manuring and working necessary for the preceding crop shall leave the ground almost ready to receive the plants without further trouble. This view of the subject, based on the recognition of a proper rotation of crops, is a most important one, as all good gardeners and agriculturists are perfectly aware ; and we hope in some future paper to go fully into the subject, as bearing on the whole garden ; such remarks will well befit our autumn labours, when we shall be better able to spare a few columns for the purpose ; for we must soon haste to the pine-apple affair, and some other most pressing matters.

Having thus opened a few of the leading considerations of this subject, we must proceed to advise about planting, and the subsequent autumn culture.

The mode of obtaining good and early runners was explained in our previous paper; we will now suppose, that such having been carried out, plenty of all the necessary kinds are available. Before describing the mode of planting, a few remarks on *kinds* will be necessary; for as they differ so much in habit of growth it is necessary that this—which must in the main influence

the distance at which they are to be planted—be taken into consideration.

In former days, those kinds which were the types or progenitors of the present numerous kinds were not only few in number but much more decided in habit, and distinct in character; their culture was, consequently, more simple. Notwithstanding this, much more abundant crops are produced in these days by the intermixture of races, although we doubt whether any decided advance in point of flavour has been made beyond the *old Pine* and the *Hautbois*.

Varieties.—Many of the kinds introduced within the last few years doubtless owe their parentage to a cross of the two latter kinds ; for the Hautbois character may be clearly traced both in the flavour and in the foliage. However to proceed, it may be observed, that most of the gross growing kinds, producing heavy foliage with long leaf-stalks, should by all means be cultivated in single rows ; whilst those the reverse in habit may, if circumstances require it, be grown in beds ; although there can be little doubt that *all are the better for single row culture.*

The *Keen's seedling* we cultivate with the greatest of success, both in beds and in rows ; the *British Queen* does not succeed in beds at all ; the *Elton* succeeds admirably in beds ; in rows we have not succeeded equally well. Indeed we feel satisfied, that the latter invaluable strawberry, for late purposes, answers best by far, if allowed to spread its runners unmolested on the sides of the plot, the ground having received a slight top-dressing, without digging, previous to the runners starting in the spring. By this mode of culture, the old plants in the centre may be dug down, thus forming an alley between two plots of young runners, right and left.

Such was the habit of that celebrated strawberry of some half score years since, and which was one of the first which bore the impress of a Hautbois cross ; the name we forget—probably *Myatt's Pine.* This was a magnificent strawberry, but few could grow it.

Mr. Robert Reid, late of Noblethorpe, suggested the above mode of culture, or nearly so ; and he has repeatedly affirmed, that by this mode he obtained superior crops to any other.

It is a common practice to grow the *Alpines* in beds, and to let them produce their runners unmolested. Much superior, however, are they in both size and quality when grown singly, or, as we prefer, in threes : each three forming a distinct and separate hillock or little bush.

Planting.—We come now to remark on the distance apart, both of the rows and of the plants in the row ; and in doing so may be permitted to quote our present practice, the result of many years' observation, and adopted after trying many plans in order to combine all the best modes of culture in one ; or, in other words, to simplify matters as much as possible. Let us suppose that a plantation has to be made of the larger kinds, that is to say, those which *ought* to be grown in rows ; and that the kinds are the *Keen's seedling* and the *British Queen.* We will also take the case of a plot of ground exhausted by a previous crop recently removed; supposing, however, that the staple or mechanical condition of the soil is pretty good, for we have in a previous paper disposed, for the present, of that portion of the subject. It may also be premised, that the plantation when made is to remain for three or four years. The ground should be deeply dug or trenched, and some new or undecomposed manure should be dug with the first "spit" into the bottom. Before removing the second spit, some manure or vegetable soil of a more decomposed character should be introduced : placing it on the surface and digging it and the soil together. By these means there will be an admixture of organic materials in the *lower level*, which will be a source of nutrition to the deeper roots for three or four years, besides being a pasture for the roots to revel in; such, at that depth, being a matter of great importance during surface droughts, which always prove exceedingly injurious to the strawberry.

The upper stratum, containing the mixture of decomposed materials, will establish the plant at once,—a matter of some importance. We hope, nevertheless, that our readers will not suppose that a great amount of manurial matter is here intended: no such thing. Too great an amount of manures will produce an invincible coarseness of foliage, and this will be found to tend to barrenness. To establish the plant speedily, and to promote durability, especially during dry periods, at the blossoming and fruiting, are the legitimate objects to aim at.

And now, the ground prepared, we come to the matter of distance. We allow three feet between the rows for all the larger kinds,—considering that when fully established the plants on either side will extend at least one foot; this of course leaves about a foot for the operator to tread upon when watering, gathering the crop, &c. Between the plants, for a permanent plantation, we give one foot only; but immediately the fruit is gathered we destroy alternate plants, thus throwing, the second year, the plants at two feet apart.

And now let us suppose the *bed-system* to be carried out. It must here be observed, that by bed culture is not meant the continuing the plants for more than two seasons by any means; indeed, we do not advise more than one, or what is termed "the frequent remove system." Beds, however planted, become so crowded, confused, and, by consequence, shaded after the second year, that flavour is out of question.

Beds for strawberries should, by no means, be more than four feet wide; indeed, if the single row system *must* be departed from, we should prefer merely double rows, or, in other words, beds—if beds it must be—with only two rows in them. The beds being forty-two inches in width, the rows may be eighteen inches apart; thus leaving one foot on each side of the rows, besides an alley of a foot or so for the operator.

Another point we would urge, both in bed culture and in single rows: let their direction be, whenever possible, north and south; this gives both sides of the row an equal amount of sunshine. Indeed, this principle applies to almost all the products of the kitchen-garden, with the exception of summer crops requiring shade; and then the plan recommended by our clever coadjutor, Mr. Barnes, of running rows of the Marrowfat peas, runners, &c., east and west, in order to furnish a shade, is excellent.

We have before stated, that we grow our *Eltons* for late purposes in a border on the north side of a wall, at about five or six feet from the wall. This is an excellent plan, and by it the table is constantly furnished until October, when the Alpines are in full perfection. Those amateurs, however, who cannot spare a wall border, may easily accomplish the same object, by so setting out their ground, that every year a row of Victoria, or Knight's Marrow Peas, may be sown on the south side in the direction before advised. As a rotation the Scarlet Runner may be used in alternate seasons, or even a row of Jerusalem Artichokes.

We have a bed of Eltons thus situated, which have stood six years, and have received no farther culture than thinning out the crowded runners in October, and scattering a top-dressing of horse droppings over the surface; these are at once a manure and a protection. The bed promises this year to be as fine as ever.

It will be borne in mind that we advised only two rows in a bed, eighteen inches apart; in these the plants may be placed eight inches apart, and each alternate plant removed after the first year's fruiting. Those who are severely limited for ground may put four rows in the bed, and remove alternate rows after the first bearing. It must, however, be remembered, that the thicker the cropping the less manure must be used, or the end in view will assuredly be defeated.

In all strawberry planting, care should be taken to get up the roots carefully with a little ball of soil if possible. Equal care must be taken that the fibres do not become dry by exposure; those who have few to plant will do well to throw them into a bucket of water as they take them up. The roots should not be planted deep, and they should be kept regularly moist until well established. Of course all weeds must be kept under. We would advise those who are planting the *British Queen*, to take care that they are somehow protected in the middle of November; any ordinary straw or litter will answer, or tree leaves of the previous year. Even the asparagus haulm, or that from the peas, might be thrown over them; fern, also, is available in some places; in others, the boughs of the spruce fir.

Much more has to be said about strawberry culture, which must pass on to another opportunity.

R. ERRINGTON.

THE FLOWER-GARDEN.

FLOWER-GARDENERS who aspire to excel in their calling, have two very strong temptations to withstand from this time to the end of September. In the first place, we all of us know that certain seedling varieties of choice plants have a strong tendency to depart from those forms or colours for which we chiefly admire them, and hence are difficult to preserve from seeds true to those points for which we cultivate them. We all acknowledge this difficulty, and yet we do not, in most instances, make proper allowance to the seedsmen for it, but rather look on them as if they were endowed with some magic spell by which they ought to overcome such natural tendencies in their seed gardens. Now comes the first temptation. We have a beautiful flower-bed in full bloom, and all from seeds which are variable in their nature—but this time the plants turn out just to the very tint desired: and if the seedsmen would but engage to supply samples so true as these for the future, who would go to the trouble of saving doubtful seeds? Seedsmen, however, may make what arrangements they think best, but they cannot always ensure many kinds of seeds to turn out quite as we, or they, want them; and, therefore, it is that we are now tempted to let a certain bed run to seed rather than hazard the chance of a failure another season. Yet, it goes a good way against the grain to see a choice flower-garden converted into a seed nursery, even to the extent of one single bed. But what is to be done in such cases is more than I can tell. If I had a bed, or a row, or even a patch, of true *blue branching Larkspur*, I would certainly let it ripen the seeds before I removed the plants, because I do not believe there is a single seedsman in Europe, or elsewhere, who can supply the genuine plant. Yet, this fine annual finds a place in every third garden in the country; and I recollect the time when no larkspur of this tall kind was to be seen but the deep blue variety. But since the eight or nine varieties of it, of different tints, which are now to be met with in every fashionable flower-garden have come into competition with that old sort, the real blue branching larkspur can hardly be seen at all; what generally goes by that name is a purplish blue plant. The tall larkspurs being now in full beauty, any one who has a bed of them, and sees this, can easily put me right if I am in error; and, moreover, if two or three pods of seeds from a genuine variety could be sent to me by post at the same time, it would be a good way of convincing me how far I have been wrong. There are, or were some years since, two sorts of the plant I want—one with the open part of the flower light blue all round, and the bottom a deep dark blue, and the other, which is the best, is dark blue all over; but seeds from either can hardly be depended on if a tall larkspur of a different colour is so near that the bees, or the wind, can carry the pollen dust from one to the other. Others, no doubt, have some favourite flowers difficult to keep, or to obtain true from seeds, and so the temptation to save seeds under one's own eye goes the whole way round the circle. I believe it to be a natural law that, if plants are divested of their seed-vessels as fast as the flowers begin to fade, they will keep much longer in flower than is natural to them. At any rate, there is no question about the soundness of the principle as far as the generality of flower-garden plants are in question, therefore, from this time to the end of the season, seed-vessels or pods should be looked on in the same light as weeds. When a head, or a bunch of flowers, falls off or fades at once, there is very little trouble about the matter—the stalk is cut, and there is an end to it; but in others, as, for instance, *Scarlet Geraniums* and *Lupines*, some of the flowers die away, and the seed-vessels stick out like beaks or bean-pods long before some of the flowers on the same stalk are ready to open, so that it becomes a tedious and a delicate operation to keep a bed of these scarlets free from seed vessels. Of all the scarlets that I have seen, *Compactum* and *Shrubland Scarlet* are the two most free from forming seeds; but both have another failing just as bad, for the flowers in the centre of their trusses die away, and are decayed, or mouldy, before the outside flowers are ripe enough to open; therefore, to keep a large bed of any of this tribe in first-rate order, they must be looked over every two or three days, and the dead flowers, or the seed-vessels, cut out carefully with a sharp knife or pair of garden scissors; and the best scissors for all garden work that I have seen are those sold as *Turner's Garden Scissors*, which are manufactured by Mr. Turner, of Neepsend, Sheffield. They cut clean, like a good knife,—not a bruised cut as by the common work-basket scissors.

We grow many *Lupines* here, and our rule is to cut off the whole spike of flowers as soon as one-third of its length is faded at the bottom—an extravagant way, certainly, and might be improved on by taking hold of the top of the flower-spike with one hand, and rubbing off the bottom pods with the other; indeed, any way of saving the flowers, and at the same time the seeds, is a good plan. Writing about lupines, reminds me that we had a new one last year from a friend, of which kind we have a good stock this season, but it has hardly got into seed catalogues yet. It belongs to the tall section of annuals to which *Lupinus mutabilis* is referred, and might be taken for *mutabilis* or *Crookshankii* before it comes into bloom; but the colour is very different, being partly cream colour with a pinkish shade; we had it for a real pink lupine, but it is not so in reality; nevertheless, it makes a good marked variety, and lasts—like its relatives—till overtaken by a smart frost. These tall lupines are not grown half so much as their merit deserves—I mean the annuals of the *mutabilis* section; and from this time to the middle of August is the best time in the year to sow them, for one particular purpose, which is, to flower them as single specimens out on the grass—one plant in a place, three plants in another, and so on, as one might choose; or if a bank or large bed of them were planted like dahlias in such princely places as Chatsworth or Windsor Castle, the effect would be magnificent; but to have them in a sober way for more ordinary situations, a dozen of them got up now, or soon, and half starved in little pots singly

through the autumn, would take up no more room in a dry pit or greenhouse than so many verbenas in single pots; and as soon as they began to move in the spring to be potted, and so encouraged to grow on and to be repotted once or twice more before the time of planting them out in May, they would become large bushes, such as one could hardly believe who has not seen the mode tried. Where there is head-room, one or two plants of them might be grown very large, just to see what good cultivation could effect before the time of planting them out; and should they even be coming into flower as early as the first of May, there would be no danger of their ceasing to bloom down to the end of October, particularly if their seed-pods are kept down. I should not be surprised to hear of a single annual lupine reaching the height of ten feet, and full and bushy in proportion; but for so large a plant, a very sheltered spot should be chosen, as a heavy wind would have great power on such a mass of succulent shoots and thin foliage. For common ordinary use they are not sown till the end of March, like other annuals.

The second great temptation is about making *cuttings from choice geraniums*. This is just the best time of the year to make cuttings of the whole race of flower-garden geraniums; but now that they are only in fine bloom after a struggle for existence, it seems hard to take off any cuttings yet. To have a fine stock of healthy plants, however, long before the winter sets in, we must begin to propagate early. Here we use as many geraniums as most people, and more kinds of them than any other place in the country. My catalogue of this class of geraniums contains 87 names, and I shall add half a dozen more to them this season. We also keep a propagating book, in which every plant we bed is entered, and the number of cuttings that are required is put after each name. These numbers are altered every season—except a few of what we call stock-plants—to suit the arrangement of the planting next season. Our first stock-plant of geraniums is our own scarlet seedling called *Punch*, and of it we annually root five thousand cuttings. This is the greatest number we strike of any one sort, and it is very seldom we put cuttings of these kinds of geraniums in pots, unless it is a very delicate or a rare sort which we can ensure better that way. The whole are rooted in the open ground, and full in the sun, and the hottest day in the year will not hinder our propagation when we once begin, and we never shade a geranium cutting. The vine and peach borders are generally the propagating beds, and it is a good old plan to put a slight coat of some light rich compost over these borders in July, when most of the liberal waterings are over for the season. The borders being first stirred with a fork to the depth of two or three inches, and then a couple of inches of the mulching compost is added. The whole is then raked, and the usual alley is marked out near the wall, and the place is ready for the cuttings. You begin at one end of the border, and plant the cuttings in rows across it, two inches between every cutting, and six inches between the rows. When two or three rows of cuttings are thus planted, and you see from the propagation book how many cuttings of that sort are to be struck this season, you can calculate what length of border will hold the whole of them; then measure off that length of the border, and then begin with the next kind, and so on for the whole collection, and by the time the propagation is finished, every sort will be found by itself. Besides the look of the thing, this is by far the best plan to ensure a systematic course of management. When a gardener first begins to propagate, the chances are that he cannot get more than a tenth of the number he requires, and not even that of many varieties, therefore, if he were to plant the first crop of cuttings in close succession on the border without leaving intervening spaces as above, he might certainly root all his stock, but they would be so huddled and mixed together as would render their management difficult. Strong and fast growing sorts would overrun the weaker ones, and some would require water much oftener than others, but if they are in close contact, how is he to proceed? and, moreover, if the propagator should forget to mark down in his book the numbers of cuttings he made at any one sitting, the whole must be counted over again; all this would look like hap-hazard.

For those who know very little of these things, I may now give the details. The border or open space of ground in a sunny aspect we shall suppose is ready, and I put most stress on having the place full in the sun, because half the world lie under a mistake on this head, and suppose that a north aspect is the best, which is, indeed, a very wrong notion. Then look over the bed or plants from which the cuttings are to be taken, and select carefully those shoots near the centre of the plant, or where they are most crowded; and in this early searching for cuttings you are to study "the look" of the plants rather than the number of cuttings, for if we "take the market on the day," we have plenty of opportunities yet for an abundant supply of them. Then, at this early period, be content with a few, and that few, if judiciously chosen, will rather improve the look of the plants, and enable them the sooner to extend sideways. The cuttings of strong growing scarlet geraniums may be six or seven inches long, as an average; three of their bottom leaves to be cut off, and the bottom of the cutting to be a clean cut just under a joint, or under the bottom leaf. Some people say that these cuttings should lay by a while to dry, so as that the fresh soil should not "damp them off," but this is hardly necessary; the soil is dry enough to suck off any moisture that may be on the cut part, and a cutting in the open ground is not at all so likely to rot as one placed in a pot. Mark off the border with a line, or string tied to two sticks, or you may leave the line stretched across the bed or border, and plant the cuttings by the side of it, and then move it on for the next row, and so on. The surface of the border ought to be even, and the planter should stand or kneel on a piece of board rather than disturb the bed by his foot. About an inch deep will be the right depth to plant the cuttings, but less than that will do if the surface of the bed is a little firm. When the whole are planted, give them a *slight* watering to damp the leaves and settle the surface of the soil about the cuttings, but by no means give so much water as to reach to the bottom of the cuttings so early; indeed, we have planted thousand of these cuttings in hot weather without giving any water at all.

D. BEATON.

GREENHOUSE AND WINDOW GARDENING.

DOUBLE FLOWERS.—The day is not yet so far distant when our scientific botanists were experiencing something like fever heat, from witnessing the growing partiality for these truly beautiful, though to them hateful, monstrosities—a fever only secondary in its evils to the nightmare antipathy with which they viewed the labours of the hybridising florist, who, in the extreme number as well as diversified forms of the varieties he introduced, seemed to make havock of nomenclature, and ride rough-shod through all their nicely drawn-up specific distinctions and definitions. Even they, however, our learned instructors—for though they were not free from prejudices any more than other men, we must not forget the debt we owe them—even they can now join the florist in expatiating upon, and defining

the merits of, a beautiful hybrid; and, what is more, can mingle with the vulgar throng and behold a peculiar beauty in these double monstrosities, altogether apart from the means which such flowers present for building up a peculiar phytological theory.

I confess that in the case of many plants, such for instance as the *Chinese Hibiscus*, the single perfect flower is to my eye far more beautiful than the double varieties; but beautiful and lovely though many even of our common plants be in their single state—such as the daisy, when slowly rolling back its pale crimson hood-like covering as the sun's rays reach it in the morning—I conceive that few, with a correct taste for the beautiful, would think of contrasting for a moment the single and the double in such plants as daisies, primroses, violets, ranunculuses, pinks, carnations, roses, stocks, wall-flowers, Sweet Williams, rockets, balsams, fever-few, catch-fly, &c.; plants which, though generally found in their highest perfection in the garden of the amateur and cottager, will never disgrace the parterre of the nobleman.

Our attention has been directed to this subject by the inquiries of a lady correspondent, as to how such flowers are at first produced. "Is it from richness of soil, as in the stock? I know that double flowers may be perpetuated by impregnation, but want to know how to get one double in the first instance." Now our difficulty here consists in the fact, that our own mind is not quite made up on the subject, though we incline to our friend's supposition, that double flowers are chiefly produced by cultivation, and, in addition, that they are perpetuated by the same means; and although aware that they *may* be perpetuated by *impregnation*, we consider that even that holds a rather secondary place to careful cultivation. Glancing, however, at one or two fallacies may lead the investigations of our friends, who have time at their command, into a channel whence more consistent and legitimate deductions may proceed.

That our correspondent is not alone in her opinion, that double flowers are perpetuated by cross fecundation, may be seen in the circumstance of saving a single flowering stock for seed that has been surrounded by double ones; the practitioners believing that the contiguity of the double flowers will influence the single ones, and thus so far affect the seeds formed that they will produce plants with double flowers. Now, in examining the matter, it will at once be found that the double state in flowers is generally produced by the stamens, and the pistils, the male and female organs, and also at times what are termed floral leaves, &c., being all changed into petals; and the more completely this has been done, the more perfect the specimen appears as a double flower. But the more effectually this was accomplished, the more unlikely would such double flowers be to exercise any influence *whatever* upon the properties of the seed produced from single flowers in their vicinity. If these double flowers contained any perfect stamens, the fertilising pollen of these stamens might be transferred to the summit of the pistil of the single flowers, and thus the properties of the double flowers might be imparted to the seeds so fecundated; Thus, in saving seed from semi-double flowers, or even from flowers containing a greater number of petals than usual, there is a greater probability of obtaining double flowers in future than from plants with perfectly single flowers, as a predisposing cause in the first case has already been in action. Whether this double flowering condition be the result of disease or merely of a full plethoric habit, superinduced by high cultivation, is a question that will not at all affect the above proposition But, if no such influence in the shape of male organs existed in the double flowers, then their neighbourhood to the single ones could exercise no power whatever upon the qualities of the seed that would naturally be produced. Future culture will determine whether the plants from such a seed shall be puny or luxuriant, but that culture for the first season will have little or no influence as to the plant possessing double or single flowers; these are qualities which would be chiefly lodged in the seed while yet remaining in the seed-vessel of its nurse-parent. What, then, are some of the principles by which we ought to be guided, when our object is to *obtain* and *preserve* double flowers?

Making allowance for exceptions, the following may be adduced as leading general propositions :—*First.* To obtain double flowers from seed, dependance must not be placed upon the influence of a stray stamen that was not converted into a petal or flower leaf, but means must be taken to make the seeds possessed of a property which otherwise they would not possess, by superinducing a highly elaborated, full, plethoric habit, in the seeds. This can only be done by stimulating the plant with high cultivation at a certain period—*after the flower-buds appear*,—and then by removing the greater portion of the seeds. If the stimulus is applied at an earlier period, the plant will increase greatly in luxuriance; by giving it thus later, a greater degree of strength is conveyed to the flowers; by thinning these flowers, or the seed vessels, as soon as formed, so as to have only a very few seeds to ripen, these, in consequence, acquire a full plethoric habit; and we know that in the vegetable and animal world alike, this state is opposed to productive fruitfulness, while in the deplethoric state it is encouraged. From a full double flower, therefore, we expect and obtain no seeds. From such plants as balsams, which, though said to be double, yet produce seeds, the rendering of them more double must be obtained by the high cultivating and seed thinning process. In their case, as well as some others, *compactness* of growth and *clearness* of colour seem to be gained by preserving the seed for several years; the fresher a seed, the sooner will it vegetate, and the stronger and more luxuriant the plant. . In double composite flowers, such as the *Dahlia*, which consist of a number of florets upon a common receptacle, though the most of these florets may have their parts of fructification changed into petals, others may be unchanged, though they remain unnoticed until the petals fall off; and from these, when seeds are produced, more double flowers may be expected than from seeds saved from more single varieties, because possessing a greater constitutional tendency in that direction. This will more especially be the result when, as in the other cases, high cultivation is resorted to whenever the seed appears. Thus something like *superfetation* is induced in the seed, which leads it afterwards, when sown, to develope itself more in leaves and petals (which the botanists tell us are the same thing), instead of flowers producing seed; and this altogether independent of the culture it receives for that season. When any of our friends, therefore, look somewhat disconsolate on their beds of stocks nearly all single, they may rest next to assured that the culture they imparted had little or nothing to do with it. The seeds they sowed would have been single in *any* circumstance. The matter is different in the perennial plants, such as the daisy and the primrose. Without resorting to seeds at all, the plant from being divided, having its soil frequently changed and stimulated by rich compost, will often gradually change from the single into the double flowering condition, upon exactly the same principles; luxuriance and fruitfulness being ever opposed to each other. Several years ago we carried out these ideas with considerable success, and such as they are, now commend them to the notice of our friends who have more time at their command.

Secondly. On much the same principle, care should be taken to preserve double flowers, when propagating them by cuttings, runners, and divisions of the root,—

by giving them the same careful cultivation, otherwise they are apt to return to the primitive single state. To secure this object effectually, two considerations should be attended to. If a rich stimulating system of cultivation is at the first resorted to, there will be the likelihood of having a luxuriant development of stem and leaves, at the expense of depriving the flowers of their requisite proportions. In all free-growing luxuriant plants, it will be wise policy not to over stimulate the plant until the bloom appears; and the increased nourishment judiciously given will then enlarge the size of the flower, while the rest of the plant would continue to maintain a comparative dwarf and stubby character. In choosing seed when it is produced, let it be selected from such plants. Then, again, if the size of the flower is to be maintained, and prevented degenerating into its primitive condition, rich composts should not only be used, but fresh soil, if possible, given to them every year.

Now is a good time to propagate all these pretty desirables, at least all that are of a comparative hardy nature. Many of them, when the flower stems are decayed, may be divided at the root; such as the *Rocket*, which with the *Wall-flower* and *Sweet William*, *Lychnis*, &c., will strike by small cuttings in light soil under a hand-light, under the same treatment as is resorted to with *Pinks*. In the case of using hard stems of Rockets and Wall-flowers, &c., it is advisable, after cutting through with a sharp knife at a joint, to run the knife upwards a short distance, through the centre of the cutting, and then to make a similar incision at right angles with the first, so that the base of the cutting shall consist of four equal divisions. This exposes a greater portion of the inner bark, and roots in consequence are more quickly and plentifully produced.

R. FISH.

HOTHOUSE DEPARTMENT.
EXOTIC FERNS.
(Continued from page 212.)

PROPAGATION BY SEED.—We described a successful mode of raising the *Gymnogramma chrysophylla* from seed at Kew. There are some other methods that it will be well to try should that one fail. Procure a brick or a piece of stone partially covered with very short moss, sprinkle the fern seed upon it, and cover it with a hand-glass in a shady part of the stove or orchid house, keeping the surface round the brick or stone very moist. In this situation the seeds, if good, will soon come up in the shape of a small roundish leaf, from the base of which the first frond will make its appearance. At that particular juncture raise the young plants with a small flattened stick, and transplant them thickly over the surface of shallow pots or pans. Cover these incipient plants again with a hand-glass, and keep the internal air moist. As they advance in growth, tilt the hand-glass on one side for a few hours every day, gradually increasing the height of the opening and the duration of the time of keeping it open, till the plants are so far advanced as to be fit to transplant singly into small pots. The size called "thumbs" will be sufficient for these tiny plants in the first instance. Continue to repot them till they reach their maximum size.

This method is, for the most difficult sorts, best for free growing kinds. The more simple way is, to brush the seeds of the fronds upon the soil in a pot, place it under a hand-glass, and when the seedlings come up transplant and repot in the usual way. The late Mr Shepherd, of the Liverpool Botanic Garden, raised numbers of ferns from fronds, collected abroad and brought home in a dry state between sheets of paper. The dust that had rubbed off during the transit he collected and scattered upon soil in pots filled to within an inch of the top : no covering was necessary upon the soil. He then laid upon the pots pieces of glass large enough to rest upon the edges and overhang them a little: this prevented evaporation; and he was rewarded by a plentiful crop. Some of the fronds had been collected several years, but it seems the seeds had the power to preserve their vitality. No doubt there were several species that never came up, but a sufficient number did make their appearance to reward him for his trouble. Our readers may inquire, "Which of these methods are we to adopt?" The answer is, try them all, if convenient, and any other your ingenuity may suggest till you succeed. Bake the soil, to destroy the seeds of weeds, or you may be deceived and disappointed by having a worthless crop instead of the beautiful foreign ferns you may wish to succeed with.

SPECIES.—We subjoin a list of such of the most beautiful exotic ferns as may be procured at nurseries cultivating them for sale. There is a very good collection at Pine Apple-place under our care. Such of our readers as may have connexions abroad would do wisely to desire their friends to collect fronds of ferns with ripe seeds on, to dry them, and pack them up between sheets of dry paper, inclosing the whole in a deal box, to be kept dry; and as soon as they arrive let the seeds be sown in some one or other of the methods we have described above. Living plants might be sent home in Wardian cases with great success. By these means new species of these elegant plants might be introduced.

Name.	Average height. Feet.	Price. s.	d.
Adiantum assimile	1	2	6
* ,, *curvatum*	1½	5	0
* ,, *concinnum*	2	5	0
* ,, *cuneatum*	1	2	6
* ,, *formosum*	1½	3	6
,, *macrophyllum*	1	5	0
* ,, *lunatum*	½	10	6
,, *lucens*	½	3	6
,, *pubescens*	1	2	6
* ,, *pedatum*	1	2	6
,, *reniforme*	¾	5	0
,, *rhomboideum*	1	5	0
* ,, *tenerum*	1½	5	0
* ,, *trapeziforme*	2	5	0
* ,, *villosum*	1	5	0
Aspidium mucronatum	2	7	6
,, *serra*	2	5	0
* ,, *indivisum*	3	7	6
,, *villosum*	3	10	6
,, *auriculum*	1	5	0
**Allantodia axillaris*	2	3	6
,, *australis*	2	5	0
Anemia flexuosa	1	5	0
,, *fraxinifolia*	1½	3	6
Asplenium ebeneum	½	2	6
,, *bulbiferum*	1	5	0
* ,, *falcatum*	2	5	0
,, *flabelliforme*	½	3	6
,, *molle*	2	2	6
,, *præmosum*	1½	5	0
,, *palmatum*	1	5	0
* ,, *nidus avis*	2	15	0
,, *Shepherdii*	1	5	0
* ,, *rhizophyllum*	2	10	6
Blechnum australe	½	3	6
* ,, *brasiliense*	2	7	6
,, *gracile*	1	3	6
,, *triangulare*	½	3	6
,, *occidentale*	1	2	6
**Cassebeera farinosa*	1	21	0
**Cheilianthes lendigera*	1	10	6
,, *micromera*	½	5	0
,, *profusa*	¾	8	6
,, *repens*	3	5	0
,, *viscosa*	1	5	0
* ,, *vestita*	1	5	0
,, *tenera*	½	7	6
**Cœnopteris cicutaria*	1	3	6
* ,, *vivipara*	1	5	0
Cibolium Barometz	2	5	0
Davallia canariensis	1	2	6
* ,, *elegans*	2	10	6
Darea odontites	1	2	6
* ,, *diversifolia*	1½	21	0
**Dicksonia antarctica*	6	21	0
* ,, *davallioides*	2	5	0
Diplazium decussatum	1	2	6
,, *plantagineum*	1½	10	6
**Doodia aspera*	½	3	6
,, *rupestris*	½	1	6
,, *Kunthiana*	¾	2	6
**Gymnogramma calomelanos*	2	3	6
* ,, *chrysophylla*	1	7	6
,, *ochracea*	1	2	6
* ,, *tartarica*	1	5	0
,, *tomentosa*	2	7	6
* ,, *dealbata*	1	5	0
Hemionitis palmata	½	3	6
Lastræa eburnea	2	10	6
,, *paludosa*	1½	5	0
Lindsæa linearis	¾	7	6
,, *falcata*	¾	7	6
**Litobrockia leptophylla*	1½	5	0
,, *denticulata*	½	5	0
Lomaria attenuata	¾	5	0
,, *Pattersonii*	½	3	6
Lygodium palmatum	climbing	7	6
* ,, *scandens*	do.	5	0
**Lycopodium circinale*	½	3	6
* ,, *cuspidatum*	¾	5	0
* ,, *cæsium*	½	2	6
,, *arboreum* (very elegant)	12	10	6
,, *flabulare*	¾	3	6
,, *schottii*	½	5	0
,, *denticulatum*	¾	1	6
* ,, *stoloniferum*	1	1	6
,, *plumosum*	½	5	0
* ,, *Wildenovii*	1	7	6
* ,, *umbrosum*	¾	3	6
Meniscium palustre	2	5	0
**Nephrodium decompositum*	½	3	6
,, *exaltatum*	3	3	6
,, *ottonis*	3	5	0
,, *pectinatum*	2	3	6
Niphobolus pertusus	creeping	3	6
,, *rupestris*	do.	3	6
,, *sinensis*	½	3	6
**Nothochlæna sinuata*	1½	21	0
,, *nivea*	¾	10	6
,, *distans*	½	5	0
,, *trichomanoides*	½	5	0
Olfersia cervina	2	7	6
Platyloma falcata	1	3	6
,, *subverticillata*	1	3	6
Physematium molle	¾	5	0
Polypodium aureum	3	2	6
,, *effusum*	3	5	0
,, *neriifolium*	2	5	0
* ,, *pectinatum*	2	5	0
,, *phymatodes*	1	3	6
,, *sepultum*	½	10	6
Polystichum drepanum	½	3	6
* ,, *proliferum*	1	5	0
Pteris chinensis	1½	3	6
* ,, *collina*	¾	5	0
,, *cretica*	1	7	6
,, *heterophylla*	1	5	0
,, *hastata*	1½	2	6
,, ,, *latifolia*	1½	5	0
,, *lata*	1½	5	0
,, *longifolia*	1	2	6
**Pteris marginata*	½	2	6
* ,, *rotundifolia*	½	3	6
* ,, *sagittæfolia*	¾	5	0
* ,, *pedata*	1	5	0
,, *palmata*	1	7	6
,, *tremula*	3	2	6
,, *vespertilionis*	2½	3	6
**Platycerium grande*	2½	42	0
,, *acrostichioides*	3	5	0
Woodwardia radicans	1½	3	6

This may seem a numerous list, but there are in cultivation a great number more; they are either very high priced or in private collections, and, therefore, not come-at-able. The garden at Kew is exceedingly rich in these elegant plants. We have marked with an * the most beautiful species in our list.

FLORISTS' FLOWERS.

DAHLIAS.—These splendid autumnal flowers will now require every due attention to bring their blooms to the greatest possible perfection. Unlike most other florists' flowers they will bear almost any quantity of stimulating food. The stronger the plant the larger and finer will the blooms be. A good mulching of very rotten dung, covering a space of half-a-yard all round each plant, will be beneficial, whether the season be dry or wet; if dry, the mulching prevents evaporation from the soil; and if wet, the rains wash down the nutritive properties of the manure, and encourage the growth of the plants Watering in dry weather with liquid manure also will be useful. Every care must be taken that each branch is properly secured by stakes and ties, to prevent the autumn winds or heavy rains from breaking them down. Thin the branches so as to throw strength into the flower-bearing ones; the flowers, too, should be thinned, in order that such as are left may have every advantage of sun, light, and air. As soon as the flowers begin to expand they will require shading and protecting from sun and rain; the best shade we ever saw was formed of a small square box, glazed on three sides, and the top, bottom, and back of wood. These were fastened firmly to a stake; a slit was sawn half way across the bottom; one of the glass sides was hung on a hinge, the flower was brought within the box and fastened securely, the window closed, and the flower was thus effectually protected from sun, wind, and rain, and also from insects. These shades are rather expensive, but with care they will last several years.

RANUNCULUS.—As soon as the leaves decay the tubers should be taken up immediately, because if rain fall in abundance they will be very apt to put forth new roots, and in time will commence growing again above the surface; this would be a very unhappy circumstance, as it would weaken the growth and bloom next year; recollect this, and take up directly the leaves are turned yellow and dead. Should any of the stalks be bearing seed it should be carefully gathered before the wind blows it away. In taking up the tubers be careful not to bruise them; lay them in a dry place where the sun will shine upon them only two or three hours each day. As soon as they are quite dry clean them and put them in drawers for the winter, till the planting time arrives again.

TULIPS ought to be also all now in winter quarters We shall shortly notice the necessary work to be done at the beds in which the ranunculus and tulip have grown this season. T. APPLEBY.

MISCELLANEOUS INFORMATION.

THE DARNING BASKET.

By the Authoress of " My Flowers."

WE perceive with regret that we have, quite unintentionally, overlooked the query of a very kind and indulgent correspondent, upon which we now hasten to remark, to the best of our ability, although with a strong sense of the difficulty of the task: "Where there is very little money to procure garments of any kind, how much time must be given to mending, darning, and darning stockings ?"

It is most important that clothes, particularly those of children, should be repaired the moment they require it; not the slightest rent or broken stitch should be overlooked, or put by until it becomes a little larger, for by this attention to trifles not only is much time gained, but one stitch will literally "save nine," and great expense will be avoided by clothes thus lasting so much longer than if mending is neglected or carelessly done.

It is not possible to lay down rules for the portion of time necessary for this purpose. The relative to whom I have before alluded, and whose example and experience aid me materially in my suggestions, was wont, in the days of her children's infancy, to fill a large basket every Monday morning with the clothes and household linen that needed repair; this basket was ever at her feet, and her needle seldom found repose from making and mending until Saturday night, when the whole of its contents were completed. Her children were taught to amuse themselves with their toys on the floor, and to give as little trouble as young children can possibly do; the baby was laid on the sofa, with a bunch of keys fixed so that its little hands could reach and play with them, close to its mother's side. When her employments permitted her to leave the house my sister seated herself beneath the shade of trees, in a field close to the pretty cottage, still with a *smaller* basket by her side, where she busied herself with her work while the little ones ran about and amused themselves. Visitors never interrupted her useful and necessary labours; even her husband's occasional expostulation, which raised a happy laugh, "my dear, *do* come and take a walk; I shall find you dead some day if you don't take exercise," was playfully parried; and certainly the effects of her care and industry were strikingly apparent.

With small means and a rising family the mother has an anxious, an important, and a self-denying task to perform—if that can ever be called self-denial which we do for those we love. She will have to renounce the amusements both of mind and taste: the fancy-work, the interesting correspondence, even the recreation of rational books must be laid aside to minister to the wants and comforts of those dependant upon her—for she will find but little time to do a thousand things that ought to be done in her little household. It is, however, as I have just remarked, *impossible* to lay down rules, because we cannot meet every case. In towns, where a mother cannot sit in a field while her children play, and where exercise is essential to general health, something must be sacrificed, unless a servant—a *trusty* servant—can be spared to accompany them in their daily walk. If a town house possesses but the smallest garden, the children should be constantly out in it; a coarse brown "blouse" or pinafore, an old bonnet or hat, and a pair of *thick* shoes, will keep a child in a great degree from dirt and wet; for to ensure health and strength no *coddling* should be permitted. My sister brought up her boys as she herself had been brought up—to disregard weather; and she cheerfully submitted to the task of changing their wet clothes whenever they came in, and seeing, *herself,* that their shoes and boots, &c., were properly dried before they were again required. How often, when her boys were sleeping, have I seen her arranging the damp jackets and trousers safely round the fire, after sponging off the mud or snow, that they might go out clean and dry in the morning, and their health not suffer! If it is *possible* to give children a run in the fields it is most desirable to do so; but if it is unattainable, it is vain to mourn over it. A sense of deep responsibility blending with fervent trust in God, and entire submission to His wise and righteous will, will so preserve the balance of the mind as to keep it in a state of watchful activity to do all that it can do, and of perfect peace when it cannot do all it would wish.

I have alluded to a subject apparently unconnected with that with which I begun my remarks, because it really concerns it very nearly; and one anxious "mother" may gain by the example of another some useful hints for the arrangement of her daily duties. While children are out at play a good deal of quiet time can be devoted to *the basket,* and this is of real moment. If clothes and linen are well and regularly mended, it is a very great saving, although it does take up time; and as much time as can be given to it will be profitably spent. This, of course, must be regulated greatly by circumstances, of which each wife and mother is the best judge; but every moment should be treasured and employed. At the breakfast and tea-table sometimes we are led by the pleasure of social intercourse to loiter away a good many valuable minutes; and at these times the admirable custom of a very charming married lady, the mother of a young family, is worthy of imitation. Even when visiting her friends she would take out her work the moment her own meal was finished, and employ herself with her needle, while joining with delightful vivacity in the general conversation around the table.

My sister found a knowledge of knitting very useful. At many odd moments she could catch it up and do a few rows; and by this means the socks of both father and children may be new-footed or tipped, which all helps to reduce expense. Cotton stockings are the most tedious of all things to darn, because they ought to be done neatly, and this takes up some time. It is an excellent plan to have the heels and feet of new stockings closely and neatly run on the inside, just where they are most liable to wear out; this strengthens them considerably. In running them, the alternate stiches should be taken up singly, which will quite prevent the look of the new stockings being injured.

The only plain work that I have heard matrons say can never be well done at home is shirt-making. Husbands and sons, who are faultless in all other ways, are ungovernable with regard to home-made shirts; they are never to be pleased or pacified in this particular; and, therefore, it is in the end the best economy to buy them ready-made.

I trust *the basket* will be found a useful appendage to the work-table of every anxious mistress of a family, from my sister's valuable experience. Every time the clothes come from the wash they should all be carefully looked over, and every defective one placed in it; at the same time, every article of wearing apparel, or household linen, that can be mended *before* it is washed should be attended to, because washing will always enlarge a rent, or so pull it out of shape as to make mending more troublesome; and starch will also prevent a darn being made very neat, particularly in what we ladies call "fine things."

To young ladies commencing housekeeping, these hints, I hope, may be useful. I cannot for an instant suppose they will benefit a more experienced class; and lest I should be deemed impertinent for offering them to all readers, I beg to be understood as aiming only to assist the *young* and *inexperienced* of "my sisters."

WILD FLOWERS OF JULY.

(*Continued from p. 229.*)

SINCE we penned the first part of our paper on the Wild Flowers of July we have had a rapid glimpse of the vegetation of the North of Scotland, under circumstances of so peculiar a kind that we feel called upon to give the readers of THE COTTAGE GARDENER some account of our wanderings before proceeding to recount the remainder of our July wildlings. The present Professor of Botany in our Edinburgh University (Dr. J. H. Balfour, the celebrated hero of Glen Tilt) usually devotes the Saturdays throughout the summer session to excursions in the neighbourhood of Edinburgh, for the purpose of enabling his students to put into practice in the fields the instructions received in the class-room. These excursions had never before been to any great distance from Edinburgh, a long Highland tour being generally undertaken at the end of the session; but on Saturday, 29th June last, the Professor, accompanied by upwards of 100 students of his class, set out on an expedition of a more extended kind than had ever before been undertaken in a single day by any party of botanists. Through the kindness of the Professor we were enabled to embrace this opportunity of getting a day's peep at northern botany, and, accordingly, we numbered one of his party. The botanical army started from Edinburgh by the Northern Railway at five on the morning of the day mentioned, and proceeded northwards, passing through the counties of Fife, Perth, Forfar, and Kincardine, to the City of Aberdeen (distant from Edinburgh about 135 miles), which was reached between 10 and 11 A.M. After breakfast in the Royal Hotel of Aberdeen, our party visited King's College, to admire the antique relics which it contains, and being there joined by Dr. Dickie, Professor of Natural History in Queen's College, Belfast, we proceeded some miles to the north, passing the picturesque bridge of Don, to the woods and moors at Denmore. Here every spud was unsheathed, and the botanists, spreading themselves through the woods, soon replenished their boxes with a goodly supply of the floral rarities which the place produced—and these were not a few nor without interest.

The first plant which attracted attention was the beautiful *Trientalis Europæa*, which was strewed through the woods in great profusion, in some cases giving birth to a small parasitic fungus, named *Tubercinia trientalis*, which generally appeared on the leaves of the plant. In close companionship with Trientalis the interesting *Pyrola minor* was found, a plant which we are glad to observe is now beginning to be cultivated in collections of *Alpines*. The rare northern Orchid, *Goodyera repens* (named in honour of John Goodyer, a botanist of Gerarde's time), was also observed in considerable profusion growing beside the plants we have mentioned; but it had not then produced its flowers. Towards the end of the present month it will well reward the researches of northern wanderers, for it will then be in fine condition; and although not found at all in the south it occurs in great profusion in some of the Highland woods. We likewise noticed the prevalence of a beautiful fungus, the *Cylindrospora deformans*, which attacks the stem and leaves of the Whortleberry, sometimes transforming the latter into beautiful round saucers or cups of a delicate cream colour, occasionally tinged with pink. But the most interesting wild flower which was found in the woods was *Linnæa borealis*, the "little northern plant, long overlooked, depressed, abject, flowering early, which Linnæus selected to transmit his own name to posterity," and which we had occasion to notice in a former paper published in THE COTTAGE GARDENER. It was out of flower, or had not flowered, at the station we visited; but fresh blossoms were brought to the Professor from another locality by an Aberdeen botanist.

On the marshy moors the beautiful *Habenaria bifolia*, and other native Orchids, were gathered, along with *Schœnus nigricans*, *Veronica scutellata*, *Sedum villosum*, and several interesting *Carices* and *Cryptogamic* plants. The highly curious Sundews, *Drosera Anglica* and *rotundifolia*, were sending up their racemes, but the blossoms were not fully developed, although they no doubt will be before the end of the month. Here the *Mimulus luteus* was found by one of the party, a plant in which we have always personally felt considerable interest, as affording one of the most conspicuous and best known instances of the complete naturalization of a foreign species in our country in the course of a few years. The *Mimulus* was originally introduced from the Western Continent about the year 1812, and very soon after that time became firmly established in some of our native streams, and has ever since continued increasing its hold on British soil, until we can now no longer look upon it as an occasional straggler, but as a completely naturalized, nay, almost a *common* plant. From a list of localities now before us it appears that the Mimulus, besides being found in England, occurs at various stations in the counties of Forfar, Perth, Fife, Kincardine, Stirling, Dumfries, Edinburgh, Aberdeen, and perhaps others.

It is highly interesting to observe the changes which take place in the flora of a country. As we have elsewhere remarked, there was a time when the soil of Britain was not touched by spade or plough, and when its flora was in a state of natural purity, unaffected and unchanged by the commerce or operations of mankind. When cultivation began, however, and was gradually extended, and the nature of the soil changed, then in like proportion would the character of the flora change. Many of the aboriginal inhabitants of our primeval forests would decrease in numbers, and some of the rarer species that were confined to a small area might be exterminated altogether. In the place of these, other plants, to which the changed conditions of the soil were suitable, would spring up from the seeds carried there by mankind and other active causes, and thus would take place a change in our country's flora of a real, because of a permanent kind. Perhaps there are not many (if there indeed be any) of the common annual weeds of cultivated grounds but have had their origin as British plants in this manner. Of late years various plants of exotic origin have been reported as accessions to our British flora, some of them belonging to the class of annuals before referred to, which would be ready again to quit the flora in the event of a cessation of cultivation; and others of a more permanent caste, which have likewise been introduced by the agency of mankind, but which have established themselves amongst the real indigenous vegetation of the land, and, as has been remarked, now bid defiance to all efforts at extermination. To the latter class does the *Mimulus luteus* belong.

But we have wandered into a bye-way, and must return to our botanical party at Aberdeen. After culling the treasures we have mentioned, and many more for which we have no room in the limited space allotted to us in these pages, our botanical army remounted the vehicles and returned to the sandy Links of Aberdeen, where a number of marine species were added to our stores. Here the *Carex incurva* and *C. arenaria* were both in fine condition. It is these, chiefly the latter, assisted by *Ammophila arenaria* and other sea-side plants, which bind the sandy downs with their extensively creeping roots, and thus prevent the sand being disturbed by the wind or the ocean waves. In districts where similar tracts of sand are cultivated, it is the practice to preserve as much as possible of the Ammophila and other species in order to give firmness to the land; and in some instances where these plants have been thoughtlessly eradicated, the result has been a sterile waste, unfit for *all* purposes of Agriculture. Among the more interesting plants collected on the Links we may mention, in addition to the above, *Cerastium atrovirens* (BAB.), a form peculiar to such situations, *Triticum junceum*, *Thalictrum minus*, and *Potamogeton pectinatus*.

Returning from the Links, we visited the Granite Polishing Works, the Marischal College, the Medical Buildings, and the new Market-place—the formidable appearance of the hundred botanists, with their noisy tin boxes, and other botanical appurtenances, creating quite a sensation in the northern city. After dinner in the Royal, we entered the return-train at 6 P.M. for Edinburgh, which was reached at a late hour. The weather being delightful, the excursion was altogether an exceedingly pleasant one; for although 270 miles were gone over by rail, any uneasiness from the long ride was prevented by the interesting character of the country through which the line lay,—embracing the fertile vale of Strathmore and other districts of agricultural celebrity, with here and there a neat little village, a range of heath-clad hills, or a placid lake with its white swans and water lilies floating on the unruffled surface. There was a profusion of showy flowers on the railway banks, such as the Viper's Bugloss (*Echium vulgare*), various trefoils and cruciferous plants, wild wall-flower, wild mignonette, &c.; and towards the north end of the line the banks were in some places whitened by the beautiful *Galium saxatile*, and at others they were of a warmer hue, from a profusion of heather bells. The editor of the *North British Journal of Horticulture* (who was one of our party) mentions in his paper of the 4th instant the profuse occurrence of *Lychnis vespertina* all the way between the stations of Stanley and

Coupar Angus, while not a plant of the *L. diurna* was observable; another instance of the curious circumstance that these two nearly-allied plants are never or very rarely to be found growing together, for, as we mentioned in a paper last month wherein we noticed them at length (p. 181), the plants prefer different situations for their growth—the White Campion loving exposure to sunshine, while the red flower seeks the silent shade of the woodland, and occurs most often by some "streamlet's marge."

Before concluding an account of the Aberdeen trip, it may be worthy of remark, that during the time of our explorations a fire broke out in Aberdeen, and a party of the students who had remained in the city lent a helping hand to extinguish the flames, which were finally got under. Their assistance was acknowledged in an Aberdeen newspaper paragraph, published before we left for the south that afternoon.　　　　G. LAWSON, F.B.S., &c., *Edinburgh.*

ROYAL BOTANIC SOCIETY'S SHOW.
REGENT'S PARK, JULY 3.

THE Exhibition was a good one for July. The orchids were in fine condition, and in average quantity. The large collections of plants showed that no care was wanting, both in the art of retardation and bringing forward fresh plants in fine order. Cape Heaths were in excellent condition, and did great credit to the growers. Specimen plants were also plentiful, and in good condition. New plants were rather scarce. In florists' flowers, the Pelargoniums were in as fine order as at any previous show, whilst the cut roses, as might be expected, were most excellent. Carnations, Picotees, Pinks, and Pansies, were shown by the different growers in good order, and attracted the admiration of the company. But the greatest attraction was the fruit tent. We may venture to say that there never was exhibited before such a quantity of well-ripened, finely-swelled, and highly-coloured fruit of all the kinds usually exhibited. There were, for instance, thirty-seven Pine-apples of various kinds, every one of which was a fair average fruit. The Queens especially, were good, handsome, and many of them uncommonly large fruit. Black Grapes were very numerous, there being fourteen dishes of excellent fruit. Peaches and Nectarines also were very fine and numerous. Strawberries extra fine, both in size, colour, and quantity. We have seen more Melons, but we were assured by the judges that the flavour was first-rate. The growers of fruit have shown that if proper encouragement is given to them, the complaint that this part of Horticultural Exhibition will be as respectably filled as either plants or flowers.

EXOTIC ORCHIDS.
COLLECTIONS OF TWENTY-FIVE.

1ST PRIZE to Mr. Mylam, gardener to S. Rucker, Esq., Wandsworth. By far the greater number of his plants were shown for the first time this year, and were, as usual, in fine order.

Vanda Batemaniana. Our readers will remember that last week we described this valuable, rare, and beautiful plant. We need only add that this specimen was three feet high, and had a noble spike of flowers, eight being fully expanded, with many more to open. *Anguloa uniflora;* with fifteen of its large pure white flowers open. *Aerides odorata major;* with thirty fine spikes of its very fragrant lovely flowers fully expanded. *Aerides crispo'vulvera;* with three long spikes of flowers. *Aerides maculosum;* a lovely high-coloured species. *Saccolabium Blumei;* three very long spikes fully-bloomed; a lovely rare species. *Lælia majalis;* this most lovely species is rarely seen in flower. The plant had two large rosy blossoms upon it. *Oncidium lanceeanum;* a large plant two feet through, had four spikes of its rich-coloured blossoms expanded. *Epidendrum serruceum;* a beautiful rare species with its blossoms of the richest pink colour; the lip has several processes upon it like warts, hence its name. *Cycnoches Egertonianæ;* a very curious species, with two long spikes of nearly black flowers. There were also two plants of *Phalænopsis grandiflora,* a *Vanda cristata,* with numerous flowers, and several other fine plants of less note.

2ND PRIZE to Mr. Williams, gardener to C. Warner, Esq. If Mr. Mylam had shown the least remissness, he would have been assuredly beaten by this collection.

Saccolabium guttatum; eight spikes. *Aerides affine;* several spikes. *Aerides rosea* (very beautiful); three spikes. *Aerides maculosum;* three spikes. The richly-coloured *Broughtonia sanguinea.* The elegant *Barkeria spectabile;* with five spikes. *Cypripedium barbatum;* five flowers. *Dendrobium densiflorum;* second time flowering this year; six spikes. A large mass of *Epidendrum striatum,* &c.

COLLECTIONS OF FIFTEEN.

1ST PRIZE to Mr. Blake, gardener to J. Schroder, Esq., Stratford. In this collection was a large mass of

Trichopilia tortilis; with numerous flowers. *Aerides odorata major;* twenty-five spikes. The beautiful *Burlingtonia venusta;* with five spikes. The rare *Caianthe mazuca;* with three spikes. The pretty *Galeandra Baueri;* three spikes. The curious *Angræcum caudatum;* with eleven flowers, and long green tails. *Cypripedium barbatum;* with eleven flowers. A large mass of the beautiful *Dendrobium chrysanthum;* with many flowers. *Cattleya mossiæ; Phalænopsis grandiflora,* &c.

2ND PRIZE to Messrs. Rollison, of Tooting. There were some extra good specimens in this collection, especially

Miltonia spectabile; 2½ feet across, well covered with its beautiful flowers. *Stanhopea tigrina superba;* the red variety, with six of its large grotesque flowers. *Oncidium lanceanum,* and *O. lanceanum violaceus.* The elegant *Dendrochilum filicaule;* and a fine plant with numerous spikes of *Caianthe furcata,* very like *C. veratrifolia.*

COLLECTIONS OF TEN.

1ST PRIZE to Mr. Barnes, gardener to R. Hanbury, Esq., The Poles, near Ware, Herts. We noted, especially, the beautiful

Oncidium lanceanum; with eight spikes. *Aerides affine;* three spikes. A noble *Stanhopea tigrina;* dark variety, with six flowers. The rare *Barkeria melanocaulon;* the lip of which has a spot of green. A large plant of *Aerides odorata;* fourteen spikes. *Brassia Wraya;* and *Saccolabium Blumei.*

NEW ORCHIDS.

1ST PRIZE to Messrs. Loddiges, of Hackney, for

Aerides suavissima (the sweetest A.). A very remarkable species. The whole flower has a pale yellow cast, with thinly scattered spots of rose colour. The flowers are larger than any other Aerides, and the spikes longer, with the exception of *Aerides affine.* A very elegant desirable species.

2ND PRIZE to the same firm for a variety of *Saccolabium Blumei.*

Messrs. Rollison exhibited *Cypripedium Javanicum,* slightly different from *C. barbatum.*

Mr. Barnes exhibited *Phalænopsis rosea,* a rare plant, but not to be compared for beauty with either of the other species of this charming genus.

COLLECTIONS OF THIRTY STOVE AND GREENHOUSE PLANTS.

1ST PRIZE to Mr. Cole, gardener to H. Collyer, Esq., Dartford. We prophesied some time ago that this cultivator was making rapid strides in his art to come up to, if not to surpass, the collection at Ealing Park. On this occasion our prophecy was fulfilled: he surpassed his formidable antagonist. The judges placed him first. We give no opinion on the matter, the fact speaks for itself. All we have to do is to give a fair description of the best plants in each, leaving our readers to judge for themselves.

Dipladenia crassinoda; 5 ft. by 2½ ft., with numerous very high-coloured large flowers. *D. splendens;* equally well flowered. *Ixora coccinea;* a noble plant, 4 ft. by 3 ft., with thirty heads of bloom in the best condition possible. *Allamanda Schottii, A. grandiflora, A. cathartica;* three fine plants well-bloomed. *Kalosanthes coccinea;* 5 ft. by 3 ft., full of large heads of highly-coloured flowers. *Vinca rosea,* and *V. rosea alba;* each 5 ft. by 4 ft., well grown, and finely bloomed. *Cyrtoceras reflexum;* a stout healthy plant, 2½ ft. by 2 ft., well bloomed. *Erica Parmentierii rosea;* one of the most beautiful of Heaths, with flowers of the deepest rosy hue, 2½ ft. by 2 ft. *Ixora crocata;* a dense bush covered with bloom, 2½ ft. by 2½ ft. *Polygala cordifolia;* finely grown, and full of flower, 4 ft. by 4 ft. *Aphelexis;* several varieties beautifully in flower.

2ND PRIZE to Mr. May, gardener to Mrs. Lawrence, Ealing Park. A noble collection of mostly large handsome plants. Many thought this ought to have been first, but the judges thought otherwise.

The gem of this collection was a beautiful plant of the splendid new *Ixora Javanica.* The beauty of this plant was indescribable, every twig bearing a bunch of orange scarlet blossoms, 2½ ft. by 2½ ft. Two large plants of *Stephanotis floribunda;* trained balloon-wise, and well bloomed, 5 ft. by 4 ft. The same number of *Allamandas* as Mr. Cole, and finer plants even, but not so well bloomed. *Sollya linearis* and *Sollya heterophylla;* each 5 ft. by 5 ft.; immense plants, full of their tiny blue blossoms. *Burchellia capensis;* a useful effective plant, with numerous heads of orange flowers. *Erica pulverulenta;* a pretty Heath, well bloomed, 2½ ft. by 3 ft. *Erica Bergiana;* well flowered, but dull in colour. *Vinca ocellata, Phæmocoma floribunda;* very large, but few flowered. *Gardoquia Hookerii;* a difficult plant to grow, but well done in this instance, 1½ ft. by 1½ ft. *Ixora coccinea;* a smaller plant than Mr. Cole's, and not so well bloomed.

COLLECTIONS OF TWENTY STOVE AND GREENHOUSE PLANTS.

1ST PRIZE to Mr. Green, gardener to Sir E. Antrobus, Cheam. Very excellent, especially

Erica Massonii; a fine Heath, 3 ft. by 3 ft. *Pleroma elegans;* large, but scarcely in bloom. Its fine large purple flowers are exceedingly handsome. *Metrosideros floribundus:* very effective, covered with its bottle-brush-like scarlet blossoms, 4 ft. by 3 ft. *Leschenaultia Baxterii major:* 2½ ft. by 2 ft. *Stephanotis floribunda:* 4 ft. by 2½ ft. *Allamanda cathartica, Echites atropurpurea:* with dark purple bell-shaped blossoms,—a plant rarely seen, 4 ft. by 3 ft.

2ND PRIZE to Mr. Taylor, gardener to J. Costar, Esq., Streatham. There were some good plants in this collection, the best were

Cyrtoceras reflexa : eleven heads of its Hoya-like blossoms. *Allamanda cathartica :* very fine. *Erica metulæflora bicolor :* an immense plant covered with bloom, 4 ft. by 4 ft. *E. Cavendishii :* 3 ft. by 3 ft. *Epiphyllum Akermannii, &c.*

COLLECTION OF TEN STOVE AND GREENHOUSE PLANTS.

1ST PRIZE to Mr. Williams, gardener to Miss Trail, Bromley. Ten plants, all well-grown, and finely-bloomed, especially

Polygala cordata : 3 ft. by 3 ft. *Kalosanthes coccinea grandiflora:* very large flowers, highly coloured, 3 ft. by 2½ ft. *Pimelea decussata :* 4 ft. by 3 ft. *Leschenaultia biloba superba :* with numerous deep blue flowers. *Phœnocoma prolifera :* 3 ft. by 2½ ft. *Rondeletia speciosa:* 2½ ft. by 2½ ft. *Pimelea Hendersonii.*

2ND PRIZE to Mr. Croxford, gardener to H. Barnes, Esq. We noted

Kalosanthes coccinea ; Clerodendrum fallax, Allamanda cathartica, Aphelexis humilis, as being in first-rate order.

NEW PLANTS.

Begonia cinnabarina. Messrs. Henderson, of Pine-apple Place, sent again this beautiful plant. The specimen was a fine one, 1½ ft. by 1½ ft., and was covered with its beautiful orange scarlet blossoms. Not new enough to obtain a prize under this class.

Ipomea limbata. Messrs. Rollison sent a pot full of a Convolvulus-looking plant, with the above name attached to it. The flowers are about 1½ inch across, cup shaded, of a deep purple colour edged with white.

1ST PRIZE was awarded to Mr. May, gardener to Mrs. Lawrence, for a very fine plant of the splendid *Ixora Javanica.*

2ND PRIZE to Messrs. Rollison, for their *Ipomea;* for *Magnolia fragrantissima,* a noble plant with one flower upon it; and for *Thyrsacanthus bracteolatus,* a Justicia-looking plant with dull red flowers.

2ND PRIZE also to Mr. Henderson, Wellington Nursery, St. John's Wood, for a small plant of *Hemiandra pungens,* a pretty pink flowered species.

3RD PRIZE to Messrs. Rollison, for a new seedling hybrid *Heath,* named *Gemmifera elegans;* and to Mr. Glendinning, Chiswick, for a new *Achimenes,* named *Tugwelliana,* a very pretty variety, with purplish large flowers.

(*To be continued.*)

THE DOMESTIC PIGEON.
GENERAL HISTORY OF PIGEONS.
(*Continued from p. 196.*)

The ancients only knew four species of pigeons—1st, the ring-dove; 2nd, the turtle-dove; 3rd, the stock-dove; and 4th, the dove-house pigeon; at least, the nomenclature of Aristotle includes only these. Those who have followed him, and Brisson among the rest, have extended this number to seven. 1st, the Roman pigeon, which furnished them with fourteen varieties of the dove-cot pigeon; 2nd, the domestic or dove-house pigeon; 3rd, the stock-dove; 4th, the rock pigeon; 5th, the wild pigeon; 6th, the ringdove; 7th, the turtle-dove. Buffon has thought that these seven species really form but three : the ring-dove, the stock-dove, and the turtle-dove. Naturalists have given an invariable rule to recognise the true species from the mere varieties; which is to ascertain if the beings which spring from two different individuals are fruitful; should they produce again, there is no doubt that the father and mother merely formed varieties; but if the young ones are mules, the father and mother were of two different species. This law of nature they say is so general, that its application not only extends to animals, but even to plants. The individuals produced by the canary and goldfinch are always unfruitful; the females sometimes lay, but the eggs are always addled. The goldfinch and canary, then, constitute two true species. Everybody knows that the mule produced by the ass and the horse is unfruitful.

Plants produced by the fecundity of the stamens of one species on the pistil of another species produce seed, but this has never been known to grow. Nature has been so careful to maintain the types of every race in all their purity, and she will, by every means possible, insure the preservation of the existing species; but it appears she will not allow any new creations.

This principle being granted, we will now follow the reasoning of Buffon, who adds,—"We must not then consider the dove-cot and dove-house pigeons—that is to say, the great and small domestic pigeons—as two different species, but limit ourselves to calling them two races of one species : one of which is more domesticated and more perfect than the other. In the same manner, the stock-dove, the rock-pigeon, and wild-pigeon, are three nominal species that we must reduce to one, which is the stock-dove ; of which the two former make but very slight varieties; since, as our nomenclators have acknowledged, these three birds are nearly the same size : that they are all migratory, accustomed to roost, have the same natural habits, and only differ from each other by some tints of colour."

According to the opinion of this naturalist, all the nominal species of the authors would be reduced to two—the ring-dove and stock-dove, or wood-pigeon. As the ring-dove does not produce with the wood-pigeon, this last would be the stock of the dove-cot pigeon ; and these would only differ more or less in their type according as they had been managed by man. He explains this supposition in the following manner :—" The fourth gradation in the order of degeneration includes the large and small dove-cot pigeon, of which the tribes, varieties, and blendings, are innumerable, because from time immemorial they have been absolutely domestic. Man, in perfecting the exterior forms, has, at the same time, altered their interior qualities, and radically destroyed every inclination for liberty ; these birds, the greater part of which are larger and handsomer than the common pigeons, have also another advantage, that of being more fruitful, larger, and better flavoured ; and it is in consequence of all these reasons that people have taken so much care of them, and sought to multiply them, in spite of the trouble their training, fecundity, and the success of their numerous productions must cause them. None of these ever return to their natural state."

(*To be continued.*)

DESCRIPTION OF THE DOVE-COT PIGEONS.
THIRD RACE.
(*Continued from page 196.*)

FEATHERED-FOOTED PIGEONS : *Columba pedibus plumosis.*—These birds, formerly so much estimated, are at present, with some near varieties, banished by the greater part of amateurs. They may be recognised by the feathers more or less thick and long, which cover the feet down to the claws; and by the absence of other characteristics which would rank them in a determinate race. They have the usual forms of the mixtures, and like them partake of all colours.

7. COMMON FEATHERED-FOOTED PIGEON : *Columba vulgaris pedibus plumosis.*—Middle size, less feather-footed than the Limosin, and not so large; it partakes of all colours common to the pigeon, but, nevertheless, it is generally varied with black or fawn colour. It is very productive, and not particular as to food or lodging, but equally satisfied with the dove-house, dove-cot, stable, or even a simple box. It is very common everywhere, but especially in the south of France. The greater part of the dove-cots in the environs of Lyons are inhabited by this variety.

8. THE LIMOSIN FEATHERED-FOOTED PIGEON : *Columba lemovicensis pedibus plumosis.*—Very large and lengthy, with long legs; and remarkable for the unusual length of the feathers which cover the feet. It is of all colours, with the head and wings white. It is very productive, but has the fault of throwing its eggs out of the nest with the feathers on its claws, in consequence of which they are obliged to be cut. If they were pulled out they would quickly grow again, and the evil would only be obviated for a short time. The

same thing was originally said of the "Limoges," from whence its name.

9. MONTHLY PIGEON: *Columba menstrua pedibus plumosis.*—Frisch calls it in Latin, Columba menstrua (Monthly pigeon), "because," he says, "it produces every month; and only waits until its young ones are able to feed themselves to lay again; we must, however, except the depth of winter, and only reckon on eight or nine broods in the year." It is, in fact, one of the most productive; and only differs from the preceding by its crest.

10. NORWEGIAN PIGEON: *Columba Norwegica pedibus plumosis.*—It is extremely large, tufted, and quite white. Some authors consider it as a species, but the greater part of them speak of it as a variety of the Dove-cot pigeon.

11. GOAT SUCKER PIGEON: *Columba caprimulga pedibus plumosis.*—This bird has a flat and square head, which gives it a little resemblance to the bird after which it is named. It has a black iris, and no filament round the eyes; its feet are ornamented with feathers, and the colour of its plumage is grey. This pretty pigeon, like all mongrels, is very productive.

12. THE PLUNGING PIGEON: *Columba urinator pedibus plumosis.*—It has received its name from the habit it has, when flying, of swimming, if I may so call it, on its throat, which it swells a little for this purpose, says M. Vieillot, although we have never been able to perceive it, in spite of our reiterated observations; but it is most certain that it hovers a very long time in the air without moving its wings, in the same manner as birds of prey. Its feet are thickly covered with feathers, and its thighs are also covered with long feathers, forming what amateurs call "breeches." The author of the article, "Dove-cot Pigeons," in the new *Dictionary of Natural History,* says, "that its plumage is silvery white, or blue with black bars," but we have never seen it anything but grey. This bird is interesting from its great fecundity.

13. THE FRIZZLED PIGEON: *Columba pedibus plumosis crispa.*—Aldrovandus considered this variety as a true species. This bird is very rough-footed, quite white, and curled all over the body; the beam feathers of its wings having their beards separated and curled, which deprives it of the faculty of flying. The female resembles the male in all respects; it is about the size of the *Tambour,* and very productive.

(*To be continued.*)

EXTRACTS FROM CORRESPONDENCE.

HEDGE-ROWS.—Those who, like myself, are fond of country rambles will have noticed, particularly in remote places. the large quantity of rank and luxuriant herbage which often grows neglected along the hedges and ditches of our fields. Here and there a farmer of the better sort will not suffer *this;* some will be at the cost and trouble of cutting, and leaving it to rot; but the greater number neglect it entirely, and then it becomes a positive evil, affording shelter to vermin, and sowing the land with weeds. My object in mentioning the subject is to convert this evil into a boon to the deserving cottager who has a cow, pony, or donkey. If a person of this description be allowed to collect the herbage upon condition of his keeping the hedge-rows clean, he would be serving the farmer and himself at the same time. This plan is partially adopted in my neighbourhood, and with good results. One man, who is a small coal-carter, keeps his donkey through the summer months by this means. Another who carts wood, and has more leisure, collects his material into a stack, at the corner of the lane, and is thus provided with provender for his horse throughout the year.—S. P., *Rushmere.*

EFFECTS OF LIGHTNING ON TREES.—At a recent meeting of the Botanical Society of Edinburgh, Mr. M'Nab, of the Royal Botanic Garden, made a communication on the effects of lightning on trees. He remarked:—"A few days ago I accidentally heard of a tree which had been struck by lightning on the 5th inst. (June, 1850), at Pitferrane, Fifeshire, the residence of Andrew Buchanan, Esq.; and, being anxious to ascertain the species, I wrote for a small branch, with any history which could be given regarding it. I have just received the leaves shown, which prove it to be the *Ulmus montana,* or Wych Elm. My object in bringing the notice before the Society, is to ascertain from its members any varieties of trees known to them as having been struck by the electric fluid. About this time last year a very large oak on the grounds of John Wauchope, Esq., of Edmonston, was shattered to pieces; and a few years previously a laburnum standing close to the oak was likewise destroyed. While on a tour over a portion of the American continent, some years ago, I had several opportunities of observing gigantic trees torn to pieces by electric influence. In every instance I observed they were oaks. During a thunder-storm I found the workmen (chiefly in Canada) resorting to the beech trees for protection, from an idea that they were not liable to be struck by lightning; certain it is, that I saw none, notwithstanding the prevalence of large sized beeches in many districts. The elm above alluded to at Pitferrane, had an iron fence standing close to it, which was supposed by the inhabitants to have had some influence in attracting the fluid. The above observations are thrown out, in the hope of ascertaining if there be anything in the composition of one species of tree rendering it less liable than another to electric influence." Several other members present at the meeting mentioned that the beech, the horse chestnut, and the ash, had all been struck by lightning.

TO CORRESPONDENTS.

₊ We request that no one will write to the departmental writers of THE COTTAGE GARDENER. It gives them unjustifiable trouble and expense; and we also request our coadjutors *under no circumstances* to reply to such private communications.

HARTLEY'S PATENT ROUGH GLASS (*A Constant Reader*).—You complain that the hardier plants, such as Geraniums, Fuchsias, Oleanders, &c., turn yellow, while Ixoras and other stove plants flourish; and as shading would be difficult, you have tried whiting and size, but it was washed off by the first shower, and you ask whether more ventilation would not be an advantage. We reply, decidedly, yes; and if you have not already formed a division between your stove and greenhouse plants, that you may give more air to the latter. If such a house had several compartments, as recommended by Mr. Fish, you would carry out your object more fully. We have had but little experience with Hartley's rough patent, but imagined one object intended was to *prevent burning.* The shade of your vines will likely assist you as respects that matter, but if you are covetous of having fine grapes, you must make up your mind to second-rate plants, unless you confine the vines to the rafters, and the sashes are wide. Mr. Fish never expected the whiting would last long, but he would cover a roof with a syringe quicker than you could cover it with any sort of blinds, unless you had one large one to cover the whole, and that would be much preferable to any mixture, as you would have all the light in a dull day. He was well aware that the mixture of size and whiting would not remain *inside,* owing to the condensation of moisture, and therefore he *decidedly* recommended its application *outside.* Hot size zinc coloured with whiting remained on his glass the whole of last summer; hot zinc put on alone, daubed, as mentioned in a late article, has already been on for a couple of months, both on upright glass, and on a sloping roof, and though subjected to heavy rains there seems no perceptible difference in its appearance; of course the glass should be quite dry when it is put on, and if in the morning, it seems to adhere best. He prefers this to any other preparation, if well done, and no whiting used. You will require to examine it, to see that there is anything on the glass at all, and yet everything like burning is perfectly done away with, while a great portion of the heating rays are excluded. *Use double zinc,* which is procured in a jelly-form, and not a cake-like substance.

FUCHSIA SPECTABILIS (*H. Bennet*).—We cannot conceive why your plant will not grow, as you succeed so well with *F. serratifolia,* for they require similar treatment. We partly agree with you that the stock must have been deteriorated by some means, as all your neighbours are in a similar predicament. We should suppose, that any nurseryman in the *south* that deals in Fuchsias would supply you with a nice little plant at a fifth part of the price that yours cost in the beginning of 1849. As a last hope, we would place the gentleman in a sweet hotbed, and set a propagating glass over him, not close, but nearly so ; stir the soil on the surface of the pot almost every day ; keep all sweet around him, and see and start him into free growth by heat and genial moisture in the atmosphere.

PRESERVING HALF-HARDY THINGS DURING WINTER (*A Constant Reader*).—See mode of raising turf pits *above* the level of the soil in last volume. This will insure their being kept dry. In *sunk* pits, damp will commit even greater ravages than the frost. The plants you name Petunias, Verbenas, &c., may thus be kept all the winter without any fire-heat, but in continued dull weather, and in severe frost, a little would be an advantage.

ROSE CUTTINGS FOR GROWING IN POTS (*J. R. Collins*).—If your standards are the kinds that propagate freely by cuttings, the spring of the year, just when the shoots are from one inch to two inches in length, is the best of all periods for striking the cuttings successfully, by placing them either under a hand-light, or in a close frame in light soil, and shaded when necessary. They may be propagated at any time however ; but if you try it late in autumn, you may make up your mind to lose a good many in winter.

CINERARIA SEED (*M. J.*).—These will vegetate nicely in an open pot in a warm window, or in a cool place either, and require no artificial heat ; but it would be as well to use light soil, and just place a square of glass over the pot, not so much for *heat,* as to prevent evaporation, and thus save frequent waterings.

CUTTINGS (*An Enquirer*).—1. You say : "Cuttings of double wall-flowers inserted in light soil on the north side of a hedge, covered with a hand-glass, and then shaded with a bag over all, do not strike well—turn yellowish." The bag was here superfluous. 2. You ask : "Is it necessary that cuttings should have no sun for the first two weeks?" Quite the reverse. In such a position we should consider all shading unnecessary. See a late article on propagating by Mr. Fish. 3. You ask : "Will soft wooded cuttings strike nearly as well under a hand-light in a frame as under a bell-glass?" Often better ; we generally use neither—quite content and happy to get the frame. 4. The double yellow scented tender rose. Smith's we presume. See answer, "Rose cuttings," above.

DOUBLE FLOWERS (*Mary H.*).—You will see you have been attended to.

IMPREGNATING FLOWERS (*Ibid*).—To insure a hybrid, the stamens of the female plant should be renewed, but it is not always necessary, for in the case of the *violet* referred to the stigma stands out beyond the anthers, and if pollen is applied to its summit before its own anthers burst, and fecundation is effected, its own pollen will have no effect afterwards. However, we think you could remove the anthers without even destroying the petals which you are so careful about, by inserting the point of a small penknife and rubbing them off. Have you noticed a peculiarity as to how the stamens open their anthers and clasp the base of the pistil ? Something more may be said on the subject ere long.

CROPPING FRUIT BORDERS (*L. R. L.*).—Your vine border is far too rich and too deep ; however, your question is, "May I, without injuring *materially* my vines, plant geraniums, &c., in the border, as it is an eye-sore from my room windows?" and we are obliged to answer, you cannot. It is not the impoverishing of the soil, which you suggest may be remedied by applying more manure annually, that renders cropping fruit-borders objectionable, but it is the disturbance of the surface-roots of the vines, and the shading them when shading is not desirable. If the objection to the bare border must be obviated by screening it with geraniums and other flowering shrubs, grow these in pots plunged in the border. Thanks for your hints, which we do not lose sight of, but we must render our pages attractive to some who otherwise would not aid in circulating them. Take a *volume,* and your objection is not valid ; take a section of a volume, and it is. Thanks also for the observations on surface stirring, which we will publish.

VIOLA CANINA (*J. S.*).—We cannot tell you where Mr. Paxton ascertained that this (Dog's Violet) is "a famous agent in removing cutaneous diseases." All the violets produce seeds which are diuretic, and their roots are purgative in drachm doses. Your *Cyclamen seedlings* are now at rest ; see their treatment at page 231 of last number.

BLACK GROUSE BANTAM (*A Subscriber*).—This, which has a difficulty in swallowing whole barley, should be fed on moist, nourishing food,—barley meal mixed with a little milk and water. If the crop is hard, give the bird a tea-spoonful of gin. If costive, give it the same quantity of castor oil.

CAGE BIRDS (*A. H. R.*).—We can only advance by degrees. We wish we could find room for everything that everybody wishes to have preference, which is somewhat difficult as tastes are so different.

NAME OF INSECT (*Verax*).—Your question was answered at page 152.

ROSES WITH GREEN CENTRES (*A. T.*).—This is an instance of what is now termed morphology, or the science of vegetable transformations, the pistils of the roses being changed into leaves. It is probably caused either by your soil being too full of moisture or too rich. Prune off all these misformed flowers from your Bourbon, Noisette, and autumn-blooming roses, for these will probably push again and produce more perfect roses.

NAME OF MOTH (*A Young Collector*).—It is the Six-spotted Burnet Moth (*Anthroceras filipendula*). Its caterpillar feeds on trefoil, plantain, and quaking grass. You may obtain good *strawberries* from seed, but they will be different from their parent.

CYRTOCERAS REFLEXUM (*F. W. T.*).—This being leggy, with only one stem, is very little worth. All plants, to make handsome bushes, should be operated upon when young. They ought, when four inches high, to have their tops nipped off ; and this should be repeated until the plant becomes bushy, compact, and shapely. It is hardly possible to make a nice bushy plant of a long-legged one, but you may try. Bend the plant down as low as you can without breaking—do this two or three times until you get the top down quite to the pot; keep it in that position. The tendency to grow upwards will induce some buds, perhaps, to break at the base of the stem. When these have got three or four leaves top them; that is, pinch out the pair of leaves last made. Just allow them to push again, and then you may safely remove the old stem, and make cuttings of it. If you cut it down at once, ten to one it will die. Cuttings of it must be planted in silver sand round the edge of the pot, placed under a hand-glass upon a heated bed of sand, in a top-heat of 70° at least. Very little water must be given, as they are very succulent (full of juice), and will be apt to damp off.

HOITZIA COCCINEA (*Ibid*).—This flowers in March or April; it loves a rich light soil and liberal treatment. It requires, also, to be frequently stopped during summer to induce a bushy habit. Cease stopping about August, as it flowers on the tops of the young shoots. It is, when well managed, a very pretty desirable plant. Cuttings root readily treated similarly to the *Cyrtoceras.*

BEES TRANSFERRED.—*M. A. B.* says :—"I have an improved cottage hive of Neighbour's, which was stocked on the 1st of July last year by fumigating a very large and promising swarm which had previously been placed in a common straw hive. This straw hive, though a large one, they had from the 1st of June almost entirely filled, and there was a great deal of brood still in the cells. I was not then aware that all the brood comb should be restored to them (being quite a novice in bee keeping. After being transferred they never seemed to thrive, and though they existed through the winter they did not appear to work with much rigour or activity when the warm weather set in ; their numbers, too, instead of increasing visibly diminished. I therefore thought it advisable to add some fresh bees, and accordingly, on the 15th of June, a strong cast was joined (by first fumigating the bees) to the old hive. For the first week or ten days all appeared to be well with the united bees ; they commenced fresh combs and seemed rapidly filling their hive, but the last week they neither seemed so numerous or to be working so much, and the thermometer in the hive shows a much lower temperature, 78°—74°." Your large and promising swarm of the 1st of June, last year, was destroyed by being fumigated and removed from the hive they had very nearly filled with honey and brood to an empty one ; we have never recommended fumigating nor transferring. As they are you must not expect them to survive the coming winter. Your better plan will be to stock the hive next year with a good and early swarm. That bees do sometimes desert their hive is certain, for we have now a hive in which a cast was put on the 20th June, and it is now deserted, leaving a few leaves of comb which the bees had made. It is very unusual for a swarm to go off without any drones, which you say you have noticed.

WEIGHT OF PEACHES.—Mr. Errington wishes to correct his statement at page 207; instead of "our fruit at that period averaging 11 ounces," he wishes to have inserted "our fruit at that period not unfrequently weighing 11 ounces."

NAMES OF PLANTS (*T. M. W.*).—If you had sent us a more perfect specimen of your *Rose* at first we could have told you the name before : it is *Rosa cinnamomea,* or Cinnamon Rose. We would say, once for all, that if it is desirable to ask us to devote our attention to a plant, it is but common courtesy to take every pains to save us from unnecessary difficulty by sending a good sized specimen of the flower and leaves in a box that cannot be crushed by the post-office punches. Your *Fuchsia* we believe to be *racemiflora,* a freely blooming old variety. (*M. C. E.*)—Your plant is *Calandrinia speciosa,* or Showy Calandrinia, from California. Your pale pink rose is, *we think, La Reine*; and the purplish one *fimbriata,* but no one can be certain in his judgment founded upon a faded flower of which there are hundreds of varieties.

LONDON: Printed by HARRY WOOLDRIDGE, Winchester High-street, in the Parish of Saint Mary Kalendar; and Published by WILLIAM SOMERVILLE ORR, at the Office, No. 2, Amen Corner, in the Parish of Christ Church, City of London.—July 18th, 1850.

M W D D	JULY 25—31, 1850.	Weather near London in 1849.		Sun Rises.	Sun Sets.	Moon R. & S.	Moon's Age.	Clock bef. Sun.	Day of Year.
25 Th	St. James. Dss. Camb. b., 1797.	T. 67°—48°.	S.W. Rain.	15 a. 4	58 a. 7	9 a.41	16	6 10	206
26 F	St. Anne. Graywing Butterfly seen.	T. 74°—47°.	S. Rain.	16	56	9 9	17	6 10	207
27 S	Blackcap's song ceases.	T. 75°—45°.	W. Rain.	18	55	9 32	18	6 10	208
28 Sun	9 Sun. Aft. Trinity. Admiral Butterfly seen.	T. 73°—57°.	S.W. Fine.	19	53	9 54	19	6 9	209
29 M	Common Grasshopper crinks.	T. 68°—52°.	S.W. Rain.	21	52	10 16	20	6 8	210
30 Tu	Wheat cut.	T. 74°—50°.	S.W. Fine.	22	50	10 39	21	6 7	211
31 W	Hoary Ragwort flowers.	T. 79°—47°.	W. Fine.	23	49	11 3	22	6 4	212

Somewhere in one of the Churchyards of Westminster, repose the remains of the best writer on Landscape Gardening—Thomas Whately. Many years since, when we first became acquainted with his work, we were so struck with the force of the language, its phrases, and eloquence, that we traced in them, to our own satisfaction, a strong resemblance to the writings of " Junius." Pursuing the idea, suspicion became almost certainty when we found that Mr. Whateley had been one of the political characters of his day—being a representative in parliament of Castle Rising, successively Secretary to the Earl of Suffolk and the Hon. George Grenville, Secretary of the Treasury and Under-secretary of State. We are not sure that we did not commence writing an essay, to add to the thousand previously published ; and should have given it probably some such title as " Junius Detected." Fortunately, however, we communicated our contemplations to Mr. Felton, author of " Gleanings on Gardens," and other works—a man with a mind abounding with universal information, and he at once directed us to Mr. Whateley's tomb. On that, he said, were inscribed the fatal words, " Died May 26th, 1772 "—fatal to our hopes of having raised the yes unmoved veil ; for Woodfall states that he received letters from Junius in 1773 ! Mr. Whateley was born during this month in the year 1726 ; and was a relative, son or brother, of the Rev. Joseph Whateley, of Nonsuch Park, near Epsom, who became possessed of that residence by the will of his uncle, Joseph Thompson, Esq., who, though a dissenter, left it to him on condition that he took priest's orders in the Church of England. When we have added that Mr. Whateley had two brothers, we have published nearly all the relative biographical information that we have gathered ; for we have already noticed that he is one of our classic authors on Landscape Gardening. The work on which his title to this fame is founded was first published in 1770, and designated, Observations on Modern Gardening, illustrated by descriptions. It was translated very speedily into French, first by Latapil, and then by Masson de Blamont—being praised, yet not above its merits, by all the continental Reviews ; though a single letter annihilated his fame among the Germans, who generally have called him Whitely ! Mr. Loudon justly pronounced these " Observations " to be " the grand

fundamental and standard work on English Gardening "—that copying of the beautiful in nature, and gathering the copies together in our pleasure-grounds and parks, that is so admired among us, and which Mr. Whateley has described in the very motto of his title-page :—

" Where wealth, enthron'd in nature's pride,
    With taste and bounty by her side,
        And holding plenty's horn,
    Sends labour to pursue the toil,
    Art to improve the happy soil,
        And beauty to adorn."

It would be ridiculous for us to attempt to analyse his work in this brief space ; but we can state confidently, that if any one needs a suggestion for shaping his grounds, conducting his waters, grouping his woods, or placing his buildings—any hints for the arrangement of an ornamental farm, a park, a garden, or a riding—if he will consult the pages of Whateley he shall not turn from them either unbenefited or undelighted. We think his descriptions of a pleasure-ground, and its parts appropriate for enjoyment in the freshness of the morning, in the excess of fervid noon, and in the fading splendour of evening, are among the most beautiful examples of English composition. Only those who know what Wright, Brown, Holland, and Eames did then as practical Landscape Gardeners, and what Shenstone and G. Mason—the only practical directors—had written, can justly estimate Mr. Whateley's merit. His is the first prose work which lays down—and illustrates whilst it teaches—rules and directions for Landscape Gardening. Pope had led the way in rhyme, and Mason in blank verse.

Meteorology of the Week.—At Chiswick, during the above seven days, from observations made during the last twenty-three years, the average highest and lowest temperatures are 73.7° and 51.7°, respectively. The greatest heat, 92°, occurred on the 25th in 1844 ; and the extreme cold, 43°, on the 29th in 1845. During the period 97 days were dry, and on 64 days rain fell.

RANGE OF BAROMETER—RAIN IN INCHES.

July		1841.	1842.	1843.	1844.	1845.	1846.	1847.	1848.	1849.
25	B.	30.127	29.902	30.221	29.955	29.932	30.067	29.947	29.794	29.478
		30.071	29.812	30.176	29.901	29.931	29.575	29.906	29.753	29.434
	R.								0.11	0.04
26	B.	30.074	30.966	30.249	30.110	29.929	30.152	30.098	29.790	29.026
		30.022	29.967	30.171	29.908	29.921	30.123	29.929	29.695	29.549
	R.	0.02	0.10			0.02			0.06	0.46
27	B.	29.999	30.156	30.055	30.181	29.850	30.202	30.075	29.950	29.973
		29.943	30.196	29.995	30.161	29.774	30.157	30.064	29.833	29.841
	R.	0.56	0.02		0.07				0.01	0.01
28	B.	29.839	30.045	30.002	30.197	29.746	30.318	30.050	30.064	30.030
		29.774	29.996	29.995	30.005	29.557	30.126	30.064	29.995	29.992
	R.			0.05		0.05				
29	B.	29.760	29.987	29.759	29.956	29.794	30.092	30.076	29.095	30.836
		29.723	29.851	29.634	29.947	29.559	29.981	30.052	29.055	29.765
	R.	0.01		0.07						0.22
30	B.	29.695	30.064	29.676	29.828	29.790	29.975	30.035	29.997	29.662
		29.621	30.018	29.636	29.474	29.577	29.937	29.997	29.654	29.614
	R.			0.07	0.14	0.33			0.18	
31	B.	29.622	30.224	29.299	29.706	29.587	29.955	30.058	29.512	29.913
		29.576	30.127	29.792	29.529	29.545	29.876	30.050	29.350	29.771
	R.	0.11		0.03	0.02	0.18			0.04	

Natural Phenomena Indicative of Weather.—Dr. Forster says that abundance of wasps are said to foretell a good fruit year ; and if so, the present should be one most abundantly productive. We never saw more queen wasps than in the May and June last past ; and the Earl of Burlington, at the other extremity of England (Holkar Hall, Cumberland), having commissioned his gardener, Mr. Wilson, to give a penny each for every wasp brought to him caught in or about his lordship's gardens, from the 23rd of April to the end of June had taken no less than 2364. As every wasp killed at this time of the year is a nest destroyed, the number thus prospectively abolished is almost incalculable. The converse of the abundance of wasps in good fruit years has also been observed ; and in 1824, one of the worst for apples and stone fruit, scarcely a wasp was seen.

Whoever is conversant with our early literature, whether in prose or verse, will find a flower mentioned variously by such discordant names as Sops-in-wine, Pagiants, Horse-flesh, and Blunket ; but more frequently as the Clove-gilloflower. This variously-titled ornament of " the year growing ancient " is the first particularized of those races now filling our lengthy lists of Carnations and Picotees. Its wild parent, known to botanists as the Dianthus caryophyllus, or Clove Pink, was introduced from southern Europe, but is now found native in many parts of England. In this uncultivated form

its petals are rose-coloured, their edges finely toothed, and their fragrance but slight. The florists' art was directed very early towards its improvement ; and Shakespeare makes Perdita observe, that

" the fairest flowers o' the season
Are our Carnations, and streak'd Gilly'vors,
Which some call Nature's bastards : of that kind
Our rustic garden's barren ; and I care not
To get slips of them. For I have heard it said,
There is an art which, in their piedness, shares
With great creating Nature."

If, like Perdita, any have the same prejudice against

hybridizing and the florists' art, they need no other refutation than the reply returned to her by Polixenes—

" This is an art
Which does mend Nature,—change it rather: but
The art itself is nature."

All the most customary names of this flower refer to its beauty and fragrance. *Dianthus* means a divine flower; *Caryophyllus* alludes to its clove-like, spicy odour; and Gillo-flower is a corruption of the French name *Giroflier*, which is also allusive to its clove-like fragrance.*

When Parkinson wrote his "Paradisus" in 1629, and in a still earlier authority, Dethycke's "Gardener's Labyrinth," published in 1586, these flowers were divided into two classes; *Carnations* being the largest in flower and leaf, and the *Gilloflower* characterized by less size in both. Parkinson says, they were then "the chiefest flowers of account in all our English gardens," and they would not be less prized in those days of "good Queen Bess," because the first improved varieties were brought hither from Flanders by the Protestant worsted manufacturers, driven thence by the persecution of Philip the Second, and settled at Norwich in 1567. The Orange-tawney, or yellow Gilloflower, was not introduced until about thirty years after; for Gerarde, in 1597, says, "a worshipful merchant of London, Master Nicholas Lete, procured it from Poland, and gave me thereof for my garden, which before that time was never seen nor heard of in these countries."

By the end of the century in which Parkinson wrote, the varieties had so vastly increased in number (Rea in 1702 enumerates 360), that florists began to classify them; and we find them arranged as: " *Flake Carnations*, having only two principal colours, disposed in broad flakes or stripes quite through the petals. *Bizarre Carnations*, having three or four different colours—red, purple, scarlet, &c., in different shades, irregularly disposed in spots and stripes. *Piquette Carnations*, having always a white ground, pounced, or finely spotted with red, scarlet, purple, or other colours; and *Painted Lady Carnations*, having the petals a bright red or purple above, and entirely white beneath."

Modern florists only retain the three first classes; and they have changed the characteristics of the third,—for a *Picotee* is no longer a spotted carnation, but is a carnation with all the colour confined to a border, of slight or extended width, round the edge of each petal.

Miller and Abercrombie, in the editions of their Dictionaries published in the concluding half of the last century, are the earliest authorities enumerating the properties required to characterize a first-rate carnation. We have compared these with those given by Hogg and others, and find them all concentrated and improved in Glenny's *Properties of Flowers*, from which, slightly altered, we extract the following:—

* Chaucer calls the Carnation *Girofler*; Shakespeare, we see, adopted another corruption, and there are others all tending to show that the name is derived from the French and not from the English words, July-flower, as many have supposed. *Carnation* alludes to the flesh-colour which characterised the earlier varieties.

PROPERTIES OF THE CARNATION.

1. The flower should be not less than two and a half inches across.

2. The guard or lower petals, not less than six in number, must be broad, thick, and smooth on the outside, free from notch or serrature on the edge, and lapping over each other sufficiently to form a circular rose-like flower; the more perfectly round the outline the better.

3. Each layer of petals should be smaller than the layer immediately under it; there should not be less than five or six layers of petals laid regularly, and the flower should so rise in the centre as to form half a ball.

4. The petals should be stiff, free from notches, and slightly cupped.

5 The ground should be pure white, without specks of colour.

6. The stripes of colour should be clear and distinct, not running into one another, nor confused, but dense, smooth at the edges of the stripes, and well defined.

7. The colours must be bright and clear, whatever they may be; if there be two colours, the darker one cannot be too dark, or form too strong a contrast with the lighter. With scarlet the perfection would be a black; with pink there cannot be too deep a crimson; with lilac, or light purple, the second colour cannot be too dark a purple.

8. If the colours run into the white and tinge it, or the white is not pure, the fault is very great, and pouncy spots or specks are highly objectionable.

9. The pod of the bloom should be long and large, to enable the flower to bloom without bursting it; but this is rare; they generally require to be tied about half-way, and the upper part of the calyx opened down

to the tie of each division; yet there are some which scarcely require any assistance, and this is a very estimable quality.

10. Decided superiority of perfume should obtain the prize when competing flowers are in other respects of balanced merit.

PROPERTIES OF THE PICOTEE.

The characteristics of good *form* are the same as for the Carnation, but with regard to *colour*,

1. It should be clear, distinct, confined exclusively to the edge of the petals, of equal breadth and uniform colour on each, and not running down (called sometimes *feathering* or *barring*), neither should the white ground run through the coloured border to the edge of any one of the petals.

2. The ground must be pure white, without the slightest spot.*

DISQUALIFICATIONS OF A CARNATION OR PICOTEE.

1. If there be any petal dead or mutilated.

2. If there be any one petal in which there is no colour.

3. If there be any one petal in which there is no white.

4. If a pod be split down to the sub-calyx.

5. If a guard petal be badly split.

6. Notched edges are glaring faults, for which no excellence in other respects compensates.

* This rule renders the name, still retained by Florists, inappropriate, for *Picote* is the French for spotted.

THE FRUIT-GARDEN.

THE PINE-APPLE ON THE HAMILTONIAN PLAN.—A few remarks were offered at page 93 on this head, and in order to enable our amateur friends to comprehend the real bearing of the subject, a few more will not be deemed out of place at this period. In order to understand the subject in Mr. Hamilton's own way, we have trespassed on his kindness by carrying on a correspondence with him, for some time, about the pine affair, and some extracts from his letters will, doubtless, not be considered altogether wide in the present remarks.

In the first place we are reminded by Mr. H., that in our anxiety to render pine culture more easy the remarks offered at page 93, as connected with the principle of shading, are somewhat incautious, and the only points from which he can dissent. He would have those remarks qualified, by observing, that whatever modification of principles becomes necessary through expediency it must ever be borne in mind that, as a general maxim, the pine requires all the light which our northern skies afford. Exceptions of course will occur; plants may have been disturbed at the root, intense sunshine may occur for many days continuously, together with other matters, and these, of course, at intervals may cause the cultivator to diverge from what may be considered first principles; still the judicious pine grower will hasten back to the main points as soon as he has attained his object.

Now, as a preliminary remark, it must be well understood in the outset, that the distinguishing feature of the Hamiltonian system is the fruiting suckers on the old stool, *whether planted out or in pots*, for a series of years. Of course in dealing with this system as applied to the wants of the amateur, we do not wish it to be understood that the advice is intended to apply to pines intended for exhibition, but more as applied to the purposes of a regular supply to an ordinary family. If we understand our position aright, the main points to be dealt with are, first, to render their culture simple by stripping away everything of an extraneous character or involving much labour; and, secondly, to make them a profitable crop, economy of labour being one of the chief essentials of the latter. It will, nevertheless, be found that when Hamilton's principles of pine culture are fully carried out, little if any sacrifice in point of size will be made; this, however, will become manifest to the tyro as he proceeds.

Not every one who attempts to carry out this system will be able to command a tank-heated chamber as a source of bottom heat. It would be very easy to say, *you must* have a bottom warmth of this character, and who will dispute the propriety of such a course? We wish, however, so to shape our advice as that persons of very moderate incomes shall not be deterred from adding a pine to their dessert through a fear of not being able to produce fruit equal to noble dukes or marquises. Under such circumstances, then, it is well to know that pine stools in pots, plunged, may remain undisturbed for several years without submitting to that imperious dictum of our knights of the prescriptive order:—"they must be taken up and repotted in order to renew the bottom-heat."

In order to be well assured on this point, we must beg leave to make extracts from letters from our worthy friend, Mr. Hamilton, to whom we popped the question for the sake of a thorough satisfaction in the affair; for it must be understood that Mr. H. has been such an enthusiast in pine culture, and has met with such success, that he has the whole matter (to use a homely saying) at his finger's ends. I addressed six queries to him a week or two since, on points closely connected with *his mode* of pine culture; I give his answers as they stand.

FIRST.—Will pines stand long by this system if not tank-heated?—"Pines may remain on old tan beds ten years (if planted out) without disturbing the plant, if planted in rows across the bed, leaving a tolerable space between the rows to fill up with new tan twice in the year, namely, spring and autumn. If they are to be grown in pots they may remain undisturbed—say five years—by adding a little fresh tan twice a year."

SECOND.—Will tan alone sustain them?—"I would recommend a little chopped turf put round their stems once a year in preference to tan alone."

THIRD.—You say they do with much less water than by the old pot culture; say how much?—"They will not want watering above four times a year if syringed and grown in a moist atmosphere."

FOURTH.—Which make the best plants for your system, stem-suckers or ground-suckers?—"Ground-suckers generally produce the best fruit, but I make a practice of taking two or three crops from the stem-suckers first, and then encourage a ground-sucker; cutting the old stem down."

FIFTH.—How is it that mossy matter is liable to be engendered on the leaf of pines on the Hamiltonian system, and what is the remedy?—"The green matter which adheres to the leaf is occasioned by constant moisture with little or no intermission. If the leaves are permitted to get dry each day only for an hour this will be prevented; ventilation is the remedy."

SIXTH.—You sent me a leaf which had produced a sucker at its base after being torn from the parent plant; was the leaf from an old stool or a "maiden plant?"— "The leaf, with the sucker attached, was taken from the bottom of an old plant."

Thus far our good friend Hamilton, to whom we feel very much obliged for so patiently and carefully answering the inquiries.

We will now offer a few comments, or advice, to young beginners who are obliged to steer their way through difficulties, promising, however, to meddle as little with the form of friend Hamilton's texts as possible.

POINT FIRST: THE RENEWAL OF BOTTOM-HEAT.—It will be found that old beds heated with fermenting material will, when of a year or two's standing, threaten at certain periods to lose their heat altogether; and in such an event an inconvenient amount of tan may be required, in order to put fresh life in the bed. Now, as gaps will occur in the bed at times, by the total clearance of perhaps three or four adjoining fruits, advantage may be taken of such a circumstance to remove a plant or two, and to excavate deeply, introducing such materials as dung and tree leaves, in a fermenting state, or even fresh tan, as the case may be; this, however, is a contingency not to be expected under the tank system, and we give it as a make-shift in extreme cases. It will be seen that Mr. H. recommends an increased amount of room between the rows, and also that the latter be straight across the bed, not in the quincunx manner. Indeed, this is obviously the only reasonable mode of proceeding, for it will thus be found that the tan may at all times be introduced with facility.

POINT SECOND.—Here it will be seen that although tan alone as top-dressing will sustain them, yet Mr. H. prefers an occasional top-dressing of turfy material. He has, nevertheless, shewn in his book on Pines, that they extend their roots with the utmost freedom in fresh tan.

POINT THIRD: WATERING.—This is a point which deserves serious consideration. A person who had been accustomed to grow Queens in pots, would be almost sure to do serious mischief with the water-pot to Black Jamaica Pines, under the Hamiltonian plan. Syringing must be closely attended to, and not only this, but much atmospheric moisture provided for, by the use of evaporating pans, or tiles; by hot water pipes in troughs, or by open tanks. This done, they will seldom require water; it must be kept in mind that they have a much greater volume of material to revel in than those confined to pots; their collar, moreover, is at a much lower level; the latter an important consideration.

POINT FOURTH.—It will be seen that Mr. H. (in his own language), makes use of the stem-suckers for a year or two, or, as he says, for two or three crops. We must admit that this is somewhat indefinite, but as we shall recur to this subject again, if all be well, opportunities will arise for us to ascertain such collateral points with some precision. We would here point to the fact, that young pine stools in general make their first efforts at reproduction up the stem, and that the throwing up suckers from below the ground level is more the habit of the mature plant, and indeed, no doubt in part points to a great amount of power, through an encouraged longevity in the earliest formed fibres, together with an increased power to range in quest of food.

POINT FIFTH.—This point refers to the matter of ventilation, and we do hope that no one will again try to disparage the Hamiltonian mode of culture, through a fancy that Mr. H., in his strong advocacy of abundance of atmospheric moisture, neglects the important point of so far aerating the pine structures, as to thoroughly dispel all stagnant and vitiated lodgments of impure air—at least once in the day. How strongly this coincides with our friend Mr. Appleby's sound and clever remarks on the management of the atmosphere for orchids; he insists, as all good cultivators do, on a thoroughly dry leaf, at least once in twenty-four hours. Indeed, nature herself in her general economy forces this great fact on the notice of all who will pay a close attention to the established order of things.

POINT SIXTH.—We would direct the attention of our readers to the great fact, that Mr. H. has produced a sucker from the leaf of an old stool; the leaf I have had possession of, and examined with much interest; no one could do so without being struck with the fact so often reiterated by Hamilton, viz.—that the whole system of the pine plant, even after one or two fruits are recently cut, is still a storehouse of surplus food of eminent service in getting on the young offspring, and thereby shortening the fruiting period by many weeks. Now, if this be a fact, and although to some apparently carrying a hypothetical appearance, it has hitherto received no contradiction of sufficient weight to invalidate its correctness.

Now this leaf, after producing a sucker somewhat after the way of a gloxinia we suppose, was, as we are informed by Mr. H., thrown in the sunshine, divested of soil in order to see whether it would still not only live but increase in substance; it did both, and herein is a fact, as we conceive, bearing with no mean strength on the point before alluded to.

Having at least a dozen letters on the table touching points in the Hamiltonian system, and which the great civility of Mr. H. has enabled us to work up, we must take leave of the pine for a week or two, promising to return to it, and to use further extracts from Mr. H's letters, which will be quite as palatable to those of our readers who feel a strong interest in understanding the bearing of the subject, as any comments that we can make. We shall then attempt to show that the Hamiltonian system need not be confined to the culture of the Black Jamaica.   R. ERRINGTON.

THE FLOWER-GARDEN.

CUTTINGS.—I have said that we often plant cuttings of Scarlet Geraniums in hot weather, and in the full sun, without giving them any water afterwards. In such cases the most of the large leaves flag down, and some of them will die, but in a week or so the cuttings stand erect and are past all danger. Nevertheless, it is a good way to give as much water at the time of planting as will settle the earth and keep the leaves from perspiring too freely. We all say that such and such practices were common in "olden times," when we mean to disapprove of them; and we also say, or rather we are taught to say, that nature has provided that leaves should perspire and inspire; and yet we go on foolishly enough to hinder all this natural process, even in recent times, by pouring water on the leaves in close houses. But in the case of cuttings, although the process of arresting perspiration is unnatural, it is beneficial so far—we break the letter of the law to obtain a certain end, and of two evils we choose the least—for it is much less injurious to stop perspiration in the leaves for a time than to allow it to go on naturally, and so dry up the cutting before it has time to form roots through which a supply of moisture, more than equivalent for that which is perspired, is obtained. Now, here is the very principle on which people prefer a north aspect for these cuttings; the sun is warded off by a wall or hedge, and then the leaves are in little danger of being too powerfully acted on, and so things pass off quietly and comfortably enough for a week or two; but after that mark the progress of a double set of cuttings, the one on a south border the other behind the wall, the nights getting longer and the power of the sun diminishing daily. One week, or at farthest ten days, will put both sets on an equality as to their capacity of bearing up against a strong sun, and those in the shade would now stand the sun as well as those that were planted there at once; but, for the rest of the season, they are deprived of that natural agent from which they derive more than one-half of their vigour. It is true they will be longer than those on the south aspect, and at the time of wintering the advocates of a north aspect will have more bushy or leggy plants than the others; but it is not either bulk or length that is most essential for a young plant of any kind, much less so for such as we have now under consideration; strength and firmness are the right qualities to face a long winter with.

Another experiment will prove conclusively which is the best way to rear a stock of bedding stuff. Let us say, a four-light box or pit is made choice of to winter autumn-struck cuttings in; let two lights be filled with such as were brought up in the shade and the rest with those reared on a southern aspect, and let us hear next spring how many "damped off" out of each lot; but I can give the verdict at once from a reasonable share of extensive practice: it is five to one, on the lowest calculation, more difficult to bring plants from cuttings on a north aspect through the winter. The way in which many gardeners manage their autumn cuttings, by delaying their propagation till September, and then getting them up in a few weeks with the power of hot-beds and glasses, is far preferable to that of the more easy way of beginning now and on a north aspect: but for one who has the means of hot-bed culture, there are ten who must be content without. For a long time I had been an advocate for quick propagation by hot-beds in September, but having proved how much better it is to begin early, and in the open air, I would not willingly return to the hot-bed system—not even with Verbenas and Petunias; but these and all small plants cannot well be propagated on a south aspect without hand-glasses, which must be shaded till the cuttings are nearly rooted, unless the weather is dull. I am persuaded there is no better way of rooting all these small soft-wooded plants for the flower-garden than under hand-glasses full in the sun, and without pots. More than one-half of the bother of wintering such things is got over by this mode of propagation.

Any one having the convenience of a hot-bed in early spring to root cuttings in, should not encumber himself with a full stock in the autumn. The trouble of wintering a host of little weakly plants will often try the skill and temper of our best gardeners, who may have all at their command to ensure success. How then is an amateur, only just beginning to see his way into gardening, to be expected, with his limited means, to do that which sometimes baffles the best of us?

There is nothing more common amongst gardeners, in first-class situations, than a sort of letter-begging correspondence, early in the spring, relating how some accident or another had finished a whole stock of *Anagallises* and *American Groundsel*—two plants which seldom miss a good standing in the chapter of accidents. The freemasonry of gardening is never better exemplified than on these occasions. One seldom hears of refusals at such times; and I often think what a good thing it would be if all classes of the community could so clearly see their dependence on each other as we gardeners do, and act accordingly. The great fault of gardeners, cottage gardeners and all, is, that they strive to winter too much stock for the flower-borders, whereas, if they could but see how easily a few really good well-grown plants in the autumn could be wintered, and how fast cuttings of them will root in the spring, and how much better a healthy young plant will start away when planted out in May, they would surely be persuaded to begin their propagation thus early; six good plants, of a given variety, of any of the soft wooded low things generally used for bedding, if struck *now*, or very soon, and potted singly into small pots, and to have six weeks in the open air before it is time to house them for the winter, are quite sufficient for any purpose; and I am justified in saying this, who use as many bedding plants as most gardeners. Instead of being contented with these six plants, I used in former years to have, perhaps, as many hundreds of the same sort; but as I get older, I learn by experience to save my time and my means; and we are none of us too old to learn what is best for our gardening interest, and I can vouch for it that this is the best time to begin. Therefore let us make a start with the *Anagallis*.

Of the different varieties of this I generally reserve half a dozen stock plants in May from the spring propagation; pot them in rather strong loam. Clean loam, except, perhaps, a little sand when the loam happens to be very strong, is what the anagallis likes, and in which it will winter better than in any kind of mixed compost; these stock plants or pots are kept all the summer in the reserve ground plunged down in sand, and they are allowed to flower, but not much; from this time we nip off the blossoms and tie down their long shoots, for they are very apt to die if their tops are cut off at once, with a view of procuring bushy specimens of young branches; but as soon as their now old branches are tied down the buds or eyes at the very bottom will start, and as soon as the new shoots are an inch or two long we begin to reduce the older shoots by cutting them back to the new wood; and when the young shoots are three inches long they are topped, and this stopping is maintained for the rest of the season, and bushy low plants are thus easily procured, and as easily wintered, for we seldom lose any of them now since we adopted this plan.

Cuttings of them are not now easily procured—the tops of the flowering shoots do not make good cuttings or healthy plants, even if rooted—little bottom shoots are the best. Gardeners generally strike them in September, in hotbeds, and keep them in the same pot all the winter; and never remove them from the cutting-pots until they have rooted a crop of cuttings from their tops in the spring, but there is not one amateur in five hundred who can manage them that way. The way I would advise these cuttings, and, indeed, all cuttings of weak flower-garden plants, to be managed is this:—I would choose a dry piece of ground on which the sun shines all day, if possible, for a nursery; and strike all the cuttings without pots under hand-glasses, that is at this early period of the season; and later I would strike them in close single cucumber-boxes, with or without a slight bottom-heat, according to the season. No bottom-heat is necessary till we get into September; and every cutting I know of will winter better if rooted without bottom-heat, or even much close confinement. But let us go on with the hand-lights: place one of these on your border next to an alley or a walk, beginning at one end, and it will leave a square mark on the ground, then take out the natural soil from within this mark just two inches deep, and lay it all round the outside of the marked parts; this will add to the depth of the bed within this glass-mark a little; but it is hardly wanted, for two inches is quite deep enough to strike cuttings of our Shrubland scarlet geraniums, the strongest of the family. Now put in one inch of any light compost, but first of all sprinkle a handful of soot on the bottom, to keep down the worms, then the compost of half sand and half leaf-mould, or any light rich refuse, and cover the whole with an inch of clean sand; water this so that the whole is damped through, and let it settle for a while to drain; then press down the sand gently with the bottom of a flower-pot, if nothing handier is at command, and your contrivance is at once fit for cuttings. I forget how many cuttings ought to be put under a common hand-glass, but one or two rows across the sand is quite enough of any one sort for a place of almost any extent after making an allowance of ten per cent. for failures between this and next spring. After planting the cuttings, and no deeper than just to hold them in their places, give them a good watering with a fine-rose pot, so as to settle the surface about them and wet the whole to the bottom. After all this let it stand without the glass for an hour or so until the leaves get dry, but the sun should not strike on them to dry them; and as I suppose the cuttings to be on a south border, it will be necessary to shade them at first, and also the glass, from ten in the morning to four in the afternoon; and for the first week the cuttings managed on this plan, that is full in the sun, ought to be damped every morning with a fine rose when the shades are put on, but no more need be given than will just wet the leaves and the surface of the sand.

Under this management verbena and petunia cuttings will root in about half the time they would require on a north aspect; and we all know the sooner a cutting of any kind roots, the more healthy the young plant will be; and another great secret in making such cuttings at this season, or, indeed, at any other, is to have them as short as it is possible to handle them; and from the very tips of the shoots, or from little side-shoots from near the bottom. If we say two or two and a half inches long for such cuttings it will be sufficient; one thing we must all avoid in choosing cuttings of soft-wooded shoots, and that is long-jointed shoots. Sometimes you will meet with a plant, say a petunia, that has all the joints up to very near the top as long as I want the whole cuttings to be; but rather than make use of such leggy things for cuttings I would be content to take an inch from the very top, above the uppermost long joint. Sometimes when one gives away a few cuttings to a neighbour the state of the shoots are never thought of, and it may happen that one can hardly get a really good cutting out of a large bundle of shoots: this is very provoking; and no less so, when you get a tin-boxful of rose shoots, to bud from, through the post, and find when you unpack them that not a bud is to be seen: the shoots being cut too young, or so old that all the buds on them are started into little shoots, and ten to one if these young shoots are old enough to make cuttings: but then the disappointment ends here; not so, however, that from the long-legged cutting—you

may plant it and it will root like the rest, and when the time comes you pot it and all of them from the cutting class, water them, and put the little pots under the hand-glass, and shade for a few days; then you take off the glass at night the first week after potting, to inure your little plants to stand the open air; by-and-bye you place the pots in a sheltered situation, and all goes on to your mind until the first high winds come to sweep over them,—then snap goes the long-legged plants, or those made from long jointed cuttings, because the tops were too heavy; and now there is not another eye below to make a fresh shoot, or if there is it is the very bottom one, and is buried with the roots, and will hardly push

D. BEATON.

GREENHOUSE AND WINDOW GARDENING.

FERTILIZATION OF SEEDS.

HYBRIDISING.—That there should be distinct male and female organs in the flowers of plants, is one of those facts that forcibly strike the attention of those just commencing the study of vegetable phenomena. A floating, half real, half mythical belief in this principle has existed since the days of Empedocles, who attributed to plants desires, passions, and feelings somewhat analogous to those existing in the animal creation; it was reserved for the great Linnæus to establish, incontrovertibly, the presence of these distinctive sexual organs, and to make the *number* and the *position* of stamens and pistils the groundwork for his famous artificial arrangement of plants into classes and orders. The knowledge of this sexual system forms the foundation for all improvements in the races of our vegetables, fruits, roots, and flowers; without the perfect action of these organs upon each other there can be no true fruit, no fertile seeds. True, what is generally termed the *fruit*—such as the eatable part of a melon, the melting pulp of a peach, the solid, useful part of a cucumber—may respectively swell and be fit for use, but unless there has been an influence exerted by the pollen dust from the anther boxes of the stamens upon the summit, or stigma, of the pistil, or upon some cellular tissued part of the pistil if the *stigma* be wanting, there can be no production of true seeds in the fruit—such seeds as afterwards will vegetate and grow. When the mere covering of the true fruit is all that is wished—such, for instance, as in a long, symmetrical, green *cucumber*, fit for the table—the desired result may be obtained as well, *often better*, without the fertilizing process as with it. Hence, when at times I wished to grow fine looking, long, symmetrical cucumbers, I used to tie a string round the female blossom of the fruit before opening, to prevent all possibility of fertilization, either by winds, or by bees or flies carrying the fertilizing pollen on their legs or wings, and I did so because in the finer races of cucumbers fertile seeds are generally attended with knobby excrescences on the fruit, which, however desirable to contemplate when seed is the object, are not very pleasing when symmetry of form is the desideratum.

One reason why peaches and nectarines drop off when the stoning process commences, in addition to allowing too many fruit to remain, is owing to a deficiency in the fertilizing process when the trees were in bloom, as in houses where the fertilization was assisted by scattering the pollen by means of fans and camel hair brushes I have scarcely ever had a fruit drop during stoning. Even here the stone will frequently be formed, and the kernel, or true seed, or fruit, be defective. When, however, in favourable circumstances, ripe pollen is shed upon a healthy pistil, it sends out a tube, which, though not more than the one-thousandth part of an inch in diameter, penetrates the style, or stalk, of the pistil, and fertilizes the ovules in the seed vessel at its base.

God has taken such care of His beautiful vegetable offspring, that wherever both of these distinctive organs exist in a perfect state seeds will be infallibly produced, perfect in their kind, and which, under favourable circumstances, will produce plants similar in type to that from which they came. Our fair correspondent, therefore, who wishes to know how she is to "avoid breaking the flower"—the blown petals of the plant she wishes to impregnate, such as the pansy, "and also if it be necessary to remove the stamen from the flower operated upon," may rest contented that, if mere fruitful seeds are her object, her attention in this respect will not be required, as in favourable circumstances nature will manage all this without her interference. But if, as we suppose, she desires to obtain not merely fertile seeds, but seeds which will produce other flowers different and more beautiful still than the one she wishes to fecundate, then her aid will be of importance in securing the desired object; that object being the producing a cross, or a hybrid or hybrids, that will have the good properties of both parents.

Though the matter has been several times referred to, we thus touch upon it again, believing that even yet great misapprehension exists. A short time ago I was visited by an enthusiast in gardening—an amateur who spends a considerable sum every year upon novelties, who is a good cucumber grower, and perfectly understands the method of fertilizing their seeds, and yet made it his especial errand to know how such things are done in the case of calceolarias, geraniums, &c., stating that he could not make out a female flower from a male flower, as he could readily do in the case of the cucumber and melon. Now, though many plants resemble the cucumber in having their male and female blossoms separate, the great bulk of our flowering plants possess both sexes in the same flower, and in such cases the female may always be readily recognised—1st. By its holding the first or central part of the flower; a fact which might teach philosophers the importance of establishing a correlative in the rational world, by giving to *woman* the first, the central, and not the secondary place in society, a position she *must* occupy before great advances are made in refinement and civilisation; and, secondly, the female part of the flower is always known by containing at its base, as in the case of the cucumber, the *embryo* of the future seed vessel. These things being known, fertilizing the female organ with the pollen of its own stamens, or cross fertilizing it, or hybridising, with the pollen of a kindred plant, becomes a mere matter of routine.

There are, indeed, some very singular phenomena connected with the position and the office of these separate organs in some tribes, which must be understood and examined before the processes can be readily seen through. Many of these have already been referred to, and one of the most striking is that of the common blue bell or campanula, as was noticed so well lately by our friend Mr. Beaton; but I have mislaid the number. A young friend enquired the other day, if the three horned-like things in the centre of a full blown bell-flower were stamen boxes fixed upon the central pistil? As these horns were covered with pollen, and as the true stamens had dwindled down into almost imperceptible threads, it is no wonder that she made such a mistake; but by showing her a flower not quite opened the mystery was at once explained. There stood the five chubby gentleman anthers, cheek by jowl, with the three pointed pistil; the anthers with slits longitudinally, while the tripartite, or three horned pistil, in each of its divisions was furnished with rows of short bristles, and only in the side next the anthers—which entering the pollen boxes cleared them out of their pollen, and thus fertilization was effected—the anthers withered and drooped, while the style of the pistil became elongated, so as to present the appearance that puzzled our young friend. Now, though not so striking, there is also something peculiar in the mode of fructification of the common *pansy*. The pistil, as in every other analogous case, is in the centre of the flower. The stigma is the point which we easily observe in the centre, connected with the germen or seed-vessel by a short slender style; while the anthers, five in number, clasp firmly the sides of the seed-vessel. Here, as in the case of the bell-flower, the stamens open *only* on the inner side, next the germen; did they open on the outside, the pollen dust might be scattered *wide* of the stigma. As it is, and owing to the slightly nodding character of the flower, the pistil in some of its parts must be covered with the pollen as it falls; and to ensure this more effectually, there is an appendage fixed to the upper point of the anther, which acts as a fan-board or shield, an appendage which is not common in hardly any other tribe of plants. Now in answer to the two questions of our friend: there will be no necessity for breaking off the bloom of the flower you would impregnate; but as we have seen that the pollen boxes are close to the side of the germen, you cannot get at the pollen dust by any other means than by turning the flower, and for this purpose it will be generally necessary to nip off the flower-buds you intend to act as males, bearing in mind that the pollen dust will be ripe for fecundation when the bloom is fully expanded. Shaking the bloom with its male parts thus ripe, or, what is better, tying it over the pistil you wish to hybridise, will generally be successful. We disapprove of destroying the blossom-petals of the plant thus intended for seed-bearing; and if it is necessary to remove the stamens, that may easily be effected before the blossom opens, by bending the petals just so much as will enable you to start them off at their base with the point of a needle or a small pen-knife.

Now, as to the second question—is it necessary to remove the stamens in such circumstances? we say, decidedly so, when any very precise and definite result is intended, and by the means specified it may easily be done; but in general cases it is not necessary, as the fecundating of the pistil with foreign pollen before the pollen cells of its own anthers burst is held to be sufficient. Our own experiments, as well as many others, would almost lead us to hold this opinion, but we confess that the data are not quite sufficient to enable us to determine definitely, In all cases of nicety, therefore, we recommend removing the stamens.

Our space has so soon filled up, that we shall have something to say in another communication of some of the results of being acquainted with the sexual system, and the principles to be kept in view in hybridising.

CHRYSANTHEMUMS.—We can say little of this splendid flower in addition to what was stated last year, only now is a good time for making layers from plants growing in the open air, so as to ensure very dwarf specimens. One of the best modes is to have pots filled with light rich soil; place the top of the chrysanthemum over it; run a knife for an inch or two along its centre; place a stone, or stick, or piece of mould, between to keep the wound open; cover it with soil; and fasten it in its place with a pebble or hook, and roots will soon be protruded if moisture is supplied. Those in pots should not have their shoots stopped any more, or the flowers will be small and scarce.   R. FISH.

HOTHOUSE DEPARTMENT.
EXOTIC ORCHIDACEÆ.

PLANTS REQUIRING BASKETS (*Concluded from page* 226.)

Vanda fusco violacea; E. India.—A handsome species, with brownish sepal and petal, and a violet-coloured lip. 168s.

V. insignis (Noble V.); Java.—A handsome species; ground-colour cream, with stripes of purplish crimson. 105s.

V. Roxburghii (Roxburgh's V.).—A fine species; sepals and petals yellowish, blotched with red; brown inside, light pink and white outside; the lip is white, with a broad blotch of pink. 63s.

V. Roxburghii cærulea.—The only difference is, that the blotch on the lip is pale blue. Both varieties are well worth growing. 63s.

V. suavis (Sweet-scented V.).—This is next to *V. Batemaniana,* if not equal to it both for beauty and noble habit. Though more plentiful in the country it is yet very dear, being slow to put out offsets. One was offered for sale at an auction in Messrs. Steven's rooms, in London, and fetched the high price of 17 guineas. The flowers are large, produced on racemes from the axils of the noble leaves, sometimes producing as many as eight of its large flowers on a stem. The sepals and petals are white, beautifully and broadly striped with purplish crimson; the lip is white, finely shaded, and blotched with red.

V. tricolor (Three coloured V.).—Much like the *V. suavis ;* the leaves are narrower and longer, and the flowers have a few stripes of yellow mixed with the white and crimson—hence its name. 210s.

V. violacea (Violet V.); Manilla.—A beautiful dwarf species, very rare. The sepals and petals are white, tinged with violet; the tip is white, also richly striped with violet-purple, hence its name. 210s.

CULTURE.—The baskets for the large growing species should be, comparatively speaking, of a large size. They should be filled with, first, a lining of sphagnum, and then with a mixture of rough fibrous peat, chopped sphagnum, and broken potsherds. They should, when small, be hung up about two or three feet from the glass, and kept in the Indian house in an atmosphere hot and moist during the growing season, which season extends from May to the end of August. After that time they should be kept rather dry and cool until the April following; then the heat should be raised to 75° by day and 65° by night, and the atmosphere kept rather dry: this will ripen the wood and induce flower-buds to make their appearance. As soon as the buds are perceived the plants should be syringed freely, and encouraged liberally with water. In the cool part of the year hang them up pretty close to the glass, that is, the top of each plant should be about two feet from the glass roof. In summer they may with advantage be placed upon pots turned upside down. This situation will afford a better opportunity to view them when in flower, and water can be applied to them more conveniently.

SECOND DIVISION.

PLANTS THAT REQUIRE TO BE GROWN ON BLOCKS.

This is a very important point in the culture of orchids. The plants we shall enumerate in this division mostly grow in exposed situations on the branches of trees. The practice of placing such on blocks of wood is imitating Nature as nearly as we possibly can, in our artificial treatment of such tropical plants. The kind of wood best adapted for this purpose, and the method of fixing the plants to the blocks, we have already described. It only remains to mention, that some require a little moss to be fastened to the blocks along with the plants; and others do not need such an addition, but are injured by it. We shall, as we describe each species, notice this peculiarity.

Angræcum bilobum (Two-lobed A.); South Africa.— This is a most lovely species; the flowers are produced on a pendulous raceme, and are slightly but sweetly fragrant. The whole flower is of a pure white, excepting a small speck of pink at the end of the sepals and petals. It will thrive better if a little moss is placed near the body of the plant to retain moisture, but the roots must be allowed to protrude beyond it. 31s 6d.

Barkeria elegans (Elegant B.); Mexico.—Sepals and petals light rose. This plant, we fear, is lost to the country.

B. Lindleyana (Dr. Lindley's B.); Costa Rica.—This species flowers in autumn like the next; sepals and petals rich purple; the lip rich dark purple, with a blotch of white in the centre; a truly elegant plant, but very scarce. The only good plant we know is in the fine collection of R. S. Holford, Esq.

B. Skinnerii (Mr. Skinner's B.); Guatimala.—This plant is considered by some to be an *Epidendrum.* It is described under that name in the *Botanical Register,* but its habit and the shape of the flowers are quite sufficient to place it under the genus Barkeria. It is a lovely species, flowering in autumn, and lasts a long time in bloom. Sepals and petals deep pink; the lip is of the same colour, with a deeper tint in the centre. 21s.

B. melanocaulon (Dark-stemmed B.); Costa Rica.— This is a rare species; exhibited for the first time at the Royal Botanic Society's Exhibition, in June, by Mr. Barnes, gardener to R. Hanbury, Esq., of the Poles, near Ware. The sepals and petals are of a lilac-pink: the labellum or lip has a curious spot of green in the centre. 42s.

B. spectabilis (Showy B.); Guatimala.—Sepals and petals pale lovely lilac, spotted a little with light purple, lip white at the base and in the middle, lilac at the edges and point, and spotted with blood-red spots. Along the middle five purple lines are placed, below the column, which greatly add to the beauty of the flower. 42s.

CULTURE.—As we have already written pretty largely on this genus in a former volume of the COTTAGE GARDENER, we shall be, in this place, very brief in our remarks on the culture they require; and it is a happy circumstance that all the species thrive best by one method. They require to be grown on blocks, without moss, hung up in the most airy part of the Mexican house; syringed freely whilst growing, but kept dry during the period of rest. They will, during that season, lose all their leaves, but, if rightly managed, the pseudo-bulbs will appear plump and fresh; and the buds at the base of each will appear plump and prominent, ready to start into active growth as soon as the longer days of spring and the invigorating influence of the sun shall increase the temperature and stimulating light of the house. As soon as that season arrives they should be freely syringed twice a day, to encourage strong growth: for in proportion to the strength of the growth will the number of the flowers on each spike be. As the summer advances give plenty of air to the plants of this genus; they will grow stronger, produce more flowers, with higher colours.

These remarks apply more particularly to all the species excepting *B. Skinnerii* and *B. Lindleyana,* which flower, as we remarked above, in the autumn; all the rest are summer flowering.

Bolbophyllum barbigerum (Bearded B.); Sierra Leone —Sepals and petals; greenish brown; the lip is covered with dark-coloured hair. 21s.

B. saltatorium (Dancing B.); South Africa.—There is not much difference between this species and the preceding one. The pseudo bulbs in the former are of a deeper green, and the leaves are greener. The labellum of the latter is larger and of a lighter colour. 21s.

CULTURE.—They thrive best on a block of wood with moss attached to it, and love, when growing, abundance of heat and moisture. They do not possess much beauty, but the labellum is the most curious part; the least air, or breath, or motion, sets them dancing up and down. On that account they are worth growing as curiosities. The genus is a tolerably large one, but the above two species are quite enough in number to cultivate.

Brassavola angustata (Narrowed B.); Demerara.—Sepals and petals pale yellowish green; lip white and fringed; a pretty species.   21s.

B. cucullatum (Hooded B.); West Indies.—Sepals and petals dark purple; lip white and fringed; hood-shape, with a reddish shade in the centre.

B. Digbyana (Mr. Digby's B.); West Indies.—Sepals and petals yellowish white; lip very large, white streaked with purple lines; the flowers measure four inches across. It is the finest of the genus yet known.   84s.

B. glauca (Glaucous B.).—Alluding to the colour of the leaves, which are of a milky green; sepals and petals yellow; lip orange, with a white throat. A very handsome fragrant species, somewhat difficult to flower, but that may be overcome by liberally growing it during the proper season, and giving it a severe dry rest.   12s.

B. tuberculata (Tubercled B.); Brazil.—This species is the most easily grown of the whole tribe; the flowers are pretty, of a greenish white, and last a long time in bloom.   15s.

B. Venosa (Veined B.); Honduras.—Sepals and petals cream; labellum white, strongly veined. A desirable plant.   21s.

CULTURE.—The whole of this family grows on trees in open glades, where the tropical sun darts upon them his burning rays, but they do not suffer from his fierce attacks. Their fleshy round leaves are not easily injured. In our stoves they require to be grown on naked blocks—that is, blocks without moss—and hung up to the roof constantly; there they will thrive and flower freely.

FLORISTS' FLOWERS.

A pressure of other matter prevents us from giving our usual essay this week on this part of our labours. We can only say to our florist readers, read over our remarks for the last week or two. We will endeavour to enter fully into the subject next week.

T. APPLEBY.

THE KITCHEN-GARDEN.

CAULIFLOWERS AND COLEWORTS.—Continue to plant out in succession, and encourage those in the various stages of growth by the application of liquid-manure and frequent surface stirrings.

CELERY.—If the early-planted celery should produce a quantity of suckers, they must all be cleared off previous to earthing, and the earthing must be attended to in a very pains-taking manner. The growth of celery in every successive stage should be encouraged by frequent stirrings, and liberal soakings of sewerage-water or liquid-manure of some kind.

CABBAGE.—The best kinds should be sown at twice, between this date and the 12th of August, on a well-prepared piece of ground. The second week in August will be found a good season for sowing the *Red Dutch cabbage* to stand over for spring planting.

ROUTINE WORK.—Sow *American* and *Normandy cress*. Plant out *Endive* in succession, and make another sowing. Sow a small portion of *Flanders spinach* for autumn consumption, and continue to fork and stir well the soil intended for sowing the winter crop next month. *Leeks* should be planted in succession on well-manured soil. *Chamomile flowers*, and herbs of any kind in flower, should be secured *for drying* in fine dry weather. The early crops of *Onions* may now have their stalks pressed down. *Parsley* should be thinned very carefully, in order to have the most curled and strongest plants; another sowing should be made, and a small portion potted for winter use. *Brocolis, Borecoles, Savoys*, and all kinds of winter stuff which have been planted between other crops, or in other ways, should be as soon as possible after they are established have the ground to themselves, and be well encouraged by hoeing and scarifying, in order to encourage a luxuriant growth. Continue to plant all such vegetables in succession; and at this season *Coleworts* especially should be planted pretty freely. *Swede turnip plants* may also be transplanted to advantage at this season, for producing spring greens, and *Turnips* of the small nimble garden kinds should be sown in full crop in succession, for the next three or four weeks, to insure a good supply until April next.

CUCUMBERS AND MELONS in pits and frames should be assisted by a little addition to the top of the linings, and as the nights become chilly after rain, a slight covering may be added to advantage. Liberal soakings of tepid liquid-manure should also be given to those now swelling a crop of fruit, and stopping, airing, thinning, and setting the fruit should be attended to as recommended previously.

MUSHROOM BEDS which are becoming rather slack in producing, should be liberally soaked with tepid clear liquid-manure, brewed from cow, sheep, or deer dung.

JAMES BARNES.

MISCELLANEOUS INFORMATION.

OUR VILLAGE WALKS.
By the Authoress of "My Flowers."

IT is a remarkable circumstance, that in England we scarcely ever possess a few days of hot summer weather that they are not snatched from us by a thunderstorm. Rain, and cold, and wind, most frequently ensue; we find our beautiful summer flowers dashed about and disfigured, and the bright green leaves lying beneath the trees, torn from the boughs in all their unfaded freshness. There is a feeling of sadness in observing the desolation caused by a sudden storm such as we have just experienced—the gardens look so wet and wild where but a few hours before the shrubs and flowers were all so neat and gay. Now the seringa blossoms are scattered on the ground, the bloom on the dark polished Portugal laurel looks dingy and drooping, and the roses are so shaken and discomfited that half their beauty for a time is taken away. How loudly are we reminded by these sights and circumstances of the uncertainty, the frailty, and the

perishable nature of all we possess, of the earthly happiness we enjoy, nay, of our own life also, for "the wind passeth over it, and it is gone; and the place thereof knoweth it no more."

The grandeur and sublimity of a slowly advancing storm is very striking; there is a majesty in its approach that awes the mind, and a terrible power which we feel that no hand but that of the Most High God can direct or restrain. As we watch the dark masses of cloud rolling heavily towards us, pile upon pile, sometimes tinged with a murky red, we are forcibly reminded of the Lord's address to the restless inhabitants of a restless world—"Be still, and know that I am God." We feel so helpless, so impotent, in the presence and beneath the power of a storm, that we are irresistably taught the nothingness of man and his utter inability to deliver himself from the hand which directs it. Human knowledge—human skill—human strength avail nothing when "the air thunders" and the "arrows" of God go abroad. Who can turn aside the bolt that darts from the electric cloud when the Lord's hand hath winged it?

A few nights ago, after several days of unusual heat, a storm swept with fearful wings over some parts of the country; upon the immediate spot where I am now passing a short time it fell,—by the mercy of God very slightly! yet within a few short miles on every side it was an alarming visitation; dark lurid clouds gathered during the day and hung heavily around the hills, and a peculiar atmospheric weight and solemn silence in the air warned us that a storm was near.

The cooling, delicious rain, for which nature seemed thirsty, fell during the night, and the thunder was distant; still, the sheets of blue lightning flashed vividly, and illumined, with awful brightness, every corner of the room. A midnight storm is peculiarly solemn, and seems more closely to address our hearts; the deep darkness—broken by the sudden flash which lights up every hill, and tree, and shrub—every room, and every object in them—warns us that the secrets of all hearts, hidden from every human eye, shall soon be made known to all the world, displayed by a light more terrible still than that of a passing storm. The thunder too, in the stillness of night, utters its voice with increased sublimity, because the earth is silent; it seems as if nothing interposed between us and "the glorious God who maketh the thunder," and whose voice sounds so impressively in every peal, as if we were then, more than ever, standing in trembling helplessness before the throne of God. Yet let us ever remember "the messenger of the covenant," the "daysman betwixt us," who layeth "his hand upon us both;" and let us, amid storm and tempest, trust simply and fearlessly on Him.

I hope that a very remarkable instance of the Lord's loud and compassionate warning to the children of men which took place during the late storm will attract the attention of my cottage readers in particular, and be a means of conveying deep spiritual instruction to their hearts; I copy, verbatim, the letter of a lady residing near the spot, for I cannot in my own words convey her ideas so well:—

"The refreshing rain you speak of was most woful in its accompaniments here. Wednesday was a most overpowering day of heat, and about six in the evening there were great indications of an approaching storm; vivid flashes of lightning, succeeded by heavy rolling thunder, warned us of coming evil. This continued, with occasional heavy rain, until about 12 o'clock at night, when the tempest became fearful, with both forked and sheet lightning, and thunder that made the houses crack and the hearts of the timid quail, and even the strong and bold felt that the Lord is Lord of all. About one o'clock there was one flash—such a flash!—and at the same moment a thunderbolt fell—not into water! not into earth! but through the roof of a large cottage, where one of the most drunken and dissipated families we have reside! The house was shattered all through, and immense beams shivered to atoms, yet has the Lord spared the inhabitants! Surely this wonderful preservation is for some wise cause, and if it does not awaken the hearts of those persons I hope at least we may all 'consider,' and feeling truly that 'the Lord He is the God,' we may watch and examine ourselves carefully, lest He come and summon us at an hour when we are unprepared."

This short extract needs no comment, yet I cannot help reminding my humbler readers that their lowly state cannot hide them from the piercing eye of God, and that His law, first delivered from Mount Sinai amid thunderings and lightnings, is still binding upon us all, and if broken will as surely bring down judgments upon our heads. Let every storm, then, that bursts over us lead our minds away to spiritual things, and teach us to cherish less fondly the things "that are ready to die." We mourn over one of our beautiful trees scathed by the storm; we stand confounded amid the ruins of our house, built by the hand of man, and we gladly turn to those who will help and comfort us; but we madly disregard the ruin that sin has caused, and we turn as madly from Him who would deliver us from it. We might have been struck down like a cedar, and shivered to atoms like the poor man's home, yet are we spared to receive this solemn warning. Let us "hear and understand," lest it should be our last.

PRESERVING.

The fruit season having commenced, I think a few remarks on preserving may not be unacceptable to some of my readers. Jellies and preserves are easily made, though they sound rather formidable to the inexperienced housekeeper; and every cottager who owns a currant or raspberry bush should abstain from eating them raw in order to keep them for winter use; in illness a little jam or jelly is most refreshing, besides, fruit eaten raw is soon gone, and does no good, whereas if boiled and converted into jam it goes much further, and often "comes in" handy when butter is scarce.

Great cleanliness should be observed with every article that is used for the preserves. The saucepan, or the preserving pan, should be brightly clean; the pots in which it is to be kept well dried. Attention also should be paid to the tying down; a piece of writing-paper, dipped in brandy, cut the size of the pot, and laid on the jam is the best plan to prevent mould from appearing; a double piece of paper should then be tied over it all, and there is then very little chance of its not keeping well. Black currant jelly is the most useful preserve that can be made; in the winter, when coughs and colds are prevalent, it will be found of great service.

The art of making good preserves is to boil the fruit well before the sugar is added, in order to allow the watery particles to evaporate. The fruit for preserving should always be picked in dry weather, or else it will soon require boiling up again.

I will begin my receipts with the one most suited to the humble home, which is

Currant Jelly.—Pick the currants when quite ripe, put them into a jar with the stalks (as it will waste time picking them off), tie it down and put it into a saucepan of boiling water, let it remain over the fire for three-quarters of an hour, bruise the currants and strain the juice through a sieve, pour it into a preserving pan or saucepan, and when it has boiled add one pound of sugar to every pint of juice. Boil it together for ten minutes, and pour it whilst hot into the pots in which it is to be kept. A pint of juice will make a very good store for winter coughs, and as a pound of sugar does not cost above sixpence, I strongly recommend any one who possesses a currant-tree to avail themselves of the opportunity of having so nice a medicine at so small a cost. A teaspoonful of this jelly mixed with a little water is a most refreshing draught in a fever. The currants from which the juice has been extracted should not be thrown away, for if mixed with a little treacle they make a very nice pudding.

Gooseberry Jam is another useful and cheap preserve; cheap because coarse sugar may be used, or even treacle, though of course it is not so palatable, nor will it keep so long as when made with white sugar. The red gooseberries are the best, but they must be picked when quite ripe and dry; when you have taken off the tops and stalks weigh them, and to every dozen pounds of fruit add one pint of currant juice. Put it into a preserving pan, boil them quickly, and when soft mash them with a fork, and add to each pound of fruit three-quarters of a pound of sugar. Boil together for three-parts of an hour, pour it whilst hot into jars, but do not tie it down till it is quite cold. Examine the jam a few days after it is made, and if the fruit appears separated from the syrup boil it again.

Blackberry Jam is an economical and wholesome preserve, but it must be boiled for half an hour before the sugar is added, and then to every pound of fruit put half a pound of sugar.

Raspberry Jam is very much improved by having a little red currant juice mixed with it, in the proportion of half a pint to a pound of fruit. This fruit also requires to be boiled for half an hour before the sugar is added. Raspberries should be used as soon as possible after they are picked, or else their flavour is very quickly gone.

Raspberry Vinegar is easily made, and is found very refreshing in case of illness. To make two quarts of the vinegar pick a quart of ripe raspberries, cover them with best vinegar, and let them stand 24 hours; strain it through a piece of flannel, make a thick syrup with one pound of sugar, mix it with the juice and boil them together for ten minutes; strain it again and bottle it. If this vinegar is kept in a cool place it will keep good for some years. Only those who have watched by sick beds can know the pleasure with which a cooling drink is received, and surely when it can be procured with so little trouble and such little expense it should not be withheld; and although, through God's mercy, sickness may have been a stranger in your dwelling, yet come it will, and as we know not what a day will bring forth, it is our interest, our duty, to prepare not only for our bodily wants but for our spiritual. "Watch, for ye know neither the day nor the hour of your Lord's coming."—A FRIEND.

ALLOTMENT FARMING FOR AUGUST.

POTATOES.—It is a painful duty to announce the re-appearance of *the potato disease ;* not the mere root-rot which may be found at times very early in the summer, without exciting any very serious apprehensions, but disease attended by the real *Botrytis infestans*—the name of a parasitic fungus, but too familiar to our readers. Such appearing in Cheshire, at the period at which these remarks are penned (July 14th), so sufficiently alarming as to induce all parties to make an endeavour, before the season is too far spent, to produce as great an amount of vegetable food as possible, which may, should a great emergency occur, act in some degree as a substitute, or at least aid, to an economical consumption of the potato. We do not wish hereby to cause unnecessary alarm; for, judging from past symptoms, it may fairly be inferred that the disease is (as was by most well-informed persons anticipated) steadily on the wane; for there can be no question but a progressive advance has been made both in the productive and the keeping qualities of the potato during the last two years. A wise general will not, however, go to sleep and dream of safety whilst the enemy is picquetting within gun-shot, but betake himself immediately to at least defensive measures. As first and best advice, we say at this period, make an effort to plant a few more Swede turnips. No root is more useful, especially after Christmas, than this.

The allotment should be carefully looked over forthwith, in order not only to search for blanks, but to see if any crop exists which is not flourishing, and which might be removed and turned to account at the present moment. Such might be the case with *late peas* which have become much mildewed, *broad beans* much infested with the fly, *cabbages* which are much clubbed, &c., &c. Now is the time to act with some real decision, for most of these things may be given to the pig or cow. *Early potatoes,* too, if more than the cottager can consume, should be sold forthwith, for these are, or ought to be, too good for the pig; and, indeed, the allotment or cottage garden ought at this time to teem with materials of no other use than to give to the pig, and to increase the bulk of the manure heap. Sometimes the *onion* crop is much grubbed, and the cottager is apt to stick tenaciously to them, although only a few patches of plants remain, which can be expected to survive the wreck; let these, we say, be pulled up forthwith, and roots introduced. The same may be said of the *carrot* beds; and, indeed, of every garden it may be affirmed, that a keen eye and a decisive mind may at all times find occasion to make some re-arrangement of this kind; and it will be found that, with a proper amount of earnestness, and a little labour, which only costs the allotment holder the sweat of his brow, enough may be produced to purchase the sacrificed store, and something to boot. And here we would say, let there be no unnecessary alarm about having too many *Swedes,* or other store roots, in case the potato disease should not spread. If too many for the cow or pig, or the cottager's family, they may always be exchanged or sold.

COMMON TURNIPS for winter, if such are needed, must be sown in the first or second week. Enough of these may be generally grown on some border or nook; not, however, beneath the shade of trees, or close to a hedge. The best

kinds are the Stone or the Dutch. The other and more keeping roots are, nevertheless, so much more profitable as well as more convenient, that we would advise only enough of these for the cottager's wife, and some to produce a few early turnip-tops in spring.

CABBAGES.—These are a somewhat important affair; they are always useful and profitable. A rather liberal sowing must be made in the second week of August; and as the ground for their reception will, in all probability, not be ready until some of the autumn root crops are removed, a bed must be got ready in a few weeks, and the seedlings must be pricked out at three or four inches apart. Those who had sown the coleworts as recommended in June, should now endeavour to get a few rows out, using a little manure. We plant our onion ground with them every year; for we so manage our onions as to get them off the ground a fortnight or more before our neighbours. However, it is impossible to dictate any given plot for them—modes of cropping are so various. We again suggest that all cabbages in heart, and getting what is termed ripe, should at once be cut and used up; for if they are intended for sprouts, the latter will be more valuable, and the plants become exhausted by allowing the old heads to remain until they burst.

WINTER GREENS, &c.—Here, again, is another section of most useful articles, for either the house, the cow, or the pig. Nevertheless, it is seldom the cottager can afford ground enough to make them a primary crop, such are generally introduced amongst the standing crops of the early summer, such as peas, beans, early potatoes, &c. A severe limitation of ground of course renders it imperative on the holder to resort to expedients or shifts; for this course nothing need be said of an apologetic character; according to the old saying, "Necessity is the mother of invention," or, as the Scotch have it, "Necessity gars the auld wives trot." Whatever be the mode of cropping, certain it is that an allotment or cottage garden, well stocked with good cabbage, the green kale, good bouncing savoys, and even a dozen or two brocolis for spring, with a patch of forward turnips, to produce early turnip-tops, presents a very different appearance to one which, regarding a first crop alone, is suffered to become a wilderness of weeds during the autumn and early spring.

The *green kale* is assuredly the first on the list as to general utility; next we may place the *savoy,* which is a most excellent companion for a small piece of the cottager's pickled pork, or what folks within a hundred miles of the Mersey call "green bacon;" to these may be added a few of the *Brussels sprouts,* on account of their extreme hardihood, as also their eligibility for standing thick on the ground; they moreover furnish a useful early food for cow or pig in March, when they are "running to seed." Of the *brocoli* tribes we say little, they are of course a luxury; still, where allotments are near railways, or close to thriving towns, we would have the allotment holder burst some of the ordinary trammels of culture, and study in some degree the markets near him; where such is the case the cultivation of *celery* is sometimes a profitable affair: we are, however, diverging from the strict line of allotment matters, and must return to our subject.

MANGOLD.—Little need be added here about this valuable root; where grown as a secondary crop between potatoes, &c., care must be taken at this period that the primary crops do not overshadow them; weeds must be kept under, and a little soil drawn to their stems we have ever found of much service.

LETTUCE, SPINACH, &c.—We do not name these as allotment crops in general, but point to them merely as being useful adjuncts, and, perhaps we may add, luxuries when attainable. Those who desire to have these things in a profitable way during the autumn, should sow a pinch of the *Brown Cos Lettuce* and the *Prickly Spinach* in the very earliest part of August, indeed, for the Northern Counties such should be done at least a fortnight earlier to be profitable.

CARROTS.—By this time at least the main winter crops of the Long Surrey and Altringham carrots will require a final thinning. As a general rule the majority of carrot crops in field culture will have received their final thinning long ago; such, however, is the horror of the carrot grub amongst cottagers, and those of the allotment class, that we frequently see this crop placed under circumstances of bad culture—as to a timely thinning—through a dread of this so frequent visitation. In the end of July, or at latest the first week of August, we say, let a final thinning be made. The thinnings by this time will be large enough for cooking, and the tops are excellent for either cow or pig. The larger carrots may be thinned, if in beds, to four or five inches apart, but the Horn carrot not to half the distance.

WEEDING.—All crops should have one more thorough cleaning in the beginning of August; this will keep them clean for the remainder of the growing season. The hoe should be deeply plied between drills of all kinds, and if any crops have become very foul with weeds, and the weather is anyways showery, it is by far the best policy to dig between the drills.

HAY GRASS.—Those who have land enough for a cow, will of course have their hay cleared off the ground; and now is a good time to apply either liquid-manure or guano, the latter should by all means be applied in a showery time, for to apply it in dry weather is to lose one-half its qualities. If there is only one plot of pasturage, the cow may be kept tied up most of the time; but many cottagers have a chance of turning out in grassy lanes, or on commons. Of course the waste thinnings of the allotment or garden will go far towards keeping the cow at this period; but if she is in full milk we would advise giving a little linseed, morning and night, until some good after-math is to be had. Those who have any corn crops, such as barley or oats, should break up their stubble betimes in the autumn, and endeavour to get in some rye and vetches for early cutting. This is of immense service in April, and the early part of May, after which such ground will be well adapted for either mangold or Swedes.

Let us again advise the cow-keeper to make a point of running over all his ground once a week, in order to collect all refuse for the cow or pig. Let crops be ever so well "set out" early in the season, there will always be something which a diligent cottager can collect.

Mangold will occasionally run to seed, and so will cabbage, and as the root crops advance it will be found that some plants take the lead, and are crowded by inferior ones, which may be drawn away when about half-grown. The outer leaves too of all the green and cabbage crops will be frequently coming to hand.

MANURE HEAP.—Now is the principle period for the cottager to keep a sharp look out for all coarse weeds and gross herbage that he can justly lay hands on. We have seen cottier's children, stout boys, attending the cow when turned out in lanes (where a danger of trespass existed), who were sauntering about the whole day in idleness, when they might have been trimming with a short sickle all the rank herbage with which such lanes commonly abound. A boy thus situated would, by a little industry, collect three or four large barrowsful in the course of the day; and this, thrown into the outlet of the pig-stye, day by day, would form a most important item in the augmentation of the manure heap. Let us advise cottagers who have not already done so, to cover their previous made manure with soil rather thickly. The loss by fermentation and drying during the hot months of summer is more considerable than people imagine. We have little doubt that nearly 30 per cent. is frequently lost by evaporation, rains, &c., during July and August. The heap should be first thrown in a sharp ridge, and the soil beat firm, to throw off the rain.

THE POULTRY-KEEPER'S CALENDAR.—AUGUST.

By Martin Doyle, Author of "Hints to Small Farmers, &c."

PEA-FOWL.

ONE of the correspondents of this periodical who has not been as successful as he hoped to have been in rearing pea-fowl, has requested to have some information respecting the management of them; this will account for the introduction of a branch of poultry-keeping on the present occasion that does not apply to the circumstances of the mere cottager, who would be a nuisance to his neighbours if he presumed to keep these aristocratic birds to the injury of their limited and ill enclosed gardens. No person without a sufficient

range of lawn, and a garden distant from the poultry-yard and secured from their depredations, should think of keeping pea-fowl. A high wall is no defence against birds one of whose habits it is to fly up to the highest trees for roosting, and over walls and houses in search of favourite food, or in mere indulgence of a wild and roving disposition, which no length of forced and unnatural domestication has subdued.

It is not surprising that a pea-hen does not rear a large progeny; first, she has to contend against the desire which her mate has to destroy her eggs, she is therefore led by her instinct to lay in out of the way places where they may be lost altogether, or to hatch in some insecure though secret place, and generally on the ground among rank grass or hedge weeds. Having no very strong desire to sit, she is easily tempted to forsake her nest if disturbed. Her habit is to lay (but not before the third summer) from four or five to seven eggs, and if she is prevented from sitting on them to lay a second time after some interval. Her proper period of incubation is from 27 to 29 days, which is also the period of a turkey's incubation. Now, the turkey being a more staid and tender nurse, the best way is to give the pea-fowl's eggs to her both for hatching and rearing. But if the pea hen already have them born, it will be better to coop her for a fortnight or more, especially if she be a young and inexperienced mother; for young pea-hens are apt, with their first brood, to be over-excited, and to crush in the nest, or trample to death afterwards, or drag about heedlessly, their first born brood; and the more they are interfered with under such circumstances, the more awkward and injurious does their over-zeal and anxiety become. As medical men might possibly express such restlessness of disposition, they are apt to labour under a sort of puerperal fever, which it is difficult to cool down, and during the course of which the unfortunate chicks are in hourly danger of untimely death in various forms. The egg of the pea-fowl is somewhat bigger than that of the turkey, but of a convenient size for the incubation of the latter bird.

THE REARING OF PEA-FOWL.—The best way of rearing pea-chicks is to follow the instructions which Mr. Dixon has given for rearing little turkeys. Give them nothing at first; let them be in the nest under the shelter of their mother's wings at least eight or ten hours; if hatched in the afternoon, until the next morning. Then place her on the grass in the sun under a roomy coop. The food should be crumbs of bread, with curd, chopped egg, boiled rice, or barley-meal. and soon afterwards chopped onions, leeks, lettuces, &c.; in short, exactly as for turkey chicks. There should also be the same care to guard them from too much sunshine, and showers, and dangers of all kinds; and in due time a free range over a lawn or field should be permitted; the search for grubs, insects, seeds, &c., is an agreeable occupation both to the foster mother and the little ones, and conducive to their healthy growth. And if the stomach of the turkey chick, which is to grow so considerably in a few months, require abundant and *frequent* filling, that of the pea fowl requires at least equal supplies of nourishing food. The poult is fit for table at nine months old, and may be fattened like turkeys, and with any turkeys with which they have been familiar. They should not be confined alone for fatting, else they will pine away. We may add Mr. Dixon's receipt for cooking pea-fowls, which if not too old are of a delicate pheasant flavour:—"They should be larded over the breast, covered with paper, roasted at a gentle fire, and served with bread sauce and brown gravy, exactly like partridges or pheasants."

TURKEYS: HATCHING.—The maternal sensibilities of the turkey are not acute. She never grieves for the loss of her brood, even if robbed of it at a very early stage, as a common hen or almost any other bird would, but begins to lay again after the shortest possible grief and a short interval of rest. She is undoubtedly a stupid bird in many respects, and seems to make no distinctions of regard for the chicks of any miscellaneous brood that she may have hatched—common chickens mingled with turkey chicks and ducklings—though of different sorts and sizes, find equal favour in her sight. Two turkey hens have this season produced, in our neighbour's poultry establishment, not medley broods, but two broods of turkey chicks. One of the mothers had fifteen little ones and the other six born at the same time. They were duly cooped, and in a few days the lesser brood went over to the larger through some mysterious influences; the bereaved mother did not take the matter to heart, and when liberated from her maternal cares seemed quite happy. The other hen took care of the united families with perfect good humour. It is curious that turkey chicks should thus transfer their affections from one mother to another, and that turkey hens should seem to have no objection to admitting under their wings the broods of other hens. Perhaps in this instance there was something harsh or forbidding in the treatment of the deserted mother, or repulsive in her voice, whereas the other hen might have possessed the contrary qualities—or it might have been a natural tendency of the lesser number to combine with the greater.

FOWLS: HATCHING.—The habits, the waywardness, and caprices of fowls, are curious subjects of observation, and even after much attention are sometimes mysterious and inexplicable. We have had two recent cases of perplexity. A young Dorking hen, manifesting a strong desire to sit, was entrusted by us with eleven eggs, which were placed in a nest in a retired corner of an unused brewhouse. She sat very steadily, sometimes without leaving the nest for four successive days. Two of the eggs were accidentally broken at an early period; there remained nine to be accounted for. Four or five days before the full time of incubation, the nest was examined, and seven eggs only were in it; the hen remained on the nest immovably until the full time for the appearance of the brood had arrived, when lo! four eggs more had entirely disappeared. There remained one broken shell, from which a chick had issued, and two addled eggs! Now, besides the obvious illustration of the proverb, "do not reckon your chickens before they are hatched," there remains an unexplained mystery, what became of the six eggs of which no trace remained? Did the hen eat them to the very last atom, or did a rat or rats remove them from under her? The hen remained on two or three occasions so many days without quitting the nest for the corn and water which was on the floor beneath, that it is not improbable she had found sustenance from the indulgence of an unnatural appetite; yet would she not have left some little evidence of her crime in a fragment of shell, a bit of yolk, or a feather or membrane of the destroyed chick? Besides, though hens may have been known to eat eggs over and above the number which they could properly cover and warm, have they been known to eat those which were not in excess, and on which they had been patiently sitting? Rats are supposed to have the power of carrying off eggs unbroken with their mouth and paw or paws; and hens, which would resist their attacks on living chicks, might not venture to contend with them when stealing their eggs. We have never seen a rat where the hen sat. But on the other hand, what then became of the eggs, which were of no value to any human robber?

THE BEE-KEEPER'S CALENDAR.—AUGUST.

By J. H. Payne, Esq., Author of "The Bee-keeper's Guide," &c.

THOSE persons who, in this unpropitious season for bees, have been so fortunate as to get their glasses filled with honey will now be preparing to take them off; but I would recommend every one to do it with great caution; and not only first to weigh the matter well in their own minds, but also to weigh their hives, and if it can be satisfactorily proved that they will contain twenty pounds of honey each when the glasses are removed, all well; but if not, let the glass or box remain upon the stock hive until the bees have emptied it of its honey,—as soon as that is ascertained let it be removed.

Some persons having found much difficulty in expelling the bees from a glass or box after having removed it from the stock-hive, and others who have complained of the time occupied in effecting this object, may adopt the following very ingenious and useful apparatus invented by Mr. Antram, a clergyman of Devonshire, and which has been kindly handed to me with his permission to make it public. It is a contrivance for emptying a hive of its occupants; it may also be applied to a bell-glass or box, either at top or attached to a board on which the removed glass is placed; he calls it his

Bee Trap; and it is, he says, "an invention for taking the honey from every description of double hive, which is not only simple, but very efficacious, and entertaining to watch. I should premise, that every extra box or hive must be furnished with a second aperture, never to be opened except when the honey is to be taken. Provide a block of wood one inch longer, and half an inch deeper than the aperture, and three or four inches wide; cut the front to an angle of 45 degrees, or less, then cut out of the under part a groove the exact size of the aperture, thus leaving a thickness of half an inch of wood at the sides and top. Get a piece of talc or very thin horn (glass is too heavy), cement or gum it to a piece of ribbon, which latter fasten to what remains of the sloping front above; divide the talc into portions about a quarter of an inch wide; a tin bottom should be affixed to the whole, to which the talc must reach, and on which it must rest.

When you wish to empty a hive place this before the opening before-mentioned, and cut off the communication between the hives; the bees seeing the light will one by one push up the small pieces of talc and escape; the talc falls back in its place, thus there is no re-entering, and your hive becomes rapidly emptied. There is here no previous removing of the hive or box, no danger of a sting, and no fear of robbers; even if the queen be there, she, finding herself deserted by her subjects, will soon depart, and re-enter the stock-hive by the accustomed entrance; it acts upon the same principle as the old wire rat trap. Two loops of tin, with holes through, are added to fasten or suspend it, when there is no alighting board. It may be placed on the top of a box, but must then have a hole in the bottom, and a slip of tin by way of a back; the tin bottom may project a little beyond the lower edge of the talc in front, and indeed it is better so."

This useful contrivance I feel assured will be adopted by many persons, for it will entirely prevent the tediousness of watching a glass of honey until the bees have left it, which without this protection is at all times necessary, and more especially so when taken late in the season and robbers are on every side. I have more than once seen a good glass of honey emptied of every drop by them when carelessly left by its owner for a few hours; now, with this trap attached, it may be left even for days with perfect safety.

I have just been seeing what to me was a very pleasing sight, and would in a measure, I am sure, be so to every one, it was the apiary of a cottager, consisting of upwards of sixty hives, all well managed upon the depriving system, for he has not destroyed any bees for many years. I saw some beautiful specimens of honey in boxes holding about six pounds each, that were taken off about the middle of June; some of them were curiously fine. The neatness and the air of comfort pervading his cottage was quite as gratifying to me as the sight of his well managed and extensive apiary. His bees, without any doubt, were the means of affording him many comforts, but there was also another source from which they flowed, for upon the table I espied the family Bible, which appeared to be but just closed after the morning's gathering around the family altar—for my visit was early. I came home much delighted, and, I trust, profited by my call; and with the determination of going on to say, as I have already done, in the words of the good old bishop—Keep bees! keep bees!

I must still go on to say, that the season here has been a very unpropitious one for bees; the sudden changes from heat to cold have been very unusual. On the 22nd of June the heat was so intense that the bees almost forsook their hives for clustering on the outsides; and on the 25th it became so cold that a frost at night was anticipated. But the season for honey-gathering has not been so bad everywhere. I am happy to find, for whilst writing this paper a letter reaches me from a kindly-disposed brother apiarian in Wiltshire, whose name I have never before seen; but who, on reading my "gloomy prospects" in the apiarian's calendar for last month, very kindly gives me a most cheering account of his own apiary, as well as of those of some of his parishioners, "to cheer me," he says, "in my gloom." His account is so very different from what I have received from many other districts, that for the encouragement of other desponding ones I will relate it.

He says, "I was in hopes that all bee-masters were re-

joicing, with myself and my parishioners, at the strength
and activity of their hives; and that their prospects, far from
being gloomy, were of the most cheering and encouraging
nature. The earliest swarm with us was on May 20th, but
the weather being cold there were only two or three swarms
before the 28th; from that day up to the past week (the last
in June) swarms have been numerous and of unusual size:
so large, indeed, that my own seemed to completely fill up
the hives in which they were put. The weather has been so
beautiful throughout the month of June, and the harvest of
honey-dews so abundant, that these hives have been filled
very rapidly, and I have been compelled to give additional
room to several.

"My first swarm was on June the 1st, and was hived into
your Improved Cottage-hive (Payne's); on the 11th the
bees began to cluster at the hole, which I attributed at first
to the heat of the hives, but its weight led me to another
conclusion. I waited, however, until the 18th, when I removed the cover and replaced it by a small hive, which on
the 24th was filled with honey. On June the 2nd I hived a
swarm into a box of a Nutt's hive, and on the 19th opened
the communication with a side-box, which by the 26th contained six combs of a fair size filled with honey, all the
honey-combs of the first box being sealed up. I can speak
encouragingly of my other swarms and casts."

The two next most productive apiaries that I have heard
of are both directly upon the sea,—the one at Deal, and the
other at Wicklow, in Ireland; indeed, throughout Ireland
bees this year have done tolerably well.

ROYAL BOTANIC SOCIETY'S SHOW.
REGENT'S PARK, July 3.
(Continued from p. 244.)

COLLECTIONS OF FIFTEEN CAPE HEATHS.

THERE were two collections exhibited of such equal merit
that the judges awarded first prizes to both. One came from
the garden of S. Rucker, Esq. (Mr. Mylam, gardener). The
other from the garden of W. Quilter, Esq., of Norwood (Mr.
Smith, gardener). Both collections were fine specimens of
good Heath culture. We shall only notice those not previously exhibited this year.

In Mr. Mylam's collection, there were

Erica oblata ; a fine heath, 2 ft. by 2 ft.   *E. tricolor major* ; 3 ft. by
3 ft.   *E. ventricosa Bothwellii*; 3 ft. by 3 ft.   *E. Vernonii* ; 2½ ft. by
2½ ft.   *E. eximea* ; 3 ft. by 3 ft.   *E. inflata* ; 2½ ft. by 3 ft.   *E. retorta
major* ; 2 ft. by 2 ft.

In Mr. Smith's collection,

Erica metulæflora, *E. retorta major* ; 2½ ft. by 2 ft.   *E. tricolor Hol-
fordiana* ; a finely grown excellent heath, 4 ft. by 3 ft.   *E. ventricosa
grandiflora* ; 3 ft. by 2½ ft.   *E. tricolor elegans* ; 3 ft. by 3 ft.   *E. tricolor
Lecana* ; 4 ft. by 3½ ft.

COLLECTIONS OF TWELVE CAPE HEATHS.—NURSERYMEN.

1st PRIZE to Mr. Epps, of Maidstone.   A fine collection.
We noted especially

Erica Shannonii, *E. haliracaba*, *E. tricolor Jacksonii*, *E. Massonii*,
E. tricolor dumosa, *E. inflata alba*.

2nd PRIZE to Messrs. Rollison, of Tooting.   This collection was nearly equal to Mr. Epps's, but some were
smaller plants and scarcely in bloom.   The following were
excellent:—

Erica oblata, *E. ampullacea nana*, *E. Eransiana*, *E. Savileana
major*, *E. ferruginea superba*, *E. pulcernienta*, and *E. jubata*.

COLLECTIONS OF SIX CAPE HEATHS.

1st PRIZE to Mr. Williams, gardener to Miss Trail,
Bromley.   The best plants in this well-grown collection were

Erica jasminiflora alba, *E. Shannonii*, *E. Cavendishii*, and *E. ventricosa superba*.

CAPE PELARGONIUMS.

By this term our readers must understand the original
species as found growing wild at the Cape of Good Hope.
1st PRIZE to Mr. Staines, for

Bicolor, *ardens major*, *quinquevulnerum*, *Blandfordianum*, *bipinnatifidum*, *ardens*, and *bicolor rosea*.

2nd PRIZE to Mr. Parker, for

Glaucifolium, *reniforme*, *flexuosum*, *tetragonum*, *erectum*, *glaucum*,
Blandfordianum, and *fulgidum*.

COLLECTIONS OF CAPE CALCEOLARIAS.

1st PRIZE to Messrs. Henderson, of Pine-apple Place, for

Nell Gwynne, *Falconbridge*, *Elegans*, *Laura*, *Catherine Seyton*, and
Black Agnes.

2nd PRIZE to Mr. Leyton, Hammersmith, for

Bianca, *Fire King*, *Diomede*, *Lady of the Lake*, *Blanche*, and
Admiral.

3rd PRIZE to Mr. Gaines, Battersea, for

Panther, *Victory*, *Regulator*, *Baron Eden*, *Princess*, and *Gertrude*.

CARNATIONS.

There were several stands of very good flowers exhibited.
1st PRIZE to Mr. Wilmer, for

Solander, *Earl Falmouth*, *John Hepworth*, *Defiance*, *Brilliant*,
Wilmer's Frederick, *Wilmer's Seedling*, *Duke of Cumberland*, *Prince
Albert*, *Mr. Moore*, *Sir R. Peel*, and *Duke of Wellington*.

2nd PRIZE to Mr. Newhall, of Woolwich, for

Prince Albert, *Squire Trove*, *Duchess of Sutherland*, *Mrs. Birkett*,
Nindos, *Orlando*, *President*, *Omnum Primo*, *Juba*, *Mrs. Moore*, and *Conquering Hero*.

PICOTEES.

1st PRIZE to Mr. Turner, of Slough, for a beautiful stand
consisting of

Dodwell's Mary (a perfect flower), *Constance*, *Seedling*, *Mary*,
Heroine, *Sylph*, *Juno*, *Ne Plus Ultra*, *General Jackson*, *Beauty*, *Prince
Arthur* (a new and perfect flower), and *Duchess of Sutherland*.

2nd PRIZE to Mr. Newhall, for

Rosalind, *Ne Plus Ultra*, *Constance*, *Duchess of Sutherland*, *New
Purple*, *Shaw's Beauty*, *Norman's Beauty*, *Prince Royal*, *Lady*, *Pool
Pry*, *Lady Fowler*, *Rose*, and *Lord Chandos*.

3rd PRIZE to Mr. Wilmer, for

Ne Plus Ultra, *Peter the Great*, *Prince Royal*, *Shaw's Beauty*, *Lion*,
Heroine, *Duchess of Sutherland*, *Trip to Cambridge*, *Norman's Beauty*,
Wilmer's Seedling, and *Miss Browning*.

PINKS.

1st PRIZE to Mr. Turner, for

Whipper-in, *Great Britain*, *Diana*, *George Glenny*, *Lola Montez*,
Newborough Buck, *Criterion*, *Sappho*, *Queen of England*, *Huntsman*,
Dr. Daubeny, and *Lord Valentia*.

2nd PRIZE to Mr. Bragg, for

Newborough Buck, *Whipper-in*, *Great Britain*, *Lola Montes*, *Young's
X X*, *Rubens*, *Lord Valentia*, *Criterion*, *Duchess of Kent*, *Henry Steers*,
and *Brilliant*.

COLLECTIONS OF VERBENAS.—CUT FLOWERS.

Mr. George Smith, of Hornsey, exhibited a collection of
twenty-four varieties.   We give their names because they
were all good sorts and worth having.

Laura, *Heroine*, *Desdemona*, *Madame Buenzoa*, *Magnificent*, *Vulcan*,
Superb, *Mrs. Mills*, *Defiance*, *Niobe*, *St. Margaret*, *Unique*, *Tricolor*,
Masterpiece, *Piccolo*, *Optimus*, *Painted Lady*, *Reine Hortense*, *Satyr*,
Seedling, *Selim*, *Psyche*, *Gem*, and *Pauline*.   A prize was awarded to
them.

A prize was also awarded to C. Lochner, Esq., for a beautiful clear white Verbena, a seedling named *Bianca*.

MISCELLANEOUS.

Under this head prizes were awarded that were not in the
schedule.   A prize was given to Mr. Wigan, of Clare House, for
a neat collection of *rare cut British flowers*.   These were much
admired, both for their beauty, rariety, and the neat manner
in which they were mounted.   A prize was awarded to Mr.
Williams, for a neatly grown collection of *Lycopodiums*;
to Mr. Puryer, gardener to E. Foster, Esq., for six well-
grown handsome *Cockscombs*; to Mr. Hunter, Islington, for
three handsome *Cucumbers*; to Mr. Turner, for a fine *seedling
Pink*, of good properties, named *Sappho*, and for a second
seedling Pink not quite so good, but which will improve, it is
named *Huntsman*.

FRUIT TENT.

This was the grand attraction of the day.   It was constantly and densely crowded, from three o'clock till half-past
six, and that not by standing-still spectators, but by a continuous column of moving visitors during the whole time; and
the sight was well worth the struggle.   The fruit filled a
bench at least 4 feet wide, and nearly 100 feet long.   We
cannot pretend to give a minute detail of the various kinds of
fruit brought together that day from all parts of the kingdom.
Our notices must be brief.

MISCELLANEOUS COLLECTION OF FRUIT.

1st PRIZE to Mr. Fleming, gardener to the Duke of Sutherland, Trentham.   This collection consisted of a handsome
Providence Pine Apple; a dish of fine *Noblesse Peaches*; a

dish of *May Duke Cherries*; a dish of *Marseilloise Figs*; and a dish of good *Grapes*.

PINE APPLES.—COLLECTIONS OF SIX.

1ST PRIZE to Mr. Bray, gardener to E. Leusada, Esq.

2ND PRIZE to Mr. G. McEwen, gardener to his Grace the Duke of Norfolk.

PROVIDENCE PINES.—SINGLE SPECIMENS.

1ST PRIZE to Mr. Fleming. Weight 7 lbs. 8 oz. This was a well-grown handsome-shaped fruit.

BLACK PINES.

1ST PRIZE to Mr. Jackson, gardener to H. Beaufoy, Esq.

RIPLEY QUEEN.

1ST PRIZE to Mrs. Bailey, 26, Belgrave-square.

GRAPES.

The *black grapes* were nearly all in good perfection, being fair sized bunches, large well-swelled berries, and of a good colour. *White grapes* were not so plentiful, and some hardly ripe. There were exhibited at least fifty dishes of all sorts. Five collections of 12 lbs. each were shown. 1ST PRIZE for this class was awarded to Mr. Henderson, gardener to Sir G. Beaumont, Bart., of Coleorton Hall. 1ST PRIZE (equal) to Mr. Venables, gardener to G. Solomon, Esq., Peckham Rye. They were Black Hamburghs, and were really handsome, well-ripened, and well-coloured fruit.

THREE DISHES OF GRAPES OF DIFFERENT KINDS.

1ST PRIZE to Mr. Bennett, gardener to J. Smith, Esq., Dulwich. The kinds were Black Hamburgh, Black Prince, and Royal White Muscadine.

THREE DISHES OF BLACK GRAPES.

1ST PRIZE to Mr. Holmes, gardener to E. Garrod, Esq., of Putney Heath. These were most excellent fruit, the berries were finely swelled, of a jet black colour, and the bunches were handsomely formed.

MUSCAT OF ALEXANDRIA.

1ST PRIZE to Mr. Macintosh, gardener, Burghley House.

WHITE FRONTIGNANS.

1ST PRIZE to Mr. Moffat, gardener to the Duke of Newcastle.

VINES IN POTS.

1ST PRIZE to Mr. Northcot, gardener to Miss Wigan, Wanstead.

PEACHES AND NECTARINES

were excellent, and reflected great credit to the growers. 1ST PRIZE for four dishes to Mr. Turnbull.

1ST PRIZE for two dishes was awarded to Mr. Macintosh.

CHERRIES.

1ST PRIZE for a splendid dish of *Purple geans*, to Mr. Snow, gardener to Earl de Grey.

MELONS.

1ST PRIZE to Mr. Barnes, gardener to H. Banbury, Esq., for *Hybrid green flesh*.

STRAWBERRIES

were exhibited in great quantities, and in high perfection, both for size and colour.

1ST PRIZE (equal) to Mr. Lydiard, market gardener, Bath, and Mr. Kimberley, of Coventry.

A prize was awarded to Mr. Ivison, for an interesting collection of *Exotic fruit*, consisting of *Vanilla planifolia*, *Carica papaya* (the Papaw), *Myristica moschata* (the Nutmeg), *Xanthochymus tinctorius*, and *Physalis peruviana* (the Peru Cherry). A prize was also awarded to Mr. Bray, gardener to Baron Goldsmid, for a large tray of *citrons*, *oranges*, and *lemons*.

Such is a very brief account of this grand exhibition of fruit, the magnitude of which may be inferred from the fact, that the judges were not able to finish their laborious task till nearly 5 o'clock.

In all the departments (much against our inclination) our restricted space has obliged us to omit the names of many prize-takers, and an enumeration of their plants, flowers, and fruits. We regret this not only because it is information useful to country exhibitors, but because in gardening, as in all other arts, it is ever beneficial to inform even the humblest practitioner of what is doing in the very highest departments.

THE DOMESTIC PIGEON.

GENERAL HISTORY OF PIGEONS.

(*Continued from page 244.*)

If Buffon had said that our dove house pigeons, our *mixtures*, and even some races of our dove-cot pigeons, descended originally from the wood-pigeon, he would not have found any one to contradict him. In short, the wood-pigeon only differs from the first in its colour, which is a little more brown. It is a migratory bird, whose migrations are periodical; which is a sufficient proof that it is not a domestic pigeon rendered free. Its habits are quite different; it dwells in the most silent woods, roosts habitually, and builds its nest in hollow trees, which would appear to separate it altogether from our domestic pigeon; but, as soon as this last abandons the dove-house to go and live in old towers and the holes of rocks, we quickly perceive in its manners and plumage the first step taken towards its regeneration. This pigeon is first called a runaway, so long as it only inhabits old buildings. Its posterity quickly becomes more obedient to the laws of nature, and will fly still farther from the presence of man and bondage; it will seek in the solitary mountains an inaccessible hole in a rock, where it may, in peace and liberty, approach still closer the laws of nature; and this is the rock-pigeon spoken of by authors. Being free from all fetters, and every strange impulsion, it will soon have regained that natural timidity which renders this species so fond of solitude. The facility with which reptiles and small voracious animals are able to surprise it and its young family in the rocks, will cause it uneasiness, and oblige it to quit the place and penetrate into the heart of the forest; it will then roost and build in hollow trees. This is what the ancient authors describe by the name of the wild pigeon. But it has almost returned to its pure origin; and if it did not retain, during two or three generations, some varied and different coloured feathers, it would no longer carry any mark of its former bondage, and would be a true wood-pigeon. We see that it returns very easily to its pure origin, but when rendered captive by the hand of man, it degenerates with the same rapidity; its posterity will quickly pass through all the blendings that we have just described—if not in manners, at least in plumage.

If all that we have just said did not prove, incontestably, that our dove-house pigeons and some mixtures are only wood-pigeons more or less changed, or, to speak in the language of the amateurs, more or less ameliorated by a long succession of ages, I would cite in support of it a fact which I had just seen when I began this work. A person inhabiting the environs of Paris possesses a dove-cot near a place where wood-pigeons abound; one of them has entered into his dove-cot and coupled with a hen. Mixture, and they have already produced several pairs of young pigeons, which do not differ in any respect from the deserters. Some one has assured me that a ring-dove has done the same thing, but the fact appears to me very doubtful, because this wild bird constantly refuses to couple even with the stock dove, besides, its specific differences are incontestable in its size, form, colour, and manners.

Some varieties, then, of the dove-cot and the dovehouse descend from the wood-pigeon. But how to explain the enormous difference which exists, for example, between the Turkey-cock Pigeon and the Warted Pigeon (Bagadais),—how to persuade oneself that these two birds, so unlike in their form, their size, and all their characteristics, descend from the same stock, the wood-pigeon, which they both differ from almost as much as they do from each other?—this is a much more difficult question to resolve, and one that Buffon himself has positively contradicted. After having advanced the opinion that we have just transcribed, it would appear we must feel this difficulty still more, and retract it; he says, in the History of the Ring-dove—"As this bird is much larger than the wood pigeon, and both are very like the domestic pigeon, one might believe that the small races of our dove-cot pigeons proceed from the stock-dove and the larger from the ring-dove, the more so as the ancients were in the habit of rearing ring-doves, of fattening and multiplying them; it may be, then, that our large dove-cot pigeons, and particularly the large rough footed, came originally from the ring-dove; the only thing which would appear to contradict this idea is, that our small domestic pigeons produce with the large ones, whereas it does not appear that the ring-dove produces with the stock-dove, since both frequent the same places without mixing together. The turtle dove, which grows familiar still more readily than the ring-dove, and which can easily be brought up and fed in the house, might have an equal title to be regarded as the stem of some of our races of domestic pigeons, if it was not, as well as the ring-dove, of a particular species, and which never mixes with the wild pigeon; but we may suppose that animals which do not mix in their natural state, because every male finds a female of his own species, might mix in a state of captivity if deprived of their own female and only a strange one was offered to them. The wood pigeon, the ring-dove, and the turtle-dove never mix in the woods, because there each one finds the female the most suitable to him, that is to say, one of his own species; but it is possible that, being deprived of their liberty and their female, they might unite with the one presented them, and as these three species are very near akin, the individuals which would result from their mixing might be found fruitful, and consequently produce lasting races or varieties."

Further on, in the Natural History of the Turtle-Dove, he speaks with less hesitation:—" The different varieties (of turtle-doves) are easily united together; they may even be paired with the pigeon, and made to produce mongrels or mules, and thus form new races or new individual varieties. 'I have seen, a credible witness writes me word, in Bugey, at a Carthusian friar's, a bird born from the mixing of a pigeon and turtle-dove; it was the colour of the French turtle-dove, and retained more of the turtle dove than the pigeon; it was restless, and disturbed the peace of the dove-cot. The father pigeon was of a very small species, perfectly white, with black wings.' This observation, which has not been followed so far as to learn if the mongrel proceeding from the pigeon and turtle-dove was fruitful, or whether it was a barren mule, proves at least the very great proximity of these two species. It is, then, very possible, as we have already insinuated, that the wood-pigeon, ring-dove, and turtle-dove, whose species appears to maintain itself separately and unmixed in the natural state, may nevertheless often be united when domesticated, and that the greater part of the races of our domestic pigeons may be the issue of their mixing, some of which are the size of the ring-dove, and others, by their smallness and figure, &c., resemble the turtle-dove, and several of them, in short, belong to the wood-pigeon, or participate in all three."

Those naturalists who, without a deep examination, have adopted the opinion that all domestic pigeons descend from the wood-pigeon, are not backward in quoting Buffon to prove this; and yet we have just seen that this great man has not dared himself to decide this question in a positive manner. Some authors, and Brisson among others, have thought that the Roman pigeon was a primitive species; and that all our races come from that and the wood-pigeon, with its three varieties. I should not only agree with this opinion, but even give a greater extension to the idea; for I think that many varieties have been produced by blending the ring-dove, turtle-dove, wood-pigeon, and other strange species, but belonging, nevertheless, to the ancient Continents. As a proof of this, some wild pigeons are found in Asia and Africa, which have a great analogy of form with tha the varieties that we possess. 1st. The pigeon from Barbary or Crete, described by Willughby and Aldrovandus, is found in the two countries of which it bears the name, both in a domestic and wild state. According to ancient authors, it has a very short beak, like our Polish pigeon, and the eyes are surrounded by a large band of naked skin. 2nd. The Guinea pigeon of Brisson, or the triangular spotted pigeon of Edwards, is about the size of the Roman pigeon, and consequently one of the largest; it has round the eyes a naked skin of a bright red, orange-coloured iris, the beak blackish, with the membrane which covers it ash-coloured. 3rd. The Norwegian pigeon, from Schwenckfeld, is tufted, rough footed, as white as snow, and larger than any of our pigeons. 4th. The pigeon of the Indies of Brisson, or Edwards' brown pigeon, has the habit of frequently moving the tail like the wagtail, which would make it resemble our shaker pigeon; furthermore, it is the same size, not being larger than a turtle-dove. 5th. According to Gemelli Carreri, pigeons are found among

the Phillippine or Manilla islands which raise and display their tail like the peacock, &c.

It may be seen by this connection, and I might carry it much further, that by blending these species with them and the wood-pigeon, one might produce, in a very short time, all the most singular races, with the exception of the Jacobine and Turbit pigeons; but these last even have, doubtless, their type also, which, perhaps, will one day be discovered.

I know that this will be objected to, as I have before said that the mongrels proceeding from two different species are unfruitful; but I should reply, that nothing will oblige me to look upon the individuals I have just named as distinct species. Why should we not admit primitive races in animals, as we are obliged to do in man, according to the reasoning of enlightened anatomists? If there are pure races of white and black men, producing by the mixture fruitful Creoles, I do not see why the white Norwegian pigeon, tufted, and rough-footed, should produce barren individuals with our wood-pigeon, which has none of its characters.

DESCRIPTION OF THE DOVE-COT PIGEONS.

FOURTH RACE.

(Continued from page 245.)

TAMBOUR PIGEONS: *Columba tympanisans.*—This race appears to be one of the most pure—since if once lost there is no means of reviving it, let us take what care we may in the crossing. These birds may be known by their extremely feathered feet, the crown on their head, and still better by their singular voice.

14. TAMBOUR PIGEON: *Columba tympanisans glouglou.*—This bird is very remarkable for its cooing, which when heard at a certain distance resembles exactly the noise of a drum, from which it derives its first name; the second is in consequence of its continually making these two sounds, "glou-glou." The iris is of a pearl white, and the eyelid red—but it has no filament round the eyes; the head is covered with scales; it has a crown of feathers across the forehead above the beak, resembling very closely the tuft of a canary; it is very rough-footed and breeched, that is to say, having long feathers on the thighs, which sometimes exceed two inches; it is thickly feathered on the feet, and is heavy of flight. There are some white ones existing, but generally they are shaded black and white.

This variety is recommendable for its great fecundity. The "glou-glou" lays every month, and only waits until its young are able to feed themselves to sit again: we may reckon on eight or nine broods a year. However, these delicate birds require some attention to succeed perfectly. In wet climates and neglected dove-cots the long feathers on its thighs, being wet and dirty, stick to the eggs while sitting, and, consequently, on quitting the nest it drags them out and breaks them; or the filth that the bird carries into the nest accumulates on the eggs, forming such a thick hard crust over the shell that the young ones cannot break it to hatch, if even it has not hurt the incubation. The moulting of this bird is also more painful and dangerous than in the other varieties. For all these reasons this valuable and singular race was entirely lost in France during several years, until M. Corbié sent for a great number from Germany. If we cross these birds with another species, even with that which appears to resemble them very closely, their young ones lose for ever their peculiar voice and tuft.

15. DRESDEN TAMBOUR PIGEON: *Columba tympanisans Dresdæ.*—M. Corbié, having heard that there were some varieties of the "glou-glou" in Saxony unknown in France, sent for some immediately. Seven of them have appeared sufficiently interesting to be described.

The "glou-glou" from Dresden differs from the preceding in its plumage, which is entirely red, with the exception of the back and shoulders, these being pure white. The young ones have an entire red plumage—no part becoming white until the first moulting. The iris of this bird is yellow.

16. YELLOW TAMBOUR PIGEON: *Columba tympanisans lutea.*—Resembling the last, but with a yellow plumage.

17. BLUE TAMBOUR PIGEON: *Columba tympanisans cærulea.* This one has the head and the beam feathers of the wing and tail white—the rest blue.

18. WHITE TAMBOUR PIGEON: *Columba tympanisans candida.*—In every respect like the preceding, but all white.

19. BLACK TAMBOUR PIGEON: *Columba tympanisans nigra.* Plumage entirely black; wings striped with white.

20. GREY-HEADED TAMBOUR PIGEON: *Columba tympanisans cometa.*—Entirely black, but with a grey head.

21. ORANGE-STRIPED TAMBOUR PIGEON: *Columba tympanisans lineata-aurea.*—Wings, tail, and head white—the rest blue; the wings striped with orange colour.

(*To be continued.*)

GARDEN WALKS.

OF the many attractions our gardens contain, certainly not the least is good walks; and a few words in the way of making such may not be out of place, especially as it is a matter everybody takes an interest in; and, before entering on the subject of making new ones, let us take a glance at the various materials used for the purpose. In the first place, we suppose we must put gravel, which, by-the-bye, includes a wide range of material; next come ashes, be they from the kitchen, the iron-foundry, or the chemical works, all differing in their character; then we have cuttings—a sort of stone crushed as small as acorns in the lead-mining operations, and, probably, a similar material may exist where copper or tin is worked; then we have brick-dust, or the refuse of a pottery of unglazed ware; then there is sand of various kinds; a kind of cockle shell found on some parts of the coast makes also a pretty and useful walk; in some places a sort of asphalte or concrete is also used. Other substances are also occasionally used as make-shifts, as tan, stonemasons' chippings, small coals, &c., &c.; but by far the most of walks are made of gravel, and to them I now address myself.

Not long ago, a great authority in such matters insisted that walks, in order to be dry in wet weather, ought to be above the level of the surrounding ground; that such a plan would secure their dryness is unquestionably true, but that it would mar their appearance in an ornamental point of view is equally apparent, as it would be impossible to clearly define the edging, which would consequently be jagged, while its ridge-like look, seen where it would have been better to conceal a walk altogether, form insuperable objections to that plan coming into general use. We shall, therefore, content ourselves with remarks relating to walks whose edges are slightly below the turf or border edging which defines them; and, before commencing operations, let us examine the nature of the ground we have to traverse, and other matters.

It cannot have escaped the observation of our gardening friends how clean and dry the public roads are, even in very wet weather, in those districts termed sandy or gravelly. Even when an inferior stone is used for those roads they still are tolerably clean, compared with those in strong loamy or clayey parts, where very likely more stone is used. In the first case, most of the rain that falls is quickly carried away by the porous nature of the ground, while the adhesive cha-

racter of the latter has a contrary tendency to retain it. It is evident, therefore, when a garden walk has to be made through such a bed of retentive matter, means must be used to abstract as much of the moisture that falls on the walk as possible; and, having had a good deal of experience in forming walks under such circumstances, I beg to lay before your readers the plan I have adopted, with tolerably good success.

When a new walk is to be made in such a retentive place, let the earth be taken out to the depth of—say seven or eight inches at the side, and perhaps a foot in the middle, which will have a sort of furrow appearance—both sides drooping to it; and along the middle, deepening such furrow, lay a course of drain-tiles, carefully covering them up (and the whole walk over) with rough stones or brick-bats; both of which are better if they have been used in a building and old mortar adhering to them; worms are not then so likely to work up through, while the rain in falling is quickly carried away by the drain, which, of course, must be made to empty itself into some handy place not far off. When walks are very wide, as 14 feet and upwards, two such drains may be put, by cutting the ground into a sort of ridge-and-gutter system. I have made an area, 150 feet each way, perfectly dry by putting a series of such drains in, cutting the ground into the required ridge-and-gutter shape, in order that the rain in falling may, after passing through the gravel and rough stones, at last come to an inclined plane, at the bottom of which is the drain waiting to receive it. That something of that sort is necessary I have the most practical proof of; and if any of your readers have a large area of gravel at their front door they want to lay dry, I can assure them they may accomplish their object by doing as I have advised. And there are many places in which such an area is at the bottom of a hill, or where the alterations may have removed all porous earth or other matter.—I have no hesitation in saying, that unless supplied with drains to carry away the water that falls, no amount of stones put in will compensate for the absence of these; as, if the clay be of that retentive character I have had to deal with, water might remain in it a month before it found its way through, unless carried away by evaporation.

We will presume the ground-work intersected by drains, as above, and the proper thickness—say three or four inches of stone or brick-bats laid on; it will be now necessary to lay on something else before putting on the gravel; refuse cinders, are called "clinkers," are good, being obnoxious to worms, and very porous; coarse gravel that may be unfit for the top will also do, or anything that will keep the top material from finding its way down through, will do likewise, provided it be open enough to allow the water to percolate freely through it. Next, of course, is the top coating of gravel, or whatever you finish off with; it is needless, however, dwelling on details which every one knows, but my purpose is, to explain the system by which the foundation of walks will be found to answer the purpose of quickly dispersing the water which falls on the strata above.

I am aware, that many good useful walks have been formed by merely covering the ground some two or three inches with good gravel, and in light, open, sandy, or gravelly soils that is really all that is wanted; in such places the ground itself forms a natural drain, by which the superfluous water is conveyed away, and the only evil in that case is the liability that worms may find their way through it, but they are less plentiful in a sandy than on a moist soil; but such a course will hardly do on a bed of blue clay or tenacious loam; here something more must be done.

Of the qualities of gravel it is almost needless to speak, because few have the means of choosing, but I may observe that the gravel which binds the firmest in dry weather clings most to the feet in wet, while that which is liable to get loose in dry weather is firmest and pleasantest in wet; the one consists of a variety of small stones, imbedded in a loamy substance, which cakes as hard as a sun-burnt brick; the other is more sandy in texture, and, consequently, gets loose in dry weather. It may be proper to add, that where the former gravel prevails it is advisable to sift a portion of the very fine matter out, so that a greater abundance of stones may exist; by so doing you get rid of that miry substance which hangs so tenaciously to the feet in wet weather, the ample provision of small stones forming a sort of pavement in miniature, on which the sole of the shoe rests, the dirt being still lower, except after frost, the expansive nature of which elevating the portions containing water above the stone work, causes that disagreeably dirty feeling that many walks have at that time; the effect after rain is the reverse, this solidifies the walk. Where it is possible to have a mixture of loose, open gravel with that of a more adhesive kind, the union will be better than either alone, and some gravels consist naturally of such a mixture; but where loose gravel alone has to be used, let the top of the walk consist of very fine matter only—nothing larger than a boy's marble, as loose pebbly stones are very unpleasant to walk amongst in summer, and rolling in such cases does very little good.

The above remarks hold good when other substances than gravel are used; and certainly other things may be used to advantage. As good and, I think, as pretty walks as ever I saw were made of ashes from an iron manufactory; they were of a bright bronze colour, and the least infected with weeds, worms, or moss of any I know of. Blue stone chippings also make a good firm walk; only when any part gets loose it sets badly again. Sand, of course, gets loose in dry weather, unless in moist places, where it does very well. But by far the best substitute for good gravel is that kind of empty and *half*-decayed cockle-shell found on the shores, in places, at the mouth of the Thames; for walks much used in wet weather this is even preferable to the best gravel, while its dazzling whiteness forms a pleasing contrast with the turf through which we presume it to pass; but it must be laid on very thin, and on a bed of something firm and level, as it never binds firmly; it is better to have but little on; every shower of rain washes it and gives it a silvery appearance, which on the whole is too glaring in bright sunshine; while the fact of it being in the best order even when rain is falling is a point in its favour; and where good gravel is not to be had, I advise those to whom water conveyance may be available to inquire after shells. I feel assured they will like them. It is needless to say they soon grind down into pieces not much larger than coarse saw-dust, but still retain the same silvery hue, which, however dirtied by long wear, is, in a great measure, restored again by the first rain that falls.

Having extended this paper to a greater length than I intended, I will reserve the observations on walks on hilly places until another opportunity; but, in the meantime, perhaps some other correspondent will favour us with his views on that point, as I must confess I have been far from successful in preventing those evils which generally attend heavy rains. If some one else would kindly report a cure for such a state of things, there is none would be more grateful than I would be.   S. N. V.

EXTRACTS FROM CORRESPONDENCE.

BEDDING-OUT PLANTS.—In looking over the plan given by your correspondent, S. N. V., it appears to me that he could have improved the arrangement of the colours there shown, by introducing some plants capable of forming a better contrast than Lobelia and Heliotrope, or Cuphea strigulosa and Silver-edged Geranium; the two former being blue and dark lilac, and the latter orange and scarlet—colours that always fail in setting off each other.—R. L.

EXCESS OF DRONES.—A stock of bees, a last year's early swarm, were put in their winter quarters, a dark cold room, with several other boxes and hives, and all were taken out about the end of February and placed in their summer situation. They at first appeared as busy and healthy as the others, but after some time I found they carried in but little farina, which continued to be the case, whilst the other stocks were increasing rapidly in numbers and store. This stock appeared to decrease in both, which would have convinced me that they had lost their queen, had I not observed some drones amongst them. At this time, the second week in June, I had a hive from which I expected a second swarm if I did not give them room, so I determined to let them swarm and attempt to unite them with the unprosperous stock, and the following was the result:—The swarm came out the next day, which I hived. In the evening I fumigated the unprosperous stock, and in a few minutes found their queen, which I killed; she appeared small. The whole

number of bees were not above two or three quarts, and amongst them were many drones. As the bees did not revive quickly, I had time to examine the combs. I found brood of every stage, but to my surprise *all* that were forward enough for me to judge of were drones, and all were in the *working bees' cells*. Each cell that contained brood forward enough to require it, was elongated, to accommodate the young drone. I cut out most of this brood, and now the bees being sufficiently revived, I sprinkled them with a little honey and water, and replaced them amongst the remaining combs. Carrying them to the spot where I had the second swarm hived, I turned upside-down an empty box the exact size of the one fumigated, then placing the new swarm over it, with two or three blows beat out all the swarm into it. I now placed the fumigated box over them, and let them all remain until 4 o'clock next morning, when, to my satisfaction, I found all united in the fumigated box and tolerably quiet. I had now only to place the box in its original place, and they are prospering as well as any stock I have. I always keep a hive or two for swarms; but I work my bees on a plan much like Mr. Nutts, but on a cheaper and, I think, more simple method with every success. I use side boxes, but the only communication between them is a passage cut in common floor boards; and I have them now fast filling the side boxes, as well as glasses. I think this plan more easily managed than the storifying system, which, by the way, I cannot condemn; for on the storifying plan I took last year from one stock a box of 64 ℔, and from another a box of 63 ℔, and all were pure virgin comb, well ventilated, and free from brood or bee bread.—J. W. W.

BLACK BEETLES.—I have found my small plants just set out much eaten, and put heaps of bran covered with cabbage leaves, supposing it to be snails, and each morning find several black beetles in each heap of bran. This may be useful to some of your readers.—A CONSTANT READER.

WHITE FORGET-ME-NOT, &c.—Our obliging correspondent has had much pleasure in forwarding plants of the "White Forget-me-not" to the different applicants for it. She has already put up two and twenty little boxes of plants, and written with each to the effect, that if they do not thrive she will, upon application in the autumn, send seeds. The dry weather is against such delicate plants being removed. Some few of the recipients have written, and handsomely acknowledged the arrival of the plants. It is not at this place (Ledbury), but at Malvern, that the "Forget-me-not so flourishes. It delights in rock work, or a gravelly soil where it sows itself. As our correspondent is only now there occasionally, she cannot promise any more plants; but all who have hitherto applied shall have some. In the May number of THE COTTAGE GARDENER an application, under the initials "A. E. D.," is made for seed of the *Myosotis alba*, or "White Forget-me-not." If the address is sent to the Editor, and forwarded, a few seeds shall be sent. The plant will thrive in most situations, she believes; but it must be treated as an annual. The *Weigela rosea*, planted out in the open border about three years since, in a sheltered situation, has grown into a fine bush, and flowered nicely this year. As soon as frosts appear in the autumn the plant is entirely covered over with dry fern. Thus treated it flourishes well. It is so beautiful, that others may be tempted by this account to cultivate it. The *Plumbago Larpentæ*, respecting which there is so much difference of opinion, has succeeded at this place (Ledbury) in the open borders; and though unprotected through the last severe winter, has stood well—dying to the ground, and shooting up in the spring. As an ornament to the greenhouse or conservatory through the autumn it is well adapted. The *Anemone japonica*, and *A. vitæfolia*, form a handsome group in a flower-bed, and spread themselves so thickly as to become almost like a weed. The hybrids, too, produced by the two varieties, and self sown, are very pretty.—M. D. D. H.

PRESERVING WALL-FRUIT FROM WASPS.—As there are many wasps this year, I send you a good receipt for preserving wall-fruit from them in the autumn, which we have tried with great success. Boil large carrots in water well sweetened with coarse brown sugar (quite a syrup). Hang these carrots on the fruit-trees, and the wasps preferring them, will eat the carrots quite away, and fall down in numbers quite tipsy under the trees, when they can be killed or buried.—W. A. E.

AYLESBURY DUCKS: PEACH-LEAF BLISTERING: PAINTING WALLS.—The person from whom my Aylesbury ducks were procured, is Richard Watkins, Haddenham Lowe, near Thame. The cause you assign for unproductiveness in duck's eggs could not well apply to my case, as my stock was one drake and three ducks; no excess of polygamy it must be allowed. I have long thought of writing to you respecting that worst of all liabilities of peach-trees—the blister. The simple immediate cause I believe to be a sudden alternation of heat and cold; the one forcing an abundance of sap into the leaves, and the other expanding it before it has time to return by its natural channels. The effect is, that it bursts its filmy integument, as frozen water bursts a glass bottle. The remedy you prescribe, although successful with your trees (some other agency being, perhaps, simultaneously at work) is not always effectual. Doubtless, humidity of soil, or any other stimulant to early and excessive root action, may help to produce the evil, by encouraging premature and crude vegetation—by, in short, hastening the formation of leaves at a season of sudden vicissitudes of temperature. My soil is naturally a dry hungry sand; so dry, indeed, that I have been obliged to improve its staple by clay. This was laid on in 1848, and dug in after being thoroughly pulverized by the winter frosts. It still errs on the side of drought; the sub soil is a pure sand, with no water within 16 feet of the surface. Added to this, the surface where the peaches are is 18 inches higher than that outside the wall. From what has occurred with me, I am led to think that the disease may be caused quite as much by a feeble as an excessive root action; I mean as a subordinate cause. My strongest trees have escaped altogether; three, which have been severely attacked, are the worst-rooted of the whole. I do not think any preventive is to be relied on but protecting the trees. What corroborates the view adopted by myself, I believe, in common with many others is, that all the cases I have had have occurred on a south wall. I am trying an experiment with the view of ripening the Black Hamburgh grape on the open wall. It is painting the wall with Carson's anticorrosive paint; colour, invisible green. The difference of heat between the painted and unpainted part, when the sun shines, is greater than one would think possible. And although it is said that darkening a wall's surface causes it to lose an equivalent by its more rapid cooling, I am disposed (antecedently, however, to any experimental test), to suspect this to be mere theory, based perhaps on a sound hypothesis, but of no practical effect. Indeed, a bold ground may be adopted by stating that, if the wall be really cooler at night (and I believe it will gain far more in the day, in any case, than it will lose by night), it may be a positive advantage. Mr. Beaton justly adverted lately upon a similar subject—to the cold mornings of the tropical latitudes. This seems nature's provision intended to refresh and invigorate vegetation. But the difference by night would not, I think, be worth speaking of. Then, again, look to the waterproof properties of the paint; the wall is always dry, and, after any amount of rain, is ready to receive the sun's rays. I am persuaded that much solar heat is wasted by the porous bricks imbibing it. The macintoshed surface repels and reflects it.—REV. ROBT. BLACKBURN.

PRESERVING EGGS.—Dip fresh eggs in boiling water, and keep them in it while you count twenty. They will keep well for a long time.

COOPS FOR FOWLS.—The best I find is an old crate, which may be bought for 1s 6d. When I wish to feed the young chickens on ground oats, &c., I place the food in a crate, and the young ones get at it, while the old ones cannot.

TO CORRESPONDENTS.

CLIANTHUS PUNICEUS (Legeolium).—The minute white spots on the leaves are caused by the Red-spider. Sponge them all over with tepid water, and keep the plant in a moister air. The sticky exudation on Geranium leaves is caused by over-luxuriance. You kept them too well, both as to food and warmth. You had better grow from cuttings. The refuse of your kitchen-garden boiled and mixed with a little bran, and your butter-milk, ought to keep your chickens in good condition. Even the boiled tops of stinging nettles are nutritive.

GOATS (Busy-body).—We shall be very much obliged by the results of your experience. Your Aquarium is under consideration.

BEES: PREVENTING SWARMING (M. J. T.).—A month since you purchased a strong hive of bees, and, as they indicated swarming, you put on a cap, and supplied a side hive to them,—yet they have swarmed. Now, "a month since" was a very improper time for removing bees, except a swarm newly hived, and it was quite enough to derange them altogether; but, remember, that a "side hive" has never in a single instance been recommended by Mr. Payne. The room you gave was not the kind effectual for preventing swarming. It should have been given by placing a small hive between the one already partially filled and the stock-hive.

PAYNE'S HIVES (A Farmer).—The hole at the top of Payne's hive need not be of any exact size, so that it be more than three inches in diameter, and not exceeding four inches. The hole in the adapters should always be four inches in diameter.

PLATE GLASS (M. R. J.).—The plants would be better if they were a foot from the window, as the rays of heat and light would thus be more diffused. As you object to a thin muslin screen, and do not seem to approve of setting the plants outside, a moveable table, so that you could place them even further from the window on a bright day, would be desirable. See what was said of the contrivances of "Mrs. Think-in-Time," in reference to window-plants, in last volume.

GERANIUM GROWING (S. R. F.).—You are quite right so far. Your mixing super-phosphate with the soil, and, at once, after potting, watering with soot and guano-water, were your great errors. You are mainly right in your proposed mode of treatment, only do not cut the plants down at once, but let them stand and get dryish; and give them little water until they have broken, then shift into light soil as you propose in September, and again into good compost early in February; but do not water for three weeks afterwards with manure-water. Give them nothing but the purest water you can get, until the pots are getting filled with roots, then give manure-water occasionally, but very sparingly, until the buds show for bloom.

GREENHOUSE BUILDING (G. P. H.).—For a house 12 feet long, by nine feet wide, your back wall, in order to give a moderate fall to the glass and prevent drip, should be five feet higher than the front one. The front may consist of glass, upon a low wall of brick; or may consist of half brick and half glass. It would be convenient if the front altogether was from six to seven feet at least, to permit walking space. But this will require to be regulated by the height you can raise at the back, as when against a dwelling-house these things must be considered. You might, it is true, make a hipped roof, having the highest point in the middle, but it would be much more expensive in such circumstances, owing to the necessary gutters, &c. We do not like the idea of heating by any sort of stove fixed in the house, as has been repeatedly stated; a small flue would be much preferable, as the leaves of plants sooner tell a tale than even the lungs of animals. Hot-water would be the best; you say you cannot afford it. Many simple methods have been recommended, but the difficulty is, to get the proper materials reasonable. We have mentioned the subject to several hot-water men and foundry-folks, and hope soon to be able to get something to suit such places as yours. Allowing £1 for the boiler, and £1 4s for piping, the expenses ought not to rise into a frightful bill, as sometimes they do. Would some London friend look at the boilers of Eley and Co., City-road, near the toll-gate, and report progress; as to fitness and price, their being so easily fixed is a recommendation. We think you had better acquaint the district surveyor, for some people are so jaundiced, that they would designate a nuisance what other pure-minded folks would term an improvement.

CACTUS (A Lover of Flowers from Childhood).—Your specimen we suppose to be one of the varieties of Ackermannii. We are sorry that you have been so disappointed. You were quite wrong in potting it when it was showing its buds; unless great care was used, it was almost certain to make the buds drop. All you can do now is to keep it full in the sun inside the glass, and keep it growing for a month, by sponging its stems, and watering its roots, and then set it against a south wall, or let it remain where it is, withholding water. Never mind if the young shoots do not grow much if well roasted in the sun, and kept dry in the winter as you used to do. The old shoots will again bloom, but, nevertheless, encourage some young shoots.

FRUIT-TREE BORDER (Northampton).—Leave only five feet of border properly constituted, and thoroughly drained, and so make the substratum of the under portion of the walk so that the roots of the trees may penetrate and enjoy it. We would sooner submit to a border four feet wide without cropping, than twelve feet with it. On your wall 166 feet long, you may plant eleven trees as follows:—three Apricots, viz.—two Moorpark, one Shipley's; two Peaches—one Royal George, one late or Walburton Admirable; two Nectarines—one Elrunge, one late Newington; one Cherry—Elton; two Pears—one Neilis, one Glout Morceaux; one Plum—Greengage.

GRAPES FOR GREENHOUSE (W.).—Supposing eight rafters, say the following grapes, viz.:—six Black Hamburgh; one Royal Muscadine; one Dutch Sweet Water. Train to the rafters on the spurring system. Why had you not taken advice before building your house? We do not like your flue. You will be plagued by dry heat over its surface, and flue cleaning will be difficult. We would have had hot water pipes in a chamber; the pipes in a cemented trench filled with water at pleasure. Cannot you throw a chamber over your flue, covered with slates or slabs?

Dividing a Forcing-house (*A. Tyro*).—If you will have two small houses (for this is the effect of a partition), let us advise you to place the boiler between the two, and to carry a greater amount of piping into one of them. Thus you will have a little stove and a little greenhouse. These tiny structures, however, require much discretion in heating. In your stove place pipes in a covered chamber, as a source of bottom-heat in a cemented trench, to carry water at pleasure; the pipes, or a portion of them in contact with the bottom. On the sides of the chamber place a slide or two to permit the chamber to give place to the atmosphere occasionally; over the chamber, of course, soil for your cucumbers, &c., or sand for striking cuttings. You will, however, need a pipe outside the chamber to warm the atmosphere. We care nothing for perforated zinc plates, only let plenty of ventilation be provided by a moderate ingress of fresh air at front, and a wiry fire-escape at back. Iron boilers are commonly used.

Circulation of Warm Air (*Tyro*).—This is desirable, and to a greater or lesser extent takes place in every hothouse, as you may easily prove by suspending any light material at different distances from the roof. You will find descriptions how still further to effect it, in the writings of the advocates of poor Polmaise. A house raised in the centre with drainage or flues below, using both at back and front, and open, may accelerate this object. The most important of all is where the fresh air is heated and moistened before it circulates, and thus you can manage by having a drain in front of your house communicating with the external atmosphere, and then with the interior by means of slides opening under or by the side of the heating medium. We are not acquainted with Arnott's ventilators for the back wall of a greenhouse; any system will do that will place enough under your command. The circulation of air beneath the roots of vines, as recommended by Mr. Errington, is desirable. A cheap mode would be to have the bottom of the border covered with rubble, cross drains deeper, terminating in a longitudinal drain deeper still, with gratings over the front drain opposite every cross one, and similar gratings over the cross ones next the house.

Verbenas (*Minnie*).—You say your Verbenas were *mismanaged*, and had hardly grown anything for the first six weeks after planting, although you supplied them with liquid-manure. We have, over and over again, pointed out the fallacy of the prevailing opinion that liquid-manure will bring sickly plants to vigour. In most cases, and very likely in yours, it acted just the other way. Soft pond, or rain water is quite strong enough for sickly or mismanaged plants. Let plants get into a free healthy state first, then, *but not till then*, apply stimulating food. Your Verbenas are by this time in free growth, if so, give them liquid-manure now and they will soon make up for lost time; also stir the soil amongst them, and damp their leaves in the evening with a rose watering-pot. See also what has been said about planting temporary things amongst Verbenas and other plants when first turned out.

Moving Yellow-edged Holly (*Wilcot*).—You ask *when* and *how* you may move a yellow-edged, variegated holly. We suppose just now your holly is growing freely, making its 12-inch annual growth. Though we should not fear removing it even now with perfect safety, yet we would advise you to let it remain where it is a month longer, that is, to about the third week in August. This is our answer as to the *when*; the *how* requires a little more consideration. As the plant does not spread it may be the more easily moved. With a small cord tie up the lower branches, then mark a circle two feet from the bole of the tree, and another circle two feet beyond the first; the space between the two circles must have all the soil dug out of it—do not be afraid of going deep down; whilst this is going on let another labourer be digging a hole larger than the ball of the tree will require, making it rather deeper; fill in some of the best soil, chopped fine, and mix it with water till it forms a puddle of the consistence of thick paint. The men who are digging round the tree must gradually undermine the ball below the roots till it stands quite loose; then wrap some garden mats round, and tie the ball firmly together with a strong rope; then wrap the stem round as near the soil as possible with some old carpet or sacking; tie to the stem at that part a stout pole eight or nine feet long; then lower the tree gently down, and let as many men as are necessary to carry it take hold of the pole and remove the tree to its place, letting it down gently into the hole amongst the puddle, taking care that it is not below but rather above the general level; fill in good soil round the ball after the tree is set upright and the mats, ties, &c., removed. Mix this soil with water till it is a puddle like the bottom; secure the tree with props to prevent the winds from shaking it. Do all this rightly and we have no fear but your favourite tree will grow and flourish as well as ever, especially if the surface is covered with moss from the time of shifting it till next spring; you may secure the moss by stretching across it some rods, fastened down with strong hooks. By this method we have removed hollies and various other trees, as high even as 30 feet, with the greatest success.

Cultivation of Ginger (*E. M. E.*).—Green ginger may be easily cultivated two ways, either in pots or in a deep pit. If in pots the plants should be procured in February, or even now if you have a stove to keep them in through winter; take the plants, shake them out of the pots when at rest in February, divide them, and pot each piece into a pot 6 inches across; plunge them, as soon as the heat is temperate, in a bark pit, or a frame heated with dung like a cucumber bed, the surface being covered with tan deep enough for the pots. As soon as the plants come up give a small supply of water, gradually increasing the quantity as the plants advance in growth. By August they will be fit to take up and preserve. If a large quantity is required a deep pit of two or three lights will be necessary, the bottom to be filled with rich soil to the depth of a foot; plant the roots in this soil and line the pit with hot dung, renewing it as the heat declines. The time for planting in the pit is February or March. Water whilst growing, give air in hot weather, and in September you will have a large supply of fine ginger roots, equal to foreign.

Retarding German Asters (*C. B.*).—Your German asters and geraniums that have had their buds nipped off with a view to flower them in September, must now be left alone, or they will not flower by the time you want them (the first week in September). Asters will flower well then because they are naturally autumn bloomers; but geraniums are different things,—we doubt all the means you can use will not induce much bloom in autumn to a spring and summer flowering plant. We should be glad to know the result of your nipping off the buds; should, contrary to our expectations, buds be formed now, and be progressing to bloom, some weak manure-water once a week will strengthen them greatly, and cause them to make finer flowers, besides stimulating them to bloom by the required time. Do not repot them, as that would throw them into growth instead of bloom.

Evergreen Oak (*E. N. S.*).—We are obliged by your complimentary letter, and are happy to find The Cottage Gardener is prized by "lady gardeners." With regard to the size of your evergreen oak, of which the trunk is 10½ feet in circumference, and the branches about 290 feet, we think it is larger than any one we have either seen or heard of, and we are not surprised you should wish to clear away any obstructions to the sight of it from your window. It is a great pity that the raised bank, marked D, is so near the house. We are always warm advocates for trees and large shrubs to stand at a respectable distance from a dwelling house, for wherever trees are close to a house they render it in some degree unhealthy; unless, however, we knew all the circumstances, and saw the place, it is almost impossible to advise what would be best to do. Our present impression is that the whole bank, trees and all, not even sparing the two yews, ought to be moved to a greater distance. Unless the yews are extraordinarily large they might be moved with safety; we have seen yews moved with stems thicker than a man's body, and 30 feet high, with perfect success. This bank, &c., being moved at least 20 yards further north, you will have then a fine view of your noble evergreen oak, and the space between it and the window may be laid down with grass without any flower beds; grass is kept in order with much less labour than beds of flowers. The boundary between the pleasure-ground and kitchen-garden might be formed with flowering and evergreen shrubs; a receding portion may be made into rockwork, and a greenhouse of a Gothic form built in the centre with good effect. For the method of forming artificial rock-work, see page 232 of the present volume. We must again repeat that it is nearly impossible to give right ideas of laying out or altering grounds with the best effect, without seeing the place.

Transferring Bees (*Apis*).—We abide by what we have said before, transferring stocks is bad practice. But autumnal unions—as recommended in "Taylor's Bee-keeper's Manual," page 131, 4th edition—cannot be too highly commended. Transferring a stock is generally understood to be taking the bees from an old or ill-shaped hive, and putting them into an empty one of a kind more suited to the taste of their owner, depriving them at once of their store of honey and brood.

Bees (*M. A.*).—The best history of this insect is in "The Honey-bee; its Natural History, Physiology, and Management," by Edward Bevan, M.D. London: Vanvoorst, Paternoster-row. For gratuitous distribution, as "Payne's Cottager's Guide" cannot be had, we recommend "A Short and Simple *Letter* to Cottagers from a Bee-preserver." London: printed for the Society for Promoting Christian Knowledge. Sold at their Depository, and by all booksellers, price 3d. To prevent the stock and super-box from slipping apart in *Taylor's single bar-hive*, cut a rabbet one-eighth of an inch on the upper side of the crown board of the stock box, to fit the inside of the super; or the rabbet may be formed by putting on with brads two pieces of the above thickness. For the other information you seek see *Taylor's Bee-keeper's Manual*, pages 44, 47, and 126, 4th edition. You cannot transfer bees now with the least chance of success. You will be much forwarder by having an early swarm next year into your box. Your best plan will be to get one of Taylor's *single* box-hives from Messrs. Neighbour, or Mr. Baxter, as a model.

Bees Swarming Late (*W. A. E.*).—"In your answer to me in vol. ii., page 169, you gave me very little hopes for my hive, so I determined to run the risk of removing the eke from beneath it, which I did very successfully last September, by smoking the bees with fungus, taking off the eke, and cutting through the combs with a wire. It was done in two minutes; and had not the labourer I employed been a little nervous, I do not think a bee would have been killed. The hive was extremely populous, full of honey, and did well all winter; carried in yellow balls in February, and plenty of young bees at the end of March, so that I expected an early swarm. On the 30th of May and following week all the cottagers round saw drones, and had swarms and casts; but though my hive had done apparently as well or better than theirs all spring, not a drone was to be seen; and the bees beginning to be idle, I put the five glasses on, on the 9th of June, which they took to directly. On the 23rd of June one drone was seen in the hive, and the following day several appeared; and an immense swarm flew off, so large that one of Mr. Golding's hives could hardly hold it. As there was old comb in the hive, I hope they may do well, though so late. I put a large glass on the top of the hive, to give them room, but they have not taken to it. When the brood hatches, and they require more room, would it be better to *put an eke under, instead of the glass over*, being so late a swarm? I took the glasses off the parent hive immediately, and found five pounds of honey in. A fortnight after the swarm flew off—viz., 8th of July—a cast of good size came. This I hived in another of Neighbour's cottage hives, and in the evening put it (after opening the holes at the top) under the parent swarm, and they have united well." It appears that bees having been stupified with fungus, &c., never do so well as those that have not been treated in that way. The "large glass" should *not* have been put on until 18 or 20 days afterwards, and not then unless room was *absolutely* wanted. *Put no eke under*, and take the glass off if there is only a few bees in it. Uniting bees in the way you have done, by placing them in a hive under the one you wish to join them to, is very bad; you risk their being all killed. Join them in future as directed at page 104, vol. ii., of THE COTTAGE GARDENER.

TAYLOR'S HIVE (*Ryde*).—Mr. Taylor having given models of his hive to Messrs. Neighbour and to Mr. Baxter, we do not feel at liberty to give working drawings. You were right in raising the part of the floor-board within the hive an eighth of an inch, to prevent the hive slipping aside. There is no objection to the thermometer you have introduced. Your elevation in the crown board as in the floor board is right. You will see how to fix the cover of the super-box at page 47 of Mr. Taylor's book. The lower edge of the super-box ought to rest on the bars. The roof should not be solid. The openings under the cornice, convey air only between the super-box and the cover. The super-box is *not* to remain on in winter. The roof should be merely placed upon the crown board of the stock box. To remove the crown board of the stock box, take out the screws, and then pass a very thin knife between the bars and the crown board. For the feeder required, see Mr. Taylor's book, page 126.

PAYNE'S HIVES (*Q. Q.*).—The drawing, No. 5, you sent, is *not* Payne's Improved Cottage Hive. His costs 1s 6d, but your No. 5 costs 33s. We recommend your waiting till next year before you purchase No. 7; it will, by that time, have undergone some very considerable alteration. A shed will render the use of pans or zinc covers unnecessary. The shed you mention had only roof and sides, open back and front; south aspect is certainly the best. Mr. Farwell, of Wolverhampton, has Payne's hives in use.

BEES (*An Unfortunate Bee-keeper*).—Your bees, without doubt, swarmed on the 28th. You had better not smear the box with honey. Your bees having swarmed, you must not expect any honey from the boxes or the glass. It is very likely that a second swarm will leave the hive, which will now be comparatively useless to you.

STEELE'S HAND-BOOK OF FIELD BOTANY.—The abbreviations we are told, for we have not a copy, are explained at page 4 of the work. The asterisks, daggers, &c., we are also told, are chiefly to mark with greater clearness the several sections.

CATERPILLARS AND ANTS (*A Constant Subscriber, Netherton*).—Dust the caterpillars, by means of a dredging-box, with the powder of white hellebore. Ants do as much good by killing the green fly (*Aphis*) as they do harm by eating the ripe fruit. We are quite sure that ants do *not* eat the leaves of the peach.

TORTOISE (*W. D. Payne*).—In hot weather the tortoise will drink, or, at all events, put its head into water if placed before it in a shallow dish. It should be fed with lettuce and dandelion leaves, and with soft fruits, such as strawberries and the flesh of cherries. It becomes torpid in the winter, and to prevent its being killed by cold, it should be taken into the house and placed in a box filled with hay. If it revives before green food can be obtained, it will eat bread sopped in milk.

LAVENDER (——).—This should be picked either for drying or for distilling just after the flowers have opened.

INDEX (*T. Lindsay*).—Thanks for your suggestions. We do not think our readers object to refer to four indexes for what they require. When we become more voluminous we will publish a general index.

QUEEN OF BEAUTY FUCHSIA (*Ystrad*).—The bloom from your cutting is paler than that from the parent, but the colour will be uniform if grown in similar soil and similarly cultivated next year.

PINE APPLE PRESERVE (*M. B.*).—Cut off the rind, and cut the pine apple into tolerably thick slices; boil the rind in half a pint of water, with a pound of powdered loaf sugar and the juice of a lemon, for twenty minutes. Strain this liquor, and then boil the slices in it for a quarter of an hour. The following day pour off the syrup and boil it again, removing the scum as it rises; put the slices into the jar where they are to remain, and pour the liquor hot over them. When cold, place a paper dipped in brandy over the preserve, and tie the jar down with bladder. You will see some valuable hints on the best and most economical modes of preserving in the present number.

SAVING STRAWBERRY SEED (*Currig Cuthol*).—The best mode is that chiefly adopted by the French. Collect a sufficient quantity of well-shaped and well-ripened berries. Put these berries upon a plate, and set them in a dry place out of the reach of mice. They will then decompose and dry up. No danger is to be apprehended from the berries becoming putrid or mouldy, for the decomposition of the pulp tends only to perfect the seeds. The strawberries thus dried are to be kept till the following spring, when, by rubbing them between the fingers, the seed may be easily separated from the remains of the pulp, which may be thrown away as useless, and then the seeds will remain unmixed and almost perfectly clean. If seed from Alpine strawberries was saved from the finest and earliest ripening berries, it ought to be as good as that from France.

Fuchsia seed is obtained by keeping the berries until quite dry, and then crushing them. In *The Cottage Gardeners' Dictionary* all the points you name will be attended to.

WORK ON AMERICAN PLANTS (*B. le B.*).—A very good and cheap one has lately been published, entitled "Waterer's System of growing the Rhododendron, &c., &c.," by W. B. M'Person. Simpkin and Marshall, publishers. We know of no separate publication on the Cedar tribe.

NAME OF PEA (*Groniensis*).—Yours is the Tamarind pea. One of those with skinless shells, and, therefore, boiled in the pod. You will see more particulars in our list at page 194 of our third volume.

BRITISH PLANTS.—A clergyman wishes for some rooted plants of such species as *Cornus Suecica, Saxifraga stellaris, Rudbeckia purpurea, Gentiana verna*, &c. We shall be obliged by information where they can be obtained.

GOATS (*T. Woolley*).—There is no book upon the management of goats, but there is a paper upon the subject in one of the volumes of the Royal Agricultural Society. You will see, to-day, that we are promised information from one who says he has long practical acquaintance with the subject.

RABBITS' DUNG (*A Constant Reader*).—A very good liquid-manure can be made from this by putting a peck of the dung to thirty gallons of water.

POTATO STEMS (*Hawthorn*).—We incline to your opinion that those inclosed by you were attacked by the potato murrain, but we cannot decide without having a doubt, they were so flattened and dry. The affection seems confined to the very top of the stems, and if so try what effect cutting off these tops will have. On no account cut off the stems to any great extent, for that will destroy the crop under any circumstances. They are late sorts, which are always most open to injury from the murrain.

PELARGONIUM UNIQUE (*J. M. B.*).—This may be obtained of any florist who advertises in our columns.

HEATING GREENHOUSE (*J. S. L.*).—So far as keeping up a sufficient temperature in a house, 14ft. by 10ft., there is no doubt that a Walker's stove of moderate size would be sufficient; but it is a mode of heating among the very worst that can be adopted.

HIMALAYAN PUMPKIN (*R. O.*).—For greater security, you may impregnate the flowers as you would those of the melon; but the bees will do it for you.

GLYCINE SINENSIS (*Ibid*).—This is now called *Wistaria Sinensis*. The best mode of propagating it is by layers, made any time after the fall of its leaf. Your plant is *Echium vulgare*, Common Viper's Bugloss.

SEEDLINGS (*M. H.*).—All these are not carnations; even the glaucous-leaved one is more like a seedling pink. The pea-green coloured seedling is a China pink, *Dianthus Chinensis*. You may have many handsome flowers from your seedlings, however, if you plant them out in some border, and can select from them when blooming.

NAMES OF PLANTS (*R. A., Barming*).—Your plant is a *Commelina*, but we cannot tell the species from your fragment. (*T. M. W.*).—Yours is *Lycium Europæum*, or European Box Thorn, called the Tea-tree by many people. We cannot tell you of any book from which you can learn the names of plants, unless you understand botany. If you do, *Loudon's Encyclopædia of Plants*.

GREEN PEAS TO PRESERVE FOR WINTER USE (*X. X. X.*).—Shell full grown peas; scald them; dry them by spreading them on cloths; harden them by putting them on dishes in a cool oven, keep them in paper bags hung up in the kitchen. To cook them, let them first be for an hour in water; then set on to boil in cold water, with a piece of butter, and boil until ready; boil a spoonful of sugar and a sprig of dried mint with them.

VARIOUS QUERIES (*Ibid*).—We do not know how Bass's *pale ale* is brewed. Any gardener will give you a cutting in November of a *Black Hamburgh* vine, to plant against your south wall. The best *ventilator for a bed-room* is a balanced trap-door opening into the chimney from near the ceiling. For the centre of your little garden have the hybrid China Rose *Adolphe*, budded as a standard.

CALENDAR FOR AUGUST.

GREENHOUSE.

AIR, give plenty night and day, especially during the former. In very hot weather, it is often advisable to keep rather close with a moist atmosphere during the day, even though the sashes should be entirely removed in the evening, to be replaced in the morning. This treatment will apply to *Heaths, Azaleas, Camellias*, &c., that are now making their growth. Those which have set their buds may be removed to a sheltered place, and have no glass protection for a time. CINERARIAS, propagate by rooted slips, and transfer the earliest to blooming pots. PELARGONIUMS; those done flowering cut down, and now pushing again may have the soil shaken from them, be placed in light soil, and in a close moist pit, to encourage free growth. In growing from cuttings, success will greatly depend in never allowing them to stand still, but keeping them constantly, but slowly, growing. BUDDING and SUMMER GRAFTING must now be finished. GREENHOUSE PLANTS IN GENERAL, if healthy and their wood made, will be better out of doors in a sheltered place than within; defending the pots from being too much heated in sunshine is even of more importance than shading the tops. ALL YOUNG STOCK growing freely begin to harden by exposure by the end of the month. CHRYSANTHEMUMS, SALVIAS, &c., for winter blooming, set in an open place fully exposed to sun and air. The former must not be stopped any more. The latter should alone receive final stopping and shifting. PROPAGATION: almost everything may now be successfully propagated. CLIMBERS, on the rafters train when over rampant, but the more natural looking the better. GATHER SEEDS of all desirable things as they ripen. The propagating of half-hardy things, such as CALCEOLARIAS, may commence about the end of the month. About the middle of the month, SOW SEED OF HERBACEOUS KINDS in a cool pit. DRESS, tie, surface stir, and keep all neat and clean. R. FISH.

ORCHARD.

BUDDING, finish and remove bandages from that done three weeks since. Remove waste shoots from stocks, especially below the bud. BLIGHT (American), apply the brush once more, using spirits of turpentine. APHIDES: still try to extirpate them in peaches, plums, &c. RED SPIDER: if this appears, dust flowers of sulphur on the back of the leaves. COCCUS, or scaly insect: if this appears, use soap-suds. FIGS, continue to disbud, and commence stopping rambling shoots. VINES, follow up stopping of laterals, and keep them thin, also thin the berries. APRICOTS, stop gross leaders, and keep down breast shoots by pinching. PEACHES and NECTARINES, stop all gross shoots, and keep under breast wood by the same process; where too thick, remove shoots altogether. PEARS, remove foreright spray, cutting one half away of moderate shoots, first selecting and tying down all short-jointed and brown-looking wood. PROTECT fruit with nets, &c. WASPS, destroy nests. Late STRAWBERRIES, water well. ALPINES, reduce runners from, and place slates or tiles beneath. STRAWBERRIES, make plantations of early and strong runners. RASPBERRIES (double-bearing), remove all barren shoots from, and carefully train those in blossom. TOMATOES, thin, stop, and train. Commence and complete, as soon as possible, all NAILING and TRAINING, whether on walls, pales, or espalier trellises. GOOSEBERRIES, still continue the extirpation of caterpillars. BUSH FRUIT, retard by shading with mats. GRAFTS, remove stock shoots from, and protect from wind waving. R. ERRINGTON.

FLOWER GARDEN.

ANEMONES, sow. ANNUALS, stick; water; clear from decayed leaves, &c. AURICULAS, shift into fresh earth; water; seedlings prick out; sow. BEDS, in which bulbous flowers have grown, fill with annuals from pots, to flower through autumn. BIENNIAL seedlings, transplant. BULBOUS-rooted flower-seeds as *Iris Xiphium*, &c., to obtain varieties, sow. BULBOUS roots, remove or transplant; remove and plant offsets; (Autumn flowering), plant. CARNATION layers cut from old root and plant; water frequently; layering may still be done, b.; card the flowers and shade from sun. DAHLIAS, stake; thin the flowers. DAISIES propagate. Put in CUTTINGS of all flower-garden plants early; keep them in the cutting-pots through winter. DOUBLE-blossomed perennials with fibrous roots, as fine double *Larkspurs*, &c., propagate by division, e. DRESS borders as required. EDGINGS of box, &c., clip in wet weather. EVERGREENS may be moved, e., if wet weather; plant cuttings. GRASS, mow and roll weekly. GRASS SEEDS may be sown, e. GRAVEL, weed and roll weekly. HEDGES, clip in moist weather, except laurel and holly hedges. HELIOTROPES, put in cuttings under glass in a gentle heat, b. MIGNONETTE sow in frame, b. PELARGONIUMS propagate by cuttings, b. PERENNIALS, in pots and elsewhere, will require water almost daily; cut down flower-stalks as they finish blooming; seedlings transplant. PIPINGS of Pinks may be planted out. POLYANTHUSES, sow. PONDS keep clear of green scum. POTTED ANNUALS will require water daily in dry weather. RANUNCULUSES, sow; plant in pots to bloom in November. ROSES, bud; prune in strong straggling shoots; cuttings of China and Tea-scented varieties plant under hand-glasses. Roses may be budded to the end of September on the Manetti and some Bourbon stocks. September is the best time to bud, unless done at the end of May. SEEDS, gather as they ripen. Even those of Heliotropes and Verbenas will frequently be found to be fertile. SHRUBBERY, cut off the bunches of seeds of Laburnums, and Lilacs, &c., to strengthen the bloom next year. SOWINGS, to obtain varieties, had better be done in boxes. TEN-WEEK stock, sow, b. TULIPS, and other bulbous-rooted flower-seeds, sow. TURF may be laid, e. VERBENAS, put in cuttings of new kinds, e. WATERING will be required generally in dry weather. WEEDING, generally attend to. *Cuttings* of Penstemons, Snapdragons, double Lychnis, and other herbaceous plants, will yet succeed, if planted and shaded under hand-glasses. Of the *China Asters*, mark the finest, and save for seed. D. BEATON.

ORCHID HOUSE.

HEAT: if the weather continues warm no fire will be needed; but should cold nights and gloomy days visit us, towards the end of the month a little artificial heat will be necessary. AIR, give in moderate quantities to the Indian house, and more freely to the cooler. DYING LEAVES AND FLOWERS remove daily, as in this department they quickly rot and give out a bad effluvium, offensive to the visitor and injurious to the plants. MOIST ATMOSPHERE must still prevail internally, as most of the plants will now be rapidly forming their new pseudo-bulbs. REST: several species will by this time have fully made their annual growth, refrain then from watering, and, if possible, remove them into a cooler house. INSECTS, look after and destroy diligently; they breed fast at this season. SYRINGE the growing plants the same as last month. T. APPLEBY.

PLANT STOVE.

ACHIMENES going out of flower place in a cold pit and give no water to. CUTTINGS of various stove plants may yet be made, and placed under bell-glasses in heat; cuttings rooted should be directly potted off, and placed in a close heat till they begin to grow again. GLOXINIAS going out of bloom set out of doors, give no water, and as soon as the leaves are quite dead remove them in their pots into the place where they are to remain till spring; do this before there is any danger of frost. GESNERIAS, treat similarly. IXORAS, finish potting for the last time. PASSIFLORAS, and all other creepers, reduce within bounds by pruning and tying in. RED SPIDER, a most tiny yet destructive insect, we wage continual war with; wherever a leaf is seen spotted the enemy will be there; frequent sponging is the best remedy. THRIPS, a scarcely less destructive enemy, may be killed by washing the flues or pipes with sulphur, and smoking the house severely with tobacco two or three nights in succession; wash the house all over with soap and brush towards the end of the month. OLD STOVE PLANTS grown straggling, cut down, and give no water till they begin to grow again. T. APPLEBY.

FLORISTS' FLOWERS.

AURICULAS AND POLYANTHUSES, continue in their summer quarters, but keep clear of weeds and slugs. CARNATIONS AND PICOTEES, finish layering the beginning of the month. DAHLIAS, shade, tie effectually, and water freely. LAYERING is a good way to propagate: layer *Pansies* and *Pinks*, and various other plants. Every attention must be paid to keep everything going at the right time. RANUNCULUSES must all be taken up immediately, and put away till spring. TULIPS must also be taken up, if not done already. SEEDS of various kinds must be carefully saved before they drop out of the seed vessel. Let neither WEEDS nor VERMIN of any kind be allowed at any time, or in any place. T. APPLEBY.

FRUIT-FORCING DEPARTMENT.

As long as the temperature will permit, admit AIR day and night. Allow the TEMPERATURE to range, with sun-heat, from 65° to 85°, and during night from 55° to 65°. Give the last shifting, early in the month, to those PINES intended for early fruiting next season; let others follow in succession; keep down superfluous suckers. Clear ripe GRAPES from all diseased and mouldy berries; admit abundance of air. Keep down, or rather keep *away*, the RED SPIDER, by lighting a fire in dull days, and brushing the pipes or flues with a thin mixture of sulphur and water. Thin freely the late crops, and water the VINES in dry weather, also use mulchings. Give to PEACH-HOUSES, from which the fruit has been gathered, copious syringing; and shut the houses rather close, to raise their temperature by sun-heat, that the wood may be hardened and ripened before ultimate exposure by removing the sashes. Stop and thin shoots in late houses. Regulate the shoots and set the fruit on MELON plants, also use manure-water liberally. Strike cuttings, or sow seeds, of CUCUMBERS intended for a late supply. Encourage the completion of growth of all PLANTS IN POTS intended for forcing, and place those fully matured by the back of a north wall. Lay STRAWBERRIES in small pots, to be shifted into larger. Turn BARK BEDS. PAINT, wash; clear out furnaces; empty and rinse out boilers; and have everything in readiness for a cold weather campaign. R. ERRINGTON.

KITCHEN-GARDEN.

ALEXANDERS and ANGELICA, sow, and earth growing crops. ARTICHOKES, cut the heads from, whether required or not; for if allowed to run to flower the roots are exhausted. ASPARAGUS, attend to (see JUNE and JULY); and should it happen that the stems be top-heavy, and fall over the pathways, tie them to sticks, rather than cut them off. BORAGE, sow; and thin out advancing crops to a foot apart. CABBAGE, continue to sow until the 12th of the month of any favourite kinds, and a little *Dutch Red*. CARROTS, sow Early Horn in warm borders, for early spring use. CAULIFLOWERS, plant out and sow about the 21st, in open warm borders, in order to have a good supply of plants to stand the winter. CELERY, plant out and earth up advancing crops. CUCUMBERS, attend to topping, thinning, and clearing away decayed leaves, either in pits, frames, or out-doors crops. Cuttings may be struck of any favourite kinds, for autumn and winter growth. ENDIVE, plant out, and sow; tie up or cover over full grown, for blanching. MELONS, attend to; give plenty of air to those ripening-off fruit; be very sparing with the water-pot among them; encourage the growth of the younger crops just swelling-off their fruit with about three liberal waterings of manure water, given from the spout of the water-pot; let these liberal waterings be given principally at the back part of the beds, and not over the crowns of the plants; sprinkle almost daily in dry weather at shutting up time. ONIONS, sow, to stand the winter, about the first week of this month, the silver-skinned kind being the most hardy sort; press down the stiff-necked among the present advancing crops, and pull up those that are full grown, and lay them on their sides to dry-off well before storing away. SPINACH, sow of the winter or prickly-seeded kind, from the 1st up to the 12th of the month, in well prepared borders or beds in the open quarters. TURNIPS, sow of the best small early kinds, and thin-out advancing crops. VEGETABLE-MARROWS attend to, thin, and train out. Keep a watchful eye to the different kinds of SEEDS, and collect them as fast as they ripen, or the birds will make havoc among them.

GENERAL SOWING.—Although *cabbage* and *endive* were sown in last month for winter and spring supply, yet August is a much more important month for general sowings; and if the season is lost, it is never regained. From the 1st to the 12th of the month nearly all the before-mentioned seeds should be sown, *cauliflower* excepted, which should be sown from the 21st to the 24th. In all cases, should the weather be dry and hot, water well before sowing the seeds, and screen through the day from hot sun. Sow in open healthy situations, rather than under walls, and such places, so that you may raise stocky, sturdy plants. Sow thin, rather than too thick, in all cases. T. WEAVER.

LONDON: Printed by HARRY WOOLDRIDGE, Winchester High Street, in the Parish of Saint Mary Kalendar, and Published by WILLIAM SOMERVILLE ORR, at the Office, No. 2, Amen Corner, in the Parish of Christ Church, City of London.—July 25, 1850.

WEEKLY CALENDAR.

M W D D	AUGUST 1—7, 1850.	Weather near London in 1849.		Sun Rises.	Sun Sets.	Moon R. & S.	Moon's Age.	Clock bef. Sun.	Day of Year.
1 Th	Lammas Day. Swallow's second brood fledged.	T. 74°—45°.	W. Fine.	25 a. 4	47 a. 7	11 a.29	☾	6 1	213
2 F	Large Egger Moth seen.	T. 74°—55°.	S.W. Fine.	26	45	morn.	24	5 57	214
3 S	Mugwort flowers.	T. 67°—39°.	N.E. Rain.	28	44	0 2	25	5 53	215
4 Sun	10 SUNDAY AFT. TRINITY.	T. 70°—41°.	N.E. Fine.	29	42	0 43	26	5 48	216
5 M	Mushrooms abound.	T. 72°—42°.	S.E. Fine.	31	41	1 33	27	5 43	217
6 Tu	PRINCE ALFRED BORN, 1844.	T. 80°—44°.	W. Fine.	33	39	3 34	28	5 37	218
7 W	Name of Jesus. Honeysuckle berries ripe.	T. 83°—50°.	W. Rain.	34	37	rises.	●	5 30	219

Even as late as the end of Henry the Eighth's reign (1546) it was the custom of the queen to send for a salad to Holland ; and his daughter, Queen Elizabeth, when endeavouring to improve our horticulture, had to rescue it from that shameful dependence, thought it wise to seek for instructors in the same country ; she obtained from thence one TREDESKIN, or TRADESKIN, to be the Royal Gardener, who, with his equally celebrated son, are especially entitled to our notice. JOHN TREDESKIN, or, as it is now usual to call him, TRADESCANT, was not gardener to Queen Elizabeth only, but probably held the same appointment in the royal households of her successors, James and Charles I., for when he died about this time in 1637 he was succeeded, as gardener to the king last named, by his son, usually known as John Tradescant *the younger*. There is no record of his burial, but in the Churchwarden's accounts for 1637-8 of the parish where he resided, St. Mary's, Lambeth, there is this funereal entry—"*Item. John Tredeskin; ye greet bell and black cloth, 5s 4d*." His wife had died three years previously, for in the same parish officer's accounts for 1634 in this acknowledgment—"June 1. Received for burial of Jane, wife of John Tradeskin, 12s." The emoluments arising from the office of Royal Gardener were considerable ; money was then five times more valuable than now, yet even then the gardener at Hampton Court who was also a foreigner, John Dinye, another of the royal establishments, received about two shillings per day, and Tradescant probably, as the head cultivator of the London establishments, would receive more. It is, moreover, certain that he had profited both in acquiring knowledge and wealth by being gardener to the Lord Treasurer Salisbury, Lord Wotton, and the Duke of Buckingham, previously to succeeding to the royal gardenership. He was devoted to his profession, and travelled far more assiduously and fearlessly in pursuit of plants than did his contemporary Gerard ; the emblematic figures still traceable upon his tomb in Lambeth churchyard seem to have reference to his visits to Greece, Egypt, and Barbary ; and he even accompanied the fleet sent against the Algerines in 1620, for no other purpose than to obtain a supply of Algier apricot trees : he was successful in his enterprise, and our gardens were also indebted to him for a new strawberry from Brussels, and a superior variety of plum from Turkey. Our pleasure grounds also were enriched by him with the deciduous Cypress, and many flowers. He lived and died, at the date we have stated, at his house in South Lambeth, and surrounded by the plants and curiosities he had collected in such abundance that the garden and establishment were known popularly as "Tradescant's Ark." His son, JOHN TRADESCANT, JUNIOR, succeeded him in his appointment, and was in every way his equal as a gardener, naturalist, and antiquary. He also was a traveller in search of plants, visiting Virginia in 1626, and bringing thence many new plants ; among these was the *Spiderwort*, and if this was named after him *Tradescantia*, in allusion to his fondness for antiquities, it is a satire not severe enough to be offensive, nor within the just reproof—"If you crown a botanist let it not be with thorns." We have before us that rarity—a perfect copy of his catalogue, with portraits of his father and himself, entitled *Museum*

Tradescantianum; or, a collection of rarities preserved at South Lambeth, near London, by John Tradescant. This was published in 1656 ; and that it did contain rarities our readers may judge when we state that one item is, "Two feathers of the Phœnix tail !" The list of plants in this catalogue is far more rich and authentic, for he was here a teacher and not a novice ; and it is gratifying that the very spot is known where they were cultivated by him ; it is close to the vinegar manufactory of Messrs. Beaufoy ; and when visited by Dr. Watson in 1749 a few plants were detected among the weeds—"manifest footsteps of the founder." That spot is yet worthy of a pilgrimage, and we wish the garden could be found there entire, to reward the research of each palmer of science, instead of being almost traceless, and associated with many details of sorrow and shame. Tradescant found himself in old age childless ; and he tells us of the departure of the last of his descendants, when, in all the simplicity of true grief, he states that his catalogue had been long before written, when "presently thereupon my only son died," and for four years it was passed aside. Mr. Ashmole, a man of congenial pursuits, lodged in Tradescant's house, and the childless couple, for Tradescant's wife was a party, by a deed of gift (we use Ashmole's own words) "bestowed upon me their closet of curiosities when they died." Tradescant died on the 22nd, and was buried on the 25th of April, 1662, and Ashmole has the boldness to record his own baseness when he enters in his Diary, under the date of May 30th—*May of the same year !*—"This Easter Term I preferred a bill in Chancery against Mrs. Tradescant for the rarities her husband had settled on me." In two years he records that his suit came to a hearing, and he evidently was foiled, for he does not state the result, and the widow remained in possession. But the antiquarian vulture was not to be baffled ; he hung upon the aged widow, and, we may be sure, importuned and dogged her, and was impatient that death did not sooner render the gift-deed operative. At length he prevailed, and tells us in his Diary—"Nov. 26, 1674. Mrs. Tradescant being willing to deliver up the rarities to me I carried several of them to my house." This (taking from the old widow three relics and remembrances of happier times seems to have continued at intervals, and then came the fearful ending, which the spoiler shall tell himself. "1678, April 4. My wife told me Mrs Tradescant was found drowned in her pond !" We have erred—this was not the end ; for next year Ashmole obtained a lease of the poor old widow's house and garden, and the name of Tradescant is but associated with that of Ashmole, though his "closet of curiosities" formed a part of what is now the Ashmolean Museum. We are aware that there is a document in the Bodleian Library purporting to be signed by Mrs Tradescant, acknowledging she had vilified Mr. Ashmole ; but who shall convince us that that signature is genuine ?

METEOROLOGY OF THE WEEK.—At Chiswick, from observations during the last 23 years, the average highest and lowest temperatures of these days are 74·4°, and 52·9°. The greatest heat, 92°, was on the 1st, in 1846, and the lowest cold, 36°, on the 6th, in 1838.

INSECTS.—About April may be seen in bake-houses and mills—especially in those not kept very dry and scrupulously clean — a pitch-black beetle, with wing-cases regularly furrowed ; antennæ,

though eleven-jointed, short ; and with feet and some of its edges rather rusty coloured. This is the *Tenebrio molitor*, the grubs or larvæ of which are the *Meal Worms* so destructive to flour kept in damp, ill-ventilated stores, and to biscuits during long sea voyages. These grubs—the favourite food of the nightingale when in an aviary—are of a dirty-white colour, 13-segmented, smooth, and soft. They are the

more destructive because they will remain two years in this form before entering the chrysalis state.

RANGE OF BAROMETER—RAIN IN INCHES.

Aug.		1841.	1842.	1843.	1844.	1845.	1846.	1847.	1848.	1849.
1	B. {	29.923 29.790	30.277 30.218	29.934 29.849	29.807 29.732	29.732 29.578	29.758 29.670	30.818 29.944	29.669 29.369	30.117 30.053
	R.	0.02	—	0.02	0.05	0.05	1.23	—	6.34	—
2	B. {	29.937 29.765	30.183 29.979	29.750 29.691	29.908 29.744	29.818 29.340	29.830 29.642	30.944 29.827	29.949 29.880	30.139 30.092
	R.	0.39	—	0.08	0.11	0.61	0.65	—	0.10	—
3	B. {	29.091 29.411	29.950 29.609	29.574 29.551	29.469 29.486	29.764 29.630	29.905 29.861	30.609 30.003	29.856 29.707	29.997 29.965
	R.	0.38	—	1.63	0.15	0.10	0.04	—	0.15	0.02
4	B. {	29.785 29.365	29.902 29.899	29.596 29.567	29.833 29.563	29.564 29.581	29.912 29.922	29.945 29.741	29.671 29.652	29.979 29.900
	R.	—	—	0.18	0.01	—	0.85	0.02	0.05	—
5	B. {	29.742 29.609	29.930 29.901	29.959 29.774	29.833 29.612	29.672 29.597	29.920 29.827	29.640 29.505	29.552 29.429	29.939 29.803
	R.	0.01	—	0.02	0.37	0.62	6.43	6.28	0.11	—
6	B. {	29.851 29.663	29.937 29.844	30.116 29.990	29.587 29.592	29.824 29.778	29.906 29.635	29.733 29.505	29.775 29.859	30.048 29.939
	R.	0.07	0.15	—	0.02	0.12	—	—	0.12	—
7	B. {	29.803 29.798	29.963 29.859	30.311 30.191	29.656 29.621	29.786 29.738	29.747 29.693	29.773 29.723	29.639 29.984	30.062 30.019
	R.	—	—	—	0.12	0.24	—	—	—	0.17

The great horticultural exhibitions of the year having now closed, we naturally pause to consider—What good have they achieved? And we respond at once, as our conviction, that their benefit has been great. We have seen gathered together, in the tents of the Regent's Park and Chiswick Shows, thousands of specimens of perfect plant culture, and there exhibited to hundreds of cultivators, who thence might learn what could and ought to be effected in their own stoves and greenhouses. Each specimen was a warning to some against neglect, and to others a stimulus to fresh exertion. Such meetings, too, bring together amateurs and gardeners from wide-apart districts : thus facilitating that interchange of ideas, that renewal of old intercourse, which does more in one hour than even the penny postage can promote in a year's correspondence. There is nothing like personal evidence and cross-examining a witness to get quickly at the whole of a truth. Then there is, also, the worthy emulation among the exhibitors—that best stimulus to good cultivation, when a gardener who loves his employment has the opportunity of seeing the specimens of his skill exhibited well-honoured among those of the best gardeners of the world, and before the critical eyes of thousands who know what ought to be the aspect of each flower and fruit. For such reasons the contest for prizes has ever been a cherished mode of promoting skill, and such contests have never ceased among civilized nations from the days of the Olympian games; nor will they cease from increasing, we hope, until every village has its cabbage and rose show. The principle is sound, therefore the results are salutary : and the more salutary, the wider it is brought into operation.

But another question presses upon us for an answer: Do these exhibitions effect all the good of which they are capable? and most emphatically do we answer—No ! We look upon the Horticultural and Royal Botanic Societies as national institutions, and we think that, instead of holding their meetings year after year at Chiswick and the Regent's Park, that each of their meetings in every year should be in some distinct district of England. The legitimate intention of such societies is to promote throughout the length and breadth of the land the onward progress of horticulture; and the prizes they have to give away, and the worthy emulation they call into activity, should be as widely diffused as possible. Why are the plants of Mrs. Lawrence and of Mr. Colyer, year after year, the only competitors for the greatest prizes? Not because there are no other collections that could bring twenty such plants into the arena, but because those praise-worthy exhibitors are near to the place of competition; and it would not be difficult to point out many counties which would turn out their thirties, twenties, fifteens, and sixes, if the Societies had their arenas opened within a come-at-able distance. It is a reply, but of no weight, to observe, that Messrs. Veitch send up plants from Exeter, and Mr. Epps from Maidstone ; for these, and such as these, are the exceptional cases—the rule is, that growers at a distance from London do not send.

What we have said about the benefits derived from such exhibitions apply with redoubled force to them held in country districts, whereby thousands of amateurs and gardeners would have the opportunity of seeing the results of the best gardening of our time, who now have no such opportunity once even in a life time. It is not for us to enter into details to show that all difficulties in the way of such country meetings might be readily obviated; but they could be so obviated, and we are quite sure that railway companies and every one else interested in the prosperity of gardening—and who is not?—would unite in facilitating so desirable an object, as they have done, and still do, to promote the similar meetings of the Royal Agricultural Society.

Lastly, we are quite sure that it is bound up with the prosperity of the two societies to hold such country meetings, for they may rest assured that their incomes will go on gradually declining if they do not. That of the London Horticultural Society fell off no less than five hundred pounds last year ! and why, but because distant subscribers grow weary of receiving but little in return for their annual payments, and of having none of the advantages enjoyed by London resident members. He knows little of human nature who expects that year after year a man, living in a distant county, will pay two guineas a year, to receive in return a quarterly journal, which he can obtain through his bookseller for half the money. But if the meetings were occasionally held within such a distance of his home that his own plants might sometimes have a chance of being placed in the floral race,—and if he could thus be enabled occasionally to exercise some of the privileges of other members resident nearer London, not only would each old subscriber continue to contribute, but largely would the list of members be strengthened. Gladly should we see this, for we know the good such societies can work out; and we also know that their power to work out that good is proportioned to the strength of their funds and the wide diffusion of their members.

So great has been the advantage which we have found, during the present year, from the use of the ammoniacal liquor of gas works to Asparagus, Rhubarb, Cabbages, and other kitchen garden crops cultivated for their production of leaves, that we wish to have a little pamphlet, advertised in our columns to-day, distributed as widely as possible, for the purpose of inducing others to give it a trial.

A correspondent (F. L.), referring to our observations at p. 234, inquires, " if there is any simple means of testing the difference between hard and soft water?" The following is a satisfactory reply to his query :—Let him dissolve a piece of white soap, the size of a nut, in a wine-glassful of alcohol (spirit of wine), and put a small teaspoonful of this into a wine-glassful of the water to be tested. In distilled water no change is apparent after this addition ; but it will cause in any other water a milkiness more white in proportion to the greater degree of its hardness. *All* spring and river water will shew some milkiness when thus tested, but by comparing together three or four the eye soon learns to detect immediately the soapy solution is added, whether the water tested is unusually hard. The milkiness is caused by the alkali of the soap quitting its oily or fatty matter, and combining with the acid of the earthy or metallic salts in the water, and constituting its hardness; whilst the earthy or metallic bases of those salts unite with the oily or fatty matter of the soap, and their being insoluble gives the milky appearance.

In connection with the subject of impure water, we may notice that leaden pipes and pumps are always to be avoided for the supply of water, and the rather because the more pure the water the more readily does it dissolve the lead. Where such metallic apparatus is employed the water previously to use should always be filtered through sand, for this has the providential power of separating from it the leaden contamination. Some year or two since the royal stag-hounds were supposed to be affected with a particular foot-lameness or paralysis from drinking water conveyed to them from Bagshot, through leaden pipes; and Professor Clark, commenting upon this, says :—

" Some of the Bagshot water alluded to had poisoned some of the Queen's hounds, and brought on *colica pictonum* in one of the huntsmen. Through the kindness of Sir James Clark, I obtained a specimen of this water, and in a few days came to the unexpected result, that filtration would separate the lead. Thus a very simple practical means for separating lead, wherever it contaminates water, was discovered. At a marine villa of Lord Aberdeen's some of the servants suffered in health from lead in water derived from pipes. Sand filters were put up under my direction at this villa, and subsequently at Haddo House. On making inquiry, recently, of his lordship's agent, in Aberdeen, I learn that the filters have been in use ever since, and that the waters have been tested from time to time, without any lead having been discovered in them. I have been told, indeed, that so satisfied has Lord Aberdeen been with the result, that on hearing of the Count de Neuilly's family at Claremont being troubled with lead in the water, he wrote, recommending the same process being tried there; and, from general rumour, I had previously heard that the process had been adopted there.

" I hold it in all cases to be dangerous to allow water to pass through any considerable length of lead pipes, or to allow water to remain for a long time even in short pipes. In the case of the marine villa before alluded to, the water came a considerable distance through lead pipes; I suppose above a quarter of a mile. The water in Aberdeen is brought from the iron mains in the streets, into the houses, by means of lead pipes; and in general without any disadvantage, because the supply from the pipes is constant, and the use of the stop-cock very frequent in a family; but in my class-rooms and laboratory I find that whenever a pipe has been out of use for a few days, the water taken from it affords a trace of lead, which disappears when the water has been allowed to run briskly from the stop-cock for a few minutes."

We now come to a consideration of the consequences of using hard water for cooking, washing, and other household purposes, and we will in the present instance confine ourselves to *tea-making.* Upon this we have the following evidence of M. Soyer, late cook of the Reform Club, and of Mr. Philip Holland, the practical chemist.

M. Soyer, examined—

"Have you made the examination as to the comparative effect of waters of different qualities in the preparation of tea?

Yes, I have. In making the experiments, as time is of importance for the effect as well as for economy, I thought it proper to take an account of it. For culinary purposes I am confident that that water which boils the quickest is the best; and I conceived that this might be ascertained in respect to tea. I took samples of the common tea in use by the population, green tea, and tea of a third class, and prepared them with equal quantities of water: I took, as the standard of soft water, distilled water, which I obtained from Apothecaries' Hall. The whole results were more striking than I had previously anticipated. The softest or distilled water had an extraordinary power in obtaining a quick extract; the result showed perhaps too high a power, for it draws out the woody flavour. Next to it was the Artesian well water, which is one-third less hard than the Thames water. I should indeed prefer that water to any other tried in these experiments: although the distilled water draws out the aromatic property of the tea more than the Reform Club water, it does not I think produce so good an extract. Each water gave its own shade, and had its own distinct extract. Finding the results so extraordinary, I solicited the assistance of two friends, Messrs. Hooper, the most eminent tea-tasters in London: the results were the same, and the following table gives the conclusions I came to :—

Kinds of Water.	Time taken to boil.	Their rank in making of Tea.	REMARKS.
Distilled water from Apothecaries' Hall	Min. 5½	2	
Covent-garden, an Artesian well*	8½	5	* Impure as if it contained iron.
Reform Club, 306 ft. deep,† and Trafalgar-square	6½	1	† This well has been sunk ten years ; the pipes are the same as at first laid down, but they are all blistered. This makes tea one-third more than any other water.
Camden Town, sunk 208 feet in the chalk‡	8		‡ This is the well sunk by the North-Western Railway Company for the supply of their locomotives. I moved the machinery for manufacturing the nectar into Whittlebury-street, close to Euston-square Station, in order to receive the advantages of this water, and paid a large sum per annum to the Company to obtain it ; but I find, that the water in passing through the iron pipes from Camden Town to the station becomes so impregnated with iron as to cause it to be considerably altered in its nature. This fact may be seen by the deposit of iron it leaves at the urinals in the station : it likewise makes deep grooves in the pipes, as if planed out with a machine.
New River, from a cistern in Bulliter-street, City	8	3	
Welleclose-square, a spring	10		
Camberwell, a sunk well 60 feet deep§	10		§ Camberwell is considered the hardest water in the vicinity of London.
Thames, from Hungerford, 2 hours after high water ..	9½	4	
Standard solutions of lime-water, reckoned according to Clark's scale of hardness :—			‖ Of the three, No. 2 is by far the best.
2°‖	7	6	¶ Very impure, and boils with a scum upon it.
9°	7½	7	
16°¶	8½	4	

" Are you confident as to the difference in the time of boiling between hard and soft water?—My experiment was with pints of water, in the same size stewpan, with a gas lamp, so that the heat was manageable, and the same in both cases; and there was certainly a difference of full two minutes in favour of the boiling of the soft water; and the same result was given in several experiments.

" From these experiments, and your extensive knowledge, will you state the general results as to the relative power of the hardest and the softest water in making tea?—I should say that whilst with the hard water three cups might be made; with the soft water about five might be made.

"What extra expenditure of tea then would the use of the Thames water incur in making tea?—Nearly one-third.

"That is on all the tea consumed in the metropolis?—Yes, I have no doubt of it."

We must reserve Mr. Holland's observations and our own comments until next week.

THE FRUIT-GARDEN.

ROOT-PRUNING.—It will appear strange to some persons to talk of root-pruning when trees are in full-growth, but in all probability a better period cannot be chosen than the end of July, for to delay longer with subjects requiring the operation, especially if trees of tender habit, is to lose a good chance of facilitating the ripening of the wood. Late growths are antagonistic in all cases to the latter process, and if any one doubts it let him note his fancy pear-trees at this very period; he will find two kinds of shoots—the young ones we mean—quite distinct in appearance and in character: the one, brown, and peculiarly short in the joints, has ceased growing, or, rather, extending; the other, pale-coloured, with the joints or internodes much longer; these shoots, probably, growing still, or they have but recently ceased. Now, it is tolerably obvious that the brown and early ripened shoots here adverted to are earlier developments; they are, moreover, in all probability, the produce of buds which had gained at least one step in advance in the previous year towards the consummation of nature's ultimate design—the fruit-bearing condition.

Some may ask, "How is it that this process of nature is frequently so indeterminate in character?" To this it may be answered, that the reproductive principle is so dependant on a given amount of light and heat, together with an immunity from those sudden impulses arising from an undue amount of moisture fitfully received at certain periods of high root action, that any serious derangement of these great conditions necessarily produces anomalous appearances. Hence the embryo blossom-bud—at least that which, through a concurrence of the above circumstances, had advanced a stage or two in the way of elaboration, and, we may add, concentration—suddenly becomes converted into a growing shoot. Who has not seen the common *Rhododendron* in such an anomalous position? Who has not seen a *Rose* shoot protruding from the centre of a blossom? These, although (it may be) not correctly classified in the eyes of our first-class men of science, are yet thrown into a position which will aptly enough illustrate the matter in hand, and plainly enough show that in such cases some of the great ends of nature are baffled for awhile, and that "circumstances (as say the lawyers) alter cases."

Thus much for the rationale of the affair; come we now to the practical application of the principle of root-pruning as applied in July or August.

The first thing to name is this: let every one count the cost before he proceeds. By this we mean, that because root-pruning is perfectly correct as a last resort, let no person root-prune indiscriminately at any period, more especially at this. Such a proceeding would be what Brother Jonathan terms "going the whole hog;" now this going the whole hog is not quite right at all times in gardening matters, it is rather too sweeping an affair. Let us put a case:—One of our worthy amateur friends has a favourite *Peach* or *Nectarine*, a tree which covers many square feet of walling, and which never yet carried a full crop; it is time, how-

ever, says experience and science, that it should do so. Certainly it has two or three dozen of fine fruit on this year. What, then, should be done? Now this is a case which requires a moderate degree of patience; and well it is that there exists no act of parliament to *compel* a worthy amateur to crop his roots in the month of August. Our advice is, forbear until the fruit is gathered, and then proceed but by degrees. Throw open a trench—a thorough excavation down as low as the roots go—but take care even then that you are at a safe distance, for we do not wish you so to mutilate the roots as that the leaves shall forthwith be cast through sheer exhaustion. This done a few days, will show whether the process has had a strong effect or not on the system of the tree. If the leaves actually flag, be assured that the tree has had enough of it for the present; if you see no difference during a hot sunshine, prepare for another instalment of punishment, by opening the trench a little closer, and by carefully searching for very deep roots, on which have no mercy.

Now, what we say of the peach and nectarine applies to all our other fruits, with some trifling modification of practice. No tree with which we are acquainted bears a more severe mutilation in this respect than the pear—its vital powers are immense. Under all circumstances of dwarfing, however, and early bearing, let no one hesitate to root-prune in a judicious way; all fruit-bearing trees which show signs of that invincible-looking coarseness in the young growth, which is the certain concomitant, or, as the case may be, precursor of barrenness.

Nor need the operation be confined to the fruit-bearing trees of the kitchen-garden. The *Mulberry*, the *Walnut*, the *Chestnut*, the *Ornamental Thorn*, with indeed a host of other things liable to an amount of luxuriance which is inimical to that early fruitfulness which (although not nature's way of proceeding) is adapted to the wants of man; all will submit to the same operation, provided it is applied *judiciously*. Judicious! Yes. How much meaning is comprised within the bounds of this simple term.

Who has not heard of persons famed for certain practices, and whose name has extended far and wide; highly esteemed in a circle capable of appreciating their merits? And, again, who has not heard of projects of note from them being either passed over as crotchets, or set aside for years after "a false start" or two? The late lamented Mr. Smith, of Deanston, how frequently has he been misunderstood in his great efforts to ameliorate and deepen the thousands of acres in Britain, which for generations have thirsted for *judicious* improvements? "Thorough draining," said Smith, "and then follow with your subsoiling; thus and thus only can the mechanical texture be altered in a permanent way." Many, however, subsoiled first and drained after. This indeed made all the difference; still it was called "Smith's plan."

We name these things merely to caution our readers as to how they carry out the principles of Mr. A. or Mr. B. A mistake, through a non-appreciation of the dictum of the above singularly gifted teachers, will mar the success of the whole proceeding.

By judicious, we not only mean correctness in the time of operation, but in the extent of it. This will have been guessed at by our previous digression. It will be far better than in the case of trees carrying a small crop of fruit, to postpone the root-pruning until the fruit is gathered; for why should the proprietor be disappointed in his few jargonelles or his greengages, when the process will do as well, or nearly so, in September or October? Still it is possible so to open a trench at such a distance from a tree carrying a little fruit, as to do little or no injury to the fruit. If such is done, we see no reason to object to it; and the trench should remain out until October, when a second portion of roots may be cut away, and the trench filled in. This practice, however, is too unsightly in dress grounds to be generally recommended, as the hillocks of soil here and there detract much from the general neatness.

It is very difficult to convey a just idea of the amount of roots necessary to be removed to persons not accustomed to the practice. We know of no better plan than classifying all fruits under four different sections, as to habit, which may stand as follows :—1st. The gross. 2nd. The luxuriant. 3rd. The thriving. 4th. The weak. Now it will be obvious that No. 4 does not belong to our present subject; it is a proper case for a rich top dressing, or renewed soil. No. 3 also requires little meddling with. We have now to come to some definition of the terms "gross" and "luxuriant," than which (although, perhaps, not perfectly satisfactory) we can find no better terms to express what we would convey. In order, then, to be understood, let us take the case of two young peaches—say the Royal George—growing side by side on a wall. The one had made shoots three feet long by midsummer, at which period all the coarsest shoots had their points pinched away. Since then they have put forth side spray, which has been pinched again, and again they are branching as fast as ever. This we call a case of grossness.

And now for subject the 2nd. This had grown also nearly a yard up to the same period, and some of the shoots were pinched; instead, however, of subdividing into a profusion of watery spray, they have remained stationary, or nearly so. This, then, is a case of luxuriance. This tree is strong and hearty; the former is what gardeners term "wild."

Any person, indeed, however ill-informed on this subject, may soon take a few lessons from Nature's self, by watching for a few weeks, in the height of summer, the growth of various trees. The indications before alluded to will soon become manifest, and a little attention will render them familiar as the alphabet.

And now as to the distance at which to operate in July or August root-pruning. Few fruit trees in kitchen gardens, under a training or dwarfing system, extend roots of any consequence above six feet from the main stem. Here, then, is a safe distance at which to commence operations. We are now speaking of trees nearly or quite full grown. In such cases the luxuriant tree may be cut at about this distance, whilst in the case of the gross tree about one-third more of the space between this point and the tree stem may be cut. This latter will be a severe operation, and will, indeed, be carried to within four feet or so of the stem.

In the case of young trees, a year or two after planting, they may generally have a trench opened to within half a yard of their stem. The vital forces are so active in the latter class, that a severe operation is much sooner recovered from than in older trees; and we must, therefore, recommend our readers to think of this when root-pruning, and to suffer their operations to be biassed in some degree by it.

Some writers on root-pruning advise that the excavation be filled with rich soil or compost. We do not advise this course. It is quite sufficient to introduce fresh turfy soil, if to spare.   R. ERRINGTON.

THE FLOWER-GARDEN.

PROPAGATION BY CUTTINGS.—No one who has experienced the annoyance of losing a host of little half-starved plants in the winter, and who is at all aware of the fact that plants from cuttings made late in the autumn are so weak in their constitution that it tries the skill of a good gardener to preserve them half alive over a long winter,—I say no one who knows all this, or

even the half of it, will assert that it is too soon now to put in all the cuttings which he may require or can procure. Hotbeds for cuttings in September, unless very slight indeed, are an abomination altogether for amateurs; and those writers who recommend this—the largest class of the community—to trust to hotbeds for a stock of plants, and say it is time enough to think of putting in your cuttings this long while yet, ought themselves to be put into these very hotbeds and nailed down till they were half stifled and gaping for breath; they would then better understand the difficulty of tending hotbed-struck plants during the winter, for they would probably find out to their cost that after being half smothered themselves in a stinking hotbed, they would have little relish, and less ability, to stand against a November fog. It is just so with little bits of soft plants that are half stifled in these beds, to get them to root late in the autumn. But I shall be told of the success that has attended late autumn propagation for years, by Messrs. So-and-so; and I allow it, and I can vouch for the fact, for in 1840 the first cutting for the flower-beds in this place, Shrubland Park, was made on the 10th of October; yet the beds were as full and gay in 1841 as they were before or since. But then look at the machinery that was put in motion to bring up lost time,—whole ranges of hot-pits with linings, hot water pipes, and what-not, and a dozen or more men to attend to them. But where is an amateur, with only the assistance he can get from the pages of a little twopenny book like this, that could manage to fill one small flower-bed next year, if he were to put off his cuttings till next October? No; amateurs ought to have all the cuttings, or rather all the plants they require for "stock" next spring, struck before the end of August, and that without any assistance whatever from hotbeds. Then, to inure the whole of them to stand out of doors through September, and as far into October as the frost would allow of, but to guard them all the time from heavy rains, to nip off the points of the shoots, and at every other joint, as fast as they grow, and after "housing" them for the winter to allow them as much air as the state of the cold will permit, and to keep the pots for the whole winter in that happy medium we call between wet and dry. Let any one who doubts the possibility of keeping these soft plants alive during a long winter try this plan, and begin it immediately, and I am sure he will never put off his autumn propagation again till September, or even to the middle of August.

The Anagallis was mentioned as a sample of what I think would be the safest course to pursue with any plants that are found difficult to manage in winter. By keeping over a few plants of such at the time of planting out in May, they are sure to be strong enough to stand rough treatment in winter, where young autumn-struck plants of the same kind would be sure to die before Christmas. The Double American Groundsel I instanced already as belonging to those tender things, and after that one's own experience, can fill up a goodly list; besides, what one man finds easy to keep another cannot keep at all—so that all of us must make our lists from our own experience, rather than from printed ones; and I should make it a standing rule that whatever plant I found ticklish to stand the winter with me, should henceforth be put on the list of troublesomes, and be propagated at the end of spring for storing, instead of in the autumn.

There is a second class of bedding plants which differ in different soils and under different management; the Heliotrope will represent this class, which includes all those plants of which it is difficult to get good cuttings in the autumn, or which root unwillingly even if they can be procured. Almost every plant will strike from cuttings in the spring, but now the case is different; the shoots are either too thick and succulent, or they are flowering shoots that do not root easily, or there is hardly any short young wood fit for cuttings on them. Whenever one meets with a case of this description, the best remedy is to keep a few reserve plants in pots all the summer, from the spring propagation. There is a section of the fancy geraniums or pelargoniums which every one thought very difficult to root in the autumn a few years back; *Queen Victoria* and *Prince of Orange* are fair examples of this class, and so is *Lady Flora Hastings*, of which I have this season the best bed I have yet seen, from plants that are four years old, which were almost neglected, as I did not use this variety for beds these three years. About this time last year I cut down these plants and shook the soil from them in the usual way, and they were kept cool all last winter and spring, so that they made very slow growth, with thick, short-jointed branches, just the reverse of what it usually is. They were planted out last May, and have done remarkably well, so much so that it is restored into the bedding catalogue again, although there is hardly an end to the varieties of these speckled geraniums for beds, and many of them are of the same class as *Queen Victoria* in respect to propagation.

There is a clever gardener now in the north of Ireland, who lived with me here some years since, and I well recollect of an argument we once had about striking cuttings. He, and another man who is still with me, maintained that every plant—no matter from what country, or of what nature—if it made shoots fit for cuttings, such cuttings could be made to grow; neither of them being then aware of the peculiarity of this section of geraniums, which were new to us at that time. To try their skill to the utmost I offered to give six cuttings to each of them, and in six weeks if one cutting out of the six was rooted I would give the lucky propagator five shillings for it; and when I told them the cuttings would be geranium cuttings I had some difficulty to persuade them to the trial. "Oh! they did not want to be bothered with things which Aunt Harriet and her maid Susan, down at ——, could do as well as any gardener." However, with a little soft reasoning, they did undertake the trial, and lost it completely; for I believe they tried many cuttings of these geraniums in various ways, but not a single one of them did they root the whole season. Now, this will sound odd to those not aware of the fact, that a section of geraniums will not strike from cuttings in summer, except in one particular way; but so it is, and this *particular* way happens to be the easiest way of all to strike geraniums—which is just as curious the other way. Not many months back two of our very best gardeners asked me very seriously if I knew how the *Unique geranium*—one of the finest of our bedding varieties—could be increased abundantly in summer, and some told me they could not strike it at all, except in the spring, and that they were obliged to keep plants in pots on purpose for spring propagation, as I have been recommended to do with the Anagallis, &c.; and not only that, but when these plants were in the prime of their bloom in September, or earlier, they were under the necessity of cutting them down like the old sorts, in order that a stock of young shoots might be made before winter, that would come in for cuttings early in the spring, and this is, by the way, a very judicious way of managing every one of this section. But yet it is not at all necessary to sacrifice one's flowers in September, and later, for the *Unique*, in particular, if stopped back two or three times in July and early in August, will go on flowering down to near Christmas.

The gardener who first wrote to me how to root *Queen Victoria geraniums* from summer cuttings, is now in charge of one of the largest gardens in the United States of America; and I hope he will see his laconic

receipt in print. It runs as follows:—" Put in the cuttings under a north wall, and do not water them or look at them for three months, and they will be sure to root by that time." And true enough they will; and that is the only way to overcome their natural disposition for blooming; and as long as they are in a flowering condition their whole strength seems to be turned that way, and they will not root. But cut off the supply from the roots, by making them into cuttings, and place these cuttings as far from stimulating agencies as can be, and immediately they cease blooming, and turn their exertion the other way and form roots. If, on the other hand, after we have detached portions of these plants and made them into cuttings,—if we continue the stimulus of high cultivation,—inclose them under hand-glasses or in close hotbeds, where the confined damp atmosphere is grateful to vegetation, we merely check their usual growth, not stop it altogether; and as long as they grow at that season they will flower and not root; for it seems foreign to their nature to carry on the two processes at one and the same time. Hence *the true cause* of the complete failures which attended the first attempts at striking cuttings from these plants while they were in blooming growth, so to speak. My friend's advice about such cuttings must not, however, be construed too literally. Although it is essential to success that an entire absence of growth be insisted on while the cuttings are forming their roots, it will be equally requisite that everything which tends to damp or otherwise injure soft cuttings should be guarded against. If we attend to these, and see that an entire cessation of growth in the leaves is maintained as long as the roots are forming, all these geraniums root as freely through the summer months as *Tom Thumb*, or any other scarlet geranium. Yet, when one has plants of any of these shy rooting sorts in pots, it is a good plan to have them cut-in by the end of August, and to grow them on freely to Christmas; to stop them in October, or November, or when they have made four joints of young wood, and after that stopping to let them grow on till a hotbed or some hothouse is at work in early spring, and then to make cuttings of all the young tops; if one could then—say in February—force them gently for a month or six weeks, another and a double crop of spring young cuttings could be procured before the end of March, that would soon root in bottom heat, and be ready to plant out in beds by the middle or end of May.

A celebrated flower gardener from Surrey called here this morning, who makes these and, indeed, all the bedding geraniums his chief bedding stock; and although he is well versed in all the leading sorts used round London, he was much surprised at the number of varieties we use here. He never saw the *White Unique* as a bedder before; and I had some white seedlings of the *Perpetual-flowering Geraniums*, with very small crumpled leaves, with which he was particularly pleased; and he agrees with me how desirable it would be to follow up these small leaved crosses. I wish I could urge on breeders to turn their attention to this class of bedders of the striped varieties. He thought *Spleenii* was my best; but to do it full justice it should be planted in poor light soil, as it is a free grower, which the other striped ones are not—I mean such as *Sidonia* and *Diadematum bicolor*.

I received many good hints from this visitor, of which I shall make use in these pages, as relating to a plant on which I lately wrote—*Tropaolum speciosum*. He told me the best way is to let it remain in the ground all the winter, and then it is as strong as *Tropaolum pentaphyllum*, and will cover a great breadth of trellis, flowering in the sun just as freely as on the north side of a wall. One is always pleased meeting with a frank, candid person, who will tell just what he thinks if his opinion is asked; because more than one-half of the gardening world think it the best policy, first, to ascertain, if possible, your own opinion on a point or subject to be discussed, and then to give their vote on your side of the question, without reference to the merit of the case, but simply with a view to please, if not to flatter you. I would not give a straw for such opinions.

My visitor was a true blue on this point; he told me plainly, before we entered the flower-garden, that he was totally at issue with me—personally a stranger to him, and an older man by a score of long years—on the subject of *annuals*. Of course he was—and so are all the great guns; but that does not alter the matter one jot; before we got over half the garden he expressed himself favourably on the way I use these annuals—and so does every one who sees them; and what everybody says must be true. And it is hardly less true that I am the only gardener in the country who puts ephemeral annuals to their legitimate purpose; with them I fill the beds brimful in May, in the spaces between the permanent plants, and in one week after planting the beds are more full than some I could name are in two months.

D. BEATON.

GREENHOUSE AND WINDOW GARDENING.

IMPREGNATING AND HYBRIDISING.—As a continuation of last week's article, and because no better time than the present can be chosen by amateurs for making their experiments, we shall, in a random manner, glance at some of the results of a knowledge of the sexual system in plants, and, secondly, allude to a few principles to be kept in view by those inclined to making hybridising experiments.

First. Most cultivators of flowers grow their plants chiefly for their bloom; in many of these the parts of fructification—the stamens and the pistils—owing to their being almost inconspicuous, present few claims upon our observation. Unattractive though they seem, however, the beautiful flower petals are the guard which nature has stationed for their protection and security. When the fertilization of the seeds has been effected, the swelling of the seed vessel is generally accompanied by the fading of the flower petals; hence some of our friends who are somewhat enthusiastic in their love of flowers, should have the openings in their plant-houses surrounded with gauze netting, which would allow air to enter and yet keep out bees and all flying insects. No sooner do these little artificers get in among your prettiest fuchsias, geraniums, &c., than the process of fecundation is prematurely, as it were, hastened, by their liberal scattering of the pollen, and, as a consequence, the bloom is prematurely shed. In cases such as we have alluded to, where the stamens and pistils are not very conspicuous, the netting may be dispensed with, by cutting them out either with a knife or a small pair of scissors; the removing of the female organ alone will be sufficient; the bloom will stand much longer in consequence. The course to be attended to when double flowers are the object has already been noticed. Is it desirable to save the seed of a certain flowering plant, or vegetable? True, it must be kept far apart from others of its kind, or, if that cannot be done, the plant as a whole, or the particular flowers selected, should be covered with gauze so open as to permit light and air to enter, and yet so thick as to prevent the intrusion of insects and pollen borne by the winds. Even in the kitchen-garden, our cauliflowers, cabbages, Brussels sprouts, and borecoles, being merely varieties of an original species, would soon revert to the primitive type if care was not thus taken in growing them for seed.

Again. Barrenness often takes place in plants even though there be plenty of flowers, because these flowers are wanting in the necessary organs of reproduction. When the principal organ, the pistil, is absent, as will frequently be found to be the case if the plant has been unduly shaded the previous season, or if there has been a cold, wet autumn, which has been more favourable for the *growing* than the maturing principle, then our knowledge will be of no avail for that season. But, on the other hand, when the stamens are either altogether wanting, or so miserably small as to be deficient in pollen, then the remedy is easy and obvious; by means of a camel hair brush, a soft feather, &c., transfer the pollen from those flowers where it is plentiful to the pistils of those where it is deficient; and, better still, where the fertile flowers would stand thinning, cut a number out when the anther boxes are opening, and place or shake them over the pistils you wish to fertilize. In the case of large trees, fertile branches might be thinned out, when in bloom, and placed in proximity to those that were imperfect. Last season we obtained a fair crop of *filberts* from trees that were next to destitute of male catkins, by cutting a quantity of hazel branches from the hedges when the male catkins were opening, and tying them among the filberts, leaving the wind to waft the pollen to the little red blossoms. "Oh! but did not you get nuts instead of filberts?" said a friend, who stoutly contended, that a melon not coming true was owing to its growing beside a different variety. No! this artificial impregnation, this hybridising, very seldom effects much apparent difference upon what is *commonly* termed the fruit—the rind and pulp of a melon, the shell and kernel of the nut, the pulpy matter of the peach, the juicy consistence of the apple or pear, the berry of a strawberry, or the seed vessel of any plant we cultivate. The appearance is generally exactly the same as if fecundation had been effected by its own appropriate pollen. It is in the seeds, the true fruit, that the change is effected; the plants and flowers raised from which may be expected to be different from both parents, and yet exhibiting features of both. Thus every man who has only a few inches of ground, such as may be set in his window-sill, or on his balcony, has it in his power to introduce improved varieties of flowers and vegetables, and thus constitute himself a public benefactor. Amateurs and cottagers have in general more opportunities for this than gardeners. Thus it is our best varieties of flowers and vegetables are produced; all that is necessary to secure a hybrid is by means of a needle, or a small pointed pair of scissors, to remove the stamens, before their anthers open, from the plant you wish to act as the mother, and then carefully to apply to the summit of the pistil the pollen from those stamens which you wish to act as the father; or leaving the desirable plants in the neighbourhood of each other, will often secure a desired result, but not so surely as when more time and attention is bestowed. Where correctness is an object each flower acted upon artificially should be labelled, shut in by a gauze covering, and a proper memorandum made.

Secondly. We shall now allude to a few principles to be kept in view, in order to guard against unnecessary failures, and ensure some measure of success.

1st. Hybridisation will not take place between plants destitute of natural relationship. Thus the many wondrous tales of the influence exerted by oranges upon apples, black currants upon roses, &c., &c., are fit only for the *good* old times that are gone for ever. Even where there is considerable natural affinity, so that both plants belong to the same genus, and where even a graft will take and grow for a time, as in the case of the pear and the apple; it has as yet been impossible to obtain a hybrid between them. Neither has a hybrid been obtained between the currant and the gooseberry.

As a general rule, distinct genera, though belonging to the same natural order, will not hybridise; there may be a few exceptions.

2nd. Hybridisation between species of plants takes place more readily than among animals, though, as in the latter case, the hybrid or mule is generally barren, as in the pretty mule *Pink*, which can only be propagated by cuttings. If, in some cases, such hybrids between distinct species do produce seeds that will grow, the plants soon lose the power to do so, unless fecundation has been again effected by one or both of the original parents.

3rd. Hybridisation is most easily effected between distinct varieties of the same species. Such hybrids are also the most valuable, because many of them if kept distinct, will reproduce themselves true from seed, such for instance as our garden varieties of the *cabbage*. They will also hybridise with other varieties, which also will be reproductive. But this reproduction can be carried only to a certain point, that point being determined by no known rules, but depending upon something constitutional in the nature of that tribe of plants. Thus, we have found that *Calceolarias* long crossed would not produce seed, though apparently possessing perfect stamens and pistils; nor yet would they do so when fecundated by another variety as high bred as themselves, though seeds would be produced when fecundated with the pollen from some of the coarser, more original, types of the species; but, of course, in that case the progeny were defective in form and beauty. Even when the seed of the variety continues fertile and they are not averse from joining issue with kindred varieties, still a deterioration of quality will *in time* ensue, similar to what takes when the breeding in-and-in system among animals is adopted. When, therefore, a superior flower—root, vegetable, fruit or grain—is obtained, care should be taken not only to keep the variety true, but experiments should be made to cross it with some other *dissimilar*, and yet desirable variety, in the hope of obtaining a fresh production which may take the place of both its parents when they are beginning to wear out.

4th and Lastly. In hybridising, many experiments would tend to confirm the idea that manner and style of growth will be chiefly regulated by the characteristics that belong to the plant that possesses the pistil, while the flower and other parts of fructification will be influenced by the plant from whence the pollen of the stamens was taken. Thus, when the beautiful *Fuchsia fulgens* was introduced by the house of *Lee*, great hopes were entertained of what could be done by hybridising it with such old varieties as *globosa*. But as most of the attempts were made by selecting *fulgens* as the mother plant, the progeny were distinguished by large leaves and small flowers, whilst what was desirable was the large flowers of *fulgens*, and the small compact foliage of *globosa*. Again, for example, our earliest *peas*, such as the *Albert* and the *Frame*, are hardy and stubby in their growth; but then no one will use them after the more tender, later, but large and sweet peas of the various *Marroufats* appear. To cross the Marrow with the Early Pea, would have the tendency to give a variety possessing the small flavourless fruit of the latter, with the tender and late habits of the former. By making the Early Pea the mother plant, and the large high-flavoured Marrow the father, there is a likelihood of obtaining early peas, hardy in their nature, large in size, and good in flavour.

From the operation of such principles, either naturally or artificially, improvements in vegetable forms have taken, and are now taking place. Glance at the diminutive *violet*, and behold in a florist's bed of *heartsease* what has been given to man as the reward of industry and care. Taste the luscious *apple* and *pear*, and contrast them with the diminutive gritty things of former

times. Look at the wiry thing upon the cliffs of Dover. the grand original of all our *cabbages* and *cauliflowers*. Observe the uncultivated *turnip*, scarcely recognisable from wild mustard, and notice the sticky, wiry *carrot* as it grows by the highway, and then just step into that jolly good farmer's fields and feast your eyes, at the proper season, on the rare turnips and carrots there, and then you will be convinced not only of what hybridisation and careful culture have already done, but that when these principles are better understood and more acted upon, additional sources of rational employment will be opened up to the industrious mind,—flowers still more beautiful will be produced; fruits, roots, and grain most suitable for particular soils and climates will be found; vegetable phenomena will be better understood and more attended to; and the consequence will be, that *practice* will not sneer at, but become the companion and the testing agent for the principles of *science*; and thus more elevated enjoyment will be realised; more food be produced; more employment provided, and a higher degree of happiness secured for all.

R. Fish.

HOTHOUSE DEPARTMENT.
STOVE PLANTS.

Stove Climbers.—As this department of plant culture is, with the exception of the orchid house, the most expensive of any, both with respect to the erection of the heating apparatus and the quantity of fuel afterwards required, it is especially desirable to make the best use of the interior to obtain an amount of enjoyment proportionate to the outlay. Every good gardener will, in addition to furnishing the stages, platforms, or pits, with suitable plants, be desirous to cover the *rafter* and cross bars with handsome and free flowering climbers. There are now in this country numbers of such plants—more than sufficient to clothe variously the roofs of the largest hothouses in Europe. Hence arises a temptation to cultivate too many, so as almost to defeat the purpose they are intended for. By crowding them too much on the roof, they not only injure the inhabitants below, but cannot flower or thrive themselves so well as if there were fewer of them, and kept thin enough to allow the light and air to circulate in the house. It is to prevent this evil, as well as to recommend their culture in a proper degree, that we propose to ourselves to give a paper or two on the subject of stove climbers; more especially for the roofs of the moist stove and the stove conservatory; proposing hereafter to describe such as are proper to be used to train to a trellis, to be placed amongst the ordinary stove plants on the stage or centre pit. As some of our readers are building, or are intending to build, a stove, we shall in the first place give a list of the very best stove climbers, that they may be at no loss what kinds to procure.

	s. d.
* *Allamanda Schottii*; large yellow, brown, striped flowers	5 0
——— *grandiflora*; small foliage, large yellow flowers	5 0
Bignonia venusta; orange	3 6
——— *Chamberlayni*; pink	3 6
* *Clerodendron splendens speciosissimum*; scarlet	3 6
* *Combretum purpureum*; bright scarlet	3 6
Dipladenia crassinoda; rose	3 6
* *Echites splendens*; rose and whitish blush	7 6
Hoya imperialis; chocolate	3 6
——— *carnosa*; white and pink	2 6
Ipomea Horsfallia; deep crimson	3 6
——— *Learii*; deep blue	3 6
Passiflora alata; crimson, purple, and white	3 6
——— *Kermisina*; red and white	3 6
——— *Lemicheviana*; blue and white	3 6
——— *quadrangularis*; crimson, purple, and white	3 6
* ——— *racemosa*; scarlet	3 6
* *Stephanotis floribunda*; white	3 6
Schubertia graveolens; white	3 6
Thunbergia grandiflora; light blue	3 6
——— *Hawtayneana*	5 0

The above is a very select list of twenty-one of the

best of stove creepers for the roof of the house. We have marked with an asterisk such as will answer best for a rather small house; and for a very small one, such as we may suppose some of our amateur friends may possess, or build, we recommend the *Stephanotis*, the *Dipladenia*, and *Passiflora racemosa*.

CULTURE.—To grow these splendid plants to perfection, so as to enable them to produce abundance of bloom, you must have a small pit eighteen inches or two feet square, or any other form of the same dimensions, but at least two feet deep. At the bottom place a layer of pieces of brick or stone, six inches thick, cover this with some pieces of turf with the grassy side downwards. The rubble is for drainage, and the turf to prevent the soil choking it up. The soil should be composed of peat, loam, and rotten leaf mould, in equal parts, mixed with a sufficient quantity of sand to keep it open and to allow the water to pass through it freely. This compost should not be sifted, but only large stones and the roots of perennial weeds picked out. The situation of these small pits may be as near to the front wall as convenient, to allow the creeper to be trained up to the roof, and along the roof over the paths. A rod of iron, kept well painted, should be suspended from the rafters at a distance of about a foot, to allow room for the shoots, leaves, and flowers, at a favourable distance from the glass. To this rod the creepers must be kept neatly tied, but not too stiffly. The taste of the cultivator must suggest a free graceful mode of performing the operation. In the stove at Pine-apple Place we use small chains running lengthwise, just over the curbstone of the pit. They are fastened up at intervals to the roof, and allowed to hang down slackly between each interval, so as to form, when covered with the creeper, graceful festoons of flowers. Managed in this way they are very ornamental.

In summer when the creepers are growing freely, and, as we hope, flowering profusely, the days being long and the sun giving abundance of light, the creepers may be allowed to grow somewhat luxuriantly; but as soon as they have done blooming, the days shortening and the light less intense, they should then be pruned in freely, to allow the greatest quantity of light to reach the plants below.

WATER.—In the summer months, when the growth is luxuriant, the creepers will require an abundant supply of soft water at their roots. The syringe, too, must be used frequently and freely to cleanse the leaves from dust, and to prevent the increase of insects; care being taken to injure the flower as little as possible. Should the *mealy bug* unfortunately find its way into the house it will soon infest the creepers, especially the *Stephanotis*, upon the flowers of which it loves to dwell. There is no way to destroy this pest effectually but by crushing it with a brush, made either of stiffish hair or bass matting; with this every cranny and joint must be diligently washed, and, if possible, not an insect left alive. It is not once or twice washing that will banish them when they have once got established; the washing must be repeated till they are overcome. Other insects, such as the *red spider* and the *thrip*, must be waged war against continually, for if once allowed to get a-head they are extremely hard to conquer or entirely clear away.

We are just now reminded by a correspondent, that it is not in all cases convenient to have pits built for creepers; when that is the case they may be planted in long boxes arranged along the front, or in large pots set in any convenient corner; but be it remembered that they will neither grow nor flower so finely as by the former mode.

PROPAGATION.—All these plants may be increased by cuttings, placed in silver sand, under bell-glasses, in heat, excepting *Ipomœa Horsfalliæ* and *Combretum pur-*

pureum. These two must be increased by grafting upon the more freely striking species; *Ipomœa Horsfalliæ* grafts easily upon *Ipomœa insignis*, and *Combretum purpureum* upon *C. Pinceanum*.

FLORISTS' FLOWERS.

TULIP AND RANUNCULUS ROOTS being now all taken up, it is often a matter of grave consideration what to do with the beds in which they have grown. They must either be planted with some autumn blooming flowers or be left empty till the planting season for the bulbs comes round again. In such situations where the beds are in sight of the windows, or even frequently seen, beds with flowers that have been reared in pots for the or in high kept grounds, it may be desirable to fill these purpose; in such a case it will be desirable, nay, necessary, to have in the compost-yard a large heap of good compost suitable for these bulbs, which, as soon as the frosts destroy the temporary occupants of the beds, should be wheeled in after the old soil has been removed to some other part of the garden, where it will be useful for other purposes. The new soil should be left now at least six inches above the level required when it is settled. When the beds are so situated that it is of no consequence leaving them empty till the planting season arrives again, the soil should be thrown out on each side of the beds, and laid up in ridges, taking up along with it the layer of dung recommended to be placed over the drainage. In this situation the soil should be frequently turned over, to expose every part of it to the sun and air, and, as there is nothing like system in doing any kind of work, or carrying on regularly any operation, we would advise a set time to be appointed for turning soils, and that time to be faithfully kept as much as the weather will allow. Once a month will be a proper time to turn over the soils of the tulip and ranunculus beds.   T. APPLEBY.

THE KITCHEN-GARDEN.

GLOBE ARTICHOKES.—The suckers of this season's planting should be well attended to by keeping the surface of the earth open; and a soaking of liquid-manure given occasionally will encourage the luxuriant growth necessary for the plentiful production of heads of good quality.

JERUSALEM ARTICHOKES merely require at this season for the earth's surface to be kept open, and in a good state, by frequent stirrings.

CABBAGE for early spring crops should now be sown in full crop; where a large quantity is required it is advisable to sow two or three successive times, at intervals of a few days. The *Red Dutch* should also be remembered if required for pickling, stewing, &c., as well as the *Flat pole*, or *Drumhead*, by those who require them for cattle.

ROUTINE WORK.—*Cauliflowers* and *coleworts* should still be planted freely for autumn and winter purposes. *American* and *Normandy cress* should be sown. *Herbs* of all kinds should be gathered while in bloom. *Chamomile* and *marigold flowers* should be collected two or three times a week. Make a sowing of *cucumbers* for early winter fruiting, and select and save for seed the likeliest fruit of the best varieties; collect all *gherkins* for pickling, and the handsome, long, green *cucumbers* for preserving. *Endive* should be sown in full crop for late planting, and the planting of the same should be weekly attended to for some time to come. Several sowings, also, of *lettuce* should be made where much is required throughout the winter and early spring; the best varieties for this purpose are the *Old Egyptian*,

Brown Coss, the *Bath Brown Coss*, and the *Hammersmith Hardy cabbage lettuce*. *Horseradish* should be kept clear from spurious suckers, and the earth's surface about it kept open and clear.

Mushroom Beds should be made in succession by collecting good stable manure. If the straw is very long some of it may be shaken out to advantage; half-dried cow, sheep, or deer dung are all very good for mushroom culture, either mixed with stable dung or made use of separately. Any of the above materials should have a sufficiency of good holding loam incorporated with it, to prevent its heating too strongly, which the dung by itself is very apt to do, and thus become dry, and exhausted of its best properties by evaporation; this the soil prevents by absorption, maintaining both a kindly temperature and moisture, the two principles that are most essential for the successful culture of mushrooms. In making a mushroom bed the materials should be well trodden or rammed, in order to make it very firm, and spawned at a very moderate temperature, cased with good holding friable loam to the thickness of about two inches when beaten down very firm; after it has been cased a week or ten days it should have another good even beating over, so as to make it very firm after setting.

JAMES BARNES.

MISCELLANEOUS INFORMATION.

HOME-BAKED BREAD.

By the Authoress of " My Flowers."

Bread is an article of extremely great importance in every household; especially where economy is rigidly required. Families must be fed; and where meat is necessarily very sparingly used, there must be a substitute for it; and what can be more nourishing, more simple and agreeable, both for old and young, than sweet, wholesome bread?

Home-made bread is so incomparably superior to that of the baker, that every endeavour should be used to obtain it; not only is the baker's profit gained, but home-made bread goes farther than an equal quantity of that which is procured from the shop. It is firmer and more satisfying in its texture; the stomach remains much longer at rest after receiving it, and does not feel that hollow craving sensation that very frequently follows the use of baker's bread. It has been said, and doubtless with much reason, that many diseases of the stomach are engendered by the adulteration of food; and scarcely any article consumed by man admits of this wicked and injurious practice to so great an extent as bread. On the point of health, therefore, if not of economy, bread should, if possible, be made at home, and thereby one very material source of discomfort will be cut off; for I have myself known cases in which real illness has been caused by the use of baker's bread. Very probably much indisposition, and general derangement of the system, arises from this unsuspected cause.

In large towns it is sometimes impossible to accomplish baking at home. There may be no oven, and no place in which to erect one, and fuel may be scarce and exorbitantly dear. In country towns, even in villages in fact, wherever wood has to be bought, it is comparatively dear; but even supposing for a moment that household bread is not eaten at a cheaper rate than that supplied by the baker, it is made of *pure flour and yeast*, which is a grand consideration; and it goes farther also; but, generally speaking, it will be absolutely cheaper.

Home-baked bread possesses this advantage, also, over that which is bought, that it can be eaten without distaste in a very stale state. Baker's bread is almost uneatable when a week old, and is sometimes very unpleasant at the end of three days. Pure household bread is excellent when a fortnight old; and the thrifty cottager usually bakes a fortnight's batch, as it saves fuel, and bread too—the more stale it is, the more quickly it satisfies hunger. This plan should be adopted by the economist of a higher sphere. When means are small, and principle is strong (which we know to be the case with some of our excellent correspondents), no taste or fancy will be allowed to interfere with that which we see to be right; and we shall soon become reconciled to the good stale loaf, and enjoy it with a keener relish than we ever did the delicate spongy bread of our more affluent days. We feel that we are doing what we can to avoid expense, and support ourselves upon the means which, either we have *undertaken* to live upon or it has pleased God in His infinite wisdom to grant us, and in both cases the conscientious mind will take pleasure in every act of self-denial. *Tastes* are sometimes very difficult to deal with; but if we always bear in mind that a *principle* is involved in nearly every thing we do, we shall overcome many difficulties; and all that is to the "natural man" distasteful, will be rendered easy and even pleasant by the holy motive on which we act.

Ladies with small incomes cannot always procure servants who understand baking; they are sometimes obliged to be dependant upon the services of an ignorant girl, who has never been taught to make bread, and probably never even saw the process carried on. In such a case it is a very great advantage to be able to direct and teach this useful branch of household duty; and yet how many ladies enter upon housekeeping without knowing the way in which it is done! And how many may, perhaps, have kept house for years without having learned or observed it! In every cookery book we open the directions how "to make bread" are given, but so imperfectly—even in those which profess to be the most simple and practical—that they are no guide whatever to a novice; and I, therefore, venture to subjoin the only plain sensible directions I ever met with, and by which any lady, however uninstructed herself, may teach a servant with ease and success. I have extracted it from a little work, by a writer whose practical knowledge and simple style, if his pen had but been guided by "the wisdom which is from above," would have made him eminently useful to the humbler classes:—

"Suppose the quantity be a bushel of flour. Put this flour into a *trough* that people have for the purpose, or it may be in a clean smooth tub of any shape, if not too deep, and sufficiently large. Make a pretty deep hole in the middle of this heap. Take (for a bushel) a pint of good fresh yeast; mix it and stir it well up in a pint of *soft* water, milk-warm. Pour this into the hole in the heap of flour. Then take a spoon and work it round the outside of this body of moisture, so as to bring into it by degrees flour enough to make it form a *thin batter*, which you must stir well about for a minute or two. Then take a handful of flour and scatter it thinly over the head of this batter, so as to *hide* it; then cover the whole over with a cloth to keep it warm; and this covering, as well as the situation of the trough as to distance from the fire, must depend upon the nature of the place, and the state of the weather as to heat and cold. When you perceive that the batter has risen enough to make *cracks* in the flour you covered it with, you begin to form the whole mass into *dough*, thus: you begin round the hole containing the batter, working the flour into the batter, and pouring in, as it is wanted, to make the flour mix with the batter, soft water, milk-warm. Before you begin this you scatter the salt over the heap, at the rate of half a pound to a bushel of flour. When you have got the whole sufficiently moist, you *knead it well*. This is a grand part of the business; for unless the dough be well worked there will be little round lumps of flour in the loaves; and besides, the original batter, which is to give fermentation to the whole, will not be duly mixed. The dough must, therefore, be well worked. The fists must go heartily into it—it must be rolled over, pressed out, folded up, and pressed out again, until it be completely mixed, and formed into a stiff and tough dough. When made, it is to be formed into a lump in the middle of the trough, and with a little dry flour scattered thinly over it, covered over again to be kept warm and to ferment; and in this state, if all be done rightly, it will not have to remain more than fifteen or twenty minutes. The oven should be hot by the time the dough has remained in the lump about twenty minutes. When both are ready, take out the fire, and wipe the oven out clean; and at nearly about the same moment take the dough out upon a clean table or large square board; cut it up into pieces, and make it up into loaves, kneading it again in these separate parcels; and as you go on, shaking a little flour over your board to prevent the dough adhering to it. The loaves should be put into the oven as quickly as possible after they are formed, upon a flat wooden shovel with a long handle; and when in, the oven-door should be fastened up quickly, and *very closely*; if all be properly managed, loaves of about the size of quartern loaves will be sufficiently baked in about two hours. But they usually open the door and look at the bread, to see how it is going on."

These directions are so minute, and yet so clear, that it is scarcely possible to err in practising them. Heating the oven is a matter of some nicety; but observing it done once or twice by an experienced hand will give the needful instruction. Most ovens, indeed, have a particular brick built into the back, which turns white when the heat is sufficiently strong. This is a safe guide.

Bread should not be cut until it is at least two days old; and for family use it is better to keep it still longer. It should be kept in a dry, cool place, as damp and heat are equally to be avoided; and where large bakings are made, the place in which it stands is of some consequence. When loaves are first taken out of the oven they should be allowed to stand on their *heads* until they are quite cold.

HISTORY OF AN APIARY.

INCREASING THE NUMBER OF STOCKS.

As I am desirous of inducing some of your readers to adopt a very interesting method of increasing their stock of bees in autumn, which I tried with perfect success last year, and as the season is fast approaching for the purpose, I shall bid farewell to the subject of my old apiary, with a very few words in addition to what I wrote in my last letter. Suffice it to say that, until last year, when I transferred it to the care of my youngest sister, and commenced a new apiary under different auspices, in a new and more favourable locality, I met with no sort of success as a bee-keeper. The same luckless hive occupied the identical position in the garden where it had stood for years without throwing off a single swarm or yielding me a single pound of honey. Its fate was ultimately similar to that of its predecessor; for, being disgusted with its unprofitableness, I drove it in the early part of last July, when on a visit home, and with the bees which I saved a good-sized swarm occupied the boxes, which had long waited in vain expectation of a swarm from it. They did very well till November, when they died in an unaccountable manner, probably owing to the old age of the queen, plenty of comb and honey being taken from the box on clearing it out.

A brief summary of my success last year with my new apiary, as well as a short account of it, will be found at pp. 202 and 203 of your third volume. Among the various colonies which I purchased, or otherwise obtained, was a stock composed of two united swarms, or rather *families*, of bees, which I had saved from a sulphurous death. Ill as I had hitherto succeeded in my attempts to preserve bees on artificial food throughout the winter, I felt confident that the thing *might* be done, if undertaken in a right manner. I therefore resolved to try what a *doubled* colony would do. My theory was, that if the population of a stock, to be formed by artificial means, were *twice* as numerous as other stocks usually are at this season of the year (August), there would be a greater probability of its doing well, because not only would there be plenty of workers *in* the hive (as well collectors of the furnished stores as wax-workers and nurses of

the young bees—for a good queen lays largely at this season), but, also, a large surplus of honey-gatherers would be at liberty *to roam the fields*, whose industry would not only *augment* the winter store, but likewise *improve the quality* of the food laid by. Whether this theory be sound or not, I succeeded in preserving my bees in admirable health through the winter and spring, and they have become, and are still working with an enormous population, as my strongest and most profitable stock, as I shall show by-and-bye. Moreover, on tasting some of this food in April last, which I scooped out with a teaspoon through a large hole in the top of the hive, I found it had a very agreeable flavour—very different from, and far superior to the original syrup with which I had supplied them—the taste of honey being distinctly perceptible though not preponderating. Another advantage connected with this *doubling* of the population I had almost forgotten to mention, namely, that if it be true, as Huber avers, that where two queens exist in the same hive *they always*, and *they alone*, seek each others' destruction, the workers being only passive spectators, perhaps instigators of the combat; if, I say, this be true, is it not probable and likely that the most vigorous queen will assert her superiority and destroy her rival ? I *know* that this was the case with me, for I picked up the conquered queen the day after the union was effected, and was enabled to compare her with her victorious enemy, who was decidedly the largest, and she has proved a most fertile mother.

It is to the method which I adopted in *uniting* these bees that I wish to call especial attention, because, not only do I claim to have discovered it (at least, nowhere in the twenty and odd bee-books which I have read have I seen even a remote hint of the knowledge of the existence of such a plan), but it is one of the simplest and most useful of bee-operations, as well as a very successful one. I discovered or rather hit upon it accidentally, as I was hesitating between the adoption of the fumigating or sugar-and-water drowning process of uniting bees, one or other of which is recommended generally by apiarians. I was quite unused to either of these plans, and somewhat dreaded the experiment. The *scene* of operation was the small nursery back-garden of some very kind friends of mine who had kindly permitted me to make what use I pleased of the population of five cottage hives, which they intended to plunder; and *the time* was 8½ p.m., on the 9th of August. After trying what I could do by fumigation with one hive, and having made a terrible mess of the affair, so that I began to wish I had never meddled with the business, I proceeded to try the sugar-and-water drowning process, to effect which, I proposed, first, to drive into separate empty hives the population of two strong stocks; and, then, after sprinkling each hive well with sugar and water, to mix the bees together. An awkward, filthy job this appeared, against which my heart revolted; however, there seemed no remedy, so to driving I went. A magnificent second-year stock, as full of bees as it could hold (the more bees the better for the success of the experiment), was successfully driven in about 15 minutes into an empty hive, which was taken off and put gently aside until wanted again. The few remaining bees in the old stock were fumigated with sulphur before being taken into the house. Another fine and populous stock was next turned up as before—an *early* cast of the current year; but, instead of placing an *empty* hive over it as before, it suddenly entered my head to try what driving into the other *already temporarily tenanted* hive would do—the empty hive I mean into which the population of the first hive had been driven. But would they not fight and destroy each other ? If they did, thought I, I have got two good stocks to fall back upon ; so in a moment the tenanted combless hive was gently placed over the now reversed cast, and to driving we went in good earnest. "Hark! what an awful buzzing!" said my companion; and, indeed, I began to dread a general massacre as the hum increased ; presently, however, our tapping having ceased, the hum died away, and a profound silence reigned within. My success was complete, for on taking off the upper hive, an *enormous mass* of bees was disclosed hanging in thick clusters from the roof, united together in great apparent harmony and tranquillity. The few remaining bees in the old hive were sulphured as before; and our united hive was suffered to remain till morning, resting over an empty bucket, and covered with a sheet. Great was the activity of our newly-formed stock the next day (but no signs of war were visible) till about 2½ o'clock p.m., when I shook them all out upon a sheet on the ground in front of the box which had been destined for their reception, into which they immediately crept after their queen. As soon as they had nearly all left the cloth the conquered queen was discovered in front of the box, *dead*, but still surrounded by an escort of bees who paid her the last tribute of respect and loyalty. The box containing the now united swarm was transferred the same evening to my own apiary, where it still remains to this day. I would observe, that on shaking out the bees from the temporary hive *two combs* were found already began, one of them being *2 inches in length*.

So much for my plan of uniting bees in autumn by means of *driving* alone, which I have tried with uniform success on several occasions since then. And, now, a few words as to the treatment of these bees. *Never* did they lack a supply of food (for which, see third vol., page 203,—where, instead of ½lb of honey, read 1½lb) in the feeder (described at page 297 of third volume) for five weeks; and if the food was not quite to their liking I made it suit. It is, I believe, *essential* to the success of this experiment, that the stock be formed *not later* than the 10th of August,—*the earlier the better*; some friends of mine tried it on the 17th, and failed: though, I believe, chiefly owing to negligence, in feeding with unwholesome food. It is well, also, so to arrange the feeder, that there be no *current* of air through the hive. I am going to form two stocks on the same principle this year,—one of them to be composed of three united swarms.

A Country Curate.

HORTICULTURAL SOCIETY'S SHOW.

CHISWICK, July 13th.

The last exhibition of the Society for the present year took place in their gardens at Chiswick on Saturday, the 13th of July; and so for this year the hopes and the fears of the exhibitors have been put an end to. Upon the whole, we may venture to say, that the shows, at both the Park and Chiswick, have been better than in any previous year. The collections of plants of every number, whether large or small, have been more equal, that is, there were fewer bad or middling grown plants than before. The Fruit part of the exhibitions has been a decided improvement, and the Florists' flowers have been more unique and more numerous. This encourages us to hope still better for the time to come. From what we know personally of the various exhibitors we anticipate they will leave no means untried, no nerves unstrung, to ensure success in their future efforts to produce still better specimens of every kind of horticultural produce. We heartily wish them every success.

The exhibition was above the average of those that take place at this season annually. The Orchids as usual, in our opinion, taking the lead. Every part, however, was respectable. The Fruit tent especially was well garnished with luscious sweets. With these few preliminary remarks we shall now briefly describe in our usual way such objects as were exhibited for the first time, or as may be useful to our readers. We judge that the mere giving the names of plants that win the awards of the judges is useful, because it proves not only that the plants were well grown and so worthy of such distinction, but also our reports prove that such plants are capable, by good culture, of being made to merit such distinction.

COLLECTIONS OF TWENTY EXOTIC ORCHIDS.

1st Prize to Mr. Mylam, gardener to S. Rucker, Esq.; making the sixth first prize Mr. M. has won this year. On this occasion we noted especially the following:—

Aerides quinquevulnera, with three long spikes fully in flower. *A. maculosum*, beautifully bloomed. *Cœlogyne speciosa*, with several flowers. The beautiful and fragrant *Cattleya citrina*, with three of its golden flowers. *Cypripedium barbatum*, with 11 flowers. The curious and handsome *Coryanthes maculata*. The rare *Aganisia pulchella*, with numerous flowers. The large flowered *Cycnoches chlorochilum*. The beautiful *Epidendrum verrucosum*. The rare *Paphinia cristata*. *Saccolabium Blumii*, with three fine well bloomed spikes. The new and beautiful *Odontoglossum hastilabium* and the truly noble *Vanda Batemaniana* in finer perfection than even when shown at the Park.

2nd Prize to Mr. Williams, gardener to C. Warner, Esq. This collection was very nearly equal to Mr. Mylam's.

Aerides affine was the best plant in it; it had three spikes 2 ft. long, with several branches on each; and two spikes nearly as long without any side shoots. *A. rosea*, with three spikes. *A. maculosum*, very neat. *Barkeria spectabilis*, in fine order. A large *Miltonia spectabilis*, with several fine flowers. A large plant of *Epidendrum radiatum*, and a good *Vanda tricolor*.

COLLECTIONS OF FIFTEEN EXOTIC ORCHIDS.

1st Prize to Messrs. Rollison, Tooting. In this collection there were several very fine specimens, especially

Cattleya crispa; a large plant with upwards of eight spikes of its fine flowers upon it. *Miltonia spectabilis*; a large mass, 2 ft. across, with numerous flowers. *Stanhopea tigrina*, with nine flowers. *S. Wardii*, with 15 flowers. *S. Devoniana*, with six of its beautiful flowers fully expanded. A good *Cattleya mossiæ*. The sweet *Odontoglossum citrosmum*; and the rare *Sobralia liliastrum*.

2nd Prize to Mr. Dobson, gardener to E. Beck, Esq., Isleworth. The gem of this collection was a dwarf plant of

Epidendrum crassifolium, and a prettier little thing we do not remember to have seen for some time. The plant was not more than 15 inches high, and 10 inches through, yet it had not less than 14 (!) spikes of its pretty pink blossoms. This plant usually attains the height of 4 ft. before it flowers. He also had in good condition the seldom-seen *Promenæa Stapelioides*; the rare *Zygopetalum rostratum*: a fine plant of *Epidendrum calochilum*: and the well known *Butterfly plant* in fine flower. The rest were plants that we have described on former occasions. There is a circumstance or property in these interesting plants that does not occur in any other, namely, the long time they remain in bloom. One of Mr. Dobson's plants has remained so long in perfect bloom, that it has enabled him to exhibit it at three successive exhibitions—we allude to the *Oncidium ampliatum major*, by far the finest plant of the kind exhibited this year; and it is not the only orchid that possesses this desirable quality. If we had leisure we could mention numbers that are equally long-lived in beauty.

COLLECTIONS OF TEN EXOTIC ORCHIDS.

1st Prize to Mr. Blake, gardener to H. Schroder, Esq. We can only notice the best:—

Aerides odoratum, with numerous spikes of its fragrant beautiful flowers. *Calanthe masuca*, with three spikes of its purple flowers. *Dendrobium chrysanthum*, with numerous spikes. *Angræcum caudatum*, beautifully bloomed. The noble *Vanda insignis*. The rarely-seen *Galeandra Bauerii*: and a good *Phalænopsis grandiflora*.

2nd Prize to Mr. Carson, gardener to F. G. Farmer, Esq. We noted especially, as being in good order,

Odontoglossum grande, with five of its large handsome flowers fully expanded. A fine specimen of *Cycnoches Loddigesii*. The rare *Zygopetalum rostratum*. *Cœlogyne speciosa*, with 10 flowers. A neat *Aerides rosea*. The dark variety of *Sobralia macrantha*: *Aerides quinquevulnera*: and the handsome *Dendrobium chrysanthum*.

COLLECTIONS OF SIX EXOTIC ORCHIDS.

1st Prize to Mr. Gorrie, gardener to Sir John Cathcart, Bart. In this collection was a good plant of the lovely

Odontoglossum citrosmum, with four spikes of its fragrant flowers highly coloured. A good *Brassia caudata*, with nine spikes of flowers, and a good plant of the rare *Dendrobium aduncum*.

2nd Prize to Mr. Woolley, gardener to H. B. Ker, Esq., Cheshunt. He had in fine order the beautiful

Oncidium leucophyllum. A large plant, with numerous drooping spikes, of the old *Cymbidium aloefolium*: *Oncidium pulvinatum*: and a finely flowered *Cattleya Forbesii*.

SINGLE SPECIMENS OF ORCHIDS.

1st Prize to Mr. Kinghorn, gardener to Earl Kilmorey, Twickenham, for a fine specimen of *Phalænopsis grandiflora*.

COLLECTIONS OF TWENTY STOVE AND GREENHOUSE PLANTS.

1st Prize to Mr. Cole, gardener to H. Collyer, Esq., Dartford. Mr. Cole exhibited his plants again in fine order, and was again successful in beating his formidable antagonist Mr. May. We shall notice the fresh plants he brought into the field.

Kalosanthes coccinea major: a well bloomed specimen, 4 ft. by 4 ft. *Sphenotoma gracile*: 3 ft. by 2 ft. *Erica arimia*: 2½ ft. by 2½ ft. *E. ampullacea*: 2½ ft. by 3 ft. *E. infundibuliformis*: 3 ft. by 3 ft.; a truly splendid specimen.

2nd Prize to Mr. May, gardener to Mrs. Lawrence. Noble plants, well grown, but several past their best. Mrs. Lawrence ought, however, to be well satisfied; her gardener has well sustained his fame, having this year won, in this class, four out of the six grand prizes offered by the two Societies. His fresh plants were

Tristania neriifolia: covered with its pretty yellow flowers; 5 ft. by 5 ft. *Relhania squarrosa*: an old plant seldom seen; 2½ ft. by 2½ ft. *Erica obtata*: 2½ ft. by 2½ ft. *E. Juliana*: 2 ft. by 2½ ft. *E. tricolor Wilsonii*: 3 ft. by 3 ft. *E. tricolor major*: 2½ ft. by 3 ft.

COLLECTIONS OF FIFTEEN STOVE AND GREENHOUSE PLANTS.

1st Prize to Mr. Green, gardener to Sir E. Antrobus, Bart., for some first-rate plants, especially

Pleroma elegans: 4 ft. by 4ft.; a circular plant covered with its rich purple blossoms. *Lisianthus Russellianus. Echites atropurpurea*, with dark rich chocolate-coloured flowers. *Erica Savileana : E. tricolor :* and *Stephanotis floribunda.*

2ND PRIZE to Mr. Carson, gardener to J. Farmer, Esq. We noted, as the best,

Leschenaultia spectabile : 2 ft. by 2½ ft. *Æschynanthus Lobbii*, with its almost black calyxes and large scarlet blossom ; the plant was covered with bunches of bloom. *Polygala oppositifolia :* 2 ft. by 2 ft. *Pimelea pubescens :* 2 ft. by 2 ft. *Stephanotis floribunda :* and *Dipladenia crassinoda.*

COLLECTIONS OF TEN STOVE AND GREENHOUSE PLANTS.

1ST PRIZE to Mr. Croxford, gardener to H. Barnes, Esq. He had in fair condition *Sollya linearis* and *Clerodendrum fallax.*

2ND PRIZE to Mr. Stanley, gardener to H. Bevens, Esq. Here was a good

Clerodendrum Kæmpferii, Euphorbia splendens, Cyrtoceras reflexus, Phymatanthus tricolor, and *Franciscea acuminata.*

COLLECTIONS OF SIX STOVE AND GREENHOUSE PLANTS.

1ST PRIZE to Mr. Bruce, gardener to Boyd Millar, Esq., Collier's Wood, Merton. Every plant was excellent ; there were—

Aotsima crinea, with nine heads of bloom. *Aphelexis humilis : Ixora coccinea : Stephanotis.* and *Erica metulæflora.*

2ND PRIZE to Mr. Kinghorn, for

Leschenaultia arcuata : L. formosa : Aphelexis humilis : Tremandra verticillata : and *Erica metulæflora bicolor.*

(To be continued.)

EXTRACTS FROM CORRESPONDENCE.

SURFACE-STIRRING.—I observed some weeks ago an article in your useful journal on the benefit of hoeing and stirring the surface of the soil. I am sure such is of no trifling benefit, and I can state a fact which proves very clearly (what may be, perhaps, known by many, but, nevertheless, will be worth the trial of those for whom I trust your journal is principally written, namely, the cottager) the benefit of frequently stirring the surface soil of plants in pots. For three years I had a small greenhouse which was *not* heated ; in this house I kept through three winters, with hardly a single loss, geraniums, verbenas, heliotropes, fuchsias, cacti, mesembryanthemums, and other tender plants ; my only plan being regularly twice a week, and sometimes oftener to stir the surface soil ; this I did more during the frosty weather than otherwise, and I believe I could trace the ill effects of frost on plants that had been unattended in this house, whilst the pots near to them, that had been surface-stirred, seemed to have suffered no harm. I name this, because it is quite applicable to the cottage flower fancier, and I believe he may keep many plants by this simple plan through a severe winter which otherwise he might have lost. —L. R. L.

TO CORRESPONDENTS.

*** We request that no one will write to the departmental writers of THE COTTAGE GARDENER. It gives them unjustifiable trouble and expense. All communications should be addressed "*To the Editor of The Cottage Gardener*, 2, *Amen Corner, Paternoster Row, London.*"

WILD FLOWERS (X. Y. Z.).—As you have not time (?) to study botany to enable you to ascertain the names of these, your only plan is to purchase a book containing drawings of them. The cheapest is *Baxter's Flowering Plants of England.* For the *Ferns* no book is so good and cheap as Moore's *Hand-Book of British Ferns* ; you can carry it in your pocket, and it is only a few pence in price. It has a drawing of each species. Frogs and toads are beneficial in a garden. They feed on insects.

GUINEA FOWLS (K. O. T.).—These having frost-bitten feet which have since ulcerated, should have them washed, and be kept in a room with a stone or boarded floor, where no grit or dirt could penetrate the wound until healed. If the wounds are inflamed, wash them with Goulard water ; if fungus or proud flesh appears touch it with blue stone. Apply creosote ointment.

HEATING SMALL GREENHOUSE (W. R. Glossop).—As this is only ten feet long and is to be heated from your kitchen boiler, you cannot do better than adopt the plan described at page 203 of our third volume.

BIND-WEED (E. O., Devon).—This, otherwise called the wild Convolvulus (*C. arvensis*), like other deep-rooting perennial weeds can only be destroyed by pulling up the stems as fast as they appear among your flowers. The weeds will struggle on for a year or two, but will die finally of exhaustion.

MOST PROFITABLE PIGEONS (*A Subscriber from the Commencement*). —None surpass the common Blue Dove-house, and common large Mixture Pigeons.

AMERICAN BLIGHT (H. F. L.).—Your trees must be in a wretched plight indeed when "their top branches and even the young shoots are literally white, so that in many places the colour of the stem cannot be seen!" We can only recommend you in this case to head-back the branches of your trees, to burn what you cut off, and, by the assiduous use of spirit of turpentine, to take care that the disease does not so get a-head again. *Ceanothus azureus* is an evergreen, and *Ceanothus cæruleus* is another name for the same plant.

CARROT MAGGOT (*W. B—— A——a*).—Your crops would not have been saved by the omitted hoeing. We trench two spits deep, turning in dung with the bottom spit and watering *that* spit with the strongest ammoniacal liquor from the gas works. The Carrot Maggot never attacks our crops. You can have for a penny *an index* for each of the former volumes ; and uniform covers for each for a *shilling.* Tell your binder to omit the advertisement pages, and he will do so without any trouble.

NAMES OF PLANTS (F. H. S.).—Your plant is a very old and too much neglected hardy garden plant, the Strawberry Blite (*Blitum virgatum.* (*Harriett.*) Yours is Shrubby Rest-harrow (*Ononis fruticosa*).

CHRYSANTHEMUM SLIPS (*Harriett*).—These which were taken off and planted in a bed last May, can be potted in September. Your other question shall be answered next week.

ROSES DISEASED (A. M.).—The cause of the stalks of your *rose-buds* decaying, just like shanking in grapes, is the want of root action. If the roots had been covered with mulch, probably, the decay would not have occurred, but we cannot prescribe without knowing the soil and situation where your roses grow. The *leaves* of your roses with little left upon them but the skin on one side and the nerves, have been eaten by the caterpillars of a small black Saw-fly (*Tenthredo æthiops*). If you had dusted the leaves with the fresh powder of white helebore as soon as brown spots appeared, you would have saved your leaves. See pages 169, 179, and 222 of vol. ii.

INFLAMED RUMP-GLAND IN POULTRY (*Kate*). — Remove the feathers from around it ; open the ulcer with a needle, press out the offensive matter, wash the place clean, and then bathe it with Goulard water. Give a teaspoonful of castor oil if needed. Dirty water and deficiency of green food are thought to cause this disorder.

WHITE FORGET-ME-NOT.—We have just received the following from the party who so kindly offered to supply this—" I will endeavour to send seed of the white ' Forget-me-not ' to those who have already applied for it, but having few plants at this place, and not intending to be at Malvern for some time, *I can send no more.*"

ECONOMISING (*Verax*).—We have forwarded your letter to the authoress of " My Flowers." The statements to which you refer are quite reconcilable. If you have to keep a man to cultivate your garden, then economy says, decidedly, give this up ; but if you can cultivate your garden during your own leisure hours, with only occasional aid, say a man's labour once a week, then economy says, as decisively, keep on your productive kitchen-garden. In the latter case it will be remunerative ; but with a man kept for its cultivation you will lose at least thirty pounds a year by its retention.

LIGHT, PEATY SOIL (R., 1850).—The best dressing for this will be chalk and clay to improve its staple ; and if put on six inches deep, and well incorporated, it will not be too much. We should put this on as the crops are cleared off, and ridge the ground to allow the frosts of winter to aid the mixing. The soot and salt may be put on in the spring just previous to sowing and planting. Half a bushel of soot and 10 lbs. of salt to every one hundred square yards is a good proportion. To drive away grubs, &c., give the soil a good soaking with gas ammoniacal liquor, just before digging for any crop.

NAMES OF MOTHS (R. L.).—The largest is the Buff-tip (*Pygæra bucephala*) ; the three smallest are the White Plume (*Pterophorus pentadactylus*) ; the others were too much injured for us to discover their names, but, moreover, we cannot undertake to name entomological specimens unless the insects are connected with injuries to plants. We think your brick furnace and earthenware flue sufficient for *heating your greenhouse.*

MILDEW ON NECTARINE-TREE (T. L., *Newton*).—This arises from excessive stagnant moisture ; your soil is badly drained, so that the wall is kept constantly damp, or there is a want of a free circulation of air. These circumstances are injurious to the health of the tree, and congenial to the growth of the minute fungi constituting the disease. These white parasitical fungi are *Oidium erysiphoides, Sporulrichum macrosphorum, Torula botryoides,* and *Erysiphe pannosa.* We have little doubt that these fungi never attack plants that are in good health, for we entertain the opinion that it is only the sap of diseased plants—sap in a state of decomposition—that is suited to be the food of the fungi. Prevention, therefore, is preferable to curative applications ; and we have no doubt that if the nectarine or peach tree is kept in due vigour by having the soil well drained, and prevented from excesses of either moisture or of dryness—and if its leaves are similarly protected from being exposed to sudden atmospheric changes—they will never be visited by mildew. We are justified in this conclusion, because with this disease our peach trees, in the whole course of our practice, have seldom or never been troubled. Mildew of all kinds generally proceeds from an impeded root action, and we have generally found that stagnation suddenly caused, whether by excessive heat or drought, is liable to produce it, more especially if succeeded by much solar light. We have little doubt that in such cases the elaboration (by overtaking or being in advance of the absorbing power) produces more highly concentrated juices, which are adapted as pabulum for this obscure class of parasites. The best preventive is a good top-dressing of rotten manure in the early part of June, and as soon as drought sets in a thorough soaking of water. If caused by bad and deep borders, the remedy must be sought in thorough drainage, or an entire renovation of the soil. When mildew appears the best application is a dusting with flowers of sulphur. The *mildew in cucumbers* arises from similar causes, and requires similar treatment. The species of fungi forming the mildew on the cucumber are *Nicotheclum roseum*, *Oidium erysiphoides*, and *O. leuconium*.

Fig (*Jannet D.*).—Any open garden soil, mixed with a little dead turfy matter and lime-rubbish, will suit it, but *the essential point is drainage*; stagnant moisture at the root is fatal to its fruitfulness. A south wall is best for it. There is an excellent essay on its culture, by Mr. Errington, at page 3 of our second volume. Thanks for your communication, which shall appear the first opportunity.

Drift Sand (*Twig*).—This, washed down from the Kent sand hills, next to silver sands, is good for potting purposes. Prune back your *Portugal laurels* next April. *Wolfsbane* is the *Aconitum lupulinum*.

Cucumbers Producing only Male Blossoms (*J. N. C.*).—What you call "false" are the male blossoms. These only being produced, although "the vines appear thriving," intimates that they have been kept too moist and too cold; give them less water and more heat. We know of nothing that you could apply to a quick hedge to render the leaves so unpalatable that sheep would not eat them; nothing would be so durable or effectual as a row of hurdles.

Mesembryanthemum Purpureum (*Fuchsia*).—This, if in a pot, will grow nicely in three parts sandy loam and one part lime rubbish, well drained. It will do well out of doors in any light soil during the summer. Cuttings of it strike freely in light sandy soil; now is a good time to insert them, allowing them to dry a little at the cut end before planting them. Set them in a frame, or in a shady place in the open air; they want no bell-glass.

Chorozema Chandleria (*Ibid*).—We do not know this. If you treat it much as was recommended in our last volume for the genus in general, and such as the genus *Epacris* was described as needing, you will succeed. If one of the tenderer kinds, the cuttings will require nearly all pure peat and sand, with scarcely any loam. *Henchmanii*, with foliage like a heath, must receive similar treatment, and, with few exceptions, the heath and epacris require the same management. *Cuttings* are best formed from small side shoots, cut off with a small heel, and inserted in pure sand, below a bell-glass, there being sandy peat below the sand; but, as we before remarked, the best plants are obtained from seeds. This applies to the genus as a whole, and may give a hint for your species.

Florist's Geranium Cuttings (*S. G. R.*).—The matter will soon be referred to, though much that is new will be impossible, after what has already been said at different times.

Eutralia Grandiflora (*Ibid*).—This we do not know. We have seen the *E. trinervis*, with purplish yellow flowers, and the *E. macrophylla*, of a brownish colour, and these are easily grown in peat and loam, requiring a temperature of 40° during winter, and to be placed in a sheltered place out of doors in summer. Cuttings will strike readily, if side shoots, or the points of shoots, are taken off now or in the spring, inserted in sand above sandy loam, covered with a bell glass, and set in a cold frame.

Ixora Javanica (*Ignoramus*).—We would advise stopping the fourth shoot at such a height that it would start level with the three shoots you have already stopped, and are going to stop again. We presume it was not so strong as the other three when it was stopped previously, and if so you acted quite correctly.

India Rubber Plant (*W. H.*, *Kensington*).—This, which we presume to be the *Ficus elastica*, and which has been wintered in a parlour, and set out of doors in summer until it has become unwieldy from its size, may be cut down a little now, but not farther than where it possesses leaves. In the beginning of summer, it might have been pruned more freely, more especially if it could have been set in a house with a little heat afterwards. It will distil its *rubber* pretty freely on being wounded. We would endeavour to compress it a little by *tying*, instead of *cutting* much, at this advanced period. Cuttings, after the cut ends have got dried, and with all their juicy leaves remaining, will root in peat and sand; and more quickly if, after a few days, the cutting pot is plunged in a mild bottom heat.

Roses (*X.*).—The best soil for roses in general is a deep strong loam, enriched with rotten cow-dung. The cause of the rose-buds falling off, whatever it may be, must be at the roots; the soil is certainly at fault. Does not the clay hold too much water?

Blue Annuals (*Ibid*).—We have given the names of all the blue flowering annuals in former numbers.

Cabbage (*Ibid*).—Growing cabbages are not injured by having the large, old outside leaves pulled off *after* the plants have "hearted;" not before if they are healthy.

Pomegranate (*Ibid*).—The climate makes all the difference to those grown on the Continent. Their whole treatment with us may be seen by referring to the indexes.

Rhododendrons (*Ibid*).—All Rhododendrons and Azaleas should be pruned, if they require it, after flowering, not before.

Kitchen-garden Crops (*Ibid*).—All kitchen-garden crops are much benefited by frequent and heavy waterings during droughts.

Arrangement of Flower-beds (*Novice*).—By the arrangement of 18 beds for the groundwork of a flower-garden, insisted on by our coadjutor, Mr. Beaton, we understood him to mean that number for a garden of the first-rate magnitude, and when three times that number would probably be necessary to fill up the design. At any rate, that plan is not applicable to the design you sent, but we approve of your plan of dividing the corner beds, and so have three distinct colours in each; but the plants ought to be of the same height, or nearly so, in all the divisions. For lists of the best plants for them, we can only refer you to our former ones.

Apples (*Ibid*).—The best apple we know for a high situation like yours at Wolverhampton, is the *Court-pendu Plat*, or Poor-man's Profit, or Garnon, as they call it in Herefordshire. It never flowers till after the 29th May, comes into use in November for table and kitchen, and lasts till next May or June. For the rest, we would recommend you to see Mr. Errington's lists in our first volume.

Artichokes Unproductive (*E. D.*).—Your plants on a light soil are healthy, but produce no heads. The only causes for this that we can imagine are want of root moisture, or being under the shade of trees. In either case the artichoke is always unproductive. Mulch round each of the stools at once, and water them over the mulch abundantly in dry weather. Remove the suckers, and winter dress them as usual. Renew the mulching in March next, and water abundantly in dry weather throughout the spring and summer, and, if not overshadowed, you will have heads next year. Other answers next week.

Verbena Cuttings (*Jane B.*).—How can we tell the cause of your failure in striking these, unless we know the mode you adopted? It is no doubt complimentary, but we do assure you that among the gifts of universal knowledge editors are thought to be gifted with, second-sight is not included. Tell us *all* that you have done, and we will endeavour to point out the source of failure.

A Lodger's Plants (*S. P. Q. R.*).—Although your landlord gave you permission to plant in his garden, yet we think you have no legal right to remove the shrubs; but your landlord's landlord will be very arbitrary if he prevents you.

Rabbit-skin Refuse (*E. Maxwell*).—There is no better way of using "the fur, feet, and ears," than by digging them fresh into the soil. The fur, like any other hair, is long in decomposing, but it does so slowly, and is proportionately a lasting manure; the flesh on the feet and ears decays much faster, and is immediately beneficial to the crop. If you were to grow a few square yards of any crop unmanured, and a similar space manured with this refuse, you would see a very sensible difference in favour of the latter.

Young Cucumbers or Gherkins for Pickling (*Cotswold Hills*).—Have them sound and fresh gathered: spread them on dishes, salt them well, and let them lie in the brine for seven days. Then drain and dry them, put them into a jar, pour over them a sufficient quantity of hot vinegar, in which some sliced horseradish, ginger, and peppercorns, have been previously boiled. Cover the jar with a cabbage-leaf and a plate, place it near the fire; and next day drain off the vinegar from the gherkins, and boil it again; pour it once more boiling hot over the gherkins. Repeat this the third day, and when quite cold cork down the jar, and tie a bladder closely over. Some recommend plenty of vine-leaves for covering the jar in preference to the cabbage-leaf and plate; and also advise the process of boiling to be repeated, covering the jar with fresh leaves every time until the gherkins are of as good a colour as you wish Let the pickles be well covered with the vinegar.

Preserved Fruits for Dessert (*Ibid*).—*Strawberries to preserve whole.* For this purpose have them picked fresh into wide-mouthed glass bottles, adding their own weight of finely powdered loaf sugar, and filling up the bottles with Malaga, sweet Malmsey, or sherry wine boiling hot. This plan is rather expensive; a cheaper mode is, by taking their own weight of powdered sugar, and after well covering each strawberry with the sugar, making a thin syrup of the remainder; but, instead of water, use red currant juice, in the proportion of one pint to every pound of strawberries, and simmer them in this until the fruit is sufficiently jellied, without being broken. The syrup may also be made with the juice of strawberries instead of currants. *Gooseberries* :—Gather the large red hairy kind when nearly ripe in dry weather, and place them singly on sieves or dishes in the sun or before the fire, until quite shrivelled and dry. Store them with sheets of white paper between each layer of fruit. A more luscious mode is, to strew two pounds of pounded loaf-sugar over six pounds of gooseberries beginning to turn red; in three days put them into a jar, cover close, put into a pan of cold water over a gentle fire, take off when water nearly boils, let them stand until next day, strain off the syrup, boil it a little, pour it on fruit while hot, let it remain a week; boil the syrup again, pour it on the fruit. Drain the fruit, rinse it with water, drain, dry before the fire, and keep in close jars in a dry closet. *Cherries* :—To six pounds of Kentish cherries, stoned, add two pounds of loaf-sugar powdered and strewed over them in a preserving-pan, in which they must simmer until they begin to shrivel, strain them from the juice and lay them on sieves, dishes, or soft cloths on a hot hearth, or in an oven cool enough to dry without baking them. The same syrup will serve for another six pounds of fruit. Keep them with sheets of paper between each layer of fruit in a dry place.

London: Printed by Harry Wooldridge, Winchester High-street, in the Parish of Saint Mary Kalendar; and Published by William Somerville Orr, at the Office, No. 2, Amen Corner, in the Parish of Christ Church, City of London.—August 1st, 1859.

WEEKLY CALENDAR.

M D	W D	AUGUST 8—14, 1850.	Weather near London in 1849.		Sun Rises.	Sun Sets.	Moon R. & S.	Moon's Age.	Clock bef. Sun.	Day of Year.
8	Tu	Swift last seen.	T. 85°—54°.	S.W. Fine.	36 a. 4	35 a. 7	8 a. 3	1	5 23	220
9	F	Linnet's song ceases. [accen.]	T. 91°—56°.	S.W. Fine.	37	33	8 35	2	5 15	221
10	S	St. Lawrence. Silver-spotted Skipper Butterfly	T. 89°—59°.	S.W. Fine.	39	32	9 8	3	5 7	222
11	Sun	11 Sun. aft. Trinity. Dog Days end.	T. 81°—57°.	S. Rain.	40	30	9 29	4	4 59	223
12	M	Swallows and Martins begin to congregate.	T. 79°—56°.	S. Rain.	42	28	9 54	5	4 49	224
13	Tu	Second brood of House Martins fledged.	T. 70°—53°.	S.W. Rain.	43	26	10 19	6	4 38	225
14	W	Goldfinch's song ceases.	T. 70°—52°.	S.W. Fine.	45	24	10 47	)	4 28	226

Antoine Laurent Lavoisier, whose birthday was the 16th of the present month, in 1743, deserves a notice on this page as being one of the first to apply his knowledge of Chemistry practically to the cultivation of the soil. We can remember the time when the farmer and the gardener scoffed at such application; and we can remember, also, many of the wild theories published by dabblers in science, which practical cultivators quoted in justification of their scoffs. How baseless were those theories and that ridicule we have also lived to see acknowledged. Because Tull, Beatson, and others, mistaking the discoveries of chemistry, have maintained that frequent hoeings will enable the cultivator to dispense with his dunghill, is no more a reason that chemistry can afford no guidance to the farmer and gardener than astronomy is proved to be useless to the navigator because some surveyors of the heavens have maintained that the sun travels round the earth. Doubtless, Lavoisier made many such mistakes, was wrong in his inferences, and consequently was disappointed when he came to the results of his experiments; yet he went on cultivating his two hundred and forty acres in La Vendée. Satisfied that his principle was right, he instituted other experiments, corrected his mistakes, gained yearly more and more knowledge of the phenomena of vegetation and of the food of plants, nor ceased until at the end of nine years his annual produce doubled that obtained per acre by the neighbouring farmers. This combination of practice with science must ever outstrip either practice or science alone. The mere practitioner goes on a blind follower of the blind; and science without practical knowledge is like a sunbeam falling on empty space. In no department of knowledge is this union of practice with science more beneficial than in that including the cultivation of the soil. It exhibits in a light the most obvious the intimate connexion of the sciences—the *mechanism* of our implements, the *physiology* of our animals and plants, the *chemistry* of their food, and the *geology* of our soils, are all subjects on which volumes have been written—volumes from which the most experienced cultivator gathers enlightening information. Lavoisier through life kept this practical use of science in view, and was engaged in researches tending to the same bright object when he voluntarily went forth to death at the call of duty; and we know of no nobler passage with which to embalm his memory. Finding that his chemical researches involved him in heavy expenses, he sought for and obtained the lucrative appointment of a Farmer-general of the revenue—not to increase his fortune, but to enable him the better to aid other students in science, and to empower him more freely to open to them his laboratory. This was on the eve of the justly named "Reign of Terror" marking the outbreak of the French Revolution. Lavoisier continued at his studies without interfering in that political convulsion, and this, coupled with the fact of his being a Farmer-general, determined his doom. In that time of "terror within terror," when "executions took place in batches, and fifty persons were sent to death daily," innocence was no safe-guard; and he was denounced on the absurd charge of mixing noxious ingredients with the tobacco supplied to the public from the warehouses within his department. To avoid arrest—for there was then rarely a passage from the prison door but to the scaffold—Lavoisier secreted himself; but hearing that his colleagues and his father-in-law were imprisoned, he surrendered, and was condemned to death. He asked for a respite to complete some experiments, the results of which would be important to mankind, but the reply was, "The Republic has no need of Chemists!" He sought no further for delay; and no victim murdered by the guillotine ascended it with more fortitude, nor died more beloved by their private friends, nor more lamented by men of science. He was beheaded on the 8th of May, 1794. This is no appropriate place for commenting upon his discoveries in science, his logical deductions, his enlightened theoretical conclusions, nor even upon his admirable chemical nomenclature. He may be said to have constructed a language for chemistry—a language so happily constituted, that the mere name of any compound at once informs of what it is constituted, and to what class of bodies it belongs. We wish most fervently that some Lavoisier would arise among botanists, and reform their nomenclature of names—names at present constituting a jargon difficult to interpret, and for the most part worthless when interpreted.

Meteorology of the Week.—At Chiswick, from observations during the last twenty-three years, the average highest and lowest temperatures of these days are 74.3° and 51° respectively. The greatest heat, 93°, occurred on the 10th in 1842; and the extreme cold, 32°, was on the 13th in 1839. Ninety-eight days were fine, and on sixty-three rain fell.

Insects—We have been asked so repeatedly to furnish information whereby the three different tenants

RANGE OF BAROMETER—RAIN IN INCHES.

Aug.		1841.	1842.	1843.	1844.	1845.	1846.	1847.	1848.	1849.
8	B.	29.716 / 29.519	30.029 / 30.035	30.226 / 30.153	29.719 / 29.614	29.831 / 29.826	29.728 / 29.701	29.731 / 29.700	29.896 / 29.763	29.960 / 29.837
	R.	—	—	—	—	0.26	—	0.10	0.13	—
9	B.	29.684 / 29.596	30.039 / 29.644	30.460 / 29.950	29.756 / 29.733	29.624 / 29.447	29.969 / 29.944	29.876 / 29.731	29.861 / 29.803	29.792 / 29.678
	R.	0.01	—	—	—	0.01	—	0.02	0.23	—
10	B.	29.800 / 29.678	29.772 / 29.621	30.177 / 29.997	29.744 / 29.591	29.877 / 29.526	30.022 / 30.009	29.881 / 29.809	30.022 / 29.952	29.873 / 29.737
	R.	0.30	1.06	—	—	0.68	—	0.05	0.15	—
11	B.	29.562 / 29.458	30.131 / 29.832	30.287 / 30.234	29.783 / 29.650	29.760 / 29.523	30.073 / 30.039	30.112 / 30.073	30.054 / 29.994	29.906 / 29.861
	R.	0.30	—	—	0.12	0.36	0.26	—	0.19	0.34
12	B.	29.923 / 29.898	30.257 / 30.200	30.237 / 30.213	29.566 / 29.374	29.929 / 29.826	30.039 / 30.039	30.110 / 30.088	30.018 / 29.963	29.764 / 29.679
	R.	—	—	—	0.33	0.01	—	—	—	0.02
13	B.	29.885 / 29.772	30.399 / 30.379	30.211 / 30.093	29.641 / 29.531	30.035 / 30.003	29.792 / 29.682	30.257 / 30.139	29.990 / 29.951	29.594 / 29.570
	R.	0.30	—	—	0.94	0.07	0.22	—	0.21	0.09
14	B.	29.710 / 29.599	30.550 / 30.214	30.074 / 29.945	29.424 / 29.331	29.952 / 29.819	29.912 / 29.879	30.316 / 30.276	29.472 / 29.411	29.762 / 29.674
	R.	0.04	—	—	0.30	—	—	—	0.68	—

of a bee-hive may be distinguished from each other, that we think it best to furnish a drawing of each, with the descriptions given of them by one who has written the most successful monograph of the bee tribe—the late Mr. Kirby. We will begin with the most numerous members of the colony—the working Hive Bee (*Apis mellifica*). Its head, triangular; *mandibles* (jaws), prominent, terminating the head in an angle, toothless, overlapping at the point; *tongue* and *maxillæ* (teeth), long and incurved; *labrum* (upper lip) and *antennæ*, black. The trunk has black *ligulæ*; wings, reach to the edge of the fourth segment of the abdomen; legs, black, with *digits* (fingers) pitch-coloured; hinder *tibiæ* (shanks), naked above, concave lengthwise on outside, inside convex, furnished with lateral recumbent hairs to form the *corbicula* (receptacle for kneaded pollen); the upper surface of the under part of the hinder *tarsi* (feet) resembles that of the *tibiæ*, furnished underneath with a stiff brush (*scopula*) of hairs in rows. The *abdomen* rather longer than both head and trunk, oblong, rather heart-shaped, clothed with pale yellowish hairs, first segment short with longer hairs, base of three intermediate segments banded with pale hairs, apex (summit) of three intermediate ventral segments tawny, and at the base of each a trapeziform *wax-pocket*, covered with a thin membrane; *sting*, or rather sheath of the sting, straight. There are two sorts of working bees—the wax makers and the nurses who attend upon the brood. An ounce of bees contains 336, and a pint holds 2160. They collect the nectar of flowers, from which they form *honey* and *wax*; the pollen or dust from the anthers, of which *bee-bread*, their food, is made; and *propolis*, a resinous substance used in the lining of the hive, and finishing the combs. The tongue of the bee laps up the nectar; and it is swallowed, passing into the first stomach or *honey-bag*. Wax is believed to be secreted in the wax-pockets. They do not attempt to collect nectar from the Trumpet Honeysuckle, because of the difficulty of access to it; but they avoid that of the Crown Imperial, probably because noxious; and the Oleander yields honey fatal to flies, but it never succeeds in tempting the bee. In each journey from the hive a bee visits but one species of flower, which is the reason we see them return with such different coloured pellets of pollen. Each bee makes about six excursions daily. In twenty-four hours they will construct a comb twenty inches long and seven wide. The bees often seen vibrating their wings so rapidly at the entrance of a hive are promoting its ventilation. They have been preserved in the same hive for thirty years; but the age to which a bee will live has not been clearly ascertained.

MANY of our readers represent to us, that from their situation in towns and other causes, they are unable to have a sufficient supply from that only true mine of fertilizing matter—the Dung-hill; and to meet their wishes, we purpose giving a series of papers upon artificial manures. We shall rarely touch upon proprietary manures, but confine ourselves for the most part to those which may be obtained of any dealer in such articles. Before commencing our observations, we would warn our readers that all artificial manures, unless rich in animal and vegetable substances—substances affording to the roots of plants carbon, hydrogen, and ammonia (the chief constituents of their whole frame, whether it be a fragile petal or a sturdy stem)—are but assistant manures. They may help a plant to vigorous growth, the same as a richer milk may supply more phosphate of lime to a rickety child, but unless there are in the soil the more essential supply of decomposing animal and vegetable remains, such as are supplied by dung-hill manures, failure in securing productive growth must ensue. An artificial manure, deficient either in such remains or their components, can do no more than supply a constituent to a plant which may promote its vigour, or it may render a soil less dry by absorbing moisture from the atmosphere, or it may make an adhesive soil more friable. It may kill weeds and vermin, and it may preserve plants from injury when exposed to drought or to frost, but these are only secondary benefits. The most important office of a manure, let us ever bear in mind, is to supply carbon, hydrogen, and ammonia to the roots of plants in such a form that they can feed upon them.

Taking a dealer in manures' list, and adopting his alphabetical arrangement, we come first to

ALUM; but let no one of our readers look towards this with any sanguine anticipations that it will brace and invigorate his plants. We have no experience of its merits ourselves, nor do we anticipate that it will act direct upon any plant with beneficial effect, though it may be of use in the mode mentioned by M. Sprengel. We will quote his statement, and leave our readers to judge for themselves. "I have found, in repeated experiments, that alum, composed of 11 parts potash, 10 parts alumina, 34 sulphuric acid, and 45 water, is a very powerful manure. It does not, like gypsum, merely advance vegetation by the sulphuric acid it contains,* but also by its potash and alumina. Alum is very soluble in water, and must not be used, therefore, except in small quantities, unless the soil contains much carbonate of lime, in which case gypsum will be formed. Forty or fifty pounds are generally sufficient for a Magdeburg acre (equal to half an acre English). Alum will chiefly improve crops belonging to the tribe of clovers, although it also benefits oats and barley. Further experiments will show whether it is advantageous to other crops; and if analogy be not deceiving, this will be the case. If much humic acid is in the soil, the alum will be decomposed, humate of ammonia formed, and the

* M. Sprengel is not quite correct here. Gypsum is a constituent of clovers, saintfoin, &c.; and it fixes ammonia, forming sulphate of ammonia the same as is done by alum.

sulphuric acid set free. On soils rich in humus (the soluble extract of decomposed vegetables), it is to be used with caution. Alum may be used as a fixer of ammonia in urine, sulphate of ammonia being formed by the mixture." It is in this last mode mentioned by M. Sprengel that it is most likely to be beneficial; and Dr. Ingle, of La Hague, in the Island of Jersey, states that if used for the purpose in a stable, it speedily removes the strong ammoniacal smell; a pailful of water, with half a pound of alum dissolved in it, being sufficient for the purpose. This must be sprinkled over the urine-moistened parts.

Alum has been employed also, with some success, to change the colour of the *hydrangea's* flowers from pink to blue. About seven years since some experiments on this subject were tried in the Chiswick Garden, and the plants submitted to the trial were exhibited at the rooms in Regent-street. One plant cultivated as usual was the most healthy, and bore its pink flowers; another, to which half an ounce of phosphate of iron had been administered, was unhealthy, its leaves yellow, and its flowers small but pink; a third plant, treated with half an ounce of caustic potash, looked similarly; but a fourth hydrangea, to which half an ounce of alum had been given, produced blue flowers. The quantity, however, was excessive, for the plant was weakly and the flowers small. Mr. Beaton finds that the best mode of obtaining blue hydrangeas is, by rooting cuttings of them in February, and potting them in loam with which iron filings have been mixed. See page 243 of our second volume.

RESUMING the subject of the comparative value of hard and soft water for culinary purposes, we come next to the evidence of a practical chemist, Mr. Philip Holland, who, in confirmation of M. Soyer's statements relative to their employment in *tea-making*, observed:—

"I find that the water softened by means of oxalate of ammonia extracts the strength of tea almost twice as well as when it is hard. I had tea made with equal quantities of the leaf and equal quantities of boiling water, with and without oxalate of ammonia. The infusion made with water softened by the oxalate was strongly and better flavoured, and had to be diluted with the addition of 80 per cent. of hot water to bring it down to the strength of the other. It follows, therefore, that with the oxalate 10 parts of tea go as far as 18 without it.

"Does that saving pay for the expense?—Over and over again; my tea costs me about 1s. a-week: if I can save eight parts out of 18, I can have as strong and better flavoured tea for less than 7d. a-week, being a saving equal to half the water rate. It is not easy, however, to get these savings effected regularly, it is apt to be forgotten, and cannot well be left to the servants. It would be far better to have a water originally soft, if it were procurable."

The reason why hard water is so inefficient for making an infusion of tea is easily understood when we consider its composition; 100 parts of green and black tea are composed as follows:—

	Black.	Green.
Tannin	40·0	34·6
Gum	6·3	5·9
Albumen	0·4	5·7
Lignin (woody fibre)	44·8	51·3
Volatile Oil., &c.	1·9	2·5
	100.0	100·0

Now the tannin, gum, albumen, and volatile oil, on which last the flavour of the tea depends, are all capable of uniting with the salts causing the hardness of water, and forming with them either insoluble or peculiar flavoured compounds. In either case they diminish the colour and taste of the infusion, and delay the process of tea-making.

To remove the hardness of the water so as to render it most suitable for the tea-urn, there is no addition so desirable as *Oxalate of Ammonia*. The oxalic acid of this salt unites with the lime, whatever may be its combination in the water, and forming an insoluble salt (oxalate of lime) falls to the bottom, while the ammonia of the oxalate of ammonia is driven off by the heat of the water. We recommend as much of this salt, powdered, as will lie on a sixpence to be put into the tea-urn or kettle rather than a proportionately smaller quantity into the tea-pot. Even if the powdered sub-carbonate of soda is used for the same purpose it should be added to the water before this reaches the tea-pot, and in much smaller quantity. If used only in a proportion but little more than necessary to decompose the calcareous salts in the water, it helps to extract a dark colour from the tea, but destroys its flavour, and makes it taste vapid, or "flat."

THE FRUIT-GARDEN.

Budding.—As the seasons revolve, each brings its duties, and amongst the rest our present subject holds an important position. As to the budding of exotic plants, roses, &c., our clever fellow labourers in the pages of The Cottage Gardener will, doubtless, give them due attention; and although the principles are identical, be it ours to assist our amateur friends in budding their fruit-trees, and for this proceeding the present period is, of all others, the most eligible.

One remark may here be permitted as worthy of special notice, and that is the character and condition of the *stock*, on which so much depends. If the bark does not "rise" well (that is, does not part freely from the wood), say our old blue aprons, the buds will not succeed, and the blue aprons are perfectly correct.

Before offering advice on budding, it will be well to give the *rationale* of the practice; and for this purpose we may be allowed to quote from "The Theory of Horticulture" this accurate and brief explanation: "Budding and grafting consists in causing an eye, or a cutting, of one plant to grow upon some other plant, so that the two, by forming an *organic union*, become a new and compound individual. The eye in these cases takes the name of *bud*, the cutting is called *scion*, and the plant upon which they are made to grow is named the *stock*."

And now as to the effects sought to be produced; we again quote, for we cannot possibly make a better case of it. "By these means we gain the important end of bringing in *close contact* a considerable surface of *young organising matter*. The organisation of wood takes place on its exterior, and that of bark on its interior surface; and these are the parts which are applied to each other in the operation of budding; in addition to which the stranger bud finds itself in its new position *as freely in communication with alimentary matter, or more so, than on its parent branch.* A union takes place of the cellular faces or horizontal system of the stock and bark of the bud, while the latter, as soon as it begins to grow, *sends down the woody matter or vertical*

system through the cellular substance. In consequence of the horizontal incision, the returning sap of the scion is arrested in its course, and *accumulates a little just above the new bud,* to which it is gradually supplied as it is required. Sometimes the whole of the wood below the bark is allowed to remain; and in that case contact between the organising surfaces of the stock and scion does not take place; and the union of the two is much less certain; as it is, however, usually practised with tender shoots *before the wood is consolidated,* the contact spoken of is of less moment."

In order to save repetition, we have placed those parts in italics which ought to form the peculiar study and receive the utmost attention from the inexperienced in budding affairs.

Many fanciful modes of budding are, and have been, practised, but we have not space to describe them; and their utility, moreover, to the readers of The Cottage Gardener is very questionable. What is termed *shield budding* is in universal practice and repute in Britain; and what our nurserymen, who are an intelligent class of the community, practice in propagation matters our readers may safely follow, until their inventive faculties can produce some other worthy to supersede it.

Once more, then, we may venture to give a detail of the proceeding, which our more experienced readers must excuse, for the sake of those who have yet much to learn that appears so familiar to some minds.

A good *budding knife* is the first thing to be provided; any respectable nurseryman will furnish this.* Next, some really good matting; we prefer the new *Cuba bast,* but the finest of the ordinary Russian mats will answer equally well, perhaps better, provided the material is very fine and very tough. In selecting a mat for this purpose, it is better for those who do not require a great amount to give an extra price for the pick of a good one. Such may be distinguished by two or three critera, which stand as follows:—First, whatever colour the bast be, it must feel silky and somewhat oily to the touch; such is generally a good character of bast. A full reliance must not be placed on this alone, however, but the strength should be tested. This is readily done by cutting off a fine-looking strand, and stripping off a narrow piece as fine as twine. This, if good, should withstand a considerable amount of tension; it is well, however, to try a second piece. As to colour, such is generally a pale straw. So much for the character of bast, for be it understood it is extremely inconvenient to have the bast frequently breaking in the hand, to say nothing of the prejudice of the bud. The bast must be cut into lengths and adapted to the size of the stocks—be they what they may. A mere novice may soon determine the length necessary, by twisting a piece round any twig of similar size, as in the act of budding.

Before describing the process itself, it will be well to speak of the condition of *the stocks* or subjects to be operated on. Budding, as before observed, is performed at various seasons; and in very early budding, as previously shewn, it is considered in the majority of cases prudential, if not absolutely necessary, to insert the whole of the shield or bud with its own system of wood attached. When the summer is far advanced, however, and the buds are become individually perfect, or nearly so, in their organization, the case alters, and the less of intervening matter there exists between the bud with its immediate appurtenances of petiole, the barks, &c., the better.

* The best budding instrument we have ever seen is made by Mr. Turner, Neepsend, Sheffield. It has a budding knife at one end and a grooved hook at the other end. This hook being inserted in the T cut made with the knife keeps it open, and allows the bud to be slipt easily down the groove into its place. It really supplies the budder with a third hand.—Ed. C. G.

Budding, then, in spring or early summer is generally accompanied, it may be presumed, by a copious current of sap; not so, however, late summer budding on all occasions; the season may have been unusually warm and dry; the stock or subject may be short of sap, or, in other words, be beset with a paralysed root action; all these are impediments. Can anything be done then to alleviate these misfortunes ? Yes. A copious watering the evening previous to the process will, indeed, promote the free rising of the bark, on which so much depends. In addition to this, a cloudy day is preferable to a sunny one, and thus, like the gardening processes of transplanting, cutting, &c., &c., a careful choice of weather, when possible, is of some importance.

In former days the chief criterion of the eligibility of a tree for the budding process was the cessation of growth, or rather of extension, in point of length in the stock. Such generally happens in fruit-trees: such as the peach, apricot, cherry, plum, &c., about the first or second week in August. The period, of course, being liable to be modified by several circumstances, as heat, drought, &c. Instead, however, of this waiting until the eleventh hour, people in those days make an earlier commencement; and, in fact, there is little occasion to delay these things after the middle of July has passed, unless the stocks or scions are subjects of late growth and excessive luxuriance.

We almost fear we shall be tedious in describing the insertion of the bud : a thing so simple that, as a mere mechanical process, a child seven years of age would soon be taught to perform with ease. Nevertheless, as many young ladies and young gentlemen condescend to listen to our practice, and to be somewhat guided thereby, we must begin at the beginning.

The exact position of the bud being determined, *the incision* is made across the stock transversely, in length sufficient to create an opening for the bud ; this slit forms the head of the incision, which, when the next slit is made, will form the letter **T**. In making this slit, or incision, a somewhat bold cut must be made,—in fact, the point of the knife must be made to reach the surface of the wood of the stock.

The perpendicular slit is made from the bottom upwards, and an experienced budder gives a peculiar flirt or jerk to the knife when he approaches the head of the **T** : this jerk at once rifts up the bark better than any slower process could do it ; and the haft of the budding-knife is in a moment turned round, and the point introduced ; and by pressing it close to the wood, right and left, the bark is, as it were, ploughed up, or liberated from the wood.

All is now ready for the reception of *the bud,* which is, indeed, by most good budders prepared first, as follows :—The cutting or shoot of the kind to be inserted being wood of the current year's growth, is generally kept in a waterpot, first cutting off all the leaves : care must, however, be taken to leave most of the petiole (leaf-stalk) to handle the bud by ; this also, doubtless, assists in forming a speedy union.

The bud, with its bark and a little of the wood of the tree, is then cut off in the form of a shield ; and the point of the knife and thumb-nail of the right hand, by a little nice handling, are made to remove the portion of woody matter from the centre. The bud is instantly introduced beneath the bark in the **T** incision of the stock, where, as before observed, it is found in the same relation to the stock or stem of its new parent as existed between it and the shoot whence it sprang. This done, it is carefully and closely, but not tightly, bound with the bast; the operator generally beginning to bind at the lower end, gives an extra tug with the mat when he comes tolerably close to the lower end of the petiole. This is an old practice, and not particularly intelligible; the meaning, we suppose—if meaning it have—being,

that the tightness of the ligature in that precise position impedes slightly the *returning sap,* thereby concentrating it about the bud.

Some persons employ a *grafting wax* to cover the parts where air may enter; the following mixture will make a very useful kind :—Sealing wax, one part, mutton fat, one part ; white wax, one part ; honey, one-eighth part. The white wax and fat are first melted, and then the sealing wax is to be added, gradually, in small pieces: the mixture being kept constantly stirred lastly, the honey must be put in, just before taking it off the fire. It should be poured into paper or tin moulds and kept slightly agitated till it begins to congeal.

We before observed, that when the season is late, and the bark rises somewhat badly, it may be excited to rise. A liberal watering with liquid-manure, of the tempera ture of 90°, the day before the operation, will in general facilitate the proceeding. When the bud or shield, after the wood is removed, appears hollow at the bud part, it is commonly rejected. Such are not always barren, but they are apt to lie dormant for a year or two.

When a choice of position offers itself, we prefer the shady side of the stock ; it is of more importance, however, to select a clear portion of the stem, free from knots; although some fancy the bud takes better if placed in a position from whence a natural bud has been removed. It should be taken as a maxim, that only those buds should be selected, the leaves of which have become fully developed; the leaf also should, if possible, be unblemished.

Cloudy weather is in all cases to be preferred to sunny periods ; and we may add that one of the chief criteria of the stock being in a condition to bud, is the premonitory sign of a speedy cessation of growth, as evinced by a sort of stationary character. This must not, however, be the only dependence ; stocks may be tried and proved in some portion about to be cut away.

R. ERRINGTON.

THE FLOWER-GARDEN.

GARDEN-WALKS. —Those awful tempests which we experienced just on the turn of St. Swithin's day, tore up garden-walks in all parts of the country where the ground was not level ; any path, or alley, or walk on the side of a bank or any sloping ground, unless made on a plan very different to the usual way, must have been washed into sloughs and gullies, and every kind of inequalities. I recollect seven or eight years since we had such another routing here with a summer storm, but this time we escaped very nearly. Mr. Rivers, the great rose-grower, called here the next day after all our walks were nearly washed away, and he was so frightened with the wreck of what he was told were fine gardens that he never came to see us since. At that time I took it into my head that we were all wrong about making garden-walks, carriage-roads and all, and I wished very much to try an experiment or two on a large scale, to see how far I could succeed in another direction—but fanciful experiments are dear toys. However, through the indulgence of my worthy employer, I did get a fair start in making a walk on a novel plan—on the level, and on all kinds of inclinations, from a gentle swell to a steep hill side, where we are under the necessity of using long flights of steps to get up and down, in several parts of the garden; and now I shall cordially shake hands with S. N. V. (see page 263), and some of these days I shall tell him how to construct a walk along the face of " Snowden," the Malvern Hills, the Peak of Derby, or from the top of Arthur's Seat to Salisbury Craigs, which will be storm proof as long as either of us live and can walk without a stick. But, like S. N. V., I should first like to hear what the experience of walk-makers among *our readers* is, as for the last six or seven months I have been patiently hearing "those on the other side."

Some of our readers will probably recollect, that some time last spring when writing about keeping grass lawns tidy, and all that sort of thing, that I said I would write a whole chapter on making walks after a new fashion, or something to that effect, and now that "murder is out," I may as well at once acknowledge that that promise was a "feeler;" and although in my younger days I fished on some of the best lochs and streams in the Highlands, and could even dress a fly-hook which a salmon could not resist by moonlight, I confess, I never knew a bait answer its purpose better than did that *feeler*, and seldom did I enjoy the sport more keenly than on this occasion.

I knew very well that there is in books and in gardener's heads a great deal of wrong ideas on the subject of making walks, and I was embued with as much of these false notions as any of them until I was driven to my wits' ends from the demolishing effects of thunderstorms on the walks here; but I was not quite sure if longer practice had not improved the system of walk-making, although we had no accounts of it in our books and journals, hence the reason for my *feeler*. No sooner did I announce my promise than a host of my own best friends and others flew into print to anticipate me—just the very thing I wanted. I shall wait a few weeks longer to see if any one will answer S. N. V., about making walks on hill sides, and will now merely remark, that the only novelty worth mentioning which the discussion on walk-making brought to light in the press this season is this, that the best gardeners who wrote on the subject have proved by their own confessions that they know less on the subject than some of their co-adjutors who never wheeled a barrowful of gravel for a walk in their lives, or thrust a spade in the ground for any thing; and I hope ere long many will answer S. N. V.'s request about making good substantial walks on sloping ground, for I am so pressed about roses and other flowers just now, that people would think me *daft* if I were to occupy space in August about making walks.

ICE.—Another subject—a singular one, by the way—has been broached to me since the beginning of the dog-days, and which I must put off for a few weeks, if only for the look of the thing, I mean the queries about *ice-houses* and preserving *ice*. Let no one think for a moment of building an ice-house; they are the most extravagant and foolish things in the whole country; and we shall have time enough to make all the necessary preparations for making walks and keeping ice after the frost has cut down the flowers. While I think of it, however, I may tell of a curiosity which is "unbeknown" to most of our readers, and that is, that there is a sheet of water within the compass of this island which is now covered with natural ice strong enough to allow a regiment of soldiers to pass over it. I never learned to skate well, but I often took a sliding exercise on this ice in the dog-days.

Let us now turn to the flowers! "*What is the best time to bud roses?*" is the most prominent question one hears throughout the rose season; and if a gardener gets into conversation on the rose subject, the next question is sure to be, "What kind of *stock* do you consider the best for roses?" And this leads to the third question, which is as likely as anything to be about the difference between roses on their own roots and those worked on stocks. Now, all these queries are so general, that one cannot give a decisive answer to them.

The best time to bud all tender roses that are liable to be hurt by frost, is at the end of May or in the middle of September; and for this reason, that it is their nature to grow as soon as they receive the juices of the plant or stock on which they are worked; and if they are put

in or budded after the end of June until as late in September as that they shall not push that season, their young growth will not have sufficient time to ripen; and if a hard winter follows, although it may not kill the young growth outright, it will so cripple them that they do little good for years afterwards. After the middle of September few roses, if any, will start or grow from buds then inserted, but remain inactive, like the rest of the buds, until the following season; and, on the whole, gardeners prefer such buds to those which start the first season—I mean buds of tender roses.

The best time to bud all the hardy roses is when one has time to do it; for all times that the bark will rise from the wood is equally good, from March to October. I have known Hybrid Perpetuals budded at the end of August begin to grow late in October when the weather was fine, and get pinched the following winter, and even a length of six inches of young growth killed; but that made little difference the following season, as little buds were formed at the bottom of the killed shoot, which grew away as if nothing was amiss with their leader.

Buds that were put in last September, or such as were budded before last midsummer, and have grown six inches, should now have the remaining portion of the branch or stock above them cut off, that the cut or wound may be covered as much as possible with the young formation of wood just now being formed rapidly by the descending sap. It is a very bad practice to leave pieces of the stock branch uncut for any length of time after the bud has grown out freely, or at any rate after the young leaves are ripe and begin the formation of wood, or, say, after the middle of July, because the descending sap will collect at the union and form a swelling of young wood, which should go partly to heal the wound; instead of which, it is interrupted just as if the shoot had been ringed, or a ring of bark taken off, or as if it had been tied with a piece of wire. The first scent which physiologists obtained of the descent of the sap and the formation of wood, was from such cause as this of stopping the natural current, when it was found that the swelling caused by the ring or tie was always on the upper side of the obstruction.

A keen amateur of my acquaintance holds out stoutly against all this "fine doctrine," as he calls it, and maintains that the convenience of tying the young head from a rose bud to the six inches of the branch in which the bud was inserted, and so avoiding the trouble of putting sticks to hold them instead far more than counterbalances the rapid covering of the cut behind the budded part; and after all, perhaps, the "best way" is that which suits our own notions best, apart from all philosophy.

As for *the best stocks* and no stocks, there has been a good deal written this very season in the different gardening works, and more particularly in *The Gardeners Chronicle*; and even nurserymen of the very highest standing and respectability have crossed swords—or, grey-goose quills—for and against different varieties of roses better fitted for stocks than any others. Now, when we hear two or three first-rate nurserymen, or as many old gardeners, of extensive practice, hold out that black is blue and that blue is white, our opinions get staggered, unless we are in the secret ourselves, and see like the juryman who exclaimed, after hearing counsel on both sides, that they were both right. I have often witnessed a keen controversy between two gardeners on a subject on which both of them were right. It had been the fashion among us gardeners, till very recently, to think that a subject would look poor indeed in print unless it was well larded with a number of long, hard dictionary words—the application, or force, or meaning of which few of us understood. This failing cannot be laid to the charge of the different writers on the subject of rose stocks; but yet "there is a tide in the affairs" of gardeners which not only leads up to, but explains the cause of the different opinions entertained by the great rose-growers on the best stocks for their staple commodity. When a young gardener, " who has a thorough knowledge of his profession," gets into his maiden place, he learns more the first season than " his thorough knowledge " will allow him to confess; still it is real useful knowledge gained—it may be by sad experience; but by and bye he begins to plant his cabbages wrong end upwards, and for this he is soon in the market again, with his " thorough knowledge," and something more this time; and by the time he rings the changes half a dozen times, say in as many counties, and, perhaps, on as many soils and situations, he is really a sound practical man—he will tell you many facts hard to be understood, yet true enough for all that. His vines at Maldo were always very fine, with very little trouble to himself, but his pinks and carnations " his thorough knowledge " could not manage at all at all! On the other hand, when he was at Parkstone, do what he could his grapes were the poorest in that part of the country, but then his pinks and carnations required no pains or trouble taken on their behalf, for they would do " anyhow;" and something in the same way influenced all his plants and crops in different degrees in each place; and so he chimes in at last with those who say, that soils which exhibit the same properties under the analysis of the chemist may still be opposite in the results they show under the hands of the gardener or farmer: in short, that there is a something still—a principle, if that suits better—in the composition of soils which has hitherto escaped the labours of the chemist, and to this day are, and can only be, known by the results they produce. It is very different with the unassuming man who begins the world with a mistrust of his own " knowledge : " he tries to do overything in the best manner, and at the right time, and he succeeds so far that at last he masters all the difficulties of his position in some way or other. Things which do not answer well in his garden he shuns, and pays more attention to those things which he finds will suit, and thus he gains the confidence of his employer, and is pronounced " a good gardener ;" but in truth he is no such thing—he is only a good gardener in a particular locality and under particular circumstances. Send him to Maldo, or to Parkstone, or to any of the half dozen other places where the " thorough knowledge of his profession" man failed, and he would fail too in all probability. The fast man has the advantage over him now, and if at this stage they were both sent into a new field, he would soon show the superiority of his knowledge; fast as he may have been formerly, he will not content himself in the new field to trust his labours under one set of rules, like the " good gardener," but will conduct his principal operations under three or four sets of rules at the same time; and thus is in possession of the capabilities of the new field the first season, and without a disappointment; for oven if some of his rules fail, as there is no doubt they will, no one knows it but himself, and his failures of one season he avoids in the following. *He*, now, is the good gardener, and the " good gardener" is discharged, because he persisted in doing everything as he used to do them, although he failed three years running. Now all this is literally drawn from real life, and within my own personal knowledge; and I adduce it to account for the strange fact, that two or three eminent rose-growers should entirely disagree as to the merits of this, that, or the other kind of *stock* best suited to work upon; and I cannot help thinking that they are doing some harm to the trade, besides disquieting the rose mind, if there is such, all over the country. They are like " the good gardener"—and I have no fear of their being angry with mo for saying so; their respective experience is formed and matured in one given

locality, and if they were to change to one very different they would find their present practice would need to be altogether remoddeled. If there is anything more firmly established in the heads of old gardeners than another, it is this—that *every kind of stock* (whether for roses, or for apples, or any other flower or fruiting plant) *will grow in one particular kind of soil better than in any other*; and as no mode has yet been discovered by which one could tell beforehand whether a certain plant will do or answer on a given soil or not, without giving it a trial, it is of very little practical use to insist exclusively on the merits or faults of any given stock. *The dog rose* is allowed by nine-tenths of the rose-growers of this country to be the best suited to work the different varieties on; now this same dog rose will not live more than five or six years in the soil of the garden here, and no variety that I have hitherto tried will look quite healthy on the dog rose more than three years. Should I, therefore, be justified to run down the dog rose, and call it a dangerous experiment to try it? Certainly not! Even where all kinds of roses answer well it will be found, that certain varieties will do better on one particular kind of stock than on any other.

I must apologise for occupying so much room, but I have had queries enough this season to convince me that more room must be spared to talk and write about roses.   D. Beaton.

GREENHOUSE AND WINDOW GARDENING.

Propagating Florists' Pelargoniums, &c.—I thought that this subject had already been sufficiently referred to, but the continued inquiries of correspondents, and the hint of our good editor, influenced by these inquiries, that something more of a simple nature would be acceptable, have led me to give the matter this prominence : though fully aware that I cannot give utterance to one idea that has not already been referred to, if not by myself, by others more qualified to do the matter full justice. Though over glad to attend to all inquiries that come in my way, I sometimes think that time and postage would be saved by a reference to the index of past numbers. I know, however, that in the case of those who do no possess past volumes it is somewhat tantalising thus to tell them, in a *quiet* way, to go to a bookseller's and get them ! The pages of a periodical work should, in some respects, resemble a well-conducted railway-train, that sets down and takes up passengers at every station—attending to the comforts of all. It is not only a harmless but a praiseworthy curiosity that leads the last admitted passengers politely to inquire about the state of the country through which the farther-travelled passengers have passed; and we should set them down as clownish churls who, because a few that started from the terminus had already observed the country, and expressed to each other their relative opinions, were snappishly to tell the new comers to go and look, and then form opinions for themselves. Older subscribers, therefore, when they meet with articles—the matter of which they are perfectly conversant with—will just be so good as skim them over with the thought, that what may be of no interest to them may yet possess attractions for many who have had less experience.

In order to simplify the matter, let us glance for a moment at what *a cutting* is. In general, it may be described as part of a healthy plant, containing one, two, or more joints, with a bud or buds either fully developed, if the wood is ripe, or with buds formed or forming in the axils of the leaves, if the wood is still green and growing. From these buds, formed or still to be formed, possessing a growing point, and connected at their bases with the pith of the shoot, all extension upwards into stems and branches must proceed. On the other hand, extension downwards in the shape of roots proceeds chiefly from cellular matter protruded from the base of the cutting, and chiefly from that part of it between the liber and alburnum—the part in all plants possessing netted-veined leaves where the living principle is most active, and where all lateral additions in girth to stem and branches have their origin.

Where a cutting possesses several joints, it is usual to cut it transversely through the lowest one, and for these reasons:—First, one or several of the lower leaves may thus be removed, and the bud at the base likewise, and thus the evaporating surface is reduced, the danger of damping-off lessened, and the fastening of the cutting in the prepared compost better secured. And, secondly, at these nodes, and especially in the case of all plants with hollow stems, there is an accumulation of vital energies, so that roots from these parts are sooner produced. The other week I mentioned cases where, when the bark or skin was getting hard, it is advisable after thus cutting through a joint to run the knife for a short distance up its centre, that more cellular matter might thus be exposed, and roots sooner and more abundantly produced. In many cases, however, where the stems are soft, it is not necessary to cut to a joint at all; one bud and part of the shoot being quite sufficient to form a rooted cutting. Mr. Beaton mentioned in the spring how this was done with *Verbenas ;* and I have long practised a similar method with bedding *Calceolarias*—any part of the stem rooting freely; and thus time in making the cuttings is saved, an increase of a desirable variety sooner obtained, and long-legged plants prevented. The same thing may be done successfully with a single bud, and part of a shoot of many plants, though the wood be indurated, as in the case of a vine raised from what is termed an *eye*, and more especially if a part of the outside has been cut away, so as to expose a good portion of liber and alburnum. Exactly the same operations will be here developed as in a cutting with many buds; and, therefore, instead of increasing and confusing our nomenclature with talking about raising plants from *buds* and *eyes*, we should term them all cuttings, *wherever* there is a bud and part of the wood, however small, connected with it. Striking plants from *leaves* is quite a different thing. There, in most cases, fresh buds must be formed by the organisable matter protruded at the base of the leaf or its footstalk, before any upward extension can take place. Many leaves will root very freely, and yet be so loath to form a bud from whence a shoot only can come, that—unless in a few cases, some of which have already been referred to—such experiments are more interesting than useful.

It will at once be obvious, that the more perfect the buds upon a cutting, the sooner will fresh shoots be produced, and thus a healthy stubby plant be formed. It will also be seen, that the principle involved in striking cuttings of plants is identical, whether they be hardy or tender, deciduous or evergreen, hard or soft wooded, possessing ripened shoots from whence the leaves have fallen, or shoots still growing and possessing healthy leaves, performing the functions of absorption, perspiration, and respiration. But the mode of working out that principle must be as varied as the circumstances. Thus, when a plant is very succulent in its nature we expose it to heat and light, give less water, and even partially dry the cutting before inserting it, lest there should be danger of the soft matter rotting and damping instead of forming roots. Again, if the shoots would be too hard, as would often be the case with *Heaths, Epacrises,* &c., we place them in a close warmish place until fresh growth is made, and nip the little bits off when they are neither so hard as to render rooting difficult, nor yet so soft as to render

damping and rotting likely. Thus, again, well-ripened shoots and green growing ones must be treated differently. In the one case, such as in the well-ripened shoot of a gooseberry or a vine—though the former may be inserted as a cutting out of doors and the latter in a hotbed—comparative little attention will be required for either, provided too many buds are not left to grow, as each cutting possesses in itself a stock of elaborated nutritious matter, which, when acted upon by the stimuli of moisture and heat, &c., will cause a nearly simultaneous pushing out of roots in the soil, and of shoots from the buds. By the manner in which we apply these exciting agents we may generally get roots in advance of the shoots, or the contrary, just as we please. But when we take a green growing shoot of any of these, or of a greenhouse or stove plant (for, with the exception of the difference in temperature needed, our necessary attentions otherwise will be similar), we have got no highly elaborated matter in the cutting to fall back upon—its tissues will be soft, its juices thin and gross, and to succeed with it we must aim at giving it some of the same properties it would have enjoyed if left upon its mother plant. Expose it with its leaves to light and air, and the quick perspiration of its juices causes it quickly to die of starvation. Absorption of moisture merely by the lower end will do but little to arrest such a result. Shade it altogether from light; and if you prevent perspiration from the leaves, you also prevent the assimilation of fresh elaborated matter to the cutting, and retard the process of rooting, until very likely, though your leaves be freshish, the stem becomes so attenuated that it cannot keep itself upright, and failure is generally the result. Hence, when we make such a cutting we insert it in light soil, well drained, so that moisture when communicated shall not stagnate about its lower end and cause the soft tissues to rot; we cover it with a bell-glass or hand-light, not only to keep out the air, but to obtain an atmosphere well saturated with moisture, so that not merely the lower end of the cutting but the stem and the leaves may have the opportunity of absorbing as well as perspiring; we shade in bright sunshine, because then otherwise the perspiring powers would exceed the absorbing, and the assimilation of carbon, or fresh solid matter, would be too quick for its peculiar position; but knowing that the maturing principle and the addition of fresh matter to the cutting (without which, in such circumstances, we have little hopes of success) can only be obtained by the elaborating processes effected by the leaves in sunlight, we remove the shading during the morning and evening, and ultimately at mid-day as soon as it will stand it; and knowing, in addition, that the close atmosphere has a tendency to expand the cutting upwards, while we chiefly want it at first to root downwards; even before we venture to give air during the day we do so during the night, and also evening and morning—first by raising the glass with a pebble or potsherd a little on one side, and then removing it altogether, but replacing it before the sun strikes it until it has rooted. By keeping the cuttings at a distance from the glass in pots, giving them *diffused* instead of *direct* light, I have been enabled, in most cases, to dispense with shading altogether. Of course the cuttings are exposed to direct light as soon as the rooting process is going on, either by elevating them or removing the glass.

If what I have stated be correct, then we may see :—

First, that having a bud at the base of a cutting is not necessary for the *protrusion* of roots, as some gardening writers state. On the contrary, unless in the case of plants that form tubers, it is a disadvantage, as that bud is as likely to grow upwards as any of the rest, and, therefore, will furnish you with ground-shoots instead of having a plant with a clear nice stem. Cutting through at the joint where the bud is situated will in general be advantageous.

Secondly : cuttings of deciduous plants are easiest raised from well-ripened shoots with perfect buds. An exception exists in the case of many herbaceous plants, which should not be over ripe.

Thirdly : hardy evergreens likewise will require least attention in the open air, when their shoots are approaching maturity ; and, therefore, cuttings should be removed and inserted towards autumn.

Fourthly : small pieces of tender evergreens, nursed under glasses, will succeed best when partaking of a medium character as to firmness—between the shrubby and the herbaceous.

Fifthly : grosser plants, such as the geranium, will succeed best when their buds are formed, and the shoots firmer and brown than otherwise.

Sixthly : the greatest nicety of all is required with soft spongy cuttings, as the fresh matter must be assimilated before you can have great hopes of success ; and, therefore, gardeners instead of choosing the points of luxuriant, sappy shoots, fix upon the small side ones that are firmer in their texture ; and contrive to slip them off close to the stem, because there, as at a joint, is an accumulation of vital energies.

We cannot now say much on Pelargonium cuttings, but these matters we trust will be interesting to those who want to make them for the first time. As these plants are liable to insects, and apt to be gross in their habits, I would advise the preparing for taking off cuttings by two things :—

First : place all your plants where you can smoke them ; and then syringe their leaves and stems the day after.

Secondly : place the plants full in the sun for the best part of a week, and keep them as dry as possible, without allowing the leaves to flag anything to speak about ; and thus you will obtain two advantages, as the result of the maturing of the stem, and the elaboration or thickening of its juices : the cuttings will succeed better, and be less likely to damp ; and the old plant when cut down will not bleed, and will break better in consequence.

Thirdly : secure some light sandy soil.   R. Fish.

HOTHOUSE DEPARTMENT.
EXOTIC ORCHIDS.
(Continued from page 255.)

PLANTS REQUIRING TO BE GROWN ON BLOCKS.

Broughtonia aurea (Golden B.) ; Mexico.—A scarce species. Sepals and petals deep yellow ; the lip has a tinge of red in the centre ; the flowers are larger than *B. sanguinea*, and are scentless. 84s.

B. sanguinea (Blood-coloured B.) ; Jamaica.—A very handsome free-growing and free-blooming species. Every collection ought to contain this charming long-blooming plant. The whole flower is, when grown near the glass, of the richest crimson colour. The bloom is on terminal racemes. 25s.

Culture.—This genus is best cultivated on blocks, without moss, and hung up near to the roof. When growing they must be freely syringed daily, and kept in the India house ; but when the annual growth is completed they must be kept moderately dry and cool.

Burlingtonia candida (White B.) ; Demerara.—A most beautiful species, but very scarce. The whole flower is of the purest white. 105s.

B. fragrans (Sweet-scented B.) ; Brazil.—Very like *B. venusta*, but distinguished from it by its delicious fragrance. Unfortunately, like the first species, it is scarce. 84s.

B. maculata (Spotted B.) ; Brazil.—Sepals and petals

pale yellow, spotted with light brown ; lip creamy white, also spotted. A fragrant species, but not very showy. 21s.

B. rigida (Stiff-stemmed B.) ; Brazil.—This is a handsome species, but difficult to flower. The flowers are produced in heads, and are of a purplish white, spotted with pink on the lip. It is the most common of the whole genus. 31s 6d.

B. venusta (Charming B.) ; Brazil.—A beautiful free flowering species. The flowers are produced in drooping racemes ; sepals and petals pure white ; the lip has a pretty spot of yellow down the centre. 42s.

Culture.—The whole of this genus thrive well on blocks, with a small quantity of green moss attached to the logs. *B. candida* will also thrive moderately well in pots. They require to be kept hot and moist whilst growing, with abundance of water from the syringe, but cool and dry when at rest. *B. rigida* may be grown in a basket, filled with a mixture of peat, chopped sphagnum, and broken potsherds. Place the plant in the centre, and keep the shoots pegged-down to the surface of the basket. Though we have flowered it on a block, yet, treated in this way, we have seen it flower freely. They should all be sheltered from the sun's rays, as they grow in the depth of the dark forests of Brazil.

Camarotis purpurea (Purple C.) ; Sylhet, India.— The sepals and petals are bright purple lilac ; the lip is deep purple. 42s.   This is a very elegant and beautiful plant. It was discovered by Mr. Gibson, growing on trees at the foot of the Khosea Hills, in Sylhet ; and brought by him to the collection at Chatsworth, in 1837. It has the appearance of a small Vanda or Saccolabium, and is distinguished from these genera by the curious form of the lip, which is distinctly chambered at the point. Our readers will remember we described a large plant of it as being exhibited at the June Show at Chiswick, by Mr. Bassett, gardener to R. S. Holford, Esq., at Weston Birt. The manner in which this plant was grown is worthy of imitation, and for the benefit of our orchid-growing readers we shall try to describe it.

First, a circular flat block, about 18 in. in diameter and 6 in. thick was made ; then a hole was cut in the centre, and into that hole an upright branch of a tree 4 ft. high, 6 in. in diameter at the base, and 4 in. at the top, was closely and firmly fitted. Green moss of a considerable thickness was fastened to this upright pillar, and the plant or plants were fastened to the moss with copper wire. The plants were so large that they entirely covered the column, so that it could scarcely be seen ; the lower branches projected a little beyond the next, and so on to the top. The plant then formed a very upright pyramid, and at the time when it was exhibited every part and every side was clothed with the beautiful pendant spikes of its lovely purple blossoms. This fine plant had been about five years in forming and arriving at this splendid state of perfection. Our readers may justly remark, where shall we be able to procure plants to form such a noble specimen ! We can only say, make a beginning on a small scale on the same plan : manage the plant judiciously by dividing and spreading it out on the block, and you will soon see that you are in a fair way to approach, if not to come up with, such a fine plant.

Catasetum.—This is a family of curious rather than beautiful flowering plants, yet we do not recommend the entire banishment of all of them even from small collections. Though the colours of the flowers are generally not bright or pleasing, yet the various forms they assume are so grotesque, that it is desirable for the sake of seeing such out-of-the-usual-way flowers to cultivate a few species. We shall make a selection of the handsomest and most interesting.

Catasetum barbatum (Bearded C.) ; Demerara.—Sepals and petals narrow, green, and blotched with purple ; the lip green and pink; the outer edge is fringed with delicate fibres of a dull white like a beard, hence its name. 31s 6d.

C. deltoideum (Triangular-lipped C.); Demerara.— Sepals, petals, and lip greenish brown, marked with bands and spots of dark brown. The lip being of a triangular shape denotes at once the species. 31s 6d.

C. laminatum (Plaited C.); Mexico.—Sepals and petals spreading: large, brown, spotted with purple; the lip white, with a deep plait or frill running down the centre. It is sometimes spotted with purple, and then forms the variety called *maculatum*. This is a rare and beautiful species. 84s.

C. longifolium (Long-leaved C.); Demerara. —The whole flower is of a bright orange colour, with a narrow border of violet. The flowers are produced on a long raceme, drooping a foot or more long, and thickly set upon it. The finest of the genus, but very rare. 105s.

C. naso (Nose-shaped C.); Caraccas.—A very curious species. Sepals and petals white, tinged with greenish yellow, spotted thickly with deep crimson purple; the lip terminates in a long snout like the elephant's trunk. 84s.

C. saccatum (Bagged C.).—One of the most extraordinary flowers ever seen. It is very large; the sepals and petals are spotted with rich purple; the lip is bright yellow, thickly covered with crimson spots. It is bored, as it were, in the middle by a narrow opening, which leads into a deep chamber or *sack*, hence its specific name. 84s.

C. tridentatum (Three-toothed C.).—There are several varieties of this species: *Claveringii, floribundum, Waileni,* and others; indeed, there seems to be no certainty in any specific distinctions, as the same plant frequently sports into them all. This monstrous propensity renders it extremely amusing to the general cultivator, but very annoying to the lover of botanical accuracy. A plant one year may be the true *C. tridentatum*, but, "presto—quick and begone," and like magic next year it may be *Monacanthus viridis*, or *Catasetum cristatum*, or some other unlikely species so called, or variety. 21s.

CULTURE.—Though this remarkable genus will grow in pots, we have always found them to thrive well on naked blocks, that is, without any moss, and live longer on them, though perhaps not flower so finely. In their native *habitats* (dwellings) they are found growing on branches of trees exposed to the burning rays of a tropical sun. In syringing the house they must frequently be omitted, as water on the young shoots is very apt to cause them to perish. When growing freely they should be kept in a moist heat, and will produce abundance of young roots and strong shoots, which will form large healthy pseudo-bulbs, if not too much syringed overhead. The blocks may be taken down when in that state and be dipped in the cistern, just up to the young shoots, with advantage. Even if the roots touch water constantly when in that state the plants will thrive all the better for it. In a torpid state, as soon as the pseudo-bulbs are fully formed, they should be kept dry and cool, even till all the leaves drop off. As they are mostly natives of the hot climate of Demerara, they require a great heat when growing; the India house is a proper habitation for them; a heat of 70° by night and 85° by day will be necessary, but in winter 60° will be sufficient.

T. APPLEBY.

FLORISTS' FLOWERS.

AURICULAS AND POLYANTHUSES.—These flowers will now require some attention. Should heavy rainy weather be prevalent, remove them from their summer quarters behind a north wall to a situation where they will obtain more sunshine, and be protected whenever the autumnal rains prevail to any extent. Cold nights and wet days will soon tell a melancholy tale upon these delicate plants, especially upon the auriculas. Do not trust them any longer to the chances of being exposed to such unfavourable circumstances, but shift them at once into a more favourable exposure. At the same time avoid any thing like coddling, or keeping them too warm. Let them have plenty of air and light but no heat, excepting such as the natural heat of our climate affords. Should there be strong sunshine in August or September, shade will be necessary to prevent premature growth or flowering.

Seedlings may yet be potted, as well as such young plants as may have been potted early in the summer, but all potting should be finished by the end of the month.

CARNATIONS AND PICOTEES.—Before this meets the eye of our flower-loving friends, all layering must positively be finished. Let all decaying flowers be immediately cut off, excepting such as are intended to *seed*, and from them remove the floral leaves as soon as they show symptoms of decay; we have seen many a promising pod of seed rotted by allowing the flowers to remain on till they began to rot. *Seedlings* will now be forming nice little plants, and should be planted out in beds four inches apart every way. These beds should be made of light rich soil, rather elevated, and in a dry open part of the garden. The plants should be put out in showery weather, so as to get established strongly before the cold weather sets in.

DAHLIAS.—Every care must now be taken of these fine autumnal flowers. Three points must be attended to. 1st—To give them plenty of nourishing food, either in the shape of *manure-water*, or by covering the roots for a considerable space round each plant with short rotten dung, the nourishing qualities of which will be washed down to the roots by the rain or water from the rose watering-pot. 2ndly.—*Tying-up* securely the branches to enable them to stand the strong equinoctial winds of autumn; and, lastly, *to protect the flower* from both wind, sun, and rain. There is also another point we had nearly forgot, and that is, to preserve the flowers from devouring *insects*—and there is none so destructive as the earwig. Various are the means that have been recommended to stay the ravages of these vermin, every one of which are useful. Small garden pots, with a little moss or hay at the bottom, turned upside down, and in that position placed upon the stakes, form an excellent trap. They should be emptied every morning, and the earwigs destroyed. Another way is to place bean-stalks amongst the plants; the insects creep into them for concealment every morning, and then they should be blown out of them into a pail of hot water. Also take a lantern, and every evening after dark look diligently over each flower. The earwigs feed at night, in the dark, and may then be caught in the act of destruction, and put to death, or your flowers will be sadly disfigured by having, perhaps, some of the finest petals half eaten, and thus spoiled for exhibition.

T. APPLEBY.

THE KITCHEN-GARDEN.

ANGELICA.—The present is a very good time for sowing, in order to have strong young plants for next season's produce. Sow the seed thinly in a drill. If more than one drill is required, four feet should be allowed between each, and two feet from plant to plant. When finally thinned, a dozen plants established on well-prepared soil, and assisted in the growing season by application of liquid-manure, will produce, in the course of the spring and summer months, many luxuriant crops of stalks, which are so much esteemed when preserved on account of their beautiful colour, their transparency, and peculiar flavour.

Asparagus, may still be encouraged by moderate applications of salt sown in showery weather.

Cabbage.—Sowing for the main crop should be well attended to up to the 12th of August; and one sowing should be made for the last time about the 20th to stand all the winter in the seed bed. The early sown plants should be pricked as soon as they can be handled.

Chervil.—A sowing should now be made in a sheltered corner for standing the winter.

Onions may be sown to stand the winter in the seed bed from the 18th to the end of August. If intended for use as young onions throughout the autumn and winter, they should be sown about the 12th. Onions now approaching maturity should have their tops gently pressed down. The back of a wooden rake is a very good article for this purpose, but it may also be very well performed with a pole, or a light soft broom. Those put for storing should not stay longer on the ground than actually needful. Our practice is (and it is one that seems to answer very well) to provide ourselves with ties of the proper length, either willow shoots or yarn, and set to work pulling and bunching, clearing and binding or tying, into moderate sized bunches; each onion gets a twist round, as it is drawn, in order that it may rise clean; and they are then at once conveyed under shelter, and hung up in open sheds or dry lofts, where they dry gradually, maintaining their silvery colour and natural flavour throughout the season. Any infected ones are at all times easily observed. A wet day, after the onions have been nicely dried, is chosen for handling and cleaning them over, when a little of the outside skin will fall off, causing them to look clean and shining, and to feel firm. We do not approve of their being exposed out of doors, or in the sun, after being ripe and drawn; for even if no rain falls on them, the dews of night and the hot sun by day discolours them, and causes their flavour to be hot and rancid.

Winter Spinach, as previously advised, should be well prepared for, and the main crop sown, by the 12th, but not later, as even one day or two later makes so much difference in the strength of this vegetable for winter and early spring production. Another sowing may be made later by a week or ten days, the produce of which will be but trifling until the spring, but which will not start to seed so soon as the main crop.

Potatoes.—Of the early varieties now taking up, the middling-sized ones may be advantageously put by for seed. We place such on the floor of lofts to harden and green. There can be but little doubt that after the late hasty rains and sultry close atmosphere, the foggy nights and some slight frosty mornings, that there will be again a general outcry about the progress and ravages of disease—more particularly amongst the late planted potatoes. As to people stating that it comes upon them all at once, that they examined their crops last week, or only a few days since, and could not observe any disease, which may be very true, but it shows, at the same time, a great blindness; and a good deal of nonsense no doubt is, and will be, uttered upon the occasion, as in former years; but we have never been able to discover, throughout the season, any one's potatoes that were entirely free from the old enemy—over which we have so long observed the sudden fluctuations of atmospheric changes to have so much influence. Those who insist on planting late, will, as a natural matter of course, have the most to complain of through their own folly. In this locality (Devonshire), through the general early planting for this last year or two, the disease has affected the potatoes but very slightly, particularly during the last season, when the crop was most abundant, of very good quality. All the early and half-early varieties, too, that were planted early this season are also producing an abundant crop of good quality. We have a piece of the old *Devonshire Red*, a variety almost lost in this locality, as strong and healthy as they were previous to the first appearance of the disease, which have bloomed and produced a fine crop of berries.

JAMES BARNES.

MISCELLANEOUS INFORMATION.

OUR VILLAGE WALKS.

By the Authoress of "My Flowers."

There is something inexpressibly striking and interesting in the white cliffs that bound and characterize our dear old Island Home! They gave to her her most ancient name; they have been the theme of song from the earliest days—and "The white cliffs of Albion" will, to the end of time, be dear and lovely in her children's eyes. There is beauty, too, in the swelling undulations that separate the restless ocean from the fertile plains and valleys that distinguish our happy land, especially in those we know by the name of Southdowns. Range after range of these soft, grassy hills stretch along our southern coast, covered with sweet herbage for innumerable flocks, and forming a bold and beautiful barrier against the storms that sweep along the shore. As we travel from the inland districts towards the coast we perceive a gradual change taking place in the aspect of the country: the trees first lessen in size, and become inelegant in their forms, from the prevalence of the strong sea breezes that pass over them so much in one particular direction as to give them a kind of hump-backed shape, never observable but in such situations; then succeeds an air of wildness, and an occasional appearance of bleakness, mingling with the rich pastoral scenery, announcing the near neighbourhood of a new and formidable feature in the world's amazing structure! At length we perceive the quiet swell of "the hills that encircle the sea," with their deep chalky chasms and bluff headlands, and the innumerable windmills that mark the presence of towns lying low in the snug valleys; and what an indescribable feeling arises when we reflect that the ocean—the restless, roaring, mysterious ocean—stretches itself at their feet! The first sight of the sea, which sometimes meets the eye like a silver edging to the horizon, and sometimes bursts upon it in all its glittering expansiveness, is always interesting and affecting, whether we view it for the first time or after a lengthened absence. It is such a wonderful portion of the earth's surface that it is impossible to contemplate it in any of its moods without deep awe, it is so beautiful—so terrible—so unquiet! Stretching from east to west—from north to south—covering so large a portion of the globe—playing so vast a part in the service of God and man—governed by such wondrous laws—and restrained by such mighty power! Can any natural object address our hearts more forcibly? Can anything speak more loudly and impressively of God? Does not every wave that breaks upon the sounding shore, as it advances farther and farther on its appointed way, declare His might? Why should that wide-spreading body of irresistible force advance and recede with so much methodical exactness? Why should it not rush onwards with overwhelming force and sweep away all before it? Why should not the gale dash the mountainous waves over hill and valley, engulfing the whole earth? Why should it suddenly, yet steadily, refuse to advance another step, even one little inch, amid all its rage and roaring? Why should it at one particular moment, in spite of its reckless fury, retire to its tossing bed as if by its own free will? Why? Can the philosopher answer? Can the man of science answer? Can "the wise" in their craftiness answer? No! Who can reply? A little child, with the oracles of God in his hand, can tell us the reason: "Because the Lord 'hath set a bound that they may not pass over: that they turn not again to cover the earth.'"

It is delightful to sit on the sea-shore and observe all that passes around us; for the simplest object and incident belonging to the sea is beautiful. The shells that lie scattered on the sands, and the ridges of sea-weed flung up from the depths of ocean—some of them exquisitely delicate in form and colour,—the pebbles that look as brightly coloured as agates when the water has washed them, and the varying tints of the waves as the clouds pass over them, are all subjects for deep thought and admiration. Sometimes a sea-gull, with its long, powerful wings, skims the surface, uttering its piercing, storm-portending cry, and settles on a wave, riding upon its own rude element as gracefully as the swan on the quiet river. Then a sail glitters on the horizon, and the coasting vessels vary and animate the scene with their busy movements. Sometimes an aristocratic-looking Revenue cutter, with her long, graceful ribbon floating on the breeze, will glide quietly round a headland, contrasting well with the heavy-built traders among whom she skims along. There is always a stir upon the waters, and when we seat ourselves upon a rock, and enter fully into the scene, we scarcely know when or how to tear ourselves away.

Some of the incidents, too, are invested with a sweet scriptural interest that a thousand-fold heightens their charm. "The Saviour of the World" oftentimes walked and "sat by the sea-side," and some of His most striking miracles, some of His most precious words, were performed and spoken upon or near the sea. It is quite impossible to watch the fisherman in his little boat, "launching out into the deep," with his light sail set, and his nets hanging over the side,—or to see him dragging them ashore, or mending them upon the beach,—or battling with the stormy tide when "the wind is contrary," without feeling a yet stronger tide rising and rushing through our hearts! We remember the teachings of Jesus—His patience—His pity—His protecting love—His mild rebuke—His outstretched hand—His instant deliverance. We see Him ever near to His disciples in all their toils and troubles; and we hear His voice—that voice that shall one day awake the dead!—bidding even the winds that baffled them "be still."

What comfort is this to the Christian's heart! How it quiets the fears that will arise, and strengthens the hope that is sometimes ready to die within us! How it sanctifies the hour we spend by the sea-side, and how it enhances all our enjoyments!

The "gallant ship" in the offing, upon which our eye rests, may also give us a word of instruction. We, too, are floating on "the waves of a troublesome world:" are we as well provided for our perilous voyage? Have we that "anchor of the soul, both sure and stedfast," which only can hold against the beating tides of life? Have we our charts on board, and do we study them? The port we profess to steer for has but a narrow channel, "and few there be that find it."

The very rock we rest upon tells us a blessed truth: firmly as it stands beneath our feet, boldly as it breasts and defies the waves, it will one day be rent and melted! It tells us that the true Rock is "Christ:" "neither is there any rock like our God." Let us take heed that our feet are planted as firmly on the Rock of ages, for none other will stand unmoved in "the cloudy and dark day." The murmuring waves add their word in season to arouse our hearts while it is yet "to-day;" they tell us "the wicked are like the troubled sea, that cannot rest," but the "peace" of God's people shall be "as a river."

Let England, as she looks down upon the ocean over which she has reigned so long, remember that only while the Saviour's name is honoured and exalted on her shores will her national prosperity exist. When she prays Him "to depart from her coasts," when she offers the right hand of fellowship to idolators and unbelievers, waves wilder than those of ocean will wash over her, and the glory of her name will cease.

RHUBARB WINE.

A FEW weeks since, in No. 88, you gave two receipts for making wine from the stalks of the rhubarb; in the first, the addition of sugar after the fermentation has ceased, and in the second, the direction to add brandy, are both wrong in principle. I have by me some notes respecting the manufacture of this wine, which are at your service, together with such commentaries as experience enables me to offer. They may not prove to be altogether useless or unacceptable to the readers of your excellent little journal, nor, perhaps, would a few words on wine making be out of place in a publication, many of whose readers must occasionally have a superabundance of fruit, which might be rendered useful if properly made into wine.

Against "home-made" wines a prejudice has long existed, and not without reason. The principles upon which the vinous fermentation should be conducted are, generally, nearly or altogether unknown, or lost sight of, in its manufacture; and a certain receipt being blindly followed, the result is left to chance, and, consequently, is generally an unwholesome compound of vinegar, sugar, carbonic acid, and water, with, or without, the flavour of the fruit used, and containing, may be, in favourable specimens, a small quantity of real wine. Now the fact is, that it is impossible to be certain of making wine by following any receipt; while, on the other hand, with a little knowledge of the subject, real good and sound wine may be made from any fruit. Sugar, water, and a ferment, with a little tartaric acid, being all the essentials to make wine—flavour being imparted by, and varied according to, the fruit used.

The juice of the grape, when properly ripe, contains all the constituents necessary to make wine. This juice when expressed and ready for fermentation, is technically termed "must." It contains sugar, vegetable matter, a ferment or yeast, water, citric, malic, and tartaric acids, in combination with potash and lime, and a peculiar flavouring essential oil; and in making an artificial "must" we endeavour to approach as nearly as possible this model. As our fruits have a deficiency of sugar, we supply it. Cane sugar differs somewhat from grape sugar, but this is of no material consequence. The fruit supplies the vegetable matter, the ferment, and a great portion of the water; tartaric acid is wanting. We supply it in the shape of argol, which is an impure bicarbonate of potash found in wine casks, precipitated during fermentation of foreign wines.

Having thus formed the "must," with the addition of more water if necessary, the next step is to conduct the fermentation properly. As home-made wines are generally made in small quantities, the fermentation is apt to decline towards the end of the process unless artificial heat be employed—temperature, then, must be attended to; the room in which the process is conducted should be at about 60 degrees. When the fermentation has proceeded as far as is required, which may be fairly guessed at by the taste, or ascertained by an instrument called a saccharometer, or measurer of sugar, further fermentation should be stopped by racking, or drawing off the clear liquor from the "lees" or deposit, and sulphuring the cask. The wine should now be placed in a cool cellar, and suffered to remain there, with an occasional inspection, for one, two, or even six or seven years, before bottling.

Bearing in mind, then, these general principles, it is obvious that in the stalks of the rhubarb, containing a quantity of juice, we have the vegetable matter, the ferment, the flavour, acid, and water, just as in currants or other fruit.

Wine may be made from these stalks either effervescent or still; in the former case, being undistinguishable from Champagne; and in the latter, of the character of the Rhine wines, especially when it is mature. Some made by myself in 1841 is very like genuine hock, and is pleasant, sound, and wholesome; and when I add that its cost, not including interest of money, is about one shilling per bottle, surely you must agree with me that some pains are well bestowed on its manufacture.

Having premised thus much, I will, though with some diffidence, enter more into detail in a future paper, should you deem the subject and my manner of handling it worthy your columns. Meanwhile, your readers must remember that I am but an amateur in the arts both of wine making and literary composition; and in the former have only had opportunities of putting theory into practice on a small scale. But I hope my communication may induce some of your readers to follow in my steps. I shall not be surprised or displeased if they soon outstrip me, and be enabled in their turn to amend and improve my suggestions.—Henry W. Livett, *Wells, Somerset.*

HORTICULTURAL SOCIETY'S SHOW, CHISWICK, July 13th.

(*Continued from page 281.*)

Cape Heaths were exhibited in considerable numbers, and never in better order.

COLLECTIONS OF TEN CAPE HEATHS.—AMATEURS.

1st Prize to Mr. Smith, gardener to W. Quilter, Esq., Norwood. The finest plant in this collection was

Erica Massonii, 3 ft. high, and as much through, profusely bloomed; also *E. infundibuliformis*, 2½ ft. by 2½ ft. *E. Bergiana*, covered with its bell-shaped purple blossoms, 3 ft. by 2½ ft. *E. oblata umbellata*, 2½ ft. by 2 ft. *E. Parmentierii rosea*, *E. tricolor Wilsonii*, *E. metulæflora*, *E. Irbyana*, and *E. retorta major*.

2nd Prize to Mr. Mylam. The best was

Erica oblata Veitchii, one of the finest of the genus; also *E. retorta major*, *E. Sevileana*, *E. infundibuliformis*, *E. Vernonii*, *E. eximia*, and *E. inflata*.

COLLECTIONS OF TEN CAPE HEATHS.—NURSERYMEN.

1st Prize to Mr. Epps, of Maidstone. Ten magnificent plants, all measuring 3 ft. by 3 ft.

Erica Parmentierii rosea, *E. Shannonii*, *E. metulæflora bicolor*, *E. inflata alba*, *E. eximia*, *E. tricolor Jacksonii*, *E. tricolor superba*, *E. tricolor Leeana*, and *E. retorta major*.

2nd Prize to Messrs. Rollison and Sons, for a scarcely inferior lot, consisting of

Erica oblata umbellata, *E. ferruginea*, 3 ft. by 3 ft.; *E. ampullacea tincta*, *E. jubata multiflora*, *E. jubata superba*, *E. Parmentierii rosea*, *E. Irbyana*, *E. Aldersonii*, *E. mutabilis*, and *E. reflexa*.

COLLECTIONS OF TEN CAPE HEATHS IN 11-INCH POTS.—NURSERYMEN.

1st Prize to Messrs. Rollison. Neat small plants, consisting of

Erica miniata, *E. oblata umbellata*, *E. Evansiana*, *E. Juliana*, *E. ampullacea major*, *E. jasminiflora*, *E. bandodiana*, and *E. tricolor Leeana*.

2nd Prize to Mr. Epps, Maidstone. He had in good order

Erica oblata, *E. tricolor Dunbariana*, *E. tricolor Wilsonii*, *E. perspicua rosea*, *E. ampullacea vellata*, and *E. Savileana*.

NEW OR RARE PLANTS.

1st Prize to Messrs. Veitch, of Exeter, for *Ixora salicifolia*, or Willow-leaved Ixora. The flowers are exceedingly like *I. Javanica*, the foliage is, however, sufficiently dissimilar to warrant a specific distinction. This specimen was not a handsome plant, being tall and thin, but it had upon it a fine head of orange scarlet blossoms.

2nd Prize to Messrs Lane and Sons, for a new *Acineta*, an orchid, with a pendulous spike of flowers of a creamy white, covered with brownish spots. Mr. Ivison had the 3rd *prize* for a handsome variety of *Cattleya Mossiæ*, with almost white sepals and petals. Besides these that obtained prizes there were exhibited by Messrs. Rollison a pretty variety of *Cattleya crispa*, named very properly *violacea*. The lip being of the deepest violet colour. They sent also the handsome *Luxemburghia ciliosa*, a greenhouse shrub of great beauty, with heads of bright yellow flowers. It is, however, not new, having been exhibited several times even in collections.

SINGLE SPECIMENS OF STOVE AND GREENHOUSE PLANTS SHOWING SUPERIOR CULTURE.

1st Prize to Messrs. Veitch and Sons, Exeter, for their *Rhododendron Javanicum*, with rich orange-coloured wax-like flowers. A very handsome and well-grown plant. A prize of the same value was awarded to Messrs. Frazer, for a splendidly bloomed plant of *Kalosanthes coccinea*.

2nd Prize to Mr. May, gardener to Mrs. Lawrence, for a noble *Stephanotis floribunda*; and to Mr. Green, gardener to Sir E. Antrobus, for an extra fine *Lisianthus Russellianus*.

3rd Prize to Mr. May, for a splendid *Ixora Javanica*; and to Mr. Dennett, gardener to H. H. Gilliatt, Esq., Clapham, for a handsome well-flowered *Erica Parmentierii rosea*.

4th Prize to Mr. May, for a large *Sollya linearis*, 5 ft. by 4½ ft.; and to Mr. Ivison, for *Curcuma Roscoana*, not well-coloured; also to Mr. Epps, for *Erica ferruginea*, 4 ft. through; a splendid plant.

MISCELLANEOUS.

Under this head the following obtained prizes:—

Mr. Glendinning, for a collection of *Statices*, consisting of *S. arborea*, *frutescens*, *mucronata*, *Fortunii*, *sinuata*, and *puberula*.

A prize was also awarded to the same for a very interesting collection of *new hardy evergreen shrubs*, mostly from California, viz.:—

Cerasus illicifolia, *Laurus regalis*, *Myrica Californica*, *Rhamnus Californicus*, *Ceanothus rigidus*, *C. dentatus*, *C. papillosus*, *C. cuneatus*, *C. integerimus*, *Berberis Leschenaultia*, and an *Arbutus*, like *procera*.

FLORISTS' FLOWERS.

CUT-ROSES.—NURSERYMEN.—COLLECTIONS OF FIFTY.

1st Prize to Messrs. Lane and Sons, Great Berkhampstead. The following were excellent:—

French Roses: *Ohl*, shaded lake; *Pharericus*, large crimson; *Madame Audiot*, creamy white centres; *General Jacqueminot*, large shaded red. Hybrid Provence: *Chenedolle*, brilliant crimson; *Coup d'Hebe*, delicate rose. Hybrid Bourbons: *Chateaubriant*, pink; *Comte de Montalivet*, rosy crimson; *Duchess de Praslin*, blush, pink centre; *Standard of Marengo*, fine rose. Hybrid Perpetual Bourbon: *Dupetit Thouars*.

2nd Prize to Messrs. Paul, Cheshunt.

Hybrid Perpetual: *La Reine*, rosy pink. Bourbon: *Souvenir de Malmaison*, clear flesh, large. Noisette: *Miss Glegg*, pure white. Hybrid China: *Chenedolle*, deep rosy crimson.

Messrs. Paul had a box of twelve new or superior roses in excellent condition. These were the best—

Julie de Krudner, *Duchess of Sutherland*, *Baronne Prevost*, *La Reine*. *Sydonie*, *Pius the Ninth*, *General Negrier*, *Duchess de Montpensier* (Hybrid Perpetuals); *General Jacqueminot*, *Lamoriciere* (Hybrid China), *Felicite*, *Parmentier* (Alba), and *Madame Hardy* (Damask).

FANCY PELARGONIUMS.

These were evidently on the decline.

1st Prize to Mr. Staines, for

Magnifica, *Hero of Surrey*, *Reine de Francais*, *Bouquet tout fait*, *Queen Superb*, and *Fairy Queen*.

2nd Prize to Mr. Gaines, for

Wintonia, *Orestes*, *Fairy Queen*, *Reine de Francais*, *Aboni*, and *Hero of Surrey*.

3rd Prize to Mr. Ambrose, Battersea, for

Enchantress, *Pride of Surrey* (new and good), *Juno* (do.), *Magnet*, *Standard*, and *Pilot*.

PELARGONIUMS.—SIX FINE SCARLET VARIETIES

were exhibited by Mr. Miller, gardener to R. Moseley, Esq., Paddington, but the heat of the day caused some of the finest flowers to fade, yet they were such noble specimens as to attract great admiration; their names were

Fire-fly, *Victoria*, *Frost's Superb*, *Compactum*, *Tom Thumb*, and *Rigby's Queen*.

FUCHSIAS.

These were by no means such fine specimens as from the advanced period of the year might reasonably have been expected.

1st Prize was awarded to Mr. Franklin, gardener to Mrs. Lawrence, Ealing Park, for

Beauty of Chelmsford, *Star*, and *Dr. Jephson*.

2nd Prize to Mr. Salter, nurseryman, Hammersmith, for *Exoniensis*, *Comte de Beaulieu*, and *Beauty of Dalston*.

3rd Prize to Mr. Gregory, nurseryman, Cirencester, for *Splendida*, *Elizabeth*, and *Dr. Jephson*.

(*To be continued.*)

TO CORRESPONDENTS.

*** We request that no one will write to the departmental writers of The Cottage Gardener. It gives them unjustifiable trouble and expense. All communications should be addressed "*To the Editor of The Cottage Gardener, 2, Amen Corner, Paternoster Row, London.*"

Myatt's Hautbois Strawberry (*Delta*).—This does not generally colour so well as the old hautbois, but then it is a sure bearer. Its colour would be improved on poorer soil, but then the fruit would not be so large.

Plants in Sitting-rooms (*Sigma*).—This will meet attention, but little can be done; want of moist air and light are, in your case, the great evils.

Cape Heaths and Bulbs from Seed (*Fanny H.*).—We should have liked better if you had received your seed earlier, but would advise sowing the most of them *now* instead of waiting for the spring. The *Heaths* should be sown on the top of sandy peat, after it has been gently pressed, and the pot more than half filled with drainage. Press the seed gently into the soil, and scatter over them the smallest dusting of silver sand. It would be better to water the compost well before instead of after sowing, and then, with a square of glass put over the pot, or a bell-glass, set in a cold frame, and kept shaded and close, little more water will be wanted until the little plants appear, which the most of them will do in a month or two, if the seed be good. When up the seedlings must be hardened off by exposure to sun and air, and allowed to stand in the seed-pot until March or April. The seed of bulbs should be used in a similar manner, but so much care will not be required. If the seeds are large, it will be as well to give no water for a short time after sowing, but allow them to swell by the moisture they absorb from the soil.

DATURA (E. D.).—This, "with large, pendant, white flowers," we suppose to be the *Brugmansia suaveolens*. This has not flowered in your greenhouse, not even when cut down, and you wish to know if putting it in a small forcing house would assist it, and, if so, when to put it in? This plant, if kept in a dormant state during winter, in a warm shed, pruned a little and put into a greenhouse in the spring, may be turned out into rich compost in the open garden, and will bloom beautifully in the end of summer and autumn; the blooming may be prolonged into the winter by pruning the roots gradually, and then transferring the ball to a tub before frost. The plant also blooms well during spring, summer, and autumn in the greenhouse; but it should enjoy a season of rest during the winter, the wood being so well ripened previously as to allow the leaves to fall. Such plants cut-in a little in the spring, top-dressed with rich compost, and placed in your small forcing house, say in February or March, would throw out a number of shoots, which should be thinned, and each of these should produce blossoms when the plant is moved to the greenhouse, say in May. Those put in the greenhouse from the shed, or from underneath the stage, where they stood during the winter, treated in the same manner, would come in a month or two later.

SWEET-SCENTED ROSES TO FORCE IN WINTER (*Ibid*).—*Moss:* The common moss, Alice Leroy, and Celine. *Hybrid Perpetuals:* Madame Laffay, Duchess of Sutherland, Baronne Prevost, William Jesse. *Bourbons:* Armosa, Paul Joseph. *Tea-scented:* Abricots, Nephetos, Belle Allemande, Sofrano, &c. The two last classes are the easiest to force, and need little preparation.

CAMPANULA CARPATICA (*Ibid*).—It is a perennial, though if the seeds are sown early, they may bloom in the autumn of the same year. It is easily propagated by divisions of the root, and these bloom better and later than when left untouched.

CARNATIONS WITH DIFFERENT COLOURED BLOOMS (*R. V.*).—This is not at all uncommon. Flowers, especially florist's flowers, are liable to *sport*, as it is termed, in this way; and when they do so frequently they are rejected by amateurs because liable to come *untrue*.

WOOD LABELS (*Ibid*).—You ask "for the most simple way of making these." Have some laths planed smooth, cut into the required lengths, and painted white; then dry write the name with a cedar pencil.

POTATO HAULM DISEASED (*O. Stevens*).—As your potato tubers "are not near being ripe" you had better leave them untouched; if August proves dry they will ripen, and the disease will not descend to the tubers. If you can nip off the diseased tops, if the disease is confined to the summits, try the effect of doing so; but on no account either cut or pull off the major part of the stems. *Let every one remember that to remove the stems or leaves is to stop the further growth of the tubers; and that the leaves being gangrened is by no means an indication that the tubers are so.*

APHIS ON RED CABBAGE (*W. Wakefield*).—The insect on your red cabbages, cauliflowers, &c., is the common Cabbage Louse (*Aphis Brassicæ*). Dusting the plants with Scotch snuff frequently, and supplying the roots abundantly with water and liquid-manure, is the treatment best calculated to destroy the enemy, and to enable your plants to withstand their attacks.

CATERPILLARS ON PEAR AND CHERRY LEAVES (*S. H. R.*).—These caterpillars, which you very graphically describe as having "eaten the leaves threadbare," are slimy grubs, the parent of which is a saw fly, *Selandria Æthiops*, which you will find figured and described at page 69 of our third volume. Try what dusting with lime will do against them. There is no reason, as your *Corallina Fuchsia* has reached the desired height, why you should not stop it by pinching off the leading bud.

AUSTRALIAN SEED (*A Lady*).—Your seeds are of species all good hardy greenhouse plants. Defer sowing the seeds till spring, say February; sow them in peat-earth, well drained; a temperature of from 55° to 65° at most will suit them well. Keep your seeds in a dry room, hung up in a canvas bag, until sowing time.

EXPENSE OF ERECTING A HOTHOUSE (*A Young Beginner*).—Ask the builders in your neighbourhood to give you an estimate, describing how you wish it built. If 20 feet long and 12 feet wide it ought to be done for something under £50. You had better heat it with a flue. If you refer to our indexes you will find abundance of information on all the modes of heating. What does for a greenhouse is equally effectual for a stove; for the latter the fire has to be kept up more frequently and longer.

ORCHARD (*A Staffordshire Inquirer*).—Drain your ground and trench it before you begin to plant. Plant on *stations*, as directed by Mr. Errington at page 87 of vol. i. *Of Apples*, plant for *Kitchen use* Keswick Codling, Monk's Codling, Blenheim Pippin, Dunclow's Seedling, Minshall Crab, Bedfordshire Foundling, Norfolk Beaufin, Hawthornden, Herefordshire Pearmain, King of Pippins and John Apple. *For Dessert:*

Early Harvest, Early Red Margaret, Kerry Pippin, Early Nonpareil, Pitmaston, Pearson's Plate, Ribston Pippin, Ross Nonpareil, Old Nonpareil, Lamb-Abbey Pearmain, Starmer Pippin, and Court pendu plat. You will find a list of the best *Pears* at page 20 of our second volume, with their times of ripening. *Of Cherries:* Early purple Griotte, Early May Duke, Black Eagle, Elton, Bigarreau, Florence, Late Duke, Morello, and Buttner's October Morello. You will find full descriptions of these, and of the most desirable *Plums*, with their times of ripening, &c., at pages 157 and 178 of our first volume. You can obtain them of any of the first-rate fruit nurserymen near London. Plant in *October* or *November* by all means, but in the month first named if possible.

SENDING FLOWERS BY POST (*T. M. W.*).—What we said at page 246 about having "the common courtesy" to send plants to us in boxes that could not be crushed, was neither said in anger nor directed against any one in particular. If a flower, or other crushable article, is put into a pasteboard box with two or three pieces of an old wine cork by the sides of the plant, cut of a thickness equal to the depth of the box, the flower, &c., is effectually protected from the post-office punch.

BUDDING CHERRY TREES (*T. Ellis*).—See what Mr. Errington has said to-day; if that is not sufficient write to us again.

STRAWBERRIES (*W. H.*).—To have them ripe by the end of April a very small amount of artificial heat is necessary. By all means use a little fermenting matter inside of your pit if possible; but let it be a little. You must by no means suffer the heat to exceed 70° on any occasion. Your plants may be either potted (the best plan) or pricked out, a foot apart, on good soil, not too rich. The plants must be set to work immediately; and you will do well to have two chances—the Keen's *Seedling* and the *British Queen*. There must be outside warmth to the pit also. Make up your bed in the end of January; let the materials be firm, to prevent sinking; and plant with balls carefully as soon as the bed has settled. Pray read our back numbers on strawberry forcing. Read *Roberts on the Vine*, but do not use the carrion he advises.

MILDEW ON GRAPE VINES (*A Constant Subscriber*).—What we said last week relative to the mildew on nectarine leaves applies equally to the vine. We should sponge every leaf with a weak solution of salt in water (say two ounces to a gallon of water), and then dust them with flowers of sulphur. To prevent its recurrence try what draining your border will do.

BEST GOOSEBERRIES (*S. R.*).—We have had the following from Mr. Turner, Neepsend, Sheffield; they are very fine, *and have not produced a sucker. Reds:* Slaughterman, Companion, London. *Yellows:* Catherine, Leader, Drill. *Greens:* Thumper, Queen Victoria, General. *Whites:* Queen of Trumps, Lady Stanley, and Freedom. For preserving and high flavour none are equal to the old Red Warrington.

VARIOUS QUESTIONS (*J. S., Kingston*).—To prevent swarming, the most effectual way is to put a second hive between the stock and the cap in which the bees have begun to work. A *workatoo* occasionally laying an egg is not a symptom of disease. Your luxuriant *Morello Cherry*, which has been neglected, will probably bear well enough next year, if you train in the young wood properly.

ROSES (*A Curate's Wife*).—Soot water may be given to roses that have done flowering. You can bud perpetual roses on pillar roses that are *not* perpetual, and you may do so any time till the end of September, or as long as the bark will rise; the *evergreen* pillar roses are the best to work on. *Fulgore* is the only one of the hybrid perpetuals that we find to do well on the Ayrshire *section*, and the pillar Boursault roses are the next best after the evergreen or sempervirens section. See what Mr. Beaton says to-day on the subject.

ROSES (*F. C.*).—Your roses are in a very bad state, indeed. How could you expect Mr. Rivers or anybody else to write books or directions, or even anticipate that such luxuriant roses as *Brennus* and *Beauty of Billiard* should be so ruined as to produce only eight inches of wood, and that quite bare at the bottom, with thin leaves and little blooms? The "best treatment" for them would be to remove them out of sight, and replace them by a fresh stock, after making proper beds for them, according to Mr. Rivers' or our own directions in former numbers. The next best plan is to prune them quite close at the end of October, and transplant them into fresh rose soil next February. With your "warm border sloping to the south," and your Irish climate, you ought to beat Mr. Rivers and all us Englishmen with roses. The brown spots on the leaves are induced by the bad soil in which they grow, or perhaps they were only planted last winter, and suffered from spring frosts.

PRESERVING ICE (*Harriet*).—Have nothing to do with building ice-houses. We shall give you, in good time, directions to keep ice much better than in the old extravagant way you propose.

FERNS (*W. H.*).—The specimen sent is *Asplenium viride*, or Green Spleenwort. We shall be very glad to receive your notes on hardy Fern culture. A wooden tank lined with lead or zinc, the size of the floor of your miniature greenhouse (4 feet 6 inches square), and covered with thick slate, to be filled with boiling water as occasion required, would be the best mode of heating it. We will think over what you say about Societies. Other answers next week.

VINES FOR A LARGE WINDOW (*T. Hill*).—The best black grape for your purpose is the *Black Hamburgh*, and the best white the *Chasselus musque*. Peaches and other wall-fruit would not do so well.

RECIPES FOR BROWN STOUT AND PORTER (*Ibid*).—A very excellent brown stout is made with the following proportions of malt and raw grain, and much better than if the liquor were brewed entirely with amber malt. Spread equally over the false bottom of the mash-tub four bushels of the best pale malt; over this place eight bushels of unmalted barley, ground in the usual manner. To this let in through the spout, 135 gallons of water at 155°. The water first catches the malt, and then flows up to the barley. Mash the whole well together during half an hour, and let the mash-tub be covered with thick cloths, and its contents allowed to infuse an hour and a half longer, when the wort may be drawn off. This quantity, allowing for soakage, will amount to about 81 gallons of wort. This should be immediately conveyed to the wort copper, if there be two boilers; if not, let it be done the moment the water for the second mashing is taken out. This water amounts to 80 gallons at 200°, rather above than under, and the mashing must be active during half an hour; the tub must then be covered, and the infusion continue without agitation an hour longer, when the second wort is drawn off, and boiled either separately or with the other. The quantity of hops should be fourteen pounds, a strong mashed infusion being first made to mix with the wort after it leaves the copper, and the strained and pressed hops then boiled an hour with the wort. The hops used may be strong Kent. While in the boiler, the following ingredients should be added:—Eight pounds of good treacle; twelve pounds of moist sugar; as much burnt sugar or essentia bina as will impart, in conjunction with the treacle, the desired colour; twelve pounds of liquorice-root; three ounces of Spanish liquorice; an ounce and a half of linseed, whole; three quarters of an ounce of capsicum seeds; an ounce of grains-of-paradise; an ounce of coriander-seed; three drachms of either stick cinnamon or cassia buds. When put to clear, add three ounces of ginger divided equally among the casks; put also into each cask before the liquor is poured in a good handful of flour, and a handful of salt, dissolved in a couple of quarts of the wort, and well beaten. After the stout has been fined, add to this quantity a drachm of sulphate of iron in powder, and a drachm of alum, dissolved together in a sufficient quantity of water, and equally divided among the casks. If not fine enough for bottling in a couple of months, it may be fined with isinglass, though time is the best finer when it can be allowed to operate. This liquor, which is full and generous, may likewise be drunk from the cask, but it is much better bottled, for which purpose the bung must be taken out during three or four days, to allow all the carbonic acid to escape from the cask, in order that the liquor may become dead, otherwise the bottles may burst. The following is an old and excellent recipe for brewing eight gallons of good sound *porter*, fit either for bottling or to drink from the tap:—A peck of the best malt properly ground is put into the mash-tub. The malt may be either pale or amber, at the choice of the operator. The porter from the former is sounder and better flavoured. Four gallons of boiling water are now cooled to the proper temperature by the addition of a gallon of cold water at 60°. This must be added gradually to the malt, working the whole well during the whole time, until it be smooth and quite free from lumps. The mixture must then be mashed a little longer, making the entire duration of the mashing to last half an hour from the time the first water was poured upon the malt. The mash-tub is now covered with sacks or coarse cloths, to prevent the escape of the steam. When it has stood two hours the wort is drawn off, if it run clear; if not, it must be poured back until its muddiness has disappeared. Four gallons of boiling water are next poured upon the malt, and the whole mashed up again during twenty minutes. The second infusion may stand an hour and a half. Whilst this is going on, the first wort should be boiled in the boiler with a quarter of a pound of hops, during an hour. The following ingredients must be added and boiled with this wort:—A pound of treacle; half a pound of moist sugar; essentia bina enough to give a very strong colour, which will be reduced by mixture with the second wort; six ounces of sliced liquorice-root; six ounces of Spanish juice; a small pod of capsicum. The second wort must be boiled in the same manner with the hops of the first: but without any other addition. The two worts when cooled, are to be mixed in the fermenting-vat, the first mashing being first set working, with half a pint of yeast. In cleansing, a dessert-spoonful of flour, half an ounce of powdered ginger, and a tea-spoonful of common salt, should be put into the cask. When the liquor is fine, add eight grains of sulphate of iron, and eight grains of alum dissolved in a little water.

ICE-HOUSE (*Ireland*).—Yes, we can give you any information you may require about ice and ice-houses. All our coadjutors manage the ice departments in their respective situations. We recollect reading an original paper last year in the pages of a contemporary on the subject of ice-houses, from the pen of Mr. Beaton, and we will request him to write an article expressly to meet your wishes.

CONSEQUENCE OF TRANSFERRING BEES (Z.).—"On the 12th of July we fumigated the old hive, which was 20 in. in diameter. Neighbour's lamp was used, and although two-thirds full of powder more smoke was required; but as the lamp had been *soldered*, not riveted, the parts adhered, and none could be introduced through that medium. We knew not what to do, and my assistant, a bee master upon the old system, applied tobacco smoke. The bees smoked were placed in the Improved Cottage Hive of Neighbours, and returned to their original position. On the following morning I lifted the hive, and swept the floor board on to a clean cloth, and to my regret I found in the evening of that day upon it no less than 2 lbs. weight of bees—a result I never contemplated, and a cruelty for which the honey from fifty stocks will never be to me a compensation. The bees seem to be at work, but not actively; on the 15th, anxious to know what weight of bees I had left, I weighed my hive, and found that they, together with the comb they may have made, from the night of the 12th when they were fumed, was 4 lbs. 11 oz. I fear from the account in your paper of Thursday that I must lose them." We thank you for favouring us with the result of your fumigating and transferring your bees; this, and many like accounts, tend to confirm us more strongly in our opinion. You say your bees are in a Neighbour's Improved Cottage Hive, therefore you are feeding them at the top, and it matters not how much barley sugar you give them at a time—certainly not *less* than a pound. Mr. Huish has told us that 5,000 bees weigh about a pound, therefore your loss may be about double that quantity but if you had on the 15th 4 lbs. 11 oz., you are pretty well off for numbers; your casts will, in all probability, require strengthening more than these; feed them by supplying 2 lbs. or 3 lbs. at a time, until you get them up to 18 lbs. or 20 lbs. The method for effecting autumnal unions Mr. Payne will give in his next calendar, which will be in good time. Mr. Payne has already done much in supplying all who asks it with hives and bee dresses, and now to ask him to open a warehouse in London for the purpose would be unfair. If you paid 2s. 11d. for carriage of your two hives, we imagine that *four or six* would not have been charged more. Indeed, that number would have been taken from Bury St. Edmund's to London for one shilling.

CITRONS TO PRESERVE (*E. C. S.*).—Cut a hole at the stalk end of the citrons the size of a shilling, and scoop out the pulp quite clean without cutting the rind. Tie the pulps and the rinds separately in muslin, and lay them in spring water for two days, changing the water twice a day; then boil them in the muslin, on a slow fire, until tender. Keep them well covered with water during the whole time, adding it hot if needed. The citrons should be weighed at first, and for every pound of fruit allow 2 lbs. of the finest loaf sugar and one pint of water, which boil together, with the juice of the citron, to a syrup, which should be well skimmed and allowed to stand until cold, when the fruit should be boiled in the syrup for half an hour. If not clear the first time of boiling, repeat the process daily until it becomes so. Then put a layer of fruit into a new sieve, and dip it suddenly into hot water, so that any syrup hanging about the fruit may be taken off. Put the fruit on a napkin before the fire to drain, whilst some more are done in the sieve. Sift over them some of the finest powdered loaf sugar until the fruit is quite white on all sides. Put them on sieves placed bottom upwards in a slightly warm oven, turning them two or three times until dry. The process requires great care throughout.

GOOSEBERRY WINE (*X. Y. O., Brentwood*).—Gather in dry weather, and when the gooseberries are only half ripe. Pick and bruise a peck of fruit in a tub, and then press them as much as you can without breaking the seeds through a cloth. When the juice is thus pressed out, add 3 lbs. of fine powdered loaf-sugar for every gallon of gooseberries, and stir it together until the sugar is dissolved. Put the liquor into the cask, which must be quite full. If a ten or twelve gallon cask, let it stand a fortnight; if twenty gallons, three weeks. Set it in a cool place, draw it off from the lees, wash these from the cask, and pour in the clear liquor again. A ten gallon cask must then stand three, and a twenty gallon four months, before the wine is bottled off.

NAMES OF PLANTS (*Boston*).—The tree from which you have taken your leaves is *Salisburia adiantifolia*, or the Maiden hair-leaved Salisburia. Its leaves are referred to by botanists to illustrate the term *fissum*, or cloven-leaved.

TAYLOR'S HIVES.—We have received the following from Mr. Taylor: "Your last publication contains a reply to a correspondent who had expressed a desire that 'working drawings' of my bee-boxes might be given in your interesting periodical. Your hesitation is most honourably based on the supposition, that I had, either for myself or on the part of others, retained some special right or monopoly in their manufacture and sale. You will, I am sure, permit me to say, that whatever I have been enabled to do for the encouragement and promotion of apiarian knowledge, gain has been the last thing in my mind. I retain no exclusive rights myself, nor have I given them to others. *Pro bono publico* is my motto. At the same time I may observe, that as the recently published edition of *The Bee-keeper's Manual* contains correct illustrations of all that is essential to the right construction of the boxes and their appurtenances, accompanied by detailed instructions to the artificer, I am at a loss to see what object would be gained by multiplying drawings beyond what any intelligent carpenter might supply for his own working guidance, on the full scale of dimensions, as recommended by me. On looking over the replies to the queries of some of your correspondents, in this connexion, I may remark, that most of them are anticipated in my book. It may be permitted me farther to observe, that I only desire to be accountable for what are laid as my own recommendations. I am always happy to recognize improvements of whatever kind, when they are really such; but have just cause of complaint where unmeaning alterations are made, retaining my name to what I should be inclined to repudiate. With the pen in my hand, it may be well to remark, that, appended to the lines given at page 161 of *The Bee-keeper's Manual*, the name of 'Southey' ought to be substituted for 'Miss Aikin.'"

LONDON: Printed by HARRY WOOLDRIDGE, Winchester High-street, in the Parish of Saint Mary Kalendar; and Published by WILLIAM SOMERVILLE ORR, at the Office, No. 2, Amen Corner, in the Parish of Christ Church, City of London.—August 8th, 1850.

WEEKLY CALENDAR.

M W D D	AUGUST 15—21, 1850.	Weather near London in 1849.			Sun Rises.	Sun Sets.	Moon R. & S.	Moon's Age.	Clock bef. Sun.	Day of Year.
15 Th	Assumption B.V.M. Large Black Staphyline	T. 76°—52°.	S.W.	Rain.	47 a. 4	22 a. 7	11 a.17	8	4 17	227
16 F	Greenfinch's song ceases. [seen.	T. 64°—42°.	S.W.	Rain.	48	20	11 52	9	4 5	228
17 S	Duchess of Kent born, 1781. Barley cut.	T. 73°—42°.	W.	Rain.	50	18	morn.	10	3 53	229
18 Sun	12 Sun. Aft. Trin. Devil's bit Scabious flowers.	T. 69°—49°.	N.	Fine.	51	16	0 22	11	3 46	230
19 M	Common Tansy flowers.	T. 72°—50°.	N.	Fine.	53	14	1 12	12	3 26	231
20 Tu	Small Copper Butterfly seen.	T. 73°—52°.	W.	Fine.	55	12	2 13	13	3 12	232
21 W	Sun's declin. 12° 10′ N.	T. 78°—58°.	W.	Fine.	56	10	3 10	14	2 58	233

Sir Benjamin Thompson, better known as Count Rumford, does not merit our notice for his taste in landscape gardening, which we are told was great, and much less for his knowledge of plants, for even the common names of the commonest plants were to him for the most part unknown,—but he deserves our especial regard for the great benefits he achieved for us by improving our furnaces, fire-places, ventilation, and cookery, and, for ever bearing in mind that man should not live for himself alone. America has cause for being proud of giving him birth ; and it was fortunate, perhaps, that his birth and childhood passed away in one of the least known of her village towns—Woburn, in Massachusets. Descended from parents not above the middle class of villagers, without the temptations that fly to the wealthy and gather round the citizen, he had to seek for in-door recreation in the society of books, those best and most unobtrusive of friends. His was not above such an education as could be acquired in his birth-place ; but he had that within him which is better than the best of tutors, and without which tuition is little more than sinking inscriptions into stone—he had a love for the labour of acquiring information ; and to his own industry and to his thirst for knowledge, more than to any instructions derived from masters, was owing the richly stored mind which guided him to the affluence and honours he attained even in early manhood. Passing over that portion of his life in which he supported the Royalist cause in the American war, and for which George III. conferred upon him in 1784 the honour of knighthood, we then find him active in the Bavarian service, in the more successful struggle to improve the social condition of the people. It is startling to us, who have so long been conversant with the merits of the potato, to find that he was the first to overcome the prejudices of the Bavarians, and to win them to its general use as a food. To aid him in this, as well as to improve the habits of the soldiers, he devised the system of military gardens—that is, " pieces of ground in or adjoining to the garrison towns, which were regularly laid out, and exclusively appropriated to the non-commissioned officers and private soldiers belonging to the regiments in garrison." In these gardens every private soldier was assigned a piece of ground, about three hundred and sixty-five square feet in extent. This piece of ground was to remain the sole property of that soldier so long as he served in the regiment ; he was to be at liberty to cultivate it in any way, and to dispose of the produce in any way, he chose ; if, however, he did not choose to work in it, but wished rather to spend his pay in idleness, he might do so ; but in that case the piece of ground was to be taken from him, and so also if he neglected it. Every means were used to attack the soldiers to their garden labour : seeds and manure were furnished them at a cheap rate ; whatever instruction was necessary was given them ; and little huts or summer-houses were erected in the gardens, to afford them shelter when it rained. " The effect of the plan," says Rumford, " was much greater and more important than I could have expected. The soldiers, from being the most indolent of mortals, and from having very little knowledge of gardening, became industrious and skilful cultivators, and grew so fond of vegetables, particularly of potatoes, that these useful and wholesome productions began to constitute a very essential part of their daily food. These improvements began also to spread among the farmers and peasants throughout the whole country. There was hardly a soldier that went on furlough that did not carry with him a few potatoes for planting, and a little collection of garden seeds ; and I have already had the satisfaction to see little gardens here and there making their appearance in different parts

of the country." He made its productiveness one of his assistants in abolishing that organised system of mendicancy which until then had been like a nightmare upon their social prosperity. Not only did Munich, but the whole country, swarm with beggars, who followed mendicity as a trade, and claimed for it prescriptive rights and privileges. The military had proudly declined all interference with these parasites ; but Sir Benjamin, having provided workhouses, sallied forth on the New Year's day of 1790, decorated with all his Bavarian orders, and at the head of a military and civil staff seized with his own hands the first mendicant. His example was promptly followed, but with the most perfect good humour ; and before nightfall every beggar of Munich was lodged in its workhouses. Sustenance and labour were supplied to all ; new manufactures—as we have seen new food—were introduced ; and gradually there was established in Bavaria that preference of industry to idleness, and of decency to filth and rags, which still characterise its people—the most prominent symptoms of lingering vagrancy being those broom girls, who can scarcely be classed among our street nuisances. For such services the sovereign of Bavaria bestowed upon him many rewards, but none more prominent than creating him Count of Rumford, the name of his title being taken from the place where he had spent some of his happiest days in his native land. In 1799 he returned to England, and here with renewed energy addressed himself to various efforts whereby to diffuse economy and comfort. For years he engaged incessantly in experiments for improving the construction of our chimnies and fireplaces, all aiming at a decreased consumption of fuel, and the memory of which is preserved in that fireplace still known as the Rumford Stove. It is impossible for us to compress into our space even an outline of the Count's improvements. It must be sufficient for us to say, that the suggestion of all our modern system of prominent grates near the floor, and of backs contrived to act as reflectors of heat, are to be found in his " Essays, Political, Economical, and Physical." The first grate in conformity with his suggestions was erected at Lord Palmerston's, in Hanover-square ; and so popular became his fireside improvements, that even Pindar sings amid much ridicule undeserved—

> Lo ! every parlour, drawing-room, I see
> Boasts of thy stoves, and talks of nought but thee.
> Yet not alone my lady and young misses—
> The cooks themselves could smother you with kisses.

The Count, however, was above the reach of ridicule, and pursued his course—his admirable course—applying science to the arts, and using his influence and his wealth to enlist others in the same beneficial object. He invested £1000, the interest of which is to be devoted for ever as a premium every second year to the discoverer of such improvements relative to the application of heat or light as the Council of the Royal Society may consider most beneficial to mankind. A still more striking monument of his useful career is the Royal Institution in Albemarle-street—that institution whose laboratory gave birth to the splendid discoveries of Faraday and Davy ; and well might it be a source of pleasurable reflection, that to himself the latter owed his appointment of lecturer on chemistry. When the results of Count Rumford's efforts are considered—his published works, his contributions to the Philosophical Transactions, and his ever progressing experiments—we are not surprised at the query, " How did he find time for all this ? " and the satisfactory answer seems to be, " No man in all his habits had more the spirit of order : everything around him was classed. No object was allowed to remain an instant out of its place when he had done with it ; and he was never behind his time to an appointment a single minute." Next to the power of concentrating attention to a subject under consideration, this regard to order is the best aid to facility of progress. We must conclude, and by merely recording that he died near Paris on the 21st of August, 1814, and that he was born in 1752. He had been twice married—the second union being with the widow of M. Lavoisier, noticed in our last number.

Meteorology of the Week.—At Chiswick, observations during the last twenty-three years show that the average highest and lowest temperature of these days are 73.1° and 51.9°, respectively. The greatest heat, 92°, occurred on the 18th in 1842 ; and the greatest cold, 37°, on the 20th in 1839. Eighty-nine days were fine, and during seventy-two days rain fell.

RANGE OF BAROMETER—RAIN IN INCHES.

Aug.		1841.	1842.	1843.	1844.	1845.	1846.	1847.	1848.	1849.
15	B.	29.746 29.687	30.204 30.153	29.923 29.894	29.744 29.552	29.800 29.728	29.740 29.716	30.229 30.163	29.896 29.846	29.919 29.865
	R.	—	—	0.51	80.3	—	9.07	6.32	—	0.01
16	B.	29.921 29.851	30.162 30.130	30.040 29.979	29.919 29.955	29.911 29.837	29.863 29.792	30.088 30.040	29.806 29.769	29.793 29.769
	R.	—	—	0.15	9.01	—	—	0.12	0.15	—
17	B.	30.055 29.969	30.112 30.092	30.100 30.097	29.880 29.762	29.901 29.797	29.855 29.746	30.044 30.040	29.905 29.801	29.045 29.873
	R.	—	—	—	—	0.27	0.34	0.02	0.01	
18	B.	30.173 30.140	29.939 29.830	29.981 29.958	30.092 30.060	29.762 29.549	29.870 29.539	30.101 30.082	30.046 29.884	30.046 29.993
	R.	—	—	—	—	0.28	0.07	0.10	—	
19	B.	30.197 30.005	29.919 29.879	29.820 29.870	30.119 30.041	29.371 29.111	29.548 29.478	30.119 30.015	29.844 29.718	30.272 30.145
	R.	—	0.81	0.01	0.01	0.42	0.01	0.05	0.06	—
20	B.	29.734 29.628	30.036 29.981	30.171 29.547	29.901 29.774	29.765 29.624	29.829 29.730	29.971 29.695	29.960 29.892	30.337 30.295
	R.	—	—	—	—	0.53	—	—	0.26	—
21	B.	29.903 29.797	29.981 29.943	29.977 29.985	29.747 29.727	30.060 29.894	29.954 29.744	29.911 29.749	29.718 29.478	30.322 30.230
	R.	—	—	—	—	0.04	0.02	0.17	—	

In this the season of DAHLIAS, we may appropriately bring before our readers the characteristics which we agree in thinking are marks of excellency in this queen of autumnal flowers. In 1847, aided by Mr. Turner, of Chalvey, near Slough, we published a small volume on this flower; and from its pages, almost without alteration, we republish the following observations :—

The first discovered species of the genus is that known now to botanists as *Dahlia superflua*, or *D. variabilis*. It was found in 1789, and named by Cavanilles, a Spanish botanist, in honour of Dahl, a Swedish pupil of Linnæus. Some objections were raised to the name of Dahlia, because it too nearly resembles that before given to a very different genus, *Dalea;* and to obviate the difficulty, Willdenow, in 1803, gave to the species the names of *Georgina pinnata*, but though these were adopted by a few distinguished botanists, the prior applied names have properly prevailed.

The plants from which three new supposed species of dahlia were described, were sent from the Botanic Garden at Mexico to the Royal Garden at Madrid, where one, called by Professor Cavanilles *Dahlia pinnata*, flowered in October, 1789; his *D. rosea* and *D. coccinea* produced flowers a few years afterwards. They do not seem to have been successfully treated, for with him they attained the height of three or four feet only, and did not flower till October. In 1802, plants of each were transferred from Madrid to the Jardin des Plantes at Paris, where they grew so well as to enable Mons. Thouin, in 1804, not only to describe and figure them, but also to treat on their cultivation. In May, 1804, seeds of the three kinds were sent from Madrid by Lady Holland to Mr. Buonainti, Lord Holland's librarian in England; from these good plants were produced, one of which, the *D. pinnata*, flowered in September following, and was figured by Andrews in the "Botanist's Repository." In the succeeding year, plants of the *D. rosea* and the *D. coccinea* also flowered in the gardens of Holland House.

Though this importation of the seeds was the most successful as to its produce (for from it nearly all the plants then in our gardens were obtained), yet the original introduction of the first species was (on the authority of the *Hortus Kewensis*) from Spain, in 1789, by the Marchioness of Bute; but it is probable that the plant so introduced was soon after lost, as we do not find any further notice taken of it. The other species, then called *Coccinea*, was actually flowered by Mr. John Frazer, who is said to have obtained it from France in 1802, the same year in which it was produced in the French gardens from seed procured from Madrid. It also appears that in the autumn of 1803, Mr. Woodford flowered, at Vauxhall, a plant of Cavanilles' *D. rosea*, which he had obtained from Paris; so that, independently of one introduced by the Marchioness of Bute, in 1789, it seems that both species had flowered in this country before the seeds were transmitted by Lady Holland.

At Madrid they were a long time in the Royal Garden without any indications of change; and after they were spread through Europe some years elapsed before any extensive variation took place.

Mons. De Candolle, it is said, obtained from Madrid the plants which he cultivated at Montpelier, about the same time they were sent to Paris. His "Memoir" was printed in 1810, and he therein describes only five varieties of *D. superflua*—viz., *Rubra*, *Purpurea*, *Lilacina*, *Pallida*, and *Flavescens*, besides three varieties of *D. Frustranea*—viz., *Coccinea*, *Crocea*, and *Flava*. Probably, when he wrote, he had not obtained any double flowers, though he evidently expected such would soon be produced.

Mons. Otto, as early as 1800, obtained from Dresden, for the Royal Garden at Berlin, a plant of the *D. Pallida* of the "Hortus Berolinensis;" and in 1802 a plant of the *D. purpurea*, of the same work, was sent to him from Madrid; but he had no new varieties from his own seed till 1806; and the chief varieties were raised between 1809 and 1817. About 1813, M. Otto began to pay more attention to their cultivation, and improved their kinds by cross impregnations. The first double flower he possessed came from Stutgard; but a complete double one of his own flowered in 1809; it was dark red, exactly similar to that from Stutgard, but had, at first, blown only semi-double. Three more double ones were raised in 1815 and 1816, and he had in 1820 no more than six with double flowers. A pure white single one was given to him in 1809, and in 1810 he raised another white one himself. He mentions, that in the Catalogues of the Nurseries at Berlin from 80 to 100 sorts are enumerated for sale, but he considers the really good ones to be about thirty.

In our own country we had an early promise of great success, and had we hit upon the right plan of management, in keeping the plants when produced, there is no doubt but we should have been as equally successful as the continental gardeners in obtaining varieties. Mr. Buonainti saved seeds from the plants raised at Holland House in 1804, the produce of which seeds he states to have given him, in the succeeding year, nine varieties of that which was called *D. pinnata*, two of which were double, one with lilac and the other with dark purple flowers; of the single flowered plants, some were certainly dark coloured, four figures were published from them at the time; the paler coloured varieties were chiefly considered as belonging to what was then called *D. rosea;* he had also two varieties of *D. coccinea*, the original deep coloured one and a paler one, which, though called by him *Crocata*, was the pale yellow variety, as is apparent from the figure of it published in the "Paradisus Londinensis."

Mr. Salisbury also obtained several varieties from the seeds which he received from Holland House in 1806; these he had particularly noticed in his paper printed in the first volume of the Transactions of the Horticultural Society. In the fifth volume of the second edition of the *Hortus Kewensis*, which was published in 1813, the varieties of *D. superflua* there named are *Purpurea*, *Lilacina*, and *Nana*; the latter being taken from a double variety, figured in Andrew's "Botanical Repository," but which is certainly not particularly entitled to be considered as a dwarf plant. No varieties of *D. frustranea* are given in the *Hortus Kewensis.*

Mons. de Candolle, in his essay on the genus, has observed, that it is not probable we shall ever see a blue one, since the variation is from purple to yellow. He considers blue and yellow to be the fundamental types of the colours of flowers, and that they mutually exclude each other: yellows pass readily into red or white, but never into blue; and, in like manner, blue flowers are changed by cultivation into red and white, but never into yellow. Until about forty years ago, no variety was known that did not possess a tinge of purple in its blossoms, and it was even doubted whether a blossom entirely untinged with purple could be produced.

When Mr. Sabine wrote on the dahlia in 1818, the single varieties only were abundant; the number of double ones was very limited, but they rapidly increased, and have now nearly expelled the single ones from gardens of repute. The extension of sorts has, however, been limited to the *D. superflua*; the varieties of *D. frustranea* have but little multiplied, and no double flowers of that species have yet been produced. The brilliancy of the colours of the blossoms of the *D. frustranea*, however, is such, that it might have been expected it would have induced some practical horticulturist to apply his skill to their improvement.

A few of the double dahlias which were raised at an early period still hold a place in the estimation of gardeners; but, in general, those of a few years' standing have yielded their places to a younger progeny, which in their turn may be deprived of their station by fresh productions.

After 1814, the dahlia was introduced to more general notice, and cultivated in most collections; but it was reserved for the intelligent cultivators of the last few years to circulate it more extensively, and make the most rapid advances towards a state of perfection. Indeed, so lately as less than twenty years since it was considered a perfectly novel sight to witness dahlias with double flowers in the garden of a tradesman or cottager; but, owing to the astonishing rapidity with which new and good sorts have since been obtained and circulated, it is now quite as rarely that we see or meet with a cottager's garden which does not contain at least a few good dahlias; and many possess plants of first-rate sorts. (*Paxton on the Dahlia,* 9.)

In taking a retrospective view of the dahlia fancy, it is pleasing to remark the gradual improvement of this autumnal favourite up to the present time. This improvement is annually progressing towards greater perfection; for of late years many of the finest varieties have been introduced; and it is notorious, that an established fine seedling at the present time will command a higher price than at any previous period. To mark the progress of the dahlia, the stand that obtained the £20 prize for the best twenty-four blooms at the Cambridge Dahlia Show in 1840, contained only one variety that was shown in the first stand of the same number of blooms at the Metropolitan Exhibition of

1846, a brief period of six years. That variety was *Springfield Rival,* a flower of 13 or 14 years' standing. Both stands were grown by Mr. Turner. The former was considered to be the best that has been produced up to that time, and the latter was certainly the best twenty-four he had shown during 1846. At Cambridge, Unique was what is termed the "bloom of the exhibition;" *Penelope, Amato, Hope, Conservative, Maid of Bath,* and many other flowers now out of date, were stars in that superior stand.

The first intelligent writer upon the characteristics of excellence in the Dahlia, we think, was Mr. Paxton, followed by Mr. Glenny and Mr. Wildman; but as Mr. Glenny's code in his *Properties of Flowers* is much fuller than Mr. Paxton's, and was prior to Mr. Wildman's, we shall adopt it with but slight alterations and additions:—

1. FORM.—Viewed in front, the flower should be a perfect circle; the petals broad at the ends, smooth at the edges, thick and stiff in substance, perfectly free from indenture or point, and should cup a little, but not enough to shew the under surface. They should be in regular rows, each row forming a perfect circle, without any vacancy between them; and all in the circle should be the same size, uniformly opened to the same shape, and not rubbed nor crumpled.

2. Looked at sideways, the flower should form two-thirds of a ball. The rows of petals should rise one above another in rows; every petal should cover the join of the two petals under it—which the florists call imbricating—by this means the circular appearance is perfected throughout.

3. The *centre* should be perfect; the unbloomed petals lying with their points towards the centre should form a button, and should be the *highest* part of the flower completing the ball.

4. The flower should be very double. The rows of petals lying one above another should cover one another very nearly; not more should be seen in depth than half the breadth; the more they are covered, so as to leave them distinct, the better in that respect; the petals, therefore, though cupped must be shallow.

5. SIZE.—The size of the flower when well grown should be not less than four inches in diameter.

6. COLOUR.—The colour should be dense, whatever it may be—not as if it were a white dipped in colour, but as if the whole flower was coloured throughout. Whether tipped or edged, it must be free from splashes or blotches, or indefinite marks of any kind; and new flowers, unless they beat all old ones of the same colour, or are of a novel colour themselves, with a majority of the points of excellence, should be rejected.

DEFECTS.—If the petals show the under side too much, even when looked at sideways,—if they do not cover each other well,—if the centre is composed of petals pointing upwards, or those which are round the centre are confused,—if the petals are too narrow, or exhibit too much of their length,—or if they show any of the green scale at the bottom of the petals,—if *the eye* is sunk,—if the shoulder is too high, the face flat, or the sides too upright,—if the petals show an indenture as if heart-shaped,—if the petals are too large and coarse, or are flimsy, or do not hold their form—in any or all these cases the flowers are objectionable; and if there be one or two of these faults conspicuous, the flower is second or third-rate.

If flowers are exhibited which show the disc, or a green scale, or have been eaten by vermin, or damaged by carriage, or are evidently decayed, the censors should reject them at once.

Characteristics of the Plant.—Although the form of the plant is quite of secondary consideration, and is only to be regarded as subservient to the more important consideration of exhibiting the flowers to more advantage as they grow, yet it is a matter worthy of some notice. Mr. Paxton's observations upon it are very judicious. He says, the general figure should be uniform and compact, that is, it should gradually enlarge from the lowest lateral shoots to the extremity of those highest, and it should be devoid of a straggling or rambling habit. Secondly, the plant should be disposed to bloom freely and numerously. Thirdly, its blossoms should stand out clearly from the foliage, on short strong flower-stalks, so as to be presented boldly and advantageously.

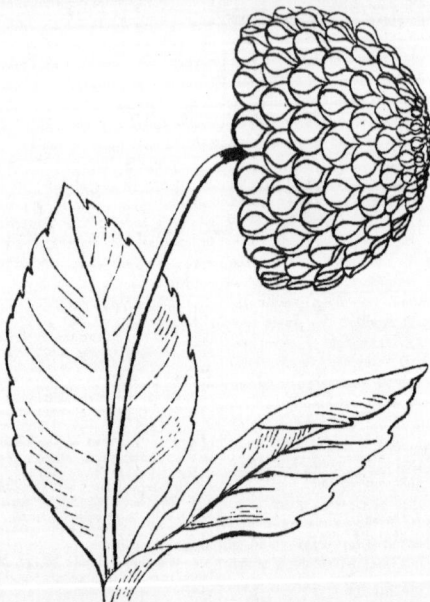

THE FRUIT-GARDEN.

RIPENING THE WOOD OF FRUIT-TREES.—According to the maxims of some of our gardeners of former days, it was time enough to think of this when the leaves first commenced decay, and consequently we find urgent recommendations by those of the old school to use the besom pretty freely in October. "Brush off the leaves to assist in ripening the wood," is an old maxim, now tolerably obsolete; but, with the repudiation of this silly idea, the fact in question should be seriously grappled with; for, perhaps, a broken crutch is better than no crutch at all.

We will not go so far as to assert, that sweeping off a few *decaying* leaves in early autumn may not have the effect of rendering the buds of those leaves still remaining more perfect, by carrying more fully out the principle of accretion; but all this only proves a previous neglect. Neglect, we repeat, for if light and heat, acting on the fully exposed surface of the leaf of tender trees, be so essential to the proper organization of the bud, (and who shall disprove it?) why should an improper amount of the annual spray be reserved during the thinning or disbudding season; only in the first place to create mutual injury, and in the second, to cause a more troublesome course of winter pruning than there is a real necessity for? It is well known what a controversy has been carried on for many months, in the pages of contemporary horticultural periodicals, about the *covering or non-covering of fruit-trees*, in order to protect the blossom, and to facilitate the "setting" or impregnation of the fruit. They say that covering does not always insure a crop. We wonder how many yards of canvass or bunting it would take to ensure a crop of fruit on a Marie Louisa Pear-tree; or, indeed, on any other tree, the embryo buds of which had been smothered in the previous summer with watery spray.

Trees are suffered to hang in a wild state from the walls until the approach of September—for the first time perhaps the future blossom-buds behold daylight—for about three weeks, and are allowed to bathe themselves in that degree of light which a darkening autumn affords; and which, after all, as to their habits, is only a kind of twilight. Well, then, in the spring, a great fuss is made about covering; it is done; the blossoms perish, and the unhappy cultivator comes forth like a lion with a fresh argument against the utility of covering or protection. What would be thought of a writer who should recommend strawberry forcers not to get their runners too soon for forcing purposes, to delay it until the end of August, and then to select them from gross and over-crowded plants with petioles or leaf-stalks dangling a foot in length? We wonder whether the best of winter protection, or the most complete and expensive pit ever invented by man, could ensure a crop of strawberries on such plants?

This is sufficiently illustrative to all who will grapple with the real bearing of the question; those who will persist in adhering with pertinacity to a set of notions which have no real foundation either in science or practice, must still be content to endure baffled efforts.

If, then, protection coverings are not to be shorn of their great utility, let the extra labour or attention requisite for tender fruits be bestowed in summer, instead of so much elaborate nonsense about winter pruning. If there be any truth in this, both common sense and economy will be found on its side; surely a man's day's labour is a more productive article in July than in **January!**

Let those, then, who deem it expedient to follow the advice of THE COTTAGE GARDENER, carefully examine all their trained trees *immediately;* there is still time on all good aspects to obtain pretty firm wood, by a careful and immediate removal of all waste spray.

In order to give our observations a definite character, in which shape they are chiefly useful to amateurs and young beginners, we will point at once to some trees with their probable condition at this period.

THE PEACH AND NECTARINE.—About this period, and a little sooner, peaches which had grown at only a reasonable rate during the early part of summer, burst forth with an improper amount of strength; and shoots which had been pinched long since, through luxuriance (or a doubt of the propriety of retaining them finally), produce a considerable amount of axillary shoots; and these shoots at once arrest and appropriate the ascending sap; they also create an injurious amount of shade to the true and bearing wood. All such should be pinched immediately; and it is not unlikely that they will require pinching again within another fortnight or three weeks. The production of such spray, at a late season, argues a too powerful action of root; and some persons would be ready, under such circumstances, to advise root pruning. Now, although strong advocates for this process, and probably the first to urge it in general practice in this country, yet we would by no means interfere with the vegetable economy, at this period, in trees bearing fruit.

It will be frequently seen in the peach and the nectarine, that fine growing young shoots may be seen over the centre of the tree, and, perhaps, on one particular side, whilst the extremities of the limbs, which are carrying a crop, are void of young shoots, or carry a stunted appearance. This frequently happens from the circumstance of such shoots having carried a heavy crop on their extreme boughs the year previously, whereby those portions had been too heavily drawn upon, and a temporary exhaustion is the consequence Now, if the ascending current of sap is not transmitted sufficiently copiously to excite these branches into young wood, a partial contraction of the sap vessels will take place; and such will have to be pruned away before long, in order to give place to a progeny which have fattened at their expense. Now, lopping off the older limbs of peaches and nectarines is but a perilous practice at the best; and it is well to know, that by an early stopping of most of the stronger young shoots below them, and stopping again if necessary, such old shoots may be reinvigorated by a fresh infusion of the ascending sap, which, as before observed, had been arrested in its passage. In other words, they will commence making young shoots with freedom; and these young shoots (as encouraging a renewed vitality) will save them from destruction, as well as cause the fruit to become better fed, or, in other words, more perfect.

As to *stopping*, our practice is to stop every shoot in the first week of August that is of sufficient length for the next year's purpose, excepting in the case of delicate or weak trees; here there is no occasion, nature or accident will stop such soon enough. An exception is also taken in favour of weak shoots on robust trees—these are left unstopped altogether. And now it is that the renewed balance of strength takes place; the weaker and unstopped shoots, at this general stopping, soon show signs of having strengthened at the expense of their proud neighbours; and before the latter can develop other buds, autumn with its chills has arrived,

and it is scarcely possible for them to do much mischief.

There can be little doubt that this general stopping (which should be performed as soon as the last swelling has fairly commenced) increases both the size and the flavour of the fruit—at least, so we have always found it. And no wonder gross young trees produce not such high-flavoured fruit as older and more solidified trees; and why? Merely because a too rapid or copious influx of the ascending sap is in antagonism to flavour. What then occurs in any given branch stopped or pinched as we describe? Why, a portion of the demand being cut off, in the character of growing spray, the supplies of the ascending current become proportionately limited. Not so, however, the elaboration, or, shall we say, concentration? This is augmented in power, inasmuch as this stopping tends to keep the original, or first-formed, leaves well distended—a thing absolutely necessary, in order that plenty of material for the elaborative processes should exist in the neighbourhood of the fruit until perfected. Therefore, let all young peach growers believe, that to keep the large leaves that cater for the fruit well fed, and to encourage a late growth at the extremities, are two very different matters.

It was by such means, and such alone, that the splendid peaches which we used to exhibit at the Societys' meetings some years since were produced, and which attracted so much notice. We frequently attend the great London " shows," as well as some of the country ones, but we have never met with any that would prove an overmatch for such, if, indeed, they would equal them. If this appears egotistic, we say, in apology, that it appeared necessary in order to illustrate the matter in hand.

THE PEAR.—This all-important fruit, so necessary to the winter dessert (for who does not covet a rich melting pear in December and January?) deserves some consideration as well as the peach. Although the principles of stopping, and the general control and equalisation of the vital fluids, are of equal application here; yet some peculiarities of habit—arising in part from modes of training—require special notice.

In the first place, then, once more put the trees under a thorough revision; that is, remove all watery spray produced since the last disbudding; "leave not a wrock behind " of this powerful witness of a pampered constitution, as well as harbinger of future barrenness. Next in order, take care that every leading shoot considered necessary for the future year be carefully tied down or nailed. This done, all that remains may be examined closely, and every short-jointed shoot of a brown and fruitful-looking character, *especially those with enlarged buds,* indicating thereby a guarantee of early and sure fruitfulness, tied down or nailed. The residue will be rejected spray; but a little caution is necessary in the disposal of this.

On the cooler aspects, and where a doubt exists in any situation in our northern counties, the better way will be to cut such all away to within two or three leaves of the base of each shoot. In doing this, regard must be paid to kind as well as aspect. Such kinds as the *Easter Beurré,* and some of the autumn-ripening kinds, will be liable to a premature ripening, if exposed too suddenly to intense sunshine; for it so happens, that what perfects the future blossom-bud is not always perfectly contributing to the highest amount of flavour. Nature, it would seem, is more bent on the former than the latter.

Let every one, therefore, take into consideration the character of the climate in which he is situate, together with the aspect, and the kind, and proceed accordingly. It will, of course, be said, that all this requires an amount of practical knowledge which will be looked for in vain in persons otherwise engaged.

Admitted; and to supply such gaps THE COTTAGE GAR-
DENER was established; but, be it understood, the points
we have adverted to require more explanation as to the
minutiæ than can be explained in a number or two.
Much may be gleaned from the van of this work; and
much more, we may add, remains in the rear.

As we may not have an opportunity, immediately, of
speaking as fully about the dressing of *plums, cherries,*
&c., we may here observe, that as soon as the more
tender kinds, as *apricots, peaches, nectarines,* and *pears,*
are completed, the cherries and plums must also undergo a revision.

As to *plums,* they may receive precisely similar treatment to the pears; and we tie down the *cherries* in a
like manner; they are not, however, so manageable by
this mode as the former fruits. The *Morello cherries*
may have their shoots laid in three times as thick as the
larger-leaved kinds.

In *apricots* the utmost care should be taken after this
period to keep down all superfluous breast-wood; the
sun must be permitted to shine on the embryo fruit-buds
without hindrance until the leaves fall. This is the
chief secret of the blossom "setting well" in the ensuing spring; and thus it is that old apricots, which
produce scarcely any breast-wood, generally succeed so
much better than young and gross trees.

　　　　　　　　　　　　　　　　　R. ERRINGTON.

THE FLOWER-GARDEN.

CALYSTEGIA PUBESCENS AND OTHER HARDY CLIMBERS.
—A few years back the London Horticultural Society
surprised the botanical world with a new double flowering Bindweed, which they introduced from the north of
China through their collector, Mr. Fortune, and which
they called *Calystegia pubescens* — that is, the downy
Bearbind. The large white Bindweed, which grows in
our own hedges, and the small white and pinkish ones
which creep among the grass by our road-sides and dry
banks, are also called *Calystegia* in books; and this new
one from China has proved a near relative to our
larger Bindweed or Bearbind. How they could make
out this relationship between the two plants from a
double flower, was a great surprise to our fresh-water
botanists—or those who only possessed a smattering
knowledge of the Linnæan classification. There were
no stamens or pistils to count over to make out even the
class or order of the Linnæan arrangement, much less
the particular genus; and the men of science, if not
surprised, were, at least, much interested in it, as being
the very first double flowering plant belonging to the
natural order of Bindweeds (*convolvulacea*) of which
they had ever heard. If any of our readers still cling to
the shades of the obsolete system by which a knowledge
of plants was obtained through the system of counting
stamens and pistils, devised by the illustrious Swede,
this Chinese Bindweed, with double flowers, should
close their account with the Linnæan Society at once;
then to turn a new leaf and begin a fresh score—not
with the old firm as formerly, but rather with the heads
of the natural system society, whose officers had no more
difficulty in finding out the proper place in their arrangement for this new flower, double as it is, than I
should in counting how many thumbs I carry about
with me. It is extremely rare that we see botanists put
to the test of determining the name or relationship of a
new plant with a double flower, because in the wild state
plants are supposed to take only after the single type.

The old *Corchorus Japonicus* is the only other instance
which occurs to me at present of a double flowering
plant being introduced, before we had any knowledge of
the single form of it; and that, too, has proved a flaw in
the system of Linnæus. This double flowering *Corchorus*
was cultivated in our gardens for more than a hundred

years under that name; but as soon as a plant of it
with single flowers only was introduced, some fifteen
years back, then it was found not to be a Corchorus at
all, and, as a matter of course, the plant had to be
named over again; for naturalists are not like poli-
ticians—they do not hold with ancient names or old
arrangements for the sake of "consistency," which is
only a polite name for obstinacy, although obstinate
people often call them hard names for this trait in their
character; and the new and proper name of our old
Corchorus is now *Kerria.*

That double Bindweed and this *Kerria japonica* and
many other "japonicas" that need not be named, prove
to us, whether we would or not, that Chinese gardeners
know as much about the art and mystery of making
double flowers from single ones as any of us, and, perhaps, a good deal more if all were known. The Bindweed under notice is certainly a production of the art of
gardening in China, and not a wild form of the plant.
There are those who see no beauty in a flower unless it
is a double one; and there are others who think just the
contrary; and there is a saying in the Highlands, when
a man undertakes to do a thing which he is not capable
of performing—to the effect, that "if he cannot make a
spoon he can spoil a horn"—spoons being made in that
wild part of the world actually from horns. The adage
may well be applied to the Chinaman who produced our
double Bindweed: he did not make the spoon, but he
spoiled a horn; from the most lovely single flower of all
the convolvuli, or bindweeds, he has produced the ugliest
of all our double flowers; but still he effected what no
one else ever managed to do before him—originated a
double convolvulus. And I have the gratifying intelligence to communicate to-day that the Chinaman's knot
is unloosed, and that *the plant has reverted to the single
form* in the flower-garden here; and a most beautiful
thing it is, nearly as large as the flower of *Ipomœa
Learii;* the colour, between salmon and French white,
with five stripes or divisions of a lighter hue; and when
we consider that the plant is as hardy as our own hedge
Bindweed, and will increase as fast as a potato, and is,
therefore, every cottager's plant, we ought to congratulate our cottage friends on the acquisition of so nice a
summer climber to train up before their doors.

I cannot make out what caused the plant to turn
single; it was planted in one of those barrels I often
have recommended, along with the new *Yellow Jasmine*
from China, against an old oak in the "Swiss Gardens,"
and facing the north. It did not see the sun these last
two seasons; and, like the rest of our out-door plants, it
received neither dew nor rain for two months this summer; but the barrel was watered with strong manure-
water once a-week, for the sake of the jasmine, which I
wished to grow fast; and which I wish was planted
against the front of cottages as extensively as the China
rose; and for the pillar of a verandah nothing could answer better. This bindweed might be planted along with
it, so that it might climb up of itself against the jasmine,
and so save the trouble of training it. Those who are
looking out for things of this sort to cover a north wall
will find these two new plants well adapted for the
purpose.

Before I close this part of my paper, I want to recommend another summer climber lately introduced by
the Horticultural Society through Mr. Fortune, as it is
not nearly so well-known as its merits deserve: I mean
Rhynchospermum jasminoides, a beautiful white flowering
sweet-scented climber, requiring about the same treatment as the lovely *Mandevilla,* flowering out of doors
from Midsummer till August, when the Mandevilla
comes in to succeed it. I am not quite sure what degree
of covering protection it requires in winter; but I should
think much about the same as the Mandevilla or any of
the new Fuchsias, just to keep it from damp and frost

It is a very good plant to train against a post or pillar, or against a back wall in a greenhouse, where it will flower in April and May; and if the wall is damp it will root into it all the way up like the ivy. A large plant of it in a pot, plunged, against a pillar out of doors, has been beautifully in bloom for the last two months with a friend of mine—a reader of these pages—to whom I am indebted for my hints on such things.

The *Solanum jasminoides*, another climber of considerable merit, has stood the last hard winter here, and in many other places, without any protection, and therefore may be put on the list of hardy climbers for the flower-garden. *Abelia rupestris*, a comparatively new plant, is also all but hardy, and for covering a low wall comes in very useful; and for a fast growing climber against an open wall, the old *Bignonia jasminoides* comes in for a first-rate place. I have it now most beautifully in flower against an east wall, and the individual blossoms are much superior to those produced under glass, but in winter the plant requires to be well protected from frosts. One good way of managing it, and many others of the half-hardy climbers, for the flower garden, is to take them up every autumn and protect them in a greenhouse over the winter. This would give them a yearly root-pruning, as Mr. Errington wishes fruit-trees to be dealt with, under certain circumstances; but, for people who are not expert at potting or transplanting large plants, perhaps the safest way would be to keep them in large pots, and to plunge, pots and all, in the ground at the time of planting in May. One good arising from plunging or planting out old half-hardy plants in their pots is, that as soon as the surface of the pot is buried in the earth the roots spread upwards from the bottom of the pot, occupy the whole of it, and then escape into the free earth over the top of the pot. There is no other way, that I know of, so effectual in keeping the roots of some plants in all parts of the pots as this of plunging them over the top, whether in a bark-bed or in an open border. We all know that roots of most plants *will* go down to the very bottom of pots, and there coil round and round rather than spread about the whole ball; but no sooner do we bury the pot in the earth, or in plunging material, than these coiled roots send up feeders in all directions. I ought, however, to tell of some dangers which attend this pot-planting in summer, in some soils, &c., *viz.*—that if put in a hole no larger than will just hold the pot, and deep enough to allow it a couple of inches under the general surface, if the soil happens to be at all strong or retentive of moisture, this hole will drain the soil for a given distance all round it, and as deep as the hole itself, and this drained water lodges round the pot, and when you come to water it, or when the rain helps, the pot cannot part with the extra water, at least for some time, and then the plants are in a much worse condition than those growing naturally on very wet land or on undrained farms. If the bottom of a border rests on a bed of clay (the most hopeless case for our pots), and that to get depth enough for burying the pot we must cut a few inches into the clay bottom, then there is no other means of security for the welfare of the plant than that of cutting a side drain from the bottom; but on any other soil a lodgment of water round the pot may be got rid of without a drain. The more common way is to make the hole six inches deeper than the pot, then to put two brick-bats in the bottom of the hole, and rest the bottom of the pot on the bats, so that it stands four inches clear from the under soil, and this allows room enough for drainage; and some make the bottom of the hole like an inverted cone, and allow a foot or more of open space below the pot; this is a good way to keep back the roots from working out of the bottom into the free soil. I believe the flower gardener from Surrey, whom I mentioned lately, told me that he

covered a long stretch of trellis, pillars, &c., with half-hardy climbers plunged in pots; but the soil of the garden he manages is so light that he needs no precaution for drainage.

Rᴏꜱᴇ Sᴛᴏᴄᴋꜱ.—I have said already that the dog rose stock will not live long on our light, chalky soils here; indeed, before "the Rosary" was properly made, three years was about the usual time that *Mrs. Elliott.* the freest grower of the perpetual roses, could look healthy on the dog rose, while on the crimson and purple Boursaults it, and all the strong growing roses, flourish to, I was going to say perfection, but, to my satisfaction is a more modest term. And yet I have heard and read of the dog rose as the best, and the Boursault stock as the worst that could be used; but, I believe, by writers whose experience of their respective merits was confined to one kind of soil—just the source from which half the mistakes and disappointments in gardening take their rise. I have said, over and over again, how to make cuttings of roses and other plants so as to prevent their ever sending up a sucker from the collar or any part of the stem, but when we meet with a plant whose natural way of increasing, or rather extending itself, is by making long underground shoots from the roots, we are baffled; and that is the habit of these Boursaults, and therefore I have been reluctantly obliged to cease budding on them. The Italian rose, called *Manetti*, introduced by Mr. Rivers, promises to be as good a grower on our soil as the Boursault; and they say it does not produce root suckers; and if that be true, I have no doubt but that it is all that has been said of it on light sandy soils, so that it fills up a void we experienced for years where the dog rose would not live. I have a rose here which I have known for ten years, and of which I entertain great hopes as a stock to work on;. it is a real cross hybrid, raised by the late Dean of Manchester, and, I believe, with the view for a stock for chalky soils; but any light soil suits it, and all that I have worked on it have done well yet.

D. Bᴇᴀᴛᴏɴ.

GREENHOUSE AND WINDOW GARDENING.

Fʟᴏʀɪꜱᴛꜱ' Pᴇʟᴀʀɢᴏɴɪᴜᴍꜱ—Cᴜᴛᴛɪɴɢꜱ, &ᴄ.—The wood being prepared by hardening, &c., as alluded to last week, the next thing is the *selecting* of the cuttings; or, if many are wanted and it is desirable to make the most of the old plant for another year, then all the shoots should be cut down at the same time, in order that fresh growth in the different parts may proceed simultaneously. If the plant is large, we cannot err in cutting low enough, provided a single joint or bud is left to each shoot. Even this is not absolutely necessary, but fresh shoots will be formed sooner than if we *stumped* the plant in to the two-year-old wood. If, however, the plant be small, and with few shoots, and you wish to have it large the following season, then several buds may be left upon each shoot; and if they break at all nicely, you will obtain a large flowering plant earlier, because much *stopping* will not afterwards be necessary.

Notwithstanding your preparing the plant, it will sometimes *bleed* after you cut it down; but that may be easily stopped by dropping a pinch of quick lime on the cut part, and this is better than resorting to watering, which often, when given in such circumstances, imparts a gouty habit, which the young shoots are long in getting free from. Instead of watering at the roots, it is preferable to dust the stems slightly with lime-water from the syringe, for a week at least, and to keep the place, pit, or frame, &c., in which the plants are situated, rather close and moist. The clear lime-water from the syringe will tend both to harden the cut points and free the stems from all impurity.

Leaving the old plants for a little, let us look after *the cuttings*. Each kind has been put by itself, labelled and tied up as the plants were cut down. The cuttings may be of any length, from two to six inches, and upwards. The medium size will generally answer best. It is advisable that every cutting should contain at least two joints; at each of these a leaf will have stood, and a bud will be formed, or forming, in its axil—the part enclosed between the footstalk of the leaf and the stem or shoot to which it is attached. For reasons previously referred to, remove the leaf from the lower part of the cutting, and cut straight through the bud at the joint with a sharp knife, allowing the leaves, if any, to remain at the upper joints, to carry on there as long as possible their peculiar functions. Other circumstances being favourable, the lower end of the shoots being best ripened will form the best cuttings; and even if they should not root so soon as those more soft and spongy, they generally make the nicest, stubbiest plants in the end. Cuttings from those parts which immediately support the flower-stalks ought to be avoided, unless it be a very rare and valuable kind, as such parts are too soft and spongy to make good plants. When it is neither desirable to remove a shoot nor yet cut a plant down, small sturdy side shoots may often be obtained, and these taken off close to the stem, placed under glass, and shaded, will make beautiful plants.

The cuttings being formed by cutting straight across the lower joint, and in a slanting manner, half an inch above the upper one, it will next be advisable to dry the lower end, for half a day at least, whilst the top end is kept moist and shaded, and then proceed to planting them. This may be done in many ways. From the end of June until the middle of August, strong cuttings might be inserted in light sandy soil in the open border, just as Mr. Beaton practises with scarlet geraniums. Numbers, I might say millions, are thus propagated in the neighbourhood of London every year. Where the soil is strong and loamy, the easiest way to do this would be to rake out shallow drills six inches apart and fill them with sandy loam, or a compost of equal parts leaf-mould and sand. If watered well when they are inserted, they will not want much, excepting *dustings* afterwards, as they will have the advantage of the moisture contained in the soil of the garden. A little shading in hot weather may be necessary; but those who have never tried such a plan would be surprised to find how little it would be required. Of course, as soon as rooting commenced it would be altogether unnecessary. The advantage of this system is, that all the labour of draining, and filling, and carrying propagating pots, glasses, &c., is avoided; and when potted in good time, before they become gross in their habits, fine hardy plants are thus obtained. The disadvantage of the system is, that beginners seeing them growing so well, are apt to be too late in potting them, and thus a grossness of habit is produced, which causes the plant to feel the change when transferred to a pot. If possible, therefore, plants so struck should be potted before subjected to the heavy autumnal rains. This grossness of habit is prevented, and an earlier development of roots effected, by planting the cuttings in light sandy soil, under a hand light, or beneath the sashes of a frame, as the heavy rains are thus excluded, and keeping the atmosphere close and shaded when necessary preserves the leaves fresh. Even here, however, air should be given liberally at night, by *tilting* or removing the lights. Placing the cuttings round the sides of a pot that previously had been well drained, and then filled with light sandy soil, transferring them then to a cold frame kept close during the day, but with air given at night, is also a good plan, especially for rare kinds; and then, in such cases, the rooting process may be accelerated by moving and plunging the pots in a slight hotbed, after they have stood in the cold frame two or three weeks.

Something of this plan is necessary when cuttings are to be struck as late as September. The best plan of all, in the case of fine kinds which you wish to rattle on, is to follow a similar system, only with the exception of putting one cutting by the side of a very small pot, technically called *thumbs*, and removing it to a larger whenever it has filled with roots. In this case the base of the cutting should either rest upon the drainage or on the bottom of the small pot; when shifted it will be an easy matter to get the stem of the plant in the centre, instead of being at the side as when first inserted. "But why not put the cutting in the centre of the pot at once?" Because gardeners have found that cuttings strike sooner when, in addition to their bases resting on a hard substance, their sides also come in contact with a hard matter. "But why is this?" Aye! there is the difficulty; the bare enumeration of the theories would take up more than my limited space: one reason, however, for the present, must suffice:—In placing a cutting in the centre of a pot it is apt to get over wet, and to damp, and, if it escaped these evils, the soft matter by which it is surrounded allows of the expansion of the cutting, and thus size, *laterally*, may actually be gained with but little disposition to protrude roots; but when placed close to the porous side of the pot, not only is the danger of *damping*, &c., lessened, but the cutting finds an *obstruction* to its expansion *laterally*, and, therefore, not to be thwarted, sends out, either at the side or the base of the cutting, that cellular matter from which roots afterwards proceed. Much the same principle is here acted upon, though worked out in a different manner, as when we slit up the base of a cutting of a hard stemmed carnation, or skin a small piece off the wood from the opposite side of the bud in a vine shoot used as a cutting; the *object* being to ensure a more free protrusion of the cambium matter between the bark and wood, and the *result* being that roots are generally more quickly produced.

But, however raised, the cuttings should be potted off shortly after they are struck; kept close in a frame or pit during the day, until they are rooting freely (giving air, however, at night), and then set in the open air; housing them in good time; stopping them; repotting those which require it in the end of October; kept slowly growing all the winter; seldom allowing the thermometer to fall below 45°, and yet giving as much air as possible in all favourable weather, recollecting that most of the evils and want of success in geranium growing arise from a close, moist, cold atmosphere; stop and shift again in March; encourage with a rise of warmth, gradually, of 10°, with plenty of air; keep the plants near the glass to mature the buds; thin out some of the larger leaves at times, and spread out the shoots; give manure water frequently after the flower-buds appear, *but not before*, and they will reward you with nice heads of bloom in June and July. If bloom is not your object the plants may be stopped again in May, the shoots well tied out and encouraged, and shifted into large pots in July and August, so as to flower the following season in April and May. If this should not be desired, those stopped in May will bloom in the autumn, if not shifted. Those which bloom in June and July may be cut down, and from them the second crop of flowers may be obtained next season. All this is not so easily done as talked about: the surface of the soil must be kept stirred, especially during winter; the foliage be refreshed with syringings, especially after February, and until the flower-buds appear; smoking with tobacco attended to whenever one green fly is seen; the plants kept near the glass, with nothing to obscure the light; and water judiciously

given; managing it so that the flower-buds do not
appear until the pot is crammed with healthy roots.

Now, glance for a moment at the *old plants* we left
getting nursed in the cold pit. In eight or ten days
after being cut down, and receiving moisture *about* the
tops rather than *among* the roots, the pots may receive
a fair watering,—asfmuch as will reach every good root.
When the buds break, gradually give air. When one
inch in length or so, take the plants to the potting-bench,
shake the soil from the roots, examine and prune the
roots a little, re-shift into similar, or, what in general
will answer better, smaller-sized pots ; place them again
in the cold pit, and keep close until the fresh roots are
running in the new soil, then give air gradually until at
length you expose them *entirely* to the atmosphere ;
steering clear, however, of cold rains and anything like
frost. Plants cut down in June and July, if transferred
to small pots, will require to be placed in blooming pots
in the end of October. Those cut down in the end of
July or during August, will not want repotting until
the new year has brought lengthened sunshine; and
from these different successions of bloom may be expected. To have it fine, cleanliness, air, light, *room*,
and a temperature seldom below 45°, must be leading
considerations. During winter, unless during sunshine,
the temperature should never be higher. After a sunny
day it may be from five to eight degrees lower at night
with impunity. In the case of large plants, little stopping will be required after repotting. Thinning instead
will often be necessary. Hence, old plants generally
produce the earliest bloom, as every general stopping of
the shoots as well as every shift given retard the
blooming period.

Cuttings inserted now would flower early enough next
season, if kept in small pots and not stopped. Young
plants when first potted, will do well in rich sandy soil;
as they get older more nutritious matter may be added
by degrees, and the best for them is two or three years
old cow dung. At the last shifting we generally use
three-parts fibry loam, one of peat, one of leaf mould,
one of cow dung, and one of silver sand. A dressing of
cow dung on the surface is often given when the flower-
buds appear.   R. Fish.

HOTHOUSE DEPARTMENT.
STOVE PLANTS.

Exotic Ferns.—To grow specimens such as are
exhibited at the metropolitan shows by Mr. Williams,
gardener to C. Warner, Esq., the following method
should be practised:—Choose in March a young healthy
plant, the roots of which have just reached the sides of
the pot, say of one five inches in diameter. Take a pot,
eight inches in diameter, and drain it well, fill it just high
enough to receive the plant with a compost of rough
fibrous peat, turfy loam, and half decayed leaf-mould,
mixed with a due proportion of river sand. Then place
the plant in the middle of the pot, leaving the drainage
attached to the ball; fill in around it with the compost,
pressing it down gently with the hand, till the pot is
full. Then give the pot a smart stroke or two upon the
bench to settle the soil. Place the plant in a position
where it will receive a due proportion of light, and as
near the glass as will allow it to receive the benefit of
the rays of the sun during the morning and afternoon,
shading it from the noonday sunshine, and giving it a
liberal supply of water after it has begun to grow freely.
The strong growing kinds will require repotting twice
before August into a pot increased in size proportionately to the growth of the ferns, using the same compost. By this liberal treatment, a plant six inches high
may be grown in one year to a bush two feet high, or
more, and as much across.

The following species bear this treatment, and flourish well in consequence :—

Adiantum formosum, A. trapeziforme, Aspidium serra,
Allantodia axillaria, Asplenium falcatum, A. præmorsum, A.
nidus-avis, A. rhizophyllum, Blechnum brasiliensis, Chei-
lanthus repens, Cibotium Barometz, Dicksonia adiantioides,
Diplazium decussatum, Gymnogramma calomelanos, G.
ochracea, Lycopodium cæsium arboreum, Meniscium palustre, Nephrodium molle, N. exaltatim, N. pectinatum,
Polypodium aureum, P. nereifolium, Pteris hastata, P.
effusa, P. tremula, P. vespertilionis, and Woodwardia
radicans.

The more delicate growers require a little different
treatment. The shifts at the potting time should be
less; that is, supposing the young healthy plant to be
in a pot three inches in diameter, a shift into a five-inch
pot will be sufficient at once. This will allow a full
inch of fresh compost (which should be a trifle finer) all
round the ball. They should have the same number of
shiftings during the summer, the last of which will
leave them in nine-inch pots. If they thrive as they
ought to do, they will then be specimens a foot or more
high, and as much through, and very beautiful objects.
The following are a few kinds that may be subjected to
this second mode of treatment :—

Adiantum curvatum, A. concinnum, A. cuneatum, A.
macrophyllum, A. tenerum, Asplenium palmatum, Casse-
beera farinosa, Cheilanthes lendigera, Cænopteris cicutaria,
C. vivipara, Gymnogramma chrysophylla, G. dealbata, Lycopodium Wildenovii, Nothocleana nivea, Polystichum proliferum, Pteris collina, P. saggitæfolia, and P. palmata.

Some *British Ferns* are much finer specimens if cultivated in the same way in the stove. The beautiful
Adiantum capillus veneris will by such treatment grow
to an amazing size. A plant of this species was exhibited by the same successful grower referred to at the
commencement of this article, which measured a foot
high and eighteen inches across. This plant had been
grown in a vinery from March up to the time it was
exhibited, and was so fine as almost to cause a doubt as
to its identity with the puny plants of the same species
cultivated in the usual way. The pretty *Asplenium
marinum*, or Sea-side fern, will scarcely exist away from
its native *habitat*, excepting when it is grown in heat,
and then it rivals in beauty and vigour its foreign
rivals. We recommend the following British ferns, in
addition to the above, to be cultivated in the stove in
the same manner, knowing from experience that they
will agreeably surprize the grower by their luxuriance
and beauty:—

Allosorus crispus, Asplenium fontanum, Cystopteris alpina,
C. dentatus, C. fragilis, Lastræa lonchitis, L. rigida, Polypodium calcareum, P. dryopteris, P. phegopteris, and P.
thalyptris.

The only point to attend to will be to keep such
specimens of hardy ferns so cultivated in a cold frame
or pit from September to March, to give them a rest
during that season, and so enable them to shoot again
with equal vigour the following season ; potting them
into fresh compost to strengthen their summer growth.

We might have given much longer lists, but we consider the above quite sufficient for a moderate collection,
or medium sized house. It is an easy matter to increase
the number, if space and inclination render such increase desirable. We shall be glad to see their culture
more attended to, because no objects in the plant world
is more interesting, or more worthy of attention and
care in cultivation.

Gesneraceæ *(Continued from page 174.)*

In our former communications we have principally
confined our remarks to the large genera of *Achimenes*
and *Gloxinia*, alluding only to one species of *Gesnera*,

namely, *G. zebrina*, a beautiful winter flowering species. There are, however, several other species of *Gesnera* that are well worthy of cultivation. We shall devote the remainder of our space this week to them.

Gesnera Merkii is one of the most beautiful of this charming family of plants. The flowers are produced in terminal spikes, and are of the brightest crimson. Individually, they are not quite so large as some, but they are produced more numerously. The root or bulb is solid, like that of a gloxinia; sending up in the spring, when three or four years' old, several strong shoots, which, with good management, will all flower, but they will also send forth several weak ones. These ought to be rubbed off, and make excellent cuttings when increase is desired. But whether used for that purpose or not, they must be removed, and only as many left as the plant is likely to flower to perfection; the number to be proportioned to the size and strength of the bulb. This species flowers in autumn, and is then very ornamental at a time when flowers are comparatively scarce. For the information of such of our readers as may not know this species in perfection, we may mention, that we have seen a plant of it with six flower-stems, each bearing at one time upwards of fifty opened blossoms, besides numerous buds to succeed them. The bulb was seven years old, and had flowered well for several seasons previously. It requires the same winter treatment as the gloxinia : that is, to be gradually dried off, and kept in a dormant state till March.

G. Cooperii and its allies, *G. Suttonii* and *G. faucialis*, are very fine varieties, well worthy of cultivation ; but they are so very little dissimilar, that it requires a very nice discrimination to detect any difference. The flowers are of a brighter, or rather lighter, scarlet than *G. Merkii*, and though much larger are by no means so numerous. Like that species they are produced at the ends of the shoots, generally in pairs when the plants are weak, but more numerous if the bulbs are old and strong. They require exactly the same treatment as we have described above. The season of flowering is much earlier than the last-named, thus giving a succession of bloom. We have had them in flower so early as May, but the general season is from June to the middle of July.

G. splendens.—This is a fine distinct species, growing much higher than any we have yet named. We have now one in flower with three flower-stems, each nearly three feet high. The colour is a bright light scarlet. The flowers are at the ends of the shoots, branching, about the size of *G. Merkii*, and are very numerous on each stem. It is one of the most ornamental plants we have now in bloom.

G. bulbosa and *G. rutila* are two distinct species, now very scarce, chiefly on account of the species previously named being so much handsomer in colour and size of bloom ; but they are by no means to be despised, as when well grown they are very fine objects.

All the above are similar in habit, have solid bulbs, and require to be kept during winter in the same way as *G. Merkii*. They may be easily increased by taking off some young shoots, when three inches long, and inserting them in sand, under a bell-glass, in heat. They will flower, but not strongly, the second year.

There is a very curious and handsome variety of *G. Suttonii*, named *Sub-alba*, the flowers of which are a clear flesh-colour. It is very handsome, and worth having. In all other respects it is exactly like *G. Suttonii*.

Gesnera oblongata.—This species has no bulb, which renders it very distinct from the foregoing. It has the advantage of producing its flowers in the dreariest months of the year, which renders it valuable for winter bloom, though its flowers are by no means so bright in colour. The plants when well grown form dense bushes,

from two to three feet high, and as much through. The flowers are very numerous, produced in short bunches from the axils of the leaves towards the extremities of the stem. They are of a brick-red colour. This plant must be kept moderately moist even when at rest. As soon as they have done flowering, cut them down to within a foot of the pot. Place them in a cool house, that is, in a heat of 45°, and give them very little water till they begin to grow again. They should then be repotted, frequently stopped to make them bushy, and placed in a close pit till they are wanted in September for the stove. Propagated by young shoots in a similar manner to the rest of the genus.

(To be continued.)

FLORISTS' FLOWERS.

Pinks are now all gone out of flower for this year. The old plants are of little use to the florist, as they seldom produce the second year first-rate bloom, but for ornamenting the border they are valuable. Remove them out of the bed ; trim off all dead flower-stems ; and plant them in the borders of the garden rather deeper than they have been before. They will make fresh roots higher up the stems, and form close compact bushes, producing the next season abundance of flowers. If it is intended to grow Pinks again in the same bed, the soil ought to be taken out a foot deep and renewed with fresh loam, and very rotten stable dung, in the proportion of three of the first to one of the latter, turning it over frequently to thoroughly mix and sweeten it. This should be done *immediately*, as the season for planting will soon be here.

Pansies.—The *early-struck cuttings* of these beautiful long blooming flowers should in a week or two be planted out in the beds where they are to flower next year. They love a good loamy soil, enriched moderately with rotten leaf-mould or hotbed manure, but not too rich, as too strong food will be apt to canker them at the time when they ought to produce their bloom in perfection. *Cuttings just rooted* had better be potted to be kept in a cold frame through winter. If kept too long in the place where they have been put in to strike root, they are apt to damp off during the wet autumn months.

T. Appleby.

THE KITCHEN-GARDEN.

Cabbage.—The season is now approaching when the ground must be prepared for the cabbage crop. The onion ground, which, from the summer surface scarifying, is sweet, wholesome, and entirely free from weeds, with us generally falls in at a convenient time for being succeeded by the early spring cabbage crop. The onion, like all other kitchen-garden crops, is cultivated with us on sloping banks, and immediately the onions are cleared, the ground is liberally manured and ridge-trenched, leaving the soil as rough and open as possible; and as soon as the earliest cabbage plants are strong enough, the strongest are selected, and a row of them planted on each side of the ridge one foot apart. The ridges being two-feet trenches, each plant is left one foot apart, which is the space we allow for the early small close-growing kinds; for the later and somewhat larger growing kinds, we allow from eighteen inches to two feet space each way, and fill up the ground with strong early growing varieties of *coleworts*. By planting a row of these one foot apart, and another plant also between each of the cabbage plants in the rows they may be pulled out as greens, &c., throughout the winter and early spring ; and by this course of cropping, with good attention to the after management, an immense produce may be taken from a moderate sized piece of land.

CARROTS.—The *Early Horn* may be sown towards the end of this month and the beginning of next, on a dry, sheltered, healthy situation; those who have lights to spare need not sow so soon by a month. Our system for obtaining early spring carrots is to cast out a shallow pit in a sheltered situation, forming the outsides with the earth, and finishing it level on the top with turf, upon which we place any old rough boards, or slabs, if they are to be had conveniently at the time. Into this pit we put any kind of refuse sweepings and rakings, leaves, &c., or, indeed, anything that we may have then to spare that will secure drainage and a little bottom warmth; upon this we place from ten to twelve inches of open sweet sandy soil, raising it quite to the top of the pit; drills are pressed into the soil eight or nine inches apart with a straight-edge, and every alternate drill is sown with Early Horn carrots, and the other drill with radishes, which, being up early, nurse and shelter the young carrots by the time they appear. These radishes, of course, being thus early and well thinned, are quickly ready for use, and when drawn out of the way, leave the carrots in rows eight or nine inches apart. We take care to make such beds the same width as the frame or pit lights, in case we should have any of them to spare for a short time when needed, but otherwise they are covered with slight protectors, the size of a light, covered with straight straw, fixed on closely and neatly; or, light protectors made in the same way, covered with asphalt felt. We can sometimes manage to have every alternate protector with glass, and shifting them daily answers the purpose very well. We have occasion for many ranges of such kind of home-made pits for carrots, lettuce, endive, radishes, cauliflowers, Neapolitan violets, and other varieties of bulbs, &c., &c.

CAULIFLOWERS.—It has been for many years a general custom to sow this vegetable under hand-glasses and in other ways for standing the winter about the 18th, or from the 18th to the 24th of August; should the autumn be mild, if sown at the foregoing date they will sometimes get large plants by November, either for hand-glasses or for other winter protection, and then in consequence of the checks they sometimes receive through the severity of the weather in the winter months, instead of their growing on again in early spring, they will frequently set the flower and button, as it is termed by gardeners, that is, showing a little flower about the month of March of the size of a button. Our practice for many years past has been, not to sow for a month or more later than the above date; indeed, we find that sowing on a gentle warmth, and close to the glass inside a frame or pit, the first week in October, sufficiently early for us to obtain very beautiful cauliflowers in the month of April following. As soon as the plants are up and can be handled, we prick them into thumb or three-inch pots, plunging them into some comfortable earth close to the glass inside a pit or frame, or temporary turf pit, where they are encouraged to maintain a sturdy growth by taking the lights entirely off on fine days, and tilting them at night. They are often surface-stirred, and are watered when they require it with tepid water; they soon require five-inch pots, from which, by New Year's Day, they are transferred into seven or eight-inch pots, and their growth encouraged until February, when an early and suitable opportunity is embraced for turning them out; four under a large hand-glass, between sloping banks, on a good preparation, where they do not fail in repaying well for the trouble previously taken about them. The required quantity of plants for spring planting on the quarter, &c., are pricked in temporary pits, sloping banks, &c., and protected in severe weather by applications of dry dust about their stems, and thatched hurdles or temporary lights, or some kind of protector.

CUCUMBERS.—To keep up a succession of autumn and winter fruit, sowings should now be made in succession. After trying many varieties for winter culture in pots, tubs, boxes, or troughs, we cannot find any variety so well adapted as the true *old Sion*, which is both hardy and prolific, at all times firm, and of excellent flavour. Those who have any favourite variety now growing may easily strike cuttings, and quickly get any desired quantity of plants.

MELONS.—Those of the late kinds should be kept thin, and the atmospheric heat kept about them pretty briskly, but not too humid.

JAMES BARNES.

MISCELLANEOUS INFORMATION.

YEAST.

By the Authoress of "My Flowers."

FAMILIES are often deterred from baking at home, on account of the bread being so often spoiled, and having to labour through a whole batch when it has turned out heavy, or bitter, or hard. Home-made bread will occasionally vary in degrees of excellence, particularly in summer, because in hot weather it will not rise so well as in cool; but so much depends upon the person who makes it, that if she is skilful and active, very little fear need be entertained for the result. I was convinced of this fact many years ago, by that which occurred in our own family. After a succession of cooks, under whose auspices the bread was almost always uneatable, heavy, or bitter, or hard, a young person undertook the situation, less qualified for it, in many ways, than any of those who had preceded her. But from the moment she commenced making bread—and with the same flour, the same yeast, and the same oven that had always been used—all annoyance ceased. Nothing could be lighter, or sweeter, or more excellent than the tempting loaves she moulded; and during her reign, the bread never failed to be good. Her method of making it was exactly like that of other people, *only* she kneaded it powerfully and briskly, being young, active, and strongly made. It seemed to me that this was the grand secret of the affair. She might, perhaps, have taken extra pains with the yeast, for certainly we never had even bitter bread while she remained in the family; but I am sure that the cause of her general success was the vigour with which she kneaded. This point cannot be too strongly impressed upon servants; it is labour certainly, and when they are unused to it, it will naturally tire the arms; but every time it is done, the fatigue will lessen, and the arms will find it easier, and the pleasure of eating light, wholesome, palatable bread will be a full reward for the effort of making it. The eye of the mistress will be especially needful on the baking day, unless her servant thoroughly understands her business, and gives herself cheerfully all the trouble the occasion calls for.

The yeast from strong beer, or even good table beer, is not so good for making bread as that which is taken from poor beer. We always found our bread lighter when we procured yeast from those among the villagers who brewed at home, than when we obtained it from the brewer or the neighbouring farms. Why this should be the case I do not know; but so it always was. In the country it is often difficult to obtain yeast, in which case it is desirable to make it at home; and for the benefit of those who are inconveniently situated for obtaining it, I subjoin some directions for that purpose, beginning with one which has often been tried and approved of in our own family:—

Take two dozen large floury potatoes and roast them well, as if for eating. Scoop out the insides, and with a rolling-pin roll them until they are quite fine and pulverized. To this add a quarter of a pound of coarse brown sugar, and as much water as will make it of the consistency of batter. Then add a pint of yeast, and let it work together. A pint of this yeast should always be kept to make a fresh stock, unless beer yeast can be obtained, which is the best to set the composition working.

Another recipe for yeast, which I believe to be a good one, but of which I cannot speak from actual experience, is the following :—Boil three quarts of water, put it into a stone jar, and let it stand until the steam is gone off. Then put in half a gallon of ground malt, and when well mixed and mashed, cover it close, and let it stand one hour; then add three quarts of boiling water, and let it stand five hours. Strain it, and work it with yeast. When worked, it should be kept in stone jars, and stopped very close. A pint of this yeast is sufficient for a bushel of flour.

Another way to make a gallon of yeast, which is said to be excellent, is to boil one ounce of hops in four quarts of water until they are reduced to three. A quarter of a pound of dry malt must then be put into a stone pan, the boiled hops strained into the malt, and the mixture covered up close. This must be left to stand until cool; then a pint of old yeast must be added, a quarter of an ounce of cream of tartar, and a good handful of flour. These must be all well mixed together, and set to work for six or eight hours. One teacupful of this yeast will be sufficient for half a stone of flour.

The writer from whom I quoted in my last paper upon the subject of bread, has given directions for making " yeast cakes," which he says will keep a whole year, and make very excellent bread. I extract the passage, as it is well worth attention :—" The materials for a good batch of cakes are as follows—3 ounces of good fresh hops, 3½ lbs. of rye flour, 7 lbs. of Indian corn-meal, and 1 gallon of water. Rub the hops so as to separate them. Put them into the water, which is to be boiling at the time; let them boil half an hour, then strain the liquor through a fine sieve into an earthen vessel. While the liquor is hot put in the rye-flour, stirring the liquor well and quickly as the flour goes into it. The day after, when it is working, put in the meal, stirring it well as it goes in. Before the meal is all in, the mess will be very stiff; and it will, in fact, be dough, very much of the consistence of the dough that bread is made of. Take this dough, knead it well as you would for pie-crust. Roll it out with a rolling-pin, as you roll out pie-crust, to the thickness of about a third of an inch. When you have it (or a part of it at a time) rolled out, cut it up into cakes with a tumbler glass turned upside down, or with something else that will answer the purpose. Take a clean board (a tin may be better), and put the cakes to *dry in the sun.* Turn them every day, let them receive no wet, and they will become as hard as ship biscuit. Put them in a bag or box, and keep them in a place *perfectly free from damp.* When you bake, take two cakes, of the thickness above mentioned, and about three inches in diameter, put them in hot water over night, having cracked them first. Let the vessel containing them stand near the fire-place all night; they will dissolve by the morning; and these you use in setting your sponge (as it is called) precisely as you would use the yeast of beer. Indian-meal is used merely because it is less adhesive than that of wheat. White pea-meal, or even barley-meal, would do just as well..... The cakes when put in the sun may have a glass-sash or a hand-light put over them. This would make their berth hotter than that of the hottest open air situation in America. In short, to a farmer's wife, or any good housewife, all the little difficulties to the attainment of such an object would be as nothing. The will only is required; and if there be not that, it is useless to think of the attempt." The yeast cakes must not be dried by the fire, and they must be dried as hard as ship biscuit, and as quickly as possible.

I hope I may not be considered tedious in my remarks and directions about yeast. Good bread is of so much consequence, both in the light of economy, wholesomeness, and individual comfort, that it is desirable to glean all possible information on the subject.

If beer yeast is bitter, the most effectual way to manage is that often practised by the poor :—Take the outer skin from a middling-sized onion, and put the onion into the yeast, when it is first added to the flour. Then let it remain until it is time to make up the dough, when the onion must be drawn out with whatever may adhere to it. Not the slightest flavour is imparted to the bread. Many persons mix a double handful of bran in the yeast, and strain it through a cloth or bag into the flour. A red-hot cinder or two is sometimes put into the yeast and strained out in a similar way, and for a similar purpose; but the use of the onion will prevent any further trouble. Some persons may object to the idea of an onion, but if it is used exactly in the way abovementioned, it is perfectly unobjectionable, and the most prejudiced or fastidious person will be unable to detect the slightest evidence of its having been present.

TO CORRESPONDENTS.

. We request that no one will write to the departmental writers of THE COTTAGE GARDENER. It gives them unjustifiable trouble and expense. All communications should be addressed " *To the Editor of The Cottage Gardener*, 2, *Amen Corner, Paternoster Row, London.*"

ALLAMANDA CATHARTICA (T. W. T.).—Yours has very long branches, and is producing some young shoots near the bottom. It is now in full bloom, but the branches are straggling, and you ask what you are to do to make it a more seemly plant next year? As soon as it has done flowering lift the pot so as to bring the plant nearer the light; bring the long branches lower down, so as to give the young shoots more light and air; the long shoots had better be shortened about the end of September to within about one foot from the old wood, leaving on all the foliage below the cut; this will encourage the young shoots to push on strongly; give considerably less water after the pruning, but do not allow the plant to flag. In February repot the plant into a rich compost of rotten leaf-mould, turfy loam, and peat in equal parts; give it then bottom-heat and liberal treatment, with water both at the root and over head; train the shoots, as they advance in growth, on a large balloon-shaped trellis, keeping the branches so thin as to allow every leaf a full exposure to the light; we have no doubt your plant will then be a complete bush, and flower satisfactorily. *Allamanda Schottii* (Henderson's variety), is much finer than A. Cathartica; the flowers frequently measure more than five inches across, and have the throat beautifully striped with rich brown. *A. grandiflora* is a beautiful species, with small foliage, and flowers of a paler yellow; but the colour is very pleasing, being clear and bright. Make no apology about asking questions; we are always happy to meet the wishes of our correspondents, and assist them with all the information they may require. The only thing we ask, is an accurate statement of the treatment that has been given to any plant previously to asking for our advice.

FERNS UNDER A GLASS SHADE (W. H.).—You wish to know what species of ferns thrive well under a glass shade, but you do not say what kind of shade, nor its size. A stove or a greenhouse is a glass shade on a large scale, as a bell-glass, six inches in diameter, is one on a small scale. In the first volume of THE COTTAGE GARDENER there are ample directions how to treat ferns in Wardian cases. The kinds we usually plant in a moderate sized one are *Adiantum pubescens, A. formosum, Asplenium ebeneum, A. planicaule, Cænopteris cicutaria, Davallia canariensis, Doodia aspera, Litobrochia leptophylla, Lycopodiums*—several species, *Nephrodium decompositum, Polystichum hispidum, Pteris chinensis, P. hastata,* and *P. palmata.* A pretty fern for a small bell-glass is *Adiantum setosum,* also *Doodia rupestris* and *Adiantum cuneatum.* For one of a large size the rare *Trichomanes speciosum,* emphatically called the Irish bristly fern, is very suitable. We have seen one growing beautifully under such a glass upon a table in a gentleman's library, in the neighbourhood of Bedford Square, in almost the heart of London.

FERNS FOR GREENHOUSE (*Ibid*).—You ask what ferns are suitable for a greenhouse? Most of our British ferns thrive better in a greenhouse than in the open air, at least such as are difficult to cultivate in the ordinary way. The following exotic species are also suitable for that purpose—*Adiantum pedatum, Allantodia australis, Aspidium coriaceum, Asplenium falcatum, A. ebeneum, Cheilanthes vestita, Cænopteris japonica, Cibotium Baromets, Davallia canariensis, Dicksonia Antarctica, Lycopodium denticulatum, L. stoloniferum, Onoclea sensibilis, Polypodium Billiardierii, P. decussiva pinnata, Pteris chinensis, P. Kingianum,* and *Woodwardia radicans.*

CUPREA STRIGILLOSA (*Ibid*).—Requires the protection of a greenhouse during winter. Your question about aloes and yuccas shall be answered shortly.

MUSK-PLANT TRANSPLANTING (W. R., Chelsea).—Dig your beds before winter, and fork them over in March when the ground is dry. Then procure lumps of the old roots of musk plants, separate these lumps, and you will see small white roots in abundance, every inch of which will make a plant; but if you have plenty of roots, take three or four little pieces for every patch; and these patches may stand six inches apart each way in your new beds.

FLOWER POTS (*S. T.*).—By an oversight your note was mislaid, and consequently our reply will be too late for the time you wanted it; but it may serve your purpose to know that excellent pots and saucers, at very moderate prices, may be obtained at Mr. Charles Philips's Pottery, Weston-super-mare, Somerset. We have seen his pots, and can vouch for their being well and neatly made, and moderate in price.

CLOTH OF GOLD ROSE (*Ibid*).—This is constitutionally a shy bloomer; no means will make it bloom freely. Obtain *Solfaterre*, it is as good in colour and flowers freely.

TWELVE PELARGONIUMS FOR EXHIBITION (*T. B.*).—The following we recommend for the purpose. *Six dark varieties*—Orion, Sikh, Victory, Gipsy Bride, Alonzo, and Negress. *Six light varieties*—Pearl, Mont Blanc, Rosetta, Ariel, Forget-me-not, and Rosamund.

BOOKS FOR CHILDREN'S PRIZES (*J. H.*).—You have offered to present to children two books on gardening for the first and second best bouquets of wild flowers at a horticultural show. We know of none so good for such a purpose as No. 2 of "*The Finchley Manuals of Industry*." It is entitled, "Gardening, or Practical and Economical Training for the Management of a School or Cottage Garden;" is published by Mr. Masters, Aldersgate-street, and is one of the most admirable little books we know. We should give a copy to each, and, in addition to the first prize, we should add "*The Flowers of the Year*," published by the Religious Tract Society, one of those little volumes which we love in childhood and do not weary of in maturer age.

POTATOES FOR AUSTRALIA (*Ibid*).— Keep the tubers in alternate layers with dry earth in a dry cool shed until the vessel sails in October, and then put them into canvas bags, and sling them in the most airy part of your cabin.

DISAPPOINTED BEE-KEEPER (*A Subscriber, Sydenham*).—We cannot give our correspondent's name; but if you send us the questions, we will have them answered.

GARDENERS' DICTIONARY (* *).—This, with which Johnson's will be incorporated, but almost entirely re-written, will appear the first Thursday in October.

HIMALAYAN PUMPKIN (*Ibid*).—You may cook this, young, like the Vegetable Marrow, or keep it until quite ripe, and then use the flesh mashed like turnips; or in making soup according to the excellent and economical recipe we formerly gave, vol. i., page 43.

URINE (*Zeta*).—To no plant can this be given undiluted without injuring it. One gallon to five gallons of water would be a good proportion.

SYRINGING GREENHOUSE VINE (*A Constant Subscriber*).—Under no circumstances should this be done in July. From the time of blooming until the time of colouring or ripening commencing, moisture should be supplied to the leaves by watering the floor, and then even that be gradually omitted until the floor becomes dry.

WHITE POWDER ON GRAPES (*J. N.*).—This, "like fine lime dust," has made its appearance upon the berries of your Black Hamburghs growing on an open wall at Brixton, Surrey. This we fear is the egg mildew (*Odium Tuckerii*), and your only chance of cure is *immediately* to dust over all the berries with flowers of sulphur.

COCOA-NUT FIBRE NETTING (*Delta*).—Our correspondent wishes to know whether such an article is made calculated for shading purposes, which he thinks desirable, on account of its durability. There is a very nice netting which we think would suit our correspondent, called "Weatherproof Burnettized Netting," which may be had at Mr. Farlow's, 5, Crooked Lane, London Bridge.

POLYGALA VULGARIS (*Ibid*).—We have never heard or seen this, the common Milkwort, improved by cultivation. We have seen it as a rock plant in gardens, and other ways grown. There are many varieties on the chalky banks of Hampshire, all about the same size of flower, only varying in colour (deep blue, purple, white, and flesh coloured). We think it a very desirable plant to keep in gardens, even without any farther improvement upon its flowers, and it would do well on banks in open situations. The plant is not very particular as to its soil in a wild state, as it is found on gravelly loam, gravelly heath, or the chalky down on sunny banks.

NEMOPHILA MACULATA (*A Parson's Wife*).—This is best sown in the open bed where it is to flower, like the blue one. Good gardeners can only grow it well in pots, and this must be done from autumn-sown seeds, to flower the following April or May.

SPRUCE FIRS (*L. F. W.*).—These require no protection. They do not, however, like the smoky air of towns; but if they are in deep loamy soil they ought to do even there. Your tree is cramped at the roots, and, with the smoky air, this causes it being stunted. No protection can remedy such conditions.

MELALEUCA LANCEOLATA (*Mark*).—Your plant, three feet high, grows freely, but has not flowered, nor will it do so until it is a little older, and wood is well ripened in autumn. Keep it short of pot room, and put it in-doors before the middle of September, so that the dews and rains do not keep it growing late.

RED SPIDER (*An Amateur*).—There is no mode of getting this from your *Solitya* but by sponging its leaves thoroughly, and submitting it to the fumes of sulphur, by putting some of the flowers of sulphur upon a hot-water plate filled with boiling water, and placing the whole under a tub or other close cover. Try what putting the plant under the same cover together with a large quantity of bruised laurel leaves will do, and let us know the result.

HOUSE SLOPS (*G. Tucker*).—To prevent these smelling, the best mode is to dilute them with water in the proportions requisite for using them as a liquid manure. We cannot tell what this should be as you do not say whether you mix *suds, &c.*, all together. See what we said above about *urine*. In addition you might mix an eighth of an ounce of alum with every gallon.

PUTTY (*Ibid*).—Glazier's putty is made of whiting and boiled linseed oil. The whiting should be well dried, and then pounded and sifted till it becomes a fine powder, and is quite free from grit. The whiting, a little warm, should be gradually added to the oil, and well mixed by means of a piece of stick, or a spatula. When it is sufficiently stiff, it should be well worked with the hand on a table, and afterwards beaten on a stone with a wooden mallet, till it becomes a soft, smooth, tenacious mass. A ball of putty when left some days becomes somewhat hard, but may be easily softened by beating.

SKYLIGHT (*Sister Anne*).—A room with only a skylight will hardly keep *Verbenas* and *Petunias* over the winter, even if you had a fire-place in it. Three things are essential for wintering all young soft plants, viz.—to be near the light; to be free from damp; and to be secure from frost. We do not know the price of the book you want.

NAMES OF PLANTS (*Juvendus*).—1. Alopecurus pratensis. 2. Scabiosa arvensis. 3. Centaurea scabiosa. 4. Lathyrus pratensis. 5. Myosotis arvensis. 6. Convolvulus arvensis. 7. Malva sylvestris. 8. Briunia dioica. (*W. W.*)—We think your miserably crushed specimen is Picridium vulgare.

RHODODENDRONS (*S. G. H.*).—A foot deep is the least peat you can give to them in making the bed described at page 148 of vol. iii., and 20 inches would be better as your peat is not good. Your situation sloping to the south is applicable; and any time, except when they are making their annual growth in May or June, will do equally well to make the bed and to plant them. Keep six feet from the stems of the Morello trees; that will not hurt them.

YELLOW JASMINES (*Ibid*).—There are several common yellow jasmines; *nudiflorum* is a new one from China, which flowers in the winter.

TROPÆOLUM PENTAPHYLLUM (*Ibid*).—It flowers very well on a north wall; but there is something the matter with yours not having grown this year. Have the roots got down too deep, or have they overrun their bounds, or have they got frosted by being too near the surface?

BLUE LARKSPURS (*Ibid*).—Many thanks; but "old plants" will not do. What Mr. Beaton wants, is seed of the *annual* blue larkspur.

GERANIUMS (*Erina*).—Aunt Harriet put her geraniums to rest after flowering full in the sun, and not plunged, and never cut them down till they began to grow again. Her "stronger compost" means, that she put less sand in it than others. The highest attainment in these things is to flower the largest possible specimens in the smallest possible pots. Aunt Harriet's largest pots were eleven inches over the mouth. We like your signature as much as that of our esteemed relative, that is, if we translate it right, "*A Daughter of Erin*."

INTERMEDIATE HIVES (*C. R. R.*).—To prevent a hive swarming, Mr. Payne directs a small hive to be placed between that partially filled (which had been previously put on) and the stock-hive. You ask, "What is the shape of the intermediate hive?" The same exactly as the small one already on your stock—flat at the top, with a two or three inch hole. The adapter prevents the top of the stock-hive being pressed in by the weight of the cups, and very much assists in their removal. See THE COTTAGE GARDENER, vol. i., page 305, and vol. ii., page 104.

TROUBLES OF BEE-KEEPERS.—*M. J. P.* writes as follows:—"I am in a peck of trouble about my bees. I told you last week of a swarm weighing 6 lbs. having left the hive, after my having given room to prevent swarming, four days after that swarm was hived into one of Payne's Cottage Hives; a great portion of the bees left the hive, clustering on a tree near like a fresh swarm; these were again hived into another Payne's Hive, unsmeared; they were found to weigh 4 lbs., leaving only 2 lbs. of bees in the first hive; and two days after they again forsook the last hive, and took possession of a hollow tree at some distance, where it was impossible to get at them. But this loss was but the *commencement* of my troubles, for, finding that two of my caps on different hives were ready to come off, I carefully separated them yesterday morning, and turned them up some little distance from the hive (but certainly too near)! one was full of the purest honey; in the other the largest portion was brood comb; although there was another hive between it and the stock-hive, and this is from a swarm of *this* year. The bees clustered so in a few minutes to the edges of the caps, that it was impossible to replace it without crushing the greater number; and my fearing the queen might be there was my reason for placing it within three yards of the parent hive. In a few moments both caps were covered with bees, and the greatest commotion existed in *every hive* (seven in number); a furious combat ensued, and in consequence the ground is to-day strewed with the killed and wounded; and, worst of all, on going in the evening to examine my caps, which I hoped by covering at any rate to preserve, I found every drop of honey gone, and the comb presented the appearance of *sawdust*, it was so mutilated. In removing my upper hive, next to the cap which contained brood, had I not better apply a ventilator for some days first, for fear the queen should be there?" There had, in all probability, been bees in the hollow tree before, and the combs they had left there pleased your bees better than the hive you had prepared for them. The caps should *not* have been turned up (see THE COTTAGE GARDENER, page 216, vol. ii.); the one with brood immediately returned (for bees will not leave their brood); and the one with pure honey should have been removed to a distance and carefully watched, and removed from place to place till the bees had left it. A cap or glass of honey when taken of should never be left for an instant till the bees have all left it (see full directions, page 105, vol. ii. of The Cottage Gardener); for it is not only the loss of the honey that is to be regretted, but the death of thousands of bees throughout the whole apiary. Ventilation is now unnecessary; swarming is over, and honey gathering also. We will give a drawing of the bee trap.

A grateful Subscriber from the Vale of Clwyd—after describing a patent hive—says: "May 23. The bees in it showed signs of swarming which we encouraged, wanting to increase our stocks, but finding they were absolutely doing nothing, May 28, we put on a glass, which was immediately taken possession of. May 29, another, with the same success, and still the appearance of swarming; and the *immense* dense population of the lower hive continuing, we put on two more, May 30, and they promised fair to be filled in a few days, when they all at once *deserted* them, and began pillaging; and, June 10, suddenly swarmed, knit, and, in a few minutes, as suddenly dispersed and returned; piping then commenced. June 19, the same attempt and result. June 20, threw off a swarm weighing four pounds; but the piping, and havoc with the honey, and idleness continuing, we took off the three entire glasses to reserve some of the honey which had been nearly filled; also three of the bell-glasses quite *emptied*. June 28, they cast again; there was no more piping and continued idleness; but in a week they resumed, though sluggishly, carrying farina and honey, which they began to do as early as February. They still continued very idle, and all the combs through the windows look empty and very scanty of bees; they have, a little, resumed in one of the glasses, but the contrast between their idleness and the ceaseless activity of the other hives is most striking. From this hive and the old straw one we have now three other flourishing colonies. The first swarm from the straw hive was on May 21—an immense one; we think the bee rather smaller than in the patent hive, which are *Cheshire* bees, while the small ones are *natives*; it was hived in a cottage hive adapted for a glass, and with Taylor's collateral floor boards, and was hard at work in a few hours; it had filled the hive in a fortnight, when a collateral one was given, which was immediately taken possession of, and now weighs at least 50 pounds; and they have also filled a flower-pot and a bell-glass 1¼ pound each, and are now filling two more. The hive from which these swarmed we prevented swarming a second time, by immediately giving a collateral hive, which they directly took possession of, and have filled also a small glass on it, and a flower-pot on the stock-hive. The cast from the patent hive, which was small, has nearly filled its hive. I should observe, we are in the middle of woods, wild flowers, and a rich agricultural district, and at the foot of the Clwydian range. I would now ask, whether it be desirable or admissible to deprive the full stock-hives of some honey?" If your hive *is* a patent one, the name of the patentee should be affixed to it; we are not at all able to say whose it is, and not knowing the hive, can give you no directions as to its management; but as it has answered no good purpose either to yourself or the person who gave it you, it would be better not to use it. We would recommend your *not* depriving your stock-hives of any of their honey. Yours must be a most excellent district for bees; and we recommend your increasing the number of your stocks, but not of *patent* hives.

Bees Unsealing Cells (*S. G.*).—If your bees are opening the cells of honey that have been sealed, and carrying it down into the stock-hive, it proves that their store is very low, and insufficient for winter's consumption; however, if you can be quite sure that the hive contains twenty pounds of honey, remove the glass immediately.

Substitute for the Puff Ball (*Ibid*).—An excellent one is *Racodium cellare*, or Mouse-skin *Byssus*. It grows in immense bunches from the roofs of large wine or beer vaults; in the London Docks' wine vaults it grows in immense quantities. It requires no drying, and ignites readily, and is more efficacious even than the puff ball.

Joining Hives of Bees (*Z.*).—It would not be good policy to join two such largely populated stocks as an old stock that has *not* swarmed and a *first* swarm of the present year. We will give a receipt for making mead, and one also for making excellent vinegar from refuse honey, washings of combs, &c., in our next calendar.

Preventing Swarming (*An Unfortunate Beekeeper*).—You will find that bees always prefer working in a box or glass placed *over* the stock than in one placed by its side. It is not merely by placing a box or glass upon the top of a stock that prevents swarming, but to induce the bees, by means of guide-combs, to establish themselves in it, and then to give free ventilation. If your bees have swarmed, which they appear to have done on the 28th, you must not expect any honey in such a season as this.

Stilton Cheese (*A Grateful Subscriber*).—The chief of this is now manufactured at Melton Mowbray, in Leicestershire; and we are informed it is thus made (of course the quantities must be proportioned to the amount of milk and cream):—Make a strong brine of salt and cold water; put into it thyme, hyssop, sweet-brier, and marjoram, a small tied bunch of each, and a few peppercorns; in three days rack off the brine, and soak the rennet in it for four days; it is then ready for use. The morning's new milk, with the cream of the previous night's milking, are mixed in a narrow deep pan, made purposely of the size and shape of the intended cheese; heat it to 90° and put in the rennetted brine, covering the pan in a warm airy room; pour off the whey; do not break the curd, but turn it without breaking into a sieve of size and shape that will

readily admit it, and apply pressure very gently until the curd is firm and dry, then transfer it to a wooden hoop, or case, fitting it exactly. When sufficiently firm take the cheese out of the hoop, bind it with a clean cloth, which is to be changed every day, and at each change bound more tight, as it becomes closer and firmer. Wipe the top and bottom daily, and often change the end on which it stands; when it can support itself without danger of breaking remove the cloth, and brush the cheese twice a day for two months, and then store. The only salt used is that in the rennet-brine.

Book on Greenhouse Plants (*W. Richardson*).—We know of no better book at present than the one you mention by Mr. Macintosh; but you will find *The Cottage Gardeners' Dictionary*, which will appear the first Thursday in October, much more useful.

Thrips on Cucumbers (*X. Y. Z.*).—See this subject fully treated at page 260 of our second volume. Try covering each young plant with a small glass, and putting under at the same time some laurel leaves cut in pieces and well bruised.

Budding (*T. Ellis*).—The delay arose from our seeking for you the best information. You will have seen the subject fully discussed in our last number. You will find it similarly treated at page 206 of our second volume, and at page 226 of our first volume are some drawings fully illustrating the process.

Crickets (*A. L. O.*).—Is it absolutely necessary to destroy "the cricket of your hearth?" We like their merry chirp, which seems like a grateful return for all the hospitality they require—the warmth of the fireside, and its crumbs. Bottles containing a little sugared liquid, placed on their sides near the crickets' haunts, trap them. It is said that a little bundle of pea-straw is an excellent trap, as they are very fond of it; and if it is plunged into boiling water every morning after being near their holes at night dozens may be thus destroyed.

Cutting off Strawberry Leaves (*Ibid*).—We know many instances in which, like you, the proprietors who love tidiness cut off the leaves of their British Queens at the end of summer, and yet had good crops next year. But the question is, would not the crop have been better if they had been left on? We can say (except, perhaps, in the case of over-luxuriant plants which require weakening) we know it would. Cut off the runners and the dead and decaying leaves, but allow the green ones to remain, and then even tidiness, that most desirable presiding genius, will be satisfied also.

Tree Pæony (*Dromore House*).—This may be propagated by *dividing the roots* in October; by *layering* some of the previous year's shoots in February; by cutting, in October, a stem into as many lengths as it has eyes; each may be buried in the soil, and is really *a cutting*.

Goat with Kid (*G. A. Clark*).—Put an advertisement into our paper and state what you require; we cannot undertake such correspondence.

Book on Poultry (*Amateur, Rotherhithe*).—"The best and cheapest" is Richardson's *Domestic Fowl*. You can obtain the Cochin China fowl of the dealers in London. Give your *hens not laying* a little more stimulating food, such as scraps of animal food, and pea-meal.

New Eschscholtzia (*J. Evans*).—Your's is certainly a new and distinct variety, creamy white, and as you say it has proved true to colour for two years, it is deserving a place in our flower-borders. Where can seed be had, and is your soil rich or poor?

Intruders in Hive (*W. O. W.*).—They are only two of the solitary bees which had intruded, and have been killed by the legal tenants.

Gas-stove in Greenhouse (*W. B. P.*).—This may be employed effectually to keep out frost in a greenhouse, 16 feet by 10 feet. Any form will do; but a pipe communicating with the outer air to supply the flames with the means of combustion, and another pipe above to carry off the deleterious gases, are indispensable. A circular pipe one foot in diameter, perforated above with holes two inches apart, will give you heat enough. The flower you have sent is entirely withered, but we find it is *Pardanthus chinensis*.

Depriving Bees (*C. C.*).—We refer you to page 279 of our present volume, where you will find the information required; and we recommend your loosing no time, but to set about depriving your hives as there directed immediately. The method is very simple, and very effectual; fumigation of any kind you will see is unnecessary.

Glass Hive (*A. D.*).—It is always advisable to fasten a piece of clean empty comb in a glass before putting it on, to induce the bees to commence working in it; a very small piece is sufficient.

Uniting and Feeding Bees (*Z.*).—You would find Mr. Payne's plan of uniting stocks very easy, but if you have not courage to follow it, adopt the method recommended at page 279 of our present volume, which is still more simple. You will also find in the same communication directions how to unite them; you may certainly put some of them to Neighbour's No. 5. You will not be able to buy barley sugar for less than 10d. per pound, but you can make it for 6d.; a receipt has been given at page 85 of the present volume. Payne's *Bee-keepers Guide* has passed three editions; the last is dated 1846. If you prefer liquid to solid food for your bees, let it be one pound of loaf sugar, a quarter of a pint of water, and a quarter of a pound of honey, boiled *two* minutes; but no salt.

London: Printed by Harry Wooldridge, Winchester High-street, in the Parish of Saint Mary Kalendar; and Published by William Somerville Orr, at the Office, No. 3, Amen Corner, in the Parish of Christ Church, City of London.—August 15th, 1850.

WEEKLY CALENDAR.

M D	W D	AUGUST 22—28, 1850.	Weather near London in 1849.			Sun Rises.	Sun Sets.	Moon R. & S.	Moon's Age.	Clock bef. Sun.	Day of Year.
22	Th	Gold Spot Moth seen.	T. 70°—57°.	S.W.	Fine.	55 a. 4	8 a. 7	rises	☾	2 44	234
23	F	Starlings flock together.	T. 76°—54°.	S.W.	Fine.	v	5	7 a. 37	16	2 38	235
24	S	St. Bartholomew.	T. 77°—53°.	N.E.	Fine.	1	4	8 0	17	2 13	236
25	Sun	11 Sun. Aft. Trinity. Winged Ants migrate.	T. 77°—58°.	S.W.	Fine.	3	1	8 22	18	1 57	237
26	M	Prince Albert born, 1819.	T. 79°—55°.	S.W.	Fine.	4	vi	8 44	19	1 40	238
27	Tu	Grey Plover comes.	T. 60°—51°.	N.W.	Fine.	6	57	9 7	20	1 23	239
28	W	St. Augustine. The Knot arrives.	T. 73°—58°.	N.W.	Rain.	7	55	9 38	21	1 6	240

It is a propensity of the unthinking to attribute to the artist faults which really are referable solely to his patrons. On returning from the Exhibition of Pictures at the Royal Academy, how usual is the outcry against artists for displaying so many portraits; yet those portraits would not be there if the painting them were not the most encouraged department of the art. So in garden designing, it is usual to laugh at the tasteless gardeners of the 17th century, who never aimed at other beauties than those attained by mathematically arranged beds and borders on either side of a central walk, where

"each alley has its brother,
And one half the garden just reflects the other."

But why was this, except that their employers had no relish for a less formal arrangement? That the answer must be acquiescent seems inevitable, if we consider that no sooner had a taste for more natural beauty been called into activity—no sooner was there a demand for such painting in which streams, hills, trees, and flowers were the materials placed in the artist's hands with which to surround the mansion with pleasing pictures—than that artist was found fully equal to the task. Addison and Pope, in the *Spectator* and *Guardian*, were the first to treat practically of such garden designing; and four couplets of the poet last named gives the outline of the art:—

"Consult the genius of the place in all;
That tells the waters where to rise or fall,
Or helps th' ambitious hill the heavens to scale,
Or scoops in circling theatres the vale;
Calls in the country, catches op'ning glades,
Joins willing woods, and varies shades from shades;
Now breaks, or now directs th' intending lines;
Paints as you plant, and, as you work, designs."

Pope at Twickenham and Addison at Bilton exemplified the style they admired and advocated; they aided to render it generally admired and sought for; and then was it found that Bridgeman and Hunt were quite competent to realise the desires of their patrons; nor have worthy successors ever failed us since, for we have had Wright, Brown, Holland, Eames, Repton, and Loudon.

Now, although it is extraordinary, as we have remarked, that artists are blamed for not effecting certain achievements, so is it more extraordinary, that no sooner have they brought them to pass than another class of the public, with minds differently constituted, immediately discover that the success has not the merit of originality, but that some one, or some nation, did the same ages before! So has it happened with Landscape Gardening; for that style so peculiar to us as to be known now to all the world besides as *English* Gardening was ridiculed by the French under the title of *Le gout Anglo-Chinois*, or Anglo-Chinese taste; and even a man so usually accurate in judgment as Dr. Joseph Spence published a work to prove that the Emperor of China's pleasure-grounds were laid out on principles similar to those of our landscape gardeners. The volume we allude to was published in 1757, and entitled, *Some account of the Emperor of China's Gardens, near Pekin, by Sir Harry Beaumond;* for the doctor discreetly avoided acknowledging the authorship. It is compounded of translations of the Jesuits' letters, who were endeavouring to diffuse Christianity in the Chinese territories; and even supposing all their statements to be true, yet we find nothing in the description of the imperial garden giving us any idea of attention being paid to nature, except a determined irregularity. It contained 200 gilt, painted, and varnished palaces, hills 60 feet high, bridges serpentine as the rivulets, and a minute town, in which the eunuchs of the court imitated the employments of Pekin for the Emperor's amusement. Here, too, adds Mr. Walpole, his Majesty plays at agriculture—there is a quarter set apart for that purpose; the eunuchs sow, reap, and carry in the harvest in the imperial presence; and his Majesty returns to Pekin persuaded that he has been in the country. Dr. Spence's practice was not an exemplification of English and Chinese gardening being identical, for we are told that the grounds about his residence at Byfleet, in Surrey, were models of taste—that best of taste where no more of art is seen than is shown by all the selections and arrangements being from nature's best. Dr. Spence was a man devoted to intellectual pursuits, of refined taste and candid judgment; and his was indeed a pure and beautiful character, if that be faithful given by Mr. Ridley in his excellent "Tales of the Genii." Our readers may be surprised to find that "the Dervise of the Groves," Phesoi Ecneps (his names reversed), was intended as a portraiture of Dr. Spence. It is not within our province to dwell upon the literary works by which he is best remembered—"An Essay on Pope's Odyssey," his "Polymetis," and his "Anecdotes of Literary Characters." His taste aided that of Shenstone in adorning the Leasowes; and the "Dervise of the Groves" appears to have been especially happy in the construction of garden seats and alcoves. "These seats," says Phesoi Ecneps, "which first I raised to rest my wearied limbs, reflection dedicated to the memory of my virtuous friends, whose loved images alternately strike my fancy as I walk." Shenstone therefore appropriately commemorated his friend by inscribing on a seat within a clump of beech trees—

JOSEPHO SPENCE,
EXIMIO NOSTRO CRITONI;
CUI DICABI VELLET
MUSARUM OMNIUM ET
GRATIARUM CHORUS
DICAT AMICITIA.*

He was born in 1698, and was accidentally drowned in his garden on the 20th of August, 1768.

METEOROLOGY OF THE WEEK.

From observations at Chiswick during twenty - three years, the average highest and lowest temperatures of these days were 71.6° and 50.1°, respectively; 95 of the days were fine, and on 66 days rain fell.

---

* To our unequalled critic
Joseph Spence;
To whom Friendship dedicates
What a chorus of all the
Muses and Graces
Would wish to be dedicated.

RANGE OF BAROMETER—RAIN IN INCHES.

Aug.		1841.	1842.	1843.	1844.	1845.	1846.	1847.	1848.	1849.
22	B. {	29.874	29.999	29.640	29.727	30.297	30.055	29.763	29.643	30.183
		29.806	29.913	29.477	29.696	30.184	29.994	29.665	29.577	30.126
	R.	6.58	—	0.32	—	—	—	0.09	0.00	—
23	B. {	29.994	29.988	29.619	29.726	30.139	30.123	30.050	29.797	30.132
		29.797	29.869	29.412	29.673	30.004	30.062	29.886	29.537	30.115
	R.	0.61	—	0.05	—	0.97	—	0.01	0.04	—
24	B. {	30.094	29.846	29.747	29.745	29.979	30.310	30.184	30.020	30.132
		30.048	29.785	29.909	29.559	29.975	30.138	30.075	29.987	30.115
	R.	0.13	0.22	—	—	—	—	—	8.03	—
25	B. {	30.079	29.725	29.889	29.976	30.004	30.210	30.113	30.634	30.112
		30.959	29.702	29.835	29.902	29.824	30.194	30.071	30.005	29.997
	R.	0.47	0.32	—	—	—	—	—	0.04	—
26	B. {	30.725	29.916	30.006	30.052	30.020	30.148	30.227	29.832	30.100
		30.181	29.818	29.929	30.007	29.850	30.051	30.146	29.815	29.985
	R.	—	—	0.01	—	—	—	—	0.04	—
27	B. {	30.344	29.940	30.130	30.082	30.182	29.996	30.207	29.839	29.983
		30.142	29.923	30.080	30.078	30.080	29.940	30.354	29.815	29.959
	R.	—	0.70	—	—	—	—	—	0.01	—
28	B. {	30.189	29.977	29.994	30.137	30.206	29.985	30.005	29.986	29.975
		30.125	29.975	29.915	30.119	30.217	29.991	30.197	29.851	29.927
	R.	—	0.14	0.05	—	—	0.02	—	0.10	—

INSECTS.—Having described the Working Bee (page 283), we will now proceed to similar particulars relative to the *Queen Bee*. Her *body* is much longer than that of either the Drone or Worker; *head*, like that of the latter, but *tongue* more slender and shorter; *under jaws* (maxillæ), straighter; *upper jaws* (mandibles), forficate, reddish pitch colour; terminating in two teeth, of which the exterior is acute, and the interior blunt; *upper lip*, tawny; and *antennæ*, reddish black. The scales defending the base of the wings, red-black; *wings* reach only to tip of third abdominal segment; *shanks* and *feet*, reddish tawny; *hind shanks*, flat above, with short hairs, but no marginal fringe of hairs (corbicula) for carrying pollen, nor *pectes*, and the *plantæ* have no hairs in situ, nor the nucleis at the base. The *abdomen*, much longer than the head and trunk together, lengthened conical, and sharp-pointed; its *dorsal segments* tawny at the top, with short pale hairs; *ventral segments*, tawny, with longer hairs; *anal segment*, black; the *sting* (properly, *vagina of the spicula*) curved. However numerous the queens produced in a hive, all but one are destroyed; the old queen always leaves the hive with the first swarm. The queen is the mother of all the bees produced; she begins laying eggs which produce workers, and continues to lay them solely for eleven months, and produces from 70 to 100,000—laying from 100 to 200 daily. In the spring she lays about 2,000 eggs, to produce drones.

Of potatoes we have tried many varieties this year. *Bark-ham's Walnut-leaved Kidney* we do not find better than the old variety of that name ; but it is as good, and like it to be grown for the earliest crop. Planted on the 21st of February the tubers were ready for boiling early in July. *Rylott's Flour Ball* is a good potato. Planted February 21st it was ready for taking up in the first week of August ; but is not an abundant bearer. *Mar-tin's Early Seedling* and the *Red Ash-leaved Kidney* planted February 21st, were taken up quite ripe on the 5th of August ; they are two of the best flavoured, mealy, and most productive varieties we have ever grown. The Martin's Early Seedling we especially re-commend to the attention of our readers. Every plant we grew of them produced from fifteen to twenty-five potatoes fit for boiling ; and a gentleman near us actually had *forty-five* tubers fit for kitchen use, besides small ones, from one plant.

We will take this opportunity to observe, that all our potatoes were stored perfectly ripe by the 9th of this month ; and though the quantity grown is but small (about twelve bushels), yet they afford us abundant evidence that they can be grown so little influenced by murrain, that if we were not sedulously searching for its appearance, the disease would pass unnoticed. There were not fifty diseased tubers accompanied those twelve bushels ; and with but five exceptions not one of the diseased ones weighed more than an ounce. So remark-able was this that the gardener who took up the crop observed—" There are none but little ones diseased." The deduction we draw from this year's, and many pre-vious years' experience, is that *the disease may be alto-gether avoided by early planting early varieties.*

We planted *Ash-leaved Kidneys* last November, and notwithstanding the severe winter that followed, we did not lose a single set. We only grew about three bushels of them, and when they were taken up on the 9th inst., not a dozen tubers were diseased, although the leaves were as ulcerated and as covered with parasitical fungi as any specimens we ever examined. Let no one suppose that we delayed designedly planting any of our potatoes until February. The delay in planting the new varieties named arose solely from our not receiving the seed until then.

We thus early record again our confirmed conviction in favour of early planting, and early varieties, because we would beg of every one of our readers to make arrangements for trying the experiment. A cry is up again that there is no dependance upon the potato as a store crop, and so successful has been the cry, and so alarmed have the cottage cultivators of Hampshire become, that the market is glutted with fine samples, at eighteenpence per bushel. These, for the most part, have been taken up before ripe ; and then, if they do not keep well, they will be quoted in confirmation of the despair-cry—" the potatoes are again all going !" That cry we firmly believe to be unfounded and unjustifiable ; and even if the late-ripening and late-planted kinds should fail, yet we are well aware, not only from obser-vation but from information furnished by others, that

the breadth of early-planted and of early varieties is so unusually great, that it will more than supply the possible failure. To all our readers we say—*store your potatoes in a dry cool shed in alternate layers with dry earth or cinder ashes, and do not fear the result.*

Since the above was written we have been favoured with the following from Mr. Weaver, gardener to the Warden of Winchester College. We are sorry to find that some of his potatoes have been destroyed by the disease ; but we think if they had been stored in earth or coal ashes, the result would have been otherwise.

" My opinion about the potato disease is just the same as at first. The low confined situation suffers first and most ; also the potato that makes the greatest bulk of haulm suffers much more than the less stemmy kinds. This I have every year found to be the case since the appearance of the dis-ease. This very season the potatoes in a quarter of the lower part of our garden began to go off about the last week in July, whilst the same kind at the upper part of the same garden were looking all well. This first quarter was planted with a favourite kind, called *Looker's Oxonian,* a very prolific and early sort, but stemmy ; therefore, it suffered so much the more from having been planted in this lower part of the garden. They were taken up the last week in July, and there did not appear much the matter with the tubers at the time of taking up, but since that time half are gone off. The diseased appearance of the stems progressing gradually up the garden, the second week in August we determined to take all up, beginning at the lower quarters first.

The next quarter bore *Herefordshire Early Purples.* These were a little touched in the haulm, but we scarcely found a diseased tuber ; crop large and fine. This is not a stemmy kind, therefore moisture did not hang about it as in the first case.

On the next quarter were *York Regents.* This quarter is situated about the middle of the garden, but lies rather low. The York Regent is a very stemmy kind, and its stems were going off fast ; but on taking up the crop we did not find many of the tubers faulty, except where we came to a root that seemed dead ripe ; that is, where the stems were dead, and there nearly the whole of the tubers were diseased ; but where the stems were strong and green, no diseased tubers appeared. These three quarters were planted in the autumn.

The fourth quarter, which reached the top of the garden in the same line, was planted with *Forty-folds,* which is not a stemmy kind. They were planted in *February.* There were slight appearances of disease in the stems, but there were very few diseased tubers. Two other large quarters of *York Regents,* also planted in *February,* at the top of the garden, were very stemmy and beginning to go off. In taking them up we found scarcely any diseased tubers, and all pretty well ripened, and looking very well up to the present time. They were taken up on the 7th and 8th of August."

THE FRUIT-GARDEN.

Vines.—We must now offer a little of what may be termed autumn advice to the amateur or cottager, for dark days are at hand, and every means must be taken to get both the fruit and the wood for the future year's crop perfected, or what gardeners term ripened ; a term which when applied to the wood, has a very different signification from its usual application to the fruit. We will commence with the

Greenhouse Vines ; supposing, what is very com-monly the case, vines in a house appropriated to the culture and display of exotics in general. Grapes here will, for the most part, be turning colour or already ripe. At this period, then, it will be necessary to ex-amine carefully if any waste or useless spray can be dispensed with ; for although such is useful in its day as promoting root-action, and, by consequence, a liberal circulation of sap, yet in our dull clime the action of

solar light on the larger leaves is of far more importance. Where the vine is indigenous, no doubt these
rambling laterals are of eminent service; there their
elaborative powers will be called fully into action, and
then their very shade will be beneficial to the larger
and first formed leaves, which, without their interposition, would be liable to scorch or prematurely dry up.
Not so, however, in Britain; here "the tables are completely turned"—every ray of solar light is demanded by
the principal leaves after the mouth of August has
passed. Indeed, at this late period all, or nearly all,
the axillary shoots may be removed as soon as the
berries change colour, for there will be no danger of
the fruiting buds of the future year bursting. Of course
the shoots will be kept carefully trained; they must not
be suffered to run into confusion. A thorough ventilation, also, must be encouraged—no coddling allowed;
air given before seven o'clock, A.M., and a little left all
night. Most of the plants being out of doors, every
facility will be afforded for carrying out the necessary
operations; and it is well, where convenient, to remove
every plant out for about two or three weeks during
the latter part of August and first week of September;
such a course is beneficial to the vines, as enabling
them to enjoy a dry and mellow air during the colouring
process—a thing they much delight in, and which cannot be thoroughly afforded whilst the house is crammed
with pots, and, of course, continually damp with the
watering requisite.

REPAIRS.—Another point of importance is concerned
in this movement, and that is, the flue cleaning, painting, wall washing, alterations, and general repairs.
Perhaps no better opportunity is afforded the amateur—
especially if he has no other general plant-house—of
carrying out such matters; for, as to the heating apparatus, such must be put in trim for the winter, whether or
not; all boilers or piping looked carefully over, in order
to remove any sedimentary obstructions, or to repair
leakages; as, also, to ascertain whether the boilers can
be relied on for another winter. All flues thoroughly
cleaned, and slightly tested, to see if they are perfectly
sound; any cracks or flaws may be speedily discovered,
if the bricklayer light a hasty fire of sticks and straw,
and then throw something over the chimney-pot. A
sharp eye inside the house will soon have proof of the
condition of the flue, which will be made to tell tales of
itself in every deficient part. Such matters as painting,
the washing of walls, &c., may be carried out with care,
or much injury may accrue to the grapes. All dust
must, of course, be avoided, by occasionally sprinkling
the floors; and as for splashing, a careful person must
be employed, and mats, &c., made use of. In the washing of walls, &c.,—a thing which should be performed
in all plant-houses twice a year, if possible—let us advise a liberal use of flowers of sulphur with the lime.
It is almost impossible to use too much in this way, for
it is at most harmless; this we have practised for years,
and our immunity from the red spider is, doubtless,
owing in the main to this. None of the insect world
known as "pests of the garden" like the smell of sulphur; all experience goes to prove this. We have
heard a gardener of long standing assert, that wasps
would not pass the ventilating apertures of hothouses if
sulphur was daubed in such positions. This is a strong
assertion, and we cannot vouch for the truth of it;
were it indeed a fact, it would prove to be one worth
knowing.

VINES WHICH HAVE BEEN FORCED EARLY.—We must
be permitted to say a few words about these for the
sake of taking our subjects in due course, and grouping
them as it were; we may, perhaps, thus be enabled "to
report progress, and ask leave to sit again." These
want a course of treatment somewhat peculiar to themselves, as well as to the season. In the first place, if

they are to be very early forced next year, try and persuade them to take an early nap. Now, it so happens,
that such vines will produce a lot of spray as a sort of
second growth under certain circumstances. This is
not always the case; vines exhausted through a heavy
crop, through age or a bad root, will seldom be guilty of
such tricks. The amateur who has not had much vine
practice will naturally say, "What is the reason of all
this?" We will endeavour to furnish one. It need
hardly be urged, that there must be a correspondent
amount of root-action, either present or of recent occurrence. Such generally arises in healthy vines about the
time the fruit is all cut; and the cause will be obvious
when it is duly considered how much a crop of grapes
exhausts the tree, and that the fruit, until shrivelled,
continues to draw on the resources of its parent. Cutting all the fruit, then, is a considerable relief to the
tree, which suddenly finds itself in possession of a sur-
plussage of sap; and the ground heat being still considerable, the vine is with difficulty induced to rest. As
before observed, the best plan is to cut such late growths
away at once, for at this season they become actual
robbers—taking from the parent what they cannot pay
back, as the season is too far gone for them to elaborate
fresh juices. Another point of good culture is, to apply
a good top-dressing of rich manure the moment they
cast their leaves; and those who can so manage it would
do well to thatch the surface, or to place a tarpaulin
over the dressing; this latter process we would delay
for three weeks longer, if it be desired to enrich the
border through the medium of rains. Pruning, too,
should be performed immediately the leaves can be
removed; this is all-important; indeed, some good cultivators in part prune their vines before the decay of
the foliage; this, we think, is carrying matters rather
too far.

VINES ON WALLS.—These will want the most scrupulous attention at this time; not a sprig of growing
spray should be allowed to shade the larger leaves, and
a good deal may be removed in order to permit the sun
to shine on the wall itself, which, by becoming heated,
will act as a reservoir of warmth for a great part of the
night. Every shoot should be closely nailed or tied
down; the neater they are trained, the more sunlight
they will obtain. If the border is dry, and the roots as
they ought to be, near the surface, a liberal watering
with manure-water may benefit them. Every protection
must be afforded the fruit, in due time, from the depredations of wasps, mice, or birds.

STRAWBERRIES FOR FORCING.—Those who have omitted
providing these at an early period must lose no time in
doing so; and if any success is to be expected, every plant
must be removed in the most careful way with a nice
ball of earth. We have known some taken thus (from
the outsides of the strawberry plantations) to succeed
nearly equal to those potted early. The best of all
plans, though, is to lay them betimes in five-inch pots—
one in a pot; plunging the pot to the rim in a position
to receive the runner, which may be loaded with a
stone, enclosing a patch of moss or mulchy manure.
Those so done in the early part of July will now be
strong plants, with a pot full of roots, and should immediately be transferred to seven-inch pots. For compost,
the following will be found excellent:—Sand and charcoal dust, one part; old leaf soil, one part; good rotten
manure, two parts; sound loam, six parts. Much depends on the character and quality of the loam, which,
be the colour what it may, should feel unctuous in the
hand. Perhaps the old criterion is as good as any, in
regard of texture. It is this:—Take a handful somewhat pulverized, and neither wet nor dry, squeeze it
close in the hand, and then let it fall on the ground
from a height of about five feet. If it does not divide
and somewhat pulverize, it is rather too adhesive, and

sand must be added accordingly. Of course, turfy loam is the best, but such should have been procured a twelvemonth or so previously; this will cause the turfy material to feed the plant better. Some cultivators use a good deal of soot in the soil; for strawberries are known to be partial to it. We would not, however, mix much with it, for its principles can be easily imparted in the character of liquid-manure. It is, nevertheless, esteemed good practice to place some soot in the bottom of the pots, over the drainage, in order to keep the earth-worm out. A good drainage must be insured, not, however, too much inorganic materials, as they are but of negative value; dry lumpy manure and turfy matter blended answer well, placed over two or three hollow crocks. The soil should be tolerably dry, at least mellow, for potting; care must be taken to press it close in the act of filling the pot, the ball being placed immediately on the drainage before described. A good watering with a rosed pot will benefit them immediately they are placed in a permanent situation, which must be in the lightest and warmest part of the garden; and there is nothing better than a hard gravel or cinder bottom for them. Some persons object to plunging them; we do not. They must, however, be plunged on or above the ordinary ground level, not below it; in fact, no water must for a moment be permitted to lodge beneath them. As soon as November arrives, some loose litter may be strewn over them, unless the weather continues mild; and henceforward they should never be allowed to freeze, if it can be avoided. The *British Queens*, it may be mentioned, require particular protection; a very little hard weather will injure them.

R. Errington.

THE FLOWER-GARDEN.

Light-soiled Flower-gardens.—From the beginning of August to about the middle of September first-rate flower-gardens, on light soils and on high dry situations, are generally more rich and gay than at any other period of the season; while such as are situated either in low damp situations, or on rich heavy land, with a damp bottom, are past their best by the end of July, or, at any rate, after the first fortnight in August. Therefore, flower-beds should be made very differently for these different situations. To make the best of a flower-garden, there is as much judgment necessary for the preparation of the beds in winter as there is in planting them and in keeping them up to the mark in summer—perhaps more so; for no matter what plants we use for gay flowering, unless the compost in which we grow them is suitable, not for the plants only, but for making the most of them in a given locality, we shall be baffled. Some people go so far as to insist on it that you can grow all kinds of flower-garden plants, with equal success, in every kind of situation where such things are likely to be wanted in this country; but this is a most absurd and erroneous fancy, and a fancy, too, which could only get hold of the brains of a set of easy-minded people, who have passed the greater part of their lives and matured their observations in one given locality.

They say "a rolling stone does not gather moss;" and, on the same principle, a rolling gardener, or one who has been shifting about up and down the country, will hardly increase in prejudice. The sharp angles on the organs of his perceptiveness have been worn down, so as to suit themselves easily to such things as he undertakes, no matter where. When he comes to lay out a flower-garden on the side of a dry chalky hill, he makes the beds as deep again as he would think it necessary for them in the bottom of the valley. The compost to fill them, too, he would use stronger and richer

on the chalk, sand, or gravel, than would be useful on clays and rich damp land. Yet, after all has been done that good gardening and sound judgment could suggest, the best of us may be defeated in many situations.

I had a letter the other day from one of the very best gardeners in England—if not the very best; he has in his charge one of the largest garden establishments in the country, yet, he says, he reads The Cottage Gardener every week with pleasure and profit—"his very teeth water at some of the lists of bedding plants which I have set forth from time to time." Some of the plants, owing to his locality, he cannot get to the expense of their propagation; he, too, expects soon to see a white flowering variety of the scarlet geranium: but he cuts his letter short in the middle of the sheet with this reflection, "What is the use of such anticipations? our muffy, murky atmosphere will never allow me to shine, like you, in the autumn. No sooner do the nights lengthen perceptibly in August than the fogs and vapours rise from the lakes, and envelope the gardens and surrounding country, and they, with the natural heat of the season, set every plant and bed growing so unnaturally, as that they produce only a crop of rank foliage; and this, I suppose, must be our fate to the end of the chapter." He then turns round with a spark of consolation—for Nature is always kind, and will never leave us in despair—and remarks, "but we beat you out and out in May and June, if not even in July." True enough, master. We have all of us heard of "beating the globe," but it remained for the schoolboy to "break it," when he let it fall from the stand in the lecture room. You may beat us any month in the year when we have our great folks from home, but "in May and June, and even in July," if we needed a fine display, I am not quite sure that you could have the success of the schoolboy, if "even" you could "beat us."

I once planted a piece of sloping ground with a selection of trees and shrubs, an *arboretum* in short, and from every pit or tree I had to cut a trench, or drain, to take off the water to an open ditch on the lower side; the clay was perfectly waterproof, and would hold it like a china bowl. Yet in that locality, and on the same kind of land, we could keep the flower-beds tolerably well till the middle or end of September, because the air was dry and no water or flat valley near to us. The flower-beds were from twenty inches to two feet deep, and filled up with rough coal ashes to within ten inches of the top, that being the best arrangement I ever found out to prevent plants "going into leaf" too much in the autumn. Now, hear the other side of the question. About six or seven years back, after having been well nigh "beaten" with some flower-beds here, I got into a fit of experimental gardening, turned a new leaf in the flower-garden, and before I received my "account for hauling," there were two hundred and eighty-three two-horse loads of rank clay put down against me; whether or not I really received so many loads is more than I now can say—I had enough and none to spare—every spadeful of which had been put into one flower-garden—"The Fountain Garden." This garden is nearly a circle, with a fountain in the centre, and on one side of it a grass terrace, six feet higher than the garden, passes, and from this terrace every bed and plant in the garden can be seen at one view; all the beds are on grass, and the greatest distance between any two of them is not more than four feet; the beds number 152 in all, and they were dug out, or rather cut out, off a solid bed of chalk. To make up for this dry bottom, the beds were made from three to four feet deep; but in practice, we soon discovered that something more than depth was necessary for the full development of a good flower-garden. In a dry season, the chalk sides and bottom of these beds actually sucked out the moisture in the soil, and left our plants in a powdery compost, that must needs be watered every other day to keep the plants alive. To get over the difficulty of watering the beds like so many flower-pots, a set of hose-leather pipes, with screws and valves, were fixed to the pipe which supplies the fountain, and with this hose one man, with a boy to lift the hose over the beds as they turned round, could water the whole garden, grass and all, in twenty minutes. This was a great help; but there may be too much watering as well as too little, and when that happens to be with "hard" spring water, as in the present instance, it is not so good as any contrivance that would lessen the need for it—hence the cause of the experiment with the clay—and a rough experiment it was, and a long one too, for it occupied the time of a dozen men for six weeks in the winter, and this is the way the work was performed. Three or four beds running in one line—"union flag like," as one of our friends would say—were emptied, and the soil piled up on similar beds not far from them; thus a trench was opened; a foot of clay was then put at the bottom of the beds in rough lumps, so as to allow water to pass, but intercept the sucking power of the chalk from below; the next and more difficult process was to plaster up the sides of the beds, beginning at the bottom with four inches thick of soft clay, and sloping up to the surface, where one inch thick was only used. These sloping sides were well plastered with the back of the spades as the work proceeded; and to make the thing more easy for the men a bucket of water was placed near them to plunge their spades in from time to time, and the wet spades would glide smoothly over the clay, and set it firmly and very even. As soon as one set of beds were finished so far, the next set behind them were emptied, and their contents more than filled the clayed ones. By this process the bottom soil of the old beds were on the top of the renewed ones; the light top soil thrown over the rough lumps of clay filled up the spaces between them, and thus secured a free passage for the water to pass through to the chalk. Unless this had been provided for, it is very likely that in time the rough clay at the bottom would "run together," and so prevent the escape of water altogether, for the sides were made waterproof. In this way all the beds were clayed, and now, after six years' trial, we are all satisfied here that the experiment has fully succeeded; but the best proof we can adduce of the truth of this is, that since then most of the flower beds all over the pleasure-grounds have been remodelled after the same manner. Had this not been done, my belief is that we should have been burnt out this summer; and even as it was I began to think at last that we must give up all hopes of saving our plants, for from the third week in May to the beginning of July we had neither rain nor dew, although at times the rain fell in torrents, as the newspapers say, within six miles of us; but with the exception that a few kinds of the geraniums are now too strong with us, we were seldom in better bloom than at this moment.

The *cause* of those *geraniums being too much in leaf* is, that as soon as they were well rooted after planting out, we gave them three or four heavy waterings with liquid manure, to cause them to get on a little faster, to make up for lost time, and now we find they are doing so rather too fast. The way we check them may be of some use to others whose geraniums are now growing too much to leaf through any cause. We merely cut out so many of their new made leaves at first, and this we continue to do from time to time, or as often as the grass is cut, and the whole trimmed for the rest of the season. If we see a necessity for it, about the middle of August we also begin to stop the plants regularly over the beds, as well as thinning the leaves; by thus exposing the older leaves, which in reality prepare the food for a large bloom, and by stopping the onward growth of the main shoots, we

cause the plants to furnish such a crop of flowers as, of itself, gives them a very great check—then to succeed this bloom a host of side branches must come, as the leading ones can go no farther; these, in their turn, have their young leaves thinned, and, perhaps, stopped also if they grow too fast. Now this will appear a tedious process to many, but it is not so in reality, but just the reverse. A man with a few grains of common sense may be entrusted with the job, and after a little practice it is "wonderful" how fast he gets over the ground; no knife or scissors need be used, only the forefinger and thumb. A circular bed, ten feet through, may be so trimmed in less than ten minutes; but it should be so managed that a stranger coming round ten minutes afterwards should not perceive that any one had been near that bed for the last month—and that should be my criterion for a good dresser in a flower-garden. No marks of his handicraft should be left behind him; every bed and border, the grass, gravel, and all should appear to a stranger just come in as if the whole had been made to suit or "to order" that very morning. The misfortune is, that not one out of a thousand ever thinks of this—we all try to do or undo too much, from the very first to the last flower-garden in this country; this is as apparent as if the fact were put up in large letters over the garden gate.

This is a good time to think about the *Mildew on Verbena beds*, and to apply the soot and sulphur, as was recommended, where any danger is apprehended. Some varieties are more subject to mildew than others. With me, *Miss Harcourt*, a fine white one, takes it first, and is, therefore, the first we dust over, or rather under; for it will be recollected that one measure of flowers of sulphur is added to three or four measures of dry soot, and that a mop-like brush is dipped in this, then pushed in between the plants and shook with a sudden jerk, so that the ground and the underside of the leaves are covered with dust.

Petunias require now, and for some time past, to be topped every week or ten days—only an inch or two taken off at one time. This will make the beds appear all bloom, and also cause the plants or shoots to advance apparently at the same rate of growth. Wherever they are liable to be beaten down by the rain or winds, small sticks, with or without side branches, should be thrust in amongst them to keep them in the right position. *Œnothera macrocarpa*, a fine large yellow flowering one of the evening primroses, ought to be looked over every day, or every second day, to pick off the dead flowers, as they are very unsightly. *Lupines* of all sorts, and many other plants, will now be seeding as fast as you pick off their seed pods; but recollect it is one of the grand secrets of keeping up a late bloom to remove seed pods as fast as the flowers fade. The beautiful yellow *Eschscholtzia*, used as an annual, and thus kept from seeding through the summer, will last in flower from the end of May to October. I wish I had a pen which, by one magic stroke, would influence all my readers at once. The first line would run thus:—*Procure a bed of the White Campanula carpatica.* It is the most beautiful white flowering plant I ever saw; and we have six beds of it here, every one of which is fit for a queen. It is also the easiest plant I know to manage; it is as hardy as a crocus, and all the care it requires for the season is to divide it in April, and to cut off the seed pods as fast as the flowers go off.   D. BEATON.

GREENHOUSE AND WINDOW GARDENING.

PLANTS IN ROOMS.—A correspondent makes several inquiries upon this subject, and states his conviction that a paper upon such a matter would be interesting to many subscribers like himself. He purchases plants when in full bloom, sets them in his room, waters, but does not over water them, finds that the bloom soon fades, that no new bloom appears, that the plants become sickly and covered with insects, generally lose even their leaves, and when in the end he turns them into the soil of the garden in June, they seldom do any good, as geraniums thus treated are looking miserable still. He wants to know how he is to keep his plants healthy? How secure a succession of bloom? and, if that cannot be done, how to secure from these bought-in plants ornaments for the flower-garden when they become untidy for the house? He attributes his want of success chiefly to the fact, that his plants are brought from greenhouses of an equal temperature, and taken to a room where the temperature varies; thinks, however, that knowledge and science may relieve him from his difficulties; and tells us in a postscript that his plants are kept not in or near the windows, but on side-boards, &c., because it is common for people "to want to stick flowers about in pots as ornaments."

As we often find in a *lady's* letter, so here in the post-script we have the most important information. The *position* of the plants in the room, rather than their *removal* from a greenhouse to it, is the chief cause of disappointment. They who adopt the custom of sticking plants anywhere and everywhere in a room, may be good friends to the plant growers, but as to cultivating them themselves, that is quite out of the question. Plants are so accommodating, that they freely consent to act as ornaments, for a short time, upon tables and side-boards, even though, as in our correspondent's case, the windows be "close curtained;" but their luxuriating or flourishing when continued in such circumstances, would be as great a wonder as the finding that a pony, suspended to a balloon, got fat and plump by feeding upon rarified air. No doubt some plants that flourish in comparative shade,—others, whose chief ornament is in their foliage, such as *ferns*,—others, again, such as evergreens, with thick leathery foliage, will submit better to such treatment for a continued period than geraniums and heliotropes, &c.; but even in *their* case the green would gradually exchange for the sickly yellow; the flowers, if produced, would lose their colour, and as to forming buds for the unfolding of more that would be impossible.

Many ladies and gentlemen who have rather clear notions as to the mode of raising bullocks for Smithfield, have very imperfect ideas as to how plants feed and grow. The best gardener is often in as great a fix as our worthy correspondent, not because he does not know better, but because he is overruled. "We are to have a party on such a night," says his worthy employer, "and I hope you will deck us out with a number of fine plants." "O yes!" says blue apron, "but I hope you will let me have them in a day or so, for though they look nicely for a short time in niches, on tables, &c., without scarcely perceiving light, continuing them there renders them fit for little but the rubbish heap." "O you shall have them back in a day or so; and to ensure their health I will attend to all their wants myself." The plants look so pretty as ornaments, and attract so much attention, and so many friends continue calling, that the gardener is told he may remove his favourites *only* when they are in such a state that he has to examine them and deliberate, whether destroying them or attempting to recover them to health would be the better wisdom; conscious all the while, that unless he has great means and a great supply, this treatment of his plants will tell adversely against him, not only for the present but the future. Much as I like to see a pretty plant in any position, I never look at them placed upon mantel-pieces and shaded side-boards, and continued there for any length of time, without either wishing that their possessors should be contented with arti-

ficial instead of real ones, or hoping that a society might be formed for preventing cruelty to plants as well as to animals. Gardeners who are required to do much in the way of room decoration, chiefly employ ephemeral things, that look beautiful but are of no value when the bloom is faded, or take care to have the opportunity of very frequently changing them if valuable.

The means for preserving plants in rooms have several times been referred to. Light, air, temperature, moisture, must be communicated according to their nature and necessities. Freedom from dust, as well as insects, must also be insured. Great things cannot in general be expected from plants bought in full bloom in April or May. You purchase it merely for its bloom; and the nurseryman reckons its value when he sells it, as in large towns he can make nearly as much of the bloom alone as of the plant, with the bloom on it. If, therefore, when you set such a plant upon a side-board, and derive a little more gratification than you would have done by the bloom being cut and placed in a vessel with water in a similar position, you have little to complain about. If you wish the plant to continue in health, to expand the bloom buds not yet opened, to form more which will unfold afterwards, or to make it fit for repaying you for the trouble of transplanting it out of doors, you must not continue it upon a side-board, but give it similar advantages, as far as possible, to that it would have enjoyed in the greenhouse of the nurseryman or gardener. Even then two things are against you, if you know but little about plants. The first is, that many of the plants sold at that early season will not bloom abundantly until the same period again returns; a few will, but the majority of florists' pelargoniums will not continue to bloom in the same pots, though many flowers and a luxuriant foliage will be obtained by turning them, in a proper manner, into the open ground. Others, however, such as the *scarlet geraniums*, if top-dressed and enriched with manure water, will continue to produce fresh buds and bloom. The second thing against you is, that though most of the plants sold at that season are what are termed greenhouse plants, and, therefore, ought to thrive with the light and shade, &c., you are able to give them in the window, more especially after the colds of winter are gone, still, as it is merely the bloom that gives a value to the plant, and as the earlier that bloom is produced the higher will be its price, the plant grower, in such circumstances, has given a higher temperature to force the bud into bloom than otherwise would be required; and, therefore, when you purchase a flowering plant in April to set in your room—a *geranium* for instance,—more care will be required as respects temperature and light, than if you purchased the plant in May and June, when the house from which it came was comparatively cool and open. Thousands of plants are lost by not paying attention to the circumstances in which they were placed before coming into the purchaser's possession, and this not among amateurs only, but also among gardeners. The nurseryman, acting merely upon the principles of competition and commercial wisdom, endeavours to get a saleable article as forward as possible; and hence thousands of greenhouse plants are propagated and grown when young in an atmosphere and a temperature that would suit Mr. Appleby's orchids. The plants are sent out nicely packed, the receiver rejoices over their luxuriance, he places them in the greenhouse, and cannot conceive why, in no great time, they assume a rusted stunted appearance. Keeping them in a higher temperature, and a closer, moister atmosphere at first, exposing them to more air and light by degrees, would have prevented the disappointment.

Precisely a similar course must be adopted with *geraniums, heliotropes, roses,* &c., bought in bloom in April or earlier. They must be kept warmer for a time than plants brought from open houses in May; obtain all the light that can be given, without flagging them, and cleanliness and moisture to the atmosphere afforded by sponging their leaves with water. Such plants, after being gradually inured to the open air and shaded for a time with an evergreen branch, &c., when transferred there will furnish anything but miserable appearances. To have given the plants from the side-board a chance out of doors, they should have been moved to the windows, shaded at first from bright sunshine, gradually inured to it, exposed by degrees to the open air, and then, but not till then, turned into the border, and watered and shaded for a time, until they had got hold of the fresh soil.

Our correspondent's failure, therefore, proceeded chiefly from neglecting the element of light; and he will find that his plants will thrive best in rooms where there are windows from different aspects. Where there is only one window, the plants should be as near it as they will bear, and they should be frequently turned, that the light may reach every side of them alike. The necessity of shading is more relative than real. The more light a plant gets the hardier it will be, the more freely will its flower buds be produced, and the fitter will it be for being transferred as an ornament to the flower-garden. R. FISH.

HOTHOUSE DEPARTMENT.
EXOTIC ORCHIDACEÆ.

PLANTS REQUIRING BLOCKS.—*(Continued from p. 291.)*
Cattleya Aclandiæ (Lady Acland's); Brazil.—This is a splendid and rare species. The sepals and petals are of a rich brown, stained with green; the lip is purple and white. 210s.

C. citrina (Citron-coloured C.); Oaxaca.—We have already described this lovely species amongst those requiring peculiar treatment. We need only state here that the way to grow this, is to place it on a block without moss, with the last made pseudo-bulb the lowest. The sepals, petals, and labellum are of the bright colour of the citron, with a shade of white in the centre of the flower. The pseudo-bulbs are short, almost white, and something like a Catesetum. The flowers are large, solitary, and pendant. 42s.

C. marginata (Bordered C.); Brazil.—A very dwarf plant not more than four inches high. The flowers are produced singly on the top of the last made pseudo-bulbs. They are large compared with the size of the plant. Sepals and petals rosy crimson; lip deep rose margined with white.

C. Pinellii and *C. pumila* are very much like this species, if not identical with it. Requires growing on a block without moss. 31s. 6d.

C. bulbosa (Bulb-like C.); Brazil.—A remarkable species sufficiently distinct from the preceding by its short club-like pseudo-bulbs, surmounted by a pair of bluntly ovate fleshy leaves, *Cattleya marginata*, &c., producing only one leaf on each pseudo-bulb. The sepals and petals are of a deep rose; the lip of the same colour, with a large blotch of deep purple in the centre. It is a very fine desirable species. 105s.

CULTURE.—These small gems of the finest tribe of orchids do not require an extraordinary amount of either heat or moisture. If kept too close and hot they will grow weakly, and never flower. If kept too moist in autumn and winter the roots will perish, and the same effect will be induced. Place them at the coolest end of the house, pretty near to the glass, and during the growing season only, syringe the blocks slightly every evening. Shade only from the midday sun. By this treatment judiciously applied, they will grow vigorously, and flower well; but never profusely; seldom, even on the stronger plants, producing more than two or three flowers at a time; but the colours are so splendid, and the flowers so large in comparison to the plants, that they are exceedingly striking and handsome. During the season of rest keep them dry and cool, syringing only just often enough to prevent the whole plant from shrivelling too much.

Cirrhopetalum auratum (Golden C.); Manilla.—A curious and pretty plant. The whole flower when expanded is like an open fan. The upper sepals and petals are fringed with golden-coloured hairs, the lateral sepals have no hair, and are stained with purple. The general colour of the flower is yellow, mottled with crimson. 42s.

C. candelabra (Chandelier-formed C.).—Another curious and ornamental plant from India. The plant when strong sends up a stoutish scape or flower-stem, to the height of nine inches; the flowers are placed in a circle round the head of the scape; the outer sepals and petals assume a downward direction, forming a fantastic resemblance to a chandelier; whence its name. These outer petals are pink; the lower sepals and petals are of a light straw, streaked with purple; the lip is fringed at the margin, and is yellow. The leaves of the plant are small, and of a purplish colour. 84s.

C. Chinensis (Chinese C.); China.—Flower larger than the rest of the genus. The upper sepals and petals are purple; the lateral sepals are yellowish; one of the lobes is like a chin and tongue, which are continually in a state of motion when in flower, rendering it very amusing. 63s.

C. Cummingii (Mr. Cumming's); Philippine Islands.—The sepals and petals rich ruby; the lip is of the same colour. It is large and conspicuous. The whole flower forms a flat head with the sepals and petals drooping. The column on being touched moves backwards and forwards for a considerable time like the pendulum of a clock. 42s.

C. Medusæ (Medusa's-head C.); Singapore.—This has a flower like the last, with a flat head from which the petals and sepals hanging down terminating in long wavy strings, so as to have a slight resemblance to a head of flowing-hair. They are of a pale straw-colour, the inner part spotted with pink. 42s.

C. Thouarsii (Thouar's C.).—Like all the genus, this is a very curious species. The sepals and petals are long and narrow, of an equal breadth; the colour is yellow, finely spotted with red, and fringed with bristle-shaped teeth, terminating in a long awl-shaped point. 31s. 6d.

Such is the description of the best known species of this curious, interesting genus. They are certainly not of a showy character like Cattleyas, Dendrobiums, or Lælias, but the exceedingly curious forms that the flowers assume, the little room they take up, and their easy culture, render them objects worthy of being in every collection, however small. The only objection against their being more generally grown is their comparative scarceness and high price; but as there are several collectors now out in their native localities, it is to be hoped they will be sent home in such quantities as to bring them within the reach of every orchid cultivator.

CULTURE.—The mode of growing these is very simple. They should be placed upon logs, of a size suitable to them, and have a little moss attached to each block. The Indian house is their proper place, in a temperature of 75° to 85°, during the season of growth. The atmosphere should be as moist as possible, and the syringe freely used every day. As soon as the year's growth is perfected they should be kept moderately dry and cool; that is, they should only be syringed when the pseudo-bulbs appear to be shrinking; and the temperature should be reduced to 60°. By such treatment they will grow and flower satisfactorily.

Comparettia coccinea (Scarlet C.); Brazil.—Sepals and petals of a brilliant scarlet; lip of the same colour, with a tinge of white at the base. The leaves are of a bright green on the upper surface, but of a beautiful purple underneath. A very elegant and beautiful species; very rare. 105s.

C. falcata (Sickle-shaped C.); Brazil.—Sepals and petals of a rich rosy purple; lip the same colour, excepting it is thickly veined with a deeper shade. Also very rare and beautiful. 105s.

C. rosea (Rose-coloured C.); Spanish Main.—This is a very small plant, but on account of its beautiful gracefully-pendant blossoms it is well worthy of cultivation. It is very like *C. falcata*, but distinct both in colour and the flowers being produced more densely on the flower-stem. 105s.

This small genus is unfortunately very rare; and is, as we have been informed, rare also in its native *habitat*. Their beauty is great, and of a delicately pleasing character; and they last a long time in bloom.

CULTURE.—Their roots are long and weak, consequently they require fastening to the block with small wire. A little moss thinly placed on the log with them will assist their growth greatly. They are rather impatient of moisture even at the season of growth, but still more so when at rest. The warmest part or nooks of the Mexican house will suit them best.

(To be continued.)

FLORISTS' FLOWERS.

AT this season of the year there are but few manual operations to perform amongst these favourites. The *Auriculas* and *Polyanthuses* should all be finished potting without delay, and placed in such a position as to be easily protected from heavy autumnal rains. Their *seedlings* should also be pricked out into shallow boxes or pans, and the earliest raised potted into small pots. Some of the strongest may flower next spring.

DAHLIAS.—These will now be in great beauty, but will require every encouragement to keep them so. In dry weather water freely, and occasionally with liquid-manure. As autumn winds may now be expected they must be kept well tied, and the best blooms protected from wind, rain, and sun. Young plants lately struck may be potted into five-inch pots, to make bulbs for next year. In those pots they survive the damps of winter better than in any other way. *Seedlings* will now be showing blooms; all such as are single, or come with pointed petals, or with forms otherwise faulty, should be pulled up and discarded at once; whilst such as have well-formed petals and are nearly double may be preserved for further trial; marking them legibly, and describing their several properties, so as to be a guide for judging them the following season. Such seedlings as are really superior to the older varieties should be preserved with the greatest care, and even cuttings put in of them immediately, which will increase the chances of keeping the variety alive for the next year.

TULIPS AND RANUNCULUSES.—Look to the roots occasionally and remove all such as may be decaying or have any mould upon them. We have known many a fine root lost for want of a little attention just after they have been put away for the winter. Attend to our remarks upon the preparation of the beds, lately given, and put them in due order, if not yet done.

T. APPLEBY.

THE KITCHEN-GARDEN.

CELERY.—To obtain this vegetable large and of good quality throughout the winter, it must be well attended to for the next two months. In the first place, the operation of applying the earth for blanching should be performed in a very systematic and careful manner, and not at too early a stage of its growth. Let a healthy luxuriance be first encouraged by frequent surface-stirrings and applications of good liquid-manure, keeping the plants entirely free from spurious suckers; and when earthing-up is first commenced, care should be taken to have all the outside leaves gathered together, and held erect by one hand, whilst the other is placing and pressing the earth round it to keep it in that position, and thus prevent the earth and rain from descending into the heart. These simple matters, if not well attended to, prove sometimes very destructive, by producing disease and decay. Dry weather, and when the celery is dry, too, should always be chosen for applying the earth.

Celery should, also, still be planted, and a few of the best plants of the several kinds, and of the most esteemed varieties, should be selected and planted where they are to stand for seed.

ROUTINE WORK.—Plant out *endive* and *lettuces* in succession, and make another sowing. The present is a good season for sowing the *American cress* and the *Black Spanish radish* for winter sallads; the *early short-topped scarlet* and *turnip radishes* may also still be sown on warm borders. Another sowing of *parsley*, too, should be made, which will be likely to come into growth in the spring, instead of starting to seed; thus keeping up the supply of this useful herb at a very needful season. *Leeks* may still be planted, and *onions* sown to stand the winter; the quick coming-in kinds of *turnips* may also still be sown; and every spare piece of ground should at once be cropped with vegetables of some kind. If any *Savoy plants* are left in the seed-bed, the present is still a good season for putting them out thickly for spring; *Green coleworts*, also, should be liberally planted; young *cabbage plants* should be pricked out in succession; and those already pricked out should be surface-stirred in due time.

Cardoons should be finally thinned, if not already done, and their growth well encouraged by surface-stirring and applications of liquid-manure. *Spinach* sown the middle of July will now require its final thinning, as well as its due allowance of surface-stirring. The main winter crop of *spinach* and *lettuce* should be carefully attended to whilst making its appearance above ground, so as to prevent the ravages of slugs and birds; a slight dredging or two of chimney-soot and lime mixed together is an excellent preventive, as well as a stimulant for assisting the growth of the plants. Encourage, also, all kinds of *cabbage-worts* planted as winter and spring crops, by frequent surface-stirrings.

Mushroom-beds.—Spawn and case such as are in condition for so doing; make another bed as previously directed, and continue to collect materials and store for small beds in succession.

JAMES BARNES.

MISCELLANEOUS INFORMATION.

WHAT IS A GARDEN?

By the Authoress of " My Flowers."

THE following remarks on gardens require neither introduction to the notice of my readers, nor apology for their insertion in a work so much devoted to the subject as our own.

It is a trite saying, that we live in an age of *knowledge*, consequently, that every thing may be defined and described; and yet how rarely can we define any thing clearly and satisfactorily! We have been led into this train of thought whilst reflecting upon the title of our unpretending little work—THE COTTAGE GARDENER. What is a garden, and how shall we define the meaning of the word? It is true that in the French, the Italian, the Welsh, and English languages, almost the same sound conveys the same meaning, which Dr. Johnson thus defines—" A piece of ground, inclosed and cultivated with extraordinary care, planted with herbs or fruits for food, or laid out for pleasure." Yet how greatly do men's minds differ in their ideas of " extraordinary care," inclosure of ground, plantation, food, and, above all, of " pleasure."

Although the fact is universally known, we cannot help recalling it to our minds, that our first parents had their primary existence in a *garden*—the Garden of Paradise; and it seems as if when they by transgression fell from it they carried with them, and handed down to posterity, a love for every similitude, even in name, to their first abode. All the earliest histories of mankind, as well from books of inspiration as otherwise, prove this. How full of allusions to what Dr. Johnson calls " pieces of ground," &c., &c., " planted with herbs and fruits," are the Holy Scriptures! It would be endless to repeat them; and how beautiful is the imagery to which they give rise! We cannot wholly pass by the hanging gardens of Babylon, brought to the highest pitch of cultivation so far back as the time of Nebuchadnezzar, about 600 years before the birth of Christ, with the aqueducts constructed for their irrigation in a manner which we cannot even attempt to imitate. In how many refreshing forms are the fruits and products of gardening noticed in Holy Writ, from " the juice of the grape " to " the garden of cucumbers." Following the subject through the varied imagery of the Old Testament to that of the New, who can forget the vine and the branches, the fig-tree, and the olive? and who would wish to forget that, as man's fall occurred in a garden, so in like manner the garden of Gethsemane, and " the new tomb " in the garden of Joseph of Arimathea, were the scenes of, and derived an undying lustre from, man's Redemption?

Although it is well to follow the serious suggestions which will and ought to be connected with the pursuits of every-day life, yet, leaving them, we are led to reflect, that the love of gardening seems to have accompanied civilization in every part of the globe. Among the Greeks and Romans it was considered worthy of their heroes and philosophers, many of whom, we learn from history, were celebrated for the magnificence of their gardens, planted with odoriferous flowers and shrubs, and embellished with fountains and statues. A love of horticulture accompanied civilization. The most civilized parts of Europe, Asia, and Africa, at very early periods showed the value attached to gardens, not merely as sources of food, but also of luxury and pleasure. The Chinese were very early cultivators of gardens; the Persians much earlier. The warmer latitudes of Europe soon learned from their southern neighbours the benefits of cultivating fruits and flowers. In England we arrived at this knowledge more slowly; we read, that previously to the 16th century, most of our vegetables and fruits were procured from the Netherlands. But shortly after this period, a taste for horticulture and botanical research sprang up in Italy and Germany, and soon extended to this country; and many varieties of flowers, plants, and roots, previously unknown, but now most common to us, were imported into this country from Flanders. After the discovery of America, plants and fruits were largely imported from tropical climates; and hothouses were constructed for the growth of pine-apples and oranges; and forcing beds of tanner's bark, introduced by the Dutch, are first mentioned in the year 1688, when they were made at Blackheath for rearing orange-trees. Man's primeval taste and love for gardening have always been progressive; and it seems as if, in every quarter of the globe, after houses were erected with any degree of knowledge of architecture, or appreciation of comfort, gardens attached to them became at once indispensable.

But after all, we do not seem to have made any progress in defining what *a garden* really is. The Duke of Devonshire has spent more money, probably, than any other individual in trying to teach the world the meaning of the word. How can we, in a few lines, do more than make the faintest allusion to the beauties of Chatsworth and Chiswick! The Duke may well point with complacency, and some feelings of pride, to Chatsworth, as manifesting what are *his* ideas of a garden. Who that has ever visited this charming spot on a fine day can forget the glory of the scene, with its woods, rocks, and waterfalls; its parterres and terraces; its orangeries, and pineries, and vineries: the extraordinary application of art and science to nature—their apparent triumph over the very seasons, and their success in bringing together at our feet plants, flowers, and fruit from every latitude and clime! And whilst the gardens and groves are enjoying generally their exposure to all the varieties of our ever-changing climate, and deriving new beauties from it, yet, as if to remind us that our beneficent Creator has placed others of our species in warmer lands, here, as if in imitation of tropical climes, we suddenly find ourselves breathing the atmosphere of the West Indies, or Cape of Good Hope, beneath a whole acre of glass in the grand conservatory! This is a garden most richly and exquisitely elaborated.

Then there are the gardens of Hampton Court, and Windsor, and of other abodes of royalty, which probably were transcendently beautiful in the days when subjects did not attempt to surpass in outward display the splendid possessions of their liege lords. The mansions of the great and noble throughout Great Britain are proverbially celebrated for their skilful appliances and beauties.

We cannot stay to particularize the large, stately, sombre, rectangular gardens and terraces of the Escurial, or of the old noblesse in Spain, Portugal, or France. For purposes of practical utility, the gardens of the Low Countries became early celebrated; and it is probable that the taste for horticulture was first taught them by the Spaniards, until Dutch gardening became proverbially excellent. The Dutch were, then, in a great degree, our own instructors. It is truly exhilarating to notice the rapid progress of vegetation in the rich alluvial soil of Holland. But what can exceed the folly of the *gardeners* when we read that one single tulip root has been sold in former times for 10,000 florins! and " the aggregate sum produced by the sale of 120 tulips was 90,000 florins, or £6750!"

The gardens of the wealthy in the vicinity of the large towns in Holland are still very interesting, even in their uniformity; and in sailing down the Armstel and other places where the rich chiefly reside, and where the river's banks are ornamented with their villas and gardens, we were much struck in reading the inscriptions over many of their summer-houses—such as " Sweet is my repose," " Glorious is the scene," " Happy is my home," &c., &c. This may be simply the language of pride, but we trust that it is some times the voice of gratitude to the Giver of all good."

(To be continued.)

RHUBARB WINE.

I will now proceed to the method of manufacturing this wine, and in doing so, will assume that the process of wine making is unknown to your readers, and that with them, as in my own case, a mere domestic apparatus only can be made available.

We will suppose the quantity to be made to be 10 gallons. This is a very convenient quantity for beginners, although it should be borne in mind that *the larger the quantity made*, the more easily and perfectly will fermentation be carried on. The articles necessary are: First—a tub capacious enough to hold rather more than this quantity; a common washing-tub will answer the purpose. Secondly—a nine gallon cask and a two gallon stone jar, both scrupulously clean, or a foreign and disagreeable flavour may be imparted to the wine. Thirdly—a convenient wooden mallet to bruise the rhubarb stalks. Fourthly—some kind of screw press, to press out the juice from the bruised stalks; a common linen-press might easily be adapted for use. I generally borrow a "tincture press" from my druggist for the purpose. Fifthly—a vial bottle fastened to a stick, so that a small portion of the wine may be conveniently dipped from the bung-hole, in order to ascertain, from time to time, the progress of the fermentation. Sixthly—although this *may* be dispensed with, although necessary when accuracy is desired—a saccharometer.

Now for " the recipe."

Take of rhubarb stalks (unpealed) 60 pounds.
    „   loaf-sugar ..   .. 30 pounds.
    „   red argol (powdered) .. 4 ounces.
    „   water, a sufficient quantity.

The rhubarb stalks should be bruised one by one with the mallet against the side or bottom of the tub. Four or five gallons of cold water should then be poured upon them, in which they should be allowed to macerate for 12 or 16 hours. The stalks should now be put into the press, and all their juice pressed out. This, with the liquor in which they were macerated, together with the sugar and the argol should be mixed in the tub, and the quantity made up to 10¼ gallons by the addition of cold water. (It would save trouble in measuring, if a mark were previously placed in the tub to indicate when this quantity was contained in it.) This mixture is the artificial "must." The tub should now be covered with a blanket, and placed in a temperature of from 55 to 60 degrees. Here it may remain, being occasionally stirred, for two or three days, according to the symptoms of fermentation it may show; it should then be poured off, straining it through flannel into the cask, which should be filled to the bung-hole, and placed across the tub, in order that the scum and yeast which will be thrown off may be caught and removed. The superabundant must, which will be 1¼ gallons, must be poured into the jar, in order that as the fermentation in the cask proceeds, and the liquor diminishes, there may be a supply in readiness to fill up the cask, which must always be kept full or nearly so. In about a fortnight the bung may, most probably, be put loosely in, and in another week firmly fixed, and the cask placed in the cellar; but this of course depends upon the state of the wine. If the sweetness has disappeared, or nearly so,—or if, on the saccharometer being placed in it, the index marks a specific gravity of about 40,—the wine has fermented far enough for cellaring; if it has not reached this point, the wine should be well stirred, and the temperature kept up to promote further fermentation. In a month or six weeks after cellaring it may be fined and drawn off into a clean cask, or the same properly cleaned and, if necessary, sulphured to stop further fermentation, before the wine is returned. The cask may now be finally stopped close, and if an effervescent wine be desired, allowed to remain until March, when it should be bottled; the corks wired, and the bottles laid down. But if a still wine, like hock, be desired, another year in the wood, or even more, will be advantageous.

The only difficulty about this process is to find out the precise period at which the fermentation has reached the desired point. The saccharometer will show this correctly. About 35, as marked on the scale of Thompson's saccharometer, would indicate proper attenuation for wine intended to be effervescent; if it is to be still and dry it may be lower—25 to 30. But the taste may be educated so as to form an approximation to truth; as long as sweetness exists to any extent the fermentation is incomplete; and after eating a small piece of crust most persons may readily detect the presence of too much sugar in the wine; in this case the wine should be shaken or stirred, that the wine may "feed," as it is termed, on the lees; fining, on the contrary, will check fermentation; and when it has gone far enough,

sulphurous acid gas stops it, as in the process of "sulphuring," which may be readily done by burning a few sulphur matches within the bung-hole, the cask being inverted.

Fining is generally performed by means of isinglass previously dissolved, or partly so, in a little of the wine. About a drachm of isinglass so dissolved and poured into the bung-hole, the *upper part* of the wine being stirred at the same time, will probably be found sufficient.

Thompson's saccharometer costs three guineas; but a friend has informed me that a simple glass one, quite sufficient for our purpose, may be procured for a few shillings. I will make enquiries respecting this, as, no doubt, to *ensure* accuracy a saccharometer is necessary, and the cost is an obstacle to its general use.

As a rule it may be observed, that the finer the sugar, the more alcohol is produced from it. It may be noted, that as the rhubarb juice will *iron mould* linen, care should be taken when the stalks are bruised.

I will append a copy of some rough notes taken by myself of the different stages of manufacture of rhubarb wine; they may serve as pegs whereupon to hang more extensive observations; and in conclusion I beg to say, that if any part of the foregoing directions be less clear than might be, I shall be happy to explain more in detail any little point; and I shall be gratified if what I have said should induce some of your readers to try the manufacture of this wine upon *correct* principles; and I am certain that they will find themselves amply repaid for the trouble and expense, in having as a result genuine, wholesome wine, instead of the compound of vinegar and sugar usually denominated "home-made wine."

NOTES.

1840. 10¼ gallons, as receipt. Made, May 29th. Put in cask, June 2nd. Stopped, June 10th. Cellared, June 23rd; saccharometer, 45. Racked and fined, August 3rd. October 25th, racked and sulphured; saccharometer 37. Bottled, January 25th, 1841. This wine turned out very good,—not to be distinguished from champagne.

1842. Rhubarb, 90 pounds. Sugar, 50 pounds. Argol, 8 ounces; quantity, 17 gallons. June 12th, made. June 19th, put in casks (a nine-gallon and a six-gallon);—fermentation commenced the 17th. June 26th, stopped. July 4th, cellared; saccharometer 43. August 15th, racked.

1843. March 17th, nine-gallon cask tested with saccharometer shewed 34 degrees; six-gallon shewed 40. Bottled nine-gallon cask. Stirred six-gallon. May 13th, fined six-gallon and sulphured; saccharometer 33.

1844. March—bottled.

1850. A good still wine.

HENRY W. LIVETT, *Wells, Somerset.*

HORTICULTURAL SOCIETY'S SHOW, CHISWICK,
JULY 13TH.
(*Concluded from page 294.*)

CARNATIONS.

These beautiful July flowers were exhibited in the best order.

AMATEURS.

1ST PRIZE to Mr. Newhall, Woolwich, for

Toon's Ringleader, Lorenzo, Prince Albert, Count Pauline, Queen of Purples, Calcutt's Brutus, Sir Jos. Reynolds, Ely's Cymba, Queen Victoria, Flora's Garland, Earl Grey, Prince Arthur, May's Conquering Hero, Harriet, Duke of Sutherland, Squire Trow, May's Orlando, Prince of Wales, Georgina, Sir Henry Hardinge, Fireball, Lady Ely, Lord Byron, and *Ely's King of Scarlets.*

2ND PRIZE to J. C. Edwards, Esq., Holloway. He had, in addition to some of the above,

Solander, Defiance, Puxley's Prince Albert, Cardinal Wolsey, Crusader, Beauty of Woodhouse, Vivid, Unique, Gem, Lady of the Lake, Ariel, Caliban, Regular, Edgar, Cradley Pet, Excellent, Earl Spencer, and *Premier.*

NURSERYMEN.

1ST PRIZE to Mr. Norman, Woolwich, for

Puxley's Prince Albert, Kny's Majestic, Lady of the Lake, Duchess of Sutherland, Martin's President, Squire's Defiance, Sampson's Queen, Cartwright's Rainbow, Hale's Prince Albert, Squire Trow, Lorenzo, Georgina, Norman's Queen, Queen of Purples, Sir Rowland Hill, Calcutt's Brutus, Earl Spencer, Sir Jos. Reynolds, Bucknall's Ulysses, Caliban, Buonaparte, Beauty of Woodhouse, Hepworth's Briton, and *Dido.*

2ND PRIZE to Mr. Ward, of Woolwich, for

Puxley's Albert, Jenny Lind, Miss Barton, Simpson's Queen, General Moore, Kay's Majestic, Conquering Hero, Martin's President, Georgina, Admiral Curzon, Hale's Prince Albert, Squire Trow, Vivid, Atterton's Fanny Gardener, Atterton's Earl Spencer, Atterton's Margaret Evans, Brutus, Sir H. Smith, Milwood's Premier, Juba, King of Scarlets, Lady of the Lake, and *Queen of Purples.*

AN EXTRA PRIZE was awarded to Mr. Bragg, of Slough. We give a few names of the best:

Cartwright's Rainbow, Duke of York, King of Scarlets, Greig's Mary, Lady of the Lake, Calcutt's Juba, May's Prince Arthur, May's Edgar, Beauty of Woodhouse, Ely's Prince of Wales, and *Village Maid.*

AN EXTRA PRIZE was also awarded to Mr. Wilmer, of Sudbury, for a fine stand, several of which were seedlings raised by himself. We noted a few of the best, namely,

Wilmer's John Hepworth, Hale's Prince Albert, Wilmer's Defiance, Martin's President, Wilmer's Solander, Strong's Duke of York, Barrenger's Premier, Hufton's Duke of Wellington, Wilson's Harriet, Ely's Duke of Bedford, Cartwright's Rainbow, and *Hepworth's Brilliant.*

PICOTEES.—AMATEURS.

1ST PRIZE to J. Edwards, Esq., Holloway, for

Alpha, Coronation, Sebastian, Constance, Mary Ann, Sophia, Duchess of Sutherland, Amethyst, Mrs. Barnard, Sally, Ne Plus Ultra, Portia, Miss B. Coutts, Sylph, Duke of Newcastle, Shaw's Beauty, Traher's Rosalind, Agitator, Emma, Norman's Beauly, Mrs. Annesley, Lady Chesterfield, Lucretia, and *Elizabeth.*

2ND PRIZE to — Newhall, Esq., for

Woolwich, Duchess of Bedford, Sebastian, Rosalind, Prince of Wales, Prince Royal, Emperor, May's Jessica, Lady Smith, Cox's Regina, Isabella, Mrs. Barnard, Hardstone's Sarah, Mrs. Bevan, Norman's Beauly, Miss B. Coutts, Princess Augusta, Brenklow's New Purple, Portia, Venus, Constance, Duchess of Sutherland, Craske's Prince Albert, and *Burrough's General Jackson.*

NURSERYMEN.

1ST PRIZE to Mr. Norman, Woolwich, for

Sir R. Peel, Ne Plus Ultra, Brinklow's Leader, Rosalind, King John, Mrs. Bevan, Lord Chandos, Portia, Mrs. Barnard, Shaw's Beauly, Emperor, Mary Ann, Emma, Elegant, Regina, Prince Albert, Duchess of Sutherland, Princess Louisa, Venus, Seedling, Garratt's Red Edge, Norman's Beauty, Duke of Newcastle, and *Isabella.*

2ND PRIZE to Mr. Ward, Woolwich, for

Exquisite, Mrs. Bevan, Duchess of Bedford, Agitator, Ne Plus Ultra, Leader, Norwich Rival, Shaw's Beauty, May's Portia, Atterton's Sunbeam, Duchess of Sutherland, Gidding's Diana, Wilmer's Prince Royal, Craske's Albert, Sharp's Elegant, Sarah, Norman's Beauty, Hudson's Nymph, Cox's Regina, Lady Chesterfield, Princess Augusta, Countess of Gray, Lord Hardinge, and *Gidding's Vespasian.*

The exhibitors of carnations and picotees have reason to be proud of their achievements at this exhibition. We are sorry that the Society does not afford better encouragement. The Silver Banksian Medal, value twenty shillings, being the highest prize, is but a sorry recompence for the great pains and labour requisite to produce a good stand of 24 carnations or picotees. Can we hope the amount of the prize will be increased next year? We are quite sure such fine stands of exquisitely beautiful flowers are worthy of better prizes.

SEEDLING FLORISTS' FLOWERS.

FANCY PELARGONIUMS.—The best were sent by Mr. Ambrose, of Battersea. *Eclipse* and *Crimson King* we considered worth growing.

CARNATIONS.—May's *Romeo*, rose flake; May's *Antonio*, ditto, are good varieties, with a clear white ground, rose edges, and fine clean stripes of clear rose colour. In scarlet flakes, Puxley's *Mars* is a superior thing, being of a fine form, substance, and colour; heavy edged.

PICOTEES. — Red edged *Dodwell's Mary*, purple edged *Alfred*, were large flowers, with clear distinct edges. These are all worth looking after.

FUCHSIAS.—Mr. G. Smith, of Hornsey-road, had his seedling, *F. Sidonia*; a good showy variety; the corolla is a deep purple; the sepals well turned up to show it to advantage. The only deficiency is in the tube, which is rather short. It is a desirable kind. *Bank's Expansion*, exhibited by Mr. Turner, is also a desirable variety, flowering profusely; colours very distinct, and the parts of the flower of good size.

FRUITS.

The fruit tent was again a great attraction, but upon the whole there was not so much as was shown at the Park ten days previously; but the *grapes*, especially the black varieties, were better coloured, and some, in other respects, superior. *Peaches, Nectarines*, and *Strawberries*, were also excellent. To give our country readers some idea of the extent of a metropolitan exhibition of fruit, we need only mention that there were exhibited on this occasion 28 *Pine Apples*, all handsome fruit; 57 dishes of *Grapes*, 24 large dishes of *Strawberries*, 17 dishes of *Peaches*, and 10 dishes of *Nectarines*, and a goodly lot of *Melons*. The weight of the heaviest *Queen Pine* was 5 ℔ 14 oz. It came from Mr. Jones, gardener to Sir J. Guest, Bart. The heaviest *Providence Pine* weighed 9 ℔ 13½ oz., from Mr. Spencer, gardener to the Marquis of Lansdowne, Bowood, near Bath. Our limited space prevents us giving more particulars of the winner's names, varieties of fruit, &c., exhibited on this occasion. Sufficient it is to state, that most of the exhibitors were the same whose productions we described in our account of the last show in the Regent's Park.

WHITE FLOWERS, AND THEIR UTILITY IN GARDEN DECORATION.

IN the various improvements which florists' flowers have undergone the last few years, it must be admitted that but little has been done to obtain things purely white; the dazzling scarlet, rich purple, or gay yellow, have been more sought after than the simple colour whose claims to our notice it is my purpose here to call attention to; and as the number of plants blooming white is no ways meagre, a few remarks on the disposal of them may not be out of place.

I should think there are few visitors of a flower-garden by twilight, but who have been struck by the gay appearance a large plant of the double white rocket has at that time; a large white campanula (whose name I cannot call to memory), is equally conspicuous, as also are all other free-blooming white flowers, while their more gay brethren of the blue, red, and other dark hues, appear little different from the foliage they wear; if you go into the greenhouse the effect is the same, the white azaleas, pale-coloured cineraria, and similar things attracting your attention. Now, my readers will be saying—" We know all that, but we seldom visit such places at that time; but what has that to do with daylight gardening?" Have patience, and we will explain. We have said that white looks better than other colours in the dark, it is because it forms such a strong contrast to all around it,—the foliage, the ground, or it may be the turf, nay, even the very atmosphere wearing a murky aspect, tend to strengthen that contrast, and show its perfection to greater advantage. Now, the same thing, or nearly so, may be done by daylight, and we will attempt to explain how and when it may be made to do so.

In very many gardens there are more or less of shrubbery borders having a front of flowers, and as such borders are generally at some distance from the house and principal walks, and their appearance at a distance is an important matter, in such borders we say, plant abundance of white flowers—as dahlias, roses, phloxes, rockets, and similar things. The reason is obvious, the back ground of shrubs, &c., being higher, show the white blooms of such things to every advantage, while it is only on closer inspection (that is, when the eye takes a more limited view), that deep-coloured flowers look well at all. Let any one dubious of this matter just examine a scarlet and a white thorn closely, and then walk a distance from them and look again; the white one which looked well even on close inspection, will look equally so as far off as the eye can discern colours at all; not so its companion, a very short distance is sufficient to confound the bloom and foliage. Now, this is just the same if a pink, red, or blue flower is planted in front of a mass of foliage of other things, the eye being unable to separate these colours from the green against which they are placed, they are consequently lost to view. Next to white are those pale colours approaching nearest to it, even yellow and white with a mixture of other colouring, but it is surprising how much the latter detracts from the effect white would have alone; how gay an orchard of cherry-trees in bloom looks at the distance of a mile, compared to one of apples at the same range of view, the mixture of pink neutralizing the latter; look also at an elder-tree, its bloom forming a strong contrast with its rich green foliage. The Guelder rose might form another example, if such were wanting, but it is hoped we have said enough to call the attention of your young friends to the subject; and if they have borders backed by shrubs or trees, or even where the eye of the spectator passing over them rests on a piece of turf or other dark body, we say plant white and other light-coloured flowers with unsparing hand. We should certainly not discard all others; what we mean, is to plant in such a situation more than the usual share of such colours, especially if appearance at a distance be an important point. The same remark holds good to massing or bedding-out in flower-gardens where the beds are cut out on grass, which forming the base or back-ground, the effect is much the same, though in a less degree than the shrubbery-border above in the flower-garden. Other circumstances render a variety of colours indispensable, but it is to be deplored that in the directions generally given as to the planting of such beds, the back-ground or rather ground-work seems to be entirely overlooked; certainly a set of geometric figures cut in grass ought not to be planted the same as if they were separated by gravel walks; in the former case white and kindred colours should be more liberally dealt out than in the latter, or, to speak more plainly, the colour approaching nearest to that of the gravel ought to be most sparingly used.

While on this subject I may remark, there is only one place where white flowers are out of character—that is, in a Dutch flower-garden, where the walks intersecting the beds are laid with white shells; in such places the walks generally occupy one-third, or even one-half, of the entire area; and the bright glare they present to a summer's sun renders anything more of that colour superfluous. In all such gardens we would say, plant deep coloured flowers in greater profusion; and if for variety's sake you must have a white bed, edge it with something dark, as scarlet verbena or blue lobelia—it will not be so likely to blend with the walks. When gravel, sand, brick-dust, or ashes are used for walks, we would say, use sparingly those colours approaching thereto; if, as we have said above, you wish to introduce one, let it have a rim of something blooming the reverse. But as this is foreign to the subject we have in hand, we shall say no more than again impress on our readers to remember, that if they want to make a flower-border (backed by anything except a chalk cliff or white-washed wall) look well at any distance exceeding fifty yards, they must plant abundance of white and other pale-coloured flowers; and where a great breadth of turf separates flower-beds on the lawn, there likewise to plant the same colours in as great profusion as attention to other matters will allow them to do.—S. N. V.

EXTRACTS FROM CORRESPONDENCE.

Bee-keeping Difficulties.—I have commenced bee-keeping this year, utterly unacquainted with the subject, and entirely directed by The Cottage Gardener. My difficulties may be of some guide to you in writing future articles. I bought one of Payne's cottage hives, but for the timely advice of a friend I should have placed it on a board so *thin* that it would have *warped*. I think you give no warning against this. You direct a glass or small hive to be placed on the parent hive in 21 days after housing the swarm. You give no reason why it should not be done sooner, and whether any harm would ensue if it was done sooner. Would placing it on sooner prevent the parent hive from being filled? would the operation in it be suspended, and all the work be transferred to the upper story? Then you do not say how the glass (if a glass is used) is to be covered. You cannot take the milk-pan or earthenware cover and place it on the glass: the glass would break, and would not be darkened enough. Under other advice than that contained in your columns, I bought a straw cover in the shape of a hive, and a circular cover open at both ends to stand on the parent hive, and for the first-mentioned cover to rest on. There was then shelter for my glass. And my pan surmounted all the mass. After a week, I raised my glass, and put a small 10 lb hive between it and the parent hive. The glass, full of comb, I found very top-heavy too on the empty straw-hive, though I used adapting boards, and I could not manage to make the two stand very straight. Then my top straw cover and my circular centre piece were not high enough for my two fold erection: I was in despair. The top cover hung on the glass, and would not reach the centre-piece. I covered the glass with brown paper, and pegged a piece of matting round the gap. Again I mounted my pan on the top. I am in mental fear of a high wind; my fabric is rather shaky, and far from perpendicular. There I shall leave my erection for the present. But, to my great consternation, I see in a recent number of your paper that sometimes a *third* hive must be placed! I really must serve an apprenticeship to a skilful architect before I dare venture upon such a Tower of Babel. Why not empty the glass and put it on again, instead of piling mountain upon mountain? Next, I want to know how I can tell when a glass or small hive is fit to be removed and the honey abstracted? You say when the "cells are all sealed up," but that is Greek to a novice. How can I tell by looking through three or four inches square of glass into my small hive when that event has happened? I think you direct no glasses or hives to be added after July. But provided those already placed on being not quite filled, how long are they to stand into the autumn? When is the parent hive to be left by itself? Should more than one swarm be taken from any stock during one summer? I suppose, after taking a swarm, if you do not wish to take a second, a glass or small hive should *immediately* be put on the parent hive. I do not think of any other difficulty at present, but when I do I shall not fail to consult you, as I am sure that the difficulties of the pupil are useful to the teacher when expressed to him, as they inform him of points which require explanation, but which, from being familiar to him, never occurred to him as being difficulties. Some people say it is best not to use glass at all on straw hives, but only on wooden ones, as glass does not stand steady on them. Is it so? I have not tried wooden boxes on my parent straw hive. I do not think I shall venture to touch my Babel till I hear from you, fearful of an upset, and not knowing whether my glass will be fit to remove when I do look at it. If the bees work away quietly, I shall let well alone.—Sigma.

[In reply to the above, it was not considered necessary to give the thickness of the floor-board; common observation would suggest that a half-inch board would not be sufficient to support a weight of, perhaps, from 40 to 80 lbs. If the moveable top of Payne's Improved Cottage Hive is taken off in less than 18 or 21 days, there is danger of the combs in the hive falling, by having their hold to the top of the hive loosened before they are firmly fixed to the sides, especially if the weather be very hot; and, again, the bees would not have established themselves sufficiently in a shorter time in the hive so as to commence working in the glass. For the best kind of cover to a glass, see The Cottage Gardener, vol. II., page 42. A box of wood deep enough to cover the glass, and to rest upon the adapting board on which the glass is placed, will do as well. When the 10 lb hive was put between the stock-hive and the glass, the adapter on which the glass and its cover rested should have been removed with them, and a fresh adapter put upon the top of the stock-hive for the 10 lb hive to stand upon, which would have rendered "brown paper and matting unnecessary." The glass must not be taken off until the cells are sealed up; in some hives, and in some seasons, the increase of bees is so rapid, that they will be seen clustering at the mouth of the hive before this is done, although a small hive has been supplied; in this case a *second small hive* must be given between the two receptacles for honey already on the stock-hive, or a swarm will be the result. A glass must not be taken off and *another* put on; the bees will not go up into it; but a small *hive* must again be placed next the stock-hive. Either a glass, a box, or small hive, is fit to be taken off when the combs are all sealed up. In The Cottage Gardener, vol. II., p. 105, the cells next the glass in the small hive are the last that are sealed up, so when you see that done, the hive is ready to be taken. The time of the final deprivation must vary with the season—this year, say the last week in August; but first ascertain if the stock-hive contains 20 lbs of honey, if not, leave the glass on until the bees have emptied it. When a stock has swarmed once, all the room you can give them will not prevent a second, nor, perhaps, a third swarm. See The Cottage Gardener, vol. II., p. 104.]

Double Flowers.—Reading with some degree of interest an article of your's of last Thursday, relative to the production of "double flowers," and agreeing with you as I do on the generality of your remarks, I was at the same time struck with one relative to the culture having little or nothing to do with the flowers being single or double. Now, the opinion I have formed, and which is entirely founded on the experience of the last few years, is, that as regards *stocks*, that by giving them rich and nourishing soil, paying attention to situation and drainage, double flowers will be produced in greater profusion, and more certainty; and that by a contrary treatment the reverse may be expected. For instance, last year I sowed seed (saved by myself from single stocks growing in the midst of double ones) upon a very rich vine-border recently made—not high gardening, you will say—facing the south and well drained, the result was about six or eight to one in favour of *double* stocks. Part of the same seed was sown in a small bed about twenty feet from the aforesaid vine-border, the situation not so open, and the soil very poor, the result was just the reverse, about six or eight to one being *single*. The same thing occurs at this present time; a portion of the seed saved by myself was sown as an edging to a rose-bed composed of old cow-dung, silver sand, and Wanstead yellow loam: of 47 stocks there were only six single, and they all together. The other portion of seed sown on the same border of poor soil as previous year, the result was about three or four to one single stock.—J.R.S. [We do not perceive where you differ from Mr. Fish in his observations at pages 238-9. He says, " double flowers are chiefly produced by cultivation, and are perpetuated by the same means." And, then, after advising that to free-growing seedlings rich manure be not given until after the bloom appears, and then to give increased nourishment. We have no doubt ourselves as to the fact, that a much richer soil than is required for the growth of a plant in a seed-bearing state, is essential for growing it with double flowers.—Eᴅ. C. G.

Gᴏᴀᴛs.—These animals are very tame, and when reared from early kidship by any one, become as much attached to their owner as dogs; and will follow him and lay at his feet in the same manner. Their habits resemble also those of the chamois: they frequent mountainous and rocky districts, where they leap fearlessly from rock to rock; their tiny feet keeping them firm on the narrowest paths, which they seem proud to tread. Their food is of the kind afforded by such situations: the rankest and most aromatic weeds and herbs being selected; as also woody herbage, chiefly of an astringent nature, such as the sloe, rose, and blackberry. Without this food (which Nature has pointed out to them) they are soon attacked with diarrhœa, or become what is termed " hoven." Grass, alone, will *kill* them in a very short time; though a chance attack may be relieved by a dose of common salt, administered in water. They delight in heat, which never produces vertigo in the goat; and the writer has seen them in tropical countries lying on rocks the most exposed to the sun, and so heated they could scarcely be touched by the human hand. They will endure cold, but not if they can avoid it. Their milk is highly nutritious, when it will agree with the stomach.—Bᴜsʏ Bᴏᴅʏ.

Tᴏ Pʀᴇᴠᴇɴᴛ Cᴀʀɴᴀᴛɪᴏɴs Bᴜʀsᴛɪɴɢ.—Take a broad bean from its pod, cut off both ends, and cut the remainder into two or three slices, according to the size. Push out the green part from one slice, and you have remaining a compressed ring of skin. Slip this over a bud of a carnation, and let it hang on the lower part of it; by the next day it will have collapsed into a tight and scarcely visible bandage. —A Pᴀʀsᴏɴ's Wɪꜰᴇ.

Pʀᴇsᴇʀᴠɪɴɢ Fʀᴜɪᴛ.—In addition to the very excellent advice given to cottagers for preserving fruit, by " A Friend," I would offer this, as more economical for cottagers or anybody else. Instead of tying the jars down with paper dipped in brandy, make some stiff paste with flour, spread it on writing-paper, and put this over the jars, while *quite hot*, and the preserve will keep for years in a dry situation. My wife has followed this plan for years, and always with success. She used some last week that had been done two years ago. —A. Aʟᴏᴇs.

Sᴛʀᴀᴡʙᴇʀʀɪᴇs.—I have amazing crops; and I never do anything to the plants except cutting off the runners. The ground in which they grow is as hard as a road, being chalky. The sorts I have principally are the Kean's Seedling, the Pine—an old sort, but the best I know. The

British Queen and Princess Alice Maude do not seem to do well; but I shall follow your directions with them another year.—W. X.

TO CORRESPONDENTS.

⁎ We request that no one will write to the departmental writers of Tʜᴇ Cᴏᴛᴛᴀɢᴇ Gᴀʀᴅᴇɴᴇʀ. It gives them unjustifiable trouble and expense. All communications should be addressed " *To the Editor of The Cottage Gardener*, 2, *Amen Corner, Paternoster Row, London.*"

Bᴇᴇ Tʀᴀᴘ (*M. J. P.*).—You and others having applied for more particulars relative to the apparatus for allowing the egress of bees, but preventing their return, recommended by Mr. Payne at page 259: we have obtained the following sketch from its inventor, R. Antram, Esq., Slapton, near Dartmouth.

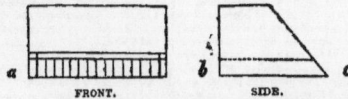

FRONT.   SIDE.

" This is drawn one-fourth the size of the original, which is four inches wide; but this width must be regulated by that of the hive's entrance. *a*, are pieces of talc, a quarter of an inch wide, and three quarters of an inch long; hinged by being cemented to a strip of narrow ribbon. *b*, the under side of the block; cut out three inches wide, forming a passage from back to front. *c*, the tin bottom.

Iᴠʏ (*Ivy Lover*).—To " cover an unsightly wooden fence with ivy as soon as possible, and at the smallest expense," plant cuttings of the broad-leaved or Irish ivy on the most shaded side of the fence in September. Plant the cuttings a foot apart. When well rooted give them manure and plenty of soft water in dry weather. You can thin out the plants when they become too thick. Each cutting should have a heel of ripe wood, and one joint buried beneath the soil after removing the leaves from that joint, and only two leaves be left above ground.

Oxꜰᴏʀᴅ Bᴇᴇ Sᴏᴄɪᴇᴛʏ (*A Subscriber*).—This dissolved long since. Mr. Cotton was its presiding genius; and when he left it was broken up.

Dɪsᴇᴀsᴇᴅ Rᴏsᴇ Lᴇᴀᴠᴇs (*F. C.*).—The leaves you enclosed are very severely mildewed. They are covered with the remains of the parasitic fungus *Puccinia rosæ*. But the leaves betray ill-management. If you mulch over the roots of the trees now, and renew the mulch next March, giving water copiously in dry weather, you will not find a repetition of such leaves.

Rʜᴜʙᴀʀʙ Wɪɴᴇ (*An Original Subscriber*).—In the second receipt, at page 154, it is intended that the fermentation should proceed in the cask. Do not add the brandy until the fermentation has ceased. Half an ounce of isinglass will clarify a large cask.

Tʀᴏᴘᴀᴇᴏʟᴜᴍ Pᴇɴᴛᴀᴘʜʏʟʟᴜᴍ (*S. H. H.*).—Let the frost cut down your now luxuriant *T. pentaphyllum*, and the roots, which have large tubers, will take care of themselves; but, in case a very hard winter should hurt them, you had better spread three or four inches deep of coal-ashes over the roots. The habit of the plant is to spread its tuberous roots laterally, and sometimes downwards, so that in a few years they depart altogether from their position, or bury their roots too deep, therefore it will be necessary to take them up like potatoes every third season; and this may be done in October or November, the tubers kept dry till next March, then to be replanted in fresh soil.

Sɪɴɢʟᴇ Pɪɴᴋs ᴀɴᴅ Cᴀʀɴᴀᴛɪᴏɴs (*Stanley*).—It is only by high cultivation that these can perchance be rendered double. Mr. Fish's observations upon the subject generally apply equally to your flowers in particular.

Pᴇᴀʀ-ᴛʀᴇᴇ Bᴀʀᴋ Sᴘʟɪᴛ (*Ibid*).—There is no better application for excluding the air and wet than Mr. Forsyth's plaster, the recipe for which is given at page 228 of the present volume. We always use clay instead of the wood-ashes, as this renders the plaster more adhesive.

Gᴜᴀɴᴏ ᴀɴᴅ Sᴇᴇᴅs (*A Clergyman*).—Our correspondent asks us urgently to recommend him some party from whom he can obtain genuine flower-seeds, because, he says, " when sowing flower-beds of particular colours, I am frequently annoyed by finding my seed not true, and, perhaps, not more than a third of the proper colour." Now, we cannot specify any particular seedsman, but we will go so far as to say, that if you will send your order to any of those who have advertised in our columns, you shall have as good seed as can be procured. We have never been disappointed in the way you have suffered, except in cases where cross-impregnation is very difficult to be avoided. We buy our guano of the London Manure Company, 40, Bridge-street, Blackfriars.

Aɴᴛɪʀʀʜɪɴᴜᴍs (*J. W. Thorne*).—We have received your box of seedling flowers. Those numbered 12, 6, and 7, are the best; but all are deficient in brilliancy of colour. Your parent plants cannot be good. We will give the characteristics you wish for.

Sᴛᴇᴀᴍɪɴɢ Aᴘᴘᴀʀᴀᴛᴜs (*Devizes*).—Thompson's Registered Portable Steaming Apparatus, which received the Royal Agricultural Society's prize, is that we should select. It is made by Messrs. Barrett, Exall, and Co., Reading, priced £16. But to steam potatoes, &c., for a few pigs, we should have a large kind of cullender made to fit upon our brewing copper, in the way that steamers are made for fitting upon a pot for steaming potatoes in the kitchen.

STRAWBERRY PLANTING (G.).—You state, upon the authority of Mr. Keen, that "*autumn* planted runners never produce so good a crop as those moved from a nursery bed in March;" and this is very probable; but certainly *summer* planted runners, that is, those well established in pots, or well rooted in compost near the parent, and planted out at the end of July or early in August, beat the spring-planted. We have tried both modes, and the summer planted were the strongest, and bore well the next year. Thanks for your comments; and we agree that there is something valid in a portion of your objection, but there is no hypocrisy in the writer.

PEACH-LEAF BLISTERING (*Ibid*).—You say you know of two instances where excess of dampness could not possibly be the cause of this disease; but we are as sure as if we had seen them that the leaves were on luxuriant trees; and whether the excess of sap in the leaves arises from damp soil, or from excessive root action, matters little. The mass of gum above the point of junction between a vigorous Elton Cherry and its Mahaleb stock arises from the vessels of the latter not being large enough to carry down the sap as rapidly as it is elaborated by the leaves. The growth of the stock does not keep pace with that of the scion.

LATE STRAWBERRIES (*M. D. Y.*).—If, in addition to your *Keen's Seedlings*, you grow the *British Queen*, *Elton*, and *White Alpine*, you may have a succession of strawberries from your open borders from June to November.

HEATING (*C.*).—We are sorry that you have been to the expense of a Polmaise structure, and are now obliged to abandon it; and it is poor comfort to know that you only share the fate common to most who have tried it. The surface of hot water pipe you propose to use is not sufficiently large for your greenhouse, and we should recommend it to be six-inch pipe instead of four-inch. For your pit, the three-inch pipe will be sufficient. Zinc piping would be cheaper at first, but infinitely dearer in the end, than cast iron, for it is perpetually out of order. The size of the boiler is of no consequence; the only material consideration being what amount of surface is exposed to the fire. A boiler, with a bottom exposing three square feet to the fire, will be sufficient for your purpose. The difference between the level of the flow and return pipe need not be more than twelve inches. Do not place the return pipe lower than the level of the bottom of your boiler.

BEDDING PLANTS (*J. R. R.*).—The very lists you request, "for laying out a garden, in enclosed plan, upon Mr. Beaton's principles," have lately been copiously supplied by that gentleman himself. It could not serve our purpose to reprint these lists, as Mr. Beaton has refused to plant gardens on paper. For ourselves we may remark, however, that such things as *zinias*, *amaranths*, and a *standard rose*, are entirely unsuited to small circles in a regular set of beds like yours; that is, they are too high. To plant the four corner large figures in the same proportion, you would require plants 12 feet high. Read what Mr. Beaton wrote about the terrace flower-garden at Kew; that is the right style for your garden.

ROOM PLANTS (*Sigma*).—You will find a detailed answer to-day.

SALVIA PATENS AND FULGENS (*Litherland*). — These, in the majority of cases, will not stand the winter without protection. We have cut them down and covered the bed with ashes and tan, and they have come strong. Those left in the beds will flower almost as soon as those taken up. The *S. patens*, having fine large tubers, may be kept in sand, like dahlias, until they begin to spring; it is best to take up some, and make sure. The *S. patens* is also freely propagated from seed, gathered when ripe, and sown in a little heat in spring; the seedlings pricked out into pots, and transplanted in May. Such make nice strong bushy plants.

MIMULUS (*Ibid*).—The most of these are hardy enough in damp situations, and sheltered, but the finer and rare kinds are generally kept in cold pits during winter. They propagate freely from seeds and cuttings; the latter mode is the only one to secure the variety true.

ECCREMOCARPUS SCABER (*Ibid*).—Instead of sowing now, we should decidedly recommend you, as you propose, to take up and pot the old plants when done flowering, which may be housed, under a stage in a greenhouse, or in a cold pit, and will break strong and flower abundantly next season. If, however, your situation is anything dry, the fleshy roots will remain in the soil well enough all the winter, with the covering of a little moss and ashes to keep off cold and wet, and exclude slugs, which are fond of feeding on them in mild weather.

PEGS FOR VERBENAS (*Ibid*).—No doubt you may get plenty of these from the ferns and they will answer well, but we never *peg* any. We prefer sticking the ground with brushwood, to keep the plants from the ground.

ALOES (*W. H.*).—These are succulent evergreen greenhouse plants of rather easy culture, provided the pots are well drained, and filled with sandy loam, peat, and a little brick rubbish; and during summer top-dressed with old cow dung, or watered with a solution of a cool kind of manure-water. Like other succulents, scarcely any water will be required in winter; and the temperature will answer well if at a medium of 40°. They will take no harm when dormant, if frost be excluded. Cuttings strike freely in loose soil.

YUCCA (*Ibid*).—With the exception of requiring a richer light soil, and more water both in winter and summer, the greenhouse species require similar treatment to the aloe. The hardy species—and all the more lovely on that account—should have the place where they are planted well drained, and a rich light compost secured, such as one part of peat, two of loam, one of old reduced cowdung, half a part of rough lime rubbish, and half a part of silver sand. They are propagated by suckers.

TURNER'S BUDDING INSTRUMENT (*E. H. T.*).—We are not aware of any agent in London for its sale. If you write to "Mr. John Turner, Neepsend, Sheffield," telling him how many you require, he will send them free by post.

FUCHSIA CUTTINGS (*T. M. W.*).—The stems of these decay whilst the leaves remain green. The soil, probably, has not enough sand mixed with it, and is kept too moist.

TRANSFERRING BEES (*Ibid*).—The box into which "A Country Curate" transferred the bees, as described at pages 279-80, was empty. You will observe he kept them constantly supplied with food. Mr. Payne promises to write upon transferring in his next calendar.

ELDER WINE (*Ibid*).—To every gallon of elder-berries, after they are picked from the stalks, add two gallons of water, and let them stand for two days. Then boil them, and when soft break the fruit, and run the liquor through a hair sieve. To every gallon of this juice add 3½ lbs. of sugar, with a bag of spice in the proportion of 1 oz. ginger, ¼ oz. cloves, and ¾ oz. allspice, with a very little cinnamon, to every four gallons of berries. Let this boil altogether for about twenty minutes, and before it is quite cold toast a piece of bread, cover it with yeast, and put it into the wine to set it working, which it must be allowed to do for two or three days; then skim it clean, and put it into the cask. The wine may be bottled, and drank at Christmas, or it will keep for years. Coarse Lisbon sugar may be used with safety; but there is so little difference now in the price that we recommend the loaf in preference.

DRIFT SAND (*G.*).—The drift sand washed down from the limestone hills would improve the staple of the clay lands in your neighbourhood. The quantity scarcely could be too large. It should be well incorporated by ridging and trenching.

VINEGAR PLANT (*Rec. P. B.*).—We never made vinegar from treacle by the aid of the plant, but consider, that if left a little longer than required when sugar is used the effect would be the same. Leave the vinegar for a few days after the plant is taken out, and it will be found to have become quite clear; at least it does so when loaf sugar is used.

HIMALAYAN PUMPKINS DROPPING (*W. D.*).—These, as well as cucumbers and melons, will fall off when about the size of pigeons' eggs, if the water given is abundant, and the temperature low. In cool weather give less water. Your *Dahlia-leaves* have probably been devoured by slugs.

SHOOTS OF NEWLY-BUDDED ROSES (*Oxoniensis*).—The roses you budded last year have made shoots five or six feet long. Do not cut them back now, but wait until February; then cut them back so as to leave only four or five buds. See page 148 of vol. iii.

TO RENDER LEATHER WATERPROOF (*M. D.*).—We should try Indian rubber dissolved in naptha; but as for this we have no experience either of ourselves or others, we give you two recipes which come from almost the opposite poles of the earth. *North American Recipe*—Boil together for half an hour one quart of linseed oil, two ounces of rosin, and half an ounce of powdered white vitriol; remove the mixture from the fire, and add four ounces of spirit of turpentine, and two ounces of very fine and very dry oak sawdust. Mix well, and apply when cold with a brush. *South American Recipe*—Dry the leather, apply a coat of tallow, dry this in by the fire, and then, by means of a brush, apply a mixture of one pint balsam of copaiba and a quart of naptha.

KILLING TREES WITH SALT (*Philocarpus*).—Boring a hole into the root or trunk of a tree, and filling it with salt, will not kill it. The only mode of killing a tree with salt, is by applying large quantities to the soil about the roots, so that they imbibe it in excess with the moisture of the earth. It must be in very great excess, or it will only partially kill it. An excess of any soluble salt will destroy either an animal or a plant.

CHAMOMILE CULTURE (*W. H. W.*).—Plant offsets, or divisions of the roots, or sow seed, in February or March. If from seed, when the seedlings are three inches high, thin them to six inches apart, and they must remain thus until the following spring, then to be planted out in rows at eighteen inches apart from plant to plant. They require no other attention than giving water at the time of planting, and frequently hoeing afterwards. Offsets are planted at the same distances, and produce flowers the same year. These are to be gathered just as they open; and they are best dried quickly and *thoroughly* before storing. A light dry soil produces flowers most potent in bitter principle.

CLEMATIS AND PASSION-FLOWER (*H. H.*).—You may cut these back in the autumn; October is as good a month as any for the operation.

NAMES OF PLANTS (*H. G. B.*).—Your plant is *Canna Indica*, or Common Indian Shot. (*F. S. B.*).—Your's is *Fragaria Indica*, or Yellow Indian Strawberry. It is not poisonous, and is closely related to the Potentilla. (*T. Mercer*).—You have named all the specimens correctly except two. 1. Is *Tagetes lucida*, and 2; is *Saponaria vaccaria*.

LONDON: Printed by HARRY WOOLDRIDGE, Winchester High-street, in the Parish of Saint Mary Kalendar; and Published by WILLIAM SOMERVILLE ORR, at the Office, No. 2, Amen Corner, in the Parish of Christ Church, City of London.—August 22nd, 1850.

WEEKLY CALENDAR.

M W D D	AUGUST 29—SEPTEMBER 4, 1850.	Weather near London in 1849.	Sun Rises.	Sun Sets.	Moon R. & S.	Moon's Age.	Clock bef. Sun.	Day of Year.
29 Th	St. John Baptist beheaded. Martins collect on	T. 79°–65°. N.W. Fine.	9 a. 5	53 a. 6	10 a. 2	22	0 49	241
30 F	Red Bryony Berries ripe. roofs.	T. 76°–60°. S. Rain.	11	51	10 38	23	0 31	242
31 S	Peaches ripe. [Butterfly seen.]	T. 75°–53°. N. Rain.	12	48	11 22	24	0 13	243
1 Sun	14 Sun. Aft. Trin. Giles. Clouded Yellow	T. 69°–52°. E. Rain.	v	vi	morn.	25	0 6	244
2 M	London burnt, 1666, O. S. Barberries ripe.	T. 77°–52°. S.W. Rain.	15	44	0 15	26	0 26	245
3 Tu	Traveller's Joy flowers.	T. 80°–53°. S. Rain.	17	42	1 29	27	0 44	246
4 W	Horticultural Society's Meeting.	T. 76°–58°. N.E. Fine.	19	40	2 36	28	1 3	247

Who ever knew a bad man fond of gardening? As far as our experience goes, we think the universal reply must be—No one. It is quite true that paid officers of societies connected with gardening, and the cultivators of any one tribe of florists' flowers, may be excepted; for we have known in both these classes of amateurs characters wicked like him who Milton describes as, while "each passion dimm'd his face," moving among the flowers of Paradise. Some of such men's love of gardening may extend no further than is necessary to retain their salary; or, as in the case of one tulip fancier we knew, may proceed only so far as a love of fine colouring and to knowing, according to his own phrase, "my neighbour has no such flowers as these." Such men are not among "the true lovers of gardening;" for these are such—and only such—as prefer to all other modes of existence, "domestic life in rural pleasure pass'd." Of these such was John Locke. What! Locke the metaphysical philosopher, the analyst of the human understanding, the regulator of our coinage, the arbiter of education, the advocate of Christianity, and the Scriptural critic? Even so: Locke was all this, and more than all, for he was that rare character—a good man ever acting up to what he considered his duty. Even he was a gardener too; he could trace out the minutest ramification of philosophic reasoning, yet took delight in "his garden with its many cares." He was naturally very active, says his biographer; he loved walking, but not being able to walk much, through the disorder of his lungs, he used to ride after dinner; and "sometimes he diverted himself with working in the garden, which he well understood." It is not this love of gardening, however, nor even his spotless worth, that would entitle him to a notice in this brief nook of our pages, if he had not written upon the cultivation of certain plants connected with our appropriate subjects.

In 1675 Mr. Locke, fearing that his asthmatic symptoms tended towards consumption, travelled to the south of France, and resided long at Montpellier. Whilst there, he noted down all his remarks and knowledge acquired whilst visiting the neighbouring vineyards, olive-yards, and mulberry plantations. These notes were eventually published, with the title, *Observations upon the growth and culture of Vines and Olives: the production of Silk . and the preservation of Fruits.* It is a very small pamphlet, but interesting, not only because from the pen of such a man, but because it is a faithful narrative of the culture of the vine at the time when he wrote. Do any of our readers know this grape which he thus describes? "*Grumeau negre,* or the Black Grumeau—an excellent large grape, very fleshy, and well enough tasted, of the fashion of a pear.

I have seen one single grape of this sort which was in compass above 3¼ inches English measure, and in compass the long way 3⅔, and weighed of their weights half an ounce, one drachm, three grains, and all the rest of the grapes of the same bunch proportionable; but I have not observed it ordinarily planted in their vineyards." It is like having to epitomise a folio volume within the circumference of a sixpence to mark the career of such a man within our brief space, but we cannot resign our pen without some further notice. His introduction to Lord Shaftesbury, by one of those events we thoughtlessly term an accident, influenced all his after life. Admitted to an intimacy with him and the leading characters of the day, they appreciated and submitted to the spirit of appropriately applied wisdom that ever characterised him. Upon one occasion, when the noblemen assembled adjourned to the card-table almost without conversation, Mr. Locke sat by them with his pencil and pocket-book before him; and the reason being asked, he replied. "My Lord, I am endeavouring to profit, as far as I am able, in your company; for having waited with impatience for the honour of being in an assembly of the greatest geniuses of this age, and at last having obtained the good fortune, I thought I could not do better than write down your conversation; and, indeed, I have set down the substance of what has been said for this hour or two." He was not called upon to read much of this record; but enjoying the jest, and feeling the justice of the ridicule, they quitted the card-table, and passed the evening more suitably. We need not here dwell upon the years of exile he endured; for whether right or wrong in his political opinions, he acted conscientiously, was certainly guilty of no crime, except in the eyes of such a king as James II., and therefore rightly declined to accept a pardon from him. "I have no occasion for a pardon," was his reply, "since I have not been guilty of any crime." Under William III. he met with such treatment as his surpassing merit deserved; but he resigned his reward—his Commissionership of Trade—as soon as he became unable to perform its duties. The king personally pressed him to retain it as a sinecure; but Mr. Locke replied that he could not reconcile this with his conscience, and persisted in his resignation. He did not survive his retirement from office more than four years; and in an Essex church, that of High Laver, this epitaph, prepared by himself, may tell the rest :—

"Stop, Traveller. Hard by lies John Locke. If you ask what kind of man he was, he answers—that he lived contented with his own mediocrity. When initiated in literature, he progressed so far as to contend for truth only. Learn this from his writings, which will shew you what remains of him more faithfully than the suspicious eulogium of an epitaph. He would set forth whatsoever virtues he had far less for his own praise than for an example to you. Let his faults only be burned. If you seek an example of morality, you have one in the Gospel,—of vices, I could wish, no-where,—of mortality, surely, one which may profit you, here and every-where. He was born A.D. 1632, August 29th; and died A.D. 1704, October 28th."

Meteorology of the Week.—From observations made at Chiswick during twenty-three years, the average highest and lowest temperatures of these days are 70.5° and 49°, respectively. The greatest heat, 88°, was on the 1st of September, 1815; and the extreme cold, 36°, on the same day, 1841. Of the days, 95 were fine, and on 66 rain fell.

RANGE OF BAROMETER—RAIN IN INCHES.

Aug.		1841.	1842.	1843.	1844.	1845.	1846.	1847.	1848.	1849.
29	B.	30.159	29.959	30.037	30.138	30.363	30.010	30.145	29.995	29.896
		29.920	29.955	29.964	30.113	30.271	29.929	30.097	29.970	29.927
	R.	—	0.52	—	—	—	—	0.01	0.03	—
30	B.	29.998	30.011	30.138	30.152	30.295	30.172	30.065	30.050	29.858
		29.940	30.003	30.003	30.127	30.262	30.095	29.976	30.022	29.823
	R.	—	—	—	—	—	—	—	—	0.06
31	B.	29.844	30.151	30.195	30.293	30.288	30.178	30.009	30.058	29.864
		29.729	30.137	30.158	30.278	30.266	30.132	29.951	30.029	29.844
	R.	0.02	0.22	—	—	—	—	—	1.31	0.26
Sept. 1	B.	30.092	30.062	30.292	30.390	30.378	30.361	29.896	30.201	29.783
		29.991	29.992	29.043	30.335	30.200	30.180	29.729	30.140	29.675
	R.	—	0.46	—	—	—	—	0.01	—	0.24
2	B.	29.843	30.175	30.333	30.322	30.179	30.287	29.967	30.382	29.745
		29.752	30.075	30.300	30.192	30.164	30.269	29.766	30.340	29.684
	R.	—	—	—	—	—	—	—	—	0.04
3	B.	29.591	30.203	30.284	30.097	30.301	30.280	29.967	30.362	29.953
		29.499	30.153	30.200	30.090	30.195	30.227	29.698	30.254	29.874
	R.	0.48	—	—	—	—	—	0.03	—	0.12
4	B.	29.775	30.197	30.330	29.977	30.395	30.233	29.879	30.174	30.064
		29.444	30.193	30.255	29.926	30.180	30.163	29.827	29.929	30.030
	R.	0.32	0.01	0.02	0.02	—	—	—	—	—

Insects.—We have to-day represented the Garden Tiger Moth (*Arctia,* or *Euprepia caja*), chiefly because some particulars concerning its caterpillar will answer more than one query relative to the voracity of such larvæ generally. The moth is given of its natural size; its fore-wings are a reddish brown, irregularly marked with creamy white; hind-wings, bright red, with blueblack spots; thorax, brown, with a red neck-band; abdomen, red, with blueblack bars. It appears in July. The caterpillar from which it arises is found in June, and is very destructive when it occasionally occurs in numbers on the strawberry and lettuce. They are dark brown, densely covered with reddish brown hairs, and so stiff and pointed are these, that it has been suggested they might be administered like Cowhage to destroy intestinal worms. The skin, when cast, is very entire—so much so, that if saved you seem to have ten different specimens of caterpillars, yet all representing the same individual. They are very voracious, and will eat fully twice their own weight daily, which is about the same as if an ordinary sized man were to eat 3 cwt. of food per day. This arises from their only retaining the juice of the leaf they eat; for if their excrement is put into water the shreds of leaf uncoil. One of these caterpillars weighing 36 grains voided daily more than 15 grains weight of excrements, yet its own weight only increased two grains daily.

THE next subject connected with the employment of *hard water*, are its prejudicial effects in cookery. Upon this point M. Soyer made the following statements to the Sanitary Commissioners in answer to their queries:—

" What was the effect of the hardness in cooking ?—That we were in many processes obliged to use potass or soda for the water, to soften it.

What were the processes ?—First, in boiling cabbage, greens, spinach, asparagus, hard water gives them a yellow tinge, especially in French beans : hard water shrivels greens and peas, and will be more particularly noticed in French beans ; the process of boiling is also longer.

That requires more fuel ?—Certainly.

What would be the difference in time ?—With dry vegetables certainly one-fourth more.

How is it with potatoes ?—I do not think it acts so much upon potatoes, but still it has an influence upon all sorts of vegetables. I do not see the same effects however upon roots generally as upon leaves generally ; the effects are very powerful.

What do you find to be the effect of hard water upon the animal foods ?—Upon salt beef the hard water is not so good, it does not open the pores of the meat so freely as soft water. On fresh meat it likewise has a prejudicial effect, but not equal to that on vegetables. It has the effect of making very white meat whiter than the soft water ; upon all delicate things it has however a more marked effect—for example, in making beef tea, chicken or veal broth, or upon lamb ; and the more delicate a substance is the greater is the influence of a hard water upon it. A hard water as it were compresses the pores, whilst a soft water dilates them and the succulent matter which they contain. It makes them more nutritious. The evil of hard water is more visible in small quantities, such as broth or beef-tea.

Then it will be the more prejudicial or expensive in domestic cookery, which must be in small quantities ?— Exactly so ; in the larger operations, where there is much boiling, the boiling itself, and for a long time, reduces the hardness. In the small quantities requisite for invalids and delicate persons the disadvantages are the most experienced. When I used Thames water at Gwydyr House, I have had quantities boiled in order to soften it, and have then let it get cool and kept it ready for use for the smaller operations.

What is the effect of hard water upon bread?—I have not had practical experience in bread-making ; but there is not the least doubt that soft water is of the greatest importance in making the best bread. This is exemplified in Paris, where the water is hard, and where that bread which is made in imitation of Gonness bread, though made with the same flour and by the same bakers, never equals that made at the place itself, where the water is soft. I am informed that part of the water at Glasgow is very soft, and that the Scotch bakers from thence, when they first come to London, cannot understand why the bread does not rise so well as in Glasgow, even though they make use of the same yeast and flour. It is well known that the addition of a small quantity of bi-carbonate of magnesia in the water renders bread lighter and whiter."

The chemistry of all this is very apparent. The reason that hard water changes the green colour of vegetables from green to yellowish brown is, that vegetable greens are always altered to the latter colour when boiled in a solution of the salts of the alkaline earths, such as lime, which is the common cause of a water's hardness. Soda and potash, on the contrary, have the property of increasing the intensity of vegetable greens, taking from the leaves boiled all the acid matter tending to turn them brown, and changing all their blue tints to a decided green. The calcareous or limy salts act upon the flesh-meat boiled in water containing them, by combining with its albumen and extractive matter, so as to render a portion of these insoluble ; and if much lime is added these components are rendered entirely insoluble. The importance of this is at once seen, when we know that on the albumen and extractive matters nearly all the nutriment and flavour of the meat depend.

There is much more philosophy in the boiling of meat than most persons, for want of thought, may recognise. In a black iron saucepan water boils much sooner than in a polished tin saucepan, of similar size and thickness of metal, simply because black surfaces absorb heat more rapidly than polished surfaces. Water in a tin or other metal saucepan will boil at 212°, under the ordinary pressure of the air, but under the same pressure in an earthen or glass vessel it requires for boiling 214°, because at the lower temperature earthenware does not conduct the heat fast enough to keep up the ebullition or boiling. Hard water requires a higher temperature to boil it than soft water, and the more of any salt that is added the higher the temperature required to boil the water. Soups and other thick liquids require a higher temperature than water for boiling for the same reason ; namely, that whatever hinders the rapid rise of the bubbles from the part of the vessel admitting the heat, requires them to be so much more heated before they acquire the requisite elasticity enabling them to rise to the surface, which rapid rise and conversion into steam constitutes boiling.

COMMON sense usually succeeds in whatever it undertakes ; and this was never better exemplified than in a letter on cow-keeping we publish to-day from the pen of the widely, and as well as widely, known Miss Martineau. This letter, we happen to know, was written at the request of the Poor Law Commissioners, and how it has reached the newspapers, from one of which we copy it, is one of the mysteries of journalism. We also happen to know that Miss Martineau continues so well satisfied with her success, that she either has taken or intends to take on lease another half acre, for the purpose of growing the potatoes required for her household and all the keep for her cows and pigs. The average produce of milk stated in her letter may seem small, but we must remember that it includes the three months during which each cow was allowed to be dry before calving. This is an unnecessarily long time ; and we shall take an early opportunity of stating in detail another instance of successful cow-management with still greater produce.

THE FRUIT-GARDEN.

FRESH SOILS, COMPOSTS, &c.—There are two reasons why no better period during the whole year can be chosen for collecting and preparing soils for the ensuing winter operations in the fruit-garden, than the early part of September, provided the weather is dry. In the first place, soils should never be handled when in a close or stagnant state : and in the second, there can be no doubt that loams and other adhesive soils are then much fuller of the gaseous matter of the atmosphere than at any other period. Soils handled in a damp state become what country folks term " livered," or, as some have it, "soured,"—their particles become forced closer together, whereby the qualifying and wholesome air contained in their interstices is forced out, and the air cavities, of course, compressed. This occurs through the tread of the foot of either man or horse, and is also continually taking place through the action of the spade or other implement employed in digging and collecting it.

Soils thus circumstanced are with difficulty pulverized again; indeed, if buried forthwith below the ground level, they will long retain these awkward properties; and if preserved in the compost yard, many months pass away, and some handling is requisite, in order to get them in a wholesome condition again. They are fuller of the invigorating and mellowing agencies of the atmosphere in the end of summer; for it is well known how pent-up and stagnant moisture becomes evaporated by the heat of summer, the place of which must of necessity be filled with air.

Strong soils, moreover, contract much by drying, and this, as is well known, causes them to rift in all directions; which mechanical action is of the utmost benefit to the soil, as ultimately promoting easy pulverising. We need scarcely add, that the latter process is absolutely essential to fertility.

Now, a winter's fallow, or exposure to the alternations of frost and thaw, will produce the same mechanical effects; but then the soil becomes filled again with moisture. Thus it will be readily seen why the end of summer is decidedly the most eligible time to collect soils. Another point recommends this course: the turfy material at this period contains a greater amount of *organic matter* than at any other period. Gross herbage will be found to prevail, and a vast accumulation of organic remains of the previous spring's growth; and we need scarcely say, that all good cultivators esteem their soils in proportion to the amount of organic matter they contain.

We would have all young gardeners pay the utmost attention to these points. Much, very much is to be learned from the study of this apparently simple affair. Of course the remarks here made apply principally to what are termed loams,—that indefinite class of soils fully understood by the practical man, the squeeze of whose thumb and finger will determine with tolerable accuracy the character of such soils.

We have given in a back number of THE COTTAGE GARDENER, a definition of what constitutes the gardener's loam; but we fear it will be almost as difficult to convey a truly satisfactory idea to the mind of a person ill informed in gardening matters, as it would to a young amateur grazier as to what constitutes "handling, feel and touch" to the old veteran grazier.

The aspirants for horticultural fame, however, of the rising generation, may fairly exult in their position in this respect, as compared with some other classes of society; for by means of such periodicals as THE COTTAGE GARDENER, they have these abstruse technicalities, conventionalities, &c., &c., made realities, and brought fairly home to them.

Now, it must not be supposed that in speaking of composts, soils, &c., that we would wish our readers to infer that we are continually harping about loam. It must be confessed that loam—good loam—is the very elixir of the compost yard; still, as we are not advising the year round about strawberry potting, melon culture, and the like, we must cast our eyes over the wants of the cottager and the amateur, and see what advice can be given them in the improvement of the staple in their respective plots, more especially as concerns fruit-tree culture.

Various, then, are the materials that may be collected for such purposes, varying, too, with districts. Besides, the question is not always what *ought* to be had, but what *can* be had; and it so happens that many self-taught amateurs, possessed of much horticultural acumen, will turn materials to account which the gardener of my Lord Duke would utterly despise. Amateurs, cottagers, &c., as well as folks already possessed of good gardens, frequently have to enclose and reclaim plots of ground where nothing of a loamy character exists. Sometimes the new plot is gravelly, sometimes very sandy, and ofttimes of a peaty, boggy, or moor soil character. It not unfrequently happens, also, that the plot is in a town or in the suburbs, where, it may be, brick rubbish and the most ordinary soil lie side by side in pell-mell confusion.

In anticipating improvements in such soils or sites, the first thing, of course, is valorously to determine on thorough drainage, if necessary. This we will take for granted. Next, to consider the general character of the plot, and if great inequalities exist in point of texture, to determine on making the clay help the sand and gravel, or *vice-versa*, as the case may be. These things concluded and plans of culture laid down, it will be readily ascertained how much and what character of improvable material is requisite to carry out the plan. Such, then, forms a legitimate course of procedure for the end of summer, provided the chance offers; and an active and thinking person will set about getting together materials according to the demand.

We need hardly remind townsfolk or suburbans of the facility that exists in general for getting together such imperishable materials as brick-rubbish, old plaster, charred material, &c., &c., by which to open the staple of soils, hitherto too retentive of moisture. On the other hand, the refuse of the carpenter's bench or workshop may be sought, for such things as shavings, sawdust, &c., all of which are available as vegetable or organic matter, to add to the embryo dung-heap.

The turfy material from ordinary commons or wastes is not to be despised because it is easily procurable. It is astonishing what an amount of nutritive qualities is contained in the surface skimmings of such places, albeit the staple of the soil beneath is below consideration. Here will be found an accumulation of vegetable matter, the work, it may be, of ages; and here by consequence, a vast amount of that pabulum, or those nutritive qualities which all organic matter in its progressive decay furnishes in a steady way to the generation of vegetables or trees by which it is superseded.

We have now been speaking of organic matter chiefly; for, indeed, many sterile plots need much in this way. We have many a time seen fresh garden enclosures, or reclaimed waste lands, in which a thorough drainage and a liberal addition of such matters, would at once set the plot a going.

Speaking of the obtaining of materials for improvements, we may here advert to the one of *charred matter*, and in so doing must beg to recommend those who wish to avail themselves of such a useful and profitable article, to direct their attention at once to its accumulation. No better time can be taken for the purpose. Nature, ever bountiful in her vegetable productions, has, by the month of September, covered every common and wild, every lane and roadside, and even the most barren moor with coarse herbage, adapted to work up in this way. Moreover, the garden itself, with its appurtenances of hedge clippings and other coarse material, yields at this period an unusual amount of stuff, capable of being made into a most useful component of a renewing compost.

Let us, then, advise strongly that this principle be attended to, and at this season; and that all weeds and rubbish be collected to one common spot, both to promote order and decency and to augment the compost heap, against the days of alterations and improvement.

We must again revert to the subject of loamy materials. Loams are used in general to give stability and consistence to shingly and incoherent soils. Now, since what the gardener terms loam, or "sound loam," contains a considerable per centage of clayey matter, it is evident that clay itself, or, what is better when procurable, marl, may be advantageously employed.

In the improvement of the staple, then. of loose or sandy soils, there is no doubt that even clay will be beneficial, provided it is laid on the land betimes in the autumn, and not blended with the soil until it has fallen to pieces, which will be the case by the month of March, if it is turned and worked occasionally. In making stations for fruit-trees on such soils, we should unhesitatingly throw masses of clay in a raw state on the proposed platform, taking care to introduce weedy or vegetable matter liberally amongst it; for the two will act well together for years as a preventive against extreme droughts, which so frequently cause fruits of various kinds to crack, as also the trees to be devoured with the red spider and other insects. Let it be remembered, nevertheless, that we are speaking of dry and light soils only; to pursue such a course on cool soils, would be a most unwise procedure.

Marl, however, whether of the clay or slate kinds, is, of course, far superior to clay; but not every one is fortunate enough to be situated in a marly neighbourhood. This may be blended liberally with all light or sandy materials for fruit-tree stations, taking care that it is divided first, and adding vegetable matter freely.

Before concluding these remarks, we may be permitted to turn our attention to the amateur's melons, pines, strawberries, and other fruits, for forcing purposes. A good loam is almost indispensable for high culture in these things. Every one should endeavour annually to procure a little fresh, for sometimes it becomes expedient to use it fresh, or to mix them, as the case may be. We have before repeatedly described the consistence of such materials; we may now add, that the more coarse herbage it possesses the better. What are termed furrowing clods are excellent; and a stipulation may sometimes be entered into with the farmer, who would exchange such for manure; or they may sometimes be had for the labour necessary to procure them.　　　　　　　　　　　　　R. ERRINGTON.

THE FLOWER-GARDEN.

MOVING LARGE EVERGREENS.—One could hardly meet with a gardener of extensive practice, "in a day's march," who could not affirm, that evergreen trees and bushes—yea, that all kinds of trees and shrubs, whether evergreen or otherwise—*might* be planted any month in the year, or "all the year round," provided that gentlemen choose to incur the expenses of the operation; and those who know little or nothing on the subject are firm in their belief, that the whole secret lies in these "expenses," on the principle, as I suppose, that "money makes the mare to go."

Much of our earliest knowledge of planting was first borrowed from nurserymen, whose more immediate business it was to remove young stock, and, as a matter of course, were supposed to have learned by experience the fittest seasons for transplanting the different families which they reared. Whether it was that nurserymen were more wise in their generation than gardeners, or whether it suited their purpose better, it would be now difficult to prove; but sure it was that they, the said nurserymen, advised, or rather convinced, a race of gardeners, that late in the spring was the safest period to remove their evergreens. "Here we are," said they, "we never arrange our quarters of evergreens till the sale for the plants is over;" and, as "early closing" was not then thought of, he who kept his nursery longest open in the spring had so much the more chance of a

longer sale; and thus the planting of evergreens in April in the course of time became a positive creed with those concerned. The consequences of this belief gave rise to another creed, which affirmed, that evergreens were difficult to transplant at the best of times. A dry May setting in on the heels of a late removal of these plants was sure to kill many of them before they got hold of the new ground; but this was overlooked when a dripping May succeeded the operation and all went on well. The scorching of the leaves, or the death of the branches, or—which as often happened—the death of the whole plant, was put down as the necessary consequence of the difficulty of removing this tribe of plants. All this, however, and more also, is now only a matter of history; evergreens, of all ages and sizes, are found to be as easily removed as deciduous ones, under the same circumstances; and it is far more difficult to remove or transplant a popular creed or prejudice than any trees whatever.

Of late years planters of evergreens have been divided into two classes: spring planters, from February to May; and late autumn planters, who would remove all kinds of evergreens in November. But the most successful planter of evergreens in England—indeed, the best planter of them in the world—Mr. Barron, gardener to Lord Harrington, at Elvaston Castle, in Derbyshire, has proved beyond a doubt, that midsummer, or between that and the end of July, is the true season in our climate for the removal of very large specimens. He would make no more "ado" about removing a few at that season that had been planted in the time of Henry VIII., than some planters would if they had to transplant ten yards of box edging round a bed of roses next Michaelmas. It is asserted by Mr. Barron's friends (for he does not write much himself), that his criterion for the proper time to remove a large evergreen is, when it ceases to make its annual growth. This may happen a few weeks earlier or later in different seasons, according to the lateness or earliness of our springs; therefore, to say that midsummer, or any given period, is preferable to a few weeks before or after it, would not be quite right. I have seen enough of plants and planting to convince me that Mr. Barron's time and criterion for this kind of planting are the true ones; and I shall go one step more—having a proof of the assertion in my pocket—and say, that when a large evergreen is so near the place where it is to be transplanted to, as that the work may be completed in a couple of hours from the time the roots are uncovered, the hotter the day and the more cloudless the sky, the more surely will the plant succeed, provided there is no screen put between it and the sun in the new situation, as has been recommended by some. But if the plant has to be removed from a distance, so that its roots and its leaves are acted on by the sun and air longer than the balance between them will hold out, the work would be more safe in cloudy or rainy weather. In either case, and in all planting of large evergreens in summer, the planting is more sure if done in water, that is, to allow an open space for the roots to be laid out at full length; and to wash in the soil amongst them with water, by first throwing the soil on the ball of earth which accompanied the roots, and then pouring water over it to wash it down among the roots. In very hot weather roots will suck up their full from this watering in a few hours, and fresh roots are made in a few days, from which, and the fresh soil, a plant from a poor soil may be better fed, and do better afterwards, than if it had not been removed at all. If we now suppose some unforeseen accident to have caused the roots to reject the water, and not to extend themselves by new growth for one week, why in that case death would ensue immediately.

Some six and thirty years since, the late Sir William Middleton brought a packet of seeds of the tree box from Box Hill, in Surrey, from which a great number of plants have been reared by Mr. Lovett, his gardener—now one of the most contented race of our old gardeners, living in "a cottage near a wood" in the middle of the park, and although in his eightieth year he enjoys a walk round the gardens as much as any of us, to see "all these new fancies," as he terms the present style of gardening. Some of those box trees which Mr. Lovett planted thirty years since on a long dry bank under large trees, now form a thick screen for a "winter garden," from which, when we want a "box," we can draw full-grown plants without being missed. Among other "new fancies," we resolved last May to make a hedge of full-grown box-trees for one side of a new terrace, which was in progress under the directions of Mr. Barry, the celebrated architect. At first, it was proposed to plant this box hedge next September, as recommended by Mr. Glendenning in the *Journal of the Horticultural Society*, who removed a hedge of large hollies for the Society last September with perfect success; but, on a second consideration, I wished to prove how far Mr. Barron's views of planting could be relied on upon a very different soil from that on which he has practised with such marked success; and as the plants were at hand, and no stint of them either, if we did fail the loss would not be felt. All this being duly considered, my worthy employers, seeing I had rather an itching for the job, gave their consent to have the hedge planted at once. The box was then in the middle of its growth, and I wished to wait until the growth was completed, which would be about the third week in June; but, owing to the arrangements of the masons and bricklayers, I must either get in the hedge at once or put it off till the middle of August. This was considered a point rather in favour of the planters, as if the box trees should die under the operation, they would have a loophole for escape, and could say "it was all owing" to their being removed at the critical time of their annual growth. A trench, twelve feet wide and four feet deep, was opened, the old soil removed, and a fresh supply carted in, and the trench was filled up to within 18 inches of the top; the whole was gently stamped down, as the soil was put in so that it could settle but very little afterwards, and when the bed was ready for the plants, that is, within eighteen inches of the top, it was stamped down quite close. There were two reasons for this last pressing of the soil: the first reason, that it should not settle as I have just said; and the second, that the water should not pass through it readily when the plants were watered. This would have been a very injudicious proceeding on some soils, although in our case it was necessary. The soil here is so light, that a fresh bed of it, like the one for this box-hedge, would let the water pass right through it to the bottom, without doing any good for the plants, unless it was thus compressed; whereas some retentive soils, if this process were applied to them, would not drain at all, which would be as injurious the other way. Now, here is one of those sources of disappointment and vexation inseparable from the system of learning how to do particular things from books. We read of so and so having been performed with great success, and we think that by following the writer step by step we must also succeed in similar attempts. Here, then, is where the "practical" man has the advantage over the book man; the book may put us on the right scent, but unless we have as much practical knowledge as will show us how far we may be justified in carrying out a set of rules under different circumstances, we may make a mess of it after all our reading. Hence the reason why I would not recommend others, under different circumstances, to follow me implicitly in the planting of large evergreens, even at any season.

To make this experiment more complete, I made it a point that none of the men engaged in the gardens should have a finger in it. I took half a dozen strong men who worked on the farm, with spades, pickaxes, and three tined strong forks, and set them to work on Monday the third of June, and in ten days the hedge was planted, which then looked as if it had been growing there these twenty years. The first five weeks passed with only one slight shower, and the sun poured his unbroken rays on the hedge all the time; in short, every thing tended to test the experiment of planting large bushes or trees at midsummer, on light soils; and no experiment could be more complete—not a single leaf drooped, and even the young growth went on without let or hindrance, just as if the plants had not been interfered with at all. If the same men had continued to plant large trees or bushes from that day to this, I can see no reason why a single leaf on all the plants removed should take any hurt; and if that be so, it is surely a safe time now to remove evergreens,—not only so, but every week that passes, from this day, will add to the disadvantages under which removed trees must more or less be liable. The Horticultural Society of London had set a very good example, by the removal of the holly hedge in their garden early in the autumn of last year; not but that gardeners were well aware of the fact, that such things *could* be done, but in a public place like their garden, and under the auspices of a public body, the thing was more likely to take the attention of the gardening world. The true time, however, to begin to transplant large evergreens, as I said before, is as early in July as their growth is finished for that season; and the credit of the discovery is undoubtedly due to Mr. Barron, at Elvaston Castle; and all that I, or, indeed, any other gardener has done in this line, is no more than picking up the crumbs from under his table.

There was nothing particular in the *modus operandi* of our proceedings in this instance; nevertheless, as amateurs like to read about the way such things are actually performed in practise, I shall in my next letter give a detailed account of how every item of the work was carried on, and, what is of more import, shall explain the reasons for every particular movement from first to last. Meantime, I would urge the great importance of the early removal of large evergreens, and now that no time be lost in preparing for immediate operation.   D. BEATON.

GREENHOUSE AND WINDOW GARDENING.

CLERODENDRUMS.—These beautiful plants are universal favourites, owing to their massive handsome foliage, and in general their large heads of scarlet blossoms. They who have stoves and propose growing them, will find a select list of the best kinds, and ample directions for culture, in a late number. With a little attention, however, some of the prettiest may be grown successfully with the assistance of a greenhouse, and such aid of bottom-heat for a short time as the common cucumber box could supply. Some of the readers of the COTTAGE GARDENER have expressed surprise at seeing fine plants used solely during summer for ornamenting the greenhouse, and other places where no artificial heat could be given; and, therefore, a few notes of our practice in this respect may render these flowers a more general luxury.

The family is native only of the tropical regions of both hemispheres. What a practical man would term the "*sight*" of the plants, would at once hint this fact; and if he knew nothing of their history, their appearance would lead him to consign them to the warm pit or stove. If kept there, he will find that they will be evergreens in their character, or a sort of *go-between* the ever green and deciduous. He finds, however, that if he treats it as an evergreen shrub, his flowers will every year become more diminutive and scanty, and that to have fine bloom it must be supported by strong, somewhat succulent, shoots. Taking other plants of a similar nature as a guide, he sees the importance—first, of thinning the shoots, to increase their luxuriance; and then, when that does not altogether answer, of pruning them back, that fresh and vigorous growth may be made by the stirred-up energies of the unmutilated roots: upon the same principle that the forester cuts down the stunted young tree through which the juices cannot pass freely, in order that he may obtain a more luxuriant sapling from the stump that is left. By-and-bye he will find, that if naturally an evergreen, the Clerodendrum may be treated as a deciduous plant, and pruned as closely as an amateur would do in the case of a rose from which he wished to obtain a few very fine, rather than a multitude of middling flowers.

Treated as a deciduous plant, the first thing of importance that presents itself is, the necessity of having the wood well ripened, at least near the base of the shoots; the second, giving the plants a season of rest; and the third, is the ability to give them a fair start in the spring, by proper attention to potting, warmth, and moisture. These things kept in mind, most of the Clerodendrums may be made subservient to greenhouse decoration from July to the middle of October, and with as little or rather less trouble than is required for an Achimenes, or even a Balsam.

The species we have found to answer best for this purpose are, *Kœmpherii, fallax, paniculatum*, and the old *fragrans flore pleno*. With the exception of the last, the first is the easiest managed. On smallish healthy plants four or five large heads of bloom may be obtained.

I shall now give the mode of treatment pursued, commencing from the present time. Wherever the plants are situated they will want a liberal supply of water; and weak liquid manure may either be given, or a dressing of rotten cowdung placed over the pot, through which the water may percolate. If close to the glass, strong sunshine will disfigure both flowers and foliage. It is better, therefore, either to place the plants farther from the glass, or give shade during the heat of the day. A little *size* put on the glass answers well with me. If kept in a good place a few seeds may ripen, which make nice little plants; but these, in your circumstances, you must keep dry during winter, and sow in a hot-bed in spring. If you could have commanded a temperature of from 55° to 65° during winter, we should have advised sowing them when gathered. The next thing is, in the autumn, to place your plants in the warmest part of the house, and in the full sunshine, and giving little or no air where they stand, and gradually lessening the supply of water, in order that your wood may be well hardened, especially near the base of the shoots; if the ends are green and spongy it will be of less consequence. By-and-bye, the ripening of the wood and the unsightly look of the plants will be effected together; and instead of staring your visitors in the face, remove them under your stage, at the end of the house where your furnace is situated. We used to leave them there unpruned; but two things must be here attended to :—First, *drippings* from the plants on the stage should not reach them to any extent, though damping the stems at times with the syringe will be advisable; a piece of glazed calico will prevent the drip. Secondly, the roots must be kept moistish, but scarcely ever watered; it is better to pack the pots loosely in moss, and damp the moss at times. Here, if the wood is moderately ripe, they will exist very well in a temperature of 45°; of course it would be higher in a bright sunny day.

About the beginning of March examine them, and prune away the shrivelled unripened wood from the ends of the shoots. If from four to six inches are left alternately it would be enough, as from three to six shoots will be enough finally to leave; but we do not recommend pruning back at first for two reasons: the first is, that the breaking of a number of buds will promote a vigorous root action; and, secondly, the young shoots themselves, when removed afterwards, will be valuable for propagating. After pruning thus partially, and stirring up the soil in the pot, place them where the plants will have more light and heat; if in a vinery, peach-house, &c., where forcing has commenced, and the temperature ranges from 55° to 60°, that will be the situation for them; if not, by one of the contrivances frequently alluded to, give less air, and more heat in the greenhouse; this would suit your geraniums, heaths, &c. When you perceive that the plant is giving signs of active vitality, remove it to a cucumber pit, and where the top heat will range from 60° to 70°, and the bottom heat will average 80°. Set the plant on the surface of the bed for a few days; then partially plunge it. When the young shoots are from half an inch to an inch in length, prepare for repotting it, by getting a mixture of peat and loam, and a little silver sand, using it in a lumpy state. Shake the most of the old soil from the roots; reshift into a similar or a smaller pot, pruning the roots a little, and laying them nicely among the fresh loam; plunge the pots in the bed, and use water at a temperature of 80°. Keep them close and shaded for a short time until fresh growth has freely commenced; then select the number of shoots you wish to have: prune back accordingly. The free growth will prevent the check being felt.

Flower-buds even now, especially on the Kœmpherii, will very likely appear; but they must be pinched off, as they will not be worth looking at until you get large leaves; the strongest bud will soon break into a shoot again, and your patience will be well rewarded. It is of no use having many shoots, as a few of the uppermost will monopolise all the strength.

If a huge head of bloom is desired, one shoot only should be left. If a compact plant with from four to six heads of bloom is wanted, then the strongest shoots will very likely require stopping, so as to get two shoots, and two flowers instead of one. In a month or six weeks the plants may be potted again—plunged; but by-and-bye when the pot is filled with roots pretty well, gradually removed from bottom-heat, and by June either removed to a warm close place in the greenhouse, or, what is better, placed in a cold-pit, where they can be kept rather close for a fortnight or three weeks. In this last potting, either use very rotten cow-dung—but dried into lumps, along with the compost—or make up your mind to top-dressing or manure waterings. As soon as the first flowers are opened they will stand anywhere under glass, provided they are shaded from very bright sunshine, and will be beautiful objects for three months, individual panicles remaining in bloom much longer than in a stove.

We return now for a moment to the young shoots adhering to the part cut off. These, of from one to three inches in length, if taken off with a *heel* close to the old stem, inserted in sand under a bell-glass, and in a good bottom-heat, and potted twice will furnish nice little plants by August and September, from one foot in height, and each with a pretty panicle of flowers. These, however, must be kept in the cucumber-bed until the flowers begin to open, and then be gradually hardened off to suit the greenhouse. The *Kœmpherii* succeeds best with us as young plants in this manner.

R. FISH.

HOTHOUSE DEPARTMENT.
STOVE PLANTS.

BROMELIACEÆ.—This is a numerous tribe of ornamental plants, numbers of which are now in cultivation. It contains also the well-known and highly esteemed fruit, *the Pine-apple*. This will, to our less informed readers, give an idea what kind of plants belong to the Natural Order Bromeliaceæ. And here we would just remark the grand advantage a very moderate knowledge of the natural system of arrangement of plants has over any artificial one whatever. The moment any one well-known plant is mentioned as belonging to a certain natural order, the mind takes cognizance of the whole tribe, as in the instance now mentioned. The *Ananassa* or Pine-apple belongs to Bromeliaceæ ; now, whenever any of our readers shall see a plant similar to a Pine-apple plant, in its mode of growth and habit, and with similar flowers produced out of the centre of the plant, they may be pretty sure it belongs to the same group of plants. We have chosen this tribe as the subject of our weekly paper, in consequence of having seen lately some very fine species in flower, and we shall treat it in such a way as will, we hope, be useful and instructive to our amateur friends.

These plants are mostly found growing in the hottest parts of the world, and consequently require artificial heat in this our cold climate. Some of them are located upon the branches of trees, growing amongst the dead leaves, twigs, and moss collected in some hollow or fork of the branch. These may be grown like orchids, upon blocks of wood, or even will thrive and flower well if a ball of moss be tied round the roots, and the plants be hung up to the glass, similar to the orchid tribes. We have some growing in this way, with the roots uppermost, and the plant underneath, just reversing the way plants generally grow; and they appear to thrive just as well as their allies who are in the upright state. But by far the greater number of these plants are found upon the ground at the edges of thickets, or even in the deepest jungle; and we must treat them accordingly. *Achmea fulgens* (Fulgent or Glowing Achmea).—*A. fulgens discolor* (dark coloured leaved ditto).—A plant growing about a foot and a half high. The flower stem springs from the centre, and is of the most intense scarlet. The calyx is also scarlet of a deeper shade, approaching crimson, and the petals are of the brightest blue; these soon fade, but the calyxes and the bright glowing stem continue in beauty for months. The leaves are pale green, a foot long, and three inches broad. The whole plant forms a kind of cup, which holds water that does not injure the plant, unless it becomes foul, to prevent which it will be necessary to empty the water out, by reversing the plant every three or four days. The water accumulates from the syringing of the house and from the deposit of dews on the leaves. In their native wildernesses this and similar plants catch the heavy night dew by means of their spreading, hollowish leaves, conducting it, condensed into water, to the centre of the plant, and serves frequently for quenching the thirst of the wanderer amongst the regions where these plants grow wild.

The soil Achmeas thrive best in is a compound of fibrous peat and rotten leaf mould in equal parts, with one sixth, or thereabouts, of good sound light loam added. In a young state, that is, during the first year, they must be rather underpotted. A flowering plant of that age will not require more than a 5-inch pot. The roots are few and wiry at that age. After the plant has flowered for the first time it dies ; that is, that part dies and sends up one or more (generally more) suckers. These suckers must be encouraged if you wish to have a fine specimen with more than one flower stem. We have seen a specimen with six spikes upon it, but it is quite possible to grow one with sixty. All that will be required is to keep repotting as soon as the flowering season is over, and when the suckers have made some growth and become pretty well furnished with leaves to remove, by cutting down the old plants just low enough not to injure the rising young plants. In fact, the management of these stocks or stools of plants, is something similar to what is called the Hamiltonian system of cultivating the Pine-apple. The best season for potting *young* plants is the spring; for *older* ones, the best season is immediately after flowering. One point must be strictly attended to, and that is thorough good drainage. The reason of this is, evidently, that the plants being half epiphytes—growing on branches of trees—the roots are never so excessively drenched with the moisture, especially stagnant moisture. Like *Cattleyas* and *Lælias*, they require, if grown in pots, excessive drainage. (The Pine-apple requires it too.) A few pieces of charcoal thrown in amongst the soil will be useful, in addition to the broken potsherds at the bottom.

Propagation.—These plants are easily propagated by division, or by taking off *the young suckers* when three inches long, and placing them in heat under bell-glasses. They are apt to damp off unless great care is taken in wiping the glasses frequently, and by a vigorous heat inducing them to send forth roots quickly. As soon as the roots are perceived, pot them off and place them in a shady part of the house for a few days, till they begin to show fresh growth. They may then be removed into a more open situation and treated in the ordinary way, as described above. Sometimes *seed* is produced upon old established plants. As this is a very lovely desirable plant, and is yet comparatively scarce and dear, we recommend such as possess it to try to save seed, or rather to induce it to produce seed. Two or three years ago we had a batch of seedlings sent over from a nurseryman on the continent. They were exceedingly small, but grew well, and several of them have flowered. They are all alike in the flower, but in the foliage considerably different : some approach near to the variety named *discolor*, having a shade of deep purple on the under side of the leaves; others are much lighter green. In one instance the flowers were evidently improved, but that plant was sold during my absence. It is evident that these plants sport, and may be greatly improved, like most other plants having that propensity. We trust our friends that grow it, or may do so hereafter, will try to induce seed by impregnation, and thus help to forward the grand end and aim of all scientific florists—the improvement of the various races of plants.

FLORISTS' FLOWERS.

ANEMONES (single) for early blooming, may now be planted advantageously in beds five inches apart every way, and in borders three or five roots in a patch. Prepare beds for the best *double varieties* similar to those recommended for the Ranunculus. Keep *seedlings* quite clear of weeds, by plucking them up whilst in the seed-leaf. A genuine lover of flowers will soon learn to distinguish weeds, even in that state, from seedlings of his favourite flowers. It is far better to pluck up weeds at that age in every part of the garden, but more especially out of the seed-beds, seed-pots, or pans of florists' flowers. If allowed to advance to a second or third stage of growth, the roots are then so numerous that they will bring up with them a portion of the soil, and, may be, some of the flowers just coming up at the same time. Perhaps a Prince of Wales, or a Duchess of Sutherland, or some other equally high sounding name, may thus be unwittingly nipped in the bud, and prevented showing the raiser how very grateful his humble dependants are, and how desirous to reward him for his pains, now unhappily frustrated, because the weeds were allowed to progress beyond the seed-leaf.   T. APPLEBY.

THE KITCHEN-GARDEN.

CELERY.—Pay attention to keeping the surface of the ground open, the plants free from spurious suckers, and the soil moist.

COLEWORTS, SAVOYS, &c.—To secure a plentiful supply of spring vegetables, every vacant piece of ground should at once be cropped with *coleworts, savoy coleworts, borecoles,* &c.—if any plants are still left in the seed-beds. All of these may be planted thickly, and will, without fail, be found useful in spring for some purpose. *Cauliflowers* and *Cape brocoli* may still be planted for winter storing. Plant fully also of *endive,* both *curled* and *Batavian;* continue to keep the earth's surface amongst the brocoli, and all kinds of winter stuff, well stirred, and the decayed leaves cleared; for the latter, if allowed to remain on the soil, afford only a refuge for slugs, &c.

SPINACH.—Encourage this vegetable by repeatedly surface stirring the soil, thinning out the plants in due season; and, if the soil has not been already pretty well manured, its growth may be stimulated by the judicious application of liquid manure, not so much as to encourage at this season too great a luxuriance, which would render it liable to get cut off by severe winter weather, and yet, at the same time, a sufficient quantity should be given to keep up a good winter gathering of strongly grown clear leaves.

KIDNEY BEANS should now be planted on warm borders, in patches the size of the spare hand-glasses and spare cucumber and melon frames, which should be placed over them previously to the arrival of the cold nights and stormy windy weather, so that a succession of this excellent vegetable may be kept up throughout the autumn months.

ONIONS will, in general, become ripe enough for harvesting by the end of this month. When drawn, they should have a twist round, in order to clear them of the soil with one hand and be placed in the other to be tied into moderate sized bunches, and at once hung up in a loft, or open shed, or other place, where they can gradually dry. The present is still a good season for sowing onions.

Ripe *capsicums* and *chillies* should be gathered and dried by those who wish to convert them into Cayenne pepper; the green fruit should be collected for pickling, &c., and *tomatoes,* both ripe and green, should be secured for sauce and pickling also.

JAMES BARNES.

MISCELLANEOUS INFORMATION.

SCALES OF EXPENDITURE.

By the Authoress of "My Flowers," &c., &c.

IN offering to the consideration of my readers some scales of expenditure for the management of limited incomes, I feel that I must claim from them even more kind indulgence than I have yet received; because the subject is one of extreme difficulty, and because I cannot, from my *own* experience, either lay down rules, or practically judge of those afforded me by others. I have benefited by the advice and calculations of some whose experience has been great, both in affluence and poverty: who not only *talk well* on the subject, but whose actions have fully corresponded with, and perhaps exceeded, the sentiments they expressed, and the directions they have given me. And I purpose to make extracts from a very useful little work entitled, "Practical Domestic Economy," which may be unknown to many of my readers, and beyond the means of others; and I shall venture to add remarks as they occur to me, or are suggested by my friends.

I think I have already said, that it is impossible to lay down accurate rules for the management of an income. The great, the important point—that *without* which nothing can be effected, and *with* which all things may be done—is stern rectitude of mind, based upon "The Rock." Circumstances and situation vary so much, that what is feasible in one case is impossible or improper in another. House-rent, for instance, is sometimes so much higher than the scale has admitted of, that a reduction must necessarily take place in some other item to make up for it. Provisions are also higher priced in some situations than in others, in which case less consumption must be permitted in those things which are not essential for the support of life; and in some cases—indeed I may say in all—many incidental expenses arise, for which there ought to be some provision made, and which, it appears to me, are not sufficiently allowed for in any scale I have hitherto met with. Journies are at times necessary, and often imperative—sickness enters our dwelling—accidents occur to furniture, china, glass, &c.—carriage of parcels and goods must be paid for: and in the country this is often a very material and unavoidable expense. Economists must therefore, in almost all cases, alter estimates to suit their own particular requirements, for they will seldom find one exactly such as they wish. Testimonies to the correctness of some of the estimates I am about to transcribe, however, have been most satisfactorily given; and if the experience of only one family attests their truth, it is a proof that whoever *will* may meet with similar success.

It may perhaps be expected that I should begin with the larger incomes, and gradually descend to those of the narrower limits; but it is so much more easy to expand our ideas than to contract them—it is so much more easy to add to our weekly expenses than to take from them—to indulge than to refrain—to spend than to save—that I begin at once from the lowest point at which a scale can conveniently be framed, and which will, indeed, be the basis of all the rest. Besides, there is, in straitened circumstances—in honest, well-bred, straitened circumstances—something so interesting to the feelings, and my own individual sympathies extend so warmly to all who are thus situated, that I have abundantly more pleasure in the task than if hundreds and thousands were concerned. As many of our readers are persons receiving weekly salaries, or of limited incomes, I shall address myself exclusively to them.

The writer of the work, to which I have already alluded, commences by giving the following rule :—

"Divide the whole income, whatever it may be, into 12 equal parts; and of the expenditure, per week, in every estimate, that of the adults or parents will be four-twelfths for each, or eight-twelfths for both; and for each child one-twelfth, or three-twelfths for the three children; the remaining twelfth will be the reserve or saving. In a less scientific but more homely language it is to be understood, that whatever is the amount of income for any given time *in shillings, so many groats* will be the expense of each parent; and so many pence will be the expense of each child, for that time; and that the saving will be one penny in the shilling." The writer, in all his estimates below £150 per annum, calculates for a family consisting of the parents and three children.

" . . . . It may be proper to say, that the quota of eight-twelfths, or two-thirds, assigned to the two parents, includes not only all the articles of provision for themselves, but every other description of household expense, together with their clothes, rent, and all extras; whilst the one-twelfth for each child consists chiefly of provisions of the following kinds:—namely, bread, flour, rice, oatmeal, sugar, treacle, milk, butter, potatoes, and some other vegetables; and a participation with their parents in a small portion of meat.

in the shape of stews, broth, or soup, &c., with the addition of clothes, washing, and schooling."

The first estimate given is the following:—

Income: 3s 6d per day—21s per week—£55 per annum.

Family: a man, and his wife, and three children.

PROVISIONS WEEKLY.	£	s.	d.
Bread and flour for five persons, 24 lbs., at 1½d. .	0	3	0
Butter, cheese, and milk	0	1	9
Sugar and treacle	0	0	9
Rice, oatmeal, salt, &c.	0	0	6
Butcher's meat or fish—say meat, 6 lb., at 4½d. .	0	2	3
Vegetables (including a ¼ cwt. of potatoes, or 4 lb. per day, at 3s 0d per cwt.), 2d per day . .	0	1	2
Table beer, 1 quart per day, at 2d	0	1	2
Coals, 1¼ bushel per week, on an average all the year round, at 1s 4d—1s 8d; and wood 1d: 3d per day	0	1	9
Candles, on an average all the year round, ½ lb. per week, at 7d	0	0	3½
Soap, starch, blue, &c., for washing	0	0	3½
Sundries, for cleaning, scouring, &c.	0	0	1
Total for household expenses	0	13	6
Clothes, haberdashery, &c.	0	3	6
Rent	0	2	3
Total expense	0	19	3
Saving one-twelfth	0	1	9
Amount of income	1	1	0

The prices of all articles vary. Meat may not always be attainable at 4½d per pound, in which case either a smaller quantity must be consumed, or some other item must be reduced to allow for the difference. Potatoes are, in these days, incalculably dearer than when "Practical Domestic Economy" was compiled; other vegetables must therefore be substituted, or bread and rice eaten in their place. A careful, sound, conscientious economist will easily discover a way of meeting a difficulty of this kind.

This estimate has been tested by several families, one of which was that of a mechanic, and found to correspond exactly with their own experience. In both cases a saving was made from the yearly income. How many families, even in the higher classes of society, possess as small an income as a humble mechanic! and upon £50 per annum how many *single* persons fancy they must starve!

ALLOTMENT FARMING FOR SEPTEMBER.

OUR readers will remember that we pointed to the re-appearance of the *potato disease* in the last allotment paper. It will also come to mind, that a prudent forecast was advised as to the planting of swede turnips, and the various greens which are so serviceable in eking out a limited supply of the root crops. We must again repeat the advice, for the danger is now become more imminent; and it is not, *even now*, too late to take measures for alleviating the distress occasioned by a serious loss in the potato crop, which is anything but impossible.

We see at the period in which those remarks are penned (August 15th), that the public press teems with alarming reports, and, like wave over wave, each leaves a deeper impress on the strand of public opinion. Our impression is just what it was at the fearful commencement of the disease, that like cases of disordered digestion in man, in proportion as the causes which induced it were long in operation, in just a corresponding ratio, or nearly so, will be the period of its departure. We do not pretend to offer any opinion here, as to whether the murrain is the cause or the effect. We would merely observe, that the constitution of the potato generally, after so many years of abuse, was prepared either to generate or to receive any of those destructive fungi, which, like the wasp, the vulture, and others of the animal or insect creation, are what have been termed nature's scavengers. These hints are given by the way, and simply as mere opinions; other matters of a more tangible character must demand our attention.

WHAT IS TO BE DONE WITH DISEASED PLOTS?—This will be immediate business, we conceive, with everybody, for no time may be lost in the affair. We believe that the majority of experimenters during the last few years will back us, when we say that it is by far the best plan to cut away the haulm before the virus has spread far. In our opinion, the sooner the tubers and the haulm part company under such circumstances the better. It is quite true that the tubers will cease to increase in size or nearly so, as might have been expected; but of what use is increase in size in a material so evanescent, or rather so perishable, as a highly diseased potato? After cutting them over we would still recommend that they be "soiled over," unless they are required for immediate use, or for sale; in either of which cases they will of course be taken up at once.

It is almost unnecessary to repeat here, that dryness is one very important condition after they are removed from the soil; the dryer the better, provided no artificial heat is used. Above all, fermentation must be avoided,—that mighty agent of decomposition in all organic matter, more especially where an incipient decay exists, and where a real gangrene has already commenced.

SEED POTATOES.—The more the potato disease threatens, the more care people should take over their potato sets, for surely no one would desire their utter extermination; and the avoidance of abuse is surely a remedial measure at least. As to the care of the seed or sets, we will take *the Ash-leaved Kidney* for a type and example. We do not think that one cultivator in ten understands the real habits of this valuable potato; invaluable I might have said. Mr. Knight, of Downton, long since showed that so far from being a shy potato, enormous crops might be obtained from it, by pursuing a mode of culture congenial to its habits.

Now, this potato, if placed under conditions of fermentation, speedily wastes its germinating powers long before the spring arrives; and it is vain to look for success from seed thus treated. Our best cultivators in these districts (Cheshire)—and we have many more cottagers who perfectly understand the humour of the Ash-leaved Kidney—take them up for seed long before they are what is termed "ripe." They then spread them on the floor of an outhouse or shed, or even beneath their beds in their sleeping rooms, where in single layers, or nearly so, they soon become green and exceedingly hard. Sprout they cannot, for lack of moisture; for mere heat alone will not cause them to bud prematurely. Dryness, therefore, is the main condition, and by the time they have become greened and "hardened," the month of September has far advanced; and now the declining temperature natural to the autumn, together with the rest that has been induced, offers no temptations to a premature germination; and many, for convenience sake, pit them in a cool and dry situation until Christmas has passed, when they are again brought from their hiding place, and once more placed in single layers in boxes beneath their beds, or on any floor or shelf that may offer; all that is requisite is to ward off frost, and to keep them dry.

Thus, by the middle or end of March, these seed kidneys are formed with short and thick sprouts not more than a quarter of an inch in length, and as firm almost as the twig of a tree. In this state they are committed to the soil, and those who plant under such conditions in March, or even in April, obtain potatoes earlier than those who plant in February seed treated according to the old or ordinary method.

AUTUMN CROPPING.—The various winter greens, as kale, savoys, and the Brussels sprouts, may still be planted on spare plots; and plenty of the coleworts or small cabbages which were sown in the end of June or in July. The latter will do on spare borders, or portions of them. All those before planted should be thoroughly cleaned, and have plenty of earth drawn to their stems; for much of their bulk, under all circumstances, is produced from surface roots thus encouraged, more especially if the club should take place. We have even heard of swede turnips being planted as late as the first week in September, and making pretty good bulbs, but we have no faith in such late work. Ordinary turnips may yet be sown in warm situations and on light soils; and for this purpose we should choose the early Dutch, although many prefer the stone. Horn or other carrots may still be sown for early spring use; they will, however, be neither very certain nor very profitable. Beyond these things we are not aware that anything else can be placed under the head of cottager's autumn cropping; for it will be time enough to speak of autumn potato planting in the next allotment paper.

Onions.—If any onions remain still on the beds in a growing state, they must immediately be bent down with a rake or broom. All those loose on the ground should be instantly removed and ripened off. The onion not only bears, but requires, a deal of heat to ripen it soundly; and we do not hold with the plan of laying them out-doors on walks, &c., at this late period. They had better be put in baskets and carried in and out, as the ant dries its winter stores, unless they can be placed in some dry room immediately over a fire place. Roping is the best plan for the cottager, and this done there will be no trouble with them afterwards. A few winter onions may be sown in the first week of September if neglected in August. These will be useful to draw young, and also to transplant next March, when, with a rich soil, they will produce onions at the very period when the winter stores are gone, and the spring sown not come to hand.

Keeping of Store Roots.—It is full soon for these to come to hand in any quantity; the time is near, however, and a little advice on the general principles connected with their sound preservation may be useful. As with the potato, so with the carrot, the parsnip, the swede, the mangold, &c., dryness is the great essential, and in addition coolness. When we say dryness, however, we do not mean subjecting the roots to an atmosphere which shall extract their own juices. We merely mean a security from rain or snow, and a dry situation beneath. We have before said that germination, or sprouting, robs the root of its stores, and that such sprouting cannot proceed in an injurious degree without moisture or much atmospheric damp.

We once knew a person pile up a large body of carrots the moment they were removed from the field, and, after a strawy covering, they were soiled or earthed over, after the manner of potatoes. The consequence was, that in a few weeks they were a mass of putrefaction, and no wonder. They were in a sufficient body to provoke a high amount of fermentation, especially being, as they were, full of the watery matter fresh imbibed from the soil. This had no means of escape commensurate with its accumulation; they were, therefore, subjected to what may be termed a stewing process.

The longest kept mangold wurtzel we ever knew was found, after lying nearly twelve months at the bottom of the pit (an in-doors one), imbedded in broken straw and dust; this mangold, taken out in November, was fresh, or nearly so, as when first placed there.

Pickles.—The Vinegar Plant.—This is the season for the cottager, or allotment holder, to lay in a stock of pickles; for why should a poor man be debarred the luxury of a zest to his piece of bacon or cheese. Of course, red cabbage, onions, ghirkins, narsturtiums, &c., will readily come to mind; but what we would here draw attention to is the immense utility of what is termed The Vinegar Plant. Our readers are many of them, doubtless, acquainted with this singular fungus—for so it is. Having, however, tried it here for nearly two years, and made our pickles with it, we can vouch for its great utility and convenience. Our plan is this :—One pound of treacle and three-quarters of a pound of sugar to about five quarts of water. These materials are placed in a jar with the vinegar plant, and remain a little more than a month. We then draw off the vinegar, and repeat the same process with the plant. But here it may be observed, as information to the novice, that the plants reproduce or increase frequently; and that such, if permitted to accumulate, are found, it would appear by experience, to absorb the vinegar. Our plan, therefore, is, to remove the oldest and, of course, thickest plants when a change is made; for these will be found to become much increased both in thickness and firmness of texture. Another point should be noted : the old plant on removal is made to repay the amount of absorption, by subjecting it to a change of water; and this not being thorough vinegar, we have deemed it expedient to add it to the jar again, in order to complete acidification. We keep a paper tied over the jar, as in pickles, and the jar stands on a shelf near the kitchen fire; the temperature, doubtless, ranging from seventy to eighty degrees on the average. Nothing can succeed better, and with us it has fairly superseded all other vinegars—the flavour being equal to most of our ordinary vinegars at least.

MISS MARTINEAU ON COW-KEEPING.

"What I want to gain is not pecuniary profit, but comfort, while, at the same time, I cannot afford to lose by my experiment. There are months of the year (and exactly the months when my friends come to see me) when I cannot be sure of being able to buy enough of meat, milk and cream, and vegetables for my table; and the vegetables, and milk and cream, can rarely be had good at any season of the year. If, without loss, I can provide myself with hams and bacon, fowls and eggs, vegetables (except winter potatoes), butter and cream, I shall be amply satisfied, as far as considerations of the purse go. A much higher consideration is, that if I can make my plan succeed, it provides for the maintenance of two honest people, who might otherwise have had no prospect but of the workhouse in their old age, and in all seasons of pressure meanwhile.

"My land amounts in the whole to less than two acres and a quarter; and of this, part is mere rock, and a good deal is occupied with the house and terrace, the drive, and some planted portions. A year and a half ago, a little more than an acre of it, in grass, was let for £4 10s. a-year to a tenant who kept a cow upon it. This tenant never took the slightest care of the pasture, and it became so lumpy and foul as to be an eyesore from the house. I paid more than six guineas a-year to an occasional gardener, who could not even keep things neat in the time he gave to it, much less render my ground productive. If I wanted a ham, I had sometimes to pay £1 for it, and for eggs I paid during three months of the year a 1d. a-piece. I never saw cream worthy of the name; and had to get butter from a distance. In the midst of this state of things, it occurred to me that it might be worth trying whether my land would not produce such comfort as I wanted, without increased expense.

"Having satisfied myself that it was worth a trial, I wrote to you to inquire whether your union would despatch hither a labourer whom you could recommend. Besides that we are underhanded in this district, I knew that my neighbours would laugh at me for proposing to keep a cow and pig on my own land, when the rule of the district is, that it takes three acres to keep a cow, and when it is the custom for one man to undertake the charge of as many acres of land as you please, and my neighbours did laugh for a time. They said that I was paying at the rate of 6d. a quart for milk; they asked how I could possibly find employment for a man on two acres of ground; they charged me first with cruelty to my cows, in not letting them range on the fell; and then of fatting them. Some, however, saw the importance of the experiment in the way of example, and have encouraged me throughout. I do not yet affirm that the experiment will answer, but I believe that it will; and I am sure that the comfort of my little household is prodigiously increased by it. I do not forget how our success mainly depends on the choice you made of a farm servant for me. He is a man of extraordinary industry and cleverness, as well as rigid honesty. His ambition is roused; for he knows that the success of the experiment mainly depends on himself. He is living in comfort, and laying by a little money, and he looks so happy that it would truly grieve me to have to give up; though I have no doubt that he would immediately find work at good wages in the neighbourhood. His wife and he had saved enough to pay their journey hither out of Norfolk. I give him 12s. a-week all the year round. His wife earns something by occasionally helping in the house, by assisting in my washing, and by taking in washing when she can get it. I allow her the use of my washhouse, copper, &c., on condition that the copper is kept clean for the boiling of the cow-food in winter. I built them an excellent cottage of the stone of the district, for which they pay 1s. 6d. per week. They know that they could not get such another off the premises for £5 a-year.

"Besides the cottage and washhouse, I had to build a cow-house, pig-house (for it is not a stye), a poultry-yard, and hay-house. I consider these under the head of invest ment, not expenditure. I could let them, with the land, at any time if I chose to give up cow-keeping.

"In planning the turning up of my ground for spade cultivation, I went on the supposition of keeping only one cow; and for seven months we kept only one. But I considered the inconvenience of the cow being dry for three months out of the twelve; and that there was room in the stable for a second, and little more trouble in keeping two than one; and a pretty certain market among my neighbours for whatever butter and milk I might have to sell. So I bought a 'spring calver' as companion to the 'autumn calver,' and we find that we very nearly maintain them both on little more than three-quarters of an acre of grass, and less than half an acre of garden. The second cow pays her way by her manure and milk.

"Our first consideration was the manure. It is as true with relation to our small concerns as to a greater, that 'the more manure, the more green crops; the more green crops, the more stock; the more stock, the more manure.' There are two tanks, well flagged and cemented, well closed, so that not a drop can ooze out. One is connected with the house, and the other with the cottage and cow-house, receiving all their drainage of every kind. A barrel on wheels stands at the back-door to receive all the slops, soap-suds, cabbage-water, &c., and this liquid manure is wheeled away, and applied where it is wanted. There is a compost pit at the back of the kitchen garden; and a compost heap behind some young trees at the bottom of the field. What with the clippings, and weedings, and sweepings, and nothing being wasted, the pit being kept clean, and the cow-house swept out twice a day, we have abundance of manure (without buying any whatever), which accounts for the abundance of our crops thus far. One instance of my servant's passion for economy amused me so much that it seems worth telling you. Early one morning, returning from my walk, I looked in upon the pig, just when his breakfast was approaching in another direction. I said to Robert, 'I think piggy looks very well, only that he wants a washing.' 'Yes, ma'am,' said Robert, 'that will be to-morrow. To-morrow is washing-day, and the suds will wash the pig first, and then be as good, and better, for manure; and then the soap serves three times over.'

"Our available ground is—of pasture, three roods twenty-eight perches; and of tilled ground, one rood fifteen perches. There are besides about twenty-six perches of grass in the little plantation, orchard, and slope, which yields some fresh grass when mowed in summer. I shall turn up a little more ground this spring in order to provide completely for the maintenance of two cows, though I cannot encroach much more on the grass, on account of the views from the windows. But for this, we should give our cows no grass or hay, which are the most expensive kinds of food. Our soil is good; neither very rich nor very light; laying at varying depths upon limestone. Much of our newly-dug portion was full of stones. Our neighbours advised us to cover them up again, but we judged differently. I thought we might as well make drains of the new path-ways we must have, so, by deep digging, we obtained drains, and the large stones were thus disposed of. Some more were carted out to mend the roads, and when my servant was in despair at there being yet more, it occurred to him to dig out good earth from corners of the plantation, and supply its place with stones. He actually dug pits breast deep for this purpose.

"His digging for crops was not less than two spits deep, dug straight down, and the whole was richly manured. The ground being ready, our method is this:—

"In August we sow cabbage-seed, and by the end of September we begin to set out the young plants, about 400 per week, for six weeks, to secure a succession. We set them in rows, the plants being eighteen inches apart, and the rows a yard apart. In March and April we sow swedes and beets in alternate rows between the rows of cabbages. By the time we are beginning to cut the cabbages, the turnips and beets are past the danger of the fly, and may be thinned—the removal of the cabbages letting in air and sunshine. We also keep a portion of ground for Belgian carrots, which afford excellent cow food. We succeeded less with these this year than with our other crops, from their not being sufficiently thinned. But we had twenty-five stone of them, and four or five carrots per day were very acceptable to the cows. By the end of March the cows can get a bite in the pasture, and the mowings of the grass in the orchard, &c.,

are brought to them fresh. While the pasture is shut up for hay the cabbages begin to ripen. They weigh from 4 lbs. to 12 lbs., and each cow eats about eighteen per day. This is their food from June to November, with such grazing as they get after our hay-making, and a handful or two per day of Indian meal, scalded and given with their grass. The pasture having been well manured in the winter and wonderfully retrieved by good care, yielded more than a ton and a half of the finest hay. This year, I think, I shall try for a second crop, as we have abundance of manure. But last year I had half the pasture hurdled off, and the cows let out for some time every fine day to graze, the one half for one fortnight, and the other the next. By the time the grass and the cabbages were done, we had laid in less than we hope to produce this year, but a fair amount of crops. For the cows one and a half ton of hay, twenty-five stone of Belgian carrots, and at least ten cwt. of swedes and beet.

"We laid out too much of our ground for household vegetables, having had a surplus after the following supply:—Fine green peas—from the 12th of June till the middle of September—peas, lettuces, radishes, spinach, turnips, and carrots, and onions, enough for the whole winter—five or six stone of early potatoes, vegetable marrow, a few cucumbers, abundance of cauliflowers, broccoli, and cabbages, and plenty of rhubarb and gooseberries. A strawberry bed is laid out, too, and we are to have plenty of apples, and pears, and cherries, and damsons, hereafter. We used enough green vegetables for a family of five persons for the whole summer and autumn.

"The average yield of the cows is about ten quarts per day each, i. e., about four pounds of butter per week. The skimmed milk is eagerly bought, being as good as I used to buy for new milk. The butter-milk improves our bread and cakes very much, and the pig has what we do not use. The cows give sixteen quarts per day for some time after calving, and are dry for about three months before. One cow calved in October, and we sold the calf (a cow-calf) for a guinea at the end of a fortnight. The same cow is to calve again in September, and the other in May, and thus a continued supply of milk is provided for. We kill two pigs in a year, and selling half each time, get our hams and as much bacon as we want for little or nothing. What we have to buy is three barrels of Indian meal in a year (at an average of 16s. each), some of which we use ourselves for puddings and cakes, and which goes far towards feeding the fowls; a few trusses of wheat-straw after harvest (when it is cheapest) to chop and mix with the cows' boiled turnip-food in winter, a few pennyworths of grains per week, and two or three loads of turnips after Midsummer, and perhaps a little (but a very little) hay. As I consider that the cows maintain the man, this expenditure is all that I have to make in return for our large supply of vegetables, pork, bacon, and hams, eggs, and a few fowls, our gardening, and the keeping of the whole ground in high order, and, moreover, through the good nature of my excellent servant, our window-cleaning and coal-shifting. It may not be out of place here to mention his other proofs of zeal and kindness. His sister is my maid, and she has care of the plate. In the short days, or in excessively bad weather, he comes up and offers to clean the plate, which is, in consequence, better kept than it ever was before. Again, the tenant of the next field besought me to take possession of the fence (by permission of the owner), as it was a great expense and trouble to him. I long refused, though the hedge was very ugly, with eight hideous pollards and eternal rows of wet linen hung on from the other side. At last my servant begged me to take the hedge, saying that he would grub and fell the whole, and that, if the wood did not pay me for a new fence, the gain in land would. I put up a cross pole fence, which is highly ornamental. My neighbour and I gain each ten square yards of ground, I am safe from sheep and trespassers, and I have wood enough for about two years' consumption, besides pea-sticks and poles as many as we want. The new fence cost £0 and a few shillings. The purpose of setting forth this man's merits is to be fair; for I am aware how essentially the success of my experiment depends on the quality of the servant who has to work it out.

"The cow-house is, as I said, swept out (into the entrance of the tank) twice a-day; and it is whitewashed twice a year. The cows are rubbed down daily, and kept almost as sleek as horses. Both are now in much finer condition than when they came. They were rather restless for a few weeks, after first coming from the fell; but they seem now perfectly happy, and when out in the field, they return to the stable of their own accord to avoid rains, heat, or flies. Their food in winter is each a stone of turnips three times a day; the turnips being shred, and boiled with chopped wheat straw, a little hay, a handful of salt, and a double handful of Indian meal, or somewhat more of bran. They may have, besides, to amuse themselves with, a few raw turnips, and two or three handfuls of hay per day.

"Harriet Martineau."

NATIVE WILD FLOWERS.
AUGUST.

By the beginning of August, the wild roses have almost entirely faded from the hedgerows, although a stray bush here and there still retains somewhat of its blooming beauty. No sooner, however, do the roses—so conspicuous in the summer landscape—begin to fade than another highly interesting family of rosaceous shrubs begin to put forth their scarcely less beautiful though less highly-coloured blossoms, and continue to adorn the hedgerows throughout the autumn months. This tribe is the brambles, a family which, in one way or other, find interest with every body. The poets sing of the beauty of their "satin-threaded flowers," the schoolboy is nowhere so delighted as in the midst of a bramble-brake; the mountain shepherd seeks the fruit of the mountain brambles as his only luxury; the artist admires the thorny shrub as one of the most successful beautifiers of nature,—covering with its long leafy stems the old ruinous wayside walls and stony hedgebanks with a fresh and flowery verdure; and the botanist—ah! no family of plants delight to distraction so well as the ever-changing *Rubi*. The fruit, called blackberries in England, but better known under their genuine name of *brambles* in Scotland, meet with very general approbation; and although the schoolboy gets the chief credit of enjoying this free and simple fruit of nature's garden, yet the hungry botanist seldom lingers in the thorny brake without indulging in gastronomic as well as botanic philosophy. The supposed species of *Rubus* have been greatly extended of late; but we fear a proposal to lead the Cottage Gardeners through the thorny mazes of the genus which have been created by botanical authors would not meet with a very grateful reception; and shall therefore only allude to one or two of the more familiar and easily known and distinguished species. The *Rubus fruticosus* may be considered the popular representative of the host of so called species distinguished by botanists, which afford the brambleberries or blackberries, a fruit which will be perfectly familiar to every reader, and which is sometimes used economically in the making of tarts and preserves. Jeremy Taylor, in allusion to the practice which prevails in some districts of binding down the sods on newly covered graves by the young shoots of the bramble, remarks: "The autumn, with its fruits, prepares disorders for us; and the winter's cold turns them into sharp diseases; and the spring brings flowers to strew upon our hearse; and the summer gives *green turf and brambles to bind upon our graves.*" *R. idæus* is the origin of our garden raspberry, and a capital fruit it is, even in its wild condition in the woods. The alpine *R. Chamæmorus*, or Cloudberry, although a small plant, affords large and juicy berries, called *Avrons* by the mountain shepherds.

The highly ornamental family of St. Johnsworts (*Hypericum*) produce their profusion of yellow blossoms during the last and present months, being generally found in woods, thickets, and bushy places. *H. pulchrum* occurs on heaths, and *H. humifusum* on old pastures; but *H. elodes* seeks the humid margin of the stream. One of the species has its leaves curiously perforated with small transparencies, hence it is called *H. perforatum*. This is the "balm of the warrior's wound;" and in allusion to the profusion of its flowers we have the following lines:—

"Hypericum, all bloom, so thick a swarm
Of flowers, like flies, clothing its slender rods
That scarce a leaf appears."

There are in all twelve wild species of Hypericum, but two of them are considered to be only naturalized plants. One of these, *H. calycinum*, may be familiar to many of our readers as a frequent ornament of the shrubbery.

One of the most beautiful of the August flowering plants is the Grass of Parnassus (*Parnassia palustris*), which occurs in the loveliest profusion on many of the northern hills and mountains, although it is by no means so common in the south.

July and August are the months for the flowering of the Dyer's Rochet, Yellow Weld, or wild Mignonette (*Reseda luteola*), which grows in extraordinary abundance on railway embankments, and on the rubbish heaps of old quarries; in fact, wherever the turf is disturbed and the subsoil thrown up. It bears a remarkable similarity of appearance to the common garden Mignonette—the *Reseda odorata* of botanists—styled by Cowper

"The fragrant weed—the Frenchman's darling;"

but the wild plant grows to a much greater size than the cultivated species; and, besides having long linear leaves whereby it may readily be recognised, it wants the agreeable odour of the garden favourite. Hooker and other writers mention that the Dyer's Rochet is used in dyeing woollen stuffs yellow; and the author of "Wild Flowers of the Year" says, "It has been used for dyeing, especially in France. The whole plant affords juice for this purpose, and its colour is good and permanent. The coloured paint, called by artists Dutch pink, is obtained from it." Lightfoot states that the plant was in his day much used for dyeing both woollen and silk of a yellow colour; the fresh herb shredded and boiled, or dried and reduced to a powder, being the ways of using it. The Base Rochet (*R. lutea*) is a much rarer species, but of no importance in an economical point of view, so far as we can learn.

The Corn Marigold (*Chrysanthemum segetum*) is a very conspicuous golden field flower during the month of August, when it is generally in full bloom. According to our own observation, it is often more profuse in potato fields than in corn fields, and certainly more conspicuous when so circumstanced. The Corn Marigold is not so very troublesome a farm pest in this country as to require a statutary enactment to enforce its eradication by the cultivator of the soil, as has been found necessary in Denmark; but it frequently occurs in tolerable abundance, especially in cold, wet, clayey land. Its peculiarity of distribution, however, renders it to some extent a local plant; for there are some districts where it is particularly scarce, among which we may notice the neighbourhood of Edinburgh.

There are a good few other plants of the Natural Order Compositæ which produce their flowers during the present month; and we may notice one or two of the more interesting. The common Chamomile (*Anthemis nobilis*) is a favourite cottage herb, the stomachic and tonic powers of which are "justly celebrated." At many of the stations where this plant may be found it is probably not indigenous, as its constant attendance at the cottage door gives it many opportunities of being introduced to different parts of the country where it may readily become naturalized. Several varieties are grown in gardens. According to Hooker, the principal virtues of this plant are supposed to reside in the *involucre*, which contains an essential oil. Sir J. E. Smith says, "Varieties with double flowers, whose yellow tubular florets are entirely or partially transformed into white ligulate ones, are common in gardens; the discoid variety, destitute of rays, is more rare. The latter, perhaps, ought to be preferred for medical use, the double white flowers being now acknowledged to be weaker than those in a natural state. Every part of the plant is intensely bitter, and gratefully aromatic, especially the flowers." The Sneezewort Yarrow (*Achillea ptarmica*) is a beautiful ornament of the ditch banks, more especially in the north, although by no means uncommon anywhere; but the common Yarrow or Millfoil (*A. millefolium*) is even more abundant, occurring chiefly by the waysides. It is said to cause bleeding at the nose if put up the nostrils; hence one of the English names, Nose-bleed. The family of Knapweeds (*Centaurea*) are exceedingly showy, more especially *C. scabiosa*, and *C. cyanus*; indeed the latter is frequently grown in gardens as an ornamental annual. The stamens of some of the species have been observed to show irritability, similar to that in the Rockrose and Barberry. It is well known that the painter in water colours takes advantage of the bright blue of the Corn-blue-bottle, the juice of the petals being used mixed with alum water. Smith mentions the interesting fact, that the separate floret in *English Botany* coloured with this, by way of experiment, had stood well for thirty years, which is no mean recommendation to this floral colour. During the month of August we have two plants in flower, which, although they are not in themselves of great interest or importance, are interesting to the botanist, as being each the single British representative of a large American genus, forming a conspicuous feature in the western wilds. The common Star Wort (*Aster tripolium*), is the only member of the extensive family of Asters which we possess; we daresay, beautiful as is our salt marsh plant, it cannot in respect of beauty be compared with the species of other lands, and there seems little sympathy betwixt it and the China Asters of our gardens. The Golden Rod—so variable in its stature—is one of our next showy northern plants; and the great family of Solidagos to which it belongs is one of the most conspicuous on the North American Continent.

G. Lawson, F.B.S., &c., Edinburgh.

THE POULTRY-KEEPER'S CALENDAR.—September.

By Martin Doyle, Author of "Hints to Small Farmers," &c.

Fowls.—Though the hatching of chickens at this late season is to be totally discouraged, on account of the exceeding difficulty of rearing them at the approach of winter, there is no reason why hens should not be at any time allowed to indulge their desire for sitting, if ducks' eggs can be provided for them. Ducklings can be reared, with moderate pains-taking, during our ordinary winters, especially by cottagers who will not object to have their kitchen occupied by the tender brood until they can bear removal to less comfortable quarters. Ducklings reared at seasons when they are very rare luxuries for the table bring a price which repays for the extra trouble of rearing them. Those poultry-keepers, then, who can provide ducks' eggs for hens, as we have recommended, in the seasons when a brood of chickens cannot be brought forth with a reasonable prospect of success, need never check the determined disposition of a hen to sit; and are altogether inexcusable if they use cruel methods (such as that of throwing the hen into a cold bath) in order to check the natural desire. As a hen cannot cover more than five *goose* eggs, it is better to let her hatch ducklings than goslings, and leave the hatching of the latter now to a Turkey hen disposed to incubation.

On account of the violent quarrels which unexpectedly arise among hens, it is requisite to have separate places in which they may be kept for a time apart. Twice within nine months a terrible outbreak has occurred in our own poultry yard, and without any apparent cause. This circumstance has led us to consider what may be the best *secondary punishments* for refractory and quarrelsome hens. The first case was as follows : six well-grown white Dorking pullets, and a cock of the same brood, were purchased in December last, and introduced to a family consisting of a few dark-coloured hens of the Dorking kind also. The new comers were kindly received by the old stagers, and the utmost harmony prevailed among them until the middle of June last, when two of the older hens assaulted two of the younger ones, pecked them until they drew blood from them, and nearly blinded one of them. The poor persecuted creatures were unable to eat, and feared to go to the common roost during two nights, or venture out of their hiding-places by day. Disliking the notion of capital punishment, by strangling, or the blade (and partly swayed by the consideration that their flesh was nearly uneatable), and wishing to ascertain the effect of imprisonment in such case, we confined the criminals, and also cut off their wings, in order to mortify their vanity, and prevent them from rising up to a roost over their heads. They were allowed dry corn and water, and a few rays of light entered their cell. After 48 hours' confinement they were discharged; and on their liberation they did not attempt to renew the assault for which they had been so justly punished. In the meantime,

the young hen who had been so sorely beaten was most tenderly nursed by the cock, who seemed as if ashamed of himself for not having interfered in the first instance to prevent the outrage. At the end of July the same white hens were beaten by the same dark feathered ones, but not severely, without any discoverable cause. It is not a war of races, for the whites and blacks were in perfect amity at the beginning of their acquaintance, and are derived from the same stock. Jealousy does not seem to have caused it : the cock has but eight wives altogether—fewer by many than those of the Nepaulese ambassador, and seems equally attentive and affectionate to all. Confinement has not altogether succeeded in this case of gross misconduct, and it may make matters worse—the offender, whether a cock or hen, at the expiration of the term of imprisonment often renews the assault, or perhaps suffers one, and interference does little more good than in other family quarrels. Perhaps the best way is to let matters settle of themselves; and if poultry cannot or will not fall into quietude, the only certain remedy (and it then becomes a just punishment) is to make a meal of them as soon as they can be rendered fat for this purpose.

Some cottagers prevent their hens from getting into their neighbours' gardens or stubble fields, through hedges, by making a sort of yoke, which is simply a stick laid horizontally across the shoulders, and fastened round the neck by a necklace of string.

Eggs.—The gleanings of harvest now afford so great supply of food to fowls that they lay abundantly. Eggs become cheaper than at any former season of the year ; and for a few weeks to come the price of them will not rise. This is the time, therefore, for thrifty housekeepers to lay in a stock of eggs for winter cooking purposes—whatever mode of preserving them they may think fit to adopt.

Preparing Fowls for the Table.—The new wheat, barley, &c., brings them speedily into such good condition, that they are fit for table without any further fatting. A barndoor fowl is undoubtedly superior in flavour to the over-fed, flabby, greasy birds which the London cooks like to have under their hands. To make fowls fat to their taste they must be prevented from taking exercise by close cooping, and kept almost in darkness to insure perfect quietude.

Turkeys and Guinea Fowls.—Great attention should be given to turkey poults now, when the tail feathers are beginning to grow ; they require good nourishment to sustain the exhaustion of strength during this period of their growth ; barley-meal mixed with their food should be abundantly afforded to them, as their future vigour and size will mainly depend on the care now taken of them. Guinea fowls are now shooting their horns, as it is termed, and will also require a full supply of food to carry them well through this important stage of their lives.

THE BEE-KEEPER'S CALENDAR.—September.

By J. H. Payne, Esq., Author of "The Bee-keeper's Guide," &c.

Autumnal Unions.—The time has now arrived for these operations, which are so strongly recommended by Gelieu and many other apiarians; and, indeed, their necessity, as well as their utility, cannot be too much insisted upon, and especially as the method which I have adopted is so very simple, and which I had pledged myself at page 295 of the present volume of The Cottage Gardener to give in this place, but which now becomes unnecessary, for my plan, as well as every other one that I have either seen or heard of, is, I am happy to say, entirely superseded by the method given by "A Country Curate" in page 279, No. 96, of The Cottage Gardener, for which communication he has my best thanks; and he deserves, also, the thanks of every apiarian in the kingdom,—his plan being so safe, so simple, and so effectual ; for here is no fumigating, no stupifying, which I have always found to be injurious, and, indeed (beyond a puff or two of tobacco-smoke, and even that only on especial occasions) unnecessary. This method, however, applies to *entire* deprivation, and is recommended to be done early in August, whilst those of Gelieu are at the end of September ;

and then it is not strong stocks that are to be deprived of their honey and united to others, but *weak* ones only. Still, if this total deprivation be performed so late as the end of September the bees may, with a little trouble, be kept through the winter, which the following anecdote related to me a short time since by a gentleman residing in the neighbourhood of Bury St. Edmunds fully proves. He said to me, that the circumstance which led to his becoming an apiarian was rather a singular one; for, passing one evening the garden of a cottager in the village where he resides, he observed some rather extraordinary preparations going on, the nature of which he could not understand, and was induced to inquire a little into the matter and the reply was, "We are going to burn the bees, sir;" and upon being assured that the stupified bees would be of no value to the cottager, and that they would be buried, he begged them, and waiting the process over, took them home with him in a large flower-pot; and after sprinkling them very gently with sugared ale put them into a box, and supplied them with a syrup made with brown sugar and ale, at the top of the box, and in a few days he had the satisfaction of finding they had formed several combs, and were proceeding rapidly in carrying on their work, which greatly increased his interest in them, and induced him to give them every possible attention, by which means he carried them safely through the winter, and obtained from them two good swarms the following summer, besides a few pounds of fine honey-comb, and for the last three or four years he has had a large and productive apiary.

THE PRESENT SEASON.—Although in this neighbourhood (Bury St. Edmunds) we have had little or no honey in boxes or glasses from the tops of the hives, I am happy to find that the *stocks* are remarkably good, with scarcely any exceptions, which will give us encouragement in looking forward to another season. Some accounts which I have lately had from the neighbourhood of London are much better than I expected; I hear of a person at Croydon having taken off a box of honey containing 30 pounds, and the box is again nearly filled by the same stock; this has afforded him the most honey, but his other stocks have done remarkably well. And I hear, also, of a person at Chiswick having had a similar good year; I wish it had been the same here.

MEAD.—I am requested to give a receipt for mead, and the following is the best that I have seen, and is certainly most excellent:—Pour five gallons of boiling water upon 20 pounds of honey, boil, and remove the scum as it rises; when it ceases to rise, add one ounce of hops, and boil for 10 minutes afterwards; put the liquor into a tub to cool; when reduced to 75° of Fahrenheit, add a slice of bread toasted and smeared over with a little new yeast; let it stand in a warm room, and be stirred occasionally; and when it carries a head, tun it, filling up the cask from time to time. When the fermentation has nearly finished bung it down, leaving a peg-hole, which may soon be closed; bottle in about a year.

HONEY VINEGAR.—A most excellent vinegar may also be made from honey: Put half a pound of honey to a quart of water, boiling hot; mix well, and expose to the greatest heat of the sun without closing the vessel containing it, but sufficiently so to keep out insects. In about six weeks this liquor becomes acid, and changes to strong vinegar, and of *excellent* quality. The broken combs, after being drained, may be put in as much water as will float them, and well washed; the linens also and sieves which have been used for draining honey, may be rinsed in the same water, and with this make the vinegar; first boil and scum it before mixing it with the honey.

HOME-MADE WINE.

THIS may appear rather an extravagance for humble households, yet when the receipts which I will give are read, the expenses of making them will be found very trifling, provided the fruit has not to be bought; and we all know how much a bottle of wine is prized!

On great occasions, such as christenings, birthdays, or weddings, instead of spending money in spirits, or wine from the wine merchants, how much better is it to have a little store of home-made wines from which to take a few bottles and welcome your guests. Though dissipation and pleasures which interfere with our duties are decidedly *wrong*, yet hospitality exercised towards our friends is a virtue which should not be neglected. Let us at the same time be careful who our *friends* are, for if not careful in their selection, we shall be led away from the narrow path of duty, and find ourselves serving that master of whom our blessed Lord himself has declared—"Ye cannot serve God and Mammon." "Lose not the world, neither the things which are in the world," is a text which, if kept constantly before our eyes, would assist us materially in all our undertakings; and we should be enabled to resist all those pleasures into which we cannot enter without danger to our eternal happiness.

Cleanliness is as essential in the act of home wine making as it is in every other branch of cookery. My receipts I intend for those who wish to make wine on a small scale, and therefore I will not insist on the necessity of having "vats," "treaders," &c., but merely say that *a cask* and *a tub* are requisite, also *a coarse sieve* to strain the juice through.

THE FRUIT from which wine is to be made must be picked in dry weather, and every unsound berry picked out as well as the stalks. The room in which the wine is made should be comfortably warm, in order that the fermentation may be assisted. Some people are in the habit of adding spirits to their home-made wines; this practice, however, spoils the flavour, and of course adds materially to the expense.

RED CURRANT WINE.—Gather the currants when quite ripe, on a dry day. Pick the stalks off, and if you wish five gallons of wine, take six gallons of fruit, put them into the tub, press them until each currant is crushed, strain the juice off, and to the crushed fruit put two quarts of cold spring water. Let it stand whilst you measure the juice which you have previously strained. Add to the juice an equal proportion of spring water, and then strain the water from the currants, and add that to the mixture of juice and water. To every gallon of liquid add two pounds and a half of good sugar, stir it till the sugar is melted, and then pour it into a cask, and to each gallon add half an ounce of "crude tartar." Place a tile on the bung-hole for a couple of months, at the end of which time it may be fastened closely down, but the wine should not be bottled for six or eight months after it is made.

BLACK CURRANT WINE is sweeter than the red currant, and when ready for drinking is very nice warmed up with spices, &c. It is made thus:—To every gallon of water allow a gallon of black currants, squeeze them, but be careful not to break the pips; put them, with the water, into a saucepan, and boil them ten minutes; strain the juice, and add to the fruit again a small quantity of water, say a quart, so as to allow for the waste which takes place in boiling. Put them on the fire for a few minutes, and add the second juice to that which you have already strained. To each gallon allow two pounds and a half of sugar and one ounce of "crude tartar," and whilst the liquid is quite hot (just hot enough to bear your finger in it) add to every five gallons a quarter of a pint of fresh yeast. Leave a tile on the bung-hole till the fermentation has ceased, and the longer it is kept in the cask before bottling the better it will be.

ELDER WINE will be found very wholesome, and as the berries belong "to all and everybody," it is a pity not to use them. To each gallon of picked berries add one gallon of water; let it stand a day and night, stirring it frequently; put it into a saucepan and boil it well for half an hour, strain it through a sieve, put the juice into a clean saucepan, and to every gallon add two pounds and a half of moist sugar, boil it for twenty minutes, and then add, tied up in a muslin bag, half an ounce of bruised ginger and allspice to each gallon of liquid; continue boiling it altogether for ten minutes; pour it into a tub, and when cool set it to "work" with some yeast spread on a piece of toast. When it has left off fermenting put it into a cask, bung it down securely, and when it has stood three or four months bottle it, though, if more convenient, the wine can be drank from the cask. Elder wine is very nice warmed with spice in the same way as the black currant wine, and on a cold winter's night it will be very much in request.

Wine may be made from almost any fruit, also from ginger and parsnips, but the three I have now given are, I think, the easiest as well as the cheapest to make of any. Ginger wine is very wholesome if taken as a medicine, but it is too heating to be useful as a constant beverage.

A FRIEND.

WINTERING BEES.

AMONG the *memorabilia* of the year which I have preserved in my note-book, I find the notice of an interview which I had on the 2nd of May with that veteran in apiarian science, Dr. Bevan. On that day he did me the honour to pay me a visit at my cottage, in consequence of a correspondence which I had with him relative to the subject of the *burial of hives* in winter. Your readers will, I am sure, be glad to hear, that he then appeared hale and hearty; and bore the weight of eighty years with cheerfulness and dignity. In proof of his activity of mind, he told me, that he had been busied of late in preparing a lecture on bees, to be delivered before some society in Hereford. Our intercourse originated in a desire on my part to be more particularly informed, touching a curious experiment which both himself and his friend Dr. Dunbar (living in Scotland) had successfully tried some years ago with a couple of hives buried in the ground, at a depth of two feet—the one for four months, the other for three. The former, which weighed at the latter end of November 37 lbs., was found to have diminished only 2 lbs. in weight, when on the 1st of April following it was resuscitated. The bees, too, were in good health; and at once, on being restored to light and liberty, set to work with all vigour, as if nothing had happened. This hive had a tube of ¼ inch bore inserted at the entrance "brought above ground with a curved extremity," and communicating with the open air. This experiment was repeated (I suppose in the same manner) the following year by Dr. Bevan; the only precaution which he (as well as Dr. D.) used, being, as he informed me by letter, to "give the hive a light covering of straw, to prevent the super-ambient earth from coming in close contact with the hive." It was dug out on the 15th of March, having been buried "as soon as the frost had fairly set in in December." The bees in this, as in the former case, were found to be in good health, with stores reduced in weight by about 4lb. He told me afterwards that this hive "continued vigorous for several years." Of Dr. D's, he heard nothing subsequent to its disinterment.

Now, in this account is to be observed the very great difference in the consumption of honey in these two hives: that buried *four* months decreased only two pounds in weight, while that interred *three* months lost as much as four pounds. If the latter were the *usual* result of the experiment, I would hardly recommend the trial of it in preference to any other plan of wintering bees—at least, my note-book tells me that my two box hives lost in the same time last winter very little more, *i.e.*, about five pounds a-piece, as they stood in my window with a S. W. aspect. But if Dr. Dunbar's statement be correct, and the result *as a usual thing* inclines to the figure which he shows, it really becomes a matter of importance to ascertain whether success would *generally* attend a more extensive adoption of this plan. Dr. B. did not repeat the experiment, because he has not since had any hives (*cottage hives*) which he could have buried; his apiary consisting of *boxes* worked on the depriving system.

A more extraordinary fact, however (if *fact* it really is), connected with this subject, appeared in the same number of the "Hereford Times" which contained Dr. Bevan's remarks. The editor of that paper has not furnished his readers with the name of the individual who professes to have verified this singular experiment, nor indeed is there any signature of any kind to the paper. It runs thus (speaking of two somewhat different experiments):—

"The first experiment was made on two hives in the autumn of 1831—32; the quantity of honey in each hive having been ascertained, as near as circumstances would permit. Both hives were then placed on a stone floor in an open shed, and were covered over with leaves to the depth of about two feet. Here they remained for five months, and

were then extricated (there are no *dates* specified). On examination the bees *presented an appearance as if dead*, and *no perceptible diminution had taken place in the honey*. The day being very fine they were removed to a warm situation. Only a few minutes elapsed before they presented the *animation of a midsummer swarm*"!

Now, strange as this may seem, I can as readily believe, that bees, which apparently die of foul or exhausted air, will come to life again on restoration to the light of day, as that they, as well as other insects which have been for a long time immersed in water or other liquids, will recover life under similar circumstances. In either case there is a mere *suspension* of animal life. But to continue—

"One of the hives swarmed on the 28th of May, the other on the 8th of June, the same season. To test the practicability of this system of wintering bees, 26 *hives* were subjected to the same treatment the following autumn, and *two were entirely divested of their honey and comb before being buried; all of them existed during the winter without any provision whatever* (!!) and ever since, this plan of preserving bees during winter has been practised with eminent success."

Now, if this be only *true*, it is a secret of the very highest importance to every bee-keeper to be acquainted with; for, in such case, the keeping of bees *must* be a most profitable concern, and there can be next to no loss in it. It is a marvel to me, however, that such a secret should be so little known. I confess myself to be somewhat incredulous as to the truth of this story. Yet such a statement would hardly have been permitted by the editor of a respectable paper to find its way into his columns without his having some assurance of the truth and authenticity of the statement. At all events, be it true or false, I am disposed not to let the matter rest until I have tried the experiment myself. Will any of the numerous, intelligent, and curious apiarians who read your pages join with me in giving these different systems of wintering bees a fair trial? If it be done on a *large scale*—if a dozen or more individuals would be magnanimous enough to sacrifice, *if need be*, one, two, three, or more hives a piece, the thing would be set at rest for ever; and if successful, we should have the merit of effecting a most wholesome and important revolution in apiarian economics, which would, indeed, deserve for us "the thanks of every apiarian in the kingdom."

It would be necessary to take careful notes in writing of the date and manner of interment, the quality of the soil, the situation and aspect of the cemetery, the weight of the hives, as well as the state of the weather at the time of interment, and the character of the after winter, at the same time noting the peculiarity of the experiment. It would be of importance, also, to ascertain as nearly as possible the age and pedigree of every queen, as an assistance in accounting for casualties which may occur. To insure uniformity and prevent mistakes, I will draw up a sort of scheme or form to be filled up, and returned to me in the spring, which may be had from the Editor of THE COTTAGE GARDENER, who will, I dare say, kindly undertake to forward it to any one who may apply for it. Progress might be reported and notes compared after the 1st of April, and towards the close of the next honey season in July; each person verifying his share in the experiment by appending his or her signature to the paper, the purport of which might be printed in THE COTTAGE GARDENER. In order to make the difficulty in the way of expense or sacrifice less formidable I would suggest that, if it be proposed to inter weighty and valuable hives, they should be buried according to Dr. Bevan's and Dr. Dunbar's plan, by which the hazard would probably be less. As for the other experiments, it would be easy to make cheap bargains with cottagers for late but *populous casts* (not for poor *stocks*—these probably would have an *old* queen, and be useless from other causes); or why not unite the population of such doomed hives together, according to the plan suggested by me in a former paper, feeding them plentifully for a week or two, till the *first frost* presented an opportunity for interring them. It would be well for them to have *some* comb—of course the more the better—and to have some bee-bread and food also (say 6 or 8 lbs weight), if only that they might start well in spring. If any of your readers have ever tried one or other of these systems of wintering bees, or any other unusual method, the testimony of their experience, in your pages, would be very gratefully received.—A Country Curate.

[We earnestly recommend the above to the attention of our readers; the experiments are easily tried, and the results may be very important. We shall be very willing distributers of the papers to any one who sends us *a ready directed and stamped envelope*.—Ed. C. G.]

ENGLISH CAGE BIRDS.

GARDEN WARBLER.

INSESSORES DENTIROSTRES. SYLVIADÆ.

Sylvia hortensis ; Motacilla hortensis ; Motacilla passerina ; Curruca hortensis : Greater Pettychaps; Garden Fauvette; Passerine Warbler; Garden Warbler; Billy Whitethroat; Nettle Creeper.

THE Garden Warbler is little inferior to the nightingale, and is considered by some to surpass the blackcap, which it much resembles, in activity, shyness, and restlessness,—secreting itself mostly amidst the dense foliage, beneath which it pours forth its melodious and often long continued song. It is not so commonly known as the two former birds, nevertheless, it is pretty general, but oftener heard than seen. It is somewhat larger than the blackcap, and its plumage is exceedingly plain and unobtrusive. If caught wild, its mode of treatment is similar to that of the blackcap, with this difference, that in addition to the bread, egg, and hempseed which should be given to it in a dry state, another portion should be mixed or moistened with hot water, a little are soft sugar and cream. Beef and egg mixed as for the nightingale; fruits of all kinds which are ripe and soft are the varieties of food on which it will thrive amazingly, and sing continuously. I need scarcely observe, he should be provided with a cup of water, and allowed to bathe if so disposed. The Garden Warbler is most easily reared from the nest, by feeding it at regular and short intervals upon fruit, such as strawberries cut in pieces small enough for the nestlings to swallow; raspberries in like manner and currants, red or white, occasionally with the paste above mentioned made with sugar and cream, and also the beef and egg. I should have observed, that grocer's currants may added when other fruit is not to be had with the dry food of bread, egg, and hempseed, &c. I have noticed that the Garden Warbler will feed most readily on the garden cabbage caterpillar, and which would be excellent food for those recently captured.—W. RAYNER.

[The Garden Warblers arrive in the south of England late in April, and gradually advance towards the north as summer approaches. They reach Sussex during the latter half of April, but in Cambridgeshire Mr. Jenyns mentions May 1st as the earliest day of their being heard in nine years. Mr. Blyth, in his excellent edition of "White's Selborne," says—"Its melody resembles somewhat the continuous note of the blackcap, but is softer, much deeper, and more flute-like in its tone, approaching to the mellifluous warble of the blackbird. I have noticed its singing with great spirit against a nightingale—determined not to be outdone. Its habits and nest exactly resemble those of the blackcap, but its eggs are grayer." It builds in a bush near the ground in a thick hedge, and usually lays four eggs. It resorts to gardens at the end of summer for the sake of the currants. Mr. Neville Wood observed it darting into the air to catch insects, in the manner of the spotted flycatcher, which it did with a loud snap of the bill, often taking its stand on a Dahlia stake, and returning thither from its hawking.]

WHITETHROATED FAUVET—WHITETHROAT.

INSESSORES DENTIROSTRES. SYLVIADÆ INSECTIVORÆ.

Sylvia cinerea ; Motacilla sylvia ; Curruca cinerea : White-throated Warbler; Common Whitethroat ; Nettle Creeper ; Peggy Whitethroat; Whey-beard; Wheetie-why; Churr; Muffott, Whattie, &c.

THIS bird is the most common and numerous of all our summer visitants. There is scarcely a hedge or a bush where it is not both seen and heard ; often rising upwards uttering its voluble and not unpleasant notes, with crest erected as if with pride, while his puffed-out throat plainly indicates the earnestness of its song. The natural food of this bird consists of insects, their larvæ, and fruit. Caterpillars are also a very favourite food with it, and when recently captured, if procurable, is the best description of food for it. When inured to confinement, it is readily kept on the nightingale's and garden warbler's food. For nestlings, which always remain exceedingly tame, and on that account are very desirable and interesting little birds, the same description of food will suit them as the young of the blackcap or garden warbler. I think it of importance with all young birds, to supply them often with a drop or two of water after feeding them. In confinement, this little bird is very pugnacious, and often quarrelsome—perfectly fearless of even a larger bird than himself ; and as if to show his consequence and prowess in driving away his antagonist, either from the food-drawer or water-cup, he immediately commences his song, erecting his crest, and distending his little throat, singing with all his might as if in defiance. The plumage of the Whitethroat is very sober and plain, and is distinguished by its chin and throat being perfectly white—hence its name.—W. RAYNER.

[The Whitethroat arrives between the 20th of April and 10th of May ; frequenting groves and hawthorn hedges. It is very vehement, and scolds with a churring voice, if you approach its nest. Its song is among the earliest during the mornings of summer; and it perseveres with its notes late into the evenings. It is found occasionally in gardens, feeding on the raspberries and currants. Its nest is usually among brambles and briars ; and is elegantly but loosely constructed of withered stalks and grass, lined with softer grass and a little hair. The eggs, usually five, are regularly oval, greenish white and speckled with purplish grey.—*Macgillivray's Brit. Birds.*]

COOLING DRINKS.

I RECOMMENDED in one of my papers, that those who had any of the common fruit in their gardens (such as strawberries, raspberries, currants, or gooseberries), should boil them with sugar and keep them for winter use. These fruits can also be turned to another account, and a very pleasant drink can be made with raspberries and currants, which will be found very useful in cases of illness. Thirst almost always accompanies disease, and those who have attended in a sick room well know with what pleasure a cool, refreshing draught is received.

If my receipts for making raspberry vinegar and currant acid should attract the attention of any who have a little time and a little money to spare (and how few have not) to lessen the discomforts of their poorer brethren, I strongly advise them to try them, and bottle a few pints for their use; it will be the means of giving a luxury to those who are unable to procure them for themselves ; and although the necessaries of life are certainly to be thought of before luxuries, yet, in sickness, any little extra is duly appreciated. Just enter the sick room of the generality of cottages. How devoid of all comfort does it appear! Illness, as we all know, is difficult to bear, but when with sickness comes poverty and neglect, how doubly painful must the dispensation of an all wise Providence be; and when the sufferer is not sustained by the never failing love of "Jesus Christ, and Him crucified," how pitiable must be his position! It is the duty of all to whom a portion of this world's goods have been given, to minister to the wants of others; and there is no time when our Christian sympathy is more wanted than in cases of sickness.

In order to make good RASPBERRY VINEGAR be careful that the fruit is picked on a dry day, and when perfectly ripe; put a quart into a large basin, and over them pour one quart of best vinegar. Let it stand 24 hours, stir it during that time occasionally, strain it through a flannel bag or thick cloth, and boil it for ten minutes with pounded loaf sugar, in the proportion of one pound to every pint of liquor. Do not squeeze the bag as it is running through, or it will be thick; and when it is boiling take off the scum as it arises. Pour it into bottles, but do not cork it down until it is quite cold, and then keep it in a cool place. When you wish to use it put a teaspoonful into a wine-glass of water.

CURRANT ACID.—Put 12 lbs. of currants that have been picked from their stems into a basin, and then melt five ounces of tartaric acid in two quarts of spring water; pour this over the currants, and let it remain for 24 hours; strain it, and to each pint of clear liquor add one pound and a half of finely powdered sugar; stir it constantly till it is dissolved, and then bottle it. This, if kept in a cool place, will keep good for years. Use it in about the same proportions as the raspberry vinegar. Raspberry acid can also be made in the same manner, merely substituting the raspberries for currants.

During the hot weather, when children require COOLING DRAUGHTS, a very pleasant and refreshing one can be made thus:—"Cream of tartar, half an ounce; white sugar, four ounces; boiling water, three pints: mix it all together and put it into a bottle." A wine-glassful drunk three or four times a-day will be found refreshing and wholesome.

SYRUP OF CURRANTS OR RASPBERRIES is a favourite beverage with many people. It is made thus:—When the red currants are quite ripe pick them from their stems, and put them into a stew-pan over the fire until they burst, then press them through a sieve, and put the liquor into a cool place until it becomes quite cold; strain it through a cloth, and sweeten with loaf sugar according to your taste. Do not boil it after the currants have burst. A little of this syrup mixed with spring water makes a very nice draught. Raspberries and cherries make an equally good syrup for those who like the flavour of those fruits; but if the latter fruit is used the kernels should be taken from the fruit, and put into the bottle when the syrup is made.—A FRIEND.

DOMESTIC MECHANISM.

PEA TRAINER.—The annexed sketch is a representation of an easily made contrivance for training peas (or other like plants, sweet peas, &c.,) upon. Take two pieces of wire, some four or five feet long, and bend their upper parts as shown in the sketch; connect the two together by means of thin wire. Insert the ends into the ground firmly, in such a manner as that the wires will form a kind of arch over the plants beneath. If the wire is made of iron, the parts inserted in the ground may be thrust into pieces of charred wood; this will prevent the damp from acting on the metal. If the wires are of zinc this will not be necessary, as the metal will not become oxidised like iron.

AMERICAN COTTAGE GATE SPRING.—Gates are generally hung so as to fall or shut close when left open. This is a great desideratum, more especially in gardens—excluding animals from them, when otherwise they might gain access through the gates, left open by the carelessness of attendants. The following plan we saw in America; it was pointed out to us as an excellent and simple contrivance:—Procure a circular elastic band some four or five inches diameter, and very strong; they can be purchased at almost every stationers; make two iron staples, such as is shown to the left of the annexed sketch. Fasten one of these near to the edge of the post to which the gate is hung, and at a height about the centre of the gate. In one of the cross bars of the gate, at the same height as the staple just mentioned, drive in the other staple. The distance between the two staples should be equal to the inside diameter of the elastic band when at rest (that is, when neither pulled one way or other), when the gate is fully open. Pass the elastic band over the two staples—the hooks will keep it in its place. When the gate is open the elastic band is at its natural state of distension. When the gate is left, instead of shutting noisily, as is generally the case, it falls gently forward, the elasticity of the band tending to pull it back, or keep it open, but the weight of the gate counterbalances it, and it arrives at the shutting point with force enough to get in the latch gently. This contrivance is greatly used in the United States; it is a useful one, and is cheaply and easily attainable. The parts of the staple on which the band rests should be smooth and well rounded; if they were left rough and angular, the band would soon be chafed and worn through. _a_ is the wall; _b_, the gate; the position of the band is shown by the thick black line.—D.

EXTRACTS FROM CORRESPONDENCE.

BIRD-SCARING.—There is one mode of keeping birds off fruit which, I believe, has not been mentioned in THE COTTAGE GARDENER, and yet it seems to be the most effectual way. I have, at this time, a kitten tied with a string three-quarters of a yard long to a ring that slips on an iron rod placed horizontally; by this means the kitten can travel over a large space up and down, without having a long string to get entangled. It was thus treated as soon as it could eat and drink, and has not known what liberty is since; I have hung an empty cotton reel to a tree close by, which serves as a plaything, and the kitten appears to be "as happy as the day is long." The old cat frequently visits it, and looks up at the birds which sit and scream with rage because they cannot come down to the strawberries. We have gathered, I should think, double the quantity of fruit in consequence of the kitten's presence. It is now removed to the raspberries, and we are likely to have a bountiful supply—thanks to puss! A large flower-pot, placed on its side at one end of the rod, serves as a shelter from heat and wet, and the old cat sleeps there with her kitten. In the description of the "Tirydail Shippen Vinery," there is no mention of a muslin screen, which might with advantage be stretched across from beam to beam, preventing the dust arising from littering straw, &c., reaching the grapes.—I am thy obliged, JANNET D.

PEAR MOTH.—The larva of this moth are very shy, hide themselves very ingeniously by spinning two leaves together, or fixing a leaf on the young fruit lengthwise. Each grub occupies its own quarry, for they are not social like the "tent moth" that attacks apple-trees, or the gooseberry caterpillar, who share a leaf together, until there is nothing left but the stalks or veins. But those are readily discovered, while the larva of the pear moth is hid in all kinds of ways, even in the crowns of the young fruit, protected by a web from which these caterpillars suddenly drop, or spin down like the most of their species when disturbed.

A writer lately stated that the cocoons of the grubs are laid up in the crowns of the fruit, while another denied it, alleging that the chrysalis would perish when the fruit rotted, or was consumed before the following season. Neither of these, however, seem to be well conversant with the economy of this pest, for their cocoons are usually found rolled up in the leaves, in general about a month from the time that they attack the trees; and if any happen to be in the crowns of the fruit they are hatched and take wing long before the fruit are either ripe or "rotten." There are doubts if the pear and apricot moth be the same species, but I have none myself, at least I never could see any difference in the grubs nor in their food. During this season I fed grubs taken from apricot trees on pear leaves, and also some of those from pear trees on apricot leaves: both parties throve alike. I kept them in small flower-pots, with wet sand at bottom, into which I stuck young shoots and leaves for food, and covered the top with gauze. Some of the prisoners commenced the silent or pupa state on the 8th of June, and were discharged or took wing about the 16th of July. I may observe that, in my long experience in gardening, I never knew a second attack by the pests during one season, consequently, I fear what Mr. Doubleday states in another quarter is not correct, namely, that the "grub forms a web in autumn, in which it passes the winter, to appear again in spring." The vigilant gardener knows that the cocoons of the pear moth are not defended by a web like those of the small "tussock moth," which also attacks pear trees. When this beautiful white moth is disturbed it "shams death" admirably, and its eggs are defended by a brown downy substance that comes from the abdomen of the insect while in the act of depositing them. I cannot speak correctly respecting the eggs of the pear moth, for I never could keep the insects long alive, at least to produce eggs; but I suspect they are laid shortly after the insects take wing, and remain in holes in the wall, or under the rough bark of the trees, until they blossom the following spring. If I am wrong in this point, and if it happens to come under the eye of Mr. Curtis, perhaps he will have the goodness to notice it: in the meantime I may observe, that the pest produced by a small brownish insect, not unlike the one that renders cloth "moth eaten," is spread broadcast all over the country, especially on wall trees in warm places; and also, that the house sparrow, and our summer visitant the red start, when not disturbed, hunt eagerly after the grubs; but hand-picking is the best remedy. I have known them very destructive in the neighbourhood of Edinburgh; and I recollect when a boy picking, or rather squeezing, the greenish worms among the leaves of my father's trees, and he used to tell me, "Laddie, be sure to nip the small hard brown ones (chrysalises), for they contain the flies that lay eggs for next spring."—J. WIGHTON.

BUDDING INSTRUMENT.—Beguiled by your interesting pages I have dabbled a little in budding roses—a process most clearly explained by you, and very simple in theory; but with me the "knack" is wanting which makes it easy to practise. "Bungling fellow!" you will say, "That's your affair." But stop, sir! I have the vanity to think I have compensated this absence of "knack," by a little mechanical ingenuity, which partial friends are wont to attribute to me. I introduce to your notice, herewith, a little contrivance which you may style "Tyro's Budding Plough." No explanation will be necessary for you, so I merely say, that the plough being very light, I leave it under the bark when in use, and have both hands at liberty for working the bud into position through the upper opening. Humble goosequill, horn, or tortoiseshell may be the material for the implement. —M. WALTHAMSTOW.

[Your "Budding Plough" was mislaid, and never came to the Editor's hands. From your description we think it must resemble "the Budding Implement" we have more than once mentioned, which may be had of Mr. Turner, Neepsend, Sheffield. His implement has a budding-knife at one end, and a hollowed plough at the other to keep the bark open, and to allow the bud to be slipped down behind. —ED. C. G.]

LAYERING CALCEOLARIAS.—As I have met with much disappointment by trying to strike cuttings of calceolarias, I tried, with success, the plan of layering, as follows :—I took the plant, with its ball of earth, out of a pot, and cut away part of root and earth, and laid it in a long dish—so every shoot becomes a plant. The above will answer for all sorts of plants I have tried that will root by cuttings, only a peg should be put down where each division is to be made, to save ruining all with the knife.—T. HILL, Pinxton.

DOUBLE STOCKS.—My attention has been directed to the article on double flowers; as I have been growing stocks these last seventeen years, I may be able to give an opinion on the subject; but I have had no occasion to puzzle my brain about the best method of getting double ones, as mine is a sort that produces more double than single every year—I should say, in the proportion of seven out of nine, invariably. They are good colour, and bloom beautifully, not spilling up in the middle and lasting but one year, but yielding a great number of fine flowers, and standing two or three years. I had one, two or three years ago, on which I counted fifty-three flowers; and the plant about three feet high. I should have been happy to have sent you some seed, but unfortunately I did not save any last year, as I removed from the neighbourhood, and the few plants that I have are all double; there are some growing in the neighbourhood, from which I hope to get some seed. About twenty-five years ago, I sowed some seed from the plants; I selected thirty-five for planting, and gave away the rest. I suppose I kept the best plants for myself; out of the thirty-five, I had seven double ones. But on enquiry, I found that the plants I gave away produced a much larger proportion of double than mine, so I concluded that to have double flowers it would be best to choose small plants. Mentioning the subject to a nurseryman several years afterwards, said he—"There was a lady here this spring for some plants, she says, 'Pick out the small plants, sir ;' I said, Madam, why do you wish to have the small ones ? 'Because,' said she, 'there is a better chance of getting double flowers from small plants.'" This mode of selecting plants may be best in some sort of stocks, but for the sort I have there is no necessity. Some people (and it is a favourite notion among most people) imagine that if you tie a single stock to a double, there is a greater chance of having double ones; but I would as soon tie it to the leg of a stool as to a double one, for the chance I should have for double ones. If a bee alights on a double stock, it will not tarry there a moment: there is nothing there for it. It may be deemed huge presumption in me to suggest to a master in the floral department, but I would just say, suppose you take seed from the last pod in the stock, which may be supposed to be the weakest seed on the plant, or seeds from the extremity of any pod, and try them next year. As to the soil they require, it should be rich and deep, but no dung, except it is well decomposed, as new manure is apt to breed worms, which very often injure the roots.—J. O. ANTHONY, *Providence Mines, near St. Ives.*

RASPBERRY ACID.—As I see directions in THE COTTAGE GARDENER of July 25 for making raspberry vinegar, I am induced to mention another way of preparing the raspberries, which produces a far more pleasant beverage than the vinegar. In lingering illnesses among the poor, especially consumptive, I have found that a small bottle of this "acid" was a gift very highly valued :—Dissolve 5 oz. of Tartaric acid in two quarts of cold water; pour it on 12 ℔ of fruit, in a *deep* pan. Let it stand twenty-four hours. Strain the liquor from the fruit, without pressing; and to every pint add 1¼ ℔ of pounded white sugar. Stir it frequently (in a cool place) till the sugar is all melted. Bottle, cork, and seal it close, and keep it in a cool place. Warmth would cause fermentation, and the bottles would perhaps burst; and, if that did not happen, the liquid would become lumpy and less agreeable. A tablespoonful of the liquid is enough to mix with half a pint of water, when it is required for use.—WILCOT.

BREAD MAKING.—Your lady contributor, in writing on the making of bread, omits one thing which long experience has proved to me to be very important. In heating an oven, a much smaller quantity of time and wood is consumed if care is taken that every part of the floor of the oven is, in its turn, kept *quite clear* of wood and ashes : it should be as clean as it can be scraped. In no other way can the bottom of the oven be heated thoroughly. I cannot tell why, but it seems to me that the heaped-up embers prevent the free circulation of hot air over every part. However that may be, the effect is certain. Heated in this way the oven will give you loaves as crisp at bottom as at top ; whereas, if this precaution is neglected you will have many loaves well baked in all parts except the bottom, which will be soft and tough, and to which every particle of ashes left on the floor will have adhered. With regard to the advice in making bread, to "knead it well," it is good for those who wish their families to consume as little as possible, for it makes the bread closer and harder; but for *luxury*, the bread should have *not one unnecessary punch.*—WILCOT.

STRENGTHENING A HIVE OF BEES.—After having written to you, I arrived at the conclusion that no second swarm might be expected from either stocks (which you confine), and in one I cut a 3¼ inch hole, affixed a board 12 inches square, and added a small box, the bees have since commenced to persecute the drones, and I presume their slaughter will soon succeed. The other hive being coated with Roman cement, with only a small hole for ventilation. I placed on a box 12 inches long, 12 inches broad, and 5 inches deep, with a two-inch aperture on the top, and from its roof the bees soon hung in a large cluster, quite inactive, although breeding was evidently going on rapidly. Yesterday evening I gently lifted off the hive, turned up the box, sprinkled the cluster with sugar-syrup, and placed over it a box containing a cast, to which I intended to add the whole stock in autumn, or any other casts that have come forth. The union was perfect, and the increased industry of the enlarged colony was evident; the old stock of course was removed a few miles away, where it also is working. By this I prevent, I hope, one from swarming, and give an early addition to the weak population of the other. Matters to you perfectly simple and easy of explanation, to an amateur are often insuperable difficulties, and I mention my proceedings (fulfilling, in part, by anticipation, the spirit of your advice kindly given), thinking it may amuse you to witness the resources of a novice in perplexity.—J. B. P.

HARDY BEAUTIFUL FLOWERS.—My flower-beds contain some plants of very great beauty, which I would recommend to the notice of those of your readers who are not already acquainted with them. The *Mimulus Robinus* has been in bloom now (July 19th), for nearly three months, and has had more than 30 flowers out at a time. I have also the *Œnothera grandiflora*, which I think unequalled in beauty, with 8 or 10 flowers out every evening. The *Calandrinia umbellata*, with its beautiful purple crimson flowers, the *Phlox Drummondii, Chelone barbata,* the *Heliophila trifida*; these, with Penstemons, Campanulas, Geraniums, Verbenas, and Fuchsias, make my garden look very gay. I have only four beds, and am therefore able to keep them in order entirely myself.—E. O., *Devon.*

COTTAGER'S HORTICULTURAL SOCIETIES.—Most delighted are we to see these so widely on the increase, and no efforts of ours shall be wanting to promote their prosperity. We have received the reports of many, but none in a form we can quote, except that of the Blithfield Horticultural Show. It has been established chiefly through the exertions of the Hon. and Rev. H. C. Bagot, and held its first meeting this month in Blithfield Park, the seat of Lord Bagot, near Rugeby.

"A large temporary room, decorated with garlands, evergreens, and flowers, was, by the kindness of Lord Bagot, erected in the centre of the avenue of spreading lime-trees, for the exhibition, through which the visitors passed into the gardens and pleasure-grounds of his lordship, which were kindly thrown open for the occasion. Previous to the opening of the show, the school children arrived in procession, each with a nosegay of wild flowers, for several of which prizes were awarded; the children seeming to vie with their parents and others in the interest they took in the proceedings. The examination of these wild nosegays by Miss Bagot, was one of the most pleasing incidents of the day; and the detection here and there of a doubtful flower caused much amusement. The prizes were distributed by Lord Bagot, assisted by the Hon. and Rev. H. C. Bagot, to whose exertions, we understand, the origin and success of the society are chiefly owing. The children afterwards engaged in a number of amusements, which greatly enlivened the scene. A brass band from Stafford was in attendance.

"We cannot but wish that such exhibitions were more frequent than they are. The occasions on which all classes meet together on a common ground of enjoyment are now so rare, and are daily becoming rarer by the modern habits of social life, that even were the object less useful and pleasing than the encouragement of gardening among the poor, we should still hail with pleasure any occasion that brought the tenant and his landlord, the farmer and his labourer, the peer and the squire, the squire and the yeoman, into an hour's disinterested and unrestrained intercourse. It was impossible not to observe the real and unaffected enjoyment in which all classes participated at the Blithfield show; there was such an utter absence of all pride, reserve, and awkwardness, that one could not but feel that as long as scenes of this description recur, so long (and perhaps no longer) will there be no fear of the kindly links of mutual respect—stronger than all laws—which now bind together the rich and the poor, being broken. We heartily wish success to this and all similar institutions, and hope that the same propitious sun, and the same good feeling, may brighten the exhibitions of many succeeding years."

BALSAM GROWING.—I find in reading my treatment of the balsam, vol. iii., page 358, there is a little mistake. Six weeks should have been eight weeks for the time between potting and blooming; and "Fedington" should have been "Toddington." I have at the present time balsams that were potted from the seed pots on May 23rd, that on July 18th measured at the base of the stem four inches in circumference and three feet two inches round near the top of the side branches. Average height one foot ten inches. They are in pots eleven inches by eleven inches.—J. HUNT, *Toddington, near Dunstable, Bedfordshire.*

ANTS.—I have read many ways of destroying these pests, but the following never. I accidentally placed an empty garden pot over an ant's track, where it remained a fortnight; on moving it I found a complete nest full of eggs, ants, and earth, which I put into a pail of boiling water and destroyed the whole. I repeated the process with equal success.—J. S., *Kingston.*

PICKLED VEGETABLE MARROW.—Cut the marrow in thick slices and salt them twelve hours, and then dry them in the sun; then boil three quarts of vinegar, with a pound of the flour of mustard, a good handful of black pepper, a few allspice and cloves, thirty-six bay leaves, and a stick of horseradish cut in slices; boil them altogether until it is the thickness of cream, and pour it hot over the marrow and cover it close. Add to the above one pound of mustard seed, half an ounce of long pepper, quarter of an ounce of mace, and nine green capsicums, boiled in a pint of vinegar with a teaspoonful of Cayenne. It will be fit for use in six months.

CURRANT JELLY.—Add to every pound of currants three-quarters of a pound of loaf sugar, and put them altogether into the preserving pan, and when the sugar is quite dissolved let it boil only six minutes, and then strain it through a fine sieve into a large bason with a lip to it; then pour it quickly into your jars. The pulps may be boiled up again for ten or fifteen minutes, with the addition of half a pound of sugar to four pounds of pulp, and a pint of fresh currants or raspberries; it makes a nice jam to be used soon, as it will not keep long. All jellies and jams should be covered with writing paper cut round and dipped in white of egg.

RASPBERRY JAM.—Boil the raspberries with a little currant juice for ten minutes, then add three-quarters of a pound of sugar to a pound of fruit, and boil it five minutes more after the sugar is dissolved and it begins to boil.

AN EXCELLENT CAKE THAT WILL KEEP GOOD A YEAR.—Three-quarters of a pound of flour, three-quarters of a pound of butter, and the same quantity of currants, raisins, and brown sugar; one ounce of almonds blanched and put to dry before the fire, five eggs well beaten, one ounce of orange peel, and the same of lemon peel; the butter to be beat up to a cream, and mixed by degrees with the flour; add a wine glass of brandy. This cake should not be cut under three months.

EVERLASTING CHEESECAKES.—To a quarter of a pound of butter put a pound of loaf sugar, the yolks of six eggs, the rind of two lemons, and the juice of three lemons, and to these add a little grated biscuit; put all into a preserving or stew-pan, and let it simmer over the fire until the sugar is dissolved and it begins to thicken like honey; you must then put it into a jar for use. Line small patty pans with puff paste and put a little in each.

344   THE COTTAGE GARDENER.   [AUGUST 29

TO CORRESPONDENTS.

TO OUR READERS.

We are very sorry, after the notice we have so publicly given, that any one should so little know what is correct conduct as to persist in writing to our coadjutors, Mr. Beaton and others. Mr. Beaton writes to us thus :—" I am overwhelmed with applications from your readers for cuttings and other things ; and one party notices and neglects your warning not to write to us privately by saying, ' I do not write to you as a writer of THE COTTAGE GARDENER, but in your private capacity.' An acute casuist this! *From this day forth Donald Beaton will take no notice of private letters, even though they contain postage stamps.*" Mr. Beaton is quite right ; and we trust, after this notice, to hear no more of such conduct, which no plea can justify.

** We request that no one will write to the departmental writers of THE COTTAGE GARDENER. It gives them unjustifiable trouble and expense. All communications should be addressed "*To the Editor of The Cottage Gardener,* 2, Amen Corner, Paternoster Row, London."

SLOPING BANKS (*J. A. M.*).—As you do not "altogether understand Mr. Barnes's account" of these most useful structures, we will give the following from *The Gardener's Almanack* of the present year. "Supposing the banks to run east and west, the south side, especially as respects all low-growing things, such as French beans, potatoes, &c., will produce eight days earlier than when cultivated on the level, while the north side will retain lettuces, &c., during summer, much longer fit for the table. The surface of the ground is also increased, notwithstanding learned assertions to the contrary. In making them at first in shallow soils, they should not be wider than six feet at the base ; but as the soil becomes improved they may be from 10 to 12 feet in width. In deep soils, the banks may be formed by trenching in the usual manner, only throwing it into shape by a line and stakes. In thin soils, care should be taken to have plenty of room in the first opening to stir the subsoil, and then replace again the surface soil on the surface. The accompanying sketch

will give some idea as to how they are formed, each ridge being 12 feet wide at the base. A B is the ground level, c the apex of the ridge, and d d paths between. Of course they could not be raised so high at first without impoverishing the other ground. If drained beneath the paths all the better—for in heavy land, without drainage and deep stirring, the moisture will be long retained. If at c there is a board fixed, or even a row of dwarf hardy peas, the south side will be rendered still warmer, and the north side more cool and late. Such banks, therefore, may not only be used for vegetables, but also those for accelerating and retarding fruits, such as the strawberry. Owing to the depth of soil thus obtained, if the surface is kept stirred, you will never need much of the water-pot, even in the driest weather. The right hand or south side should be the longest, and, in a succession of ridges, the northernmost one should be the highest."

LINUM CATHARTICUM (*Rusticus*).—This weed, commonly known as Purging Flax or Mill Mountain, can only be eradicated by constantly cutting it down. Mowing off the tops, and sowing salt thickly over the place, if repeated two or three times, will usually eradicate it. The grass, also, will be destroyed *at the time,* but will eventually yield a greener and better herbage. The black-seeded melon from Malta, we have little doubt, is the common *water melon* ; and, if so, worthless in our climate.

BUDDING ROSES (*D. W. G*).—July is the best month for budding those planted in November.

LIQUID-MANURE (*Ibid*).—Half a pound of oil of vitriol poured into your 40 gallons of pig-stye and water-closet drainage, will fix all the ammonia ; and one gallon of the compound mixed with five gallons of water will be quite strong enough for your kitchen-garden crops. Weak liquid-manure is beneficial to cabbages, celery, &c. ; but if strong, it kills or greatly injures them.

GOOSEBERRY-TREES NEGLECTED (*Ibid*).—Without seeing them, it is impossible to give a positive judgment whether it would be best to uproot them and plant young ones. We should recommend you to thin out the old branches, and reduce the young shoots on those left both in number and to half their length. From the cuttings of the young shoots (rather than suckers), after *cutting out down into the very wood* all buds to be planted beneath the soil, we should raise young trees to succeed the old ones ; for these will bear some fruit, but your cuttings not for two or three years.

CALYSTEGIA PUBESCENS (*T. T. T.*).—You cannot obtain seed either of this or of the *Kerria japonica* of the seedsmen. The latter may be readily grown from young cuttings. If by " flies on geraniums " you mean the green fly or aphis, give them a good fumigating with tobacco-smoke, whilst each plant is covered over with a sheet propped up by a stake to keep it from breaking the plant.

UNITING HIVES (*W. O. W.*).—You will see what Mr. Payne says to-day upon this subject. We are sorry that you should have postponed trying " the Country Curate's " plan.

BLUE GLASS FOR GERMINATING SEEDS (*A Lover of Flowers*).—It is quite true, as Mr. Hunt and others testify, that seeds germinate more rapidly under blue glass than under colourless glass ; but we are quite sure that they do not germinate so strongly, and the moment the leaflets appear it does positive harm. If you wish to try the experiment turn a blue finger-glass over some of the seed. For striking cuttings such coloured glass is useless ; it has no influence over the production of roots.

KITCHEN-GARDEN CROPS WITHERING (*J. W., Leith*).—You need seek for no other reason for this failure beyond the fact you state, that you have only " ten inches of light soil, with a sandy gravelly subsoil." The remedy you are adopting of trenching the subsoil two feet deep is the best remedy you can adopt ; and we should turn in with it abundance of sea-weed, which you have at command. You will find mulch about your crops, with a little earth covered over it, the best mode of manuring your crops ; it would keep their roots moist. Your *rhubarb* will be benefited especially by this, and the frequent application of liquid manure. All the leaves whilst green should never be taken off rhubarb, for they have to prepare the sap and ripen the buds for next year's growth ; when the leaves are dead they may be removed, because then their usefulness is over.

HARES AND WILD RABBITS (*J. M. U.*).—These will not thrive if kept in coops or hutches. Cowper the poet's account of keeping tame hares is most interesting ; but they were allowed to frisk about in the house and garden. *Poultry* may be kept in a shed enclosed with wire, and will thrive. It is impossible to say how much water is sufficient for a *strawberry plant* ; it must depend so much upon the soil and temperature ; twice the quantity you mention, given every night, on a light soil, and in dry weather would not be too much.

WALL TREES (*Ibid*).—Plant three-year old well balanced trees of the following : *Apricots* — Shipley's, Breda, Moorpark. *Peaches* — Acton Scott, Royal George, Bellegarde. *Nectarines* — Early Newington, Pitmaston Orange, Violette Hative.

VERBENAS (*F. H.*).—You are right, it is best to keep only a few *good* plants of the different verbenas and petunias over the winter, and to begin to work from them early in the spring. All of them should be topped till the new year, if they are growing freely.

AIMEE VIBERT ROSE (*Ibid*).—This will root from cuttings either in pots or in the open ground. Now is a good time ; but the cuttings may be made from March to October. It is the only rose we know which smells offensively, but being dwarf and a free bloomer it makes a good white bed or edging.

FORTUNE'S PIT (*Subscriber*).—All the dimensions given of this pit may be so reduced as to fit your requirements ; but without knowing in what respects you fail to apply it, we cannot be of use to you.

VINERY (*Novice*).—You will have length sufficient for two nice houses, each twenty-four feet long. You may thus make one the early house, and the other a late or winter one. Do not make them an inch higher—back or front—than is really wanted for head room. In order to keep them low, there is no real necessity for a person to have height enough to stand upright at the front inside ; about a yard in depth may suffice at front, and about ten feet at back. The interior arrangement must vary according to the use you intend making of the interior area. Growing pines beneath the vines depends on whether you are determined to have some, and whether you will build a house or pit specially for them. Pines may be grown beneath vines, but it would be far better and more economical in the end to grow them in a separate place. For the early grapes, a provision must be made inside for their roots, and the front wall on arches, to let the roots go out as they like. In the late house, the roots may be entirely outside. The hot-water pipes must, of course, be placed inside the pits or houses.

CARNATION CUTTINGS (*M. J.*).—Unless your cuttings are very young we should have preferred cutting them across at the first or second joint, instead of the third. If slit up the centre for a short space, as recommended by Mr. Fish lately, they would root all the sooner if the wood was hard ; if soft, it would not be needed ; and your cutting at the third joint will answer. Your inserting them in a hand-light will answer if you can continue the mild bottom heat you gave them. They will generally show a swelling of cellular matter at the base in from a fortnight to a month. If, after that, roots are not quickly formed, raise them carefully, and without touching the bottom part place them round the sides of well drained pots, and plunge these in a mild bottom heat. From the first shade in bright sunshine and give air at night. Your shortening of the leaves was a matter of little consequence, provided you could keep them from flagging ; roots would sooner have been formed by the leaves being left entire.

LEMON PLANT (*Novice*).—Cuttings of the *Aloysia citriodora* strike most freely in spring in a little heat, such as a cucumber box ; ripened shoots strike freely in autumn in a warm shady place ; small half-ripened side shoots will strike freely now in sand, covered with a hand-light or bell-glass, kept close during the day, with a little air at night, and without bottom heat. If you find they do not strike fast enough, place the pot in a little bottom heat in two or three weeks, but the plants will be more tender in consequence.

FORCING FLOWERS FOR A GREENHOUSE IN SPRING (*L. E. S.*).—If you would tell us what you chiefly want we should better be able to meet your wishes. With pits that can be artificially heated, you may almost have anything you like, such as violets, bulbs, geraniums, calceolarias, cinerarias, azaleas, camellias, &c. If you will be more precise as to your wants, we will endeavour to meet the case.

ROSES FOR TRELLIS (*B. C.*).—With the exception of *Russellians*, the roses you mention, such as *Chenedolle, Great Western*, &c., are *not* climbing roses, but they are strong growing, and very beautiful, and will soon cover your arch, unless it is very high, and be more brilliant than climbing roses generally are. Every rose grower will supply them.

STONE JARS (*Ibid.*).—These filled with hot water, and often enough renewed, will keep oranges from frost during the winter in a small greenhouse, three yards and a half square, and four yards high. In very severe weather use a little protection besides.

LILIUM LANCIFOLIUM (*A New Subscriber*).—All the varieties are desirable. They are quite hardy in most places. They, however, make fine ornaments for a greenhouse in autumn ; and for this purpose they should be potted shortly after they have done flowering, placing four or six large bulbs in a twelve or fourteen-inch pot, three inches below the rim of the pot, using equal portions of loam, peat, and leaf-mould dried, and half quantities of old cow-dung and silver sand, and kept either in a cold pit during the winter, or covered up with ashes or tan similar to hyacinths. If you obtain small bulbs, you must not expect much bloom for a year or two ; bulbs, according to the size and varieties, will average in price from 2s. 6d. to 4s. ; but these matters we cannot enter into, nor yet to recommend nurserymen.

BRICK PIT (*J.*).—We suspect your heat from the dung failed, because you either had not enough of dung, it had not been sufficiently worked and sweetened, or the heat failing, you had no means of renewing it by linings. Less trouble will be given by using tan, because it will soon be sweet, and will retain heat longer than dung, unless well made. It is often advisable, in the case of plunging plants, to have a little tan laid over the surface of fermented dung. We presume you planted your cucumbers and melons in appropriate soil, though you speak of placing manure in the *centre* of the tan-bed. Your cucumbers may have failed from other causes than the want of heat in the bed, as little would be required. Greenhouse plants may be preserved in such a pit, but more by attending to coverings than to any heat the bed may retain.

MYRTLES (*Clara*).—We give our myrtles and pomegranates two month's gentle forcing in a vinery, or, say, during April and May, and both flower well from July. We turn them out on the first of June.

SCARLET GERANIUMS (*Erina*).—Follow Aunt Harriet's plan by all means ; those you refer to were intended for a particular purpose, which might not suit you, even if you could follow it up.

NEW GROUND (*T. P.*).—The piece of new ground attached to your house at Islington is likely to be of stiff earth. It will require no manure the first season ; trench it before winter, and as the work goes on try and put in a few drains, two feet deep. Leave the top very rough and the frost will mellow it. In March, when it is dry, fork it over and over five or six inches deep, and if you find it stiff put a quantity of fine coal-ashes or sand on it, to lighten it, and after that flowers and shrubs will grow well on it next year. Almost all the evergreens we mentioned in former numbers will grow on the shaded parts.

WEIGELA ROSEA (*C. W. B.*).—You have done perfect justice to this plant ; the reason why it did not bloom last spring was, that last season's growth was finished too late in the autumn, and the late hard winter injured the tips of the immature wood, from which the flowers should issue. Now that you have it a yard high, and as much across, we should think it could not fail to flower late next spring ; if you see any more signs of growth extending this autumn, push a sharp spade down through the roots, at two feet or 30 inches from the stem, that will stop it, and cause it to flower better.

DOUBLE-BLOSSOMED GORSE OR FURZE (*C. J. M.*).—Plant cuttings of the young shoots in a shady border under a hand-light. The single-blossomed is best raised from seed.

GENTIANELLA SOWING (*Ibid.*).—Sow in pots of light sandy loam, in March, and keep in a cold-pit, giving the seedlings plenty of air. They may be transplanted into a bed of light earth very early in the autumn.

RACODIUM CELLARE (*Ibid.*).—It is very possible if this is moved from the old cask to the side or roof of your cellar, that it may grow. It likes a mild damp air, but not a *wet* wall. We should put it upon a piece of rotten wood and fasten this to the wall. If you will refer to our indexes, you will find all you require about *pits*. We will answer your other question next week.

RYLOTT'S FLOUR-BALL POTATOE (*W. L.*).—This is a perfectly *white* potato, flattish round, deeply sunk eyes, and roughish skin. It is one of the most mealy and best flavoured potatoes we know. It has no pink colour about it anywhere. It ripens in the first week of August, but with us, though a good bearer, not so prolific as Martin's Early Seedling ; the latter, however, is scarcely so mealy or so good flavoured. We shall be glad to receive your promised communication.

BEES (*G. Ambler*).—If you put your neighbour's stupified bees, the tenants of two or three hives, into one, and feed them with barley sugar as much as they can consume, you *possibly* may save them. "A Country

Curate" (whom we know to be a good authority), says it should be done by the 10th of August. But try the experiment. We have given a recipe for *barley sugar* at page 55 of our present volume. Answers to other queries next week.

BOOKS ON SMALL FARMING, &c. (*J. C. M.*).—Farming from books you will find a difficulty. They give suggestions, but practice must teach how to carry them into effect. *Rham's Dictionary of Farming, Spooner on Sheep*, and *Cobbett's Cottage Economy*, will suit you. These and Martin Doyle's *Hints to Small Farmers* may be all had for about sixteen shillings.

NAMES OF PLANTS (*Subscriber, Bury St. Edmunds*).—1. *Rhus Cotinus*, or American Sumach. 2. *Euphorbia Cyparissias*, or Cypress Spurge. 3. A *Veronica*, probably *V. spicata*, but no one could tell from such a specimen.

BOOKS (*T. O.*).—There is no book better than Mackintosh's. Wait for *The Cottage Gardener's Dictionary*, which will contain all the information you require. (*A Young Naturalist*).—Dr. Lindley's *Introduction to Botany and Vegetable Kingdom*, especially the latter, will best put you in possession of the generic characters according to the natural system.

UNDER-HIVING BEES (*P. S. B.*).—This, which it appears you have adopted, is very bad practice ; you can never in this way have any fine honey. You should have placed the additional hive on the top ; room being given will never prevent a second swarm. Let your hives remain as they are until February, and then on a mild day separate them ; the bees will then be found to be in the upper hives, and the honey as well. Had you followed the advice given in our paper, by placing your hives above instead of below, you might now have taken from No. 1 25 lbs. of fine honey, and from the swarm 15 lbs. The east as it is will make you an excellent stock.

HALF-FORMED BEES (*C.*).—These which you have seen put out of the hive are drones not matured, which are always torn from the cells at the time of the general massacre. The bees on the floor board indicates its strength and prosperity.

HUMMING IN HIVE (*J. S.*).—The loud humming noise in your Taylor's hive during the hot days of July indicated its prosperous and healthy state; and when it became cooler it ceased, and the bees appeared reduced in number till a hot day came. It is not at all unusual for them to remove the honey from unsealed combs at the side of the hive. A prime swarm of June 19th should have done more than yours appears to have done. The slides were withdrawn at a proper time, but the season has not been sufficiently good for them to work up into the box. You have done right in replacing the slides. As you will feed at the top begin immediately, and feed until you have twenty pounds in the stock box. The box with glass top must always be uppermost, and when a third is required it is placed between the two already full, because the bees will take to it more readily, being in the centre of the colony, than if placed empty on the top.

CALENDAR FOR SEPTEMBER.

ORCHID HOUSE.

AIR must now be given, but sparingly when the sun is bright, to dry the damp off the young pseudo-bulbs. BLOCKS, look to ; if much decayed remove the plants from, and renew. FIRES, light now every night, especially in the India house ; but do not raise the night temperature so high as the day by 10°. DENDROBIUMS, and similar plants that have finished their summer growth, remove to a cooler and drier house ; giving very little water at the root,—twice during the month will be enough. NEWLY-IMPORTED PLANTS place upon logs, and keep rather dry and cool ; vegetation must be very slowly induced, for the young and old shoots or pseudo-bulbs will perish if too quickly excited. SHADES may be almost entirely dispensed with, especially on span-roofed houses, facing east and west. WATER, apply sparingly, even in bright weather; in dull sunless days give none, either in the shape of water or atmospheric moisture.

T. APPLEBY.

STOVE PLANT HOUSE.

AIR, give freely during the day, especially when the sun shines; this will keep the plants from spindling up, and will preserve the leaves. ACHIMENES done blooming remove into a cold pit ; keep them perfectly dry, but not too much exposed to the sun. BARK-BEDS, where any, should now be renewed, and the worms and other insects found in them destroyed. It is important to do this now, so as to obtain a moderate bottom heat before winter—at that season it is dangerous. CLEANLINESS and order must be constantly attended to; the plants should have their leaves sponged ; the pots must have all the moss and dirt thoroughly scrubbed off ; the earth on the surface ought to be removed and some fresh put on; and the whole of the collection should be arranged for the winter campaign. AUTUMN AND WINTER BLOOMING PLANTS, such as Begonias, Gesnera zebrina, picta and oblongata, Justicias, Salvias, and Sericographis, should have a moderate supply of water, occasionally mixed with liquid-manure. *Plants* that have been set out in *frames* or in the greenhouse to harden their growth bring now into the stove PRUNE severely all straggling plants, creepers, &c., so as to reduce their size and cause short branchy habit. POTTING, very little needed, excepting by very young plants of vigorous habit of growth ; these pot and place close to the glass. Regulate the plants, so as to give all an equal share of *light* ; place them thin, even if some have to be thrown away. Of all mistakes that is the greatest, of keeping more plants than will stand at a right distance from each other. Even in winter no one plant should interlace with or even touch another. SUCCULENTS bring in and place in the driest part of the house. WATER sparingly, and that in a morning, so as to have the damp dried up before the evening. Temperature—by day 65°, by night 55°.　　　　　　T. APPLEBY.

FLORISTS' FLOWERS.

AURICULAS and POLYANTHUSES, protect from heavy rains; remove into winter quarters about the last week in the month. CINERARIAS, repot twice during the month; carefully protect them from early frosts, as they are very impatient of cold, yet do not like heat. A cold frame or pit is the best place for them. CARNATIONS and PICOTEES, take off rooted layers; pot, and place under a shade for a while till fresh roots are made. CHRYSANTHEMUMS, pot for the last time, and still keep them in the open air, watering occasionally with liquid-manure. DAHLIAS, keep well tied, and the best blooms sheltered from wet, sunshine, and insects; supply with liquid-manure in dry weather. HYACINTHS, a few for very early blooming may be potted at the end of the month. IRISES (bulbous), plant at the end of the month. PINKS, plant out about middle of month where they are to bloom. PANSIES, plant, when strong; if weak, pot four in a pot five inches wide; to be protected in a pit through winter. TULIP and RANUNCULUS beds renew and turn over frequently.
　　　　　　T. APPLEBY.

GREENHOUSE.

AIR, give freely night and day, unless when very stormy. BULBS, pot for early blooming, such as Hyacinths, Narcissus, Tulips, &c., also Lachenalias, Brodiæas, &c. CAMELLIAS, still expose, but defend from heavy rains. CINERARIAS, sow, prick off seedlings, shift into flower pots for winter. CALCEOLARIAS, sow seed; propagate by cuttings under hand-lights, and shift. ERICAS and AZALEAS, get under shelter, ready to be housed by the end of the month. GERANIUMS, MYRTLES, SALVIAS, &c., propagate by cuttings, shift into larger pots, to be established before winter, and prepare for taking up out of the open border by cutting round the roots, doing only one half at a time. Where there is not plenty of room cuttings struck early will answer better. GLASS, PLUGS, &c., clean and repair. PLANTS, clean, tie, arrange. POTS, free from moss and filth, and fresh surface with suitable compost. SEEDLINGS of all kinds, prick out as soon as they can be handled. PROPAGATE all half-hardy things, such as Geraniums, Fuchsias, Salvias, and especially Calceolarias, Petunias, Verbenas, &c.; the last three named will do better than if struck earlier, the smallest pieces will do best. WATER will still be abundantly required for plants growing freely, and those intended to bloom in winter, such as Primroses, Cinerarias, and Chrysanthemums, should have manure-water given freely. Whenever you observe the first flower bud of a Chrysanthemum, though no larger than a pin-head, you may give the clear manure-water freely. Water should be given sparingly to plants that are to be put into a state of rest; give very little water until the pot is getting filled with roots, as they cannot bear sour sodden soil; let the pots be well drained. CLIMBERS will soon require cutting that have been growing rather naturally, in order that more light may be given to the plants below.
　　　　　　R. FISH.

FLOWER-GARDEN.

ACONITE (Winter), plant, e. ANEMONES, plant best, e.; sow, b. ANNUALS (Hardy), sow, b. AURICULAS not shifted in August now remove; water and shade; prepare awning to protect in autumn and winter; sow, b. BULBOUS-ROOTS, plant for early blooming, e.; sow, b. CARNATION layers remove, b. CHRYSANTHEMUMS, plant cuttings, &c., b. CUT ROUND THE ROOTS of large specimens intended to be taken up next month, b. Cut in large specimens of geraniums, &c., in the beds to be potted, as soon as they break, to make specimens of, b. DAHLIAS, number and make list of whilst in perfection: describing their colour, height, &c. DRESS borders assiduously. EDGINGS, trim, plant. EVERGREENS, plant, b.; make layers. FIBROUS-ROOTED perennials, propagate by slips, parting roots, &c. FORK over vacant compartments. GRASS, mow and roll; sow, b. GRAVEL, weed and roll. GUERNSEY LILIES, pot. HEARTSEASE, plant cuttings; trim old. HEDGES, clip, e.; it is the best time. MIGNONETTE, sow in pots, to shelter in frames. ROOTED PIPINGS, pipings of pinks, &c., plant out for blooming. PLANTING, generally commence, e. POLYANTHUSES, plant. RANUNCULUSES, plant best, e.; sow, b. DOUBLE ROCKETS, divide and transplant. SEEDLINGS, plant out. SEEDS, gather as ripe. TRANSPLANT perennials, e. TUBEROUS-ROOTED plants, transplant. TURF, lay. VERBENAS, cut the roots of favourite sorts, six inches from the stem; water them, and in three weeks they may be removed safely to be kept in pots; a few plants thus treated are better than many cuttings. WATER Annuals and other plants in dry weather.　　D. BEATON.

ORCHARD.

LOAMY COMPOSTS prepare for planting fruit-trees, Commence and continue GATHERING fruits as they ripen. GRAPES, bag or cover from wasps, whether on walls or in houses. Of SUPERFLUOUS SHOOTS on trained trees make a general removal, or shorten them where gross. NETS, apply to fruit-trees, to secure from birds. NEW FRUIT PLANTATIONS, make preparations for as soon as leisure occurs; planting may commence, e., with some fruits, provided the wood is ripened. STRAWBERRIES, remove in moist weather; strawberry-beds, dress from waste runners, b. STONES of fruit for stocks, save. WALL-TREES in general, look over once more. WASPS, entrap by hanging bottles; wasps' nests still destroy. RASP-

BERRIES, cut away the old bearing wood and train suckers. ALPINE STRAWBERRIES, still remove weak runners from. BUSH-FRUIT, retard with coverings, and examine occasionally. FIGS, make a final thinning, and stop. FRUIT-ROOM, prepare and cleanse. TRAINING, let all shoots be nailed close.　　R. ERRINGTON.

FRUIT FORCING DEPARTMENT.

AIR, admit freely during the day but more sparingly at night; da temperature, with sun, from 65° to 80°; night ditto, 55° to 60°. BARE-BEDS, turn and renew, if chilled; but beware of too much heat, as, instead of excitement, plants should be gradually hardened and ripened; an exception may be made in those plants fresh potted, as they should be encouraged to fill their pots with roots. CLEAN from all decaying leaves, insects, and mossy surfaces; and dress with fresh suitable compost. VINES: proportion is to the weather and the demands of your plants; shut at all times the dribbling system. PINES, finish shifting; shut up early in an afternoon, but give a little air in the night. PEACH-HOUSE: spare no attention to obtain the wood healthy and well ripened; give plenty of air to those now ripening their fruit. VINERIES: look after the grapes in early houses; ripen the wood; and in late houses, forward the colouring process, by closing much solar heat. FIGS, PEACHES, and all trees or shrubs in pots for early forcing, should have their wood well ripened, and then removed to the coldest, shadiest place you can command, protecting or plunging the pots. MELONS and CUCUMBERS in frames must be banked up with fermenting materials; stir the surface of the soil, but give scarcely any water after this period; a slight syringe early in the afternoon after a hot day will be useful. Pot off seedlings and cuttings of CUCUMBERS for winter: for this purpose none excels the Sion House or Kenyon. Finish potting STRAWBERRIES for forcing.
　　　　　　R. ERRINGTON.

KITCHEN-GARDEN.

ANGELICA, thin out, and earth-stir in the seed-bed where the plants may remain until the spring. AROMATIC POT HERBS, finish gathering. ARTICHOKES, break down stems, and keep clear of weeds. ASPARAGUS-BEDS, weed. BALM, cut, and dry. BEANS, keep clear of weeds, and seed collect, and dry off well; store them away in the pods. BEET, take up as wanted. BORAGE, earth-stir amongst, and seed collect. BORA-COLE, plant out, and use the hoe freely amongst. BROCOLI, plant. BURNET, plant. CABBAGES, plant out; keep the seed-beds free from weeds, and earth-stir. Red Dutch Cabbages are ready for pickling. CARDOONS, earth up well in dry weather. CARROTS, attend to thinning and earth stirring the August sown crops. CAULIFLOWER PLANTS, prick out in rich, open, warm borders, so as to have a good choice of plants to stand the winter. CELERY, earth up freely in dry weather, and plant out successional crops which will be found very useful to the cook during the winter and spring months. CHERVIL, sow. COLEWORTS, plant out. CORIANDER, sow. CORN SALAD, sow. CRESS (American), sow and plant. WATERCRESS, plant. CUCUMBERS, attend to in pits and frames, top and clear away all decayed leaves, &c.; strike cuttings of favourite kinds, or sow seeds, for winter and spring growth. ENDIVE, plant out; tie up or otherwise cover up to blanch. FENNEL, plant and cut down. HOEING, attend to in all cases in dry weather. HYSSOP, plant. JERUSALEM ARTICHOKES, keep clear of weeds; do not injure the stems; take up roots if required for use. KIDNEY-BEANS, earth-stir among, and collect seeds; put away dry in pods. LEEKS, plant and earth-stir. LETTUCES may still be sown in warm borders, but attend to those which were sown at proper time; prick out from the seed-beds; keep them clear from weeds, so as to have a good winter supply of sturdy plants; tie up full grown. MELONS, be sparing with water at this season; give plenty of air to ripening fruit; keep up warmth by backing up with linings, &c.; shut up early. MINT, still cut and dry. MUSHROOM SPAWN, collect; which is often found when breaking up old hotbeds; put it away in close dry sheds until wanted. MUSHROOM-BEDS, make; this is the best season in the whole year for making mushroombeds in any way, from the proper mushroom-house to the common appanrof bed in the open air to be covered with straw. NASTURTIUMS, gather as they become fit for use. ONIONS, press down to promote their bulbing, and take up those that are ripe; dry well before stored away for winter; attend to the August-sown; weed and earth-stir. POTATOES, take up and store away. PARSLEY, cut down and transplant in some warm corner for winter supply. PEAS, look after birds and collect seed of, dry them well, and store them away in their pods. PENNYROYAL, cut and dry. MARJORUM, the same. RADISHES, sow in warm borders. RHUBARB, clear from weeds. SAGE and SAVORY may be planted. SAVOYS, plant and earth-stir. SEA-KALE-BEDS, keep clear from weeds. SEEDS, gather of all kinds as they ripen. SMALL SALADING, sow. SORREL, plant. SPINACH, sow in warm border; attend to thinning out the August-sown crops from eight to ten inches apart. TANSY AND TARAGON, attend to if required. THYME, plant. TURNIPS, sow of the best little early kinds; thin and hoe advancing crops. ATTEND TO earthing up, earth stirring, and hoeing in general, in dry weather; the rake may be advantageously used in many cases after the hoe at this catching season of the year. Many good managers only plant CABBAGES in one week of the whole year, and that in the first week in September, and from plants sown about the 21st of July; the soil to receive them should be made thoroughly rich. Others make a good planting at this time, and another in March, which will give an excellent supply for the whole year.　　　　　　T. WEAVER.

LONDON: Printed by HARRY WOOLDRIDGE, Winchester High-street, in the Parish of Saint Mary Kalendar; and Published by WILLIAM SOMERVILLE ORR, at the Office, No. 2, Amen Corner, in the Parish of Christ Church, City of London.—August 29th, 1850.

WEEKLY CALENDAR.

M W D	W D D	SEPTEMBER 5—11, 1850.	Weather near London in 1849.			Sun Rises.	Sun Sets.	Moon R. & S.	Moon's Age.	Clock bef. Sun.	Day of Year.
5	Th	Old Bartholomew.	T. 77°–52°.	E.	Fine.	30 a. 5	37 a. 6	3 57	29	1 23	248
6	F	Gossamer floats.	T. 78°–49°.	N.E.	Fine.	32	35	sets.	●	1 43	249
7	S	Enurchus. Red-under-wing Moth seen.	T. 67°–45°.	E.	Fine.	33	33	7 a. 28	1	2 2	250
8	Sun	15 Sun. aft. Trinity. Nativity B. V. M.	T. 65°–52°.	N.E.	Fine.	35	30	7 54	2	2 22	251
9	M	Dog Rose casts leaves.	T. 76°–49°.	N.E.	Fine.	37	28	8 18	3	2 43	252
10	Tu	Yew berries ripe.	T. 70°–51°.	S.	Rain.	38	26	8 46	4	3 3	253
11	W	Scotch Fir leaves fall.	T. 66°–48°.	S.W.	Rain.	30	24	9 16	5	3 24	254

It is not asserting more than can be justified when we say, that mere practice can advance the cultivation of plants to no greater perfection than it has attained at present. This was the opinion, also, of the last President of the Horticultural Society, Mr. Knight; for when writing to us some twenty years since he gave as his opinion—"Physiological knowledge can alone now direct the gardener to improvement, for he possesses all that mere practice is likely to give." If we look back over the improved modes of cultivation—if we trace to their origin the changes in the times and details of our gardening practices—we shall find in every instance that each beneficial alteration took its rise from the stronger light gradually diffused over the cultivation of plants by chemistry and physiology—sciences which reveal the changes going on in, and the structure of, the organs and vessels of all organised bodies. In these fields of science are rich harvests yet to be reaped; for notwithstanding the golden returns that have been thence gathered, yet richer, incalculably richer, products remain to reward the future husbandmen of these sciences; and we may still use the words of the Christian philosopher, Dr. Stephen Hales, when he said, "We must be content in this our infant state of knowledge, while we know in part only, to imitate children, who, for want of better skill and more proper materials, amuse themselves with slight buildings. Yet the farther advances we make in the knowledge of nature the more probable and the nearer to truth will our conjectures approach—so that succeeding generations, having the advantage of their own observations and those of preceding generations, may then make considerable advances—when many shall run to and fro, and knowledge shall be increased (Dan. xii. 4)." Dr. Hales saw as clearly as any man that it is by such experimental researches—by the "asking questions of nature"—alone can progress be made in the cultivation of plants; and he bowed implicitly to the forcible observation, that "All the real knowledge we have of nature is purely experimental, inasmuch that we may lay this down as the first fundamental rule in physics—it is not within the compass of the human understanding to assign a purely speculative reason for any one phenomenon of nature."

If we were asked to select the object in this world most deserving and, indeed, most commanding veneration, we should place our finger upon one not rarely blessing our land—the pastor of a rural district sedulous in his care of the spiritual welfare of his flock, and occupying his leisure by employing his acquired knowledge for the benefit of the world at large. Such a man was Dr. Hales. Early in life he accepted the living of Teddington, near Hampton Court—accepted it for the purpose of fulfilling its duties; and, therefore, loving and loved by those over whom he presided, he firmly rejected all offers that tempted him to leave the spot where he knew he was being useful. Hearing that he was nominated to a Canonry of Windsor, he hastened to the Princess of Wales, and obtained her promise that the nomination should be cancelled. "My circumstances," he said, "are such as entirely satisfy me, and a better income would only be a greater incumbrance." Natural philosophy—that study so consonant with and so conducive to quiet virtuous happiness—was his favourite amusement, even in early youth. A student of Cambridge, and

with Ray's "Catalogue of Cambridge Plants" in his pocket, he searched the Gogmagog Hills and the bogs of Cherryhunt Moor, in its vicinity, in pursuit of their vegetable rarities. Insects also obtained a portion of his study, and "he contrived a curious instrument for catching such as could fly." Chemistry, geology, astronomy, were also familiar to him; nor were these acquirements merely flowers of the study, but were so cultivated by him as to be fruitful of benefits to his fellow men. His ventilators extirpated the "gaol fever" from our prisons, for in Newgate alone by their use the deaths were reduced to two annually, whereas previously they varied between 50 and 100. But we must proceed to notice the work which especially entitles him to our notice here—Vegetable Staticks, or an account of some statical experiments on the sap in vegetables. This was published in 1727, and soon passed through several editions. It is the first work giving correct views of vegetable physiology, and is yet a standard authority relative to the motion of the sap, the force with which it ascends, the progress and mode of a plant's growth, and the amount of air and moisture it imbibes and perspires—the whole applied by the author so as to be "of use to those who are curious in the culture and improvement of gardening." The honesty and simplicity of his character is apparent even in his preface; for instead of leaving it to be inferred that his genius led him to the experiment he pursued, he avows—"by mere accident I hit upon it, while I was endeavouring by several ways to stop the bleeding of an old stem of a vine cut too near the bleeding season, which I feared might kill it." There are but few epocha in the life of such a searcher after truth but those usually marking life's boundaries in an epitaph, and Dr. Hales' is not an exception. His brief monumental memorial stands thus in the vestry of Teddington church, and within its tower, which he built at his own expense:—" Here is interred the body of Stephen Hales, D.D., Clerk of the Closet to the Princess of Wales, and Minister of this parish for 51 years. He died on the 4th of January, 1761, in the eighty-fourth year of his age," being born on the 7th of September, 1677. We need append no more than this, translated from an additional epitaph by the friend of moral excellence, Dr. Jortin:

> "Candour, sweet inmate of the generous breast;
> Virtue, sound morals, truth, religious zeal;
> A hand most prompt to succour the distrest,
> A head inventive for the public weal;
> These gifts were thine; the court's, the senate's voice,
> Applauds the long career thou well hast trod;
> A nation's panegyric crowns their choice,
> And but anticipates the praise of God."

Meteorology of the Week.—At Chiswick, from observations during the last twenty-three years, the average highest and lowest temperatures of these days are 69.2° and 48.6°, respectively. The greatest heat, 83°, occurred on the 5th in 1848; and the extreme cold, 31°, on the 6th in 1847. There were 82 fine days, and 79 on which rain fell, during the period.

Insects.—Recently we had brought to our notice a heap of wheat which had been entirely destroyed, owing to neglect in pro-

RANGE OF BAROMETER—RAIN IN INCHES.

Sept.		1841.	1842.	1843.	1844.	1845.	1846.	1847.	1848.	1849.
5	B.	29.823	30.195	30.388	29.926	30.140	30.126	29.878	29.838	30.180
		29.733	30.086	30.312	29.801	30.103	30.064	29.849	29.754	30.075
	R.	0.04	—	—	0.03	0.01	—	0.01	0.10	—
6	B.	29.795	30.028	30.398	29.934	30.149	29.954	29.994	29.984	30.122
		29.704	29.942	30.261	29.837	30.131	29.898	29.845	29.791	30.054
	R.	—	—	—	—	0.04	—	0.01	0.01	—
7	B.	29.794	29.896	30.370	29.913	30.137	29.909	29.984	30.055	30.181
		29.186	29.497	30.046	29.804	30.010	29.819	29.970	29.976	30.111
	R.	0.17	0.34	—	0.01	—	0.03	—	—	—
8	B.	29.951	30.616	30.367	26.873	30.115	29.985	29.977	30.085	30.138
		29.717	30.396	30.192	29.749	30.698	29.891	29.807	29.954	30.092
	R.	—	0.04	—	0.28	—	—	0.08	—	—
9	B.	30.019	29.537	30.183	29.747	30.142	30.079	30.099	29.919	29.884
		29.969	29.427	30.096	29.717	30.002	29.999	30.058	29.829	29.540
	R.	0.06	—	—	0.34	—	—	—	—	—
10	B.	30.008	29.377	30.023	29.934	30.085	30.304	30.133	29.746	30.466
		29.985	29.335	29.956	29.820	29.971	30.262	30.035	29.594	30.255
	R.	—	0.07	0.52	—	—	—	—	0.33	0.18
11	B.	30.052	29.663	30.075	30.014	30.038	30.372	30.122	30.228	30.164
		29.976	29.655	29.942	29.995	29.956	30.343	30.010	29.937	29.111
	R.	—	—	—	T	—	—	—	—	0.32

perly turning and airing, by the Wheat Weevil, or Corn Chafer (Calandra granaria, or Curculio, or Rhynchophorus granarius). To our readers a few particulars relative to this pest may not be unacceptable. The whole of its body and limbs are a dull red or tile colour; and its thorax is so unusually elongated as to equal in length the rest of the body. The thorax is pitted all over with minute indentations, and the wing cases are

furrowed. The female employs her long beak to bore a hole into each grain of corn before she deposits in it an egg. In its beetle form, as well as in its grub state, it feeds upon the flour of the corn. The extent of this weevil's ravages is no longer a subject for surprise when we know that a single pair of them may originate 6000 descendants in one year.

THE potato murrain, and the immense loss it occasions not only to individuals but to the nation, calls upon us to repeat again and again our warning—*store your potatoes in layers alternately with dry earth, sand, or coal-ashes, and in a dry cool building.*

We have received a sufficient number of inquiries, relative to our recommendation, to enforce upon us the importance of being still more explicit relative to this mode of storing potatoes.

1. Each layer of potatoes should be only one potato deep, and they should not touch each other.

2. Each layer of earth, sand, or ashes, should be sprinkled in between the tubers, and cover the whole about a quarter of an inch deep; and then another layer of potatoes should be placed upon it, and so alternately until the whole are piled together.

3. The most easy way of thus storing potatoes, is by having boards fixed across one end of the building, so as to form a bin or box for them; the front edges of the layers being thus kept from slipping down.

4. A cellar, shed, stable, or any other building in which the temperature never rises above 45°, nor falls below 33°, is suitable, provided rain is excluded, and the floor is not damp. It does not signify whether the floor be brick, stone, earth or wood, so that the layers of potatoes and their packing stuff be kept dry.

We have received various communications upon the subject, the contents of which singularly refute themselves. One from Essex, after lamenting " the loss sustained annually," asks—" Do you not think pitting potatoes is as good as the plan you recommend?" " Pitting!" that is, digging out a spade's depth of earth, putting the potatoes in a conical heap within the hole thus made, covering them with straw and then with the earth dug out, is one of the very worst modes of storing potatoes : they ferment, heat, and consequently accelerate decay, and the result is told in " the loss sustained annually."

Another gentleman, writing from Taunton, regrets " the bushels" he has lost each year during " the last five years," and yet he thinks his mode of " storing in a dry cool outhouse, without any other covering, as good as that recommended in THE COTTAGE GARDENER." Now, if " bushels" have been lost by following this plan, it cannot be good ; and as we have stored our's during the years enumerated without any such loss, the plan is not so good as that we have adopted and recommended.

The question, if we come to theory, simply is this—Whether the decay of the tuber is caused by a fungus or merely by gangrene or putrefaction, are not coolness, dryness, and the exclusion of the air effective checks to its progress? Now, we will undertake to say, that not a practical gardener nor a man of science in all Europe will answer in the negative; and if so, then the plan we recommend is that most consonant with reason, as in practice we have found it most effectual.

PROCEEDING with our notes upon the list of artificial manures, commenced by us at page 284, we next come to BLEACHING POWDER, or *Chloride of Lime.* This is composed of about 63 parts *Chlorine*—which used to be called spirit of salt, being obtained from our common table salt—united to 37 parts *Lime ;* and it has been employed as an assistant to plants in various ways. When exposed to the air, as when poured dissolved in water over the soil, it parts with a portion of its Chlorine and is changed to *Muriate of Lime,* a salt which absorbs moisture from the air very rapidly. This has been found alike beneficial to crops on light and clayey soils, for it keeps light soils moist during dry weather, and it prevents the clods on clayey soils becoming baked during drought, so as to be unbreakable by the hoe.

The plants we have applied it to with most advantage are *Asparagus,* the *Cabbage tribe,* and *Sea-kale,*—all natives of the sea-shore, where they obtain this salt from the waters of the ocean.

Chloride of Lime, from its property of giving off its Chlorine slowly, is largely employed for bleaching purposes ; and the same property adapts it for promoting the germination of seeds, the destruction of vermin, and the removal of noxious smells.

Mr. F. Fincham, of Manchester, states that he employed Chloride of Lime in his garden with good effect, for *hastening the growth of Turnip-seed.* Half of some Turnip-seed was steeped for thirty-six hours in a solution composed of one pound of Chloride of Lime and 48 pints of water. Both the halves of the seed were sown under precisely similar circumstances of soil and aspect. The plants from the steeped seed came up much sooner, were never attacked by the fly, the produce was half as much more, and the leaves more luxuriant. He observes, that in some instances Sir H. Davy and others found the application of Chlorine to seeds too highly stimulating, which he attributes to its being used uncombined with Lime, and that wherever it has failed of doing good this has arisen from the mode of application rendering failure certain.

Great care is required in the employment of Chloride of Lime as a stimulant for seeds, for though Mr. Fincham found Turnip seed was benefited by being soaked for thirty-six hours in a solution of one pound to 48 pints of water, yet in another instance *Mustard-seed* is said to have been destroyed by being soaked for six hours in a solution of only one pound to 60 pints of water. Seeds of *Strelitzia regina,* on the other hand, were uninjured by being soaked in it for twenty-four hours.

For *destroying vermin,* Chloride of Lime has also been employed very effectively. Mr. Fincham employed a solution of the same strength as for his Turnip-seed to destroy the insects (he does not say whether caterpillars or green-flies) which attacked his rose, gooseberry, and currant trees ; watering over them by means of a rose water-pot, " by which they were effectually cleared from the vermin."

A gardener writing in the *Gardeners' Chronicle,* in 1843, says—" I was very much annoyed by the worms getting into the flower-pots, of which I have between five and six hundred, and not a place where I can set them in the summer season, except round the edges of the grass plot ; so I have used for this last three years Chloride of Lime, and I have found it quite to my wishes The quantity I use is about an ounce to eight gallons of water, and I have never found it hurt or discolour a leaf, though I have frequently watered the beds, plants, and grass plot all over. It kills the moss on the latter; but what I find it the most useful for is, about every month, to water round the pots that it may run underneath them, which it quickly does, the garden being on a descent ; and by applying the water a little stronger, and applying the brush gently to cause it to go over every part at the same time, it effectually destroys all the green on the flag-stones."

As *a fixer of Ammonia*, Chloride of Lime is one of the most effectual applications. Half a pound dissolved in two and a half gallons of water, kept corked in a stone bottle, and a little twice daily sprinkled over the places wetted with the excrements, &c., of horses, cows, pigs, and poultry, will almost entirely remove the offensive fumes, and at the same time prevent the escape of the ammonia.

THE FRUIT-GARDEN.

EARLY AUTUMN PLANTING.—We advise those of our readers who have fruit-trees to plant, to lose no time in making the necessary preparations. The first step of all others which we practise, when possessed of an opportunity, is to cut round the trees intended for removal. This pre-supposes that the trees are already in possession ; and, indeed, refers more to trees of some size than young stock from the nursery.

This cutting round we consider somewhat important; and it should be performed in the first week of September at latest : if a little earlier so much the better. Its effects will be, to bring on an immediate disposition to produce a much increased amount of young fibres ; and we need scarcely observe, that such will the sooner establish the tree ; for it must be understood, that most of our hardy deciduous trees and shrubs carry on a continuous root action all the winter ; they are, probably, *never* entirely dormant, whilst the ground temperature is as high as from 40 to 50 degrees.

Root action, then, being in some degree dependant on warmth in the soil, how important early autumn planting must be to those who would gain time, which is generally the great object whether in planting for ornament or for utility. It may also be noticed, as a point in this argument, that trees cut round will of necessity be forced into a somewhat earlier rest : the supplies to the leaf being in a great measure cut off for a time, the action of the foliage is almost entirely elaborative, and the latter functions soon become carried out or completed. Such being the case, a tree cut round in the first week of September may be considered fit for removal by the end of the month ; and at this period there still remains a considerable amount of ground-heat, even until the middle of October or later,—enough to set the small fibres in action ready for the returning spring.

Such are some of the reasons why early autumn planting is to be recommended ; but there remain others, the weight of which being fairly added to the scale will cause a great preponderance, we think, in favour of the practice.

Let any one acquainted with gardening observe the immense pressure of business which spring invariably brings, a pressure doubtless double that which exists in September and October. How important, then, is it to do all that can be done at this period, in order to ease the coming spring ! The young gardener who does not know or rightly estimate this has much to learn.

Again, all soils are handled much easier now than in February, and are thereby left in a condition much more congenial to vegetation. Added to this, a day's labour is a much more productive article at this period than in early spring—the days being longer, and the chances of bad weather much less.

More need scarcely be said as to the expediency of early autumn planting : we will now, therefore, proceed to offer advice connected therewith. And, first, let us draw attention to *thorough drainage*, without which all other labours are vain. Of course we mean on soils of a stagnant character ; such may be readily known to the veriest tyro by various symptoms. If unreclaimed or new enclosures from commons, wastes, or road-sides, the very character of the herbage produced should point to its condition. Such land, if of a damp or "gouty" character, will produce grasses of a peculiarly coarse habit, together with the *Polygonum* family, the lakeweed, rushes, &c., &c., most of which things we feel persuaded are known at sight to the majority of the readers of THE COTTAGE GARDENER.

Sometimes plots of ground are partially damp, and require but partial drainage. Such may be readily distinguished by the colour of the surface, provided that no herbage exists on it ; for if portions of such plots remain of a dark colour for days after other portions have become dusty on the surface, there can be little doubt that such portions require drainage. Let then, we say, no person esteem this as a light affair. How many pounds loss and years of disappointment have we known through ignorance or neglect of this fundamental principle. Where, however, plots evince by their general character that all is right below, the improvement necessary with regard to fruit trees, lies in a narrow compass. One of the first points is to examine *the subsoil* in its relation to the surface soil. By this we mean not only its mechanical character—that is to say, its power of transmitting superfluous moisture downwards with facility,—but its proximity to the surface ; in other words, the average depth of the surface soil in its unimproved state. What we have now observed bears reference to the *general* improvement of any given plot, and we are hereby supposing that the object of the cultivator who may be enclosing a piece of unreclaimed land, and converting it at once into a vegetable and a fruit-garden, is to effect general and economical improvements at the least possible amount of expense.

With regard to the introduction of a tree here and there in existing gardens, the case is quite different. Here, if the soil be of a mellow character or improved state, nothing is wanted but *the stations* suggested in previous numbers of THE COTTAGE GARDENER. Still, we would say, let a small amount of jealousy be exercised as to the existence of stagnation below. We have known many old kitchen-gardens, which might fairly lay claim to a mellow and pulverised soil on the surface, charged, it may be, with a regular surfeiting of manures, yet anything but sound beneath. Let not the possessors of such gardens imagine that because fruits have been somehow or other cultivated in such plots for very many years, that they ought to rest satisfied with them. Let us again and again assure them, that even our hardiest fruits will not thrive in a satisfactory way, if an enemy exist beneath in the character of stagnating moisture.

As THE COTTAGE GARDENER circulates north as well as south, we would here remark on the culture of tender fruits in the cooler parts of Scotland, as also in the soft and damp atmosphere of the north of Ireland. If a regular cockney gardener—one who had never gardened twenty miles from Battersea, or, it may be, the warm county of Kent, or the precincts of Wimbledon Common—were to be duly packed and transferred in the character of head gardener to some nobleman, in either of the northern districts above alluded to, how astounding—as say our great writers—would be the change. Adieu to all successful fruit culture, if he began his Battersea tricks of planting fruit-trees on the ordinary ground level! And the evil would be still farther aggravated if he had a Battersea market gardener's manure-heap to go to. Within a couple of years we should hear of peaches making shoots six feet long, four feet of which would go black in October, to the great dismay of the Battersea man, who would of course talk of peculiar conditions of the atmosphere, electrical currents, &c., &c.; having imbibed such notions in his early training, and being persuaded that such doctrine was a mere " march of intellect" affair.

But, to turn the tables, suppose that this metropolitan prodigy had a gardening neighbour, who at once took a bold and common-sense view of such matters; and who, believing that the ripening of the wood, through the conjoint influences of light and heat acting on a proportionate amount of the "raw material" (if we may be permitted so to use common-place phrases), had great influence in this affair; suppose, we say, that this man was content with a much less amount of luxuriance, and what would be the consequence ? Why, the wood of his trees would become better ripened, and the fruit-buds better perfected; need we say that superior success would follow? How then, it will be said, is all this to be accomplished ? Why by eschewing all deep borders or beds of earth, *especially if below the ground level*; and herein lies the real gist of the affair.

Had we to act in a position of the kind, we should plant the majority of our trained trees *on or above the ordinary surface.* No man should dig a hole for a tree in such climes for us. There can be no doubt, therefore, that most of our superior fruits could be very well cultivated in such climates, if those entrusted with their management could but be brought to believe, that shoots of moderate growth ripen both better and earlier in the season than free growing trees; and that the *fruit* in all its stages partakes of this precocity, to say nothing of the much greater certainty of a crop, through more perfect blossoms.

So that we may see it is not a question of mere depth alone; for a bed of earth, a foot or so above the ordinary ground level, is a very different thing from one a foot below such level; and those who will try the experiment in our more northerly counties will soon have demonstration enough. Indeed, it will be at once obvious, that if long-continued underground damp is an evil—destroying or preventing that mellowing of the soil which renders it easily permeable to the atmosphere—that an elevated border is one of the surest safeguards.

There is, however, no necessity to elevate a whole border thus much above the ordinary ground level; stations may be made on what we term the platform mode; only taking care that the platforms are gradually widened as the trees become well established; or, indeed, as soon as they show symptoms of receiving an overcheck from the drought of hot summers. This is easily managed, for if the stations be about five or six feet square, little more would be necessary in such cases than to apply a coating of half-rotten leaves, or vegetable matters—even grass mowings would do—over and round the exterior of the platform; merely to ward off extreme drought. Such might be applied in June, and might, if requisite, be removed and dug in for vegetables in the end of August, in order to let the solar rays fairly penetrate the soil. Such remarks equally apply to stations connected with walls, and to those in the open garden. in all cases where stagnant moisture is sus-

pended; and, in conclusion, we again repeat our advice, that this work be proceeded with as soon as possible: first cutting round trees to be removed, and then proceeding with the preparation of the stations, the draining, and the preparation or procuration of soils.

In cutting round specimens for removal, the distance may be ruled by the size of the tree; indeed, a trench may at once be excavated in the position it would be, if the tree was to be removed forthwith. This trench may be left out, and thus there will be extra inducement to the tree to produce fibres in the interior of the ball of earth.   R. Errington.

THE FLOWER-GARDEN.

Planting Evergreens, and other Planting Matters.—Last week I promised to say how the large plants were taken up, and how planted; this part will only be useful to very young planters. The operation was conducted nearly in the way recommended by the Editor, in a leading article, last spring; but as a good tale is never the worse for being twice told, I shall keep to my promise, and say how the first plant was removed. We selected such plants as spread a great way; not the tallest that we could find, because the hedge was not required to be more than eight feet high; the first plant was about ten feet through it at the bottom; and with such plants as yews and hollies it would have been safe gardening to open a trench at the outside of this circumference, that is, at five feet distance from the stem; but box-trees do not run their roots far away, but produce them in great abundance nearer home; so the first thing we did was to tie up the lower branches, by running a strong cord all round the plant, by which the branches were well pulled in, broom-fashion. We had thus a command of the space covered by the branches; and at four feet from the stem a ring was marked on the ground, and on the outside of this ring the men set to work to open a trench all round, and about 18 inches wide; the depth was regulated by the depth of the roots. They went no farther down than 18 inches, as the soil was very hard and poor; but the trench was made two feet deep, in case we should find tap-roots under the centre part. Now, here was a ball of earth eight feet in diameter, with a huge bush stuck in the middle of it; and if we could remove it, bush and all, to the site of the hedge, half the gardening world would think we had done wisely; but the truth is, if we had done so the chances are that not one plant in ten would have lived out the month of June, then in its infancy; and this is the most curious part of the whole concern, and on it lay the foundation of our success; indeed, some would say, that a *principle* was involved here; but I never could make out what that word meant; and if they will allow the word in our forthcoming Dictionary, we must have a consultation as to how we can best explain it for gardening language; and as that consultation might cause all of us to meet in London for discussion, I shall save myself the journey by giving my definition of it now, which is this—*any-thing to suit your ideas or convenience.* Well, here then is a set of men at work on a *principle*; and it must be plain enough that it would not suit our *convenience* to remove such a large lump of earth on so hot a day. Then, as to our *ideas*—if we had any at all on the subject—they must have been very confused, if they could not lead us to perceive that if this ball of very hard earth, and which then was as dry as Welch snuff, were removed and placed in the midst of a newly prepared border of moist loose earth, it could only be a repetition, but on a large scale, of potting a geranium with a hard dry ball into a " one shift" large pot; and all the gardeners would say that is a bad plan; because, water as you may, the dry ball in the centre of the pot could not receive any moisture—the water would run off it into the fresh soil as off a duck's back. So here is another *principle*, and a very bad principle it is; for all the gardeners in the country could not wet it. Therefore it would never do to plant large box-trees in June on this principle. On the other hand, if the work had to be performed in November, when the face of the earth is well moistened with the autumn rains, this ball of it would be moist also, and then would be in a fit and proper state to be removed, with care, for the benefit of the roots which held it together. We shall call this the wet or moist side of the *principle*; and on this view of it we find writers on planting large trees recommending a ball to be removed with large and small trees. Now, when one's head gets full of *principles*, he might say on principle, that what was good for the goose should do for the gander; that what was essential for the good of a tree on removing it in November should not, on principle, be otherwise in June; but here the principle breaks down,—the case, as we have seen, is just the reverse, and my definition of a principle is right after all; therefore it was that this huge ball of earth was reduced bit by bit with three-pronged forks, and with the greatest possible precaution, so that the roots received as little damage as could be; the loose soil thus picked or forked off the ball was removed from the trench as fast as it was loosed, and the trench itself was getting wider and wider in consequence, so that by the time we reached where we expected, and where we found some tap roots, the trench was large enough to allow the men to look about them and see how best to deal with these tap roots. When they found one as large as the little finger, they digged lower down by the side of it, and when they could dig no farther, the root was cut clean off with a knife: it is true, that on the principle of convenience, this root might be thrust through with a spade as low down as it could reach, and then pulled up and the bruised end cut off with a knife; but here the *idea* part of the principle comes against that part of it which is founded on convenience; for the moment we begin to work among principles, they thicken around us. If the root were hit hard with a spade, the principle of *tension* or *strain* is immediately involved, for roots, like other parts of plants, are made of long fibres and tubes, something after the manner of a rope; and every one of these members has a part to play in the economy of the plant; if, therefore, you strain a root so that it must break, all the damage you cause it may not be just at the point of breakage; in all probability some of the fibres of the root are broken far back nearer the stem, although held together by the bark, so that cutting off the jagged end of a root on the principle of convenience is not the best way. The better plan is never to put a firm root to the test of straining at all, but to cut it off at once with a sharp knife. In the whole circle of gardening there is not a more mischievous act, or the result of which is less understood, than this of straining the roots; I have known plants die from it two years after the operation. There is a race of the *Cactus* family in Mexico, and in other parts of Central and South America, having their stems compressed into round heavy lumps of soft matter, like our melons or turnips, and they root from the bottom just like a turnip; and in hot countries these roots go down a long way to find moisture, so that it is hard to pull them up when one wishes to remove any of the plants. I have known some of these plants received in this country to all appearance perfectly sound, and remain so for many months afterwards, but to have died after awhile, because their roots were too much strained in pulling up the plants, the fleshy portion in the heart of the plants began first to decay from the tender ends of the roots having given way there and caused an internal fracture; mortification proceeded slowly, till at last it reached the outside, and people

began to wonder what ailed the plants, " that they died so." Farmers cry out when their turnips do not keep in heaps, after they are torn by main force from hard dry ground, and their roots strained at all points; and so do those who think themselves very cunning, who pull up bulbs abroad after the same manner, when they find after all their care of them they die by inches before their eyes. The same happens with fruit and forest-trees, and sometimes with box-trees also, but our boxes escaped that kind of principle, all the large roots that could not be dug out were cut clean off by the knife. An oak-tree should no more be pulled by the root than a melon cactus.

After all this, and by the time the whole of the roots were separated from the under soil, the ball was so reduced that three stout men could lift the plant on to a low truck, and what earth was left close to the stem of the plant was pierced through and through with the pronged forks, or with a sharp pointed stick, so that water could get into it at the first touch; the plant was then set down on the surface of the new border, not in a hole made to receive it, but on the bare surface, which it will be recollected we left eighteen inches lower than the surface of the terrace; then a ring or bank of fresh soil was made outside the end of the roots, and a foot or so in height; this ring was to confine the water to the space occupied by the roots, and for washing it down amongst them with the water-pot as the work proceeded. Some recommend, first, to make a puddle of earth and water, and then to put in the plant. I never plant that way.

Now, three men with spades, at equal distances round the plant, began to throw loose sand and earth up to the stem of the box-tree, not on the bare roots: and two men with large watering-pots, with the rose on, stood opposite each other pouring water on the stem, which washed down the soil as fast as the three men could throw it on; one man did no more than keep the plant steady, and if a strong pole or stake were first driven in the border before the water planting commenced, and the bush tied to it, this man's time might be saved, and the plant be the better for it afterwards; but in our case we were planting a close hedge, and stakes were not needed; but in planting singly, one or three stakes should first be placed where they would best support the plant. When all the hollow parts under the bottom roots were thus filled up with what I may call mud, a third watering-pot was put to work on the bank outside the roots; this pot had a rose to it so that it should not break through the bank, but merely wear down the inside of it gently against the roots. In this way the roots were soon covered, and when the water drained away every root must have been encased as closely as the wick inside a " dip " candle; and to prevent evaporation an inch or two of very dry soil was placed over the whole, and we all returned to the " box bank " for another subject; and after all were planted, the whole were damped every evening for the first month with a garden engine, and not one single leaf failed.

Now, is there any reason to suppose that the same men, country labourers, with the same care, and under similar circumstances could not be as successful with a thousand or ten thousand large box-trees as with a few scores, and that if they had continued to plant all the summer, the same results would be obtained. I am not quite so sure, however, that from this time to Christmas the success should be so complete, because after this time the active power of the plants to form new roots will be on the decline, and go on so in the same ratio as the degrees of temperature. In November large plants can be removed and look very well, without giving them so much water as we did—indeed, without giving them any water; but that is not the question at all, or whether it is better to plant in November at one third less cost than in July or August—for these are certainly the best two months in the year to remove evergreens in our climate,—but what is the best time for making the largest number of new roots in the shortest time; and when that is ascertained, as it undoubtedly is among the present race of gardeners, the cheapest mode of planting them will, like everything else, be that which is the cheapest in the long-run. More money, or, what is the same thing, more care and more water will be necessary to insure summer planting than would be required in November; but then look at the results in both periods, not one of a hundred of summer planted evergreens need lose a leaf, or be the least crippled in any way by the operation; but in November it is not so, and in the nature of things it is not possible that it should be so, for then success depends as much on the kind of winter which follows as on the skilfulness with which the planting is performed. It is true, that the effects of late autumn planting, or the effects of a hard winter on the plants, are not seen much till next April or May; and that a hundred reasons, and not one of them the true one, can then be assigned for the failure: high winds, bad land, water lodgement, late spring, and what not, can be brought forward, had done it all; whereas they had only helped to finish that which was begun at the wrong end of the story.

To show the subject under another view, let us give another turn to it. One of the best props for holding up the credit due to skilful planting is, the age of the tree itself. I have heard it applied over and over again this very season; and even thirty years were put down as something to boast of in the case of our own hedge plants: one visitor remarked, that he had seen box-trees as large as ours at half their age; inferring at the same time, that age cast more difficulty in the way of removing trees than size did,—that he had, himself, some box-trees full ten feet high, and from thirty to forty feet round, but they were quite young compared to ours; and, of course, could be moved at any time next season with half the risk that we incurred; and he did intend to transplant some of them. Now, I could not conscientiously allow this gentleman to depart thus confirmed in an erroneous idea, by what he had seen of our planting, neither could I drop the subject without showing this side of it; indeed, at the time I determined, if ever I told or wrote the history of this little job, that I would endeavour to put the saddle on the right horse, and disabuse the minds of young planters on this point.

Who ever heard of the removal of a very large tree, evergreen, or otherwise, who did not at the same time hear of how many toll-bars had to be broken through—how many corners of streets, or how many houses or windows, had been damaged by the vegetable wonder; and all this unavoidable damage is made to tell in favour of the great wonder of removing very old trees? Whereas the age and size of a tree to be transplanted, in nine cases out of ten, ought to be set down in favour of the planter, not against him, as at present. It is three to one more difficult to transplant a vigorous, healthy, young full-grown tree than the same tree would be a hundred years hence; and the reason is this—"vigorous and healthy" bespeak good soil and situation, circumstances under which trees make fast progress in a comparatively short space of time; and when they are removed from such favourable conditions it is seldom in the power of the planter to find a better, or even as good, a soil for them; besides, every fibre or part, from the ends of the roots to the topmost branch, is distended to the full in a "healthy vigorous" tree; and all the planters in the world could not remove a tree in this condition without impairing the system, more or less—a root not bigger than the little finger would tell against such tree, if cut off injudiciously; and all this is so well understood by nurserymen, and by the planters of young stock, that the nurseryman advertises, as a recommendation, that such and such trees are, or were, growing on such poor soil that there can be no fear about their doing well anywhere, after they are removed; and the planter is satisfied that all this is right. He is also aware, that when he plants from a new nursery with deep rich soil the chances are against him, because the young plants, like the healthy vigorous full-grown tree, are distended to the full, and in that condition are more susceptible of injury than if they were in a slow stunted growth, when a change to a fresh soil could not fail to be of much benefit to them. All this about young nursery stock is so well understood, that we call it a principle; and the very next day we violate this principle by implication, when we come to treat of transplanting large trees. We give great credit to a planter who has been successful in removing a tree a hundred or two hundred years old, which may have been living for the half of its time on the scantiest pasture; its own roots, or those of neighbouring trees, having long since exhausted the soil around it, so that its annual growth for years past could only be counted by inches—in short, has arrived at that condition most favourable for the credit of the planter; because if the size or bulk of this tree will allow of its being removed at all, it can hardly be placed under more unfavourable conditions than it has been in for years, and the change to better soil, if ordinary care is taken with the roots, is sure to be in its favour rather than otherwise. In the case of our box-trees, therefore, their age was much in their favour; for the last twenty years they were struggling on under the disadvantages incident to old trees; and instead of suffering from being removed, they were rather very much the gainers—removed in the height of the growing season into a fresh bed of soil, they struck fresh roots into it immediately.　　　　　　　　　　　　　D. Beaton.

GREENHOUSE AND WINDOW GARDENING.

Lantana.—This family of plants is chiefly to be found in South America and the West India Islands. It belongs, like the Clerodendron, to which I lately alluded, to the natural group of verbenas, though at a first glance the different varieties and species present little resemblance to that beautiful family. The flowers are produced very abundantly all over the shrubby plant, the pretty compact corymbs continuing to start in pairs, from opposite sides of the stem, as long almost as a suitable temperature is maintained, and showing off to the best advantage owing to their longish but stiff, firm, footstalks. Some of these corymbs of flowers are so flat, as to resemble in appearance the generality of our common bedding-out verbenas; other species again have their heads of flowers so rounded as to resemble in form a guelder rose in miniature.

From the localities whence they have been introduced, it has been usual to treat the most of them as denizens of our plant stoves; and this is necessary if the character given to them as stove evergreens is to be maintained. I have, however, long used them for decorating the greenhouse, by treating them as deciduous plants, giving them their season of rest in winter just as we do in the case of a vine or a fuchsia. Several kinds, such as *Lantana mutabilis*, *Crocea superba*, *Aculeata*, &c., will flourish in the common soil of the flower-garden during summer, if the place be well sheltered. In high and exposed situations the wind and the rains are too much for the beauty of the flowers. The best of all the species for this purpose is the beautiful crimson, *Sellowi*, a dwarf plant with small leaves but large corymbs of flowers; but unlike all the others which flourish in peat and loam, it must have a preponderance of loam, if the plants are to be robust and bushy. The pretty *Sellowii*, whether in a pot or in a bed in the flower-garden, must be planted chiefly in peat, in order that it may be healthy and produce its flowers plentifully.

There are many species, such as *Coccinea*, with red; *Violacea*, with purple; and *Nivea*, with white flowers; but the species incidentally alluded to above are as interesting as any; the *Crocea superba* being a great improvement in habits, colour, and free blooming upon the old *Crocea*, whilst *mutabilis*, with its yellowish pale rose flowers, ever changing until they become almost white, contrasted with its deep green foliage, is an object that ladies seldom pass without admiring. Many are likewise partial to the strong aromatic odour of the leaves when handled, though I confess, for myself, it is too strong to be pleasant.

Supposing, then, that some of our friends have already obtained, or propose getting, a few of these plants for their greenhouse, the following is the outline of treatment they will require :—During September the plants may be set anywhere, so as to be seen to the best advantage; but towards the end of the month, if still flowering freely, they should be set on the front shelf in order to obtain more light; and less water should be gradually given, the object being not so much continuous growth, but the hardening and ripening of the wood already made. If their beauty should already be on the wane, the front of a south wall, full in the sun, and where the pots may be protected from heavy rains, will answer a similar purpose. By the end of October the plants from either position, and before they have been injured by frost, if they stood out of doors, should be removed beneath the stage of the greenhouse, giving them similar, but not so particular, treatment as was recommended for the Clerodendron. The leaves remaining, when placed in the winter quarters, will soon fall; a temperature of from 40° to 45° will preserve the vitality of the stems. A slight dusting from the syringe frequently, will also be of advantage, the roots being kept by covering, &c., in that medium state that may be described as neither wet nor dry.

By the middle or end of March, the increasing heat and light will tell upon the poor looking Lantanas ; the extreme points of the shoots, when the wood was green and unripened, may be shrivelled up—but what then? after these pieces are removed, buds in plenty will be bursting from each side of the nodes of the young shoots where the wood was moderately ripe, giving sufficient promise for a fine headed plant. The surface soil of the pot not troubled during the winter is now broken, that air may more freely penetrate to the roots ; water several degrees above the temperature of the house is more freely given; on a dull day the plants are removed to the stage, that full light may not strike them too suddenly ; they will want but little room, though the closest and warmest part at first. When the shoots are about one inch in length, the plants may have part of their old soil removed, and be transferred to fresh pots and new lumpy soil that has previously been aerated over a furnace ; few things being more prejudicial at an early period for pot plants than transferring them to *cold* soil. By attention to watering and liquid manure occasionally after the flower-buds appear, giving more room, and dusting at times with the syringe, you will obtain fine plants in July, to take the place of geraniums, &c., getting out of bloom.

The above is the method to pursue by those who have only one glass structure. Where, in addition, there is a forcing-pit, or even a cucumber frame, cuttings one inch in length, taken off in the end of April, or sooner, inserted in heat under a bell-glass, potted as soon as struck into 3-inch pots, returned to the bed for a fort-night or three weeks, potted again into 6-inch pots, and gradually inured to the greenhouse, will make pretty luxuriant plants for the whole of the autumn.

When, in addition, there is a forcing house, where the temperature is raised even so late as March, we would only save one or two plants of a species of Lantana during the winter ; transfer them to the forcing house—say a vinery or a peach house—as soon as its temperature is 5° or 10° above the greenhouse, take off as many young shoots as you may require when one inch and upwards in length ; insert them as described above in bottom-heat; when struck, throw away the old plants; shift quickly and successively into 3, 6, and 12-inch pots ; the plants after the first, and if possible after the second, shifting being set for a short time in the cucumber or melon pit, and continued in the forcing house a short time after the third, until the roots begin to work in the new soil, and thus you may obtain fine luxuriant large plants for ornamenting the greenhouse from July to the end of October. Where there are the conveniences, we prefer this last method to all others; and though it involves considerable trouble, the look of the plants will repay it.

CALCEOLARIA.—Now is a good time to sow the large flowering kinds for blooming in spring and early summer. It would be as well to have had a few sown towards the end of August, but small plants generally stand the winter better than larger ones, and they may be rattled on easily after the turn of the day. Some of our friends fail in raising plants, owing to *burying* the seed. The following directions, therefore, may be useful :—Take equal proportions of loam, peat and leaf mould, and half a portion of sand; dry them over a furnace sufficiently hot to set the smallest worms a scampering; expose it then for a day to become well aerated; pass it through a half-inch sieve; pass the finest again through a very fine wire sieve; fill the pots or pans nearly half full with drainage; cover the drainage with a layer of the rougher portions from the first riddling, then another layer reserved from the second riddling, then a layer of the soil riddled through at the first sifting, and then within a quarter of an inch of the top with the fine soil; press rather firmly down, and set the pots over-head in a tub of water; when fully soaked take out and set to drain. In a day, or less, smooth the surface a second time, then evenly scatter the seed; dust over them a little fine silver sand; place a square of glass over each pot, and set them in a shady place in a cold-pit or frame, not moving the glass, or seldom doing so, until the plants appear.   R. FISH.

HOTHOUSE DEPARTMENT.
EXOTIC ORCHIDACEÆ.

PLANTS REQUIRING BLOCKS *(Continued from page 318).*

Dendrobium amœnum (Charming D.); Nepaul.—Sepals and petals white, spotted with yellow ; the lip has a border of green round a yellow spot. A charming species, delightfully fragrant; unfortunately, it is very scarce. 10s.

D. amplum (Large-flowered D.); Bombay.—A very curious species, with a triangular-shaped solitary flower. The ground colour of the sepals and petals is yellowish, stained and spotted with pink; the lip is yellow, curiously barred with rich brown ; very rare. 10s.

D. aureum and *D. aureum pallidum* (Golden D.) ; Ceylon.—The whole flower is of a rich golden hue, and is very handsome ; but its chief recommendation is its delightful fragrance, particularly towards the evening : two or three flowers will scent the whole house. The perfume is equal to the scent of a large bed of violets. 8s.

D. Cambridgensis (Duchess of Cambridge's); Khoosea

Hills.—This is a truly magnificent species. Sepals and petals of a fine golden colour; lip of the same hue, with a large blotch in the centre of the richest purple chocolate. They are produced in pairs, on short thick drooping pseudo-bulbs, sometimes as many as four pairs on a stem; each flower measuring two inches across. It is the finest of all the yellow Dendrobes. 63s.

D. Jenkinsii (Capt. Jenkins's); India.—A neat growing species, clinging close to the block; the pseudo-bulbs are produced close together, overlapping each other like the tiles of a house. The flowers are produced singly, and are very large in proportion to the rest of the plant. The colour is a pale buff, with a shade of orange towards the centre. A very pretty little plant. 21s.

D. longicornu (Long-horned D.); Nepaul.—A handsome species. The stems are covered thickly with short purplish hair; sepals and petals white: lip large, shaped like a half moon. It is yellow, with orange-red stripes. 42s.

D. pulchellum (Pretty D.); Sylhet.—A desirable species found growing on trees. As it is of a dwarf habit and branches freely, it may be so managed as to cover very soon a large upright log. The sepals are white, edged with green; the petals of the same colour, edged with delicate rose; the lip finely fringed at the edge, and has a blotch in the centre of bright orange red. There is a variety with the rose on the petals of a deep purplish hue. Every collection ought to have in it a good plant of this very pretty, easily-managed species. 15s.

D. tetragonum (Four-angled D.); Moreton Bay, New Holland.—Excepting *D. speciosum*, this is the handsomest of all the New Holland species. The sepals and petals are yellowish, bordered with red; lip pale yellow, striped with narrow bands of crimson. The sepals and petals are much lengthened, so as to give them a strap-like appearance. 42s.

This section of Dendrobium, that we have selected as proper to grow on logs of wood, might have been considerably extended. There are from New Holland a large number of dwarf-growing curious species belonging to this genus, but as they are more objects of botanical curiosity than fine ornamental plants, if compared with the rest of the tribe, we have thought it best to omit them altogether. Such as we have described are really beautiful or otherwise interesting species, and are all worth growing. There are several handsome varieties that would grow and flower well on blocks, but they grow much finer in pots. We mention this to give our readers to understand that we have not overlooked such handsome species, but have reserved them to be described in the next section amongst those that do best in pots.

The Culture on blocks is, first, to procure them of suitable sizes, in proportion to the plants; to fasten a little moss (thin green flakes are the best) on the blocks; and then to fasten the plants to the blocks upon the moss with some zinc wire: we think this better than copper, because it is softer, and not so liable to injure the plant. Then hang them up in the house pretty near to the glass; and whilst they are growing syringe them gently twice a-day, keeping up a high temperature and moist atmosphere in the house. When their new pseudo-bulbs are fully formed, gradually lessen the syringing, moisture, and heat of the house. This will induce rest, and enable them to fill up the buds with flowers. If they are kept constantly growing they will not bloom, hence this resting is a point of culture that is indispensible; indeed the growth itself will be stronger for having a period of cessation of growth. In the regions where these plants are found there are three seasons, quite distinct: a season that is hot and dry, during which orchids generally bloom; a rainy season—the rains in those tropical regions compared with ours being perfect deluges, long continued, and this is the season of growth to the orchids; lastly, there is a cold season—and this is the season of rest. The cold season of India is, however, warm compared with ours; therefore, we must not subject our orchids from that country to too low a temperature, but induce rest by withholding moisture, in conjunction with a reduced moderate heat. These observations apply to all plants of this tribe as well as to those on blocks, and we trust our readers will exercise that judgment and discretion in supplying the three seasons at such proper periods as will be most conducive to the health and well-being of the plants.

Epidendrum aloifolium (Aloe-leaved E.); Mexico.—Sepals and petals greenish yellow, changing to a deeper colour; lip large, pure white, and shaped like the head of a lance. The flowers are produced, as it were, out of the bosom of the leaves, sometimes in fives, but generally in threes. When large and well grown this species is very handsome, particularly in the latter stage of blooming. They continue a long time in bloom, and are fragrant. 31s 6d.

E. bicornutum (Two-horned); Trinidad.—This is a very handsome species, vieing with the famed *Phalænopsis*. The flowers are large, and when the plant is healthy and strong are produced numerously in upright panicles. Sepals and petals pure white; the lip is the same colour but beautifully spotted with crimson dots. 42s.

E. lamellatum (plated); Honduras.—Sepals and petals delicate pink; the lip rose-colour and very bright. It has a row of scale-like plates of a yellow colour, whence its name; very rare. 84s.

E. macrochilum (Large-lipped); Mexico.—A very fine species and very fragrant. The sepals and petals are of a curious colour, difficult to describe—greenish brown will perhaps come nearest to it. The labellum or lip is the prettiest part of the flower, being pure white, with a bright rosy purple spot at the base. The whole flower will frequently measure three inches across. 31s. 6d.

E. macrochilum, var. *roseum* (Rose-coloured variety); Guatimala.—A very distinct and beautiful variety, having the sepals and petals of a deeper hue, and the lip of a rich rose-colour streaked with crimson. A very desirable plant. 42s.

E. vitellinum (Yolk-of-egg coloured); Mexico.—This is a splendid species, on account of its brilliant colour. It is, indeed, very lovely. The leaves are glaucous (milky green), the sepals and petals rich orange scarlet, the lip is of a clear bright yellow.

The above are the epidendrums that do best on blocks of wood. *E. bicornutum* is a difficult plant to keep, but may be managed by being placed on a log without moss and kept close to the glass, moistened when growing with the syringe, and kept quite dry through the winter and whilst at rest. The same treatment will suit the beautiful *E. vitellinum*. The others should have a portion of moss placed round their roots on the block, and will bear a much more free application of water, especially whilst growing. As they are all, excepting *E. bicornutum*, natives of cooler parts of South America, they are suitable inhabitants of the Mexican house, and will thrive well and flower finer in such a house than if kept warmer. *E. macrochilum*, and its variety *roseum*, will grow in pots in a mixture of rough peat and broken potsherds; but there is always danger of the roots perishing in winter, and, therefore, we recommend placing them on blocks.   T. APPLEBY.

(To be continued.)

FLORISTS' FLOWERS.

CARNATIONS AND PICOTEES.—If our directions about layering have been followed, the layers will now be rooted, and ought to be taken off and potted in pairs in five-inch pots. By putting them in pairs in pots your frames will hold double the number. If, however, you have plenty of room, they will undoubtedly be better single, though not very much so, as they are only put in these pots to keep them through the winter more conveniently. In taking up the layers be careful not to injure the roots or break off the part beyond the tongue or slit; we have seen frequently a finely rooted layer deprived of its roots entirely by lifting it up too high previously to cutting it off from the parent plant. The soil to pot the layers in need not be very rich. Light friable loam, mixed with one-sixth of very decayed leaf-mould or dung, with a due portion of sand added, will be suitable for them.

PINKS.—If your bed is not ready for the pipings no time ought to be lost in preparing it; they ought to be planted in their blooming situation early in September. By planting early they get good hold of the soil before the severe frost sets in; while on the other hand, if planted late, the frost is almost sure to throw them out of the ground, and thus frequently destroy them.

T. APPLEBY.

THE KITCHEN-GARDEN.

ANGELICA.—To obtain plants for planting out permanently next spring, the present will be found a good season for sowing this vegetable. New seed should be chosen, the old seed of Angelica being very liable to fail in germinating.

GLOBE ARTICHOKES.—Those that have been some time in bearing, will at once require the old stalks and old leaves to be taken from them, which will encourage the growth of the suckers; and in order to get these strong against winter they should also be thinned by taking away the spurious and weak ones, and leaving only a few of the strongest to each stool. By such management, and the addition of a simple methodical winter protection, a good foundation is laid for ensuring an abundant crop for the next season.

spring planted Artichokes, if previous directions have been attended to, are now in full bearing. To assist them in swelling out their heads handsome and large, good liquid manure should be liberally applied; care should be taken in cutting the first head not to cut the stalk lower down than the first joint or leaf, as by due encouragement they will continue to produce heads from those joints; and although they will not be so large as the first or summit head, they may still be obtained of a pretty and useful size.

ROUTINE WORK: Celery.—The earthing-up should be attended to, and another small planting made for late spring use; plant also early Cabbage, and encourage the growth of Coleworts by frequent surface stirrings. Early Horn Carrots may still be sown on dry healthy soil in sheltered situations, or in temporary made pits, where they are likely to get some kind of winter protection. Cardoons should still be encouraged by liquid manure, and the forwardest by applications of earth when the weather is dry. Sow Corn Salad, American and Normandy Cress, and replant a portion of the Watercress bed. Attend to the planting and pricking-out of Endive and Lettuce. If Onions are not already sown for spring planting, this may still with safety be done. Those who esteem the very large Onion should sow the Tripoli, White Spanish and Deptford varieties.

POTATOES.—All that are ripe should be taken up in dry weather and stored in dry situations. Those who have at command any dry dust, charred earth, or charred saw or wood dust, or charred old tan, will find such materials excellent for storing this useful tuber.

A portion of the best curled Parsley should be potted for the every day's supply when we have snow and frost, and the short days of winter. Thin out in due season the winter crop of Spinach; keeping it at all times clear from dead leaves and weeds. Vermin will not be troublesome if previous directions are fully carried out with regard to the regular performance of surface-stirring.

JAMES BARNES.

MISCELLANEOUS INFORMATION.

WHAT IS A GARDEN?

By the Authoress of " My Flowers," &c., &c.

(Concluded from page 319.)

THEN our minds wander to gardens of another kind—the Botanical Gardens, which are to be found in the neighbourhood of London, Paris, and many other large cities. No doubt they greatly aid the cause of knowledge in most places; but to our minds there is something very dull and uninteresting in seeing long rows and borders of shrubs and plants labelled in their blooming in a chemist's shop, with all kinds of unpronounceable names; but we are not botanists.

Near these, again, in the suburbs of large cities, are found such gardens as those of Vauxhall and Ranelagh, where few seeds are found and matured but those of vice, the better seed being taken elsewhere. Then we may advert to those other appendages of well-peopled cities—the Zoological Gardens. As gardens they sometimes verge on the line of beauty (as at Paris) without attaining it; but as places of intellectual amusement and instruction, they are highly commendable, and useful both to rich and poor,—to the old and young.

The gardens, like the mansions of the middling classes in easy circumstances, are perhaps, after all, the most to be admired in this country, where art, science, a reasonable command of money and time, lend their aid to nature, and make the teeming earth develop those supplies of beauty, fruit, and flowers, which in less favourable circumstances

are not to be expected. How truly enviable are the gardens and conservatories of the wealthy in the neighbourhood of London, and of most large towns! Cowper says,—

" Who loves a garden loves a greenhouse too ! "

A garden of one acre is usually considered to be of the fairest proportions, for all purposes of practical utility and family economy. Descending in the " sliding scale " of horticulture, we cannot help noticing the endless variety of little gardens attached to great houses, or of great gardens attached to small houses, where a small show of evergreens and a few borders of flowers form the whole product to delight the eyes and nose, but without any provision for the mouth.

It is too much the custom to ridicule those little quadrangular spots of cultivated ground in front of the endless rows of houses in the approaches to London and most other cities, where we find three or four square yards of earth covered or intersected with bright gravel, white pavement, and brown grass, with rows of box, and a few dingy roots and shrubs, endeavouring to extricate themselves from the tight embrace, forming what is pleasantly called the " front garden;" but we hail with fulness of respect this tribute to the God of nature, as being the only approach to the living vegetable world, which stern necessity allows to many sons and daughters of toil and of affliction. Endless and diversified indeed are the various forms of what are called gardens in and near towns, until we arrive at almost the last and humblest link in the horticultural chain,—that dismal spot, half garden and half drying-ground, where nought rises from the ground but a few patches of grass, overshadowed by those "hanging woods" called drying-posts.

Who can forget, as he walks along the streets of a city, how often his thoughts are unexpectedly recalled to other scenes by the sight of a few flowers growing in pots, or bulbous roots is phials of water, fondly cherished by those who have no garden at all? Who has not seen in the filthiest parts of a town the inmates of attics

> "overhead
> Suspend their crazy boxes, planted thick
> And watered duly. There the pitcher stands,
> A fragment; and the spoutless teapot there:
> Sad witnesses how close-pent man regrets
> The country; with what ardour he contrives
> A peep at nature, when he can no more."

We must not, however, in our hasty view of the various links in our chain, pass over one of them, though lowly, yet much cherished by the readers of this little work—the cottage garden. Here, as in a mirror, we may read with tolerable accuracy the owner's character. If it be well laid out, well fenced, well drained, well cultivated, how loudly it speaks of his industry and skill. If it be all devoted to cabbages and potatoes, it proclaims the master one who leaves all to nature, bestowing the least possible quantity of his own exertions on it. If it be a garden of flowers only, it marks improvidence. If it be all fruits and vegetables, it marks a too calculating spirit, which forgets that some of the fair flowers of nature may inspire an air of comfort, and bestow as much of ornament as God permits; whilst a few well selected herbs of medicinal qualities afford a simple remedy for many of the ailments and wounds of humble life; whilst footpaths neglected, and doors and gates dilapidated, speak of idle habits and ill-conducted children. The bee-hive, that emblem of industry and source of a poor man's wealth, should always find a place in his garden, where flowers would thereby bring back a reward in golden treasures.

The cottager sometimes, with the best intentions, errs in undertaking too large a garden, forgetting that his time and labour are usually his master's property, and that a very small portion of ground ought to engage his moments of leisure, which, as well as his hours of toil, belong (for bodily refreshment) to the earthly master whom God has placed over him; always excepting that day on which he is charged to do "no manner of work."

We have particularised, as far as our limits will permit, the varieties of garden ground which conduce to man's health or wealth upon the soil; and we have also cursorily alluded to the "crazy boxes" and "spoutless tea-pots" suspended in mid-air in the name of gardening. But man's unextinguishable love for the pursuit is carried with him to the very surface of the sea. In proof of this, let any one sail down the Thames, or into Portsmouth, or any other harbour, and there, from the very windows and port-holes of the shipping, whether homeward-bound, outward-bound, or at anchor, still the "crazy boxes," &c., present themselves in every variety, in evidence that even many waters cannot drown our inherent love for vegetable life.

Having traced this natural and innocent feeling over earth, and air, and water, we still find the name of garden adopted, as expressive of beauty, where no vegetable life remains. When the botanist has ransacked every part of the habitable globe in collecting rare specimens of dried fruits, flowers, herbs, seeds, leaves, reeds, and mosses, and has arranged them in scientific order in glass cases, from want of a more expressive name, he calls the collection a "Hortus siccus," or dry garden—and there is something both poetical and beautiful in the idea.

When Noah was anxiously awaiting his release from the ark, how joyfully must he have recognised the olive branch presented to him, as a fit emblem of the goodness of God in permitting him to return to a world, once more to be beautified by fruits and flowers, and trees and herbage, some springing spontaneously into perfection, but others (to remind man ever of his "fall") procurable only by "the sweat of his brow."

May we not say that the earth itself is one vast garden, nourished and tended by the Hand Divine? What a field for thought, for adoration, and praise, is the simple cottage garden!

HISTORY OF AN APIARY.

Let me say a few words more on the subject of my last communication, before I pass on to my report of this year's res gestæ in my apiary. In recommending the adoption of the plan there proposed of increasing a stock of bees, let me not be misunderstood. I do not propose it either as a cheaper or a better plan than the good and old-fashioned method, by purchase of swarms in May or June. It has too much of hazard to be generally recommended, requiring, as it does, perpetual attention during the feeding-time. I would advise none but amateur apiarians, who make it their hobby and amusement to keep bees, to undertake it. Few persons in active business would have the necessary leisure, or the inclination, to carry it through with perseverance. And it is very little less expensive than would be the purchase of a prime swarm in the height of the season. I speak, of course, according to my own experience, for I do not pretend to specify the minimum quantity or the precise quality of the food requisite to ensure the success of the experiment. I simply recommend the plan (as I have tried it myself) for the amusement and interest which attends it,—an interest which is carried on so much later than is usual in some localities. For instance, in my own neighbourhood no addition is made to bee stores after July is over. From this time my hives cease to interest me: the drones are killed; the bees become remiss; the temperature of the hive sinks many degrees; and the weight diminishes gradually day by day. In places, however, where ling and heather abound, or other late blooming plants, it is very different; then from 5 to 20 lbs. of honey may yet be gathered. No strict rule, therefore, can be laid down; but when the circumstances of a locality are similar to those of my own, I do highly recommend my plan to all who love bees and their interesting habits. Only let them be careful to feed regularly and liberally, to use good and wholesome beer as an ingredient in the syrup, and to keep their bees as warm as possible the while. To this I add,—the more bees the better; the stronger and fuller the hives whose population is saved, the greater the chance of success. To those who can meet all these requisites, I can promise a due reward and great gratification.

And now to resume the long-suspended story of my second start in bee-keeping. You will be curious to know the ultimate fate of my various stocks, and the results of my projected experiments, as spoken of when I first had the honour, in January last, to communicate with you on the subject. It has been a very busy year with me, and not, on the whole, an unsuccessful one, although in general, in this as in other localities, there are sad complaints among the cottagers of the unkindliness of the season. I should say however, that but for the evil spring and the ignorance of those said cottagers as to some of the mysteries of bee-keeping, to which I alluded in a former paper, the season has been, in this part of the country at least, an average good one. My stock, "A," for instance, which I plundered rather too freely, as you doubtless thought at the time, and which I really feared had begun to perish in March, is now as strong a stock as I could wish. I took from it a beautiful bell-glass containing 8½ lbs. of perfectly pure honeycomb, on the 15th July, and a second, containing 2 lbs., on the 6th inst., besides 8 lbs. equally pure from the side-box, on the 19th July. This stock, therefore, has yielded me this year in all 18½ lbs., and I shall be careful not to touch the contents of the stock-box, as I did foolishly last October, though its weight is at least 30 lbs. I doubt whether I should have reared it, but for a judicious supply of food in March and April, when the weather was sufficiently warm to tempt the bees up into my feeder, and for the addition to them, on the 5th of April, of about 1000 bees taken from another hive. The second hive (B) was very strong in February and March—as strong as any of my others; but its population seems to have been larger than the supply of food, for they perceptibly, though gradually, fell off in numbers till the beginning of June, when they rallied, and have thriven well since. On the 15th of that month the weight of the hive was but 18¼ lbs., i.e., only 3¼ lbs. heavier than it was on the 24th of April. The hive itself and appurtenances weighs 9 lbs. Since then, however, it has much improved; the drones appeared soon after, and the weight of it at the present moment is 32 lbs.—sufficient, I hope, to ensure its future prosperity. I removed it the other day (July 30th) from the window, where it had remained since September last, to its old stand in my friend's garden, to make way for one of my experimental stocks, which took its place yesterday evening (August 7th). Not more than about 200 bees in all seem to have returned to their old quarters, though my friend's house is not half a mile off. I am sceptical as to the great harm of shifting bees, if it be not done in the early and cold spring, and the busy season. My hive "B," seems to be doing as well as before. One thing, however, I have learnt from the turn-up of this speculation—not to keep late casts. I must wait till the third, or perhaps the fourth, year for any profit from it. This hive is not even now more than two-thirds full of comb; but it is very large.

My most profitable stock has turned out to be the identical one united last August, and fed on artificial food (C), in the manner which was stated and recommended in my last paper. I have taken from it in all 3½ lbs. of undefiled honeycomb, viz., a bell-glass containing 6 lbs. on the 27th June; a second, containing 4 lbs., on the 28th; and a third, containing upwards of 11 lbs., on the 27th July; besides 11b. from a small fourth glass, and 12 lbs. from the side-box on the 20th of the same month; and it now weighs 29 lbs.

A COUNTRY CURATE.

THE DOMESTIC PIGEON.

(Continued from page 262.)

CROSSING OF BREEDS.

THIS chapter—the most interesting of all—relating to the means of obtaining varieties more desirable for their beauty and utility, will be found the most incomplete, because amateurs have always neglected to note down their observations, and the bird sellers or trainers have not published the manner in which they have obtained some varieties on which they speculate. We shall mark with an asterisk the previous observations of authors that we think false, or at least very doubtful. We must warn amateurs, that in crossing their varieties, if they do not immediately obtain such as they wish, they must not in consequence renounce their hopes; for it very frequently happens that we do not attain the desired end until the third or fourth generation.

*1. The Pouters produce with the Mixtures the Blue-spotted, and their speckled varieties. This note of M. Vieillot appears to us altogether wrong, for the spots do not exist either in the Pouters or in the Mixtures; it can only be the production of a happy chance, and in this case would it transmit itself to the young pigeons?

2. The Pouters crossed with the Jacobin produce the Cavaliers.

*3. The Pouters and the Jacobin produce the Hooded pigeon. M. Corbie has often crossed these two birds, to discover the justice of that observation of M. Vieillot, but has never obtained anything but worthless pigeons.

4. The Chamois Pouter and the Jacobin may produce the Spotted Chamois or the dark variety.

5. The Pouter and the large Mixture produce the Cavalier.

6. The Spotted Jacinthe and the Red-spotted produce the Spotted Tawney.

7. The Jacinthe and the Tawny produce the Red-spotted.

8. The Blue Pouter and the Black-banded Pouter produce the Grey.

9. The Spotted Grey Pouter and the Black-banded Pouter produce the Grey-dotted.

10. The Chamois Pouter and the Blue produce the slate-coloured.

11. The Black-banded Pouter and the Blue produce sometimes the Red Pouter; but this production is very uncertain.

12. The Lisle crossed with the Feather-footed has furnished the Plunging pigeon, and the Lisle snapping pigeon.

*13. A male of the Tambour and a female of the Broad-tailed Shaker produce, according to Ray and Willulghby, the Shaker pigeon with a straight tail. We have not been able to test this by experience.

14. A Tambour and a Carrier produce the Goat-sucker pigeon.

15. The Bastard Bagdad and Mixture produce the Large-headed Bastard Bagdad.

16. The Bagdad with a large white mushroom excrescence with the Black Bastard Bagdad produce the Short Bagdad.

17. The Mixed Bagdad or Swan pigeon and the Common Cavalier produce the Proud Cavalier.

18. The Common Runt mixed with the Bastard Bagdad produce the Mixed Runt.

19. The Black Runt and the Grey Runt produce the Grey-spotted.

20. The mixing of the Silky Shaker pigeon with other races produces Silky pigeons of every form and colour; if it is crossed with pigeons that have bars on the wings they produce individuals bearing handsome fringes of varied colours.

21. The female of the Hooded Jacobin with the male of the Red Jacobin produce the Spotted Red Jacobin.

22. The Spotted Red Jacobin with the Dun-coloured Jacobin produce the Spotted Dun Jacobin.

23. The Common Jacobin and the Mixture produce the Hooded Jacobin.

*24. The English Tumbler and the small Mixture, if very rich in colour, may produce the Swiss pigeon with a golden collar, says M. Vieillot.

*25. The Common Carrier and the Peacock pigeon produce, according to the opinion of some authors, the Black Carrier, with a white tail.

26. The common Polish pigeon and the Turbit produce the Gentle Polish.

This is nearly all that is known of the results obtained by crossing pigeons. As to the blending of colours, we now give their probable result; for nature often produces tints altogether unlooked for.

1. A blue male and a red female will produce pigeons of a golden colour, or yellowish—sometimes black.

2. A red pigeon and a black will produce birds of a deep red, but frequently lead colour.

3. A red with a dun colour will often produce a very beautiful red, but sometimes dull.

4. A blue and a fawn colour will sometimes reproduce individuals all blue, or all fawn, or mixed with both colours.

5. A fawn and a black, or a blue and a black, may produce a pinkish grey.

6. A black and a blue will sometimes produce pigeons of a dark colour with black bars—perhaps red, or black, or sparkling.

7. A yellow and a black will produce dark colours streaked with yellow.

8. Finally, a female of a sparkling red with a male of a blue sparkling black might produce a dark gold colour spangled with red.

The amateurs who attempt to breed new varieties of pigeons will always be recompensed for their trouble, whether they obtain or not their immediate object; for it has been proved that mongrels are more fruitful than pigeons of a pure race, and they are so much the more so according as the varieties from which they have been obtained had least analogy between them. As to the general forms and characters, it is necessary to know that the male alone transmits them.

We will now show by an example the manner in which we must proceed to insure success. I will suppose that we wish to establish a race of the Peacock, of which we only have one male: we would choose a female that has some resemblance to it in size and form; we would also choose its colour according to the variety we wished to reproduce in the race, and couple them together. The mongrels produced by them would already have from 13 to 28 feathers in the tail, and this, without being yet so raised as that of its father, would still place it already much above its wings. We would then choose a female from their young, and couple it the following year with the old male; and the tail of these mongrels of the second generation would be furnished with from 17 to 28 feathers, having the faculty of raising and displaying it in the same manner as the father. We would then couple the old male a third time with one of these new females, and the young pigeons springing from them would have all the beauty of the pure race; but yet we must not rely on the purity of their offspring until three or four new generations have well confirmed the crossing.

It is more difficult to produce a variety of which we do not possess any individual, because it requires more time and attention. Let us suppose that we wish to have the Proud Cavalier, not possessing any Cavalier. We should choose those individuals which have the greatest analogy with them. The Proud Cavalier is large, of a handsome figure, swelling out its note, high on its legs, and has a ribbon round the eyes, as well as a kind of mushroom on the beak. When this is known the choice is easily made. As it is a Pouter, we should take a Pouter and couple it with a Runt, to obtain the size. From this will spring a Cavalier that we have classed among those of a pure race, because it transmits all its qualities to its posterity. We shall already have a bird with long legs, having thick membranes on the nostrils, and a small ribbon round the eyes; but it cannot swell its crop so much as the Pouter. We should couple this Cavalier with the Mixed Bagdad or Swan pigeon, and thus obtain a true tubercle about the bill, a larger ribbon round the eyes, a swelling throat, and, in short, a true Proud Cavalier.

We must not conclude from these two examples, that new varieties can easily be obtained by combining judiciously races and varieties without remarking, that nature sometimes refuses to produce interesting birds, in spite of all our patience and sagacity. For example, it rarely happens that we can obtain from crossing the Swiss Tumblers and Carriers anything but true Stock doves, without beauty or any other merit. Several varieties crossed together produce young ones much more ugly even than the parents were handsome. But, by way of recompense, it also happens that these very insignificant birds produce by crossing them a handsome posterity. The amateur must never grow weary, because sooner or later he will be recompensed for his pains; neither must he cease to try experiments because the first attempts may not have succeeded.

"If one reflects," says M. Vieillot, "on the number of races considered pure, on the possibility of coupling them among themselves, obtaining young ones from them, of pairing these, either with their own race or that of their parents, or with their brothers of another brood or another crossing, we shall perceive how easy it is to obtain varieties almost innumerable, since the first blending produces 144 varieties." The author only speaks here of the blending of those varieties he has described; for the first mixing of ours would produce more than 3,300 varieties.

(*To be continued.*)

PIG-FATTING AND BACON-CURING.

A few weeks since we received a letter from near New Galloway, in Scotland, from which we make the following extract:—

"The practice here is to let pigs run loose till they have come to their full size, and then to give them a quantity of potatoes till within a short time of their being killed. Since potatoes have failed, I believe turnips have been used, the effect being pretty much the same to produce a great quantity of fat, and make the flesh very coarse food. The only thing done to improve the quality of the meat, is to give the pigs some bruised oats or oatmeal for a few weeks before they are killed. The bacon and hams are considered very inferior to those of Sligo, which are held in high estimation; and you would confer an important benefit upon us were you to make known the mode of management adopted there. Our plan of curing too is very defective, while that adopted in Sligo is most successful; and upon this point also, we should be exceedingly obliged by your affording us information."

In consequence of this application we have sought for information in the best pig-fatting and bacon-curing districts of England, and the following are the results.

From *Norfolk* our correspondent writes thus:—

"I have been in the habit of fatting pigs for nearly forty years; and from experience, and from the knowledge of the growth of animals, I find that to fat a pig in the shortest time, and with the least expense, the animal must first have acquired its full growth. I have bought them in young, allowed them to roam about my ground, and fed them night and morning with swill and grains, with potato-peelings, &c., until they have been fit from growth to put up; by this time perhaps the pig may weigh eight stones, being a large pig for full growth. My stye is a good one,—*warm*, well ventilated, and not capacious. The hog is then fed upon barley-meal three times daily, just sufficient to be eaten; the stye is kept well littered and very clean; and one sack of meal is sufficient to make it from 10 to 11 stone—quite large enough for any family; they have always thrived well by running about, and pick up many things congenial to their digestive powers before being put up. The animal should have just sufficient for consumption at a time; if more it is apt to ferment, and it is then carried off too quickly by the bowels, and no benefit derived; the meat by this method is better, more firm, and does not waste by boiling; whereas if brank, peas, or rye are given you lose much in cooking, besides the hardness, &c. If you will refer to the analysis of the latter food, it is not equal to barley-meal; it is apt to run off by the bowels, except the brank, which intoxicates, and produces stupor. The barley-meal has all the properties to make fat, and renders the meat tender and well-flavoured. Perhaps these observations may not be very satisfactory to many, but I have found the plan the least expensive, and farmers perfectly agree with me."

From *Suffolk* we have the following answers to our queries from one of the best farmers of that county:—

"What is the best age of a hog to put up to fat, with a view to profit?—All pigs require to finish their growth before they are put up to fatten, as if not full grown, growth and fatting must go on at the same time, and that is a disadvantage. The Suffolk pigs take nine months to grow, and then they are fit to fatten. What food at first, and what changes of it, during fattening?—Peas and a small quantity of turnips at first; after the hog gets large, that is, when it is seen that it is perceptibly getting fat, peas only; and *then* the peas should be ground. How often fed?—From five to six times a day, and only small quantities at a time; a fatting pig should leave off with an edge to its appetite. How much food is required to increase each stone in weight?—The Suffolk rule is one bushel of peas or peas-meal to every stone of pork; or six pecks of barley-meal."

In *Hampshire* we find the best authorities agree that it is not profitable to put up a hog to fat until it has attained its full growth, and at this time it should be of a breed to weigh about seven or eight score pounds, because when fattened to 10 or 12 score it finds the readiest market. Barley-meal is the most profitable food; warmth, cleanliness, and even scrubbing with warm water every week, and feeding four times a-day at regular intervals, are the essentials for fattening.

For curing bacon, one of the best curers in Hampshire informs us, that as soon as the hog is quite cold, that is the day after killing, it is cut into halves, and rubbed with a mixture of salt and saltpetre; 28lb of salt being required for a hog of ten score pounds, mixed with an ounce of saltpetre, pounded, for every score pounds of pork. The sides of the hog are laid upon a stone-floor, and for the first week turned daily, and some of the salt mixture rubbed in; but for the second and third weeks the turning and rubbing need be repeated only each second day; at the end of the three weeks it will be sufficiently salted. If the bacon is not immediately required the salted sides are put on *edge* in a bin, and salt put between them so that they cannot touch, and it is also heaped over them, so as to exclude the air and to keep the next tier of sides from touching them. If the sides are placed flat-ways they become too salt. They are taken out for smoking (making into bacon) as required, and thus they quite avoid that rustiness which will occur in bacon which is stored for any length of time.

To convert the pork thus salted into bacon the sides are taken out, the salt wiped from them, and they are hung up by hooks fixed across the roof of a brick-built room made so high that the lower end of the side of a hog is about eight feet from the floor. If nearer the floor the heat would melt the fat. On the floor a little saw-dust is lighted and kept smouldering on constantly day and night for ten days, which is long enough for the side of a hog weighing ten score pounds. The door of the smoking-room shuts quite close, but there is a hole through the wall on a level with the floor to admit air enough for keeping the saw-dust burning, and the only escape for the smoke is through the tiles, for it is the confinement of the smoke about the pork which so soon baconizes it.

A most important point is *the quality of the saw-dust* ; oak, elm, and birch are best. Our informant prefers that of the oak; and there are two other facts not to be forgotten :— First—*The saw-dust cannot be too old nor too dry* ; and Secondly—*No fir, larch, deal, nor other saw-dust containing turpentine must be used or it will spoil the bacon.*

TO CORRESPONDENTS.

⁎ We request that no one will write to the departmental writers of THE COTTAGE GARDENER. It gives them unjustifiable trouble and expense. All communications should be addressed "*To the Editor of The Cottage Gardener, 2, Amen Corner, Paternoster Row, London.*"

ELDER WINE (*X. Y. Z.*).—This can be made in the same manner as directed for rhubarb wine, at page 326, but the proportions of the ingredients must differ. Recipes will be seen at pages 324 and 338.

BLACKBERRY WINE (*Ibid*).—Wine can be made of this fruit. We have obtained the following recipe, but perhaps some of our correspondents will furnish us with others :—When the blackberries are fully ripe put them into a cask set on end, open at the top, and with a tap fixed in it ; pour on the berries as much boiling water as will cover them, and then, as soon as the hand can be put among them, crush every berry ; let them remain until the refuse of the berries begin to rise to the top, which will be in three or four days ; then draw off the clear liquor into another vessel, and to every ten quarts add one pound of loaf-sugar ; stir it until quite dissolved, and let it remain for ten days to work in the first vessel ; draw it off by the tap, through a jelly bag, into a larger vessel ; steep one ounce of isinglass for twelve hours in a pint of the liquor, then boil it upon a slow fire until all dissolved, then add a gallon of the liquor, and boil again for a minute or two ; mix the whole together, let it remain a few days to clear, then draw it off and keep it in a cool place.

TRENCHING (*Ibid*).—The good kitchen soil, resting on a clayey subsoil, will be benefited by trenching, especially if the bottom spit is mixed with limy rubbish and coal ashes, to render it more porous. We are no friends to letting ground lie fallow, which is only another term for doing nothing ; trench as we have said, manure as a kitchen-garden should be manured, and keep the hoe going, and then there will be no need of fallowing.

DIAMETER OF POTS (*Novice*).—When a 5-inch, or any other sized pot is thus spoken of, the number of inches are meant which the pot measures inside across, just below the rim.

STRAWBERRIES FOR FORCING (*Ibid*).—Your plants in 4-inch pots move into 7-inch when well rooted. Do not begin forcing by moving them into the house until the middle of February. You will find Mr. Errington's very full and excellent directions for treating the plants, and for forcing, in our third volume.

ALSTRŒMERIAN (*Queen Mab*).—We recommend you to plant these as soon as you can get them. Several kinds, such as *Acutifolia, Hirtella, Ovata, Psittacina, Pelegrina, &c.,* will do well out of doors, planted six inches deep, in a mixture of sandy peat and loam, on a warm border ; others, such as *Aurantiaca, Occulata, Pallida, &c.,* are better potted two or three inches deep in well drained pots, and kept during the winter in a frame or cold pit ; and a third set, more tender still, require even more heat, though most of them will succeed under that treatment. Very likely those you have received are the hardiest kind, but even them we would recommend you to pot them for the first season. They will do anywhere secure from frost until they begin to grow.

VARIOUS (*A Constant Reader*).—Your Yucca, with its roots above the pot, may be repotted now in sandy loam and peat. See the week before last. White Lilies growing in large bunches had better be separated, and they will flower better. Your Grapes and Vines are mildewed, and washing with weak salt and water has done no good : puff the afflicted parts with flowers of sulphur, and a little fine quick-lime mixed with the sulphur ; it will not require to be put on thick, though it may need repeating to effect a cure. *Araucaria Cunninghami* and *Excelsa* are not hardy enough for our winters in common circumstances. *Strawberries* planted two years ago ought to have borne well ; those put out last year ought to bear better next year than runners of this season, unless you give them extra kind attention, such as layering them in pots, or pricking them out into beds before planting ; if so most kinds will bear the first season, and plentifully the second. They are partial to a strong soil if there is not too much clay. As to kinds, that will depend upon your taste—the Black Prince is early ; Keen's is first-rate for bearing plentifully, early, and from young plants ; British Queen is large and fine flavoured ; Elisa is smaller but high flavoured ; and Elton, though

rather tart, is valuable as a late large sort. If you fancy the *Hautbois* get the *Prolific.*

TRAINING PLANTS IN POTS (*F. W. T.*).—This will meet with notice ere long, but the difficulty of the matter is, that few feel as you do the necessity for revision in this matter. It is often a serious thing to hint at a man's want of taste, and still more difficult to prove he is wrong, a principle of taste being rather a fluctuating thing.

VINES TRAINED OVER A SLATE ROOF (*A. B., Camberwell*).—If there is plenty of strength in your vines this will answer. The vines, being on a trellis, during the day will not be too hot, because the slates will absorb heat and not reflect it ; at night, or when the atmosphere is colder than the slate, the heat will be radiated from the latter to the former, and the vines will derive the benefit of it as it passes. Through this radiation the slates will become very cold at night towards the end of autumn, because heat will be dispersed more quickly than from an upright wall. We have no doubt but the plan would answer well in your locality if your roof has a good aspect. As to covering the roof above the vines with glass we doubt its propriety, as without great attention to moisture in the atmosphere, and the giving of air, the enclosed atmosphere would be too hot and dry ; putting glass on towards the end of autumn would be advantageous, but, altogether, it would cost you less trouble to place the glass over part of your vine wall.

MARVEL OF PERU (*Susannah*).—It mattees not whether you take the roots out of the pots or not, provided you keep them dry and free from frost during winter.

STOVE CLIMBERS, PITS FOR (*E. F.*).—No doubt our friend, Mr. Appleby, will perfectly satisfy you on the subject ; in the meantime we imagine, that instead of merely sinking a hole he wishes these little pits to be formed of solid materials, and for two reasons,—First, to keep the roots of the different climbers separate, and thus have them under command ; and, Secondly, to give them merely as much room as will secure a certain degree of luxuriance, and yet an abundance of bloom, by telling the roots "thus far you may go, but no farther." In your stove, with the pipes only ten inches from the fruit wall, you could not have such little pits, or large pots, or brick boxes you may term them, there with any degree of propriety ; but any part of the house, such as against a pillar or support, will answer equally well. If, however, the position of the pit is far from the glass, it will be necessary to have your plants a good size before planting, as recommended for conservatory climbers some time ago.

IPOMŒA LEARII (*Ibid*).—This, planted in the greenhouse, has reached the rafters, and is flourishing, but has not flowered ; we would leave it alone instead of thinking of moving it to the stove, and, with common attention, we shall be much deceived if next season its splendour in the greenhouse does not lead you to thank us for the advice. We have had one ranging wildly over the roof of such a house for a number of years that continues blooming abundantly the whole of the summer and autumn.

BLUE FLOWER FOR BEDDING (*Minnie*).—Three-pennyworth of seeds of *Lobelia ramosa* will plant a bed six yards long and ten feet wide ; and it is the finest blue bedder in England or elsewhere, and about a foot or 15 inches high, and will flower all summer and autumn, just as you require.

SOIL FOR ROSES (*Ibid*).—Now is a good time to make up a new bed for roses, and the end of October is the best time to plant it ; roses will do very well in any fresh soil that is neither light, that is, with too much sand in it, nor heavy, that is, having too much clay ; and if you add a barrowful of old rotten dung to every five or six barrows of that kind of soil, the roses will thrive on it all the better. Have the bed 18 inches or two feet deep, drained, and do not raise it much in the centre as some people do, for if you do, when the bed is very dry, your watering and that from the rain will pass off it as from the roof of the house. To make the best of it plant none but perpetuals, but in them we include every rose, no matter what section it belongs to, that will flower in the autumn.

ROSE-BED (*C. J. M.*).—You say :—"I am about to make a rose-bed of about seven or eight yards in circumference (it may be oval). I propose having three or four pillar-roses, of different colours, in the centre, surrounding these with tall standards, and these again with half standards, and filling up the interstices between the standards with dwarfs, leaving sufficient room round the edges for pegging down such roses as Persian Brier, &c., and bedding out Scarlet Geraniums, Verbenas, Petunias, &c. Will this be a good arrangement ? If so, what roses would you recommend ?" The idea is not a bad one, but the outside row of Persian Brier, or, what is equally good, *Rosa Harrisii*, need not be pegged down ; we object altogether to pegging down roses, for reasons already insisted on ; these briers may be kept low by pruning out the tallest of the centre shoots annually after the bloom is over in May. We would place three poles in the centre, and in a triangle to meet at the top, for supporting the climbers and standards of *Madame Lafay, Geant des Batailles, Baronne Prevost, Duchess of Sutherland,* or, indeed, others of the best autumnal roses, both for standards and dwarfs ; the colours, names, and degrees of strength, may be found in our former volumes. An outside row of scarlet geraniums or verbenas, with spring bulbs, would answer and compensate the want of flowers in the briers after May.

ROSES (*A Lady Subscriber, Ireland*).—Your account now is very different from your former one about your roses. There is not a "rosary" in England free from the black spots and blotches exhibited on the leaves you sent, the cause of which is little known, and a cure for it still less; but from your statement about the preparation of the ground and feeding we have no doubt but your roses will give you very great satisfaction next year. The cold spring, the long journey, and the sudden turn to sultry weather at the end of May, sufficiently account for your disappointment this time; pray do not prune them too close, but have it done next November, and after that smear them over, stems and all, with a thick paint of fresh lime and soot; repeat this again next spring, before the buds are too forward, and you may say good-bye to black blotches, but give them neither manure nor strong drinks till the flower-buds are well formed next May, as high feeding aggravates the disposition to "green centres."

BEES.—If J. B. P. will send his address to J. H. Payne, Esq., Bury St. Edmunds, inclosing *four postage stamps*, he will send him a packet of the *Racodium Crilare*, which he can compare with that found in the Dublin Custom House vaults. Your "two fine first swarms united on the 13th of June, and weighing at this time only 17½ lbs. gross, and your best stocks being equally deficient," is on a par with us in England, with very few exceptions.

BEES (*A Lady Subscriber*).—Your third swarm should have been united to the second on the day of its swarming, as recommended in THE COTTAGE GARDENER, page 104, vol. ii.; it will now be very difficult to get them out of the cap without fumigation. In driving, a napkin should have been tied very tightly round the hives at the point of junction, to prevent the escape of the bees. Bell-glasses of all sizes may be had of Messrs. Neighbour and Son, 127, Holborn, London, at about 1s 6d per pound.

POTATO STORING (*Rev. H. R. D. P.*).—Your chief query is answered editorially. *Walnut leaved Kidneys* are not at all forwarded, but rather retarded by being planted in the autumn, otherwise they may be safely inserted. For autumn field planting we should recommend a depth of seven inches.

SPANISH POULTRY (*A Naval Officer*).—Can any one say where the real breed of these can be obtained. Thanks for your drawing, it has been sent to the engraver. Your list of roses is good.

CARDON DE TOURS (*A Subscriber*).—This is considered by the French the best kind of Cardoon, because it has ribs thicker, more tender, and more delicate than the common Cardoon. It is of the same botanical genus as the artichoke (*Cynara*). Sow four together, in patches 18 inches apart, about the middle of April, in trenches six inches deep and 22 inches wide, into which a little good dung has been dug previously. When the plants have four or five leaves remove all but one at each patch; water frequently and abundantly. At the end of October, when the plants are full grown and quite dry, tie up the leaves carefully with pieces of bass matting, then wind a hay-band round each, after which earth them up like celery. When blanched they are ready for cooking. The flavour is very agreeable. Reject all the stalks which are tough, fibrous, or hollow; cut the good into four-inch lengths, cleansing them from all prickles; put them into boiling water and parboil them, boiling the heart less time than the outer stalks; as soon as the slime upon them will come off by dipping them in cold water and wiping them with a cloth, they are done enough; clean them all from the slime in that way, then stew them in a little rich gravy, and just before taking off the fire add a piece of butter rolled in flour. This is the best mode of dressing, but they sometimes, after being cleared of the slime, are again put into boiling water and sent to table like sea-kale.

COVERING PRESERVES (*A Young Housekeeper*).—The paste must be put on the inside of the paper, according to the plan at page 333, for the paper has to be pasted over the mouth of the preserve-pot. The object is to exclude the air. Paste spread thinly dries and does not mould.

FERNS AND ROCK PLANTS (*W. F.*).—You wish for twelve of these for a shaded border beneath your dining-room window, and we recommend—of FERNS: *Polypodium driopteris*, *Onoclea sensibilis*, *Asplenium filix fœmina*, and *Aspidium lonchitis*. Of ROCK PLANTS: *Cheiranthus alpinus* (yellow), *Dianthus alpestris* (white), *Gnaphalium dioicum* (pink), *Vinca herbacea* (blue), *Myosotis rupicola* (blue), *Phlox procumbens* (lilac), *Soldanella alpina* (purple), and *Potentilla reptans pleno* (yellow).

THE COTTAGE GARDENERS' DICTIONARY (*Ibid*).—It will be sufficiently copious. The first number will appear on the 3rd of October.

POTATOES (*Beta—W. Blood*).—We had our Martin's Early Seedlings and Red Ash-leaved Kidneys from Mr. Hairs, 109, St. Martin's Lane, Charing Cross. From November to January is a good time for pruning *the yew*.

PITS (*W. Barnely*).—We know of no separate work upon the erection of these with working drawings, &c.

CHRYSANTHEMUMS (*French*).—The *Compte de Rantzau* is a fine show flower, large and crimson; *Lucidum* is very double, large, and white; and *Pilot* is also a good show flower, large, and pink. If you stop them now they will not bloom this season. Six-inch pots are large enough for you this year. You had better not try a peach-tree in your greenhouse. You had better have a Black Hamburgh vine. The eastern aspect will suit it well.

HEN (*Rev. H. L. J.*).—We have more than once known a hen to have a brood of small chickens and to lay at the same time.

LANDSCAPE GARDENING (*W. H.*).—You will find the *first* part of Practical Mathematics in "Chambers's Educational Course," and the Key to it of great use. It will teach you all the geometry and land-surveying that you require.

PLANTS TRUE TO STOCK (*W. R.*).—Some kitchen-garden varieties produce seed that give birth to seedlings like their parent, but quite as many, and rhubarb is among these, do not. Your Victoria rhubarb seedlings will be all more or less unlike their parent. An answer to your bee question next week.

SAVOYS, &c., CLUB-ROOTED (*W. W. H.*).—Your garden probably had been over-cropped with cabbage-worts before you had it. If the case were our own, and our savoys, &c., were club-rooted "to a dreadful extent," we should pull them all up, soak the ground with ammoniacal liquor from a gas-work, give a good coating of dung, and plant again fresh undiseased savoys, Brussels sprouts, &c. If you obtain vigorous plants, and move them carefully, you will be in time.

MANURE FOR AN ACRE (*J. S.*).—If you have plenty of soot, and the mowings off three-quarters of an acre of lawn, some leaves, and charred rubbish, you will have enough manure for your acre, provided you can have a supply of ammoniacal liquor from the Canterbury gas-works to soak your ground previously to digging it for each crop.

SOLDANELLA ALPINA (*Barkestone Vicarage*).—This is best treated as a pot plant in winter, giving it the protection of a cold frame. The plant you sent is *Verbena venosa*, so often mentioned by Mr. Beaton as the most useful and hardiest of our bedding verbenas.

NAMES OF PLANTS (*R. R., Birmingham*).—Yours is *Agathoæa ciliata*, a native of the Cape of Good Hope. (*A Durham Reader*).—We do not know of such a plant as *Phlox depressa*.

ALPINE PLANTS (*A Durham Reader*).—To drive the worms away from these you may water them with lime water at any time when the worms are troublesome.

MANY QUERIES (*Philocarpus*).—We do not know any chemical substance more effectual for destroying vegetable life than some of the salts; nor should we like to impart the knowledge by which the evil-disposed might injure others covertly. We have given all the knowledge we possess relative to the *blistering of peach and nectarine leaves*. We believe it to arise from too much moisture at the root, or from some other cause of too much sap being furnished to the leaves. A top-dressing of gas-lime and ashes has been found a good application against the *Turnip fly*. A very little gas-lime is sufficient, applied a day or two after sowing. *Flowers of Sulphur* are a good application to the mildew on peaches, or any other plant. We do not know what you mean by *root-pruning strawberries* to renew them. You cannot disturb their root without injuring them. Spring is the best time for *planting artichokes*.

FOWLS (*R. L. H.*).—When they have been driven by workmen from their usual haunts they are some time before they again become reconciled, especially when, as in your case, they roam to a distance during the disturbance. Give them a little more stimulating food, such as chopped meat, brank or buck-wheat, and sun-flower seeds.

LARGE FUNGUS (*J. Brotchie*).—Your globular fungus twenty-seven inches in circumference is nothing extraordinary in size. It is probably a species of *Boletus*.

BEES (*G. Ambler*).—*Racodium Cellare* is frequently used for stupifying bees, and with better success than the puff ball. It grows abundantly in the London Docks' wine vaults. See, about *feeding*, the Calendar for September, in last number: feed them copiously until they weigh 29 lbs. The *bee dress* is described at page 66 of THE COTTAGE GARDENER, present volume. The use of the *adapting board* is two-fold; it renders the removal of a box much easier than it would otherwise be; and, secondly, it prevents the crown of the stock-hive being pressed in by the weight of boxes and glasses that from time to time are placed upon it. Make *sheds* for your bees, if you please, but they are quite unnecessary; the earthern milkpan is sufficient protection.

BEE-HIVES (*Crewensis*).—The small hive, glass, or box is required for early swarms the *first year*; and in a good season 30 lbs. is frequently taken from a new swarm, leaving about the same quantity in the hive for winter store. The tops will be forwarded at 1s. 6d. each. Mr. Payne's hive is certainly not complete without either a small hive (or indeed two), box, or glass.

LIQUID MANURE (*A Staffordshire Inquirer*).—There cannot be a better manure than the mingled drainage from your pigs, cows, and horses. It is good for any plant when *diluted* with water, but especially for kitchen-garden crops.

GRAPES (*J. C., Winchester*).—Do not put bags over your grapes until they are nearly ripe; the best material is net, such as women's caps are made of. Mr. Maund, of Bromsgrove, says that glass over the bunches hastens their ripening; but Mr. Weaver says that it only preserves them by keeping off the wet and insects. No injury need occur to your vine by building a greenhouse over it; the foundation would be too far from the roots.

CUCUMBER PLANTS (*Minnie*).—These trained against a south wall suddenly flag and wither. The reason for this is that the root action is not equal to the demand of "the remarkably healthy leaves." Let the soil over their roots be covered with mulch, and uncovered during hot days, but covered again every night.

LONDON: Printed by HARRY WOOLDRIDGE, Winchester High-street, in the Parish of Saint Mary Kalendar; and Published by WILLIAM SOMERVILLE ORR, at the Office, No. 2, Amen Corner, in the Parish of Christ Church, City of London.—September 5th, 1850.

WEEKLY CALENDAR.

M D	W D	SEPTEMBER 12—18, 1850.	Weather near London in 1849.		Sun Rises.	Sun Sets.	Moon R. & S.	Moon's Age.	Clock bef. Sun.	Day of Year.
12	Th	House Flies swarm in windows.	T. 60°—43°.	S.W. Rain.	31 a. 5	21 a. 5	9 49	6	3 45	255
13	F	Sycamore leaves dirty brown.	T. 61°—47°.	N.W. Rain.	33	19	10 29	7	4 6	256
14	S	Holy Cross.	T. 61°—51°.	S.W. Fine.	35	17	11 14	8	4 27	257
15	Sun	16 Sun. Aft. Trinity. Vapourer Moth seen.	T. 66°—49°.	S. Fine.	36	14	morn.	9	4 48	258
16	M	Lime leaves yellow.	T. 70°—42°.	N.E. Fine.	38	12	0 5	10	5 9	259
17	Tu	Lambert. [leaves fall.]	T. 63°—38°.	N.E. Fine.	39	10	1 1	11	5 30	260
18	W	Ember Week. Geo. I. and II. landed. Sycamore	T. 57°—38°.	N. Fine.	41	8	2 1	12	5 51	261

It used to be true, even to a proverb, that the best writers upon farming and gardening were the worst practical cultivators. This is not surprising when we reflect, that even as late as the commencement of the present century very few of the lords of the plough and the spade were sufficiently educated to be qualified for venturing out of their own fields and gardens into those of literature, and that writing devolved exclusively upon the more amateur. Take, as examples, Professor Bradley, Jethro Tull, Arthur Young, and William Marshall, all of whom were men whose writings are perused and consulted at the present time, yet not one of whom rose even to mediocrity when they attempted to cultivate the soil. That their works should be full of sound information, though they themselves were deficient in the art of applying it properly, is only another illustration of the truth forced upon us at each step of every-day life—that the most trustworthy guide-poets may be unable to advance a step along the road to which they truly point. Men who, like Arthur Young and William Marshall, have their time fully occupied in preparing for publication the stores of knowledge they have gathered, may be excused if they fail in keeping that eye upon the works and workmen upon their own land which alone can secure regularity and efficiency. To such men the farming and gardening community are deeply indebted, for it is to their published works that that community are beholden for such an interchange of ideas and practices as enables the gardener and the farmer, who rarely pass a boundary of which their market town is the extreme limit, to be conversant with the cultivation, and the implements employed in all other parts of the British dominions. "I like Mr. Marshall's books," said a small farmer near Diss, "because they tells we what they do down in the sheers" (shires—other counties). Let this Mr. Marshall be our theme to-day; and we will similarly comment on Mr. Arthur Young next week.

William Marshall is an instance of the futility of that proverb which tells us that we may "bend the sapling" to whatever direction we please. To use his own expression, he was "born to the plough;" his childhood was passed among those "whose talk is of bullocks;" and his heart was occupied with their pursuits; but his friends would not yield to his wishes, and he was required to apply to the unravelling of the mysteries of the linen trade. In the furtherance of this commercial occupation he visited the West Indies, but even here he turned aside into the more favoured path, and became a planter. Returning thence, he became the occupant of a farm near Croydon, in Surrey, but it was more for the sake of testing certain opinions; so that he held it only for four seasons, left it when his experiments were concluded, and published them under the title of *Minutes in Agriculture made on a farm of 300 acres*. Between the years 1786 and 1808 he passed his winters in London, digesting and preparing for the press the agricultural knowledge he accumulated during his annual summer tours. The publication of these embraced full particulars relative to the agriculture of Yorkshire, Gloucestershire, the Midland and Southern Counties, the west of England, and the rural economy of Norfolk. During this time he kept constantly in view the amassing and arranging of three other great works on *Planting and Rural Ornament*, on *The Landed Property of England*, and *A System of Agriculture*—the first and second of which he lived to publish, but the third remained incomplete at his death. Not one of the least honourable testimonies to his firmness and perseverance under difficulties, was his courtship of twenty-five years, terminating in his marriage with the object of his adherence. Being then in more affluent circumstances, he purchased a large estate in the Vale of Cleveland, in his native county, Yorkshire; and died there, after a retirement of eleven years, on the 18th of September, 1818. We have not particularised the prominent part he took in the formation of the Board of Agriculture, an institution on which we shall remark next week; nor have we given even the titles of all his publications, among which is *A Review of The Landscape* (Mr. Knight's poem), *with practical remarks on Rural Ornament*; but we must give a brief extract from one of those works, because it is eloquently coincident with our own opinions upon a subject much more deeply operative upon the peace and happiness of our native land than those who glance over the surface even of grave subjects may appreciate. We allude to *Cottage Gardens*. "Wholesome and comfortable habitations," says Mr. Marshall, "with sufficient Garden Grounds to employ the leisure hours of themselves and their families, and to furnish them with a change of wholesome food at little cost, are what labourers might well have a right to demand of their country. No farm labourer with a wife and family ought to have less than a quarter of an acre laid to his cottage, to afford him that variety of food which comfort, if not health, requires; to supply him with fresh vegetables in summer, and with roots in winter." "Then, while the important works of husbandry were prosecuted without interruption, the labourer would have nothing to allure him from the path of industry. His whole attention would be paid to his work, and all his comforts looked for at home." We rejoice in this testimony, and hope that it will from year to year be more effectual, for it is the unbiassed testimony of one who had witnessed the state of the labourer and its consequences in every county of England.

Meteorology of the Week.—From observations at Chiswick, during the last twenty-three years, the average highest and lowest temperatures of these days are 67.4° and 46.6°, respectively. The greatest heat, 84°, was on the 17th in 1843; and the extreme cold, 29°, on the 17th in 1840. During the period 86 days were fine, and on 73 rain fell.

RANGE OF BAROMETER—RAIN IN INCHES.

Sept.		1841.	1842.	1843.	1844.	1845.	1846.	1847.	1848.	1849.
12	B.	29.923	29.930	30.206	30.080	29.955	30.582	29.917	30.319	29.094
		29.599	29.788	30.183	30.011	29.934	30.575	29.884	30.272	29.011
	R.	—	—	—	—	—	—	—	—	0.36
13	B.	29.943	30.196	30.135	30.159	29.910	30.50	29.788	30.255	29.385
		29.815	30.071	29.931	30.138	29.750	30.281	29.762	30.210	29.281
	R.	—	—	—	—	0.04	—	0.27	—	0.01
14	B.	29.863	30.167	29.847	30.078	29.599	30.257	29.911	30.800	30.166
		29.589	30.149	29.834	30.030	29.470	30.235	29.663	30.319	30.095
	R.	—	—	0.01	0.03	6.92	—	0.01	—	—
15	B.	29.896	30.144	29.956	29.857	29.611	30.238	29.889	30.409	30 170
		29.847	30.101	29.795	29.830	29.355	30.204	29.708	30.359	30.139
	R.	0.06	—	—	0.05	0.45	—	0.16	—	—
16	B.	29.876	30.087	30.055	29.848	29.699	30.210	29.712	30.432	30.164
		29.920	29.918	29.994	29.838	29.487	30.115	29.391	30.377	30.128
	R.	0.01	—	—	—	0.47	—	0.01	—	—
17	B.	29.967	29.787	30.126	29.729	29.476	30.050	29.453	30.361	30.383
		29.913	29.730	30.062	29.708	29.397	29.909	29.389	30.280	30.296
	R.	—	0.29	—	0.47	0.19	—	0.22	—	—
18	B.	29.903	29.787	30.148	29.989	29.492	29.889	29.797	30.260	30.415
		29.892	29.611	30.090	29.729	29.271	29.559	29.455	30.122	30.343
	R.	—	0.10	0.30	0.11	0.87	—	0.03	—	—

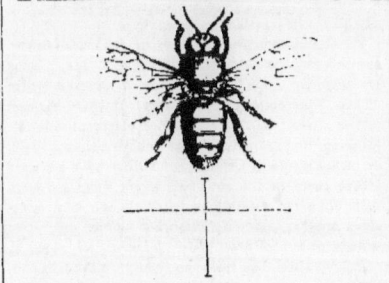

Insects.—Having in previous numbers figured and described the working and queen bees, we have lastly to treat similarly of the *Drone*, or male bee. Spence describes him as the very reverse of his royal paramour—being thick, short, clumsy, and very blunt at each extremity. *Head*, depressed and round; *tongue*, shorter and more slender than the females; *mandibles* (upper jaws), smaller; *eyes*, very large, and meeting at back of the head. *Trunk*, large; *wings*, longer than body; *legs*, short and slender; *hind tibiæ* (shanks), long, club-shaped, hairy; *hind plantæ* (under part of the feet), brushy, for rubbing their bodies; *abdomen*, heart-shaped, short, tawny, having seven segments. It is destitute of sting. There are usually 700 or 800 drones produced in a hive annually. The eggs producing them are laid in April and May, and the drones are all killed by the working bees in July and August.

A SCIENTIFIC correspondent (a physician residing in Norfolk) writes to us as follows :—

"I think I mentioned that my potatoes were perfectly sound. I had about eight rods of the Ash leaved kind, which we took up as we wanted them for the table. The tops of the remainder, about six rods, having died off, I had them taken up, and I am sorry to say the greater part of them are diseased. The outer skin in brown patches, and when cut into, it extends in some from one-sixth of an inch to the middle of the potato. This disease must have come very suddenly and quickly, as I examined them daily in different parts of the bed and none were found touched with it. The crop is very great, there being rather more than a sack to the rod. In the same piece of ground I have a large space with the Cambridge Red Kidney, and a round white potato, the name of which I know not. In the stalks of many I find brown patches, as if they were naturally dying off, and upon examining the tubers they appear perfectly sound, and seemingly full grown, but the skin easily abraded by the finger. I have had the tops mown off close to the ground. I wish to ask you, under the present state of the tubers (which I am told are hardly fit to be taken up, and if taken up they will not keep), what is to be done? The disease may attack them as the others, and to let them remain until the middle of next month—when I took them up last year—I fear the loss may be greater: what would you advise me to do? This disease appears to baffle every one, and until we know its real nature, we shall remain unable to prevent it. The first thing to understand is the construction of the plant and circulation of the sap, and a chemical examination of a diseased stalk, and also a healthy one; the result may lead to some conclusions, whether or not the disease takes its origin from atmospheric causes or from the soil. It seems singular that it should occur yearly; this is not the law of epidemic diseases; and the same law exists in the vegetable tribe as in the animal. For those potatoes I now have cut off, the land was well limed when set, and to this I attributed the escape last year, when my neighbours did not. From your experience as a practical gardener you can inform me, whether lime has a beneficial effect on the present occasion. In examining the principal root of a diseased tuber, I find it brown and pulpy, while that of a healthy one is white and somewhat finer. This has induced me to think the soil has something deleterious to the plant; but why should it not attack all the tubers of the same plant? so that it is a most puzzling complaint. Has the degeneration of the plant any influence? And do we not require a new stock? However, I could fill sheets by inquiries; and shall shake your patience and waste your time; I shall, therefore, conclude by requesting at your leisure your observations and advice."

Immediately upon the receipt of this letter we wrote to our correspondent, and recommended him to take up all his potatoes, and store them as fully directed in our last number. By leaving them in the ground they are more liable to the access of moisture, and to occasional high temperature, than they are when stored between layers of earth, &c., under cover.

It so happened that immediately previously to the receipt of our correspondent's letter, we had been reading Mr. Cuthill's very excellent pamphlet, *Practical Instructions for the Cultivation of the Potato*, just published, and some comments we have to offer upon it will serve to answer our correspondent's inquiries.

Mr. Cuthill commences by observing :—

"It seems to be agreed that we must look upon atmospheric influences, of the nature of which we are able to give no account, as largely concerned in the production of the evil; yet, as I believe I can show in the following pages, improper modes of cultivation have greatly aggravated, if they did not even give the first occasion to, the destructive visitation which has fallen upon the plant."

Now, how much we agree with this will appear from the following extract from a pamphlet we published in 1846, entitled *The Potato Murrain and its Remedy :—*

"It has been [suggested that either fungi or insects are the cause of the disease; but I think both these are excluded by the fact that it appears in every quarter and latitude of the globe,—in the frigid climate of North America, in the temperate locality of Devonshire, and between the tropics at St. Helena. Now, I know of no fungus or insect that has it habitat alike uninfluenced by heat or cold; and even less conceivable is it that a fungus or insect is just created for the purpose of destroying the potato crop. The fungus or insect, it is more rational to conclude, must have existed throughout time, and its ravages have only been felt by increasing degrees, as the potato has gradually reached a state of disease fitted for the nutriment of the parasite. The same and other facts preclude unfavourable seasons from being the *cause* of the disease, though they may hasten its progress. The disease is said to be as prevalent this year (1846) as last, yet no two years could have had seasons more different. It is quite clear that no local cause—such as the employment of any particular manure, the staple of the soil, or the mode of culture—can be the origin of the disease, for the crop has been grown on all possible varieties of arable soil, with and without manures, and in various modes; the sets have been dug in, and dibbled in,—the plants have been earthed up and left unearthed,—yet in all and in each has the disease appeared. The cause, then, must be one of universal applicability, for the disease is epidemic in the widest sense of the term. Does it arise from the vital powers of the varieties being exhausted? No; for, in many instances, the most recently raised from seed are as productive of diseased tubers as the oldest cultivated kinds. Does it arise from the almost universal practice of taking up the tubers as soon as the stems are dying or dead, and keeping those tubers out of the soil for four, five, or more months? I am of opinion that this is the cause. The practice is nearly universal; it is the practice throughout Europe, as it is in America, St. Helena, and the hill districts of Hindostan; and in all those regions the disease prevails. It is not the practice in New Zealand, and there the disease is unknown. Now, has the withdrawal of bulbs and tubers from the soil the effect of gradually rendering them and their progeny diseased? I think no horticulturist or vegetable physiologist will answer in the negative. A writer in the *Gardener's Chronicle* of the present year (p. 478), most correctly observes, that the bulbs of hyacinths, tulips, and crocuses, keep well in the ground, but, if taken up, have a strong tendency to decay. But what effect has this treatment upon the plants to which they give birth? Why, it imparts to them disease. The strain, the beauteous variegation of the tulip's petals, are the effects of disease. Leave the bulb in the soil throughout the year, and it returns to its natural vigour and simple colours. No variety occasioned and preserved by such artificial treatment will endure a few years. It is no effectual objection that seedling potatoes are now affected with the same disease, for such diseases are hereditary in vegetables as well as animals, and the seedling's tubers have been subjected to the same keeping out of the soil for months as were its parents. Neither is it an effectual objection to say that only recently the disease has prevailed, for it has been noticed for full fifteen years, and it is only by such detention from the soil through a series of years [that the disease is advanced to its prevailing malignant form."

Mr. Cuthill then proceeds to detail his mode of culture, and this requires no other statement than this, "during ten years my crops have never been attacked by the disease," to command from every cultivator the most serious attention. An epitome of his practice is this: thinking that the potato ought to have a change of soil, he buys his sets in October, before they have sprouted; greens them in the sun; and stores them and keeps them quite dry, "with their heads all one way, to preserve order at taking up time when planted out," under a stage in a cool greenhouse. About the middle of January, when they have shoots an inch long, they are covered with earth, are watered, and left without being further touched until planting time, about the middle or end of February. They have then strong stems and a mass of roots; these, without being injured, are planted in rows from eighteen inches to thirty inches apart, and from nine to twelve inches from set to set in the rows, according to the habit of the variety. The ground for them is trenched and laid in ridges during the winter, being then also manured with two tons of salt and thirty bushels of soot per acre. The potatoes (all whole) are put into the trenches, and the earth from the old ridges dug down in ridges upon them. In May, if very dry weather, they are watered twice a-week until rain occurs.

It will be seen that in what we consider the chief requisites for successfully storing the potato, we for the most part agree with Mr. Cuthill. We agree that dryness and coolness are essential, but we deprecate the unnatural greening of the tubers by exposure to the light, and we advocate the exclusion from them of those great promoters of putrefaction, occasional exposure to warmth, and a free exposure to the air. For cooking purposes potatoes cannot be stored as Mr. Cuthill recommends, because a greened potato is rendered waxy and unwholesome. Let our reader try both modes of storing their *seed* potatoes, and we shall be most ready to record the results, whatever they may be.

Mr. Cuthill has some statements from which we totally differ, and among them is this—"The flat system is quite unnatural, for it is unreasonable to plant a potato upon a flat surface; and after allowing it to grow a foot high, to draw earth over the stems and leaves." It is, on the contrary, the natural way to plant on a flat surface ,and not to earth up; for this earthing up, we quite agree with Mr. Cuthill in thinking, weakens the plants and retards the production of the tubers.

The cutting off the stems when the bloom is passed is quite condemned, and very properly, by Mr. Cuthill. "I have tried it," he says "and have found that the same kind of potato grown on the same ground, produced very inferior tubers when so treated; they contained very little starch, while those left to nature were very mealy." Such potatoes, also, are more liable to be attacked by the murrain, a result to be anticipated from the analysis of diseased tubers, which are found to differ from the sound ones only by containing more water and less starch. The experiments of Dr. Lyon Playfair and Professor Johnston agree in showing that the increase of water is from two to eleven per cent.

In conclusion, let us recommend Mr. Cuthill's pamphlet to the attention of our readers; it is well stored with facts gathered together by an overy-way trustworthy practical man. Neither let our readers suppose that the pages are devoted to the potato alone. On the contrary, they will have much and very useful information relative to Asparagus, Sea-kale, Rhubarb, the Strawberry, and other garden produce.

We beg from our readers a perusal of the following gratifying letter. The writer has confided to us his name, and we hold him up as an example, hoping that many will follow it; not only in the superior cultivation of flowers, but in sending a report of their progress:—

You have taken so much pains in THE COTTAGE GARDENER, to communicate to your readers the best and easiest methods of managing their flowers, that I cannot doubt that you will be pleased to hear the success which has attended my labours in that pleasing employment. Indeed, as I consider myself your pupil, it seems to me only an act of gratitude to you to relate my progress, in order that you may judge thereby of the amount of interest your efforts have excited; and also that you may make my experience a fresh source of interest to others.

For some years I have had a small cottage and garden in one of the suburban villages, and during the summer months my chief pleasure has been to spend my mornings—the only time I could take from business—in adorning my little plot with a few annuals and perennials. But when October came my employment, and with my employment my pleasure, in a great measure ceased: I saw my beauties one by one fall away, until at last my only amusement was in keeping the paths smooth and the borders clean, longing for the winter to pass that I might commence anew.

The summer of 1849 was to me the commencement of a new era; in THE COTTAGE GARDENER I read of beautiful beds of scarlet geraniums; the richness and splendour of the verbena and the petunia, the heliotrope and the cuphea, also came under my notice; and by dint of begging—very common with amateur florists—by the end of July I found myself possessed of some hundreds of plants, all vieing with each other in gratifying my senses. Let me confess that, amidst all my joy in possessing this store—greatly heightened by the praise I received from my friends—there was in my mind a hidden sorrow. These must all perish, thought I, before the blast of the wintry winds. I talked the matter over with my wife. We read in your book how slight a covering might preserve them. We longed for a greenhouse, but the expense seemed so great. I could get nothing built under £20 or £30. I began to consider whether I could not manage to raise something by my own hands. I meditated and calculated, and, having entered deeply into the design, I found, by examination, that the materials were not so very costly, if I could find time to use them. I did not doubt my ability to form a habitation for my favourites, if the materials were within my reach. Many times of an evening I drew out plans suitable for my garden, marked out the position of the building, and went to bed to dream of the preservation of my plants. Surely, where there is a will there is a way! One fine evening a friend, used to bricks and mortar, heard my longings for a greenhouse, and willing to gratify my wish offered to lay the foundation. He had seen my plan, we had even marked out the dimensions: and about my premises lay, as luck would have it, some 300 bricks and a moderate supply of mortar. We went to bed, and my friend rose early. At six o'clock I walked down the garden, where I found the foundation dug out, and nine inches of brick-work already laid. Eighteen inches of wall were raised that morning, and there the work stayed. The foundation measured 11 feet by seven; and our plan was, that the front should be four feet high altogether, rising to seven feet at the back. How the plates (I began to learn builders' terms now)—how these were laid, all unplaned; how the frames were rabbited, and the glazing accomplished (upwards of 150 feet of glass puttied in by myself), and the whole painted inside and out, and a nice sliding sash in the roof, and a swinging one in the front, and a little narrow door in one corner,—how these were all done it seems now quite a mystery; yet before the middle of September I could shut the door of my little building, and say, "Here is a home for my tender nurslings!" A wide shelf in the front, and a stage leaning against the back, completed my furnishings; and I counted room for 250 pots, or more, of 60's and 48's. The beginning of October warned us that the time was come when the plants must be housed; carefully we took them from the ground, potted them, shaded them for some days under your directions, and when they were removed to their winter quarters few showed any signs of decay. None can know, but by experience, the inward joy I felt at the result of a little industry. My house had cost me less than £5.

At length the frost came, and my next thought was, how to

keep him out. I matted the top : being low this was not difficult ; but still my thermometer told me that I was too cold
within. I determined to find a stove, and after some consideration I purchased one at Cadman's, Newgate-street, for 18s.,
and a sack of fuel for 5s.; this, with the exception of a slight
smell, answered the purpose admirably, as it would keep a
light, by management, for twelve hours easily, but the fuel
was expensive. When this prepared fuel was gone I procured some charcoal dust, almost useless in commerce, and
having sifted the very fine away I charged my stove with
this. To my great pleasure this burned quite as well as the
more expensive coal, with little, if any, more smell, and cost
me next to nothing. Now, then, I saw my plants in safety,
and henceforward I entertained no fear; five shillings more
than covered the expense of all the winter months, and many
times the fire continued untouched for twenty-four hours. I
never lost a single plant all the winter. One drawback there
was, especially if my plants had been in delicate flower,
namely, there was more dust than I could have wished; but
my object was to preserve my plants, and in this I succeeded
to my utmost wish.

Winter now yielded as much pleasure in gardening almost
as summer. Every morning my wife and I visited our
greenhouse, and inquired diligently of each, almost daily,
how they fared. The geraniums continued in full leaf; the
petunias continued to flower; the verbenas mildewed a little;
our phloxes also continued in bloom ; and every day almost
some flower would greet our eyes. Then came the various
experiments suggested by you, all which we put into practice.
Thus the greater part of the winter passed, and about
February we found our geraniums making way. Then came
the idea given us by you of striking cuttings of verbenas and
petunias for bedding out in spring. This we managed in a
way peculiar, I think, to ourselves, and which I think worthy
of recording. When I purchased my stove, I had an iron
pan made to fit the top, so that when I wished I could take
away the usual cover or lid, by which aperture the stove is
fed, and substitute as a cover my iron pan, holding water to
create a moisture; this was about five inches deep and fourteen inches square. We filled this for about three inches
with broken charcoal and gravel, and above this one inch of
pure sand, and having well watered it and prepared eighty-
one cuttings of verbenas about two inches long, we placed
them in the sand in nine rows. They looked like a little
forest. The stove gave out its heat to the house, and generated sufficient heat to the sand, so that in ten days I found
my pretty little slips starting freely at the top. I scarcely
dared to disturb one. However, about the twelfth day, I
ventured to look at one of the most healthy, and judge of my
surprise to find that the roots had shot out on all sides,
three-quarters of an inch long in some of them. No time
was lost. Some small 60's were prepared with common
garden mould, four of the cuttings placed in each, carefully
shaded and kept comfortably warm until they grow to six
and eight-inch plants, and at length when May appeared
took their place in a neat bed, heart-shape—for this was very
near my heart—and soon produced such a grand and dazzling appearance as almost to intoxicate me with delight.
This was my first effort, and from that moment to this when
I write, August 31, they have never failed to obtain the
admiration of my friends ; nay more, my neighbour, a gardener of some experience, paid me the compliment of saying,
" You beat me at verbenas."

No sooner were my verbenas out of the pan than in went
about the same number of petunias; these seemed to strike
still easier than the verbenas. They also took their place in
another bed, and although at times the drenching rains
shrivel the delicate bloom, they are still in most luxuriant
flower. My geraniums I watched with great anxiety to see
the flower buds ; at length they came, threw up their long
stems, and, at the proper time, some in pots and others
bedded out, have made my garden look, to my eye, quite
like a paradise. Often after the labours of the day when I
have returned to my little retirement, my wife and I seated
at our tea-table, overlooking our handywork, and with
hearts rejoicing in the goodness of God, who has so wonderfully beautified the face of creation, have with unfeigned
gratitude thanked Him for His love, and you for leading
us how to admire and train these, the exhibitions of His
wondrous and Divine power! J. B.

THE FRUIT-GARDEN.

THE HORTICULTURAL STRUCTURES OF THE AMATEUR.—
Having conducted our readers—safely, we trust—through
the busy part of the year, as regards the summer management of fruits, we intend availing ourselves of the
breathing time afforded during the next four or five
weeks, to offer a few remarks on greenhouses, hothouses,
&c., as well as on those generally subordinate structures—
the pit and the frame.

In taking a retrospective view of the past fruit
season—for by the time this reaches our readers it will
be nearly past—we are more than ever assured of the
importance of attending closely to the principles of fruit
culture, set forth in the past pages of THE COTTAGE
GARDENER. Principles we say, and advisedly too ; for
we have not been busied in recommending a set of
mere " blue apron " rules, conceived and perpetuated
with an equal amount of ignorance of those great first
principles which, indeed, constitute nature's own laws,—
laws, to use the language of Pope—" bound fast in fate ;"
and which may never be transgressed with impunity,
however specious what are termed systems may appear.

We introduce these remarks here, to try and coax our
readers into a bestowal of their confidence, which we
assuredly desire to possess ; and, indeed, without which
the goose quill will be handled in vain. We can boldly
affirm, taking occasion to boast for a moment, in order
to give a substance to our claims for confidence, that we
never experienced so fortunate a fruit season as the
present in its results, during the thirty years that we
have had the charge of gardens. Gardeners who have
visited here (Oulton Park), have been astonished at the
crops of fruit of all kinds ; whilst one-half of the kingdom has teemed with complaints of the ungenial
character of the season.

Peaches and nectarines have been especially complained of ; ours are excellent; the trees, too, in the
most perfect health, not a leaf amiss ; no gum, no blister,
no insect,—not a single naked branch on the whole of
the trees. These seem bold affirmations, but they are
literally true. Our pears, too, are capital ; our plums
enormous ; and, indeed, all but apples, which are only
half a crop. Surely this is not to be referred to the
chapter of accidents. Our management has been precisely that laid down in THE COTTAGE GARDENER ; we
use comparatively shallow soils, and are advocates for
protecting blossoms. As this statement will necessarily
bear a vaunting appearance, we beg to say that we deem
it of importance, as bearing on the coming season for
alterations ; for, like other mortals, we would fain pro-
selytise as many as possible. Many persons who have
admired the crops here insisted that we must have had
milder weather than themselves, and that our locality
must be a very snug one. Now, differing from all this,
we have always fancied ourselves very ill used; for being
on the edge of Delamere Forest, or, as Nickson the Cheshire Prophet termed it, " the forest of grey," we have
cold winds at least two-thirds of the year ; and we are
exposed, moreover, to the ungentle zephyrs of the wild
Atlantic, or, perhaps, we ought to say, the Irish Channel.
We, moreover, had a thermometer of sixteen degrees
(sixteen degrees below freezing) in the last days of
March. What less could mortal desire ?

And now having done with this self-gratulation, we
will proceed to the subject with which we set out.

FORM OF HOTHOUSES.—Herein lies a wide subject for
consideration, for hitherto there has generally prevailed
but one notion—a lean-to. Not but that " span-roofs"
have been in use chiefly among nurserymen, but the
amateur, and, we may add, the general gardener, has
scarcely as yet availed himself of the advantages which
such would seem to offer. Now, in scanning over the
proceeding as to hothouse building during the last score

years, it does seem surprising that the lean-to form of building should still prevail. It may be right; it may be wrong; but the fact is, that three-fourths of our gardening gentlemen who, in acquiring a competence, seek for relief from the incessant turmoils of mercantile pursuits in horticultural pleasures, in putting up a greenhouse or hothouse, at once adopt the lean-to form of building. Such persons, we know, have scarcely the time, and, it may be added, have hardly skill enough to grapple with the question, as to what form should prevail; they have seen Mr. A.'s nice greenhouse, or Sir Wm. B.'s, full of nice Fuchsias, Geraniums, and Achimenes, and what could be better? Very well—this is all good so far; but the question, as before observed, has wide bearings.

We do think, nevertheless, that when a house is to be *entirely* appropriated to *vines, peaches*, or *figs*, that a southern lean-to is quite as good—perhaps better—as any other. But, then, how few are content to cultivate these things singly; indeed, many amateurs possess but one house for all purposes; and a few grapes must be obtained, and, if possible, without any sacrifice of the plants beneath them; and here it is that a consideration arises, as to whether any other form of roof would be more eligible.

Now a span roof—the span running longitudinally north and south, and thus presenting one side to the morning sun, and the other to the evening—would, perhaps, be found a more convenient plan than any other, provided that vines above and plants below were the object. In this arrangement a neat little stage, or level bench of slate or stone, might be placed down the centre; this stage, about six feet in width, would prove very convenient to lady amateurs, who would be enabled to reach any given plant or flower with facility. Of course, a walk should be all round the stage, of about 30 inches in width; and this would give a total width to the house of about 11 feet. In such a house we should consider it indispensable to make the lights or sashes of the roof as wide as possible, otherwise the shadow produced by the frequency of the rafters, in the case of narrow lights, would prove very injurious; especially in winter, when the solar rays would strike in an excessively oblique direction.

In such a house we should depart from the ordinary mode of planting the *vines*, planting two at each end; and train one (main) stem, on the spurring system, down the centre of each side of the span: running north and south, as the house itself stands. Thus but a moderate amount of shade would be produced, and the vines would at all times be reached with facility. Some may think that there would be a loss of grapes by this arrangement; but this could not be the case, or, at least, there would be as many as would be compatible with the well-being of the plants; and in a house of this kind, 30 feet in length, about seventy pounds of good grapes might annually be expected; or rather more than one pound to a lineal foot; or, indeed, we might say, at least, a third more, if the vines were as thriving as they ought to be. Where the primary object has been to grow *pot plants*, we do think that the proprietor ought to rest content with this produce.

As to ventilation, the escape of heated or corrupted air should be made at the angle of the ridge, where flaps at almost every sash-top, having a connecting rod, might be worked with great facility, by what has been termed "the sympathetic mode;" such may be seen beautifully applied in Her Majesty's gardens at Frogmore. The admission of air should take place just above the floor-level, on each side of the house, where hinged flaps, long and narrow, and capable of graduation, should admit the fresh air immediately opposite the hot-water pipes: thus the air would in severe weather be warmed at its entrance. The bottom, or return pipe or pipes,

might rest on a cemented floor or enclosure forming a sort of trough; and this might be furnished with water on fitting occasions.

Although we set out at the commencement of this paper with the intention of dealing with the form of roofs *generally*, it appeared expedient to go into detail as the matter proceeded; we must now beg to revert to the point from whence began a suggestion for a span-roof-house.

There is an old fashioned house to be found here and there possessing what are called "north lights;" this is what may be termed "one of the olden time;" but we trust that the intelligent readers of THE COTTAGE GARDENER will be prepared to embrace objects new or old, or, it may be, both in combination, provided they can be backed by common sense and a little philosophy. This kind of house I feel anxious to recommend, inasmuch as some of the most successful courses of culture, where objects of a mixed character are sought, have been carried out by this old fashioned plan. In pointing to this it will be well to observe, before proceeding farther, that we do not act on the supposition that our amateur friends aim at no other objects but vines and plants. There are those who require *melons*, it may be *figs*, as also *strawberries*, forced; and are also desirous of *cucumbers* nearly all the year round; and *pine apples*, if possible. We shall, therefore, hold it a duty to endeavour to be useful in offering advice in these respects.

Before proceeding farther, it will be well to see how these objects group together, as to habit and economy of room. The best use we have known made of such a form of house, is when pines occupied a bed-tank heated beneath the south lights and cucumbers were trained beneath the north lights; and when, moreover, a walk being carried all round, a nice narrow shelf obtained a place all along the front—the principal of the piping to warm the atmosphere being beneath this shelf. At the back, too, a shelf may be obtained; and even a portable little shelf of six inches in width, suspended by iron brackets, beneath the apex of the ridge. The front shelf in such a house constitutes the nicest place in the world for dainty stove plants—the *achimenes* and *gesneraceous* plants in general, *orchids*, &c.; whilst the shelf against the back wall is peculiarly adapted for *propagating matters*, young and fresh potted stock, &c., &c. The suspended shelf is well fitted for *strawberries*, received from dung-beds or other and more airy structures, after the blossom is well set; and, indeed, for many other purposes.

Such a house we will undertake to recommend to the especial notice of those amateurs who desire to cultivate a few choice stove plants, as well as the ordinary greenhouse kinds; and, in so doing, may at once combine their culture with that of the pine-apple and cucumber. To accomplish all this in the most certain and economic way, we do not know of any structure superior to this.

Now, as the meaning of this north light may not be obvious to all our readers at first sight, we may as well offer a remark or two. In the first place, it is proved by experience, that the cucumber will do well in such a situation most of the year. It is quite at home, of course, all the summer; has just as much light as it requires during spring and autumn, and even succeeds tolerably well through the winter, provided that plenty of atmospheric moisture is given. Indeed, a house about thirty-five feet long would keep any family supplied with salad cucumbers without another plant in frame or pit; here, then, is economy and simplicity at once, enabling the cultivator to put his pits or frames to other purposes, and setting his mind at rest for the whole year on the score of cucumbers. Again; who does not know of the difficulties experienced by amateurs—not to mention gardeners—of coaxing on young and fancy stock, and also of carrying on propagation matters?

Such placed in any ordinary structure require much fuss in shading, &c., and are liable to many mishaps; but here, the "man of all work" may at once place his newly-potted stock or his cuttings on the back shelf, not fearing a sudden glare of light, and the ceremony of shading and unshading dispensed with, except in extreme cases; for the majority of such things get just as much light as they require.

We would, in building such a house, place it a little out of the cardinal points, giving it a slight turn to the south-east; this turn must, however, be *slight*. This will have the effect of throwing the mild rays of the evening sun into the north part, which will be of immense benefit, not only in point of a mild light, but as enabling the cultivator to "put his plants to bed warm"—a homely gardening phrase, signifying the indulgence in the maximum point of temperature when all danger from scorching is over. This practice we have always consi dered one of the fundamental principles of good forcing.

R. ERRINGTON.

THE FLOWER-GARDEN.

ANNUALS.—The "Exhibition of 1851," in Mr. Paxton's beautiful glass house, on a slice of Hyde Park, bids fair to set people thinking about the best and simplest methods of erecting their plant houses in future. Instead of leaning them against walls for support, as at present, we shall find that it is possible to make them stand on their own legs, and still be as cheaply heated, and far better, for plants, grapes, peaches, and all. But those are not the only reasons for my thus referring to the Exhibition of 1851, but, rather, to ask the great London gardeners, who have been at issue with me on the subject of annuals for years past, how are they going to dress up their flower-gardens next May and June? For, depend on it, these *expositors* of arts and sciences from foreign parts will swarm over the country like locusts; and, although they may do no more harm to our crops than butterflies, it will go hard against the grain with us, if they go home and tell their wives that we had no flower crops worth speaking of. And let it not be thought for one moment that two or three hundreds of railroad miles will hinder them from going down to distant parts of the provinces. The Caledonian Lochs, and the Lakes of Killarney, and all the intervening places of note will not escape their prying curiosity; and, as if to prove the adago, "that it never rains but it pours," here, in Ipswich, we are to have the "British Association" next summer; so that, between one gathering or another, our flower-gardens all over the country are in a fair way of being visited by strangers, who, no doubt, have heard much of our gardening skill in this country from the reports of our great exhibitions, and from travellers who have visited us on purpose to see our style and mode of gardening.

I am persuaded that, in the country at least, we shall learn more substantial gardening—that is, in the way of dressing our pleasure grounds in May and June—during the next year or two, through the influence of this great exhibition, than we have done for the last ten years, notwithstanding all our books, exhibitions, and medals; indeed, these great competitions in London in the months of May, June, and July in each year, have just done as much to hinder the progress of our art in many of its most essential branches, as they have done in raising that of growing plants in pots far above all other attempts in any other part of the world. Even this department of pot plant culture suffers tremenduously through the very patronage which has expended its thousands upon thousands to rear it to its present standard of excellence. None of the great spirits, who have carried off medals enough to fill an ordinary sized

barrow, care a single straw for the best plant in the catalogue unless they can, with a little cooking, get it into flower to stand one of the great competitions; and after the exhibition season is over, the competition plants have all the force and indulgence of the master and man expended on them for the rest of the year. Not only that, but their pockets are generally well lined with money, and they can thus encourage the best country gardeners to flock to London for higher wages, to the disadvantage of country establishments; and, after all this, there are those in distant parts of the country who know so little of the spirit and machinery, and the loss to gardening too, by which these London exhibitions are "got up," that they partly believe the London style could be carried out in the provinces; and sure enough it could, if country people would forego the pleasures and refinements of country gardening for nine or ten months in the year, in order to "get up" a score or two of huge bushes so covered with blossoms as to make their neighbours stare for a day or two, or for as many weeks, in the height of summer. Those of us, therefore, who have so far imbibed this false taste of growing plants so far beyond their natural capacities that no art can save many of them more than a few weeks after they have been "exhibited," will now, or, rather, will find out next summer, that flower-gardening, and the decorations of our home—sweet home!—are, after all, the best and most elegant branches of our art. Let us, therefore, prove to all the world how well we understand this out-door gardening of ours. Who would have thought, when we first heard of the "Exhibition of 1851," that it would have created all this stir throughout the country? The writer feels the force of all this: he, too, has got his foot into the tight boot, and has only one good leg to stand on.

There is no other means of having a full flower-garden in May, according to our present style of decoration, than that of using *annuals*, sown about this time, to stand over the winter as best they may in the open ground, and to be transplanted into the beds from the beginning or middle of March to the end of April, according to the forwardness or lateness of the season, and as the beds are ready for them. As most of these annuals do not hold in bloom above a month, another set of them should be sown by the end of February, also in the open ground, and again in the first and second week in April; but not one of them to be sown where they are to flower, if summer bedding plants are to succeed them. The whole must be transplanted from time to time in regular rows, and then in May the bedding stuff must be planted out in the intervening spaces between the annuals. This is neither new nor dangerous. I have done so over and over again. Indeed, for *anagallis* and very weak plants of that habit, and for *verbenas* that have been struck in a hurry late, I prefer this plan of sheltering them at first turning out, to the usual way of exposing them on the naked beds. Some people put boughs of evergreens round the beds for a few days after planting out, and I have done so occasionally, and when no one was expected to see the garden in the mean time, we made a shift with them; but I must confess the practice is too slovenly and *namby pamby*.

In the winter, when the dead leaves are flying in all directions, and one can hardly find more hands than will keep the walks clean, I have for years past used evergreen boughs stuck here and there in the naked flower-beds, to break their raw appearance; and I like the plan much, although I have had to stand a good many raps from critics, who ought to know better, for recommending it to others; but save me from planting evergreen boughs next May along with the *verbenas* and *petunias*. The worst of this plan is, that in a long bad winter and a late spring, such as the last, many of these annuals are liable to go off, and to think of preserving them in frames, except for limited use, is all out of the question. We must, therefore, sow with a liberal hand, and let them take their chance.

I have so often told the best way to sow them, and the best sorts for the purpose, that referring to our indexes is all that is left for me to do now. I may remark, however, that the small siftings from coal ashes is an excellent dressing for seed-beds of any kind in the autumn, where the plants or seedlings are intended to be left in them over the winter; and that autumn seed-beds should not be dug deep; to break the surface with a hoe an inch or two, then to strew the ashes over it, and to rake the whole backwards and forwards to mix the ashes well with the soil, is about as good a way as any we can adopt.

All the Californian annuals, and they are many, seem to answer better from autumn-sown seeds than from seed put in in the spring. They present the same magic effect in the warm valleys of California which the *Ixias* and other irids do in our Cape Colony on the approach of the periodical rains. In California the annuals take a range different from anything else we know of in other countries. There one species occupies some hundreds of acres in succession, to the almost exclusion of all other plants. Then another and another follows exactly in the same way—a flower-garden, in short, on a magnificent scale, like all the works of nature on those vast regions. In April, the whole valleys are thus luxuriantly clothed from one end to the other, but return thither by the end of May, and all is as barren and naked as a wilderness; the annuals are scorched to cinders, and the seeds, self-sown, remain on the baked crust until the autumnal rains, acting, hot-bed like, on the heated surface, bring them into instantaneous growth; after that, they progress slowly through the mild winters for four or five months. Not as in South Africa, where the bulbs are up and done with in half that time. Hence their suitableness for autumn sowing with us. Late in the spring whole beds may be entirely devoted to annuals alone, such as *Clarkias, Collinsias, Nemophilas,* and others, which may be gathered from our former lists as early flowers, that would help on from the end of April through May; others, and they have been all mentioned already, that grow taller and come in later, should be planted out in regular rows in April, and the spaces between them left so as to admit of the usual planting of "bedding out" plants in the old regular way. One grand object should be kept in view, and that is, that all the dug beds should be full; anything better than mere weeds will look more cheering than naked earth. Then there are many old border plants that can be used as annuals, of which the double varieties of *rockets* are a good example of early flowers. They, the rockets, come in in May, and as soon as they are over can be removed for a succession of other things; and where is a finer flower than the double lilac *Delphinium* and the tall single perennial *Poppies (Papaver bractiatum* and *orientale)*; and there is a variety or two of each with the edge or bottom of the flower more or less marked with dark or lighter shades. The dwarf *mimuluses* are also very gay in April and May, and there are many very beautiful varieties of them, and of the taller *mimulus* too, of which *rosea* is, or was, the head of the section. The *narcissus* family supply many useful varieties for May, and the English and Spanish bulbous *irises* come in after them in June; but by far the best, the gayest, and the cheapest way to make a blaze in May and early June, is with the much neglected annuals.

I have, over and over again, in these pages, insisted on this; and regretted the prevailing fashion of having so few plants in flower in our best gardens early in the season. We should, also, begin at once to lay a good foundation, not only to succeed these annuals, but to have our bedding plants more forward than usual for planting out

next May; and the best way to do that is, to lay in a larger stock of store pots of all the *verbenas, petunias, anagallis, senecio,* and such things, so that a first crop of cuttings of them may be had in quantities by the middle of January; or, at any rate, that we should have plants enough in store to provide all the spring cuttings before the middle of February; for, although the old plants from the autumn propagation make stronger plants, they do not come into flower so early in May as young stuff, provided it is propagated and ready to pot off by the first week in March. I long had an idea, which was then prevalent among gardeners, that these soft plants were better from autumn-struck cuttings; and now I have no doubt but they would be the best, provided we could give them proper justice all through the winter and spring, but there is not one place in a thousand where sufficient room can be provided for such a stock. In the most favoured places such plants are too much crowded by one half to pass over the winter without suffering in health; and if once they get into ill health, good bye to them. It is a hopeless task to strive to recruit them again in time to be of much use early that season. All this having been proved and brought out in practice, we now, or at least most of us, plant these low soft plants from spring propagation.

I have said before, that the planter ought also to be the propagator; that is the way I manage here, and I am very fortunate in having one of the very best of that class to attend to this department. His name is Henry Faires, and a more industrious fellow never lived. Some great spirit—perhaps Linnæus himself—found him at the Suffolk plough and cast his mantle over him, and here he is; and there is not a flower-bed, or box, or vase, in the whole garden, but he can tell you at once how many plants—of any sort—it will take to fill it "chuck full," as he calls it. I have been consulting him, for the last fortnight, as to the best means of getting the flower-garden in bloom next May and June, as for some years past we only required to be up to the mark by the beginning or middle of July, when the "London season" was over. He says it is all plain enough; but I shall give him another week to consider his plans, and then I shall give a true and particular account of all his plans; and it is hard if, between us, we do not hit on something that will be useful to many who are placed under less favourable circumstances.

Now all this brings me to a point which has never yet been properly mooted in any of our periodicals, and as our Editor has now more room in his pages, and is never angry with me for what I say, I cannot do better than fill the rest of my letter with a statement of what I mean. When we are engaged on any work, if only planting cabbages, if we require the assistance of a second party, and expect to benefit to the fullest extent by his or her assistance, we ought to allow him or them a kind of self-interest in the undertaking; or, as we say in the country, "let them have a finger in the pie." By doing this we may get more work done, and done better too, than if we go on a different tack, and say—"such and such things must be done by such and such a time, at all hazards; and if so and so cannot do it, why some others must." By this kind of overawing we may get the letter of the law complied with; but, depend upon it, that is not the right way to make the best of your man, even if he is a stupid fellow. Self-pride, of which no human being is quite free, is not thus subdued, or made the most of. No matter how low the natural capacity or the intelligence of your assistant may be, let him but clearly understand that the issue of an experiment or job, rests as much upon his exertions in carrying it out as on your judgment in planning it, and you are sure, not only of your instructions being literally complied with, but of all that is in him to the bargain; and we all know that two heads are better than one, even if they are only ordinary ones. We gardeners, who have to carry on complicated concerns by the assistance of under gardeners, know well the value of this system, or principle; and we could never succeed as we do, unless we acted on it. We set every one, who has charge of a department under us, thinking for himself; and, although we may be disappointed at times, in the long run we are sure to benefit both ourselves and our assistants. D. BEATON.

GREENHOUSE AND WINDOW GARDENING.

ARRANGEMENT—FITNESS—NEATNESS—DOING THINGS IN TIME.—In the case of some of our cottage gardeners, attention to those seeming trifles upon which success depends, come upon them by fits and starts. The greatest pleasure and enjoyment can only be derived when that attention is continuous; a day's neglect will often destroy the labours of previous months. When the dreariness of winter is passing, and the lengthening day is diffusing cheerfulness, and eliciting fresh vegetable liveliness, there are few who possess anything in the shape of plants, or gardens, however small, but feel a desire, ending in the practical resolution to put their gardening something in harmony with the freshness of nature around them. Hence, plants in windows and greenhouses are cleaned, the pots are scoured, and possibly ornamented for the season, fresh earth either as a top-dressing, or as a reshifting, is imparted; seeds are sown in profusion; the ground outside receives its spring dressing; edgings are clipped; walks gravelled and rolled; and all bespeak the determination, that whatever previous seasons may have been, the ensuing one shall be distinguished for untiring assiduity and attention to the means of excelling. Few things are more exciting than an evening stroll where all these operations are proceeding at railroad pace. Creatures so far of circumstances and example, the diligence becomes contagious; the drones in the human hive—even those whose chief ambition is to be thought the *big wigs* of the public parlour—are aroused for once; example and activity combined (and for the manifestation of both in a right direction we are more responsible than we often think), have transferred rural homes and city window-gardens into scenes of loveliness, that lead our thoughts back to the happiness and innocence of paradisaical times. And why should such well-directed care be often solely exhibited during the early months of spring and summer? Is the love of flowers a civilising influence—and we maintain it is—then we inquire why that love should not be as potent in September as it is in April? We are told somewhere, that "order is heaven's first law;" and never do plants look so well as when neatly trained and scrupulously clean, they are arranged in circumstances most suitable to their own nature, and so as to command the greatest degree of attention. Such *order*, not only testifies at once to a certain degree of mental discipline, and appreciation of the beautiful, but furnishes an index of the regularity, punctuality, and attention to trifles, manifested by a man or woman in the various departments of life. *If* such attention is so desirable, why should it not be lasting?

The evils inseparable from a growing carelessness are every where perceptible, though a vast improvement has taken place within a few years—so far as the range of my observation extends. I am not vain enough to suppose that I had any thing much to do with it, though frequent were the notes I received as to the hard hits I had been giving; but hard or soft, the writers of these notes in every case amended their own practice. I hope there are no readers of THE COTTAGE GARDENER that need apply these remarks to themselves; if the coat

does not fit, there is no occasion for wearing it; but a word "fitly spoken," a hint kindly given, may be of much importance to some of their less favoured, and less attentive neighbours. When direct attack, open opposition, a sly sneer, or a biting sarcasm would utterly fail, it is amazing the effect often produced by a quiet hint, seen to be prompted by benevolence and good will; and until our human nature is changed we all prefer being *led* instead of being *driven*.

Leaving, therefore, for the present, to our friends to lessen the contrast presented by many cottage gardens in spring and autumn, at one time marked by true neatness, and at the other by slovenly neglect—leaving them to effect the necessary remedy in those windows well filled with nice flowering plants during the *fashionable* period, and now either empty or worse than empty, studded with leggy, lanky specimens of diseased and insect-covered vegetation. Allow us at random to peep into the greenhouses of several of those who once looked upon the possession of one of these structures as the summit of their ambition, resolving that in *their* case, such structures should be patterns of neatness and order : merely premising that each and every one of them might have been taken as patterns, in the early months of summer, for attentive gardening.

We call upon friend A.: his house, so beautiful in May and June with geraniums, cinerarias, &c., is now completely empty, but perfectly clean,—no, not empty, for depending from the roof were a number of fine bunches of grapes, with which he is to do great things in September and October. Now, here we at once see the propriety of the course adopted. The house is intended as a greenhouse in winter and spring, and as a vinery in the end of summer and beginning of autumn. Every plant introduced at this season would, less or more, interfere with the good condition of the grapes. Many would like even then to see a few ornamental plants; but they could not complain, because *utility and fitness for the end contemplated* would be at once apparent.

We look in upon friend B. This house is seen from the principal sitting-room, and therefore is a striking object in the little garden, ornamented now with some nice beds of tender flowers, which the greenhouse had protected during the winter. Admiring them, we pass on, expecting to see something prettier still in the greenhouse, but find it completely empty, with the exception of some starved-like creepers, which have been neglected since the other plants were all removed.

Disappointed as we were, we became much more so when in looking in upon a similar structure belonging to C., we beheld, instead of plants, the interior covered with lettuce seed, onions, and peas' haulm, drying before they could be sorted and stored. Now the disappointment here was perfectly natural. The house was made for plants, and not for the drying of seeds. If out of sight, and in the kitchen-garden, the inconsistency would not have been so apparent. As it was, *fitness* for its object was interfered with. Seen from the window, expectations would be raised. The finer the lawn—the prettier the flower-beds before you reached it—the higher would these expectations be; and, consequently, the deeper would be the disappointment. The blank expression on the face of your visitors would at once tell you of your mistake. Surprise people, if you will, by bringing them suddenly upon some beautiful object which they did not expect, and from this unexpected pleasure every thing else will derive an additional lustre. Erect a plant-house in a conspicuous part of your grounds, and—whatever you may have in the open air—there your visitors will expect to see something nicer, and different from what is outside, and this may easily be done with little groups of *balsams, achimenes, fuchsias, clerodendrums*, &c. Disappoint them, by showing an empty space enclosed by glass, and your other plants elsewhere will seem less beautiful than they really are. There is no occasion for cramming such a house in summer; the plants may either be set thinly and mixed, or, what will look better, arranged into separate groups, according to kind, or colour, and spaces left between.

Not to weary you, we shall solicit your company a few steps farther, just to visit our kind, bustling friend D. His glass is not extensive, but it is amazing what he gets out of it in a roughish way. By means of screens, divisions, &c., he obtains grapes, cucumbers, French beans, strawberries, and good flowering plants into the bargain. It is pleasant to look upon any man's countenance when he is pleased, but there is something of the super-delightful in witnessing D. arresting your attention before something that he knows to be good—crossing his arms over his breast, gaining rather than losing in height, and exclaiming "*There now!*" No one can give a sly poke with better grace, and, what is rarer still, none can be quizzed and joked in turn with better humour. Nevertheless, our friend D. has some failings in his gardening, just to keep him from perfection. The first, noticed in the early part of the season, is his contempt of *weeds;* with him, a fresh surfaced plant, or a fresh potted one, are the same every day for months after. As to little weeds they are never seen, it is only when they become large enough to threaten to rival the chief plant that extermination is thought about; pulling them out as soon as seen, grubbing them up and placing them in his pocket or apron with his left hand, while he wields the watering pot in his right, is a matter not to be thought of in his philosophy! Approach the house in spring and you might almost go blindfolded; but now, in the second place, it is very different: the smooth rolled walk *then* is *now* so crammed with pots that have been turned out of the house, some fresh, some withered, and some so full of weeds as to defy all notion as to what they were intended to contain, and force you to pick your way at every step. And why? because D. has either such a love for pots that once stood in his house that he cannot put them out of sight, or cannot make up his mind what to do with them; and there they remain, turning a beautiful part into an eyesore, and exhibiting such a mass of confusion *without* as detracts from the merits of what is *within.* Hint that old French bean plants are scattering thrip, and green fly, and spider in the neighbourhood, or that strawberry pots have their plants dead or dying. "Ah! yes; but then I thought about planting out in the open garden, and could not quite make up my mind whether to do so or not." All who are similarly circumstanced whose determination is not prompt and clear—who cannot decide at once whether plants that are used for certain purposes shall be retained, or sent to the rubbish heap—ought to have a piece of ground set apart, and not much in view, where all such things should be kept. As a greenhouse is built for plants, so a walk is made for walking on. *Unitdy,* and *untasteful,* and *unfitful* as they always look when applied to other purposes, these are concentrated into downright ugliness when the walk that leads to a greenhouse is flanked and blocked up with discarded flower-pots, conveying the idea that the possessor could manage to get them outside the door, but was incapable of moving them farther.   R. FISH.

HOTHOUSE DEPARTMENT.

STOVE PLANTS.

BROMELIACEÆ (continued): *Guzmannia tricolor* (Three-coloured G.); South America.—Green, red, and white flowers. Very handsome when in flower; grows about a foot high. The leaves are light green, the longest measure nine inches long, and about two inches wide. The flowers, at first, spring up in the centre of the leaves in the form of a spathe of bracts or floral leaves. These open when about a foot high, and the real flowers appear out of the bosom, as it were, of each bract. Though handsome, they have the drawback of being of short duration, but each spike produces a large number of flowers in succession, thus prolonging the bloom for a considerable period. This plant is the only one of the genus, and may be propagated and managed in the same way as *Achmea fulgens,* described at page 331.

Puya Altensteinii; South America. — Rich scarlet flowers. This is a noble species, continuing a long time in bloom. The flower spike frequently rises to the height of three feet, the leaves average two feet long, and are arranged in the shape of a fan; the flower-spike springs up in the centre, and consists of highly coloured bracts or floral leaves; the real flowers rise about two inches above each bract, and appear in succession. They are pure white, excepting the anthers, which are a pale yellow. The contrast between the rich crimson, or deep scarlet bracts, and the white flowers is very pleasing, and renders this plant very effective as an ornament to the stove.

Puya undulæfolia (Wave-leaved P.); South America.— This also is a very handsome and very desirable plant. The flower-stems are two and a half feet high. The whole flower is of the richest crimson. The leaves are about one and a half foot long, and six inches broad at the widest part, gradually tapering off to a point. The edges are wavy, whence its specific name.

CULTURE.—Both these *Puyas* are easily cultivated, requiring a very moderate stove heat. The *soil* should consist of rather strong loam and very rotten dung, in the proportion of two of loam and one of dung. As they are of strong free growing habits, they require liberal pot room; a strong full grown plant (when in flower) ought to be in a pot eleven inches in diameter. Good *drainage* is essential to success with these as with all the family. For large plants, two to three inches of broken potsherds or other equally effectual draining material will not be too much. *Water.*—As these plants have a large surface of foliage, and consequently evaporate a large quantity of moisture from the pores, especially in a young state, they require to be liberally treated with water through the growing months. In winter the quantity ought to be lessened considerably, but not entirely withheld. The grand rule in all watering operations is to supply the plants, of whatever kind they may be, with just enough to keep them fresh when in a comparative state of rest, and more abundantly when in a state of growth. The quantity to be given in the latter state depends entirely upon the habit of the plant. From the great number of plants now in cultivation of such various habits, with regard to the amount of foliage, and from the changeful nature of our climate, sometimes rejoicing in bright clear sunshine for a short period, and then changing to a dull gloomy wet and cloudy atmosphere, the treatment of plants, with respect to the giving of water, must of necessity be somewhat difficult, requiring from the operator a considerable amount of discrimination. Of all the operations and grand points in plant culture in pots, the properly watering them is the most important, and at the same time the most difficult to teach. Therefore we say to our readers, *never water a plant until it requires it.* We have been often asked how many times a day a plant wants water! It is for the benefit of such inquirers that we have penned the above remarks on watering plants, and we trust they will be useful.

PROPAGATION.—Both these species of plants send out suckers, which will put out roots for themselves in process of time. As soon as that has taken place to some extent they may be carefully divided from the main plant, potted into small pots, and placed in a shady place for a time, to establish themselves by making fresh roots. They may then be placed in a more open situation, and subjected to the usual routine of culture.

Tillandsia stricta (Stiff-leaved T.); Brazil.—A small plant, seldom attaining more than half a foot in height; the leaves are glaucous (milky green), rather narrow, very rigid, and recurved; the flowers are produced on a scape four inches high; they are small, but of the most intense and lovely blue, which renders them very attractive and desirable.

CULTURE.—The best way to cultivate this little gem is to fasten it to a block with some moss attached to it; syringing it freely, and sometimes taking it down and dipping it in the cistern, holding it there until every part of the plant, block, moss, and roots are thoroughly saturated. This plant is very scarce on account of the difficulty of propagating it; the only certain way is by division, but care must be taken that each division has some roots to it, or it may be expected to perish.

Vriesia psittacina (Parrot-beaked V.); Brazil.—A splendid plant when in blossom. The plants grow to a foot in height; the leaves are of a light green, and form at the base a kind of cup, like *Achmea fulgens*, which holds water; the flower-scape rises up in the centre of the plant, and attains the height of two feet; the bracts are placed on each side of the scape, at a distance of three or four inches from each other; the flowers are produced out of the bracts. The beauty of the plant consists in the extreme brilliant scarlet colour of the stem and bracts; there is a finish and a polish about them quite wonderful. The flowers are white.

Vriesia splendens (Splendid V.); Brazil.—The leaves of this plant are exceedingly beautiful, they are elegantly marked in bands of chocolate colour, very strongly and clearly defined; the flower-scape rises to the height of two feet; and the bracts are scarlet, closely piled over each other. The flowers are white. Decidedly worth growing.

CULTURE.—The same as *Achmea fulgens*.

T. APPLEBY.

FLORISTS' FLOWERS.

DAHLIAS.—There is no flower that shows so clearly the advantages of a rather elevated site for a garden as the dahlia. Frequently in the valley or lowland it will be cut off even in this month, so as completely to destroy its beauty for this year, whilst in a garden more happily situated on a rising ground it frequently escapes till the end of October; the reason is obvious enough, even to the commonest observer, the heavy fogs descend to the lower garden and drive up the warm air to the higher one; thus, if the cold amounts to the freezing point the flowers in the lower garden suffer from it, whilst the others escape. Of course this only can take place to a certain extent; if the frost is very severe it will also reach the higher parts, and destroy all tender flowers in every garden; but it frequently happens that there is a slight frost in September, just severe enough to spoil the blooms in gardens so unhappily situated. A very slight protection would prevent such ill effects; we have used, with great success, common garden mats, just stretched over the plants upon stakes high enough to clear them. Should the weather prove dry it will still be desirable to water dahlias freely at the roots. This is a good time to make remarks and notes upon the different varieties, setting forth their good and bad qualites, so as to be able to regulate them next year.

TULIPS, RANUNCULUSES, AND OTHER BULBS.—Attention must be paid to the different beds these fine flowers are to be planted in for next year. Turn over the soil and mix it with enriching materials as soon as possible.

GLADIOLI.—These fine summer flowers have now finished their bloom and growth for the year. They require to be taken up, dried, and kept in a cool place till spring. Should any of the *G. psittacina* still continue green in their foliage, take a spade and just lift them up; this will have the effect of checking the growth of such late plants. T. APPLEBY.

THE KITCHEN-GARDEN.

CELERY plant out, and water well at the time of planting; earth stir among the growing crops, and earth up the forward. That which is full grown, bury up well, so that it may be well bleached, and soon fit for use. In earthing up the younger crops, first loosen the soil with a fork, and then go along the rows with the hand, and holding the plants in one hand, draw up the earth round the plant with the other; then, with the spade, give it a deeper earthing, but not so as to bury the hearts while the plants are growing. The earthing should be done a little and often, but the finishing touch should bury it up well. These earthings should always be done in dry afternoons; and the previous forking in the forenoon.

This is just the season for extensive CABBAGE and COLEWORT planting, only the soil to receive them should be made thoroughly good with plenty of manure. Water at the time of planting. Also prick out seedlings in beds from the seed-beds, so as to have good stocky plants for future planting.

Plant out any kinds of BORECOLES, or SAVOYS, or even BROCOLIS, if any remain unplanted—all may be found useful.

It is late for sowing TURNIPS, although I have sown as late as the 16th of September, yet I have had a very useful crop of this vegetable: both of nice little bulbs, and an abundant supply of greens, too, in the spring months. The young growing crops should be well thinned out in time, and the hoe passed among them often.

The August-sown CARROTS in the open borders should be well fingered out, and the earth stirred among them often. Carrots (Early Horn kind) may now be sown in either old melon or cucumber-bed frames, first stirring up the earth, and adding a little more, so as to bring the crop up nearer to the glass.

CARDOONS, earth up when thoroughly dry.

CAULIFLOWERS, prick out, as soon as they are large enough to finger, into a good rich bed, in an open situation, so as to have the required number of good healthy sturdy plants for planting out under hand-glasses, and otherwise to protect through the winter. When a little better bed than common is required, it may be done in this way:—Trench or well dig up any small plot of ground, pulverize well as the work goes on, line it out in the usual way; and then, to make it a little better than common, give the whole bed a surface-covering of either leaf-mould and loam, or well-rotted dung and loam, well broken and mixed together, and run through a coarse riddle or sieve. The mould from an old hot-bed is just the thing, with a little of the old rotten bed mixed up with it. Put from one to two inches thick of this mixture over the whole surface of the bed. It is surprising how the roots of the young plants will run along in beds made up in this way.

ENDIVE, plant out, and prick out, of both kinds, and tie up for blanching; also LETTUCES the same, and prick out in open beds, so as to have a good supply to choose from next month.

MELONS AND CUCUMBERS.—Back up with linings; be sparing with the water-pot, and shut up early.

MUSHROOM-BEDS, make, and look after spawn, as an abundance is often to be found in either breaking up an old mushroom-bed or old hotbeds, which should be stored away in some close dry shed for use when required.

ONIONS, pull up, dry well, and store away.

CARROTS.—Where the leaves begin to look yellowish would be better taken up and stored away in some dry cool place.

RADISHES AND MUSTARD AND CRESS.—Sow in succession.

SPINACH, thin out 10 inches from plant, and earth stir often.

TOMATOS, or LOVE APPLES, should be continually topped, in order that the fruit may have the whole benefit of the sap. Let the fruit-laden branches be all nailed up securely, so that the fruit may be as much as possible exposed to the rays of the sun, but keep all the ripe fruit closely gathered in, and should there be an appearance of severe weather set in for a night or two, collect in the unripe before frost-bitten, and place it either in a warm kitchen, or on a dry shelf in the hothouse, or in any such kind of place, where nearly the whole would ripen off well, if the fruit be full grown.

CAPE BROCOLI AND CAULIFLOWERS nearly full grown and heading in, water with liquid manure.

T. WEAVER.

MISCELLANEOUS INFORMATION.

SCALES OF EXPENDITURE.

By the Authoress of "My Flowers," &c., &c.

THE second estimate given, is for a man, his wife, and three children, receiving an income of 24s per week, or £62 per annum.

PROVISIONS WEEKLY.	£	S.	D.
Bread and flour for five persons, 24 lbs., at 1½d..	0	3	0
Butter, 1lb., at 1s.	0	1	0
Cheese, ½lb., at 6d.	0	0	3
Milk	0	1	0
Tea—once a day—2 ozs., at 3s. 6d.	0	0	5¼
Sugar, 2 lbs., at 4d.	0	0	8
Grocery—chiefly rice, oatmeal, and condiments..	0	0	7
Meat, fish, &c.—say meat at 5d.—6 lbs.	0	2	6
Vegetables	0	1	2
Beer	0	1	6
Coals and wood	0	1	10
Candles—average ½ lb., at 6d	0	0	3
Soap, starch, blue, &c.	0	0	3½
Sundries, for cleaning, scouring, &c.	0	0	2
Total for household expenses	0	14	8
Clothes, haberdashery, &c.	0	4	0
Rent	0	2	6
Total expense	1	1	2
Saving	0	2	10
Amount of income	1	4	0

In this estimate I have made one or two trifling alterations as regards the price of articles, which is, of course, somewhat different now to that which prevailed when the calculation was formed; but the quantities I have given exactly as they are stated, with the exception of butter, which I have reduced from two pounds to one, as in the case of children, where milk is plentiful butter is not required, and a little treacle is a good and cheap substitute for it in cases where something is needed to moisten the bread. I have also allowed a few pence more per week for milk, as I do not consider (from the experience of others) that one penny per day is sufficient for this useful and wholesome beverage, where there are little children; and besides it may furnish a meal on many occasions for the parents also.

Tea only once a-day, appears a serious grievance to those who truly enjoy that unequalled refreshment; but I can only assure them, that what is right, and acted upon in a right spirit, will prove an easier undertaking than can be imagined by those who suffer themselves to murmur at every little inconvenience that befals them. Many a cup of tea has, I know, been drank and relished too, when warmed up again for a second meal. If drained from the leaves, put by in a clean jug, and warmed in a clean saucepan, with a table nicely laid out, and thankful hearts, we shall not make a much less comfortable meal than if we had the best and strongest infusion that money and skill can produce. I have stated the price of tea at 3s 6d per pound, which is a fraction less than 2¾d per ounce, but I have placed it at that amount for convenience sake. It is a low price I admit, but our food must be in proportion to our finances. Such excellent tea can be purchased at the large establishments in London at 3s 8d per pound, that a trifling reduction in price may be made with little discomfort by those to whom every penny is an object, and who will contentedly enjoy that which their narrow means afford. I beg particularly to direct the attention of such of my readers as can procure it to the tea at 3s 8d per pound, sold at the Messrs. Twining's, in London. It is far superior to that purchased from country shops at 4s and 5s per pound, and amply repays the carriage in *goodness*, to those who can indulge in a trifling additional expense. The larger the house at which we deal, the cheaper we shall make our purchases, of all articles of grocery, cheese, &c. Small country shops are invariably the highest priced.

I have stated sugar at 4d per pound. Excellent brown sugar can be bought in London, I *know*, at 3d; but in the country it is always dearer. We should *prefer* a finer, more *lady-like* sample at 5d, but we are struggling with the world, and even an extra penny must be resisted.

I may be considered too low in the price I have allowed for meat, both in my first estimate and the present; but I write for the poor, and not for the rich, and many contrivances can be made to bring down the butcher's account to my level. In towns, if meat is bought in the evening, after the business of the day is over, it is procured cheaper than at an earlier hour. Nice little bits of different sorts of meat—fit for puddings, pies, soups, &c.,—will be sold cheap, because they are trimmings cut from joints, and are usually set aside for small customers; but they are prime meat, and better adapted for puddings, stews, &c., than other parts. It always appears a pity to cut up a nice joint of meat into bits for those purposes. If a lady takes her little basket to the butcher's shop late in the afternoon or evening, she will find many excellent little pieces that will be sold cheap, rather than suffered to remain on hand; and the shin-bones of beef are always low in price, and make most nourishing, relishing soup; or baked in a brown dish in the oven form a capital stew. Cow-heels are excellent and nutritious, so are ox-tails and cheeks; bullocks' liver is very cheap, and yet, fried in slices, as calves' liver is dressed, is little inferior to it; although we are accustomed to consider it beneath our notice. Poverty teaches us many wholesome lessons; and if supported with child-like docility and faith in Him who appoints for us our "portion of meat," as well as "the bounds of our habitation," will *invariably* prove a blessing in disguise. Many tastes, many prejudices, many fine and foolish notions will be exposed, or uprooted, or subdued; and in every instance we shall find ourselves wiser or happier than we were before. Even if we only feel that, instead of worsted-work and crotchet we are doing a useful work in our daily existence, we shall benefit in no small degree, and feel more real satisfaction in ourselves. Our hands may not perhaps be quite so delicate, but our minds will be kept from many cogitations that do us no good; and will be busy about useful things at least, if not refined ones. We shall prepare and relish many simples that in richer days would have been thrown aside, or considered unfit for the table of gentility;

and we shall probably in our low estate wonder at the trifling amount of the medical bill, and look round to find the ailments that attended us in our higher and more luxurious mode of life. When in the providence of God one blessing is withheld or withdrawn, many spring up in its place. When a mighty tree has fallen, does not the barren soil beneath it mantle presently with herbs and flowers ! Is the hand of the Lord *ever* "shortened ? "

I find I have quitted somewhat abruptly the subject upon which I commenced my remarks. In a future paper I will resume them, soliciting the continuance of the indulgence I have ever received, for the introduction of matter which I feel to be closely connected with our daily duties, and therefore with our general happiness and welfare. When we are laying out our smallest pittance, or busying ourselves in the kitchen and the nursery, or setting apart the simplest trifle for " our poor brother," or doing a thousand things that perhaps we were never born to do, we are fulfilling a duty as decidedly, and obeying God's will as devotedly, as the highest, and wisest, and richest in the land.

MARKET-GARDENING.

HAVING had twelve years' experience in the management and entire superintendance of several of the most extensive and well-kept market-gardens in the vicinity of London, from the floral to the field culture, in its many and various branches, I will endeavour to give (in answer to your correspondents) a few practical, but humble, hints how I should commence had I a four-acre field of good stapled soil, and now in grass, to break up and convert into a vegetable, fruit, and flower-garden, for market purposes.

If not already *well-drained* naturally, or other ways, by all means secure at once this most essential foundation-stone for all future good culture; for, without this point is properly attended to, much disappointment is sure to occur in the consequent slow and tardy growth of vegetation, the immature growth of fruit-trees, and the blighting, cankering, and failure of crops. Indeed, unless the soil is thoroughly drained, it is impossible to maintain it, as it ought to be at all seasons in a good condition, fit for cropping, and keeping each successional crop in perfect health ; for, unless the soil is kept in this state, it will be of but little value, and cannot possibly be expected to remunerate the cultivator. Your correspondent A. B.'s field, lying on a good slope to the west, there will be no difficulty in draining it, should it be found necessary to do so.

As a *market-garden*, no more ground should be wasted in forming roads and walks than is actually necessary for conveying the manure on to the soil, and carrying the produce off. A cart-road through the middle would be essential, if the field is bounded by a wall, wooden fence, or high earth bank and hedge, or a close hedge without a bank. A border should be formed all round the garden, of a corresponding width, for the convenient production of early vegetables and salads on the most sheltered and warmest sides, and a shady part for the production of late vegetables, herbs, and salads, in the heat of summer, and for sowing and pricking plants preparatory to their being planted out. Next to the borders, should be a path to divide them from the quarters, which would be a convenience for both. Such a walk would not be required above the width of four feet. If any more cross walks are required for the convenience of dividing and passing from one quarter to the other, such could be adopted as most convenient. The glass and homestead sheds would be best placed near the dwelling; all glass structures for the market-trade, whether for early fruit forcing, vegetable, or plant culture, should be span-roofed, and no higher than actually necessary for the convenience of performing the requisite operations.

Deep culture is the next consideration, previous to which, on breaking up grass land for the culture of vegetables, three cwt. of salt should be sown over it per acre, in order to give the slug and wire-worm a scourging. The latter pest we have always found particularly obnoxious the first season after grass land has been broken up. Deep culture, to commence with, requires a little consideration. Should the soil not have been previously drained, or should the subsoil be poor and hungry, or of a very sandy or stiff clay nature, by no means should it be exposed to the day-light in too great abundance on the first trenching, or disappointment will

certainly follow with regard to the obtaining of first-rate crops for the first year or two. Much extra labour will also be required in working it, so as to get it at all in a healthy friable condition, and sufficiently intermixed and worked together for the reception of seed and small plants, the healthy and quick progress of which is so essential for making a ready return for the outlay expended.

Our system of commencing the *trenching* of such a piece of soil as above described, would be to take out a two-foot trench in width the whole length, or, rather, width of a quarter or border, 14 inches deep, then, with a strong long tined fork break up the subsoil at the bottom of the trench to the full depth that the fork can be thrust, and let it remain at the bottom of the trench in as rough and open a state as possible, this would add 10 inches more of trenched soil to the 14 surface inches, and would make about two feet of trenched soil altogether. I would then have the turf or grass buried to a sufficient depth ; about four inches of it should be tumbled into the trench first, and then a good spit of 10 inches, which is the depth a good spade, well managed, will clear, should be next taken and placed on the top of the turf in a ridge, in as rough and open a state as possible. This work should be performed in the latter part of the autumn, so that the soil should have the full benefit of the winter's frost, and thus be in a fit condition for the early spring cropping. The next time it is trenched, a portion of the subsoil may be mixed up advantageously with the surface, and again forked to a greater depth.

By following such a course, any desired depth of soil may in time be procured ; and if a liberal dressing of *manure* can be obtained or afforded the first time of trenching, and cast in over the turf or top spit, it would add greatly to its future value, or the manure may be added at the cropping season. by placing it between the ridges where there is a suitable width for crops to be planted on it when the ridges are tumbled or forked loosely down over it, or for a seed crop, the ground should be first laid down with the fork, and the manure applied on the surface, and forked in. If artificial manure is to be applied, it should, by all means, be drilled in with the seeds.

If a portion of the ground is to planted with *fruit trees,* such as the best varieties of apples, pears, plums, cherries, &c., the ground should be well trenched for them first. Standards and half standards should be planted from 20 to 24 feet apart each way, and the bush fruit, such as the gooseberry, currant, raspberry, filbert, &c., should be planted between, in rows, at six feet distances. The raspberries may at first be planted in the rows at two feet apart ; the currants and gooseberries at five or six feet apart ; and the filberts at eight feet ; the after pruning will keep all uniform and within proper bounds. Strawberries kept to single plants or stools two feet apart, may be profitably cultivated for the first two or three years between the bush fruit. By such a system of culture I have observed a very profitable return made, there being in succession, after the various fruits are got into a bearing state, something for market from the fruit plantation every day, from the commencement of the green gooseberry gathering, till the store apples and pears are gone. The different varieties of fruit require much judgment in choosing.

With regard to *vegetable cropping,* the different varieties must be to some extent cultivated according to the capabilities of the soil, and the demand of the locality. The time of sowing and after management will be treated on in future papers.

I have already said that glass structures for market purposes should be erected near the dwelling, and be also placed at a convenient distance from the high road ; and my idea also is, that for general business, as well as for the sake of economy, the usual mode of structure should be span-roofed, but no higher than is actually necessary for the operations to be performed therein; for of what use can a lofty house be to a man who has his living to make out of the produce ; a structure for business is what we require, not for show; a lofty house is inconvenient for the purposes of giving air, watering, &c., besides the extra expense when forcing, or at any other season, when fire is required to heat a superfluous quantity of air. From my own practical observations, I am satisfied that for general purposes, whether for pine, grape, peach, plant, early vegetable, or salad culture, moderate-sized convenient structures only are required for the production of such things in the best and most economical manner. Whether they are constructed east and west, or north and south, we find such as I am now recommending the best and most economical. Formerly, great fear was entertained of exposing a surface of glass to any other than a southern aspect; but experience gained by those who have proved its fallacy, and the improvement of glass and glazing, have to some extent uprooted such ancient notions.

The structures intended for peach and grape culture should have the foundation wall, the whole way round, arched to the surface of the intended border the trees are to be planted on, which will afford their roots space without limitation, so needful for the production of first-rate grapes for many successive years. The vines, peaches, and nectarines, or any kind of fruit trees intended for house culture, should by all means be planted inside; by having arches in the walls, their roots could be allowed to range outside.

The system to be kept in view for market gardening, or, indeed, for any other gardening purposes, whether public or private, may be summed up in a few words—adopt at the commencement of cultivation thorough drainage; deep culture, regulated as mentioned in the foregoing directions; liberal manuring, so applied that the crop may at once obtain the greatest benefit from it; not as we have often seen in garden practice, more particularly amongst the old school in former days, to trench deep, burying the manure deep, and casting the sour stagnated bottom spit of subsoil over it, there to let the soil remain, instead of casting it into rough open ridges, so that it should receive the benefit of atmospheric influences. In the after management, take every opportunity, in suitable weather, of using the pick-axe or strong fork; and do not let the soil remain to get washed and run together by heavy rains, which will cause it to become surface bound, hard, and in every way unkind, causing much extra labour and future disappointment. The main spring of all good culture after the foregoing system is adopted, is constant and systematic surface stirring, hoeing, and forking the earth's surface amongst and about all the crops, which it is impossible to perform too often in suitable weather.

Sow everything you cultivate in drills; and shallow hoeing may be performed as soon as the plants can be seen; continue to follow up this most essential operation of surface-stirring, and deeper scarifying as the crops advance, as long as there can be found room for the operation with spirit; weeds have then no chance of appearing, and slugs, wire-worms, and other obnoxious garden pests are so constantly routed out of their hiding places, that they and their broods are either destroyed with the constant operation, or fall a prey to birds &c.; the labour of the water-pot is saved in dry weather, the destructive ravages of frost are thereby much prevented, and every kind of vegetable is by such treatment advanced quickly in size and forwardness, as may very soon be proved by any one putting into practice the foregoing rules on one part of any kind of crop and leaving the other part undone.

By thus keeping an open loose surface-soil amongst all kinds of crops, securing, at the same time, a good preparation for all succeeding ones, there is no need at any time or season for rest, or fallowing the land, which is never exhausted by cropping if our instructions are well attended to, neither do the crops ever materially suffer either from drought, moisture, from severe frost, or vermin. Keeping also in view the trenching and forking over every spare piece of ground the moment the crop is off, and having at all times seed and plants waiting for a vacancy, instead of the soil waiting for seed or plants, it is astonishing how rich a return may be secured for our labour.   JAMES BARNES.

A CONSULTATION ON BEE-KEEPING.

I HAVE derived so many enjoyments from a perusal of, and attention to, the instructions of THE COTTAGE GARDENER, that I feel it right, when the difficulties it has unwittingly occasioned to others have been stated, to mention those pleasures which it has opened to myself.

When a lad, I was always fond of gardening; the early portion of manhood was so fully occupied, that I could not give to it the requisite time, and of late years having no permanent abode, I deferred its pursuit until I was settled upon my own land. Your publication, however, so revived and invigorated my love for the early employment of my leisure hours, that at its commencement, although as far from being settled as ever, I set to work in good earnest, and for the last two seasons have had, for its size, as gay and pretty a garden as any in my neighbourhood, that have not had the advantage of a greenhouse or warm-pit.

Respecting the management of *bees*, I have been very troublesome to you, and feel, therefore, obligated to give you some account of the success which has attended my progress in this delightful pursuit. For many years I have been desirous of keeping these interesting creatures, but as I knew of no other way of obtaining their honey, except by their destruction, I never gratified my wish. Your periodical this year set me to work with a zeal and diligence perhaps even greater than it did to my garden, being not only myself much interested, but anxious to prevent the wanton destruction of life in my neighbourhood. Accordingly, in the spring of this year, I purchased two stocks (No. 1, and No. 2), for which I paid 10s each. The hives and boards were in a very bad state; boards cracked and warped; hives nearly falling to pieces. I had purchased them unseen. From No. 2, I have obtained 12½ lb of comb, worked in small super hives; from No. 1, 4½ lb, in the same manner. The board of this hive, as well as the hive itself, were so bad, that contrary to your advice, but with that of an old bee-master, I determined to transfer it. This was done by fuming after the Oxford method, and its result, a loss of 2 lb weight of bees, almost disheartened me, but having other hives doing well, I was encouraged to proceed. From this hive I obtained 15 lb of raw honey. The bees saved, were placed on the 12th July, in Neighbour's No. 5 hive, which, by-the-bye, when I purchased it, *I took* for "Payne's Improved Cottage." They have since—feeding with about half a pint of liquid brown sugar every night—been doing well. The hive is now three parts full of comb, and on the 22nd of August I added to it the bees given me by a neighbour, from a stock that had swarmed, cast, and colted. To No. 2, I have given a new floor-board, and am just about to remove an empty box that was placed between the hive and one partially filled, and to leave this stock, now weighing, I am told, including board, about 56 lb in its old hive for swarming next season. This hive swarmed on the 9th June, but not placing the swarm on its stand at once, it rose in about three hours and took up its abode in a tree, and when dislodged was so mutilated as to be of no use. On the 11th of June, I procured another large swarm in its place (No. 5), and set it upon a doubling board; in eighteen days the hive was full of comb; on the second of July, I gave it a second hive, the cold weather just then prevented the bees taking to it, and in ten days it was removed and a glass placed upon the top of the hive. This partially filled, I took off, finding the bees were eating the honey. It contained 1½ lb. Did I do right in removing it? (*Yes.*) On the 29th July, this hive, exclusive of hive and board, weighed 29½ lb. Do you think I need weigh them again before winter, I cannot do it conveniently? (*No.*)

Anxious to know more about their work and to manage bees in the best manner, I was desirous of obtaining one of Taylor's hives. Three guineas, however, was more than I could afford, and finding the inventor not interested in their sale, with the help of his very useful book, 4th edition, and a good joiner, I constructed a stock box, super cover and pedestal, such as I think would do credit to the joiner who made the original. The only difference seems to be, that we have used the common screws for the crown board, and have not, what I took to be on inspecting the hive at Neighbour, a half-crown board to answer the purpose, I presume, of an adapting board; I could not, however, see exactly its use, as my time was limited. For this hive, as no swarm could be procured, I spoke for two casts. On the 2nd of July, the first came in a common straw hive; on the 9th, the second, a very strong one, that arose the 16th day, came in the same way; this latter one I transferred into the bar-hive the same evening, intending to put the other to it, but was overpersuaded by my old friend the bee-master to retain it in its own straw-hive, as my box would do credit to the two. I have now convinced him we both were in error. As soon as I could procure a feeder, I began feeding it with liquid sugar and honey, and have been delighted for some time to find the hive full of comb, and those cells near the windows, although not closed up, containing a large portion of honey, which the bees are now eating. (*They are and eating but removing it.*) How may this be prevented, for if continued it will sadly diminish the store they have obtained for winter from the food I have given them. Do you think I need fear their standing the winter? (*No.*) The bees get between the thermometer and the window, and almost render it useless. Can I in any way remove the propolis, I presume it is, which they place upon them? (*No.*) I had no opportunity this season to paint this hive. When may it be done with safety to the bees? (*Immediately.*) It stands in an open shed. I have now given over feeding it.

(*To be continued.*)

TO CORRESPONDENTS.

*** We request that no one will write to the departmental writers of The Cottage Gardener. It gives them unjustifiable trouble and expense. All communications should be addressed "*To the Editor of The Cottage Gardener, 2, Amen Corner, Paternoster Row, London.*"

POTATOES (*J. Willis*).—We have communicated with the party, and will advise you of the result.

MANURING FOREST TREES (*A Country Subscriber*).—Beyond all doubt "Guano water," or animal or vegetable manure of any kind, is highly beneficial to young forest trees, not only for accelerating their growth, but for improving the beauty of form and excellence of timber. A vigorous tree is always the most handsome; and it is an old fallacy, that the slowest grown timber is the most durable. Ground well drained, well trenched, and well manured, will grow the finest timber.

NETTLES (*Presbyter*).—These impair the neat appearance of your churchyard; and though you have them continually cut down, they as constantly reappear where some old buildings stood. Your only resource to get rid of this persevering "follower of man's footsteps," is to have its roots forked out of the soil, and then to water the place with diluted oil of vitriol, to remove the saltpetre, without which the nettle will not thrive. After this, you must fork out every piece which may have escaped, as it reappears.

GUINEA FOWLS AND DUCKS (*Subscriber from No. 1*).—Can any of our readers say what is the usual marketable value of Guinea fowls; and whether there is any mark whereby the drake of the Aylesbury breed can be distinguished when about ten weeks old?

WHEAT SOWING (*W. K. W.*).—You should tell us whereabouts you live, and what is the character of your soil. Michaelmas is a good time for sowing. Put on guano just previously to the last ploughing. Dibble your wheat in rows nine inches apart, and six inches from hole to hole; two inches is deep enough. As you have an unlimited supply of manure and labour, you may grow potatoes and wheat alternately for an unlimited number of years. We know land in Essex that within the memory of man has never grown anything but beans and wheat. Keep the hoe going.

BOOKS (*W. H. W.*).—Buy Spooner on *Sheep*, Johnson's *Modern Dairy and Cow-keeping*, and Richardson on *Horses* and *Pigs*.

NAMES OF PLANTS (*K. O. T.*).—Your grape is, we think, the *Grizzly Frontignan*; your plant, *Cuphea platycentra*; the *Fuchsins* we could not recognise. (*T. M. W.*).—Yours are *Petunia nyctaginiflora*, one of the parents of all our garden varieties. The berries are those of the Black Bryony (*Tamus communis*), a poisonous plant. (*F. G. D.*).—1, *Inula Dysenterica*; 2, *Lychnis divica*; 3, *Myosotis palustris*; 4, *Verbascum nigrum*; 5, *Tormetilla officinalis*; 6, *Galeopsis ladanum*; 7, *Impatiens* (not English); 8, *Erhium vulgare*; 9, *Impatiens glandulifera* (not English); 10, *Euphrasia officinalis*; 11, *Scutellaria galericulata*; 12, *Lythrum Salicaria*. (*W. P. H.*).—We do not know for certain what your bulbs are, but no doubt they are hardy. Plant them in pots in sandy loam and leaf-mould, and treat them as frame plants; and when they put forth plenty of leaves send us one in a perfect state. We think they are a species of *Scilla*, probably *Scilla Peruviana*.

GREENHOUSE AND VINERY (*M. D.*).—By all means prepare for a new vinery, as you propose. Your plan in general is eligible, but you are inclined to embrace too many objects; this will lead to confusion, and a compromise of principles in culture. We do not say that the whole of your plan cannot be carried out; but, to do so, you had best eschew flues, and betake yourself to hot-water piping. In any event, you should have your fire-place and chimney *between* the two houses, as you will be compelled by your present proposal to heat the vinery, whether or no, in keeping the frost out of your greenhouse; and this at certain periods will not be proper. Get your vines as soon as you like, and next February plant them in large pots or baskets (the latter we should prefer), and cultivate highly through next summer. Do not make your vine border until wanted, but provide materials soon, keeping them in sharp ridges to exclude rain. Vines and peaches seldom agree well together; we dare not recommend them to be mixed up under the care of a "man of all work"—such is enough for a clever gardener to manage. Eight vines may be—2 Hambro', 1 Dutch Sweet Water, 2 Royal Muscadine; 1 the true West's St. Peter's, 1 Muscat of Alexandria, 1 Black Prince, placing the Muscat at the hottest end, next the Sweet Water, then the St. Peter's, then Muscadine, and last Hambro'. You had better write again if you need more information.

BUDDED ROSES (*Rev. P. V. M. F.*).—Rose buds put in lately, and now started into growth, should have the shoots of the stocks cut back to a foot above the bud, and so remain till next May or June. This will assist the growing bud to grow stronger, and will not check the stock too much. If there are more shoots on the stock than are budded on, let them remain as they are, and cut them right out in winter; but leave those having the buds on till the plant is in active growth next season, then cut close behind the bud, and tie the young shoot to a stick fastened to the stock.

INDIA RUBBER PLANT (*J. N. Blackett*).—Do not be afraid of wearying us. Four feet long, as a cutting, was rather too long, especially when kept in a window; you will perceive that perspiration from the plant would so far exceed its possible absorbing powers that a shrivelled appearance was almost inevitable. You had better try and get it placed for a month or six weeks in a hothouse, where bottom-heat could be given, and where, from being kept close, the whole plant, if not too far gone, would absorb moisture strongly.

STEPHANOTIS FLORIBUNDA (*Peter Pindar*).—This, potted in sandy peat, and grown in a succession pine pit, has never flowered. It had better have a little loam mixed with the peat at the next shifting, and during winter, and especially the spring, and, in fact, at all times, you must keep the wood rather thin, so that the buds may be swelled and plump; keep it rather cool during the winter, say 45° to 50°; raise the temperature to 60° and 70° in the spring, and shortly afterwards, if the buds were well ripened, the flower-buds will appear.

CORRCEA SPECIOSA (*Ibid*).—We are not surprised you failed to raise this from cuttings; it does best grafted, or inarched, on the *Corraea alba*. The first number of the current volume is No. 79.

EVERLASTING FLOWERS (*A Cheshire Clergyman*).—We presume you mean *Xeranthemums* and *Gnaphaliums*, &c. We have seen these preserved for years merely by drying them in a room, laid on sheets of paper, and then tied in bundles.

MOUNTAIN ASH BERRIES (*Ibid*).—These, we think, might be kept until Christmas, by sticking their branches in damp soil and keeping the birds from them.

MOVING HIVES (*W. R.*).—You ask,—"What time of the year we recommend for removing three hives of bees to a position about ten feet in advance of their present one?" Do it immediately, and if the hives are brought forward a foot every other evening, till they reach the proposed position, their removal will be attended with less loss.

MARKET GARDENING (*A. B.*).—You will see that we have attended to your request.

FRAME (*R. P.*).—By some accident your drawing has been mislaid. Use rough glass for glazing it.

TOBACCO (*J. N.*).—Your tobacco just about to flower has been allowed to grow too long; it should have been cut before the flower-stem began to rise. Cut it immediately, but during dry weather, cutting it just within the soil; let it lie on the ground during dry days, but house it in a heap at night. When quite dry store it in a dry place, and take a leaf as you require it for fumigating purposes. *Water melons* are worthless. *Himalaya pumpkins, gourds*, and *vegetable marrow* may be boiled when as large as an ostrich egg, and eaten like sea-kale, or the flesh of the ripe ones may be mashed like turnips.

LONGEST CUCUMBER (*G. T., York*).—Allen's Victory of England is the longest we know; it is frequently grown two feet long. *Hollyhocks* are best sown in June, the seedlings to be transplanted as soon as large enough to where they are to remain. They may, however, be sown in pots in March, and plunged in a gentle hot-bed; the seedlings must be gradually hardened, and planted out in September. *The Cottage Gardeners' Dictionary* will begin publishing the 3rd of next month.

RAKING BEDS (*T. O.*).—Some of our most able coadjutors discard the rake entirely, and there is no doubt that an adroit gardener will lay the surface of a bed as smooth with a hoe as with a rake, but we question whether this is to be expected of an ordinary gardener. There is no harm in your trying, and there is no doubt that the surface kept tidy by the hoe only, allows the air to penetrate better to the roots of plants. To improve the staple of your light soil you had better put on the clay unburnt.

VINE TRAINING (*Vitis*).—You are not the only one who has complained of this tendency in the vine trained by Hoare's system, to have strong shoots at the ends of the main branches and weak shoots nearer the stem. We had thought that Mr. Hoare advocated three stages or lengths in the shoots; at any rate, such would be better than two, we think. The best mode of equalising strength, under any circumstances, is by summer stopping, and when your gross leaders have produced shoots about a couple of feet long, we should say, off with their heads. To carry on this, we fear you will have to deviate a little from Mr. H.'s system.

JOSLING'S ST. ALBAN'S GRAPE (*X. Y.*).—This variety is not for a limited selection. There can be no doubt of the *August Muscat* ripening with less heat than the *Muscat of Alexandria*, as the latter requires more heat than any grape we know. The *Pitmaston White Cluster* is unknown to us, but the Catalogue of the Horticultural Society says it is first-rate, and will ripen on a wall.

LONDON: Printed by HARRY WOOLDRIDGE, Winchester High-street, in the Parish of Saint Mary Kalendar; and Published by WILLIAM SOMERVILLE ORR, at the Office, No. 2, Amen Corner, in the Parish of Christ Church, City of London.—September 12th, 1860.

WEEKLY CALENDAR.

M W D D	SEPTEMBER 19—25, 1850.	Weather near London in 1849.		Sun Rises.	Sun Sets.	Moon R. & S.	Moon's Age.	Clock bef. Sun.	Day of Year.
19 Th	Chiffchaff's song over.	T. 64°—46°.	N.E. Fine.	42 a. 5	5 a. 6	3 5	13	6 12	262
20 F	Sun's declination 1° 8' N.	T. 52°—46°.	N.E. Rain.	44	3	4 10	14	6 33	263
21 S	St. Matthew.	T. 64°—49°.	N.E. Rain.	46	1	rises.	◉	6 54	264
22 Sun	17 Sun. aft. Trinity. Autumn commences.	T. 66°—50°.	E. Fine.	47	58 a. 5	6 a.48	16	7 15	265
23 M	Beech mast falls.	T. 66°—50°.	E. Rain.	49	56	7 11	17	7 36	266
24 Tu	Ash leaves lemon colour.	T. 66°—42°.	N. Fine.	51	54	7 35	18	7 57	267
25 W	Ivy flowers.	T. 71°—39°.	S.W. Fine.	52	51	8 4	19	8 18	268

On the 7th of September, 1741, was born Arthur Young, of whose writings it has been justly said, that "they produced more private losses and more public benefit than those of any other author." They occasioned those losses by tempting the unpractised to become farmers, and the farmers to try unprofitable experiments; and they occasioned public benefit even by the wisdom gained from those failures, but still more by diffusing agricultural knowledge among the cultivators of the soil. "We will not assert," said Mr. Kirwan, "that in all cases his conclusions were correct, or his judgment unimpeachable, but even his blunders, if he committed any, have tended to the benefit of agriculture, by evciting discussion and criticism." Let us add, that every gardener, every farmer, and every amateur confers a benefit upon his fellow cultivators by recording his failures as well as his successful experiments,—just the same as a lighthouse is equally valuable whether it shows the rock to be avoided or the harbour for which we are to steer. From childhood Mr. Young had a great fondness for farming, and exhibited at least an equal power for literary composition; yet the great mistake was made of spending some hundreds of pounds, and as effectually wasting a still greater number of his days, in endeavouring to break down his mind to the craft of a wine-merchant. Nature was invincible; so that instead of devoting his thoughts to the topography of the European vineyards, and the art of rendering their produce agreeable to British palates, he wrote novels and a political pamphlet, the reward for which—ten pounds worth of books from the publisher—was always remembered as causing a most memorable pleasure. Now occurred the death of his father; and he found himself, his apprenticeship being expired, his own master, with a freehold of 80 acres, producing as many pounds annually, and his mother in possession of 80 more acres, at Bradfield, near Bury St. Edmunds. She urged one willing to assent when she asked him to reside with her, and undertake the cultivation of her farm. He accepted her proposal, and the result may be told in his own words: "Young, eager, and totally ignorant of every necessary detail, it is not surprising that I squandered large sums under golden dreams of improvement." It is the less surprising, because he had a thirst for experiment without a knowledge of what is required to secure success. Undaunted by failure, and unsobered by experience, he married unsuitably, and undertook the cultivation of Sampford Hall, in Essex. It embraced 300 acres of good arable land, yet want of capital, want of practical knowledge, and that still more bitter want—the want of " a help mete for him," drove him from the farm; yet the tenant, to whom he gave £100 to take the lease off his hands, realised upon it a fortune. Still unshaken from his love of the soil, he sought for another farm, and the search furnished materials for his *Six Weeks' Tour through the Southern Counties*—a work popular, and passing through several editions, yet resulting to himself in no greater good at the time than beguiling him into taking a Hertfordshire

farm of 100 acres, by seeing it in a favourable season, and by its having a good residence attached. This farm he has thus described—"I know not what epithet to give this soil,—sterility falls short of the idea of such a hungry vitriolic gravel. I occupied for nine years the jaws of a wolf. A nabob's fortune would sink in the attempt to raise good arable crops in such a country." Finding that it would not return him a subsistence, he accepted an engagement as Parliamentary Reporter for the *Morning Post*, a most incongruous employment for a farmer, because it compelled his absence from home during six days of the week. Yet he retained it for several years—walking 17 miles down to his farm every Saturday evening, and returning to London every Monday morning. "I worked," are his own words, "more like a coalheaver, though without his reward, than like a man acting from a predominant impulse." Passing over the publication of several of his agricultural tours, we come to the year 1784, when he commenced his *Annals of Agriculture*, in which he appeared both as editor and author throughout its 45 volumes, until blindness closed his literary labours. It had this guarantee of trustworthiness—no essay was admitted without the name and address of the writer. Its correspondents, consequently, are singularly eminent; and even George III. contributed to his seventh volume a report, under the name of *Ralph Robinson*, of Mr. Ducket's farm at Petersham. Undaunted by failure, Mr. Young was about to embark in the cultivation of a vast tract of waste land in Yorkshire, when in 1793 he was appointed to the Secretaryship of the newly established Board of Agriculture. "What a change," he writes, "in the destination of a man's life! Instead of entering, as I proposed, the solitary lord of 4000 acres, in the keen atmosphere of lofty rocks and mountain torrents, with a little creation rising gradually around me, making the desert smile with cultivation, and grouse give way to industrious population, behold me at a desk, in the smoke, the fog, and the din of Whitehall. Society has charms,—true, and so has solitude to a mind employed. The die, however, is cast; and my steps may still be, metaphorically, said to be in the furrow." But to "the furrow" the society did not exclusively attend. Its transactions were disfigured by political dissertations, and it consequently so lost the support and respect of a large portion of the agriculturists who differed from its political tenets, that it ceased to be useful. Government then withdrew from it the annual grant of £3000; and in 1816 the Society ceased to exist. Mr. Young had not been able to perform the duties of Secretary for some years previously; and he did not long survive its failure, for he died in 1820, in the 80th year of his age. His characteristics have appeared as our brief narrative has proceeded; and we may add that his agricultural attainments were estimated more highly by foreigners than in his own land, for when the Duke of Bedford once breakfasted with Mr. Young, at Bradfield, there were also at the table pupils from Russia, France, America, Naples, Poland, Sicily, and Portugal. We cannot conclude without holding forward prominently that feature of his character, never found among the attributes of the vicious—his pure unwavering affection for his mother. Whithersoever inclination prompted him still inclination was invariably sacrificed to satisfy the wishes of his parent. In every way she was worthy of his affection, and may be added to the thousands of instances in which we know that it was the remembrance of the mother's gentleness, the mother's precepts, and the mother's example, that biassed man to the right path, long after the form with which they were associated had passed to the grave.

METEOROLOGY OF THE WEEK.—The observations made at Chiswick during the last twenty-three years show that the average highest and lowest temperatures of these days are 66 3° and 45.9° respectively. The greatest heat, 82°, occurred on the 25th in 1842. During the twenty-three years 87 of the days were fine, and on 74 days rain fell.

RANGE OF BAROMETER—RAIN IN INCHES.

Sept.	1841.		1842.	1843.	1844.	1845.	1846.	1847.	1848.	1849.
19	B.	{ 30.037 29.972	29.583 29.543	30.153 30.148	30.068 29.933	29.996 29.681	29.790 29.614	29.067 29.757	29.999 29.792	30.460 30.443
	R.	—	0.08	—	0.01	—	—	0.50	—	—
20	B.	{ 30.109 30.056	29.522 29.478	30.107 30.034	30.028 29.997	29.982 29.690	29.908 29.476	29.024 29.790	29.766 29.617	30.407 30.996
	R.	—	0.02	—	0.01	0.29	—	0.03	—	0.05
21	B.	{ 29.969 29.700	29.464 29.438	30.215 30.131	30.091 30.048	29.538 29.315	29.537 29.555	30.108 30.011	29.798 29.764	30.178 30.123
	R.	0.10	0.02	—	0.01	0.12	—	0.19	0.03	0.03
22	B.	{ 29.617 29.613	29.494 29.460	30.445 30.363	30.036 29.921	29.946 29.582	29.657 29.581	30.058 30.023	29.795 29.767	30.082 30 030
	R.	0.30	0.01	—	—	0.08	—	—	—	—
23	B.	{ 29.617 29.578	29.494 29.346	30.509 30.460	29.741 29.592	30.998 30.011	20 444 29.935	30.008 29.935	29.564 29.531	29.915 29 807
	R.	0.23	0.36	—	—	—	1.21	—	0.22	0.16
24	B.	{ 29.526 29.480	29.424 29.341	30.467 30.375	30.081 29 803	30.242 30.016	29.811 29.403	30.199 30.141	29.341 29.396	29.866 29.899
	R.	0.23	0.05	—	—	—	0.01	—	—	—
25	B.	{ 29.481 29.398	29.642 29.536	30.259 30.101	30.234 30.174	29.852 29.592	29.813 29.682	30.088 29.954	29.476 29.381	29.830 29.834
	R.	0.30	0.26	—	—	0.01	—	—	0.10	—

The Chrysanthemum is usually considered as being first mentioned by Kœmpfer in 1712, under the title of *Matricaria*; but we think it had been previously described by Ray, in the third volume of his *Historia Plantarum* (page 225), published in 1704, and who quotes for his authorities the *Hortus Malabaricus*, and specimens in *Petiver's Museum* He describes it under the name of *Matricaria indica latiore folio, flore pleno*, and under the native name of *Tsjetti-Pu*. Linnæus in 1753 first placed it as a distinct species, with two varieties, in his *Species Plantarum*, giving it the name of *Chrysanthemum indicum*, the title it has ever since retained. *Rumphuis*, in his *Plants of Amboyna*, published in 1750, and Thunberg, in his *Flora Japonica*, published in 1784, were the first to describe it fully, and to detail the success with which it is cultivated by the Chinese and Japanese. It is a native of their respective countries, and is their especial favourite. "The Chrysanthemum," says Mr. Fortune, who resided in China two or three years, "is the Chinese gardener's favourite flower. There is no other with which he takes so much pains, or which he cultivates so well. His Camellias, Azaleas, and Roses are well grown and well bloomed, but in growing all these we beat him in England. In the cultivation of the Chrysanthemum he stands unrivalled. The plants themselves seem to meet him half way, and grow just as he pleases. Sometimes I met with them trained in the form of animals, and at other times they were made to resemble the pagodas so common in their country. Whether they were trained into these fanciful forms, or grown as simple bushes, they were always in high health, full of fresh green leaves, and never failing to bloom most profusely in the autumn and winter."

It was cultivated in England in 1764, by Mr. Philip Miller, in the Apothecary Company's Garden at Chelsea, being one of the new plants presented by him in that year to the Royal Society, in accordance with the will of Sir Hans Sloane, but it did not acquire much attention from English gardeners until far into the first quarter of the present century. It is true that some of the Chinese varieties were imported into France in 1789,

and were brought here the year following; but it was not until eight new varieties were introduced about the year 1808, by Sir Everard Home and Mr. Evans, and seventeen more varieties had been imported between that year and 1823, that the flower became popular and established in our florists' lists. We scarcely need say, that the very numerous varieties of this flower are now the most prevalent ornaments of our borders in late autumn, whether those borders are about a cottage, or are enamelling the pleasure grounds of a palace; and in this, too, we resemble the Chinese, for Mr. Fortune says, "it is everybody's plant,—blooming alike in the garden of the lowly Chinese cottager as in that of the blue-buttoned mandarian; and when in bloom is in great request for the decoration of court-yards, halls, and temples."

"Although we are indebted to China," says the same talented writer, "for the parents of those varieties of Chrysanthemums which now enliven our gardens during the dull months of winter, yet, strange to say, the progeny is more numerous in Europe than in China itself. Some of those beautiful kinds raised by Mr. Salter in France would be much admired even by the Chinese florist. It is a curious fact, however, that many of those kinds, such as *formonum* and *lucidum*, originally raised from seed in Europe, are also met with in the north of China."

No one attempted to define the desirable characteristics of a good Chrysanthemum until Mr. Glenny undertook the task in 1843, and those characteristics, though with considerable modification, we have adopted as follows :—

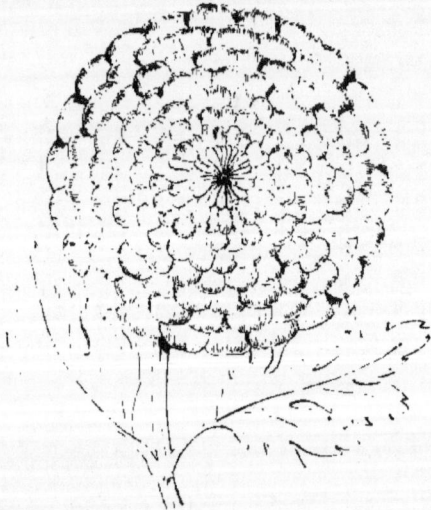

1. The plant should be dwarf, shrubby, well covered with green foliage to the bottom of the stems ; the leaves broad and bright ; the flowers well displayed, abundant, and well supported by the stems. If the stems are more than eighteen inches high they are gawky, and show too much green in comparison with the bloom.

2. The flower should be round, double, high in the crown, perfect in the centre, without disk or confusion, and of the form of a segment of a ball.

3. The petals should be thick, smooth, broad, circular at the ends, and the point where they meet hardly perceptible. They must not show their undersides by quilling, and should be of such firm texture as to retain themselves well in their places.

4. The flowers to be large in proportion to the foliage, but the size only to be considered when plants are in all other respects equal.

5. The colour, if a self, is superior in proportion to its purity and brightness; if the colours are more than one they should be well defined and distinct. The worst of all colours are those which are mixed or clouded together ; and we are inclined to place more than usual emphasis upon colour in the case of the Chrysanthemum, because many flowers now admitted even into exhibition stands are odious in this respect.

We have given no rules for judging either *the quilled* or *the tasselled* varieties, because these should never be admitted to be shown except in a separate class as "Fancy Chrysanthemums;" and in that class we can only say, that those least offensive to the eye should receive the prize.

It is usual to grow the Chrysanthemum so as to have flowers only on the tops of the stems, but there is no occasion for this, and it is only a consequence of bad cultivation. Indeed, so leggy are Chrysanthemums usually grown, that various ingenious contrivances are required to exhibit them in a state as if clothed with leaves throughout their length. We repeat, there is no occasion for this, for we have seen the Chrysanthemum grown not only bearing leaves naturally along the whole length of the stem, but that stem having laterals almost from the ground upwards crowned with flowers. So much is the beauty of the plant increased by this, that we think it would be judicious to have a rule, that other properties being equal, the first prize should be awarded to the Chrysanthemums with the greatest number of well-placed and well-bloomed laterals.

THE FRUIT-GARDEN.

PEACHES AND NECTARINES.—Those who live in cold situations should now pay the utmost attention to both wood and fruit. Where trees have been growing strongly, every shoot may now be stopped, and any waste laterals or superfluous spray entirely removed : we would not have a shoot more than requisite for the next year's crop. Where any leaves cover the fruit, they should be pinched in two, so that the sun may shine on about one-third of the fruit ; for we do not think it well to fully expose it, as two or three continuously sunny days, with a high temperature, would ripen

them prematurely : the consequence of which would be a loss of flavour.

Some of the best and most highly flavoured peaches we ever grew were retarded; that is to say, a canvass shade was applied just before they were thoroughly ripe. Now this was not done on principle, but as an expedient, in order to keep up a long succession : the trees being in the peach-house, and the ripening taking place in the end of June and through July. We thus had peaches for five weeks successively, and better fruit were never sent to table. Now, what was done on expediency is now adopted on principle with us ; nevertheless, the practice must be applied out of doors with some caution, as gross trees in deep borders would have difficulty in ripening their wood in some seasons.

We would strongly advise that all luxuriant trees be root-pruned the moment the last peach is gathered ; this will check the root action, and bring on the solidifying principle, by checking the ascent of watery matters. Those who want to plant young peaches, or remove larger ones, will find the end of the month a capital time for the operation. Let no one fear for the leaves flagging a little, which will do little harm. Still, we would advise a slight shading, if the weather is very bright, during the middle of the day. The trees, too, should have a moderate ball of earth, if possible ; and they may be thickly mulched immediately, as this will shut in some ground heat, a consideration of importance ; for it must be remembered, that the earth has already commenced repaying to the atmosphere the warmth it received during May, June, July, and August. We dare say, that fresh sawdust would be a good thing—being a powerful non-conductor of heat.

FIGS.—Here we have another late ripener, and one which requires a little assistance in the north. To be sure, figs may be found along the line of our southern counties in the character of trees ; and little, if any, pains bestowed on them. This, however, merely proves the importance of two or three degrees of latitude, in the ripening of tender fruits or vegetables, to which the ordinary climate of England is not quite equal. We must freely confess to an envious feeling—living as we do in a northern corner of the kingdom ; a county in which the atmospheric conditions have eminently fitted it for the produce of cheese, for many generations (and which conditions, in about a proportionate ratio, *unfit it* for the production of tender fruits)—an envious feeling we repeat, when we hear or read of the great figs about Arundel, Worthing, and other highly-favoured localities.

An idea irresistibly rises in the mind, as to the amount of excellence most of our tender *pears*, &c., ought to attain in such climes, if placed under proper culture ; and how little impediments lie in the way, as compared with our northern counties, the land of tall chimnics, &c. No doubt our Sussex friends must either smile or stare vastly at our urgent and oft-repeated recommendations about ripening the wood, &c. ; and, doubtless, frequently consider such directions too fussy by half. It ought to be remembered, however, that our Devonshire or Sussex readers do not require a tithe of the advice that is *absolutely requisite* for those in the north.

To return to the figs. Most good cultivators practise stopping about this period, the tendency of which is, to cause the embryo fruits of the following year to become more decided in character ; for we frequently see developments towards the points of free growing figs—especially young trees—which are neither figs nor woodbuds, but seem to partake of the character of both. This, we believe, occurs through a too powerful action of root, too late continued ; and the best way to stay proceedings, next to root-pruning, is to stop the growing principle. One squeeze of the finger and thumb will suffice to effect this. Still, as there is no more fitting subject for root-pruning than a gross fig-tree, in localities not famed for capital climate, we advise the immediate application of this principle, remembering that the vital powers of the fig are immense; indeed, it is a somewhat difficult matter to kill this singular tree, without the aid of fire.

STRAWBERRIES.—We hope that the readers of THE COTTAGE GARDENER have rejected the false practice of mowing down their strawberries, although it is expedient to reduce the amount of runners at this season; at least, such is our practice. We have, indeed, gone farther this season, having, after dressing away all runners, applied and dug in the manures considered requisite. The strawberry stools are thirty inches apart between the rows, and the plants about two feet apart in the row; we, however, merely dig one spade's width down the centre between the rows, levelling a little fresh soil about the crowns. Every care is taken not to trim any leaves away in the operation, or to bury them; and the runners being removed, the principal leaves fall on each side, and thus admit sunlight to the interior of each stool, which is of considerable benefit.

RASPBERRIES.—The autumn-bearing kinds now require a little extra attention. No barren shoots should be permitted, and the bearing ones should be carefully tied or trained. Plenty of sunlight is the desideratum; and much care should be exercised in gathering the produce when dry. Thus managed, and placed in a dry room on clean paper, they will keep for three days, provided a slight amount of ventilation may be permitted.

WASPS.—We are exceedingly fortunate this season, for we have now (Sept. 2nd) scarcely a wasp to be seen. We have, however, laboured indefatigably for several seasons, both in getting the spring wasps caught and also in having the nests taken; especially those very near the gardens. We are tolerably well persuaded, that most of the depredations committed by the wasps are by those from nests within half a mile of the garden in question. Like some others of the animal or insect creation, we do think they become attached to certain neighbourhoods, and if this opinion be correct, it shows that a person in following up their destruction is not working so much for his neighbours as for himself; that is to say, in country places where gardens are a good way apart. Where these terrible pests take to vineries, no time may be lost in taking precautionary or preventive measures. The old practice of bagging the grapes is not so well approved as in former times. The fact is, that a "good bloom" is now-a-days considered indispensable, and the bagging plan is by no means *favourable* to a good "bloom." The preventive *principle* is the best, and if the case is not excessively severe, ordinary canvass, woollen netting, or such things as book muslin, are used in covering those openings of the house where the ventilation is carried on. One great fault of these materials is, that they much impede ventilation. Caution, therefore, must be exercised in this matter, or the vines may yet be injured in late houses, by what is termed burning. We have more than once known what is termed a "run" of warm and sunny weather, even in September, although we much fear the converse is more likely to be the case. Speaking of wasps, we regret we did not offer advice about them a fortnight sooner. So many objects, however, connected with horticultural matters are perpetually arising, that the best of us is at times liable to be rather "too late for the train."

GATHERING FRUIT.—It is scarcely necessary to urge the importance of an almost daily attention to the gathering and duly storing of our hardy fruits. This requires a prudent forecast, for, to have a given kind as long in succession as possible, or so to economise as to secure a regular succession to the table, both knowledge and watchfulness become necessary.

To carry out such matters, recourse must be had at times to retarding principles. Thus, we will suppose

that the proprietor is partial to the King Pippin apple, or the Jargonelle pear; it becomes a question, then, how to commence early with them, and how to arrest the decay of the remaining portion. As to early maturity, a few of the very best swelled fruits may be plucked a little before they are quite ripe, and such covered close in a warm room will be ready in a few days. There is an old practice with some country fruiterers, of placing fruit under such requirements in boxes or tubs among layers of nettle leaves. Why nettle leaves are selected, we can scarcely say; but we believe it is understood that they impart neither flavour nor smell. The main principles involved in the operation are, doubtless, increased temperature, and an immunity from shrivelling, by warding off atmospheric action. The retarding principle is somewhat different; among the main features of which may be named, the shading the fruit, or a portion of it, on the tree; commencing the operation about the period that the fruit is changing or completing the ripening process. These things are always accomplished at the expense of some loss of flavour. Still it is often worth while to pay this penalty, for the sake of convenience and regularity of supply.   R. ERRINGTON.

THE FLOWER-GARDEN.

LAST year, while the other writers in THE COTTAGE GARDENER were diligently engaged trenching and draining, enclosing and planting, all kinds of gardens for the cottager, from the orchard garden to the vegetable garden, and so on to flower, rock, pond, and fern gardens, and I forget how many more gardens besides—I say, when all this was going on I was kept at home to clean the cottage windows, and to keep things straight and tidy about the door, and thus had more opportunities of making the cottager's acquaintance than some of them, and thus, by close contact, I soon gained on his confidence. By-and-bye, he began to show me his letters,—and queer letters some of them were; and not only that, but he wished me to teach him—or, rather, I had seen his want of knowing how much he needed to be taught, how to write business letters himself—and I showed him that it would never do to write such long letters as he used then to receive from Dublin—that it was a waste of paper, and that no one could waste time in reading over a sheet or two of post paper merely to know what *class* a *Batchelor's Button* belonged to, or what time of the moon's age a bed of cabbages should be planted out; and now he writes much more to the purpose than some of his betters. From letter-writing he began to be curious about the spelling and pronouncing, and the meaning, of the hard names they give to plants; and this I taught him also, so far, that he had a great mind to have a book made up for "his ownself," as he would call it, in which he could learn these things for himself, without bothering me so much. Now, although his *rent* was not then all paid up, owing to the expenses of having done so much for his garden grounds, we saw enough of him to believe that all his arrears would be paid up, and that he could be trusted with a new book to the bargain. About that time people began to say, that no book could be made better than THE COTTAGE GARDENER's "weekly twopenny," and that if it could, it would trespass on the province of the "twopenny" itself; but that was a wrong idea altogether, for good books are like money, the more we get of them the more we want to have. If there had not been a COTTAGE GARDENER, there never would have been this call for a COTTAGE GARDENER's DICTIONARY—for a dictionary, as all the world knows by this time, this new book is to be. But I would not have so good a book confined to the cottager; if he had it all to himself, the next thing he would do would be to turn head-gardener himself, and, goodness knows, we have heads enough already on that string. There is now a race of young men learning gardening and botany all over the kingdom, to whom this new dictionary will be quite a treasure, and it is on their account, and for them only, that I, an old gardener, have thus broken out of my weekly tract to say so, and to advise them most earnestly to study the new way of giving English finishings to the names of plants, and the orders to which they belong; for of all the improvements in gardening books, in my time, this is by far the greatest; and if Dr. Lindley had done no more for gardening and botany by his books but this very thing, the next generation would call him a great reformer, who had done more for us gardeners in his day and generation than all his contemporaries—just as we talk at present of the great Linnæus, who, although he did not live to see our days, had seen them afar off. This great man was *certainly* the worldly cause of my ever being a gardener; for when I was a little fellow they intended to make a gentleman of me, but before I left school, I got hold of a book—and such a book—written by Linnæus himself, and translated into English. It went by the name of "Lee's Botany," and when I think of it even now my hair stands on end! there were a thousand words in it as long as the handle of my pen, and as hard to be pronounced as the language of the Cossacks, and yet I very nearly got it all "by heart;" and it so fired my young Highland spirits, that I disdained to be made a gentleman of. I would be a philosopher some day. But I soon found out that the first step in the progress of a philosopher of this stamp was to get down into a "stoke-hole" to make up the fires, and to clean out the stoke-hole and all about the fire every Saturday, to screen the ashes, and to return the cinders to the old stoke-hole again to be ready to "damp down" the fires with the last thing at night. And they did damp the fires, and damped *something else* besides; but no matter—the young philosopher, in course of time, was trusted "to give air," and to look at the thermometers. As to making cuttings, he knew all about them already—he rooted two Balm of Gilead cuttings out of three before he left school; what he wanted was a book beyond "Lee's Botany," in short, a dictionary, like this that we are now getting ready for the cottager. But at that time they could no more write such a book, than they could lay down railroads or sink telegraphic wires under the English Channel. They have a custom in the Highlands, and in other wild parts of the world, that, where a great chief or some one of consequence had fallen in battle, every one who passed by that way should cast a stone into his "cairn," and a heap of stones was thus collected together: and that is just the way that the best books are produced, and more particularly plant dictionaries and catalogues, and in this manner the cairn has accumulated from the days of Linnæus to this, from which materials are obtained which we now recast, and to which we add the mites from our own experience to form a most useful gardening dictionary. Indeed, natives of all climes, who have written down their thoughts or their experience on matters connected with this book, have, in fact, cast their stone into the common cairn, and the book itself will, in its turn at some future day, be as one of these stones—a unit in the accumulating heap. Linnæus laid the concrete, Jussieu and Decandolle were the master-mason and bricklayer, and Dr. Lindley the chief architect of this our dictionary, and we, whose names have been advertised as the humble bees, are, in fact, only the bricklayers, hodmen, and thatchers of the firm; and when we get the roof covered in, the editor must do the painting and polishing. But amongst us all, if we do not produce a first-rate article, we ought to be ashamed of ourselves, and some of us, at least, be sent back to the stoke-hole again, to dampers and all.

ROSES.—For many years past I have gone over all our *Perpetual roses* about the middle of September, with a pair of gloves and a sharp knife, and give every one a particular kind of pruning; and I find the plan so very useful, that I would no more put it off, or do it earlier in the season, than I would give up pruning roses altogether. I believe one half the best rose growers do the same, but, somehow or other, the thing has not become fashionable enough to be treated of in books or magazines; but I rejoice to see that many more things which we treat of for the first time in this—our friend THE COTTAGE GARDENER—soon take root, and wings and spread among our brethren—on *principle*, no doubt—for the good of others. If for no other reason, therefore, I would strongly recommend this subject to all gardeners, from the palace down to ourselves, as one of the most useful joints in the machinery for growing good late roses; we cut roses here from the open ground generally up to or down to Christmas; and I am quite sure that with a little pains now, there are many rose lovers who may gratify their taste, by taking a leaf out of our book.

Like every thing else that is done in a garden, this should be performed, year by year, on some fixed plan. If you put a man to count straws only, you ought to make him do it, or tell him how to do it, systematically; and not allow him to put the counted ones in the bundle heads and tails. Money is no more the root of all evil than system is the root and branches of good gardening, and of good everything else that we do. Well, then, this system of managing to have lots of roses late in the season, is to begin about the end of May, when the flower-buds are three parts grown, and you can see which of them promise to have the finest blown roses; many of the "green centres" can then be detected; and if an insect or grub has nibbled the buds, that also can be seen, with other imperfections, if there be any. All such buds are pulled, or rather cut clean out with a knife—for I dislike very much pulling about any plant or part of a plant—after that those buds that have only small shoots to support them are done away with, and by this time perhaps one-third of the whole crop is gone, and that is enough on good rose soil, where the plants grow very well; but on thin land, and where roses do but moderately, one half of the flower-buds ought to be taken off, and the other half left on the best and strongest shoots to flower. Some people say, that if you want good late flowers, and to spare your plants, all the first show of flower-buds should be destroyed; and I have tried that many a time, but I do not believe in the doctrine at all, for I never could make out that half a crop in June did any harm to that of the October following. Others, again, cut back the shoots at the end of May, to get late roses, but that is an extraordinary bad fashion, which no one would indulge in who knew any thing of vegetable life. It is just as if a farmer were to let his calves suck the cows dry, and expect to have cream and fresh butter nevertheless. The leaves being the representatives of the cows, the gardener who cuts down his roses in the middle of the growing season is that of the sucking calves, and the buds and full blown roses the cream and butter. Instead of two crops of roses by this system of cutting back the shoots at the end of May, the fact is, that the poor plants are forced to give three crops of moderate bloom instead of two good ones. At that early season the next bud or two below the cut part are in leaf in ten days, and in bloom by the end of June, so that cutting back hinders the autumnal crop very much, instead of easing the plants, as some knowing folks suppose.

The first crop is put off only three weeks in some seasons, and not more than a month or five weeks at any time; and cut as we may we cannot alter the nature of a rose-tree more than that of any other plant; and it is in the nature of Perpetual roses to make a fresh growth of wood as soon as a crop of roses is ready to cut for the button-hole or bouquets and glasses—no matter what time, that is from the end of May to the middle or end of August—by not cutting off any of the leaves in May and June; and by reducing the vigour of the plants a little, with having a crop of flowers, we kill three instead of two birds with the same stone.—We have so many flowers; the leaves digest the proper food for the next crop at the proper time, the height of their growing season; and the plant is made to take a longer time before it makes a second growth; for the merest observer can perceive, that after a rose-bush has flowered it rests awhile, before it makes another attempt at growing; whereas when a plant is cut early in the summer it will not rest, as we have just seen, but makes a second growth in a hurry, flowers in a hurry, and will be ready by the middle of July to make a third instead of a second growth. It is true, that where roses do well, and where there are plenty of them, if one does not flower well after a few seasons of bad management, another with which escaped the ordeal, or which had a stronger constitution, and the cause of failure in the first plant is overlooked; but when one's ground is very small, and the best is to be made of a limited number of plants, attention to small matters like this is really of some consequence.

I do not mean to say that the bad effects of a wrong system is to be seen the first or even in the next season, but depend upon it, sooner or later, it must and will tell; and that is the reason why we are so particular in asking our correspondents for the past history of such plants as they write to us about for cause and cure. By the time a rose-bush has finished its growth, and put off a crop of flowers, the bottom of the young growth gets hard or ripe; as then we say, or find, that the bark will not "run," if we want to bud on it; and at this stage, no matter what time of the season, the bottom leaves get hard and dry also: their office is in a great measure fulfilled, and *black specks* and *blotches* tell the fact; and here the young grower takes alarm: he thinks it must be something inimical to the health of the plant has caused the leaves to look so, but the healthiest oak-leaf in the forest shows exactly the same symptoms at the proper time, and we think nothing of it; the frost is at hand, and down they come. Well, in August and September we do get frost at times, but not hard enough to cast down the ripened leaves on the lower parts of our rose-bushes; then it is that we ourselves should be so frosty-natured as to do the work instead—that is, pull off all the ripened leaves with the hand. We thus get rid of the contagion from the black and yellow blotches, and also let in the sun and air to play among the branches, by which they are ripened still more; and the fresh leaves above have also a better chance of doing their part more effectually. This, then, is the first process of September dressing:—the old useless dry blotched leaves are stripped off, and we see where all the shoots have sprung from; also which of them are strong, and which are not. Such as are below a medium size are now cut right out: this gives still more light and air to the strong ones, and the sap that would go into the little ones must from hence find its way into the large ones; and if it does not make them still larger, it will add to their strength to flower better. Now we must look up among the branches, and find out those places where the first June blossoms were made, and here two or three weak or little shoots will be found also; and one or more strong ones which issued from a stronger bud lower down has taken the lead, and left the weak ones completely in the shade, and of course they can be of no use; therefore, the best plan is to cut them off also—cutting close to the bottom of the best leaders. This, in its turn, throws more sap, more air, and more light into and against all the strong leading

shoots; and surely under all these advantages they must flower better in the autumn, and ripen better for next year; and so they will. But we have not done with them yet: look now from above down among the branches, and if you cannot see the earth below, right through the bush, the branches are too thick, and you must thin them; and here a little knowledge of the sort of rose would be necessary to guide one. There are some of these autumn roses so strong—such as *Madame Laffay* and *Mrs. Elliot*—that if you were to cut out the smallest of their shoots, at this final stroke the very strong ones might not blossom; therefore, two or three of the very strongest shoots of such must be cut out, and the rest will blossom all the better; whereas the more dwarf varieties require the weaker taken off, and the strongest left to bloom.   D. Beaton.

GREENHOUSE AND WINDOW GARDENING.

Training Plants in Pots.—Several correspondents having wished for hints upon this subject, we shall shortly advert to some of the leading ideas to be kept in mind; leaving for the present figured illustrations in wood cuts, as requested by some, because it would occupy more time and space than we can at present spare, and also, because in the long run such representations would be of little value, unless in the case of those who admire the art displayed in the prettiness of the trainer more than the plant, which ought entirely to conceal it. Even in these simple matters such varieties of taste will be found, that if people are not satisfied with any wire trainers that the wire-workers possess, these will in a few moments embody your ideas into shape.

The first thing here to be remembered is, that whatever be its form or material, whether an iron trellis or a wooden stake, this ought ever to be looked upon as a secondary object. A second idea is, that *fitness* for its purpose should at once be apparent. A climber or a twiner may be taught to ramble over a flat surface, and to most people, when the trellis is covered with dependant festoons, it would appear an object of great interest; but the idea of *fitness* will not be so apparent as if the plant had been trained upon a roundish, barrel-shaped trellis, whether consisting of wire, wood-stakes, or, better still, something resembling a tree; in each case ultimately concealing the medium of support by its foliage and bloom. This *fitness* when seen, will not only please, but reconcile us to that which otherwise would appear unfit and incongruous. Thus, there is the *Euphorbia jacquiniflora*, to which some time ago attention was directed; bearing its fine masses of crimson flowers at the points of its shoots; the finer and stronger these shoots are, the more splendid will be the flowers; the strength of the plant is naturally directed into a few instead of many shoots, and hence the next to impossibility of making the plant bushy or pretty to look at when growing. The tying of the slender shoots loosely to a single stake in the centre of the pot would seem the most fit for such plants, unless, indeed, you could suspend the pot, and allow the shoots to hang over its sides; the branches when in bloom being just below the level of the eye. Of all things the surrounding such a plant with a round barrel-shaped, very open wire trellis would seem the most *unfit*, and yet with such a contrivance I have seen a splendid exhibition of the flowers of the above plant. The cultivator studied its nature; instead, therefore, of growing a single plant in a pot, he congregated a number of plants into one large pot. He cut back these plants to different heights, the lowest to supply the bottom of the trellis with strong shoots, and the middle and highest plants for these parts of his trellis respectively. When growing freely, the shoots were brought out and fastened in the desired place to the slender wires, and when the blooming season came, a mass of bloom was thus presented that I have never seen by any other method. Here the nature of the plant being known, and a peculiar system being adopted, enabled the cultivator to render apparent the *fitness* of a medium of training, which otherwise would have seemed the most unfit. Hence the difficulty of stating, as some friends wish us to do, the best form and method of training different plants, as that will be more variously and also effectually done by studying the nature and capabilities of the plant, than by attending to anything like a prescribed stereotyped form, however beautiful it may be. Variety in mode and form is ever pleasing; imitation soon becomes insipid.

The third element to be attended to is *apparent utility*. We have already noticed that the medium of support should ever appear a secondary, not a primary object. When in perfection a plant should conceal the framework, which has set it off to the best advantage. That frame-work, whether it be a wire trellis or a stake or stakes of wood, should never, therefore, be of a *colour* glaring or attractive in their appearance. A dull lead, a dark stone, or a sombre brown colour, are among the best. Hence, to our eye, there is no comparison between a well seasoned hazel rod, with its brown bark on, and a painted stick of any kind, or one cut out of double laths, as is so prevalent in our nurseries. The latter only becomes tolerable when the freshness, the result of the "whittling," has disappeared by exposure and use. A correspondent complains that neither he nor his gardener can manage, to his mind, the *Chironia floribunda*, because "the smallest sticks show." Now this is just one of many plants with respect to which a number of small sticks are not necessary. The tying of the progressing shoots to one upright stake until they reached a certain height, in the present case one or two feet, and then allowing them to bend and hang downwards, or the fastening of the shoots to a slender wire trellis, and dispensing with stakes altogether, would, in such cases, confer satisfaction upon the cultivator. But then, for all that, when the plant is growing there is no fault to be found with seeing either stake or trellis, provided they do "show" rather conspicuously. Their seen *utility* marks their *appropriateness*. Even in or around the precincts of a garden common delicacy, without any overstrained sentimental refinement, suggests the importance of some objects and operations being concealed from general view; just as in the various departments of the garden it is desirable that we should be able to contemplate one series of objects, without being disturbed by viewing a totally different class of objects in their immediate vicinity. But making allowance for such like exceptions as these, I honestly affirm, that where there is a seen utility, it can never be associated with the ugly or the unnecessary. Small plants when beginning to be fastened to their stake or trellis, may seem somewhat incongruous when placed among other plants that have arrived at perfection. Here, in the case of those who wish to preserve *unity* of expression, there may be a necessity for dividing their house, however small, into an exhibiting and a growing department, as I have several times recommended; but the seeing a large part of a stake or a trellis unoccupied by a young growing plant, cannot be construed into the ugly or the unnecessary, except by those minds that cannot perceive what the plants are desired, and ultimately destined, to accomplish. Hence, much as we disapproved of seeing *geraniums* and *calceolarias* stilted up with a forest of sticks, and rejoicing as we do in witnessing a better taste prevailing, still, upon the principle of utility and fitness, a degree of allowance ought to be made in these matters for plants that have to be con-

veyed to exhibition tables, over all kinds of roads, that there would be no necessity for tolerating in the case of plants that were never removed from the garden.

For all creeping, climbing, twisting, and very slender growing plants, where it is not intended that the shoots should hang over the sides of the pot or basket, from either of these being suspended, most people who are admirers of great neatness will patronise slender wire trainers. For slender things, the main supporting wires need not be made more than one-eighth of an inch in diameter, and the binding wire which forms the open network less than the sixteenth of an inch. For strong growing plants the main wire should be from a quarter to three-eighths of an inch in diameter, and bound and twisted with wire proportionately stronger than for the smaller trainers. For an *upright round trainer*, all that is necessary is to take two or three wires of the requisite thickness, bend them into a semicircular form in the middle, fasten them there together, and then you have four or six supporting legs, which you must keep at equal distances, and fill up between with smaller wire in a manner to suit your fancy. The bottom of these legs may go into the soil, and thus serve the purpose of feet; or, what is better, they may be bent over the rim of the pot, and descend halfway down its sides outside; while a ring brought up from the bottom and securely fastened over them would keep the trellis firm. A *flat trellis* is made in a similar manner, only two side pieces and a centre one of strong wire will be required. It is better to fasten on a cross piece at bottom, that there may be four feet instead of two. When these flat or round trainers are not fastened externally by the side of the pot, but descend among the soil inside, a wire should be fastened round the rim of the pot outside, and to this the trellis should be firmly secured by wire in various places, as nothing injures plants or trellises more than the liability of these trellises to be moved and knocked from their places. Various blocks for bending the wire and a pair of wire pincers will be necessary; but the nearest worker in wire will make them cheaper and better than you will be able to do yourselves, and the slightest sketch you may give him will be attended to even to the very minutiæ.

But some do not like wire,—would rather have something more simple, that would give work and cost little or nothing. Well, the same methods may be adopted with long rods of wood, such as brier and bramble, and crossed and recrossed with waxed string. Slender things may be attached to a branch of a tree with all its twigs remaining. The branch of a larch or a spruce, when peeled in spring, answers well for this purpose. Young trees of the spruce and the larch thus peeled we have often used for such plants as *Thunbergia*, *Torrenia*, *Tropæolum*, &c.; and as they were fastened to, and allowed to run among the slender twigs until they completely covered them, the effect was very pleasing, and looked perhaps more *natural* than could be done by attaching them to a trellis. In that case it was particularly necessary that the young peeled tree should be attached by wires to the wire round the rim of the pot, to prevent its being shaken.

For plants that may be grown in something of a pyramidal form, one stake in the centre will generally be sufficient, if a system of what may be termed *hasping* is resorted to. Thus the lower branches are fastened horizontally to the wire round the rim of the pot, the last and succeeding layers are kept in the desired place by a small thread fastened to the stake on one side, and to a lower tier of branches on the other. In the process of growth the threads are not seen, and the branches soon retain of themselves the position thus given them, and thus a paraphernalia of sticks is got rid of. Plants grown rather flat-headed may be treated in a similar manner, even such as *geraniums* and *calceolarias*. I have had the latter, some years ago, when some of the finer large kinds were a favourite hobby, so large in size that it required two men to move them, and yet no stakes were seen as, with the exception of one in the centre and six round the side, the whole of which were hid by the stems; the flowers were kept in their places by hasping with thread and fastening to fine wire or thread, which was crossed and recrossed from the different stakes to each other, and all of which was concealed by the heads of bloom. When in the case of *geraniums*, a more pyramidal shape becomes fashionable, the tying down to a wire at the rim of the pot, and the hasping by thread of the alternate branches to keep them in their place, will render a multitude of stakes wholly unnecessary. Until that takes place, and also for all other little things that require *neat little stakes* or twigs, I may mention, that I have found nothing more useful or more easily procured than the shoots of *fuchsias*. Independently of their beauty, *Fuchsia Thompsoniana* or *Coccinea* are as much, if not more profitable for this purpose than a plantation of willows. After being cut down at the commencement of winter, after being frosted, they may be stripped and tied up into bundles of different sizes in the worst weather.

R. FISH.

HOTHOUSE DEPARTMENT.

EXOTIC ORCHIDACEÆ.

PLANTS REQUIRING BLOCKS *(Continued from page 318.)*

Lælia accuminata (Pointed-tipped L.); Guatimala.—Sepals and petals delicate blush colour; the lip is of the same colour with a blotch of rich brownish purple; the flowers are produced on a spike, four or five in number. It is a free-growing desirable species. 15s.

Lælia albida (Whitish L.); Oaxaca.—Sepals and petals white, tinged with yellow; lip of the same colour, with a reddish-purple streak or spot. It has a scent like the primrose; very pretty. 15s.

Lælia anceps (Two-edged L.); Mexico.—A splendid species that ought to be in every collection. Sepals and petals of a rich rosy lilac colour; the lip is of a rich velvety purple outside; the inside is marked with crimson and yellow veins, and has on the broadest part a deep purple spot. The flowers are large, measuring when well grown four inches across. They are produced on long footstalks, gracefully bending with the weight of the flowers. 21s.

Lælia autumnalis (Autumnal-flowering L.); Mexico and Guatimala.—Sepals and petals pale blush, shaded with rose. The lip is nearly white, with a deep rich purple spot at the end. Equally handsome, and in one respect superior, to *L. anceps*, which seldom has more than three flowers on each stem, whilst *L. autumnalis* will, when strongly grown, produce on each flower scape eight or twelve of its splendid flowers. 15s.

Lælia furfuracea (Scurfy-stalked L.); Oaxaca.—Very like *L. autumnalis*, but slenderer in all its parts. A beautiful delicate species, well worth growing. Rather scarce. 42s.

Lælia majalis (May-flowering L.); Oaxaca.—A very handsome dwarf growing plant. It is the *Flor de Maya*, or May-flower, of the natives; and is much esteemed even there. The flowers are produced singly on short footstalks; they are very large, being nearly six inches across. Sepals and petals blush, beautifully spotted and veined with pale purple. The lip is of the same colour, but the spots and veins much more numerous. It is rather difficult to flower, but may be successfully bloomed by growing it upon a log, without moss, in the coolest part of the Mexican house, where it can have a long rest in winter. In the spring, when it begins to grow, syringe it freely till it has completed its annual

growth, which ought to be effected by the end of August; then refrain from syringing by degrees, and keep it dry and cool till March. By this simple treatment it will produce its magnificent flowers in May or June. 21s.

Lælia rubescens (Blushing L.); Mexico.—Sepals and petals cream colour, delicately shaded with pink, tinged with green at the edges; the lip is of the same colour, with a yellow blotch in the centre, and a rich plum coloured one at the base. A very pretty desirable species. 31s. 6d.

Lælia superbiens (Most superb L.); Guatimala. This is indeed a truly magnificent plant. We have in a former volume described the noble plant of this kind in the gardens of the London Horticultural Society, at Chiswick, as it appeared when in bloom last year. Like most Lælias, it is found in the higher altitudes of the western hemisphere, consequently, does not require a high temperature. It will thrive well in a common stove, but will not flower till the pseudo-bulbs acquire a considerable size. Great care must be taken in syringing it, so as not to allow water to lodge in the sheaths of the young growing pseudo-bulbs, or it will be apt to cause them to rot, and thus destroy the growth for that year. The young roots, too, are liable to decay if kept always wet; syringe, therefore, in the morning, and the moisture will be dried up before the evening. Give plenty of air during the day, even in the growing season, and keep the plant dry and cool after the growths are complete in the autumn. It flowers at a time of the year when flowers are most welcome, namely, in winter and early spring. The temperature of Chautla, in the province of Guatimala, averages from 55° to 65° generally The flowers are produced on long stems, in clusters at the end, and frequently number 14 to 16 on each stem. The sepals and petals are rich rosy pink; the lip is light crimson and yellow striped with dark crimson, each flower measuring from four to five inches across. Small plants may be purchased for 42s., but strong flowering ones cannot be had under 105s. On account of its great beauty and easy culture, it ought to be in every collection, however small. Although all the species of this beautiful genus may be grown well on blocks, we have reserved a few that we find grow more finely in pots. These we shall mention and describe hereafter.

CULTURE.—All the species of Lælia do best in the Mexican house. Mr. Bateman says, "being found at a considerable elevation they all thrive best in a moderate temperature, and require to be kept high potted, as by this means the roots are more likely to be retained in a healthy state; during the winter they should be sparingly watered and kept in an almost dormant state." This is sound advice, but we have found the placing of the greater part on logs a much safer plan to preserve the roots in winter. The kind of log we need not dwell upon, which lasts the longest is the best. Use no moss, as it retains too much moisture. The size of the block must be proportioned to the size of the plants. The plants should be suspended from the roof of the house, but not far from the glass: a foot to 18 inches will be a proper distance, excepting when in flower. The stems of some species then rise to such a height as to make it necessary to lower the blocks, which may be easily done by longer or shorter wire hooks, as each plant may require.

T. APPLEBY.

(To be continued.)

FLORISTS' FLOWERS.

TULIPS.—The beds for these must now be attended to. Old ones should have some fresh loam added, and fresh dung at the bottom next the drainage. Look over the roots and remove all decayed ones; separate also the young bulbs and plant them immediately, so as to enable them to make plenty of roots to strengthen the spring growth, and so increase the size of the bulbs, and bring them to such state of maturity as will enable them to flower.

RANUNCULUSES.—The same care must be bestowed upon the beds intended for planting with these flowers; but there is no need of so much hurry. The tulip ought to be planted in the month of November, and, as near as the weather will allow, the 10th day of that month. This date suits all the counties south of Birmingham. Those to the north had better be planted a little earlier. The roots of the ranunculuses should be frequently examined and all insects destroyed, and decaying bulbs removed. For the treatment of the rest of florists' flowers see the preceding numbers of THE COTTAGE GARDENER.

T. APPLEBY.

THE KITCHEN-GARDEN.

MUSHROOM-BEDS make. This is just the season for this kind of work. Use dryish, husky materials. The grand thing is to use such materials as will heat themselves dry, and continue warm the greatest length of time. Beds made with such materials, attended to when required with the finest showery waterings with tepid water, and with due attention to coverings, will continue in bearing a very long time. Let the materials be turned over several times previously to making up the beds; and horse droppings should form the principal part of the materials used, particularly if for boxes and shelves; but for the common ridge beds out of doors, half horse droppings and half dry husky litter, mixed up well together, will form excellent materials for these kinds of beds. The beds should be spawned as soon as the heat is a little on the decline, and covered with a light loamy soil, neither too wet nor too dry, from one and a half inch to two inches thick. It should be watered with a very fine rose waterpot, and covered equally all over, and beat down with the back of a smooth spade; then sprinkled again, and beat down again and again until the whole face of the bed is quite smooth and even. Let the whole dry off a little before it is covered with any thing. The coverings should be very thin at first, so as not to draw up too much heat, &c. Refuse hay is the best material for covering the beds with; but, in the case of out-door beds, thatched hurdles, or the like, would be found useful to throw off the rain.

ASPARAGUS. — Where plenty of strong plants have been prepared for keeping up a regular supply of this vegetable, from the middle of October until the next spring, a preparation should now be made for commencing its gentle forcing; and those who are provided with tank heat, or the means of obtaining hot-water pipe heat, have nothing more to do than to clear out the structure, lime-white its walls, &c., and well furnish it with the requisite quantity of light soil, leaf-mould, or decomposed sweet old tan, the leaf-mould we have long found the best, but the chief point is to secure a well-regulated genial warmth, particularly when the plants are first placed on the bed. Those who have the command of tank or hot-water pipe heating have this essential requisite fully at hand, but those who have entirely to depend on fermenting materials should always give this matter a little consideration, and reflect how they may best make a beginning that will secure a satisfactory ending; and for this purpose great care must be taken not to apply too strong a bottom-heat at first. Such a mode of proceeding being sure to hurry up the crop in an unnatural manner, and produce asparagus of a small and flavourless kind.

The foundation of the hotbed, whether in pit or frame, should be made of a quantity of rubbish, prunings, trimmings, bush faggots, or anything of a similar kind that can be spared; on this a slight hotbed should be placed made with well wrought materials, or what is better, with old half-decayed hotbed linings, upon this place six inches of decayed old tan, leaf-mould, or light earth, on which the plants should be placed as thick together as they can be put, after having been taken up very carefully with all their roots to them, and without being bruised; care should be taken too, that the buds at their crowns are not bruised, or the shoots will appear deformed and rusty; over the crowns of the plants when first placed, about two inches of either of the foregoing materials should be put carefully all over them; a command of bottom-heat at the commencement from 75° to 80° is quite sufficient, increasing it a little by the application of linings in about a fortnight, but the principal aim in applying linings should be to command a surface or interior *atmospheric* heat of from 60° to 65°, instead of the strong burning bottom heat which was formerly aimed at, by leaving flues in the hot-beds and boring holes through them to admit all the possible heat that could be commanded underneath the plants. If the *interior atmosphere* is thus kept warm and genial, there will be no fear but that the *bottom heat* will be sufficient. For this purpose, place at the foundation of the linings some open rubbish or faggots, as recommended for the foundation of the hotbed, hanging over the outside of it any kind of refuse litter to prevent the cold air entering; on this should be placed the fermenting materials for commanding the top or interior heat, which is more in imitation of the sun shining; and by protecting the outside of the lining with thatched hurdles, furze faggots, or faggots made of evergreen prunings, bean, or artichoke stalks, or any kind of handy refuse, and occasionally topping it up, a beautiful uniform heat may be commanded with little trouble or expense for the length of time required. This atmospheric temperature of 60° or 65° should not, however, be applied until the asparagus has fairly started its buds, which may be ascertained by examination, or by observing them making their appearance through the light shallow covering, which should then have three or four inches more added to its surface.

CARDOONS.—A part of the earliest should have a thorough soaking of liquid manure, and when dry the leaves should be tied up round the heart of each plant, and then bandaged with hay or straw bands, and earthed up to blanch. The tube or growing crop should be duly encouraged by surface stirring, and the application of liquid manure.

CAULIFLOWERS.—Those already up should at an early opportunity be pricked out; if mildew prevails in the seed-bed they should be dredged all over with flowers of sulphur whilst damp. Those who intend sowing their cauliflowers at the end of the month should have a little good fermenting material in their mind's eye.

CUCUMBERS should be sown for winter crops in a kindly heat; the plants early pricked into small pots placed close to the glass, and kept well aired to keep them healthy and strong, which will ensure their giving satisfaction when placed in their proper quarters.

KIDNEY BEANS.—The growth of kidney beans should be encouraged in spare pits and grounds where they are up and growing, by having the lights shut close at night, being sprinkled down early on sunny afternoons with tepid water, and then shut up. As melon and cucumber pits and frames become vacant more should be planted in succession. As the nights get colder, add also a little extra heat by linings and slight coverings, at night, if found necessary.

ROUTINE WORK.—*Celery* : earth up ; see last week. *Cabbages* : plant ; let the soil be made rich to receive them. The quarters where the onions are taken off in general come in well for the cabbage crop. Continue *pricking out* all kinds of young plants into nursery-beds three or four inches distant every way from plant to plant, such as *lettuces* of sorts, *cauliflowers*, *endives*, and *cabbage* plants of different kinds. All these things should be brought forward out in the clear open quarters, so as to have good stocky healthy plants to finally plant out, or for planting in frames under walls or other places for winter protection. In preparing these *nursery-beds*, if the weather should be dry, always well water previously to planting, and again after planting : such work should be done in the afternoon. A little shading with a mat the next day, if the sun should be very powerful, is of great importance in this work; and about the third day go over the little nursery-beds with a pointed stick, or something of the kind, and open the earth: this gives new life to them; also remove any decayed leaves, &c. *Sea-kale, asparagus*, and *rhubarb* keep clear from weeds; and remove decayed leaves, which are a great harbour for vermin. *Onions*, take up and dry off, previously to storing away. Any quantity of the August-sown may be transplanted into three or

four feet wide beds, to stand the winter for early summer bulbs, that is to say, May and June, which will be found very useful should the stored crop run short. The beds should be lined out neatly, with just a few crumbs thrown up from the alleys, leaving the beds a little higher than the alleys, which will be all the better. The onions should be planted about seven inches from plant to plant every way, and if planted lengthways, by line, the beds will look neat and tidy through the winter and spring months. *Seeds*, of any kinds, collect as they become ripe; let them be dried off well, and stored away in a dry situation. This is a good season for potting off any quantity of *parsley-roots* for winter protection, as the plants, by being potted now, will become well established before they need any protection at all. The stored away *potatoes* should be looked to, to see that there are no defaulters among them. Apply good soakings of manured water to *Cape* and *other Brocoli* now coming in for use; also to *Cauliflowers* the same.

J. BARNES & T. WEAVER.

MISCELLANEOUS INFORMATION.

OUR VILLAGE WALKS.

By the Authoress of " My Flowers," &c., &c.

WHAT animation the face of the country now again displays ! What a life and stir there is among the crops; and how the village seems deserted during the busy day ! The whole population appears to go forth at the time of harvest : the parents to reap, and the little ones to glean. It is a beautiful sight, and can never lose its interest to an English eye. Although the sounds connected with it are not so joyous as those of the merry hay field, yet the sentiment it awakens is deeper, sweeter, and more thankful. The harvest is emphatically the provision of bread. The sweet household loaf of the British farmer, the crust of the honest, valuable labourer, and the delicate roll that is placed on the table of the palace, are all stored up in those rich, golden sheaves that are heaped together in the stack-yard and the barn. Should not this give our corn-fields—our sun-burnt reapers—and all the busy operations of the farm, a powerful interest in our eyes ? Should they not raise our hearts, above all, to the " Lord of the harvest," to Him who satisfies " the poor with bread ; " without whose blessing the fields could not " yield their increase ; " without whose mercy no man could gather it in !

I frequently return from a late evening walk through a stack-yard close to my own home ; and occasionally during harvest time the important work proceeds long after the labouring hour. I have stood to enjoy the scene when a bright moon has been lighting the earth : the yard full of men, and horses, and waggons—the farmer on the rick, heading the operations,—all busy, but steady, and silent as the hour, and scarcely a sound heard but the rustling of the sheaves as they were thrown up, and the rumble of approaching wheels with another load. Nothing could be more calm and beautiful than the dark blue sky, with its sparkling stars and large resplendent moon—or more full of stirring interest than the earthly scene beneath it.

I am at this moment admiring a picture of autumnal beauty which few sights can exceed. As I glance through the window I see on the one hand a noble wheat-rick standing quietly upon the newly cleared stubble, all safe and well ; and near it stretches a sheepfold upon the rich after-grass, where the flock are banquetting. The tinkle of the sheep-bell sounds sweetly and peacefully ; and all is still, while the shepherd is busily assisting in the harvest. In the distance, through the groups of trees, harvest fields every where appear, and for the next few days there will be little rest either for man or horse.

On the other hand, there is an oat-field in full activity; the waggon loading—men and women busily at work—the fore-horse waiting to be hooked on when the load is completed—

and the empty waggon returning from the farm, and rattling lightly over the stony road. A little beyond, the eye catches a large portion of allotment ground, with its long strips of green and gold ; but this year the gold prevails. The donkey carts are all at work : the cottagers are as busy with their little harvest as the farmer with his fields and teams ; and it is a more interesting sight too, and comes home even more closely to our feelings. It is delightful to see and hear the contentment with which the poor man views his crops. Very seldom does a murmur escape his lips, even when the depredations of the mischievous rabbits rob him of half his gain ; but when the Almighty Hand " presses him sore " his patience and submission beneath the stroke teaches a wholesome lesson to his richer neighbour.

I like to see the gleaners returning home in the evening, with their long trailing treasure, and the little children each with its tiny handful—all burnt brown, wearied, and sleepy ; and I have been deeply distressed at the cruelty—I may say the ungodliness—of farmers, who actually *raked the stubbles* before the poor were permitted to begin. It happened, I rejoice to say, but in one season, as far as I have ever heard ; but then it was done in more instances than one ; and it seemed to me as if a judgment must fall upon the head of him who did it—for was it not robbing the poor ? The Lord himself has said, " And when ye reap the harvest of your land, thou shalt not wholly reap the corners of thy field, neither shalt thou gather the gleanings of thy harvest." Let the farmers ponder upon this ; for who among the people of our land leaves the *corners of his field* for the poor ?

The rapidly passing, but heavy showers of the last month have been continually beautified by rainbows. Sometimes a perfect arch appeared, sometimes only broken fragments, and sometimes a second bow of fainter hue appeared for an instant by the side of its companion. It is always a matter of surprise to me, that professing Christians—those who believe the Word of God and study it—should be so indifferent as they are to this most beautiful, most heart-affecting appearance in the sky. My own apathy astonishes and confounds me. We know that the Father of Spirits created all things—the glorious sun, the moon, the stars, the thunder cloud, the darting lightning, are all made, sustained, impelled by Him, and all are " good " and beautiful; but in the bright resplendent bow there is a " token " that none other of God's works possesses : " I do set my bow in the cloud, and it shall be for a token of a covenant between me and the earth. And it shall come to pass, when I bring a cloud over the earth, that the bow shall be seen in the cloud;

and I will remember my covenant, which is between me and you, and every living creature of all flesh; and the waters shall no more become a flood, to destroy all flesh."

When we see the bow in the cloud, we are reminded of a cheering and faithful promise; we know that He "will look upon it," and remember His covenant; and it ought to be to the Christian's heart an object of the deepest and sweetest interest. It should remind us, too, of the *hope* that cheers and supports the people of God, in every age and clime, under the many darkenings of their earthly pilgrimage. There is a bow in every cloud that overshadows us as *Christians*. The hand of the Lord sends us a "token" under every dispensation, that He looks upon us and remembers us for the sake of Him who bought us "with a price," and that the troubles and trials of life shall not be suffered to overwhelm us. There is, too, "a rainbow round about the throne, like unto an emerald," the throne upon which sitteth Him who liveth for ever! How closely does the earthly sign connect us with the heavenly vision, and how full of deep scriptural interest is the sight we so often see! yet how little do we consider it, beyond its beauty, and how dead are we to its spiritual voice!

We often watch the dark threatening storm-clouds spreading themselves above the horizon, throwing the tall trees brightly and pointedly forward; we mark the increasing blackness, and expect every moment to see the flash, or hear the distant roll of the storm—but as we gaze, the graceful glittering rainbow spans the earth, and speaks volumes at once to the heart. Let us ever remember, that God Himself has set " the bow in the cloud."

A CONSULTATION ON BEE-KEEPING.
(Continued from page 374.)

The cast in the straw hive I have been and am feeding as above, and on the 8th of August it weighed, exclusive of board and hive, 8½ ℔. I have added to it on the 23rd inst. the bees from a colt. Can I do anything more to preserve it? (*Only feed it.*)

I have, as you know, made inquiry relative to the best way of preserving, in an empty hive, the bees that would be destroyed by my cottage neighbours, and finding that if I waited for the September Calendar I should not obtain bees, as they were fast taking them up hereabout, I spoke to my old cottage friend, who said, "I am taking up three hives, one of which that has not swarmed I am going to drive into a hive full only of comb; the bees from the other two you are quite welcome to; they are of no use to me, and I should only burn them, poor things." On the 8th inst. we drove the bees from a hive that had not swarmed into an empty hive; on the following evening we drove another, that had swarmed and cast, into another empty hive—we had not the courage of " The Country Curate," to drive the two into one hive. On the 9th, we turned the last driven bees upon a cloth, and placing the first driven bees over them, they all ascended, and were placed the next morning upon their stand. They have had food every night (3 ℔ of sugar, 1½ ℔ of honey, 1 quart of water, boiled two minutes), one pint at a time. I have placed them out, and adopted the shade Mr. Taylor recommends. I fancy, however, it is too cold a covering, as I have found several bees dead in the feeder on several frosty mornings. In this entire operation, including what may have been killed in fighting, I do not think more than 200 were lost. The conquered queen we have searched for but in vain. The heat of this hive is greater than any of my three others that are furnished with thermometers. Should these bees have food in the day? (*Yes, if given at the top of the hive, but not otherwise.*) And ought the four-inch entrance to be now diminished? (*Narrow the entrance.*) If I succeed in preserving them, I propose working them in the way recommended by Mr. Taylor, page 37. They have already eaten ten quarts. Three gallons, as named by "The Country Curate," will not, I think, be enough. How much longer should they be fed? (*Till they have a store of 20℔.*) I was greatly delighted to find, on removing, the 16th day, the window shutter, to see not only comb but honey within it.

Being offered the bees from an old stock, and also from a colt that was to be taken up last week, about a mile distant, I obtained the assistance of my old friend, who, wedded to his experience of 40 years, was very doubtful, after the result he had witnessed of the transfer of No. 1, of the success of

the experiment by *fuming*. Determined, if possible, that it should succeed, I procured everything requisite beforehand: a copper lamp brazed—a small light tub—12 inches across and five deep, with a three-inch rim on a level with the top, and a sheet of zinc for its cover. We introduced a considerable quantity of smoke into the hive, where it stood, which caused a great uproar at first; after a few minutes' tapping of the hive a deep silence prevailed. My old friend removed the hive, and found, to his astonishment, nearly all the bees lying on the floor-board—a very awkward one, being the immovable stump of a tree; we got them off, as well as we could, into the tub, fixed the pierced zinc cover to it, and conveyed them one mile. When at home we rubbed over the zinc a considerable quantity of sugared ale, which seemed to quiet their restlessness for a time; then lifted No. 1 (Neighbour's cottage hive) and placed it on the tub, the sheet of zinc was then withdrawn, and they were left for the night, air being given them through one of the holes at the top. At five o'clock the next morning we removed the hive to its old floor-board, and found only 137 bees in the tub; these we took for dead, but many I think would have recovered had they been placed in the sun, as I have since discovered. My aged friend was amazed, and promises never again to " burn his bees, since I have made known to him a plan which he is now convinced will answer." He has also been much pleased with the plan of feeding at top, which I induced him to adopt by giving him a feeder, and, after his 40 years experience, he confesses he has " much to learn in bee-keeping." The hive, No. 1, thus augmented, is doing well; I have been and am still feeding it. We have not found her conquered majesty. The following evening I took the bees from the colt in the same way, and happily succeeded in adding them to the cast before named. Only 80 bees were found dead in the tub, 30 apparently revived on being placed in the sun. The conquered queen in this case, also, we have not been able to find, although we have looked for her most sedulously, being very anxious to compare her with the worker bee.

I have now what I may call six stocks, all doing well; that they should all continue to do so is perhaps more than I ought to expect. (*Not at all, if your attentive treatment continues.*) Their treatment has afforded me numerous pleasures, all introduced to me by your interesting periodical, and I therefore cannot allow myself to omit thanking you for the great kindness you have manifested in answering my many inquiries.

P.S.—It just occurs to me to ask, whether I might with advantage, if bees could be procured, add them to the cast in Taylor's hive. (*Yes, certainly.*) I have now saved the bees from four hives, and trust in some degree atoned for the destruction of such numbers in my first transfer.—*Z.*

ENGLISH CAGE BIRDS.
THE LESSER WHITETHROAT.

INSESSORES DENTIROSTRES. SYLVIADÆ INSECTIVORÆ.

Sylvia sylviella; Motacilla sylviella; Curruca sylviella; Curruca garrula; Sylvia curruca; Ficadula garrula: Garrulous Fauvet; Brake Warbler; Babbling Warbler; White-breasted Warbler; Babillard.

THIS is a very lively and elegant little bird, easily known by its peculiar call-note, which it utters continually, and seldom ends its song without it; it is, in fact, an everlasting chatterer. It is most frequently found in woody districts; its food consisting of insects, their larva, and small fruits. It is as easily kept in confinement as its congeners, feeding on the same food and, in a large aviary, out of the same dish. It is also very readily reared from the nest, by adopting the means resorted to as in that of the blackcap, &c., as previously directed.   W. RAYNER.

[This species is very closely allied to the whitethroat noticed in our last number, but is not so common. Its chief apparent difference is, that besides the throat, the breast and belly are also of a purer white, the last named part being tinged with red, and the feet dark bluish grey. The following is the best description of it, and is given by Mr. Blyth, in his excellent edition of *White's Selborne*, of which a new edition is just published:—]

"It is an elegant little bird, arriving generally towards the close of the month of April, and departing in September, though a few stragglers are often met with for some weeks afterwards. This species has most erroneously been described to keep wholly to the closest underwood, whereas it passes its time chiefly upon trees, often at a considerable height from the ground, and is nowhere found but in their immediate vicinity. It is a bird little known, considering its abundance, and also the familiarity of its habits, the general character of its haunts much resembling those of its musical congener the blackcap. It is particularly common about little cottage gardens, and indeed everywhere affects gardens and neighbourhoods, often building in ornamental shrubs close to the house. It is also plentiful about tall and thick hawthorn hedges, but is never found (like the whitethroat) in open and exposed places, nor does it ever mount singing into the air (like that species), though its notes may be occasionally heard, as it flutters, in a vacillating manner, from tree to tree. Its song is very low and weak, and may be easily recognised by the frequent recurrence of a note like *sip, sip, sip*; but, after warbling in this strain continuously for a few seconds, it always terminates with a loud and shrill shivering cry, which is monotonous and unpleasing, though analogous to the lively whistle of the blackcap. Not unfrequently it emits this cry without any previous warble, and it utters also the same *check* as its congeners, and sometimes also a peculiar inward rolling note, which it has in common with the furzelin, or Dartford warbler, to which species it is allied (and immediately connected by means of an exotic congener), and which at least in confinement it considerably resembles in its manners, both these little birds sometimes climbing up the wires of their cage in a manner that is not observable in the other fauvets. An individual I formerly kept in captivity, in a spacious cage, was exceedingly active in its habits, sometimes darting about so rapidly that the eye could scarcely follow; and it used frequently, and many times in succession, to perform quick somersets in the air, throwing itself over backwards, a habit which I have noticed in others of the same species in a captive state. It is a determined fruit-eater in the season, hardly inferior in this respect to the blackcap, and in the spring is very expert in the capture of winged insects, though it never leaves its perch in order to seize them, but snaps at them the moment they are within reach. It also feeds a good deal, like the pettychaps genus, upon small caterpillars, and like them is a great destroyer of aphides. It also resembles them in the extreme pugnacity of its disposition, which I have observed, not only in confinement, but in the wild state, a quality in which it much differs from its British congeners. The male and female are quite alike in plumage, and some of the older individuals have the irides of a beautiful and conspicuous pearly white, which adds much to the handsomeness of their appearance; many have also a delicate blush on their under parts, which is likewise frequently observable in the male whitethroat. The nest is smaller than that of the last-mentioned species, and is always lined with fibrous rootlets; the eggs, four or five in number, are also of less size than those of that bird, but have the markings more defined, and larger.

"The sexes are very much alike; and, for the information of those who may wish to keep one in confinement, I may state, that the only difference I could ever perceive between them, consisted in the more rufous tint of the under surface of the wing in the cock bird. Its melody resembles somewhat the continuous note of the blackcap, but is softer, much deeper, and more flute-like in its tone, approaching to the mellifluous warble of the blackbird. As it proceeds, it increases gradually in spirit and loudness, and often ends with a rich and dulcet melodious flourish, though never so clear and loud as the lively, spirit-stirring music of its congener the blackcap. I have noticed it to sing with great spirit against a nightingale, determined not to be outdone; and indeed the peculiar sweetness of its lay must ever render it a prime favourite with those who love to listen to the wild music of the groves. Its habits are exactly similar to those of the blackcap, which it also resembles in its nidification; but differs in being one of the latest to arrive of all our summer birds of passage, whence probably it is, generally speaking, so little known. It is seldom heard much before the beginning of May, but does not, as has been said, depart earlier than its congeners. Its eggs are of a grayer tinge than those of the blackcap."

WINTERING BEES.

To save trouble, and for the sake of greater publicity, we now print the table which "A Country Curate" wishes to have filled up by those who try the desired and desirable experiment of burying one or more hives this winter. The hives to be buried should be bound round with straw, somewhat thickly; and they should be plastered down with clay or cement to a bottom-board—if of stone, so much the better,—saving only the small hole, wherein the tube is inserted.

What sort of Hives buried, whether swarms, casts, or old stocks, or preserved bees.	If preserved bees, was any comb or food allowed to them.	Date of interment.	Whether in earth, or in a shed or outhouse, on a stone, and under leaves.	State of weather when interred.	Probable age of weather Queen.	Estimated weight of contents of hives at time of interment.	Estimated weight of contents when disinterred.	At what time were the hives disinterred.	State of hives on disinterring disinterred.	What consumption Observations of food.	Further

N.B.—It is requested that a paper copied from this be forwarded to the Editor of THE COTTAGE GARDENER, some time in the interval between the 1st and 10th of April in the ensuing spring. And it is recommended as *the safest plan*, that no hive be interred save in *cold* (and, if possible, *frosty*) weather, either very early in the morning or *late at night*, when the bees will be found in a half-torpid state, and close huddled up together. They should be handled gently, so as not to be disturbed. A metal tube of a ½ or ⅜ inch bore should certainly be applied either to the entrance or top of the hive (whether buried or stored in leaves), communicating with the open air above.

NATIVE WILD FLOWERS.

September.

THE falling leaves that rustle in our path tell of the rapid approach of winter; and the bare harvest fields and almost flowerless meadows of September present few attractions to the botanist. Still, however, some of the mountain flowers are fresh and lovely—such as the glowing purple heather and the golden Rod (*Solidago Virgaurea*), both of which have been in blossom for several months; the latter, although rare in England, is a common plant in some of the Highland districts of Scotland.

One of the most conspicuous plants in pasture lands, and by hedgerows and waysides, at the present time, is the Ragwort (*Senecio Jacobæa*), which has proved itself highly prejudicial to the farmer on account of its drain-obstructing propensities, and thus draws our attention to a subject of considerable importance to the cottage gardener. Draining has now established itself as one of the most profitable and essential departments of agricultural as well as horticultural improvement, and whatever tends to affect its success is of importance to the cultivator. We will, therefore, venture a few remarks on the obstruction of drainage by those weeds and wild flowers which make their unwelcome appearance on the farm and in the garden, and injure the legitimate crops of the soil. Such obstructions are not now noticed for the first time in agricultural history, but with the increase of draining they have recently become quite alarming in extent, and in many cases threaten to nullify the exertions and improvements of the diligent cultivator, and, indeed, in many instances to lessen the inducement to judicious improvement. The plants hitherto observed, whose roots form the obstructions referred to, are chiefly the following:—The elm, poplar, willow, ash, and larch trees; the gooseberry; the polygonum amphibium, field horsetail, docks, thistles, and the ragwort to which we have already referred, which in one remarkable instance, recorded on the authority of Dr. Neill, had insinuated its roots into a drain by a very small orifice, and completely filled it up for about 20 ft. of its length! It would appear from the limited number of facts which have come before us, that the evil is of much more ready occurrence in wet heavy soils, with moist climate (where drainage is most wanted), than in soils of a lighter and drier nature. That such is the case is the more unfortunate for the farmer; but not at all to be wondered at when we consider that those semi-aquatic plants most likely to insinuate their roots into drains and seek nourishment there, are the very plants which thrive in and form the field-pests of such lands. And the equally cogent reason is not to be lost sight of, that drains laid in such wet and heavy lands are, in very many cases, kept running with water, more or less, throughout the entire year; thus forming a continued support and encouragement for the extension of the drain infesting roots, instead of allowing them to be dried up, or their growth arrested, in the dry season, as would be the case in a light sandy soil.

That drainage is much disturbed by the roots of the legitimate crops of the land, we do not think to be the case, although instances may occur, more especially where the drains have not been placed at a sufficient depth, and this will form a reason for placing drains beyond the mere depth of the plough, even where subsoil ploughing has not attained to its proper rank, as an essential element of cultivation. The roots to be mainly feared are those of the weeds which naturally infest the soil; and the timeous and systematic destruction of these has now become more than ever of the first importance. Our fields, in general, present a less weedy aspect than they did some twenty years ago; but it is a fact, undeniable, though lamentable, that attention to the eradication of such cumberers of the soil has not increased in an equal ratio with improved cultivation. It is no common thing to see a good crop of weeds on a farm where cultivation is otherwise unexceptionable, and we could point out fields wholly crimsoned with poppies, and whitened with ox-eye flowers. Weeds of a *perennial* kind are those

to be mostly feared, and special care should be bestowed on the eradication of such semi-aquatics as horsetails, polygonums, tussilago, &c., which form excessively troublesome, almost *ineradicable*, weeds in some parts of the country. Perhaps no argument more powerful than the occurrences to which we refer, has yet appeared in condemnation of the absurd practice which obtains, in some districts, of leaving large margins of the fields for the growth of perennial weeds. These, with the entire host of open ditches, hedge banks, and marsh wastes, will now surely be all but abolished, and their remnants only left in the rudest wilds of Ireland, to be pointed out to students of agricultural history as the barbarous practices of a barbarous age. There are two points of considerable importance to the farmer as well as to the landed proprietor, which have been long under consideration, and which have formed the subjects of many an able argument, both *pro* and *con*. We refer to the question of the advantages and disadvantages of hedges as field enclosures, and of hedge row trees; and upon these questions, we think, the discoveries of drain obstructions may bear heavily. We are not aware of its having been shown by actual observation that the roots of hawthorn and other hedging plants are amongst the drain pests; but, reasoning from analogy, we are entitled to entertain the provisional supposition that such is the case; and here, then, is a fruitful source of drain obstructions.

According to facts already shown respecting other plants, it is quite reasonable to conclude, that the roots proceeding from a hedge-row are capable of completely obstructing the drains on either side of the hedge to an extent of 20 ft. throughout its entire length. Such would be the case were the radical powers of hawthorn similar to those of the ragwort; and it is more probable that they will be much greater, the former being the more permanent of the two. If such facts hold good with regard to hedges, what must be the case with large hedge-row trees? Without any breach of probability we may safely say, that where an ordinary sized field is surrounded with hedge-row trees, the roots of the latter may be capable of completely filling up and obstructing the drains throughout the entire length and breadth of the field (unless checked by deep trenchings, or otherwise), besides extending considerably to adjoining fields. The roots of forest trees have, in many instances, been found to extend to astonishingly great distances in the soil; and when they enter a drain there is no saying how far they may go. We should be sorry to think that the safety of drains should require the removal of many of the beautiful forest trees which, scattered here and there, add shelter and picturesque beauty to the cultivated land of rich agricultural districts where these seem to be required; but if the interests of agriculture demand it, then, of course, our wishes give way. We have regretted the loss of many an old hawthorn hedge, aged tree, and piece of waste headland; but the consideration of rural improvement risen with us above all other claims; and, beautiful as may be a bramble brake, we rank not amongst those who would regret to see it cleared away to give place to a cottage garden or a field of golden grain.

    (To be continued.)   G. W. LAWSON, F.B.S.

TO CORRESPONDENTS.

INSECTS ON VINE LEAVES (*B. Watson*).—They are the *thrips*, and miserably are the leaves affected. Your only remedy now is to fumigate daily with tobacco smoke, in the hope of destroying the pest. We should in the autumn clean out the vinery thoroughly, and lime-wash it with some flowers of sulphur mixed with the lime. In the spring we should scrape off all the loose bark, and similarly paint the entire vine, stems and shoots. Your border must be poor, if the leaf sent is an average size. Put some mulch upon it at once as you propose, and in the spring point in with a fork some rich compost. Keep your air moister during the forcing season; dry air promotes the thrips. Have you not allowed the vine to bear too heavy crops?

STORING WALNUTS (*Zero*).—These will not bear storing away in the green husks the same as filberts. They sprout, and acquire a most acrid flavour. We are eating filberts now which have been kept exactly a year in their husks in a damp cellar, without any addition, and they are nearly as juicy as those now gathering. Take your walnuts from their green coats, wipe them dry, put them in a jar between layers of sand, so that no two walnuts touch, and keep them in a cool damp cellar. When required for use, soak them for an hour in warm water, changing it as it cools. They will eat crisp, and will peel nearly as easily as fresh ones.

FOREST TREES (*A. T. B.*).—These will not flourish with a less depth of soil than two feet. On such light elevated soil as yours, we should not attempt to grow any other trees than birch and larch. Some of the new conifers, such as the Deodar cedar, would also suit, and this is a very desirable tree. Your soil would do for a nursery of such trees, we think; but we speak doubtingly when you say it is "a clayey loam"—this can hardly be "lying high" and on "a subsoil of shale." Your garden should have eighteen inches depth of soil. *Loudon's Arboretum Britannicum,* and his edition of *Repton's Landscape Gardening,* are books which would suit. No one ever acquired a just taste for landscape gardening by reading. A landscape gardener is born so, not made by education.

WALLS OF SLATES (*W. H.*).—We have heard of, but never seen, walls made of large thick slates, let into wooden uprights, and well jointed together. The trees upon them were trained to iron netting or other trellis put close to the slates. Thus constructed, with a bank of earth behind, and a coping projecting six inches on each side, we think that a very superior wall for fruit-trees would be obtained. There would be no friction of the young wood, if it were fastened to the wire trellis as we do with narrow slips of very thin lead, which can be twisted tightly with the greatest facility. In such a wall greater heat might be accumulated if shades were used at night to prevent radiation; there would be no nail holes to harbour insects; and it would be very neat. There would not be too much heat accumulated, as we can testify from having a wall painted black facing the south.

POTATOES (*Percontator*).—Do not manure for them at all, or, at the most, give a top dressing of soot and salt just previously to digging for planting. We recommend *Martin's Early Seedling,* the *Red Ash-leaved Kidney,* and *Rylott's Flour Ball*; they are the three best varieties we ever grew. A peck will hold about 400 small tubers sufficiently large for planting, therefore it is easy for you to calculate the quantity you will require after you have determined at what distances you will plant.

PLAN FOR FLOWER GARDEN (*M. B. R.*).—We invariably must decline to furnish such plans. So much depends upon situation, associations, and peculiarity of taste, to say nothing of soil, cultivation, &c., that though we might perchance give satisfaction the chances are infinitely in favour of our failing to do so.

TRELLIS FOR FRONT OF HOUSE (*Ibid.*).—We prefer galvanized iron wire netting to any other: it is so much easier for training against, is so much more durable, and may be painted so as to be invisible.

CLUB-ROOTED SAVOYS, &c. (*W. W. H.*).—For pouring over your soil *previously* to digging use the ammoniacal gas liquor as strong as you can obtain it.

FOREST-TREE SEEDS (*T. M.*).—Autumn is the best season for sowing; sow thickly, in drills a foot apart, and with a path between every five rows. The outer *leaves of Cabbages* flag more than the inner leaves, because the evaporation from them is greater; and when they become thus relaxed their greater length acts as a lever to weigh them down. The *Grubs* you enclose are the larvæ of the Daddy-long-legs (*Tipula oleracea*), at least we think so; but the specimens were crushed. Water your cabbage plants two or three times with diluted ammoniacal gas liquor.

BOOK ON BIRDS (*G. D.*).—Macgillivray's *British Birds* will suit you. It gives all the land birds. Yarrell's work includes water birds, but is dearer.

HOTHOUSE (*C——, Hull*).—You will have seen what Mr. Errington said at page 364, and we agree with him. Use rough glass both for your vinery and forcing-house.

PASTING-DOWN PRESERVES.—Will "*A. Alora*" answer these queries; we have several of them. "What we want to know is whether the pasted paper is to be placed *on the preserve,* or stretched *over the edges of the jar*; and if lying on the preserve whether the pasted side of the paper is to be next the preserve?"—*T. S. P., &c.*

KIND OF IRIS (*M. J. C.*).—You have the seeds and bulbs of "a white kind of Iris." They are a variety either of the *Iris Xiphium* or *I. Xiphioides.* Sow the seeds now, and put in the bulbs immediately three inches deep, in a light rich border; the seedlings will flower the third season and produce blue, and yellow, and brown flowers, notwithstanding they were gathered from a white one.

HYACINTHS (*S. Y. R.*).—You ask for the names of ten that will look well together in a glass bowl, the price not to exceed one shilling each. *Bruidkloeed,* double rose, 8d. *La belle Alliance,* single, deep red, 1s. *Aringaris,* double, light blue, 6d. *Lawrens Koster,* double, dark blue, 1s. 6d. *La grand Vedette,* single, blue. *La Tour d'Auvergne,* pure double white, 1s. 6d. *Vuinquer,* single, white, 8d. *Victoria regina,* single, white, 1s. *L'Or du Perou,* double, yellow, 3s. *Heroine,* bright citron, single, 1s.

EARWIGS (*Ibid.*).—Any "sticky composition" to put round Dahlia stems for preventing the ascent of earwigs, is an imposition, for they have wings. The mode of treating *potatoes,* adopted by your brother in Essex, is not new. He had better take them up and store them *strictly* as we have directed.

DEPRIVING BEES (*W. X. W.*).—You say:—"I have two hives, a first and second swarm, both strong and doing well, standing side by side, which I will call A and B. Now, I wish to unite these and get the produce from one hive. Now, I want to know if it would answer to drive, first, A into an empty hive, and then drive B into the same hive with A, and then drive the *united* A and B into one of the stored hives, either belonging to A or B. I think this would be better than having artificial feeding, and I suppose that this might be done safely any time this month, September." Feeding may be done with the least possible trouble, if done at the top

of the hive, giving about 2 lbs. of food at a time, and which may be done daily until each hive contains 20 lbs.; or you may drive in the way you propose, but then you will have but one, instead of two stocks, for which the little honey thus obtained will be a very inadequate compensation.

ALWAYS GAY (*Incognita*).—Your excellent communication shall appear next week.

NAME OF PLANT (*M. A. P., Staffordshire*).—It would save much trouble if all correspondents would send their specimens in as good order as this came to hand. Your plant is the common hemp, *Cannabis sativa.* Your plant is the female plant; they are diœcious plants. Do you not keep a bird and feed it with hemp-seed?

CALYSTEGIA PUBESCENS (*T. M. W.*).—It will grow well in good garden ground, for it is not at all particular about soil, but it does not like growing in a pot; only very clever gardeners can do anything with it in pots. There is no fear that any degree of cold we experience in England will injure it, that is, the roots, for, like our native bindweeds, it dies down to the roots every year. However, in case you should lose it this winter, if planted out now, from some one dressing the garden and digging it out, the best plan is to bury it, pot and all, in some safe corner of a border until your garden is put in order next spring, and then to turn it out of the pot, and, meantime, you can think where you would like to see it best. No one, we think, has ever said in our pages anything so erroneous as that *seedling petunias* never produce fine flowers! Why, raising seedlings is the only mode of improving them!

FLOWER-BED PLAN (*Elise*).—Very good, indeed, for the size; true in principle, and easy to work. You need not have the points of the grass diamond in the centre so sharp as they are now. It is not at all necessary, or even in good taste, when a flower-garden like yours is placed on gravel, that all parts of the gravel should be of the same width. The gravel forms the ground colour of such a garden, and that need not be laid out in regular stripes as walks any more than the ground colour of a dress, although in very regular symmetrical figures it cannot well be otherwise. You need not, therefore, be afraid of having a little more breadth of gravel opposite the corner of the diamond bed, and no other figure would answer better.

UNITING HIVES (*Z*).—Our correspondent writes thus (Aug. 31):—"It may be satisfactory to you to know the result of the experiment I tried at the suggestion of "A Country Curate." The two colonies of bees which were placed in an empty hive this day three weeks, now weigh exactly twenty-two pounds. I have made a little variation from the kind of food recommended. The beer and wine I wholly omitted, and substituted water; and finding, after feeding with two or three quarts, that the brown sugar caused the feeder to become very foul, I have since used white, and they have used nearly 11 quarts (three pounds of loaf-sugar, one and a half pound of honey, one quart of water, boiled two minutes, this makes rather more than two quarts). I have given them about one pint a day. The heat of this hive I observe is 12° hotter than three of my other hives. Ought they to be fed longer? (*Not if they weigh twenty-two pounds without the hive.*) I intend working them on Mr. Taylor's plan (p 23 and 27) next summer, with his shade, but now I have it on, I am at a loss to know how a *super* can be removed, as it is to stand outside the inner rim. (*No, the super, be it small hive or glass, must stand inside the rim; the upper hive is intended only as a cover to the super.*) I ought, perhaps, to remark that the weather has, on the whole, been favourable, and they have had the advantage of a good bed of mignonette. When should these plants, recommended for bees, be set or sown:—crocus, hepatica, helleborus niger, tussilago petasites, salvia nemorosa, origanum humile, anacampseros populifolia. (*Any time this autumn*).

NAME OF ROSE (*W. W. B.*).—We think your rose must be *Renoncule pourpre,* more frequently called *Mrs. Wood.* If so, it is a Hybrid moss, red, shaded with purple, large, and double. Answer to your other query next week,

HAIR-DYE (*J. W. C., Manchester*).—Can any of our readers furnish us with one? For our part, we have ceased to notice these splashings by time as he passes us; but, if we did, we should try the French Pomatum, called *Pommade de la jeunesse.* It is made by mixing thoroughly a small quantity of pearl white (sub-nitrate of bismuth), with any common pomatum, and brushing a little daily into the hair. It is said to make the hair dark, and certainly would do no harm. Dr. Willich, who was opposed to all cosmetical applications to the hair, says, that the hair will assume a darker colour by having it cut close, and passing a leaden comb through it every morning and evening.

SHEEP-SKIN MATS (*A Grateful Subscriber*).—Take a spoonful of alum, and two of saltpetre, pulverise and mix well together; after sprinkling the powder on the flesh side of the skin, lay the two flesh sides together (leaving the wool outside), and fold up as tight as you can and hang in a dry place. In two or three days (as soon as it is dry) take it down and scrape it with a blunt knife till clean and supple: this completes the process. Other skins which you desire to cure with the fur or hair on may be treated in the same way. To dye them buff colour, wash the wool thoroughly with soap and water; rinse out all the soap, and then let them soak for some days, until the dye is imparted, in a cool liquor, made by boiling one pound of logwood chips and madder in each gallon of water.

LONDON: Printed by HARRY WOOLDRIDGE, Winchester High-street, in the Parish of Saint Mary Kalendar; and Published by WILLIAM SOMERVILLE ORR, at the Office, No. 2, Amen Corner, in the Parish of Christ Church, City of London.—September 19th, 1850.

WEEKLY CALENDAR.

M D	W D	SEPT. 26—OCT. 2, 1850.	Weather near London in 1849.		Sun Rises.	Sun Sets.	Moon R. & S.	Moon's Age.	Clock bef. Sun.	Day of Year.
26	Tu	St. Cyprian. Elm leaves orange.	T. 67°—55°.	E. Fine.	54 a. 5	49 a. 5	6 37	20	8 38	269
27	F	Hawthorn leaves tawny yellow.	T. 70°—51°.	E. Fine.	55	47	9 18	21	8 58	270
28	S		T. 66°—51°.	S.W. Rain.	57	44	10 7	☾	9 18	271
29	Sun	16 Sun. Aft. Trinity. Michaelmas Day.	T. 66°—55°.	S.W. Rain.	59	42	11 8	23	9 38	272
30	M	St. Jerome.	T. 62°—59°.	S.W. Rain.	60	40	morn.	24	9 57	273
1	Tu	Hornbeam leaves yellow. Remigius.	T. 57°—48°.	N.E. Rain.	vi	v	0 16	25	10 17	274
2	W	Walnut leaves fall.	T. 55°—38°.	N.E. Rain.	4	35	1 32	26	10 36	275

On the 1st of October, in the year 1819, and in the 86th year of his age, died one of the best of practical gardeners—WILLIAM SPEECHLEY. His name is associated with the superior cultivation of the pine-apple and the grape vine, and with no more than justice, because those who know the volume he wrote upon the proper modes of growing them, and who also know the essays upon the same plants that had been published previously, will readily appreciate how much the gardening world were indebted to him. The fruit of the pine-apple had been made known in England in 1657; for an embassage returning from China, in that year, appears to have brought pine-apples thence as a present to Oliver Cromwell. John Nieuhoff, who was secretary to the embassy, describes the fruit very correctly; and Evelyn, in his "Diary," under the date of 9th August, 1661, says, "I first saw the famous Queen pine brought from Barbadoes, and presented to his Majesty (Charles II.); but the first that were ever seen in England were those sent to Cromwell four years since." It may be that from the crowns of this, and of others mentioned by Evelyn as sent to the king from the West Indies in 1669, that Mr. John Rose, his Majesty's gardener, succeeded in raising a fruit of the pine-apple in this country. We say it may be, because there is a portrait in oil colours of Rose, at Kensington Palace, representing him giving a pine-apple to Charles II. Rose was then gardener to the Duchess of Cleveland, and the garden in which the present is being made was that at her Grace's seat, Downey Court, Buckinghamshire. If Rose was thus successful, the culture of the pine-apple soon became a lost art; and it was not until 1718 that it was really established in this country by Mr. H. Telende, gardener to Sir Matthew Decker, at Richmond, in Surrey. In 1767, John Giles, at one time gardener to Lady Boyd, at Lewisham, in Kent, and afterwards foreman to Messrs. Russell, nurserymen in that village, published "Ananas, or a Treatise on the Pine-apple;" and in 1769 appeared another on the same subject, entitled, "A Treatise on the Ananas or Pine-apple," the author of which was Mr. Adam Taylor, gardener to J. Sutton, Esq. of New York, near Devizes. He claims for himself the merit of being the first who brought the fruit to an improved size and excellence without the aid of fire heat. A coloured engraving of the pine-apple is prefixed to the volume; and if this be the improved size then attained its predecessors must have been small indeed, for it is only six pips high. That this was so we may conclude from the drawing of a pine-apple, published in 1733 by a gardener at Kensington named Furber, and this is only four pips in height.

In 1779 appeared Mr. Speechley's *Treatise on the Culture of the Pine-apple*, and is so far superior in every respect to the two preceding publications, that until within these few years it was the best guide to which the amateur could refer, and certainly led the way to the improved pine culture now practised. The same may be said of his work on the grape vine. Here, as in the case of the pine-apple, the leader was John Rose, gardener to Charles II., for he published his "English Vineyard Vindicated," in 1675. It is dedicated to the "merry monarch;" and in the dedication Rose says, "I know your Majesty can have no great opinion of our English wines as hitherto they have been ordered, but it is not altogether from defect of the climate, at least not in all places; and that if my directions be followed that precious liquor may once again recover its just estimation, though the product of your Majesty's dominions." Switzer, in his "Practical Fruit Gardener," published in 1724, incorporates the chief part of Rose's work already noticed, but adds much valuable information from his own practice and knowledge. He says that it is to Lord Capel and Sir William Temple we are indebted for the introduction from the Continent of some of our best varieties of the grape—Sir William having brought into England the Chasselas, Parsley-leaved, Frontignac, Amboyse, Burgundy, Black Muscat, and Grizly Frontignac. The building of sloping walls about this time, Switzer says, led the world to the improvement of "glassing and forcing grapes." The Duke of Rutland had the walls heated by flues, and "glassed them all before as you do stoves, which penned in the heat to a great degree; and from this they had good success." Switzer suggested that the roots also should be kept warmer, and this was immediately effected by a flue passed under the border. The success was then more complete.

It is needless to trace in detail the progress of vine culture further, for we have now brought its history down to the time of Miller and others, who still rank among modern horticultural authorities. The first edition of Miller's Dictionary appeared in 1731, and contains moderately full directions for the cultivation of the vine. In the following year Sir Alexander Murray published "The Nature and Method of Planting, &c., a Vineyard," a work containing much useful information. Hitt's standard work on "Fruit Trees" appeared in 1755; Abercrombie's "Hothouse Gardener," and other works, between 1774 and 1790, and these, with some others of minor note, gave way to Speechley's *Treatise on the Culture of the Vine*, which issued from the press in 1789. This is still a work of good authority. These were his principal works, and of a third, the offspring of his old age—*Practical Hints in Domestic Rural Economy*—we may hereafter have occasion to speak. One who seems to have been a relative has furnished the few particulars usually found in the biography of one "who knows no care beyond the garden walls." He was born at a village near Peterborough, in Northamptonshire, the son of a respectable farmer, who gave him that best of dowries, a sound education; and the seed was cast upon good ground, for he had the first essentials of success—a powerful mind and strenuous industry. From early youth he selected gardening as his path to competency; and after being made free of "the stole hole" at Milton Abbey, now Earl Fitzwilliam's, advancing to a better position at Castle Howard, Earl Carlisle's, and being head gardener to Sir W. St. Quentin, he finally attained the same office at Welbeck, in Nottinghamshire, the Duke of Portland's. He resigned this situation to occupy a farm at Woodborough Hall, left vacant by the death of his younger son; this was followed by the death of his elder son in 1804; and soon after Mr. Speechley adjourned to nearer London, to be in the vicinity of the last survivor of his family. He died at Great Milton, in Oxfordshire.

RANGE OF BAROMETER—RAIN IN INCHES.

Sept.		1841.	1842.	1843.	1844.	1845.	1846.	1847.	1848.	1849.
26	B.	29.480 / 29.422	29.906 / 29.795	30.038 / 29.947	30.370 / 30.198	29.985 / 29.740	29.736 / 29.700	30.237 / 30.130	29.650 / 29.514	29.843 / 29.507
	R.	0.27	0.08	—	—	0.05	—	0.24	—	
27	B.	29.567 / 29.471	29.922 / 29.859	29.781 / 29.681	30.179 / 30.096	29.914 / 29.790	29.763 / 29.723	30.276 / 30.269	29.792 / 29.655	29.763 / 29.729
	R.	0.57	0.27	—	—	0.02	0.25	—	0.01	
28	B.	29.581 / 29.310	30.059 / 30.047	29.834 / 29.735	30.047 / 29.984	29.947 / 29.454	29.557 / 29.513	30.323 / 30.397	29.738 / 29.723	29.825 / 29.739
	R.	0.15	—	0.05	—	0.09	—	0.80	0.07	
29	B.	29.267 / 29.167	30.093 / 30.026	29.968 / 29.937	30.219 / 29.961	29.949 / 29.753	29.447 / 29.391	30.310 / 30.235	29.677 / 29.669	29.078 / 29.497
	R.	0.35	0.04	0.24	0.01	0.01	—	0.27	0.40	
30	B.	29.413 / 29.172	30.150 / 30.138	29.893 / 29.748	30.280 / 30.242	29.800 / 29.704	29.800 / 29.018	30.247 / 30.117	29.790 / 29.691	30.216 / 30.184
	R.	0.11	0.01	0.01	—	0.01	—	—	0.49	0.37
Oct. 1	B.	29.598 / 29.434	30.257 / 30.200	29.999 / 29.976	30.169 / 29.962	29.946 / 29.844	29.929 / 29.866	30.050 / 29.905	29.681 / 29.673	29.598 / 29.427
	R.	0.20	—	—	—	0.93	—	—	0.02	
2	B.	29.773 / 29.730	30.300 / 30.149	30.099 / 29.999	29.783 / 29.561	29.874 / 29.680	29.795 / 29.610	30.110 / 30.039	29.699 / 29.564	29.727 / 29.586
	R.	—	—	0.11	—	0.07	0.44	—	0.03	0.13
3	B.	29.792 / 29.745	30.069 / 30.010	30.138 / 30.061	29.830 / 29.758	29.854 / 29.510	29.700 / 29.637	30.164 / 30.194	29.910 / 29.711	29.540 / 29.206
	R.	0.13	—	0.01	—	0.17	0.02	—	0.04	1.01

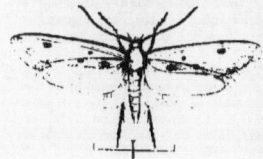

INSECTS.—Such destruction was recently occasioned to some valuable carpets of a friend, by what housekeepers emphatically call "The Moth," that we determined to give some relative particulars, more especially as we are able to add a most simple preventive of their ravages, namely, spreading a thin layer of hay between the floor and the carpet. There are two moths the larvæ of which are thus destructive—*Tinea tapetzella*, the tapestry, or black-cloaked woollen moth; and *T. pellionella*, the fur, or single-spotted woollen moth. They both are destructive to carpets and other woollens, but the larvæ of the latter moth is especially fond of ladies' furs, "paying no more respect to the regal ermine than to the woollen habiliments of the poor." This moth is represented magnified in our drawing. Its fore-wings are ashy brown, slightly clouded, glossy, with a black dot on the disc before the middle; hind-wings, pale ashy brown.

METEOROLOGY.—We give eight days this time to complete the year. The average highest and lowest temperatures, from observations at Chiswick during the last twenty-three years, are 64.4° and 45°, respectively. During the period there were 89 fine days, and 95 on which rain fell. The greatest heat during the time was 90°, and greatest cold 24°.

HAVING had opportunities during the concluding year of visiting many provincial horticultural exhibitions, and of perusing the prize lists of a still greater number of horticultural societies, we are induced to put to their managers this question—*What do you consider is the object to be aimed at by a Horticultural Society?*

However variously expressed, the substance of the replies which the good sense of those managers will suggest is, that a horticultural society's chief object should be to improve, to the utmost of its power, the gardening of the district where it is established. To such a reply no exception can be taken, and we then must ask the managers we have referred to, severely and scrupulously to test each prize they offer, by pausing over each and considering, "Is this prize calculated to improve the gardening of this neighbourhood?"

We do not wish to be severe, but we deliberately and painfully have come to the conclusion, that the vast majority of horticultural prize-lists would be decimated, if submitted uncompromisingly to such an ordeal.

It is impossible to set up a standard of rules fitted for all societies, because soil, climate, and the pecuniary resources of the members at large are controlling circumstances. But we can remind *all* managers of such societies, that they do not "improve to the utmost the gardening of the district," by having prizes for such plants, or such numbers of plants, as are certain to be won by a very few exhibitors. If year after year the same prizes of a society go to the same parties, and almost for the same plants, the finger of death is upon that society; it may be a lingering death, but ere many years are passed the circulation of its life-blood—its subscriptions—will cease. Subscribers grow weary of having annuitants upon the funds.

To remedy such an engrossing of the prizes by a few competitors, the prizes should be more numerous, of smaller amount, and for flowers and other objects of cultivation that will let in a more numerous class of exhibitors. Why do we see prizes so generally omitted for auriculas, pansies, polyanthuses, and gooseberries, whilst roses in pots, pelargoniums, chrysanthemums, and grapes are as generally highly rewarded?

Again, in the lists of prizes for greenhouse plants; why do we see such varied prizes for dozens and twenties of these, but none for three or six that have been cultivated in the sitting-room? In other words, why are there no prizes for window plants? Moreover, why is any exhibitor allowed to have a prize for a single specimen of a class in which he is exhibiting a collection? For example, why is Mr. A. allowed to exhibit twelve greenhouse plants, and two or three single specimens of greenhouse plants? There is no just reason for this; inasmuch as that, if those single specimens are very superior, they ought to have been included in the collection to secure for it the first prize; whereas, Mr. A. will be contented to have a second prize for his collection, if he can have prizes for the single specimens more than equivalent to the difference between the first and second prizes. Now, this has no tendency "to im-

prove to the utmost the gardening of the district;" but it most effectually consumes the Society's income.

In concluding these suggestions, which we make for the purpose of rousing attention to a consideration most important for the prosperity of each and every Horticultural Society, we will add what we consider a golden rule to be constantly kept in mind when forming its prize list:—

Give many and small prizes, rather than a few large ones.

The object is to secure numerous exhibitors, and this can only be effected by success being certain to more than a few.

WE understand that a popular account of the Royal Lily (*Victoria regina*), with a detail of the history and habits of the Water Lilies of our own land, may soon be expected from the pen of our contributor, Mr. Lawson, of Edinburgh. We shall postpone some observations we have to make upon this flower until after Mr. Lawson's work has been published.

THE FRUIT-GARDEN.

THE GOOSEBERRY.—It being the period for planting this very useful fruit, which is, indeed, a favourite with everybody, and, what is more, equally within the reach of the peer and the peasant, we will offer a few remarks, first premising that our main purpose will not be to discuss the merits of what are termed "show gooseberries," but to point to some of the best kinds for cultivating in the amateur or cottager's garden. Of course, flavour is the great consideration with regard to dessert kinds; without this being first-rate, it is sheer nonsense to cultivate them; as high-flavoured kinds are to be had amongst *all* the colours, and of both *early* and *late* sorts. Fineness of skin is, moreover, a recommendation; and for this reason most of the huge kinds emanating from the Lancashire growers are rejected by all good gardeners, so many of them proving exceedingly coarse, albeit many possess very good flavour. They are, however, very liable to burst in rainy seasons, and being mostly middle season berries, the birds are apt to make sad havoc amongst them.

Next to flavour we must consider how to provide distinct colours—a few of each class; for it is scarcely necessary to add that those who like to enjoy a daily dessert, will naturally like a change of colour, which, indeed, generally involves change of flavour. It sometimes happens, too, that when several dishes of fruits are required on the table, there may be room for a couple of dishes of gooseberries; how nice, then, to have two kinds, decidedly distinct both in flavour and in colour, and the latter of a decided character. Thus, suppose a dish of the fine yellow Rockwood's and a dish of the Green gage, or, it may be, the Red champagne; which latter is, indeed, equal, if not superior, to some grapes.

Thus much for colour; but we have another most important matter for consideration—how to have as long a gooseberry season as possible. We this season commenced getting the early green hairy on the fifteenth of July, and we shall finish our last berries about the first week of October.

We have not, however, done all that may be done;

and we will boldly affirm that those who can spare time and a trifling amount of expense, may with certainty produce them from the first week in July until the middle, if not the end, of October. Here, then, we have a constant supply from one sort of fruit only, and that a good flavoured one, and produced with great economy and certainty. Still, one more consideration remains in making a proper selection, and that is, to procure a few proper sorts for preserving and for bottling. Having now stated the principle objects in gooseberry culture, as connected with moderate sized gardens, we may proceed to suggest points of culture, and, before we finish, will add a list of truly good and useful kinds classified.

The principles of accelerating and retarding are applicable to the gooseberry as well as to most of our other fruits. They are, indeed, sometimes forced in hothouses, but not with that degree of success to entitle them to general consideration. They are trained on the southern aspect of walls in some gardens, in order to produce early berries, as also on northern or colder aspects, in order to obtain late berries. Both these are good practice when an opportunity offers. As it is, however, few amateurs can spare room for them; for an ample demand exists in such situations on behalf of the pears, peaches, nectarines, and apricots.

We now desire to suggest a mode which we feel persuaded would, if properly carried out, prove superior to most now in practice, at least for prolonging the season of the more valuable late kinds. Such would consist in adopting trellises, such as we frequently find apples and pears trained on in the gardens of the wealthy, only somewhat more diminutive in character, for four feet in height would, perhaps, be sufficient for them. These might be formed of strained wire, in parallel lines, running north and south. The lines of wire should be about six inches apart. Now, as we have to recommend the adoption of a sort of pent-house or coping covering, as, also, a little canvass applied at certain periods, we must endeavour to show how the greatest amount of gooseberries can be obtained on a given space, in order that the expense incurred may not outrun the value of the produce. Perhaps, then, a double trellis would be the best; that is to say, such a one as would be formed by leaning two iron hurdles against each other, forming an acute-angled triangle, with a base of about one foot, or, in other words, the two sides a foot apart at the bottom, and meeting within a couple of inches at the top. Plants may then be planted along *both* sides, and trained and kept separate, allowing no shoots to occupy the interior, which should be kept free for a thorough circulation of air. As some kinds grow very upright, such as the Champagne kinds, whilst others have a constant tendency to spread almost at right angles, such as the Warrington, we would plant alternately an upright and a spreading kind, and encourage the upright kind to assume a longer stem, in fact, a stem nearly half the height of the trellis, and suffer the dwarf and spreading kinds to occupy all the lower portion of the trellis. As to distance, about six feet would be preferable; thus allowing three feet on each side of the stem of any given plant for the extension of the side branches.

We will now suppose the arrangement completed, and the trellis covered with fruit, the next point will be the covering or protection from both bad weather and also from birds and wasps.

We before said, that the two sides of the trellis might be two inches apart at the top; we would now place a wooden spout on the top, running horizontally, both in order to carry off water, to guard from severe frosts during the blooming season, and to suspend canvass curtains from—the latter working like ordinary bed curtains, with rings sliding along an iron rod.

The following will represent the end section of the trellis:—

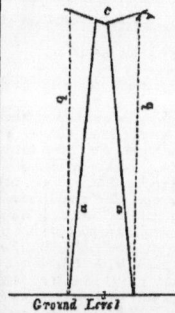

Ground Level

It will be seen that *a a* are the two wire sides; *b b* the curtain; and *e* the spout, at the extreme points of which the curtain rod commences. The curtain of gauze or canvass should be in divisions adapted for covering and uncovering with facility. Now, the water which may collect can be carried down little zinc pipes at the ends, and a little drain should be provided to meet them. The spout at top may be just wide enough to throw the drip beyond the foot of the trellis; and thus dryness—a great essential—is secured.

The curtain would be of great use in February, March, and April, in warding off late frosts; and equally useful in the end of June, to arrest, if necessary, the ripening a little; and during September, October, and November, its uses are equally manifest. With such a simple contrivance we would engage to preserve gooseberries until nearly Christmas, and fruit of the very highest flavour, merely taking care to have them *perfectly ripe* by the end of August; for we would retard them a fortnight in the spring, and another week just before the ripening period. Indeed, the character of the trellis will of itself throw them many days later, for they would not be hurried by the mid-day sun; from eleven until one o'clock of each day they would be in comparative shade. Such a plan would surely pay as a commercial speculation; and we cannot but fancy the astonishment of our London fruiterers, should they by such a system one day receive fine gooseberries by bushels in October and November. An acre of ground thus disposed would yield a vast amount; for the lines of trellises need not be more than about six feet apart in a parallel way.

The gardens of the wealthy, too, or those who have extensive establishments, would possess much more interest if such formed part of a system for increasing the amount of retarded fruits; indeed, here something appears indispensable. Our late gooseberries now (the 12th of September), as fine as can be, are matted up, but this is merely because we have it not in our power at present to adopt a better plan; for doubtless under the matting system there will be few remaining even in another fortnight.

Having thus delivered our ideas of, at least, one economical and sure plan of producing, for a greater length of time, a very useful adjunct to good dessert, the next consideration will be an enumeration and classification of some well-known and truly good kinds. We will commence with those for *special* purposes :—

LATE HANGING KINDS, OR THOSE FIT FOR THE TRELLIS.

1. *Warrington;* hairy red; known also as Aston seedling.
2. *Pitmaston Greengage;* green; this is noted for shrivelling in the raisin character on the tree.
3. *Taylor's Bright Venus;* white; also a shriveller.
4. *Coe's Late Red;* accounted a good late berry.
5. *Champagne Red;* very rich, and of upright growth.
6. *Champagne Yellow;* very rich, and upright.

The above we can safely recommend for trellis purposes, or, indeed, for general culture, as dessert fruit.

KINDS OF GENERAL UTILITY.

7. *Rockwood's Hairy Yellow;* early.

8. *Leigh's Rifleman;* red hairy; rather late; great bearer.
9. *Green Walnut;* green smooth; great bearer.
10. *Whitesmith* (Woodward's); white; good flavour.
11. *Keen's Seedling;* much like Warrington, and rather earlier.
12. *Roaring Lion;* red smooth; great bearer.
13. *Glenton Green;* a very good hairy green.
14. *Heart of Oak* (Massey's); green smooth; good bearer.

Now, we are perfectly aware that there are many other good and useful kinds in the country; these, however, we have grown—most of them for years; they may, therefore, be relied on for general use. It may be remarked, that they are not exhibition berries; that is to say, not fit to compete in point of mere size. We would recommend particular regard being paid to Nos. 1, 4, 9, 11, 12, 14, as great bearers, and generally adapted to kitchen use. Although No. 1 is always a good table fruit, No. 12 is particularly adapted for early tarts or puddings; we would not, however, grow many bushes, as they soon burst or decay. Perhaps of all the kinds known, none are so generally useful as the Warrington. We must here observe, that we had forgotten to name the old *Rumbullion*, which is still the favourite with many for bottling purposes—possessing much fleshy pulp in proportion to the amount of seeds, which appears to be the necessary qualification with our clever housewives.

R. Errington.

THE FLOWER-GARDEN.

Roses.—The next division of this subject—and then I close it for the present—is this: after the September or autumn dressing of the plants, as I recommended last week, and as we manage them here, the earth is broken round every bush separately with a fork, and liquid-manure is given to each once a week as long as flower-buds can be seen. Whether the autumn is wet or dry, we consider (indeed we have found it out) that rain water, whether direct from the clouds or from the watering-pots, is not of itself strong enough to enable the plants to open the flowers properly. They are much in the position of weary travellers at or near the end of a long toilsome journey: they have been hard at it since last May, growing and flowering and putting by a little for another season. To this add the shorter days and cooler nights lowering the heat and light, which are the grand stimulants for keeping up their spirits, and you make out a case, and a deserving case too, for artificial support in the shape of liquids. All this time, as I have just said, the borders may be wet enough for ordinary plants, but "wet enough" is not the thing, but whether there is strength enough in it to cause the flowers to open. We often say, that such-and-such new roses are unsuited for our climate; they do not open freely in the autumn with us; and then comes the old consequence of giving a dog a bad name. Now, if roses and all other plants would do what we wanted without the aid of art and science, what would become of us poor gardeners? There would then be no "profession" for us to get bread and cheese by, and we might all go to Bath or New Zealand, and so might the book-makers; but things are much better ordered, and we must order and improve our practice in blooming roses late in the autumn, and when we do we shall find more sorts "fitted for our climate" than some of us would like to acknowledge. Let it be, at any rate, a weekly allowance; and if twice a week all the better; the earth is a good "fixer" of good things, and the watery parts will find their way into the draining. High feeding is one of the grand secrets of getting fine autumn flowers; but it is of little use now to say, that we had given them "such a dressing" of manure last spring: *now* is the time;

but unless the clear-out of weak shoots and useless old leaves be attended to, little weak shoots can only furnish mere apologies for roses.

There is one more point that, if one could attend to it, would go a long way to establish the credit of autumnal roses; but this point is so difficult, that I am almost afraid to say any thing about it—besides, the ladies will be against me. The point I allude to is the top point or end of the flowering shoot, which they find so convenient to have along with the rose itself, to stick in their water-glasses; but now that the mornings are getting cold they must have roses in their rooms. I would never grudge after this time to have all the roses that were fit cut every morning, but I do grudge, most seriously, to have the best three or four buds at the top "clipped off," as if they were of no more use; whereas if left on the plant they would soon produce other roses in half the time that the next lower set of buds can do. The way I get over this is not in the power of most people instead of scores I plant out hundreds of rose-bushes, in all sorts of out-of-the-way corners about the kitchen-garden. For the last few years I have been getting up a stock of the finest hybrid perpetual roses for the rosary; and, if I live so long, I hope to do away with all those roses which only bloom once in the season; and to have none but climbers and perpetual roses in the regular rosary; and I suppose the gardeners of many of the large country families will do the same: for as the fashion goes now, the great families are up in London during the old rose season, and never see their summer roses at all except as cut flowers, and by the middle of July their rosaries are the least interesting parts of their garden establishments.

There are two roses, and two only that I know of, which ought to be grown on their own roots every where, if cut roses are to be looked for to Christmas time: one of them is *Gloire de Rosamene*, which by a particular management, is by far the most brilliant of all the autumn roses, beating *Geant des Batailles* itself in producing ten flowers to his one, and fully as dark fiery crimson. After the end of October, if this rose is cut when it is half blown, it will keep a week or ten days in the glass, and no one can tell but it is a double rose—whereas it is nearly a single one. The particular management required by this rose is, to make a biennial, that is, a two-yearling of it, to make the best of it for a Christmas rose—I mean, it must be cut right down to the ground every second year—any time in April, and after a few years no one, who has not seen it treated that way, could believe the enormous quantities of roses it can furnish. But the liquid-manure tank should be stirred up for it every week, from this time, to make the best of it. Another peculiarity of it is, that it must not be worked on any other stock, only grown on its own roots, and it will root as freely as a geranium. I know as much about rose-stocks as Mr. Rivers himself. I have been put to my wits'-end for them, and out of 50 sorts of stocks that I tried this *Gloire de Rosamene* on, it only succeeded on one; but for that one stock I have no name; it was a sucker from a standard rose, which I budded near the ground, and for the last seven years both did very well indeed—the standard above, and *Gloire de Rosamene* as a bush round the stem.

There is a hedge of *Gloire de Rosamene* growing on its own roots in a very light piece of ground in this garden, and only a yard away from another hedge of the common laurel. This rose hedge has, therefore, not much to boast of for a good bed; but it grows most healthily, and flowers enormously in June, and from September till Christmas; and I believe that it would not refuse to do well in a bed of sand, if it had three or four good waterings of liquid manure in the course of the season. Our gardeners here say the hedge lives entirely on "pot victuals," meaning the watering-pot: and when it is in full bloom against the laurel hedge, and seen at a distance on a dull morning or in the dusk off the evening, one might imagine the hedge was on fire. Now, every other plant in this hedge is cut down close to the ground every year, late in April, and by this time the fresh shoots are from three to five feet long, after being once stopped in July to cut away the first blossoms, so that the cut-down plants are only used for the autumn bloom. Next year these shoots will be trained against wire, almost at full length, only the small side shoots being cut out, or very close, and the next set of plants out in their turn. A stranger passing along this hedge could hardly perceive that anything particular is done to it, because the new shoots are trained as fast as they grow against the shoots of last year. Two points are thus gained—the hedge is not allowed to grow beyond a certain height, five feet, a plan which is necessary for that situation, and the enormous quantities of cut flowers it would yield. I have seen our boys make bouquets of roses in bud from this hedge, with a couple of rows of the buds of the old *White China* round the outside of it, and I am ashamed to say the diameters of them, they make them so large.

Here, now, is a fair sample of how a gardener gets entangled in roses when he wants to work among them or write of them. Farther back I thought I *would* keep to the two roses on their own roots, the hedge rose and *Fulgore*, but here the *White China* appears as an edging for a silly bouquet, and if I do not say something about it on the spot, I shall be besieged with letters. This is always the way when we let the pen slip, and mention a plant incidentally. This *White China rose* had the good fortune to come into the world before they found out the way to give roses such hard names, and, like old gardeners, very few people care anything about it; in short, I do not know if the nurserymen grow it at all, it is so old; but this I do know, that they grow no China rose half so useful. It is in full flower every day from May to December, and late in the season it is the only white rose one can pick to make a variety in the glasses. In November the buds of it are as hard as acorns, and as pointed as a bayonet, and if it is wet weather, the out side row of petals look much faded, and nine persons out of ten would pass it as gone; but strip off the faded covering and you have the nicest white rose bud you ever saw, and it will keep ten days fresh in a dry warm room. All the autumn roses for house decoration ought to be cut before the buds are more than half blown; they will keep all the longer, and look as well if not better than if they were quite open; they escape the damp, and will open in the glasses.

It often happens, that one's garden in front or behind the house is a long narrow piece of ground, and the end farthest from the house is often taken up with choice vegetables, so that the flower and kitchen-gardens are almost all in one. Now, with that arrangement, this *Gloire de Rosamene* would be the very thing to make a hedge of to divide the two gardens from each other; and where the walks interfere, I would make an archway over them of a different rose for variety—say the *Felicite Perpetuelle*, the best of the evergreen section, and also the best of them to bud others on. Then, in June, how well the delicately white blossoms of this beautiful rose would contrast with the fiery red of the *Gloire de Rosamene*. Besides, one might well amuse oneself of an evening to bud perpetual roses all round the archway; for every rose in the catalogues will grow famously on the *Felicite perpetuelle*. To make this hedge thick, and to allow of every other plant of it, or every third plant, to be cut down, if that was thought advisable, the plants should stand a foot apart; and then on the flower-garden side of this splendid hedge I would plant a whole row of the old white China rose,

and about two feet from the bottom of the hedge. This arrangement would provide more roses at less cost of space in a small garden than any one could believe who did not see the plan tried. To keep the hedge in its proper place, a row of stakes would be required the second season after planting; and for the first two years the stakes need not be higher than a yard; because all that would be necessary would only be to keep the lower part of the hedge in a straight line; and though it might lean over on either side a little, and look all the more graceful; but as soon as the plants are of full strength, I think they would look best trained regularly as a hedge from "top to bottom"—as the mason built his house. There is no speculation in all this; I have had such a hedge under my control these seven years, and I am quite sure of the plan, and that there is nothing in the garden looks better. The stakes need not stand nearer than from six to nine feet apart, and small wires to pass from stake to stake, and eighteen inches from stretch to stretch. Very small wire will do, and a pound of it, for very little money, will run a long way.

Another plan, which would add greatly to the pleasure of having such a beautiful hedge to divide one's garden, would be to plant the *Fulgore* rose as every fourth or fifth plant in the hedge; and, if one could get them so, the plants would do much better on their own roots. This *Fulgore* does not do well, I believe, anywhere worked on another plant, after the first few years. It would grow better on the *Gloire de Rosamene* itself than on any other rose, and might safely be budded on it as it stands in the hedge; and so might *Madame Laffay*, the third best rose for such a hedge. *Fulgore* is gone much out of fashion for the last few years, because it does not grow well on the dog-rose stock, at least, it will not live long on it if pruned close; but of all the late autumn roses it is by far the sweetest, and comes nearest the old *Cabbage rose* in shape, and blooms as late as *Madame Laffay*; but the true way to manage it is to get it from cuttings, and to cut it right down to the ground every second or third year, and then after thinning the flower buds, and with "pot victuals," you might cut dozens of full blown roses of it that the people in London could not make out from regular cabbage roses, and nearly, if not altogether, as sweet. Sometimes it will make three or four shoots as many feet in length, and then flower at the ends, while the rest of the head is languishing for want of nourishment; and when that happens away go the weak parts by the first hard winter, and of course an under bark disease follows; and the sweetest of the autumn roses is pronounced to be bad to keep, and, as there is no lack of sorts, it is thrown aside. It is true, that bad habits of this nature are a good deal under the control of the gardener—the long shoots might have been stopped when it was seen that they meant to have it all their own way; but then they would turn sulky, get hide-bound, and you must either assist them to follow the bent of their own nature, and not allow them a foster-parent, but to grow on their own roots, when by an occasional cutting down to the ground they will make the best autumn bloomers we have.

Now, in my experiments with *rose stocks*—for I have been driven to make all sorts of trials with them—I have found out more secrets than this of managing the *Fulgore*. There are twelve or fifteen other perpetual roses that will grow on their own roots much better than when they are worked on the dog stocks; and, what is of far more consequence, they will succeed on poor land where the dog-rose could not keep a leaf after the first fortnight of dry weather; and if I had to grow beautiful bushes of the dog-rose, I must reverse the present custom, and bud it on *Madame Laffay*, which is perhaps the best stock of all for the whole race of hybrid perpetuals on all soils inimical to the race. I have had bushes of this exquisite rose which made shoots six feet long the second season from the cutting, indeed, in the cutting bed, which was of the lightest sandy soil, and no strong water was given them. I have budded a few other sorts on it some years back, by way of trial, with which I am pleased. I have transplanted them three times, which is a good test to find out if the variety is given to form root suckers; and I believe it is not—mine showed none yet; and as to suckers from the stem of any stock that was reared by hand, I would not allow garden room for any one who could not prevent that after reading that useful work, The Cottage Gardener. I have this last month put in some hundreds of cuttings of *Madame Laffay*, with a view to make use of them to work a collection—or rather a selection—of hybrid perpetuals on. I wish I could get rid of this stupid prefix, *hybrid;* how it came to be applied to these more than to other roses I cannot tell; there is not a rose worth growing in the whole country which is not a hybrid; and as we call the natural monthly roses " China's," the perpetuals had no more need of supports by hybrid stakes than I have of " seven mile boots." Mr. Appleby has given the best receipts for making cuttings of the hardy shrubs that I have seen, in the first volume of The Cottage Gardener.

Pruning Perpetual Roses.—At the risk of having the Editorial whistle in my ears to warn me of the space I occupy, I must say two or three words, more in season, about roses, as very likely I cannot turn to them again for a long time. I have just pruned a row of perpetual roses that are growing on their own roots. I cut them very close, all except one or two of the very weakest shoots, which I left at full length. The reason I left these little shoots is, that they might take the still rising sap and keep it for themselves, instead of letting it be wasted by " bleeding;" and this they have done, for none of the cut shoots bled. Now I shall watch these cut down roses, and when I see the bottom eyes are swollen, like those of a man blowing the bagpipes, I mean to transplant them to another part of the garden. By this simple process of cutting off the shoots, I shall gain many advantages: the roses can be removed a month sooner than the usual time, by which they will be well rooted in the new place before Christmas, every cell and tube being full of sap before winter, as they must be by this plan; they will burst into leaf next spring as if they were not disturbed in the autumn, and having made good roots before this time, there is no fear but this vigour will be amply sustained, and that before the end of May no one could make out that they were transplanted for years past. I have explained all this over and over again; yet people who read constantly keep sending to us, week after week, for instructions about roses and other things, as if they had never opened a gardening book; so that we must, as it were, hammer out our instructions upon many points repeatedly before we can make the thing familiar to the million; and there is no point in gardening which seems to require more hammering than that of the due preparation of plants for removal to make the best of them. Cutting the roots all round some time before the tree or shrub is removed, as Mr. Errington recommends, is one grand step gained, and cutting the branches as I insist on is no less so; but the two operations must not be performed at the same time, otherwise the good effects of pruning to get the bottom buds plump and full of sap is interfered with in a particular degree; still, I would much rather do that than follow the common herd, and prune at the time of removing a plant; for there is no more effectual means for crippling its energies.

D. Beaton.

GREENHOUSE AND WINDOW GARDENING.

Training : Verbenas.—In speaking upon training last week, among other things I mentioned, that the nature of the plant and the mode of its growth should be carefully noted; and that in opposition to these no manner of training the plant should be adopted, unless that which a clear understanding of the subject would enable you to perceive would be an improvement upon a more nature-like system. As an illustration, I would for a moment direct attention to the management of the *Verbena*, because this is a tribe of plants with which every reader is acquainted. When first introduced it was greatly prized as a greenhouse plant, but now it is used almost solely for the decoration of the flower-borders and beds; though if grown in pots, few flowers would be more attractive either in the greenhouse or sitting-room; and for this purpose might be rendered available during the whole of the spring and summer months.

We say nothing now of the varieties, for they are endless, as the shade of a shade of a difference, requiring something like microscopic vision to discern it, is held sufficient claim for some high-sounding addition to verbena nomenclature. Nearly all of them are distinguished by the property of emitting roots from the joints, and other parts of the stems, when trailing over a damp surface. Taking advantage of this, in order to fill the bed sooner, and likewise to keep the plants in their allotted space securely, gardeners fasten these stems down with pegs, and so much stress is laid upon this pegging and training system, that when old brooms or pea-sticks cannot be got for the purpose, our correspondents wisely hunt the fern-brakes for pegs, or cutting up bass matting, or any other tying material, into pieces of six or eight inches in length, place the middle of the string over the stem, and joining the ends together fasten them securely in the earth, either with the finger or a small dibber. Now, here, the course adopted is that which the nature of the plants would at once point out as proper and desirable; and in very poor hungry chalky or sandy soil it would be followed with success, because the roots emitted from the stem would just draw up enough of nourishment, to ensure as much luxuriance as would secure a profusion of bloom, and especially in dry seasons.

But take this habit of the plant—this hint from *nature*, which some folk talk as much about as if it was wrong to display art and science even in what was artistic—and make these the guide for your training process, in soil that is heavy and rich, and need we wonder that complaints should pour in that verbena beds were not clusters of bloom—that luxuriance and size of the foliage swamped the brilliancy of the flowers, while their grossness of habit rendered them liable to be swept by winds into unseemly bundles. To obtain masses of bloom in such circumstances the beds should be raised; instead of *pegging down*, the plants should be *pegged up* with brushwood twigs, such as old birch brooms, and prunings of any kind, in length proportionate to the growth of the plant, so that the stems shall run among them and be held firm, whilst the medium of support shall be wholly concealed by the time the beds are in bloom, though it would require something like a hurricane to force them from their moorings.

Similar attention to circumstances, as well as a knowledge of the natural mode of growth, must be attended to in the case of all plants grown in pots, in order to ensure the greatest satisfaction. Keeping to the verbena as an example, many of the most beautiful varieties, with large petals, and fine heads of bloom, are next to worthless for the flower-garden, unless in the most sheltered situations. A slight shower, a brisk breeze, bleach and crumple the petals, while others seldom present a corymb of flowers with the florets all expanded, and thus exhibit a large green centre. What is, therefore, so much prized by the fastidious florist is often not so useful to the flower gardener as the less perfect formed but smaller-flowered, dwarfer-growing varieties, which after passing through the ordeal of showers and wind look up as briskly and as beautifully as before. But high breeding here, just as in other cases, produces a degree of *tenderness*. For example, we see it realised in the large herbaceous calceolarias which, though useless for the flower-garden, are great ornaments when protected by glass. All the verbenas are beautiful in pots, but the larger-flowered, more tender varieties are well worthy such care. In spring and summer, and even autumn, few things are more splendid in sitting-rooms, windows, greenhouses, or balconies, when well managed, and looked upon by those who can discover beauty in gorgeousness of colour, independently of commercial-value speculations. Instead of detracting from, the ease with which a pretty object may be obtained by the masses of society adds to its real value and usefulness.

I have tried many methods in my time for training verbenas in pots. For instance, after stopping a young shoot so as to produce two or three shoots, or encouraging one shoot to grow without stopping, I have trained these several, or that single shoot, to a stout stake, stopping or picking out every side shoot that appeared, until the main shoot or shoots reached the top of the stake, which for most kinds was eighteen inches or two feet above the surface of the pot. Here, by means of cross wires, a top was formed something of the shape and size of our new fashionable parasols—not greatly larger than the pretty faces they are intended to defend from the sun's rays. The shoots were here stopped and stopped again several times, flowering being discouraged until the shoots hung down in festoons, and when in full bloom concealing trellis, stake, and pot with their brilliancy. A similar plan was adopted with a flat upright wire trellis, only the plants were stopped more at first, to furnish a sufficiency of main shoots, the side shoots being always deprived of their bloom buds until the trellis was covered with wood, so that all might have an equal start; but by this method I never could please myself, as if set below the eye the *stilting* system resorted to was too apparent; and if placed on a stage above the eye, the flowers were not seen to the best advantage. With strong growing kinds—such as the old *Incisa*, and the comparatively more splendid *Robinson's Defiance*—I have used round, or balloon-shaped wire trellises, from three to four feet in height, and as much in diameter; and when not examined too closely, the frame-work was hid by the mass of bloom, and they were a great improvement in appearance in the flat one-sided plants.

But here, though very beautiful, unless you had plenty of room all round the plant, and could look down upon it, the effect as a whole was inferior to that produced by a bed of the same kind out of doors, raised a foot or eighteen inches above the surface; and that chiefly owing to the fact, that the plants having the liberty of following, to a certain extent, their natural inclinations, all the flowers stood upright, alike to meet the sun and the recognition of your admiring eye. Here, then, the lesson to be learned is, that verbenas grown in pots to produce the best effect, should be trained so as to resemble raised flower-beds in miniature. As in the raised bed, the pendant shoots would, in most cases, meet the surrounding medium, whether grass, gravel, or pavement; so in the pot, most of the shoots should not only point upwards, but others should fall over the pot, concealing by their flowers its appearance altogether, or nearly so, unless when growing in a vase so beautiful,

that a few flowers only hanging over to contrast with its colour might be deemed more desirable.

To attain this more natural mode of exhibiting the verbena in pots, requires no extraordinary care nor expense. For compact growing kinds with the dwarfness of the old but very useful *Charlwoodii*, nothing would be required but pegs for the side, and twigs for the middle. For those of a medium growth, such as the old *Tweediana*, a similar plan, or better still, flat rounded trainers of wire network may be used, and about eighteen inches in height. The trainer should be made to fit the rim of the pot, and then cover the pot itself, being secured in its place by a hoop of wire, made to fit it tight. For strong growing ones, like *Defiance*, the trainers should be from two to three feet in height, and as wide in diameter as you could easily manage and of any fanciful shape—round, oblong, or curved, though the first will be the best. I mentioned last week how these things are easily formed, and by hooking the strong wire round the rim of the pot, you may remove all at your pleasure, and fit to another pot. With such a rim and two or three wires bent over and attached to it in the desired shape, as a frame, nothing could answer better for verbenas than the cheap wire netting so frequently advertised, to fasten to the frame; and if galvanised, no painting would be required. If all went on well, every shoot and flower would thus be kept in their place, and yet the medium of training would be concealed from the view.

Taking these and previous remarks for what they are worth, our kind readers will perceive, that in order to excel, they must study the nature and capabilities of the plant to be trained, more than any particular directions; and I think they will also come to the conclusion, that however fashionable it may be, and however striking the effect, there is also something of the *unsatisfactory* in beholding plants, naturally of a bushy character, fixed to a flat trellis. As the verbena has been the base of our remarks, it may be mentioned that to bloom in the beginning of May the plants should be raised and potted off in September. To bloom at a later period, those struck in the end of September or in March will answer well. To bloom fine at an early season, and to be large plants likewise, the plants must be kept in a temperature of from 45° to 50°, with plenty of air, watering and syringing from the end of February; shifted several times until they are placed in six-inch pots, after which they may be transferred to pots of twelve or fourteen inches, and have the flat rounded trellises affixed. They require a rich, lumpy, light soil well drained. When we had nothing but dung and strong loam to choose from, we have used lime rubbish and broken bricks liberally with great advantage. It may also be as well to state, that when verbenas are to be kept in their cutting pots during winter, the middle of September is a good time to insert them round the side of a pot filled with light soil, and either set in a cold pit or in a window, to be shaded from the sun. For the latter position, small side shoots, with part of the stem attached, and showing incipient roots, answer best.

Our friends who wish to know all about keeping their plants in winter, will be attended to ere long. Meanwhile, let geraniums, calceolarias, &c., intended to be taken up, have some of their large leaves removed, and their roots cut round as recommended last year by Mr. Beaton.　　　　　　　　　　　　　　　　R. Fish.

HOTHOUSE DEPARTMENT.
STOVE PLANTS.

Aphelandra Aurantiaca (Orange flowered A.).—The well-known *A. cristata* is a beautiful, fine, autumnal flowering plant, and is pretty generally distributed throughout the country; but our present subject is not so well-known, nor cultivated so successfully, nor to such an extent, yet it is a fine foliaged and handsome flowered species, well worthy of the attention it requires. It has also the advantage of flowering at a time when floral beauty is scarce in our stoves, thus rendering it a grand acquisition to our early species of blooming stove plants. It is, indeed, more difficult to manage, and, therefore, requires more skill to produce good well-bloomed specimens. The leaves, when healthy, are large, and of a deep green colour. The flowers are produced in terminal racemes, and are of a deep rich orange-scarlet colour, continuing a long time in flower. It has the advantage of being of a dwarf habit, hence it is suitable for small collections.

Culture.—This fine plant requires to be kept in the warmest part of the stove. If there is a bark-bed in it it will be all the better for being plunged in it up to the rim of the pot. The compost most suitable for it is loam, fibrous-peat, and leaf-mould, in equal parts, with the addition of a liberal quantity of sand to keep the soil open; for no plant suffers more than this from too close soil. It is also necessary to use a good quantity of drainage—more, in fact, than usual; for, as we observed above, this fine plant requires, to grow it well, a little extra care and attention. In potting, throw in upon the drainage a few pieces of charcoal; it will be useful. The size of the pot depends, of course, upon the size of the plant. In this case, however, we recommend the use of smaller pots than is usually given to plants of this order. For a plant a foot high, a pot six inches wide will be amply sufficient; for less or for larger plants pots must be used of proportionate sizes. The best time for potting is in early spring, just before the plant begins to grow. If the soil the plant has been growing in previously be close and hard, so much so that it will not easily shake off, take a small sharp-pointed stick and gently pick off small portions of soil all round the ball, being careful not to bruise, tear, or otherwise injure the living roots. Should the plant be sickly, continue this operation till the ball is considerably reduced, perhaps as much as two-thirds of its former size, then put in fresh compost, and plunge in a brisk tan-bed, shading it for a while from the sun till it begins to grow again, and is able to bear more light. This fine plant must also be carefully watered; not in the all-alike method too commonly practised, but just enough for its wants and no more. It will bear syringing over head when in a growing state and not in flower, but ought to be refrained from when the plant is comparatively at rest and in bloom.

Propagation.—This is pretty easy by cuttings. Take off the top of a young shoot, insert it in silver sand in a small pot under a bell-glass, in heat, and with the requisite attention of shading and watering, just enough to keep it from flagging, it will quickly root, and make a good plant. It is encouraging to try to propagate such a plant, because it will flower at twelve months' old in a forty-eight (4-inch) pot, and is then very attractive, with its three or four fine leaves, and a spike five or six inches long of its brilliant coloured flowers.

APHELANDRA CRISTATA (Crested A.).—Though we have written above highly in praise of A. aurantica, yet A. cristata is by no means to be despised. It is a very handsome species, requiring, it is true, more room than its compeer, yet it is, where there is space to grow it, even more desirable. We have lately seen a plant with no less than eight branching spikes of its fine showy flowers. The way to obtain such a plant, is to commence stopping it at an early age, and persevering with it, repotting and nipping off all flower-buds till the requisite number of branches has been obtained; then to give the last potting in the month of March, and a free supply of water, moderate heat and air, so as to give a robust sturdy habit to your plant; and in the month of September following, you will have a truly grand object of horticultural skill and beauty. This species is much easier to grow than the preceding, being of a more robust habit, and not requiring so much heat and strict attention. The same compost, potting, watering, and method of propagation are suitable for it. No stove of moderate size ought to be without these two really fine plants.

CYRTOCERAS REFLEXUS (Reflexed C.).—This is a plant of a bushy habit when well managed, with flowers much like the still much-admired Hoya carnosa, or, as it is often called, "the honey plant." The flowers are of a creamy white, with a tinge of yellowish green in the centre. They are produced in corymbs (or heads) on footstalks, three or four inches long, out of the axils of the leaves. The leaves are four inches long and one inch wide, of a dark green when healthy. It flowers freely in June and July, and is a good plant for exhibition purposes.

Culture.—It requires a warm stove to grow it well, being apt to have the leaves turn yellow if kept too cool; a heat of 60° in winter, and 70° in summer, is the right temperature for it. As it is like the Hoya, rather of a succulent nature, the compost for it ought to be light and porous. In addition to the compost above described for the Aphelandra, mix amongst it a few pieces of charcoal and small pieces of broken potsherds. This will keep the soil open, and allow the water to pass off freely. The drainage must be kept in a perfect state, so as to do its work well and regularly. Should the surface of the soil show a disposition to become mossy, it is an indication that the drainage is stopped up, and the consequence will be yellow leaves, poor growth, and poorer flowers. In such a case, should it unfortunately occur, turn the plant out of the pot, reduce the ball of earth, renew the drainage, and put it into a less pot, giving less water, more shade, and greater heat for a time, until health, and the right colour indicating it, returns. By this treatment we have frequently recovered a plant that otherwise would have perished.

Propagation.—This plant may be increased by cuttings taken from the tops of the shoots. These ought not to be more than from two to three inches long. It will propagate also by leaves taken off with a bud at the base. Both kinds of cuttings should be put into small pots, filled first with one inch of drainage, then with the compost to within an inch of the top, and the remainder with silver sand. Place the cuttings, whether of young shoots or leaves, round the edge of the cutting pot, placing the leaves inwards, so as not to touch the glass of the hand-light. Set them upon a heated bed, and the hand-glass over them. The bell-glass is rather too close for them; where it is used it ought to be wiped dry every morning. Shade during the middle of the day; and in six weeks or two months they will be rooted. As soon as that is the case, pot them off immediately into two-inch pots; replace them under the hand-glass for a week or two, until they are fairly established, when they should have more air and light, and be managed the same as the older plants.

T. APPLEBY.

FLORISTS' FLOWERS.

THE weather lately has been propitious for late flowers. The *dahlias* have been excellent this year generally. We have witnessed in the north of England, at exhibitions in different places, some very fine stands of twenty-fours, better than we ever remember to have seen before. We hope soon to find leisure to publish a list of them, which will guide our amateur and other friends in making a selection for next year. In regard to the operations necessary to be done now, with the exception of taking off the layers of *carnations* as fast as they root, there is nothing but what we have already alluded to. We beg of our friends to look back for three or four numbers and see that preparations are going on to make the beds ready for *tulips, hyacinths, ranunculuses,* and *anemones,* as the time for planting is fast approaching. *Pink pipings* may yet be planted in their blooming beds, if not already done; but do not delay this work longer than the end of the month.

T. APPLEBY.

THE KITCHEN-GARDEN.

CABBAGE.—The main early spring crop, as before recommended, should now be planted on soil, well prepared by the application of good manure, trenching, and forming the ground into sloping banks. Sturdy and even-sized plants should be selected from the beds first pricked out, taking care to take them up with a trowel or small hand-fork, so that the fibrous roots may not, to any extent, be injured. As the late crops of peas, kidney-beans, &c., are cleared, lose no time in forming sloping banks for pricking out plenty of cabbage-plants, to stand the winter, as well as *cauliflowers, lettuce, endive,* &c.

RHUBARB, so useful for tarts, &c., through the winter and early spring months, may easily be obtained by almost every cottager who can procure a few roots of any early variety, and who has a cellar, a warm fuel-house, or any other warm corner, with the aid of an old butter firkin, with a few gimlet holes bored through the end to afford drainage; or an old water pail, deep pan, or rough box of any kind, or even a few rough boards to nail together for the purpose. Any kind of garden soil would do put in about the roots. In the after-management the principal point to attend to is, always when requiring water, to be particular in applying it pretty warm; and if the crowns of the plants are covered over with a piece of flannel, or any other warm article, until they have fairly started into growth, it will forward the production of the rhubarb considerably.

SEA-KALE, so much esteemed when well produced, may also be obtained at a very little expense through the late autumn and winter months by a similar contrivance; and any one who has a dark warm cellar, or other dark room or passage, may, by procuring some strong roots, obtain several cuttings from the same plants, during the short days of the winter season, from late autumn till early spring. Those who have large gardens generally have a large piece of sea-kale; and the custom usually is, to cover a piece at a time with blanching pots, covered to a sufficient thickness with fermenting materials, for the purpose of commanding heat enough to start it into growth, which it is almost impossible at an early season to do with sufficient regularity so as to insure a sturdy well-blanched growth, on account of the drenching rains, snow storms, and searching winds which commonly occur. Indeed, if obtained at all by such means, it requires much labour and watching—covering the tops with dry materials, and protecting the sides with thatched hurdles, &c., all of which augments the labour and expense, to say nothing

of the time and care required in frosty, windy, or cold weather, in searching to cut what is ready for table, and thus exposing the plants to sudden checks, and after all the trouble and expense, the sea-kale cannot be produced either in quantity or quality through the months of November, December, and January, equal to that which may be produced as above directed.

WINTER SPINACH should have its final thinning, if not already done; and encouragement should be given for its healthy growth by frequent surface-stirrings.

CAULIFLOWERS.—Advancing crops should be liberally supplied with manured water, as well as any other kinds of Brocoli that may be near heading-in; and attend, also, to the turning a few of the larger leaves down over the young heads, particularly on any frosty-looking evening, for the merely doing this will protect the young heads from quite a sharp frost. Attend to the earth stirring also of the Cauliflower plants; remember, too, that a good open quarter will be wanted towards the middle of next month, for finally planting out the hand-glass crop to stand the winter. This may be trenched-up at least two feet deep, and well manured in readiness; the quarters from which the hand-glass crops of Cucumbers are cleared, are generally considered an excellent situation for the winter crops of Cauliflowers.

ASPARAGUS-BEDS.—Where the stalks and seed are ripe they may be cut down close to the ground; but should seeds be required, collect them first, and put them away in a dry place for the present, as they may be washed out on any wet day during the winter months, and the stems may be all tied up in moderate sized bundles for some purpose or other, and put away in a tidy manner, until, perhaps, wanted for coverings or protection. Should there be any weeds to be seen when the stems are all cut off, let them all be hoed up lightly on a nice dry day and raked off; all such refuse may be put upon another quarter, to be trenched or dug in, and then let the beds be carefully forked up, and give them a good coat of manure regularly all over the beds. Fork up the alleys without injury to any of the roots that may have strayed out in them; then, for the sake of neatness, set down a line to form out the alleys, by just making up the edges, and neatly chop them out, throwing up any crumbs from the alleys upon the beds over the manure, and the work will be completed and all tidy for some months to come.

ROUTINE WORK: *Onions.*—Pull up, dry-off well, and store away. *Carrots.*—Attend to thinning-out and earth stirring, and taking up the main crops for winter store.

CUCUMBERS now preparing for winter use should be kept liberally aired, keeping up as hardy a growth as possible. Cut away all flower stems and decayed leaves from the *artichokes,* hoeing and clearing away all weeds from among them, and giving them a good mulching with such materials as an old mushroom bed; let them be well heaped up, and a little earth thrown over to keep all up snug together round each crown. *Celery* earth up and attend to. *Endive* plant out and tie up for blanching. *Lettuces,* earth-stir amongst them, and prick out and tie up the full-grown ones for use. *Spinach* and *Turnips* thin out. *Potatoes* take up, selecting the best for winter store, the middle sized for seed, and the refuse for the pigs.

JAMES BARNES AND T. WEAVER.

MISCELLANEOUS INFORMATION.

ALWAYS GAY.

IT is the usual aim of THE COTTAGE GARDENER, and a very good aim it is, to excite its pupils, even the humblest, to the cultivation of each flower in its perfection. But this endeavour has its disadvantages where space is small and appliances defective; no cottagers, of any rank in life, can succeed in all flowers; and if we choose two or three, some accident may cause failure in our endeavours, or, at the best, our hard-won treasures are out of bloom sometimes, and the beds are dull. My own fancy takes another line. I have no greenhouse, no better gardener than myself. I have no show plants, and take no prizes at our horticultural exhibitions. But the frequent remark of my friends is, that call when they will, except at Christmas, my garden is *always gay*. No empty beds, few vacant spaces; and if any one would like to attempt the same and improve upon my plans, he or she is very welcome to know them.

The time of all others when I like to be admired is in the early spring, when my wealthy neighbours, luxuriating in their conservatories, think it needful to let their flower garden look like the Lybian desert. Mine is filled full in the autumn with all the early flowerers I can procure, suggested by your pages or otherwise; the new ones I try first in my snug border under the house, at the foot of my myrtle and magnolia, both by the bye in full flower now. When they are gone by, I move almost all carefully away, and fill up the place with *scarlet geraniums*.

The pride of my heart in June is my *rose basket*. It stands on the lawn, and is, in truth, a bed surrounded with wire-work, which is covered all round and over the handle with creeping roses (each shoot tied down, never twisted in and out, which would certainly kill it), and the inside filled with low standards. From the time the leaves appear it is very pretty. But why should it not be pretty sooner? The ground is filled with *crocus* roots, and round the outside is a circle of wind flowers (*Anemone hortensis*). After these are gone *mignonette* is sown for the autumn.

Another bed is surrounded with a hare fence; here, therefore, are the *carnations*. But those charming flowers are deficient in one thing, leaves of real green. My hare fence forms the support of a low hedge of *French honeysuckles*, which flower at the same time with the carnations, and are green and pretty all the year round. In the spring this bed is filled with flowers among the carnation plants, and with some autumn-sown annuals for May; and about this same merry month of May are sown patches of other annuals just tall enough to peep over the hedge in the autumn, while in the middle are planted three or four *chrysanthemums*. The routine, then, for this bed is, mixed flowers till July, then carnations surrounded by French honeysuckles, afterwards late annuals, concluding with chrysanthemums.

On the lawn are several *tree roses*, which have the turf cut from them to the distance of a foot all round. These little beds contain each four successive flowers. Round the edge a circle of some early bulbs—*aconites, single snowdrops, hyacinths, Van Thol tulips*, or others. After these the roses open, and nothing more can be desired; but before they are all cut off, each stem is the support of some *low creeper* or *tall flower*; and round this, over and among the concealed bulbs, flourishes some gay little annual of a different colour, as *portulaccas* round a white *petunia*. One tree rose has round it a wreath of *double primroses* (white, crimson, sulphur, and lilac); but as their leaves appear again in the summer, instead of planting other things among them, I sow *major convolvulus*, and train them up strings fixed from the ground to the top of the stock to form a pyramid. The *canary plant* makes a pretty low hedge, supported on bent sticks round a purple *petunia*. If any one fears to injure the rose by drawing too much nourishment from its soil, I can only say that one of mine, an *Attalaine de Bourbon*, has at least 230 flowers every year.

Another bed is in the form of a Maltese cross, the centre of which forms a circular bed itself. In this centre is placed an *Œnothera macrocarpa*, whose large sulphur flowers contrast well with every thing. But the plant is invisible all the

spring, so, round it is first a ring of *crocuses* for March, then *hyacinths* for April, then *tulips* for May, and lastly, an edge

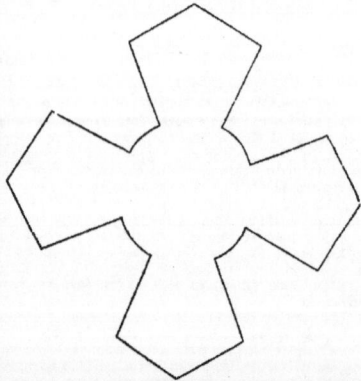

of *pinks* for June, while the *Œnothera* grows on all the time, and covers the territory of each as it fades away, till it opens its own large flowers with the inoffensive plants of the pink, by way of border. The arm of the cross which is farthest from the house, is filled with *fuchsias*, with a border of the blue and the white *Campanula pumila* in alternate masses. But amongst the fuchsias are *sweet williams*, which form a rich object earlier in the year, and are easily cut down when their taller successors claim attention. The opposite arm must be kept low, or it would hide the rest from the windows; it has a border of *pansies* for May, and is then filled with *verbenas*, pegged down—white, scarlet, and purple.

One side arm has an edge of *ranunculuses*; and while these are in flower, the plants of *Salvia patens* are spreading within, pegged down, deprived of their buds till the space is filled, and they are allowed to expand in all their loveliness. The opposite arm is bordered by *anemones*, and within them may be any other blue flower—*Campanula carpatica, Lobelia ramosa*, &c.

The summer arrangement, then, is—*yellow* in the middle; two opposite, *blues*; two opposite, *reds*, with variations. But in the early spring all the arms are full of mixed flowers and bulbs, and these are taken away as they fade; the former divided and placed in reserve beds till the autumn; the latter, if the leaves are dead, stored away; if not, moved with as much earth as they choose to take with them, to a nice airy place out of sight. The *Gentianella* alone, is too great a favourite, and too capricious to be moved about so readily; but there is a bed of *dwarf roses* to which it forms an edging, and remains green and unobtrusive afterwards, beneath the blaze of its queen.   INCOGNITA.

ALLOTMENT FARMING FOR OCTOBER.

BUSINESS OF THE SEASON.—We need scarcely say that the cottager or allottees' harvesting period is at hand—at the very door,—as to his various root crops; for these are the things wherewith to withstand the chance of a partial famine, should potatoes at any time fall away; and no man can say that these things can never be worse than they have been.

The unexpected virulence of the blight this season, when most persons flattered themselves it was progressively wearing away, is enough to alarm the most sanguine, and will have the effect of preventing a full amount of confidence in this root for many years. Still, we would be among the last to endeavour to have it superseded; only, we would implore all parties to be in great earnest about the selection and preservation of their seed; for assuredly there is no crop in which care will sooner manifest a corresponding amount of success than in the potato. We can say this much from experience, for we were amongst the first on the original appearance of the disease to advise the farmers to this course, and though it was long before we could make any impression, yet it is plainly seen now that the advice and the arguments on which it was based were not in vain. So much was said about potatoes in last month's paper, that it is unnecessary to add more now, but merely to repeat, that dryness, above all things, is essential to the potato in its present condition.

It is time now to commence using the lower leaves of the *mangold* or *beet*; this, indeed, may commence in the end of September, or even sooner. The only thing requisite is to slip them off as soon as they begin to discolour, beginning of course at the bottom of the stem and working upwards. They will bear this once a week until taken up to store. At the last trimming, our practice is to trim a great portion of the crown leaves away, for such must unavoidably be done soon on account of convenience of storing. Indeed, if very sharp frosts occur, it is well to commence this operation earlier, as much valuable fodder is contained in these tops, which the cow eats greedily; and if no cow, they can be given to the pig.

In housing or pitting the mangold, a dry day, if possible, during a dry period, should be chosen; the roots should be pulled betimes in the morning, and thrown on the surface, when, if any wind as well as sun, they will be ready to scrape by two o'clock P.M. The roots should then be passed through the hand, and the rough of the soil cleared away by means of a wooden scraper; and if they are tolerably dry, the sooner they are removed the better, otherwise it may be worth while to let them lie all night, provided the weather is safe; the latter, however, is but a gambling transaction at best, the weather being so variable and uncertain at this period. They will keep very well piled up in a sharp ridge on a high and dry plot of ground, throwing a coating of thatch over them. We prefer putting them in a shed or outhouse, if such can be had, or, indeed, anywhere where they are perfectly dry, and where a thorough circulation of air can be had; for this root does not shrivel, like the carrot, on exposure to the air. One thing must be observed in pitting them—they must not be placed in too large a body. We would not have the mound more than four feet wide at the base, but as high as they can be piled, putting all their crowns outward, at least as much as possible, and piling all *above the ground level*. The term "pitting," therefore, is not strictly applicable here.

What has been said of the mangold applies equally to *carrots, parsnips, &c.*, with some trifling exceptions. The latter roots, however, it must be understood, are not of so succulent a character as the mangold, and therefore will not endure much exposure to the atmosphere without shrivelling. Carrots keep exceedingly well in sand or ordinary soil which is nearly dry, putting alternate layers of roots and soil. Carrots, however, are very excitable as to sprouting, if anyways damp or warm; and for this reason many good cultivators cut the crowns "into the quick," or rather cut beneath them, when preparing them for storing. We have practised this mode for several years, and believe that it preserves them plump and tender longer than by the old plan.

As to parsnips, we have before said, what we must again repeat, that there is no better plan of husbanding the parsnip than to leave them in the ground, trenching them out as wanted. In this case, we merely determine on the crops which shall succeed them in the ensuing season, and this, of course, points to the amount or character of the manuring. This done, the manure is applied, and serves a double purpose—namely, to protect the crowns, and to prepare for the subsequent crop. Those who cannot find time must of necessity store them; and we may observe, that any plan which succeeds with the carrot will do for the parsnip; indeed, they may very fairly be mixed together, if need be.

SWEDES.—These are so well known that little comment is needed here. We may merely observe, that it becomes the allotment man and the cottager to make the most of their tops, as soon as the season has fairly declined.

THE VARIOUS GREENS.—Nothing remains now but to collect occasionally the half-decaying leaves, and to work them up as cow or pig food. It may seem a small thing to large holders to talk of collecting weekly, or otherwise, the decaying leaves of these crops; let them remember that "little things are great to little men," and that, indeed, without a very severe economy, which many in easy circumstances would despise, the cottager or allottee could not hope to succeed. Nevertheless, with it, with industry, perseverance, and a feeling of independence, he may, and will, succeed in placing himself beyond the pale of pauperism, which, indeed, is the wish of the majority of our countrymen, and, in the main, distinguishes them from such as the mobs of Paris and the Lazzaroni of Naples. It so happens, that the savoys and the various brocolis are tender as to their endurance of frost, just in proportion as they are luxuriant. An old and very good practice prevails among gardeners of laying or falling strong plants of these things towards the middle or end of October. Now, we opine that the mere cottager is not much in the brocoli way; nevertheless, as we would fain give breadth as well as length to our advice, and as THE COTTAGE GARDENER now and then creeps into the parlour, we must take the liberty of giving now and then a collateral turn for a moment, and swift back again to our old beat. The "falling," then, we strongly recommend; and by all means fall the *greens with their heads to the north*. There is, certainly, something very tempting in a genial sunshine to ladies'-maids, butterflies, sunflowers, &c., &c., but these brocolis, having produced their utmost bulk, require a sort of rest, during which, the vegetable extension being as it were suspended, nature is busied in forming the blossom-bud, which, when fairly developed, we term a brocoli or a cauliflower, as the case may be. This is easily accomplished by opening a trench on one side of the plant, rather deep, and preparing a sloping facing to receive it; a deep cut or two on the opposite side liberates the plant, which falls gently against the opposite slope. The plants being thus sunk, soil should be piled up to their very necks, or as high as the leaves will permit; at the same time drawing away any wounded and all half-decaying leaves.

CABBAGE.—The first week of this month is the best time to plant out those cabbages which were sown in August, and which will produce the largest of any in the ensuing summer. These require half a yard between the rows, and rather more than a foot in the row; if, however, the soil is rich and the kind large, they should have more room still. Our practice is, after planting the larger kinds at their permanent distance, to introduce a row of the small early kinds betwixt every two rows, and also a plant of the same betwixt every two plants in the row. We prefer the Matchless for this purpose; the Early York, however, will do, or any early hearting and dwarf kind. These latter will come in for use early in April if strong plants, and may be used daily until the middle of May, when they must be all cleared off, and the ground cleared for the summer cabbage, which will then require well soiling up.

All late cabbage plants not wanted to plant out permanently this autumn, should be immediately pricked out on raised beds, in an OPEN situation. These will be very valuable in spring, should a hard winter ensue; and surplus stock may be sold at nearly one shilling per hundred. Whilst on this subject it may be well to name that some of the cottagers near at hand grow many thousands in this way; and we know of one or two who have nearly paid their rental occasionally by growing the Drumhead cabbage for the farmers. We do think that every cottager should turn his attention to this point, for where he has a stout boy or two the pricking out may be done entirely by them; and this is the only tedious part of the business.

Where plenty of green-kale sprouts are desired through the winter, we advise that a portion of the crowns be used up betimes in this month; this will cause them to sprout much earlier. The too common practice is, to leave them on until February, when, of course, the heads and sprouts come all of a glut. This is neither expedient nor economical

LETTUCE.—We would have every cottager prick out a few hundred lettuces in the early part of this month; if he has not raised them, he may buy a few of some civil gardener. These form admirable pig food, to say the least of them, in the ensuing May and June, especially for breeding sows. They, moreover, attain a larger size than spring-sown lettuce, and the ground can be better spared for them than in the spring.

RHUBARB.—As soon as the leaves are decaying remove them, and apply a thick coating of rotten manure over their crowns, using the very slutch of the midden. This must be partly removed and partly dug in round the exterior of the plants in February.

COMMON TURNIPS will want one thorough clearing, and perhaps a slight thinning, in the early part of this month. Those who want good swede tops for cooking purposes early in spring, should leave a drill or two in the ground, cutting off their tops, not quite so low as the bulb, in the beginning of this month, and then soiling them over six inches deep. The young shoots may be gathered in February, March, and April, beautifully blanched, and tender as the finest sea-kale. No person should be without this useful and profitable article.

WINTER TREATMENT OF ALLOTMENTS.—Let no man fancy that when his roots are stored, and his greens, &c., dressed according to foregoing instructions, that he has done for the winter, and may henceforth stand with his arms folded. Every man worthy of holding so useful a thing as a plot of land, capable of producing all his vegetables, should every season try to enhance its value, by rendering it capable of a higher course of culture. That this is possible in three-fourths of the cases, we are assured by long observation. Many plots that we have seen are scoured by stagnant moisture; some are composed of a too stubborn soil, inclining to clay; and others possess a peaty or elastic texture. In regard to the first, nothing short of thorough drainage can ever make it what it ought to be. The stubborn loams must be broken up by a winter's fallow, and their texture altered by applying sandy materials, or even cinder ashes or old lime rubbish; the latter well pounded is an excellent thing. Peaty soils require both sandy materials and the loamy or clayey principle. Above all things we say, let every inch of available ground be fallowed, and by all means drain where the least suspicion exists.

THE LOAF OF BREAD.

By the Authoress of " My Flowers," &c.

THE remarks I think it advisable to make upon the estimates in my last papers, oblige me to touch again upon the subject of bread. My readers may consider me desultory and careless in the arrangement of my subjects, and would prefer one matter being fully discussed before the introduction of another. I am myself quite of their way of thinking, and fully aware of the deficiencies of my own mode of writing; but as I am no scientific author, and matter rises up before me when I least expect it, from various and unlooked for incidents, I must solicit their leave to do my utmost in their service, in the confused, unsatisfactory way which I am grieved to call *my best* Having thus far apologised for my short-comings, I will endeavour for the future to amend.

The estimates I have transcribed allow 24 pounds of bread and flour for five persons; that is to say, six pounds for each of the parents, and four pounds for each of the children per week. Many good managers allow only four pounds of bread per head for the family, old and young together, and find it sufficient; because some persons are not great eaters of bread, which leaves more for those who are. Many persons have naturally smaller appetites than others; some friends of my own, a gentleman and his daughter, *never* consumed a quartern loaf between them in the week; and many I have known whose habits in this particular have been the same. Others again, whose means permit it, eat a larger proportion of meat, &c., in preference to bread. Families most frequently dine late, and their luncheons consist of tart, pudding, fruit, &c., which lessens the consumption of bread, particularly as very little is eaten at tea when the dinner is late in the day; and the male portion of the household eat less bread than might be expected, because they consume more animal food than the female portion of it. But, generally speaking, where bread is a principal article of diet, and when the members of a family have hearty appetites, six pounds per week for adults will not be found much beyond the fair

allowance. Flour, too, is included in the calculation of bread, and in some cases must take considerably from it, as pies and puddings, both of meat and fruit, particularly the former, made with a plain crust, are useful in the family; and a good sized pie requires a pound of flour at least. The careful economist will soon discover the exact quantity of bread consumed in her household, and if it exceeds the limit which the estimate gives, will either substitute some other article in place of the extra quantity, or reduce on some other point to make up for it.

Early rising, early dining, and a relish for the social evening meal, after the labours and separation of the day, promote the appetite; and when baker's bread is used, it cuts away sadly fast, without affording the *stay* to the stomach which sound household bread invariably gives. When substantial meals are made upon bakers bread, in a couple of hours we feel hungry again, which is never the case even when a less quantity of sweet home-made bread has been eaten; and I am sure that some little trouble to effect home baking among the labouring population would be well repaid in comfort as well as in saving. I know too much of the inconvenience, privations, and poverty of the poor in a rural district to suppose that this can be carried out except in some few cases; but where it can be done—where flour can be bought, and yeast obtained, and the cottage possesses an oven—it is most desirable that bread should be made at home. Even if taken to be baked in the baker's oven, it would answer to the cottager to pay a halfpenny, or penny per loaf, according to its size, rather than buy bread from the shop.

I remember the large, sweet, hospitable-looking loaves at the house of a clergyman, who lived close to the village. The bread was made of wheat grown on his farm, but was kneaded and baked at the shop; and it was always well baked and light, and wholesome. Nothing looks more comfortable and hospitable than a large loaf of good sweet bread. It is not so elegant certainly as the small, delicate, shop loaf, but it cuts much more to advantage and goes much further. In the days of need we must not think of elegancies, but of that which is useful and essential. Many persons live in the near neighbourhood of a baker's oven, and might thus be accommodated at little expense.

The price of bread might be considerably reduced, if we mixed other flour with it, and it would be equally good. The writer from whom I have always quoted says, on the subject of bread, "The finest flour is by no means the most wholesome; and, at any rate, there is more nutritious matter in a pound of household bread than in a pound of baker's bread. Besides this, rye, and even barley, especially when mixed with wheat, makes very good bread. Few people upon the face of the earth live better than the Long Islanders; yet nine families out of ten seldom eat wheaten bread. Rye is the flour they principally make use of. Now rye is seldom more than two-thirds the price of wheat, and barley is seldom more than half the price of wheat. Half rye and half wheat, taking out a little more of the offal, make very good bread. Half wheat, a quarter rye, and a quarter barley,—nay, one-third of each,—make bread that I could be very content to live upon all my life-time; and even barley alone, if the barley be good, and none but the finest flour taken out of it, has in it, measure for measure, ten times the nutrition of potatoes."

Now, to the poor of a high station as well as to those of a low one, cheap bread is a grand consideration; and I think there is less prejudice to overcome in the former than in the latter. The poor are very prejudiced and cannot bear an inferior, or simply a *cheaper* article, to which they have not been accustomed. Now the higher classes can much sooner adopt a prudent measure, and reconcile themselves to what is right. I speak of each *as a class;* there are many exceptions on the one side, and many also on the other; but I think when the higher classes set an example, the poor would speedily follow.

There is a particular bread in the north of England, or there *was,* for it is many years since my father lived there, of which I have always heard him speak in the highest praise. He said it was far superior, in his opinion, to wheaten bread,—sweeter, and more moist. It was made of certain proportions of wheat and rye, which were grown and thrashed, and ground together. I *think* the quantities were equal, but I am not clear upon the subject, and I have not any north-country friend to whom I can apply for correct information. I shall feel deeply indebted to any reader of THE COTTAGE GARDENER who is able to give me the name and proportions of this excellent bread, who would kindly do so through the Editor. The name I have so often heard my father use, I have now but an imperfect recollection of; it was like *Massegeon*, or *Masselgeon*, bread.*

Where means are small, and little mouths are many, a cheap and *good* loaf is indeed a blessing; and I shall be thankful if any hints I have gathered may prove of use to the *higher poor*, who are so interesting in their trials and struggles. Yet the cheapest loaf, the closest economy, the watchful eye, and the skilful hand, will all produce nothing but restlessness, anxiety, and fatigue, without the "fixed heart," and the "mind" that "is stayed" on God. The bread " which endureth " must be fed upon, to enable that " which perisheth " to refresh and sustain us. " Oh, that " we "were wise, that" we " understood this, that" we "would consider our latter end !"

MY FARM-YARD.

THE season of the year has now arrived when those who wish to begin PIG KEEPING, or those who are about to increase their stock, should look about them, count over their little store, and see what they can spare for replenishing their " piggery." The age at which I should recommend the cottager to purchase his pig is from three to four months old. The gardens are now full of refuse vegetables. The commons will supply you with fern, which must be dried and ricked for litter during the ensuing winter. The gleaners have left the fields, and in many places, by paying a trifle, your pig can get a run amongst the wheat stubble, which will materially assist the process of fattening, by laying a good foundation before commencing the "stall-feeding." Acorns and beech-nuts will soon be falling from their lofty abodes, and by employing your children to pick them up, or by driving your pigs amongst them, you will soon see how much they improve in appearance under such judicious treatment. Thus, you see, all nature points out that something should be kept to eat the refuse of the gardens, the fields, and the woods. Nothing can be so useful, so profitable, as a pig; it is the "household god" of the poor man. It saves him and his family from many a heart-ache. It pays the rent; you need not, if you own a pig, dread the approach of Lady-day and Michaelmas, or Christmas and Midsummer, as the case may be. No! you may come forward with a bold heart to meet your landlord, the money in your hand, and, may be, even a welcome on your lips. It also gives a new winter gown to the wife, and a pair of new boots to the *master*. It provides several delicacies for the supper-table, and it has frequently been known to act as a charm, in preventing its owner from frequenting the ale-house. What more can I say for it? Surely such an animal must be a treasure, and should be found belonging to every cottage, however humble.

Farmers have always a drove of pigs ready to turn into their stubble directly their wheat is carried; of course this is as it should be, but I am sorry to say, in some parishes they forbid the poor from gleaning, in order to secure a larger amount of food for their swine. They cannot surely have read the beautiful history of " Ruth," or they could not grudge their poorer neighbours that privilege, which has been given them from time immemorial : " He that hath pity on the poor lendeth to the Lord."

Farmers, also, who live near large woods, should make a point of having a drove of swine by the time the acorns are ripe; they can be fatted sufficiently for market by sending them into those woods which abound in acorns, and on their return to the sty giving them skim milk. Pork thus fatted is very good; it makes particularly good bacon, having a peculiar " nutty " flavour, and is highly prized by epicures. I suspect in a few years, farmers who now look upon swine as secondary stock will, by finding the profits arising from them so great, place them amongst the first occupants of the farm-yard. The manure from the pigsty is of great value, particularly for turnips. I saw the other day in an essay, written by one who

* *Maslin*, or *Mascelin*, bread made of wheat and rye flour, is that referred to by " My Flowers."—ED. C. G.

well knew the value of pigs, that an acre of Swedes can be brought to the highest state of cultivation by the refuse from three pigstys. To those who grow turnips on a small scale, in a garden, I should recommend the following method of applying it :—Mix the manure thoroughly with ashes; dig the ground well, mark out the ridges deeply, and in them place the manure; over this sow the seeds, and you may anticipate a first-rate crop.

GEESE are also very profitable if bought about this time, and fatted on the stubble. In fact, poultry of all sorts should be at hand, to pick up the corn that has been spilt during the reaping and carting. You will find that if when turned into the field they are quite poor and thin, they will shortly become fit for the table, merely from picking up what would otherwise have been wasted. These little points may appear trifling, yet if they add to the comfort of home they should not be neglected; besides "a penny saved is a penny gained;" and in these hard times farmers are glad enough to save their pennies—"Take care of the pence, and the pounds will take care of themselves."   A FRIEND.

NATIVE WILD FLOWERS.
SEPTEMBER.

(*Continued from page* 387.)

To return to the favourite wild flowers, which are not so prejudicial to the cultivator as those we have enumerated as tile-drain intruders, we have first to notice the marine plant known under the name of Michaelmas daisy, or blue chamomile, but designated by botanists *Aster tripolium*, although its *apparent* resemblance to those showy China asters so well known in the gardens is very slight. It is, however, a showy plant, and highly beautiful when growing in great profusion, as we have often seen it on the flat turfy beaches of quiet bays, associated with the sea plantain and the *Salice armeria* or common thrift.

The wild teasel (*Dipsacus sylvestris*) may still be found in flower in the places which it inhabits. The fuller's teasel, as it is termed, is a very nearly allied plant, the flower-heads of which, furnished with numerous "hooked scales," are used for the dressing of cloth. Hooker and Arnott, in the new edition of the " British Flora," express an opinion that *D. fullonium* is but a variety of *D. sylvestris*, mentioning that "the hooks become obsolete by long cultivation on a poor soil." The Devil's-bit scabious (*Scabiosa succisa*) is also still in flower, and is remarkable for the peculiar appearance which its root presents of being cut or bitten off abruptly. This præmorse root gave ground for the belief, in early times, that the devil's teeth were the instruments employed in the shortening of the root, the reason assigned being his satanic majesty's " envie because it had so many excellent vertues," and, "unhappily," as a learned botanist remarks, " this malice has been found so successful, that no virtues can be now found in the remainder of the root or herb." This is the first instance on record of the exercise of the now fashionable operation of root-pruning; but now-a-days, being applied by hands more skilful than the teeth of its inventor, the results are more beneficial and satisfactory.

Let us conclude our scanty autumn wreath with a brief quotation from our late lamented laureate :—

> "Summer ebbs—each day that follows
>   Is a reflex from on high,
> Tending to the darksome hollows,
>   Where the frosts of winter lie.
>
> He who governs the creation,
>   In his providence assign'd,
> Such a gradual declination
>   To the life of human kind.
>
> Yet we mark it not ;—fruits redden,
>   Fresh flowers blow as flowers have blown,
> And the heart is loath to deaden
>   Hopes that else so long hath known."
>
>   G. LAWSON, F.B.S., *Edinburgh*.

THE APIARIAN'S CALENDAR.—October.

By J. H. Payne, Esq., Author of " The Apiarian's Guide."

My apiarian friends who are readers of THE COTTAGE GARDENER, (and who that loves a garden is not?) will naturally be desirous of receiving some communication from me at *the close of the bee season*—this untoward close, I am sorry to say, so far as many of my friends and myself are concerned; for non-swarming and migratory swarming have been the order of the day. Anxious, myself, to people one of Mr. Taylor's box-hives of the latest construction, I obtained the promise of a first swarm from several cottagers, that by so doing I might insure a good one, by having four or five to choose from; but, to my great disappointment, neither from them nor from any of my own stocks could I get one, for the few that did swarm located themselves in chimneys, in the roofs of houses, in hollow trees, and such like places from which they could not be taken; swarms have been repeatedly seen flying in different directions over the town (Bury St. Edmunds), and in our Botanic Garden they have been observed partially alighting, and shifting about from place to place, but not remaining stationary sufficiently long to be hived. Yet, after all the unusual and perplexing circumstances of this most unpropitious season, the *stocks* generally appear to be good and sufficiently heavy to go through the winter without feeding; but the *swarms*, what few there are, are *very, very* poor, and without copious feeding must perish; as to honey in glasses or small hives, in this neighbourhood, there is none.

A gentleman writing to me from Dublin the other day says, that on the 18th of May, he united two strong first swarms (to stock a favourite hive, I suppose), and upon weighing them a fortnight ago, the gross weight of the hive was only seventeen pounds and a half; and that the like is very common in the neighbourhood around him.

Wasps, also, appear to have been affected in a very unusual manner by the season, for although we had a very large number of queen wasps in the spring, scarcely a wasp has been seen since that time. I have seen but one myself, and upon making inquiry amongst the confectioners and the grocers, I can hear of only two having made their appearance; whereas, at this time of the year they usually have them by thousands, so that we have nothing to fear for our little favourites from this class of their enemies.

Autumnal Unions.—This process is now become so simplified, that the greatest novice in bee-management may accomplish it with ease, and with the most certain success; for at the conclusion of the honey season it appears that the bees may be driven from old worn-up hives, and from weak second and third swarms that have not been joined at the time of swarming, and that by putting three or four of these families together in an empty hive, and feeding them carefully, combs will speedily be formed; and that in this manner good stocks may be made for the ensuing season. The several methods for all these operations, with their results, have already been given in the pages of THE COTTAGE GARDENER; and surely, now, as Mr. Taylor says, " enough has been said of the folly, or rather *wickedness*, of killing bees," to prevent its ever being resorted to again; but should the trouble of feeding in this manner be objected to, let the bees be driven from the weak hives into a tolerably strong stock, by inverting the weak hive and placing the other over it, mouth to mouth, and tying a napkin round where the hives meet, so as to make the escape of a single bee impossible, and then gently tapping the lower hive continuously for ten or fifteen minutes, when the bees will be found to have left the lower for the upper hive; and this doubled population, however paradoxical it may at first appear (for it has been proved again and again), will consume a less quantity of honey during the winter than if the driven bees had not been joined to it.

Making-up.—The time has now arrived for *making-up* stocks, as it is termed amongst apiarians, that is, joining the bees of late swarms or casts together; and when united, to feed them until they weigh twenty pounds without the hive or box which contains them, thus making-up good stocks for the next year; indeed, no hive should be suffered to pass through the month of October without being made to weigh twenty pounds beyond the weight of the hive, for by so doing the danger as well as the trouble of feeding during the winter months will be avoided; and should the winter prove a favourable one for them, a little barley sugar only, in March and April, will be all that they require.

WINTERING BEES.

Your correspondent, " A Country Curate," has directed the attention of the apiarian public to some remarks as to the best mode of preserving bees in winter; a matter of great importance in our variable climate. It will be allowed that the experiments cited by him are of far too indefinite a character to be followed without a more accurate account of place, dates, &c. I never doubted the possibility of preserving life in a hive of bees through the winter, by covering it up from the influence of the atmosphere, either under or above the ground. The main question is whether this extra trouble and expense is actually called for. I am an old bee master, and believe that it is not; and that bees may pass the winter with the smallest possible consumption of food in their usual positions. Repeated experiments have convinced me that nothing more is needed than the entire screening of the hives from the influence of the sun in the cold months. My practice is the same as that recommended by Mr. Taylor, in his " Bee-keeper's Manual " (illustrated at page 147, fourth edition). If the bees are attracted from the hive by every gleam of winter sun or reflection of snow on the ground, the most disastrous consequences may ensue. Keep them quiet and torpid, and little or no food is wanted. In the contrary event their store is rapidly consumed; disease and death assuredly following. The little additional expense of such screens is as nothing compared with the certain advantage. But I have yet another plan, which I hope to be enabled to carry into execution; and I trust others of your correspondents will try it with me. I mean to face a few of my hives entirely to the north, throughout the year. I am convinced that the bees in leaving home are guided solely by the outer atmospheric temperature at all seasons, preferring shade for their domicile, where the choice is offered. White informs us that bees thrive well to the north. Gelieu always screened his hives from the sun. Mr. Taylor says, that " an apiarian of great celebrity placed his hives around the interior of an octagon erection, without perceiving any sensible difference in their well-doing." A friend of my own last year had a stock, the best in his apiary, which never faced otherwise than due north. The " Country Curate " appeals to the " intelligent and curious apiarians who read your pages," for assistance in carrying on a series of winter experiments. Will some of these make a trial of my proposition, by placing a few stocks altogether to the north (well sheltered of course), and compare them with those worked in other aspects? I would advise their permanent removal in November. THE COTTAGE GARDENER has rendered invaluable aid to apiarian science and practice; and I feel confident that its columns would be open to receive well-authenticated details of useful and interesting experiments. Will any correspondent favour us by saying whether he has already witnessed the adoption of my proposed scheme; and with what result?   AN OLD BEE MASTER.

ARTIFICIAL SWARMS.

PERMIT me to occupy a space in your valuable paper with a few remarks, by way of supplement, to my former letter on the subject of my plan of effecting autumnal unions, and forming artificial stocks, which seem called for by some observations of Mr. Payne upon both, and my knowledge that several of your readers are trying, or have tried, my method as recommended in THE COTTAGE GARDENER of August the 1st. But first, let me thank Mr. Payne for the cordiality and frankness with which he has acknowledged the utility as well as the simplicity of my plan of uniting bees. I have only to say, that it is adapted to every purpose of this kind, whether it be to effect autumnal unions, to transfer stocks, or to strengthen working hives in the breeding or honey gathering seasons. It has this advantage over the fumigating system, that whereas in the latter case several days are generally wasted before the bees recover their wonted energy, in the former instance there is no interruption whatever to their labours beyond the momentary interruption necessary to the operation itself. Every intelligent apiarian will at once perceive the capabilities of the plan; but I may mention, for the instruction of the uninitiated, how, on one occasion last autumn, I effected the addition of two weak stocks to one strong one. With the greatest ease imaginable, the population of all three stocks were driven into one and the same empty hive, and when united, were driven back again the same evening into the stock which was to be strengthened. This, however, as I have since discovered, was quite an unnecessary waste of time and labour. It would have been sufficient to have driven the two weak stocks together, and to have then placed the temporarily occupied hive *over* the stock to be strengthened, carefully stopping up every crevice by which the bees in the upper hive might have egress into the open air, except from below. By this means they would have been forced to descend into the lower hive, which, of course, is supposed to have a hole at its top. If this be done *at night* when the bees are quiet, the junction will be very speedily and safely effected. I have often removed a bell-glass full of bees from one hive to another, without the least apparent discord between them. It is different *by day*, when the bees are active; though even here the interposition of a perforated zinc plate for four or five hours (which can be easily done where the top of a hive is flat) has been found to obviate all danger of fighting. The upper hive should not be removed for three or four days.

One observation of Mr. Payne's, of some importance, I would wish to correct. It has reference to my method of forming artificial stocks. He says, that it is "not *strong* stocks that are to be deprived of their honey and united to others, but *weak* ones only." Very true, where *autumnal unions alone* are in question; but in the case of *entire deprivation*, and the *transfer of bees* according to my peculiar plan, it is necessary that at least *one* of the stocks to be deprived and transferred should be strong (*i.e.* populous), because the queen of such a stock being a prolific and vigorous one, there will be so much greater chance of success, as, in all probability, *she* would come off the victor in the conflict of queens. And here I may state my belief that the weakness of stocks is to be *generally* attributed to some defect in the queen, except in the case of *very old hives* (where contraction of space, as well as dirt and vermin, would mar her capabilities), and also in the case of *late casts*, whose population is distracted between attention to breeding and anxiety to procure a sufficient store of food at a time when it begins to fail. I cannot, therefore, promise much to him who has saved the bees of weak stocks *only*, how many soever he may have united together. Be careful to ensure the presence of *one good queen* (or, in other words, let *one* of the stocks be very strong), and unite as many weak ones with it as possible (consistently with the size of the hive), and there need be very little doubt of success. I do not, of course, recommend any one to destroy his established stocks for the sake of furthering such an experiment; this he need not do; but if he has any weak stocks which he desires to save, and he has a mind to try my plan, he need not, I am sure, seek far from home among his cottage friends for a strong stock that is doomed to the brimstone pit.

Again, I have mentioned the 10th of August as the latest time for the formation of artificial stocks, simply because I *have successfully* secured a stock formed as late as that time; whereas I know of the *failure* of a similar experiment which was only begun a week later. I could account for this, perhaps, in another way, but I should not like to induce any one to venture on an experiment recommended by me, without the sanction of my own experience, guarding them at the same time against the chances of failure. I do not, however, pretend to say that a stock so formed, even as late as the middle or even the *end* of September, would not succeed very well. Mr. Payne has given us lately an instance of such success, but it must have been, though an interesting, yet a somewhat troublesome experiment. Now, I *ceased* feeding my own bees about that time, nor have I given them any more food from that time to this day, except about five or six ounces of honey on one occasion in the spring. I had, therefore, no trouble whatever with them in the winter. The weight of *contents* of this hive (*i.e.* independent of box alone), when I ceased supplying them with food, was about 17 lbs., which proved amply sufficient; while I do not think much of it was left in store for another year (a matter of some consequence

I should think), before honey abounded. To what extent this system of forming artificial stocks may be carried it is impossible to say. It were desirable that it should be tried as extensively and diversely as possible. I throw this out as a hint to those who are curious in such matters, and have leisure for bestowing the requisite attention on experiments of this kind. With a *good queen* and *plenty of bees*, I am persuaded anything may be done; even *breeding* may be carried on at Christmas in mild winters almost as actively as at midsummer; but it stands to reason that, as every stock is more populous in August than in October, double or treble the number of stocks must be united in the latter month, to equalise an experiment instituted with a third or half the number united in August.

One word more as to feeding such stocks. I have somewhat improved my feeder (as described vol. iii., p. 297), by discarding the perforated zinc plate, which is made to float with difficulty. Instead of it I now use a float of half-inch wood (the harder the better), which fits loosely in the feeder, allowance being made for its expansion; a circular hole in it allows space for the cylindrical tube; besides which there are three or four holes, half an inch broad, cut through the float, and extending from side to side. To keep the wood float from sticking to the bottom when the liquid gets low, I pass three or four brads through the float, of such length that the bees cannot get under it, while it is kept clear of the bottom. My feeder is now complete. I do not find many bees drowned, and they do not soil themselves, as before, to speak of. I have further improved it by inserting, instead of the spiral wire, a cylinder of pasteboard—an exact fit, inside the tube of ascent. It is astonishing what a quantity of food they will consume in this improved feeder. Let it be only kept strictly clean, by washing it out once a week; and let the food be made of wholesome table-beer, and it will astonish the experimentalist how rapidly they will work. The best augury of success is the working of the combs down to the bottom board, which at this season of the year is significant of a vigorous and prolific queen. Such combs would on examination be found filled with eggs and brood of all ages.　　　　　　　　　　A COUNTRY CURATE.

THE POULTRY-KEEPER'S CALENDAR.—OCTOBER.

By Martin Doyle, Author of "Hints to Small Farmers," &c.

THE POULTRY-YARD GENERALLY.—The season for producing any fresh additions to the stock of poultry has now passed away, excepting the hatching and rearing of ducks and geese for the markets in January and February. These birds may yet be successfully reared late in autumn, and they will be found highly remunerative for the extra trouble they may occasion. All old or superfluous poultry which are not intended to be either for winter fatting or for breeding in the spring, should now be sold off or consumed in the form of pies and soup. The recipes for goose or duck pies and fowl soup should be consulted in the simple and useful books of cookery which treat of such subjects.

FOWLS.—Hens which are in the list of the doomed ought to be allowed to complete their moulting before they are consigned to the cook's tender mercies. Food for poultry is now so abundant, that it is better not to loose the advantage which the gleanings of harvest afford, by prematurely killing any description of poultry, and more particularly when the moulting fever in any degree affects the victims of man's gluttony. The flesh in such state is unwholesome. The feeding during its continuance, and to the moment when the knife is to be used, should, of course, be of the most generous kind, so as to improve the condition of the bird as much as possible. Besides the corn which is now so abundant in many fields, barley-meal, mixed tolerably stiff with water or milk, varied now and then with cheap rice boiled into a granular, not a sloppy state, will be the best dietary. To fowls fed in confinement on raw grain, it is almost needless to say, that gravel should be given to help them to digest the corn. For ailments of a mysterious nature, pills of calomel and colocynth, in the proportions and in the doses prescribed for adult human creatures, are recommended. It should be remembered by poultry-keepers, that a hen-ladder is useful to enable the fowls to mount to their roosting-perches. The want of it is inconvenient, and sometimes dangerous, and yet this is very common.

We had proposed to give a sketch of a good fowl coop, but it is really unnecessary to do so, as a coop is an appendage so common and so simple. A few words here, however, on this subject may not be superfluous. A coop, four feet long and three feet high, standing on legs, and divided into three compartments, will be found sufficiently commodious for fowls. It is better, generally, not to have one story over another; for, in such case, drawers will be necessary under the rounded cross-bars on which the prisoners stand to receive the excrements; and the accumulation of these will be offensive to the smell. By having an open space under the bars of a one-storied coop, the excrements fall to the ground, and can be at once removed. The bars, which are in fact perches, should be ranged parallel with the troughs, otherwise the fowls will not be in the proper position to feed without turning to the front, and scrambling for a hold on their perch, which, if at right angles to the trough, affords them no standing room. We have seen such coops. Single cells are undoubtedly desirable, except on the score of increased cost, because a bird can be taken out and examined without disturbing the others; and combats, which so often occur when gangs are put together, are prevented by the system of solitary confinement; but with two or three compartments it is always probable that the prisoners may be so assorted as to live in peace, and fatten comfortably. Some people have boarded floors for the fowl, and put straw on them, but straw is heating and generates fleas; and besides this, the natural repose of fowls is only on a perch. The fowl houses should be white-washed in every corner and cranny to kill fleas. A good fumigation with peat smoke, if it can be done without danger of fire, will be useful to purify the houses from any remains of summer effluvia.

In our last number, it was intimated that a bottle holding water, and placed in an inverted position over a pan nearly filled with liquid, is sufficient mechanism for supplying water to chickens. The diagram here presented will illustrate our meaning.

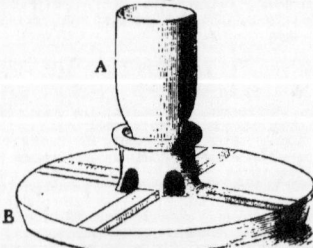

A is a bottle. B a shallow bowl with a centre piece, which is made to hold the neck of the bottle a little above the level of the pan, and having flood-gates to each compartment, as shown in the above plate.

An earthen pan, with a bottle suspended by strings or tape, would answer the purpose equally well, and is exceedingly simple, as here represented. The bottle filled with water is closed with the thumb while being inverted over the pan, and suspended with its mouth a little below the upper rim. On withdrawing the thumb, the water will rush out until it stands in the pan at the level of the mouth of the bottle.

The third plate shows a description of an earthen pan made at the pottery of Inkpen (Berks) for the safety of little chicks, which could not possibly drown themselves in the circular troughs, which are too narrow to admit their bodies—they may scramble across the partitions, but cannot fall into the spaces between them.

This plate needs no descriptive comment, except that the centre A is merely a handle for raising the pan, not a reservoir for water, as might be supposed.

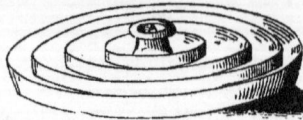

TURKEYS AND DUCKS should be encouraged to search for oak and beech mast as fast as they fall from the trees; though not in itself a delicate fattening diet, it will be an excellent foundation on which a course of barley-meal and milk diet may be laid.

GEESE should be prepared for the Michaelmas market. Very fat and heavy ones are, perhaps, more in request at Christmas than at this festival; but if the birds are not particularly young, they are much improved both in tenderness and flavour by a month's confinement and fatting with oats. In many families the dripping from the roast goose is almost as valuable as the goose itself. The fatter the goose, the more economical a diet it constitutes. For the sake of the feathers, the confined birds should be well supplied with clean straw.

Put away nursing coops now, that are no longer wanted for this year, in their proper stowage places; and on rainy days repair whatever things may require renovation. Take care of fowl stealers who may be prowling about your premises in the nights, which are becoming long and dark.

STORING VEGETABLES.

A great deal of the comfort of winter housekeeping depends on the way vegetables and fruit are kept. Many people who have an abundance of these things during the summer and autumn are obliged either to purchase or to go without in the winter, merely because they do not know the best method of preserving them. Few gardens are so small but that a surplus of vegetables and fruit are at some time or another grown, and therefore I do not imagine a few remarks on the subject would be out of place. So much has lately been said and written about *potatoes* that I dare say every one has made up their mind ere this as to the best way of keeping them. I have always found the old-fashioned plan of digging a hole in the earth about five feet deep the best. Strew this hole rather thickly with straw, and then throw the potatoes in; and when within a foot of the top, cover them over, and heap the earth up in the centre so as to form a " grave." These " pits" ought to be looked over every two months, and any potatoes that are at all diseased should be given to the pigs. This opening, however, should not take place when there is any frost, or the whole " pit " is very likely to suffer.

Onions are, next to potatoes, the vegetables I like to see cultivated in a cottage garden; no dish is palatable without one, and they are very sustaining and nourishing. The French have found this out long ago; and the labourer's dinner in that country continually consists of a couple of raw onions, some black bread, and a little jug of broth smelling most potently of garlic! September is the proper month for taking up onions; it should be done on a dry day, and then they should be laid separately on the ground in the " eye of the sun." Turn them twice a day until they are thoroughly dried, and then store them in some dry well-aired place. They may either be strung together and hung up to the ceiling, or laid on the floor, care being taken that they do not touch one another. The former plan is the best where room is of consequence. Should they begin to sprout, touch the roots with a hot iron, which will effectually prevent it, without injuring the onion. *Carrots* should be kept in sand, in a dry but not a warm place. If an old cask is at hand, you will find it very useful for the purpose—putting layers of sand and carrots alternately. This plan also answers well for parsnips and beetroot.

French beans may be kept till Christmas, at which time they will be considered great delicacies. For this purpose they must be picked when quite young. Provide a jar or butter-keg for them, and strew some salt at the bottom, and then put a layer of beans about four inches deep, sprinkle again with salt, and continue thus until the cask is full. Tie it well down, and on the top place a weight, in order to exclude every particle of air; keep it in a cellar till you require it. *Green peas* can also be eaten in the winter, but not with such success as the beans. To do so you must proceed thus :— shell, and put them into boiling water, hold them over the fire for three minutes; put them into a sieve, and when quite dry bottle them; pour a little melted suet into the mouth of the bottle, cork them down very tight, and keep them in a dark cellar. Some people bury the bottles in earth, but that is more troublesome, and I do not think more effectual. When required for table they must be treated as if they had been just picked. To prevent herbs (such as mint, thyme, sage, &c.,) from losing their flavour, they should be kept in the following manner :—Pick them on a dry day, and spread them in a warm shady place until quite dry, then tie them up into small bundles and pack them closely in a box, each sort separately; cover them over with white paper, and tie the box down; keep it in a dry and rather warm place, and you will find them very superior to those that have been kept in paper bags.

Herbs are very useful, especially to the cottager, and care should be taken to preserve them well. Although many new medicines have been discovered, which are valuable in real illness, yet I am sure if herbs were as much thought of as they were in our grandmother's time, many a bill would be avoided, and many a long walk to the parish doctor saved! If herbs were as difficult to be procured as "*pills and draughts*" are, we should soon hear of "pennyroyal tea," "chamomile tea," and all the various "simples" which were so well known one hundred years ago, but which now are despised and neglected (in many cases), merely because they are common and cheap. In matters of the greatest importance, how often is this the case! The injunction of our Lord, "Come buy wine and milk without money, and without price," is often disregarded, *because* nothing is to be paid for such luxuries, whilst the creed of penances and mortifications finds many a worshipper, because by such acts our vanity is fed, and our self-righteousness, alas! exalted.

A FRIEND.

ENGLISH CAGE BIRDS.

MISSEL THRUSH.

INSESSORES DENTIROSTRES. MERULIDÆ.

Turdus viscivorus; Merula viscivora: Misseltoe Thrush; Storm Cock; Holm Thrush.

THE Missel Thrush is one of the largest of our thrushes, and the earliest in song—commencing his strains very frequently as early as February. He generally occupies the topmost branch of the highest tree in or near the woods, where he pours forth his loud clear notes in constant succession. There is very little or no variety in it, nevertheless it is associated with our feelings of rejoicing at the departure of winter and the near approach of spring. His song is

frequently heard while on the wing chasing his mate during the pairing or breeding season; and I have noticed his song to be more frequent just before a storm of rain, and from this I doubt not he takes the name of Storm Cock. When taken wild he should be placed in a large cage covered in such a way that he cannot see any person, or by its fears and frequent attempts to escape it will destroy its plumage, if not its life. Being secured in a large cage, and supplied with a cup of water made secure as not to be easily upset in its attempts to escape, he should have a few worms, or snails, or pieces of meat (raw), thrown at the bottom of his cage; and although sulky at first, impelled by hunger (if left quiet) he will at length pick up the pieces of worms or meat. After the first few days fed upon this kind of food, I then place a dish of oatmeal mixed up into a paste with water, and stick therein pieces of meat and worms; these he will pluck out, and adhering to them portions of the paste, to which, at length, he will have recourse as readily as the worms and meat. But I prefer bringing up the young birds from the nest to old birds, as they become perfectly tame, bear handling well, will come to you by your call, and readily recognise your voice and person, are easily reared, and will breed in an enclosed place. When taken in the nest, I feed them upon worms, snails, and the paste above mentioned alternately, until they are able to feed themselves, which will often be in a month—keeping them and their nest scrupulously clean. This is indispensable; for if the feathers become dirty and matted together with filth they mostly die. They are subject to cramp; to obviate this I mix for the young birds a quantity of road grit in their paste of oatmeal, which has a very beneficial effect, and affords them a sufficiency of phosphate of lime to form feathers. The soil should be taken from each bird by the aid of a pair of pliers resembling a bird's bill, immediately it is discharged from the bird, which generally happens upon the first mouthful of food given it—the little bird rising on its legs, and elevating its hinder part over the nest—thus exhibiting the ancient moral, "that it is a dirty bird that soils its own nest." Nature has amply provided against such a contingency by encasing the excrement as it is discharged in a sort of gelatinous bag, so tough and tenacious that the parent bird can take it readily up and convey it in its bill to a considerable distance. The same treatment will do for all the thrush tribe, except that I give in addition berries of various kinds taken from the hedges. W. RAYNER.

[This bird, Macgillivray says, is a permanent resident, but the native birds of the species are supposed to be joined by others from the continent towards the end of October. They fly about in loose flocks, composed of a few individuals, seldom more than twenty, and at this season betake themselves to the open fields, especially those recently ploughed, where they search for worms, larvæ, and seeds. On alighting, the bird stands for some time with the body and tail inclined, the head raised, the wings slightly drooping. Should it descry symptoms of danger, it alarms its companions by a low harsh scream, when they all remain attentive for a while, and fly off, or should they judge themselves safe, commence their search, in prosecuting which they scatter about more than the Fieldfares or Redwings. If you watch the motions of one, you see it hop smartly along, stop to pick up an object, then resume the attitude of attention, hop forward, dig up a worm, break it to pieces, and swallow it, then stand again, and thus continue until satiated or put to flight. In this manner, which is precisely that of the Fieldfare and Common Thrush, they continue feeding for hours, unless disturbed, generally keeping at a considerable distance from each other, so that two can very seldom be shot at once. They are extremely vigilant, and the moment one is alarmed it emits a low *churr*, which is repeated by the rest, when they either fly to the trees in the neighbourhood, or flit to a distant field. In an open place, they hardly consider themselves safe at the distance of two hundred yards; and although they remain while a person passes them, they fly off if he stands to watch them. When perched on trees they seldom allow a nearer approach than a hundred yards. If they are feeding near a low wall, you may occasionally obtain a shot by going to the place and suddenly starting up, but you have little chance of catching them unawares by slowly raising your head and gun between the stones. I once shot a fine specimen in a field near Edinburgh, through a hole at the bottom of a wall, just as, having observed me, it was about to fly off.

The Missel Thrush, during winter and spring, is thus more vigilant and suspicious than even the Fieldfare, and, for this reason, as well as because it is much rarer, is seldom shot. It sometimes associates with that species in the fields; but rarely flies with it. Its flight, which is rather heavy, is performed by a series of flappings, with short intervals of cessation, like that of the Fieldfare, and has very little undulation. On occasion, however, it becomes rapid; and, when at full speed, a Missel Thrush bears a considerable resemblance to a Sparrow-Hawk or Merlin; and small birds are sometimes seen pursuing it, as they are wont to fly after a bird of prey. It is seldom that the individuals of a flock fly low or close together. While proceeding, they now and then utter a low scream, and when they find an eligible place, they either alight abruptly at a distance from each other, or fly over the field for some time.

The song of this bird resembles that of the Blackbird, but its notes are less mellow and modulated, although equally loud. It commences very early in spring, or even in winter, when the weather is fine, and is continued until the middle of summer; but, as the species is comparatively scarce in most parts, it is seldom heard, and when it is, is usually mistaken for that of the Blackbird or Song Thrush. Several individuals have heard it sing when flying from one place to another, but on such occasions I have only heard it utter its harsh scream.

The flocks break up in March, and about the end of that month, or towards the middle of April, the different pairs commence their building operations, selecting a natural wood, a plantation, or frequently an orchard, for their summer residence, whence they make excursions into the neighbouring fields and gardens. The nest, which is placed in the fork of a tree, or on a branch, generally at an inconsiderable height, is very bulky, and more rudely constructed than that of the other species which build with us. It is composed externally of twigs, straws, and grasses of various kinds, intermixed with leaves and mosses; within this is a rudely formed cup of mud, generally in pellets, mixed with grass or fibrous roots. The interior is a more carefully arranged layer of finer grasses, roots, and moss, or frequently of grass alone. Sometimes the exterior is partially covered with grey lichens and mosses; but at other times it is similar to that of the Blackbird's nest. The internal diameter of one now before me is four and a half inches, its depth two and three-fourths, and the thickness of its walls an inch and three-quarters. The eggs, usually four, or from three to five, are of a regular oblong-oval form, an inch and three-twelfths in length, by ten-twelfths, flesh-coloured, or purplish-white, marked with irregular scattered spots of light brownish-red and more obscure spots of purplish red.—*Macgillivray's History of British Birds.*]

POULTRY-HOUSE.

I now enclose you a plan of my little hen-house. I must, however, tell you that my original hen-house was up *stairs*, close to the slates, and with a skylight facing the north. It was bitter cold, so much so, that last winter my Spanish hens did not lay at all.

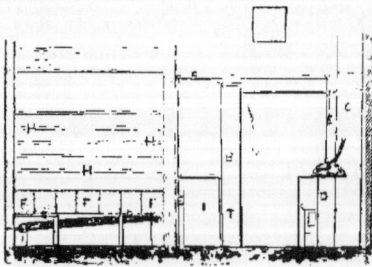

a Sunk water tank in boiling-house, &c.
b Pump—to supply regulating cistern.
c Regulating cistern.
d Boiler and stove.
e Steam-pipe for warming hen-house, and steaming tubs.
f Hen boxes.
g Platform to hen boxes.
h Roosting poles.
i Steaming tubs sunk in ground; j other steaming box.
k Entrance for poultry.

My present house was a loose box facing south. I chose it not for its capabilities, but because joining the boiler-house. In many ways I would alter the arrangement were I to fit it again, especially in having the laying-boxes under the roosting perches. As at present I believe it will answer, and at only the expense of the iron pipes, as when I am steaming food for my pigs I have nothing to do but turn the tap, and let it run off through the hen-house.

A Naval Officer.

EXTRACTS FROM CORRESPONDENCE.

The Potato Murrain.—On taking up some Ash-leaved Kidneys, that had been left in the ground, to see whether they would remain freer from disease than the rest of the crop which was taken up some weeks before, I found that the tubers under some of the plants which had been much trodden on in the course of the summer were good, without exception, whilst of the remainder nine-tenths or more were spoiled. Being on a border before a south wall, a sort of path was made over the plants nearest the wall, across the ends of the drills, by people going to the fruit-trees, &c.: and the haulm of those plants was injured, and its growth dwarfed; and their tubers though sound and good were smaller than those under the rest of the plants. Does, then, closeness of soil protect from disease? I should have thought so, had I not constantly seen this summer that the tuber deepest in the earth rots sooner than those at the surface, where, when partly greened by the air, they are hardy and well. Again, I should have said, that checking the luxuriance of the foliage might have had a good effect, but that I have seen some of the most luxuriant plants with a plentiful crop underneath, unhurt to the last—so that I can draw no conclusion. May it not be useful to learn, if it has been generally remarked, that plants trodden, as by a path, &c., have uniformly escaped disease?—Hy. Helyar, Jun., *Hardington, near Yeovil.*

[These facts coincide with the opinion we have always entertained, that *dryness* is one of the best preventives of the disease.—Ed. C. G.]

Destroying Ants.—A gentleman in this neighbourhood (Kingston-on-Thames), whose field was overrun with ants, after having tried every imaginable thing to destroy them, at last pursued the following method, and at this time there is scarcely one to be seen where before there were thousands :—Having chosen dry weather, in July last, for the purpose, he set a man to work, with a heavy block of wood in the shape of a pavior's hammer, to hammer the earth down on them, and pouring in hot water at the same time ; by these means he destroyed numbers. After this first operation three Guinea fowls were put into the field to eat what remained. By constant ramming in wet weather, and when dry assisting the operation by hot water, and this followed by two Guinea fowls (one having died), he has completely got rid of the pests ; but whether they will return next year remains to be proved.—K. O. T.

Boiling Peas.—We frequently hear our cottage friends complain of peas being "bad boilers," and taking many hours stewing before they break, and sometimes not doing so at all. Now, under the following treatment, peas that would take twelve hours to break them in the usual way, may be broken in less than one :—Pick them and clean them, if necessary, by rubbing them in a *dry* cloth ; have a vessel containing a sufficient quantity of water to cover them, boiling very hard, strew the peas into it from the hand, a few at a time, so as not in the least to check the boiling of the water, and when boiled nearly dry add cold water, and after boiling a few minutes they will break. If the water be very hard, a bit of washing soda may be put in.—J. H. P.

Soot as a Manure for Potatoes.—Will you allow me to mention that to-day I had dug up some second early potatoes—six rows. The seed was the same of all ; to two rows I put as tillage a mixture of lime and soot, to two of soot alone, and to the remaining two superphosphate of lime. All were planted the same week. The produce from the seed having the soot tillage alone was about one-third greater than that with the superphosphate of lime, and nearly a fourth greater than with the mixture of lime and soot. There were scarcely any diseased ; not one, so far as I have yet seen, from the sooted ground. I tried in another place plain soot against plain lime, and I found the produce nearly equal ; the tubers a little finer from the soot. The lime I had had under cover for many months. It was air slacked.—A. T. B., *Chesterfield.*

Runner Kidney Beans.—I now proceed to make good my promise about the Scarlet Runner Kidney beans ; in doing so, I shall just state what I have *seen,* and what we are *trying to do* here. It was in the garden of a person with whom I happened to be acquainted in the small town of Llanrhiadr (County of Montgomery), where I saw this useful vegetable trained in a manner different to what I have seen either before or since ; although I have travelled about a good deal in the northern and midland counties, I have seen *no other instance of this method of training them,* indeed, my friend told me he had borrowed the idea from the Continent, where he had seen them thus cultivated. The two rows of Kidney beans which I saw were parallel, running north and south, and probably six feet apart ; and, by means of two posts, a rail stretching from one of these posts to the other, a suitable number of wooden pegs (hooked) driven into the ground, and of good thick twine, which latter formed the connecting link betwixt the hooked pegs and the rail above, the whole had the appearance of the steep roof of a house ; the plants having made their growth, both sides showed a uniform face of leaves, flowers, and pods, and the whole formed the greatest attraction in the garden, as it had a really handsome appearance ; the crop, too, was very abundant and early. The argument in favour of this method is, that the sun's rays reach the west side of the row long before noon, and continue on the east side of it for a similar time afterwards. When the sun is perpendicular, however, and exerting its greatest power, a much larger portion of the plants are receiving the benefits of its rays than if they were trained perpendicularly, since, by the latter method, the upper part of the plants considerably shade the lower part. In districts where "poles" are scarce and dear, this plan would also be found decidedly the cheapest, and this is another recommendation. Our experiments this season, I am sorry to say, are incomplete ; for the spring frosts unfortunately took our first sowing of the beans, and the second crop of plants have never yet reached the rail, nor are likely to do now ; however, we hope to escape such calamities in future. I may mention, that instead of the hooked pegs, we used

pieces of deal the length of the rows, each three inches wide and one inch thick, fixed at the ends into upright posts only a few inches high, and had the twine laced backwards and forwards between the upper rail and the lower ones, allowing a space between of about six inches. I perceive, however, that our method might be improved upon ; if the lower rails were one inch deeper and an aperture made at every six inches distance along their lower side, with a saw sufficiently wide to admit the twine, it would prevent a possibility of the latter getting displaced ; and if knotted at intervals (the knots to be made close to the rail), there would be no risk of the fabric giving way should the twine get broken by any means. I should mention, that we used three-fold twine previously dipped in boiled linseed oil ; this strengthens and preserves it, and at the same time prevents contraction or expansion.—W. L.

Cramp in Poultry.—Having had several young ducks seized with the cramp, and the birds being completely rigid and unable to swallow, it occurred to me that a warm bath might be of service. I accordingly placed their feet in warm water, and with a sponge kept constantly squeezing the water over them for about ten minutes, which partially revived them. I then wrapped them in flannel and placed them in a basket in the warm kitchen, when they soon showed signs of recovery, and the following morning they were in perfect health.—W. B.

Polmaise Heating.—Alas ! poor polmaise ! how hard you are upon it ; you "are sorry 'C' has been to the expense of such a structure," and say, that "in being obliged to abandon it, he only shows the fate common to most who have tried it." Your favourable notice of my cow-house vinery encourages me to give you a short account of my small doings with the much abused but admirable polmaise. I am quite a tyro, and four years ago had not the slightest idea how to heat a forcing house, or to cultivate the pine-apple. Polmaise appeared and took my fancy. I have heated by it two hothouses, a pit, and greenhouse, containing at this moment fruiting and succession pines growing *most luxuriantly.* A Queen, I am told by a gardener well qualified to judge, would be worthy of the exhibition at Chiswick, and a Cayenne he expects will weigh 8 lb. In the same houses large crops of grapes on three year old vines have been gathered this season, one bunch of Muscats weighed 3½lb. Large crops of grapes also, have ripened on vines in pots ; of figs, too, in pots, there has been a good and constant supply. Stove plants have been growing so well, that many have been quite " specimen plants." So much for my horticultural polmaise ; then comes my dwelling house polmaise, for I have polmaised that too ! Five rooms are warmed by one stove ; the bedrooms have been pronounced to be in the winter most delightful, there is no feeling that would indicate that the room is heated by warm air ; all you perceive is that your room is like summer. Last, not least, comes the polmaise closet in which all the linen and wet clothes of a large family is dried quickly, without attention or risk of fire. So much for the doings of a tyro with polmaise, to whom not a single instance of failure has occurred at—Tirydail.

[We are glad to hear this, and should like to have the particulars of your arrangement, for we are the friends of any mode of heating that is effectual and economical.—Ed. C. G.]

TO CORRESPONDENTS.

₊ We request that no one will write to the departmental writers of The Cottage Gardener. It gives them unjustifiable trouble and expense. All communications should be addressed "*To the Editor of The Cottage Gardener,* 2, *Amen Corner, Paternoster Row, London.*"

Keeping Plants over the Winter (C. J. P.).—This will be treated of more fully ere long ; mean time examine last year's numbers at this time.

Scarlet Geraniums (*Ibid*).—These now growing freely and intended to be lifted, should have some of the most luxuriant foliage removed, in order to let the sun and air harden the stems, and the roots should be cut round with a trowel three or four inches from the stem, then take them up before injured by frost.

Cactus (*Ibid*).—The over-grown Cacti may be removed now, but having no greenhouse you would have more chance of making a plant of it by removing it in March and placing it in a pot, in a mixture of sand, loam, and lime rubbish.

PROPAGATING FUCHSIA FULGENS (*Ibid*).—This is easily struck in spring or summer; in the one case under a bell-glass or tumbler, in the other, under a hand-light. As its leaves are large, if you did not use a glass of any kind the evaporation from the foliage would destroy the cutting. It is also easily raised from seed. Sown in April in a pot, and a square of glass put over it and kept as hot as you can in your window. If you had a cucumber-box, it would come more quickly. The moss put over your pots has drawn many roots to the surface. If you wish for greater luxuriance, put some rotten dung thinly over the roots, and then replace the moss. You may move the *Scarlet Japonica* (we presume, *Pyrus Japonica*), any time next month or before winter.

PITS FOR CLIMBERS (*W. D. Paine*).—These made at the back of your conservatory, three feet by one foot six inches, and from two to three feet deep, will answer well—but see you give them sufficient drainage. With nothing but a small portable stove to heat it, and covering up the windows in cold weather, the *Clematis azurea grandiflora*, and the *Cobea scandens*, will answer well. *Passiflora Herbertii*, will also do. The *Passiflora edulis*, though we have grown it in a common greenhouse, we should not recommend you to plant, unless you have considerable experience, as it is a native of the West Indies, and has little to strike attention in its flowers. If you plant now, you must be careful of watering during winter. It would be as well to defer until March.

SEEDLING GERANIUMS (*Ibid*).—These, if kept over nicely during the winter, will flower early next season; do not shift them into larger pots however. Much obliged for the sketch, and wish others would be as definite; must refrain from giving anything like legal advice, but if you could devise any simple means of heating your little house, either by flue, water, or stove, so as not to be inside the house, your plants would flourish better. Much may be done by having water over and around your stove, but still the air *will be dried and robbed of its oxygen*.

FUCHSIA SERRATIFOLIA (*Alpha*).—This, three feet high, with many side branches, but which has not bloomed, do not stop; expose it as much as you can to sun and air, and it will be likely to bloom in winter and spring.

SIX FUCHSIAS FOR SITTING-ROOM WINDOW (*Ibid*).—The following old ones are good for such a purpose:—Exoniensis, Cassandra, Sir Henry Pottinger, Carolina, Napoleon, and Dr. Jephson.

FUCHSIA SPECTABILIS (*Ibid*).—We cannot tell you where to get a *slip*. Any nurseryman will either supply you or procure it for you, and it is cheap enough now.

ERYSIMUM CHEIRANTHOIDES (*Ibid*).—This is a wild flower, and raised from seed. *Snapdragons* may be propagated now by cuttings under a hand-light, but earlier would have been better. Seed also may be sown early in spring. *Cuphea*.—How many varieties are there? This we can scarcely tell, there being between one and two dozen of species; it is likely, however, you may be able to keep the one you have got in your window, if you keep it rather dry and secure from frost during winter. *Vanack cabbage* and *cauliflower* for spring planting, under a hand-light. It is too late for the former, unless you consent to coddle it. *Dianthus*.—Sow in spring, or early in autumn.

GOOSEBERRIES (*S. J. B.*).—Your gooseberry wants will, we trust, be met by a paper in the present number. Your experience, that the *Black Hamburg* vine is very liable to mildew, coincides with all we hear. Your "glasshouse" is surely short of copious front ventilation; pray knock some larger holes in the front wall, and you will then find that a liberal ingress will prevent the necessity of resorting to keep draughts. If you get the wood well ripened of such things as the *olea, fig, oleander, &c.*, there need be little fear of their wintering. Dryness and shade are the essentials; and, under such circumstances, they endure a much lower temperature in the north of Italy than is usual in an English winter. As to *coating pots* with a non-conducting medium, we would try powdered moss, applied after a dressing of some adhesive material. Double potting is, however, a safer plan.

MOVING MULBERRY (*M. M. G.*).—We much wish you had asked advice a month sooner; we would then have said—care not for the present crop; try to ripen your wood by root pruning, leaving the trench of operations open until the beginning of March; then to move it on a bottom prepared according to our platform mode, which has been described over and over again in past numbers.

WEAK VINE (*D. S., Camberwell*).—Allow as many shoots to remain as are needed for covering the available space, but prune them back to the ripened part indicated by brownness and hardness. Training is but a subordinate affair; only keep the wood thin enough during the growing season to let sunshine in.

DRIVING BEES (*W. W. B.*).—Our correspondent says, "On 19th August we drove two stocks of bees, as recommended by 'A Country Curate,' but suffocated about three quarts of them, which remained in the hives. The united stocks appropriated about 25 lbs. of food (3 lbs. sugar, ½ pint water, 1 lb. honey) in about sixteen days, when we ceased to feed them. They weigh now, exclusive of the hives, 20 lbs.; *will they require more?* I have a stock painted in 1847 or 1848; the contents of the hive now weigh 20 lbs. I suppose that is not enough, as you recommend 20 lbs. of *honey* to be left. I do not wish to overfeed them, nor do I mean to higgle with them, as they have afforded me 18 lbs. of fine honey this season. Perhaps Mr. Payne will give a table of the estimated weight which should be allowed for the comb and bees in hives of the first year, and when two, three, four, or five years old." Three quarts were,

indeed, too many too lose; and they certainly might have been saved. In driving, it is necessary to have the hive into which the bees are driven exactly of the same size at the mouth as the one they are driven from; for if there be any inequality of size at the junction the bees will not readily pass over it. Twenty pounds of *honey* are sufficient. Mr. Payne will give a table of the estimated weight which should be allowed for the comb and bees in hives of the one, two, three, four, and five years old.

CAPE BULBS (*J. E. A.*).—*Brunsvigia multiflora* (the true Candelabra plant), *B. Josephinæ*, *B. Ciliaris*, and *Falcata*—received from the Cape last spring—would have blossomed this month, or at furthest in October. *If the flower-bud* in the heart of the bulb had been formed before the bulbs were gathered; but as it is not so, all the gardeners in the country could not possibly flower them before September, 1852; but after that they ought to flower every year. Turn to the index of the first vol., and you will find ample directions about them; and if you want more instruction, write again about these charming bulbs. *Hæmanthus tigrinus* and *coccineus* are not worth cultivating. We have grown them, and have some now in flower; but the best of them are mere botanical curiosities. Some *Watsonias* are pretty things, and they require exactly the same treatment as the common *Ixias*. We must hear from you again after you read and digest what is said of these bulbs in former volumes.

GAILLARDIA PICTA (*R. F. W.*).—This plant is too gross for a neat bedder; but a large mass of it near tall plants looks well, and it is a good plant for a mixed border. Any good garden soil will do for it, and it can very easily be divided in the spring by taking up the old plants. Indeed, it does best if taken up every second or third year and fresh transplanted.

SAXIFRAGES (*Ibid*).—*S. hypnoides* is one of the low dense ones, and rock-work is just the place for it, if not too dry. *S. incurvifolia*, and, indeed, the whole family, are suitable plants for your rock-work. Mr. Appleby can supply a large collection. Your plant is the *Corydalis lutea*, and if you allow it to shed its seeds, you will soon have more than enough of it; but it is a good rock plant nevertheless.

PLANTING PINKS (*F. L.*).—You ask, "Is it true, as I have been informed, that some prize pinks of superior kind loose their natural lacing by being planted out in February instead of October?" The statement is not true, and belongs to the era of sowing and planting at different states of the moon's age to gain particular ends. However, February is a better time to plant out pinks than October.

LOBELIA RAMOSA (*F. H.*).—This must be sown on a slight hotbed, or in a warm frame, any time in April; but for a late crop, a cold close frame would do.

CAMPANULA CARPATICA ALBA (*Ibid*).—A good plant or two of this bought from a nursery, would take two or three years to make a bed by dividing the roots. The best way is to put a pot of it in heat at the end of January, and make cuttings of the young tops, as fast as they come up, till the beginning of May, just like making cuttings of the verbenas.

TOM THUMB GERANIUM (*Ibid*).—Do not pinch off the tops of the shoots made by your rooted cuttings. This dwarf variety does not require stopping at any time or for any purpose.

MOVING WALNUT-TREE (*L. L. L.*).—A walnut-tree 17 years old is just in the best age for transplanting; you cannot fail with it, if you do not spoil the roots. The end of October is the best time to remove it. Mind to stake it well with three long poles set triangle-ways.

ROSES (*Peregrinus*).—A vigorous plant of *Felicite perpetuelle* (evergreen climbing rose—and the best of that section) has grown luxuriantly but not blossomed with you; and you want to know how to deal with it. In the absence of any knowledge of the age or history of this rose, we can only give a guess answer, and say, do not touch a twig of it till after the flowering season is over next June; and unless it is a very young plant it will flower and please you. You may bud any other favourite sort on it until the middle of October; or, indeed, as long as the bark on the young shoots will "rise," or part freely from the wood. It is not necessary that the bark of the *bud plant* should rise, because a very thin slice of the young wood behind the bud will only insure its safety, although some people do not think so. If the plant is old and has refused to flower through over-luxuriance, you ought to root-prune it in October.

CAPE JASMINE (*W. H. D.*).—This is the deliciously-scented *Gardenia radicans*. It must be grown in peat only, with a sixth-part of white sand mixed with it. The plant will do in a greenhouse or room nine months in the year, if you can force it in a damp hot-bed for the other three months, say from the first of March; without some forcing in a damp atmosphere you cannot flower it very well. The time to pot it is March, and the size of the pot to be one size larger than the present one.

FUCHSIAS (*Lady Bird*).—A frame is rather too good to winter large fuchsias in, but if you can spare it, by all means do so. Look in our index for their usual winter treatment, and for flowers to furnish the greenhouse in winter, till Mr. Fish makes up his lists. The same for *Ferns*, until Mr. Appleby comes round to them again. Generic names are not *Latin*, as you will see by our forthcoming DICTIONARY; nevertheless, "the Latin name" of the Hare's-foot fern is *Davallia canariensis*, and stands in our Dictionary thus—DAVALLIA. Named after Davali, a Swiss botanist. Natural order *Ferns* (Polypodiaceæ). Linnean system, 24th Class *Cryptogamia*, and 1st Order *Filices*. The second name means that it was first found in the Canary Islands, and the English name is very appropriate. The ends of the creeping stems hang over the pot, and when the leaves are gone, and the plant is at rest, one might be excused for mistaking them for "Mauky's paws," or hare's feet.

PLANTING EVERGREENS (W. H. G.).—Mr. Beaton said his was a case of necessity, and he also said that "after the growth is finished" is the proper time to transplant evergreens.

WEIGHT OF HIVE (R. A.).—The state you describe your hive to be in, "plastered all over," renders it quite impossible to ascertain the weight of its contents. Driving cannot be done with advantage till August, when you will have two or three swarms from it. Whether the bees want it or not (which you cannot ascertain), feed them well in the spring.

DAHLIA-BUDS (J. D. H. S.).—The "grey-coloured insect" eating your Dahlia flower-buds is probably the Thrips ochraceus. Tobacco smoke and tobacco water will destroy it, but your own ingenuity must suggest how to apply these remedies. You will find a list of Fuchsias to suit you, in an answer to another correspondent to-day. The Cauliflower Brocoli you have, is probably the Walcheren variety of brocoli. Coleworts are small cabbages that have not hearted. You may put cuttings into the soil of a hotbed as soon as the heat has become mild. Sow your Auricula and Polyanthus seed next April. Weigela rosea is quite hardy. You may winter your Cupheas in your sitting-room. Apply for the seeds you require to any first-rate seedsman, and if you wish to obtain the means of ascertaining the scientific names of plants, you must learn botany.

VARIEGATED LEAVES (M. D. Y.).—All the tints except green assumed by leaves, appear to arise from the parts so coloured absorbing an excess of oxygen gas from the air, or in the process of decomposing water. If a portion of a leaf is submitted to the action of chlorine, a gas which powerfully absorbs hydrogen, and leaves free the oxygen, that portion of the leaf will be found changed to a pallid colour. Apply to a London seedsman for the flower-seeds you require. Which of the Sphinx Moths do you mean? See what is said at page 387 about storing Filberts. Your other question shall be answered next week.

GERANIUM CUTTINGS (Jane).—The unripened shoots strike most freely. Old geraniums stored away for the winter in a hay-loft should be placed upright, and not on their sides in a box "on top of each other." THE COTTAGE GARDENERS' DICTIONARY will contain epitomes of cultivation.

MANURE FOR POTATOES (W. F.).—On no account put stable manure upon any portion of the ground you purpose planting with potatoes. We do not think that crushed bones will be of benefit to them; and we recommend you to give the ground a dressing with soot and salt just previously to digging for planting. Universal experience shows that dungs of any kind applied to this crop promote disease in the tubers. Vegetable Marrows when ripe may be stored, and their flesh boiled and mashed like turnips. To preserve them through the winter no other care is necessary than keeping them dry and cool.

WINTERING PLANTS (R. R. G.).—"Please to inform me the best way to keep petunias, verbenas, heliotropes, pansies, and geraniums, through the winter, having no greenhouse, pit, or cold frame, but a spare room facing the south, with a dark dry closet in it. And also the best way to keep Fuchsia macrantha." These questions have been answered at least a dozen times. Young plants, such as yours, can hardly be kept without some better convenience than you have. The geraniums and the fuchsia may be kept in the spare room if the frost is kept from them, and the pansies will do better without protection in the open garden.

ANNUALS FOR AUTUMN SOWING (Georgina Herbert).—Clarkias, Godetias, Collinsias, Delphinums, Nemophilas, Virginian Stocks for edgings, Navelwort, Eucaridium, Erysimum, Platystemon, Leptosiphon, Gilias, and Candy tufts, are amongst the best annuals to sow in the autumn.

ROLLED GLASS (E. C. B.).—The specimen you have sent would answer admirably for vineries, or any other structure for the protection of plants. Whoever manufactures it, would consult their own interest by advertising its price, &c., in our columns.

BOOKS (J. B., Wortley).—The "Modern Dairy" is published by Ridgway, Piccadilly; and "Spooner on Sheep," by Longman and Co.

SAVIN (Cravensis).—The only savin we know is the Juniperus Sabini, and its variegated variety. One of the Cæsalpinia genus has been called sometimes the "Indian Savin."

LEEK OPERATIVE FLORAL SOCIETY.—We are glad that this society is flourishing, but it is quite impossible for us to report its shows, or those of any other local society; for if we admitted one, we could not refuse admission to one of the many hundreds now flourishing over the face of "gardening Britain."

CHINA-ASTERS (G. H. Patterson).—The best mode of raising these is by seed sown in the spring, and the seedlings transplanted in the autumn where they are to remain. But we may have something more to say upon the subject.

PEACH-TREE (J. French).—It was not the eastern aspect that induced us to warn you from planting one in your greenhouse, but our knowledge that you will never find it repay you for your trouble. We have peaches and grapes also ripening well on an eastern wall, and recommend you to plant an Acton Scot peach on that aspect. Your heath is Erica lactiflora, and requires a greenhouse; and your bedding-out plant is Ageratum mexicanum. The chrysanthemums trained according to Mr. Weaver's plan, have the stems tied round and round outside the sticks. The Victoria plum is oval, red, large, moderate in quality, and fit for dessert at the end of September.

MALT WINE (Ibid).—Will some of our readers furnish us with a recipe for making this.

MELONS (T. P.).—It is not necessary for the earth to rest upon the manure furnishing the heat; and the fermenting mass, by the soil not resting upon it, can be more easily renewed. It is a very common plan. We have no doubt that the Albert will bear if trained as an espalier, but remember that the nuts are borne at the ends of the twigs.

STORING DAHLIA ROOTS (A Subscriber).—As soon as the stems are rendered lifeless by the frosts, take up the tubers without injuring them, cut off the stems at about six inches above the tubers, and then put these into tubs, covering them well with either sand, earth, or coal-ashes, and place them in a dry cool place, but where no frost can get at them.

ROUGH PLATE GLASS (W. W. B.).—We consider this and the rolled glass mentioned in another answer, perfectly adapted for a small greenhouse. It is quite impossible for us to say whether a greenhouse built against the back wall of your kitchen chimney would be kept sufficiently warm to protect greenhouse plants through the winter. It depends upon the fire kept there, the thickness of brickwork, aspect, &c. A pipe heated by your kitchen fire might inoculate hot water round the inside of your greenhouse. We have sent to J. B. for you.

CHARGE FOR GLAZING (J. S. L).—Why not employ any working man to do it; and make your own putty?

GINGER WINE (A Newly-married Yeoman).—Six gallons of water, 14 lbs. of loaf sugar, 24 large lemons, and half a pound of white ginger bruised. Boil the ginger in the water for half an hour. Strain the liquor when quite cold, and dissolve in it the sugar; pour it upon the peels of the lemons, and let it remain for twenty-four hours; then strain, and add the juice of the lemons. Let it ferment; and treat it in all respects as directed for rhubarb wine at page 390.

WINE FROM UNRIPE GRAPES (Ibid).—The proportions for this are 40 lbs. of grapes, and 30 lbs. of loaf sugar, to four gallons of water. Vines trained as espaliers on a sheltered slope facing the south would grow you grapes fitted for this use. The Black Cluster, White Cluster, and White Riesling varieties are most suitable for the purpose. We have sent to obtain information about the hire.

PRIZE VOLUME OF COTTAGE GARDENER.—We have received so many applications for this lately that we must give this general answer—We have no more to give away at present. The offer was made last year; and a large number were given, being applied for within the time we limited. Now many of our back numbers are nearly or quite out of print; and we cannot risk disappointing new subscribers by having only imperfect volumes to supply them with.

WOODLICE (M. C. K.).—Your only remedy is to trap them by laying on their sides flower-pots half filled with moss. The woodlice creep under the moss, and may be destroyed every morning and evening. We know of no plant "called Clotemore in the Isle of Wight, used for curing boils, with a leaf resembling rhubarb in shape, and the dock in colour." The description agrees best with that of the Burdock (Arctium lappa); and old herbalists write that it is beneficial to boils and sores. It is known also as the Clot-bur. May you not have misunderstood the pronunciation?

MILDEW ON VINES (S. W.).—You are not singular in finding "the Black Hamburg much mildewed, in a house where the Sweet-water and Muscadet are not so bad." We wish we could point out the cause; but in your case we should this autumn clear the roots; cut away all that have grown down deep into the soil, and bring all the horizontal roots to within 12 or 13 inches of the surface. Mulch the surface through the winter, and next spring and summer; and paint the entire house, both this autumn and in the spring, with lime and sulphur; at the same time scraping off all the loose bark, and painting the stems and branches of the vines.

CUTTINGS (Verax).—Many good gardeners cut through a joint in taking off a cutting, but in most cases the safest way is to make the cut just below a joint.

SOIL FOR PETUNIAS (Ibid).—These and verbenas require a deep rich soil, or one well manured if poor.

CUTTINGS OF MELONS (Ibid).—April, May, and June are the months to make cuttings of melon plants that have been sown in the spring; and plants so raised come sooner into fruit, and are less rank in growth, than seedlings.

AUTUMN-PLANTING POTATOES (A Constant Reader).—There is no fear of the sets suffering from frosts during the winter in Lancashire, for they bear those of Yorkshire and Scotland. The winter on the sea-coast, too, is always milder than in the interior. You will have seen where the potatoes you ask about may be obtained. Ashes mingled with the potatoes in your clamps would be of service just in proportion to the effectual way in which they were made to keep the tubers separate, and thus help to check heating, and the admission of the air.

UNRIPE-GRAPE VINEGAR (A. Watts).—To each quart of bruised berries add three quarts of cold water; after frequent stirring during twenty-four hours strain the liquor; add one pound and a half of sugar to each gallon; and let it remain in a warm place with a piece of thin canvass tied over the mouth of the stone-jar, or bottle, for twelve months.

MILDEW ON VINES (Herbert).—Salt and water you find of no avail in removing this, and we are much obliged by your statement of the result. The mildew is a parasitical fungus. You may shift your Geraniums into smaller pots now.

OXFORD BRAWN (T. W.).—Can any of our correspondents give a good recipe for making this?

SAND FROM BISHOP'S WALTHAM (*T. M. W.*).—This is a black sand of no particular use. It is not sharp enough to supersede silver sand for potting purposes.

NAMES OF PLANTS (*M. P.*).—Your's is *Celsia sublanata.* (*W. F.*).—Your fern is *Cystopteris fragilis,* or Brittle Bladder-fern. (*A. B.*).—We cannot be certain from the *leaf* (!) you sent. It is, perhaps, *Menispermum canadense;* send us a specimen in flower. (*Queen Mab*).—Your pink shrub is *Spiraea bella,* and the others *Œnothera serotina, Borkhausia rubra,* and *Rosa cinnamomea.*

CALENDAR FOR SEPTEMBER.

ORCHID HOUSE.

SHADING must now be entirely dispensed with. AIR, give in less quantities, and only when the sun shines. CYCNOCHES, and other allied species, will now have ripened their pseudo-bulbs, and should be placed upon a shelf near to the glass, and be kept quite dry. DENDROBIUMS will also have finished their growth towards the end of the month, and must be kept moderately dry and cool. If kept moist after that time the roots will perish, which will be injurious to them, both preventing their flowering and growing well next season. INDIAN HOUSE.—The temperature should now be lowered 10°; 70° by day and 60° by night will be the proper heat. LÆLIAS will now be showing flower; wet the blocks about twice a week, in the morning, to bring out the blooms large and fine. MOISTURE, both at the root and in the air, reduce greatly, so as to induce the plants to enter gradually into a state of rest. WATER, still give to plants in a growing state, but in less quantities and not so often. ZYGOPETALUMS, now growing, pot to encourage strong growth.
T. APPLEBY.

PLANT STOVE.

AIR, admit freely during the day to dry up damp and prevent premature growths, which would perish during severe weather. AMARYLLIS AULICA showing bloom bring now out of pits; pot others, and place in gentle heat, to bring them forward; aim at exciting the roots to push before the leaves or flowers. Clear all plants from INSECTS, now more especially, so as to keep them down through the winter. GLOXINIAS, and allied plants, place in a position to rest where no water or frost can reach them. IXORAS, give less water to indulge a cessation of growth, and ripen the wood to flower well next year. LUCULIAS, take part into the stove to flower early. LYCOPODIUMS, divide and repot, to look green all winter. Keep every thing NEAT and CLEAN, not only the plants but the wood, stone, and brick-work of the building, and the pots both at the outside and on the surface. JASMINUM GRANDIFLORUM and other species place to force into flower early. SOLANDRA GRANDIFLORA should now be showing bloom; give plenty of water too at the root. SHRUBS, HARDY, bring in to force, &c. WATER freely winter blooming plants, drying up the spilled water with a mop.
T. APPLEBY.

FLORISTS' FLOWERS.

AURICULAS, place in winter quarters, top dress previously, and destroy worms, slugs, &c. WATER, a little in very dry weather; remove all dead leaves as they occur. CARNATION LAYERS, finish potting, and place in frame or pit towards the latter end of the month. COMPOST, prepare, turn over, and procure fresh. DAHLIAS, take up where the frost has killed the tops. IRISES (bulbous), plant in open beds in rich soil. POLYANTHUSES, place in frames, shelter from wet, destroy slugs amongst. RANUNCULUSES, Scarlet Turban and other varieties of Turban, plant, e. ROSES, transplant, e. TULIP-BEDS, turn over. WEEDS, every where pluck up as soon as visible.
T. APPLEBY.

GREENHOUSE.

AIR, admit freely during the day, but sparingly at night. ALSTROEMERIAS, shift, or rather pot in rich light soil, and place where they will be secure from frost. AZALEAS, remove into the house, especially those that bloomed early, as the least frost will discolour their leaves. BULBS, pot for early blooming. CINERARIAS, forward ones give manure water, and have secured. CAMELLIAS (See AZALEAS). CALCEOLARIAS, strike cuttings; pot forward plants; prick off seedlings. CHRYSANTHEMUMS for winter blooming, provide with shelter from cold rains and early frost. CLIMBERS on rafters now praise in, to give light to the plants beneath. CLERODENDRONS, GESNERAS, LANTANA, ACHIMENES, &c., keep in the warmest end of the house. AZALEAS, CAMELLIAS, FUCHSIAS, &c., at the coolest. CYTISUS and GENISTA, scourge well with soap-suds, and then with clean water, to remove all traces of Red spider, and then place where they can be sheltered, before being housed at the end of the month. GERANIUMS, keep clear from fly; and slowly growing; forward ones may be repotted, and fresh struck ones potted off. GLADIOLUS, pot. HEATHS and EPACRISES, get under shelter, and give them abundance of air, when temperature above 40°. EARLY FUCHSIAS may be put past into sheds before their stems have been injured by frost. SALVIA SPLENDENS, encourage with manure waterings, and syringing with soot water, to banish the Red spider before housing it in the conservatory. PLANTS to be raised from the flower beds should previously have their roots cut round, and then after potting should have a little bottom heat, to encourage fresh roots, while the too temperature is kept cool. They will not require to be often watered for a time, but syringing the tops in sunny days will be serviceable. ALL PLANTS should be thoroughly CLEANED, and houses and glass washed and put in good order. WATER should also now be given with a careful hand, and only when necessary. A plant may not require it above once or twice a week now, that would have wanted refreshing twice, in the dog days, during a forenoon's sunshine.
R. FISH.

FLOWER-GARDEN.

ANEMONES, plant for earliest bloom. AURICULAS and POLYANTHUSES, put under shelter. BULBOUS ROOTS, finish planting in dry weather; pot for latest forcing, and for plunging in flower beds, &c. CARNATION layers, finish planting and potting; secure the pot ones from rains. CLIMBERS of all sorts, plant, prune, and train. COMPOST, prepare and turn in dry weather. DAHLIAS, cut down after frost, and let the roots remain as long as it is safe; when taken up, dry them in open sheds, &c., before storing, where frost and damp cannot reach them. DRESS the beds and borders, and put mark-sticks to bulbs and other roots to guide you when digging. EDGINGS, plant. EVERGREENS, finish planting, b. FIBROUS-ROOTED PLANTS, finish dividing and planting, b. FORK over borders, &c. GRASS, cut very close the last time; keep clear of leaves; and roll. GRAVEL, weed and roll. HEDGES, plant, clip, and clear at bottom. HOE and rake shrubberies, and bury the leaves, &c., between the plants. LAYERING, perform generally. LEAVES, gather for compost, &c. MARVEL OF PERU, take up and store like dahlias. MULCH round trees and shrubs lately planted. PLANT perennials and biennials. PLANTING, perform generally. POTTED PLANTS, for forcing, plunge in the earth of a well-sheltered border, facing the sun. PRUNE shrubs and trees generally. RANUNCULUSES, plant for earliest bloom. Seedlings of them, in boxes, &c., remove to a warm situation. SHRUBS of all kinds plant, stake, and mulch. SUCKERS, from roses and other shrubs, separate and plant. TIGRIDIAS, save from frost as long as possible; should not be dried till January or February. TULIPS, finish planting, b.
D. BEATON.

FORCING DEPARTMENT.

AIR, admit as freely as the season allows. BARK-BEDS, renew or turn over, to keep up the required bottom heat. DRESS the borders by forking and raking, to keep a dry porous surface. FIRE-HEAT, by whatever means it may be distributed, must now be daily employed, to keep the temperature from 55° to 60°. LEAVES, keep clean with sponge, &c., and remove decayed ones. PINES require a dry temperature of 60° to 65°. PROTECT outside borders, in which forcing trees are planted, from rains and frost. PEACH, prune; wash with diluted ammonia-water from the gas-works before training. TOBACCO-FUMIGATION, employ, if insects appear. VINES, strip the old bark off, and clean, as the peach, before commencing to force; begin with a day temperature of 50°. WATER (tepid), apply with the syringe on clear days.
R. ERRINGTON.

ORCHARD.

PLANTING of all kinds carry out. STAKE newly planted trees for fear of wind. MULCH newly planted trees as soon as planted. PRUNING, commence. CURRANTS and GOOSEBERRIES, prune, b. APPLES, prune, m. PLUMS and CHERRIES, prune, e. PEARS, prune, e. LARGE ORCHARD TREES, prune, e. RASPBERRIES, prune and dress, e. FIGS, pull off all young fruit large as a horse-bean, b.; protect from frost, m. NECTARINES and APRICOTS, clear away the remaining leaves from, m. NAILS and screws, draw out superfluous or rotten ones from all wall-trees, m. Pick and prepare ditto for renailing. SUCKERS, clear away, m. VINES, prune, m. ESPALIERS, prune, m. MULBERRIES, plant, b. MEDLARS, plant, b. RASPBERRIES, plant, m. STRAWBERRIES, plant, b. STONES of fruits, sow, b. TRENCH or otherwise prepare ground for planting, b. WALNUTS, plant, b. FORK out ground about fruit-trees, slightly, b.
R. ERRINGTON.

KITCHEN-GARDEN.

ANGELICA, keep clear of weeds. ASPARAGUS beds, dress and plant for forcing. BALM, plant. BEET, take up for storing. BORECOLE, plant, earth up, &c. BROCCOLI, keep clear of weeds, and attend those heading in, to protect from frost, &c. BURNET, plant. CABBAGES, plant out, prick out, and earth-stir among. CARDOONS, earth up. CARROTS, take for winter store; leave or plant for seed; attend to the young growing crops. CAULIFLOWERS, plant out under hand-glasses about the middle of the month; also in frames, for winter protection. CELERY, plant and earth up. CHIVES, plant. COLEWORTS, plant. CRESS (Water), plant. CUCUMBERS, plant out; keep up heat of beds, by linings, &c.; water sparingly. DILL, plant. DUNG, prepare for hot-beds. EARTHING-UP and earth-stirring, attend to. ENDIVE, attend to planting and blanching. FENNEL, plant. HERBARY, dress. HORSE-RADISH, plant. HYSSOP, plant. JERUSALEM ARTICHOKES, keep clear of weeds, and take up as wanted. LEAVES fallen, remove frequently. LEEKS, earth-stir among. LETTUCES, plant and prick out under walls, &c. MELONS (late), keep up heat, by linings, or otherwise; no water must be given. MUSHROOM-BEDS make, and attend to those in bearing, &c. NASTURTIUMS, gather for seed, if not done before. ONIONS, attend to those in store, and earth-stir or thin out the autumn-sown. PARSLEY, attend to potting for use in winter. PARSNIPS, take up towards the end of the month for winter storing; leave in the ground for seed. PEAS, sow towards the end of the month, PENNYROYAL, plant. POTATOES, attend to. RADISHES, sow. RHUBARB, plant in pots for early forcing, end of the month. SALSAFY, take up for winter storing. SAVOYS, plant out for seed. SCORZONERA, take up for winter storing. SEEDS, gather of any kinds as they ripen. SMALL SALADING, sow as wanted. SPINACH, keep clear of weeds; thin out, and attend to in dry weather. TANSY, TARRAGON, and THYME, plant, if required. TOMATOS, gather; if not quite ripe place them in some warm dry situation where they will soon ripen off. TURNIPS, clear of weeds, and thin out young crops. VACANT GROUND, rough up, or ridge.
T. WEAVER.

LONDON: Printed by HARRY WOOLDRIDGE, Winchester High-street, in the Parish of Saint Mary Kalendar; and Published by WILLIAM SOMERVILLE ORR, at the Office, No. 2, Amen Corner, in the Parish of Christ Church, City of London.—September 26th, 1850.

DEN.

AURICULAS and POLY
OUS ROOTS, finish pot
and for planting at l
planting and potting ev
sorts, plant, prune &c
T. DAHLIAS, cut down c
it is safe; when take c
where frost and damp ca
and put mark along su
&c. EDGINGS, plant &c
TED PLANTS, finish th
GRASS, cut very sm
l. GRAVEL, weed an
HOE and rake everwher
LAYERING, perform
GRAVEL of Past, an
and shrubs lately pan
TING, perform &c
the earth of a well-r
and trees of several
eddings of choice, s le
all kinds plant, &
rubs, separate and se
rubs, should not be don

b.   D. BEATON